A-Z Geographers' London Atlas

CONTENTS

REFERENCE

Motorway	**M1**
Motorway *under construction*	
Dual Carriageway	
'A' Road	A40
'A' Road *under construction*	
'B' Road	B106
One Way Street — One way traffic flow is indicated on 'A' roads by a heavy line on the drivers left.	traffic flow →
British Rail Line and Station	
Underground Station	●
County Boundary	
District & Borough Boundary	
Postal District Boundary — By arrangement with the Post Office	Southall
Fire Station	■
Hospital	Ⓗ
House Numbers *'A' & 'B' Roads only*	2 45
Information Centre	ℹ
Map Continuation	130
National Grid Reference	578
Place of Worship	＋
Police Station	▲
Post Office	★

The representation on the maps of a road, or footpath is no evidence of the existence of a Right of Way.

Every possible care has been taken to ensure that the information given in this Atlas is accurate and whilst the publishers would be grateful to learn of any errors, they regret they can accept no responsibility for any expense or loss thereby caused.

The maps in this Atlas are based upon the Ordnance Survey 1:10,560 and 1:10,000 Maps with the sanction of the Controller of Her Majesty's Stationery Office. Crown Copyright Reserved.

The grid on this Map is the National Grid taken from the Ordnance Survey map with the permission of the Controller of Her Majesty's Stationery Office.

An A to Z publication   ISBN 0 85039 000 1   Edition 10A

SCALE

1:20,438
3.1 inches to 1 mile

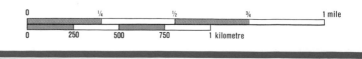

0	¼	½	¾	1 mile
0	250	500	750	1 kilometre

Geographers' A-Z Map Company Ltd.

Head Office : Vestry Road, Sevenoaks, Kent   TN14 5EP
Telephone : 0732-451152

Showrooms : 44 Gray's Inn Road, London   WC1X 8LR
Telephone : 01-242 9246

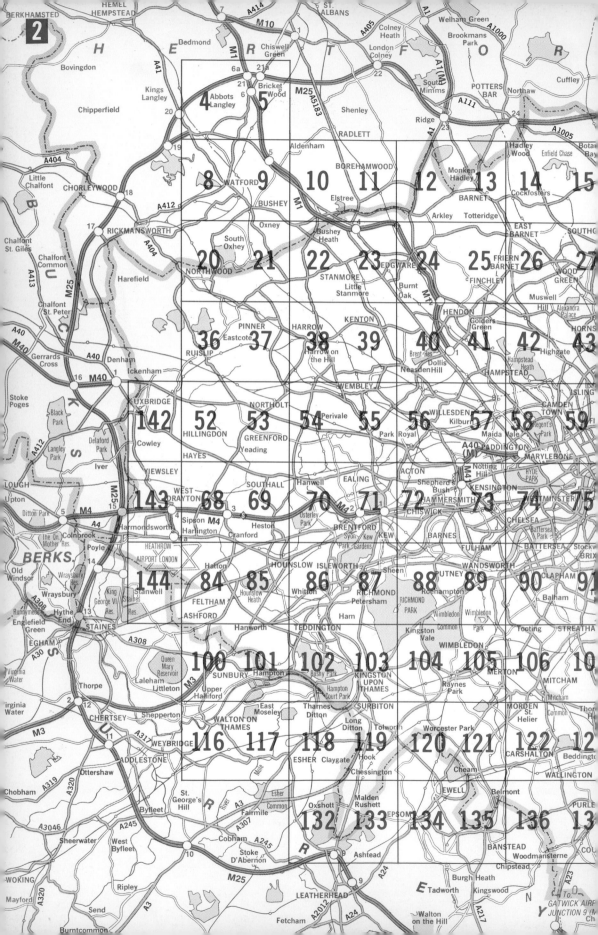

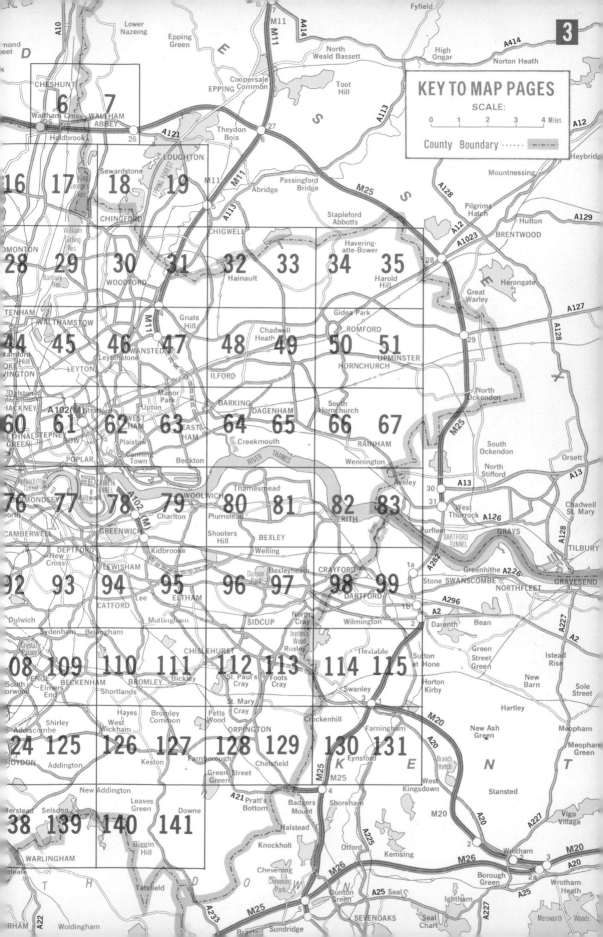

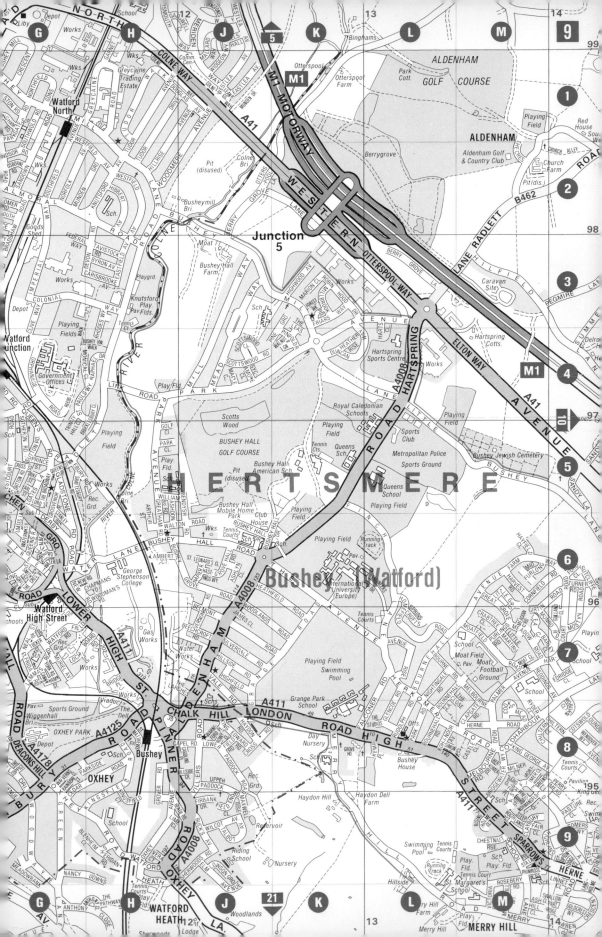

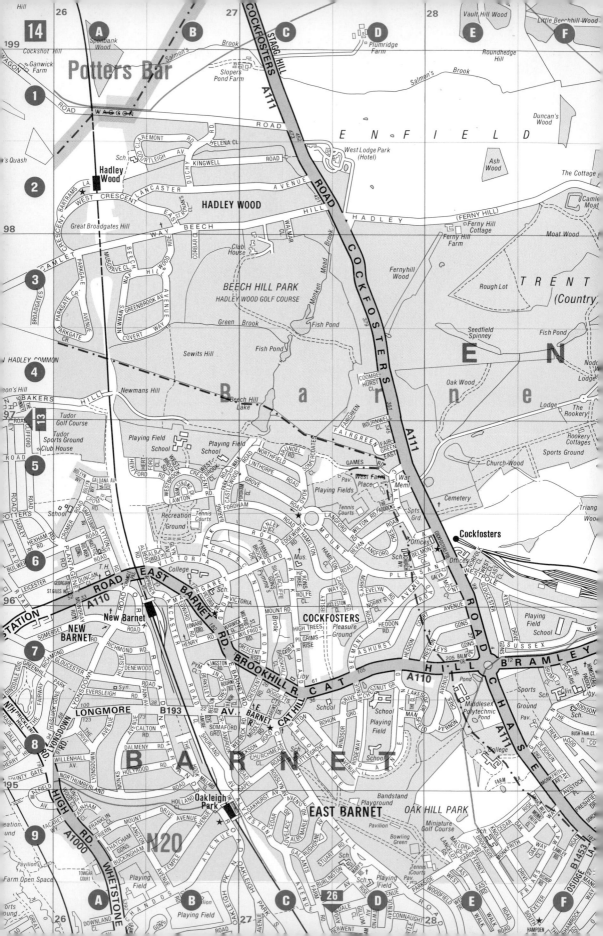

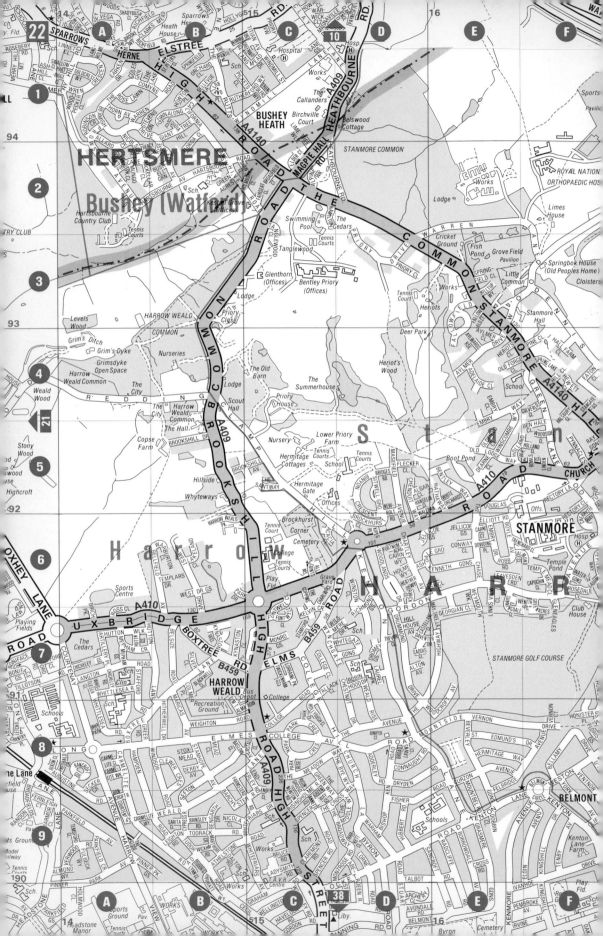

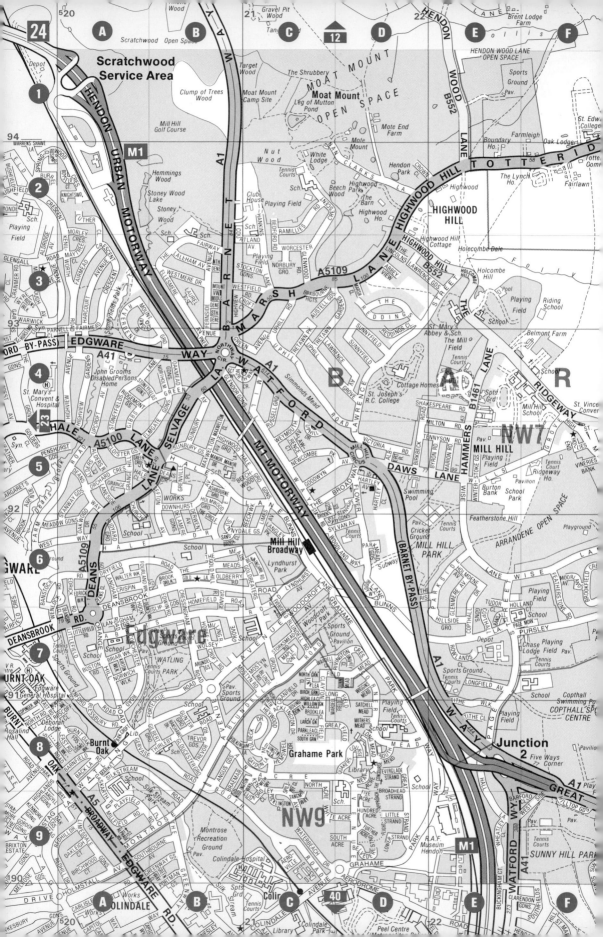

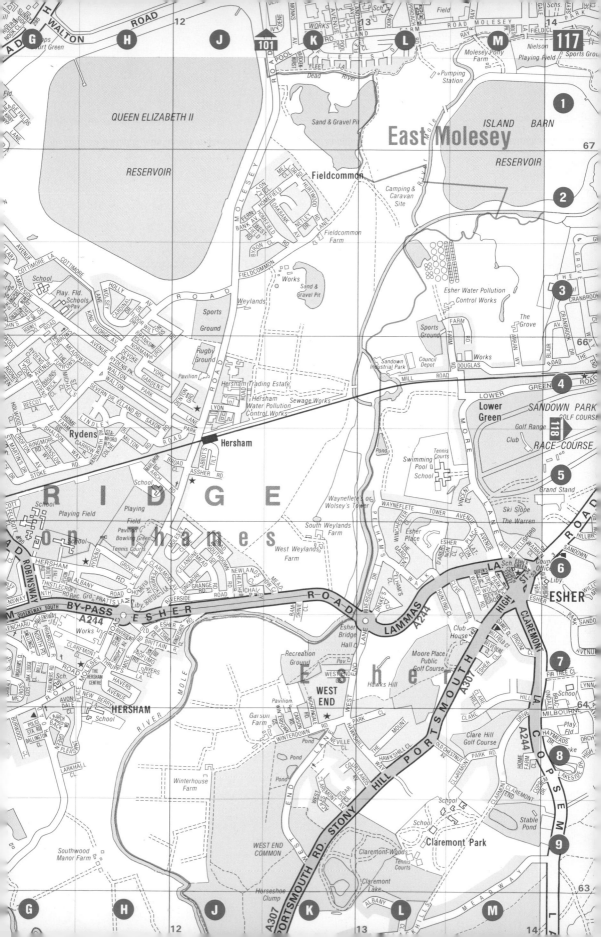

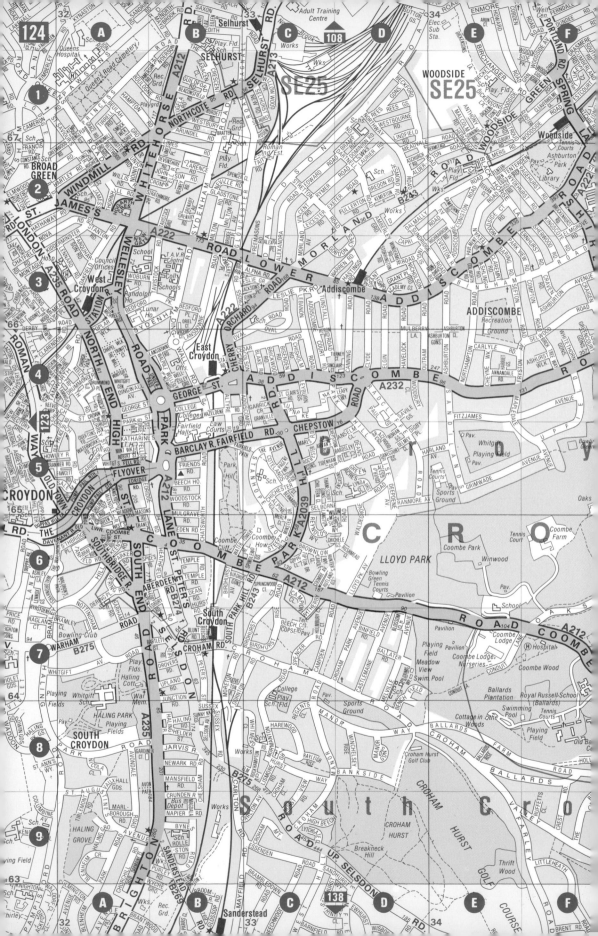

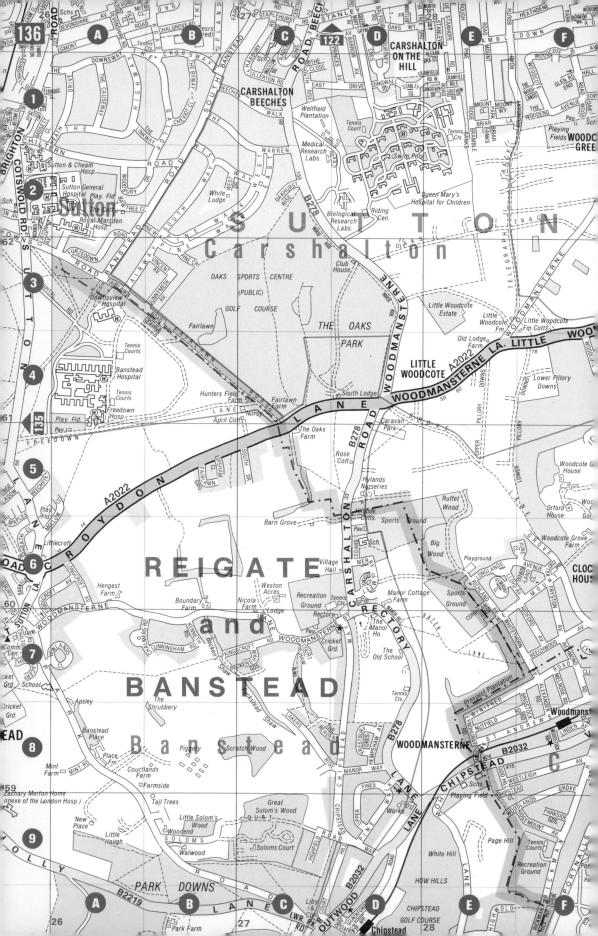

INDEX TO STREETS

HOW TO USE THIS INDEX

1. Each street name is followed by its Postal District (or, if outside the London Postal Districts, by its Post Town), and then by its map page reference; e.g. Abbess Clo. SW2—7M 91 is in the South West 2 Postal District and it is to be found in square 7M on page 91. However, with the now general usage of Postal Coding, it is not recommended that this index should be used as a means of addressing mail.

2. A strict alphabetical order is followed in which Av., Rd., St. etc. (even though abbreviated) are read in full and as part of the street name; e.g. Abbeydale Rd. appears after Abbey Cres., but before Abbey Est. and Abbeyfield Clo.

GENERAL ABBREVIATIONS

All: Alley
App: Approach
Arc: Arcade
Av: Avenue
Bk: Back
Boulevd: Boulevard
Bri: Bridge
B'way: Broadway
Bldgs: Buildings
Chu: Church
Chyd: Churchyard

Circ: Circle
Cir: Circus
Clo: Close
Comn: Common
Cotts: Cottages
Ct: Court
Cres: Crescent
Dri: Drive
E: East
Embkmt: Embankment
Est: Estate

Gdns: Gardens
Ga: Gate
Gt: Great
Grn: Green
Gro: Grove
Ho: House
Junct: Junction
La: Lane
Lit: Little
Lwr: Lower
Mnr: Manor

Mans: Mansions
Mkt: Market
M: Mews
Mt: Mount
N: North
Pal: Palace
Pde: Parade
Pk: Park
Pas: Passage
Pl: Place
Rd: Road

S: South
Sq: Square
Sta: Station
St: Street
Ter: Terrace
Up: Upper
Vs: Villas
Wlk: Walk
W: West
Yd: Yard

POST TOWN and PLACE NAME ABBREVIATIONS

Abb L: Abbots Langley
Ashf: Ashford
Asht: Ashtead
Bans: Banstead
Bark: Barking
Barn: Barnet
Beck: Beckenham
Bedd: Beddington
Belv: Belvedere
Bex: Bexley
Bexh: Bexleyheath
Borwd: Borehamwood
Bren: Brentford
Brtwd: Brentwood
Brom: Bromley
Buck H: Buckhurst Hill
Bush: Bushey
Cars: Carshalton
Chess: Chessington
Chig: Chigwell
Chst: Chislehurst

Cob: Cobham
Coul: Coulsdon
Croy: Croydon
Dag: Dagenham
Dart: Dartford
E Mol: East Molesey
Edgw: Edgware
Enf: Enfield
Epp: Epping
Eps: Epsom
Eri: Erith
Esh: Esher
Eyns: Eynsford
F'ham: Farningham
Felt: Feltham
Gnfd: Greenford
Grnh: Greenhithe
Hmptn: Hampton
Harr: Harrow
Hav: Havering atte Bower
Hay: Hayes

Horn: Hornchurch
Houn: Hounslow
Ilf: Ilford
Iswth: Isleworth
Kenl: Kenley
Kes: Keston
K Lan: King's Langley
King: Kingston upon Thames
Lea: Leatherhead
Lou: Loughton
Mitc: Mitcham
Mord: Morden
N Mald: New Malden
N'holt: Northolt
N'wd: Northwood
Orp: Orpington
Pinn: Pinner
Pot B: Potters Bar
Purf: Purfleet
Purl: Purley
Rad: Radlett

Rain: Rainham
Rich: Richmond upon Thames
Rick: Rickmansworth
Romf: Romford
Ruis: Ruislip
St Alb: Saint Albans
Sev: Sevenoaks
Shen: Shenley
Shep: Shepperton
Sidc: Sidcup
S Croy: South Croydon
S Dar: South Darenth
S Ock: South Ockendon
Stai: Staines
Stan: Stanmore
Sun: Sunbury on Thames
Surb: Surbiton
Sutt: Sutton
S at H: Sutton at Hone
Swan: Swanley

Tad: Tadworth
Tedd: Teddington
Th Dit: Thames Ditton
T Hth: Thornton Heath
Upm: Upminster
Uxb: Uxbridge
Wall: Wallington
Wal A: Waltham Abbey
Wal X: Waltham Cross
W on T: Walton on Thames
Warl: Warlingham
Wat: Watford
Well: Welling
Wemb: Wembley
W Dray: West Drayton
West: Westerham
W Wick: West Wickham
Wey: Weybridge
Whyt: Whyteleafe
Wfd G: Woodford Green
Wor Pk: Worcester Park

INDEX TO STREETS

Abberton Wlk. Rain—4D 66
Abbess Clo. SW2—7M 91
Abbeville Rd. N8—2H 43
Abbeville Rd. SW4—5G 91
Abbey Av. Wemb—5J 55
Abbey Clo. N'holt—6K 53
Abbey Clo. Pinn—1F 36
Abbey Ct. Wal A—7H 7
Abbey Cres. Belv—5L 81
Abbeydale Rd. Wemb—4K 55
Abbey Est. NW8—4M 57
Abbeyfield Clo. NW10—5L 55
Abbeyfield Rd. SE16—5G 77
(in two parts)
Abbey Gdns. NW8—5A 58
Abbey Gdns. W6—7J 73
Abbey Gdns. M. NW8—5A 58
Abbey Gro. SE2—5F 80
Abbey Hill Rd. Sidc—8G 97
Abbey La. E15—5A 62
Abbey La. Beck—4L 109
Abbey Manufacturing Est.
Wemb—4K 55
Abbey Orchard St. SW1—4H 75
Abbey Pde. NW10—6K 55
Abbey Pk. Beck—4L 109
Abbey Rd. E15—5B 62
Abbey Rd.—4M 57
NW8 1-117 & 2-98
NW6 remainder
Abbey Rd. NW10—5M 55
Abbey Rd. SW19—4A 106
Abbey Rd. Bark—4M 63
Abbey Rd. Belv—5H 81
Abbey Rd. Bexh—3J 97
Abbey Rd. Croy—5M 123
Abbey Rd. Enf—7C 16
Abbey Rd. Ilf—3B 48
Abbey Rd. S Croy—2H 139
Abbey Rd. Wal X—4A 6
Abbey St. E13—7E 62
Abbey St. SE1—4D 76
Abbey Ter. NW10—5K 55
Abbey Ter. SE2—5B 80
Abbey View. NW7—3D 24
Abbey View. Wal A—6H 7
Abbey Wlk. E Mol—7M 101

Abbey Wood La. Rain—5H 67
Abbey Wood Rd. SE2—5F 80
Abbotsbury Clo. E15—5A 62
Abbotsbury Clo. W14—3K 73
Abbotsbury Gdns. Pinn—4G 37
Abbotsbury Rd. W14—3J 73
Abbotsbury Rd. Brom—4D 126
Abbotsbury Rd. Mord—9M 105
Abbots Clo. Orp—3A 128
Abbots Clo. Rain—5G 67
Abbots Clo. Ruis—8H 37
Abbots Clo. Uxb—8B 142
Abbotsford Av. N15—2A 44
Abbotsford Gdns. Wfd G—7E 30
Abbotsford Rd. Ilf—7E 48
Abbots Gdns. N2—2B 42
Abbot's Grn. Croy—8H 125
Abbotshall Av. N14—3G 27
Abbotshall Rd. SE6—7B 94
Abbots La. SE1—2C 76
Abbots La. Kenl—8A 138
Abbotsleigh Clo. Sutt—9M 121
Abbotsleigh Rd. SW16—1G 107
Abbot's Mnr. Est. SW1—6F 74
Abbotsmede Clo. Twic—8D 86
Abbots Pk. SW2—7L 91
Abbot's Pl. NW6—4M 57
Abbot's Rd. E6—4H 63
Abbots Rd. Abb L, Wat—4A 4
Abbots Rd. Edgw—7A 24
Abbots Ter. N8—4J 43
Abbot's Tilt. W on T—5J 117
Abbotstone Rd. SW15—2G 89
Abbot St. E8—2D 60
Abbots Way. Beck—9J 109
Abbotswell Rd. SE4—4K 93
Abbotswood Gdns. Ilf—1K 47
Abbotswood Rd. SW16—9H 91
Abbott Av. SW20—5H 105
Abbott Clo. Hmptn—3J 101
Abbott Clo. N'holt—2K 53
Abbott Rd. E14—9A 62
(in two parts)
Abbotts Clo. N1—2A 60
Abbotts Clo. Romf—1M 49
Abbotts Clo. Swan—8E 114
Abbotts Cres. E4—4B 30

Abbotts Cres. Enf—4M 15
Abbotts Dri. Wemb—7F 38
Abbotts Pk. Rd. E10—5A 46
Abbotts Rd. Barn—6M 13
Abbotts Rd. Mitc—8G 107
Abbotts Rd. S'hall—2J 69
Abbotts Rd. Sutt—6J 121
Abbott's Wlk. Bexh—8H 81
Abbs Cross. Horn—6G 51
Abbs Cross Gdns. Horn—6G 51
Abbs Cross La. Horn—8G 51
Abchurch La. EC4—1B 76
Abdale Rd. W12—2F 72
Abenglen Industrial Est. Hay
—3B 68
Aberavon Rd. E3—6J 61
Abercairn Rd. SW16—4G 107
Aberconway Rd. Mord
—8M 105
Abercorn Clo. NW7—7J 25
Abercorn Clo. NW8—6A 58
Abercorn Clo. S Croy—4H 139
Abercorn Cres. Harr—6M 37
Abercorn Gdns. Harr—5H 39
Abercorn Gdns. Romf—4F 48
Abercorn Pl. NW8—6A 58
Abercorn Rd. NW7—7J 25
Abercorn Rd. Stan—7G 23
Abercorn Trading Est. Wemb
—5H 55
Abercrombie St. SW11—1C 90
Aberdare Clo. W Wick—4A 126
Aberdare Gdns. NW6—3M 57
Aberdare Gdns. NW7—7H 25
Aberdare Rd. Enf—6G 17
Aberdeen La. N5—1A 60
Aberdeen Pde. N18—5F 28
Aberdeen Pl. NW8—7B 58
Aberdeen Rd. N5—9A 44
Aberdeen Rd. N18—5F 28
Aberdeen Rd. NW10—1D 56
Aberdeen Rd. Croy—6R 124
Aberdeen Rd. Harr—9D 22
Aberdeen Ter. SE3—1B 94

Aberdour Rd. Ilf—8F 48
Aberdour St. SE1—5C 76
Aberfeldy St. E14—9A 62
(in two parts)
Aberford Gdns. SE18—9J 79
Aberford Rd. Borwd—4L 11
Aberfoyle Rd. SW16—4H 107
Abergeldie Rd. SE12—5F 94
Abernethy Rd. SE13—3C 94
Abersham Rd. E8—1D 60
Abery St. SE18—5C 80
Abingdon Clo. NW1—2H 59
Abingdon Clo. SW19—3A 106
Abingdon Clo. Uxb—4D 142
Abingdon Rd. N3—9A 26
Abingdon Rd. SW16—6J 107
Abingdon Rd. W8—4I 73
Abingdon St. SW1—4J 75
Abingdon Vs. W8—4L 73
Abinger Av. Sutt—2H 135
Abinger Clo. Bark—9E 48
Abinger Clo. Brom—7J 111
Abinger Clo. Wall—7J 123
Abinger Gdns. Iswth—2C 86
Abinger Gro. SE8—7K 77
Abinger M. W9—7L 57
Abinger Rd. W4—4C 72
Aboyne Dri. SW20—6E 104
Aboyne Rd. NW10—8C 40
Aboyne Rd. SW17—9B 90
Abridge Clo. Wal X—8D 6
Abridge Gdns. Romf—6L 33
Abridge Way. Bark—5F 64
Abyssinia Clo. SW11—3C 90
Acacia Av. N17—7B 28
Acacia Av. Bren—8F 70
Acacia Av. Hay—9D 52
Acacia Av. Horn—7D 50
Acacia Av. Rich—1K 87
Acacia Av. Ruis—6E 36
Acacia Av. Wemb—1J 55
Acacia Av. W Dray—1K 143
Acacia Clo. SE20—6E 108
Acacia Clo. Orp—9B 112
Acacia Clo. Stan—6C 22
Acacia Dri. Bans—6H 135

Acacia Dri. Sutt—3L 121
Acacia Dri. Upm—9L 51
Acacia Gdns. NW8—5B 58
Acacia Gdns. W Wick—4A 126
Acacia Gro. SE21—8B 92
Acacia Gro. N Mald—7C 104
Acacia Pl. NW8—5B 58
Acacia Rd. E11—7C 46
Acacia Rd. E17—4J 45
Acacia Rd. NW8—5B 58
Acacia Rd. SW16—5J 107
Acacia Rd. W3—1A 72
Acacia Rd. Beck—7K 109
Acacia Rd. Dart—7H 99
Acacia Rd. Enf—3B 16
Acacia Rd. Hmptn—3I 101
Acacia Rd. Mitc—6E 106
Acacia Wlk. Swan—6B 114
Academy Gdns. Croy—3D 124
Academy Gdns. N'holt—5H 53
Academy Pl. SE18—9N 79
Academy Rd. SE18—9K 79
Acanthus Rd. SW11—2E 90
Accommodation Rd. NW11
—6K 41
Acer Av. Rain—6H 67
Acer Rd. West—8H 141
Acers. St Alb—1M 5
Acfold Rd. SW6—9M 73
Achilles Rd. NW6—1L 57
Achilles St. SE14—8K 77
Achilles Way. W1—2F 74
Acklam Rd. W10—8J 57
Acklington Dri. NW9—8C 24
Ackmar Rd. SW6—9L 73
Ackroyd Dri. E3—8K 61
Ackroyd Rd. SE23—6H 93
Acland Cres. SE5—2B 92
Acland Rd. NW2—2F 56
Acme Rd. Wat—2E 8
Acol Cres. Ruis—1F 52
Acol Rd. NW6—3M 57
Aconbury Rd. Dag—4F 64
Acorn Clo. E4—5M 29
Acorn Clo. Chst—2A 112
Acorn Clo. Enf—3M 15

145

Acorn Ct. Ilf—4C 48
Acorn Gdns. SE19—5D 108
Acorn Gdns. W3—8B 56
Acorn Gro. Ruis—9D 36
Acorn Industrial Est. Dart
—4D 98
Acorn Pde. SE15—8F 76
Acorn Pl. Wat—1E 8
Acorn Rd. Dart—4D 98
Acorns, The. Chig—4C 32
Acorn Wlk. SE16—2J 77
Acre La. SW2—3J 91
Acre La. Cars & Wall—6E 122
Acre Rd. SW19—3B 106
Acre Rd. Dag—3M 65
Acre Rd. King—5J 103
Acre Way. N'wd—8D 20
Acris St. SW18—4A 90
Acton Clo. Wal X—4E 6
Acton La. NW10—6A 56
Acton La.—3A to 5A 72
  W4 1-287 & 2-280
  W3 remainder
Acton M. E8—4D 60
Acton Pk. Industrial Est. W3
—3B 72
Acton St. WC1—6K 59
Acuba Rd. SW18—8M 89
Acworth Pl. Dart—5G 99
Ada Gdns. E14—9B 62
Ada Gdns. E15—4D 62
Adair Rd. W10—7J 57
Adam & Eve M. W8—4L 73
Adams Clo. NW9—7M 39
Adams Ct. EC2—9C 60
Adams Gdns. SE16—3G 77
Adamson Rd. E16—9E 62
Adamson Rd. NW3—3B 58
Adams Pl. N7—1K 59
Adamsrill Clo. Enf—8B 16
Adamsrill Rd. SE26—1H 93
Adams Rd. N17—9B 28
Adams Rd. Beck—9J 109
Adam's Row. W1—1E 74
Adams Sq. Bexh—2J 97
Adam St. WC2—1J 75
Ada Pl. E2—4E 60
Adare Wlk. SW16—9K 91
Ada Rd. SE5—8C 76
Ada Rd. Wemb—8H 39
Ada St. E8—4F 60
Adcock Wlk. Orp—6D 128
Adderley Gdns. SE9—1L 111
Adderley Gro. SW11—4E 90
Adderley Rd. Harr—8D 22
Adderley St. E14—9A 62
Addington Dri. N12—6B 26
Addington Gro. SE26—1J 109
Addington Heights. Croy
—3A 140
Addington Rd. E3—6L 61
Addington Rd. E16—7C 62
Addington Rd. N4—4L 43
Addington Rd. Croy—3L 123
Addington Rd. S Croy—3E 138
Addington Rd. W Wick—6A 126
Addington Sq. SE5—7B 76
Addington St. SE1—3K 75
Addington Village Rd. Croy
—8K & 7M 125
Addis Clo. Enf—3H 17
Addiscombe Av. Croy—3E 124
Addiscombe Clo. Harr—3G 39
Addiscombe Ct. Rd. Croy
—3C 124
Addiscombe Gro. Croy—4C 124
Addiscombe Rd. Croy—4C 124
Addiscombe Rd. Wat—6F 8
Addison Av. N14—8F 14
Addison Av. W11—2J 73
Addison Av. Houn—9A 70
Addison Bri. Pl. W14—5K 73
Addison Clo. N'wd—8E 20
Addison Clo. Orp—1A 128
Addison Cres. W14—4J 73
Addison Gdns. W14—4H 73
Addison Gdns. Surb—8K 103
Addison Gro. W4—4C 72
Addison Pl. SE25—8E 108
Addison Pl. W11—2J 73
Addison Pl. S'hall—1L 69
Addison Rd. E11—4E 46
Addison Rd. E17—3M 45
Addison Rd. SE25—8E 108
Addison Rd. W14—3J 73
Addison Rd. Brom—9H 111
Addison Rd. Enf—3G 17
Addison Rd. Ilf—8A 32
Addison Rd. Tedd—3F 102
Addisons Clo. Croy—4K 125
Addison Way. NW11—2K 41
Addison Way. Hay—9E 52
Addison Way. N'wd—8D 20

Addle Hill. EC4—9M 59
Addle St. EC2—9A 60
Adecroft Way. E Mol—7A 102
Adela Av. N Mald—9F 104
Adelaide Av. SE4—3K 93
Adelaide Clo. Enf—2C 16
Adelaide Clo. Stan—4E 22
Adelaide Cotts. W7—3D 70
Adelaide Ct. Beck—4L 109
Adelaide Gdns. Romf—3J 49
Adelaide Gro. W12—2E 72
Adelaide Pl. Wey—6B 116
Adelaide Rd. E10—8A 46
Adelaide Rd. NW3—3B 58
Adelaide Rd. W13—2E 70
Adelaide Rd. Chst—2M 111
Adelaide Rd. Houn—9J 69
Adelaide Rd. Ilf—7M 47
Adelaide Rd. Rich—3K 87
Adelaide Rd. S'hall—5J 69
Adelaide Rd. Surb—9J 103
Adelaide Rd. Tedd—3D 102
Adelaide Rd. W on T—5E 116
Adelaide St. WC2—1J 75
Adelaide Ter. Bren—6H 71
Adelaide Wlk. SW9—3L 91
Adela St. W10—7J 57
Adelina Gro. E1—8G 61
Adeline Pl. WC1—8H 59
Adelphi Cres. Hay—6D 52
Adelphi Cres. Horn—7E 50
Adelphi Rd. Eps—5B 134
Adelphi Ter. WC2—1J 75
Adelphi Way. Hay—6D 52
Adeney Clo. W6—7H 73
Aden Gro. N16—9B 44
Adenmore Rd. SE6—6L 93
Aden Rd. Enf—6J 17
Aden Rd. Ilf—5A 48
Aden Ter. N16—9B 44
Adhara Rd. N'wd—5D 20
Adie Rd. W6—4G 73
Adine Rd. E13—7F 62
Adler St. E1—9E 60
Adley St. E5—1J 61
Admaston Rd. SE18—8A 80
Admirals Clo. E18—2F 46
Admiral Seymour Rd. SE9
—3K 95
Admiral St. SE8—9L 77
Admirals Wlk. NW3—8A 42
Admiralty Rd. Tedd—3D 102
Adnams Wlk. Rain—2E 66
Adolf St. SE6—1M 109
Adolphus Rd. N4—6M 43
Adolphus St. SE8—8K 77
Adomar Rd. Dag—8J 49
Adpar St. W2—8B 58
Adrian Av. NW2—6F 40
Adrian M. SW10—7M 73
Adrian Rd. Abb L, Wat—4C 4
Adrienne Av. N'holt—6K 53
Ady's Rd. SE15—2D 92
Aerodrome Rd. NW9 & NW4
—1D 40
Aerodrome Way. Houn—7G 69
Aeroville. NW9—9C 24
Affleck St. N1—5K 59
Afghan Rd. SW11—1C 90
Agamenon Rd. NW6—1K 57
Agar Gro. Surb—4K 119
Agar Gro. NW1—3H 59
Agar Gro. Est. NW1—3H 59
Agar Pl. NW1—3G 59
Agar St. WC2—1J 75
Agate Rd. W6—4G 73
Agates La. Asht—9H 133
Agatha Clo. E1—2F 76
Agaton Rd. SE9—8A 96
Agave Rd. NW2—9G 41
Agdon St. EC1—7M 59
Agincourt Rd. NW3—9D 42
Agister Rd. Chig—5E 32
Agnes Av. Ilf—9L 47
Agnes Clo. E6—1L 79
Agnes Gdns. Dag—9H 49
Agnes Rd. W3—2D 72
Agnes St. E14—9K 61
Agnew Rd. SE23—6H 93
Agricola Pl. Enf—7D 16
Aidan Clo. Dag—9J 49
Aileen Wlk. E15—3D 62
Ailsa Av. Twic—4E 86
Ailsa Rd. Twic—4F 86
Ailsa St. E14—8A 62
Ainger Rd. NW3—3D 58
Ainsdale Cres. Pinn—1L 37
Ainsdale Rd. W5—7H 55
Ainsdale Rd. Wat—3G 21
Ainsley Av. Romf—4M 49
Ainsley Clo. S Croy—6F 138
Ainsley St. E2—6F 60
Ainslie Wlk. SW12—6F 90

Ainslie Wood Cres. E4—5M 29
Ainslie Wood Gdns. E4—5M 29
Ainslie Wood Rd. E4—5L 29
Ainsty St. SE16—3G 77
Ainsworth Clo. NW2—8E 40
Ainsworth Rd. E9—3G 61
Ainsworth Rd. Croy—4M 123
Ainsworth Way. NW8—4A 58
Aintree Av. E6—4J 63
Aintree Clo. Uxb—9F 142
Aintree Cres. Ilf—9A 32
Aintree Gro. Upm—8K 51
Aintree Rd. Gnfd—5F 54
Aintree St. SW6—8J 73
Airdrie Clo. N1—3K 59
Airedale Av. W4—5D 72
Airedale Av. S. W4—6D 72
Airedale Rd. SW12—6D 90
Airedale Rd. W5—4H 71
Airfield Way. Horn—2F 66
Airlie Gdns. W8—2L 73
Airlie Gdns. Ilf—6M 47
Airlinks Industrial Est. Houn
—6G 69
Airport Industrial Est. West
—7H 141
Air St. W1—1G 75
Airthrie Rd. Ilf—7F 48
Aisgill Av. W14—6K 73
Aisher Rd. SE28—1G 81
Aislibie Rd. SE12—3C 94
Aitken Clo. E8—4E 60
Aitken Rd. SE6—8M 93
Aitken Rd. Barn—7G 13
Aize Av. Ilf—9M 47
Ajax Av. NW9—1C 40
Ajax Rd. NW6—1L 57
Akehurst St. SW15—6E 88
Akenside Rd. NW3—1B 58
Akerman Rd. SW9—1M 91
Akerman Rd. Surb—1G 119
Alabama St. SE18—8B 80
Alacross Rd. W13—3G 71
Alan Clo. Dart—3G 99
Alandale Dri. Pinn—8F 20
Alan Dri. Barn—8J 13
Alan Gdns. Romf—5L 49
Alan Rd. SW19—2J 105
Alanthus Clo. SE12—5E 94
Alaska St. SE1—2L 75
Alba Clo. Hay—7H 53
Albacore Cres. SE13—5M 93
Alba Gdns. NW11—4J 41
Albain Cres. Ashf—8C 144
Alban Cres. Borwd—3M 11
Alban Cres. F'ham, Dart
—3L 131
Albans View. Wat—6F 4
Albany Clo. N15—2M 43
Albany Clo. SW14—3M 87
Albany Clo. Bex—6G 97
Albany Clo. Bush, Wat—8B 10
Albany Clo. Esh—9L 117
Albany Clo. Uxb—1E 142
Albany Cres. Edgw—7L 23
Albany Cres. Esh—8C 118
Albany M. King—3H 103
Albany Pde. Bren—7J 71
Albany Pk. Av. Enf—3G 17
Albany Pk. Rd. King—3H 103
Albany Pas. Rich—4J 87
Albany Pl. N7—9L 43
Albany Pl. Bren—7J 71
Albany Rd. E10—5L 45
Albany Rd. E12—9H 47
Albany Rd. E17—4J 45
Albany Rd. N4—4L 43
Albany Rd. N18—5F 28
Albany Rd. SE5—7B 76
Albany Rd. SW19—2M 105
Albany Rd. W13—1F 70
Albany Rd. Belv—7K 81
Albany Rd. Bex—6G 97
Albany Rd. Bren—7H 71
Albany Rd. Chst—2M 111
Albany Rd. Enf—1H 17
Albany Rd. Horn—6E 50
Albany Rd. N Mald—8B 104
Albany Rd. Rich—4K 87
Albany Rd. Romf—4K 49
Albany Rd. W on T—6H 117
Albany St. NW1—5F 58
Albany, The. Wfd G—4D 30
Albany View. Buck H—1E 30
Alba Pl. W11—9K 57
Albatross Gdns. S Croy—3H 139
Albatross St. SE18—8C 80
Albemarle App. Ilf—4M 47
Albemarle Av. Twic—7K 85
Albemarle Av. Wal X—1C 6
Albemarle Gdns. Ilf—4M 47
Albemarle Gdns. N Mald
—8B 104

Albemarle Pk. Stan—5G 23
Albemarle Rd. Barn—9C 14
Albemarle Rd. Beck—5M 109
Albemarle St. W1—1G 75
Albemarle Way. EC1—7M 59
Alberon Gdns. NW11—2K 41
Alberta Av. Sutt—7J 121
Alberta Rd. Enf—8D 16
Alberta Rd. Eri—9A 82
Alberta St. SE17—6M 75
Albert Av. E4—4L 29
Albert Av. SW8—8K 75
Albert Bri. SW3 & SW11—7C 74
Albert Bri. Rd. SW11—8C 74
Albert Carr Gdns. SW16
—2J 107
Albert Clo. N22—8H 27
Albert Ct. SW7—3B 74
Albert Cres. E4—4L 29
Albert Dri. SW19—8J 89
Albert Embkmt. SE1—6J 75
  (in two parts)
Albert Gdns. E1—9H 61
Albert Ga. SW1—3D 74
Albert Gro. SW20—5H 105
Albert M. W8—4A 74
Albert Pl. N3—8L 25
Albert Pl. N17—1D 44
Albert Pl. W8—4M 73
Albert Rd. E10—7A 46
Albert Rd. E16—2J 79
Albert Rd. E17—3L 45
Albert Rd. E18—1F 46
Albert Rd. N4—6K 43
Albert Rd. N15—4C 44
Albert Rd. N22—8G 27
Albert Rd. NW4—2H 41
Albert Rd. NW6—5K 57
Albert Rd. NW7—5D 24
Albert Rd. SE9—9J 95
Albert Rd. SE20—3H 109
Albert Rd. SE25—8F 108
Albert Rd. W5—7F 54
Albert Rd. Barn—6B 14
Albert Rd. Belv—6K 81
Albert Rd. Bex—5L 97
Albert Rd. Brom—9H 111
Albert Rd. Buck H—2H 31
Albert Rd. Dag—6L 49
Albert Rd. Dart—9G 99
Albert Rd. Eps—5D 134
Albert Rd. Hmptn—2A 102
Albert Rd. Harr—1A 38
Albert Rd. Hay—4C 68
Albert Rd. Houn—3L 85
Albert Rd. Ilf—8A 48
Albert Rd. King—6K 103
Albert Rd. Mitc—7D 106
Albert Rd. N Mald—8D 104
Albert Rd. Orp—7E 128
  (Chelsfield)
Albert Rd. Orp—1F 128
  (St Mary Cray)
Albert Rd. Rich—4J 87
Albert Rd. Romf—4D 50
Albert Rd. S'hall—4H 69
Albert Rd. Sutt—7B 122
Albert Rd. Tedd—3D 102
Albert Rd. Twic—7D 86
Albert Rd. Warl—9K 139
Albert Rd. W Dray—2J 143
Albert Rd. Est. Belv—6K 81
Albert Rd. N. Wat—5F 8
Albert Rd. S. Wat—5F 8
Albert Sq. E15—1C 62
Albert Sq. SW8—8K 75
Albert St. N12—5A 26
Albert St. NW1—4F 58
Albert St. Wat—6G 9
Albert Studios. SW11—9D 74
Albert Ter. NW1—4E 58
Albert Ter. NW10—4A 56
Albert Ter. Buck H—2J 31
Albert Ter. M. NW1—4E 58
Albert Wlk. E16—3L 79
Albion Av. N10—8E 26
Albion Av. SW8—1H 91
Albion Bldgs. EC1—8A 60
Albion Clo. W2—1C 74
Albion Clo. Romf—4B 50
Albion Dri. E8—3D 60
Albion Gdns. W6—5F 72
Albion Gro. N16—9C 44
Albion Hill. Lou—7G 19
Albion M. N1—3L 59
Albion M. NW6—5K 57
Albion M. W2—1C 74
Albion Pk. Lou—7H 19
Albion Pl. EC1—8B 60
Albion Pl. EC2—8M 59
Albion Pl. SE25—7E 108
Albion Rd. E17—1A 46

Albion Rd. N16—9B 44
Albion Rd. N17—9E 28
Albion Rd. Bexh—3L 97
Albion Rd. Hay—9C 52
Albion Rd. Houn—3L 85
Albion Rd. King—5A 104
Albion Rd. Sutt—8B 122
Albion Rd. Twic—7C 86
Albion Sq. E8—3D 60
Albion St. SE16—3G 77
Albion St. W2—9C 58
Albion St. Croy—3M 123
Albion Ter. E8—3D 60
Albion Vs. Rd. SE26—9G 93
Albion Way. SE13—3A 94
Albion Way. Wemb—8L 39
Abrighton Rd. SE5—2C 92
Albuera Clo. Enf—3L 15
Albury Av. Bexh—1J 97
Albury Av. Iswth—8D 70
Albury Av. Sutt—1G 135
Albury Clo. Hmptn—3M 101
Albury Dri. Pinn—8G 21
Albury Gro. Rd. Wal X—3D 6
Albury Ride. Wal X—4D 6
Albury Rd. Chess—7J 119
Albury Rd. W on T—8C 116
Albury St. SE8—7L 77
Albury Wlk. Wal X—4D 6
Albyfield. Brom—7K 111
Albyn Rd. SE8—9L 77
Albyns Clo. Rain—3E 66
Alcester Cres. E5—7F 44
Alcester Rd. Wall—6F 122
Alcock Clo. Wall—9H 123
Alcock Rd. Houn—8H 69
Alconbury Rd. E5—7E 44
Alcorn Clo. Sutt—4L 121
Alcott Clo. W7—8D 54
Aldam Pl. N16—7D 44
Aldborough Rd. Dag—2A 66
Aldborough Rd. Upm—7K 51
Aldborough Rd. N. Ilf—3D 48
Aldborough Rd. S. Ilf—6C 48
Aldbourne Rd. W12—2D 72
Aldbridge St. SE17—6C 76
Aldbury Av. Wemb—3M 55
Aldbury Clo. Wat—9H 5
Aldbury M. N9—9B 16
Aldeburgh Clo. E5—7F 44
Aldeburgh Pl. Wfd G—4E 30
Aldeburgh St. SE10—6E 78
Alden Av. E3—6D 62
Aldenham Av. Rad—1E 10
Aldenham Dri. Uxb—7F 142
Aldenham Rd. Wat & Borwd
—3C 10
Aldenham Rd. Wat & Bush, Wat
Aldenham St. NW1—5H 59
Aldenholme. Wey—8C 116
Aldensley Rd. W6—4F 72
Alder Av. Upm—9K 51
Alderbrook Rd. SW12—5F 90
Alderbury Rd. SW13—7E 72
Alder Clo. SE15—9F 76
Alder Clo. St Alb—1M 5
Alder Croft. Coul—8K 137
Alder Gro. NW2—7E 40
Aldergrove Gdns. Houn—1J 85
Aldergrove Wlk. Horn—2G 67
Alderholt Way. SE15—8C 76
Alderman Av. Bark—6E 64
Aldermanbury. EC2—9A 60
Aldermanbury Sq. EC2—8A 60
Alderman Judge Mall. King
—6J 103
Aldermans Hill. N13—4J 27
Alderman's Wlk. EC2—8C 60
Aldermary Rd. Brom—5E 110
Aldermaston St. W10—9H 57
Alder M. N19—7G 43
Alderminster Rd. SE1—6E 76
Aldermour Rd. SE6—9K 93
Alderney Av. Houn—8M 69
Alderney Gdns. N'holt—3K 53
Alderney Rd. E1—7H 61
Alderney Rd. Eri—8E 82
Alderney St. SW1—6F 74
Alder Rd. SW14—2B 88
Alder Rd. Sidc—9D 96
Alder Rd. Uxb—2A 142
Alders. Av. Wfd G—6C 30
Aldersbrook Av. Enf—4C 16
Aldersbrook Dri. King—3A 103
Aldersbrook La. E12—8K 47
Aldersbrook Rd.—7F 46
  E11 1-13
  E12 remainder
Alders Clo. E11—8F 46
Alders Clo. Edgw—5A 24
Aldersey Gdns. Bark—2B 64
Aldersford Clo. SE4—3H 93
Aldersgate St. EC1—8A 60

Aldersgrove. E Mol—9B 102
Aldersgrove. Wal A—7L 7
Aldersgrove Av. SE9—9H 95
Aldershot Rd. NW6—4K 57
Aldersmead Av. Croy—1H 125
Aldersmead Rd. Beck—4J 109
Alderson St. W10—7J 57
Alders Rd. Edgw—5A 24
Alders, The. N21—8M 15
Alders, The. Felt—1J 101
Alders, The. Houn—7K 69
Alders, The. W Wick—4M 125
Alderton Clo. Lou—6L 19
Alderton Cres. NW4—3F 40
Alderton Hall La. Lou—6L 19
Alderton Hill. Lou—7J 19
Alderton Rise. Lou—6L 19
Alderton Rd. SE24—2A 92
Alderton Rd. Croy—2D 124
Alderton Way. Lou—7K 19
Alderville Rd. SW6—1K 89
Alder Way. Swan—6B 114
Alderwick Dri. Houn—2B 86
Alderwood Rd. SE9—5B 96
Aldford St. W1—2E 74
Aldgate. EC3—9D 60
Aldgate High St. EC3—9D 60
Aldine Pl. W12—3G 73
Aldine St. W12—3G 73
Aldingham Gdns. Horn—1E 66
Aldington Rd. SE18—4H 79
Aldis M. SW17—2C 106
Aldis Rd. SW17—2C 106
Aldred Rd. NW6—1L 57
Aldren Rd. SW17—9A 90
Aldrich Cres. Croy—1A 140
Aldriche Way. E4—6A 30
Aldrich Ter. SW18—8A 90
Aldridge Av. Edgw—3M 23
Aldridge Av. Enf—2L 17
Aldridge Av. Ruis—7G 37
Aldridge Av. Stan—8J 23
Aldridge Rise. N Mald—2C 120
Aldridge Rd. Vs. W11—8K 57
Aldridge Wlk. N14—9J 15
Aldrington Rd. SW16—2G 107
Aldsworth Clo. W9—7M 57
Aldwick Clo. SE9—9B 96
Aldwick Rd. Croy—5K 123
Aldworth Rd. E15—3C 62
Aldwych. WC2—9K 59
Aldwych Av. Ilf—2A 48
Aldwych Clo. Horn—7F 50
Alers Rd. Bexh—4H 97
Alexander Av. NW10—3F 56
Alexander Clo. Brom—3E 126
Alexander Clo. Sidc—5C 96
Alexander Clo. Twic—8D 86
Alexander M. W2—9M 57
Alexander Pl. SW7—5C 74
Alexander Rd. N19—8J 43
Alexander Rd. Bexh—1H 97
Alexander Rd. Chst—3M 111
Alexander Rd. Coul—7F 136
Alexander Sq. SW3—5C 74
Alexander St. W2—9M 57
Alexandra Av. N22—8H 27
Alexandra Av. SW11—9E 74
Alexandra Av. W4—8B 72
Alexandra Av. Harr—6K 37
Alexandra Av. S'hall—1K 69
Alexandra Av. Sutt—5L 121
Alexandra Av. Warl—9K 139
Alexandra Clo. Ashf—4B 100
Alexandra Clo. Harr—8L 37
Alexandra Clo. Swan—6C 114
Alexandra Clo. W on T—4E 116
Alexandra Cotts. SE14—9K 77
Alexandra Ct. N14—7G 15
Alexandra Cres. Brom—3D 110
Alexandra Dri. SE19—2C 108
Alexandra Dri. Surb—2L 119
Alexandra Gdns. N10—2F 42
Alexandra Gdns. W4—8C 72
Alexandra Gdns. Cars—1E 136
Alexandra Gdns. Houn—1M 85
Alexandra Gro. N4—6M 43
Alexandra Gro. N12—5M 25
Alexandra M. SW19—3K 105
Alexandra Pk. Rd.—9F 26
    N10 1-121 & 2-126c
    N22 remainder
Alexandra Pl. NW8—4A 58
Alexandra Pl. SE25—9B 108
Alexandra Pl. Croy—3C 124
Alexandra Rd. E6—6L 63
Alexandra Rd. E10—8A 46
Alexandra Rd. E17—5K 45
Alexandra Rd. E18—1F 46
Alexandra Rd. N8—1L 43
Alexandra Rd. N9—9F 16

Alexandra Rd. N10—8F 26
Alexandra Rd. N15—3B 44
Alexandra Rd. NW4—2H 41
Alexandra Rd. NW8—4A 58
Alexandra Rd. SE26—3H 109
Alexandra Rd. SW14—2B 88
Alexandra Rd. SW19—3K 105
Alexandra Rd. W4—3B 72
Alexandra Rd. Ashf—4B 100
Alexandra Rd. Borwd—3B 12
Alexandra Rd. Bren—7H 71
Alexandra Rd. Croy—3C 124
Alexandra Rd. Enf—6H 17
Alexandra Rd. Eps—5D 134
Alexandra Rd. Eri—7D 82
Alexandra Rd. Houn—1M 85
Alexandra Rd. King—4L 103
Alexandra Rd. Mitc—4C 106
Alexandra Rd. Rain—4D 66
Alexandra Rd. Rich—1K 87
Alexandra Rd. Romf—4D 50
Alexandra Rd. Romf—4H 49
    (Chadwell Heath)
Alexandra Rd. Th Dit—9D 102
Alexandra Rd. Twic—5G 87
Alexandra Rd. Uxb—5B 142
Alexandra Rd. Warl—9K 139
Alexandra Rd. Wat—4E 8
Alexandra Sq. Mord—9L 105
Alexandra St. E16—8E 62
Alexandra St. SE14—8J 77
Alexandra Wlk. SE19—3C 108
Alexandra Way. Wal X—7F 6
Alexandria Rd. W13—1F 70
Alexis St. SE16—5E 76
Alfan La. Dart—2B 114
Alfearn Rd. E5—9G 45
Alford Grn. Croy—8B 126
Alford Pl. N1—5A 60
Alford Rd. SW8—9H 75
Alford Rd. Eri—6A 82
Alfoxton Av. N15—2M 43
Alfreda St. SW11—9F 74
Alfred M. W1—8H 59
Alfred Pl. WC1—8H 59
Alfred Rd. E15—1D 62
Alfred Rd. SE25—9E 108
Alfred Rd. W2—8L 57
Alfred Rd. W3—2A 72
Alfred Rd. Belv—6K 81
Alfred Rd. Buck H—2H 31
Alfred Rd. Dart—1K 115
Alfred Rd. Felt—8G 85
Alfred Rd. King—7K 103
Alfred Rd. Sutt—7A 122
Alfred's Gdns. Bark—5C 64
Alfred St. E3—6K 61
Alfred St. E16—1D 78
Alfreds Way. Bark—6M 63
Alfreton Clo. SW19—9H 89
Alfriston. Surb—1K 119
Alfriston Av. Croy—2J 123
Alfriston Av. Harr—4L 37
Alfriston Clo. Surb—1K 119
Alfriston Rd. SW11—4D 90
Algar Clo. Iswth—2E 86
Algar Clo. Stan—5D 22
Algar Rd. Iswth—2E 86
Algarve Rd. SW18—7M 89
Algernon Rd. NW4—4E 40
Algernon Rd. NW6—4L 57
Algernon Rd. SE13—3M 93
Algers Clo. Lou—7H 19
Algers Mead. Lou—7H 19
Algers Rd. Lou—7J 19
Algiers Rd. SE13—3L 93
Alibon Gdns. Dag—1L 65
Alibon Rd. Dag—1L 65
Alice St. SE1—4C 76
Alington Cres. NW9—5A 40
Alington Gro. Wall—1G 137
Alison Clo. Croy—3H 125
Aliwal Rd. SW11—3C 90
Alkerden Rd. W4—6C 72
Alkham Rd. N16—7D 44
Allan Clo. N Mald—9B 104
Allandale Av. N3—1J 41
Allandale Pl. Orp—5H 129
Allandale Rd. Enf—9D 6
Allandale Rd. Horn—5D 50
Allan Way. W3—8A 56
Allard Clo. Orp—2G 129
Allard Cres. Bush, Wat—2A 22
Allardyce St. SW4—3K 91
Allbrook Clo. Tedd—2C 102
Allcroft Rd. NW5—1E 58
Allenby Av. S Croy—1A 138
Allenby Clo. Gnfd—6L 53

Allenby Dri. Horn—6J 51
Allenby Rd. SE23—9J 93
Allenby Rd. S'hall—9L 53
Allenby Rd. West—9J 141
Allen Clo. Sun—5F 100
Allendale Av. S'hall—9L 53
Allendale Clo. SE5—9B 76
Allendale Clo. SE26—2H 109
Allendale Rd. Gnfd—2F 54
Allen Edwards Dri. SW8—9J 75
Allen Pl. Twic—7E 86
Allen Rd. E3—4K 61
Allen Rd. N16—9C 44
Allen Rd. Beck—6H 109
Allen Rd. Croy—3L 123
Allen Rd. Rain—6G 67
Allen Rd. Sun—5F 100
Allensbury Pl. NW1—3H 59
Allenswood Rd. SE9—2J 95
Allerford Ct. Harr—3A 38
Allerford Rd. SE6—9M 93
Allerton Clo. Borwd—2K 11
Allerton Rd. N16—7A 44
Allerton Rd. Borwd—2J 11
Allerton Wlk. N7—7K 43
Allestree Rd. SW6—8J 73
Alleyn Cres. SE21—8B 92
Alleyn Pk. SE21—8B 92
Alleyn Pk. S'hall—6L 69
Alleyn Rd. SE21—9B 92
Allfarthing La. SW18—5M 89
Allgood Clo. Mord—1H 121
Allgood St. E2—5D 60
Allhallows La. EC4—1B 76
All Hallows Rd. E6—8H 63
All Hallows Rd. N17—8C 28
Alliance Rd. E13—0G 63
Alliance Rd. SE18—7E 80
Alliance Rd. W3—7M 55
Allingham Clo. W7—1D 70
Allingham St. N1—5A 60
Allington Av. N17—6C 28
Allington Clo. SW19—2H 105
Allington Ct. Enf—7H 17
Allington Rd. NW4—4F 40
Allington Rd. W10—5J 57
Allington Rd. Harr—3A 38
Allington Rd. Orp—4B 128
Allington St. SW1—4F 74
Allison Clo. SE10—9A 78
Allison Clo. Wal A—5M 7
Allison Gro. SE21—7C 92
Allison Rd. N8—3L 43
Allison Rd. W3—9A 56
Allitsen Rd. NW8—5C 58
Allnutt Way. SW4—4H 91
Alloa Rd. SE8—6J 77
Alloa Rd. Ilf—7E 48
Allonby Gdns. Wemb—6G 39
Alloway Rd. E3—6L 61
All Saints Clo. N9—2E 28
All Saints Clo. Chig—3E 32
All Saints Cres. Wat—6H 5
All Saints Dri. SE3—1C 94
All Saints Dri. S Croy—4D 138
All Saints M. Harr—6C 22
All Saints Pas. SW18—4A 90
All Saint's Rd. SW19—4A 106
All Saints Rd. W3—4A 72
All Saints Rd. W11—8K 57
All Saints Rd. Sutt—5M 121
All Saints St. N1—5K 59
Allsop Pl. NW1—7D 58
All Souls Av. NW10—5F 56
All Soul's Pl. W1—8F 58
Allum Clo. Borwd—6J 11
Allum La. Borwd—7J 11
Allum Way. N20—1A 26
Allwood Clo. SE26—1J 109
Alma Av. E4—7A 30
Alma Av. Horn—9J 51
Almack Rd. E5—9G 45
Alma Ct. Borwd—2K 11
Alma Cres. Sutt—7J 121
Alma Gro. SE1—5D 76
Alma Pl. NW10—6F 56
Alma Pl. SE19 4D 108
Alma Pl. Sun—4E 100
Alma Pl. T Hth—9L 107
Alma Rd. N10—7F 26
Alma Rd. SW18—3A 90
Alma Rd. Cars—7C 122
Alma Rd. Enf—2J 17
Alma Rd. Esh—3C 118
Alma Rd. Orp—4H 129
Alma Rd. Sidc—9E 96
Alma Rd. S'hall—1J 69
Alma Row. Harr—8B 22
Alma Sq. NW8—5A 58
Alma St. E15—2B 62

Alma St. NW5—2F 58
Alma Ter. SW18—6B 90
Almeida St. N1—4M 59
Almeric Rd. SW11—3D 90
Almer Rd. SW20—4E 104
Almington St. N4—6K 43
Almond Av. W5—4J 71
Almond Av. Cars—4D 122
Almond Av. Uxb—8A 36
Almond Av. W Dray—4L 143
Almond Clo. SE15—1E 92
Almond Clo. Brom—2L 127
Almond Clo. Hay—1C 68
Almond Clo. Ruis—8D 36
Almond Clo. Shep—6A 100
Almond Dri. Swan—6B 114
Almond Gro. Bren—8F 70
Almond Rd. N17—2E 28
Almond Rd. SE16—5F 76
Almond Rd. Eps—3B 134
Almonds Av. Buck H—2E 30
Almond Way. Borwd—6M 11
Almond Way. Brom—2L 127
Almond Way. Harr—9A 22
Almond Way. Mitc—9H 107
Almorah Rd. N1—3B 60
Almorah Rd. Houn—9H 69
Almshouse La. Chess—1H 133
Almshouse La. Enf—1F 16
Alnwick Av. E16—9H 63
Alnwick Gro. Mord—8M 105
Alnwick Rd. E16—9G 63
Alnwick Rd. SE12—6F 94
Alperton La. Gnfd—6G 55
Alperton St. W10—7K 57
Alpha Clo. NW1—7C 58
Alpha Gro. E14—3L 77
Alpha Pl. NW6—5L 57
Alpha Pl. SW3—7C 74
Alpha Rd. E4—3L 29
Alpha Rd. N18—6E 28
Alpha Rd. SE14—9K 77
Alpha Rd. Croy—3C 124
Alpha Rd. Enf—6J 17
Alpha Rd. Surb—1K 119
Alpha Rd. Tedd—2B 102
Alpha Rd. Uxb—7J 142
Alpha St. SE15—1E 92
Alpine Av. Surb—4A 120
Alpine Clo. Croy—5C 124
Alpine Copse. Brom—6L 111
Alpine Rd. SE16—5G 77
Alpine Rd. W on T—2E 116
Alpine Wlk. Stan—2C 22
Alpine Way. E6—8L 63
Alric Av. NW10—3B 56
Alric Av. N Mald—7C 104
Alroy Rd. N4—5L 43
Alsace Rd. SE17—6C 76
Alscot Rd. SE1—4D 76
Alscot Way. SE1—5D 76
Alsike Rd. SE2 & Eri—4H 81
Alsom Av. Wor Pk—6E 120
Alston Clo. Surb—2F 118
Alston Rd. N18—5F 28
Alston Rd. SW17—1B 106
Alston Rd. Barn—5J 13
Altair Clo. N17—6D 28
Altair Way. N'wd—4D 20
Altash Way. SE9—8K 95
Altenburg Av. W13—4F 70
Altenburg Gdns. SW11—3D 90
Alt Gro. SW19—4K 105
Altham Rd. Pinn—7J 21
Althea St. SW6—1M 89
Althorne Gdns. E18—2D 46
Althorne Way. Dag—7L 49
Althorpe M. SW11—9B 74
Althorpe Rd. Harr—3A 38
Althorp Rd. SW17—7D 90
Altmore Av. E6—3K 63
Alton Av. Stan—7D 22
Alton Clo. Bex—2J 97
Alton Clo. Iswth—1D 86
Alton Gdns. Beck—4L 109
Alton Gdns. Twic—6B 86
Alton Rd. N17—1B 44
Alton Rd. SW15—7E 88
Alton Rd. Croy—5L 123
Alton Rd. Rich—3J 87
Alton St. E14—9M 61
Altyre Clo. Beck—9K 109
Altyre Rd. Croy—4B 124
Altyre Way. Beck—9K 109
Alvanley Gdns. NW6—1M 57
Alva Way. Wat—2H 21
Alverstoke Rd. Romf—7J 35
Alverstone Av. SW19—8L 89
Alverstone Av. Barn—9C 14
Alverstone Gdns. SE9—8K 95
Alverstone Rd. E12—9L 47
Alverstone Rd. NW2—3G 57
Alverstone Rd. N Mald—8D 104

Alverstone Rd. Wemb—6K 39
Alverston Gdns. SE25—9C 108
Alverton St. SE8—6K 77
Alveston Av. Harr—1F 38
Alvey St. SE17—6C 76
Alvington Cres. E8—1D 60
Alway Av. Eps—7B 120
Alwold Cres. SE12—5F 94
Alwyn Av. W4—6B 72
Alwyn Clo. Borwd—7K 11
Alwyn Clo. Croy—9M 125
Alwyne La. N1—3M 59
Alwyne Pl. N1—2A 60
Alwyne Rd. N1—3A 60
Alwyne Rd. SW19—3K 105
Alwyne Rd. W7—1C 70
Alwyne Sq. N1—2A 60
Alwyne Vs. N1—3M 59
Alwyn Gdns. W3—9M 55
Alyth Gdns. NW11—4L 41
Amalgamated Rd. Bren—7F 70
Amanda Clo. Ilf—6B 32
Amazon St. E1—9E 60
Ambassador Clo. Houn—1J 85
Amber Av. E17—8J 29
Amberden Av. N3—1L 41
Ambergate St. SE17—6M 75
Amberley Clo. Orp—7D 128
Amberley Clo. Pinn—1K 37
Amberley Ct. Sidc—2G 113
Amberley Gdns. Enf—9C 16
Amberley Gdns. Eps—6D 120
Amberley Gro. SE26—2F 108
Amberley Gro. Croy—2D 124
Amberley Rd. E10—5M 45
Amberley Rd. N13—2K 27
Amberley Rd. SE2—7H 81
Amberley Rd. W9—8L 57
Amberley Rd. Buck H—1G 31
Amberley Rd. Enf—9B 16
Amberley Way. Houn—4G 85
Amberley Way. Mord—2K 121
Amberley Way. Romf—2M 49
Amber St. E15—2B 62
Amberwood Rise. N Mald—1C 120
Amblecote Clo. SE12—9F 94
Amblecote Rd. SE12—9F 94
Ambler Rd. N4—8M 43
Ambleside. Brom—3B 110
Ambleside Av. SW16—1H 107
Ambleside Av. Beck—9J 109
Ambleside Av. Horn—1F 66
Ambleside Av. W on T—3G 117
Ambleside Clo. E9—1G 61
Ambleside Cres. Enf—5H 17
Ambleside Gdns. SW16—2H 107
Ambleside Gdns. Ilf—3J 47
Ambleside Gdns. S Croy—2H 139
Ambleside Gdns. Sutt—8A 122
Ambleside Gdns. Wemb—6H 39
Ambleside Rd. NW10—3D 56
Ambleside Rd. Bexh—1L 97
Ambrey Way. Wall—1H 137
Ambrooke Rd. Belv—4L 81
Ambrosden Av. SW1—4G 75
Ambrose Av. NW11—4K 41
Ambrose Clo. Orp—5D 128
Ambrose St. SE16—5F 76
Ambrose Wlk. E3—5L 61
Amelia St. SE17—6A 76
Amen Corner. EC4—9M 59
Amen Corner. SW17—3D 106
Amen Ct. EC4—9M 59
America Sq. EC3—1D 76
America St. SE1—2A 76
Amerland Rd. SW18—5M 89
Amersham Av. N18—6B 28
Amersham Clo. Romf—6K 35
Amersham Dri. Romf—6K 35
Amersham Gro. SE14—8K 77
Amersham Rd. SE14—9M 77
Amersham Rd. Croy—1A 124
Amersham Rd. Harr—4C 38
Amersham Rd. Romf—6K 35
Amersham Vale. SE14—8K 77
Amersham Wlk. Romf—6K 35
Amery Gdns. NW10—4F 56
Amery Gdns. Romf—1H 51
Amery Rd. Harr—7E 38
Amesbury Av. SW2—8J 91
Amesbury Clo. Wor Pk—3G 121
Amesbury Dri. E4—8M 17
Amesbury Rd. Brom—7H 111
Amesbury Rd. Dag—3H 65
Amesbury Rd. Felt—8H 85
Amethyst Rd. E15—9B 46
Amhen Way. SE22—4C 92
Amherst Av. W13—9G 55
Amherst Clo. Orp—8F 112

Amherst Dri. Orp—8D 112
Amherst Rd. W13—9G 55
Amhurst Gdns. Iswth—1E 86
Amhurst Pk. N16—5B 44
Amhurst Pas. E8—1E 60
Amhurst Rd.—9D 44
  E8 1-233 & 2-240
  N16 remainder
Amhurst Ter. E8—9E 44
Amidas Gdns. Dag—9F 48
Amiel St. E1—7G 61
Amies St. SW11—2D 90
Amina Way. SE16—4E 76
Amis Av. Eps—8M 119
Amity Gro. SW20—5G 105
Amity Rd. E15—3D 62
Amner Rd. SW11—5E 90
Amor Rd. W6—4G 73
Amos Est. SE16—2H 77
Amott Rd. SE15—2E 92
Amoy Pl. E14—1L 77
Ampleforth Rd. SE2—3F 80
Ampthill Est. NW1—5G 59
Ampton Pl. WC1—6K 59
Ampton St. WC1—6K 59
Amroth Clo. SE23—7F 92
Amwell Clo. Enf—7B 16
Amwell Ct. Wal A—6M 7
Amwell St. EC1—6L 59
Amwell View. Ilf—5F 32
Amyand Cotts. Twic—5F 86
Amyand La. Twic—6F 86
Amyand Pk. Gdns. Twic—6F 86
Amyand Pk. Rd. Twic—6E 86
Amyruth Rd. SE4—4L 93
Anatola Rd. N19—7G 43
Ancaster Cres. N Mald—1E 120
Ancaster Rd. Beck—7H 109
Ancaster St. SE18—8C 80
Anchorage Clo. SW19—2L 105
Anchor & Hope La. SE7—4F 78
Anchor Bay Industrial Est. Eri
  —7E 82
Anchor Clo. Wal X—1D 6
Anchor Ct. Enf—7C 16
Anchor Dri. Rain—7F 66
Anchor M. SW12—5F 90
Anchor St. SE16—5F 76
Anchor Yd. EC1—7A 60
Ancill Clo. W6—7H 73
Ancona Rd. NW10—5E 56
Ancona Rd. SE18—6B 80
Andalus Rd. SW9—2J 91
Ander Clo. Wemb—9H 39
Anderson Clo. Eps—4M 133
Anderson Dri. Ashf—1A 100
Anderson Pl. Houn—3M 85
Anderson Rd. E9—2H 61
Anderson Rd. Wey—5B 116
Anderson Rd. Wfd G—1H 47
Anderson St. SW3—6D 74
Anderson Way. Belv—3M 81
Anderton Clo. SE5—2B 92
Andorra Ct. Brom—5G 111
Andover Clo. Eps—3B 134
Andover Clo. Gnfd—7M 53
Andover Clo. Uxb—5A 142
Andover Pl. NW6—5M 57
Andover Rd. N7—7K 43
Andover Rd. Orp—3C 128
Andover Rd. Twic—7B 86
Andreck Ct. Beck—6A 110
Andre St. E8—1E 60
Andrew Borde St. WC2—9H 59
Andrew Clo. Bex—4B 98
Andrew Clo. Ilf—6B 32
Andrewes Clo. E6—9J 63
Andrews Clo. Buck H—2G 31
Andrew's Clo. Eps—6D 134
Andrew's Clo. Orp—6H 113
Andrews Clo. Wor Pk—4H 121
Andrew's La. Wal X—1A 6
  (in two parts)
Andrew's Rd. E8—4F 60
Andrew St. E14—9A 62
Andrews Wlk. SE17—7M 75
Andromeda Ct. Romf—6G 35
Andwell Clo. SE2—3F 80
Anerley Gro. SE19—3D 108
Anerley Hill. SE19—3D 108
Anerley Pk. SE20—4E 108
Anerley Pk. Rd. SE20—4F 108
Anerley Rd.—4E 108
  SE19 19-69 & 54-120
  SE20 remainder
Anerley Sta. Rd. SE20—5F 108
Anerley St. SW11—1D 90
Anerley Vale. SE19—3D 108
Aneurin Bevan Ho. N11—7H 27
Anfield Clo. SW12—6G 91
Angas Ct. Wey—7A 116
Angel All. E1—9D 60

Angel Centre, The. N1 & EC1
  —5L 59
Angel Clo. N18—4D 28
Angel Ct. EC2—9B 60
Angel Ct. SW1—2G 75
Angelfield. Houn—3M 85
Angel Hill. Sutt—5M 121
Angelica Gdns. Croy—3H 125
Angel La. E15—2B 62
Angell La. Hay—8B 52
Angell Pk. Gdns. SW9—2L 91
Angell Rd. SW9—2L 91
Angel M. N1—5L 59
Angel Pas. EC4—1B 76
Angel Pl. N18—5E 28
Angel Pl. SE1—3B 76
Angel Rd. N18—5E 28
Angel Rd. Harr—4C 38
Angel Rd. Th Dit—2E 118
Angel St. EC1—9A 60
Angel Wlk. W6—5G 73
Angel Way. Romf—3C 50
Angerstein La. SE3—9D 78
Angle Clo. Uxb—4E 142
Angle Grn. Dag—6G 49
Anglers Clo. Rich—1G 103
Angler's La. NW5—2F 58
Anglesea Av. SE18—5M 79
Anglesea Rd. SE18—5M 79
Anglesea Rd. King—8H 103
Anglesea Rd. Orp—1G 129
Anglesea St. E1—7E 60
Anglesey Clo. Ashf—9E 144
Anglesey Ct. Rd. Cars—8E 122
Anglesey Dri. Rain—7E 66
Anglesey Gdns. Cars—8E 122
Anglesey Rd. Enf—6F 16
Anglesey Rd. Wat—5G 21
Anglesmede Cres. Pinn—1L 37
Anglesmede Way. Pinn—1L 37
Angles Rd. SW16—1J 107
Anglo Rd. E3—5K 61
Angus Clo. Chess—7L 119
Angus Dri. Ruis—9G 37
Angus Gdns. NW9—8B 24
Angus Rd. E13—6G 63
Angus St. SE14—8J 77
Anhalt Rd. SW11—8C 74
Ankerdine Cres. SE18—8M 79
Anlaby Rd. Tedd—2C 102
Anley Rd. W14—3H 73
Anmersh Gro. Stan—8H 23
Annabel Clo. E14—9M 61
Anna Clo. E8—4D 60
Annandale Gro. Uxb—8A 36
Annandale Rd. SE10—7D 78
Annandale Rd. W4—6C 72
Annandale Rd. Croy—4E 124
Annandale Rd. Sidc—6C 96
Annan Way. Romf—8C 34
Anne Boleyn's Wlk. King
  —2J 103
Anne Boleyn's Wlk. Sutt
  —9H 121
Anne of Cleves Rd. Dart—4H 99
Annesley Av. NW9—1B 40
Annesley Clo. NW10—8C 40
Annesley Dri. Croy—5K 125
Annesley Rd. SE3—9F 78
Annesley Wlk. N19—7G 43
Anne St. E13—7E 62
Annett Clo. Shep—8C 100
Annette Clo. Harr—9C 22
Annette Rd. N7—8K 43
Annett Rd. W on T—2E 116
Annett's Cres. N1—3A 60
Anne Way. E Mol—8M 101
Anne Way. Ilf—6A 32
Annie Besant Clo. E3—4K 61
Anning St. EC2—7C 60
Annington Rd. N2—1D 42
Annis Rd. E9—2J 61
Ann La. SW10—7B 74
Ann St. SE18—6A 80
  (in two parts)
Annsworthy Av. T Hth—7B 108
Annsworthy Cres. SE25
  —6B 108
Ansdale Clo. Orp—3B 128
Ansdell Rd. SE15—1G 93
Ansdell St. W8—4M 73
Ansdell Ter. W8—4M 73
Ansell Gro. Cars—3D 122
Ansell Rd. SW17—9C 90
Anselm Clo. Croy—5D 124
Anselm Rd. SW6—7L 73
Anselm Rd. Pinn—7K 21
Ansford Rd. Brom—2A 110
Anson Clo. Romf—9M 33
Anson Rd. N7—9H 43
Anson Rd. NW2—1F 56
Anson Ter. N'holt—2M 53

Anson Wlk. N'wd—4A 20
Anstead Dri. Rain—5E 66
Anstey Rd. E16—8F 62
Anstey Rd. SE15—2E 92
Anstey Wlk. N15—2M 43
Anstice Clo. W4—8C 72
Anstridge Path. SE9—5B 96
Anstridge Rd. SE9—5B 96
Antelope Rd. SE18—4K 79
Anthony Clo. Wat—1G 21
Anthony La. Swan—5E 114
Anthony Rd. SE25—1E 124
Anthony Rd. Borwd—4K 11
Anthony Rd. Gnfd—6C 54
Anthony Rd. Well—9E 80
Anthony St. E1—9F 60
Anthus M. N'wd—7C 20
Antill Rd. E3—6J 61
Antill Rd. N15—2E 44
Antlers Hill. E4—7M 17
Anton Cres. Sutt—5L 121
Antoneys Clo. Pinn—9H 21
Anton St. E8—1E 60
Antrim Gro. NW3—2D 58
Antrim Rd. NW3—2D 58
Antrobus Clo. Sutt—7K 121
Antrobus Rd. W4—5A 72
Anvil Rd. Sun—7E 100
Anworth Clo. Wfd G—6F 30
Apeldoorn Dri. Wall—1J 137
Aperfield Rd. Eri—7D 82
Aperfield Rd. West—9J 141
Apex Clo. Beck—5M 109
Apex Clo. Wey—5B 116
Aplin Way. Iswth—9C 70
Apollo Av. Brom—5F 110
Apollo Av. N'wd—5E 20
Apollo Clo. Horn—7F 50
Apollo Pl. SW10—8B 74
Apothecary St. EC4—9M 59
Appach Rd. SW2—5L 91
Appleby Clo. E4—6A 30
Appleby Clo. N15—3B 44
Appleby Clo. Twic—8B 86
Appleby Dri. Romf—5G 35
Appleby Grn. Romf—5G 35
Appleby Rd. E8—3E 60
Appleby Rd. E16—9D 62
Appleby St. E2—5D 60
Applecroft. St Alb—1M 5
Appledore Av. Bexh—9A 82
Appledore Av. Ruis—8G 37
Appledore Clo. SW17—8D 90
Appledore Clo. Brom—9E 110
Appledore Clo. Edgw—8L 23
Appledore Clo. Romf—8G 35
Appledore Cres. Sidc—9C 96
Appleford. Rd. W10—7J 57
Apple Garth. Bren—5H 71
Applegarth. Croy—9M 125
  (in two parts)
Applegarth. Esh—7D 118
Applegarth Dri. Ilf—2D 48
Applegarth Rd. SE28—2F 80
Applegarth Rd. W14—4H 73
Apple Gro. Chess—6J 119
Apple Gro. Enf—5C 16
Apple Mkt. King—6H 103
Appleton Gdns. N Mald—1E 120
Appleton Rd. SE9—2J 95
Appleton Rd. Lou—5M 19
Appleton Way. Horn—7H 51
Apple Tree Av. Uxb & W Dray
  —8D 142
Appletree Wlk. Wat—7F 4
Apple Tree Yd. SW1—2G 75
Applewood Clo. NW2—8F 40
Appleyard Ter. Enf—1G 17
Appold St. EC2—8C 60
Appold St. Eri—7D 82
Approach Rd. E2—5G 61
Approach Rd. SW20—6G 105
Approach Rd. Ashf—3A 100
Approach Rd. Barn—6B 14
Approach Rd. E Mol—9L 101
Approach Rd. Purl—4M 137
Approach, The. NW4—3H 41
Approach, The. W3—9B 56
Approach, The. Enf—4F 16
Approach, The. Orp—4D 128
Approach, The. Upm—8M 51
Aprey Gdns. NW4—2G 41
April Clo. W7—1C 70
April Clo. Felt—9E 84
April Clo. Orp—7D 128
April Glen. SE23—9H 93
April St. E8—9D 44
Apsley Clo. Harr—3A 38
Apsley Rd. E17—3K 45
Apsley Rd. SE25—8F 108
Apsley Rd. N Mald—7A 104
Apsley Way. W1—3E 74

Aquarius Way. N'wd—5E 20
Aquila Clo. N'wd—4E 20
Aquila St. NW8—5B 58
Aquinas St. SE1—2L 75
Arabella Dri. SW15—3C 88
Arabia Clo. E4—9B 18
Arabin Rd. SE4—3K 93
Aragon Av. Eps—2F 134
Aragon Av. Th Dit—9D 102
Aragon Clo. Croy—2C 140
Aragon Dri. Ilf—7A 32
Aragon Dri. Ruis—6H 37
Aragon Rd. King—2J 103
Aragon Rd. Mord—1H 121
Arandora Cres. Romf—4F 48
Aran Dri. Stan—4G 23
Arbery Rd. E3—6J 61
Arbor Clo. Beck—6M 109
Arbor Rd. E4—3B 30
Arbour Rd. Enf—5H 17
Arbour Sq. E1—9H 61
Arbour Way. Horn—1F 66
Arbroath Grn. Wat—3F 20
Arbroath Rd. SE9—2J 95
Arbrook Clo. Orp—7E 112
Arbrook La. Esh—8A 118
Arbuthnot La. Bex—5J 97
Arbuthnot Rd. SE14—1H 93
Arbutus St. E8—4D 60
Arcade Pl. Romf—3C 50
Arcadia Av. N3—9L 25
Arcadian Av. Bex—5J 97
Arcadian Clo. Bex—5J 97
Arcadian Gdns. N22—7K 27
Arcadian Rd. Bex—5J 97
Arcadia St. E14—9L 61
Archbishop's Pl. SW2—6K 91
Archdale Rd. SE22—3D 92
Archel Rd. W14—7K 73
Archer Rd. SE25—8F 108
Archer Rd. Orp—9E 112
Archers Dri. Enf—4G 17
Archer St. W1—1H 75
Archer Way. Swan—6D 114
Archery Clo. W2—9C 58
Archery Clo. Harr—1D 38
Archery Rd. SE9—4K 95
Arches, The. Harr—7M 37
Archibald M. W1—1E 74
Archibald Rd. N7—9H 43
Archibald Rd. Romf—8L 35
Archibald St. E3—6L 61
Arch Rd. W on T—5H 117
Arch Way. Romf—6F 34
Archway Clo. N19—7G 43
Archway Clo. SW19—9M 89
Archway Clo. W10—7J 57
Archway Mall. N19—7G 43
Archway Rd.—4E 42
  N19 1-43 & 2-92
  N6 remainder
Archway St. SW13—2C 88
Arcola St. E8—1D 60
Arctic St. NW5—1F 58
Arcus Rd. Brom—3C 110
Ardbeg Rd. SE24—4B 92
Arden Clo. Bush, Wat—9D 10
Arden Clo. Harr—8B 38
Arden Ct. Gdns. N2—4B 42
Arden Cres. Dag—3G 65
Arden Est. N1—5C 60
Arden Mhor. Pinn—2F 36
Arden Rd. N3—1K 41
Arden Rd. W13—1G 71
Ardent Clo. SE25—7C 108
Ardesley Wood. Wey—6C 116
Ardfern Av. SW16—7L 107
Ardfillan Rd. SE6—7B 94
Ardgowan Rd. SE6—6C 94
Ardilaun Rd. N5—9A 44
Ardleigh Clo. Horn—1H 51
Ardleigh Gdns. Sutt—2L 121
Ardleigh Grn. Rd. Horn—3H 51
Ardleigh M. Ilf—8M 47
Ardleigh Rd. E17—8K 29
Ardleigh Rd. N1—2C 60
Ardleigh Ter. E17—8K 29
Ardley Clo. NW10—8C 40
Ardley Clo. SE6—9J 93
Ardley Clo. Ruis—5A 36
Ardlui Rd. SE27—8A 92
Ardmay Gdns. Surb—9J 103
Ardmere Rd. SE13—5B 94
Ardmore La. Buck H—1F 30
Ardoch Rd. SE6—8B 94
Ardrossan Gdns. Wor Pk
  —5E 120
Ardross Av. N'wd—5C 20
Ardshiel Clo. SW15—2H 89
Ardwell Av. Ilf—3A 48
Ardwell Rd. SW2—8J 91
Ardwick Rd. NW2—9L 41
Argall Av. E10—5H 45
Argon M. SW6—8L 73

Argosy La. Stai—6B 144
Argus Clo. Romf—8M 33
Argus Way. W3—4M 71
Argus Way. N'holt—6J 53
Argyle Av. Houn—5L 85
Argyle Av. S'hall—2M 69
Argyle Clo. W13—7E 54
Argyle Pl. W6—5F 72
Argyle Rd. E1—7H 61
Argyle Rd. E15—9C 46
Argyle Rd. E16—9G 63
Argyle Rd. N12—5M 25
Argyle Rd. N17—8E 28
Argyle Rd. N18—4E 28
Argyle Rd. Barn—6G 13
Argyle Rd. Gnfd & W13—6D 54
Argyle Rd. Harr—4M 37
Argyle Rd. Houn—4M 85
Argyle Rd. Ilf—7L 47
Argyle Rd. Tedd—2D 102
Argyle Sq. WC1—6J 59
Argyle St. WC1—6J 59
Argyll Gdns. Edgw—9M 23
Argyll Rd. SW9—2K 91
Argyll Rd. W8—3L 73
Argyll St. W1—9G 59
Arica Rd. SE4—3J 93
Ariel Rd. NW6—2L 57
Ariel Way. W12—2G 73
Aristotle Rd. SW4—2H 91
Arkell Gro. SE19—4M 107
Arkindale Rd. SE6—9A 94
Arkley Cres. E17—3K 45
Arkley Dri. Barn—6E 12
Arkley La. Barn—5E 12
Arkley Rd. E17—3K 45
Arkley View. Barn—6F 12
Arklow Rd. SE14—7K 77
Arkwright Rd. NW3—1A 58
Arkwright Rd. S Croy—2D 138
Arlesey Clo. SW15—4J 89
Arlesford Rd. SW9—2J 91
Arlingford Rd. SW2—4L 91
Arlington. N12—3L 25
Arlington Av. N1—4A 60
Arlington Clo. Sidc—6C 96
Arlington Clo. Sutt—4L 121
Arlington Clo. Twic—5G 87
Arlington Ct. Hay—6C 68
Arlington Cres. Wal X—7E 6
Arlington Dri. Cars—4D 122
Arlington Dri. Ruis—4B 36
Arlington Gdns. W4—6A 72
Arlington Gdns. Ilf—6L 47
Arlington Gdns. Romf—8J 35
Arlington M. Twic—5G 87
Arlington Pas. Tedd—1D 102
Arlington Rd. N14—2F 26
Arlington Rd. NW1—4F 58
Arlington Rd. W13—9F 54
Arlington Rd. Rich—8H 87
Arlington Rd. Surb—1H 119
Arlington Rd. Tedd—1D 102
Arlington Rd. Twic—5G 87
Arlington Rd. Wfd G—7F 30
Arlington Sq. N1—4A 60
Arlington St. SW1—2G 75
Arlington Way. EC1—6L 59
Arliss Way. N'holt—4G 53
Arlow Rd. N21—1L 27
Armada Ct. SE8—7L 77
Armadale Clo. N17—2F 44
Armadale Rd. SW6—7L 73
Armadale Rd. Felt—4E 84
Armagh Rd. E3—4K 61
Armand Clo. Wat—2D 8
Armfield Clo. E Mol—9K 101
Armfield Cres. Mitc—6D 106
Armfield Rd. Enf—3B 16
Arminger Rd. W12—2F 72
Armitage Rd. NW11—6J 41
Armitage Rd. SE10—6D 78
Armour Clo. N7—2K 59
Armoury Way. SW18—4L 89
Armstead Wlk. Dag—5L 65
Armstrong Av. Wfd G—6C 30
Armstrong Clo. E6—9K 63
Armstrong Clo. Pinn—4E 36
Armstrong Cres. Barn—5B 14
Armstrong Rd. W3—2D 72
Armstrong Rd. Felt—2J 101
Armstrong Way. S'hall—3M 69
Armytage Rd. Houn—8H 69
Arnal Cres. SW18—6J 89
Arndale Centre. SW18—5M 89
Arndale Centre. Dart—6J 99
Arndale Wlk. SW18—4M 89
Arne Gro. Orp—5D 128
Arne St. WC2—9J 59
Arne Wlk. SE3—3D 94
Arneways Av. Romf—1H 49
Arneway St. SW1—4H 75

Arnewood Clo. SW15—7E 88
Arnewood Clo. Lea—6A 132
Arneys La. Mitc—1E 122
Arngask Rd. SE6—6B 94
Arnhem Av. S Ock—2M 83
Arnhem Dri. Croy—3B 140
Arnison Rd. E Mol—8B 102
Arnold Av. E. Enf—2L 17
Arnold Av. W. Enf—2K 17
Arnold Cir. E2—6D 60
Arnold Clo. Harr—5K 39
Arnold Cres. Iswth—4B 86
Arnold Gdns. N13—5M 27
Arnold Rd. E3—6L 61
Arnold Rd. N15—1D 44
Arnold Rd. SW17—4D 106
Arnold Rd. Dag—3K 65
Arnold Rd. N'holt—2J 53
Arnold's La. S at H, Dart
—3L 115
Arnos Gro. N14—4H 27
Arnos Rd. N11—4G 27
Arnott Clo. SE28—2G 81
Arnott Clo. W4—5B 72
Arnould Av. SE5—3B 92
Arnside Gdns. Wemb—6H 39
Arnside Rd. Bexh—9L 81
Arnside St. SE17—7B 76
Arnulf St. SE6—1M 109
Arnulls Rd. SW16—3M 107
Arodene Rd. SW2—5K 91
Arragon Gdns. SW16—4J 107
Arragon Gdns. W Wick
—5M 125
Arragon Rd. Twic—6E 86
Arragon Way. E6—4H 63
Arran Clo. Eri—7B 82
Arran Clo. Wall—6G 123
Arran Dri. E12 7H 47
Arran M. W5—2K 71
Arran Rd. SE6—8M 93
Arran Wlk. N1—3A 60
Arran Way. Esh—4M 117
Arras Av. Mord—9A 106
Arrol Rd. Beck—7G 109
Arrow Rd. E3—0M 61
Arrowscout Wlk. N'holt—6J 53
Arrowsmith Clo. Chig—5D 32
Arrowsmith Pl. Chig—5D 32
Arrowsmith Rd. Chig—5D 32
Arsenal Rd. SE9—1K 95
Arterberry Rd. SW20—4G 105
Arterial Av. Rain—7F 66
Arterial Rd. Purfleet, Purf
—4L 83
Artesian Clo. Horn—4D 50
Artesian Rd. W2—9L 57
Arthingworth St. E15—4C 62
Arthur Gro. SE18—5A 80
Arthur Rd. E6—5K 63
Arthur Rd. N7—9K 43
Arthur Rd. N9—2D 28
Arthur Rd. SW19—1K 105
Arthur Rd. King—4L 103
Arthur Rd. N Mald—9F 104
Arthur Rd. Romf—4H 49
Arthur Rd. West—7G 141
Arthur St. EC4 1B 76
Arthur St. Bush, Wat—6H 9
Arthur St. Eri—8D 82
Artichoke Hill. E1—1F 76
Artillery Clo. Ilf—4A 48
Artillery La. E1—8C 60
Artillery Pl. SE18—5L 79
Artillery Pl. Harr—7A 22
Artillery Row. SW1—4H 75
Artington Clo. Orp—6A 128
Arun Ct. SE25—9E 108
Arundel Av. Eps—2F 134
Arundel Av. Mord—8K 105
Arundel Av. S Croy—2E 138
Arundel Clo. E15—9C 46
Arundel Clo. SW11—4C 90
Arundel Clo. Bex—5E 97
Arundel Clo. Croy—5M 123
Arundel Clo. Hmptn—2M 101
Arundel Clo. Wal X—1C 6
Arundel Ct. N12—6C 26
Arundel Ct. Brom—6C 110
Arundel Dri. Borwd—6A 12
Arundel Dri. Harr—9K 37
Arundel Dri. Orp—7F 128
Arundel Dri. Wfd G—7E 30
Arundel Gdns. N21—1L 27
Arundel Gdns. W11—1K 73
Arundel Gdns. Edgw—7B 24
Arundel Gdns. Ilf—7E 48
Arundel Gro. N16—1C 60
Arundel Pl. N1—2L 59
Arundel Rd. Barn—5C 14
Arundel Rd. Croy—1B 124

Arundel Rd. Houn—2G 85
Arundel Rd. King—6M 103
Arundel Rd. Romf—7K 35
Arundel Rd. Sutt—9K 121
Arundel Rd. Uxb—5A 142
Arundel Sq. N7—2L 59
Arundel St. WC2—1K 75
Arundel Ter. SW13—7F 72
Arvon Rd. N5—1L 59
Ascalon St. SW8—8G 75
Ascension Rd. Romf—6A 34
Ascham Dri. E4—7M 29
Ascham End. E17—8J 29
Ascham St. NW5—1G 59
Aschurch Rd. Croy—2D 124
Ascot Clo. Borwd—7L 11
Ascot Clo. Ilf—6C 32
Ascot Gdns. Enf—1G 17
Ascot Gdns. Horn—9J 51
Ascot Gdns. S'hall—8K 53
Ascot Rd. E6—6K 63
Ascot Rd. N15—3B 44
Ascot Rd. N18—4E 28
Ascot Rd. SW17—3E 106
Ascot Rd. Felt—2E 84
Ascot Rd. Orp—8D 112
Ascot Rd. Wat—7C 8
Ascott Av. W5—3J 71
Aseing Clo. E6—1L 79
Ashbourne Av. E18—2F 46
Ashbourne Av. N20—2D 26
Ashbourne Av. NW11—3K 41
Ashbourne Av. Bexh—8J 81
Ashbourne Av. Harr—7B 38
Ashbourne Clo. N12—4M 25
Ashbourne Clo. W5—8L 54
Ashbourne Gro. NW7—5B 24
Ashbourne Gro. SE22—3D 92
Ashbourne Gro. W4—6C 72
Ashbourne Rise. Orp—6C 128
Ashbourne Rd. W5—7K 55
Ashbourne Rd. Mitc—4E 106
Ashbourne Rd. Romf—4G 35
Ashbourne Sq. N'wd—6C 20
Ashbourne Ter. SW19—4L 105
Ashbourne Way. NW11—2K 41
Ashbridge Rd. E11—5D 46
Ashbridge St. NW8—7C 58
Ashbrook Rd. N19—6H 43
Ashbrook Rd. Dag—8M 49
Ashburn Gdns. SW7—5A 74
Ashburnham Av. Harr—4D 38
Ashburnham Clo. N2—1B 42
Ashburnham Clo. Wat—3E 20
Ashburnham Dri. Wat—3E 20
Ashburnham Gdns. Harr
—4D 38
Ashburnham Gdns. Upm
—6M 51
Ashburnham Gro. SE10—8M 77
Ashburnham Pl. SE10—8M 77
Ashburnham Retreat. SE10
—8M 77
Ashburnham Rd. NW10—6G 57
Ashburnham Rd. SW10—8A 74
Ashburnham Rd. Belv—5A 82
Ashburnham Rd. Rich—9F 86
Ashburn M. SW7—5A 74
Ashburn Pl. SW7—5A 74
Ashburton Av. Croy—3F 124
Ashburton Av. Ilf—1C 64
Ashburton Clo. Croy—3E 124
Ashburton Ct. Pinn 1H 37
Ashburton Gdns. Croy—4E 124
Ashburton Gro. N7—9L 43
Ashburton Rd. E16—9E 62
Ashburton Rd. Croy—4E 124
Ashburton Rd. Ruis—7E 36
Ashburton Ter. E13—5E 62
Ashbury Dri. Uxb—8A 36
Ashbury Gdns. Romf—3H 49
Ashbury Rd. SW11—2D 90
Ashby Av. Chess—8L 119
Ashby Clo. Horn—6L 51
Ashby Gro. N1—3A 60
Ashby Rd. N15—3E 44
Ashby Rd. SE4—1N 93
Ashby Rd. Wat—2E 8
Ashby St. EC1 6M 59
Ashby Wlk. Croy—1A 124
Ashby Way. W Dray—8L 143
Ashchurch Ct. W12—4E 72
Ashchurch Gro. W12—4E 72
Ashchurch Pk. Vs. W12—4E 72
Ashchurch Ter. W12—4E 72
Ash Clo. SE20—6G 109
Ash Clo. Abb L, Wat—5B 4
Ash Clo. Cars—4D 122
Ash Clo. N Mald—6B 104
Ash Clo. Orp—9B 112
Ash Clo. Romf—7M 33
Ash Clo. Sidc—9F 96

Ash Clo. Stan—6E 22
Ash Clo. Swan—6A 114
Ashcombe Av. Surb—2H 119
Ashcombe Gdns. Edgw—4L 23
Ashcombe Pk. NW2—8C 40
Ashcombe Rd. SW19—2L 105
Ashcombe Rd. Cars—8E 122
Ashcombe Sq. N Mald—7A 104
Ashcombe St. SW6—1M 89
Ash Ct. SW19—4J 105
Ash Ct. Eps—6A 120
Ash Croft. Pinn—6L 21
Ashcroft Av. Sidc—5E 96
Ashcroft Cres. Sidc—5E 96
Ashcroft Rise. Coul—8J 137
Ashcroft Rd. E3—6J 61
Ashcroft Rd. Chess—5K 119
Ashcroft Sq. W6—5G 73
Ashdale Clo. Twic—6A 86
Ashdale Gro. Stan—6D 22
Ashdale Rd. SE12—7F 94
Ashdale Way. Twic—6M 85
Ashdene. Pinn—1G 37
Ashdene Clo. Ashf—4A 100
Ashdon Clo. Wfd G—6F 30
Ashdon Rd. NW10—4D 56
Ashdon Rd. Bush, Wat—5H 9
Ashdown Clo. Beck—6M 109
Ashdown Cres. NW5—1E 58
Ashdown Cres. Wal X—1E 6
Ashdown Dri. Borwd—4K 11
Ashdown Est. E11—9B 46
Ashdown Gdns. S Croy—7F 138
Ashdown Rd. Enf—4G 17
Ashdown Rd. Eps—5E 134
Ashdown Rd. King—6J 103
Ashdown Rd. Uxb—5E 142
Ashdown Wlk. Romf—8M 33
Ashdown Way. SW17—8E 90
Ashen Dri. Dart—5E 98
Ashen Gro. SW19—9L 89
Ashen Vale. S Croy—1H 139
Ashfield Av. Bush, Wat—8M 9
Ashfield Av. Felt—7F 84
Ashfield Clo. Rich—7J 87
Ashfield La. Chst—3A 112
Ashfield Pde. N14—1H 27
Ashfield Rd. N4—4A 44
Ashfield Rd. N14—3G 27
Ashfield Rd. W3—2D 72
Ashfields. Lou—4K 19
Ashfields. Wat—8D 4
Ashfield St. E1 8F 60
Ashford Av. N8—2J 43
Ashford Av. Hay—9H 53
Ashford Clo. E17—4K 45
Ashford Cres. Ashf—9C 144
Ashford Cres. Enf—4G 17
Ashford Grn. Wat—6H 21
Ashford Industrial Est. Ashf
—1A 100
Ashford Rd. E6—3L 63
Ashford Rd. E18—9F 30
Ashford Rd. NW2—9H 41
Ashford Rd. Ashf—4A 100
Ashford Rd. Felt—1B 100
Ashford St. N1—6C 60
Ash Grn. Lou—4K 19
Ash Gro. E8—4F 60
Ash Gro. N13—3A 28
Ash Gro. NW2—9H 41
Ash Gro. SE20—6G 109
Ash Gro. W5 3J 71
Ash Gro. Enf—9C 16
Ash Gro. Felt—7C 84
Ash Gro. Hay—1B 68
Ash Gro. Houn—9H 69
Ash Gro. S'hall—8L 53
Ash Gro. Wemb—9E 38
Ash Gro. W Dray—1K 143
Ash Gro. W Wick—4A 126
Ashgrove Rd. Ashf—2A 100
Ashgrove Rd. Brom—3B 110
Ashgrove Rd. Ilf—6D 48
Ash Hill Clo. Bush, Wat—1M 21
Ash Hill Dri. Pinn—1G 37
Ashingdon Clo. E4—3A 30
Ashington Rd. SW6—1K 89
Ashlake Rd. SW16 1J 107
Ashland Pl. W1—8E 58
Ash La. Horn—2L 51
Ash La. Romf—6E 34
Ashlar Pl. SE18—5M 79
Ashleigh Gdns. Sutt—4M 121
Ashleigh Rd. SE20—7F 108
Ashleigh Rd. SW14—2C 88
Ashley Av. Eps—5B 134
Ashley Av. Ilf—9M 31
Ashley Av. Mord—9L 105
Ashley Centre. Eps—5B 134
Ashley Clo. NW4—9G 25
Ashley Clo. Pinn—9F 20

Ashley Clo. W on T—3D 116
Ashley Ct. Eps—5B 134
Ashley Cres. N22—9L 27
Ashley Cres. SW11—2E 90
Ashley Dri. Bans—6L 135
Ashley Dri. Borwd—7A 12
Ashley Dri. Twic—7M 85
Ashley Dri. W on T—5E 116
Ashley Gdns. N13—4A 28
Ashley Gdns. Orp—7C 128
Ashley Gdns. Rich—8H 87
Ashley Gdns. Wemb—7J 39
Ashley La. NW4—9G 25
Ashley La. Croy—6M 123
Ashley Pk. Av. W on T—4D 116
Ashley Pk. Cres. W on T
—3E 116
Ashley Pk. Rd. W on T—4E 116
Ashley Pl. SW1—4G 75
Ashley Rise. W on T—6D 116
Ashley Rd. E4—6L 29
Ashley Rd. E7—3G 63
Ashley Rd. N17—1E 44
Ashley Rd. N19—6J 43
Ashley Rd. SW19—3M 105
Ashley Rd. Enf—4G 17
Ashley Rd. Eps—5B 134
Ashley Rd. Hmptn—5L 101
Ashley Rd. Rich—2J 87
Ashley Rd. Th Dit—1D 118
Ashley Rd. T Hth—8K 107
Ashley Rd. Uxb—5A 142
Ashling Rd. Croy—3E 124
Ashlin Rd. E15—9B 46
Ashlone Rd. SW15—2H 89
Ashlyn Clo. Bush, Wat—6J 9
Ashlyn Gro. Horn—1H 51
Ashlyns Way. Chess—8H 119
Ashmead. N14—7G 15
Ashmead Rd. SE8—1L 93
Ashmead Rd. Felt—7E 84
Ashmere Av. Beck—6B 110
Ashmere Clo. Sutt—7H 121
Ashmere Gro. SW2—3J 91
Ashmill St. NW1—8C 58
Ashmole Pl. SW8—7K 75
Ashmole St. SW8—7K 75
Ashmore Ct. Houn—7L 69
Ashmore Gro. Well—2B 96
Ashmore La. Kes—3G 141
Ashmore Rd. W9—6K 57
Ashmount Rd. N15—3D 44
Ashmount Rd. N19—5G 43
Ashmount Ter. W5—5H 71
Ashmour Gdns. Romf—9B 34
Ashneal Gdns. Harr—8B 38
Ashness Gdns. Gnfd—2F 54
Ashness Rd. SW11—4D 90
Ashridge Clo. Harr—4G 39
Ashridge Cres. SE18—8A 80
Ashridge Dri. St Alb—3J 5
Ashridge Dri. Wat—5G 21
Ashridge Gdns. N13—5H 27
Ashridge Gdns. Pinn—2J 37
Ashridge Rd. Mord—8K 105
Ashridge Way. Sun—3E 100
Ashri Rd. E15—1C 62
Ash Rd. Croy—4L 125
Ash Rd. Dart—7H 99
Ash Rd. Dart—1K 115
(Hawley)
Ash Rd. Orp—9D 128
Ash Rd. Sutt—3K 121
Ash Row. Brom—2L 127
Ashtead Gap. Lea—8F 132
Ashtead Rd. E5—5E 44
Ashtead Woods Rd. Asht
—9G 133
Ashton Clo. Sutt—6L 121
Ashton Clo. W on T—8F 116
Ashton Gdns. Houn—3A 86
Ashton Gdns. Romf—4J 49
Ashton Rd. E15—1B 62
Ashton Rd. Enf—9E 6
Ashton Rd. Romf—7H 35
Ashton St. E14—1A 78
Ash Tree Clo. Croy—1J 125
Ash Tree Clo. Surb—4J 119
Ashtree Dell. NW9—3B 40
Ash Tree Rd. Wat—9F 4
Ash Tree Way. Croy—9H 109
Ashurst Clo. SE20—5F 108
Ashurst Clo. Dart—2D 98
Ashurst Clo. Kenl—7B 138
Ashurst Clo. N'wd—7C 20
Ashurst Dri. Ilf—4M 47
Ashurst Rd. N12—5C 26
Ashurst Rd. Barn—7D 14
Ashurst Wlk. Croy—4F 124

Ashvale Gdns. Romf—5B 34
Ashvale Rd. SW17—2D 106
Ashville Rd. E11—7B 46
Ashwater Rd. SE12—7E 94
Ashwell Clo. E6—9K 63
Ashwin St. E8—2D 60
Ashwood Av. Rain—7F 66
Ashwood Av. Uxb—9E 142
Ashwood Cres. Hay—5D 68
Ashwood Gdns. Croy—8M 125
Ashwood Rd. E4—3B 30
Ashworth Clo. SE5—1B 92
Ashworth Industrial Est. Croy
—3J 123
Ashworth Rd. W9—6M 57
Ashworth Rd. Bexh—3H 97
Aske St. N1—6C 60
Askew Cres. W12—3D 72
Askew Rd. W12—3D 72
Askew Rd. N'wd—2B 20
Askham Rd. W12—2E 72
Askill Dri. SW15—4J 89
Askwith Rd. Rain—6B 66
Asland Rd. E15—4C 62
Aslett St. SW18—6M 89
Asmara Rd. NW2—1J 57
Asmar Clo. Coul—7J 137
Asmuns Hill. NW11—3L 41
Asmuns Pl. NW11—3K 41
Aspen Clo. N19—7G 43
Aspen Clo. W5—3K 71
Aspen Clo. Orp—7E 128
Aspen Clo. Swan—5B 114
Aspen Copse. Brom—6K 111
Aspen Dri. Wemb—8E 38
Aspen Gdns. W6—6F 72
Aspen Gdns. Mitc—9E 106
Aspen Grn. Eri—4K 81
Aspen Gro. Upm—9L 51
Aspen La. N'holt—6J 53
Aspenlea Rd. W6—7H 73
Aspen Way. Bans—6H 135
Aspen Way. Enf—8D 6
Aspinall Rd. SE4—2H 93
Aspinden Rd. SE16—5F 76
Aspley Rd. SW18—4M 89
Asplins Rd. N17—8E 28
Assam St. E1—9F 60
Assembly Pas. E1—8G 61
Assembly Wlk. Cars—2C 122
Assher Rd. W on T—5J 117
Ass Ho. La. Harr—4M 21
Astall Clo. Harr—8C 22
Astbury Rd. SE15—9G 77
Astell St. SW3—6C 74
Aste St. E14—3A 78
Astey's Row. N1—3A 60
Asthall Gdns. Ilf—2A 48
Astle St. SW11—1E 90
Astley Av. NW2—1G 57
Aston Av. Harr—5G 39
Aston Clo. Sidc—9E 96
Aston Grn. Houn—1G 85
Aston M. Romf—5G 49
Aston Rd. SW20—6G 105
Aston Rd. W5—9H 55
Aston Rd. Esh—7C 118
Astons Rd. N'wd—3A 20
Aston St. E14—9J 61
Astonville St. SW18
—7L 89
Aston Way. Eps—7D 134
Astor Av. Romf 4A 50
Astor Clo. King—3M 103
Astoria Wlk. SW9—2L 91
Astra Clo. Horn—2F 66
Astrop M. W6—4G 73
Astrop Ter. W6—3G 73
Atwood M. SW7—5A 74
Asylum Rd. SE15—8F 76
Atalanta St. SW6—8H 73
Atbara Rd. Tedd—3F 102
Atcham Rd. Houn—3A 86
Atcost Rd. Bark—8E 64
Atheldene Rd. SW18—7A 90
Athelney St. SE6—9L 93
Athelstan Clo. Romf—9K 35
Athelstane Gro. E3—5K 61
Athelstane M. N4—6L 43
Athelstan Rd. King—8K 103
Athelstan Rd. Romf—9K 35
Athelstone Rd. Harr—9B 22
Athena Clo. Harr—7B 38
Athenaeum Pl. N10—1F 42
Athenaeum Rd. N20—1A 26
Athenlay Rd. SE15—4H 93
Aberden Rd. E5—9G 45
Atherfold Rd. SW9—2J 91
Atherley Way. Houn—6K 85
Atherstone M. SW7—5A 74
Atherton Clo. Stai—5B 144
Atherton Dri. SW19—1H 105

Atherton Heights. Wemb
—2G 55
Atherton M. E7—2D 62
Atherton Pl. Harr—1B 38
Atherton Pl. S'hall—1F 69
Atherton Rd. E7—2D 62
Atherton Rd. SW13—8E 72
Atherton Rd. Ilf—9J 31
Atherton St. SW11—1C 90
Athlone. Esh—8C 118
Athlone Clo. E5—1F 60
Athlone Rd. SW2—6K 91
Athlone St. NW5—2E 58
Athlon Rd. Wemb—5H 55
Athol Clo. Pinn—8F 20
Athole Gdns. Enf—7C 16
Athol Gdns. Pinn—8F 20
Atholl Rd. Ilf—5E 48
Athol Rd. Eri—6A 82
Athol St. E14—9A 62
Athol Way. Uxb—6E 142
Atkinson Clo. Orp—7E 128
Atkinson Rd. E16—8G 63
Atkins Rd. E10—4M 45
Atkins Rd. SW12—6G 91
Atlantic Rd. SW9—3L 91
Atlas Gdns. SE7—5G 79
Atlas M. N7—2K 59
Atlas Rd. E13—5E 62
Atlas Rd. NW10—6C 56
Atlas Rd. Wemb—9A 40
Atley Rd. E3—4L 61
Atney Rd. SW15—3J 89
Atria Rd. N'wd—5E 20
Atterbury Rd. N4—4M 43
Atterbury St. SW1—5J 75
Attewood Av. NW10—8C 40
Attewood Rd. N'holt—2J 53
Attfield Clo. N20—2B 26
Attle Clo. Uxb—5E 142
Attlee Clo. Hay—6F 52
Attlee Dri. Dart—4L 99
Attlee Rd. SE28—1F 80
Attlee Rd. Hay—6E 52
Attneave St. WC1—6L 59
Attwell's Yd. Uxb—3B 142
Attwood Clo. S Croy—6F 138
Atwater Clo. SW2—7L 91
Atwell Rd. SE15—1E 92
Atwood Av. Rich—1L 87
Atwood Rd. W6—5F 72
Atwoods All. Rich—9L 71
Aubert Ct. N5—9M 43
Aubert Pk. N5—9M 43
Aubert Rd. N5—9M 43
Aubretia Clo. Romf—8J 35
Aubrey Pl. NW8—5A 58
Aubrey Rd. E17—1L 45
Aubrey Rd. N8—3J 43
Aubrey Rd. W8—2K 73
Aubrey Wlk. W8—2K 73
Aubyn Hill. SE27—1A 108
Aubyn Sq. SW15—4E 88
Auckland Av. Rain—6D 66
Auckland Clo. SE19—5D 108
Auckland Clo. Enf—1F 16
Auckland Gdns. SE19—5C 108
Auckland Hill. SE27—1A 108
Auckland Rise. SE19—5C 108
Auckland Rd. E10—8M 45
Auckland Rd. SE19—5D 108
Auckland Rd. SW11—3C 90
Auckland Rd. Ilf—6M 47
Auckland Rd. King—8K 103
Auckland St. SE11—6K 75
Auden Pl. NW1—4E 58
Audleigh Pl. Chig—6L 31
Audley Clo. SW11—2E 90
Audley Clo. Borwd—5L 11
Audley Ct. E18—2D 46
Audley Ct. Pinn—9G 21
Audley Dri. Warl—7G 139
Audley Gdns. Ilf—7D 48
Audley Gdns. Wal A—7J 7
Audley Pl. Sutt—9M 121
Audley Rd. NW4—4E 40
Audley Rd. W5—8K 55
Audley Rd. Enf—4M 15
Audley Rd. Rich—4K 87
Audley Sq. W1—2E 74
Audley Wlk. Orp—1G 129
Audrey Clo. Beck—1M 125
Audrey Gdns. Wemb—7F 38
Audrey Rd. Ilf—8M 47
Audrey St. E2—5E 60
Audric Clo. King—5L 103
Audwick Clo. Wal X—1E 6
Augurs La. E13—6F 62
Augusta Rd. Twic—8A 86
Augusta St. E14—9M 61
Augustine Rd. W14—4H 73
Augustine Rd. Harr—8A 22
Augustine Orp—7H 113

Augustus Clo. Bren—8G 71
Augustus Rd. SW19—7J 89
Augustus St. NW1—5F 58
Aultone Way. Cars—5D 122
Aultone Way. Sutt—4M 121
Aulton Pl. SE11—6L 75
Aurelia Gdns. Croy—9K 107
Aurelia Rd. Croy—1J 123
Auriel Av. Dag—2B 66
Auriga M. N1—1B 60
Auriol Clo. Wor Pk—5C 120
Auriol Dri. Gnfd—3B 54
Auriol Dri. Uxb—2E 142
Auriol Pk. Rd. Wor Pk—5C 120
Auriol Rd. W14—5J 73
Austell Gdns. NW7—3C 24
Austen Clo. SE28—2F 80
Austen Rd. Harr—7M 37
Austin Av. Brom—9J 111
Austin Clo. SE23—6K 93
Austin Clo. Coul—9M 137
Austin Rd. SW11—9E 74
Austin Rd. Hay—3D 68
Austin Rd. Orp—1E 128
Austin's La. Uxb—8A 36
Austin St. E2—6D 60
Austin Waye. Uxb—4A 142
Austral Clo. Sidc—9D 96
Austral Dri. Horn—5H 51
Australia Rd. W12—1F 72
Austral St. SE11—5M 75
Austyn Gdns. Surb—3M 119
Autumn Clo. Enf—3E 16
Autumn St. E3—4L 61
Avalon Clo. W13—8E 54
Avalon Clo. Enf—4L 15
Avalon Clo. Orp—5H 129
Avalon Rd. SW6—9M 73
Avalon Rd. W13—7E 54
Avalon Rd. Orp—4G 129
Avard Gdns. Orp—6A 128
Avarn Rd. SW17—3D 106
Avebury Pk. Surb—2H 119
Avebury Rd. E11—6B 46
Avebury Rd. SW19—5K 105
Avebury Rd. Orp—5B 128
Avebury St. N1—4B 60
Aveley By-Pass. S Ock—1M 83
Aveley Rd. Romf—2C 50
Aveley Rd. Upm—2M 67
Aveline St. SE11—6L 75
Aveling Clo. Purl—5K 137
Aveling Pk. Rd. E17—9L 29
Avelon Rd. Rain—4E 66
Avelon Rd. Romf—6B 34
Ave Maria La. EC4—9M 59
Avenell Rd. N5—8M 43
Avening Rd. SW18—6L 89
Avening Ter. SW18—6L 89
Avenons Rd. E13—7E 62
Avenue Clo. N14—8G 15
Avenue Clo. NW8—4C 58
Avenue Clo. Houn—9F 68
Avenue Clo. Romf—7K 35
Avenue Clo. W Dray—4H 143
Avenue Cres. W3—3M 71
Avenue Cres. Houn—9F 68
Avenue Elmers. Surb—9J 103
Avenue Gdns. SE25—6E 108
Avenue Gdns. SW14—2C 88
Avenue Gdns. W3—3M 71
Avenue Gdns. Houn—8F 68
Avenue Gdns. Tedd—4D 102
Avenue Industrial Est. Romf
—9H 27
Avenue M. N10—1F 42
Avenue Pk. Rd. SE27—8M 91
Avenue Rise. Bush, Wat—7L 9
Avenue Rd. E7—9F 46
Avenue Rd. N6—5G 43
Avenue Rd. N12—4A 26
Avenue Rd. N14—9G 15
Avenue Rd. N15—3B 44
Avenue Rd.—3B 58
  NW8 1-95 & 2-86
  NW3 remainder
Avenue Rd. NW10—5D 56
Avenue Rd.—5G 109
  SE20 1-55 & 2-50
  Beck remainder
Avenue Rd. SE25—6E 108
Avenue Rd. SW16—6H 107
Avenue Rd. SW20—6F 104
Avenue Rd. W3—3M 71
Avenue Rd. Bans—7M 135
Avenue Rd. Belv—5A 82
Avenue Rd. Bexh—2J 97
Avenue Rd. Bren—6G 71
Avenue Rd. Eps—6B 134

Avenue Rd. Eri—8A 32
Avenue Rd. Felt—9D 84
Avenue Rd. Hmptn—5M 101
Avenue Rd. Iswth—9D 70
Avenue Rd. King—7J 103
Avenue Rd. N Mald—8C 104
Avenue Rd. Pinn—1J 37
Avenue Rd. Romf—5G 49
  (Chadwell Heath)
Avenue Rd. Romf—7K 35
  (Harold Wood)
Avenue Rd. S'hall—2K 69
Avenue Rd. Sutt—2L 135
Avenue Rd. Tedd—4E 102
Avenue Rd. Wall—9G 123
Avenue Rd. Wfd G—6G 31
Avenue S. Surb—2L 119
Avenue Ter. N Mald—7A 104
Avenue, The. E4—4C 30
Avenue, The. E11—3F 46
Avenue, The. N3—9L 25
Avenue, The. N8—1L 43
Avenue, The. N10—9G 27
Avenue, The. N11—5F 26
Avenue, The. N17—9C 28
Avenue, The. NW6—4J 57
Avenue, The. SE7—6G 79
Avenue, The. SE9—5K 95
Avenue, The. SE10—8B 78
Avenue, The. SW4—4F 90
Avenue, The. SW18 & SW11
—6C 90
Avenue, The. W4—4C 72
Avenue, The. W13—1F 70
Avenue, The. Barn—5J 13
Avenue, The. Beck—5M 109
Avenue, The. Bex—6H 97
Avenue, The. Brom—7H 111
Avenue, The. Bush, Wat—7K 9
Avenue, The. Cars—9E 122
Avenue, The. Coul—7H 137
Avenue, The. Croy—5C 124
Avenue, The. Eps & Sutt
—9H 121
Avenue, The. Esh—7C 118
Avenue, The. Hmptn—3K 101
Avenue, The. Harr—8D 22
Avenue, The. Horn—7H 51
Avenue, The. Houn—4M 85
Avenue, The. Houn—9E 68
  (Cranford)
Avenue, The. Kes—5H 127
Avenue, The. Lea—4D 132
Avenue, The. Lou—8J 17
Avenue, The. N'wd—6A 20
Avenue, The. Orp—4D 128
Avenue, The. Orp—5F 112
  (St Pauls Cray)
Avenue, The. Pinn—6K 21
  (Hatch End)
Avenue, The. Pinn—5K 37
  (Rayners Lane)
Avenue, The. Rich—1K 87
Avenue, The. Romf—2B 50
Avenue, The. Sun—7F 100
Avenue, The. Surb—2L 119
Avenue, The. Sutt—2K 135
Avenue, The. Twic—4F 86
Avenue, The. Uxb—7B 142
  (Cowley)
Avenue, The. Wat—4E 8
Avenue, The. Wemb—6J 39
Avenue, The. W Wick—1C 126
Avenue, The. Wor Pk—4D 120
Averil Gro. SW16—3M 107
Averill St. W6—7H 73
Avern Gdns. E Mol—8M 101
Avern Rd. E Mol—8M 101
Avery Farm Row. SW1—5F 74
Avery Gdns. Ilf—3K 47
Avery Hill Rd. SE9—5B 96
Avery Row. W1—1F 74
Avey La. Wal A & Lou—9K 7
Aviary Clo. E16—8D 62
Aviemore Clo. Beck—9K 109
Aviemore Way. Beck—9J 109
Avignon Rd. SE4—2H 93
Avington Gro. SE20—4G 109
Avington Way. SE15—8D 76
Avior Dri. N'wd—4D 20
Avis Sq. E1—9H 61
Avoca Rd. SW17—1E 106
Avocet M. SE28—4B 80
Avon Clo. Hay—7G 53
Avon Clo. Sutt—6A 122
Avon Clo. Wat—7G 5
Avon Clo. Wor Pk—4E 120
Avondale Av. N12—5M 25
Avondale Av. NW2—8C 40
Avondale Av. Barn—1D 26
Avondale Av. Esh—5E 118
Avondale Av. Wor Pk—3D 120
Avondale Clo. Lou—9K 19

Avondale Clo. W on T—7G 117
Avondale Ct. E16—8C 62
Avondale Ct. E18—8F 30
Avondale Cres. Enf—5J 17
Avondale Cres. Ilf—3H 47
Avondale Dri. Hay—2E 68
Avondale Dri. Lou—9K 19
Avondale Gdns. Houn—4K 85
Avondale Pk. Gdns. W11
—1J 73
Avondale Pk. Rd. W11—1J 73
Avondale Rise. SE15—2D 92
Avondale Rd. E16—8C 62
Avondale Rd. E17—5L 45
Avondale Rd. N3—8A 26
Avondale Rd. N13—2L 27
Avondale Rd. N15—3M 43
Avondale Rd. SE9—8J 95
Avondale Rd. SW14—2B 88
Avondale Rd. SW19—2M 105
Avondale Rd. Ashf—9B 144
Avondale Rd. Brom—3C 110
Avondale Rd. Harr—1D 38
Avondale Rd. S Croy—8A 124
Avondale Rd. Well—1G 97
Avondale Sq. SE1—6E 76
Avonley Rd. SE14—8G 77
Avon M. Pinn—8K 21
Avonmore Rd. W14—5K 73
Avonmouth St. SE1—4A 76
Avon Path. S Croy—8A 124
Avon Pl. SE1—3A 76
Avon Rd. E17—1B 46
Avon Rd. SE4—2L 93
Avon Rd. Gnfd—7L 53
Avon Rd. Sun—4D 100
Avon Way. E18—1E 46
Avril Way. E4—5A 30
Avro Way. Wall—9J 123
Awlfield Av. N17—8B 28
Awliscombe Rd. Well—1D 96
Axe St. Bark—4A 64
Axholme Av. Edgw—8L 23
Axminster Cres. Well—9G 81
Axminster Rd. N7—8J 43
Axtaine Rd. Orp—2H 129
Axwood. Eps—7A 134
Aybrook St. W1—8E 58
Aycliffe Clo. Brom—8K 111
Aycliffe Rd. W12—2E 72
Aycliffe Rd. Borwd—3J 11
Aylands Rd. Enf—9D 6
Aylesbury Clo. E7—2D 62
Aylesbury Rd. SE17—6B 76
Aylesbury Rd. Brom—7E 110
Aylesbury St. EC1—7M 59
Aylesbury St. NW10—8B 40
Aylesford Av. Beck—9J 109
Aylesford St. SW1—6H 75
Aylesham Rd. Orp—2D 128
Ayles Rd. Hay—6F 52
Aylestone Av. NW6—3H 57
Aylett Rd. SE25—8F 108
Aylett Rd. Iswth—1C 86
Ayley Croft. Enf—7E 16
Aylmer Clo. Stan—4E 22
Aylmer Dri. Stan—4E 22
Aylmer Rd. E11—6D 46
Aylmer Rd. N2—3C 42
Aylmer Rd. W12—3D 72
Aylmer Rd. Dag—8J 49
Ayloffe Rd. Dag—2K 65
Ayloffs Clo. Horn—2H 51
Ayloffs Wlk. Horn—3H 51
Aylsham Dri. Uxb—7A 36
Aylsham La. Romf—4G 35
Aylward Rd. SE23—8H 93
Aylward Rd. SW20—6K 105
Aylwards Rise. Stan—4E 22
Aylward St. E1—9H 61
Aylward St. E1
Aylwin Est. SE1—4C 76
Aynhoe Rd. W14—5H 73
Aynho St. Wat—7F 8
Aynscombe Angle. Orp
—2E 128
Aynscombe Path. SW14
—1A 88
Ayot Path. Borwd—2L 11
Ayres Clo. E13—6E 62
Ayres Cres. NW10—3B 56
Ayres St. SE1—3A 76
Ayr Grn. Romf—8C 34
Ayrsome Rd. N16—8C 44
Ayr Way. Romf—8C 34
Aysgarth Rd. SE21—6C 92
Aytoun Pl. SW9—1K 91
Aytoun Rd. SW9—1K 91
Azalea Clo. W7—2D 70
Azalea Ct. Wfd G—7C 30
Azalea Dri. Swan—8B 114
Azalea Wlk. Pinn—3F 36

Azenby Rd. SE15—1D 92
Azof St. SE10—5C 78

Baalbec Rd. N5—1M 59
Babbacombe Clo. Chess
—7H 119
Babbacombe Gdns. Ilf—2J 47
Babbacombe Rd. Brom
—5E 110
Baber Dri. Felt—5G 85
Babington Rise. Wemb—2M 55
Babington Rd. NW4—2F 40
Babington Rd. SW16—2H 107
Babington Rd. Dag—1G 65
Babington Rd. Horn—6F 50
Babmaes St. SW1—1H 75
Bache's St. N1—6B 60
Bk. Church La. E1—9E 60
Back Hill. EC1—7L 59
Back La. N8—3J 43
Back La. NW3—9A 42
Back La. Bex—6L 97
Back La. Bren—7H 71
Back La. Edgw—8A 24
Back La. Rich—9G 87
  (in two parts)
Back La. Romf—5H 49
Back Rd. Sidc—1E 112
Back St. W3—2M 71
Bacon Gro. SE1—4D 76
Bacon La. NW9—2M 39
Bacon La. Edgw—8L 23
Bacon Link. Romf—6M 33
Bacons La. N6—6E 42
Bacon St.—7D 60
  E1 1-21 & 2-22
  E2 remainder
Bacton St. E2—6G 61
Badburgham Ct. Wal A—6M 7
Baddow Clo. Dag—4L 65
Baddows Clo. Wfd G—6H 31
Baden Pl. SE1—3B 76
Baden Powell Clo. Surb
—4K 119
Baden Rd. N8—2H 43
Baden Rd. Ilf—1M 63
Bader Clo. Kenl—7B 138
Bader Way. Rain—2E 66
Badger Clo. Felt—9F 84
Badger Clo. Houn—2G 85
Badgers Clo. Enf—5M 15
Badgers Clo. Harr—4B 38
Badgers Clo. Hay—1C 68
Badgers Copse. Orp—4D 128
Badgers Copse. Wor Pk
—4D 120
Badgers Croft. N20—1J 25
Badgers Croft. SE9—9L 95
Badgers Hole. Croy—6H 125
Badgers Wlk. N Mald—6C 104
Badlis Rd. E17—1L 45
Badlow Clo. Eri—8C 82
Badminton Clo. Borwd—4L 11
Badminton Clo. Harr—2C 38
Badminton Clo. N'holt—2L 53
Badminton Rd. SW12—5E 90
Badsworth Rd. SE5—9A 76
Bagford St. N1—4B 60
Bagley Clo. W Dray—3J 143
Bagley's La. SW6—9M 73
Bagleys Spring. Romf—2J 49
Bagot Clo. Asht—8K 133
Bagshot Ct. SE18—9J 79
Bagshot Rd. Enf—8D 16
Bagshot St. SE17—6C 76
Bahram Rd. Eps—2B 134
Baildon St. SE8—8K 77
Bailey Pl. SE26—3H 109
Baillie Clo. Rain—7F 66
Baillies Wlk. W5—3H 71
Bainbridge Rd. Dag—9K 49
Bainbridge St. WC1—9H 59
Baird Av. S'hall—1M 69
Baird Clo. Bush, Wat—8M 9
Baird Gdns. SE21—1C 108
Baird Rd. Enf—6F 16
Baird St. EC1—7A 60
Bairstow Clo. Borwd—3J 11
Baizdon Rd. SE3—1C 94
Baker Boy La. Croy—5J 139
Baker La. Mitc—6E 106
Baker Rd. NW10—4C 56
Baker Rd. SE18—8J 79
Bakers Av. E17—4M 45
Bakers Ct. SE25—7C 108
Bakers End. SW20—6J 105
Baker's Field. N7—9H 43
Bakers Hall Ct. EC3—1C 76
Bakers Hill. E5—6G 45
Bakers Hill. Barn—4M 13

Bakers La. N6—4D 42
Baker's M. W1—9E 58
Baker's Rents. E2—6D 60
Bakers Rd. Uxb—3B 142
Bakers Rd. Wal X—3B 6
Baker's Row. E15—5C 62
Baker's Row. Ec1—7L 59
Baker St.—7D 58
  W1 1-133 & 2-136
  NW1 remainder
Baker St. Enf—4B 16
Baker St. Wey—6A 116
Baker's Yd. Uxb—3B 142
Bakewell Way. N Mald—6C 104
Balaams La. N14—2H 27
Balaam St. E13—7E 62
Balaclava Rd. SE1—5D 76
Balaclava Rd. Surb—2G 119
Balben Path. E9—3G 61
Balcaskie Rd. SE9—4K 95
Balchen Rd. SE3—1H 95
Balchier Rd. SE22—5F 92
Balcombe St. NW1—7D 58
Balcon Way. Borwd—3A 12
Balcorne St. E9—3G 61
Balder Rise. SE12—8F 94
Balderton St. W1—9E 58
Baldock St. E3—5M 61
Baldock Way. Borwd—3K 11
Baldry Gdns. SW16—3J 107
Baldwin Cres. SE5—9A 76
Baldwin's Gdns. EC1—8L 59
Baldwins Hill. Lou—4K 19
Baldwin's La. Rick—6A 8
Baldwin St. EC1—6B 60
Baldwin Ter. N1—5A 60
Baldwyn Gdns. W3—1B 72
Baldwyn's Pk. Bex—8B 98
Baldwyn's Rd. Bex—8B 98
Bales Ter. N9—3D 28
Balfern Gro. W4—6C 72
Balfern St. SW11—1C 90
Balfe St. N1—5J 59
Balfont Clo. S Croy—5E 138
Balfour App. Ilf—7M 47
Balfour Av. W7—2D 70
Balfour Gro. N20—3D 26
Balfour M. N9—3E 28
Balfour M. W1—2E 74
Balfour of Burleigh Est. W10
  —8H 57
Balfour Pl. SW15—3F 88
Balfour Pl. W1—1E 74
Balfour Rd. N5—9A 44
Balfour Rd. SE25—8E 108
Balfour Rd. SW19—4M 105
Balfour Rd. W3—8A 56
Balfour Rd. W13—3E 70
Balfour Rd. Brom—9H 111
Balfour Rd. Cars—9D 122
Balfour Rd. Harr—3B 38
Balfour Rd. Houn—2M 85
Balfour Rd. Ilf—7M 47
Balfour Rd. S'hall—4H 69
Balfour St. SE17—5B 76
Balfour Ter. N3—9M 25
Balgonie Rd. E4—1B 30
Balgores Cres. Romf—1F 50
Balgores La. Romf—1F 50
Balgores Sq. Romf—2F 50
Balgowan Clo. N Mald—8C 104
Balgowan Rd. Beck—7J 109
Balgowan St. SE18—5D 80
Balham High Rd.—9E 90
  SW12 1-197 & 2-222
  SW17 remainder
Balham New Rd. SW12—6F 90
Balham Pk. Rd. SW12—7D 90
Balham Rd. N9—2E 28
Balham Sta. Rd. SW12—7F 90
Ballamore Rd. Brom—9E 94
Ballance Rd. E9—2H 61
Ballantine St. SW18—3A 90
Ballard Clo. King—4B 104
Ballards Clo. Dag—4M 65
Ballards Farm Rd. S Croy &
  Croy—8E 124
Ballards La.—8L 25
  N3 1-265 & 2-240
  N12 remainder
Ballards Rise. S Croy—8E 124
Ballards Rd. NW2—7E 40
Ballards Rd. Dag—4M 65
Ballards Way. S Croy & Croy
  —8E 124
Ballast Quay. SE10—6B 78
Ballater Clo. Wat—4G 21
Ballater Rd. SW2—3J 91
Ballater Rd. S Croy—7D 124
Ballenger Ct. Wat—5F 8

Ballina St. SE23—6H 93
Ballingdon Rd. SW11—5E 90
Balliol Av. E4—4C 30
Balliol Rd. N17—8C 28
Balliol Rd. W10—9G 57
Balliol Rd. Well—1F 96
Balloch Rd. SE6—7B 94
Ballogie Av. NW10—9C 40
Ballow Clo. SE5—8C 76
Balls Pond Rd. N1—2B 60
Balmain Clo. W5—2H 71
Balmer Rd. E3—5K 61
Balmes Rd. N1—4B 60
Balmoral Av. Beck—8J 109
Balmoral Clo. SW15—5H 89
Balmoral Ct. Wemb—8K 39
Balmoral Cres. E Mol—7L 101
Balmoral Dri. Borwd—7B 12
Balmoral Dri. Hay—7C 52
Balmoral Dri. S'hall—7K 53
Balmoral Gdns. W13—4E 70
Balmoral Gdns. Ilf—6D 48
Balmoral Gro. N7—2K 59
Balmoral M. W12—4D 72
Balmoral Rd. E7—9G 47
Balmoral Rd. E10—7M 45
Balmoral Rd. NW2—7F 56
Balmoral Rd. Enf—9D 6
Balmoral Rd. Harr—9L 37
Balmoral Rd. Horn—8H 51
Balmoral Rd. King—8K 103
Balmoral Rd. Romf—3F 50
Balmoral Rd. S at H, Dart
  —4M 115
Balmoral Rd. Wat—2G 9
Balmoral Rd. Wor Pk—4F 120
Balmoral Way. Sutt—2L 135
Balmore Cres. Barn—7E 14
Balmore St. N19—7F 42
Dalmuir Gdns. SW15—3G 89
Balnacraig Av. NW10—9C 40
Balquhain Clo. Asht—9H 133
Baltic Clo. SW19—4B 106
Baltic St. EC1—7A 60
Baltimore Pl. Well—1D 96
Balvernie Gro. SW18—6K 89
Bamborough Gdns. W12—3G 73
Bamford Av. Wemb—4K 55
Bamford Rd. Bark—2A 64
Bamford Rd. Brom—2A 110
Bamford Way. Romf—5M 33
Bampfylde Clo. Wall—5G 123
Bampton Rd. SE23—9H 93
Bampton Rd. Romf—8J 35
Banavie Gdns. Beck—5A 110
Banbury Ct. Sutt—9L 121
Banbury Rd. E9—3H 61
Banbury St. SW11—1C 90
Banbury St. Wat—7E 8
Banchory Rd. SE3—8F 78
Bancroft Av. N2—3C 42
Bancroft Av. Buck H—2E 30
Bancroft Ct. N'holt—4G 53
Bancroft Gdns. Harr—8A 22
Bancroft Gdns. Orp—2D 128
Bancroft Rd. E1—6H 61
Bancroft Rd. Harr—9A 22
Bandon Rise. Wall—7H 123
Bangalore St. SW15—2H 89
Dangor Clo. N'holt—1M 53
Banim St. W6—5F 72
Banister Rd. W10—6H 57
Bank Av. Mitc—6B 106
Dank Ct. Dart—5J 99
Bank End. SE1—2A 76
Bankfoot Rd. Brom—1C 110
Bankhurst Rd. SE6—6K 93
Bank La. SW15—4C 88
Bank La. King—4J 103
Banksian Wlk. Iswth—9C 70
Bankside. SE1—1A 76
Bankside. S Croy—8D 124
Bankside. Enf—3M 15
Bankside. S'hall—2H 69
Bankside. S Croy—8D 124
Bankside Av. N'holt—5E 52
Bankside Clo. Bex—1B 114
Bankside Clo. Cars—8C 122
Bankside Clo. West—9G 141
Bankside Dri. Th Dit—3F 118
Bankside Way. SE19—3C 108
Banks La. Bexh—3K 97
Bankton Rd. SW2—3L 91
Bankwell Rd. SE13—3C 94
Banner St. EC1—7A 60
Banning St. SE10—6C 78
Bannister Clo. Gnfd—1B 54
Bannister Rd. SW2—7L 91
Bannockburn Rd. SE18—5C 80
Banstead Gdns. N9—3C 28
Banstead Rd. Cars—1B 136
Banstead Rd. Eps & Bans
  —3G 135

Banstead Rd. Purl—3L 137
Banstead Rd. S. Sutt—3A 136
Banstead Way. Wall—7J 123
Banstock Rd. Edgw—6M 23
Banton Clo. Enf—4F 16
Bantry St. SE5—8B 76
Banwell Rd. Bex—5H 97
Banyard Rd. SE16—4F 76
Banyards. Horn—2J 51
Bapchild Pl. Orp—8G 113
Baptist Gdns. NW5—2E 58
Barandon Wlk. W11—1H 73
Barbara Clo. Shep—9A 100
Barbauld St. N16—8C 44
Barber Clo. N21—9L 15
Barberry Clo. Romf—7G 35
Barbers All. E13—6F 62
Barbers Rd. E15—5M 61
Barbican. EC2—8A 60
Barbican Rd. Gnfd—9M 53
Barb M. W6—4G 73
Barbon Clo. WC1—8K 59
Barbot Clo. N9—3E 28
Barchard St. SW18—4M 89
Barchester Clo. W7—2D 70
Barchester Clo. Uxb—7A 142
Barchester Rd. Harr—9B 22
Barchester St. E14—8M 61
Barclay Clo. SW6—8L 73
Barclay Oval. Wfd G—4E 30
Barclay Rd. E11—6D 46
Barclay Rd. E13—7G 63
Barclay Rd. E17—3A 46
Barclay Rd. N18—6B 28
Barclay Rd. SW6—8L 73
Barclay Rd. Croy—5B 124
Barcombe Av. SW2—8J 91
Barden St. SE18—8C 80
Bardfield Av. Romf—1H 49
Bardney Rd. Mord—8M 105
Bardolph Av. Croy—1K 139
Bardolph Rd. N7—9J 43
Bardolph Rd. Rich—2K 87
Bard Rd. W10—1H 73
Bardsey Pl. E1—7G 61
Bardsey Wlk. N1—2A 60
Bardsley Clo. Croy—5D 124
Bardsley La. SE10—7A 78
Barfett St. W10—7K 57
Barfield. S at H, Dart—5M 115
Barfield Av. N20—2D 26
Barfield Rd. E11—6D 46
Barfield Rd. Brom—7L 111
Barfields. Lou—6L 19
Barfields Gdns. Lou—6L 19
Barfields Path. Lou—6L 19
Barford Clo. NW4—9E 24
Barford St. N1—4L 59
Barforth Rd. SE15—2F 92
Barfreston Way. SE20—5F 108
Bargate Clo. SE18—6D 80
Bargate Clo. N Mald—2E 120
Barge Ho. Rd. E16—3M 79
Barge Ho. St. SE1—2L 75
Bargery Rd. SE6—7M 93
Barge Wlk. E Mol & King
  —1E 118
Barge Wlk. King—7B 102
  to 7H 103
Bargrove Clo. SE20—4E 108
Bargrove Cres. SE6—8K 93
Barham Av. Borwd—5K 11
Barham Clo. Drom—3J 127
Barham Clo. Chst—2M 111
Barham Clo. Romf—9M 33
Barham Clo. Wemb—2F 54
Barham Clo. Wey—6A 116
Barham Rd. SW20—4E 104
Barham Rd. Chst—2M 111
Barham Rd. Dart—6L 99
Barham Rd. S Croy 7A 124
Baring Clo. SE12—8E 94
Baring Rd. SE12—6E 94
Baring Rd. Barn—5B 14
Baring Rd. Croy—3E 124
Baring St. N1—4B 60
Barker Dri. NW1—3G 59
Barker St. SW10—7A 74
Barker Wlk. SW16—9H 91
Barkham Rd. N17—7C 28
Bark Hart Rd. Orp—2F 128
Barking Rd.—8D 62
  E16 1-233 & 2-242
  E13 remainder
Barkis Way. SE16—6F 76
Bark Pl. W2—1M 73
Barkston Gdns. SW5—5M 73
Barkston Path. Borwd—2L 11
Barkworth Rd. SE16—6G 77
Barlborough St. SE14—8H 77
Barlby Gdns. W10—7H 57
Barlby Rd. W10—8G 57

Barlee Cres. Uxb—8A 142
Barley Clo. Bush, Wat—7M 9
Barleycorn Way. E14—1K 77
Barleycorn Way. Horn—4K 51
Barley La. Ilf & Romf—5E 48
Barley Mow Pas. W4—6B 72
Barlow Clo. Wall—8J 123
Barlow Rd. NW6—2K 57
Barlow Rd. W3—2M 71
Barlow Rd. Hmptn—4L 101
Barlow St. SE17—5B 76
Barmeston Rd. SE6—8M 93
Barmor Clo. Harr—9M 21
Barmouth Av. Gnfd—5D 54
Barmouth Rd. SW18—5A 90
Barmouth Rd. Croy—4H 125
Barnabas Rd. E9—1H 61
Barnaby Way. Chig—3M 31
Barnacre Clo. Uxb—9B 142
Barnard Clo. SE18—4L 79
Barnard Clo. Chst—5B 112
Barnard Clo. Sun—4F 100
Barnard Clo. Wall—9H 123
Barnard Gdns. Hay—7F 52
Barnard Gdns. N Mald—8E 104
Barnard Gro. E15—3D 62
Barnard Hill. N10—8F 26
Barnard M. SW11—3C 90
Barnardo Dri. Ilf—2A 48
Barnardo St. E1—9H 61
Barnard Rd. SW11—3C 90
Barnard Rd. Enf—4F 16
Barnard Rd. Mitc—7E 106
Barnards Pl. S Croy—1M 137
Barnby Sq. E15—4C 62
Barnby St. E15—4C 62
Barnby St. NW1—5G 59
Barn Clo. N'holt—5G 53
Barn Cres. Purl—5B 138
Darn Cres. Stan—6G 23
Barncroft Clo. Lou—7L 19
Barncroft Clo. Uxb—8F 142
Barncroft Rd. Lou—7L 19
Barnehurst Av. Eri & Bexh
  —9A 82
Barnehurst Clo. Eri—9A 82
Barnehurst Rd. Bexh—1A 98
Barn Elms Pk. SW15—2G 89
Barn End Dri. Dart—9G 99
Barn End La. Dart—1G 115
Barnes All. Hmptn—6A 102
Barnes Av. SW13—8E 72
Barnes Clo. E12—9H 47
Barnes Ct. E16—8G 63
Barnes Ct. Wfd G—5H 31
Barnes Cray Rd. Dart—3E 98
Barnes End. N Mald—9E 104
Barnes High St. SW13—1D 88
Barnes Pikle. W5—1H 71
Barnes Rd. N18—4G 29
Barnes Rd. Ilf—1A 64
Barnes St. E14—9J 61
Barnet By-Pass. NW7 & NW4
  —6D 24
Barnet By-Pass. Rd. Borwd,
  Barn & Pot B—8B 12
Barnet Dri. Brom—4J 127
Barnet Ga. La. Barn—8D 12
Barnet Gro. E2—6E 60
Barnet Hill. Darn—GK 13
Barnet La. N20 & Barn—1K 25
Barnet La. Borwd—8J 11
Barnet Rd. Barn—8C 12
Barnett Clo. Eri 1D 98
Barnett St. E1—9F 60
Barnett Wood La. Lea & Asht
  —9H 133
Barnet Way. NW7—3B 24
Barnet Wood Rd. Brom—4G 127
Barney Clo. SE7—6G 79
Barnfield. Bans—6M 135
Barnfield. N Mald 1C 120
Barnfield Av. Croy—4G 125
Barnfield Av. King—1H 103
Barnfield Av. Mitc—7F 106
Barnfield Clo. Swan—2A 130
Barnfield Gdns. King—1J 103
Barnfield Rd. SE18—7M 79
  (in two parts)
Barnfield Rd. W5 7C 55
Barnfield Rd. Belv—7K 81
Barnfield Rd. Edgw—8A 24
Barnfield Rd. Orp—7H 113
Barnfield Rd. S Croy—1C 138
Barnfield Wood Clo. Beck
  —1B 126
Barnfield Wood Rd. Beck
  —1B 126
Barnham Rd. Gnfd—6A 54
Barnham St. SE1—3C 76
Barnhill. Pinn—3G 37
Darn Hill. Wemb—6L 39
Barnhill Av. Brom—9D 110

Barnhill La. Hay—6F 52
Barnhill Rd. Hay—7F 52
Barnhill Rd. Wemb—8A 40
Barnhurst Path. Wat—5G 21
Barnlea Clo. Felt—8J 85
Barnmead Gdns. Dag—1K 65
Barnmead Rd. Beck—5H 109
Barnmead Rd. Dag—1K 65
Barn Rise. Wemb—6L 39
Barnsbury Clo. N Mald—8A 104
Barnsbury Cres. Surb—3A 120
Barnsbury Gro. N7—3K 59
Barnsbury La. Surb—4M 119
Barnsbury M. N1—3L 59
Barnsbury Pk. N1—3L 59
Barnsbury Rd. N1—4L 59
Barnsbury Sq. N1—3L 59
Barnsbury St. N1—3L 59
Barnsbury Ter. N1—3K 59
Barnscroft. SW20—7F 104
Barnsdale Cres. Orp—1E 128
Barnsdale Rd. W9—7K 57
Barnsfield Pl. Uxb—3A 142
Barnsley Rd. Romf—7K 35
Barnsley St. E1—7F 60
Barnstaple Path. Romf—5H 35
Barnstaple Rd. Romf—5G 35
Barnstaple Rd. Ruis—8G 37
Barn St. N16—7C 44
Barn Way. Wemb—6L 39
Barnwell Rd. SW2—4L 91
Barnwood Clo. W9—7M 57
Barnwood Clo. Ruis—7B 36
Barnwood Ct. E16—2F 78
Baron Clo. N1—5L 59
Baroness Rd. E2—6D 60
Baronet Gro. N17—8E 28
Baronet Rd. N17—8E 28
Baron Gdns. Ilf—1A 48
Baron Gro. Mitc—8C 106
Baron Rd. Dag—6H 49
Baronsclere Ct. N6—5H 43
Baron's Ct. Rd. W14—6J 73
Baronsfield Rd. Twic—5F 86
Baron Ga. Barn—8C 14
Baron's Hurst. Eps—8A 134
Barons Keep. W14—6J 73
Barons Mead. Harr—2C 38
Baronsmead Rd. SW13—9E 72
Baronsmede. W5—3K 71
Baronsmere Rd. N2—2C 42
Baron's Pl. SE1—3L 75
Barons, The. Twic—5F 86
Baron St. N1—5L 59
Baron's Wlk. Croy—1J 125
Baron Wlk. E16—8D 62
Baron Wlk. Mitc—8C 106
Barque M. SE8—7L 77
Barrack Rd. Houn—3H 85
Barra Hall Cir. Hay—1C 68
Barra Hall Rd. Hay—1C 68
Barratt Av. N22—9K 27
Barratt Industrial Pk. S'hall
  —2L 69
Barratt Way. Harr—1B 38
Barrenger Rd. N10—8D 26
Barrets Grn. Rd. NW10—6A 56
Barrett Rd. E17—2A 46
Barrett's Gro. N16—1C 60
Barrett St. W1—9E 58
Barrhill Rd. SW2—8J 91
Barrie Clo. Coul—8G 137
Barriedale. SE14—1J 93
Barrier App. SE7—4H 79
Barringer Sq. SW17—1E 106
Barrington Clo. NW5—1E 58
Barrington Grn. Lou—6M 19
Barrington Rd. E12—2L 63
Barrington Rd. N8—3H 43
Barrington Rd. SW9 2M 91
Barrington Rd. Bexh—1H 97
Barrington Rd. Lou—6M 19
Barrington Rd. Purl—4G 137
Barrington Rd. Sutt—4L 121
Barrington Vs. SE18—9L 79
Barrosa Dri. Hmptn—5L 101
Barrow Av. Cars—9D 122
Barrow Clo. N21—3M 27
Barrowdene Clo. Pinn—9J 21
Barrowell Grn. N21—2M 27
Barrowfield Clo. N9—3F 28
Barrowfield La. N9—3F 28
Barrowgate Rd. W4—6A 72
Barrow Hedges Clo. Cars
  —9C 122
Barrow Hedges Way. Cars
  —9C 122
Barrow Hill. Wor Pk—4C 120
Barrow Hill Clo. Wor Pk
  —4C 120
Barrow Hill Rd. NW8—5C 58

Barrow La. Wal X—3A 6
(in two parts)
Barrow Point Av. Pinn—9J 21
Barrow Point La. Pinn—9J 21
Barrow Rd. SW16—3H 107
Barrow Rd. Croy—7L 123
Barrowsfield. S Croy—4E 138
Barrs Rd. NW10—3B 56
Barry Av. N15—4D 44
Barry Av. Bexh—8J 81
Barry Clo. Orp—5C 128
Barry Rd. E6—9J 63
Barry Rd. NW10—3A 56
Barry Rd. SE22—5E 92
Barset Rd. SE15—2G 93
Barston Rd. SE27—9A 92
Barstow Cres. SW2—7K 91
Barter St. WC1—8J 59
Bartholomew Clo. EC1—8A 60
Bartholomew Clo. SW18
—3A 90
Bartholomew Ct. Enf—1J 17
Bartholomew La. EC2—9B 60
Bartholomew Rd. NW5—2G 59
Bartholomew Sq. EC1—7A 60
Bartholomew St. SE1—4B 76
Bartholomew Vs. NW5—2G 59
Bartholomew Way. Swan
—7C 114
Barth Rd. SE18—5C 80
Bartle Av. E6—5J 63
Bartle Rd. W11—9J 57
Bartlett Ct. EC4—9L 59
Bartlett St. S Croy—7B 124
Bartlow Gdns. Romf—8B 34
Barton Av. Romf—6M 49
Barton Clo. E6—9K 63
Barton Clo. E9—1G 61
Barton Clo. SE15—2F 92
Barton Clo. Bexh—4J 97
Barton Clo. Chig—2A 32
Barton Clo. Shep—1A 116
Barton Grn. N Mald—6B 104
Barton Meadows. Ilf—2M 47
Barton Rd. W14—6J 73
Barton Rd. Horn—6E 50
Barton Rd. Sidc—3J 113
Barton Rd. S at H, Dart—5M 115
Bartons, The. Borwd—8H 11
Barton St. SW1—4J 75
Barton Way. Borwd—4L 11
Bartram Clo. Uxb—7F 142
Bartram Rd. SE4—4J 93
Bartrams La. Barn—2A 14
Barwell Trading Est. Chess
—9H 119
Barwick Rd. E7—9F 46
Barwood Av. W Wick—3M 125
Basden Gro. Felt—8L 85
Basedale Rd. Dag—3F 64
Bashley Rd. NW10—7B 56
Basil Av. E6—6J 63
Basildene Rd. Houn—2H 85
Basildon Av. Ilf—8L 31
Basildon Clo. Sutt—1M 135
Basildon Rd. SE2—6E 80
Basil Gdns. Croy—3H 125
Basilon Rd. Bexh—1J 97
Basil St. SW3—4D 74
Basing Clo. Th Dit—2D 118
Basing Ct. SE15—9D 76
Basingdon Way. SE5—3B 92
Basing Dri. Bex—5K 97
Basingfield Rd. Th Dit—2D 118
Basinghall Av. EC2—9B 60
Basinghall Gdns. Sutt—1M 135
Basinghall St. EC2—9B 60
Basing Hill. NW11—6K 41
Basing Hill. Wemb—7K 39
Basing Ho. Yd. E2—6C 60
Basing Pl. E2—6C 60
Basing Rd. Bans—6K 135
Basing St. W11—9K 57
Basing Way. N3—1L 41
Basing Way. Th Dit—2D 118
Basire St. N1—4A 60
Baskerville Rd. SW18—6C 90
Basket Gdns. SE9—4J 95
Baslow Clo. Harr—8B 22
Basnett Rd. SW11—2E 90
Bassano St. SE22—4D 92
Bassant Rd. SE18—7D 80
Bassein Pk. Rd. W12—3D 72
Bassett Clo. Sutt—1M 135
Bassett Gdns. Iswth—8A 70
Bassett Rd. W10—9H 57
Bassett Rd. Uxb—3A 142
Bassett's Clo. Orp—6M 127
Bassett St. NW5—2E 58
Bassett's Way. Orp—6M 127
Bassett Way. Gnfd—9M 53
Bassingham Rd. SW18—6A 90

Bassingham Rd. Wemb—2H 55
Basswood Clo. SE15—2F 92
Bastable Av. Bark—5D 64
Bastion Rd. SE2—6E 80
Baston Mnr. Rd. Brom—6F 126
Baston Rd. Brom—4F 126
Bastwick St. EC1—7A 60
Basuto Rd. SW6—9L 73
Batavia Clo. Sun—5F 100
Batavia M. SE14—8J 77
Batavia Rd. SE14—8J 77
Batavia Rd. Sun—5F 100
Batchelor St. N1—4L 59
Batchwood Grn. Orp—7E 112
Batchworth La. N'wd—5A 20
Bateman Clo. Bark—2A 64
Bateman Rd. E4—6L 29
Bateman's Row. EC2—7C 60
Bateman St. W1—9H 59
Bates Cres. Croy—7L 123
Bates St. SE18—5C 80
Bates Rd. Romf—7L 35
Bate St. E14—1K 77
Bath Clo. SE15—9G 77
Bathgate Rd. SW19—9H 89
Bath Gro. E2—5E 60
Bath Ho. Rd. Croy—3J 123
Bathhurst Rd. Ilf—6M 47
Bath Pl. EC1—6C 60
Bath Pl. Barn—5K 13
Bath Rd. E7—2H 63
Bath Rd. N9—2G 29
Bath Rd. W4—5C 72
Bath Rd. Dart—6F 98
Bath Rd. Mitc—7B 106
Bath Rd. Romf—4J 49
Bath Rd.—9G 143 to 2L 85
W Dray—9G 143
Hay—9M 143
Houn—9E 68
Baths Rd. Brom—8H 111
Bath St. EC1—6A 60
Bath Ter. SE1—4A 76
Bathurst Av. SW19—5M 105
Bathurst Gdns. NW10—5F 56
Bathurst M. W2—1B 74
Bathurst St. W2—1B 74
Bathway. SE18—5L 79
Batley Pl. N16—8D 44
Batley Rd. N16—8D 44
Batley Rd. Enf—3A 16
Batman Clo. W12—2F 72
Batoum Gdns. W6—4G 73
Batson St. W12—3E 72
Batsworth Rd. Mitc—7B 106
Battenberg Wlk. SE19—3C 108
Batten Clo. E6—9K 63
Batten St. SW11—2C 90
Battersby Rd. SE6—8B 94
Battersea Bri. SW3 & SW11
—8B 74
Battersea Bri. Rd. SW11—8C 74
Battersea Chu. Rd. SW11
—9B 74
Battersea High St. SW11
—9B 74
Battersea Pk. Rd.—1C 90
SW8 1-179 & 2-18
SW11 remainder
Battersea Rise. SW11—4C 90
Battery Rd. SE28—3B 80
Battishill St. N1—3M 59
Battle Bri. La. SE1—2C 76
Battle Bri. Rd. NW1—5J 59
Battle Clo. SW19—3A 106
Battledean Rd. N5—1M 59
Battle Rd. Belv & Eri—5A 82
Battlers Grn. Dri. Rad—1C 10
Batty St. E1—9E 60
Baudwin Rd. SE6—8C 94
Baugh Rd. Sidc—2G 113
Baulk, The. SW18—6L 89
Bavant Rd. SW16—6J 107
Bavaria Rd. N19—7J 43
Bavent Rd. SE5—1A 92
Bawdale Rd. SE22—4D 92
Bawdsey Av. Ilf—2D 48
Bawtree Clo. Sutt—2A 136
Bawtree Rd. SE14—8J 77
Bawtree Rd. Uxb—2B 142
Bawtry Rd. N20—3D 26
Baxendale. N20—2A 26
Baxendale St. E2—6E 60
Baxter Clo. Uxb—6F 142
Baxter Rd. E16—9G 63
Baxter Rd. N1—2B 60
Baxter Rd. N17—1E 44
Baxter Rd. N18—4F 28
Baxter Rd. Ilf—1M 63
Bayfield Rd. SE9—4K 95
Bayford Rd. NW10—6H 57
Bayford St. E8—3F 60
Bayham Pl. NW1—5G 59

Bayham Rd. W4—4B 72
Bayham Rd. W13—1F 70
Bayham Rd. Mord—8M 105
Bayham St. NW1—4G 59
Bayhurst Dri. N'wd—6D 20
Bayley St. WC1—8H 59
Bayley Wlk. SE2—6J 81
Baylin Rd. SW18—5M 89
Baylis Rd. SE1—3L 75
Bayliss Av. SE28—1H 81
Bayly Rd. Dart—5L 99
Bayne Clo. E6—9K 63
Baynes Clo. Enf—3E 16
Baynes M. NW3—2B 58
Baynes St. NW1—3G 59
Bayonne Rd. SW6—7J 73
Bayston Rd. N16—8D 44
Bayswater Rd. W2—1M 73
Baythorne St. E3—8K 61
Baythorne St. E3
Baytree Rd. SW2—3K 91
Bay Tree Wlk. Wat—2D 8
Baywood Sq. Chig—4F 32
Bazalgette Clo. N Mald—9B 104
Bazalgette Gdns. N Mald
—9B 104
Bazely St. E14—1A 78
Bazile Rd. N21—8L 15
Beacham Clo. SE7—7H 79
Beachborough Rd. Brom
—1A 110
Beachcroft Rd. E11—8C 46
Beachcroft Way. N19—6H 43
Beach Gro. Felt—8L 85
Beachy Rd. E3—3L 61
Beacon Clo. Bans—8H 135
Beacon Clo. Uxb—1B 142
Beacon Gro. Cars—6E 122
Beacon Hill. N7—1J 59
Beacon Hill. Purf—6M 83
Beacon Rd. SE13—5B 94
Beacon Rd. Eri—8F 82
Beacon Rd. Houn—5E 144
Beaconsfield Clo. N11—5E 26
Beaconsfield Clo. SE3—7E 78
Beaconsfield Clo. W4—6A 72
Beaconsfield Pl. Eps—4C 134
Beaconsfield Rd. E10—8A 46
Beaconsfield Rd. E16—7D 62
Beaconsfield Rd. E17—4K 45
Beaconsfield Rd. N9—3E 28
Beaconsfield Rd. N11—3E 26
Beaconsfield Rd. N15—2C 44
Beaconsfield Rd. NW10—2D 56
Beaconsfield Rd. SE3—8D 78
Beaconsfield Rd. SE9—8J 95
Beaconsfield Rd. SE17—6C 76
Beaconsfield Rd. W4—4B 72
Beaconsfield Rd. W5—3H 71
Beaconsfield Rd. Bex—8C 98
Beaconsfield Rd. Brom
—7H 111
Beaconsfield Rd. Croy—1B 124
Beaconsfield Rd. Enf—1H 17
Beaconsfield Rd. Esh—9C 118
Beaconsfield Rd. Hay—2G 69
Beaconsfield Rd. N Mald
—6B 104
Beaconsfield Rd. S'hall—2H 69
Beaconsfield Rd. Surb—2K 119
Beaconsfield Rd. Twic—5F 86
Beaconsfield Ter. Romf—4H 49
Beaconsfield Ter. Rd. W14
—4J 73
Beaconsfield Wlk. SW6—9L 73
Beacons, The. Lou—2L 19
Beacontree Rd. E11—5D 46
Beacon Way. Bans—8H 135
Beadlow Clo. Cars—1B 122
Beadman St. SE27—1M 107
Beadnell Rd. SE23—7H 93
Beadon Rd. W6—5G 73
Beadon Rd. Brom—8E 110
Beaford Gro. SW20—7J 105
Beagle Clo. Felt—1F 100
Beagle Clo. Rad—1D 10
Beagles Clo. Orp—4H 129
Beak St. W1—1G 75
Beal Clo. Well—9E 80
Beale Clo. N13—5M 27
Beale Pl. E3—5K 61
Beale Rd. E3—4K 61
Beal Rd. Ilf—7L 47
Beam Av. Dag—4M 65
Beaminster Gdns. Ilf—1M 47
Beamish Dri. Bush, Wat—1A 22
Beamish Ga. NW1—3H 59
Beamish Rd. N9—1E 28
Beamish Rd. Orp—2G 129
Beamway. Dag—3B 66
Beanacre Clo. E9—2K 61
Bean Rd. Bexh—3H 97
Beanshaw. SE9—1L 111

Beansland Gro. Romf—1J 49
Bear All. EC4—9M 59
Beardell St. SE19—3D 108
Beardow Gro. N14—8G 15
Beard Rd. King—2K 103
Beardsfield. E13—5E 62
Beard's Hill. Hmptn—5L 101
Beard's Hill Clo. Hmptn
—5L 101
Beardsley Way. W3—3B 72
Beard's Rd. Ashf—3C 100
Bearfield Rd. King—4J 103
Bear Gdns. SE1—2A 76
Bearing Clo. Chig—4E 32
Bearing Way. Chig—4E 32
Bear La. SE1—2M 75
Bear Rd. Felt—1H 101
Bearstead Rise. SE4—4K 93
Bearsted Ter. Beck—5L 109
Bear St. WC2—1H 75
Beasley's Ait La. Sun—1D 116
Beatrice Av. SW16—6K 107
Beatrice Av. Wemb—1J 55
Beatrice Clo. E13—7E 62
Beatrice Clo. Pinn—2E 36
Beatrice Rd. E17—3L 45
Beatrice Rd. N4—5L 43
Beatrice Rd. N9—9G 17
Beatrice Rd. SE1—5E 76
Beatrice Rd. Rich—4K 87
Beatrice Rd. S'hall—2K 69
Beatson Wlk. SE16—2J 77
Beattock Rise. N10—2F 42
Beatty Rd. N16—9C 44
Beatty Rd. Stan—6G 23
Beatty St. NW1—5G 59
Beattyville Gdns. Ilf—2L 47
Beauchamp Pl. SW3—4C 74
Beauchamp Rd. E7—3F 62
Beauchamp Rd. SE19—5B 108
Beauchamp Rd. SW11—3C 90
Beauchamp Rd. E Mol—9M 101
Beauchamp Rd. Sutt—6L 121
Beauchamp Rd. Twic—6E 86
Beauchamp St. EC1—8L 59
Beauchamp Ter. SW15—2F 88
Beauclerc Ct. Sun—6G 101
Beauclerc Rd. W6—4G 73
Beauclerk Clo. Felt—7F 84
Beaudesert M. W Dray—4J 143
Beaufort Av. Harr—2E 38
Beaufort Clo. SW15—6F 88
Beaufort Clo. W5—8K 55
Beaufort Clo. Romf—2A 50
Beaufort Ct. Rich—1G 103
Beaufort Dri. NW11—2L 41
Beaufort Gdns. NW4—4G 41
Beaufort Gdns. SW3—4C 74
Beaufort Gdns. SW16—4K 107
Beaufort Gdns. Houn—9J 69
Beaufort Gdns. Ilf—6L 47
Beaufort Rd. W5—8K 55
Beaufort Rd. King—8J 103
Beaufort Rd. Rich—1G 103
Beaufort Rd. Ruis—7B 36
Beaufort Rd. Twic—6G 87
Beaufort St. SW3—7B 74
Beaufort Way. Eps—9E 120
Beaufoy Rd. N17—7C 28
Beaufoy Wlk. SE11—5K 75
Beaulieu Av. SE26—1F 108
Beaulieu Clo. NW9—2C 40
Beaulieu Clo. SE5—2B 92
Beaulieu Clo. Mitc—5E 106
Beaulieu Clo. Twic—5H 87
Beaulieu Clo. Wat—1G 21
Beaulieu Dri. Pinn—4H 37
Beaulieu Gdns. N21—9A 16
Beauly Way. Romf—6C 34
Beaumanor Gdns. SE9—1L 111
Beaumaris Dri. Wfd G—7H 31
Beaumont Av. W14—6K 73
Beaumont Av. Harr—4M 37
Beaumont Av. Rich—2K 87
Beaumont Av. Wemb—1G 55
Beaumont Clo. King—4L 103
Beaumont Clo. Romf—9G 35
Beaumont Cres. W14—6K 73
Beaumont Cres. Rain—2E 66
Beaumont Dri. Ashf—2B 100
Beaumont Gdns. NW3—7L 41
Beaumont Gro. E1—7H 61
Beaumont M. W1—8E 58
Beaumont Pl. W1—7G 59
Beaumont Pl. Barn—3K 13
Beaumont Rise. N19—6H 43
Beaumont Rd. E10—5M 45
(in two parts)
Beaumont Rd. E13—6F 62
Beaumont Rd. SE19—3A 108
Beaumont Rd. SW19—6J 89
Beaumont Rd. W4—4A 72
Beaumont Rd. Orp—1B 128

Beaumont Rd. Purl—5L 137
Beaumont Sq. E1—8H 61
Beaumont St. W1—8E 58
Beaumont Wlk. NW3—3D 58
Beauvais Ter. N'holt—6H 53
Beauval Rd. SE22—5D 92
Beaverbank Rd. SE9—7B 96
Beaver Clo. SE20—4E 108
Beaver Clo. Hmptn—5M 101
Beavercote Wlk. Belv—6K 81
Beaver Rd. Ilf—5G 33
Beavers Cres. Houn—3G 85
Beavers La. Houn—2G 85
Beaverwood Rd. Chst—2C 112
Beavor La. W6—5E 72
(in two parts)
Bebbington Rd. SE18—5C 80
Beblets Clo. Orp—7D 128
Beccles Dri. Bark—2C 64
Beccles St. E14—1K 77
Bec Clo. Ruis—8H 37
Beckenham Gdns. N9—3C 28
Beckenham Gro. Brom—6B 110
Beckenham Hill Est. Beck
—2M 109
Beckenham Hill Rd.—3M 109
SE6 1-95 & 2-62
Beck remainder
Beckenham La. Brom—6C 110
Beckenham Pl. Pk. Beck
—4M 109
Beckenham Rd. Beck—5H 109
Beckenham Rd. W Wick
—2A 126
Beckenshaw Gdns. Bans
—7C 136
Becket Av. E6—6L 63
Becket Clo. SE25—1E 124
Becket Fold. Harr—3D 38
Becket Rd. N18—4G 29
Becket St. SE1—4B 76
Beckett Av. Kenl—7M 137
Beckett Clo. NW10—2C 56
Beckett Clo. SW16—8H 91
Becketts Clo. Orp—5D 128
Becketts Pl. Tedd—5H 103
Beckett Wlk. Beck—3J 109
Beckford Pl. SE17—6A 76
Beckford Rd. Croy—1D 124
Beck La. Beck—7H 109
Becklow Rd. W12—3D 72
Beck River Pk. Beck—5L 109
Beck Rd. E8—4F 60
Becks Rd. Sidc—9E 96
Beckton Rd. E16—8D 62
Beckway. Beck—7K 109
Beckway Rd. SW16—6H 107
Beckway St. SE17—5C 76
(in two parts)
Beckwith Rd. SE24—4B 92
Beclands Rd. SW17—3E 106
Becmead Av. SW16—1H 107
Becmead Av. Harr—3F 38
Becondale Rd. SE19—2C 108
Becontree Av. E17—8B 30
Becontree Av. Dag—9F 48
Bective Pl. SW15—3K 89
Bective Rd. E7—9E 46
Bective Rd. SW15—3K 89
Becton Pl. Eri—9M 81
Bedale Rd. Enf—2A 16
Bedale Rd. Romf—5L 35
Bedale St. SE1—2B 76
Bedale Wlk. Dart—7M 99
Beddington Farm Rd. Croy
—2J 123
Beddington Gdns. Cars
—8E 122
Beddington Gdns. Wall—8F 122
Beddington Grn. Orp—5D 112
Beddington Gro. Wall—7H 123
Beddington La. Croy—1G 123
Beddington Path. Orp—5D 112
Beddington Rd. Ilf—5D 48
Beddington Rd. Orp—5C 112
Beddlestead La. Warl—9D 140
Bede Clo. Pinn—8H 21
Bedens Rd. Sidc—3J 113
Bede Rd. Romf—4G 49
Bedfont Clo. Felt—5A 84
Bedfont Clo. Mitc—6E 106
Bedfont Ct. Stai—2A 144
Bedfont La. Felt—6D 84
Bedfont Rd. Felt—7A 84
Bedfont Rd. Stai—5C 144
Bedford Av. WC1—8H 59
Bedford Av. Barn—7K 13
Bedford Av. Hay—9F 52
Bedfordbury. WC2—1J 75
Bedford Clo. N10—7E 26
Bedford Ct. WC2—1J 75
Bedford Cres. Enf—8E 6
Bedford Gdns. W8—2L 73

Bedford Gdns. Horn—7G 51
Bedford Hill—7F 90
SW12 1-203 & 2-210
SW16 remainder
Bedford Pk. Croy—3A 124
Bedford Pk. Corner. W4—5C 72
Bedford Pas. W1—8G 59
Bedford Pl. WC1—8J 59
Bedford Pl. Croy—3B 124
Bedford Rd. E6—4L 63
Bedford Rd. E17—9L 29
Bedford Rd. E18—9E 30
Bedford Rd. N2—1C 42
Bedford Rd. N8—4H 43
Bedford Rd. N9—9F 16
Bedford Rd. N15—2C 44
Bedford Rd. N22—9J 27
Bedford Rd. NW7—2C 24
Bedford Rd. SW4—3J 91
Bedford Rd. W4—4B 72
Bedford Rd. W13—1F 70
Bedford Rd. Dart—6L 99
Bedford Rd. Harr—4A 38
Bedford Rd. Ilf—8M 47
Bedford Rd. N'wd—4A 20
Bedford Rd. Orp—4F 128
Bedford Rd. Ruis—9D 36
Bedford Rd. Sidc—9C 96
Bedford Rd. Twic—9B 86
Bedford Rd. Wor Pk—4G 121
Bedford Row. WC1—8K 59
Bedford Sq. WC1—8H 59
Bedford St. WC2—1J 75
Bedford St. Wat—3F 8
Bedford Way. WC1—7H 59
Bedgebury Gdns. SW19—8J 89
Bedgebury Rd. SE9—3H 95
Bedivere Rd. Brom—9E 94
Bedlow Way. Croy—6K 123
Bedmond Grn. Abb L, Wat—1D 4
Bedmond Rd. Abb L, Wat—2D 4
Bedonwell Rd.—7J 81
SE2 365-397 & 402-434
Belv & Bexh remainder
Bedser Dri. Gnfd—1B 54
Bedster Gdns. E Mol—6M 101
Bedwardine Rd. SE19—4C 108
Bedwell Gdns. Hay—6C 68
(in two parts)
Bedwell Rd. N17—8C 28
Bedwell Rd. Belv—6L 81
Bedwin Way. SE16—6F 76
Beeby Rd. E16—8F 62
Beech Av. N20—1C 26
Beech Av. W3—2C 72
Beech Av. Bren—8F 70
Beech Av. Buck H—2F 30
Beech Av. Ruis—6F 36
Beech Av. Sidc—6E 96
Beech Av. S Croy—3B 138
Beech Av. Swan—8D 114
Beech Av. Upm—8M 51
Beech Clo. N9—8F 16
Beech Clo. SW15—6E 88
Beech Clo. SW19—3G 105
Beech Clo. Ashf—2B 100
Beech Clo. Cars—4D 122
Beech Clo. Horn—8F 50
Beech Clo. Sun—6H 101
Beech Clo. W on T—6G 117
Beech Clo. W Dray—4L 143
Beech Copse. Brom—6K 111
Beech Copse. S Croy—7C 124
Beech Ct. E17—1B 46
Beech Ct. Surb—2H 119
Beechcroft. Chst—4L 111
Beechcroft Av. NW11—5K 41
Beechcroft Av. Bexh—9B 82
Beechcroft Av. Harr—5L 37
Beechcroft Av. Kenl—7B 138
Beechcroft Av. N Mald—6A 104
Beechcroft Av. Rick—8A 8
Beechcroft Av. S'hall—2K 69
Beechcroft Clo. Houn—8J 69
Beechcroft Clo. Orp—6B 128
Beech Croft Ct. N5—9M 43
Beechcroft Gdns. Wemb —8K 39
Beechcroft Manor. Wey —5B 116
Beechcroft Rd. E18—9F 30
Beechcroft Rd. SW14—2A 88
Beechcroft Rd. SW17—8C 90
Beechcroft Rd. Bush, Wat—7J 9
Beechcroft Rd. Chess—5K 119
Beechcroft Rd. Orp—6B 128
Beechdale. N21—2K 27
Beechdale Rd. SW2—5K 91
Beech Dell. Orp—6K 127
Beech Dri. N2—9D 26
Beech Dri. Borwd—4K 11
Beechen Cliff Way. Iswth —1D 86
Beechen Gro. Pinn—1K 37
Beechen Gro. Wat—5F 8
Beechenlea La. Swan—8E 114
Beechen Pl. SE23—8H 93
Beeches Av. Cars—9C 122
Beeches Rd. SW17—9C 90
Beeches Rd. Sutt—3J 121
Beeches, The. Bans—8M 135
Beeches, The. Croy—7B 124
Beeches Wlk. Cars—1B 136
Beechfield. Bans—5M 135
Beechfield Gdns. Romf—5A 50
Beechfield Rd. N4—4A 44
Beechfield Rd. SE6—7K 93
Beechfield Rd. Brom—6G 111
Beechfield Rd. Eri—8C 82
Beechfield Wlk. Wal A—8K 7
Beech Gdns. W5—3J 71
Beech Gdns. Dag—3A 66
Beech Gro. Eps—9F 134
Beech Gro. Ilf—6C 32
Beech Gro. Mitc—9H 107
Beech Gro. N Mald—7B 104
Beech Gro. S Ock—3M 83
Beech Hall Cres. E4—7B 30
Beech Hall Rd. E4—7A 30
Beech Hill. Barn—2B 14
Beech Hill Av. Barn—3A 14
Beech Hill Gdns. Wal A—1F 18
Beech Ho. Rd. Croy—5B 124
Beechill Rd. SE9—4L 95
Beech La. Buck H—2F 30
Beech Lawns. N12—5B 26
Beechmont Clo. Brom—2C 110
Beechmore Gdns. Sutt—4H 121
Beechmore Rd. SW11—9D 74
Beechmount Av. W7—8B 54
Beecholme. Bans—6J 135
Beecholme Av. Mitc—5F 106
Beechpark Way. Wat—1C 8
Beech Rd. N11—6J 27
Beech Rd. SW16—7K 107
Beech Rd. Dart—7H 99
Beech Rd. Eps—7D 134
Beech Rd. Felt—6C 84
Beech Rd. Orp—9F 128
Beech Rd. Wat—1E 8
Beech Rd. West—9F 140
Beech Rd. Wey—6B 116
Beechrow. King—1J 103
Beech St. EC2—8A 60
Beech St. Romf—2A 50
Beechtree Clo. Stan—5G 23
Beech Tree Glade. E4—1D 30
Beechvale Clo. N12—5C 26
Beech Wlk. NW7—6C 24
Beech Wlk. Dart—3E 98
Beech Wlk. Eps—3E 134
Beech Way. NW10—3B 56
Beechway. Bex—5H 97
Beech Way. Eps—7D 134
Beech Way. S Croy—5H 139
Beech Way. Twic—9L 85
Beechwood Av. N3—1K 41
Beechwood Av. Coul—7F 136
Beechwood Av. Gnfd—6M 53
Beechwood Av. Harr—8M 37
Beechwood Av. Hay—1B 68
Beechwood Av. Orp—8C 128
Beechwood Av. Rich—9L 71
Beechwood Av. Ruis—7D 36
Beechwood Av. Sun—3E 100
Beechwood Av. T Hth—8M 107
Beechwood Av. Uxb—9E 142
Beechwood Av. Wey—6C 116
Beechwood Circ. Harr—8A 38
Beech Wood Clo. NW7—5C 24
Beechwood Clo. Surb—2H 119
Beechwood Clo. Wey—6C 116
Beechwood Ct. Sun—3E 100
Beechwood Cres. Bexh—2J 97
Beechwood Dri. Kes—6H 127
Beechwood Dri. Wfd G—5D 30
Beechwood Gdns. NW10—6K 55
Beechwood Gdns. Harr—8M 37
Beechwood Gdns. Ilf—3K 47
Beechwood Gdns. Rain—8F 66
Beechwood Mnr. Wey—6C 116
Beechwood Pk. E18—1E 46
Beechwood Rise. Wat—9F 4
Beechwood Rd. E8—2D 60
Beechwood Rd. N8—1H 43
Beechwood Rd. S Croy—1C 138
Beechworth Clo. NW3—7M 41
Beecot La. W on T—4G 117
Beecroft Rd. SE4—4J 93
Beehive Clo. Borwd—8H 11
Beehive La. Ilf—3K 47
Beehive Pl. SW9—2L 91
Beeken Dene. Orp—6A 128
Beeleigh Rd. Mord—8M 105
Beesfield La. F'ham, Dart —2L 131
Beeston Clo. Wat—4H 21
Beeston Ct. E8—1E 60
Beeston Dri. Wal X—1D 6
Beeston Pl. SW1—4F 74
Beeston Rd. Barn—8B 14
Beeston Way. Felt—5G 85
Beethoven Rd. Borwd—8H 11
Beethoven St. W10—6J 57
Beeton Clo. Pinn—7L 21
Begbie Rd. SE3—9G 79
Beggars Hill. Eps—9D 120
Beggars Hollow. Enf—1B 16
Begonia Pl. Hmptn—3L 101
Begonia Wlk. W12—9D 56
Beira St. SW12—6F 90
Bekesbourne St. E14—9J 61
Belasis Av. SW2—8J 91
Belcroft Clo. Brom—4D 110
Beldham Gdns. E Mol—7M 101
Belfairs Dri. Romf—5G 49
Belfairs Gdns. Wat—5H 21
Belfast Gdns. SE3—7D 78
Belfast Rd. N16—7D 44
Belfast Rd. SE25—8F 108
Belfield Rd. Eps—1B 134
Belfont Wlk. N7—9J 43
Belford Gro. SE18—5L 79
Belford Rd. Borwd—2K 11
Belfort Rd. SE15—1G 93
Belgrade Rd. N16—9C 44
Belgrade Rd. Hmptn—5M 101
Belgrave Av. Romf—1G 51
Belgrave Av. Wat—7D 8
Belgrave Clo. N14—7G 15
Belgrave Clo. W3—3M 71
Belgrave Clo. Orp—8G 113
Belgrave Clo. W on T—6F 116
Belgrave Cres. Sun—5F 100
Belgrave Dri. K Lan—1A 4
Belgrave Gdns. N14—6H 15
Belgrave Gdns. NW8—4M 57
Belgrave Gdns. Stan—5G 23
Belgrave M. Uxb—7B 142
Belgrave M. N. SW1—3E 74
Belgrave M. S. SW1—4E 74
Belgrave M. W. SW1—4F 74
Belgrave Pl. SW1—4E 74
Belgrave Rd. E10—6A 46
Belgrave Rd. E11—7E 46
Belgrave Rd. E13—7G 63
Belgrave Rd. E17—3L 45
Belgrave Rd. SE25—8D 108
Belgrave Rd. SW1—5F 74
Belgrave Rd. SW13—8D 72
Belgrave Rd. Houn—2K 85
Belgrave Rd. Ilf—6K 47
Belgrave Rd. Mitc—7B 106
Belgrave Rd. Sun—5F 100
Belgrave Sq. SW1—4E 74
Belgrave St. E1—9H 61
Belgrave Ter. Wfd G—3E 30
Belgrave Wlk. Mitc—7B 106
Belgravia Gdns. Brom—3C 110
Belgravia M. King—8H 103
Belgrove St. WC1—6J 59
Belham Wlk. SE5—9B 76
Belhaven Ct. Borwd—3K 11
Belinda Rd. SW9—2M 91
Belitha Vs. N1—3K 59
Bellamy Clo. W14—6K 73
Bellamy Clo. Wat—3E 8
Bellamy Dri. Stan—8F 22
Bellamy Rd. E4—6M 29
Bellamy Rd. Enf—4B 16
Bellamy Rd. Wal X—2E 6
Bellamy St. SW12—6F 90
Bell Av. Romf—8F 34
Bell Av. W Dray—4K 143
Bell Clo. Abb L, Wat—1D 4
Bell Clo. Pinn—1G 37
Bell Clo. Ruis—8D 36
Bellclose Rd. W Dray—3J 143
Bell Corner. Upm—7M 51
Bell Dri. SW18—6J 89
Bellefield Rd. Orp—9F 112
Bellefields Rd. SW9—2K 91
Bellegrove Clo. Well—1D 96
Bellegrove Rd. Well—1C 96
Bellenden Rd. SE15—1D 92
Bellestaines Pleasaunce. E4 —2L 29
Belleville Rd. SW11—4C 90
Belle Vue. Gnfd—4B 54
Bellevue La. Bush, Wat—1B 22
Bellevue Pk. T Hth—7A 108
Bellevue Pl. E1—7G 61
Belle Vue Rd. E17—9B 30
Bellevue Rd. N11—4E 26
Belle Vue Rd. NW4—2G 41
Bellevue Rd. SW13—1E 88
Bellevue Rd. SW17—7C 90
Bellevue Rd. W13—7F 54
Bellevue Rd. Bexh—4K 97
Bellevue Rd. Horn—6K 51
Bellevue Rd. King—7J 103
Belle Vue Rd. Orp—2L 141
Bellevue Rd. Romf—6A 34
Bellew St. SW17—9A 90
Bell Farm Av. Dag—8A 50
Bellfield. Croy—1J 139
Bellfield Av. Harr—6B 22
Bellflower Path. Romf—7G 35
Bell Gdns. Orp—9G 113
Bellgate M. NW5—9F 42
Bell Grn. SE26—1K 109
Bell Grn. La. SE26—2K 109
Bell Hill. Croy—4A 124
Bell Ho. Rd. Romf—6A 50
Bellingham Grn. SE6—9L 93
Bellingham Rd. SE6—9M 93
Bell Inn Yd. EC3—9B 60
Bell Junct. Houn—2M 85
Bell La. E1—8D 60
Bell La. E16—2E 78
Bell La. NW4—2G 41
Bell La. Abb L, Wat—1D 4
Bell La. Enf—2H 17
Bell La. Twic—7E 86
Bell Meadow. SE19—2C 108
Bellmount Wood Av. Wat—3C 8
Bellot St. SE10—6C 78
Bellring Clo. Belv—7L 81
Bell Rd. E Mol—9B 102
Bell Rd. Enf—3B 16
Bell Rd. Houn—2M 85
Bells All. SW6—1L 89
Bells Hill. Barn—7H 13
Bell St. NW1—8C 58
Bell Trees Gro. SW16—2K 107
Bell Water Ga. SE18—4L 79
Bell Wharf La. EC4—1A 76
Bellwood Rd. SE15—3H 93
Bell Yd. WC2—9L 59
Belmont Av. N9—1E 28
Belmont Av. N13—5K 27
Belmont Av. N17—1A 44
Belmont Av. Barn—7D 14
Belmont Av. N Mald—9E 104
Belmont Av. S'hall—4L 69
Belmont Av. Upm—7K 51
Belmont Av. Well—2C 96
Belmont Av. Wemb—4K 55
Belmont Circ. Harr—8F 22
Belmont Clo. N20—1M 25
Belmont Clo. SW4—2G 91
Belmont Clo. Barn—6D 14
Belmont Clo. Uxb—2B 142
Belmont Clo. Wfd G—4F 30
Belmont Gro. SE13—2B 94
Belmont Hill. SE13—2B 94
Belmont La. Chst—2A 112
Belmont La. Stan—7G 23
Belmont Pk. SE13—3B 94
Belmont Pk. Clo. SE13—3C 94
Belmont Pk. Rd. E10—4M 45
Belmont Rise. Sutt—9K 121
Belmont Rd.—2A 44
N15 1-47 & 2-46
N17 remainder
Belmont Rd. SE25—9F 108
Belmont Rd. SW4—2G 91
Belmont Rd. W4—5B 72
Belmont Rd. Beck—6K 109
Belmont Rd. Bush, Wat—7J 9
Belmont Rd. Chst—2M 111
Belmont Rd. Eri—8L 81
Belmont Rd. Harr—1D 38
Belmont Rd. Horn—8H 51
Belmont Rd. Ilf—8A 48
Belmont Rd. Sutt—2L 135
Belmont Rd. Twic—8B 86
Belmont Rd. Uxb—3B 142
Belmont Rd. Wall—7F 122
Belmont St. NW1—3E 58
Belmor. Borwd—7K 11
Belmore Av. Hay—9E 52
Belmore La. N7—1H 59
Belmore St. SW8—9H 75
Belsham St. E9—2G 61
Belsize Av. N13—6K 27
Belsize Av. NW3—2B 58
Belsize Av. W13—4F 70
Belsize Ct. NW3—1B 58
Belsize Cres. NW3—1B 58
Belsize Gdns. Sutt—6M 121
Belsize Gro. NW3—2C 58
Belsize La. NW3—2B 58
Belsize M. NW3—2B 58
Belsize Pk. NW3—2B 58
Belsize Pk. M. NW3—2B 58
Belsize Pl. NW3—1B 58
Belsize Rd. NW6—4M 57
Belsize Rd. Harr—7B 22
Belsize Sq. NW3—2B 58
Belsize Ter. NW3—2B 58
Belson Rd. SE18—5K 79
Beltane Dri. SW19—9H 89
Belthorn Cres. SW12—6G 91
Beltinge Rd. Romf—1K 51
Beltona Gdns. Wal X—1D 6
Belton Rd. E7—3F 62
Belton Rd. E11—9C 46
Belton Rd. N17—1C 44
Belton Rd. NW2—2E 56
Belton Rd. Sidc—1E 112
Belton Way. E3—8L 61
Beltran Rd. SW6—1M 89
Beltwood Rd. Belv—5A 82
Belvedere Av. SW19—2J 105
Belvedere Av. Ilf—9M 31
Belvedere Bldgs. SE1—3M 75
Belvedere Clo. Esh—7M 117
Belvedere Clo. Tedd—2C 102
Belvedere Dri. SW19—2J 105
Belvedere Gdns. E Mol—9K 101
Belvedere Gro. SW19—2J 105
Belvedere Pl. SE1—3M 75
Belvedere Rd. E10—6J 45
Belvedere Rd. SE1—3K 75
Belvedere Rd. SE2—2G 81
Belvedere Rd. W7—4D 70
Belvedere Rd. Bexh—2K 97
Belvedere Rd. Brom—4D 108
Belvedere Rd. West—9K 141
Belvedere Sq. SW19—2J 105
Belvedere Strand. NW9—9D 24
Belvedere Way. Harr—4J 39
Belvoir Clo. SE9—9J 95
Belvoir Rd. SE22—6E 92
Belvue Clo. N'holt—3L 53
Belvue Rd. N'holt—3L 53
Bembridge Clo. NW6—3J 57
Bembridge Gdns. Ruis—7B 36
Bemerton St. N1—4K 59
Bemish Rd. SW15—2H 89
Bempton Dri. Ruis—7F 36
Bemsted Rd. E17—1K 45
Benares Rd. SE18—5D 80
Benbow Rd. W6—4F 72
Benbow St. SE8—7L 77
Benbow Waye. Uxb—8A 142
Benbury Clo. Brom—2A 110
Bench Field. S Croy—7D 124
Bench, The. Rich—9G 87
Bencombe Rd. Purl—6L 137
Bencroft Rd. SW16—4G 107
Bencurtis Pk. W Wick—5B 126
Bendemeer Rd. SW15—2H 89
Bendish Rd. E6—3J 63
Bendmore Av. SE2—6E 80
Bendon Valley. SW18—6M 89
Bendysh Rd. Bush, Wat—5J 9
Benedict Clo. Orp—5C 128
Benedict Dri. Felt—6B 84
Benedict Rd. SW9—2K 91
Benedict Rd. Mitc—7B 106
Benedict Way. N2—1A 42
Benenden Grn. Brom—9E 110
Benets Rd. Horn—6L 51
Benett Gdns. SW16—6J 107
Benfleet Clo. Sutt—5A 122
Bengal Rd. Ilf—8M 47
Bengarth Dri. Harr—9B 22
Bengarth Rd. N'holt—4J 53
Bengeworth Rd. SE5—2A 92
Bengeworth Rd. Harr—8E 38
Ben Hale Clo. Stan—5F 22
Benham Clo. SW11—2B 90
Benham Rd. W7—8C 54
Benhill Av. Sutt—6M 121
(in two parts)
Benhill Rd. SE5—8B 76
Benhill Rd. Sutt—5A 122
Benhill Wood Rd. Sutt—5A 122
Benhilton Gdns. Sutt—5M 121
Benhurst Av. Horn—8F 50
Benhurst Clo. S Croy—2H 139
Benhurst Ct. SW16—2L 107
Benhurst Gdns. S Croy—2G 139
Benin St. SE13—6B 94
Benjafield Clo. N18—4F 28
Benjamin Clo. E8—4E 60
Benjamin Clo. Horn—4E 50
Benjamin St. EC1—8M 59
Ben Jonson Rd. E1—8J 61
Benledi St. E14—9B 62
Bennerley Rd. SW11—4C 90
Bennets Copse. Chst—3J 111
Bennet's Hill. EC4—1A 76
Bennet St. SW1—2G 75
Bennett Clo. King—5G 103
Bennett Clo. N'wd—7D 20
Bennett Clo. Well—1E 96
Bennett Gro. SE13—9M 77
Bennett Pk. SE3—2D 94
Bennett Rd. E13—7G 63
Bennett Rd. Romf—5J 49
Bennetts Av. Croy—4J 125
Bennetts Av. Gnfd—4C 54

Bennett's Castle La. Dag
—7G 49
Bennetts Clo. N17—6E 28
Bennett St. W4—7C 72
Bennetts Way. Croy—4J 125
Bennett's Yd. SW1—4H 75
Bennett's Yd. Uxb—3A 142
Benningholme Rd. Edgw
—6C 24
Bennington Rd. N17—8C 28
Bennington Rd. Wfd G—7C 30
Bennions Clo. Horn—2H 67
Benn's All. Hmptn—6M 101
Benn St. E9—2J 61
Benns Wlk. Rich—3J 87
Benrek Clo. Ilf—7A 32
Bensbury Clo. SW15—6F 88
Bensham Clo. T Hth—8A 108
Bensham Gro. T Hth—6A 108
Bensham La. Croy & T Hth
—2M 123
Bensham Mnr. Rd. T Hth
—8A 108
Benskin Rd. Wat—7E 8
Benskins La. Hav, Romf & Brtwd
—1H 35
Bensley Clo. N11—5D 26
Benson Av. E6—5H 63
Benson Clo. Houn—3L 85
Benson Clo. Uxb—8C 142
Benson Rd. SE23—7G 93
Benson Rd. Croy—5L 123
Bentfield Gdns. SE9—9H 95
Benthal Rd. N16—8E 44
Bentham Rd. E9—2H 61
Bentham Rd. SE28—2F 80
Bentham Wlk. NW10—1A 56
Ben Tillet Clo. Bark—3E 64
Bentinck M. W1—9E 58
Bentinck Rd. W Dray—2H 143
Bentinck St. W1—9E 58
Bentley Dri. Ilf—4A 48
Bentley Rd. N1—2C 60
Bentley Way. Stan—5E 22
Bentley Way. Wfd G—3E 30
Benton Rd. Ilf—6B 48
Benton Rd. Wat—5H 21
Bentons La. SE27—1A 108
Bentons Rise. SE27—2B 108
Bentry Clo. Dag—7J 49
Bentry Rd. Dag—7J 49
Bentworth Rd. W12—9F 56
Benwell Rd. N7—1L 59
Benworth St. E3—6K 61
Berberis Wlk. W Dray—5J 143
Berber Rd. SW11—4D 90
Berceau Wlk. Wat—3C 8
Bercta Rd. SE9—8A 96
Berens Rd. NW10—6H 57
Berens Rd. Orp—9H 113
Berens Way. Chst—8D 112
Beresford Av. N20—2D 26
Beresford Av. W7—8B 54
Beresford Av. Surb—3M 119
Beresford Av. Twic—5G 87
Beresford Av. Wemb—4K 55
Beresford Dri. Brom—7J 111
Beresford Dri. Wfd G—4G 31
Beresford Gdns. Enf—6C 16
Beresford Gdns. Houn—4K 85
Beresford Gdns. Romf—3J 49
Beresford Rd. E4—1C 30
Beresford Rd. E17—8M 29
Beresford Rd. N2—1C 42
Beresford Rd. N5—1B 60
Beresford Rd. N8—3L 43
Beresford Rd. Harr—3B 38
Beresford Rd. King—5K 103
Beresford Rd. N Mald—8A 104
Beresford Rd. S'hall—2H 69
Beresford Rd. Sutt—9K 121
Beresford Sq. SE18—5M 79
Beresford St. SE18—4M 79
Beresford Ter. N5—1A 60
Berestede Rd. W6—6D 72
Bere St. E1—1H 77
Berger Clo. Orp—1B 128
Berger Rd. E9—2H 61
Bergholt Av. Ilf—3J 47
Bergholt Cres. N16—5C 44
Bergholt M. NW1—3G 59
Berkeley Av. Bexh—9H 81
Berkeley Av. Gnfd—2C 54
Berkeley Av. Houn—1E 84
Berkeley Av. Ilf—9L 31
Berkeley Av. Romf—7A 34
Berkeley Clo. Borwd—7L 11
Berkeley Clo. Orp—2C 128
Berkeley Clo. Ruis—8E 36
Berkeley Clo. Upm—7M 51
Berkeley Ct. N14—8G 15
Berkeley Ct. Surb—2H 119

Berkeley Ct. Swan—7C 114
Berkeley Ct. Wey—4B 116
Berkeley Cres. Barn—7B 14
Berkeley Cres. Dart—7K 99
Berkeley Dri. E Mol—7K 101
Berkeley Dri. Horn—6L 51
Berkeley Gdns. N21—9B 16
Berkeley Gdns. W8—2L 73
Berkeley Gdns. Esh—9E 118
Berkeley Gdns. W'on T—2D 116
Berkeley M. W1—9D 58
Berkeley Pl. SW19—3H 105
Berkeley Rd. E12—1J 63
Berkeley Rd. N8—3H 43
Berkeley Rd. N15—4B 44
Berkeley Rd. NW9—2L 39
Berkeley Rd. SW13—9E 72
Berkeley Rd. Bren—7E 70
Berkeley Rd. Uxb—3A 52
Berkeley Sq. W1—1F 74
Berkeley St. W1—2F 74
Berkeley Waye. Houn—7H 69
Berkhampstead Rd. Belv
—6L 81
Berkhamsted Av. Wemb
—2K 55
Berkley Av. Wal X—7D 6
Berkley Gro. NW1—3E 58
Berkley Rd. NW1—3D 58
Berkshire Gdns. N13—6L 27
Berkshire Gdns. N18—5F 28
Berkshire Rd. E9—2K 61
Berkshire Way. Horn—3L 51
Berkshire Way. Mitc—8J 107
Bermans Way. NW10—9C 40
Bermondsey Sq. SE1—4C 76
Bermondsey St. SE1—3C 76
Bermondsey Wall E. SE16
—3F 76
Bermondsey Wall W. SE16
—3E 76
Bernal Clo. SE28—1H 81
Bernard Av. W13—4F 70
Bernard Cassidy St F16
—8D 62
Bernard Gdns. SW19—2K 105
Bernard Rd. N15—3D 44
Bernard Rd. Romf—5A 50
Bernard Rd. Wall—6F 122
Bernard St. WC1—7J 59
Bernays Clo. Stan—6G 23
Bernay's Gro. SW9—3K 91
Bernel Dri. Croy—5K 125
Berne Rd. T Hth—9A 108
Berners M. W1—8G 59
Berners Pl. W1—9G 59
Berners Rd. N1—4M 59
Berners Rd. N22—9L 27
Berners St. W1—8G 59
Berney Rd. Croy—2B 124
Bernville Way. Harr—3K 39
Bernwell Rd. E4—3C 30
Berridge Grn. Edgw—7L 23
Berridge Rd. SE19—2B 108
Berriman Rd. N7—8K 43
Berriton Rd. Harr—6K 37
Berry Av. Wat—9F 4
Berry Clo. N21—1M 27
Berry Clo. NW10—3C 56
Berrydale Rd. Hay—7J 53
Berryfield Clo. E17—2M 45
Berryfield Clo. Brom—6J 111
Berryfield Rd. SE17—6M 75
Berry Gro. La. Wat—2J 9
(in two parts)
Berryhill. SE9—3M 95
Berry Hill. Stan—4H 23
Berryhill Gdns. SE9—3M 95
Berrylands. SW20—7G 105
Berrylands. Orp—5G 129
Berrylands. Surb—1K 119
Berry La. SE21—1B 108
Berryman Clo. Dag—8G 49
Berryman's La. SE26—1H 109
Berry Meade. Asht—9K 133
Berrymead Gdns. W3—3A 72
Berrymede Rd. W4—4B 72
Berry Pl. EC1—6M 59
Berry's Grn. Rd. West—8M 141
Berry's Hill. West—7M 141
Berry St. EC1—7M 59
Berry Way. W5—4J 71
Bertal Rd. SW17—1B 106
Berther Rd. Horn—5J 51
Berthon St. SE8—8L 77
Bertie Rd. NW10—2E 56
Bertie Rd. SE26—3H 109
Bertram Cotts. SW19—4L 105
Bertram Rd. NW4—4E 40
Bertram Rd. Enf—6E 16
Bertram Rd. King—4L 103
Bertram St. N19—7F 42
Bertram Way. Enf—6D 16

Bertrand St. SE13—2M 93
Bertrand Way. SE28—1G 81
Bert Rd. T Hth—9A 108
Berwick Av. Hay—9H 53
Berwick Clo. Stan—6D 22
Berwick Clo. Wal X—7C 72
Berwick Cres. Sidc—6C 96
Berwick Pond Clo. Rain—5H 67
Berwick Pond Rd. Rain & Upm
—5J 67
Berwick Rd. E16—9F 62
Berwick Rd. N22—8M 27
Berwick Rd. Borwd—2K 11
Berwick Rd. Rain—5H 67
Berwick Rd. Well—9F 80
Berwick St. W1—9G 59
Berwick Way. Orp—3E 128
Berwyn Av. Houn—9M 69
Berwyn Rd. SE24—7M 91
Berwyn Rd. Rich—3M 87
Beryl Rd. W6—6H 73
Berystede. King—4M 103
Besant Rd. NW2—9J 41
Besant Wlk. N7—7K 43
Besant Way. NW10—1A 56
Besley St. SW16—3G 107
Bessborough Gdns. SW1
—6H 75
Bessborough Pl. SW1—6H 75
Bessborough Rd. SW15—7E 88
Bessborough Rd. Harr—5B 38
Bessborough St. SW1—6H 75
Bessemer Rd. SE5—1A 92
Bessingby Rd. Ruis—7F 36
Besson Rd. SE14—9H 77
Bessy St. E2—6G 61
Bestwood St. SE8—5H 77
Beswick M. NW6—1M 57
Betam Rd. Hay—3B 68
Betchworth Clo. Sutt—7B 122
Betchworth Rd. Ilf—7C 48
Betchworth Way. Croy
—1A 140
Betham Rd. Gnfd—7B 54
Bethany Waye. Felt—6C 84
Bethecar Rd. Harr—3C 38
Bethel Av. Ilf—5L 47
Bethell Av. E16—7D 62
Bethel Rd. Well—2G 97
Bethersden Clo. Beck—4K 109
Bethnal Grn. Rd.—7D 60
E1 1-99 & 2-94
E2 remainder
Bethune Av. N11—4D 26
Bethune Clo. N16—6C 44
Bethune Rd. N16—5B 44
Bethune Rd. NW10—7B 56
Bethwin Rd. SE5—8M 75
Betjeman Clo. Pinn—2L 37
Betley Ct. W on T—5F 116
Betony Clo. Croy—3H 125
Betoyne Av. E4—4C 30
Betsham Rd. Eri—8D 82
Betstyle Cir. N11—4F 26
Betstyle Rd. N11—4F 26
Betterton Dri. Sidc—8J 97
Betterton Rd. Rain—6C 66
Betterton St. WC2—9J 59
Bettles Clo. Uxb—5A 142
Bettons Pk. E15—4C 62
Bettridge Rd. SW6—1K 89
Betts Clo. Beck—6J 109
Betts Rd. E16—1F 78
Betts St. E1—1F 76
Betts Way. SE20—5F 108
Betts Way. Surb—3F 118
Betula Clo. Kenl—7B 138
Betula Wlk. Rain—6H 67
Beulah Av. T Hth—6A 108
Beulah Clo. Edgw—3M 23
Beulah Cres. T Hth—6A 108
Beulah Gro. Croy—1A 124
Beulah Hill. SE19—3M 107
Beulah Rd. E17—3M 45
Beulah Rd. SW19—4K 105
Beulah Rd. Horn—8G 51
Beulah Rd. Sutt—6L 121
Beulah Rd. T Hth—7A 108
Beult Rd. Dart—3E 98
Bevan Av. Bark—3E 64
Bevan Ct. Croy—7L 123
Bevan Pl. Swan—8D 114
Bevan Rd. SE2—6F 80
Bevan Rd. Barn—6D 14
Bevan St. N1—4A 60
Bevan Way. Horn—9K 51
Bevenden St. N1—6B 60
Beveridge Rd. NW10—3C 56
Beverley Av. SW20—5D 104
Beverley Av. Houn—3K 85
Beverley Av. Sidc—6D 96
Beverley Clo. N21—1A 28

Beverley Clo. SW11—3B 90
Beverley Clo. SW13—1E 88
Beverley Clo. Chess—6G 119
Beverley Clo. Enf—6C 16
Beverley Clo. Eps—3G 135
Beverley Clo. Horn—5K 51
Beverley Clo. Wey—4C 116
(Oatlands Park)
Beverley Ct. SE4—2K 93
Beverley Ct. W4—6A 72
Beverley Cres. Wfd G—8F 30
Beverley Dri. Edgw—1L 39
Beverley Gdns. NW11—5J 41
Beverley Gdns. SW13—2D 88
Beverley Gdns. Horn—5K 51
Beverley Gdns. Stan—8E 22
Beverley Gdns. Wal X—3A 6
Beverley Gdns. Wemb—6K 39
Beverley Gdns. Wor Pk—3E 120
Beverley La. SW15—9D 88
Beverley La. King—4C 104
Beverley Path. SW13—1D 88
Beverley Rd. E4—6B 30
Beverley Rd. E6—6H 63
Beverley Rd. SE20—6F 108
Beverley Rd. SW13—2D 88
Beverley Rd. W4—6D 72
Beverley Rd. Bexh—1A 98
Beverley Rd. Brom—4J 127
Beverley Rd. Dag—9J 49
Beverley Rd. King—5G 103
Beverley Rd. Mitc—8H 107
Beverley Rd. N Mald—8E 104
Beverley Rd. Ruis—7F 36
Beverley Rd. S'hall—5J 69
Beverley Rd. Sun—5D 100
Beverley Rd. Whyt—9C 138
Beverley Rd. Wor Pk—4G 121
Beverley Way. King & SW20
—5D 104
Beversbrook Rd. N19—8H 43
Beverstone Rd. SW2—4K 91
Beverstone Rd. T Hth—8L 107
Bevill Allen Clo. SW17—2D 106
Bevin Clo. SE16—2J 77
Bevington Rd. W10—8J 57
Bevington Rd. Beck—6M 109
Bevington St. SE16—3E 76
Bevin Rd. Hay—6E 52
Bevin Way. WC1—5L 59
Bevis Marks. EC3—9C 60
Bewcastle Gdns. Enf—6J 15
Bewdley St. N1—3L 59
Bewick St. SW8—1F 90
Bewley Clo. Wal X—4D 6
Bewley St. E1—1G 77
Bewlys Rd. SE27—2M 107
Bexhill Clo. Felt—8J 85
Bexhill Rd. N11—5H 27
Bexhill Rd. SE4—5K 93
Bexhill Rd. SW14—2A 88
Bexhill Wlk. E15—4C 62
Bexley Gdns. N9—3B 28
Bexley High St. Bex—6L 97
Bexley La. Dart—4C 98
Bexley La. Sidc—1G 113
Bexley Rd. SE9—4M 95
Bexley Rd. Eri—8A 82
Beynon Rd. Cars—7D 122
Bianca Rd. SE15—7E 76
Bibsworth Rd. N3—9K 25
Bibury Clo. SE15—7C 76
Bicester Rd. Rich—2L 87
Bickenhall St. W1—8D 58
Bickersteth Rd. SW17—3D 106
Bickerton Rd. N19—7G 43
Bickley Cres. Brom—8J 111
Bickley Pk. Rd. Brom—7J 111
Bickley Rd. E10—5M 45
Bickley Rd. Brom—6H 111
Bickley St. SW17—2C 106
Bicknell Rd. SE5—2A 92
Bicknoller Clo. Sutt—2M 135
Bicknoller Rd. Enf—3D 16
Bicknor Rd. Orp—2D 128
Bidborough Clo. Brom—9D 110
Bidborough St. WC1—6J 59
Biddenden Way. SE9—1L 111
Biddenham Turn. Wat—8G 5
Bidder St. E16—8C 62
(in two parts)
Biddestone Rd. N7—9K 43
Biddulph Rd. W9—6M 57
Biddulph Rd. S Croy—1A 138
Bideford Av. Gnfd—5F 54
Bideford Clo. Edgw—8L 23
Bideford Clo. Felt—9K 85
Bideford Clo. Romf—8G 35
Bideford Gdns. Enf—9C 16
Bideford Rd. Brom—9D 94
Bideford Rd. Enf—2K 17
Bideford Rd. Ruis—8F 36

Bideford Rd. Well—8F 80
Bidwell Gdns. N11—7G 27
Bidwell St. SE15—9F 76
Bigbury Clo. N17—7C 28
Biggerstaff Rd. E15—4A 62
Biggerstaff St. N4—7L 43
Biggin Av. Mitc—5D 106
Biggin Hill. SE19—4M 107
Biggin Way. SE19—4M 107
Bigginwood Rd. SW16—4M 107
Biggs Row. SW15—2H 89
Big Hill. E5—6F 44
Bigland Est. E1—9F 60
Bigland St. E1—9F 60
Bignell Rd. SE18—6M 79
Bignold Rd. E7—9E 46
Bigwood Rd. NW11—3H 41
Billet Clo. Horn—6H 51
Billet Clo. Romf—1H 49
Billet La. Horn—6H 51
Billet Rd. E17—8H 29
Billet Rd. Romf—1F 48
Billingford Clo. SE4—3H 93
Billing Pl. SW10—8M 73
Billing Rd. SW10—8M 73
Billing St. SW10—8M 73
Billington Rd. SE14—8H 77
Billison St. E14—5A 78
Billiter St. EC3—9C 60
Billockby Clo. Chess—8K 119
Bilsby Gro. SE9—1H 111
Bilton Rd. Eri—8E 82
Bilton Rd. Gnfd—4E 54
Bilton Way. Enf—3J 17
Bilton Way. Hay—3F 68
Bina Gdns. SW5—5A 74
Bincote Rd. Enf—5K 15
Binden Rd. W12—4D 72
Bindon Grn. Mord—8M 105
Binfield Rd. SW4—9J 75
Binfield Rd. S Croy—7D 124
Bingfield St. N1—4J 59
(in two parts)
Bingham Pl. W1—8E 58
Bingham Rd. Croy—3E 124
Bingham St. N1—2B 60
Bingley Rd. E16—9G 63
Bingley Rd. Gnfd—7A 54
Bingley Rd. Sun—4E 100
Binney St. W1—9E 58
Binns Rd. W4—6C 72
Binsey Wlk. SE2—3G 81
Binyon Cres. Stan—5D 22
Birbetts Rd. SE9—8K 95
Birchanger Rd. SE25—9E 108
Birch Av. N13—3A 28
Birch Av. W Dray—9D 142
Birch Clo. E16—8C 62
Birch Clo. N19—7G 43
Birch Clo. SE15—1E 92
Birch Clo. Bren—8F 70
Birch Clo. Buck H—3H 31
Birch Clo. Romf—1M 49
Birch Clo. Shep—6C 100
Birch Clo. Tedd—2E 102
Birch Copse. St Alb—3J 5
Birch Ct. N'wd—6A 20
Birch Cres. Horn—2J 51
Birch Cres. Uxb—4D 142
Birchdale Gdns. Romf
—5H 49
Birchdale Rd. E7—1G 63
Birchen Clo. NW9—7B 40
Birchen Gro. NW9—7B 40
Birches Clo. Eps—7C 134
Birches Clo. Pinn—3J 37
Birches, The. SE7—7F 78
Birches, The. N21—8K 15
Birches, The. Bush, Wat—7A 10
Birches, The. Orp—6L 127
Birchfield Clo. Coul—8K 137
Birchfield Gro. Eps—2G 135
Birchfield Rd. Wal X—2B 6
Birchfields. E14—1L 77
Birch Gdns. Dag—8A 50
Birch Grn. NW9—7C 24
Birch Gro. SE12—6D 94
Birch Gro. W3—2L 71
Birch Gro. Shep—6C 100
Birch Gro. Well—3E 96
Birch Hill. Croy—7H 125
Birchington Clo. Bexh—9M 81
Birchington Clo. Orp—3G 129
Birchington Rd. N8—4H 43
Birchington Rd. NW6—4L 57
Birchington Rd. Surb—2K 119
Birchin La. EC3—9B 60
Birchlands Av. SW12—6D 90
Birch La. Purl—3J 137
Birchmead. Orp—4L 127
Birchmead. Wat—2D 8
Birchmead Av. Pinn—2G 37
Birchmere Row. SE3—1D 94

Birchmore Wlk.—Boeing Way

Birchmore Wlk. N5—8A 44
(in two parts)
Birch Pk. Harr—7A 22
Birch Rd. Felt—2H 101
Birch Rd. Romf—1M 49
Birch Row. Brom—2L 127
Birch Tree Av. W Wick—7D 126
Birch Tree Wlk. Wat—1D 8
Birch Tree Way. Croy—4F 124
Birch Wlk. Borwd—3L 11
Birch Wlk. Eri—7A 82
Birch Wlk. Mitc—5F 106
Birchway. Hay—2E 68
Birch Way. Warl—9J 139
Birchwood. Wal A—7L 7
Birchwood Av. N10—1E 42
Birchwood Av. Beck—8K 109
Birchwood Av. Sidc—9F 96
Birchwood Av. Wall—5E 122
Birchwood Ct. N13—5M 27
Birchwood Ct. Edgw—9A 24
Birchwood Dri. NW3—8M 41
Birchwood Dri. Dart—1C 114
Birchwood Gro. Hmptn—3L 101
Birchwood La. Esh & Lea —1B 132
Birchwood Pk. Av. Swan —7C 114
Birchwood Rd. SW17—2F 106
Birchwood Rd. Orp—8B 112
Birchwood Rd. Swan & Dart —5A 114
Birchwood Way. St Alb—1M 5
Birdbrook Clo. Dag—3A 66
Birdbrook Rd. SE3—2G 95
Birdcage Wlk. SW1—3G 75
Birdham Clo. Brom—9J 111
Birdhouse La. Orp—7L 141
Birdhurst Av. S Croy—6B 124
Birdhurst Gdns. S Croy —6B 124
Birdhurst Rise. S Croy—7C 124
Birdhurst Rd. SW18—4A 90
Birdhurst Rd. SW19—3C 106
Birdhurst Rd. S Croy—7C 124
Bird-in-Bush Rd. SE15—8E 76
Bird in Hand La. Brom—6H 111
Bird-in-Hand Pas. SE23—8G 93
Birdlip Clo. SE15—7C 76
Birds Farm Av. Romf—8M 33
Birds Hill Dri. Lea—5B 132
Birds Hill Rise. Lea—5B 132
Birds Hill Rd. Lea—4B 132
Bird St. W1—9E 58
Bird Wlk. Twic—7K 85
Birdwood Clo. S Croy—3H 139
Birdwood Clo. Tedd—1C 102
Birkbeck Av. W3—1A 72
Birkbeck Av. Gnfd—4A 54
Birkbeck Gdns. Wfd G—2E 30
Birkbeck Gro. W3—3B 72
Birkbeck Hill. SE21—7M 91
Birkbeck Pl. SE21—8A 92
Birkbeck Rd. E8—1D 60
Birkbeck Rd. N8—2J 43
Birkbeck Rd. N12—5A 26
Birkbeck Rd. N17—8D 28
Birkbeck Rd. NW7—5D 24
Birkbeck Rd. SW19—2M 105
Birkbeck Rd. W3—2B 72
Birkbeck Rd. W5—5G 71
Birkbeck Rd. Beck—6G 109
Birkbeck Rd. Enf—3B 16
Birkbeck Rd. Ilf—3B 48
Birkbeck Rd. Romf—6B 50
Birkbeck Rd. Sidc—9E 96
Birkbeck St. E2—6F 60
Birkbeck Way. Gnfd—4B 54
Birkdale Av. Pinn—1L 37
Birkdale Av. Romf—7L 35
Birkdale Clo. Orp—2B 128
Birkdale Gdns. Wat—3H 21
Birkdale Rd. SE2—5E 80
Birkdale Rd. W5—7J 55
Birkenhead Av. King—6K 103
Birkenhead St. WC1—6J 59
Birken M. N'wd—5A 20
Birkhall Rd. SE6—7B 94
Birkwood Clo. SW12—6H 91
Birley Rd. N20—2A 26
Birley St. SW11—1E 90
Birling Rd. Eri—8B 82
Birnam Rd. N4—7K 43
Birnbeck Ct. NW11—3K 41
Birnbeck Ct. Barn—6H 13
Birse Cres. NW10—8C 40
Birstall Grn. Wat—4H 21
Birstall Rd. N15—3C 44
Birtley Path. Borwd—3J 11
Biscay Rd. W6—6H 73
Biscoe Clo. Houn—7L 69
Biscoe Way. SE13—2B 94
Bisenden Rd. Croy—4C 124
Bisham Clo. Cars—3D 122
Bisham Gdns. N6—6E 42
Bishop Butt Clo. Orp—5D 128
Bishop Craven Clo. Enf—3M 15
Bishop Duppas Pk. Shep —2C 116
Bishop Ken Rd. Harr—9D 22
Bishop King's Rd. W14—5J 73
Bishop Rd. N14—9F 14
Bishop's Av. E13—4F 62
Bishop's Av. SW6—1H 89
Bishops Av. Borwd—7K 11
Bishops Av. Brom—6G 111
Bishops Av. N'wd—4C 20
Bishops Av. Romf—4G 49
Bishops Av., The. N2—4B 42
Bishop's Bri. Rd. W2—9M 57
Bishops Clo. E17—2M 45
Bishop's Clo. SE9—8A 96
Bishops Clo. Barn—8H 13
Bishop's Clo. Coul—9L 137
Bishops Clo. Enf—4F 16
Bishops Clo. Rich—9H 87
Bishop's Clo. Sutt—5L 121
Bishops Clo. Uxb—5E 142
Bishops Ct. Rich—2J 87
Bishopsford Rd. Mord—2A 122
Bishopsgate. EC2—9C 60
Bishopsgate Chu. Yd. EC2 —9C 60
Bishops Gro. N2—4C 42
Bishop's Gro. Hmptn—1K 101
Bishop's Hall. King—6H 103
Bishop's Pk. Rd. SW6—1H 89
Bishops Pk. Rd. SW16—5J 107
Bishops Rd. N6—4E 42
Bishop's Rd. SW6—9K 73
Bishop's Rd. SW11—8C 74
Bishop's Rd. W7—3C 70
Bishop's Rd. Croy—2M 123
Bishop's Rd. Hay—9A 52
Bishop's Ter. SE11—5L 75
Bishopsthorpe Rd. SE26 —1H 109
Bishop St. N1—4A 60
Bishops Wlk. Chst—5A 112
Bishops Wlk. Croy—7H 125
Bishops Wlk. Pinn—1J 37
Bishop's Way. E2—5F 60
Bishops Way. NW10—3C 56
Bishopswood Rd. N6—5D 42
Biskra Flats. Wat—3E 8
Bisley Clo. Wal X—6D 6
Bisley Clo. Wor Pk—3G 121
Bispham Rd. NW10—6K 55
Bisson Rd. E15—5A 62
Bisterne Av. E17—1B 46
Bittacy Clo. NW7—6H 25
Bittacy Hill. NW7—6H 25
Bittacy Pk. Av. NW7—5H 25
Bittacy Rise. NW7—6G 25
Bittacy Rd. NW7—6H 25
Bittern Pl. N22—9K 27
Bittern St. SE1—3A 76
Bittoms, The. King—7H 103
Bixley Clo. S'hall—5K 69
Blackall St. EC2—7C 60
Blackberry Clo. Shep—8C 100
Blackberry Farm Clo. Houn —8J 69
Blackbird Hill. NW9—7A 40
Blackbirds La. Wat—7M 5
Blackborne Rd. Dag—2L 65
Black Boy La. N15—3A 44
Black Boy Wood. St Alb—3L 5
Blackbrook La. Brom—9L 111
Blackburne's M. W1—1E 74
Blackburn Rd. NW6—2M 57
Blackbush Av. Romf—3H 49
Blackbush Clo. Sutt—9M 121
Black Ditch Rd. Wal A—9J 7
Blackett St. SW15—2H 89
Blackfen Rd. Sidc—4C 96
Blackford Clo. S Croy—1M 137
Blackford Rd. Wat—5H 21
Blackford's Path. SW15—6E 88
Blackfriars Bri. SE1 & EC4 —1M 75
Black Friars La. EC4—9M 59
Blackfriars Pas. EC4—1M 75
Blackfriars Rd. SE1—3M 75
Black Gates. Pinn—1K 37
Blackheath Av. SE10—8B 78
Blackheath Gro. SE3—1D 94
Blackheath Hill. SE10—9A 78
Blackheath Pk. SE3—2D 94
Blackheath Rise. SE13—1A 94
Blackheath Rd. SE10—9M 77
Blackheath Vale. SE3—1C 94
Blackheath Village. SE3—2D 94
Blackhills. Esh—9L 117
Blackhorse La. E17—9H 29
Black Horse La. Croy—2E 124
Blackhorse Rd. E17—2H 45
Blackhorse Rd. SE8—7J 77
Blackhorse Rd. Sidc—1E 112
Blacklands Dri. Hay—7A 52
Blacklands Rd. SE6—1A 110
Blacklands Ter. SW3—5D 74
Blackley Clo. Wat—1D 8
Black Lion La. W6—5E 72
Blackman's La. Warl—6D 140
Blackmore Av. S'hall—2B 70
Blackmore Rd. Buck H—9J 19
Blackmore's Gro. Tedd—3E 102
Blackmore Way. Uxb—2B 142
Blackness La. Kes—1H 141
Black Path. E10—5H 45
Blackpool Gdns. Hay—7C 52
Blackpool Rd. SE15—1F 92
Black Prince Rd. SE1 & SE11 —5K 75
Black Rod Clo. Hay—4D 68
Blackshaw Pl. N1—3C 60
Blackshaw Rd. SW17—1A 106
Blacksmiths Hill. S Croy —5F 138
Blacksmith's La. Orp—9G 113
Blacksmith's La. Rain—4D 66
Blacks Rd. W6—5G 73
Blackstock Rd.—7M 43
N4 3-175 & 2-156a
N5 remainder
Blackstone Rd. NW2—1G 57
Black Swan Yd. SE1—3C 76
Blackthorn Av. W Dray—5L 143
Blackthorn Clo. Wat—5F 4
Blackthorn Ct. Houn—8J 69
Blackthorne Av. Croy—3G 125
Blackthorne Dri. E4—4B 30
Blackthorn Gro. Bexh—2J 97
Blackthorn Rd. West—8H 141
Blackthorn St. E3—7L 61
Blacktree M. SW9—2L 91
Blackwall La. SE10—6C 78
Blackwall Tunnel—2B 78
Blackwall Tunnel App. E14 —1A 78
Blackwall Tunnel Northern App. E3 & E14—5M 61
Blackwall Tunnel Southern App. SE10—4C 78
Blackwall Way. E14—1A 78
Blackwater Rd. Sutt—6M 121
Blackwater St. SE22—4D 92
Blackwell Clo. E5—9H 45
Blackwell Clo. Harr—7B 22
Blackwell Dri. Wat—8G 9
Blackwell Gdns. Edgw—4L 23
Blackwood St. SE17—6B 76
Bladen Clo. Wey—8C 116
Bladindon Dri. Bex—6G 97
Bladon Gdns. Harr—4M 37
Blagdens Clo. N14—2H 27
Blagdens La. N14—2H 27
Blagdon Rd. SE13—5M 93
Blagdon Rd. N Mald—8D 104
Blagdon Wlk. Tedd—3G 103
Blagrove Rd. W10—8J 57
Blair Av. NW9—5C 40
Blair Av. Esh—4A 118
Blair Clo. N1—2A 60
Blair Clo. Sidc—4C 96
Blairderry Rd. SW2—8J 91
Blairhead Dri. Wat—3F 20
Blair St. E14—9A 62
Blake Av. Bark—4C 64
Blake Clo. Rain—4D 66
Blake Clo. Well—9C 80
Blakeden Dri. Esh—8D 118
Blake Gdns. SW6—9M 73
Blake Gdns. Dart—3K 99
Blake Hall Cres. E11—6E 46
Blake Hall Rd. E11—5E 46
Blakehall Rd. Cars—8D 122
Blakeley Cotts. SE10—3B 78
Blakemore Rd. SW16—9J 91
Blakemore Rd. T Hth—9K 107
Blakeney Av. Beck—5K 109
Blakeney Clo. E8—1E 60
Blakeney Clo. N20—1A 26
Blakeney Clo. Eps—3B 134
Blakeney Rd. Beck—4K 109
Blakenham Rd. SW17—1D 106
Blake Rd. E16—7D 62
Blake Rd. N11—7G 27
Blake Rd. Croy—4C 124
Blake Rd. Mitc—7C 106
Blaker Rd. E15—4A 62
Blakes Av. N Mald—9D 104
Blakes Grn. W Wick—3A 126
Blakes La. N Mald—9D 104
Blakesley Av. W5—9G 55
Blakesley Wlk. SW20—6K 105
Blakes Rd. SE15—8C 76
Blakes Ter. N Mald—9E 104
Blakesware Gdns. N9—9B 16
Blakewood Clo. Felt—1G 101
Blanchard Clo. SE9—9J 95
Blanchard Way. E8—2E 60
Blanch Clo. SE15—8G 77
Blanchedowne. SE5—3B 92
Blanche St. E16—7D 62
Blanchland Rd. Mord—9M 105
Blandfield Rd. SW12—6E 90
Blandford Av. Beck—6J 109
Blandford Av. Twic—7M 85
Blandford Clo. N2—2A 42
Blandford Clo. Croy—5J 123
Blandford Clo. Romf—2L 49
Blandford Cres. E4—9A 18
Blandford Rd. W4—4C 72
Blandford Rd. W5—3H 71
Blandford Rd. Beck—6H 109
Blandford Rd. S'hall—5L 69
Blandford Rd. Tedd—2B 102
Blandford Sq. NW1—7C 58
Blandford St. W1—8E 58
Blandford Waye. Hay—9G 53
Bland St. SE9—3H 95
Blaney Cres. E6—6M 63
Blanmerle Rd. SE9—7M 95
Blann Clo. SE9—5H 95
Blantyre St. SW10—8B 74
Blashford St. SE13—6B 94
Blawith Rd. Harr—2C 38
Blaydon Clo. N17—7F 28
Blaydon Clo. Ruis—3C 36
Blaydon Wlk. N17—7F 28
Bleak Hill La. SE18—7D 80
Blean Gro. SE20—4G 109
Bleasdale Av. Gnfd—5E 54
Blechynden St. W10—1H 73
Bleddyn Clo. Sidc—5G 97
Bledlow Clo. SE28—1G 81
Bledlow Rise. Gnfd—5A 54
Blegborough Rd. SW16 —3G 107
Blendon Dri. Bex—5H 97
Blendon Path. Brom—4D 110
Blendon Rd. Bex—5H 97
Blendon Ter. SE18—6A 80
Blendworth Way. SE15—8C 76
Blenheim Av. Ilf—4L 47
Blenheim Clo. N21—1A 28
Blenheim Clo. SW20—7G 105
Blenheim Clo. Dart—5G 99
Blenheim Clo. Gnfd—5B 54
Blenheim Clo. Romf—2A 50
Blenheim Clo. Wall—9G 123
Blenheim Clo. Wat—9G 9
Blenheim Ct. N19—7J 43
Blenheim Ct. Horn—1G 67
Blenheim Ct. Sidc—9B 96
Blenheim Cres. W11—1J 73
Blenheim Cres. Ruis—7B 36
Blenheim Cres. S Croy—9A 124
Blenheim Dri. Well—9D 80
Blenheim Gdns. NW2—2G 57
Blenheim Gdns. SW2—5K 91
Blenheim Gdns. King—4M 103
Blenheim Gdns. S Croy—4E 138
Blenheim Gdns. S Ock—2M 83
Blenheim Gdns. Wall—9G 123
Blenheim Gdns. Wemb—8J 39
Blenheim Pk. Rd. S Croy —1A 138
Blenheim Pas. NW8—5A 58
Blenheim Rise. N15—2D 44
Blenheim Rd. E6—6H 63
Blenheim Rd. E15—9C 46
Blenheim Rd. E17—1H 45
Blenheim Rd. NW8—5A 58
Blenheim Rd. SE15—1E 92
Blenheim Rd. SE20—4G 109
Blenheim Rd. SW20—7G 105
Blenheim Rd. W4—4C 72
Blenheim Rd. Barn—5H 13
Blenheim Rd. Brom—8J 111
Blenheim Rd. Dart—5G 99
Blenheim Rd. Eps—3B 134
Blenheim Rd. Harr—4M 37
Blenheim Rd. N'holt—2M 53
Blenheim Rd. Orp—4G 129
Blenheim Rd. Sidc—7G 97
Blenheim Rd. Sutt—5M 121
Blenheim Shopping Centre. SE20 —4G 109
Blenheim St. W1—9F 58
Blenheim Ter. NW8—5A 58
Blenkarne Rd. SW11—5D 90
Bleriot Rd. Houn—8G 69
Blessbury Rd. Edgw—8A 24
Blessington Clo. SE13—2B 94
Blessington Rd. SE13—3B 94
Bletchley St. N1—5A 60
Bletchmore Clo. Hay—6B 68
Bletsoe Wlk. N1—5A 60
Blincoe Clo. SW19—8H 89
Blind La. Bans—7C 136
Blind La. Lou—4C 18
Blindman's La. Wal X—3D 6
Bliss Cres. SE13—1M 93
Blissett St. SE10—9A 78
Blithbury Rd. Dag—2F 64
Blithdale Rd. SE2—5E 80
Blithfield St. W8—4M 73
Blockley Rd. Wemb—7F 38
Bloemfontein Av. W12—2F 72
Bloemfontein Rd. W12—1F 72
Blomfield Rd. W9—8M 57
Blomfield St. EC2—8B 60
Blomfield Vs. W2—8M 57
Blomville Rd. Dag—8K 49
Blondel St. SW11—1E 90
Blondin Av. W5—5G 71
Blondin St. E3—5L 61
Bloomburg St. SW1—5H 75
Bloomfield Cres. Ilf—4M 47
Bloomfield Rd. N6—4E 42
Bloomfield Rd. SE18—6M 79
Bloomfield Rd. Brom—9H 111
Bloomfield Rd. King—7J 103
Bloomfield Ter. SW1—6E 74
Bloom Gro. SE27—9M 91
Bloomhall Rd. SE19—2B 108
Bloom Pk. Rd. SW6—8K 73
Bloomsbury Clo. W5—1K 71
Bloomsbury Clo. Eps—2B 134
Bloomsbury Ct. Pinn—1K 37
Bloomsbury Pl. WC1—8J 59
Bloomsbury Sq. WC1—8J 59
Bloomsbury St. WC1—8H 59
Bloomsbury Way. WC1—8J 59
Blore Clo. SW8—9H 75
Blossom Clo. W5—3J 71
Blossom Clo. S Croy—7D 124
Blossom La. Enf—3A 16
Blossom St. E1—7C 60
Blossom Way. Uxb—3D 142
Blossom Way. W Dray—5L 143
Blossom Waye. Houn—7J 69
Blount St. E14—9J 61
Bloxhall Rd. E10—6K 45
Bloxham Cres. Hmptn—4K 101
Bloxham Gdns. SE9—4J 95
Bloxworth Clo. Wall—5G 123
Blucher Rd. SE5—8A 76
Blue Anchor La. SE16—5E 76
Blue Anchor Yd. E1—1E 76
Blue Ball Yd. SW1—2G 75
Bluebell Clo. SE26—1D 108
Bluebell Clo. Orp—4A 128
Blueberry Gdns. Coul—8K 137
Bluefield Clo. Hmptn—2L 101
Bluehouse Rd. E4—3C 30
Blundell Rd. Edgw—8B 24
Blundell St. N7—3J 59
Blunt Rd. Croy—7B 124
Blunts Av. W Dray—8L 143
Blunts Rd. SE9—4L 95
Blurton Rd. E5—9G 45
Blythe Clo. SE6—6K 93
Blythe Hill. SE6—6K 93
Blythe Hill. Orp—5D 112
Blythe Hill La. SE6—6K 93
Blythe Rd. W14—4H 73
Blythe St. E2—6F 60
Blythe Vale. SE6—7K 93
Blyth Rd. E17—5K 45
Blyth Rd. SE28—1G 81
Blyth Rd. Brom—5D 110
Blyth Rd. Hay—3C 68
Blythswood Rd. Ilf—6E 48
Blythwood Rd. N4—5J 43
Blythwood Rd. Pinn—8H 21
Boade's M. NW3—9B 42
Boadicea St. N1—4K 59
Boar Clo. Chig—5E 32
Boardman Av. E4—7M 17
Boarer's Manorway. Belv —4J 81
Boars Head Yd. Bren—8H 71
Boathouse Wlk. SE15—8E 76
Bobbin Clo. SW4—2G 91
Bob Marley Way. SE24—3L 91
Bobs La. Romf—7E 34
Bockhampton Rd. King —4K 103
Bocking St. E8—4F 60
Boddicott Clo. SW19—8J 89
Bodiam Clo. Enf—4C 16
Bodiam Rd. SW16—4H 107
Bodley Clo. N Mald—9C 104
Bodley Mnr. Way. SW2—6L 91
Bodley Rd. N Mald—1B 120
Bodmin Clo. Harr—8K 37
Bodmin Gro. Mord—9M 105
Bodmin St. SW18—7L 89
Bodnant Gdns. SW20—7E 104
Bodney Rd. E8—1F 60
Boeing Way. S'hall—4F 68

Boevey Path. Belv—6K 81
Bogey La. Orp—9L 127
Bognor Gdns. Wat—5G 21
Bognor Rd. Well—9H 81
Bohemia Pl. E8—2G 61
Bohun Gro. Barn—8C 14
Boileau Rd. SW13—8E 72
Boileau Rd. W5—9K 55
Bolden St. SE8—1M 93
Boldero Pl. NW8—7C 58
Bolderwood Way. W Wick
—4M 125
Boldmore Rd. Pinn—5G 37
Boleyn Av. Enf—3F 16
Boleyn Av. Eps—2F 134
Boleyn Dri. E Mol—7K 101
Boleyn Dri. Ruis—7H 37
Boleyn Gdns. Dag—3A 66
Boleyn Gdns. W Wick—4M 125
Boleyn Gro. W Wick—4A 126
Boleyn Rd. E6—5H 63
Boleyn Rd. E7—3E 62
Boleyn Rd. N16—1C 60
Boleyn Way. Barn—5A 14
Boleyn Way. Ilf—6A 32
Bolina Rd. SE16—6G 77
Bolingbroke Gro. SW11—4C 90
Bolingbroke Rd. W14—4H 73
Bolingbroke Wlk. SW11—9C 74
Bolingbroke Way. Hay—2B 68
Bollo Bri. Rd. W3—4M 71
Bollo La.—3M 71
  W4 1-95 & 2-100
  W3 remainder
Bolney Ga. SW7—3C 74
Bolney St. SW8—8K 75
Bolney Way. Felt—9J 85
Bolsover St. W1—7F 58
Bolstead Rd. Mitc—5F 106
Bolt Ct. EC4—9L 59
Bolters La. Bans—6K 135
Boltmore Clo. NW4—1H 41
Bolton Clo. SE20—6E 108
Bolton Clo. Chess—8H 119
Bolton Cres. SE5—8M 75
Bolton Gdns. NW10—5H 57
Bolton Gdns. SW5—6M 73
Bolton Gdns. Brom—3D 110
Bolton Gdns. Tedd—3E 102
Bolton Gdns. M SW10—6A 74
Bolton Rd. E15—2D 62
Bolton Rd. N18—5D 28
Bolton Rd. NW8—4M 57
Bolton Rd. NW10—4C 56
Bolton Rd. W4—8A 72
Bolton Rd. Chess—8H 119
Bolton Rd. Harr—2A 38
Bolton's La. Hay—8A 68
Boltons, The. SW10—6A 74
Boltons, The. Wemb—9D 38
Bolton St. W1—2F 74
Bombay St. SE16—5H 76
Bomer Clo. W Dray—8L 143
Bomore Rd. W11—1J 73
Bonar Pl. Chst—4J 111
Bonar Rd. SE15—8E 76
Bonchester Clo. Chst—4L 111
Bonchurch Rd. W10—8J 57
Bonchurch Rd. W13—2F 70
Bond Ct. EC4—1B 76
Bondfield Rd. Hay—6E 52
Bondfield Wlk. Dart—2K 99
Bond Gdns. Wall—6G 123
Bond Rd. Mitc—6C 106
Bond Rd. Surb—4K 119
Bond Rd. Warl—9J 139
Bond St. E15—1C 62
Bond St. (New) W1—9F 58
Bond St. (Old) W1
Bond St. W5—1H 71
Bond Way. SW8—7J 75
Boneta Rd. SE18—4K 79
Bonfield Rd. SE13—3A 94
Bonham Gdns. Dag—7H 49
Bonham Rd. SW2—4K 91
Bonham Rd. Dag—7H 49
Bonheur Rd. W4—3B 72
Bonhill St. EC2—7B 60
Boniface Gdns. Harr—7M 21
Boniface Rd. Uxb—8A 36
Boniface Wlk. Harr—7M 21
Bonington Rd. Horn—1H 67
Bon Marche Ter. SE27—1C 108
Bonner Rd. E2—5G 61
Bonnersfield Clo. Harr—4D 38
Bonnersfield La. Harr—4D 38
Bonner St. E2—5G 61
Bonneville Gdns. SW4—5G 91
Bonney Gro. Wal X—3A 6
Bonney Way. Swan—6C 114
Bonnington Sq. SW8—7K 75

Bonny St. NW1—3G 59
Bonser Rd. Twic—8D 86
Bonsey's Yd. Uxb—3B 142
Bonsor St. SE5—8C 76
Bonville Rd. Brom—2D 110
Booker Clo. E14—8K 61
Booker Rd. N18—5E 28
Boones Rd. SE13—3C 94
Boone St. SE13—3C 94
Boord St. SE10—4C 78
Boothby Rd. N19—7H 43
Booth Clo. SE28—2F 80
Booth Rd. NW9—9B 24
Booth Rd. Croy—4M 123
Booth's Pl. W1—8G 59
Boot La. N1—6C 60
Bordars Rd. W7—8C 54
Bordars Wlk. W7—8C 54
Borden Av. Enf—8B 16
Border Cres. SE26—2F 108
Border Gdns. Croy—6M 125
Bordergate. Mitc—5D 106
Border Rd. SE26—2F 108
Border's La. Lou—6L 19
Bordesley Rd. Mord—8M 105
Bordon Wlk. SW15—6E 88
Boreham Av. E16—9E 62
Boreham Clo. E11—6A 46
Boreham Holt. Borwd—6K 11
Boreham Rd. N22—9A 28
Borgard Rd. SE18—5K 79
Borkwood Pk. Orp—6D 128
Borkwood Way. Orp—6C 128
Borland Rd. SE15—3G 93
Borland Rd. Tedd—4F 102
Borneo St. SW15—2G 89
Borough High St. SE1—3A 76
Borough Hill. Croy—5M 123
Borough Rd. SE1—4M 75
Borough Rd. Iswth—9C 70
Borough Rd. King—5L 103
Borough Rd. Mitc—6C 106
Borrett Clo. SE17—6A 76
Borrodaile Rd. SW18—5M 89
Borrowdale Av. Harr—9E 22
Borrowdale Clo. Ilf—2J 47
Borrowdale Clo. S Croy
—5D 138
Borrowdale Dri. S Croy
—4D 138
Borthwick M. E15—9C 46
Borthwick Rd. E15—9C 46
Borthwick Rd. NW9—4D 40
Borthwick St. SE8—6L 77
Borwick Av. E17—1K 45
Bosanquet Clo. Uxb—7B 142
Bosbury Rd. SE6—9A 94
Boscastle Rd. NW5—8F 42
Boscobel Pl. SW1—5E 74
Boscobel St. NW8—7B 58
Bosco Clo. Orp—6D 128
Boscombe Av. E10—5B 46
Boscombe Av. Horn—5H 51
Boscombe Clo. E5—1J 61
Boscombe Gdns. SW16—3J 107
Boscombe Rd. SW17—3E 106
Boscombe Rd. SW19—5M 105
Boscombe Rd. W12—3E 72
Boscombe Rd. Wor Pk—3G 121
Bosgrove. E4—2A 30
Boss St. SE1—3D 76
Bostall Hill. SE2—6E 80
Bostall Hill Rd. SE2—7G 81
Bostall La. SE2—6F 80
Bostall Mnr. Way. SE2—5F 80
Bostall Pk. Av. Bexh—8J 81
Bostall Rd. Orp—4F 112
Bostal Row. Bexh—2K 97
Boston Gdns. W4—7C 72
Boston Gdns. W7—5E 70
Boston Gdns. Bren—5E 70
Boston Gro. Ruis—4A 36
Boston Mnr. Rd. Bren—5F 70
Boston Pk. Rd. Bren—6G 71
Boston Pl. NW1—7D 58
Boston Rd. E6—6J 63
Boston Rd. E17—4L 45
Boston Rd. W7—3D 70
Boston Rd. Croy—1K 123
Boston Rd. Edgw—7A 24
Boston St. E2—5E 60
Bostonthorpe Rd. W7—3C 70
Boston Vale. W7—5E 70
Boswell Clo. Orp—1G 129
Boswell Ct. WC1—8J 59
Boswell Path. Hay—5D 68
Boswell Rd. T Hth—8A 108
Boswell St. WC1—8J 59
Bosworth Clo. E17—8K 29
Bosworth Cres. Romf—6G 35
Bosworth Rd. N11—6H 27
Bosworth Rd. W10—7J 57
Bosworth Rd. Barn—5L 13

Bosworth Rd. Dag—8L 49
Botany Bay La. Chst—6A 112
Boteley Clo. E4—2B 30
Botha Rd. E13—8F 62
Bothwell Clo. E16—8D 62
Bothwell Rd. Croy—2A 140
Bothwell St. W6—7H 73
Botolph La. EC3—1C 76
Botsford Rd. SW20—6J 105
Bott Rd. Dart—1K 115
Botts M. W2—9L 57
Botwell Comn. Rd. Hay—1B 68
Botwell Cres. Hay—9C 52
Botwell La. Hay—1C 68
Boucher Clo. Tedd—2D 102
Bouchier Wlk. Rain—2E 66
Boughton Av. Brom—2D 126
Boughton Rd. SE28—4C 80
Boulcott St. E1—9H 61
Boulevard, The. Pinn—2L 37
Boulmer Rd. Uxb—6A 142
Boulogne Rd. Croy—1A 124
Boulter Gdns. Horn—1E 66
Boulton Rd. Dag—8K 49
Boultwood Rd. E6—9K 63
Bounces La. N9—2F 28
Bounces Rd. N9—2F 28
Boundaries Rd. SW12—8D 90
Boundaries Rd. Felt—7G 85
Boundary Av. E17—5K 45
Boundary Clo. SE20—6E 108
Boundary Clo. Ilf—9C 48
Boundary Clo. King—7M 103
Boundary Clo. S'hall—6L 69
Boundary La. E13—7H 63
Boundary La. SE17—7A 76
Boundary Pas. E2—7D 60
Boundary Rd. E13—5G 63
Boundary Rd. E17—5K 45
Boundary Rd. N9—8G 17
Boundary Rd. N22—1M 43
Boundary Rd. NW8—4A 58
Boundary Rd. SW19—3B 106
Boundary Rd. Bark—5A 64
(in two parts)
Boundary Rd. Pinn—5H 37
Boundary Rd. Romf—4E 50
Boundary Rd. Sidc—4C 96
Boundary Rd. Upm—8L 51
Boundary Rd. Wall—8F 122
Boundary Rd. S. Wall & Cars
—1E 136
Boundary Row. SE1—3M 75
Boundary St. E2—6D 60
(in two parts)
Boundary St. Eri—8D 82
Boundary Way. Croy—7L 125
Boundary Way. Wat—5F 4
Boundfield Rd. SE6—9C 94
Bounds Grn. Industrial Est.
N11—6G 27
Bounds Grn. Rd.—6G 27
  N22 1-107
  N11 remainder
Bourchier St. W1—1H 75
Bourdon Rd. SE20—6G 109
Bourdon St. W1—1F 74
Bourke Clo. NW10—2C 56
Bourke Clo. SW4—5J 91
Bourn Av. Uxb—7E 142
Bournbrook Rd. SE3—2H 95
Bourne Av. N14—2J 27
Bourne Av. N15—2B 44
Bourne Av. Barn—7B 14
Bourne Av. Hay—4A 68
Bourne Av. Ruis—1G 53
Bournebridge La. Romf—1A 34
Bourne Ct. Ruis—1F 52
Bourne End. Horn—5L 51
Bourne End Rd. Nwd—4C 20
Bournefield Rd. Whyt—9E 138
Bourne Gdns. E4—4M 29
Bournehall Av. Bush, Wat—7L 9
Bournehall La. Bush, Wat—8L 9
Bournehall Rd. Bush, Wat—8L 9
Bourne Hill. N13—2K 27
Bourne Industrial Pk. Dart
—4C 98
Bourne Mead. Bex—4B 98
Bournemead Av. N'holt—5E 52
Bournemead Clo. N'holt—6E 52
Bournemead Way. N'holt
—5F 52
Bournemouth Rd. SE15—1E 92
Bournemouth Rd. SW19—5L 105
Bourne Pk. Clo. Kenl—8C 138
Bourne Pl. W4—6B 72
Bourne Rd. E7—8D 46
Bourne Rd. N8—4J 43
Bourne Rd. Bex—6M 97
Bourne Rd. Brom—8H 111
Bourne Rd. Bush, Wat—7L 9
Bourne St. SW1—5E 74

Bourne St. Croy—4M 123
Bourne Ter. W2—8M 57
Bourne, The. N14—2J 27
Bourne Vale. Brom—3D 126
Bournevale Rd. SW16—1J 107
Bourne View. Gnfd—1D 54
Bourne View. Kenl—7B 138
Bourneville Rd. SE6—6L 93
Bourne Way. Brom—4D 126
Bourne Way. Eps—6A 120
Bourne Way. Sutt—7K 121
Bourne Way. Swan—7A 114
Bournewood Rd. SE18—8E 80
Bournewood Rd. Orp—2G 129
Bournwell Clo. Barn—5D 14
Boutflower Rd. SW11—3C 90
Bouverie Gdns. Harr—4H 39
Bouverie M. N16—7C 44
Bouverie Pl. W2—9B 58
Bouverie Rd. N16—7C 44
Bouverie Rd. Harr—4A 38
Bouverie St. EC4—9L 59
Bouvier Rd. Enf—2G 17
Bovay Pl. N7—9K 43
Bovay St. N7—9K 43
Boveney Rd. SE23—6H 93
Bovill Rd. SE23—6H 93
Bovingdon Av. Wemb—2L 55
Bovingdon Clo. N19—7G 43
Bovingdon Cres. Wat—7H 5
Bovingdon La. NW9—8C 24
Bovingdon Rd. SW6—9M 73
Bow Arrow La. Dart—5L 99
Bowater Clo. NW9—3B 40
Bowater Clo. SW2—5J 91
Bowater Pl. SE3—8F 78
Bowater Rd. SE18—4H 79
Bow Bri. Est. E3—6M 61
Bow Comn. La. E3—7J 61
Bowden Dri. Horn—6J 51
Bowden St. SE11—6L 75
Bowditch. SE8—6K 77
Bowdon Rd. E17—5L 45
Bowen Dri. SE21—9C 92
Bowen Rd. Harr—5A 38
Bowen St. E14—9M 61
Bowens Wood. Croy—1K 139
Bower Av. SE10—9C 78
Bower Clo. N'holt—5G 53
Bower Clo. Romf—7B 34
Bower Farm Rd. Hav, Romf
—3A 34
Bower La. Eyns, Dart & Sev
—5J 131
Bowerman Av. SE14—7J 77
Bower Rd. Swan—4E 114
Bower St. E1—9H 61
Bowers Wlk. E6—8K 63
Bowes Clo. Sidc—5F 96
Bowes Rd.—5G 27
  N13 1-153 & 2-138
  N11 remainder
Bowes Rd. W3—1C 72
Bowes Rd. Dag—4G 49
Bowes Rd. W on T—4F 116
Bowford Av. Bexh—9J 81
Bowie Clo. SW4—6H 91
Bowland Rd. SW4—3H 91
Bowland Rd. Wfd G—5G 31
Bow La. EC4—9A 60
Bow La. N12—7A 26
Bow La. Mord—1J 121
Bowl Ct. EC2—7C 60
Bowles Grn. Enf—9B 6
Bowles Rd. SE1—7E 76
Bowley La. SE19—2D 108
Bowley St. E14—1K 77
Bowling Grn. Clo. SW15—6F 88
Bowling Grn. La. EC1—7L 59
Bowling Grn. Pl. SE1—3B 76
Bowling Grn. Row. SE18—4J 79
Bowling Grn. St. SE11—7L 75
Bowling Grn. Wlk. N1—6C 60
Bowls Clo. Stan—5F 22
Bowls, The. Chig—4C 32
Bowman Av. E16—1D 78
Bowmans Clo. W13—2F 70
Bowmans Grn. Wat—9J 5
Bowmans Lea. SE23—6G 93
Bowmans Meadow. Wall
—5F 122
Bowman's Pl. N7—8J 43
Bowman's Rd. Dart—6D 98
Bowmead. SE9—8K 95
Bowmore Wlk. NW1—3H 59
Bowness Cres. SW15—2C 104
Bowness Dri. Houn—3J 85
Bowness Rd. SE6—6M 93
Bowness Rd. Bexh—1M 97
Bowness Way. Horn—1E 66

Bowood Rd. SW11—4E 90
Bowood Rd. Enf—4H 17
Bowring Grn. Wat—5G 21
Bow Rd. E3—6K 61
Bow St. E15—1C 62
Bow St. WC2—9J 59
Bowyer Pl. SE5—8A 76
Bowyers Clo. Asht—9K 133
Bowyer St. SE5—8A 76
Boxall Rd. SE21—5C 92
Boxford Clo. S Croy—4H 139
Boxgrove Rd. SE2—4G 81
Boxley Rd. Mord—8A 106
Boxley St. E16—2F 78
Boxmoor Rd. Harr—2F 38
Boxmoor Rd. Romf—5A 34
Buxoll Rd. Dag—9K 49
Box Ridge Av. Purl—4K 137
Boxted Clo. Buck H—5C 26
Boxtree La. Harr—8A 22
Boxtree Rd. Harr—7B 22
Box Tree Wlk. Orp—3H 129
Boxwood Way. Warl—9H 139
Boxworth Gro. N1—4K 59
Boyard Rd. SE18—6M 79
Boyce Clo. Borwd—3J 11
Boyce Way. E13—7E 62
Boycroft Av. NW9—4A 40
Boyd Av. S'hall—2K 69
Boyd Clo. King—4L 103
Boydel Ct. NW8—3B 58
Boyd Rd. SW19—3B 106
Boyd St. E1—9E 60
Boyfield St. SE1—3M 75
Boyland Rd. Brom—2D 110
Boyle Av. Stan—6E 22
Boyle Clo. W4—8B 72
Boyle Farm Rd. Th Dit—1E 118
Boyle St. W1—1G 75
Boyne Av. NW4—2H 41
Boyne Rd. SE13—2A 94
Boyne Rd. Dag—8L 49
Boyne Ter. M. W11—2K 73
Boyseland Ct. Edgw—2A 24
Boyson Rd. SE17—7A 76
Boythorn Rd. SE16—6F 76
Boythorn Way. SE16—6F 76
Boyton Clo. E1—7G 61
Boyton Clo. N8—1J 43
Boyton Rd. N8—1J 43
Brabant Rd. N22—9K 27
Brabazon Av. Wall—9J 123
Brabazon Rd. Houn—8G 69
Brabazon Rd. N'holt—5L 53
Brabazon St. E14—8M 61
Brabourne Clo. SE19—2C 108
Brabourne Cres. Bexh—7K 81
Brabourne Heights. NW7
—3C 24
Brabourne Rise. Beck—9A 110
Brabourn Gro. SE15—1G 93
Bracewell Av. Gnfd—2E 54
Bracewell Rd. W10—8G 57
Bracewood Gdns. Croy
—5D 124
Bracey St. N4—7J 43
Bracken Av. SW12—6E 90
Bracken Av. Croy—5M 125
Brackenbridge Dri. Ruis
—8H 37
Brackenbury Gdns. W6—4F 72
Brackenbury Rd. N2—1A 42
Brackenbury Rd. W6—4F 72
Bracken Clo. Twic—6L 85
Brackendale. N21—2K 27
Brackendale Clo. Houn—9M 69
Brackendale Gdns. Upm
—9M 51
Brackendene. Dart—1C 114
Bracken Dene. St Alb—3K 5
Bracken Dri. Chig—6M 31
Bracken End. Iswth—4B 86
Brackenfield Clo. E5—8F 44
Bracken Gdns. SW13—1E 88
Bracken Hill Clo. Brom—5D 110
Bracken Hill La. Brom—5D 110
Bracken Industrial Est. Ilt
—7D 32
Bracken M. Romf—4M 49
Bracken Path. Eps—5M 133
Brackens. Beck—4L 109
Brackens, The. Enf—9C 16
Brackens, The. Orp—7E 128
Brackenwood. Sun—5E 100
Brackley. Wey—7B 116
Brackley Clo. Wall—9J 123
Brackley Rd. W4—6C 72
Brackley Rd. Beck—4K 109
Brackley Sq. Wfd G—7H 31
Brackley St. EC1—7A 60
Brackley Ter. W4—6C 72

Bracklyn St. N1—5B 60
Bracknell Clo. N22—8L 27
Bracknell Gdns. NW3—9M 41
Bracknell Way. NW3—9M 41
Bracondale. Esh—7A 118
Bracondale Rd. SE2—5E 80
Bradbourne Rd. Bex—6L 97
Bradbourne St. SW6—1L 89
Bradbury St. N16—1C 60
Braddon Rd. Rich—2K 87
Braddyll St. SE10—6C 78
Bradenham Av. Well—3E 96
Bradenham Rd. Harr—2F 38
Bradenham Rd. Hay—6C 52
Braden St. W9—7M 57
Bradfield Dri. Bark—1E 64
Bradfield Rd. E16—3E 78
Bradfield Rd. Ruis—1J 53
Bradford Clo. SE26—1F 108
Bradford Clo. Brom—3K 127
Bradford Dri. Eps—8D 120
Bradford Rd. W3—3C 72
Bradford Rd. Ilf—6B 48
Bradgate Rd. SE6—5M 93
Brading Cres. E11—7F 46
Brading Rd. SW2—6K 91
Brading Rd. Croy—1K 123
Bradiston Rd. W9—6K 57
Bradley Clo. N7—2J 59
Bradley Gdns. W13—9F 54
Bradley Rd. N22—9K 27
Bradley Rd. SE19—3A 108
Bradley Rd. Enf—2J 17
Bradley's Clo. N1—5L 59
Bradmead. SW8—8F 74
Bradmore Pk. Rd. W6—5F 72
Bradmore Way. Coul—9J 137
Bradshawe Waye. Uxb
—8D 142
Bradshaw Rd. Wat—3G 9
Bradstock Rd. E9—2H 61
Bradstock Rd. Eps—7E 120
Brad St. SE1—2L 75
Bradwell Av. Dag—7L 49
Bradwell Clo. E18—2D 46
Bradwell Clo. Horn—2F 66
Bradwell M. N18—4E 28
Bradwell Rd. Buck H—1J 31
Brady Av. Lou—4M 19
Brady St. E1—7F 60
Braemar Av. N22—8J 27
Braemar Av. NW10—8B 40
Braemar Av. SW19—8L 89
Braemar Av. Bexh—3A 98
Braemar Av. S Croy—2A 138
Braemar Av. T Hth—7M 107
Braemar Av. Wemb—3H 55
Braemar Gdns. NW9—8B 24
Braemar Gdns. Horn—4L 51
Braemar Gdns. Sidc—9B 96
Braemar Gdns. W Wick
—3A 126
Braemar Rd. E13—7D 62
Braemar Rd. N15—3C 44
Braemar Rd. Bren—7H 71
Braemar Rd. Wor Pk—5F 120
Braeside. Beck—2L 109
Braeside Av. SW19—5J 105
Braeside Clo. Pinn—7L 21
Braeside Cres. Bexh—3A 98
Braeside Rd. SW16—4G 107
Braes St. N1—3M 59
Braesyde Clo. Belv—5K 81
Brafferton Rd. Croy—6A 124
Braganza St. SE17—6M 75
Braham St. E1—9D 60
Braid Av. W3—9C 56
Braid Clo. Felt—8K 85
Braidwood Rd. SE6—7B 94
Braidwood St. SE1—2C 76
Brailsford Rd. SW2—5L 91
Brainton Av. Felt—6F 84
Braintree Av. Ilf—2J 47
Braintree Rd. Dag—8L 49
Braintree Rd. Ruis—9F 36
Braintree St. E2—6G 61
Braithwaite Av. Romf—5L 49
Braithwaite Gdns. Stan—8G 23
Bramah Grn. SW9—9L 75
Bramalea Clo. N6—4E 42
Bramall Clo. E15—1D 62
Bramber Rd. N12—5C 26
Bramber Rd. W14—7K 73
Bramble Banks. Cars—1E 136
Bramblebury Rd. SE18—6A 80
Bramble Clo. Croy—5K 125
Bramble Clo. Shep—7B 100
Bramble Clo. Stan—7H 23
Bramble Clo. Uxb—9D 142
Bramble Clo. Wat—7E 4
Bramble Croft. Eri—5A 82
Brambledown Clo. Brom
—9C 110

Brambledown Rd. Cars & Wall
—9E 122
Brambledown Rd. S Croy
—9C 124
Bramble Gdns. SW16—7K 107
Bramble Rd. SW12—1D 72
Brambles Clo. Bren—8F 70
Brambles Farm Dri. Uxb
—6E 142
Brambles, The. Chig—5A 32
Brambles, The. W Dray—5J 143
Bramble Wlk. Eps—6M 133
Bramblewood Clo. Cars
—3C 122
Bramblings, The. E4—4B 30
Bramcote Av. Mitc—8D 106
Bramcote Gro. SE16—6G 77
Bramcote Rd. SW15—3F 88
Bramdean Cres. SE12—7E 94
Bramdean Gdns. SE12—7E 94
Bramerton Rd. Beck—7K 109
Bramerton St. SW3—7C 74
Bramfield Rd. SW11—5C 90
Bramford Rd. SW18—3A 90
Bramham Gdns. SW5—6M 73
Bramham Gdns. Chess
—6H 119
Bramhope La. SE7—7F 78
Bramlands Clo. SW11—2C 90
Bramleas. Wat—6D 8
Bramley Av. Coul—7G 137
Bramley Clo. E17—9J 29
Bramley Clo. N14—7F 14
Bramley Clo. Hay—1E 68
Bramley Clo. Orp—3M 127
Bramley Clo. S Croy—7A 124
Bramley Clo. Swan—8C 114
Bramley Clo. Twic—5A 86
Bramley Ct. Well—9F 80
Bramley Cres. Ilf—4L 47
Bramley Gdns. Wat—5G 21
Bramley Hill. S Croy—7M 123
Bramley Pde. N14—6H 15
Bramley Pl. Dart—3E 98
Bramley Rd. N14—7F 14
Bramley Rd. W10—1H 73
Bramley Rd. W5—4G 71
Bramley Rd. Sutt—7B 122
Bramley Rd. Sutt—1H 135
(East Ewell)
Bramley Shaw. Wal A—6M 7
Bramley St. W10—9H 57
Bramley Way. Asht—9K 133
Bramley Way. W Wick—4M 125
Brampton Clo. E5—7F 44
Brampton Clo. Wal X—1A 6
Brampton Gdns. N15—3A 44
Brampton Gdns. W on T
—7G 117
Brampton Gro. NW4—2F 40
Brampton Gro. Harr—2E 38
Brampton Gro. Wemb—6L 39
Brampton La. NW4—2G 41
Brampton Pk. Rd. N8—1L 43
Brampton Rd. E6—6H 63
Brampton Rd. N15—3A 44
Brampton Rd. NW9—2L 39
Brampton Rd. Bexh & SE2
—2H 97
Brampton Rd. Croy—1D 124
Brampton Rd. Uxb—5F 142
Brampton Rd. Wat—3E 20
Bramshaw Gdns. Wat—5H 21
Bramshaw Rise. N Mald
—1C 120
Bramshaw Rd. E9—2H 61
Bramshill Clo. Chig—5C 32
Bramshill Gdns. NW5—8F 42
Bramshill Rd. NW10—5C 56
Bramshot Av. SE7—7E 78
Bramshot Way. Wat—2E 20
Bramston Rd. NW10—5E 56
Bramwell Clo. Sun—6H 101
Brancaster La. Purl—3A 138
Brancaster Rd. E12—9K 47
Brancaster Rd. SW16—9J 91
Brancaster Rd. Ilf—4C 48
Brancepeth Gdns. Buck H
—2E 30
Branch Hill. NW3—8A 42
Branch Hill Ho. NW3—8M 41
Branch Pl. N1—4B 60
Branch Rd. E14—1J 77
Branch Rd. Ilf—5F 32
Brancker Clo. Wall—9J 123
Brancker Rd. Harr—1H 39
Brandbury Clo. S'hall—5L 69
Brandlehow Rd. SW15—3K 89
Brandon Est. SE17—7M 75
Brandon Rd. E17—2A 46
Brandon Rd. N7—5A 59
Brandon Rd. Dart—6L 99
Brandon Rd. S'hall—6K 69

Brandon Rd. Sutt—6M 121
Brandon St. SE17—5A 76
(in two parts)
Brandram Rd. SE13—2C 94
Brandreth Rd. E6—9K 63
Brandreth Rd. SW17—8F 90
Brandries, The. Wall—5H 123
Brand St. SE10—8A 78
Brandville Gdns. Ilf—2M 47
Brandville Rd. W Dray—3J 143
Brandy Way. Sutt—9L 121
Branfill Rd. Upm—7M 51
Brangbourne Rd. Brom
—2A 110
Brangton Rd. SE11—6K 75
Brangwyn Cres. SW19—6A 106
Branksea St. SW6—8J 73
Branksome Av. N18—5D 28
Branksome Clo. W on T
—4H 117
Branksome Rd. SW2—4J 91
Branksome Rd. SW19—5L 105
Branksome Way. Harr—4K 39
Branksome Way. N Mald
—5A 104
Bransby Rd. Chess—8J 119
Branscombe Gdns. N21—9L 15
Branscombe St. SE13—2M 93
Bransdale Clo. NW6—4L 57
Bransell Clo. Swan—1A 130
Bransgrove Rd. Edgw—8K 23
Branston Cres. Orp—3B 128
Branstone Rd. Rich—9K 71
Brants Wlk. W7—7C 54
Brantwood Av. Eri—8A 82
Brantwood Av. Iswth—3E 86
Brantwood Clo. E17—1A 46
Brantwood Gdns. Enf—6J 15
Brantwood Gdns. Ilf—2J 47
Brantwood Rd. N17—6E 28
Brantwood Rd. SE24—4A 92
Brantwood Rd. Bexh—1M 97
Brantwood Rd. S Croy—1A 138
Brantwood Way. Orp—7G 113
Brasher Clo. Gnfd—1B 54
Brassey Rd. NW6—2K 57
Brassey Sq. SW11—2E 90
Brassie Av. W3—9C 56
Brasted Clo. SE26—1G 109
Brasted Clo. Bexh—4H 97
Brasted Clo. Orp—4E 128
Brasted Rd. Eri—8C 82
Brathway Rd. SW18—6L 89
Bratley St. E1—7E 60
Bratten Ct. Croy—1B 124
Braund Av. Gnfd—7M 53
Braundton Av. Sidc—7D 96
Bravington Pl. W9—7K 57
Bravington Rd. W9—6K 57
Braxfield Rd. SE4—3J 93
Braxted Pk. SW16—3K 107
Brayards Rd. SE15—1F 92
Braybrook St. W12—9D 56
Brayburne Av. SW4—1G 91
Braycourt Av. W on T—2F 116
Braydon Rd. N16—6E 44
Bray Dri. E16—1D 78
Brayfield Ter. N1—3L 59
Brayford Sq. E1—9G 61
Bray Pas. E16—1E 78
Bray Pl. SW3—5D 74
Bray Rd. NW7—6H 25
Brayton Gdns. Enf—6H 15
Braywood Rd. SE9—3B 96
Breach La. Dag—6L 65
Bread St. EC4—9A 60
Breakfield. Coul—8J 137
Breakspeare Clo. Wat—2F 8
Breakspeare Rd. Abb L, Wat
—4C 4
Breakspear Rd. Ruis—4A 36
Breakspears Dri. Orp—5E 112
Breakspears Rd. SE4—3K 93
Bream Gdns. E6—6L 63
Breamore Clo. SW15—7E 88
Breamore Rd. Ilf—7D 48
Bream's Bldgs. EC4—9L 59
Bream St. E3—3L 61
Breamwater Gdns. Rich—9F 86
Brearley Clo. Uxb—2C 142
Breasley Clo. SW15—3F 89
Brechin Pl. SW7—5A 74
Brecknock Rd. N19—8G 43
N7 1-113 & 2-142
N19 remainder
Brecon Clo. Mitc—7J 107
Brecon Rd. W6—7J 73
Brecon Rd. Enf—6G 17
Brede Clo. E6—6L 63

Bredgar Rd. N19—7G 43
Bredhurst Clo. SE20—3G 109
Bredon Rd. SE5—2A 92
Bredon Rd. Croy—2D 124
Bredune. Kenl—7B 138
Breer St. SW6—2M 89
Breezer's Hill. E1—1E 76
Brember Rd. Harr—7A 38
Bremner Clo. Swan—8E 114
Bremner Rd. SW7—4A 74
Brenchley Clo. Brom—1D 126
Brenchley Clo. Chst—5L 111
Brenchley Gdns. SE23—5G 93
Brenchley Rd. Orp—6D 112
Brendans Clo. Horn—6J 51
Brenda Rd. SW17—8D 90
Brende Gdns. E Mol—8M 101
Brendon Av. NW10—1C 56
Brendon Clo. Eri—9C 82
Brendon Clo. Esh—8A 118
Brendon Dri. Esh—8A 118
Brendon Gdns. Harr—9M 37
Brendon Gdns. Ilf—3C 48
Brendon Rd. SE9—8B 96
Brendon Rd. Dag—6L 49
Brendon St. W1—9C 58
Brendon Way. Enf—9C 16
Brenley Clo. Mitc—7E 106
Brenley Gdns. SE9—3H 95
Brent Clo. Bex—7J 97
Brent Clo. Dart—5M 99
Brentcot Clo. W13—7F 54
Brent Cres. NW10—5K 55
Brent Cross Fly-Over. NW2
—5H 41
Brent Cross Shopping Centre.
NW4—5G 41
Brentfield. NW10—3M 55
Brentfield Clo. NW10—2B 56
Brentfield Gdns. NW2—5H 41
Brentfield Rd. NW10—2B 56
Brentfield Rd. Dart—5L 99
Brentford Clo. Hay—7H 53
Brent Grn. NW4—3H 41
Brent Grn. Wlk. Wemb—8A 40
Brentham Way. W5—7H 55
Brenthouse Rd. E9—2G 61
Brenthurst Rd. NW10—2D 56
Brentlands Dri. Dart—7L 99
Brent La. Dart—6K 99
Brent Lea. Bren—8G 71
Brentmead Clo. W7—1C 70
Brentmead Gdns. NW10—5K 55
Brentmead Pl. NW11—4H 41
Brenton St. E14—9J 61
Brent Pk. Rd. NW4—5F 40
(in two parts)
Brent Pl. Barn—7K 13
Brent Rd. E16—9E 62
Brent Rd. SE18—8M 79
Brent Rd. Bren—7G 71
Brent Rd. S'hall—4G 69
Brent Rd. S Croy—1F 138
Brent Side. Bren—7G 71
Brentside Clo. W13—7E 54
Brent Ter. NW2—6G 41
Brent, The. Dart—6M 99
Brent Trading Centre. NW10
—1C 56
Brentvale Av. S'hall—2H 69
Brentvale Av. Wemb—4K 55
Brent View Rd. NW9—5E 40
Brent Way. N3—6L 25
Brent Way. Bren—8H 71
Brent Way. Dart—5M 99
Brent Way. Wemb—2M 55
Brentwick Gdns. Bren—5J 71
Brentwood Clo. SE9—7A 96
Brentwood Rd. Romf—4D 50
Brereton Rd. N17—7D 28
Bressenden Pl. SW1—4G 75
Bressey Gro. E18—9D 30
Brett Clo. N16—7C 44
Brett Clo. N'holt—6H 53
Brett Cres. NW10—4B 56
Brettell St. SE17—6B 76
Brettenham Av. E17—8L 29
Brettenham Rd. E17—9L 29
Brettenham Rd. N18—4E 28
Brett Gdns. Dag—3J 65
Brettgrave. Eps—2A 134
Brett Ho. Clo. SW15—6H 89
Brett Pl. Wat—1E 8
Brett Rd. E8—1F 60
Brett Rd. Barn—7G 13
Brewer's Field. Dart—1G 115
Brewers La. Rich—4H 87
Brewer St. W1—1G 75
Brewery La. Twic—6D 86
Brewery Rd. N7—3J 59
Brewery Rd. SE18—6B 80
Brewery Rd. Brom—3J 127

Brewhouse La. E1—2F 76
Brewhouse Rd. SE18—5K 79
Brewhouse St. SW15—2J 89
Brewhouse Wlk. SE16—2J 77
Brewhouse Yd. EC1—7M 59
Brewood Rd. Dag—2F 64
Brewster Gdns. W10—8G 57
Brewster Rd. E10—6M 45
Brian Av. S Croy—4C 138
Brian Clo. Horn—9F 50
Briane Rd. Eps—2B 134
Brian Rd. Romf—3G 49
Briants Clo. Pinn—9K 21
Briant St. SE14—9H 77
Briar Av. SW16—4K 107
Briarbank Rd. W13—9E 54
Briar Banks. Cars—1E 136
Briar Clo. N2—1M 41
Briar Clo. N13—3A 28
Briar Clo. Buck H—2H 31
Briar Clo. Hmptn—2K 101
Briar Clo. Iswth—4D 86
Briar Clo. Wal X—2C 6
Briar Ct. Sutt—6G 121
Briar Cres. N'holt—2M 53
Briardale Gdns. NW3—8L 41
Briarfield Av. N3—9M 25
Briar Gdns. Brom—3D 126
Briar Gro. S Croy—5E 138
Briar Hill. Purl—3J 137
Briar La. Cars—1E 136
Briar La. Croy—6M 125
Briar Rd. NW2—9G 41
Briar Rd. SW16—7J 107
Briar Rd. Bex—9B 98
Briar Rd. Harr—3G 39
Briar Rd. Romf—7G 35
Briar Rd. Twic—7C 86
Briar Rd. Wat—7E 4
Briars Clo. N17—7F 28
Briars Ct. Lea—6B 132
Briars, The. Wal X—4E 6
Briars Wlk. Romf—9K 35
Briarswood Way. Orp—7D 128
Briar Wlk. SW15—3F 88
Briar Wlk. W10—7J 57
Briar Wlk. Edgw—7A 24
Briar Way. W Dray—3L 143
Briar Wood Clo. NW9—4A 40
Briarwood Dri. N'wd—9E 20
Briarwood Rd. SW4—4H 91
Briarwood Rd. Eps—8E 120
Briary Clo. NW3—3C 58
Briary Ct. Sidc—2F 112
Briary Gdns. Brom—2F 110
Briary La. N9—3D 28
Briavels Ct. Eps—7C 134
Brick Ct. EC4—9L 59
Brickenden Ct. Wal A—6M 7
Brickett Clo. Ruis—3A 36
Brick Farm Clo. Rich—9M 71
Brickfield Clo. Bren—8G 71
Brickfield Cotts. SE18—7D 80
Brickfield La. Barn—8G 12
Brickfield La. Hay—7B 68
Brickfield Rd. E3—7M 61
Brickfield Rd. SW19—1M 105
Brickfield Rd. T Hth—5M 107
Brickfields Cotts. Borwd
—5K 11
Brick La.—7D 60
E1 1-165 & 2-226
E2 remainder
Brick La. Enf—4F 16
Brick La. Stan—7H 23
Brick St. W1—2F 74
Brickwall La. Ruis—6C 36
Brickwood Clo. SE26—9F 92
Brickwood Rd. Croy—4C 124
Bride La. EC4—9M 59
Bride St. N7—2K 59
Bridewell Pl. EC4—9M 59
Bridford M. W1—8F 58
Bridge App. NW1—3E 58
Bridge Av. W6—5G 73
Bridge Av. W7—8B 54
Bridge Av. Upm—5L 51
Bridge Clo. Enf—4F 16
Bridge Clo. Romf—4C 50
Bridge End. E17—8A 30
Bridgefield Clo. Bans—7G 135
Bridgefield Rd. Sutt—8L 121
Bridge Foot. SE1—6J 75
Bridge Foot. Sun—5D 100
Bridgeford St. SW18—9A 90
Bridge Gdns. Ashf—4A 100
Bridge Gdns. E Mol—8B 102
Bridge Ga. N21—9A 16
Bridgeland Rd. E16—9E 62
Bridge La. NW11—3J 41
Bridge La. SW11—9C 74
Bridgeman Rd. N1—3K 59
Bridgeman Rd. Tedd—3E 102

Bridgeman St.—Bronson Rd.

Bridgeman St. NW8—5C 58
Bridgend Rd. SW18—3A 90
Bridgend Rd. Enf—8C 6
Bridgenhall Rd. Enf—3D 16
Bridgen Rd. Bex—6J 97
Bridge Pl. SW1—5F 74
Bridge Pl. Croy—3B 124
Bridge Pl. Wat—7H 9
Bridger Clo. Wat—6H 5
Bridge Rd. E6—3K 63
Bridge Rd. E15—4B 62
Bridge Rd. E17—5K 45
Bridge Rd. N9—3E 28
Bridge Rd. N22—8J 27
Bridge Rd. NW10—2C 56
Bridge Rd. Beck—4K 109
Bridge Rd. Bexh—1J 97
Bridge Rd. Chess—7J 119
Bridge Rd. E Mol—8B 102
Bridge Rd. Eps—4D 134
Bridge Rd. Eri—9D 82
Bridge Rd. Houn & Iswth —2B 86
Bridge Rd. K Lan—6A 4
Bridge Rd. Orp—1F 128
Bridge Rd. Rain—7E 66
Bridge Rd. S'hall—3K 69
Bridge Rd. Sutt—8M 121
Bridge Rd. Twic—5F 86
Bridge Rd. Uxb—5A 142
Bridge Rd. Wall—7G 123
Bridge Rd. Wemb—8L 39
Bridge Row. Croy—3B 124
Bridges Ct. SW11—2B 90
Bridges La. Croy—6J 123
Bridges M. SW19—3M 105
Bridges Pl. SW6—9K 73
Bridges Rd. SW19—3M 105
Bridges Rd. Dart—4M 99
Bridges Rd. Stan—5D 22
Bridge St. SW1—3J 75
Bridge St. W4—5B 72
Bridge St. Pinn—1J 37
Bridge St. Rich—4H 87
Bridge St. W on T—3C 116
Bridge Ter. E15—3B 62
Bridge, The. Harr—2D 38
Bridge View. W6—6G 73
Bridgeview Ct. Ilf—6C 32
Bridgewater Clo. Chst—7C 112
Bridgewater Gdns. Edgw —9K 23
Bridgewater Rd. Ruis—9E 36
Bridgewater Rd. Wemb—2G 55
Bridgewater Rd. Wey—8B 116
Bridgewater Sq. EC2—8A 60
Bridgewater St. EC2—8A 60
Bridgewater Way. Bush, Wat —8M 9
Bridge Way. N11—3G 27
Bridge Way. NW11—3K 41
Bridgeway. Bark—3D 64
Bridge Way. Twic—6A 86
Bridge Way. Uxb—1F 142
Bridge Way. Wemb—3K 55
Bridgeway St. NW1—5H 59
Bridgewood Clo. SE20—4F 108
Bridgewood Rd. SW16—4H 107
Bridgewood Rd. Wor Pk —6E 120
Bridgman Rd. W4—4A 72
Bridgwater Clo. Romf—5H 35
Bridgwater Rd. E15—4A 62
Bridgwater Rd. Romf—5G 35
Bridgwater Wlk. Romf—5H 35
Bridle Clo. Enf—1K 17
Bridle Clo. Eps—7B 120
Bridle Clo. King—8H 103
Bridle Clo. Sun—7E 100
Bridle End. Eps—6D 134
Bridle La. W1—1G 75
Bridle La. Cob & Lea—7A 132
Bridle Path. Croy—5J 123
Bridle Path. Wat—4F 8
Bridle Path, The. Wfd G—7C 30
Bridlepath Way. Felt—6C 84
Bridle Rd. Croy—5L 125
(in two parts)
Bridle Rd. Eps—5D 134
Bridle Rd. Esh—8F 118
Bridle Rd. Pinn—4G 37
Bridle Rd. S Croy—1E 138
Bridle Rd., The. Purl—2J 137
Bridle Way. Croy—5L 125
(in two parts)
Bridle Way. Orp—6A 128
Bridle Way, The. Croy—2K 139
Bridle Way, The. Wall—7G 123
Bridlington Rd. N9—9F 16
Bridlington Rd. Wat—3H 21
Bridport Av. Romf—4M 49
Bridport Pl. N1—4B 60
(in two parts)
Bridport Rd. N18—5C 28
Bridport Rd. Gnfd—4M 53
Bridport Rd. T Hth—7L 107
Bridport Ter. SW8—9H 75
Bridstow Pl. W2—9L 57
Brief St. SE5—9M 75
Brierley. Croy—8M 125
(in two parts)
Brierley Av. N9—1G 29
Brierley Clo. SE25—8E 108
Brierley Clo. Horn—4G 51
Brierley Rd. E11—9B 46
Brierley Rd. SW12—8G 91
Brierly Gdns. E2—6G 61
Brigade Clo. Harr—7B 38
Brigade St. SE3—1D 94
Brigadier Av. Enf—3A 16
Brigadier Hill. Enf—2A 16
Briggeford Clo. E5—7E 44
Brightfield Rd. SE13—4C 94
Brightling Rd. SE4—5K 93
Brightlingsea Pl. E14—1K 77
Brightman Rd. SW18—7B 90
Brighton Clo. Uxb—3F 142
Brighton Dri. N'holt—2L 53
Brighton Gro. SE14—9J 77
Brighton Rd. E6—6L 63
Brighton Rd. E17—3K 45
Brighton Rd. N2—9A 26
Brighton Rd. N16—9C 44
Brighton Rd. Red, Coul, Purl, & S Croy—9G 137
Brighton Rd. Surb—1G 119
Brighton Rd. Tad, Bans & Sutt —9K 135
Brighton Rd. Wat—2E 8
Brighton Ter. SW9—3K 91
Brights Av. Rain—7F 66
Brightside Rd. SE13—5B 94
Brightside, The. Enf—3J 17
Bright St. E14—9M 61
Brightwell Cres. SW17—2D 106
Brightwell Rd. Wat—7E 8
Brig M. SE8—7L 77
Brigstock Rd. Belv—5M 81
Brigstock Rd. Coul—8F 136
Brigstock Rd. T Hth—9L 107
Brim Hill. N2—2A 42
Brimsdown Av. Enf—4J 17
Brimstone Clo. Orp—9G 129
Brindles, The. Bans—9K 135
Brindley St. SE14—9K 77
Brindley Way. S'hall—1M 69
Brindwood Rd. E4—3L 29
Brinkburn Clo. SE2—5E 80
Brinkburn Clo. Edgw—1M 39
Brinkburn Gdns. Edgw—1L 39
Brinkley Rd. Wor Pk—4F 120
Brinklow Cres. SE18—8M 79
Brinkworth Rd. Ilf—1J 47
Brinkworth Way. E9—2K 61
Brinley Clo. Wal X—4D 6
Brinsdale Rd. NW4—1H 41
Brinsley Rd. Harr—9B 22
Brinsley St. E1—9F 60
Brinsmead Rd. Romf—9L 35
Brinsworth Clo. Twic—8B 86
Brion Pl. E14—8A 62
Brisbane Av. SW19 —5M 105
Brisbane Rd. E10—7M 45
Brisbane Rd. W13—3E 70
Brisbane Rd. Ilf—5M 47
Brisbane St. SE5—8B 76
Briscoe Clo. E11—8D 46
Briscoe Rd. SW19—3B 106
Briscoe Rd. Rain—5G 67
Briset Rd. SE9—2H 95
Briset St. EC1—8M 59
Briset Way. N7—7K 43
Bristol Clo. Stai—5C 144
Bristol Gdns. SW15—6G 89
Bristol Gdns. W9—7M 57
Bristol M. W9—7M 57
Bristol Pk. Rd. E17—2J 45
Bristol Rd. E7—2G 63
Bristol Rd. Gnfd—4M 53
Bristol Rd. Mord—9A 106
Briston Gro. N8—4J 43
Bristow Rd. SE19—2C 108
Bristow Rd. Bexh—9J 81
Bristow Rd. Croy—6J 123
Bristow Rd. Houn—2A 86
Britannia Clo. SW4—3H 91
Britannia Clo. N'holt—6H 53
Britannia La. Twic—6A 86
Britannia Rd. N12—3A 26
Britannia Rd. SW6—8M 73
Britannia Rd. Ilf—8M 47
Britannia Rd. Surb—2K 119
Britannia Rd. Wal X—7F 6
Britannia Row. N1—4M 59
Britannia St. WC1—6K 59
Britannia Wlk. N1—6B 60
(in two parts)
Britannia Way. NW10—7M 55
Britannia Way. Stai—6B 144
British Gro. W4—6D 72
British Gro. Pas. W6—6D 72
British Gro. S. W6—6D 72
British Legion Rd. E4—2D 30
British St. E3—6K 61
Briton Clo. S Croy—3C 138
Briton Cres. S Croy—3C 138
Briton Hill Rd. S Croy—2C 138
Brittain Rd. Dag—8J 49
Brittain Rd. W on T—7H 117
Britten Clo. NW11—6M 41
Britten Clo. Borwd—8H 11
Brittenden Clo. Orp—8D 128
Britten Dri. S'hall—9L 53
Britten's Ct. E1—1E 76
Britten St. SW3—6C 74
Britton St. EC1—7M 59
Brixham Cres. Ruis—6E 36
Brixham Gdns. Ilf—1C 64
Brixham Rd. Well—9H 81
Brixham St. E16—2L 79
Brixton Est. Edgw—9M 23
Brixton Hill. SW2—6J 91
Brixton Hill Pl. SW2—6J 91
Brixton Rd. SW9—2L 91
Brixton Rd. Wat—3F 8
Brixton Sta. Rd. SW9—2L 91
Brixton Water La. SW2—4L 91
Broad Acre. St Alb—3J 5
Broadbent Clo. N6—6F 42
Broadbent St. W1—1F 74
Broadbridge Clo. SE3—8E 78
Broadbury Ct. N18—6F 28
Broad Clo. W on T—5J 117
Broadcoombe. S Croy—9H 125
Broad Ct. WC2—9J 59
Broadcroft Av. Stan—9H 23
Broadcroft Rd. Orp—2B 128
Broadfield Clo. NW2—8G 41
Broadfield Clo. Romf—3D 50
Broadfield Ct. Bush, Wat—2C 22
Broadfield La. NW1—3H 59
Broadfield Rd. SE6—6C 94
Broadfields. E Mol—1C 118
Broadfields. Harr—9M 21
Broadfields Av. N21—9L 15
Broadfields Av. Edgw—4M 23
Broadfields La. Wat—1F 20
Broadfield Sq. Enf—4F 16
Broadfield Way. Buck H—3G 31
Broadgate. Wal A—6M 7
Broadgates Av. Barn—3M 13
Broadgates Rd. SW18—7B 90
Broad Grn. Av. Croy—2M 123
Broadhead Strand. NW9 —9D 24
Broadheath Dri. Chst—2K 111
Broadhinton Rd. SW4—2F 90
Broadhurst. Asht—8J 133
Broadhurst Av. Edgw—4M 23
Broadhurst Av. Ilf—9D 48
Broadhurst Clo. NW6—2A 58
Broadhurst Clo. Rich—4K 87
Broadhurst Gdns. NW6—2M 57
Broadhurst Gdns. chig—4A 32
Broadhurst Gdns. Ruis—7G 37
Broadhurst Wlk. Rain—2E 66
Broadlands Av. SW16—8J 91
Broadlands Av. Enf—5F 16
Broadlands Av. Shep—1A 116
Broadlands Clo. N6—5E 42
Broadlands Clo. SW16—8J 91
Broadlands Clo. Enf—5G 17
Broadlands Clo. Wal X—7D 6
Broadlands Rd. N6—5D 42
Broadlands Rd. Brom—1F 110
Broadlands, The. Felt—9L 85
Broadlands Way. N Mald —1D 120
Broad La. N8—3K 43
Broad La. N15—2D 44
Broad La. Dart—1E 114
Broad La. Hmptn—4K 101
Broad Lawn. SE9—8L 95
Broad Lawns Ct. Harr—8D 22
Broadley St. NW8—8B 58
Broadley Ter. NW1—7C 58
Broadmead. SE6—9L 93
Broadmead. Asht—9K 133
Broadmead Av. N Mald —2E 120
Broadmead Clo. Hmptn —3L 101
Broadmead Clo. Pinn—7J 21
Broadmead Rd. Hay & N'holt —7J 53
Broadmead Rd. Wfd G—6E 30
Broad Oak. Wfd G—5F 30
Broadoak Av. Enf—8D 6
Broadoak Rd. Eri—8B 82
Broadoaks. Surb—4M 119
Broadoaks Way. Brom—9D 110
Broad Sanctuary. SW1—3H 75
Broadstone Pl. W1—8E 58
Broadstone Rd. Horn—7E 50
Broad St. Dag—3L 65
Broad St. Tedd—3D 102
Broad St. Av. EC2—8C 60
Broadstrood. Lou—2L 19
Broad View. NW9—4L 39
Broadview Rd. SW16 —4H 107
Broadwalk. E18—1D 46
Broad Wlk. N21—2K 27
Broad Wlk. NW1—5E 58
Broad Wlk. SE3—1G 95
Broadwalk. Harr—3L 37
Broad Wlk. Houn—9H 69
Broad Wlk. Orp—5H 129
Broad Wlk. Rich—8K 71
Broad Wlk. La. NW11—5K 41
Broad Wlk., The. W8—2M 73
Broad Wlk., The. E Mol—8D 102
Broadwalk, The. N'wd—9A 20
Broadwall. SE1—2L 75
Broadwater Clo. W on T —7E 116
Broadwater Gdns. Orp—6M 127
Broadwater Rd. N17—9C 28
Broadwater Rd. SE28—4B 80
Broadwater Rd. SW17—1C 106
Broadwater Rd. N. W on T —7D 116
Broadwater Rd. S. W on T —7D 116
Broadway. E13—5F 62
Broadway. E15—3B 62
Broadway. SW1—4H 75
Broadway. W7 & W13—2D 70
Broadway. Bark—4A 64
Broadway. Bexh—3J 97
Broadway. Eps—7E 120
Broadway. Gnfd—7A 54
Broadway. Rain—7E 66
Broadway. Romf—9E 34
Broadway. Surb—3M 119
Broadway. Swan—1A 130
Broadway Av. Croy—9B 108
Broadway Av. Twic—5F 86
Broadway Clo. S Croy—6F 138
Broadway Clo. Wfd G—6F 30
Broadway Ct. SW19—3L 105
Broadway Ct. Beck—7A 110
Broadway Gdns. Mitc—8C 106
Broadway Mkt. E8—4F 60
Broadway M. N13—5K 27
Broadway M. N21—1M 27
Broadway Pde. Harr—3M 37
Broadway Pl. SW19—3K 105
Broadway Shopping Centre. Bexh—3L 97
Broadway, The. E4—6B 30
Broadway, The. N8—4J 43
Broadway, The. N9—3E 28
Broadway, The. N22—9L 27
Broadway, The. NW7—5C 24
Broadway, The. SW19—4L 105
Broadway, The. W5—1H 71
Broadway, The. Croy—6J 123
Broadway, The. Dag—7L 49
Broadway, The. Esh—3C 118
Broadway, The. Harr—9C 22
Broadway, The. Horn—9F 50
Broadway, The. Lou—6M 19
Broadway, The. Pinn—7K 21
Broadway, The. S'hall—3J 69
Broadway, The. Stan—5G 23
Broadway, The. Sutt—8J 121
Broadway, The. Wat—5G 9
Broadway, The. Wemb—8J 39
Broadway, The. Wfd G—6F 30
Broadwick St. W1—1G 75
Broadwood Av. Ruis—4C 36
Broad Yd. EC1—7M 59
Brocas Clo. NW3—3C 58
Brockdish Av. Bark—1D 64
Brockenhurst. E Mol—1K 117
Brockenhurst Av. Wor Pk —3C 120
Brockenhurst Gdns. NW7 —6C 24
Brockenhurst Gdns. Ilf—1A 64
Brockenhurst Rd. Croy—2F 124
Brockenhurst Way. SW16 —6H 107
Brocket Clo. Chig—4D 32
Brocket Way. Chig—5C 32
Brockham Clo. SW19—2K 105
Brockham Cres. Croy—9B 126
Brockham Dri. SW2—6K 91
Brockham Dri. Ilf—3A 48
Brockham St. SE1—4A 76
Brockhurst Clo. Stan—6D 22
Brockill Cres. SE4—3J 93
Brocklebank Rd. SW18—6A 90
Brocklehurst St. SE14—8H 77
Brocklesby Clo. Wat—5H 9
Brocklesby Rd. SE25—8F 108
Brockley Av. N. Stan—3J 23
Brockley Av. S. Stan—3J 23
Brockley Clo. Stan—4J 23
Brockley Combe. Wey—6B 116
Brockley Cres. Romf—7A 34
Brockley Cross. SE4—2J 93
Brockley Footpath. SE4—4J 93
Brockley Footpath. SE15 —3G 93
Brockley Gdns. SE4—1K 93
Brockley Gro. SE4—4K 93
Brockley Hall Rd. SE4—4J 93
Brockley Hill. Stan—1G 23
Brockley Pk. SE23—6J 93
Brockley Rise. SE23—7J 93
Brockley Rd. SE4—4J 93
Brockleyside. Stan—4J 23
Brockley View. SE23—6J 93
Brockley Way. SE4—4J 93
Brockman Rise. Brom—1B 110
Brock Pl. E3—7M 61
Brock Rd. E13—8F 62
Brocks Dri. Sutt—5J 121
Brockshot Clo. Bren—6H 71
Brock St. SE15—2G 93
Brockwell Clo. Orp—9D 112
Brockwell Pk. Gdns. SE24 —6M 91
Brockworth Clo. SE15—7C 76
Broderick Gro. SE2—5F 80
Brodewater Rd. Borwd—4M 11
Brodia Rd. N16—8C 44
Brodie Rd. E4—1A 30
Brodie Rd. Enf—2A 16
Brodlove La. E1—1H 77
Brodrick Rd. SW17—8C 90
Brograve Gdns. Beck—6M 109
Brograve Rd. N17—1E 44
Broken Wharf. EC4—1A 76
Brokesley St. E3—6K 61
Broke Wlk. E8—4E 60
Bromar Rd. SE5—2C 92
Bromborough Grn. Wat—5G 21
Bromefield. Stan—8G 23
Bromefield Ct. Wal A—6M 7
Bromells Rd. SW4—3G 91
Brome Rd. SE9—2K 95
Bromet Clo. Wat—2D 8
Bromfelde Rd. SW4—2H 91
Bromfelde Wlk. SW4—1J 91
Bromfield St. N1—5L 59
Bromhall Rd. Dag—2F 64
Bromhedge. SE9—9K 95
Bromholm Rd. SE2—4F 80
Bromleigh Clo. Wal X—1E 6
Bromley Av. Brom—4C 110
Bromley Comn. Brom—8G 111
Bromley Cres. Brom—7D 110
Bromley Cres. Ruis—9D 36
Bromley Gdns. Brom—7D 110
Bromley Gro. Brom—6B 110
Bromley Hall Rd. E14—8A 62
Bromley High St. E3—6M 61
Bromley Hill. Brom—3C 110
Bromley La. Chst—4A 112
Bromley Pl. W1—8G 59
Bromley Rd. E10—4M 45
Bromley Rd. E17—1L 45
Bromley Rd. N17—8E 28
Bromley Rd. N18—3B 28
Bromley Rd.—7M 93
SE6 1-427 & 2-394
Brom remainder
Bromley Rd. Beck—5M 109
Bromley Rd. Beck & Brom —6M 109
Bromley Rd. Chst—5M 111
Bromley St. E1—9H 61
Brompton Clo. SE20—6E 108
Brompton Clo. Houn—4K 85
Brompton Dri. Eri—8F 82
Brompton Gro. N2—2C 42
Brompton Pl. SW3—4D 74
Brompton Rd. SW3 & SW1 —5C 74
Brompton Sq. SW3—4C 74
Brompton Ter. SE18—9L 79
Bromwich Av. N6—7E 42
Bromyard Av. W3—1C 72
Brondesbury M. NW6—3L 57
Brondesbury Pk.—3G 57
NW6 1-97 & 2-64
NW2 remainder
Brondesbury Rd. NW6—5K 57
Brondesbury Vs. NW6—5K 57
Bronsart Rd. SW6—8J 73
Bronson Rd. SW20—6H 105

Bronte Clo. Ilf—2L 47
Bronte Gro. Dart—3K 99
Bronti Clo. SE17—6A 76
Bronze St. SE8—8L 77
Brook Av. Dag—3M 65
Brook Av. Edgw—5M 23
Brook Av. Wemb—8L 39
Brookbank Av. W7—7B 54
Brookbank Rd. SE13—2L 93
Brook Clo. NW7—7J 25
Brook Clo. SW20—7F 104
Brook Clo. Buck H—1E 30
Brook Clo. Romf—8D 34
Brook Clo. Ruis—5C 36
Brook Clo. Stai—6D 144
Brook Cres. E4—4L 29
Brook Cres. N9—4F 28
Brookdale. N11—4G 27
Brookdale Av. Upm—8L 51
Brookdale Clo. Upm—8M 51
Brookdale Rd. E17—1L 45
Brookdale Rd. SE6—6M 93
Brookdale Rd. Bex—5J 97
Brookdene Av. Wat—9F 8
Brookdene Dri. N'wd—7D 20
Brookdene Rd. SE18—5D 80
Brook Dri. SE11—4L 75
Brook Dri. Harr—2A 38
Brook Dri. Ruis—5C 36
Brook Dri. Sun—3C 100
Brooke Av. Harr—8A 38
Brookehowse Rd. SE6—8L 93
Brookend Rd. Sidc—7C 96
Brooke Rd. E17—2A 46
Brooke Rd.—8D 44
  N16 1-147 & 6-160
  E5 remainder
Brooke Rd. N18—3C 28
Brooker Rd. Wal A—/J 7
Brookers Clo. Asht—9H 133
Brooke's Ct. EC1—8L 59
Brooke Way. Bush, Wat—9A 10
Brookfield. N6—8E 42
Brookfield Av. E17—2A 46
Brookfield Av. NW7—6F 24
Brookfield Av. W5—7H 55
Brookfield Av. Sutt—5C 122
Brookfield Clo. NW7—6F 24
Brookfield Ct. Gnfd—6A 54
Brookfield Cres. NW7—6F 24
Brookfield Cres. Harr—3J 39
Brookfield Gdns. Wal X—1D 6
Brookfield Gdns. Esh—8D 118
Brookfield La. Wal X—1B 6
  (in two parts)
Brookfield Pk. NW5—8F 42
Brookfield Path. Wfd G—6C 30
Brookfield Rd. E9—2J 61
Brookfield Rd. N9—3E 28
Brookfield Rd. W4—3B 72
Brookfields. Enf—6H 17
Brookfields Av. Mitc—9C 106
Brook Gdns. E4—4M 29
Brook Gdns. SW13—2D 88
Brook Gdns. King—5A 104
Brook Ga. W1—1D 74
Brook Grn. W6—4H 73
Brook Hill Clo. SE18—6M /9
Brookhill Clo. Barn—7C 14
Brookhill Rd. SE18—6M 79
Brookhill Rd. Barn—7C 14
Brook Ho. Gdns. E4—4C 30
Brooking Rd. E7—1E 62
Brookland Clo. NW11—2M 41
Brookland Garth. NW11
  —2M 41
Brookland Hill. NW11—2M 41
Brookland Rise. NW11—2L 41
Brooklands App. Romf—2B 50
Brooklands Av. SW19—8M 89
Brooklands Av. Sidc—8B 96
Brooklands Clo. Romf—2B 50
Brooklands Clo. Sun—5C 100
Brooklands Dri. Gnfd—4G 55
Brooklands Gdns. Horn—4G 51
Brooklands La. Romf—2B 50
Brooklands Pk. SE3—2E 94
Brooklands Rd. Romf—2B 50
Brooklands Rd. Th Dit—3D 118
Brooklands St. SW8—9H 75
Brook La. SE3—1F 94
Brook La. Bex—5H 97
Brook La. Brom—3E 110
Brook La. N. Bren—6H 71
  (in two parts)
Brooklea Clo. NW9—8C 24
Brooklyn Av. SE25—8F 108
Brooklyn Av. Lou—6J 19
Brooklyn Gro. SE25—8F 108
Brooklyn Rd. SE25—8F 108
Brooklyn Rd. Brom—9H 111

Brooklyn Way. W Dray
  —4H 143
Brook Mead. Eps—8C 120
Brookmead Av. Brom—9K 111
Brookmead Clo. Orp—2F 128
Brookmead Industrial Est. Croy
  —1G 123
Brook Meadow. N12—3M 25
Brookmead Rd. Croy—1G 123
Brookmead Way. Orp—1F 128
Brook M. N. W2—1A 74
Brookmill Rd. SE8—9L 77
Brook Pde. Chig—3M 31
Brook Path. Lou—6J 19
Brook Pl. Barn—7L 13
Brook Rise. Chig—3L 31
Brook Rd. N8—2J 43
Brook Rd. N22—9K 27
Brook Rd. NW2—7D 40
Brook Rd. Borwd—3L 11
Brook Rd. Buck H—2E 30
Brook Rd. Ilf—4C 48
Brook Rd. Lou—7J 19
Brook Rd. Romf—9D 34
Brook Rd. Surb—4J 119
Brook Rd. T Hth—8A 108
Brook Rd. Twic—5E 86
Brook Rd. Wal X—7F 6
Brook Rd. S. Bren—7H 71
Brooks Av. E6—7K 63
Brooksbank St. E9—2G 61
Brooksby M. N1—3L 59
Brooksby St. N1—3L 59
Brooksby's Wlk. E9—1H 61
Brooks Clo. SE9—8L 95
Brookscroft. Croy—2K 139
Brookscroft Rd. E17—8M 29
Brookshill. Harr—5B 22
Brookshill Av. Harr—5B 22
Brookshill Dri. Harr—5B 22
Brookside. N21—8K 15
Brookside. Barn—8C 14
Brookside. Cars—7E 122
Brookside. Horn—3J 51
Brookside. Ilf—6A 32
Brookside. Orp—2D 128
Brookside. Uxb—3D 142
Brookside. Wal A—5L 7
Brookside. Wat—9F 8
Brookside Clo. Barn—8J 13
Brookside Clo. Harr—3H 39
  (Kenton)
Brookside Clo. Harr—9J 37
  (South Harrow)
Brookside Cres. Wor Pk
  —3E 120
Brookside Gdns. Enf—1G 17
Brookside Rd. N9—4F 28
Brookside Rd. N19—7G 43
Brookside Rd. NW11—4J 41
Brookside Rd. Hay—1G 69
Brookside S. Barn—9E 14
Brookside Wlk. N3—1J 41
Brookside Wlk. N12—6L 25
Brookside Wlk. NW11—2K 41
Brookside Way. Croy—1H 125
Brooks La. W4—7L 71
Brooks Rd. E13—4E 62
Brooks Rd. W4—6L 71
Brook St. N17—9D 28
Brook St. W1—1F 74
Brook St. W2—1B 74
Brook St. Belv & Eri—6M 81
Brook St. King—6J 103
Brooksville Av. NW6—4J 57
Brooks Way. Orp—6G 113
Brookvale. Eri—9M 81
Brookview Ct. Enf—7C 16
Brookview Rd. SW16—2G 107
Brookville Rd. SW6—8K 73
Brook Wlk. N2—8B 26
Brook Wlk. Edgw—6B 24
Brookway. SE3—2E 94
Brook Way. Chig—3L 31
Brookway. Rain—8F 66
Brookwood Av. SW13—1D 88
Brookwood Clo. Houn—1M 85
Brookwood Rd. SW18—7K 89
Broom Av. Orp—6F 112
Broom Clo. Brom—1J 127
Broom Clo. Esh—7M 117
Broom Clo. Tedd—4H 103
Broomcroft Av. N'holt—6G 53
Broome Rd. Hmptn—4K 101
Broome Way. SE5—8B 76
Broomfield. E17—5K 45
Broomfield. Sun—5E 100
Broomfield Av. N13—5K 27
Broomfield Av. Lou—8K 19
Broomfield La. N13—4J 27
Broomfield Pl. W13—2F 70

Broomfield Ride. Lea—4B 132
Broomfield Rise. Abb L, Wat
  —5B 4
Broomfield Rd. N13—5J 27
Broomfield Rd. W13—2F 70
Broomfield Rd. Beck—7K 109
Broomfield Rd. Bexh—4L 97
Broomfield Rd. Rich—9K 71
Broomfield Rd. Romf—5H 49
Broomfield Rd. Surb—3K 119
Broomfield Rd. Tedd—3G 103
Broomfield St. E14—8M 61
Broom Gdns. Croy—5L 125
Broom Gro. Wat—2E 8
Broomgrove Gdns. Edgw
  —8L 23
Broomgrove Rd. SW9—1K 91
Broom Hall. Lea—6B 132
Broomhall Rd. S Croy—1B 138
Broomhill Rise. Bexh—4L 97
Broomhill Rd. SW18—4L 89
Broomhill Rd. Dart—5F 98
Broomhill Rd. Ilf—7E 48
Broomhill Rd. Orp—2E 128
Broomhill Rd. Wfd G—6E 30
  (in two parts)
Broomhill Wlk. Wfd G—7D 30
Broomhouse La. SW6—1L 89
Broomhouse Rd. SW6—1L 89
Broomloan La. Sutt—4L 121
Broom Lock. Tedd—3G 103
Broom Mead. Bexh—4L 97
Broom Pk. Tedd—4H 103
Broom Rd. Croy—5L 125
Broom Rd. Tedd—2F 102
Broomsleigh St. NW6—1K 57
Broomstick Hall Rd. Wal A
  —6L 7
Broom Water. Tedd—3G 103
Broom Water W. Tedd—2G 103
Broom Way. Wey—6C 116
Broomwood Rd. SW15—5D 90
Broomwood Rd. Orp—6F 112
Broseley Gdns. Romf—4J 35
Broseley Rd. Romf—4J 35
Brougham Rd. E8—4E 60
Brougham Rd. W3—9A 56
Brough Clo. SW8—8J 75
Broughinge Rd. Borwd—4M 11
Broughton Av. N3—1J 41
Broughton Av. Rich—9F 86
Broughton Dri. SW9—3M 91
Broughton Gdns. N6—4G 43
Broughton Rd. SW6—1M 89
Broughton Rd. W13—1F 70
Broughton Rd. Orp—4B 128
Broughton Rd. T Hth—1L 123
Broughton St. SW8—1F 90
Brouncker Rd. W3—3A 72
Brow Clo. Orp—2H 129
Brow Cres. Orp—3G 129
Browells La. Felt—8F 84
Brown Clo. Wall—9J 123
Browne Clo. Romf—5M 33
Brownfield St. E14—9A 62
Browngraves Rd. Hay—8A 68
Brown Hart Gdns. W1—1E 74
Brownhill Rd. SE6—6M 93
Browning Av. W7—9D 54
Browning Av. Sutt—6C 122
Browning Av. Wor Pk—3F 120
Browning Clo. W9—7A 58
Browning Clo. Well—9C 80
Browning M. W1—8E 58
Browning Rd. E11—5D 46
Browning Rd. E12—1K 63
Browning Rd. Dart—3K 99
Browning Rd. Enf—2B 16
Browning St. SE17—6A 76
Browning Way. Houn—9H 69
Brownlea Gdns. Ilf—7E 48
Brownlow M. WC1—7K 59
Brownlow Rd. E8—4E 60
Brownlow Rd. N3—7M 25
Brownlow Rd. N11—6J 27
Brownlow Rd. NW10—3C 56
Brownlow Rd. W13—2E 70
Brownlow Rd. Borwd—6L 11
Brownlow Rd. Croy—6C 124
Brownlow St. WC1—8K 59
Brown's Bldgs. EC3—9C 60
Brown's Ct. W2—9C 58
Brownspring Dri. SE9—1M 111
Browns Rd. E17—1L 45
Brown's Rd. Surb—2K 119
Brown St. W1—9D 58
Brownswell Rd. N2—9B 26
Brownswood Rd. N4—7M 43
Brow, The. Wat—6F 4
Broxash Rd. SW11—5E 90
Broxbourne Av. E18—2F 46

Broxbourne Rd. E7—8E 46
Broxbourne Rd. Orp—3D 128
Broxhill Rd. Hav, Romf—3D 34
Broxholm Rd. SE27—9L 91
Broxted Rd. SE6—8K 93
Broxwood Way. NW8—4C 58
Bruce Av. Horn—7G 51
Bruce Av. Shep—1A 116
Bruce Castle Rd. N17—8D 28
Bruce Clo. Well—9F 80
Bruce Dri. S Croy—1H 139
Bruce Gdns. N20—3D 26
Bruce Gro. N17—9D 28
Bruce Gro. Orp—3E 128
Bruce Gro. Wat—2G 9
Bruce Hall M. SW17—1E 106
Bruce Rd. E3—6M 61
Bruce Rd. SE25—8B 108
Bruce Rd. Barn—5J 13
Bruce Rd. Harr—9C 22
Bruce Rd. Mitc—4E 106
Bruce Way. Wal X—6D 6
Bruckner St. W10—6K 57
Brudenell Rd. SW17—9D 90
Bruffs Meadow. N'holt—2J 53
Brumfield Rd. Eps—7A 120
Brummel Clo. Bexh—2A 98
Brumwill Rd. W5—5J 55
Brunel Clo. SE19—3D 108
Brunel Clo. Houn—8F 68
Brunel Clo. N'holt—6K 53
Brunel East. W2—5D 58
Brunel Pl. S'hall—9M 53
Brunel Rd. SE16—3G 77
Brunel Rd. W3—8C 56
Brunel Rd. Wfd G—5K 31
Brunel St. E16—9D 62
Brunel Wlk. N15—2C 44
Brunel Wlk. Twic—6L 85
Brune St. E1—8D 60
Brunner Clo. NW11—3A 42
Brunner Rd. E17—3J 45
Brunner Rd. W5—7H 55
Brunswick Av. N11—3E 26
Brunswick Centre. WC1—7J 59
Brunswick Clo. Bexh—3H 97
Brunswick Clo. Pinn—4J 37
Brunswick Clo. Th Dit—3D 118
Brunswick Clo. W on T—4G 117
Brunswick Ct. SE1—3C 76
Brunswick Cres. N11—3E 26
Brunswick Gdns. W5—7J 55
Brunswick Gdns. W8—2L 73
Brunswick Gdns. Ilf—4A 32
Brunswick Gro. N11—3E 26
Brunswick M. W1—9D 58
Brunswick Pk. SE5—9C 76
Brunswick Pk. Gdns. N11
  —2E 26
Brunswick Pk. Rd. N11—2E 26
Brunswick Pl. N1—6B 60
Brunswick Pl. SE19—4E 108
Brunswick Rd. E10—6A 46
Brunswick Rd. E14—9A 62
Brunswick Rd. N15—3C 44
  (in two parts)
Brunswick Rd. W5—7H 55
Brunswick Rd. Bexh—3H 97
Brunswick Rd. King—5L 103
Brunswick Rd. Sutt—6M 121
Brunswick Sq. N17—6D 28
Brunswick Sq. WC1—7J 59
Brunswick St. E17—3A 46
Brunswick Vs. SE5—9C 76
Brunswick Way. N11—4F 26
Brunton Pl. E14—9J 61
Brushfield St. E1—8C 60
Brussels Rd. SW11—3B 90
Bruton Clo. Chst—4K 111
Bruton La. W1—1F 74
Bruton Pl. W1—1F 74
Bruton St. W1—1F 74
Bruton Way. W13—8E 54
Bryan Av. NW10—3F 56
Bryan Clo. Sun—4E 100
Bryan Rd. SE16—3K 77
Bryanston Av. Twic—7M 85
Bryanston Clo. S'hall—5K 69
Bryanstone Rd. N8—4H 43
Bryanston M. E. W1—8D 58
Bryanston M. W. W1—9D 58
Bryanston Pl. W1—8D 58
Bryanston Sq. W1—9D 58
Bryanston St. W1—9D 58
Bryant Av. Romf—8H 35
Bryant Clo. Barn—7K 13
Bryant Rd. N'holt—6G 53
Bryant St. E15—3B 62
Bryantwood Rd. N7—1L 59
Brycedale Cres. N14—3H 27
Bryce Rd. Dag—9G 49

Bryden Clo. SE26—2J 109
Brydges Pl. WC2—1J 75
Brydges Rd. E15—1B 62
Brydon Wlk. N1—4J 59
Bryett Rd. N7—8J 43
Brynmaer Rd. SW11—9D 74
Brynmawr Rd. Enf—6D 16
Bryony Clo. Uxb—8D 142
Bryony Rd. W12—1E 72
Buchanan Clo. S Ock—2M 83
Buchanan Gdns. NW10—5F 56
Buchan Clo. Uxb—7A 142
Buchan Rd. SE15—2G 93
Bucharest Rd. SW18—6A 90
Buckbean Path. Romf—7G 35
Buckden Clo. SE12—5E 94
Buckettsland La. Borwd
  —2B 12
Buckfast Rd. Mord—8M 105
Buckfast St. E2—6E 60
Buck Hill Wlk. W2—1B 74
Buckhold Rd. SW18—5L 89
Buckhurst Av. Cars—3C 122
Buckhurst St. E1—7F 60
Buckhurst Way. Buck H—4H 31
Buckingham Av. N20—9A 14
Buckingham Av. E Mol
  —6M 101
Buckingham Av. Felt—5F 84
Buckingham Av. Gnfd—4E 54
Buckingham Av. T Hth—5L 107
Buckingham Av. Well—3C 96
Buckingham Clo. W5—8G 55
Buckingham Clo. Enf—4C 16
Buckingham Clo. Hmptn
  —2K 101
Buckingham Clo. Horn—4H 51
Buckingham Clo. Orp—2C 128
Buckingham Ct. NW4—1E 40
Buckingham Cl. Sutt—1L 135
Buckingham Gdns. E Mol
  —6M 101
Buckingham Gdns. Edgw
  —7J 23
Buckingham Gdns. T Hth
  —6L 107
Buckingham Ga. SW1—3G 75
Buckingham Gro. Uxb—5E 142
Buckingham La. SE23—6J 93
Buckingham M. NW10—5D 56
Buckingham Pal. Rd. SW1
  —5F 74
Buckingham Pde. Stan—5G 23
Buckingham Pl. SW1—4G 75
Buckingham Rd. E10—8M 45
Buckingham Rd. E11—3G 47
Buckingham Rd. E15—1D 62
Buckingham Rd. E18—8D 30
Buckingham Rd. N1—2C 60
Buckingham Rd. N22—8J 27
Buckingham Rd. NW10—5D 56
Buckingham Rd. Borwd—6B 12
Buckingham Rd. Edgw—7K 23
Buckingham Rd. Hmptn
  —2K 101
Buckingham Rd. Harr—3B 38
Buckingham Rd. Ilf—7B 48
Buckingham Rd. King—8K 103
Buckingham Rd. Mitc—9J 107
Buckingham Rd. Rich—8H 87
Buckingham Rd. Wat—1G 9
Buckingham St. WC2—1J 75
Buckingham Way. Wall
  —1G 137
Buckland Cres. NW3—2B 58
Buckland Rise. Pinn—8G 21
Buckland Rd. E10—7A 46
Buckland Rd. Chess—7K 119
Buckland Rd. Orp—6C 128
Buckland Rd. Sutt—2G 135
Bucklands Rd. Tedd—3G 103
Buckland St. N1—5D 60
Buckland Wlk. W3—3A 72
Buckland Wlk. Mord—8A 106
Buckland Way. Wor Pk
  —3G 121
Buck La. NW9—3B 40
Buckleigh Av. SW20—7K 105
Buckleigh Rd. SW16—3H 107
Buckler Gdns. SE9—9K 95
Bucklers All. SW6—7K 73
Bucklersbury. EC4—9B 60
Buckler's Way. Cars—5D 122
Buckles Way. Bans—8J 135
Buckley Clo. Dart—1D 98
Buckley Rd. NW6—3K 57
Buckmaster Rd. SW11—4C 90
Bucknalls Clo. Wat—5J 5
Bucknalls Dri. St Alb—4K 5
Bucknalls La. Wat—5H 5
Bucknall St. WC2—9J 59
Buckner Rd. SW2—3K 91

Byatt Wlk. Hmptn—3J 101
Bycroft Rd. S'hall—7L 53
Bycroft St. SE20—4H 109
Bycullah Av. Enf—5M 15
Bycullah Rd. Enf—4M 15
Byegrove Rd. SW19—3B 106
Bye, The. W3—9C 56
Bye Ways. Twic—9M 85
Byeways, The. Surb—9L 103
Byeway, The. SW14—2A 88
Byeway, The. Eps—6D 120
Bye Way, The. Harr—8D 22
Byfeld Gdns. SW13—9E 72
Byfield Pas. Iswth—2E 86
Byfield Rd. Iswth—2E 86
Byford Clo. E15—3C 62
Byford Ho. Barn—6H 13
Bygrove. Croy—9M 125
Bygrove St. E14—9M 61
Byland Clo. N21—9K 15
Bylands Clo. SE2—4F 80
Byne Rd. SE26—3G 109
Byne Rd. Cars—4C 122
Bynes Rd. S Croy—9B 124
Byng Pl. WC1—7H 59
Byng Rd. Barn—4H 13
Byng St. E14—3L 77
Bynon Av. Bexh—2K 97
Byrne Rd. SW12—7F 90
Byron Av. E12—2J 63
Byron Av. E18—1D 46
Byron Av. NW9—2M 39
Byron Av. Borwd—7L 11
Byron Av. Coul—7J 137
Byron Av. Houn—1E 84
Byron Av. N Mald—9E 104
Byron Av. Sutt—6B 122
Byron Av. Wat—3H 9
Byron Av. E. Sutt—6B 122
Byron Clo. E8—4E 60
Byron Clo. N2—4B 42
Byron Clo. SE28—2G 81
Byron Clo. Hmptn—1K 101
Byron Clo. W on T—3J 117
Byron Ct. Enf—4M 15
Byron Ct. Wal X—1B 6
Byron Gdns. Sutt—6B 122
Byron Hill Rd. Harr—6B 38
Byron Mans. Upm—8M 51
Byron Rd. E10—6M 45
Byron Rd. E17—1L 45
Byron Rd. NW2—7F 40
Byron Rd. NW7—5E 24
Byron Rd. W5—2K 71
Byron Rd. Dart—3M 99
Byron Rd. Harr—4C 38
(Greenhill)
Byron Rd. Harr—9D 22
(Wealdstone)
Byron Rd. S Croy—2F 138
Byron Rd. Wemb—7G 39
Byron St. E14—9A 62
Byron Way. Hay—7D 52
Byron Way. N'holt—6J 53
Byron Way. Romf—8G 35
Byron Way. W Dray—5K 143
Bysouth Clo. Ilf—8M 31
By the Wood. Wat—2H 21
Bythorn St. SW9—2K 91
Byton Rd. SW17—3D 106
Byward Av. Felt—5G 85
Byward St. EC3—1C 76
Bywater St. SW3—6D 74
Byway. E11—3G 47
Byway, The. Sutt—1B 136
Bywood Av. Croy—1G 125
Bywood Clo. Kenl—7M 137
Byworth Wlk. N19—6J 43

Cabbell St. NW1—8C 58
Cabinet Way. E4—5K 29
Cable St. E1—1E 76
Cabot Way. E6—4H 63
Cabul Rd. SW11—1C 90
Cactus Wlk. W12—9D 56
Cadbury Clo. Iswth—9E 70
Cadbury Clo. Sun—4C 100
Cadbury Rd. Sun—4C 100
Cadbury Wlk. SE16—5D 76
Cadbury Way. SE16—5E 76
Caddington Clo. Barn—7C 14
Caddington Rd. NW2—8J 41
Caddis Clo. Stan—7D 22
Cadell Clo. E2—5D 60
Cade Rd. SE10—9B 78
Cader Rd. SW18—5A 90
Cadet Pl. SE10—6C 78
Cadiz Rd. Dag—3A 66
Cadiz St. SE17—6A 76
Cadley Ter. SE23—8G 93
Cadmer Clo. N Mald—8C 104
Cadmore Ct. Wal X—1D 6

Cadmore La. Wal X—1D 6
Cadogan Clo. E9—3K 61
Cadogan Clo. Beck—5B 110
Cadogan Clo. Harr—9M 37
Cadogan Clo. Tedd—2C 102
Cadogan Ct. Sutt—8M 121
Cadogan Gdns. E18—1F 46
Cadogan Gdns. N3—8M 25
Cadogan Gdns. N21—7L 15
Cadogan Gdns. SW3—5D 74
Cadogan Ga. SW1—5D 74
Cadogan La. SW1—4E 74
Cadogan Pl. SW1—4D 74
Cadogan Rd. Surb—9H 103
Cadogan Sq. SW1—4D 74
Cadogan St. SW3—5D 74
Cadogan Ter. E9—2K 61
Cadoxton Av. N15—4D 44
Cadwallon Rd. SE9—8M 95
Caedmon Rd. N7—9K 43
Caerleon Clo. Sidc—2G 113
Caerleon Ter. SE2—5F 80
Caernarvon Clo. Horn—6L 51
Caernarvon Clo. Mitc—7J 107
Caernarvon Dri. Ilf—8L 31
Caesars Wlk. Mitc—9D 106
Caesars Way. Shep—1B 116
Cahill St. EC1—7A 60
Cahir St. E14—5M 77
Cain's La. Felt—4C 84
Caird St. W10—6J 57
Cairn Av. W5—2H 71
Cairndale Clo. Brom—4D 110
Cairnfield Av. NW2—8C 40
Cairns Av. Wfd G—6K 31
Cairns Clo. Dart—4H 99
Cairns Rd. SW11—4C 90
Cairn Way. Stan—6D 22
Cairo New Rd. Croy—4M 123
Cairo Rd. E17—2L 45
Caishowe Rd. Borwd—3M 11
Caistor M. SW12—6F 90
Caistor Pk. Rd. E15—4D 62
Caistor Rd. SW12—6F 90
Caithness Gdns. Sidc—5D 96
Caithness Rd. W14—4H 73
Caithness Rd. Mitc—4F 106
Calabria Rd. N5—2M 59
Calais Ga. SE5—9M 75
Calais St. SE5—9M 75
Calbourne Av. Horn—1F 66
Calbourne Rd. SW12—6D 90
Calcott Wlk. SE9—1J 111
Caldbeck. Wal A—7K 7
Caldbeck Av. Wor Pk—3F 120
Caldecote Gdns. Bush, Wat
—9C 10
Caldecote La. Bush, Wat—8D 10
Caldecot Rd. SE5—1A 92
Caldecott Way. E5—8H 45
Calder Av. Gnfd—5D 54
Calder Clo. Enf—5C 16
Calder Gdns. Edgw—1L 39
Calderon Pl. W10—8G 57
Calderon Rd. E11—9A 46
Calder Rd. Mord—9A 106
Caldervale Rd. SW4—4H 91
Calderwood St. SE18—5L 79
Caldew St. SE5—7B 76
Caldwell Rd. Wat—4H 21
Caldwell St. SW9—8K 75
Caldwell Yd. EC4—1A 76
Caldy Rd. Belv—4M 81
Caldy Wlk. N1—2A 60
Caleb St. SE1—3A 76
Caledonian Rd.—5J 59
N1 1-351 & 2-400
N7 remainder
Caledonia Rd. Stai—7C 144
Caledonia St. N1—5J 59
Caledon Rd. E6—4K 63
Caledon Rd. Wall—6E 122
Cale St. SW3—6C 74
Caletock Way. SE10—6D 78
Calfstock La. S Dar, Dart
—9K 115
California La. Bush, Wat—1B 22
California Rd. N Mald—7A 104
Callaghan Clo. SE13—3C 94
Callander Rd. SE6—8M 93
Callard Av. N13—4M 27
Callcott Rd. NW6—3K 57
Callcott St. W8—2L 73
Calley Down Cres. Croy
—2B 140
Callingham Clo. E14—8K 61
Callis Farm Clo. Stai—5C 144
Callis Rd. E17—4K 45
Callow Field. Purl—5L 137
Callow St. SW3—7B 74
Calmington Rd. SE5—7C 76
Calmont Rd. Brom—3B 110
Calmore Clo. Horn—1G 67

Calne Av. Ilf—8M 31
Calonne Rd. SW19—1H 105
Calshot Rd. Houn—1E 144
(in two parts)
Calshot St. N1—5K 59
Calshot Way. Enf—5M 15
Calthorpe Gdns. Edgw—5J 23
Calthorpe Gdns. Sutt—5A 122
Calthorpe St. WC1—7K 59
Calton Av. SE21—5C 92
Calton Rd. Barn—8A 14
Calverley Clo. Beck—3M 109
Calverley Cres. Dag—7L 49
Calverley Gdns. Harr—5H 39
Calverley Gro. N19—6H 43
Calverley Rd. Eps—8E 120
Calvert Av. E2—6D 60
Calvert Clo. Belv—5L 81
Calvert Clo. Sidc—3J 113
Calverton Rd. E6—4L 63
Calvert Rd. SE10—6D 78
Calvert Rd. Barn—4H 13
Calvert St. NW1—4E 58
Calvin Clo. Orp—7H 113
Calvin St. E1—7D 60
Calydon Rd. SE7—6F 78
Camac Rd. Twic—7B 86
Cambalt Rd. SW15—4H 89
Camberley Av. SW20—6F 104
Camberley Av. Enf—6C 16
Camberley Rd. Houn—2E 144
Cambert Way. SE3—3F 94
Camberwell Chu. St. SE5
—9B 76
Camberwell Glebe. SE5—9C 76
Camberwell Grn. SE5—9B 76
Camberwell Gro. SE5—9B 76
Camberwell New Rd. SE5
—8L 75
Camberwell Pas. SE5—9A 76
Camberwell Rd. SE5—7A 76
Camberwell Sta. Rd. SE5
—9A 76
Cambeys Rd. Dag—1M 65
Camborne Av. W13—3F 70
Camborne Av. Romf—7J 35
Camborne M. W11—9J 57
Camborne Rd. SW18—6L 89
Camborne Rd. Croy—2E 124
Camborne Rd. Houn—2E 144
Camborne Rd. Mord—9H 105
Camborne Rd. Sidc—9G 97
Camborne Rd. Sutt—9M 121
Camborne Rd. Well—1D 96
Camborne Way. Houn—9L 69
Camborne Way. Romf—7J 35
Cambourne Av. N9—9H 17
Cambourne Wlk. Rich—5H 87
Cambray Rd. SW12—7G 91
Cambray Rd. Orp—2D 128
Cambria Clo. Houn—3L 85
Cambria Clo. Sidc—7B 96
Cambria Gdns. Stai—6C 144
Cambrian Clo. SE27—9M 91
Cambrian Rd. E10—6L 45
Cambrian Rd. Rich—5K 87
Cambria Rd. SE5—2A 92
Cambria St. SW6—8M 73
Cambridge Av. NW6—5L 57
Cambridge Av. Gnfd—1D 54
Cambridge Av. N Mald—6C 104
Cambridge Av. Romf—1G 51
Cambridge Av. Well—3D 96
Cambridge Barracks Rd. SE18
—5K 79
Cambridge Cir. WC2—9H 59
Cambridge Clo. SW20—5F 104
Cambridge Clo. Houn—3J 85
Cambridge Clo. Wal X—2C 6
Cambridge Clo. W Dray
—7H 143
Cambridge Cotts. Rich—7L 71
Cambridge Cres. E2—5F 60
Cambridge Cres. Tedd—2E 102
Cambridge Dri. SE12—4E 94
Cambridge Dri. Ruis—7G 37
Cambridge Gdns. N17—7B 28
Cambridge Gdns. N21—9B 16
Cambridge Gdns. NW6—5L 57
Cambridge Gdns. W10—9H 57
Cambridge Gdns. Enf—4E 16
Cambridge Gdns. King—6L 103
Cambridge Ga. NW1—7F 58
Cambridge Ga. M. NW1—7F 58
Cambridge Grn. SE9—7M 95
Cambridge Gro. SE20—5F 108
Cambridge Gro. W6—5F 72
Cambridge Gro. Rd. King
(in two parts) —7L 103
Cambridge Heath Rd.—7F 60
E1 1-183 & 2-154a
E2 remainder

Cambridge Lodge Vs. E8
—4F 60
Cambridge Pde. Enf—3E 16
Cambridge Pk. E11—5E 46
Cambridge Pk. Twic—5G 87
Cambridge Pl. NW6—6L 57
Cambridge Pl. W8—3M 73
Cambridge Rd. E4—1B 30
Cambridge Rd. E11—4D 46
Cambridge Rd. NW6—6L 57
(in two parts)
Cambridge Rd. SE20—7F 108
Cambridge Rd. SW11—9D 74
Cambridge Rd. SW13—1D 88
Cambridge Rd. SW20—5E 104
Cambridge Rd. W7—3D 70
Cambridge Rd. Ashf—4A 100
Cambridge Rd. Bark—3A 64
Cambridge Rd. Brom—4E 110
Cambridge Rd. Cars—8C 122
Cambridge Rd. Hmptn—4K 101
Cambridge Rd. Harr—3L 37
Cambridge Rd. Houn—3J 85
Cambridge Rd. Ilf—6C 48
Cambridge Rd. King—6K 103
Cambridge Rd. Mitc—7G 107
Cambridge Rd. N Mald—8C 104
Cambridge Rd. Rich—8L 71
Cambridge Rd. Sidc—1C 112
Cambridge Rd. S'hall—2K 69
Cambridge Rd. Tedd—1E 102
Cambridge Rd. Twic—5H 87
Cambridge Rd. Uxb—2B 142
Cambridge Rd. W on T—1F 116
Cambridge Rd. Wat—6G 9
Cambridge Rd. N. W4—6M 71
Cambridge Rd. S. W4—6M 71
Cambridge Row. SE18—6M 79
Cambridge Sq. W2—9C 58
Cambridge St. SW1—5F 74
Cambridge Ter. N9—9D 16
Cambridge Ter. NW1—6F 58
Cambridge Ter. M. NW1—6F 58
Cambus Rd. E16—8E 62
Camdale Rd. SE18—8D 80
Camden Av. Felt—7G 85
Camden Av. Hay—1H 69
Camden Clo. Chst—5A 112
Camden Gdns. NW1—3F 58
Camden Gdns. Sutt—7M 121
Camden Gdns. T Hth—7M 107
Camden Gro. Chst—3M 111
Camden High St. NW1—4F 58
Camden Hill Rd. SE19—3C 108
Camdenhurst St. E14—9J 61
Camden La. N7—1H 59
Camden Lock Pl. NW1—3F 58
Camden M. NW1—2H 59
Camden Pk. Rd. NW1—2H 59
Camden Pk. Rd. Chst—4K 111
Camden Pas. N1—4M 59
Camden Rd. E11—4F 46
Camden Rd. E17—4K 45
Camden Rd.—3G 59
NW1 1-227 & 2a-282
N7 remainder
Camden Rd. Bex—7K 97
Camden Rd. Cars—6D 122
Camden Rd. Sutt—7M 121
Camden Row. SE3—1C 94
Camden Row. Pinn—1G 37
Camden Sq. NW1—2H 59
Camden St. SE15—9D 76
Camden St. NW1—3G 59
Camden Ter. NW1—2H 59
Camden Wlk. N1—4M 59
Camden Way. Chst—4L 111
Camden Way. T Hth—7M 107
Camelford Ct. W11—9J 57
Camelford Wlk. W11—9J 57
Camellia Clo. Romf—8J 35
Camellia Pl. Twic—6M 85
Camellia St. SW8—8J 75
Camelot Clo. SW19—1L 105
Camelot Clo. West—8G 141
Camel Rd. E16—2J 79
Camera Pl. SW10—7B 74
Cameron Clo. N18—4F 28
Cameron Clo. N20—2B 26
Cameron Clo. Bex—9C 98
Cameron Dri. Wal X—7D 6
Cameron Pl. E1—9F 60
Cameron Rd. SE6—8K 93
Cameron Rd. Brom—9E 110
Cameron Rd. Croy—1M 123
Cameron Rd. Ilf—6C 48
Cameron Ter. SE12—9F 94
Camerton Clo. E8—2D 60
Camilla Rd. SE16—5F 76
Camlan Rd. Brom—1D 110
Camlet Rd. E2—7D 60
Camlet Way. Barn—4L 13
Camley St. NW1—3H 59

Camm Gdns. King—6K 103
Camm Gdns. Th Dit—2D 118
Camomile Av. Mitc—5D 106
Camomile St. EC3—9C 60
Campana Rd. SW6—9L 73
Campbell Av. Ilf—2A 48
Campbell Clo. SE18—9L 79
Campbell Clo. Romf—6C 34
Campbell Clo. Ruis—4E 36
Campbell Clo. Twic—8B 86
Campbell Croft. Edgw—5L 23
Campbell Rd. E3—6L 61
Campbell Rd. E6—4J 63
Campbell Rd. E15—9D 46
Campbell Rd. E17—2K 45
Campbell Rd. N17—8D 28
Campbell Rd. W7—1C 70
Campbell Rd. Croy—1M 123
Campbell Rd. E Mol—7C 102
Campbell Rd. Twic—8B 86
Campdale Rd. N7—8H 43
Campden Clo. SW19—8J 89
Campden Cres. Dag—9F 48
Campden Cres. Wemb—8F 38
Campden Gro. W8—3L 73
Campden Hill. W8—3L 73
Campden Hill Gdns. W8—2L 73
Campden Hill Pl. W11—2K 73
Campden Hill Rd. W8—2L 73
Campden Hill Sq. W8—2K 73
Campden Rd. S Croy—7C 124
Campden St. W8—2L 73
Camperdown St. E1—9D 60
Campfield Rd. SE9—6H 95
Campion Clo. E6—1K 79
Campion Clo. Croy—6C 124
Campion Clo. Uxb—8D 142
Campion Cres. SE26—1J 109
Campion Pl. SE28—2F 80
Campion Rd. SW15—4G 89
Campion Rd. Iswth—9D 70
Campions. Lou—2L 19
Campions Clo. Borwd—1M 11
Campion Ter. NW2—8H 41
Camplin Rd. Harr—3J 39
Camplin St. SE14—8H 77
Camp Rd. SW19—2G 105
(in two parts)
Campsbourne Rd. N8—1J 43
(in two parts)
Campsbourne, The. N8—2J 43
Campsey Gdns. Dag—3F 64
Campsey Rd. Dag—3F 64
Campsfield Rd. N8—1J 43
Campshill Pl. SE13—4A 94
Campshill Rd. SE13—4A 94
Campus Rd. E17—4K 45
Camp View. SW19—2F 104
Cam Rd. E15—4B 62
Camrose Av. Edgw—9K 23
Camrose Av. Eri—7M 81
Camrose Av. Felt—1G 101
Camrose Clo. Mord—6L 105
Camrose Clo. SE2—6E 80
Canada Av. N18—6A 28
Canada Cres. W3—8A 56
Canada Rd. SE16—3H 77
Canada Rd. W3—8A 56
Canada Way. W12—1F 72
Canadian Av. SE6—7M 93
Canal Clo. E1—7J 61
Canal Gro. SE15—7E 76
Canal Head. SE15—9E 76
Canal Rd. E3—7J 61
Canal St. SE5—7B 76
Canal Wlk. N1—4B 60
Canal Wlk. SE26—2G 109
Canary Wharf. E14—2L 77
Canberra Clo. Dag—4B 66
Canberra Clo. Horn—1G 67
Canberra Cres. Dag—3B 66
Canberra Dri. N'holt—6G 53
Canberra Rd. E6—4K 63
Canberra Rd. SE7—7G 79
Canberra Rd. Bexh—7H 81
Canberra Rd. Houn—2E 144
Canbury Av. King—5K 103
Canbury M. SE26—9E 92
Canbury Pk. Rd. King—5J 103
Canbury Pas. King—5J 103
Canbury Path. Orp—8E 112
Canbury Pl. King—5J 103
Cancell Rd. SW9—9L 75
Candahar Rd. SW11—1C 90
Candler St. N15—4B 44
Candover Clo. W Dray—8H 143
Candover Rd. Horn—6F 50
Candover St. W1—8G 59
Candy St. E3—4K 61
Cane Clo. Wall—9J 123
Caneland Ct. Wal A—7M 7
Canfield Dri. Ruis—1F 52
Canfield Gdns. NW6—3M 57

Canfield Pl.—Castlecombe Rd.

Canfield Pl. NW6—2A 58
Canfield Rd. Rain—4D 66
Canfield Rd. Wfd G—7J 31
Canford Av. N'holt—4K 53
Canford Clo. Enf—4L 15
Canford Gdns. N Mald—1C 120
Canford Rd. SW11—4E 90
Canham Rd. SE25—7C 108
Canham Rd. W3—3C 72
Canmore Gdns. SW16—4G 107
Cann Hall Rd. E11—9C 46
Canning Cres. N22—8K 27
Canning Cross. SE5—1C 92
Canning Pas. W8—4A 74
Canning Pl. W8—4A 74
Canning Rd. E15—5B 62
Canning Rd. E17—2J 45
Canning Rd. N5—8M 43
Canning Rd. Croy—4D 124
Canning Rd. Harr—1D 38
Cannington Rd. Dag—2G 65
Cannizaro Rd. SW19—2G 105
Cannonbury Av. Pinn—4H 37
Cannon Clo. SW20—7G 105
Cannon Clo. Hmptn—3M 101
Cannon Dri. E14—2L 77
Cannon Hill. N14—3J 27
Cannon Hill. NW6—1L 57
Cannon Hill La. SW20—9H 105
Cannon Hill M. N14—3J 27
Cannon La. NW3—8B 42
Cannon La. Pinn—3J 37
Cannon Pl. NW3—8B 42
Cannon Pl. SE7—6J 79
Cannon Rd. N14—3J 27
Cannon Rd. Bexh—9J 81
Cannon Rd. Wat—7G 9
Cannon Row. SW1—3J 75
Cannon St. EC4—9A 60
Cannon St. Rd. E1—9F 60
Cannon Trading Est. Wemb —9M 39
Cannon Way. E Mol—8L 101
Canon Av. Romf—3G 49
Canon Beck Rd. SE16—3G 77
Canonbie Rd. SE23—6G 93
Canonbury Gro. N1—3A 60
Canonbury La. N1—3M 59
Canonbury Pk. N. N1—2A 60
Canonbury Pk. S. N1—2A 60
Canonbury Pl. N1—2M 59
Canonbury Rd. N1—2M 59
Canonbury Rd. Enf—3C 16
Canonbury Sq. N1—3M 59
Canonbury St. N1—3A 60
Canonbury Vs. N1—3M 59
Canon Rd. Brom—7G 111
Canon's Clo. N2—5B 42
Canons Clo. Edgw—6K 23
Canons Corner. Edgw—4J 23
Canons Dri. Edgw—6J 23
Canons Hill. Coul—9L 137
Canonsleigh Rd. Dag—3F 64
Canons Pk. Stan—6H 23
Canon St. N1—4A 60
Canon's Wlk. Croy—5H 125
Canopus Way. N'wd—4E 20
Canopus Way. Stai—6C 144
Canrobert St. E2—5F 60
Cantelowes Rd. NW1—2H 59
Canterbury Av. Ilf—5J 47
Canterbury Av. Sidc—8G 97
Canterbury Clo. E6—9K 63
Canterbury Clo. Beck—5M 109
Canterbury Clo. Chig—3F 32
Canterbury Clo. Dart—6L 99
Canterbury Clo. Gnfd—8M 53
Canterbury Cres. SW9—2L 91
Canterbury Gro. SE27—1L 107
Canterbury Pl. SE17—5M 75
Canterbury Rd. E10—5A 46
Canterbury Rd. NW6—5L 57
Canterbury Rd. Borwd—4L 11
Canterbury Rd. Croy—2K 123
Canterbury Rd. Felt—8J 85
Canterbury Rd. Harr—3M 37
Canterbury Rd. Mord—2M 121
Canterbury Rd. Wat—4F 8
Canterbury Ter. NW6—5L 57
Canterbury Way. Rick—5A 8
Cantley Gdns. SE19—5D 108
Cantley Gdns. Ilf—4A 48
Cantley Rd. W7—4E 70
Canton St. E14—9L 61
Cantrell Rd. E3—7K 61
Cantwell Rd. SE18—8M 79
Canvey St. SE1—2A 76
Cape Clo. Bark—3M 63
Capel Av. Wall—7K 123
Capel Clo. N20—3A 26
Capel Clo. Brom—3J 127
Capel Gdns. Ilf—9D 48
Capel Gdns. Pinn—2K 37
Capella Rd. N'wd—4D 20
Capel Pl. Dart—1G 115
Capel Rd.—9F 46
E7 1-165
E12 remainder
Capel Rd. Barn—8C 14
Capel Rd. Enf—9B 6
Capel Rd. Wat—8J 9
Capelvere Wlk. Wat—3C 8
Capern Rd. SW18—7A 90
Cape Rd. N17—1E 44
Capital Interchange Way. Bren —6L 71
Capitol Industrial Est. NW9 —1A 40
Capitol Way. NW9—1A 40
Capland St. NW8—7B 58
Caple Rd. NW10—5D 56
Capper St. WC1—7G 59
Caprea Clo. Hay—8H 53
Capri Rd. Croy—3D 124
Capstan Ride. Enf—4L 15
Capstan Sq. E14—3A 78
Capstan Way. SE16—2J 77
Capstone Rd. Brom—1D 110
Capthorne Av. Harr—6J 37
Capuchin Clo. Stan—6F 22
Capworth St. E10—6L 45
Caractacus Cottage View. Wat —9E 8
Caractacus Grn. Wat—8D 8
Caradoc Clo. W2—9L 57
Caradoc St. SE10—6C 78
Caradon Way. N15—2B 44
Caravel M. SE8—7L 77
Carberry Rd. SE19—3C 108
Carbery Av. W3—3K 71
Carbis Clo. E4—1B 30
Carbis Rd. E14—9K 61
Carbuncle Pas. Way. N17 —9E 28
Carburton St. W1—8F 58
Carbury Clo. Horn—2H 67
Cardale St. E14—4A 78
Carden Rd. SE15—2F 92
Cardiff Rd. W7—4E 70
Cardiff Rd. Enf—6F 16
Cardiff Rd. Wat—7F 8
Cardiff St. SE18—8C 80
Cardigan Gdns. Ilf—7E 48
Cardigan Rd. E3—5K 61
Cardigan Rd. SW13—1E 88
Cardigan Rd. SW19—3A 106
Cardigan Rd. Rich—5J 87
Cardigan St. SE11—6L 75
Cardinal Av. Borwd—5M 11
Cardinal Av. King—2J 103
Cardinal Av. Mord—1J 121
Cardinal Cap All. SE1—2A 76
Cardinal Clo. Chst—5C 112
Cardinal Clo. Mord—1J 121
Cardinal Clo. Wor Pk—6E 120
Cardinal Cres. N Mald—6A 104
Cardinal Dri. Ilf—6A 32
Cardinal Dri. W on T—3H 117
Cardinal Pl. SW15—3H 89
Cardinal Rd. Felt—7F 84
Cardinal Rd. Ruis—6H 37
Cardinals Wlk. Hmptn—4A 102
Cardinals Wlk. Sun—3C 100
Cardinals Way. N19—6H 43
Cardinal Way. Rain—5H 67
Cardine M. SE15—8F 76
Cardington Rd. Houn—2F 144
Cardington Sq. Houn—3H 85
Cardington St. NW1—6G 59
Cardozo Rd. N7—1J 59
Cardrew Av. N12—5B 26
Cardrew Clo. N12—5C 26
Cardross St. W6—4F 72
Cardwell Rd. N7—9J 43
Cardwell Rd. SE18—5L 79
Carew Clo. N7—7K 43
Carew Rd. N17—9E 28
Carew Rd. W13—3G 71
Carew Rd. Ashf—3A 100
Carew Rd. Mitc—6E 106
Carew Rd. N'wd—6C 20
Carew Rd. T Hth—8M 107
Carew Rd. Wall—8G 123
Carew St. SE5—1A 92
Carey Ct. Bexh—4M 97
Carey Gdns. SW8—9G 75
Carey La. EC2—9A 60
Carey Pl. Wat—6G 9
Carey Rd. Dag—9J 49
Carey St. WC2—9K 59
Carfax Pl. SW4—3H 91
Carfax Rd. Hay—6D 68
Carfax Rd. Horn—9D 50
Carfree Clo. N1—3L 59
Carganey Wlk. SE28—1G 81
Cargill Rd. SW18—7A 90
Cargreen Rd. SE25—8D 108
Carholme Rd. SE23—7K 93
Carillon Ct. W5—1H 71
Carisbrook Clo. Stan—9H 23
Carisbrooke Av. Bex—7H 97
Carisbrooke Av. Wat—3H 9
Carisbrooke Clo. Enf—3D 16
Carisbrooke Clo. Horn—6L 51
Carisbrooke Gdns. SE15 —8D 76
Carisbrooke Rd. E17—2J 45
Carisbrooke Rd. Brom—8G 111
Carisbrooke Rd. Mitc—8J 107
Carker's La. NW5—1F 58
Carleton Av. Wall—1H 137
Carleton Gdns. N19—1G 59
Carleton Rd. N7—1H 59
(in two parts)
Carleton Rd. Dart—6L 99
Carleton Rd. Wal X—1E 6
Carlile Clo. E3—5K 61
Carlingford Gdns. Mitc—4E 106
Carlingford Rd. N15—1M 43
Carlingford Rd. NW3—9B 42
Carlingford Rd. Mord—1H 121
Carlisle Av. EC3—9D 60
Carlisle Av. W3—9C 56
Carlisle Clo. King—5L 103
Carlisle Gdns. Harr—5H 39
Carlisle Gdns. Ilf—4J 47
Carlisle La. SE1—4K 75
Carlisle M. NW8—8B 58
Carlisle M. King—5L 103
Carlisle Pl. N11—4F 26
Carlisle Pl. SW1—4G 75
Carlisle Rd. E10—6L 45
Carlisle Rd. N4—5L 43
Carlisle Rd. NW6—4J 57
Carlisle Rd. NW9—1A 40
Carlisle Rd. Dart—5L 99
Carlisle Rd. Hmptn—4M 101
Carlisle Rd. Romf—3E 50
Carlisle Rd. Sutt—8K 121
Carlisle St. W1—9H 59
Carlisle Wlk. E8—2D 60
Carlos Pl. W1—1E 74
Carlow St. NW1—5G 59
Carlton Av. N14—7H 15
Carlton Av. Felt—5G 85
Carlton Av. Harr—3F 38
Carlton Av. Hay—5C 68
Carlton Av. S Croy—9C 124
Carlton Av. E. Wemb—7H 39
Carlton Av. W. Wemb—7F 38
Carlton Clo. NW3—7L 41
Carlton Clo. Borwd—6B 12
Carlton Clo. Chess—8H 119
Carlton Clo. Edgw—5L 23
Carlton Clo. Esh—3B 118
Carlton Clo. N'holt—1A 54
Carlton Clo. Upm—7M 51
Carlton Ct. SE20—5F 108
Carlton Ct. Ilf—1B 48
Carlton Cres. Sutt—6J 121
Carlton Dri. SW15—4J 89
Carlton Dri. Ilf—1B 48
Carlton Gdns. SW1—2H 75
Carlton Gdns. W5—9G 55
Carlton Grn. SW9—9M 75
Carlton Gro. SE15—9F 76
Carlton Hill. NW8—5M 57
Carlton Ho. Ter. SW1—2H 75
Carlton Pde. Orp—2F 128
Carlton Pk. Av. SW20—6H 105
Carlton Rd. E11—6D 46
Carlton Rd. E12—9H 47
Carlton Rd. E17—8J 29
Carlton Rd. N4—5L 43
Carlton Rd. N11—5E 26
Carlton Rd. N15—1D 44
Carlton Rd. SW14—3A 88
Carlton Rd. W4—3B 72
Carlton Rd. W5—1G 71
Carlton Rd. Eri—7M 81
Carlton Rd. N Mald—6C 104
Carlton Rd. Romf—3E 50
Carlton Rd. Sidc—2D 112
Carlton Rd. S Croy—9B 124
Carlton Rd. Sun—4D 100
Carlton Rd. W on T—2F 116
Carlton Rd. Well—2F 96
Carlton Sq. E1—7H 61
(in two parts)
Carlton St. SW1—1H 75
Carlton Ter. E11—3F 46
Carlton Ter. N18—3B 28
Carlton Ter. SE26—9G 93
Carlton Vale. NW6—5K 57
Carlwell St. SW17—2C 106
Carlyle Av. Brom—7H 111
Carlyle Av. S'hall—1K 69
Carlyle Clo. N2—4A 42
Carlyle Clo. NW10—4B 56
Carlyle Clo. E Mol—6M 101
Carlyle Gdns. S'hall—1K 69
Carlyle Rd. E12—9J 47
Carlyle Rd. SE28—1F 80
Carlyle Rd. W5—5G 71
Carlyle Rd. Croy—4E 124
Carlyle Sq. SW3—6B 74
Carlyon Av. Harr—9K 37
Carlyon Clo. Wemb—4J 55
Carlyon Rd. Hay—8G 53
Carlyon Rd. Wemb—5J 55
Carmalt Gdns. SW15—3G 89
Carmalt Gdns. W on T—7G 117
Carmelite Clo. Harr—8A 22
Carmelite Rd. Harr—8A 22
Carmelite St. EC4—1L 75
Carmelite Wlk. Harr—8A 22
Carmelite Way. Harr—9A 22
Carmen St. E14—9M 61
Carmichael Clo. SW11—2B 90
Carmichael Clo. Ruis—9E 36
Carmichael Rd. SE25—9E 108
Carminia Rd. SW17—8F 90
Carnaby St. W1—9G 59
Carnac St. SE27—1B 108
Carnanton Rd. E17—8B 30
Carnarvon Av. Enf—5D 16
Carnarvon Dri. Hay—4A 68
Carnarvon Rd. E10—3A 46
Carnarvon Rd. E15—2D 62
Carnarvon Rd. E18—8D 30
Carnarvon Rd. Barn—5J 13
Carnation St. SE2—6F 80
Carnecke Gdns. SE9—4J 95
Carnegie Clo. Surb—4K 119
Carnegie Pl. SW19—9H 89
Carnegie St. N1—4K 59
Carnforth Clo. Eps—8M 119
Carnforth Gdns. Horn—1E 66
Carnforth Rd. SW16—4H 107
Carnie Hall. SW17—9F 90
Carnoustie Dri. N1—3K 59
Carnwath Rd. SW6—2L 89
Carolina Rd. T Hth—6M 107
Caroline Clo. N10—9F 26
Caroline Clo. Croy—6C 124
Caroline Clo. Iswth—8C 70
Caroline Clo. W Dray—3H 143
Caroline Ct. Ashf—3A 100
Caroline Ct. Stan—6E 22
Caroline Gdns. E2—6C 60
Caroline Pl. SW11—1E 90
Caroline Pl. Wat—8J 9
Caroline Pl. M. W2—1M 73
Caroline Rd. SW19—4K 105
Caroline St. E1—9H 61
Caroline Ter. SW1—5E 74
Caroline Wlk. W6—7J 73
Carol St. NW1—4G 59
Carolyn Dri. Orp—5E 128
Carpenders Av. Wat—3J 21
Carpenter Gdns. N21—2M 27
Carpenters Pl. SW4—3H 91
Carpenter's Rd. E15—2L 61
Carpenters Rd. Enf—9C 6
Carpenter St. W1—1F 74
Carrara Wlk. SW9—3L 91
Carriage Dri. E. SW11—8E 74
Carriage Dri. N. SW11—8D 74
Carriage Dri. S. SW11—9D 74
Carriage Dri. W. SW11—8D 74
Carrick Gdns. N17—7C 28
Carrick Ga. Esh—5A 118
Carrick M. SE8—7L 77
Carrington Av. Borwd—7M 11
Carrington Av. Houn—4M 85
Carrington Clo. Borwd—7A 12
Carrington Clo. Croy—2J 125
Carrington Rd. Dart—5L 99
Carrington Rd. Rich—3L 87
Carrington St. W1—2F 74
Carrol Clo. NW5—9F 42
Carroll Clo. E15—1D 62
Carroll Hill. Lou—5K 19
Carroun Rd. SW8—8K 75
Carroway La. Gnfd—6B 54
Carrow Clo. E14—9M 61
Carrow Rd. Dag—3F 64
Carrow Rd. W on T—5H 117
Carr Rd. E17—9L 29
Carr Rd. N'holt—2L 53
Carrs La. N21—7A 16
Carr St. E14—8J 61
(in two parts)
Carshalton Gro. Sutt—7B 122
Carshalton Pk. Rd. Cars —8D 122
Carshalton Pl. Cars—7E 122
Carshalton Rd. Bans—6D 136
Carshalton Rd. Mitc—9E 106
Carshalton Rd. Sutt & Cars —7A 122
Carsington Gdns. Dart—8H 99
Carslake Rd. SW15—5G 89
Carson Rd. E16—7E 62
Carson Rd. SE21—8B 92
Carson Rd. Barn—6D 14
Carstairs Rd. SE6—9A 94
Carston Clo. SE12—4D 94
Carswell Clo. Ilf—2H 47
Carswell Rd. SE6—6A 94
Carter Clo. Romf—7M 33
Carter Clo. Wall—9H 123
Carter Dri. Romf—7M 33
Carteret St. SW1—3H 75
Carteret Way. SE8—5J 77
Carterhatch La. Enf—3D 16
Carterhatch Rd. Enf—4G 17
Carter La. EC4—9M 59
Carter Pl. SE17—6A 76
Carter Rd. E13—4F 62
Carter Rd. SW19—3B 106
Carters Clo. Wor Pk—3H 121
Cartersfield Rd. Wal A—7J 7
Carters Hill Clo. SE9—7G 95
Carters La. SE23—8J 93
Carters Rd. Eps—7D 134
Carter St. SE17—7A 76
Carter's Yd. SW18—4L 89
Carthew Rd. W6—4F 72
Carthew Vs. W6—4F 72
Carthusian St. EC1—8A 60
Carting La. WC2—1K 75
Cart La. E4—1C 30
Cartmel Clo. N17—7F 28
Cartmell Gdns. Mord—9A 106
Cartmel Rd. Bexh—9L 81
Cart Path. Wat—6G 5
Cartwright Gdns. WC1—6J 59
Cartwright Rd. Dag—3K 65
Cartwright St. E1—1D 76
Carver Rd. SE24—5A 92
Carville Cres. Bren—5J 71
Cary Rd. E11—9C 46
Carysfort Rd. N8—3H 43
Carysfort Rd. N16—8B 44
Cascade Av. N10—2G 43
Cascade Clo. Buck H—2H 31
Cascade Clo. Orp—7G 113
Cascade Rd. Buck H—2H 31
Cascades Way. Croy—2K 139
Casella Rd. SE14—8H 77
Casewick Rd. SE27—2L 107
Casimir Rd. E5—8F 44
Casino Av. SE24—4B 92
Caspian St. SE5—8B 76
Caspian Wlk. E16—9H 63
Casselden Rd. NW10—3B 56
Cassidy Rd. SW6—8L 73
(in two parts)
Cassilda Rd. SE2—5E 80
Cassilis Rd. Twic—5F 86
Cassiobridge Rd. Wat—6C 8
Cassiobury Av. Felt—6D 84
Cassiobury Dri. Wat—3C 8
Cassiobury Pk. Av. Wat—5C 8
Cassiobury Rd. E17—3J 45
Cassio Rd. Wat—5F 8
Cassland Rd. E9—3H 61
Cassland Rd. T Hth—8B 108
Casslee Rd. SE6—6K 93
Casson St. E1—8E 60
Casstine Clo. Swan—4D 114
Castalia Sq. E14—3A 78
Castano Ct. Abb L, Wat—4C 4
Castellain Rd. W9—7M 57
Castellan Av. Romf—1F 50
Castellane Clo. Stan—7D 22
Castello Av. SW15—4G 89
Castell Rd. Lou—3M 19
Castelnau. SW13—9E 72
Castelnau Gdns. SW13—7F 72
Castelnau Pl. SW13—7F 72
Castelnau Row. SW13—7F 72
Casterbridge Rd. SE3—2E 94
Castile Rd. SE18—5L 79
Castile Way. Eps—1E 134
Castillon Rd. SE6—8C 94
Castlands Rd. SE6—8K 93
Castle Av. E4—5B 30
Castle Av. Eps—1E 134
Castle Av. Rain—3C 66
Castle Av. W Dray—1J 143
Castlebar Ct. W5—8G 55
Castlebar Hill. W5—8G 55
Castlebar M. W5—8G 55
Castlebar Pk. W5—8F 54
Castlebar Rd. W5—9G 55
Castle Baynard St. EC4—1M 75
Castle Clo. E9—1J 61
Castle Clo. SW19—9H 89
Castle Clo. Brom—7C 110
Castle Clo. Bush, Wat—8M 9
Castle Clo. Sun—4C 100
Castlecombe Dri. SW19—6H 89
Castlecombe Rd. SE9—1J 111

Castledine Rd. SE20—4F 108
Castle Dri. Ilf—4J 47
Castle Farm Rd. Sev—9D 130
Castleford Av. SE9—7M 95
Castlegate. Rich—2K 87
Castle Grn. Wey—5C 116
Castlehaven Rd. NW1—3F 58
Castle Hill Av. Croy—1M 139
Castle La. SW1—4G 75
Castleleigh Ct. Enf—7B 16
Castlemaine Av. Eps—1F 134
Castlemaine Av. S Croy
—7D 124
Castle M. NW1—2F 58
Castle Pde. Eps—9E 120
Castlereagh St. W1—9D 58
Castle Rd. N12—5A 26
Castle Rd. NW1—3F 58
Castle Rd. Dag—4F 64
Castle Rd. Enf—3J 17
Castle Rd. Eps—7M 133
Castle Rd. Iswth—1D 86
Castle Rd. N'holt—2M 53
Castle Rd. Sev & Eyns, Dart
—8F 130
Castle Rd. S'hall—4K 69
Castle Rd. Wey—5C 116
Castle St. E6—5H 63
Castle St. King—6J 103
Castleton Av. Bexh—9B 82
Castleton Av. Wemb—9J 39
Castleton Clo. Bans—7L 135
Castleton Dri. Bans—6L 135
Castleton Gdns. Wemb—8J 39
Castleton Rd. E17—9B 30
Castleton Rd. SE9—1H 111
Castleton Rd. Ilf—6E 48
Castleton Rd. Mitc—8H 107
Castleton Rd. Ruis—6H 37
Castletown Rd. W14—6J 73
Castle View. Eps—6M 133
Castleview Gdns. Ilf—4J 47
Castle View Rd. Wey—6A 116
Castle Wlk. Sun—7G 101
Castle Way. SW19—9H 89
Castle Way. Felt—1G 101
Castlewood Dri. SE9—1K 95
Castlewood Rd.—5E 44
N16 1-121 & 2-102
N15 remainder
Castlewood Rd. Barn—5B 14
Castle Yd. N6—5E 42
Castle Yd. SE1—2M 75
Castle Yd. Rich—4H 87
Caterham Av. Ilf—9K 31
Caterham Ct. Wal A—7M 7
Caterham Rd. SE13—2B 94
Catesby St. SE17—5B 76
Catford B'way. SE6—6M 93
Catford Hill. SE6—7K 93
Catford Rd. SE6—6L 93
Cathall Rd. E11—7B 46
Cathay St. SE16—3F 76
Cathcart Dri. Orp—4C 128
Cathcart Hill. N19—8G 43
Cathcart Rd. SW10—7M 73
Cathcart St. NW5—2F 58
Cathedral Piazza. SW1—4G 75
Cathedral St. SE1—2B 76
Catherall Rd. N5—8A 44
Catherine Ct. N14—7G 15
Catherine Dri. Sun—3D 100
Catherine Gdns. Houn—3B 86
Catherine Gro. SE10—9M 77
Catherine Pl. SW1—4G 75
Catherine Rd. Enf—1J 17
Catherine Rd. Romf—3F 50
Catherine Rd. Surb—9H 103
Catherines Clo. W Dray
—3H 143
Catherine St. WC2—1K 75
Catherine Wheel All. E1—8C 60
Catherine Wheel Yd. Bren
—8H 71
Cat Hill. Barn—7C 14
Cathles Rd. SW12—5F 90
Cathnor Hall Ct. W12—3F 72
Cathnor Rd. W12—3F 72
Catisfield Rd. Enf—1J 17
Catlin Cres. Shep—9B 100
Catling Clo. SE23—9G 93
Catlins La. Pinn—1F 36
Catlin St. SE16—6E 76
Cator Clo. Croy—3C 140
Cator Cres. Croy—3C 140
Cator La. Beck—5K 109
Cato Rd. SW4—3H 91
Cator Rd. SE26—3H 109
Cator Rd. Cars—7D 122
Cator St. SE15—7D 76
(in two parts)
Cato's Hill. Esh—6M 117

Cato St. W1—9C 58
Catsey La. Bush, Wat—9A 10
Catsey Woods. Bush, Wat
—9A 10
Catterick Way. Borwd—3K 11
Cattistock Rd. SE9—2J 111
Catton St. WC1—8K 59
Caudwell Ter. SW18—5B 90
Caulfield Rd. E6—3K 63
Caulfield Rd. SE15—1F 92
Causeway, The. N2—2C 42
Causeway, The. SW18—3M 89
Causeway, The. SW19—2G 105
Causeway, The. Cars—4E 122
Causeway, The. Chess—6J 119
Causeway, The. Esh—9D 118
Causeway, The. Felt & Houn
—2F 84
Causeway, The. Sutt—1A 136
Causeway, The. Tedd—3D 102
Causeyware Rd. N9—9G 17
Causton Rd. N6—5F 42
Causton St. SW1—5H 75
Cautley Av. SW4—4G 91
Cavalier Clo. Romf—2H 49
Cavalier Ct. Surb—1K 119
Cavalier Gdns. Hay—9B 52
Cavalry Cres. Houn—3H 85
Cavaye Pl. SW10—6A 74
Cavell Cres. Dart—3L 99
Cavell Dri. Enf—4L 15
Cavell Rd. N17—7B 28
Cavell Rd. Wal X—1A 6
Cavell St. E1—8F 60
Cavendish Av. N3—9L 25
Cavendish Av. NW8—5B 58
Cavendish Av. W13—8E 54
Cavendish Av. Eri—7A 82
Cavendish Av. Harr—9B 38
Cavendish Av. Horn—2F 66
Cavendish Av. N Mald—8F 104
Cavendish Av. Ruis—1F 52
Cavendish Av. Sidc—6E 96
Cavendish Av. Well—2D 96
Cavendish Av. Wfd G—7F 30
Cavendish Clo. N18—5F 28
Cavendish Clo. NW6—2K 57
Cavendish Clo. NW8—6B 58
Cavendish Clo. Hay—8C 52
Cavendish Clo. Sun—3D 100
Cavendish Cres. Borwd—6L 11
Cavendish Cres. Horn—2F 66
Cavendish Dri. E11—6B 46
Cavendish Dri. Edgw—6K 23
Cavendish Dri. Esh—7C 118
Cavendish Gdns. Bark—1C 64
Cavendish Gdns. Ilf—6L 47
Cavendish Gdns. Romf—3J 49
Cavendish M. N. W1—8F 58
Cavendish M. S. W1—8F 58
Cavendish Pl. W1—9F 58
Cavendish Rd. E4—6A 30
Cavendish Rd. N4—4M 43
Cavendish Rd. N18—5F 28
Cavendish Rd. NW6—3J 57
Cavendish Rd. SW12—5G 91
Cavendish Rd. SW19—4B 106
Cavendish Rd. W4—9A 72
Cavendish Rd. Barn—5G 13
Cavendish Rd. Croy—3B 123
Cavendish Rd. N Mald—8D 104
Cavendish Rd. Sun—3D 100
Cavendish Rd. Sutt—9A 122
Cavendish Rd. Wey—9A 116
Cavendish Sq. W1—9F 58
Cavendish St. N1—5B 60
Cavendish Ter. Felt—8E 84
Cavendish Way. W Wick
—3M 125
Cavenham Gdns. Horn—3G 51
Cavenham Gdns. Ilf—8B 48
Caverleigh Way. Wor Pk
—3E 120
Cave Rd. E13—6F 62
Cave Rd. Rich—1G 103
Caversham Av. N13—3L 27
Caversham Av. Sutt—4J 121
Caversham Ct. N11—2E 26
Caversham Rd. N15—2A 44
Caversham Rd. NW5—2G 59
Caversham Rd. King—6K 103
Caversham St. SW3—7D 74
Caverswall St. W12—9G 57
Caveside Clo. Chst—5L 111
Cawdor Cres. W7—5E 70
Cawnpore St. SE19—2C 108
Caxton Dri. Uxb—5B 142
Caxton Gro. E3—6L 61
Caxton Rd. N22—9K 27
Caxton Rd. SW19—2A 106
Caxton Rd. W12—3H 73
Caxton Rd. S'hall—4H 69
Caxton St. SW1—4H 75

Caxton St. N. E16—9D 62
Caxton St. S. E16—1D 78
Caxton Way. Wat—8B 8
Caygill Clo. Brom—8D 110
Cayley Clo. Wall—9J 123
Cayton Rd. Gnfd—5C 54
Cayton St. EC1—6B 60
Cazenove Rd. E17—8L 29
Cazenove Rd. N16—7D 44
Cearns Ho. E6—4H 63
Cearn Way. Coul—7K 137
Cecil Av. Bark—3B 64
Cecil Av. Enf—6D 16
Cecil Av. Horn—1J 51
Cecil Av. Wemb—1K 55
Cecil Clo. Ashf—4A 100
Cecil Clo. Chess—6H 119
Cecil Ct. WC2—1J 75
Cecil Ct. Barn—5H 13
Cecile Pk. N8—4J 43
Cecilia Clo. N2—1A 42
Cecilia Rd. E8—1D 60
Cecil Pk. Pinn—2J 37
Cecil Pl. Mitc—9D 106
Cecil Rd. E11—8D 46
Cecil Rd. E13—4E 62
Cecil Rd. E17—8L 29
Cecil Rd. N10—9F 26
Cecil Rd. N14—1G 27
Cecil Rd. NW9—1C 40
Cecil Rd. NW10—4C 56
Cecil Rd. SW19—4M 105
Cecil Rd. W3—8A 56
Cecil Rd. Ashf—4A 100
Cecil Rd. Croy—1K 123
Cecil Rd. Enf—6A 16
Cecil Rd. Harr—1B 38
Cecil Rd. Houn—1A 86
Cecil Rd. Ilf—9M 47
Cecil Rd. Romf—5H 49
Cecil Rd. Sutt—8K 121
Cecil St. Wal X—5E 6
Cecil St. Wat—2F 8
Cedar Av. Barn—9C 14
Cedar Av. Enf—4G 17
Cedar Av. Hay—9E 52
Cedar Av. Romf—3J 49
Cedar Av. Ruis—1G 53
Cedar Av. Sidc—6E 96
Cedar Av. Twic—5M 85
Cedar Av. Upm—9L 51
Cedar Av. Wal X—6D 6
Cedar Av. W Dray—1K 143
Cedar Clo. SW15—1B 104
Cedar Clo. Borwd—6M 11
Cedar Clo. Brom—6K 111
(Bickley)
Cedar Clo. Brom—5J 127
(Keston Mark)
Cedar Clo. Buck H—2H 31
Cedar Clo. E Mol—8C 102
Cedar Clo. Eps—6D 134
Cedar Clo. Esh—8K 117
Cedar Clo. Romf—2A 50
Cedar Clo. Swan—6A 114
Cedar Ct. N1—3A 60
Cedar Ct. N11—5G 27
Cedar Ct. SW19—9H 89
Cedar Cres. Brom—5J 127
Cedarcroft Rd. Chess—6K 119
Cedar Dri. N2—2C 42
Cedar Dri. Pinn—6L 21
Cedar Dri. S at H, Dart—6M 115
Cedar Gdns. Sutt—8A 122
Cedar Grange. Enf—7C 16
Cedar Gro. W5—4J 71
Cedar Gro. Bex—5H 97
Cedar Gro. S'hall—8L 53
Cedar Gro. Wey—6A 116
Cedar Heights. Rich—7J 87
Cedarhurst Dri. SE9—4G 95
Cedar Lawn Av. Barn—7J 13
Cedar Mt. SE9—7H 95
Cedarne Rd. SW6—8M 73
Cedar Pk. Gdns. Romf—5H 49
Cedar Pk. Rd. Enf—2A 16
Cedar Rise. N14—9E 14
Cedar Rd. N17—8D 28
Cedar Rd. NW2—9G 41
Cedar Rd. Brom—6G 111
Cedar Rd. Croy—4C 124
Cedar Rd. Dart—7H 99
Cedar Rd. E Mol—8C 102
Cedar Rd. Enf—2M 15
Cedar Rd. Eri—9E 82
Cedar Rd. Felt—7B 84
Cedar Rd. Horn—8G 51
Cedar Rd. Houn—1G 85
Cedar Rd. Romf—2A 50
Cedar Rd. Sutt—8A 122
Cedar Rd. Tedd—2E 102

Cedar Rd. Wat—8G 9
Cedars. Bans—6D 136
Cedars Av. E17—3L 45
Cedars Av. Mitc—8E 106
Cedars Clo. NW4—1H 41
Cedars Ct. N9—2C 28
Cedars Dri. Uxb—5D 142
Cedars M. SW4—3F 90
Cedars Rd. E15—2C 62
Cedars Rd. N9—2E 28
Cedars Rd. N21—2M 27
Cedars Rd. SW4—2F 90
Cedars Rd. SW13—1E 88
Cedars Rd. W4—7A 72
Cedars Rd. Beck—6J 109
Cedars Rd. Croy—5J 123
Cedars Rd. King—5G 103
Cedars Rd. Mord—8L 105
Cedars, The. Buck H—1E 30
Cedars, The. Tedd—3D 102
Cedar Ter. Rich—3K 87
Cedar Tree Gro. SE27—2M 107
Cedarville Gdns. SW16—3K 107
Cedar Vista. Rich—1J 87
(in two parts)
Cedar Wlk. Kenl—8A 138
Cedar Wlk. Wal A—7K 7
Cedar Way. NW1—3H 59
Cedar Way. Sun—4C 100
Cedra Ct. N16—6E 44
Cedric Av. Romf—1C 50
Cedric Rd. SE9—9A 96
Celandine Clo. E3—8L 61
Celandine Dri. SE28—2F 80
Celandine Rd. W on T—6J 117
Celandine Way. E15—6C 62
Celia Rd. N19—9G 43
Celtic Av. Brom—7C 110
Celtic St. E14—8M 61
Cemetery La. SE7—7J 79
Cemetery Rd. E7—9D 46
Cemetery Rd. N17—7C 28
Cemetery Rd. SE2—8F 80
Cenacle Clo. NW3—8L 41
Centaur St. SE1—4K 75
Centenary Rd. Enf—6K 17
Central Av. E11—7B 46
Central Av. N2—9B 26
Central Av. N9—3C 28
Central Av. SW11—8D 74
Central Av. E Mol—8K 101
Central Av. Enf—4F 16
Central Av. Hay—2D 68
Central Av. Houn—3A 86
Central Av. Pinn—4K 37
Central Av. S Ock—3M 83
Central Av. Wall—7J 123
Central Av. Wal X—6E 6
Central Av. Well—1D 96
Central Cir. NW4—3F 40
Central Dri. Horn—8J 51
Central Hill. SE19—2B 108
Central Pde. Croy—2A 140
Central Pde. Gnfd—6E 54
Central Pk. Av. Dag—8M 49
Central Pk. Est. Houn—4H 85
Central Pk. Rd. E6—5H 63
Central Rd. Dart—4J 99
Central Rd. Mord—1L 121
Central Rd. Wemb—1F 54
Central Rd. Wor Pk—3E 120
Central School Path. SW14
—2A 88
Central Sq. NW11—4M 41
Central Sq. Wemb—2J 55
Central St. EC1—6A 60
Central Way. SE28—2E 80
Central Way. Cars—9C 122
Central Way. Felt—4E 84
Centre Av. W3—2B 72
Centre Comn. Rd. Chst—4A 112
Centre Rd. E11 & E7—4E 46
Centre Rd. Dag—5M 65
Centre St. E2—5F 60
Centre, The. Felt—8E 84
Centre, The. W on T—3D 116
Centre Way. E17—7A 30
Centre Way. N9—2G 29
Centre Way. Ilf—7A 48
Centre Way. Wal A—8J 7
Centric Clo. NW1—4F 58
Centurion Clo. N7—3K 59
Centurion Way. Purf—5K 83
Centuryan Pl. Dart—3F 98
Century Rd. E17—1J 45
Cephas Av. E1—7G 61
Cephas St. E1—7G 61
Ceres Rd. SE18—5D 80
Cerise Rd. SE15—1E 92
Cerne Clo. Hay—1G 69
Cerne Rd. Mord—1A 122
Cervantes Ct. N'wd—7D 20
Ceylon Rd. W14—4H 73

Chadacre Av. Ilf—1K 47
Chadacre Rd. Eps—8F 120
Chadbourn St. E14—8M 61
Chadd Dri. Brom—7J 111
Chad Grn. E13—4E 62
Chadville Gdns. Romf—3H 49
Chadway. Dag—6G 49
Chadwell Av. Romf—5F 48
Chadwell Av. Wal X—1C 6
Chadwell Heath La. Romf
—2F 48
Chadwell St. EC1—6L 59
Chadwick Av. E4—4B 30
Chadwick Clo. Tedd—3E 102
Chadwick Rd. E11—5C 46
Chadwick Rd. NW10—4D 56
Chadwick Rd. SE15—1D 92
Chadwick Rd. Ilf—8F 62
Chadwick St. SW1—4H 75
Chadwick Way. SE28—1H 81
Chadwin Rd. E13—8F 62
Chaffers Mead. Asht—8K 133
Chaffinch Av. Croy—1H 125
Chaffinch Clo. Croy—1H 125
Chaffinch La. Wat—9D 8
Chaffinch Rd. Beck—5J 109
Chafford Wlk. Rain—5G 67
Chafford Way. Romf—2G 49
Chagford St. NW1—7D 58
Chailey Av. Enf—4D 16
Chailey Pl. W on T—6J 117
Chailey St. E5—8G 45
Chalbury Wlk. N1—5K 59
Chalcombe Rd. SE2—4F 80
Chalcot Clo. Sutt—9L 121
Chalcot Cres. NW1—4D 58
Chalcot Gdns. NW3—2D 58
Chalcot Rd. NW1—3E 58
Chalcot Sq. NW1—3E 58
Chalcott Gdns. Surb—3G 119
Chalcroft Rd. SE13—4C 94
Chaldon Ct. SE19—5B 108
Chaldon Rd. SW6—8J 73
Chaldon Way. Coul—9J 137
Chale Rd. SW2—5J 91
Chalet Clo. Bex—1B 114
Chale Wlk. Sutt—1M 135
Chalfont Av. Wemb—2M 55
Chalfont Ct. NW9—1D 40
Chalfont Grn. N9—3C 28
Chalfont Rd. N9—3C 28
Chalfont Rd. SE25—7D 108
Chalfont Rd. Hay—3E 68
Chalfont Wlk. Pinn—9G 21
Chalfont Way. W13—4F 70
Chalford Clo. E Mol—8L 101
Chalforde Gdns. Romf—2F 50
Chalford Rd. SE21—1B 108
Chalford Wlk. Wfd G—8H 31
Chalgrove Av. Mord—9L 105
Chalgrove Cres. Ilf—9J 31
Chalgrove Gdns. N3—1J 41
Chalgrove Rd. E9—2G 61
Chalgrove Rd. N17—8F 28
Chalgrove Rd. Sutt—9B 122
Chalice Clo. Wall—8H 123
Chalkenden Clo. SE20—4F 108
Chalk Farm Rd. NW1—3E 58
Chalk Hill. Wat—8J 9
Chalkhill Rd. W6—5H 73
Chalkhill Rd. Wemb—8M 39
Chalklands. Wemb—8A 40
Chalk La. Barn—5D 14
Chalk La. Eps—7B 134
Chalk Paddock. Eps—7B 134
Chalk Pit Av. Orp—7G 113
Chalk Pit Rd. Bans—9L 135
Chalk Rd. E13—8F 62
Chalkwell Pk. Av. Enf—6C 16
Chalky La. Chess—2H 133
Challenge Rd. Ashf—9B 84
Challice Way. SW2—7K 91
Challin St. SE20—5G 109
Challis Rd. Bren—6H 71
Challock Clo. West—8G 141
Challoner Clo. N2—9B 26
Challoner Cres. W14—6K 73
Challoners Clo. E Mol—8B 102
Challoner St. W14—6K 73
Chalmers Rd. Ashf—2A 100
Chalmers Rd. Bans—7B 136
Chalmers Rd. E. Ashf—2A 100
Chalmers Way. Felt—4F 84
Chalsey Rd. SE4—3K 93
Chalton Dri. N2—4B 42
Chalton St. NW1—5H 59
Chamberlain Cotts. SE5—9B 76
Chamberlain Cres. W Wick
—3M 125
Chamberlain La. Pinn—2E 36
Chamberlain Rd. N2—9A 26
Chamberlain Rd. N9—3E 28

Chamberlain Rd. W13—3E 70
Chamberlain St. NW1—3D 58
Chamberlain Wlk. Felt—1J 101
Chamberlain Way. Pinn—1F 36
Chamberlain Way. Surb
—2J 119
Chamberlayne Rd. NW10
—4G 57
Chambers Gdns. N2—8B 26
Chambers Rd. N7—9J 43
Chambers St. SE16—3E 76
Chamber St. E1—1D 76
Chambord St. E2—6D 60
Champion Gro. SE5—2B 92
Champion Hill. SE5—2B 92
Champion Pk. SE5—1B 92
Champion Rd. SE26—1J 109
Champion Rd. Upm—7M 51
Champness Clo. SE27—1B 108
Champneys Clo. Sutt—9K 121
Chancel Industrial Est. NW10
—2D 56
Chanctonbury Way. N12
—4K 25
Chandler Av. E16—8E 62
Chandler Clo. Hmptn—5L 101
Chandler Rd. Lou—3M 19
Chandler St. E1—2F 76
Chandlers Way. SW2—6L 91
Chandlers Way. Romf—3C 50
Chandos Av. E17—9L 29
Chandos Av. N14—3G 27
Chandos Av. N20—1A 26
Chandos Av. W5—5G 71
Chandos Clo. Buck H—2F 30
Chandos Cres. Edgw—7K 23
Chandos Pl. WC2—1J 75
Chandos Rd. E15—1B 62
Chandos Rd. N2—9B 26
Chandos Rd. N17—9C 28
Chandos Rd. NW2—1G 57
Chandos Rd. NW10—7C 56
Chandos Rd. Borwd—4K 11
Chandos Rd. Harr—3A 38
Chandos Rd. Pinn—5H 37
Chandos St. W1—8F 58
Chandos Way. NW11—6M 41
Change All. EC3—9B 60
Channel Clo. Houn—9L 69
Channelsea Rd. E15—4B 62
Channing Clo. Horn—5K 51
Chanton Dri. Sutt—2G 135
Chantrey Rd. SW9—2K 91
Chantry Clo. Enf—2A 16
Chantry Clo. Harr—3K 39
Chantry Clo. Sidc—2J 113
Chantry Clo. W Dray—1H 143
Chantry Hurst. Eps—7B 134
Chantry La. Brom—9H 111
Chantry Pl. Harr—8M 21
Chantry Rd. Chess—7K 119
Chantry Rd. Harr—8M 21
Chantry St. N1—4M 59
Chantry, The. Uxb—6D 142
Chantry Way. Rain—5B 66
Chant Sq. E15—3B 62
Chant St. E15—3B 62
Chapel Clo. Dart—4C 98
Chapel Clo. Wat—7D 4
Chapel Clo. N2—1C 42
Chapel Ct. SE1—3B 76
Chapel Farm Rd. SE9—9K 95
Chapel Hill. Dart—4C 98
Chapel Ho. St. E14—6M 77
Chapel La. Chig—3D 32
Chapel La. Houn—2L 85
Chapel La. Pinn—1H 37
Chapel La. Romf—5H 49
Chapel La. Uxb—9E 142
Chapel Link. Ilf—8L 47
Chapel Mkt. N1—5L 59
Chapel Pl. N1—5L 59
Chapel Pl. N17—7D 28
Chapel Pl. W1—9F 58
Chapel Rd. SE27—1M 107
Chapel Rd. W13—2F 70
Chapel Rd. Bexh—3L 97
Chapel Rd. Houn—2M 85
Chapel Rd. Twic—6F 86
Chapel Rd. Warl—9H 139
Chapel Side. W2—1M 73
Chapel St. E15—3B 62

Chapel St. NW1—8C 58
Chapel St. SW1—4E 74
Chapel St. Enf—5B 16
Chapel St. Uxb—4A 142
Chapel Ter. Lou—1J 19
Chapel View. S Croy—8G 125
Chapel Wlk. NW4—2F 40
(in two parts)
Chapel Wlk. Croy—4A 124
Chapel Way. N7—8K 43
Chapel Way. Brom—6E 110
Chaplaincy Gdns. Horn—6J 51
Chaplin Clo. SE1—3M 75
Chaplin Cres. Sun—3C 100
Chaplin Rd. E15—5D 62
Chaplin Rd. N17—1D 44
Chaplin Rd. NW2—2E 56
Chaplin Rd. Dag—3J 65
Chaplin Rd. Wemb—2G 55
Chapman Clo. W Dray—4K 143
Chapman Cres. Harr—4J 39
Chapman Rd. E9—2K 61
Chapman Rd. Belv—6M 81
Chapman Rd. Croy—3L 123
Chapman's La. SE2 & Belv
—5H 81
Chapman's La. Orp—6H 113
Chapman St. E1—1F 76
Chapmans Yd. Wat—6H 9
Chapter Clo. Uxb—3D 142
Chapter Rd. NW2—1E 56
Chapter Rd. SE17—6M 75
Chapter St. SW1—5H 75
Chapter Ter. SE17—7M 75
Chapter Way. Hmptn—1L 101
Chara Pl. W4—7B 72
Charcroft Gdns. Enf—6H 17
Chardin Rd. W4—5C 72
Chardmore Rd. N16—6E 44
Chard Rd. Houn—1F 144
Chardwell Clo. E6—9K 63
Charecroft Way. W12—3H 73
Charford Rd. E16—8E 62
Chargate Clo. W on T—8D 116
Chargeable La. E13—7D 62
Chargeable St. E16—7D 62
Charing Clo. Orp—6D 128
Charing Cross Rd. WC2—9H 59
Charlbert St. NW8—5C 58
Charlbury Av. Stan—5H 23
Charlbury Clo. Romf—6G 35
Charlbury Cres. Romf—6G 35
Charlbury Gdns. Ilf—7D 48
Charlbury Gro. W5—9G 55
Charldane Rd. SE9—9M 95
Charlecote Gro. SE26—9F 92
Charlecote Rd. Dag—8J 49
Charlemont Rd. E6—6K 63
Charles Av. Ilf—8M 47
Charles Clo. Sidc—1F 112
Charles Ct. Eri—7C 82
Charles Cres. Harr—5B 38
(in two parts)
Charlesfield. SE9—9G 95
Charles Grinling Wlk. SE18
—5L 79
Charles La. NW8—5C 58
Charles Pl. NW1—6G 59
Charles Rd. E7—3G 63
Charles Rd. SW19—5L 105
Charles Rd. W13—9E 54
Charles Rd. Dag—2B 66
Charles Rd. Romf—4H 49
Charles II St. SW1—2H 75
Charles Sq. N1—6B 60
Charles St. E16—2G 79
Charles St. SW13—1C 88
Charles St. W1—2F 74
Charles St. Enf—7D 16
Charles St. Houn—1K 85
Charles St. Uxb—7F 142
Charles St. Trading Est. E16
—2G 79
Charleston St. SE17—5A 76
Charles Utton Ct. E8—9E 44
Charleville Cir. SE26—2E 108
Charleville Rd. W14—6J 73
Charlieville Rd. Eri—8A 82
Charlmont Rd. SW17—3C 106
Charlock Way. Wat—8D 8
Charlotte Despard Av. SW11
—9E 74
Charlotte Gdns. Romf—6M 33
Charlotte M. W1—8G 59
Charlotte Pl. W1—8G 59
Charlotte Pl. EC2—6C 60
Charlotte Rd. SW13—9D 72
Charlotte Rd. Dag—2M 65
Charlotte Rd. Wall—8G 123
Charlotte Row. SW4—2G 91
Charlotte Sq. Rich—5K 87
Charlotte St. W1—8G 59
Charlotte Ter. N1—4K 59

Chaseley St. E14—9J 61
Charlton Av. W on T—6F 116
Charlton Chu. La. SE7—6G 79
Charlton Cres. Bark—5D 64
Charlton Dene. SE7—8G 79
Charlton Dri. West—9H 141
Charlton Kings. Wey—5C 116
Charlton King's Rd. NW5
—1H 59
Charlton La. SE7—5H 79
Charlton La. Shep—7A 100
Charlton Pk. La. SE7—8H 79
Charlton Pk. Rd. SE7—7H 79
Charlton Pl. N1—5M 59
Charlton Rd. N9—1H 29
Charlton Rd. NW10—4C 56
Charlton Rd.—8E 78
SE3 1-121 & 2-78
SE7 remainder
Charlton Rd. Harr—2H 39
Charlton Rd. Shep—7A 100
Charlton Rd. Wemb—6K 39
Charlton Way. SE3—9C 78
Charlwood. Croy—1K 139
Charlwood Clo. Harr—6C 22
Charlwood Dri. Lea—7B 132
Charlwood Pl. SW1—5G 75
Charlwood Rd. SW15—3H 89
Charlwood St. SW1—6G 75
Charlwood Ter. SW15—3H 89
Charmian Av. Stan—1H 39
Charminster Av. SW19—6L 105
Charminster Ct. Surb—2H 119
Charminster Rd. SE9—1H 111
Charminster Rd. Wor Pk
—3H 121
Charmouth Rd. Well—9G 81
Charnock. Swan—8C 114
Charnock Rd. E5—8F 44
Charnwood Av. SW19—6L 105
Charnwood Clo. N Mald
—8C 104
Charnwood Dri. E18—1F 46
Charnwood Pl. N20—3A 26
Charnwood Rd. SE25—9B 108
Charnwood Rd. Enf—9B 6
Charnwood Rd. Uxb—5E 142
Charnwood St. E5—7F 44
Charrington Rd. Croy—4A 124
Charrington St. NW1—5H 59
Charsley Rd. SE6—8M 93
Chart Clo. Brom—5C 110
Chart Clo. Croy—1G 125
Charter Av. Ilf—6B 48
Charter Ct. New Mald—7C 104
Charter Cres. Houn—3J 85
Charter Dri. Bex—6J 97
Charterhouse Av. Wemb—1G 55
Charterhouse Bldgs. EC1
—7A 60
Charterhouse M. EC1—8M 59
Charterhouse Rd. Orp—5E 128
Charterhouse Sq. EC1—8M 59
Charterhouse St. EC1—8M 59
Charteris Rd. N4—6L 43
Charteris Rd. NW6—4K 57
Charteris Rd. Wfd G—7F 30
Charter Pl. Wat—5G 9
Charter Rd. King—7M 103
Charter Rd., The. Wfd G—6C 30
Charters Clo. SE19—2C 108
Charter Sq. King—6M 103
Charter Way. N3—2K 41
Charter Way. N14—8H 15
Chartfield Av. SW15—4F 88
Chartfield Sq. SW15—4H 89
Chartham Gro. SE27—9M 91
Chartham Rd. SE25—7F 108
Chartley Av. NW2—8C 40
Chartley Av. Stan—6D 22
Charton Clo. Belv—7L 81
Chart St. N1—6B 60
Chartwell Clo. SE9—8B 96
Chartwell Clo. Wal A—6M 7
Chartwell Pl. Eps—6C 134
Chartwell Pl. Sutt—5K 121
Chartwell Rd. N'wd—6D 20
Chartwell Way. SE20—5F 108
Charville La. Hay—6A 52
Charville La. W. Uxb—6F 142
Charwood. SW16—1L 107
Chase Ct. Gdns. Enf—5A 16
Chase End. Eps—4B 134
Chasefield Rd. SW17—1D 106
Chase Gdns. E4—4L 29
Chase Gdns. Twic—6B 86
Chase Grn. Enf—5A 16
Chase Grn. Av. Enf—4M 15
Chase Hill. Enf—5A 16
Chase Ho. Gdns. Horn—3K 51
Chase La. Chig—3E 32
Chase La. Ilf—3B 48
(in two parts)

Chaseley St. E14—9J 61
Chasemore Gdns. Croy
—7L 123
Chase Ridings. Enf—4L 15
Chase Rd. N14—7G 15
Chase Rd. W3—8B 56
Chase Rd. Eps—4B 134
Chase Side. N14—8E 14
Chase Side. Enf—5A 16
Chaseside Av. SW20—6J 105
Chase Side Av. Enf—4A 16
Chaseside Clo. Romf—6C 34
Chase Side Cres. Enf—3A 16
Chase Side Pl. Enf—5A 16
Chase, The. E12—9H 47
Chase, The. SW4—3F 90
Chase, The. SW16—4L 107
Chase, The. SW20—5J 105
Chase, The. Bexh—2M 97
Chase, The. Brom—7F 110
Chase, The. Chig—4A 32
Chase, The. Coul—6H 137
Chase, The. Edgw—8M 23
Chase, The. Lea—7A 132
(Oxshott)
Chase, The. Pinn—4G 37
Chase, The. Pinn—4G 37
(Eastcote)
Chase, The. Romf—1C 50
Chase, The. Romf—4J 49
(Chadwell Heath)
Chase, The. Romf—8C 50
(Rush Green)
Chase, The. Stan—6E 22
Chase, The. Sun—5F 100
Chase, The. Uxb—1F 142
Chase, The. Wall—7K 123
Chase, The. Wat—5C 8
Chaseville Pde. N21—7K 15
Chaseville Pk. Rd. N21—7J 15
Chase Way. N14—2F 26
Chasewood Av. Enf—4M 15
Chastilian Rd. Dart—6D 98
Chaston St. NW5—1E 58
Chatfield Rd. SW11—2A 90
Chatfield Rd. Croy—3M 123
Chatham Av. Brom—2D 126
Chatham Clo. NW11—3L 41
Chatham Clo. Sutt—2K 121
Chatham Pl. E9—2G 61
Chatham Rd. E17—1J 45
Chatham Rd. E18—9D 30
Chatham Rd. SW11—4D 90
Chatham Rd. King—6L 103
Chatham Rd. Orp—7A 128
Chatham St. SE17—5B 76
Chatsfield. Eps—2E 134
Chatsfield Pl. W5—9J 55
Chatsworth Av. NW4—9G 25
Chatsworth Av. SW20—5J 105
Chatsworth Av. Brom—1F 110
Chatsworth Av. Sidc—7E 96
Chatsworth Av. Wemb—1K 55
Chatsworth Clo. NW4—9G 25
Chatsworth Clo. Borwd—5L 11
Chatsworth Cres. Houn—3B 86
Chatsworth Dri. Enf—9E 16
Chatsworth Gdns. W3—2M 71
Chatsworth Gdns. Harr—6M 37
Chatsworth Gdns. N Mald
—9D 104
Chatsworth Pl. Tedd—1E 102
Chatsworth Rise. W5—7K 55
Chatsworth Rd. E5—8G 45
Chatsworth Rd. E15—1D 62
Chatsworth Rd. NW2—2H 57
Chatsworth Rd. W4—7A 72
Chatsworth Rd. W5—7K 55
Chatsworth Rd. Croy—6B 124
Chatsworth Rd. Dart—3G 99
Chatsworth Rd. Hay—7F 52
Chatsworth Rd. Sutt—7H 121
Chatsworth Way. SE27—9M 91
Chatteris Av. Romf—6G 35
Chattern Hill. Ashf—1A 100
Chattern Rd. Ashf—1A 100
Chatterton Rd. N4—8M 43
Chatterton Rd. Brom—8H 111
Chatto Rd. SW11—4D 90
Chaucer Av. Hay—8E 52
Chaucer Av. Houn—1F 84
Chaucer Av. Rich—2L 87
Chaucer Clo. N11—5G 27
Chaucer Gdns. Sutt—5L 121
Chaucer Grn. Croy—2G 125
Chaucer Rd. E7—2E 62
Chaucer Rd. E11—4E 46
Chaucer Rd. E17—9A 30
Chaucer Rd. SE24—4L 91
Chaucer Rd. W3—2A 72
Chaucer Rd. Romf—7F 34
Chaucer Rd. Sidc—7G 97
Chaucer Rd. Sutt—6L 121

Chaucer Rd. Well—9C 80
Chaucer Way. Dart—3L 99
Chauncey Clo. N9—3E 28
Chaundrye Clo. SE9—5K 95
Chave Rd. Dart—9J 99
Cheam Comn. Rd. Wor Pk
—4F 120
Cheam Pk. Way. Sutt—8J 121
Cheam Eps & Sutt—2E 134
Cheam Rd. Sutt—8K 121
Cheam St. SE15—2G 93
Cheapside. EC2—9A 60
Cheapside. N13—4A 28
Cheddar Rd. Houn—1E 144
Chedder Waye. Hay—9F 52
Cheddington Rd. N18—4C 28
Chedworth Clo. E16—9D 62
Cheeseman Clo. Hmptn
—3J 101
Cheeseman's Ter. W14—6K 73
Chelford Rd. Brom—2B 110
Chelmer Cres. Bark—5F 64
Chelmer Rd. E9—1H 61
Chelmsford Av. Romf—7B 34
Chelmsford Clo. E6—9K 63
Chelmsford Clo. W6—7H 73
Chelmsford Dri. Upm—8K 51
Chelmsford Gdns. Ilf—5J 47
Chelmsford Rd. E11—6B 46
Chelmsford Rd. E17—4L 45
Chelmsford Rd. E18—8D 30
Chelmsford Rd. N14—9G 15
Chelmsford Sq. NW10—4G 57
Chelsea Bri. SW1 & SW8—7F 74
Chelsea Bri. Rd. SW1—6E 74
Chelsea Clo. Edgw—9L 23
Chelsea Clo. Hmptn—2A 102
Chelsea Embkmt. SW3—7C 74
Chelsea Mnr. Gdns. SW3
—6C 74
Chelsea Mnr. St. SW3—6C 74
Chelsea Pk. Gdns. SW3—7B 74
Chelsea Sq. SW3—6B 74
Chelsfield Av. N9—9H 17
Chelsfield Gdns. SE26—9G 93
Chelsfield Hill. Orp—9G 129
Chelsfield La. Orp—2H 129
Chelsfield La. Orp & Sev
—9L 129
Chelsfield Rd. Orp—1G 129
Chelsham Comn. Rd. Warl
—8L 139
Chelsham Ct. Rd. Warl—9B 140
Chelsham Rd. SW4—2H 91
Chelsham Rd. S Croy—8B 124
Chelsham Rd. Warl—9K 139
Chelston App. Ruis—7E 36
Chelston Rd. Ruis—6E 36
Chelsworth Clo. Romf—8K 35
Chelsworth Dri. SE18—7B 80
Chelsworth Dri. Romf—8K 35
Cheltenham Av. Twic—6E 86
Cheltenham Clo. N'holt—2M 53
Cheltenham Gdns. E6—5J 63
Cheltenham Gdns. Lou—8J 19
Cheltenham Pl. W3—2M 71
Cheltenham Pl. Harr—2J 39
Cheltenham Rd. E10—4A 46
Cheltenham Rd. SE15—3G 93
Cheltenham Rd. Orp—5E 128
Cheltenham Ter. SW3—6D 74
Chelverton Rd. SW15—3H 89
Chelwood Gdns. Rich—1L 87
Chelwood Gdns. Pas. Rich
—1L 87
Chelwood Wlk. SE4—3J 93
Chenappa Clo. E13—6E 62
Chenduit Way. Stan—5D 22
Cheney Rd. N1—5J 59
Cheney Row. E17—8K 29
Cheneys Rd. E11—8C 46
Cheney St. Pinn—3G 37
Chenies M. WC1—7H 59
Chenies Pl. NW1—5H 59
Chenies St. WC1—8H 59
Chenies, The. Dart—1C 114
Chenies, The. Orp—1C 128
Cheniston Gdns. W8—4M 73
Chepstow Av. Horn—8J 51
Chepstow Clo. SW15—5J 89
Chepstow Cres. W11—1L 73
Chepstow Cres. Ilf—4C 48
Chepstow Gdns. S'hall—9K 53
Chepstow Pl. W2—1L 73
Chepstow Rise. Croy—5C 124
Chepstow Rd. W2—9L 57
Chepstow Rd. W7—4E 70
Chepstow Rd. Croy—5C 124
Chepstow Vs. W11—1K 73
Chepstow Way. SE15—9D 76

Choats Mnr. Way. Dag—5K 65
Choats Rd. Dag—6J 65
Chobham Gdns. SW19—8H 89
Chobham Rd. E15—1B 62
Cholmeley Cres. N6—5F 42
Cholmeley Pk. N6—6F 42
Cholmley Gdns. NW6—1L 57
Cholmley Rd. Th Dit—1F 118
Cholmondeley Av. NW10
    —5E 56
Cholmondeley Wlk. Rich
    —4G 87
Choppin's Ct. E1—2F 76
Chorleywood Cres. Orp
    —6D 112
Choumert Gro. SE15—1E 92
Choumert Rd. SE15—2D 92
Choumert Sq. SE15—1E 92
Chrislaine Clo. Stai—5B 144
Chrisp St. E14—9M 61
Christchurch Av. N12—6A 26
Christchurch Av. NW6—4H 57
Christchurch Av. Eri—7C 82
Christchurch Av. Harr—2D 38
Christchurch Av. Rain—6D 66
Christchurch Av. Tedd—2E 102
Christchurch Av. Wemb—2J 55
Christchurch Clo. SW19
    —4B 106
Christchurch Cres. Rad—1E 10
Christchurch Gdns. Eps
    —3M 133
Christchurch Gdns. Harr
    —2E 38
Christchurch Grn. Wemb
    —2J 55
Christchurch Hill. NW3—8B 42
Christchurch La. Barn—4J 13
Christchurch Mt. Eps—4M 133
Christchurch Pk. Sutt—9A 122
Christchurch Pas. NW3—8A 42
Christchurch Pas. Barn—4J 13
Christchurch Path. Hay—4A 68
Christchurch Pl. SW8—1H 91
Christchurch Pl. Eps—3M 133
Christchurch Rd. N8—4J 43
Christchurch Rd. SW2—7K 91
Christ Chu. Rd. SW14—4M 87
Christchurch Rd. SW19
    —5B 106
Christ Chu. Rd. Beck—6L 109
Christchurch Rd. Dart—5G 99
Christ Chu. Rd. Eps—4J 133
Christchurch Rd. Houn—1E 144
Christchurch Rd. Ilf—6M 47
Christchurch Rd. Purl—3M 137
Christchurch Rd. Sidc—1D 112
Christchurch Rd. Surb—1K 119
Christchurch St. SW3—7D 74
Christchurch Way. SE10
    —6C 78
Christian Fields. SW16—4L 107
Christian St. E1—9E 60
Christie Ct. N19—7J 43
Christie Gdns. Romf—4F 48
Christie Rd. E9—2J 61
Christina St. EC2—7C 60
Christopher Av. W7—4E 70
Christopher Clo. Sidc—5D 96
Christopher Gdns. Dag—1H 65
Christopher Pl. NW1—6H 59
Christopher Rd. S'hall—5F 68
Christopher St. EC2—7B 60
Christopher Way. Horn—9H 51
Christy Rd. West—7G 141
Chryssell Rd. SW9—8L 75
Chubworthy St. SE14—7J 77
Chudleigh Cres. Ilf—9C 48
Chudleigh Gdns. Sutt—5A 122
Chudleigh Rd. NW6—3H 57
Chudleigh Rd. SE4—4K 93
Chudleigh Rd. Romf—4J 35
Chudleigh Rd. Twic—5C 86
Chudleigh St. E1—9H 61
Chudleigh Way. Ruis—6E 36
Chulsa Rd. SE26—2F 106
Chumleigh St. SE5—7C 76
Chumleigh Wlk. Surb—8K 103
Church All. Croy—3L 123
Church All. Wat—2A 10
Church App. SE21—9B 92
Church App. Stai—5B 144
Church Av. E4—6B 30
Church Av. NW1—2F 58
Church Av. SW14—2B 88
Church Av. Beck—5L 109
Church Av. N'holt—3K 53
Church Av. Pinn—4J 37
Church Av. Ruis—6B 36
Church Av. Sidc—2E 112
Church Av. S'hall—4J 69
Churchbury Clo. Enf—4C 16
Churchbury La. Enf—5B 16

Churchbury Rd. SE9—6H 95
Churchbury Rd. Enf—4C 16
Church Clo. N20—3C 26
Church Clo. Edgw—5A 24
Church Clo. Hay—8B 52
Church Clo. Lou—4K 19
Church Clo. N'wd—7D 20
Church Clo. Uxb—5A 142
Church Clo. W Dray—4J 143
Church Ct. Rich—4H 87
Church Cres. E9—3H 61
Church Cres. N3—8K 25
Church Cres. N10—2F 42
Church Cres. N20—3C 26
Churchcroft Clo. SW12—6E 90
Churchdown. Brom—1C 110
Church Dri. NW9—6B 40
Church Dri. Harr—4L 37
Church Dri. W Wick—5C 126
Church Elm La. Dag—2L 65
Church End. E17—2M 45
Church End. NW4—1F 40
Church Farm Clo. Swan
    —1A 130
Church Farm La. Sutt—8J 121
Churchfield Av. N12—6B 26
Churchfield Clo. Harr—2A 38
Churchfield Clo. Hay—1D 68
Church Field Path. Wal X—2C 6
(in two parts)
Churchfield Rd. W3—2A 72
Churchfield Rd. W7—3C 70
Churchfield Rd. W13—2F 70
Churchfield Rd. W on T—3E 116
Churchfield Rd. Well—2E 96
Churchfields. E18—8E 30
Churchfields. SE10—7A 78
Churchfields. E Mol—7L 101
Churchfields. Lou—6J 19
Churchfields Av. Felt—9K 85
Churchfields Av. Wey—7A 116
Churchfields Rd. Beck—6H 109
Church Gdns. W5—3H 71
Church Gdns. Wemb—9E 38
Church Ga. SW6—2J 89
Churchgate. Wal X—2B 6
Churchgate Rd. Wal X—2B 6
Church Grn. Hay—9D 52
Church Grn. W on T—8G 117
Church Gro. SE13—4M 93
Church Gro. King—5G 103
Church Hill. E17—2L 45
Church Hill. N21—9K 15
Church Hill. SE18—4K 79
Church Hill. SW19—2K 105
Church Hill. Cars—7D 122
Church Hill. Dart—8H 99
Church Hill. Dart—3C 98
(Crayford)
Church Hill. Harr—6C 38
Church Hill. Lou—5K 19
Church Hill. Orp—2E 128
Church Hill. Purl—2J 137
Church Hill. Sev—7M 141
Church Hill Rd. E17—2M 45
Church Hill Rd. Barn—8C 14
Church Hill Rd. Surb—9J 103
Church Hill Rd. Sutt—5H 121
Church Hill Wood. Orp—9D 112
Church Hyde. SE18—7C 80
Churchill Av. Harr—4F 38
Churchill Av. Uxb—6F 142
Churchill Clo. Uxb—6F 142
Churchill Clo. Warl—9G 139
Churchill Ct. W5—7K 55
Churchill Dri. Wey—6A 116
Churchill Gdns. W3—9L 55
Churchill Gdns. Est. SW1
    —6G 75
Churchill Gdns. Rd. SW1
    —6F 74
Churchill Pl. Harr—2C 38
Churchill Rd. E16—9G 63
Churchill Rd. NW2—2F 56
Churchill Rd. NW5—9F 42
Churchill Rd. Edgw—6K 23
Churchill Rd. S Croy—9A 124
Churchill Ter. E4—3L 29
Churchill Wlk. E9—1G 61
Churchill Way. Sun—3E 100
Church La. E11—6C 46
Church La. E17—2M 45
Church La. N2—1B 42
Church La. N8—2K 43
Church La. N9—2E 28
Church La. N17—8C 28
Church La. NW9—4A 40
Church La. SW17—2D 106
Church La. SW19—5L 105
Church La. W13—3G 71
Church La. Brom—3J 127
Church La. Chess—8K 119
Church La. Chst—5A 112

Church La. Dag—3A 66
Church La. Enf—5B 16
Church La. Eps—9H 135
(Great Burgh)
Church La. Harr—8D 22
Church La. Lou—5K 19
Church La. Pinn—1J 37
Church La. Purf—6L 83
Church La. Rain—9H 67
Church La. Romf—2C 50
Church La. Tedd—2D 102
Church La. Th Dit—1D 118
Church La. Twic—7E 86
Church La. Uxb—5A 142
Church La. Wall—5H 123
Church La. Wal X—2C 6
Church La. Warl—9H 139
Church La. Warl—8M 139
(Chelsham)
Churchley Rd. SE26—1F 108
Church Manorway. SE2—5E 80
Church Manorway. Eri—4B 82
Churchmead Clo. Barn—8C 14
Church Meadow. Surb—4G 119
Churchmead Rd. NW10—2E 56
Churchmore Rd. SW16—5G 107
Church Mt. N2—3B 42
Church Pas. Barn—6J 13
Church Pas. Surb—9J 103
Church Pas. Twic—7F 86
Church Path. E11—3E 46
Church Path. E17—2M 45
Church Path. N5—1M 59
Church Path. N12—4A 26
Church Path. N17—8C 28
Church Path. NW10—3C 56
Church Path. SW14—2B 88
(in two parts)
Church Path. SW19—6K 105
Church Path. W4—4A 72
Church Path. W7—2C 70
Church Path. Croy—4A 124
Church Path. Mitc—7C 106
(in two parts)
Church Path. Romf—3C 50
Church Path. S'hall—2L 69
Church Path. S'hall—4K 69
(in three parts)
Church Pl. SW1—1G 75
Church Pl. W5—3H 71
Church Pl. Mitc—7C 106
Church Rise. SE23—8H 93
Church Rise. Chess
    —8K 119
Church Rd. E10—6L 45
Church Rd. E12—1J 63
Church Rd. E17—9J 29
Church Rd. N6—4E 42
Church Rd. N17—8C 28
Church Rd. NW4—2F 40
Church Rd. NW10—3C 56
Church Rd. SE19—5C 108
Church Rd. SW13—1D 88
Church Rd. SW19—2J 105
Church Rd.—5B 106
SW19 311-413 & 338-406
Mitc remainder
Church Rd. W3—2A 72
Church Rd. W7—1B 70
Church Rd. Ashf—9D 144
Church Rd. Asht—9H 133
Church Rd. Bark—2A 64
Church Rd. Bexh—1K 97
Church Rd. Brom—6E 110
Church Rd. Brom—7C 110
(Shortlands)
Church Rd. Buck H—1F 30
Church Rd. Croy—5A 124
(in two parts)
Church Rd. E Mol—8B 102
Church Rd. Enf—8G 17
Church Rd. Eps—5C 134
Church Rd. Eps—9B 120
(West Ewell)
Church Rd. Eri—6B 82
Church Rd. Esh—8D 118
Church Rd. Felt—2H 101
Church Rd. Hav. Romf—1G 35
Church Rd. Hay—2D 68
Church Rd. Houn—6F 68
(Cranford)
Church Rd. Houn—8L 69
(Heston)
Church Rd. Ilf—4C 48
Church Rd. Iswth—8C 70
Church Rd. Kenl—7B 138
Church Rd. Kes—9H 127
Church Rd. King—6K 103
Church Rd. Lou—5E 18
Church Rd. N'holt—5H 53
Church Rd. N'wd—7D 20
Church Rd. Orp—9G 129
(Chelsfield)

Church Rd. Orp—7A 128
(Farnborough)
Church Rd. Purl—2J 137
Church Rd. Rich—3J 87
Church Rd. Rich—1J 103
(Ham)
Church Rd. Romf—8L 35
(Harold Wood)
Church Rd. Shep—2A 116
Church Rd. Sidc—1E 112
Church Rd. S'hall—4K 69
Church Rd. Stan—5F 22
Church Rd. Surb—3G 119
Church Rd. Sutt—8J 121
Church Rd. S at H, Dart—4J 115
Church Rd. Swan—2B 130
(Crockenhill)
Church Rd. Swan—5H 115
(Swanley Village)
Church Rd. Tedd—1C 102
Church Rd. Uxb—7B 142
Church Rd. Wall—5H 123
Church Rd. Warl—9H 139
Church Rd. Wat—3E 8
Church Rd. Well—1F 96
Church Rd. W Dray—4H 143
Church Rd. West—9H 141
(Biggin Hill)
Church Rd. Whyt—9D 138
Church Rd. Wor Pk—3C 120
Church Row. NW3—9A 42
Church Row. Chst—5A 112
Church Side. Eps—5M 133
Churchside Clo. West—9G 141
Church Sq. E9—4G 61
Church St. E15—4C 62
Church St. E16—2M 79
Church St. N9—9B 16
Church St.—8B 58
  NW8 1-127 & 2-142
  W2 remainder
Church St. W4—7D 72
Church St. Croy—4A 124
Church St. Dag—2M 65
Church St. Enf—5A 16
Church St. Eps—5C 134
Church St. Eps—1E 134
(Ewell)
Church St. Esh—6M 117
Church St. Hmptn—5A 102
Church St. Iswth—2F 86
Church St. King—6H 103
Church St. Sun—7F 100
Church St. Sutt—7M 121
Church St. Twic—7E 86
Church St. W on T—3E 116
Church St. Wat—6G 9
Church St. N. E15—4C 62
Church St. Pas. E15—4C 62
Church Stretton Rd. Houn
    —4A 86
Church Ter. NW4—1F 40
Church Ter. SE13—2C 94
Church Ter. Rich—4H 87
Church Trading Est. Eri—8E 82
Church Vale. N2—1D 42
Church Vale. SE23—8H 93
Church View. Upm—7M 51
Churchview Rd. Twic—7B 86
Church Wlk. N6—8E 42
Church Wlk. N16—9B 44
Church Wlk. NW2—8K 41
Church Wlk. NW4—1G 41
Church Wlk. NW9—7B 40
Church Wlk. SW13—9E 72
Church Wlk. SW15—4F 88
Church Wlk. SW16—6G 107
Church Wlk. SW20—7G 105
Church Wlk. Bren—7G 71
Church Wlk. Dart—9H 99
Church Wlk. Hay—9C 52
Church Wlk. Rich—4H 87
Church Wlk. Th Dit—1D 118
Church Wlk. W on T—3E 116
Church Way. N20—3C 26
Churchway. NW1—6H 59
Church Way. Barn—6D 14
Church Way. Edgw—6L 23
Church Way. S Croy—2D 138
Churchwell Path. E9—1G 61
Churchyard Row. SE11—5M 75
Churston Av. E13—4F 62
Churston Dri. Mord—9H 105
Churston Gdns. N11—6G 27
Churton Pl. SW1—5G 75
Churton St. SW1—5G 75
Chusan Pl. E14—9K 61
Chyngton Clo. Sidc—9D 96
Cibber Rd. SE23—8H 93
Cicada Rd. SW18—5A 90
Cicely Rd. SE15—9E 76

Cinderford Way. Brom—1C 110
Cinema Pde. W5—7K 55
Cinnamon St. E1—2F 76
Cintra Pk. SE19—4D 108
Circle Gdns. SW19—6L 105
Circle, The. NW2—8C 40
Circle, The. NW7—6B 24
Circuits, The. Pinn—2G 37
Circular Rd. N17—1D 44
Circular Rd. SE1—4A 76
Circular Way. SE18—7K 79
Circus Pl. EC2—8B 60
Circus Rd. NW8—6B 58
Circus St. SE10—8A 78
Cirencester St. W2—8M 57
Cissbury Ho. SE26—9E 92
Cissbury Ring N. N12—5K 25
Cissbury Ring S. N12—5K 25
Cissbury Rd. N15—3B 44
Citizen Rd. N7—9L 43
City Garden Row. N1—5M 59
City Rd. EC1—5M 59
Civic Way. Ilf—2A 48
Clabon M. SW1—4D 74
Clack La. Ruis—6A 36
Clack St. SE16—3G 77
Clacton Rd. E6—6H 63
Clacton Rd. E17—4J 45
Clacton Rd. N17—9D 28
Claigmar Gdns. N3—8M 25
Claire Ct. N12—4A 26
Claire Ct. Pinn—7K 21
Clairvale. Horn—5J 51
Clairvale Rd. Houn—9J 69
Clairview Rd. SW16—2F 106
Clairville Gdns. W7—2C 70
Clammas Waye. Uxb—8A 142
Clamp Hill. Stan—4B 22
Clancarty Rd. SW6—1L 89
Clandon Clo. W3—3M 71
Clandon Clo. Eps—8D 120
Clandon Gdns. N3—1L 41
Clandon Rd. Ilf—7C 48
Clandon St. SE8—1L 93
Clanfield Way. SE15—8D 76
Clanricarde Gdns. W2—1L 73
Clapgate Rd. Bush, Wat—8M 9
Clapham Comn. N. Side. SW4
    —3E 90
Clapham Comn. S. Side. SW4
    —5F 90
Clapham Comn. W. Side. SW4
    —3D 90
(in three parts)
Clapham Cres. SW4—3H 91
Clapham High St. SW4—3H 91
Clapham Junct. App. SW11
    —3C 90
Clapham Mnr. St. SW4—2G 91
Clapham Pk. Rd. SW4—3H 91
Clapham Rd. SW9—2J 91
Clap La. Dag—7M 49
Claps Ga. La. Bark—7M 63
Clapton Comn. E5—5D 44
Clapton Pk. Est. E5—9H 45
Clapton Pas. E5—1G 61
Clapton Sq. E5—1G 61
Clapton Ter. N16—6E 44
Clapton Way. E5—9E 44
Clara Pl. SE18—5L 79
Clare Clo. N2—1A 42
Clare Clo. Borwd—8K 11
Clare Corner. SE9—6M 95
Clare Ct. Enf—8E 6
Claredale St. E2—5E 60
Clare Gdns. E7—9E 46
Clare Gdns. W11—9J 57
Clare Gdns. Bark—2D 64
Clare Gdns. Stan—5G 23
Clare Hill. Esh—8M 117
Clare La. N1—3A 60
Clare Lawn Av. SW14—4B 88
Clare Mkt. WC2—9K 59
Claremont. St Alb—4L 5
Claremont. Shep—1A 116
Claremont. Wal X—2A 6
Claremont Av. Esh—8K 117
Claremont Av. Harr—3J 39
Claremont Av. N Mald—9F 104
Claremont Av. Sun—5F 100
Claremont Av. W on T—6H 117
Claremont Clo. E16—2L 79
Claremont Clo. N1—5L 59
Claremont Clo. Orp—6L 127
Claremont Clo. S Croy—7F 138
Claremont Clo. W on T—7H 117
Claremont Cres. Dart—3C 98
Claremont Cres. Rick—7A 8
Claremont Dri. Esh—8M 117
Claremont End. Esh—8M 117
Claremont Gdns. Ilf—7C 48
Claremont Gdns. Surb—9J 103

Claremont Gro. W4—8C 72
Claremont Gro. Wfd G—6G 31
Claremont La. Esh—7M 117
Claremont Pk. N3—8J 25
Claremont Pk. Esh—8M 117
Claremont Rd. E7—1F 62
Claremont Rd. E11—8B 46
Claremont Rd. E17—9J 29
Claremont Rd. N6—5G 43
Claremont Rd. NW2—6H 41
Claremont Rd. W9—5K 57
Claremont Rd. W13—8E 54
Claremont Rd. Barn—1B 14
Claremont Rd. Brom—8J 111
Claremont Rd. Croy—3E 124
Claremont Rd. Esh—9C 118
Claremont Rd. Harr—9C 22
Claremont Rd. Horn—4E 50
Claremont Rd. Surb—9J 103
Claremont Rd. Swan—4C 114
Claremont Rd. Tedd—2D 102
Claremont Rd. Twic—5G 87
Claremont Sq. N1—5L 59
Claremont St. E16—2L 79
Claremont St. N18—6E 28
Claremont St. SE10—7M 77
Claremont Way. NW2—6G 41
Clarence Av. SW4—6H 91
Clarence Av. Brom—8J 111
Clarence Av. Ilf—4L 47
Clarence Av. N Mald—6A 104
Clarence Av. Upm—7L 51
Clarence Clo. Bush, Wat—9D 10
Clarence Clo. W on T—6F 116
Clarence Cres. SW4—5H 91
Clarence Cres. Sidc—9F 96
Clarence Gdns. NW1—6F 58
Clarence La. SW15—5C 88
Clarence M. E5—1F 60
Clarence Pas. NW1—5J 59
Clarence Pl. E5—1F 60
Clarence Rd. E5—9F 44
Clarence Rd. E12—1H 63
Clarence Rd. E16—7C 62
Clarence Rd. E17—9H 29
Clarence Rd. N15—3A 44
Clarence Rd. N22—7J 27
Clarence Rd. NW6—3K 57
Clarence Rd. SE9—8J 95
Clarence Rd. SW19—3M 105
Clarence Rd. W4—6L 71
Clarence Rd. Bexh—3J 97
Clarence Rd. Brom—7H 111
Clarence Rd. Croy—2B 124
Clarence Rd. Enf—7G 17
Clarence Rd. Rich—9K 71
Clarence Rd. Sidc—9F 96
Clarence Rd. Sutt—7M 121
Clarence Rd. Tedd—3D 102
Clarence Rd. Wall—7F 122
Clarence Rd. W on T—6F 116
Clarence St. King—6H 103
Clarence St. Rich—3J 87
Clarence Ter. NW1—7D 58
Clarence Ter. Houn—3M 85
Clarence Wlk. SW4—1J 91
Clarence Way. NW1—3F 58
Clarendon Av. SE5—8A 76
Clarendon Clo. W2—1C 74
Clarendon Clo. Orp—7E 112
Clarendon Cres. Twic—9B 86
Clarendon Cross. W11—1J 73
Clarendon Dri. SW15—3G 89
Clarendon Gdns. NW4—1F 40
Clarendon Gdns. W9—7A 58
Clarendon Gdns. Ilf—5K 47
Clarendon Gdns. Wemb—8H 39
Clarendon Grn. Orp—8E 112
Clarendon Gro. NW1—6H 59
Clarendon Gro. Mitc—7D 106
Clarendon Gro. Orp—8E 112
Clarendon M. W2—1C 74
Clarendon Pde. Wal X—2D 6
(in two parts)
Clarendon Pl. W2—1C 74
Clarendon Rise. SE13—3A 94
Clarendon Rd. E11—6B 46
Clarendon Rd. E17—4M 45
Clarendon Rd. E18—1E 46
Clarendon Rd. N8—1K 43
Clarendon Rd. N15—2A 44
Clarendon Rd. N18—6E 28
Clarendon Rd. N22—9K 27
Clarendon Rd. SW19—4C 106
Clarendon Rd. W5—7J 55
Clarendon Rd. W11—1J 73
Clarendon Rd. Borwd—5L 11
Clarendon Rd. Croy—4M 123
Clarendon Rd. Harr—4C 38
Clarendon Rd. Hay—3D 68

Clarendon Rd. Wall—8G 123
Clarendon Rd. Wal X—2D 6
Clarendon Rd. Wat—7C 24
Clarendon St. SW1—6F 74
Clarendon Ter. W9—7A 58
Clarendon Wlk. W11—9J 57
Clarendon Way. N21—8A 16
Clarendon Way. Chst & Orp
—7D 112
Clarens St. SE6—8K 93
Clare Rd. E11—4B 46
Clare Rd. NW10—3E 56
Clare Rd. SE14—1K 93
Clare Rd. Gnfd—2B 54
Clare Rd. Houn—2K 85
Clare Rd. Stai—7B 144
Clare St. E2—5F 60
Claret Gdns. SE25—7C 108
Clareville Gro. SW7—5A 74
Clareville Rd. Orp—4A 128
Clareville St. SW7—5A 74
Clare Way. Bexh—9J 81
Clarewood Wlk. SW9—3L 91
Clarges M. W1—2F 74
Clarges St. W1—2F 74
Claribel Rd. SW9—1M 91
Clarice Way. Wall—1J 137
Claridge Rd. Dag—6H 49
Clarissa Rd. Romf—5H 49
Clarissa St. E8—4D 60
Clark Clo. Eri—9E 82
Clarke Path. N16—6E 44
Clarke Av. Wor Pk—3H 121
Clarke Way. Wat—8E 4
Clarks Mead. Bush, Wat—9A 10
Clarkson Rd. E16—9D 62
Clarksons, The. Bark—5A 64
Clarkson St. E2—6F 60
Clark's Pl. EC2—9C 60
Clarks Rd. Ilf—7B 48
Clark St. E1—8G 61
Clark Way. Houn—8H 69
Claston Clo. Dart—3C 98
Claude Rd. E10—6A 46
Claude Rd. E13—4F 62
Claude Rd. SE15—2F 92
Claude St. E14—5L 77
Claudia Pl. SW19—7J 89
Claughton Rd. E13—5G 63
Clausen Way. Gnfd—5E 54
Clauson Av. N'holt—1M 53
Clavell St. SE10—7A 78
Claverdale Rd. SW2—6K 91
Claverhambury Rd. Wal A
—2M 7
Clavering Av. SW13—7F 72
Clavering Clo. Twic—1E 102
Clavering Rd. E12—7H 47
Claverley Gro. N3—8M 25
Claverley Vs. N3—8M 25
Claverton St. SW1—6G 75
Clave St. E1—2G 77
Claxton Gro. W6—6H 73
Claybridge Rd. SE12—1G 111
Claybrook Rd. W6—7H 73
Claybury. Bush, Wat—9M 9
Claybury B'way. Ilf—1J 47
Claybury Rd. Wfd G—7J 31
Clay Farm Rd. SE9—8A 96
Claygate Clo. Horn—9E 50
Claygate Cres. Croy—8A 126
Claygate La. Esh & Th Dit
—5E 118
Claygate La. Wal A—3L 7
Claygate Lodge Clo. Esh
—9C 118
Claygate Rd. W13—4F 70
Clayhall Av. Ilf—9J 31
Clay Hill. Enf—1A 16
Clayhill. Surb—9J 103
Clayhill Cres. SE9—1H 111
Claylands Pl. SW8—8L 75
Claylands Rd. SW8—7K 75
Clay La. Bush, Wat—9C 10
Clay La. Edgw—2L 23
Clay La. Stai—6D 144
Claymore Clo. Mord—2L 121
Claypit Hill. Wal A—1G 19
Claypole Rd. E15—5A 62
Clayponds Av. W5 & Bren
—5J 71
Clayponds Gdns. W5—5H 71
Clayponds La. Bren—6J 71
Clay Ride. Lou—3H 19
Clayside. Chig—5A 32
Clays La. E15—1M 61
Clay's La. Lou—3L 19
Clays La. Clo. E15—1M 61
Clay St. W1—8D 58
Clayton Av. Upm—1M 67
Clayton Av. Wemb—3J 55
Clayton Clo. E6—9K 63

Clayton Cres. Bren—6H 71
Clayton Croft Rd. Dart—8E 98
Clayton Field. NW9—7C 24
Clayton Rd. SE15—9E 76
Clayton Rd. Chess—6G 119
Clayton Rd. Eps—5C 134
Clayton Rd. Hay—3C 68
Clayton Rd. Romf—6A 50
Clayton St. SE11—7L 75
Clayton Ter. Hay—8J 53
Clayton Way. Uxb—7B 142
Claywood Clo. Orp—2C 128
Clayworth Clo. Sidc—5F 96
Cleall Av. Wal A—7J 7
Cleanthus Clo. SE18—9M 79
Cleanthus Rd. SE18—9M 79
Clearbrook Way. E1—9G 61
Clearwell Dri. W9—7M 57
Cleave Av. Hay—5C 68
Cleave Av. Orp—8C 128
Cleaveland Rd. Surb—9H 103
Cleaverholme Clo. Croy
—1F 124
Cleaver Sq. SE11—6L 75
Cleaver St. SE11—6L 75
Cleeve Hill. SE23—7F 92
Clegg St. E1—2F 76
Clegg St. E13—5E 62
Cleland Path. Lou—3M 19
Clematis Clo. Romf—7G 35
Clematis St. W12—1E 72
Clem Attlee Ct. SW6—7K 73
Clemence St. E14—8K 61
Clement Clo. NW6—3G 57
Clement Clo. W4—5B 72
Clement Clo. Purl—8M 137
Clementhorpe Rd. Dag—2G 65
Clementina Rd. E10—6K 45
Clementine Clo. W13—3F 70
Clement Rd. SW19—2J 105
Clement Rd. Beck—6H 109
Clement Rd. Wal X—1E 6
Clement's Av. E16—1E 78
Clement's Ct. Houn—3H 85
Clement's Inn. WC2—9K 59
Clement's La. EC4—1B 76
Clements La. Ilf—8M 47
Clements Pl. Bren—6H 71
Clements Rd. E6—3K 63
Clement's Rd. SE16—4E 76
Clements Rd. Ilf—8M 47
Clement Rd. W on T—4G 117
Clement St. Swan & S at H,
Dart—3H 115
Clement Way. Upm—8K 51
Clendon Way. SE18—5B 80
Clennam St. SE1—3A 76
Clensham La. Sutt—4L 121
Clenston M. W1—9D 58
Clephane Rd. N1—2A 60
Clere Pl. EC2—7B 60
Clere St. EC2—7B 60
Clerkenwell Clo. EC1—7L 59
Clerkenwell Grn. EC1—7M 59
Clerkenwell Rd. EC1—7L 59
Clerks Piece. Lou—5K 19
Clermont Rd. E9—4G 61
Clevedon. Wey—7B 116
Clevedon Clo. N16—8D 44
Clevedon Gdns. Hay—4B 68
Clevedon Gdns. Houn—9F 68
Clevedon Rd. SE20—5H 109
Clevedon Rd. King—6L 103
Clevedon Rd. Twic—5H 87
Cleveland Av. SW20—6K 105
Cleveland Av. W4—5D 72
Cleveland Av. Hmptn—4K 101
Cleveland Clo. W on T—5F 116
Cleveland Cres. Borwd—7A 12
Cleveland Gdns. N4—3A 44
Cleveland Gdns. NW2—7H 41
Cleveland Gdns. SW13—1D 88
Cleveland Gdns. SW20—9A 58
Cleveland Gdns. Wor Pk
—4C 120
Cleveland Gro. E1—7G 61
Cleveland M. W1—8G 59
Cleveland Pk. Av. E17—2L 45
Cleveland Pk. Cres. E17—2L 45
Cleveland Pl. SW1—2G 75
Cleveland Rise. Mord—2H 121
Cleveland Rd. E18—1E 46
Cleveland Rd. N1—3B 60
Cleveland Rd. N9—9F 16
Cleveland Rd. SW13—1D 88
Cleveland Rd. W4—4A 72
Cleveland Rd. W13—8E 54
Cleveland Rd. Ilf—8M 47
Cleveland Rd. Iswth—3E 86
Cleveland Rd. N Mald—8C 104
Cleveland Rd. Uxb—7B 142

Cleveland Rd. Well—1D 96
Cleveland Rd. Wor Pk—4C 120
Cleveland Row. SW1—2G 75
Cleveland Sq. W2—9A 58
Cleveland St. W1—7F 58
Cleveland Ter. W2—9A 58
Cleveland Way. E1—7G 61
Cleveley Clo. SE7—5H 79
Cleveley Cres. W5—5J 55
Cleveleys Rd. E5—8F 44
Cleve Rd. NW6—3M 57
Cleve Rd. Sidc—9H 97
Cleves Av. Eps—1F 134
Cleves Cres. Croy—3A 140
Cleves Rd. E6—4H 63
Cleves Rd. Rich—9G 87
Cleves Wlk. Ilf—7A 32
Cleves Way. Hmptn—4K 101
Cleves Way. Ruis—6H 37
Cleves Wood. Wey—6C 116
Clewer Cres. Harr—8B 22
Clichy Est. E1—8G 61
Clifden Rd. E5—1G 61
Clifden Rd. Bren—7H 71
Clifden Rd. Twic—7D 86
Cliff End. Purl—4M 137
Cliffe Rd. S Croy—7B 124
Clifford Av. SW14—2M 87
Clifford Av. Chst—3K 111
Clifford Av. Ilf—9M 31
Clifford Av. Wall—6G 123
Clifford Clo. N'holt—4J 53
Clifford Dri. SW9—3M 91
Clifford Gdns. NW10—5G 57
Clifford Gro. Ashf—9E 144
Clifford Rd. E16—7D 62
Clifford Rd. E17—9A 30
Clifford Rd. N9—8G 17
Clifford Rd. SE25—8E 108
Clifford Rd. Barn—5M 13
Clifford Rd. Houn—2H 85
Clifford Rd. Rich—8H 87
Clifford Rd. Wemb—3H 55
Clifford St. W1—1G 75
Clifford St. Wat—6G 9
Clifford Way. NW10—9D 40
Cliff Rd. NW1—2H 59
Cliff St. SE16—8D 62
Cliff Ter. SE8—1L 93
Cliffview Rd. SE13—2L 93
Cliff Vs. NW1—2H 59
Cliff Wlk. E16—8D 62
Clifton Av. E17—1H 45
Clifton Av. N3—8K 25
Clifton Av. W12—2D 72
Clifton Av. Felt—9G 85
Clifton Av. Stan—9F 22
Clifton Av. Sutt—3M 135
Clifton Av. Wemb—2K 55
Clifton Clo. Orp—7B 128
Clifton Clo. Wal X—2E 6
Clifton Cres. SE15—8G 77
(in two parts)
Clifton Est. SE15—9F 76
Clifton Gdns. N15—4D 44
Clifton Gdns. NW11—4K 41
Clifton Gdns. W4—5B 72
Clifton Gdns. W9—7A 58
Clifton Gdns. Enf—6J 15
Clifton Gdns. Uxb—5F 142
Clifton Gro. E8—2E 60
Clifton Hill. NW8—5M 57
Clifton Pk. Av. SW20—6G 105
Clifton Pl. W2—9B 58
Clifton Pl. Bans—7L 135
Clifton Rise. SE14—8J 77
Clifton Rd. E7—2H 63
Clifton Rd. E16—8C 62
Clifton Rd. N3—8A 26
Clifton Rd. N8—4H 43
Clifton Rd. N22—8G 27
Clifton Rd. NW10—5E 56
Clifton Rd. SE25—8C 108
Clifton Rd. SW19—3H 105
Clifton Rd. W9—7A 58
Clifton Rd. Coul—7F 136
Clifton Rd. Gnfd—7A 54
Clifton Rd. Harr—2K 39
Clifton Rd. Horn—4E 50
Clifton Rd. Ilf—4B 48
Clifton Rd. Iswth—1C 86
Clifton Rd. King—4K 103
Clifton Rd. Lou—6J 19
Clifton Rd. Sidc—1C 112
Clifton Rd. S'hall—5J 69
Clifton Rd. Tedd—1C 102
Clifton Rd. Wall—7F 122
Clifton Rd. Wat—7F 8
Clifton Rd. Well—2G 97
Clifton St. EC2—8C 60
Clifton Ter. N4—7L 43
Clifton Vs. W9—8A 58

Clifton Way. SE15—8G 77
Clifton Way. Wemb—4J 55
Clinch Ct. E16—8E 62
Cline Rd. N11—6G 27
Clinger Ct. N1—4C 60
Clink St. SE1—2B 76
Clinton Av. E Mol—8A 102
Clinton Av. Well—3E 96
Clinton Cres. Ilf—6C 32
Clinton Rd. E3—6J 61
Clinton Rd. E7—9E 46
Clinton Rd. N15—2B 44
Clipper Way. SE13—3A 94
Clippesby Clo. Chess—8K 119
Clipstone M. W1—8G 59
Clipstone Rd. Houn—1L 85
Clipstone St. W1—8G 59
Clissold Clo. N2—1D 42
Clissold Ct. N4—7A 44
Clissold Cres. N16—8B 44
Clissold Rd. N16—8B 44
Clitheroe Gdns. Wat—3H 21
Clitheroe Rd. SW9—1J 91
Clitheroe Rd. Romf—5A 34
Clitherow Av. W7—4E 70
Clitherow Pas. Bren—6G 71
Clitherow Rd. Bren—6F 70
Clitterhouse Cres. NW2—6G 41
Clitterhouse Rd. NW2—6G 41
Clive Av. N18—6E 28
Clive Av. Dart—5D 98
Cliveden Clo. N12—4A 26
Cliveden Pl. SW1—5E 74
Cliveden Pl. Shep—1A 116
Cliveden Rd. SW19—5K 105
Clivedon Ct. W13—8F 54
Clivedon Rd. E4—5C 30
Clive Pas. SE21—9B 92
Clive Rd. SE21—9B 92
Clive Rd. SW19—3C 106
Clive Rd. Belv—5L 81
Clive Rd. Enf—6E 16
Clive Rd. Esh—6M 117
Clive Rd. Felt—5E 84
Clive Rd. Romf—8F 50
Clive Rd. Twic—1D 102
Clivesdale Dri. Hay—2F 68
Clive Way. Enf—6E 16
Clive Way. Wat—3G 9
Cloak La. EC4—1A 76
Clockhouse Av. Bark—4A 64
Clockhouse Clo. SW19—8G 89
Clockhouse Industrial Est.
Felt—7F 144
Clockhouse La. Ashf & Felt
—9E 144
Clockhouse La. Romf—7M 33
Clock Ho. Mead. Lea—6A 132
Clockhouse Pde. N13—5L 27
Clock Ho. Rd. Beck—7J 109
Clock Pde. Enf—7B 16
Clock Tower M. N1—4A 60
Clock Tower Pl. N7—2J 59
Clock Tower Rd. Iswth—2D 86
Cloister Gdns. Croy—1F 124
Cloister Gdns. Edgw—5A 24
Cloister Rd. NW2—8K 41
Cloister Rd. W3—8A 56
Cloisters Av. Brom—9K 111
Cloisters, The. SW9—9L 75
Clonard Way. Pinn—6L 21
Clonbrook Rd. N16—9C 44
Cloncurry St. SW6—1H 89
Clonmel Clo. Harr—7B 38
Clonmell Rd. N17—1B 44
Clonmel Rd. SW6—9K 73
Clonmel Rd. Tedd—1B 102
Clonmore St. SW18—7K 89
Cloonmore Av. Orp—6D 128
Clorane Gdns. NW3—8L 41
Closemead Clo. N'wd
—6A 20
Close, The. E4—7A 30
Close, The. N14—2H 27
Close, The. N20—2K 25
Close, The. Barn—8D 14
Close, The. Beck—8J 109
Close, The. Bex—5L 97
Close, The. Bush, Wat—8L 9
Close, The. Cars—1C 136
Close, The. Dart—9H 99
Close, The. Harr—9A 22
Close, The. Iswth—1B 86
Close, The. Mitc—8D 106
Close, The. N Mald—6A 104
Close, The. Orp—1C 128
Close, The. Pinn—5G 37
(Eastcote)
Close, The. Pinn—5K 37
(Rayners Lane)
Close, The. Purl—2M 137
(Pampisford Rd.)

Close, The. Purl—2K 137
(Russell Hill)
Close, The. Rich—2M 87
Close, The. Romf—4J 49
Close, The. Sidc—1F 112
Close, The. Sutt—2K 121
Close, The. Uxb—3C 142
Close, The. Uxb—4E 142
(Hillingdon)
Close, The. Wemb—8A 40
(Barnhill Rd.)
Close, The. Wemb—2J 55
(Lyon Pk. Av.)
Cloth Fair. EC1—8M 59
Clothier St. E1—9C 60
Cloth St. EC1—8A 60
Cloudberry Rd. Romf—6H 35
Cloudesdale Rd. SW17—8F 90
Cloudesley Pl. N1—4L 59
Cloudesley Rd. N1—4L 59
Cloudesley Rd. Bexh—9K 81
Cloudesley Rd. Eri—9D 82
Cloudesley Sq. N1—4L 59
Cloudesley St. N1—4L 59
Clouston Clo. Wall—7J 123
Clova Rd. E7—2D 62
Clovelly Av. NW9—2D 40
Clovelly Av. Uxb—9A 36
Clovelly Clo. Uxb—9A 36
Clovelly Ct. Horn—7L 51
Clovelly Gdns. Enf—9C 16
Clovelly Gdns. Romf—8M 33
Clovelly Rd. N8—2H 43
Clovelly Rd. W4—3B 72
Clovelly Rd. W13—3G 71
Clovelly Rd. Bexh—7J 81
Clovelly Rd. Houn—1L 85
Clovelly Way. E1—9G 61
Clovelly Way. Harr—7K 37
Clovelly Way. Orp—1D 128
Clover Clo. E11—7B 46
Cloverdale Gdns. Sidc—5D 96
Clove St. E13—7E 62
Clowders Rd. SE6—9K 93
Cloysters Grn. E1—2E 76
Cloyster Wood. Edgw—7H 23
Club Gdns. Rd. Brom—2E 126
Club Row—7D 60
E1 1-11 & 2-10
E2 remainder
Clumps, The. Ashf—1B 100
Clunas Gdns. Romf—1H 51
Clunbury Av. S'hall—6K 69
Clunbury St. N1—5B 60
Cluny M. SW5—5L 73
Cluny Pl. SE1—4C 76
Clutton St. E14—8M 61
Clydach Rd. Enf—6D 16
Clyde Av. S Croy—7F 138
Clyde Cir. N15—2C 44
Clyde Pl. E10—5M 45
Clyde Rd. N15—2C 44
Clyde Rd. N22—8H 27
Clyde Rd. Croy—4D 124
Clyde Rd. Stai—7B 144
Clyde Rd. Sutt—7L 121
Clyde Rd. Wall—8G 123
Clydesdale. Enf—6H 17
Clydesdale Av. Stan—1H 39
Clydesdale Clo. Borwd—7B 12
Clydesdale Ct. N20—1B 26
Clydesdale Gdns. Rich—3M 87
Clydesdale Rd. W11—9K 57
Clydesdale Rd. Horn—5D 50
Clyde St. SE8—7F 77
Clyde Ter. SE23—8G 93
Clyde Vale. SE23—8G 93
Clyde Way. Romf—7C 34
Clydon Clo. Eri—7C 82
Clyfford Rd. Ruis—9D 36
Clymping Dene. Felt—6F 84
Clyston Rd. Wat—8D 8
Clyston St. SW8—1G 91
Coach & Horses Yd. W1—1G 75
Coach Ho. La. SW19—1H 105
Coach Ho. La. N5—9M 43
Coaldale Wlk. SE21—6A 92
Coalecroft Rd. SW15—3G 89
Coaley Row. Dag—5K 65
Coal Wharf Rd. W12—3H 73
Coates Dell. Wat—6J 5
Coates Hill Rd. Brom—6L 111
Coates Rd. Borwd—9H 11
Coate St. E2—5E 60
Coates Wlk. Bren—6J 71
Coates Way. Wat—6H 5
Cobbett Rd. SE9—2J 95
Cobbett Rd. Twic—7L 85
Cobbetts Av. Ilf—3H 47
Cobbetts Hill. Wey—9A 116
Cobbett St. SW8—8K 75
Cobb Grn. Wat—5F 4
Cobbins, The. Wal A—6L 7

Cobbler's Wlk. Hmptn & Tedd
—4A 102
Cobbold Est. NW10—2D 56
Cobbold Rd. E11—8D 46
Cobbold Rd. NW10—2D 56
Cobbold Rd. W12—3C 72
Cobb's Rd. Houn—3K 85
Cobb St. E1—8D 60
Cob Clo. Borwd—7B 12
Cobden Clo. Uxb—4A 142
Cobden Hill. Rad—1F 10
Cobden Rd. E11—8C 46
Cobden Rd. SE25—9E 108
Cobden Rd. Orp—6B 128
Cobham Av. N Mald—9E 104
Cobham Clo. SW11—5C 90
Cobham Clo. Brom—2J 127
Cobham Clo. Wall—8J 123
Cobham Rd. E17—8A 30
Cobham Rd. Houn—8G 69
Cobham Rd. Ilf—7C 48
Cobham Rd. King—6L 103
Cobill Clo. Horn—2G 51
Cobland Rd. SE12—1G 111
Coborn Rd. E3—6K 61
Coborn St. E3—6K 61
Cobourg Rd. SE5—7D 76
Cobourg St. NW1—6G 59
Coburg Cres. SW2—7K 91
Cochrane M. NW8—5B 58
Cochrane Rd. SW19—4K 105
Cochrane St. NW8—5B 58
Cockayne Way. SE8—5J 77
Cockerhurst Rd. Sev—8B 130
Cocker Rd. Enf—9B 6
Cockfosters Pde. Barn—6E 14
Cockfosters Rd. Barn—5D 14
Cockfosters Rd. Pot B & Barn
—1C 14
Cock Hill. E1—8C 60
Cock La. EC1—8M 59
Cockmannings La. Orp
—3H 129
Cockmannings Rd. Orp
—2H 129
Cockpit Yd. WC1—8K 59
Cocks Cres. N Mald—8D 104
Cocksett Av. Orp—8C 128
Cockspur Ct. SW1—2H 75
Cockspur St. SW1—2H 75
Cocksure La. Sidc—9L 97
Code St. E1—7D 60
Codicote Dri. Wat—7H 5
Codrington Hill. SE23—6J 93
Codrington M. W11—9J 57
Cody Clo. Harr—1H 39
Cody Clo. Wall—9H 123
Cody Rd. E16—7C 62
Coe's All. Barn—6J 13
Cofers Circ. Wemb—8M 39
Cogan Av. E17—8J 29
Coin St. SE1—2L 75
Coity Rd. SE21—7B 92
Cokers La. SE21—7B 92
Coke St. E1—9E 60
Colbeck M. SW7—5M 73
Colbeck Rd. Harr—5A 38
Colberg Pl. N16—5D 44
Colborne Way. Wor Pk—5G 121
Colbrook Av. Hay—4B 68
Colbrook Clo. Hay—4B 68
Colburn Av. Pinn—6J 21
Colburn Way. Sutt—5B 122
Colby Rd. SE19—2C 108
Colby Rd. W on T—3E 116
Colchester Dri. Pinn—3H 37
Colchester Rd. E10—5A 46
Colchester Rd. E17—4L 45
Colchester Rd. Edgw—7A 24
Colchester Rd. N'wd—9E 20
Colchester Rd. Romf & Brtwd
—8H 35
Colchester St. E1—9D 60
Colcokes Rd. Bans—8L 135
Coldbath Sq. EC1—7L 59
Coldbath St. SE13—9M 77
Cold Blow Cres. Bex—7B 98
Coldblow La. SE14—8H 77
Cold Blows. Mitc—7D 106
Coldershaw Rd. W13—2E 70
Coldfall Av. N10—9E 26
Coldham Gro. Enf—1J 17
Coldharbour. E14—2A 78
Coldharbour La.—3L 91
SE5 1-199 & 2-200
SW9 remainder
Coldharbour La. Bush, Wat
—8M 9
Coldharbour La. Hay—2E 68
Coldharbour La. Purl—2L 137

Coldharbour Rd. Croy—7L 123
Coldharbour Way. Croy
—7L 123
Coldstream Gdns. SW18
—5K 89
Colebeck M. N1—2M 59
Colebert Av. E1—7G 61
Colebrook Clo. SW15—6H 89
Colebrooke Av. W13—9F 54
Colebrooke Dri. E11—5G 47
Colebrooke Rise. Brom
—6C 110
Colebrooke Rd. SW16—5J 107
Colebrooke Row. N1—5M 59
Colebrook Gdns. Lou—4M 19
Colebrook La. Lou—4M 19
Colebrook Path. Lou—4M 19
Colebrook Way. N11—5F 26
Coleby Path. SE5—8B 76
Cole Clo. SE28—2F 80
Coledale Dri. Stan—8G 23
Coleford Rd. SW18—4A 90
Cole Gdns. Houn—8E 68
Colegrave Rd. E15—1B 62
Colegrove Rd. SE15—7D 76
Coleherne Ct. SW5—6M 73
Coleherne M. SW10—6M 73
Coleherne Rd. SW10—6M 73
Colehill Gdns. SW6—9J 73
Colehill La. SW6—9J 73
Coleman Fields. N1—4A 60
Coleman Rd. SE5—8C 76
Coleman Rd. Belv—5L 81
Coleman Rd. Dag—2J 65
Colemans Heath. SE9—9M 95
Coleman St. EC2—9B 60
Colenso Rd. E5—9G 45
Colenso Rd. Ilf—6C 48
Cole Pk. Gdns. Twic—4E 86
Cole Pk. Rd. Twic—5E 86
Colepits Wood Rd. SE9—4B 96
Coleraine Rd. N8—1L 43
Coleraine Rd. SE3—7D 78
Coleridge Av. E12—2J 63
Coleridge Av. Sutt—6C 122
Coleridge Clo. SW8—1F 90
Coleridge Gdns. NW6—3A 58
Coleridge La. N8—4J 43
Coleridge Rd. E17—2K 45
Coleridge Rd. N4—7L 43
Coleridge Rd. N8—4H 43
Coleridge Rd. N12—5A 26
Coleridge Rd. Ashf—9D 144
Coleridge Rd. Croy—2G 125
Coleridge Rd. Dart—3M 99
Coleridge Rd. Romf—7F 34
Coleridge Wlk. NW11—2L 41
Coleridge Way. Hay—9E 52
Coleridge Way. Orp—9L 23
Coleridge Way. W Dray
—5K 143
Cole Rd. Twic—5E 86
Cole Rd. Wat—3F 8
Colesburg Rd. Beck—7K 109
Coles Cres. Harr—7M 37
Colescroft Hill. Purl—7L 137
Coles Grn. Bush, Wat—1A 22
Coles Grn. Lou—3L 19
Coles Grn. Rd. NW2—6E 40
Coleshill Rd. Tedd—3C 102
Colestown St. SW11—1C 90
Cole St. SE1—3A 76
Colet Gdns. W14—5H 73
Coley St. WC1—7K 59
Colfe Rd. SE23—7J 93
Colham Av. W Dray—2J 143
Colham Grn. Rd. Uxb—8E 142
Colham Mill Rd. W Dray
—3H 143
Colham Rd. Uxb—7D 142
Colina M. N15—2M 43
Colina Rd. N15—3M 43
Colin Clo. NW9—2C 40
Colin Clo. Croy—5K 125
Colin Clo. Dart—5M 99
Colin Clo. W Wick—5D 126
Colin Cres. NW9—2D 40
Colindale Av. NW9—1B 40
Colindeep Gdns. NW4—2E 40
Colindeep La.—1C 40
NW4 2-28
NW9 remainder
Colin Dri. NW9—3D 40
Colinette Rd. SW15—3G 89
Colin Gdns. NW9—2D 40
Colin Pk. Rd. NW9—2C 40
Colin Rd. NW10—2E 56
Colinton Rd. Ilf—7F 48
Collamore Av. SW18—7C 90
Collapit Clo. Harr—4M 37
College App. SE10—7A 78
College Av. Eps—6D 134
College Av. Harr—8C 22

College Clo. E5—1G 61
College Clo. N18—5D 28
College Clo. Harr—7C 22
College Clo. Twic—7B 86
College Ct. Wal X—3C 6
College Cres. NW3—2B 58
College Cross. N1—3L 59
College Dri. Ruis—5E 36
College Gdns. E4—9M 17
College Gdns. N18—5E 28
College Gdns. SE21—7C 92
College Gdns. SW17—8C 90
College Gdns. Ilf—3J 47
College Gdns. N Mald—9D 104
College Gdns. Rd. Enf—3B 16
College Grn. SE19—4C 108
College Gro. NW1—4H 59
College Hill. EC4—1A 76
College Hill Rd. Harr—7C 22
College La. NW5—9F 42
College Pk. Clo. SE13—3B 94
College Pk. Rd. N17—6D 28
College Pl. E17—2C 46
College Pl. NW1—4G 59
College Rd. E17—3A 46
College Rd. N17—6D 28
College Rd. N21—1L 27
College Rd. NW10—5G 57
College Rd.—6C 92
SE21 1-111 & 2-120
SE19 remainder
College Rd. SW19—3B 106
College Rd. W13—9F 54
College Rd. Abb L, Wat—4D 4
College Rd. Brom—5E 110
College Rd. Croy—4B 124
College Rd. Eps—6D 134
College Rd. Harr—4C 38
College Rd. Harr—8C 22
(Harrow Weald)
College Rd. Iswth—9D 70
College Rd. Swan—5C 114
College Rd. Wal X—3C 6
College Rd. Wemb—6H 39
College Row. E9—1H 61
College Slip. Brom—5E 110
College St. EC4—1A 76
College Ter. E3—6K 61
College Ter. N3—9K 25
College View. SE9—7H 95
College Wlk. King—7J 103
Collent St. E9—2G 61
Colless Rd. N15—3D 44
Collett Clo. Wal X—1G 6
Collett Gdns. Wal X—1D 6
Collett Rd. SE16—4F 76
Collett Way. S'hall—3M 69
Collier Clo. Eps—8L 119
Collier Dri. Edgw—9L 23
Collier Row La. Romf—8M 33
Collier Row Rd. Romf—8K 33
Colliers Shaw. Kes—7H 127
Collier St. N1—5K 59
Colliers Water La. T Hth
—9L 107
Collingbourne Rd. W12—2F 72
Collingdale Av. Sidc—7E 96
Collingham Gdns. SW5—5M 73
Collingham Pl. SW5—5M 73
Collingham Rd. SW5—5M 73
Collingtree Rd. SE26—1G 109
Collingwood Av. N10—1E 42
Collingwood Av. Surb—3A 120
Collingwood Clo. SE20—5F 108
Collingwood Clo. Twic—6L 85
Collingwood Pl. W on T—5E 116
Collingwood Rd. E17—4L 45
Collingwood Rd. N15—2C 44
Collingwood Rd. Mitc—7C 106
Collingwood Rd. Sutt—5L 121
Collingwood Rd. Uxb—7F 142
Collingwood St. E1—7F 60
Collins Av. Stan—9J 23
Collins Ct. E8—2E 60
Collins Dri. Ruis—7G 37
Collinson St. SE1—3A 76
Collinson Wlk. SE1—3A 76
Collins Path. Hmptn—3K 101
Collins Rd. N5—9A 44
Collins St. SE3—1C 94
Collin's Yd. N1—4M 59
Collinwood Av. Enf—5G 17
Collinwood Gdns. Ilf—3K 47
Collis All. Twic—7C 86
Colls Rd. SE15—9G 77
Collyer Av. Croy—6J 123
Collyer Pl. SE15—9D 76
Collyer Rd. Croy—6J 123
Colman Clo. Eps—9G 135
Colman Rd. E16—8G 63
Colmar Clo. E1—7H 61
Colmer Pl. Harr—7B 22

Colmer Rd. SW16—5J 107
Colmore Rd. Enf—6G 17
Colnbrook By-Pass. Slou &
W Dray—8G 143
Colnbrook St. SE1—4M 75
Colne Av. Wat—8F 8
Colne Av. W Dray—3G 143
Colne Ct. Eps—6A 120
Colnedale Rd. Uxb—1B 142
Colne Dri. Romf—6K 35
Colne Dri. W on T—5H 117
Colne Rd. E5—9J 45
Colne Rd. N21—9B 16
Colne Rd. Twic—7C 86
Colne St. E13—6E 62
Colne Way. Wat—1H 9
Colney Hatch La.—6D 26
N10 1-187 & 2-270
N11 remainder
Colney Rd. Dart—5K 99
Cologne Rd. SW11—3B 90
Colombo Rd. Ilf—5A 48
Colombo St. SE1—2M 75
Colomb St. SE10—6C 78
Colonel's Wlk., The. Enf—5M 15
Colonial Av. Twic—5A 86
Colonial Dri. W4—5A 72
Colonial Rd. Felt—6C 84
Colonial Way. Wat—3G 9
Colonnade. WC1—7J 59
Colonnade, The. SE8—5K 77
Colson Gdns. Lou—6M 19
Colson Path. Lou—6L 19
Colson Rd. Croy—4C 124
Colson Rd. Lou—6M 19
Colson Way. SW16—1G 107
Colsterworth Rd. N15—2D 44
(in two parts)
Colston Av. Cars—6C 122
Colston Pas. SW18—6L 89
Colston Rd. E7—2H 63
Colston Rd. SW14—3A 88
Coltishall Rd. Horn—2G 67
Coltness Cres. SE2—6F 80
Colton Gdns. N17—1A 44
Colton Rd. Harr—3C 38
Coltsfoot Path. Romf—7G 35
Columbia Av. Edgw—8M 23
Columbia Av. Wor Pk—2D 120
Columbia Rd. E2—6D 60
Columbia Rd. E13—7D 62
Columbia Sq. SW14—3A 88
Columbine Av. S Croy—9M 123
Columbine Way. SE13—1A 94
Columbine Way. Romf—8J 35
Colva Wlk. N19—7F 42
Colvestone Cres. E8—1D 60
Colview Ct. SE9—7H 95
Colville Gdns. W11—9K 57
Colville Houses. W11—9K 57
Colville M. W11—9K 57
Colville Pl. W1—8H 59
Colville Rd. E11—8A 46
Colville Rd. E17—9J 29
Colville Rd. N9—1F 28
Colville Rd. W3—4M 71
Colville Rd. W11—9K 57
Colville Sq. W11—9K 57
Colville Sq. M. W11—9K 57
Colville Ter. W11—9K 57
Colvin Clo. SE26—2G 109
Colvin Gdns. E4—3A 30
Colvin Gdns. E11—2F 46
Colvin Gdns. Ilf—8A 32
Colvin Gdns. Wal X—8D 6
Colvin Rd. E6—3J 63
Colvin Rd. T Hth—9L 107
Colwell Rd. SE22—4D 92
Colwick Clo. N6—5H 43
Colwith Rd. W6—7G 73
Colwood Gdns. SW19—4B 106
Colworth Gro. SE17—5A 76
Colworth Rd. E11—4C 46
Colworth Rd. Croy—3E 124
Colwyn Av. Gnfd—5D 54
Colwyn Cres. Houn—9A 70
Colwyn Rd. NW2—8F 40
Colyer Clo. N1—5K 59
Colyer Clo. SE9—8M 95
Colyers Clo. Eri—9B 82
Colyers La. Eri—9A 82
Colyers Wlk. Eri—9C 82
Colyton Clo. Well—9H 81
Colyton Clo. Wemb—2G 55
Colyton Rd. SE22—4F 92
Colyton Way. N18—5E 28
Combe Av. SE3—8D 78
Combedale Rd. SE10—6E 78
Combe Lodge. SE7—7G 79
Combemartin Rd. SW18—6J 89
Combe M. SE3—8D 78
Comber Clo. NW2—7F 40
Comber Gro. SE5—8A 76

Combermere Rd. SW9—2K 91
Combermere Rd. Mord
　　　　　—1M 121
Combe Rd. Wat—8D 8
Comberton Rd. E5—7F 44
Combeside. SE18—8D 80
Combwell Cres. SE2—4E 80
Comely Bank Rd. E17—3A 46
Comeragh M. W14—6J 73
Comeragh Rd. W14—6J 73
Comerford Rd. SE4—3J 93
Comet Clo. Purf—5L 83
Comet Clo. Wat—7D 4
Comet Pl. SE8—8L 77
Comet Rd. Stai—6B 144
Comet St. SE8—8L 77
Commerce Rd. N22—8K 27
Commerce Way. Croy—4K 123
Commercial Dock Pas. SE16
　　　　　—4K 77
Commercial Rd.—9E 60
E1 1-601a & 2-554
E14 remainder
Commercial Rd. N18—6C 28
Commercial St. E1—8D 60
Commercial Way. NW10
　　　　　—5M 55
Commercial Way. SE15—8D 76
Commerell St. SE10—6C 78
Commodore St. E1—7J 61
Commondale. SW15—2G 89
Commonfield La. SW17
　　　　　—2C 106
Commonfield Rd. Bans—6L 135
Common La. Dart—8E 98
Common La. Esh—1E 132
Common La. Wat & Rad—3C 10
Commonmeadow La. Wat
　　　　　—6M 5
Common Rd. SW13—2F 88
Common Rd. Esh—8E 118
Common Rd. Stan—4B 22
Commonside. Kes—6G 127
Commonside E. Mitc—7E 106
Commonside W. Mitc—7D 106
Common, The. W5—2J 71
Common, The. Rich—9H 87
Common, The. S'hall—5H 69
Common, The. Stan—3D 22
Commonwealth Av. W12
　　　　　—1F 72
Commonwealth Av. Hay
　　　　　—9B 52
Commonwealth Rd. N17—7E 28
Commonwealth Way. SE2
　　　　　—6F 80
Community Clo. Uxb—8A 36
Community Rd. E15—1B 62
Community Rd. Gnfd—4A 54
Como Rd. SE23—8J 93
Como St. Romf—3B 50
Compass Hill. Rich—5H 87
Compayne Gdns. NW6—3M 57
Comport Clo. Croy—4C 140
Comport Grn. Croy—4C 140
Compton Av. E6—5H 63
Compton Av. N1—2M 59
Compton Av. N6—5C 42
Compton Av. Romf—1G 51
Compton Clo. W13—9E 54
Compton Clo. Esh—8B 118
Compton Ct. SE19—3C 108
Compton Cres. N17—7A 20
Compton Cres. W4—7A 72
Compton Cres. Chess—8J 119
Compton Cres. N'holt—4H 53
Compton Pas. EC1—7M 59
Compton Pl. WC1—7J 59
Compton Pl. Eri—7D 82
Compton Pl. Wat—3J 21
Compton Rise. Pinn—3J 37
Compton Rd. N1—2M 59
Compton Rd. N21—1M 27
Compton Rd. NW10—6H 57
Compton Rd. SW19—3K 105
Compton Rd. Croy—3F 124
Compton Rd. Hay—1C 68
Compton St. EC1—7M 59
Compton Ter. N1—2M 59
Comreddy Clo. Enf—3M 15
Comus Pl. SE17—5C 76
Comyne Rd. Wat—9D 4
Comyn Rd. SW11—3C 90
Comyns Clo. E16—8D 62
Comyns Rd. Dag—3L 65
Comyns, The. Bush. Wat—1A 22
Conaways Clo. Eps—2E 134
Concanon Rd. SW2—3K 91
Concert Hall App. SE1
Concord Clo. N'holt—6J 53
Concorde Clo. Houn—1M 85
Concorde Clo. Uxb—5C 142

Concord Rd. W3—7M 55
Concord Rd. Enf—7G 17
Concourse, The. NW9—8D 24
Condell Rd. SW8—9G 75
Conder St. E14—9J 61
Conderton Rd. SE5—2A 92
Condor Wlk. Rain—3F 66
Condover Cres. SE18—8M 79
Conduit La. N18—4B 28
Conduit La. Enf—8H 17
Conduit La. S Croy & Croy
　　　　　—7E 124
Conduit M. W2—9B 58
Conduit Pl. W2—9B 58
Conduit Rd. SE18—6M 79
Conduit St. W1—1F 74
Conduit Way. NW10—3A 56
Conewood St. N5—8M 43
Coney Acre. SE21—7A 92
Coney Burrows. E4—2C 30
Coney Gro. Uxb—6E 142
Coney Hill Rd. W Wick—4C 126
Coney Way. SW8—7K 75
Conference Rd. SE2—5G 81
Congleton Gro. SE18—6A 80
Congo Rd. SE18—6B 80
Congress Rd. SE2—5G 81
Congreve Ct. SE11—5L 75
Congreve Rd. SE9—2K 95
Congreve St. SE17—5C 76
Congreve Wlk. E16—8H 63
Conical Corner. Enf—4A 16
Conifer Av. Romf—5M 33
Conifer Clo. Orp—6B 128
Conifer Gdns. SW16—9K 91
Conifer Gdns. Enf—8C 16
Conifer Gdns. Sutt—4M 121
Conifer Rd. Swan—5A 114
Conifers. Wey—6C 116
Conifers Clo. Tedd—4F 102
Coniger Rd. SW6—1L 89
Coningesby Dri. Wat—3C 8
Coningham M. W12—2E 72
Coningham Rd. W12—3F 72
Coningsby Cotts. W5—3H 71
Coningsby Gdns. E4—6A 30
Coningsby Rd. N4—5M 43
Coningsby Rd. W5—3H 71
Coningsby Rd. S Croy—1A 138
Conington Rd. SE13—1A 94
Conisbee Ct. N14—7G 15
Conisborough Cres. SE6
　　　　　—9A 94
Coniscliffe Rd. N13—3A 28
Coniston Av. Bark—3C 64
Coniston Av. Gnfd—6F 54
Coniston Av. Upm—9M 51
Coniston Av. Well—2C 96
Coniston Clo. N20—3A 26
Coniston Clo. SW20—1H 121
Coniston Clo. W4—8A 72
Coniston Clo. Bark—3C 64
Coniston Clo. Bexh—9A 82
Coniston Clo. Dart—7F 98
Coniston Clo. Eri—8C 82
Coniston Gdns. N9—1G 29
Coniston Gdns. NW9—3B 40
Coniston Gdns. Ilf—2J 47
Coniston Gdns. Pinn—2E 36
Coniston Gdns. Sutt—8B 122
Coniston Gdns. Wemb—6C 38
Coniston Rd. N10—0F 26
Coniston Rd. N17—6E 28
Coniston Rd. Bexh—9A 82
Coniston Rd. Brom—3G 111
Coniston Rd. Coul—8G 137
Coniston Rd. Croy—2E 124
Coniston Rd. Twic—5M 85
Coniston Wlk. E9—1G 61
Coniston Way. Chess—5J 119
Coniston Way. Horn—1E 66
Conlan St. W10—7J 57
Conley Rd. NW10—2C 56
Conley St. SE10—6C 78
Connaught Av. E4—9B 18
Connaught Av. SW14—3A 88
Connaught Av. Ashf—9C 144
Connaught Av. Barn—1D 26
Connaught Av. Enf—4C 16
Connaught Av. Houn—3J 85
Connaught Av. Lou—6H 19
Connaught Clo. E10—7J 45
Connaught Clo. Enf—4C 16
Connaught Clo. Uxb—4A 52
Connaught Clo. Sutt—4B 122
Connaught Dri. NW11—2L 41
Connaught Gdns. N10—3F 42
Connaught Gdns. N13—4M 27
Connaught Hill. Lou—6H 19
Connaught La. Ilf—7A 48
Connaught Pl. W2—1D 74

Connaught Rd. E4—9C 18
Connaught Rd. E11—6B 46
Connaught Rd. E16—1G 79
Connaught Rd. E17—3L 45
Connaught Rd. N4—5L 43
Connaught Rd. NW10—4C 56
Connaught Rd. SE18—6M 79
Connaught Rd. W13—1F 70
Connaught Rd. Barn—8H 13
Connaught Rd. Harr—8D 22
Connaught Rd. Horn—8H 51
Connaught Rd. Ilf—7B 48
Connaught Rd. N Mald—8C 104
Connaught Rd. Rich—4K 87
Connaught Rd. Sutt—4B 122
Connaught Rd. Tedd—2B 102
Connaught Sq. W2—9D 58
Connaught Sq. W2—9C 58
Connaught Way. N13—4M 27
Connell Cres. W5—7K 55
Connemara Clo. Borwd—8B 12
Connington Cres. E4—3B 30
Connop Rd. Enf—2H 17
Connor Rd. Dag—9K 49
Connor St. E9—4H 61
Conolly Rd. W7—2C 70
Conrad Dri. Wor Pk—3G 121
Consfield Av. N Mald—9E 104
Consort M. Iswth—4B 86
Consort Rd. SE15—9F 76
Cons St. SE1—3L 75
Constable Clo. NW11—4M 41
Constable Clo. Hay—5A 52
Constable Cres. N15—3E 44
Constable Gdns. Edgw—8L 23
Constable Gdns. Iswth—4B 86
Constable Wlk. SE21—9C 92
Constance Cres. Brom—2D 126
Constance Rd. Croy—2M 123
Constance Rd. Enf—8C 16
Constance Rd. Sutt—6A 122
Constance Rd. Twic—6M 85
Constance St. E16—2J 79
Constantine Rd. NW3—9D 42
Constitution Hill. SW1—3F 74
Constitution Rise. SE18—9L 79
Content St. SE17—5B 76
Contessa Clo. Orp—7C 128
Control Tower Rd. Houn
　　　　　—2E 144
Convair Wlk. N'holt—6H 53
Convent Gdns. W5—5G 71
Convent Gdns. W11—9J 57
Convent Hill. SE19—3A 108
Convent Way. S'hall—5G 69
Conway Clo. Rain—3E 66
Conway Clo. Stan—6E 22
Conway Cres. Gnfd—5C 54
Conway Cres. Romf—4G 49
Conway Dri. Ashf—3A 100
Conway Dri. Hay—4A 68
Conway Gdns. Enf—2C 16
Conway Gdns. Mitc—8J 107
Conway Gdns. Wemb—5G 39
Conway Gro. W3—8B 56
Conway Rd. N14—3J 27
Conway Rd. N15—3M 43
Conway Rd. NW2—7G 41
Conway Rd. SE18—5B 80
Conway Rd. SW20—5G 105
Conway Rd. Felt—2H 101
Conway Rd. Houn—6K 85
Conway Rd. Houn—2F 144
(Heathrow Airport)
Conway St. W1—7G 59
(in two parts)
Conway Wlk. Hmptn—3K 101
Conybeare. NW3—4C 58
Conyers Clo. W on T—7H 117
Conyers Clo. Wfd G—6C 30
Conyer's Rd. SW16—2H 107
Conyers Way. Lou—5M 19
Cooden Clo. Brom—4F 110
Cookes Clo. E11—7D 46
Cookes La. Sutt—8J 121
Cookham Hill. Orp—5L 129
Cookham Rd. Sidc, Orp & Swan
　　　　　—5L 113
Cookhill Rd. SE2—4F 80
Cooks Hole Rd. Enf—2M 15
Cooks Mead. Bush, Wat—8M 9
Cook's Rd. E15—5M 61
Cook's Rd. SE17—7M 75
Coolfin Rd. E16—9E 62
Coolgardie Av. E4—5B 30
Coolgardie Av. Chig—3L 31
Coolgardie Rd. Ashf—2A 100
Coolhurst Rd. N8—4H 43
Cool Oak La. NW9—6C 40
Coomassie Rd. W9—7K 57
Coombe Av. Croy—6C 124

Coombe Bank. King—5C 104
Coombe Clo. Edgw—9K 23
Coombe Clo. Houn—3L 85
Coombe Corner. N21—1M 27
Coombe Cres. Hmptn—4K 101
Coombe Dri. Ruis—6F 36
Coombe End. King—4B 104
Coombefield Clo. N Mald
　　　　　—9C 104
Coombe Gdns. SW20—6E 104
Coombe Gdns. N Mald—8D 104
Coombe Hill Glade. King
　　　　　—4C 104
Coombe Hill Rd. King—4C 104
Coombe Ho. E4—6L 29
Coombe Ho. Chase. N Mald
　　　　　—5B 104
Coombehurst Clo. Barn—4D 14
Coombe La. SW20—6E 104
Coombe La. Croy—7F 124
Coombe La. W. King—5M 103
Coombe Lea. Brom—7J 111
Coombe Neville. King—4B 104
Coombe Pk. King—2A 104
Coombe Ridings. King—2A 104
Coombe Rise. King—5A 104
Coombe Rd. N22—9L 27
Coombe Rd. NW10—8B 40
Coombe Rd. SE26—1F 108
Coombe Rd. W4—6C 72
Coombe Rd. W13—4F 70
Coombe Rd. Bush, Wat—9B 10
Coombe Rd. Croy—6B 124
Coombe Rd. Hmptn—3K 101
Coombe Rd. King—5L 103
Coombe Rd. N Mald—6C 104
Coombe Rd. Romf—1K 51
Coombe Way. Croy—2H 123
Coombes Rd. Dag—4K 65
Coombe Wlk. Sutt—5M 121
Coombe Wood Dri. Romf
　　　　　—4K 49
Coombe Wood Hill. Purl
　　　　　—5A 138
Coombewood Rd. King
　　　　　—2A 104
Coombs St. N1—5M 59
Coomer M. SW6—7K 73
Coomer Pl. SW6—7K 73
Cooperage Clo. N17—6D 28
Cooper Av. E17—8J 29
Cooper Clo. SE1—3L 75
Cooper Cres. Cars—5D 122
Cooper Mead Clo. NW2—8G 41
Cooper Rd. NW4—4H 41
Cooper Rd. NW10—1E 56
Cooper Rd. Croy—6M 123
Coopersale Clo. Wfd G—7G 31
Coopersale Rd. E9—1H 61
Coopers Clo. Chig—2F 32
Coopers La. E10—6M 45
Coopers La. NW1—5H 59
Cooper's La. SE12—8F 94
Cooper's Rd. SE1—6D 76
Cooper St. E16—8D 62
Coopers Wlk. Wal X—1D 6
Cooper's Yd. SE19—3C 108
Coote Gdns. Dag—8K 49
Coote Rd. Bexh—9K 81
Coote Rd. Dag—8K 49
Copeland Rd. E17—4M 45
Copeland Rd. SE15—1E 92
Copenhagen Pl. E14—9K 61
Copenhagen St. N1—4J 59
Copenhagen Way. W on T
　　　　　—5F 116
Copen Rd. Dag—5K 49
Cope Pl. W8—4L 73
Copers Cope Rd. Beck—4K 109
Copesfield. E Mol—7L 101
Cope St. SE16—5H 77
Copford Clo. Wfd G—6J 31
Copinger Wlk. Edgw—8M 23
Copland Av. Wemb—1H 55
Copland Clo. Wemb—1G 55
Copland Rd. Wemb—2J 55
Copleston Pas. SE15—1C 92
Copleston Rd. SE15—2D 92
Copley Clo. SE17—7A 76
Copley Dene. Brom—5H 111
Copley Pk. SW16—3K 107
Copley Rd. Stan—5G 23
Copner Way. SE15—8D 76
Coppelia Rd. SE3—3D 94
Copperas St. SE8—7M 77
Copperbeech Clo. NW3—1B 58
Copper Beech Clo. Orp—9G 113
Copper Beech Ct. Lou—3L 19
Copper Beeches Ct. Iswth
　　　　　—9B 70

Copperdale Rd. Hay—3E 68
Copperfield. Chig—5B 32
Copperfield Av. Uxb—8E 142
Copperfield Clo. S Croy
　　　　　—3A 138
Copperfield M. N18—5C 28
Copperfield Rd. E3—8J 61
Copperfields Ct. E3—3L 71
Copperfield St. SE1—3M 75
Copperfields Way. Romf
　　　　　—8H 35
Copper Field Way. Chst
　　　　　—3A 112
Copperfield Way. Pinn—2K 37
Coppermill La. E17—3H 45
Copper Mill La. SW17—1A 106
Coppetts Clo. N12—7C 26
Coppetts Rd. N10—7D 26
Coppice Clo. SW20—7G 105
Coppice Clo. Ruis—4B 36
Coppice Dri. SW15—5F 88
Coppice Path. Chig—4F 32
Coppice, The. Ashf—3A 100
Coppice, The. Enf—6M 15
Coppice, The. Wat—8G 9
Coppice, The. W Dray—9C 142
Coppice Wlk. N20—3L 25
Coppice Way. E18—2D 46
Coppies Gro. N11—4F 26
Coppins, The. Croy—8M 125
Coppins, The. Harr—6C 22
Coppock Clo. SW11—1C 90
Copse Av. W Wick—5M 125
Copse Clo. N'wd—9A 20
Copse Clo. W Dray—4H 143
Copse Edge Av. Eps—5D 134
Copse Glade. Surb—2H 119
Copse Hill. SW20—5E 104
Copse Hill. Sutt—9M 121
Copsem Dri. Esh—8M 117
Copsem La. Esh & Lea—8A 118
Copse, The. E4—1D 30
Copse, The. Wat—5J 5
Copse View. S Croy—1H 139
Copsewood Rd. Wat—3F 8
Copse Wood Way. N'wd—8A 20
Copthall Av. EC2—9B 60
(in two parts)
Copthall Clo. EC2—9B 60
Copthall Dri. NW7—7E 24
Copthall Gdns. NW7—7E 24
Copthall Gdns. Twic—7D 86
Copthorne Av. SW12—6H 91
Copthorne Av. Brom—4K 127
Copthorne Av. Ilf—6M 31
Copthorne Clo. Shep—1A 116
Copthorne Gdns. Horn—3L 51
Copthorne M. Hay—5C 68
Copthorne Rise. S Croy
　　　　　—5B 138
Coptic St. WC1—8J 59
Copwood Clo. N12—4C 26
Coral Clo. Romf—2G 49
Coralline Wlk. SE2—3G 81
Coral St. SE1—3L 75
Coram St. WC1—7J 59
Coran Clo. N9—9H 17
Corban Rd. Houn—2L 85
Corbar Clo. Barn—3B 14
Corbet Clo. Wall—3E 122
Corbet Ct. EC3—9B 60
Corbet Pl. E1—8D 60
Corbet Rd. Eps—2C 134
Corbets Tey Rd. Upm—9M 51
Corbett Gro. N22—1J 27
Corbett Rd. E11—4G 47
Corbett Rd. E17—1A 46
Corbett's La. SE16—5G 77
Corbett's Pas. SE16—5G 77
Corbiere Ct. SW19—3H 105
Corbins La. Harr—8M 37
Corbridge Cres. E2—5F 60
Corby Cres. Enf—6J 15
Corbylands Rd. Sidc—7C 96
Corbyn St. N4—6J 43
Corby Rd. NW10—5B 56
Corby Way. E3—7L 61
Cordelia Gdns. Stai—6C 144
Cordelia Rd. Stai—6C 144
Cordelia St. E14—9M 61
Cordell Clo. Wal X—1E 6
Cordingley Rd. Ruis—7B 36
Cording St. E14—8M 61
Cordova Rd. E3—6J 61
Cordrey Gdns. Coul—7J 137
(in two parts)
Cord Way. E14—4J 77
Cordwell Rd. SE13—4C 94
Corelli Rd. SE3—1J 95
Corfe Av. Harr—9L 37

Corfe Clo.—Cranbrook Rd.

Corfe Clo. Asht—9G 133
Corfield St. E2—6F 60
Corfton Rd. W5—9J 55
Corinium Clo. Wemb—9K 39
Corinne Rd. N19—9G 43
Corinthian Manorway. Eri —5B 82
Corinthian Rd. Eri—5B 82
Corinthian Way. Stai—6B 144
Corkers Path. Ilf—7A 48
Corker Wlk. N7—7K 43
Corkran Rd. Surb—2H 119
Corkscrew Hill. W Wick —4A 126
Cork St. W1—1G 75
Corlett St. NW1—8C 58
Cormont Rd. SE5—9M 75
Cormorant Wlk. Rain—2F 66
Cornbury Rd. Edgw—7H 23
Cornel Gdns. Swan—6B 114
Cornelia Pl. Eri—7C 82
Cornelia St. N7—2K 59
Cornell Clo. Sidc—3J 113
Cornell Way. Romf—5M 33
Corner Grn. SE3—1E 94
Corner Mead. NW9—7D 24
Cornerside. Ashf—4A 100
Corney Rd. W4—7C 72
Cornfield Clo. Uxb—5B 142
Cornfield Rd. Bush, Wat—6M 9
Cornflower La. Croy—3H 125
Cornflower Ter. SE22—5F 92
Cornflower Way. Romf—8J 35
Cornford Clo. Brom—9E 110
Cornford Gro. SW12—8F 90
Cornhill. EC3—9B 60
Cornish Gro. SE20—5F 108
Cornmill. Wal A—6H 7
Corn Mill Dri. Orp—2E 128
Cornmill La. SE13—2A 94
Cornshaw Rd. Dag—6H 49
Cornthwaite Rd. E5—8G 45
Cornwall Av. E2—6G 61
Cornwall Av. N3—7L 25
Cornwall Av. N22—8J 27
Cornwall Av. Esh—9D 118
Cornwall Av. S'hall—8K 53
Cornwall Av. Well—2C 96
Cornwall Clo. Bark—2D 64
Cornwall Clo. Horn—2L 51
Cornwall Clo. Wal X—6E 6
Cornwall Cres. W11—9J 57
Cornwall Dri. Orp—4G 113
Cornwall Gdns. NW10—2F 56
Cornwall Gdns. SW7—4M 73
Cornwall Gdns. Wlk. SW7 —4M 73
Cornwall Gro. W4—6C 72
Cornwallis Av. N9—2G 29
Cornwallis Av. SE9—9B 96
Cornwallis Gro. N9—2G 29
Cornwallis Rd. E17—2H 45
Cornwallis Rd. N9—2F 28
Cornwallis Rd. N19—7J 43
Cornwallis Rd. Dag—9H 49
Cornwallis Wlk. SE9—2K 95
Cornwall M. S. SW7—4A 74
Cornwall M. W. SW7—4M 73
Cornwall Rd. N4—5L 43
Cornwall Rd. N15—3B 44
Cornwall Rd. N18—5E 28
Cornwall Rd. SE1—2L 75
Cornwall Rd. Croy—4M 123
Cornwall Rd. Harr—4A 38
Cornwall Rd. Pinn—7K 21
Cornwall Rd. Ruis—7D 36
Cornwall Rd. Sutt—9K 121
Cornwall Rd. Twic—7E 86
Cornwall Rd. Uxb—2B 142
Cornwall St. E1—1F 76
Cornwall Ter. NW1—7D 58
Cornwood Clo. N2—2B 42
Cornwood Dri. E1—9G 61
Cornworthy Rd. Dag—1G 65
Corona Rd. SE12—6E 94
Coronation Clo. Bex—5H 97
Coronation Clo. Ilf—2A 48
Coronation Dri. Horn—1F 66
Coronation Rd. E13—6G 63
Coronation Rd. NW10—6K 55
Coronation Rd. Hay—5D 68
Coronation Wlk. Twic—7L 85
Coronet St. N1—6C 60
Corporation Av. Houn—3J 85
Corporation Row. EC1—7L 59
Corporation St. E15—5C 62
Corporation St. N7—1J 59
Corrance Rd. SW2—3J 91
Corri Av. N14—4H 27
Corricum. E11—5C 46
Corrigan Av. Coul—7E 136
Corringham Rd. NW11—5L 41
Corringham Rd. Wemb—7L 39
Corringway. NW11—5M 41
Corringway. W5—7L 55
Corsair Clo. Stai—6B 144
Corsair Rd. Stai—6C 144
Corscombe Clo. King—2A 104
Corsehill St. SW16—3G 107
Corsham St. N1—6B 60
Corsica St. N5—2M 59
Corsley Way. E9—2K 61
Cortayne Rd. SW6—1K 89
Cortis Rd. SW15—5F 88
Cortis Ter. SW15—5F 88
Corunna Rd. SW8—9G 75
Corunna Ter. SW8—9G 75
Corvette Sq. SE10—7B 78
Corwell Gdns. Uxb—9A 52
Corwell La. Uxb—9A 52
Coryton Path. W9—7K 57
Cosbycote Av. SE24—4A 92
Cosdach Av. Wall—9H 123
Cosedge Cres. Croy—7L 123
Cosgrove Clo. Hay—7J 53
Cosmo Pl. WC1—8J 59
Cosmur Clo. W12—4D 72
Cossall Wlk. SE15—1F 92
Cosser St. SE1—4L 75
Costa St. SE15—1E 92
Costons Av. Gnfd—6B 54
Costons La. Gnfd—6B 54
Cosway St. NW1—8C 58
Cotall St. E14—8L 61
Coteford Clo. Lou—4M 19
Coteford Clo. Pinn—3E 36
Coteford St. SW17—1D 106
Cotelands. Croy—5C 124
Cotesbach Rd. E5—8G 45
Cotesmore Gdns. Dag—9G 49
Cotford Rd. T Hth—8A 108
Cotham St. SE17—5A 76
Cotheritone. Eps—2B 134
Cotherstone Rd. SW2—7K 91
Cotleigh Av. Bex—8H 97
Cotleigh Rd. NW6—3L 57
Cotleigh Rd. Romf—4B 50
Cotman Clo. NW11—4A 42
Cotman Clo. SW15—5H 89
Cotmandene Cres. Orp—6F 112
Cotman Gdns. Edgw—9L 23
Cotmans Clo. Hay—2E 68
Coton Rd. Well—2E 96
Cotsford Av. N Mald—9A 104
Cotswold Av. Bush, Wat—8A 10
Cotswold Clo. Bexh—1C 98
Cotswold Clo. King—3A 104
Cotswold Clo. Uxb—4A 142
Cotswold Ct. N11—4E 26
Cotswold Gdns. E6—6H 63
Cotswold Gdns. NW2—7H 41
Cotswold Gdns. Ilf—5B 48
Cotswold Ga. NW2—6J 41
Cotswold Grn. Enf—6K 15
Cotswold Rise. Orp—1D 128
Cotswold Rd. Hmptn—3L 101
Cotswold Rd. Romf—9K 35
Cotswold Rd. Sutt—2M 135
Cotswold St. SE27—1M 107
Cotswold Way. Enf—5K 15
Cottage Av. Brom—3J 127
Cottage Clo. Ruis—6B 36
Cottage Field Clo. Sidc—7G 97
Cottage Grn. SE5—8B 76
Cottage Gro. SW9—2J 91
Cottage Gro. Surb—1H 119
Cottage Pl. SW3—4C 74
Cottage Rd. Eps—9B 120
Cottage St. E14—1M 77
Cottage Wlk. SE15—9D 76
Cottage Wlk. SW1—4D 74
Cottenham Dri. SW20—4F 104
Cottenham Pk. Rd. SW20 —5E 104
(in two parts)
Cottenham Pl. SW20—4F 104
Cottenham Rd. E17—2K 45
Cotterill Rd. Surb—4J 119
Cottesbrook St. SE14—8J 77
Cottesmore Av. Ilf—9L 31
Cottesmore Gdns. W8—4M 73
Cottimore Av. W on T—3F 116
Cottimore Cres. W on T—2F 116
Cottimore La. W on T—2F 116
Cottimore Ter. W on T—2F 116
Cottingham Chase. Ruis —8E 36
Cottingham Rd. SE20—4H 109
Cottingham Rd. SW8—8K 75
Cottington Clo. SE11—6M 75
Cottington Rd. Felt—1H 101
Cottington St. SE11—6M 75
Cotton Av. W3—9B 56
Cottongrass Clo. Croy—3H 125
Cotton Hill. Brom—1A 110
Cottons App. Romf—3B 50
Cottons Ct. Romf—3B 50
Cotton's Gdns. E2—6C 60
Cotton St. E14—1A 78
Couchmore Av. Esh—4C 118
Couchmore Av. Ilf—9K 31
Coulgate St. SE4—2J 93
Coulsdon Ct. Rd. Coul—8K 137
Coulsdon Rise. Coul—9J 137
Coulsdon Rd. Coul & Cat —7K 137
Coulson St. SW3—6D 74
Coulston Rd. SW18—6L 89
Coulter Clo. Hay—7J 53
Coulter Rd. W6—4F 72
Councillor St. SE5—8A 76
Countess Rd. NW5—1G 59
Countisbury Av. Enf—9D 16
Country Way. Felt—3F 100
County Gdns. Bark—5C 64
County Ga. SE9—9A 96
County Ga. Barn—8M 13
County Gro. SE5—9A 76
County Rd. E6—8M 63
County Rd. T Hth—6M 107
County St. SE1—4A 76
Coupland Pl. SE18—6A 80
Courage Clo. Horn—4G 51
Courcy Rd. N8—1L 43
Courland Gro. SW8—9H 75
Courland St. SW8—1H 91
Course, The. SE9—9L 95
Courtauld Rd. N19—6J 43
Court Av. Belv—6K 81
Court Av. Romf—7L 35
Court Clo. Harr—1J 39
Court Clo. Twic—9M 85
Court Clo. Wall—9H 123
Court Clo. Av. Twic—9M 85
Court Cres. Chess—8H 119
Court Cres. Swan—8C 114
Court Downs Rd. Beck—6M 109
Court Dri. Croy—6K 123
Court Dri. Stan—4J 23
Court Dri. Sutt—6C 122
Court Dri. Uxb—4D 142
Courtenay Av. N6—5C 42
Courtenay Av. Harr—7A 22
Courtenay Gdns. Harr—9A 22
Courtenay Pl. E17—3J 45
Courtenay Rd. E11—8D 46
Courtenay Rd. E17—2H 45
Courtenay Rd. SE20—3H 109
Courtenay Rd. Wor Pk—5G 121
Courtenay Sq. SE11—6L 75
Courtenay St. SE11—6L 75
Court Farm Av. Eps—7B 120
Court Farm La. N'holt—3L 53
Court Farm Rd. SE9—8H 95
Court Farm Rd. N'holt—3L 53
Court Farm Rd. Warl—9E 138
Courtfield Av. Harr—3D 38
Courtfield Cres. Harr—3D 38
Courtfield Gdns. SW5—5M 73
Courtfield Gdns. W13—9E 54
Courtfield Gdns. Ruis—7D 36
Courtfield M. SW7—5A 74
Courtfield Rise. W Wick —5B 126
Courtfield Rd. SW7—5A 74
Courtfield Rd. Ashf—3A 100
Court Gdns. Romf—6L 35
Court Haw. Bans—7C 136
Court Hill. Coul—9C 136
Court Hill. S Croy—4C 138
Courthill Rd. SE13—3A 94
Courthope Rd. NW3—9D 42
Courthope Rd. SW19—2J 105
Courthope Rd. Gnfd—5B 54
Courthope Vs. SW19—4J 105
Court Ho. Gdns. N3—6L 25
Courthouse Rd. N12—6M 25
Courtland Av. E4—2D 30
Courtland Av. NW7—3C 24
Courtland Av. SW16—4K 107
Courtland Av. Ilf—7K 47
Courtland Dri. Chig—3M 31
Courtland Rd. E6—4J 63
Courtlands. Rich—4L 87
Courtlands Av. SE12—4F 94
Courtlands Av. Brom—3D 126
Courtlands Av. Esh—8K 117
Courtlands Av. Hmptn—3K 101
Courtlands Av. Rich—1M 87
Courtlands Clo. Ruis—5D 36
Courtlands Clo. S Croy—2D 138
Courtlands Cres. Bans—8L 135
Courtlands Dri. Eps—8C 120
Courtlands Dri. Wat—1C 8
Courtlands Rd. Surb—2L 119
Court La. SE21—5C 92
Court La. Eps—5A 134
Court La. Gdns. SE21—6C 92
Courtleet Dri. Eri—9M 81
Courtleigh Av. Barn—2B 14
Courtleigh Gdns. NW11—2J 41
Courtman Rd. N17—7A 28
Court Mead. N'holt—6K 53
Courtmead Clo. SE24—5A 92
Courtnell St. W2—9L 57
Courtney Clo. SE19—3C 108
Courtney Cres. Cars—9D 122
Courtney Pl. Croy—5L 123
Courtney Rd. N7—1L 59
Courtney Rd. SW19—4C 106
Courtney Rd. Croy—5L 123
Courtney Rd. Houn—2E 144
Courtrai Rd. SE23—5J 93
Court Rd. SE9—5K 95
Court Rd. SE25—6D 108
Court Rd. Bans—8L 135
Court Rd. Orp—2F 128
Court Rd. S'hall—6K 69
Court Rd. Uxb—1F 142
Courtside. N8—4H 43
Court St. E1—8F 60
Court St. Brom—6E 110
Court, The. Ruis—9J 37
Court Way. NW9—2C 40
Court Way. W3—8A 56
Court Way. Ilf—1A 48
Court Way. Romf—9J 35
Court Way. Twic—6D 86
Court Way. Wfd G—5G 31
Courtway, The. Wat—2J 21
Court Wood La. Croy—3K 139
Court Yd. SE9—5K 95
Courtyard, The. N1—3K 59
Courtyard, The. NW1—3E 58
Cousin La. EC4—1B 76
Couthurst Rd. SE3—8F 78
Coutts Av. Chess—7J 119
Coval Gdns. SW14—3M 87
Coval La. SW14—3M 87
Coval Pas. SW14—3A 88
Coval Rd. SW14—3A 88
Covent Garden. WC2—1J 75
Coventry Clo. E6—9K 63
Coventry Clo. NW6—5L 57
Coventry Rd. E1 & E2—7F 60
Coventry Rd. SE25—8E 108
Coventry Rd. Ilf—7M 47
Coventry St. W1—1H 75
Coverack Clo. N14—8G 15
Coverack Clo. Croy—2J 125
Coverdale Clo. Stan—5F 22
Coverdale Gdns. Croy—5D 124
Coverdale Rd. NW2—3H 57
Coverdale Rd. W12—3F 72
Coverdales, The. Bark—5B 64
Coverley Clo. E1—8E 60
Coverton Rd. SW17—2C 106
Covert Rd. Ilf—6D 32
Coverts Rd. Esh—9D 118
Covert, The. N'wd—8A 20
Covert, The. Orp—1C 128
Covert Way. Barn—4A 14
Covington Gdns. SW16 —4M 107
Covington Way. SW16—3K 107
(in two parts)
Cowan Clo. E6—8J 63
Cowan St. SE5—7C 76
Cowbridge La. Bark—3M 63
Cowbridge Rd. Harr—2K 39
Cowcross St. EC1—8M 59
Cowdenbeath Path. N1—4K 59
Cowden Rd. Orp—2D 128
Cowden St. SE6—1L 109
Cowdray Rd. Uxb—4A 52
Cowdray Way. Horn—9E 50
Cowdrey Clo. Enf—4C 16
Cowdrey Ct. Dart—6F 98
Cowdrey Rd. SW19—2A 106
Cowdry Rd. E9—2J 61
Cowen Av. Harr—7B 38
Cowgate Rd. Gnfd—6B 54
Cowick Rd. SW17—1D 106
Cowings Mead. N'holt—2J 53
Cowland Av. Enf—6G 17
Cow La. Gnfd—5B 54
Cow La. Wat—9G 5
Cowleaze Rd. King—5J 103
Cowles. Wal X—1A 6
Cowley Clo. S Croy—2G 139
Cowley Cres. Uxb—8A 142
Cowley Cres. W on T—6G 117
Cowley Hill. Borwd—1M 11
Cowley La. E11—8C 46
Cowley Mill Rd. Uxb—5A 142
Cowley Rd. E11—3F 46
Cowley Rd. SW9—9L 75
Cowley Rd. SW14—2C 88
Cowley Rd. W3—2D 72
Cowley Rd. Ilf—5K 47
Cowley Rd. Romf—7F 34
Cowley Rd. Uxb—5A 142
Cowley St. SW1—4J 75
Cowling Clo. W11—2J 73
Cowper Av. E6—3J 63
Cowper Av. Sutt—6B 122
Cowper Clo. Brom—8H 111
Cowper Clo. Well—4E 96
Cowper Ct. Wat—1E 8
Cowper Gdns. N14—8F 14
Cowper Gdns. Wall—8G 123
Cowper Rd. N14—1F 26
Cowper Rd. N16—1C 60
Cowper Rd. N18—5E 28
Cowper Rd. SW19—3A 106
Cowper Rd. W3—2B 72
Cowper Rd. W7—1D 70
Cowper Rd. Belv—5L 81
Cowper Rd. Brom—8H 111
Cowper Rd. King—2K 103
Cowper Rd. Rain—7E 66
Cowper St. EC2—7B 60
Cowper Ter. W10—8H 57
Cowslip Rd. E18—9F 30
Cowthorpe Rd. SW8—9H 75
Cox La. Chess—6K 119
Cox La. Eps—7M 119
Coxley Rise. Purl—5A 138
Coxmount Rd. SE7—6H 79
Coxson Pl. SE1—3D 76
Cox's Wlk. SE21 & SE26—7E 92
Coxtie Grn. Rd. Brtwd—1L 35
Coxwald Path. Chess—9J 119
Coxwell Rd. SE18—6B 80
Crabbs Croft Clo. Orp—7A 128
Crab Hill. Beck—4B 110
Crab La. Wat—8M 5
Crabtree Av. Romf—2H 49
Crabtree Av. Wemb—5K 55
Crabtree Clo. Bush, Wat—7M 9
Crabtree La. SW6—8G 73
Crabtree Manorway. Belv —4A 82
Crace St. NW1—6H 59
Craddock Rd. Enf—5D 16
Craddocks Av. Asht—9J 133
Craddocks Pde. Asht—9J 133
Craddock St. NW5—2E 58
Cradley Rd. SE9—7B 96
Cragg Av. Rad—1D 10
Craigdale Rd. Horn—4D 50
Craig Dri. Uxb—9F 142
Craigen Av. Croy—3F 124
Craigerne Rd. SE3—8F 78
Craig Gdns. E18—9D 30
Craigholm. SE18—1L 95
Craigmuir Pk. Wemb—4K 55
Craignair Rd. SW2—6L 91
Craignish Av. SW16—6K 107
Craig Pk. Rd. N18—5F 28
Craig Rd. Rich—1G 103
Craig's Ct. SW1—2J 75
Craigs Wlk. Wal X—1D 6
Craigton Rd. SE9—3K 95
Craigweil Clo. Stan—5H 23
Craigweil Dri. Stan—5H 23
Craigwell Av. Felt—9E 84
Crail Row. SE17—5B 76
Cramer St. W1—8E 58
Crammerville Wlk. Rain—7F 66
Cramond Clo. W6—7J 73
Crampton Rd. SE20—3G 109
Crampton St. SE17—5A 76
Cranberry Clo. N'holt—5H 53
Cranberry St. E1—7E 60
Cranborne Av. S'hall—5L 69
Cranborne Av. Surb—5L 119
Cranborne Gdns. Upm—7M 51
Cranborne Rd. N10—9F 26
Cranborne Rd. Bark—4B 64
Cranborne Rd. Wal X—5D 6
Cranborne Waye. Hay—9F 52
Cranbourne Av. E11—2F 46
Cranbourne Clo. SW16—7J 107
Cranbourne Dri. Pinn—3H 37
Cranbourne Gdns. NW11 —3J 41
Cranbourne Gdns. Ilf—1A 48
Cranbourne Rd. E12—1J 63
Cranbourne Rd. E15—9A 46
Cranbourne Rd. N'wd—1D 36
Cranbourn Pas. SE16—3F 76
Cranbourn St. WC2—1H 75
Cranbrook Clo. Brom—1E 126
Cranbrook Dri. Esh—3A 118
Cranbrook Dri. Romf—2G 51
Cranbrook Dri. Twic—7M 85
Cranbrook Est. E2—5H 61
Cranbrook M. E17—3K 45
Cranbrook Pk. N22—8L 27
Cranbrook Rise. Ilf—4K 47
Cranbrook Rd. SE3—2H 95
Cranbrook Rd. SE8—9L 77
Cranbrook Rd. SW19—4J 105
Cranbrook Rd. W4—6C 72

Cranbrook Rd. Barn—8B 14
Cranbrook Rd. Bexh—9K 81
Cranbrook Rd. Houn—3K 85
Cranbrook Rd. Ilf—5L 47
Cranbrook Rd. T Hth—6A 108
Cranbrook St. E2—5H 61
Cranbury Rd. SW6—1M 89
Crane Av. W3—1A 72
Crane Av. Iswth—4E 86
Cranebrook. Twic—8A 86
Crane Clo. Dag—2L 65
Crane Ct. EC4—9L 59
Crane Ct. Eps—6A 120
Cranefield Dri. Wat—5J 5
Craneford Clo. Twic—6D 86
Craneford Way. Twic—6C 86
Crane Gdns. Hay—5D 68
Crane Gro. N7—2L 59
Crane Lodge Rd. Houn—7F 68
Cranemead. SE16—5H 77
Crane Pk. Rd. Twic—8M 85
Crane Rd. Twic—7C 86
Cranes Dri. Surb—8J 103
Cranes Pk. Surb—8J 103
Cranes Pk. Av. Surb—8J 103
Cranes Pk. Cres. Surb—8K 103
Crane St. SE10—6B 78
Craneswater. Hay—8D 68
Craneswater Pk. S'hall—6K 69
Cranes Way. Borwd—7A 12
Crane Way. Twic—6A 86
Cranfield Clo. SE27—9A 92
Cranfield Dri. NW9—7C 24
Cranfield Rd. SE4—2K 93
Cranfield Rd. E. Cars—1E 136
Cranfield Rd. W. Cars—1E 136
Cranford Av. N13—5J 27
Cranford Av. Stai—6C 144
Cranford Clo. SW20—4F 104
Cranford Clo. Stai—6C 144
Cranford Dri. Hay—5D 68
Cranford La. Hay—7B 68
Cranford La. Houn—2D 84
(Hatton)
Cranford La. Houn—8F 68
(Heston)
Cranford Pk. Rd. Hay—5D 68
Cranford St. E1—1H 77
Cranford Way. N8—2K 43
Cranhurst Rd. NW2—1G 57
Cranleigh Clo. SE20—6F 108
Cranleigh Clo. Bex—5M 99
Cranleigh Clo. Orp—5E 128
Cranleigh Clo. S Croy—4E 138
Cranleigh Dri. Swan—8C 114
Cranleigh Gdns. N21—7L 15
Cranleigh Gdns. SE25—7C 108
Cranleigh Gdns. Bark—3B 64
Cranleigh Gdns. Harr—3J 39
Cranleigh Gdns. King—3K 103
Cranleigh Gdns. Lou—8K 19
Cranleigh Gdns. S'hall—9K 53
Cranleigh Gdns. S Croy
Cranleigh Gdns. Sutt—4M 121
Cranleigh Rd. N15—3A 44
Cranleigh Rd. SW19—7L 105
Cranleigh Rd. Esh—3A 118
Cranleigh Rd. Felt—1D 100
Cranleigh St. NW1—5G 59
Cranley Dene Ct. N10—2F 42
Cranley Dri. Ilf—5A 48
Cranley Dri. Ruis—7D 36
Cranley Gdns. N10—2F 42
Cranley Gdns. N13—3K 27
Cranley Gdns. SW7—6A 74
Cranley Gdns. Wall—9G 123
Cranley M. SW7—6A 74
Cranley Pl. SW7—5B 74
Cranley Rd. E13—8F 62
Cranley Rd. Ilf—4A 48
Cranley Rd. W on T—7D 116
Cranmer Av. W13—4F 70
Cranmer Clo. Mord—1H 121
Cranmer Clo. Ruis—6H 37
Cranmer Clo. Stan—7G 23
Cranmer Clo. Warl—9J 139
Cranmer Ct. SW3—5C 74
Cranmer Ct. SW4—2H 91
Cranmer Farm Clo. Mitc
—8D 106
Cranmer Gdns. Dag—9A 50
Cranmer Gdns. Warl—9J 139
Cranmer Rd. E7—9F 46
Cranmer Rd. SW9—8L 75
Cranmer Rd. Croy—5M 123
Cranmer Rd. Edgw—3M 23
Cranmer Rd. Hmptn—2M 101
Cranmer Rd. King—2J 103
Cranmer Rd. Mitc—8D 106
Cranmer Ter. SW17—2B 106

Cranmore Av. Iswth—8A 70
Cranmore Rd. Brom—9D 94
Cranmore Rd. Chst—2K 111
Cranmore Way. N10—2G 43
Cranston Clo. Houn—1J 85
Cranston Clo. Uxb—7B 36
Cranston Est. N1—5B 60
Cranston Gdns. E4—6M 29
Cranston Pk. Av. Upm—9M 51
Cranston Rd. SE23—7J 93
Cranswick Rd. SE16—6F 76
Crantock Rd. SE6—8M 93
Cranwell Clo. E3—7M 61
Cranwell Rd. Houn—1F 144
Cranwich Av. N21—9B 16
Cranwich Rd. N16—5B 44
Cranwood St. EC1—6B 60
Cranworth Cres. E4—1B 30
Cranworth Gdns. SW9—9L 75
Craster Rd. SW2—6K 91
Crathie Rd. SE12—5F 94
Crathorn St. SE13—2A 94
Craven Av. W5—1G 71
Craven Av. S'hall—8K 53
Craven Clo. Hay—9E 52
Craven Gdns. SW19—2M 105
Craven Gdns. Bark—5C 64
Craven Gdns. Ilf—9B 32
Craven Gdns. Romf—5L 33
(Havering Park)
Craven Hill. W2—1A 74
Craven Hill Gdns. W2—1A 74
Craven Hill M. W2—1A 74
Craven M. SW11—2E 90
Craven Pk. NW10—4B 56
Craven Pk. M. NW10—4C 56
Craven Pk. Rd. N15—4D 44
Craven Pk. Rd. NW10—4C 56
Craven Rd. NW10—4B 56
Craven Rd. W2—9B 58
Craven Rd. W5—1G 71
Craven Rd. Croy—3F 124
Craven Rd. King—5k 103
Craven Rd. Orp—5H 129
Craven St. WC2—2J 75
Craven Ter. W2—1A 74
Craven Wlk. N16—5E 44
Crawford Av. Wemb—1H 55
Crawford Clo. Iswth—1C 86
Crawford Gdns. N13—3M 27
Crawford Gdns. N'holt—6K 53
Crawford M. W1—8D 58
Crawford Pas. EC1—7L 59
Crawford Pl. W1—9C 58
Crawford Rd. SE5—9A 76
Crawford St. W1—8D 58
Crawley Rd. E10—6M 45
Crawley Rd. N22—4A 28
Crawley Rd. Enf—9C 16
Crawshay Ct. SW9—9L 75
Crawthew Gro. SE22—3D 92
Cray Av Orp—1F 128
Craybrooke Rd. Sidc—1F 112
Craybury End. SE9—8A 96
Cray Clo. Dart—3E 98
Craydene Rd. Eri—9D 82
Cray Av. Asht—8J 133
Crayford High St. Dart—4C 98
Crayford Rd. N7—9J 43
Crayford Rd. Dart—4D 98
Crayford Way. Dart—4D 98
Crayke Hill. Chess—9J 119
Craylands. Orp—7G 113
Craymill Sq. Dart—1D 98
Crayonne Clo. Sun—5C 100
Cray Rd. Belv—7L 81
Cray Rd. Sidc—3G 113
Cray Rd. Swan—1A 130
Crayside Industrial Est. Dart
—3F 98
Cray Valley Rd. Orp—9E 112
Crealock Gro. Wfd G—5D 30
Crealock St. SW18—5M 89
Creasy St. SE1—4C 76
Crebor St. SE22—5E 92
Credenhall Dri. Brom—3K 127
Credenhill St. SW16—3G 107
Credenhill Way. SE15—8F 76
Crediton Hill. NW6—1M 57
Crediton Rd. E16—9E 62
Crediton Rd. NW10—4H 57
Crediton Way. Esh—7E 118
Credon Rd. E13—5G 63
Credon Rd. SE16—6F 76
Creechurch La. EC3—9C 60
Creed La. EC4—9M 59
Creek Rd. E9—2G 61
Creek Rd. SE8 1-201 & 2-194
SE10 remainder
Creek Rd. Bark—6D 64
Creek Rd. E Mol—8C 102
Creekside. SE8—8M 77

Creekside. Rain—7D 66
Creek, The. Sun—9E 100
Creeland Gro. SE6—7K 93
Cree Way. Romf—7C 34
Crefeld Clo. W6—7J 73
Creffield Rd.—1K 71
W5 1-51 & 2-56
W3 remainder
Creighton Av. E6—5H 63
Creighton Av. N2 & N10
N2 1-42
N10 1-79 & 2-78
N2 remainder
Creighton Rd. N17—7C 28
Creighton Rd. NW6—5H 57
Creighton Rd. W5—4H 71
Cremer St. E2—5D 60
Cremorne Gdns. Eps—2B 134
Cremorne Rd. SW10—8B 74
Crescent Av. Horn—7D 50
Crescent Ct. Surb—9H 103
Crescent Dri. Orp—1M 127
Crescent E. Barn—2A 14
Crescent Gdns. SW19—9L 89
Crescent Gdns. Ruis—5F 36
Crescent Gdns. Swan—6A 114
Crescent Gro. SW4—3G 91
Crescent Gro. Mitc—9C 106
Crescent La. SW4—3G 91
Crescent Pl. SW3—5C 74
Crescent Rise. N22—8H 27
Crescent Rise. Barn—7C 14
Crescent Rd. E4—9C 18
Crescent Rd. E6—4G 63
Crescent Rd. E10—7M 45
Crescent Rd. E13—4E 62
Crescent Rd. E18—8G 31
Crescent Rd. N3—8K 25
Crescent Rd. N8—4H 43
Crescent Rd. N9—1F 28
Crescent Rd. N11—4D 26
Crescent Rd. N15—1M 43
Crescent Rd. N22—8H 27
Crescent Rd. SE18—6M 79
Crescent Rd. SW20—5M 105
Crescent Rd. Barn—6B 14
Crescent Rd. Beck—6M 109
Crescent Rd. Brom—4E 110
Crescent Rd. Dag—8M 49
Crescent Rd. Enf—6M 15
Crescent Rd. Eri—7D 82
Crescent Rd. King—4L 103
Crescent Rd. Shep—9A 100
Crescent Rd. Sidc—9D 96
Crescent Rd. S Ock—3M 83
Crescent Row. EC1—7A 60
Crescent St. N1—3K 59
Crescent, The. E17—3J 45
Crescent, The. N11—4E 26
Crescent, The. NW2—8F 40
Crescent, The. SW13—1E 88
Crescent, The. SW19—9L 89
Crescent, The. W3—9C 56
Crescent, The. Abb L, Wat—3D 4
Crescent, The. Barn—4M 13
Crescent, The. Beck—5L 109
Crescent, The. Bex—6G 97
Crescent, The. Croy—1D 124
Crescent, The. E Mol—8L 101
Crescent, The. Eps—6L 133
(in two parts)
Crescent, The. Harr—6A 38
Crescent, The. Hay—8B 68
Crescent, The. Ilf—4L 47
Crescent, The. Lou—8J 19
Crescent, The. N Mald—6D 104
Crescent, The. St Alb—3L 5
Crescent, The. Shep—2D 116
Crescent, The. Sidc—1D 112
Crescent, The. S'hall—3K 69
Crescent, The. Surb—9J 103
Crescent, The. Sutt—7B 122
Crescent, The. Sutt—3L 135
(Belmont)
Crescent, The. Wat—6G 9
Crescent, The. Wat—2M 9
(Aldenham)
Crescent, The. Wemb—7F 38
Crescent, The. W Wick—1C 126
Crescent View. Lou—8H 19
Crescent Way. N12—6C 26
Crescent Way. SE4—2L 93
Crescent Way. SW16—4K 107
Crescent Way. Orp—7C 128
Crescent W. Barn—2A 14
Crescent Wood Rd. SE26
—9E 92
Cresford Rd. SW6—9M 73
Crespigny Rd. NW4—4F 40
Cressage Clo. S'hall—7L 53
Cresset Rd. E9—2G 61
Cresset St. SW4—2H 91
Cressfield Clo. NW5—1E 58
Cressida Rd. N19—6G 43

Cressingham Gdns. Est. SW2
—6L 91
Cressingham Gro. Sutt
—6A 122
Cressingham Rd. SE13—2A 94
Cressingham Rd. Edgw—6B 24
Cresswell Gdns. SW5—6A 74
Cresswell Pk. SE3—2D 94
Cresswell Pl. SW10—6A 74
Cresswell Rd. SE25—8E 108
Cresswell Rd. Felt—9J 85
Cresswell Rd. Twic—5H 87
Cresswell Way. N21—9L 15
Cressy Ct. E1—8G 61
Cressy Pl. E1—8G 61
Cressy Rd. NW3—1D 58
Crestbrook Av. N13—3M 27
Crest Dri. Enf—2G 17
Crestfield St. WC1—6J 59
Crest Gdns. Ruis—8G 37
Creston Way. Wor Pk—3H 121
Crest Rd. NW2—7E 40
Crest Rd. Brom—2D 126
Crest Rd. S Croy—9F 124
Crest, The. N13—4L 27
Crest, The. NW4—3G 41
Crest, The. Surb—9J 103
Crest View. Pinn—2H 37
Crest View Dri. Orp—9M 111
Crestway. SW15—5E 88
Creswick Rd. W3—1M 71
Creswick Wlk. E3—6L 61
Creswick Wlk. NW11—2K 41
Creton St. SE18—4L 79
Crewdson Rd. SW9—8L 75
Crewe Pl. NW10—6D 56
Crewe's Av. Warl—8G 139
Crewe's Clo. Warl—9G 139
Crewe's Farm La. Warl
—9H 139
Crews St. E14—5L 77
Crewys Rd. NW2—7K 41
Crewys Rd. SE15—1F 92
Crichton Av. Wall—7H 123
Crichton Gdns. Romf—5K 49
Crichton Rd. Cars—9D 122
Cricketers Arms Rd. Enf
—4A 16
Cricketers Clo. Chess—6H 119
Cricketfield Rd. E5—9F 44
Cricket Field Rd. Uxb—4B 142
Cricketfield Rd. W Dray
—5G 143
Cricket.Grn. Mitc—8D 106
Cricket Ground Rd. Chst
—5M 111
Cricket Way. Wey—4C 116
Cricklade Av. SW2—8J 91
Cricklade Av. Romf—6H 35
Cricklewood B'way. NW2
—8H 41
Cricklewood La. NW2—9H 41
Cricklewood Trading Est. NW2
—8J 41
Cridland St. E15—4D 62
Crieff Ct. Tedd—4G 103
Crieff Rd. SW18—5A 90
Criffel Av. SW2—8H 91
Crimscott St. SE1—4C 76
Crimsworth Rd. SW8—8H 75
Crinan St. N1—5J 59
Cringle St. SW8—8G 75
Cripplegate St. EC2—8A 60
Cripps Grn. Hay—7F 52
Crispen Rd. Felt—1J 101
Crispian Clo. NW10—9C 40
Crispin Clo. Asht—9K 133
Crispin Clo. Croy—4J 123
Crispin Cres. Croy—5H 123
Crispin Rd. Edgw—6A 24
Crispin St. E1—8D 60
Crisp Rd. W6—6G 73
Cristowe Rd. SW6—1K 89
Criterion M. N19—7H 43
Crockenhill La. Swan & Eyns,
Dart—2E 130
Crockenhill Rd. Orp & Swan
—9H 113
Crockerton Rd. SW17—8D 90
Crockham Way. SE9—1L 111
Crocus Clo. Croy—3H 125
Crocus Field. Barn—8K 13
Crocus Wlk. W12—9D 56
Croft Av. W Wick—3A 126
Croft Clo. NW7—3C 24
Croft Clo. Belv—6K 81
Croft Clo. Chst—2K 111
Croft Clo. Hay—4A 68
Croft Clo. Uxb—3E 142
Croftdown Rd. NW5—8E 42
Crofters Clo. Iswth—4B 86
Crofters Mead. Croy—1K 139

Crofters Rd. N'wd—4C 20
Crofters Way. NW1—4H 59
Croft Gdns. Ruis—6D 36
Croft Gdns. W7—3E 70
Croftleigh Av. Purl—8M 137
Croft Lodge Clo. Wfd G—6F 30
Crofton Av. Bex—6H 97
Crofton Av. Croy—4A 128
Crofton Av. W on T—5G 117
Crofton La. Orp—3B 128
Crofton Pk. Rd. SE4—5K 93
Crofton Rd. E13—7F 62
Crofton Rd. SE5—9C 76
Crofton Rd. Orp—5L 127
Crofton Ter. E5—1J 61
Crofton Ter. Rich—3K 87
Crofton Way. Barn—8M 13
Crofton Way. Enf—4L 15
Croft Rd. SW16—5L 107
Croft Rd. SW19—4A 106
Croft Rd. Brom—3E 110
Croft Rd. Enf—3J 17
Croft Rd. Sutt—7C 122
Crofts Rd. Harr—4E 38
Crofts St. E1—1E 76
Crofts, The. Shep—8C 100
Croft St. SE8—5J 77
Croft, The. NW10—5D 56
Croft, The. W5—8J 55
Croft, The. Barn—6J 13
Croft, The. Houn—8J 69
Croft, The. Lou—4L 19
Croft, The. Pinn—5K 37
Croft, The. Ruis—9G 37
Croft, The. Swan—7A 114
Croft, The. Wemb—1G 55
Croftway. NW3—9L 41
Croftway. Rich—8F 86
Croft Way. Sidc—9C 96
Crogsland Rd. NW1—3E 58
Croham Clo. S Croy—8C 124
Croham Mnr. Rd. S Croy
—9C 124
Croham Mt. S Croy—9C 124
Croham Pk. Av. S Croy—7D 124
Croham Rd. S Croy—7B 124
Croham Valley Rd. S Croy
—8E 124
Croindene Rd. SW16—5J 107
Cromartie Rd. N19—5H 43
Crombie Clo. Ilf—3K 47
Crombie Rd. Sidc—7B 96
Cromer Clo. Uxb—9A 52
Cromer Pl. Orp—3B 128
Cromer Rd. E10—5B 46
Cromer Rd. N17—9E 28
Cromer Rd. SE25—7F 108
Cromer Rd. SW17—3E 106
Cromer Rd. Barn—6A 14
Cromer Rd. Horn—5H 51
Cromer Rd. Houn—1E 144
Cromer Rd. Romf—4A 50
Cromer Rd. Romf—4J 49
(Chadwell Heath)
Cromer Rd. Wat—2G 9
Cromer Rd. Wfd G—4E 30
Cromer Rd. W. Houn—2E 144
Cromer St. WC1—6J 59
Cromer Ter. E8—1E 60
Cromer Vs. Rd. SW18—5K 89
Cromford Clo. Orp—5C 128
Cromford Path. E5—9H 45
Cromford Rd. SW18—4L 89
Cromford Way. N Mald
—5B 104
Cromlix Clo. Chst—6M 111
Crompton St. W2—7B 58
Cromwell Av. N6—6F 42
Cromwell Av. Brom—8F 110
Cromwell Av. N Mald—9D 104
Cromwell Av. Wal X—3B 6
Cromwell Clo. N2—2B 42
Cromwell Clo. Brom—8F 110
Cromwell Clo. W on T—3F 116
Cromwell Cres. SW5—5L 73
Cromwell Gdns. SW7—4B 74
Cromwell Gro. W6—4G 73
Cromwell La. W6—6F 72
Cromwell M. SW7—5B 74
Cromwell Pl. N6—6F 42
Cromwell Pl. SW7—5B 74
Cromwell Pl. SW14—2A 88
Cromwell Rd. E7—3G 63
Cromwell Rd. E17—3A 46
Cromwell Rd. N3—8A 26
Cromwell Rd. N10—7E 26
(in two parts)
Cromwell Rd.—5M 73
SW7 1-147 & 2-156
SW5 remainder
Cromwell Rd. SW9—9M 75
Cromwell Rd. SW19—2L 105
Cromwell Rd. Beck—6J 109

Cromwell Rd. Borwd—3J 11
Cromwell Rd. Croy—2B 124
Cromwell Rd. Felt—7F 84
Cromwell Rd. Hay—9B 52
Cromwell Rd. Houn—3L 85
Cromwell Rd. King—5J 103
Cromwell Rd. Tedd—3E 102
Cromwell Rd. Wal X—1B 6
Cromwell Rd. W on T—3F 116
Cromwell Rd. Wemb—5J 55
Cromwell Rd. Wor Pk—5B 120
Cromwells Mere. Romf
　　　　　　　　—6B 34
Cromwell St. Houn—3L 85
Crondace Rd. SW6—9K 73
Crondall St. N1—5C 60
Crooked Billet. SW19—3G 105
Crooked Billet Yd. E2—6C 60
Crooked Mile. Wal A—3J 7
Crooked Usage. N3—1J 41
Crooke Rd. SE8—6J 77
Crookham Rd. SW6—9K 73
Crook Log. Bexh—2H 97
Crookston Rd. SE9—2L 95
Croombs Rd. E16—8G 63
Croom's Hill. SE10—8A 78
Croom's Hill Gro. SE10—8A 78
Cropath Rd. Dag—9L 49
Cropley St. N1—5B 60
Crosby Clo. Felt—9J 85
Crosby Ct. Chig—3E 32
Crosby Rd. E7—2E 62
Crosby Rd. Dag—5M 65
Crosby Row. SE1—3B 76
Crosby Sq. EC3—9C 60
Crosby Wlk. E8—2D 60
Crosby Wlk. SW2—6L 91
Crosier Rd. Uxb—9A 36
Crosier Way. Ruis—8C 3b
Cross Av. SE10—7C 78
Crossbow Rd. Chig—5D 32
Crossbrook Rd. SE3—2J 95
Crossbrook St. Wal X—4D 6
Cross Deep. Twic—8D 86
Cross Deep Gdns. Twic—8D 86
Crossfield Rd. N17—1A 44
Crossfield Rd. NW3—2B 58
Crossfields. Lou—7M 19
Crossfield St. SE8—8L 77
Crossford St. SW9—1K 91
Cross Ga. Edgw—3L 23
Crossgate. Gnfd—2F 54
Crossharbour. E14—4M 77
Cross Keys Clo. W1—8E 58
Cross Keys Ct. EC2—9B 60
Cross Lances Rd. Houn—3M 85
Crossland Rd. T Hth—1M 123
Crosslands Av. W5—2K 71
Crosslands Av. S'hall—6K 69
Crosslands Rd. Eps—8B 120
Cross La. EC3—1C 76
Cross La. N8—1K 43
(in two parts)
Cross La. Bex—6K 97
Crosslet St. SE17—5B 76
Crossley Clo. West—7H 141
Crossley St. N7—2L 59
Crossmead. SE9—7K 95
Crossmead. Wat—8F 8
Crossmead Av. Gnfd—6L 53
Crossness Footpath. Eri
　　　　　　　—3K 81
Crossness Rd. Bark—6D 64
Cross Rd. E4—1C 30
Cross Rd. N8—1J 43
Cross Rd. N11—5F 26
Cross Rd. N22—7L 27
Cross Rd. SE5—1C 92
Cross Rd. SW19—4L 105
Cross Rd. Brom—4J 127
Cross Rd. Croy—3B 124
Cross Rd. Dart—5G 99
Cross Rd. Dart—1K 115
(Hawley)
Cross Rd. Enf—6C 16
Cross Rd. Felt—1J 101
Cross Rd. Harr—2B 38
(Headstone)
Cross Rd. Harr—8M 37
(South Harrow)
Cross Rd. King—4K 103
Cross Rd. Orp—9F 112
Cross Rd. Purl—5M 137
Cross Rd. Romf—1L 49
Cross Rd. Romf—5G 49
(Chadwell Heath)
Cross Rd. Sidc—1F 112
Cross Rd. Stan—9E 22
Cross Rd. Sutt—7B 122
Cross Rd. Sutt—2L 135
(Belmont)
Cross Rd. Wal X—6E 6
Cross Rd. Wat—8J 9

Cross Rd. Wey—5B 116
Cross Rd. Wfd G—6K 31
Cross Roads. Lou—4F 18
Cross St. N1—4M 59
Cross St. N18—5E 28
Cross St. SW13—1C 88
Cross St. Eri—7C 82
Cross St. Hmptn—2A 102
Cross St. Uxb—3A 142
Cross St. Wat—5G 9
Crossthwaite Av. SE5—3B 92
Crosswall. EC3—1D 76
Crossway. N12—6B 26
Crossway. N16—1C 60
Crossway. NW9—2D 40
Cross Way. SE28—1G 81
Crossway. SW20—8G 105
Crossway. W13—7E 54
Crossway. Dag—8G 49
Crossway. Enf—9C 16
Crossway. Hay—2E 68
Crossway. Orp—8B 112
Cross Way. Pinn—9F 20
Crossway. Ruis—9G 37
Crossway. W on T—4F 116
Cross Way. Wfd G—4G 31
Crossways. N21—8A 16
Crossways. Romf—1F 50
Crossways. S Croy—9J 125
Crossways. Sun—4D 100
Crossways. Sutt—1B 136
Crossways Rd. Beck—8L 109
Crossways Rd. Mitc—7F 106
Crossways, The. Houn—8K 69
Crossways, The. Surb—3M 119
Crossways, The. Wemb—7L 39
Crossway, The. N22—7M 27
Crossway, The. SE9—8H 95
Cross Way, The. Harr—9C 22
Crossway, The. Uxb—5D 142
Crosswell Clo. Shep—6A 100
Croston Rd. E8—4E 60
Crouch Av. Bark—5F 64
Crouch Clo. Beck—3L 109
Crouch Croft. SE9—9L 95
Crouch End Hill. N8—5H 43
Crouch Hall Rd. N8—4H 43
Crouch Hill—4J 43
N4 1-75 & 2-58
N8 remainder
Crouchman's Clo. SE26—9D 92
Crouch Rd. NW10—3B 56
Crowborough Clo. Warl
　　　　　　　—9J 139
Crowborough Dri. Warl
　　　　　　　—9J 139
Crowborough Path. Wat
　　　　　　　—4H 21
Crowborough Rd. SW17
　　　　　　　—3E 106
Crowden Way. SE28—1G 81
Crowder St. E1—1F 76
Crowhurst Clo. SW9—1L 91
Crowhurst Way. Orp—9G 113
Crowland Av. Hay—5C 68
Crowland Gdns. N14—9J 15
Crowland Rd. N15—3D 44
Crowland Rd. T Hth—8B 108
Crowlands Av. Romf—4M 49
Crowland Ter. N1—3B 60
Crowland Wlk. Mord—1A 122
Crow La. Romf—5K 49
Crowley Cres. Croy—7L 123
Crowlin Wlk. N1—2B 60
Crown Arc. King—6H 103
Crown Ash Hill. West—6F 140
Crown Ash La. Warl & West
　　　　　　　—8E 140
Crown Clo. E3—4L 61
Crown Clo. NW6—2M 57
Crown Clo. NW7—2D 24
Crown Clo. Hay—3D 68
Crown Clo. Orp—7E 128
Crown Clo. W on T—2G 117
Crown Ct. SE12—5F 94
Crown Ct. WC2—9J 59
Crown Dale. SE19—3M 107
Crowndale Rd. NW1—5G 59
Crownfield Av. Ilf—4C 48
Crownfield Rd. E15—9B 46
Crown Hill. Croy—4A 124
Crown Hill Rd. NW10—4D 56
Crownhill Rd. Wfd G—7J 31
Crown La. N14—1G 27
Crown La. SW16—2L 107
Crown La. Brom—9H 111
Crown La. Chst—5A 112
Crown La. Mord—8L 105
Crown La. Gdns. SW16—2L 107
Crown La. Spur. Brom—1H 127
Crownmead Way. Romf
　　　　　　　—2M 49
Crown Office Row. EC4—1L 75

Crown Pas. SW1—2G 75
Crown Pas. Wat—6G 9
Crown Pl. NW5—2F 58
Crown Rise. Wat—7G 5
Crown Rd. N10—7E 26
Crown Rd. Borwd—3L 11
Crown Rd. Enf—6F 16
Crown Rd. Ilf—2B 48
Crown Rd. Mord—8M 105
Crown Rd. N Mald—5A 104
Crown Rd. Orp—7E 128
Crown Rd. Sutt—6M 121
Crown Rd. Twic—5F 86
Crownstone Rd. SW2—4L 91
Crown St. SE5—8A 76
Crown St. W3—2M 71
Crown St. Dag—2A 66
(in two parts)
Crown St. Harr—6B 38
Crown Ter. Rich—3K 87
Crowntree Clo. Iswth—7D 70
Crown Wlk. Uxb—3A 142
Crown Wlk. Wemb—8K 39
Crown Way. W Dray—2K 143
Crown Woods La. SE18—1M 95
Crown Woods Way. SE9
　　　　　　　—4B 96
Crowshott Av. Stan—9G 23
Crows Rd. E15—6B 62
Crowther Av. Bren—5J 71
Crowther Rd. SE25—8E 108
Crowthorne Clo. SW18—7K 89
Crowthorne Rd. W10—9H 57
Croxdale Rd. Borwd—4K 11
Croxden Clo. Edgw—1L 39
Croxden Wlk. Mord—1A 122
Croxford Gdns. N22—7M 27
Croxford Way. Romf—6B 50
Croxley Clo. Orp—6F 112
Croxley Grn. Orp—5F 112
Croxley Rd. W9—6K 57
Croxley View. Wat—8C 8
Croxted Clo. SE21—6A 92
Croxted Rd.—6A 92
　　SE21 1-293 & 2-198
　　SE24 remainder
Croyde Av. Gnfd—6A 54
Croyde Av. Hay—5C 68
Croyde Clo. Sidc—6B 96
Croydon Flyover, The. Croy
　　　　　　　—5A 124
Croydon Gro. Croy—3M 123
Croydon La. Bans—6A 136
Croydon Rd. E13—7D 62
Croydon Rd. SE20—6F 108
Croydon Rd. Beck—8H 109
Croydon Rd. Houn—1F 144
Croydon Rd. Mitc—8E 106
Croydon Rd. Wall & Croy
　　　　　　　—6F 122
Croydon Rd. W Wick, Brom, Kes
　　　　& Orp—5C 126
Croyland Rd. N9—1E 28
Croylands Dri. Surb—2J 119
Croysdale Av. Sun—7E 100
Crozier Dri. S Croy—2F 138
Crozier Ter. E9—1H 61
Crucifix La. SE1—3C 76
Cruden St. N1—4M 59
Cruikshank Rd. E15—9C 46
Cruikshank St. WC1—6L 59
Crummock Gdns. NW9—3C 40
Crumpsall St. SE2—5G 81
Crundale Av. NW9—3L 39
Crunden Rd. S Croy—9B 124
Crusader Clo. Purf—5L 83
Crusader Gdns. Croy—5C 124
Crusoe Rd. Eri—6B 82
Crusoe Rd. Mitc—4D 106
Crutched Friars. EC3—1C 76
Crutchfield La. W on T—4F 116
Crutchley Rd. SE6—8C 94
Crystal Av. Horn—9J 51
Crystal Pal. Pde. SE19—3D 108
Crystal Pal. Pk. Rd. SE26
　　　　　　　—2E 108
Crystal Pal. Rd. SE22—5D 92
Crystal Pal. Sta. Rd. SE19
　　　　　　　—3E 108
Crystal Ter. SE19—3B 108
Crystal Way. Harr—3D 38
Cuba Dri. Enf—4G 17
Cuba St. E14—3L 77
Cubitt St. WC1—6K 59
Cubitt St. Croy—7K 123
Cubitt Ter. SW4—2G 91
Cuckoo Av. W7—7C 54
Cuckoo Dene. W7—8B 54
Cuckoo Hall La. N9—9G 17
Cuckoo Hill. Pinn—1G 37
Cuckoo Hill Dri. Pinn—1G 37
Cuckoo Hill Rd. Pinn—2G 37
Cuckoo La. W7—1C 70

Cuckoo Pound. Shep—9C 100
Cudas Clo. Eps—6D 120
Cuddington Av. Wor Pk
　　　　　　　—5D 120
Cuddington Way. Sutt—4H 135
Cudham La. N. Sev & Orp
　　　　　　　—9C 128
Cudham Rd. Orp—3L 141
Cudham St. SE6—6A 94
Cudworth St. E1—7F 60
Cuff Cres. SE9—5H 95
Cuffley Av. Wat—7H 5
Culford Gdns. SW3—5D 74
Culford Gro. N1—2C 60
Culford M. N1—2C 60
Culford Rd. N1—3C 60
(in two parts)
Culgaith Gdns. Enf—6J 15
Cullen Way. NW10—7A 56
Cullera Clo. N'wd—6D 20
Cullesden Rd. Kenl—7M 137
Culling Rd. SE16—4G 77
Cullings Ct. Wal A—6M 7
Cullington Clo. Harr—2E 38
Cullingworth Rd. NW10—1F 56
Culloden Rd. Enf—4M 15
Culloden St. E14—9A 62
Cullum St. EC3—1C 76
Culmington Rd. W13—2G 71
Culmington Rd. S Croy—1A 138
Culmore Cross. SW12—7F 90
Culmore Rd. SE15—8G 77
Culmstock Rd. SW11—4E 90
Culpeper Clo. Ilf—6M 31
Culpeper St. N1—5L 59
Culross Clo. N15—2A 44
Culross St. W1—1E 74
Culsac Rd. Surb—4J 119
Culverden Rd. SW12—8G 91
Culverden Rd. Wat—3F 20
Culver Gro. Stan—9G 23
Culverhay. Asht—8J 133
Culverhouse Gdns. SW16
　　　　　　　—9K 91
Culverlands Clo. Stan—4F 22
Culverley Rd. SE6—7M 93
Culvers Av. Cars & Wall
　　　　　　　—4D 122
Culvers Retreat. Cars—4D 122
Culverstone Clo. Brom—1D 126
Culvers Way. Cars—4D 122
Culvert La. Uxb—5A 142
Culvert Pl. SW11—1E 90
Culvert Rd. N15—3C 44
Culvert Rd. SW11—1D 90
(in two parts)
Culworth St. NW8—5C 58
Cumberland Av. NW10—6M 55
Cumberland Av. Horn—8J 51
Cumberland Av. Well—2C 96
Cumberland Clo. E8—2D 60
Cumberland Clo. SW20
　　　　　　　—4H 105
Cumberland Clo. Eps—2C 134
Cumberland Clo. Horn—8J 51
Cumberland Clo. Twic—5F 86
Cumberland Cres. W14—5J 73
Cumberland Dri. Chess
　　　　　　　—5K 119
Cumberland Dri. Dart—6K 99
Cumberland Dri. Esh—4E 118
Cumberland Gdns. NW4—9H 25
Cumberland Gdns. WC1—6L 59
Cumberland Ga. W2 & W1
　　　　　　　—1D 74
Cumberland Ho. King—4M 103
Cumberland Mkt. NW1—6F 58
Cumberland Pk. W3—1A 72
Cumberland Pl. NW1—6F 58
Cumberland Pl. Sun—8E 100
Cumberland Rd. E12—9H 47
Cumberland Rd. E13—8F 62
Cumberland Rd. E17—9J 29
Cumberland Rd. N9—1G 29
Cumberland Rd. N22—9K 27
Cumberland Rd. SE25—1F 124
Cumberland Rd. SW13—9D 72
Cumberland Rd. W3—1A 72
Cumberland Rd. W7—3D 70
Cumberland Rd. Ashf—9B 144
Cumberland Rd. Brom—8C 110
Cumberland Rd. Harr—3M 37
Cumberland Rd. Rich—8L 71
Cumberland Rd. Stan—1K 39
Cumberlands. Kenl—7B 138
Cumberland St. SW1—6F 74
Cumberland Ter. NW1—5E 58
Cumberlow Av. SE25—7D 108
Cumbernauld Gdns. Sun
　　　　　　　—2D 100
Cumberton Rd. N17—8B 28
Cumbrae Gdns. Surb—4H 119

Cumbria Ct. Felt—6F 84
Cumbrian Av. Bexh—1C 98
Cumbrian Gdns. NW2—7H 41
Cumbrian Way. Uxb—3B 142
Cummings Hall La. Romf
　　　　　　　—3G 35
Cumming St. N1—5K 59
Cumnor Gdns. Eps—8E 120
Cumnor Rise. Kenl—9A 138
Cumnor Rd. Sutt—8A 122
Cunard Rd. NW10—6B 56
Cundy Rd. E16—9G 63
Cundy St. SW1—5E 74
Cunliffe Rd. Wor Pk—6D 120
Cunliffe St. SW16—3G 107
Cunningham Av. Enf—9E 6
Cunningham Clo. W Wick
　　　　　　　—4M 125
Cunningham Pk. Harr—3A 38
Cunningham Pl. NW8—7B 58
Cunningham Rd. N15—2E 44
Cunningham Rd. Bans—7B 136
Cunningham Rd. Wal X—1E 6
Cunnington St. W4—5A 72
Cupar Rd. SW11—9E 74
Cupola Clo. Brom—2F 110
Cureton St. SW1—6H 75
Curlew Clo. SE28—1H 81
Curlew Clo. S Croy—3H 139
Curlew St. SE1—3D 76
Curnick's La. SE27—1A 108
Curran Av. Sidc—4D 96
Curran Av. Wall—5E 122
Curran Clo. Uxb—7A 142
Currey Rd. Gnfd—2B 54
Curricle St. W3—2C 72
Currie Hill Clo. SW19—1K 105
Curry Rise. NW7—6H 25
Cursitor St. EC4—9L 59
Curtain Rd. EC2—7C 60
Curthwaite Gdns. Enf—6H 15
Curtis Field Rd. SW16—1K 107
Curtismill Clo. Orp—7F 112
Curtismill Way. Orp—7F 112
Curtis Rd. Eps—6A 120
Curtis Rd. Horn—6K 51
Curtis Rd. Houn—6K 85
Curtis St. SE1—5D 76
Curtis Way. SE1—5D 76
Curtis Way. SE28—1F 80
Curvan Clo. Eps—2D 134
Curve, The. W12—1E 72
Curwen Av. E7—9F 46
Curwen Rd. W12—3E 72
Curzon Av. Enf—7H 17
Curzon Av. Stan—8E 22
Curzon Clo. Orp—6B 128
Curzon Cres. NW10—3C 56
Curzon Cres. Bark—6D 64
Curzon Ga. W1—2E 74
Curzon Pl. W1—2E 74
Curzon Pl. Pinn—3G 37
Curzon Rd. N10—9F 26
Curzon Rd. W5—7F 54
Curzon Rd. T Hth—1L 123
Curzon St. W1—2F 74
Cusack Clo. Twic—1D 102
Cussons Clo. Wal X—2A 6
Cutcombe Rd. SE5—1A 92
Cuthbert Rd. E17—1A 46
Cuthbert Rd. N18—5E 28
Cuthbert Rd. Croy—4M 123
Cuthbert St. W2—7B 58
Cuthill Wlk. SE5—9B 76
Cutler St. E1—9C 60
Cut, The. SE1—3M 75
Cutthroat All. Rich—8G 87
Cuxton Clo. Bexh—4J 97
Cyclamen Clo. Hmptn—3L 101
Cyclamen Rd. Swan—8B 114
Cyclamen Way. Eps—7A 120
Cygnet Av. Felt—6G 85
Cygnet Clo. NW10—9A 40
Cygnet Clo. N'wd—6A 20
Cygnets, The. Felt—1J 101
Cygnet St. E1—7D 60
Cynthia St. N1—5K 59
Cypress Av. Twic—6A 86
Cypress Clo. Wal A—7K 7
Cypress Gro. Ilf—6C 32
Cypress Path. Romf—7H 35
Cypress Pl. W1—7G 59
Cypress Rd. SE25—6C 108
Cypress Rd. Harr—9B 22
Cypress Rd. Sun—5C 100
Cypress Way. Bans—6H 135
Cyprus Av. N3—9J 25
Cyprus By-Pass. E6 & E16
　　　　　　　—9L 63
Cyprus Gdns. N3—9J 25
Cyprus Pl. E2—5G 61
Cyprus Pl. E6—1L 79
Cyprus Rd. N3—9K 25
Cyprus Rd. N9—2D 28

Debenham Rd. Wal X—1B 6
Debnams Rd. SE16—5G 77
De Bohun Av. N14—8F 14
Deborah Clo. Iswth—9C 70
Debrabant Clo. Eri—7B 82
De Burgh Pk. Bans—8M 135
De Burgh Rd. SW19—4A 106
Decima St. SE1—4C 76
Decoy Av. NW11—3J 41
De Crespigny Pk. SE5—1B 92
Deeley Rd. SW8—9H 75
Deena Clo. W3—9K 55
Deepdale. SW19—1H 105
Deepdale Av. Brom—8D 110
Deepdene. W5—7K 55
Deepdene Av. Croy—5D 124
Deepdene Clo. E11—2E 46
Deepdene Ct. N21—8M 15
Deepdene Gdns. SW2—6K 91
Deepdene Path. Lou—6M 19
(in two parts)
Deepdene Rd. SE5—3B 92
Deepdene Rd. Lou—6L 19
Deepdene Rd. Well—2E 96
Deepfield Way. Coul—8J 137
Deepwell Clo. Iswth—9E 70
Deepwood La. Gnfd—6B 54
Deerbrook Rd. SE24—7M 91
Deerdale Rd. SE24—3A 92
Deere Av. Rain—2E 66
Deerfield Cotts. NW9—3D 40
Deerhurst Rd. NW2—2H 57
Deerhurst Rd. SW16—2K 107
Deerleap Gro. E4—7M 17
Dee Rd. Rich—3K 87
Deer Pk. Clo. King—4M 103
Deer Pk. Gdns. Mitc—8B 106
Deer Pk. Rd. SW19—6M 105
Deeside Rd. SW17—9B 90
Dee St. E14—9A 62
Dee Way. Eps—2C 134
Dee Way. Romf—7C 34
Defiance Wlk. SE18—4K 79
Defiant Way. Wall—9J 123
Defoe Av. Rich—8L 71
Defoe Clo. SW17—3C 106
Defoe Rd. N16—8C 44
Defoe Way. Romf—6L 33
De Frene Rd. SE26—1H 109
Degema Rd. Chst—2M 111
Dehar Cres. NW9—5D 40
De Havilland Rd. Edgw—9M 23
De Havilland Rd. Houn—8G 69
De Havilland Rd. Wall—9J 123
De Havilland Way. Stai
—5C 144
Dekker Rd. SE21—5C 92
Delacourt Rd. SE3—8F 78
Delafield Rd. SE7—6F 78
Delaford Rd. SE16—6F 76
Delaford St. SW6—8J 73
Delamare Cres. Croy—1G 125
Delamere Gdns. NW7—6B 24
Delamere Rd. SW20—5H 105
Delamere Rd. W5—3J 71
Delamere Rd. Borwd—3M 11
Delamere Rd. Hay—1H 69
Delamere Ter. W2—8M 57
Delancey St. NW1—4F 58
Delaporte Clo. Eps—4C 134
De Lapre Clo. Orp—2H 129
De Laune St. SE17—6M 75
Delaware Rd. W9—7M 57
Delawke Cres. SE24—5A 92
Delcombe Av. Wor Pk—3G 121
Delft Way. SE22—4C 92
Delhi Rd. Enf—9D 16
Delhi St. N1—4J 59
Delia St. SW18—6M 89
Delius Clo. Borwd—8H 11
Della Path. E5—8E 44
Dellbow Rd. Felt—4F 84
Dell Clo. E15—4B 60
Dell Clo. Wall—6H 123
Dell Clo. Wfd G—2F 30
Dell Farm Rd. Ruis—3B 36
Dellfield Clo. Beck—5A 110
Dellfield Clo. Wat—4E 8
Dellfield Cres. Uxb—7B 142
Dell La. Eps—7E 120
Dellmeadow. Abb L. Wat—3C 4
Dellors Clo. Barn—7H 13
Dellow Clo. Ilf—5B 48
Dellow St. E1—1F 76
Dell Rd. Enf—2G 17
Dell Rd. Eps—8E 120
Dell Rd. Wat—1E 8
Dell Rd. W Dray—5K 143
Dell Side. Wat—1E 8
Dell, The. SE2—6E 80
Dell, The. SE19—5D 108
Dell, The. Bex—7C 98

Dell, The. Bren—7G 71
Dell, The. Felt—6F 84
Dell, The. N'wd—2C 20
Dell, The. Pinn—9H 21
Dell, The. Wemb—1F 54
Dell, The. Wfd G—3F 30
Dell Wlk. N Mald—6C 104
Dell Way. W13—9G 55
Dellwood Gdns. Ilf—1L 47
Delmare Clo. SW9—3K 91
Delme Cres. SE3—1F 94
Delmey Clo. Croy—5D 124
Deloraine St. SE8—9L 77
Delorme St. W6—7H 73
Delta Clo. Wor Pk—5D 120
Delta Gain. Wat—2H 21
Delta Gro. N'holt—6H 53
Delta Rd. Wor Pk—5C 120
Delta St. E2—6E 60
De Luci Rd. Eri—6A 82
De Lucy St. SE2—5F 80
Delvan Clo. SE18—8L 79
Delvers Mead. Dag—9A 50
Delverton Rd. SE17—6M 75
Delvino Rd. SW6—9L 73
Demesne Rd. Wall—6H 123
Demeta Clo. Wemb—8A 40
De Montfort Rd. SW16—8J 91
De Morgan Rd. SW6—2M 89
Dempster Clo. Surb—3G 119
Dempster Rd. SW18—4A 90
Denberry Dri. Sidc—9F 96
Denbigh Clo. NW10—3C 56
Denbigh Clo. W11—1K 73
Denbigh Clo. Chst—3K 111
Denbigh Clo. Horn—2L 51
Denbigh Clo. Ruis—7D 36
Denbigh Clo. S'hall—9K 53
Denbigh Clo. Sutt—7K 121
Denbigh Dri. Hay—3A 68
Denbigh Gdns. Rich—4K 87
Denbigh Pl. SW1—6G 75
Denbigh Rd. E6—6H 63
Denbigh Rd. W11—1K 73
Denbigh Rd. W13—1F 70
Denbigh Rd. Houn—1M 85
Denbigh Rd. S'hall—9K 53
Denbigh St. SW1—5G 75
Denbigh Ter. W11—1K 73
Denbridge Industrial Est. Uxb
—3A 142
Denbridge Rd. Brom—6K 111
Den Clo. Beck—7B 110
Dendridge Clo. Enf—1F 16
Dendy St. SW12—7E 90
Dene Av. Houn—2K 85
Dene Av. Sidc—6F 96
Dene Clo. SE4—2J 93
Dene Clo. Brom—3D 126
Dene Clo. Dart—1C 114
Dene Clo. Wor Pk—4D 120
Denecroft Cres. Uxb—4F 142
Dene Dri. Orp—5F 128
Denefield Dri. Kenl—7B 138
Dene Gdns. Stan—5G 23
Dene Gdns. Th Dit—4E 118
Denehurst Gdns. NW4—4G 41
Denehurst Gdns. W3—2M 71
Denehurst Gdns. Rich—3L 87
Denehurst Gdns. Twic—6B 86
Denehurst Gdns. Wfd G—4F 30
Dene Rd. Barn—1D 26
Dene Rd. Buck H—1J 31
Dene Rd. Dart—6K 99
Dene Rd. N'wd—6A 20
Dene, The. W13—8F 54
Dene, The. Croy—6H 125
Dene, The. E Mol—9K 101
Dene, The. Sutt—3K 135
Dene, The. Wemb—9J 39
Denewood. Barn—7A 14
Denewood Clo. Wat—1D 8
Denewood Rd. N6—4D 42
Denham Clo. Well—2G 97
Denham Cres. Mitc—8D 106
Denham Dri. Ilf—4A 48
Denham Rd. N20—3D 26
Denham Rd. Eps—4D 134
Denham Rd. Felt—6G 85
Denham St. SE10—6D 78
Denham Way. Bark—4D 64
Denholme Rd. W9—6K 57
Denholm Wlk. Rain—2D 66
Denison Clo. N2—1A 42
Denison Rd. SW19—3B 106
Denison Rd. W5—7G 55
Denison Rd. Felt—1D 100
Deniston Av. Bex—7J 97
Denleigh Gdns. N21—9L 15
Denleigh Gdns. Th Dit—1C 118
Denman Dri. NW11—3L 41
Denman Dri. Ashf—3A 100
Denman Dri. Esh—7E 118

Denman Dri. N. NW11—3L 41
Denman Dri. S. NW11—3L 41
Denman Rd. SE15—9D 76
Denman St. W1—1H 75
Denmark Av. SW19—4J 105
Denmark Ct. Mord—1L 121
Denmark Gdns. Cars—5D 122
Denmark Hill. SE5—3B 92
Denmark Hill Dri. NW9—1E 40
Denmark Path. SE25—9F 108
Denmark Pl. WC2—9H 59
Denmark Rd. N8—2L 43
Denmark Rd. NW6—5K 57
(in two parts)
Denmark Rd. SE5—9A 76
Denmark Rd. SE25—9E 108
Denmark Rd. SW19—3H 105
Denmark Rd. W13—1F 70
Denmark Rd. Brom—5F 110
Denmark Rd. Cars—5D 122
Denmark Rd. King—7J 103
Denmark Rd. Twic—9B 86
Denmark St. E11—8C 46
Denmark St. E13—8F 62
Denmark St. N17—7F 28
Denmark St. WC2—9H 59
Denmark St. Wat—4F 8
Denmark Wlk. SE27—1A 108
Denmead Rd. Croy—3M 123
Dennan Rd. Surb—3K 119
Denner Rd. E4—2L 29
Denne Ter. E8—4D 60
Dennett Rd. Croy—2L 123
Dennett's Gro. SE14—9G 77
Dennett's Rd. SE14—1H 93
Denning Av. Croy—6L 123
Denning Clo. NW8—6A 58
Denning Clo. Hmptn—2K 101
Denning Rd. NW3—9B 42
Dennington Clo. E5—7G 45
Dennington Pk. Rd. NW6
—2L 57
Dennis Av. Wemb—1K 55
Dennis Clo. Ashf—4B 100
Dennis Gdns. Stan—5G 23
Dennis La. Stan—3F 22
Dennis Pde. N14—1H 27
Dennis Pk. Cres. SW20—5J 105
Dennis Reeve Clo. Mitc—5D 106
Dennis Rd. E Mol—8A 102
Dennis Rd. Gnfd—5F 54
Denny Av. Wal A—7K 7
Denny Clo. E6—8J 63
Denny Cres. SE11—6L 75
Denny Gdns. Dag—3F 64
Denny Rd. N9—1F 28
Denny St. SE11—6L 75
Den Rd. Brom—7B 110
Densham Rd. E15—4C 62
Densole Clo. Beck—5J 109
Densworth Gro. N9—2G 29
Denton Clo. Barn—7G 13
Denton Gro. W on T—4J 117
Denton Rd. N8—3K 43
Denton Rd. N18—4C 28
Denton Rd. NW10—3A 56
Denton Rd. Bex—8C 98
Denton Rd. Dart—6C 98
Denton Rd. Twic—5H 87
Denton Rd. Well—8G 81
Denton St. SW18—5M 89
Denton Ter. Bex—8C 98
Denton Way. E5—8H 45
Dents Rd. SW11—5D 90
Denver Clo. Orp—1C 128
Denver Rd. N16—5C 44
Denver Rd. Dart—6E 98
Denyer St. SW3—5C 74
Denziloe Av. Uxb—6F 142
Denzil Rd. NW10—1D 56
Deodar Rd. SW15—3J 89
Depot App. N3—8M 25
Depot Rd. Eps—5C 134
Depot Rd. Houn—2B 86
Deptford Bri. SE8—9L 77
SE8 1-17 & 2-24
SE10 remainder
Deptford B'way. SE8—9L 77
Deptford Chu. St. SE8—8L 77
Deptford Ferry Rd. E14—5L 77
Deptford Grn. SE8—7L 77
Deptford High St. SE8—7L 77
Deptford Strand. SE8—5K 77
De Quincey Rd. N17—8B 28
Derby Arms Rd. Eps—9D 134
Derby Av. N12—5A 26
Derby Av. Harr—8B 22
Derby Av. Romf—4A 50
Derby Av. Upm—8K 51
Derby Ga. SW1—3J 75
Derby Hill. SE23—8G 93
Derby Hill Cres. SE23—8G 93
Derby Rd. E7—3H 63

Derby Rd. E9—4H 61
Derby Rd. E18—8D 30
Derby Rd. N18—5G 29
Derby Rd. SW14—3M 87
Derby Rd. SW19—4L 105
Derby Rd. Croy—3M 123
Derby Rd. Enf—7F 16
Derby Rd. Gnfd—4M 53
Derby Rd. Houn—3M 85
Derby Rd. Surb—3L 119
Derby Rd. Sutt—8K 121
Derby Rd. Uxb—5A 142
Derby Rd. Wat—6G 9
Derbyshire St. E2—6E 60
Derby Stables Rd. Eps—9D 138
Derby St. W1—2E 74
Dereham Pl. EC2—6C 60
Dereham Rd. Bark—1D 64
Derek Av. Eps—8L 119
Derek Av. Wall—6F 122
Derek Av. Wemb—3M 55
Deri Av. Rain—7F 66
Dericote St. E8—4F 60
Deridene Clo. Stai—5C 144
Dering Pl. Croy—6A 124
Dering Rd. Croy—6A 124
Dering St. W1—9F 58
Dering Yd. W1—9F 58
Derinton Rd. SW17—1D 106
Derley Rd. S'hall—4G 69
Dermody Gdns. SE13—4B 94
Dermody Rd. SE13—4B 94
Deronda Est. SW2—7M 91
Deronda Rd. SE24—7M 91
Derrick Av. S Croy—2A 138
Derrick Gdns. SE7—5G 79
Derrick Rd. Beck—7K 109
Derry Downs. Orp—1G 129
Derry Rd. Croy—5J 123
Derry St. W8—3M 73
Dersingham Av. E12—9K 47
Dersingham Rd. NW2—8J 41
Derwent Av. N18—5B 28
Derwent Av. NW7—5B 24
Derwent Av. NW9—3C 40
Derwent Av. SW15—1C 104
Derwent Av. Barn—1D 26
Derwent Av. Pinn—6J 21
Derwent Clo. Dart—7F 98
Derwent Clo. Esh—8C 118
Derwent Cres. N20—3A 26
Derwent Cres. Bexh—1L 97
Derwent Cres. Stan—9G 23
Derwent Dri. Hay—8C 52
Derwent Dri. Orp—2B 128
Derwent Dri. Purl—5B 138
Derwent Gdns. Ilf—2J 47
Derwent Gdns. Wemb—5G 39
Derwent Gro. SE22—3D 92
Derwent Rise. NW9—4C 40
Derwent Rd. N13—4K 27
Derwent Rd. SE20—6E 108
Derwent Rd. SW20—9H 105
Derwent Rd. W5—4G 71
Derwent Rd. S'hall—9L 53
Derwent Rd. Twic—5M 85
Derwent St. SE10—6C 78
Derwent Wlk. Wall—9F 122
Derwentwater Rd. W3—2A 72
Derwent Way. Horn—1F 66
De Salis Rd. Uxb—7A 52
Desenfans Rd. SE21—5C 92
Desford Ct. Ashf—8E 144
Desford Rd. E16—7C 62
Desford Way. Ashf—8D 144
Desmond Rd. Wat—9D 4
Desmond St. SE14—8J 77
Despard Rd. N19—6G 43
Detling Clo. Horn—1G 67
Detling Rd. Brom—2E 110
Detling Rd. Eri—8B 82
Detmold Rd. E5—7G 45
Devalls Clo. E6—1M 79
Devana End. Cars—5D 122
Devas Rd. SW20—5G 105
Devas St. E3—7M 61
Devenay Rd. E15—3D 62
Devenish Rd. SE2—3E 80
Deventer Cres. SE22—4C 92
De Vere Gdns. Ilf—7K 47
Deverell St. SE1—4B 76
Devereux Dri. Wat—2C 8
Devereux Rd. SW11—5D 90
De Vere Wlk. Wat—4C 8
Deveron Way. Romf—8C 34
Devitt Clo. Asht—8L 133
Devoke Way. W on T—4H 117
Devon Av. Twic—7C 86
Devon Clo. N17—1D 44
Devon Clo. Buck H—2F 30
Devon Clo. Gnfd—4G 55
Devon Clo. Kenl—8D 138

Devon Ct. S at H, Dart—5M 115
Devoncroft Gdns. Twic—6E 86
Devon Gdns. N4—4M 43
Devonia Gdns. N18—6A 28
Devonia Rd. N1—5N 59
Devonport Gdns. Ilf—4K 47
Devonport Rd. W12—3F 72
Devonport St. E1—9G 61
Devon Rise. N2—2B 42
Devon Rd. Bark—4C 64
Devon Rd. Sutt—1J 135
Devon Rd. S at H & S Dar, Dart
—5M 115
Devon Rd. W on T—6G 117
Devon Rd. Wat—3H 9
Devons Est. E3—6M 61
Devonshire Av. Dart—5F 98
Devonshire Av. Sutt—9A 122
Devonshire Clo. E15—9C 46
Devonshire Clo. N13—3L 27
Devonshire Clo. W1—8F 58
Devonshire Cres. NW7—7H 25
Devonshire Dri. SE10—8M 77
Devonshire Dri. Surb—3H 119
Devonshire Gdns. N17—6A 28
Devonshire Gdns. N21—9A 16
Devonshire Gdns. W4—8A 72
Devonshire Gro. SE15—7F 76
Devonshire Hill La. N17—6A 28
Devonshire M. N13—4L 27
Devonshire M. W4—6C 72
Devonshire M. N. W1—8F 58
Devonshire M. S. W1—8F 58
Devonshire M. W. W1—7E 58
Devonshire Pas. W4—6C 72
Devonshire Pl. NW2—8L 41
Devonshire Pl. W1—7E 58
Devonshire Pl. Horn—6C 72
Devonshire Pl. M. W1—8E 58
Devonshire Rd. E15—9C 46
Devonshire Rd. E16—9F 62
Devonshire Rd. E17—4L 45
Devonshire Rd. N9—1G 29
Devonshire Rd. N13—4L 27
Devonshire Rd. N17—6A 28
Devonshire Rd. NW7—7H 25
Devonshire Rd. SE9—8J 95
Devonshire Rd. SE23—7G 93
Devonshire Rd. SW19—4C 106
Devonshire Rd. W4—6C 72
Devonshire Rd. W5—4G 71
Devonshire Rd. Bexh—3J 97
Devonshire Rd. Croy—2B 124
Devonshire Rd. Felt—9J 85
Devonshire Rd. Harr—4B 38
Devonshire Rd. Horn—7G 51
Devonshire Rd. Ilf—5C 48
Devonshire Rd. Orp—2E 128
Devonshire Rd. Pinn—5G 37
(Eastcote)
Devonshire Rd. Pinn—8K 21
(Hatch End)
Devonshire Rd. S'hall—8L 53
Devonshire Rd. Sutt—9A 122
Devonshire Rd. Wall—6E 122
Devonshire Row. EC2—8C 60
Devonshire Sq. EC2—9C 60
Devonshire Sq. Brom—8F 110
Devonshire St. W1—8E 58
Devonshire St. W4—6C 72
Devonshire Ter. W2—9A 58
Devonshire Way. Croy—4J 125
Devonshire Way. Hay—9F 52
Devons Rd. E3—8L 61
Devon St. SE15—7F 76
Devon Way. Chess—7G 119
Devon Way. Eps—7M 119
Devon Way. Uxb—5D 142
Devon Waye. Houn—8K 69
De Walden St. W1—8E 58
Dewar St. SE15—2E 92
Dewey Path. Horn—2G 67
Dewey Rd. N1—5L 59
(in two parts)
Dewey Rd. Dag—2M 65
Dewey St. SW17—2D 106
Dewgrass Gro. Wal X—8C 6
Dewhurst Rd. W14—4H 73
Dewhurst Rd. Wal X—2C 6
Dewlands Av. Dart—6M 99
Dewsbery Clo. Pinn—4J 37
Dewsbury Clo. Pinn—4J 37
Dewsbury Clo. Romf—6J 35
Dewsbury Ct. W4—5A 72
Dewsbury Gdns. Romf—6H 35
Dewsbury Gdns. Wor Pk
—5E 120
Dewsbury Rd. NW10—1E 56
Dewsbury Rd. Romf—6J 35
Dewsbury Ter. NW1—4F 58
Dexter Rd. Barn—8H 13
Deyncourt Gdns. E11—2G 47
Deyncourt Gdns. Upm—7M 51

Deyncourt Rd. N17—8A 28
D'Eynsford Rd. SE5—9B 76
Diamedes Av. Stai—6B 144
Diameter Rd. Orp—1A 128
Diamond Rd. Ruis—9H 37
Diamond Rd. Wat—2E 8
Diamond St. SE15—8C 76
Diamond Ter. SE10—9A 78
Diana Clo. E18—8F 30
Diana Ct. Eri—7C 82
Diana Gdns. Surb—4K 119
Diana Ho. SW13—9D 72
Diana Pl. NW1—7F 58
Diana Rd. E17—1K 45
Diana Way. Ilf—8M 47
Dianthus Clo. SE2—6F 80
Diban Av. Horn—9F 50
Dibden St. N1—4A 60
Dibden Clo. Sutt—5L 121
Dibdin Rd. Sutt—5L 121
Dibdin Row. SE1—4L 75
Diceland Rd. Bans—8K 135
Dicey Av. NW2—9G 41
Dickens Av. N3—8A 26
Dickens Av. Dart—3L 99
Dickens Av. Uxb—9F 142
Dickens Clo. Harr—7M 37
Dickens Clo. Hay—5C 68
Dickens Clo. Rich—8J 87
Dickens Dri. Chst—3A 112
Dickens La. N18—5C 28
Dickenson La. SE25—1E 124
Dickensons Pl. SE25—1E 124
Dickenson St. NW5—2F 58
Dickens Rise. Chig—3M 31
Dickens Rd. E6—5H 63
Dickens Sq. SE1—4A 76
Dickens St. SW8—1F 90
Dickerage La. N Mald—7A 104
Dickerage Rd. King—5A 104
Dickson. Wal X—1A 6
Dickson Fold. Pinn—2H 37
Dickson Rd. SE9—2J 95
Dick Turpin Way. Felt—3D 84
Didsbury Clo. E6—4K 63
Digby Cres. N4—7A 44
Digby Gdns. Dag—4L 65
Digby Pl. Croy—5D 124
Digby Rd. E9—2H 61
Digby Rd. Bark—3D 64
Digby St. E2—6G 61
Digby Wlk. Horn—2G 67
Digdens Rise. Eps—7C 134
Dighton Rd. SW18—4A 90
Dignum St. N1—5L 59
Digswell St. N7—2L 59
Dilke St. SW3—7D 74
Dillon Pl. N7—8K 43
Dillwyn Clo. SE26—1J 109
Dilston Clo. N'holt—6G 53
Dilton Gdns. SW15—7F 88
Dimes Pl. W6—5F 72
Dimmock Dri. Gnfd—1B 54
Dimond Clo. E7—9E 46
Dimsdale Dri. NW9—6A 40
Dimsdale Dri. Enf—8E 16
Dimsdale Wlk. E13—5E 62
Dingle Gdns. E14—1L 77
Dingle Clo. Ashf—2A 100
Dingle, The. Uxb—6F 142
Dingley La. SW16—8H 91
Dingley Pl. EC1—6A 60
Dingley Rd. EC1—6A 60
Dingonhill Clo. Hay—1F 68
Dingwall Av. Croy—4A 124
Dingwall Gdns. NW11—4L 41
Dingwall Rd. Cars—1D 136
Dingwall Rd. Croy—4B 124
Dinmont Est. E2—5E 60
Dinmont St. E2—5F 60
Dinsdale Gdns. SE25—9C 108
Dinsdale Gdns. Barn—7M 13
Dinsdale Rd. SE3—7D 78
Dinsmore Rd. SW12—6F 90
Dinton Rd. King—4K 103
Diploma Av. N2—2C 42
Dirdene Clo. Eps—4D 134
Dirdene Gdns. Eps—4D 134
Dirdene Gro. Eps—4C 134
Dirleton Rd. E15—4D 62
Disbrowe Rd. W6—7J 73
Dishforth La. NW9—8C 24
Disney Pl. SE1—3A 76
Disney St. SE1—3A 76
Dison Clo. Enf—3H 17
Disraeli Clo. SE28—2G 81
Disraeli Clo. W4—5B 72
Disraeli Ct. E7—2E 62
Disraeli Rd. NW10—5B 56
Disraeli Rd. SW15—3J 89

Disraeli Rd. W5—2H 71
Diss St. E2—6D 60
Distaff La. EC4—1A 76
Distillery La. W6—6G 73
Distillery Rd. W6—6G 73
Distillery Wlk. Bren—7J 71
District Rd. Wemb—1F 54
Ditch All. SE10—9M 77
Ditchburn St. E14—1A 78
Ditches Ride, The. Lou & Epp
—1L 19
Dittisham Rd. SE9—1J 111
Ditton Clo. Th Dit—2E 118
Ditton Grange Clo. Surb
—3H 119
Ditton Grange Dri. Surb
—3H 119
Ditton Hill. Surb—3G 119
Ditton Hill Rd. Surb—3G 119
Ditton Lawn. Th Dit—3E 118
Ditton Pl. SE20—5F 108
Ditton Reach. Th Dit—1F 118
Ditton Rd. Bexh—4J 97
Ditton Rd. S'hall—6K 69
Ditton Rd. Surb—4H 119
Divis Way. SW15—5F 88
Dixon Clo. E6—9K 63
Dixon Pl. W Wick—3M 125
Dixon Rd. SE14—9J 77
Dixon Rd. SE25—7C 108
Dixon's All. SE16—3F 76
Dobbin Clo. Harr—9E 22
Dobell Rd. SE9—4K 95
Dobree Av. NW10—3F 56
Dobson Clo. NW6—3B 58
Dockhead. SE1—3D 76
Dockland Est. E16—2L 79
Dockley Rd. SE16—4E 76
Dock Rd. E16—1D 78
Dock Rd. Bren—8H 71
Dock St. E1—1E 76
Dockwell Clo. Felt—3E 84
Doctor Johnson Av. SW17
—9F 90
Doctors Clo. SE26—2G 109
Docwra's Bldgs. N1—2C 60
Dodbrooke Rd. SE27—9L 91
Doddington Gro. SE17—6M 75
Doddington Pl. SE17—7M 75
Dodsley Pl. N9—3G 29
Dodson St. SE1—3L 75
Dod St. E14—9L 61
Doel Clo. SW19—4A 106
Doggett Rd. SE6—6L 93
Doggetts Courts. Barn—7C 14
Doghurst Av. Hay—8M 143
Doghurst Dri. W Dray—8M 143
Dog Kennel Hill. SE5—2C 92
Dog La. NW10—9C 40
Doherty Rd. E13—7E 62
Dolben St. SE1—2M 75
(in two parts)
Dolby Rd. SW6—1K 89
Dole St. NW7—7G 25
Dollis Av. N3—8K 25
Dollis Brook Wlk. Barn—8J 13
Dollis Cres. Ruis—6G 37
Dollis Hill Av. NW2—8F 40
Dollis Hill La. NW2—9D 40
Dollis Pk. N3—8K 25
Dollis Rd.—7J 25
    N3 1-89 & 2-66
    NW7 remainder
Dollis Valley Way. Barn—8K 13
Dolman Rd. W4—5B 72
Dolman St. SW4—3K 91
Dolphin App. Romf—2D 50
Dolphin Clo. Surb—9H 103
Dolphin La. E14—1M 77
Dolphin Rd. N'holt—5K 53
Dolphin Rd. Sun—5C 100
Dolphin Rd. N. Sun—5C 100
Dolphin Rd. S. Sun—5C 100
Dolphin Rd. W. Sun—5C 100
Dolphin Sq. SW1—6G 75
Dombey St. WC1—8K 59
Dome Hill Pk. SE26—1D 108
Domett Clo. SE5—3B 92
Domingo St. EC1—7A 60
Dominion Dri. Romf—6M 33
Dominion Rd. Croy—2D 124
Dominion Rd. S'hall—4J 69
Dominion St. EC2—8B 60
Dominion Way. Rain—6E 66
Domitian Pl. Enf—7D 16
Domonic Dri. SE9—1M 111
Domville Clo. N20—2D 40
Domville Gro. SE5—6D 76
Donald Dri. Romf—3G 49
Donald Rd. E13—4F 62
Donald Rd. Croy—2K 123
Donaldson Rd. NW6—4K 57

Donaldson Rd. SE18—9L 79
Doncaster Dri. N'holt—1K 53
Doncaster Gdns. N4—4A 44
Doncaster Gdns. N'holt—1K 53
Doncaster Grn. Wat—5G 21
Doncaster Rd. N9—9F 16
Doncaster Way. Upm—8K 51
Donegal St. N1—5K 59
Doneraile St. SW6—1H 89
Dongola Rd. E13—6F 62
Dongola Rd. N17—1C 44
Dongola Rd. W. E13—6F 62
Donington Av. Ilf—3A 48
Donkey La. Enf—4E 16
Donkey La. Dart
—4M 131
Donkey La. W Dray—5G 143
Donne Ct. SE24—5A 92
Donnefield Av. Edgw—7J 23
Donne Pl. SW3—5C 74
Donne Pl. Mitc—8F 106
Donne Rd. Dag—7G 49
Donnington Rd. NW10—3F 56
Donnington Rd. Harr—3G 39
Donnington Rd. Wor Pk—4E 120
Donnybrook Rd. SW16—4G 107
Donovan Av. N10—9G 27
Donovan Clo. Eps—2B 134
Don Phelan Clo. SE5—9B 76
Don Way. Romf—7C 34
Doone Clo. Tedd—3E 102
Doon St. SE1—2L 75
Dorado Gdns. Orp—5H 129
Doral Way. Cars—7D 122
Doran Gro. SE18—8C 80
Doran Wlk. E15—3A 62
Dora Rd. SW19—2L 105
Dora St. E14—9K 61
Dorchester Av. N13—4A 28
Dorchester Av. Bex—7H 97
Dorchester Av. Harr—4A 38
Dorchester Clo. Dart—7K 99
Dorchester Clo. Felt—5C 84
Dorchester Clo. N'holt—1M 53
Dorchester Clo. Orp—4F 112
Dorchester Ct. N14—9F 14
Dorchester Dri. SE24—4A 92
Dorchester Gdns. E4—4L 29
Dorchester Gdns. NW11—2L 41
Dorchester Gro. W4—6C 72
Dorchester M. N Mald—8B 104
Dorchester M. Mord—2M 121
Dorchester Rd. N'holt—1M 53
Dorchester Rd. Wor Pk—3G 121
Dorchester Way. Harr—4K 39
Dorchester Way. Hay—9F 52
Dorcis Av. Bexh—1J 97
Dordrecht Rd. W3—3C 72
Dore Av. E12—1L 63
Doreen Av. NW9—6B 40
Dore Gdns. Mord—2M 121
Dorell Clo. S'hall—8K 53
Dorian Rd. Horn—6E 50
Doria Rd. SW6—1K 89
Doric Way. NW1—6H 59
Dorien Rd. SW20—6H 105
Dorinda St. N7—2L 59
Doris Av. Eri—9A 82
Doris Emmerton Ct. SW11
—3A 90
Doris Rd. E7—3E 62
Doris Rd. Ashf—3B 100
Doritt M. N18—5C 28
Dorking Clo. SE8—7K 77
Dorking Clo. Wor Pk—4H 121
Dorking Rise. Romf—4H 35
Dorking Rd. Eps—7M 133
Dorking Rd. Romf—5H 35
Dorking Wlk. Romf—4H 35
Dorlcote Rd. SW18—6C 90
Dorling Dri. Eps—4D 134
Durly Clo. Shep—9C 100
Dorman Pl. N9—2E 28
Dormans Clo. N'wd—7B 20
Dorman Wlk. NW10—1B 56
Dorman Way. NW8—4B 58
Dormay St. SW18—4M 89
Dormer Clo. E15—2D 62
Dormer Clo. Barn—7H 13
Dormer's Av. S'hall—9L 53
Dormers Rise. S'hall—9M 53
Dormer's Wells La. S'hall
—9L 53
Dormywood. Ruis—3D 36
Dornberg Clo. SE3—8E 78
Dorncliffe Rd. SW6—1J 89
Dorney Rise. Orp—8D 112
Dornfell St. NW6—1K 57
Dornton Rd. SW12—8F 90
Dornton Rd. S Croy—7B 124
Dorothy Av. Wemb—3J 55
Dorothy Evans Clo. Bexh
—3M 97

Dorothy Gdns. Dag—9F 48
Dorothy Rd. SW11—2D 90
Dorrell Pl. SW9—3L 91
Dorrien Wlk. SW16—8H 91
Dorrington Ct. SE25—6C 108
Dorrington Gdns. Horn—6H 51
Dorrington St. EC1—8L 59
Dorrit Way. Chst—3A 112
Dorrofield Clo. Rick—7A 8
Dorryn Ct. SE26—2H 109
Dors Clo. NW9—6B 40
Dorset Av. Hay—6C 52
Dorset Av. Romf—1B 50
Dorset Av. S'hall—5L 69
Dorset Av. Well—3D 96
Dorset Bldgs. EC4—9M 59
Dorset Clo. NW1—8D 58
Dorset Clo. Hay—6C 52
Dorset Dri. Edgw—6K 23
Dorset Gdns. Mitc—8K 107
Dorset M. SW1—4F 74
Dorset Pl. E15—2B 62
Dorset Rise. EC4—9M 59
Dorset Rd. E7—3G 63
Dorset Rd. N15—2B 44
Dorset Rd. N22—8J 27
Dorset Rd. SE9—8J 95
Dorset Rd. SW8—8J 75
Dorset Rd. SW19—5L 105
Dorset Rd. W5—4G 71
Dorset Rd. Ashf—9B 144
Dorset Rd. Beck—7H 109
Dorset Rd. Harr—4A 38
Dorset Rd. Mitc—6C 106
Dorset Rd. Sutt—2L 135
Dorset Sq. NW1—7D 58
Dorset Sq. Eps—2B 134
Dorset St. W1—8D 58
Dorset Way. Twic—7R 86
Dorset Way. Uxb—5D 142
Dorset Waye. Houn—8K 69
Dorville Cres. W6—4F 72
Dorville Rd. SE12—4D 94
Dothill Rd. SE18—8A 80
Douai Gro. Hmptn—5A 102
Doughty M. WC1—7K 59
Doughty St. WC1—7K 59
Douglas Av. E17—8K 29
Douglas Av. N Mald—8F 104
Douglas Av. Romf—9J 35
Douglas Av. Wat—1J 9
Douglas Av. Wemb—3J 55
Douglas Clo. Stan—5E 22
Douglas Clo. Wall—8J 123
Douglas Cres. Hay—7G 53
Douglas Dri. Croy—5L 125
Douglas Pl. E14—6A 78
Douglas Pl. SW1—5H 75
Douglas Rd. E4—1C 30
Douglas Rd. E16—8E 62
Douglas Rd. N1—3A 60
Douglas Rd. N22—8L 27
Douglas Rd. NW6—4K 57
Douglas Rd. Esh—4M 117
Douglas Rd. Horn—4D 50
Douglas Rd. Houn—2M 85
Douglas Rd. Ilf—5E 48
Douglas Rd. King—6M 103
Douglas Rd. Stai—5C 144
Douglas Rd. Surb—4K 119
Douglas Rd. Well—9F 80
Douglas Sq. Mord—1L 121
Douglas St. SW1—5H 75
Douglas Way. SE8—8K 77
Dounesforth Gdns. SW18
—7M 89
Douro Pl. W8—4M 73
Douro St. E3—5L 61
Douthwaite Sq. E1—2E 76
Dove App. E6—8J 63
Dove Clo. NW7—7H 25
Dove Clo. N'holt—7H 53
Dove Clo. S Croy—3H 139
Dovecote Av. N22—1L 43
Dovedale Av. Harr—4G 39
Dovedale Av. Ilf—9L 31
Dovedale Clo. Well—1E 96
Dovedale Rise. Mitc—4D 106
Dovedale Rd. SE22—4F 92
Dove Ho. Gdns. E4—2L 29
Dovehouse Grn. Wey—6C 116
Dovehouse Mead. Bark—5B 64
Dovehouse St. SW3—6B 74
Dove M. SW5—5A 74
Doveney Clo. Orp—7G 113
Dove Pk. Pinn—7L 21
Dove Rd. N1—2B 60
Dove Row. E2—4E 60

Dover Pk. Dri. SW15—5F 88
Dover Rd. E12—7G 47
Dover Rd. N9—2G 29
Dover Rd. SE19—3B 108
Dover Rd. Romf—4J 49
Dover St. W1—1F 74
Dover Way. Rick—6A 8
Doves Clo. Brom—4J 127
Doveton Rd. S Croy—7B 124
Doveton St. E1—7G 61
Dowanhill Rd. SE6—7B 94
Dowdeswell Clo. SW15—3C 88
Dowding Pl. Stan—6E 22
Dowding Rd. Uxb—3D 142
Dowding Rd. West—7H 141
Dower Av. Wall—1F 136
Dowgate Hill. EC4—1B 76
Dowin St. E Mol—9L 101
Dowland St. W10—6J 57
Dowlas St. SE5—8C 76
Dowlerville Rd. Orp—8D 128
Dowman Clo. SW19—4M 105
Downage. NW4—1G 41
Downalong. Bush, Wat—1B 22
Downbank Av. Bexh—9B 82
Down Barns Rd. Ruis—8H 37
Down Clo. N'holt—5F 52
Downderry Rd. Brom—9B 94
Downe Clo. Well—8G 81
Down End. SE18—8M 79
Downe Rd. Kes—1J 141
Downe Rd. Mitc—6D 106
Downe Rd. Sev—6M 141
Downers Cotts. SW4—3G 91
Downes Clo. Twic—5F 86
Downes Ct. N21—1L 27
Downes Pl. SE15—7E 76
Downe Ter. Rich—5J 87
Downfield. Wor Pk—3D 120
Downfield Clo. W9—7M 57
Downfield Rd. Wal X—4E 6
Down Hall Rd. King—5H 103
Downham Clo. Romf—7L 33
Downham Rd. N1—3B 60
Downham Way. Brom—2B 110
Downhills Av. N17—1B 44
Downhills Pk. Rd. N17—1A 44
Downhills Way. N17—1A 44
Downhurst Av. NW7—5B 24
Downing Clo. Harr—1A 38
Downing Dri. Gnfd—4C 54
Downing Rd. Dag—3K 65
Downing St. SW1—3J 75
Downland Clo. N20—1A 26
Downland Clo. Coul—6F 136
Downland Gdns. Eps—9F 134
Downlands. Wal A—7M 7
Downlands Rd. Purl—5J 137
Downland Way. Eps—9F 134
Downleys Clo. SE9—8K 95
Downman Rd. SE9—2J 95
Down Pl. W6—5F 72
Down Rd. Tedd—3F 102
Downs Av. Chst—2K 111
Downs Av. Dart—6L 99
Downs Av. Eps—6C 134
Downs Av. Pinn—4K 37
Downsbridge Rd. Beck—5B 110
Downs Ct. Rd. Purl—4M 137
Downsell Rd. E15—9B 46
Downsfield Rd. E17—4J 45
Downshall Av. Ilf—4C 48
Downs Hill. Beck—4B 110
Downs Hill Rd. Eps—6C 134
Downshire Hill. NW3—9B 42
Downside. Eps—6C 134
Downside. Twic—9D 86
Downside Clo. SW19—3A 106
Downside Cres. NW3—1C 58
Downside Cres. W13—7E 54
Downside Rd. Sutt—8B 122
Downside Wlk. N'holt—6K 53
Downs La. E5—9F 44
Downs Pk. Rd.—1D 60
    E8 1-73 & 2-90
    E5 remainder
Downs Rd. E5—9E 44
Downs Rd. Beck—6M 109
Downs Rd. Coul—9H 137
Downs Rd. Enf—6C 16
Downs Rd. Eps—7C 134
Downs Rd. Purl—3M 137
Downs Rd. Sutt—2M 135
Downs Rd. T Hth—5A 108
Downs Side. Sutt—3K 135
Downs, The. SW20—4H 105
Down St. W1—2F 74
Down St. M. W1—2F 74
Downs View. Iswth
—9D 70

Downsview Gdns. SE19
—4M 107
Downsview Rd. SE19—4A 108
Downs Way. Eps—8D 134
Downsway. Orp—7C 128
Downsway. S Croy—3C 138
Downsway. Whyt—8D 138
Downsway, The. Sutt—1A 136
Downs Wood. Eps—9F 134
Downton Av. SW2—8J 91
Downtown Rd. SE16—3J 77
Down Way. N'holt—5F 52
Dowrey St. N1—4L 59
Dowsett Rd. N17—9D 28
Dowson Clo. SE5—3B 92
Doyce St. SE1—3A 76
Doyle Gdns. NW10—4E 56
Doyle Rd. SE25—8E 108
D'Oyley St. SW1—5E 74
Doynton St. N19—7F 42
Draco St. SE17—7A 76
Dragmire La. Mitc—7B 106
Dragoon Rd. SE8—6K 77
Dragor Rd. NW10—7A 56
Drakefell Rd.—1H 93
  SE14 1-87 & 2-134
  SE4 remainder
Drakefield Rd. SW17—9E 90
Drakeley Ct. N5—9M 43
Drake Rd. SE4—2L 93
Drake Rd. Chess—7L 119
Drake Rd. Croy—2K 123
Drake Rd. Harr—7K 37
Drake Rd. Mitc—1E 122
Drake's Clo. SE6—6L 117
Drakes Clo. Wal X—1D 6
Drake St. WC1—8K 59
Drake St. Enf—3B 16
Drakes Wlk. E6—5K 63
Drakewood Rd. SW16—4H 107
Draper Clo. Belv—5K 81
Draper Ct. Brom—8J 111
Draper's Gdns. EC2—9B 60
Drapers Rd. E15—9B 46
Drapers Rd. N17—1D 44
Drapers Rd. Enf—4M 15
Drappers Way. SE16—5E 76
Drawdock Rd. SE10—3B 78
Drawell Clo. SE18—6C 80
Drax Av. SW20—4E 104
Draxmont App. SW19—3J 105
Draycot Rd. E11—4F 46
Draycot Rd. Surb—3L 119
Draycott Av. SW3—5C 74
Draycott Av. Harr—4F 38
Draycott Clo. Harr—4F 38
Draycott Pl. SW3—5D 74
Draycott Ter. SW3—5D 74
Drayford Clo. W9—7K 57
Dray Gdns. SW2—4K 91
Drayson M. W8—3L 73
Drayson Av. W13—1E 70
Drayton Av. Lou—9E 19
Drayton Av. Orp—3M 127
Drayton Bri. Rd. W7 & W13
—1D 70
Drayton Gdns. N21—9M 15
Drayton Gdns. W4—6A 74
Drayton Gdns. W13—1E 70
Drayton Gdns. W Dray—3J 143
Drayton Grn. W13—1E 70
Drayton Grn. Rd. W13—1F 70
Drayton Gro. W13—1E 70
Drayton Pk. N5—9L 43
Drayton Rd. E11—6B 46
Drayton Rd. N17—9C 28
Drayton Rd. NW10—4D 56
Drayton Rd. W13—1F 70
Drayton Rd. Borwd—6L 11
Drayton Rd. Croy—4M 123
Drayton Waye. Harr—4F 38
Dreadnought St. SE10—4C 78
Drenon Sq. Hay—1D 68
Dresden Clo. NW6—2M 57
Dresden M. NW6—2M 57
Dresden Rd. N19—6H 43
Dresden Way. Wey—7A 116
Dressington Av. SE4—5L 93
Drew Av. NW7—6H 25
Drew Gdns. Gnfd—2D 54
Drewitts Ct. W on T—3D 116
Drew Rd. E16—2J 79
Drewstead Rd. SW16—8H 91
Driffield Rd. E3—5J 61
Drift, The. Kes—5H 127
Driftway, The. Bans—7G 135
Driftway, The. Mitc—5E 106
Driftwood Dri. Kenl—9A 138
Drinkwater Rd. Harr—7M 37
Drive Mead. Coul—6J 137
Drive, The. E4—9B 18
Drive, The. E17—1M 45
Drive, The. E18—1E 46

Drive, The. N3—7L 25
Drive, The. N7—2K 59
Drive, The. N11—6H 27
Drive, The. NW11—5J 41
Drive, The. SW16—7K 107
Drive, The. SW20—4G 105
Drive, The. W3—9A 56
Drive, The. Ashf—4B 100
Drive, The. Bans—8K 135
Drive, The. Bark—3D 64
Drive, The. Barn—5J 13
  (High Barnet)
Drive, The. Barn—8A 14
  (New Barnet)
Drive, The. Beck—6L 109
Drive, The. Bex—6H 97
Drive, The. Buck H—9G 19
Drive, The. Chst—7D 112
Drive, The. Coul—6J 137
Drive, The. Edgw—5L 23
Drive, The. Enf—3B 16
Drive, The. Eps—8D 120
Drive, The. Eri—7M 81
Drive, The. Esh—3A 118
Drive, The. Felt—6G 85
Drive, The. Harr—5L 37
Drive, The. Houn & Iswth
—1B 86
Drive, The. Ilf—5K 47
Drive, The. King—4A 104
Drive, The. Lou—6J 19
Drive, The. Mord—9B 106
Drive, The. N'wd—8C 20
Drive, The. Orp—4D 128
Drive, The. Purf—7M 83
Drive, The. Romf—7B 34
  (Collier Row)
Drive, The. Romf—8K 35
  (Harold Wood)
Drive, The. Sidc—1F 112
Drive, The. Surb—2J 119
Drive, The. Sutt—3L 135
Drive, The. T Hth—8B 108
Drive, The. Uxb—1C 142
Drive, The. Wall—1H 137
Drive, The. Wat—1B 8
Drive, The. Wemb—7A 40
Drive, The. W Wick—2B 126
Droitwich Clo. SE26—9E 92
Dromey Gdns. Harr—7D 22
Dromore Rd. SW15—5J 89
Dronfield Gdns. Dag—1G 65
Droop St. W10—6J 57
Drop La. St Alb—4M 5
Drovers Rd. S Croy—7B 124
Droveway. Lou—4M 19
Druce Rd. SE21—5C 92
Druid St. SE1—3C 76
Druids Way. Brom—8B 110
Drumaline Ridge. Wor Pk
—4C 120
Drummond Av. Romf—2B 50
Drummond Cres. NW1—6H 59
Drummond Dri. Stan—7D 22
Drummond Gdns. Eps—3M 133
Drummond Ga. SW1—6H 75
Drummond Ho. N2—9A 26
Drummond Pl. Shopping Centre.
  Croy—4A 124
Drummond Rd. E11—4G 47
Drummond Rd. SE16—4F 76
Drummond Rd. Croy—4A 124
Drummond Rd. Romf—2B 50
Drummonds, The. Buck H
—2F 30
Drummond St. NW1—7G 59
Drum St. E1—9D 60
Drury La. WC2—9J 59
Drury Rd. Harr—5A 38
Drury Way. NW10—1B 56
Dryad St. SW15—2H 89
Dryburgh Gdns. NW9—1L 39
Dryburgh Rd. SW15—2F 88
Dryden Av. W7—9D 54
Dryden Clo. Ilf—6D 32
Dryden Ct. SE11—5M 75
Dryden Rd. SW19—3A 106
Dryden Rd. Enf—8C 16
Dryden Rd. Harr—8D 22
Dryden Rd. Well—9D 80
Dryden St. WC2—9J 59
Dryden Way. Orp—3E 128
Dryfield Clo. NW10—2A 56
Dryfield Rd. Edgw—6A 24
Dryfield Wlk. SE8—7L 77
Dryhill Rd. Belv—7K 81
Dryland Av. Orp—6D 128
Drylands Rd. N8—4J 43
Drynham Pk. W on T—5C 116
Drysdale Av. E4—9M 17
Drysdale Clo. N'wd—7C 20
Drysdale Pl. N1—6C 60
Drysdale St. N1—6C 60

Du Burstow Ter. W7—3C 70
Ducal St. E2—6D 60
Du Cane Ct. SW12—7E 90
Du Cane Rd. W12—9D 56
Duchess M. W1—8F 58
Duchess of Bedford's Wlk. W8
—3L 73
Duchess St. W1—8F 58
Duchy Pl. SE1—2L 75
Duchy Rd. Barn—2B 14
Duchy St. SE1—2L 75
Ducie St. SW4—3K 91
Duckett Rd. N4—4M 43
Ducketts Rd. Dart—4D 98
Duckett St. E1—7H 61
Ducking Stool Ct. Romf—2C 50
Duck Lees La. Enf—6J 17
Duck's Hill Rd. N'wd & Ruis
—8A 20
Ducks Wlk. Twic—4G 87
Du Cros Dri. Stan—6H 23
Du Cros Rd. W3—2C 72
Dudden Hill La. NW10—9D 40
Duddington Clo. SE9—1H 111
Dudley Av. Harr—1G 39
Dudley Av. Wal X—5D 6
Dudley Dri. Mord—3J 121
Dudley Dri. Ruis—1F 52
Dudley Gdns. W13—3F 70
Dudley Gdns. Harr—6B 38
Dudley Gdns. Romf—6H 35
Dudley Gro. Eps—6A 134
Dudley Rd. E17—9L 29
Dudley Rd. N3—9M 25
Dudley Rd. NW6—5J 57
Dudley Rd. SW19—3L 105
Dudley Rd. Felt—7A 84
Dudley Rd. Harr—7A 38
Dudley Rd. Ilf—9M 47
Dudley Rd. King—7K 103
Dudley Rd. Rich—1K 87
Dudley Rd. Romf—6H 35
Dudley Rd. S'hall—3H 69
Dudley Rd. W on T—1E 116
Dudley St. W2—8B 58
Dudlington Rd. E5—7G 45
Dudsbury Rd. Dart—5F 98
Dudsbury Rd. Sidc—3F 112
Dudset La. Houn—9E 68
Dufferin St. EC1—7A 60
Duffield Clo. Harr—3D 38
Duff St. E14—9M 61
Dufour's Pl. W1—9G 59
Duke Gdns. Ilf—2B 48
Duke Humphrey Rd. SE3—9C 78
Duke of Cambridge Clo. Twic
—5B 86
Duke of Edinburgh Rd. Sutt
—4B 122
Duke of Wellington Pl. SW1
—3E 74
Duke of York St. SW1—2G 75
Duke Rd. W4—6B 72
Duke Rd. Ilf—2B 48
Dukes Av. N3—8M 25
Duke's Av. N10—1F 42
Duke's Av. W4—6B 72
Dukes Av. Edgw—6K 23
Dukes Av. Harr—4K 37
  (North Harrow)
Dukes Av. Harr—2C 38
  (Wealdstone)
Dukes Av. Houn—3J 85
Dukes Av. N Mald—7D 104
Dukes Av. Rich & King—1G 103
Dukes Clo. Ashf—1A 100
Dukes Clo. Hmptn—2K 101
Dukes Ct. E6—4L 63
Dukes Head Pas. Hmptn
—4A 102
Duke's La. W8—3M 73
Dukes Orchard. Bex—7A 98
Duke's Pl. EC3—9C 60
Dukes Rd. E6—4L 63
Dukes Rd. W3—7L 55
Dukes Rd. WC1—6H 59
Dukes Rd. W on T—7H 117
Dukesthorpe Rd. SE26—1H 109
Duke St. W1—9E 58
Duke St. Rich—4H 87
Duke St. Sutt—6B 122
Duke St. Wat—5G 9
Duke St. Hill. SE1—2B 76
Duke St. Saint James's. SW1
—2G 75
Dukes Way. Brom—7D 110
Dukes Way. W Wick—5C 126
Duke's Yd. W1—1E 74
Dulas St. N4—6K 43
Dulford St. W11—1J 73
Dulka Rd. SW11—4D 90

Dulverton Rd. SE9—8B 96
Dulverton Rd. Romf—6H 35
Dulverton Rd. Ruis—6E 36
Dulverton Rd. S Croy—2G 139
Dulwich Comn. SE21—7C 92
Dulwich Rd. SE24—4L 91
Dulwich Village. SE21—5C 92
Dulwich Wood Av. SE19
—1C 108
Dulwich Wood Pk. SE19
—1C 108
Dumbarton Av. Wal X—7D 6
Dumbarton Rd. SW2—5J 91
Dumbleton Clo. King—5M 103
Dumbreck Rd. SE9—3K 95
Dumfries Clo. Wat—3D 20
Dumont Rd. N16—8C 44
Dunally Pk. Shep—2B 116
Dunbar Av. Beck—8J 109
Dunbar Av. Dag—8L 49
Dunbar Clo. Hay—9F 52
Dunbar Ct. W on T—3G 117
Dunbar Gdns. Dag—1M 65
Dunbar Rd. E7—2E 62
Dunbar Rd. N22—8L 27
Dunbar Rd. N Mald—8A 104
Dunbar St. SE27—9A 92
Dunblane Rd. SE9—1J 95
Dunboe Pl. Shep—2A 116
Dunboyne Rd. NW3—1D 58
Dunbridge St. E2—7E 60
Duncan Clo. Barn—6A 14
Duncan Grn. W3—9C 56
Duncannon St. WC2—1J 75
Duncan Rd. E8—4F 60
Duncan Rd. Rich—3J 87
Duncan St. N1—5M 59
Duncan Ter. N1—5M 59
Duncan Way. Bush, Wat—4K 9
Dunch St. E1—9F 60
Duncombe Hill. SE23—6J 93
Duncombe Rd. N19—6H 43
Duncrievie Rd. SE13—5B 94
Duncroft. SE18—8C 80
Dundalk Rd. SE4—2J 93
Dundas Rd. SE15—1G 93
Dundee Rd. E13—5F 62
Dundee Rd. SE25—9F 108
Dundee St. E1—2F 76
Dundela Gdns. Wor Pk—6F 120
Dundonald Clo. E6—9J 63
Dundonald Rd. NW10—4H 57
Dundonald Rd. SW19—4J 105
Dundry Ho. SE26—9E 92
Dundus Gdns. E Mol—7M 101
Dunedin Rd. E10—8M 45
Dunedin Rd. Ilf—6A 48
Dunedin Rd. Rain—6D 66
Dunedin Way. Hay—7G 53
Dunelm St. E1—9H 61
Dunfield Gdns. SE6—2M 109
Dunfield Rd. SE6—2M 109
  (in two parts)
Dunford Rd. N7—9K 43
Dungarvan Av. SW15—3E 88
Dunheved Clo. T Hth—1L 123
Dunheved Rd. N. T Hth—1L 123
Dunheved Rd. S. T Hth—1L 123
Dunheved Rd. W. T Hth—1L 123
Dunholme Grn. N9—3D 28
Dunholme La. N9—3D 28
Dunholme Rd. N9—3D 28
Dunkeld Rd. SE25—8B 108
Dunkeld Rd. Dag—7F 48
Dunkery Rd. SE9—1H 111
Dunkin Rd. Dart—3L 99
Dunlace Rd. E5—9G 45
Dunleary Clo. Houn—6K 85
Dunlem Gro. SE27—9A 92
Dunley Dri. Croy—9M 125
Dunloe Av. N17—1B 44
Dunloe St. E2—5D 60
Dunlop Pl. SE16—4D 76
Dunmail Dri. Purl—6C 138
Dunmore Rd. NW6—4J 57
Dunmore Rd. SW20—5G 105
Dunmow Clo. Felt—1J 101
Dunmow Clo. Lou—8J 19
Dunmow Dri. Rain—4D 66
Dunmow Rd. E15—9B 46
Dunnage Cres. SE16—5J 77
Dunnimans Rd. Bans—6K 135
Dunningford Clo. Horn—1D 66
Dunn Mead. NW7—7D 24
Dunnock Rd. E6—9J 63
Dunnow Clo. Romf—3G 49
Dunn St. E8—1D 60
Dunollie Rd. NW5—1G 59
Dunoon Rd. SE23—6G 93
Dunraven Dri. Enf—4L 15
Dunraven Rd. W12—2E 72
Dunraven St. W1—1D 74
Dunsany Rd. W14—4H 73

Dunsbury Clo. Sutt—1M 135
Dunsfold Rise. Coul—5H 137
Dunsfold Way. Croy—9M 125
Dunsmore Clo. Bush, Wat
—8B 10
Dunsmore Clo. Hay—7J 53
Dunsmore Rd. W on T—1F 116
Dunsmore Way. Bush, Wat
—8B 10
Dunsmure Rd. N16—6C 44
Dunspring La. Ilf—9M 31
Dunstable Clo. Romf—6H 35
Dunstable M. W1—8E 58
Dunstable Rd. E Mol—8K 101
Dunstable Rd. Rich—3J 87
Dunstable Rd. Romf—6H 35
Dunstall Rd. SW20—3F 104
Dunstall Way. E Mol—7M 101
Dunstall Welling Est. Well
—1F 96
Dunstan Clo. N2—1A 42
Dunstan Rd. NW11—6K 41
Dunstan Rd. Coul—9H 137
Dunstan's Gro. SE22—5F 92
Dunstan's Rd. SE22—6E 92
Dunster Av. Mord—3H 121
Dunster Clo. Barn—6H 13
Dunster Clo. Romf—9A 34
Dunster Ct. EC3—1C 76
Dunster Cres. Upm—7M 51
Dunster Dri. NW9—6A 40
Dunster Gdns. NW6—3K 57
Dunsterville Way. SE1—3B 76
Dunster Way. Ruis—8J 37
Dunston Rd. E8—4D 60
Dunston Rd. SW11—2E 90
Dunston St. E8—4D 60
Dunton Clo. Surb—3J 119
Dunton Rd. E10—5M 45
Dunton Rd. SE1—5D 76
Dunton Rd. SW19—3B 106
Dunton Rd. Romf—2C 50
Duntshill Rd. SW18—7M 89
Dunvegan Clo. E Mol—8L 101
Dunvegan Rd. SE9—3K 95
Dunwich Rd. Bexh—9K 81
Dunworth M. W11—9K 57
Duplex Ride. SW1—3D 74
Dupont Rd. SW20—6H 105
Dupont St. E14—8J 61
Duppas Av. Croy—6M 123
Duppas Clo. Shep—9B 100
Duppas Hill La. Croy—6M 123
Duppas Hill Rd. Croy—6L 123
Duppas Hill Ter. Croy—5M 123
Duppas Rd. Croy—5L 123
Dupree Rd. SE7—6F 78
Dura Den Clo. Beck—4M 109
Durand Clo. Cars—3D 122
Durand Gdns. SW9—9K 75
Durands Wlk. SE16—3J 77
Durand Way. NW10—3A 56
Durant Rd. Swan—3E 114
Durants Pk. Av. Enf—6H 17
Durants Rd. Enf—6G 17
Durant St. E2—6E 60
Durban Gdns. Dag—3A 66
Durban Rd. E15—6C 62
Durban Rd. E17—8K 29
Durban Rd. N17—6C 28
Durban Rd. SE27—1A 108
Durban Rd. Beck—6K 109
Durban Rd. Ilf—6C 48
Durban Rd. E. Wat—6E 8
Durban Rd. W. Wat—6E 8
Durbin Rd. Chess—6J 119
Durdans Rd. S'hall—9K 53
Durell Gdns. Dag—1H 65
Durell Rd. Dag—1H 65
Durford Cres. SW15—7F 88
Durham Av. Brom—8D 110
Durham Av. Houn—6K 69
Durham Av. Romf—2G 51
Durham Av. Wfd G—5H 31
Durham Clo. SW20—6F 104
Durham Hill. Brom—1D 110
Durham Rise. SE18—6A 80
Durham Rd. E12—9H 47
Durham Rd. E16—7C 62
Durham Rd. N2—1C 42
Durham Rd. N7—7K 43
Durham Rd. N9—2E 28
Durham Rd. SW20—5F 104
Durham Rd. W5—4H 71
Durham Rd. Borwd—5A 12
Durham Rd. Brom—7D 110
Durham Rd. Dag—1A 66
Durham Rd. Felt—6G 85
Durham Rd. Harr—3M 37
Durham Rd. Sidc—2F 112
Durham Row. E1—8H 61
Durham St. SE11—7K 75
Durham Ter. W2—9M 57

Durham Wharf. Bren—8G 71
Durley Av. Pinn—5J 37
Durley Rd. N16—5C 44
Durlston Rd. E5—7E 44
Durlston Rd. King—3J 103
Durnell Way. Lou—5L 19
Durnford St. N15—3C 44
Durnford St. SE10—7A 78
Durning Rd. SE19—2B 108
Durnsford Av. SW19
—8L 89
Durnsford Rd. N11—8H 27
Durnsford Rd. SW19—8L 89
Durrants Clo. Rain—5G 67
Durrants Dri. Rick—5A 8
Durrant Way. Orp—7B 128
Durrell Rd. SW6—9K 73
Durrell Way. Shep—1B 116
Durrington Av. SW20—4G 105
Durrington Pk. Rd. SW20
—5G 105
Durrington Rd. E5—9J 45
Dursley Clo. SE3—1G 95
Dursley Gdns. SW9—8H 79
Dursley Rd. SE3—1G 95
Durward St. E1—8F 60
(in two parts)
Durweston St. W1—8D 58
Dury Falls Clo. Horn—6K 51
Dury Rd. Barn—3K 13
Dutch Yd. SW18—4L 89
Duthie St. E14—1A 78
Dutton St. SE10—9A 78
Duxford Clo. Horn—2G 67
Dye Ho. La. E3—4L 61
Dyer's Bldgs. EC1—8L 59
Dyers Hall Rd. E11—7C 46
Dyers La. SW15—2F 88
Dyers Way. Romf—7F 34
Dyke Dri. Orp—2G 129
Dykewood Clo. Bex—9B 98
Dylan Rd. Belv—4L 81
Dylways. SE5—3B 92
Dymchurch Clo. Ilf—9L 31
Dymchurch Clo. Orp—6C 128
Dymes Path. SW19—8H 89
Dymock St. SW6—2M 89
Dymoke Rd. Horn—5D 50
Dyneley Rd. SE12—9G 95
Dyne Rd. NW6—3J 57
Dynevor Rd. N16—8C 44
Dynevor Rd. Rich—4J 87
Dynham Rd. NW6—3L 57
Dyott St. WC1—9H 59
Dyrham La. Barn—1E 12
Dysart Av. King—2G 103
Dysart St. EC2—7C 60
Dyson Rd. E11—4C 46
Dyson Rd. E15—2D 62
Dysons Clo. Wal X—6D 6
Dysons Rd. N18—5F 28

Eade Rd. N4—5A 44
Eagle Av. Romf—4J 49
Eagle Clo. Enf—6G 17
Eagle Clo. Rain—2F 66
Eagle Ct. EC1—8M 59
Eagle Hill. SE19—3B 108
Eagle La. E11—2E 46
Eagle Rd. Wemb—3H 55
Eagles Dri. West—9H 141
Eaglesfield Rd. SE18—9M 79
Eagle St. WC1—8K 59
Eagle Ter. Wfd G—7F 30
Eagle Wharf Rd. N1—5A 60
Eagons Clo. N2—1B 42
Ealdham Sq. SE9—3G 95
Ealing B'way Centre. W5
—1H 71
Ealing Clo. Borwd—3B 12
Ealing Grn. W5—2H 71
Ealing Pk. Gdns. W5—5G 71
Ealing Rd. Bren—6H 71
Ealing Rd. N'holt—4L 53
Ealing Rd. Wemb—2J 55
Ealing Village. W5—9J 55
Eamont St. NW8—5C 58
Eardemont Clo. Dart
—3D 98
Eardley Cres. SW5—6L 73
Eardley Rd. SW16—2G 107
Eardley Rd. Belv—6L 81
Earl Cotts. SE1—6D 76
Earldom Rd. SW15—3G 89
Earle Gdns. King—4J 103
Earlham Gro. E7—1D 62
Earlham Gro. N22—7K 27
Earlham St. WC2—9J 59
Earl Rise. SE18—5B 80
Earl Rd. SE1—6D 76
Earl Rd. SW14—3A 88
Earls Ct. Gdns. SW5—5M 73

Earls Ct. Rd.—4L 73
W8 1-109 & 4-138
SW5 remainder
Earls Ct. Sq. SW5—6M 73
Earls Cres. Harr—2C 38
Earlsferry Way. N1—3K 59
Earlsfield Rd. SW18—7A 90
Earlshall Rd. SE9—3K 95
Earlsmead. Harr—9K 37
Earlsmead Rd. N15—3D 44
Earlsmead Rd. NW10—6G 57
Earl's Path. Lou—4G 19
Earls Ter. W8—4K 73
Earlsthorpe M. SW12—5E 90
Earlsthorpe Rd. SE26—1H 109
Earlstoke St. EC1—6M 59
Earlston Gro. E9—4F 60
Earl St. EC2—8B 60
Earl St. Wat—5G 9
Earls Wlk. W8—4L 73
Earls Wlk. Dag—9F 48
Earlswood Av. T Hth—9L 107
Earlswood Clo. SE10—6C 78
Earlswood Gdns. Ilf—1L 47
Earlswood St. SE10—6C 78
Early M. NW1—4F 58
Earnshaw St. WC2—9H 59
Earsby St. W14—5J 73
Easby Cres. Mord—1M 121
Easebourne Rd. Dag—1G 65
Easedale Dri. Horn—1E 66
E. Acton La. W3—2C 72
E. Arbour St. E1—9H 61
East Av. E12—3J 63
East Av. E17—2M 45
East Av. Hay—2D 68
East Av. S'hall—1K 69
East Av. Wall—7K 123
East Bank. N16—5C 44
Eastbank Rd. Hmptn—2A 102
E. Barnet Rd. Barn—6B 14
Eastbourne Av. W3—9B 56
Eastbourne Gdns. SW14
—2A 88
Eastbourne M. W2—9A 58
Eastbourne Rd. E6—6L 63
Eastbourne Rd. E15—4C 62
Eastbourne Rd. N15—4C 44
Eastbourne Rd. SW17—3E 106
Eastbourne Rd. W4—7A 72
Eastbourne Rd. Bren—6H 71
Eastbourne Rd. Felt—8H 85
Eastbourne Ter. W2—9A 58
Eastbournia Av. N9—3F 28
Eastbrook Av. N9—9G 17
Eastbrook Av. Dag—9A 50
Eastbrook Dri. Romf—8C 50
Eastbrook Rd. SE3—9F 78
Eastbrook Rd. Wal A—6L 7
Eastbury Av. Bark—4C 64
Eastbury Av. Enf—3D 16
Eastbury Av. N'wd—5D 20
Eastbury Ct. Bark—4C 64
Eastbury Gro. W4—6C 72
Eastbury Rd. E6—7L 63
Eastbury Rd. King—4J 103
Eastbury Rd. N'wd—6C 20
Eastbury Rd. Orp—1B 128
Eastbury Rd. Romf—4B 50
Eastbury Rd. Wat—9F 8
Eastbury Sq. Bark—4D 64
Eastbury Ter. E1—7H 61
Eastcastle St. W1—9G 59
Eastcheap. EC3—1C 76
E. Churchfield Rd. W3—2B 72
Eastchurch Rd. Houn—2C 84
East Clo. W5—7L 55
East Clo. Barn—6E 14
East Clo. Gnfd—5A 54
East Clo. Rain—7F 66
Eastcombe Av. SE7—7F 78
Eastcote. Orp—3D 128
Eastcote Av. E Mol—9K 101
Eastcote Av. Gnfd—1E 54
Eastcote Av. Harr—7M 37
Eastcote High Rd. Pinn—4E 36
Eastcote La. Harr—9K 37
Eastcote La. N'holt—1K 53
Eastcote La. N. N'holt. 1J 53
Eastcote Rd. Harr—8A 38
Eastcote Rd. Pinn—3H 37
Eastcote Rd. Ruis—5C 36
Eastcote Rd. Well—1B 96
Eastcote St. SW9—1K 91
Eastcote View. Pinn—2G 37
East Ct. Wemb—7G 39
East Cres. N11—4D 26
East Cres. Enf—7D 16
Eastcroft Rd. Eps—9C 120
Eastdean Av. Eps—5M 133
E. Dene Dri. Romf—5H 35
Eastdown Pk. SE13—3B 94
East Dri. Cars—1C 136

East Dri. N'wd—2C 20
East Dri. Orp—1F 128
East Dri. Wat—9F 4
E. Dulwich Gro. SE22—4C 92
E. Dulwich Rd. SE22—3D 92
(in two parts)
East End Rd.—9L 25
N3 1-55 & 2-120
N2 remainder
E. End Way. Pinn—1J 37
E. Entrance. Dag—5M 65
Eastern Av.—4F 46 to 2H 49
E11 61-75 & 48-120
Ilf & Romf remainder
Eastern Av. Pinn—5H 37
Eastern Av. Wal X—6E 6 .
Eastern Av. E. Romf—1B 50
Eastern Av. W. Romf—2J 49
Eastern Industrial Est. Eri
—3L 81
Eastern Perimeter Rd. Houn
—1D 84
Eastern Rd. E13—5F 62
Eastern Rd. E17—3A 46
Eastern Rd. N2—2D 42
Eastern Rd. N22—8J 27
Eastern Rd. SE4—3L 93
Eastern Rd. Romf—3C 50
Eastern View. West—9G 141
Easternville Gdns. Ilf—4A 48
Eastern Way. SE28—3E 80
E. Ferry Rd. E14—5M 77 .
Eastfield Av. Wat—3H 9
Eastfield Gdns. Dag—9L 49
Eastfield Rd. E17—2L 45
Eastfield Rd. N8—1J 43
Eastfield Rd. Bexh—2A 98
Eastfield Rd. Dag—9K 49
Eastfield Rd. Enf—2H 17
Eastfield Rd. Wal X—5F 6
Eastfields. Pinn—3G 37
Eastfields Rd. W3—8A 56
Eastfields Rd. Mitc—6E 106
East Gdns. SW17—3C 106
Eastgate. Bans—6K 135
Eastglade. N'wd—5D 20
Eastglade. Pinn—1K 37
E. Hall La. Rain—9H 67
E. Hall Rd. Orp—2J 129
East Ham and Barking By-Pass.
Bark—5C 64
East Ham Mnr. Way. E6—8L 63
E. Harding St. EC4—9L 59
E. Heath Rd. NW3—8A 42
East Hill. SW18—4M 89
East Hill. Dart—6J 99
East Hill. S Croy—2C 138
East Hill. Wemb—7L 39
E. Hill Dri. Dart—6K 99
Eastholm. NW11—2M 41
East Holme. Eri—9B 82
East Holme. Hay—2E 68
E. India Dock Rd. E14—9L 61
E. India Dock Wall Rd. E14
—1B 78
Eastlake Rd. SE5—1A 92
Eastlands Cres. SE21—5D 92
East La. SE16—3E 76
Fast La. Abb L. Wat—1D 4
(in two parts)
East La. King—7H 103
East La. Wemb—8F 38
Eastlea Av. Wat—1J 9
Eastleigh Av. Harr—7M 37
Eastleigh Clo. NW2—8C 40
Eastleigh Clo. Sutt—9M 121
Eastleigh Wlk. SW15—6E 88
E. Lodge La. Enf—1H 15
Eastman Rd. W3—3B 72
East Mead. Ruis—8H 37
Eastmead Av. Gnfd—6M 53
Eastmead Clo. Brom—6J 111
Eastmearn Rd. SE21—8A 92
Eastmont Rd. Esh—4D 118
Eastmoor Pl. SE7—4H 79
Eastmoor St. SE7—4H 79
Eastney Rd. Croy—3M 123
Eastney St. SE10—6B 78
Eastnor Rd. SE9—7A 96
Easton Gdns. Borwd—6C 12
Easton St. WC1—7L 59
E. Park Clo. Romf—3J 49
East Pier. E1—2E 76
E. Poultry Av. EC1—8M 59
East Ramp. Houn—9M 143
East Rd. E15—4E 62
East Rd. N1—6B 60
East Rd. SW19—3A 106
East Rd. Barn—1E 26
East Rd. Edgw—8M 23
East Rd. Enf—2G 17
East Rd. Felt—6B 84

East Rd. King—5J 103
East Rd. Purf—7M 83
East Rd. Romf—3J 49
(Chadwell Heath)
East Rd. Romf—5B 50
(Rush Green)
East Rd. Well—1F 96
East Rd. W Dray—5C 143
East Rd. Wey—9B 116
E. Rochester Way. Sidc & Bex
—4C 96
East Row. E11—4E 46
East Row. W10—7J 57
Eastry Av. Brom—1D 126
Eastry Rd. Eri—8L 81
E. Sheen Av. SW14—4B 88
E. Smithfield. E1—1D 76
East St. SE17—6A 76
East St. Bark—4A 64
East St. Bexh—3L 97
East St. Bren—8G 71
East St. Brom—6E 110
East St. Eps—5C 134
E. Surrey Gro. SE15—8D 76
E. Tenter St. E1—9D 60
East Towers. Pinn—3H 37
East View. E4—5A 30
East View. Barn—4K 13
Eastview Av. SE18—8C 80
Eastville Av. NW11—4K 41
East Wlk. Barn—9E 14
East Wlk. Hay—2E 68
Eastway. E9—2K 61
East Way. E11—3F 46
East Way. Brom—2E 126
East Way. Croy—4J 125
Eastway. Eps—3B 134
East Way. Hay—2E 68
Eastway. Mord—9H 105
East Way. Ruis—6E 36
Eastway. Wall—6G 123
Eastway Commercial Centre
E15—1L 61
Eastwell Clo. Beck—4J 109
Eastwick Rd. W on T—8F 116
Eastwood Clo. E18—9E 30
Eastwood Dri. Rain—9F 66
Eastwood Rd. E18—9E 30
Eastwood Rd. N10—9E 26
Eastwood Rd. Ilf—5E 48
E. Woodside. Bex—7J 97
Eastwood St. SW16—3G 107
Eatington Rd. E10—3B 46
Eaton Clo. SW1—5E 74
Eaton Clo. Stan—4F 22
Eaton Dri. SW9—3M 91
Eaton Dri. King—4L 103
Eaton Dri. Romf—7M 33
Eaton Gdns. Dag—3J 65
Eaton Ga. SW1—5E 74
Eaton Ga. N'wd—6A 20
Eaton La. SW1—4F 74
Eaton M. N. SW1—4E 74
Eaton M. S. SW1—5E 74
Eaton M. W. SW1—5E 74
Eaton Pk. Rd. N13—2L 27
Eaton Pl. SW1—4E 74
Eaton Rise. E11—3G 47
Eaton Rise. W5—8H 55
Eaton Rd. NW4—3G 41
Eaton Rd. Enf—6C 16
Faton Rd. Houn—3B 86
Eaton Rd. Sidc—8H 97
Eaton Rd. Sutt—8B 122
Eaton Row. SW1—4F 74
Eatons Mead. E4—2L 29
Eaton Sq. SW1—5E 74
Eaton Ter. SW1—5E 74
Eatonville Rd. SW17—8D 90
Eatonville Vs. SW17—8D 90
Ebbas Way. Eps—7M 133
Ebbisham Dri. SW8—7K 75
Ebbisham Rd. Eps—6M 133
Ebbisham Rd. Wor Pk—4G 121
Ebbsfleet Rd. NW2—1J 57
Ebdon Way. SE3—2F 94
Ebenezer St. N1—6B 60
Fhenezer Wlk. SW16—5G 107
Ebley Clo. SE15—7D 76
Ebner St. SW18—4M 89
Ebor St. E1—7D 60
Ebrington Rd. Harr—4H 39
Ebsworth St. SE23—6H 93
Eburne Rd. N7—8J 43
Ebury Bri. SW1—6F 74
Ebury Bri. Est. SW1—6F 74
Ebury Clo. Kes—5J 127
Ebury Clo. N'wd—5A 20
Ebury M. SW1—5F 74
Ebury M. E. SW1—4F 74
Ebury Rd. Wat—5G 9
Ebury Sq. SW1—5F 74

Ebury St. SW1—5E 74
Ecclesbourne Clo. N13—5L 27
Ecclesbourne Gdns. N13
—5L 27
Ecclesbourne Rd. N1—3A 60
Ecclesbourne Rd. T Hth
—9A 108
Eccles Rd. SW11—3D 90
Eccleston Bri. SW1—5F 74
Eccleston Clo. Barn—6D 14
Eccleston Clo. Orp—3B 128
Eccleston Cres. Romf—5F 48
Ecclestone Ct. Wemb—1J 55
Ecclestone M. Wemb—1J 55
Ecclestone Pl. Wemb—1K 55
Eccleston Rd. W13—2E 70
Eccleston M. SW1—4E 74
Eccleston Pl. SW1—5F 74
Eccleston Sq. SW1—5F 74
Eccleston Sq. M. SW1—5G 75
Eccleston St. SW1—4F 74
Echo Heights. E4—1M 29
Eckersley St. E1—7D 60
Eckford St. N1—5L 59
Eckstein Rd. SW11—3C 90
Eclipse Rd. E13—8F 62
Ector Rd. SE6—8C 94
Edam Ct. Sidc—9E 96
Edbrooke Rd. W9—7L 57
Eddington St. N4—6L 43
Eddisbury Ho. SE26—9E 92
Eddiscombe Rd. SW6—1K 89
Eddy Clo. Romf—4M 49
Eddystone Rd. SE4—4J 93
Eddystone Wlk. Stai—6C 144
Ede Clo. Houn—2K 85
Edenbridge Clo. Orp—8H 113
Edenbridge Rd. E9—3H 61
Euenbridge Rd. Enf—8C 16
Eden Clo. Bex—1B 114
Eden Clo. Wemb—4H 55
Edencourt Rd. SW16—3F 106
Edendale Rd. Bexh—9B 82
Edenfield Gdns. Wor Pk
—5D 120
Eden Gro. E17—3M 45
Eden Gro. N7—1K 59
Edenhall Clo. Romf—5G 35
Edenhall Glen. Romf—5G 35
Edenhall Rd. Romf—5G 35
Edenham Way. W10—7K 57
Edenhurst Av. SW6—2K 89
Eden Pk. Av. Beck—8K 109
Eden Rd. E17—3M 45
Eden Rd. SE27—2M 107
Eden Rd. Beck—8J 109
Eden Rd. Bex—1A 114
Eden Rd. Croy—6B 124
Edensor Gdns. W4—8C 72
Edensor Rd. W4—8C 72
Eden St. King—6H 103
Edenvale Rd. Mitc—4E 106
Edenvale St. SW6—1A 90
Eden Way. King—6J 103
Eden Way. Beck—9K 109
Ederline Av. SW16—7K 107
Edgar Clo. Swan—7D 114
Edgar Ho. E11—5E 46
Edgarley Tor. SW6—9J 73
Edgar Rd. E3—6M 61
Edgar Rd. Houn—6K 85
Edgar Rd. Romf—5H 49
Edgar Rd. S Croy—1B 138
Edgar Rd. W Dray—2J 143
Edgbaston Rd. Wat—3F 20
Edgeborough Way. Brom
—5H 111
Edgebury. Chst—1M 111
Edgebury Wlk. Chst—1A 112
Edgecombe Rd. E11—6D 46
Edgecoombe. S Croy—9C 125
Edgecote Clo. W3—2A 72
Edgecot Gro. N15—3C 44
Edgefield Av. Bark—3D 64
Edgefield Clo. Dart—7M 99
Edge Hill. SE18—7M 79
Edge Hill. SW19—4H 105
Edgehill Av. N3—2L 41
Edgehill Gdns. Dag—9L 49
Edgehill Rd. W13—8G 55
Edgehill Rd. Chst—1A 112
Edgehill Rd. Mitc—5F 106
Edgehill Rd. Purl—2L 137
Edgeley La. SW4—2H 91
Edgeley Rd. SW4—2H 91
Edgel St. SW18—3M 89
Edgepoint Clo. SE27—2M 107
Edge St. W8—2L 73
Edgewood Dri. Orp—7E 128
Edgewood Grn. Croy—3H 125
Edgeworth Av. NW4—3E 40
Edgeworth Clo. NW4—3E 40

Edgeworth Cres. NW4—3E 40
Edgeworth Rd. SE9—3G 95
Edgeworth Rd. Barn—6C 14
Edgington Rd. SW16—3H 107
Edgwarebury Gdns. Edgw
—5L 23
Edgwarebury La. Borwd
—9J 11
Edgwarebury La. Edgw—2L 23
Edgware Rd. NW2—6F 40
Edgware Rd. NW9—9A 24
Edgware Rd. W2—7B 58
Edgware Way. Edgw—1H 23
Edinburgh Cres. Wal X—6E 6
Edinburgh Dri. Uxb—9A 36
Edinburgh Ga. SW1—3D 74
Edinburgh Rd. E13—5F 62
Edinburgh Rd. E17—3L 45
Edinburgh Rd. N18—5E 28
Edinburgh Rd. W7—3D 70
Edinburgh Rd. Sutt—4B 122
Edington Rd. SE2—4F 80
Edington Rd. Enf—4G 17
Edison Av. Horn—6D 50
Edison Clo. Horn—6D 50
Edison Dri. S'hall—9M 53
Edison Gro. SE18—8D 80
Edison Rd. N8—4H 43
Edison Rd. Brom—6E 110
Edison Rd. Well—9D 80
Edis St. NW1—4E 58
Edith Gdns. Surb—2M 119
Edith Gro. SW10—7A 74
Edithna St. SW9—2J 91
Edith Rd. E6—3H 63
Edith Rd. E15—1B 62
Edith Rd. N11—7H 27
Edith Rd. SE25—9B 108
Edith Rd. SW19—3M 105
Edith Rd. W14—5J 73
Edith Rd. Orp—7E 128
Edith Rd. Romf—5H 49
Edith Row. SW6—9M 73
Edith Ter. SW10—8A 74
Edith Vs. W14—5K 55
Edith Yd. SW10—8A 74
Edmanson's Clo. N17—8D 28
Edmund Rd. Mitc—7C 106
Edmund Rd. Orp—1G 129
Edmund Rd. Rain—5C 66
Edmund Rd. Well—2E 96
Edmunds Av. Orp—7H 113
Edmunds Clo. Hay—8G 53
Edmund St. SE5—8B 76
Edmunds Wlk. N2—2C 42
Edna Rd. SW20—6H 105
Edna St. SW11—9C 74
Edrick Rd. Edgw—6A 24
Edrick Wlk. Edgw—6A 24
Edric Rd. SE14—8H 77
Edridge Clo. Bush, Wat—7A 10
Edridge Rd. Horn—1H 67
Edridge Rd. Croy—5A 124
Edulf Rd. Borwd—3M 11
Edward Av. E4—6M 29
Edward Av. Mord—9B 106
Edward Clo. N9—9D 16
Edward Clo. Hmptn—2A 102
Edward Clo. N'holt—5G 53
Edward Clo. Romf—1G 51
Edward Ct. E16—8E 62
Edward Ct. Wal A—6M 7
Edwardes Sq. W8—4K 73
Edward Gro. Barn—7B 14
Edward M. W1—9E 58
Edward Pl. SE8—7K 77
Edward Rd. E17—2H 45
Edward Rd. SE20—3H 109
Edward Rd. Barn—7B 14
Edward Rd. Belv—5L 81
Edward Rd. Brom—4F 110
Edward Rd. Chst—2M 111
Edward Rd. Coul—7H 137
Edward Rd. Croy—2C 124
Edward Rd. Felt—4B 84
Edward Rd. Hmptn—2A 102
Edward Rd. Harr—1A 38
Edward Rd. N'holt—5G 53
Edward Rd. Romf—4J 49
Edward Rd. West—9J 141
Edward's Av. Ruis—2F 52
Edward's Clo. Wor Pk—4H 121
Edward's Cotts. N1—2M 59
Edwards Gdns. Swan—8B 114
Edward's La. N16—7B 44
Edward Sq. N1—4K 59
Edward St. E16—7E 62
Edward St. J—8J 77
SE8 1-95 & 2-86
SE14 remainder
Edward Temme Av. E15—3D 62
Edward Way. Ashf—8D 144
Edwick Ct. Wal X—2D 6

Edwina Gdns. Ilf—3J 47
Edwin Av. E6—6L 63
Edwin Clo. Bexh—7K 81
Edwin Clo. Rain—6D 66
Edwin Pl. Croy—3B 124
Edwin Rd. Dart—9F 98
Edwin Rd. Edgw—6B 24
Edwin Rd. Twic—7C 86
Edwin's Mead. E9—9J 45
Edwin St. E1—7G 61
Edwin St. E16—8E 62
Edwin Ware Ct. Pinn—9G 21
Edwyn Clo. Barn—8G 13
Effie Pl. SW6—8L 73
Effie Rd. SW6—8L 73
Effingham Clo. Sutt—9M 121
Effingham Rd. N8—3L 43
Effingham Rd. SE12—4C 94
Effingham Rd. Croy—2K 123
Effingham Rd. Surb—2F 118
Effort St. SW17—2C 106
Effra Pde. SW2—4L 91
Effra Rd. SW2—4L 91
Effra Rd. SW19—3M 105
Egan Way. SE16—6F 76
Egan Way. Hay—1C 68
Egbert St. NW1—4E 58
Egerton Av. Swan—4D 114
Egerton Clo. Dart—7F 98
Egerton Clo. Pinn—2E 36
Egerton Cres. SW3—5C 74
Egerton Gdns. NW4—2F 40
Egerton Gdns. NW10—4G 57
Egerton Gdns. SW3—4C 74
Egerton Gdns. W13—9F 54
Egerton Gdns. Ilf—8D 48
Egerton Gdns. M. SW3—4C 74
Egerton Pl. SW3—4C 74
Egerton Pl. Wey—8A 116
Egerton Rd. N16—5D 44
Egerton Rd. SE25—7C 108
Egerton Rd. N Mald—8D 104
Egerton Rd. Twic—5G 87
Egerton Rd. Wemb—3K 55
Egerton Rd. Wey—8A 116
Egerton Ter. SW3—4C 74
Egham Clo. SW19—8J 89
Egham Clo. Sutt—4J 121
Egham Cres. Sutt—5H 121
Egham Rd. E13—8F 62
Eglantine La. F'ham &
S Dar, Dart—2L 131
Eglantine Rd. SW18—4A 90
Egleston Rd. Mord—1M 121
Eglington Rd. E4—9B 18
Eglinton Hill. SE18—7M 79
Eglinton Rd. SE18—7L 79
Eglise Rd. Warl—9J 139
Egliston M. SW15—2G 89
Egliston Rd. SW15—2G 89
Egmont Av. Surb—3K 119
Egmont Rd. N Mald—8D 104
Egmont Rd. Surb—3K 119
Egmont Rd. Sutt—9A 122
Egmont Rd. W on T—2F 116
Egmont St. SE14—8H 77
Egremont Rd. SE27—9L 91
Eighteenth Rd. Mitc—8J 107
Eighth Av. E12—9K 47
Eighth Av. Hay—2E 68
Eileen Rd. SE25—9B 108
Eisenhower Dri. E6—8J 63
Elaine Gro. NW5—1E 58
Elam Clo. SE5—1M 91
Elam St. SE5—1M 91
Eland Pl. Croy—5M 123
Eland Rd. SW11—2D 90
Eland Rd. Croy—5M 123
Elba Pl. SE17—5A 76
Elberon Av. Croy—1G 123
Elbe St. SW6—1A 90
Elborough Rd. SE25—9E 108
Elborough St. SW18—7L 89
Elbury Dri. E16—9E 62
Elcho St. SW11—8C 74
Elcot Av. SE15—8F 76
Elder Av. N8—3J 43
Elderbek Clo. Wal X—1A 6
Elderberry Gro. SE27—1A 108
Elderberry Rd. W5—3J 71
Elder Ct. Bush, Wat—2C 22
Elderfield Rd. E5—9G 45
Elderfield Wlk. E11—3F 46
Elder Oak Clo. SE20—5F 108
Elder Oak Ct. SE20—5F 108
Elder Rd. SE27—2A 108
Elderslie Clo. Beck—1M 125
Elderslie Rd. SE9—4L 95
Elder St. E1—7D 60
Elderton Rd. SE26—1J 109
Eldertree Pl. Mitc—5G 107
Eldertree Way. Mitc—5G 107

Elder Way. Rain—6H 67
Elderwood Pl. SE27—2A 108
Eldon Av. Borwd—4L 11
Eldon Av. Croy—4G 125
Eldon Av. Houn—8L 69
Eldon Gro. NW3—1B 58
Eldon Pk. SE25—8F 108
Eldon Rd. E17—2K 45
Eldon Rd. N9—1G 29
Eldon Rd. N22—8M 27
Eldon Rd. W8—4M 73
Eldon St. EC2—8B 60
Eldonwall Trading Est. NW2
—6E 40
Eldon Way. NW10—6M 55
Eldred Dri. Orp—4G 129
Eldred Rd. Bark—4C 64
Eldridge Clo. Felt—7E 84
Eleanor Av. Eps—2B 134
Eleanor Cres. NW7—5H 25
Eleanor Cross Rd. Wal X—7E 6
Eleanor Gdns. Barn—7H 13
Eleanor Gdns. Dag—8K 49
Eleanor Gro. SW13—2C 88
Eleanor Rd. Uxb—8A 36
Eleanor Rd. E8—2F 60
Eleanor Rd. E15—2D 62
Eleanor Rd. N11—6J 27
Eleanor Rd. Wal X—6E 6
Eleanor St. E3—6L 61
Eleanor Wlk. SE18—5J 79
Electric Av. SW9—3L 91
Electric La. SW9—3L 91
Electric Pde. Surb—1H 119
Elephant & Castle. SE1—5M 75
Elephant La. SE16—3G 77
Elephant Rd. SE17—5A 76
Elers Rd. W13—3G 71
Elers Rd. Hay—5B 68
Eleven Acre Rise. Lou—5K 19
Eley Rd. N18—4G 29
Eley's Est. N18—5H 29
Elfindale Rd. SE24—4A 92
Elfin Gro. Tedd—2D 102
Elford Clo. SE3—3G 95
Elfort Rd. N5—9L 43
Elfrida Cres. SE6—1L 109
Elfrida Rd. Wat—7G 9
Elf Row. E1—1G 77
Elfwine Rd. W7—8C 54
Elgal Clo. Orp—7M 127
Elgar Av. SW16—7J 107
Elgar Av. W5—3J 71
Elgar Av. Surb—3L 119
Elgar Clo. SE8—8L 77
Elgar Clo. Borwd—9H 11
Elgar St. SE16—4J 77
Elgin Av. W9—7L 57
Elgin Av. Ashf—3A 100
Elgin Av. Harr—9F 22
Elgin Av. Romf—6M 35
Elgin Av. Wey—7M 57
Elgin Cres. W11—1J 73
Elgin Cres. Houn—1C 84
Elgin Dri. N'wd—7C 20
Elgin Est. W9—7L 57
Elgin M. W11—9J 57
Elgin M. N. W9—6M 57
Elgin M. S. W9—6M 57
Elgin Rd. N22—9G 27
Elgin Rd. Croy—4D 124
Elgin Rd. Ilf—6C 48
Elgin Rd. Sutt—5A 122
Elgin Rd. Wall—8G 123
Elgin Rd. Wal X—3C 6
Elgood Av. N'wd—6E 20
Elgood Clo. W11—1J 73
Elham Clo. Brom—4H 111
Elia M. N1—5M 59
Elias Pl. SW8—7L 75
Elia St. N1—5M 59
Elibank Rd. SE9—3K 95
Elim Est. SE1—4C 76
Elim Way. E13—6D 62
Eliot Bank. SE23—8F 92
Eliot Cotts. SE3—1C 94
Eliot Dri. Harr—7M 37
Eliot Hill. SE13—1A 94
Eliot Ho. Rich—5K 87
Eliot Pk. SE13—1A 94
Eliot Pl. SE3—1C 94
Eliot Rd. Dag—9H 49
Eliot Rd. Dart—4M 99
Eliot Sq. NW3—3C 58
Eliot Vale. SE3—1B 94
Elizabethan Clo. Stai—6B 144
Elizabethan Way. Stai—6B 144
Elizabeth Av. N1—3B 60
Elizabeth Av. Enf—5M 15
Elizabeth Av. Ilf—7B 48
Elizabeth Bri. SW1—5F 74
Elizabeth Clo. E14—9M 61
Elizabeth Clo. W9—7A 58

Elizabeth Clo. Barn—5H 13
Elizabeth Clo. Romf—8M 33
Elizabeth Clyde Clo. N15
—2C 44
Elizabeth Cotts. Rich—9K 71
Elizabeth Ct. Wat—2D 8
Elizabeth Gdns. W3—2D 72
Elizabeth Gdns. Stan—6G 23
Elizabeth Gdns. Sun—7G 101
Elizabeth M. NW3—2D 58
Elizabeth Pl. N15—2B 44
Elizabeth Ride. N9—9F 16
Elizabeth Rd. E6—4H 63
Elizabeth Rd. N15—3C 44
Elizabeth St. SW1—5E 74
Elizabeth Ter. SE9—5K 95
Elizabeth Way. SE19—4B 108
Elizabeth Way. Felt—1G 101
Elizabeth Way. Orp—9G 113
Elkington Rd. E13—7F 62
Elkins, The. Romf—9C 34
Elkstone Rd. W10—8K 57
Ellaline Rd. W6—7H 73
Ellanby Cres. N18—5F 28
Elland Rd. SE15—3G 93
Elland Rd. W on T—4H 117
Ella Rd. N8—5J 43
Ellement Clo. Pinn—3H 37
Ellenborough Pl. SW15—3E 88
Ellenborough Rd. N22—8A 28
Ellenborough Rd. Sidc—2H 113
Ellenbridge Way. S Croy
—1C 138
Ellen Clo. Brom—7H 111
Ellen Ct. N9—2G 29
Ellen St. E1—9E 60
Elleray Rd. Tedd—3D 102
Ellerby St. SW6—9H 73
Ellerdale Clo. NW3—9A 42
Ellerdale Rd. NW3—1A 58
Ellerdale St. SE13—3M 93
Ellerdine Rd. Houn—3B 86
Ellerker Gdns. Rich—5J 87
Ellerman Av. Twic—7K 85
Ellerslie Gdns. NW10—4E 56
Ellerslie Rd. W12—2F 72
Ellerslie Sq. Industrial Est.
SW2—4J 91
Ellerton Gdns. Dag—3G 65
Ellerton Rd. SW13—9E 72
Ellerton Rd. SW18—7B 90
Ellerton Rd. SW20—4E 104
Ellerton Rd. Dag—3G 65
Ellerton Rd. Surb—4K 119
Ellery Rd. SE19—4B 108
Ellery St. SE15—1F 92
Ellesborough Clo. Wat—5G 21
Ellesmere Av. NW7—3B 24
Ellesmere Av. Beck—6M 109
Ellesmere Clo. E11—3D 46
Ellesmere Clo. Ruis—5A 36
Ellesmere Dri. S Croy—6F 138
Ellesmere Gdns. Ilf—4J 47
Ellesmere Gro. Barn—7K 13
Ellesmere Rd. E3—5J 61
Ellesmere Rd. NW10—1E 56
Ellesmere Rd. W4—7B 72
Ellesmere Rd. Gnfd—7A 54
Ellesmere Rd. Twic—5G 87
Ellesmere Rd. Wey—9C 116
Ellesmere St. E14—9M 61
Elleswood Ct. Surb—2H 119
Ellingfort Rd. E8—3F 60
Ellingham Rd. E15—9B 46
Ellingham Rd. W12—3E 72
Ellingham Rd. Chess—8H 119
Ellington Rd. N10—2F 42
Ellington Rd. Felt—1D 100
Ellington Rd. Houn—1M 85
Ellington St. N7—2L 59
Elliot Clo. E15—3C 62
Elliot Rd. NW4—4F 40
Elliot Rd. Brom—8H 111
Elliott Clo. Wemb—8L 39
Elliott Gdns. Romf—8F 34
Elliott Rd. SW9—8M 75
Elliott Rd. W4—5C 72
Elliott Rd. Stan—6E 22
Elliott Rd. T Hth—8M 107
Elliotts Row. SE11—5M 75
Ellis Av. Rain—8E 66
Ellis Clo. SE9—8A 96
Elliscombe Rd. SE7—7G 79
Ellis Ct. W7—8D 54
Ellisfield Dri. SW15—6E 88
Ellis M. SE7—7G 79
Ellison Gdns. S'hall—5K 69
Ellison Rd. SW13—1D 88
Ellison Rd. SW16—4H 107
Ellison Rd. Sidc—7B 96
Ellis Rd. Mitc—1D 122
Ellis St. SW1—5E 74
Ellmore Clo. Romf—8F 34

Ellora Rd. SW16—2H 107
Ellsworth St. E2—6F 60
Ellwood Gdns. Wat—7G 5
Elmar Rd. N15—2B 44
Elm Av. W5—2J 71
Elm Av. Ruis—6E 36
Elm Av. Upm—8M 51
Elm Av. Wat—9J 9
Elm Bank. N14—9J 15
Elmbank Av. Barn—6G 13
Elm Bank Gdns. SW13—1C 88
Elmbank Way. W7—8B 54
Elmbourne Dri. Belv—5M 81
Elmbourne Rd. SW17—9F 90
Elmbridge Av. Surb—9M 103
Elmbridge Clo. Ruis—4E 36
Elmbridge Dri. Ruis—3D 36
Elmbridge Rd. Ilf—6E 32
Elmbridge Wlk. E8—3E 60
Elmbrook Gdns. SE9—3J 95
Elmbrook Rd. Sutt—6K 121
Elm Clo. E11—4F 46
Elm Clo. N19—7G 43
Elm Clo. NW4—3H 41
Elm Clo. SW20—8G 105
Elm Clo. Buck H—2H 31
Elm Clo. Cars—3D 122
Elm Clo. Dart—7G 99
Elm Clo. Harr—4M 37
Elm Clo. Hay—9E 52
Elm Clo. Romf—8M 33
Elm Clo. S Croy—8C 124
Elm Clo. Surb—2A 120
Elm Clo. Twic—8M 85
Elm Clo. Wal A—7K 7
Elm Clo. Wal~Wrf—9M 139
Elm Ct. Wat—5F 8
Elmcourt Rd. SE27—8M 91
Elm Cres. W5—2J 71
Elm Cres. King—5J 103
Elmcroft Av. E11—3F 46
Elmcroft Av. N9—8F 16
Elmcroft Av. NW11—5K 41
Elmcroft Av. Sidc—5E 96
Elmcroft Clo. E11—2F 46
Elmcroft Clo. W5—9H 55
Elmcroft Clo. Chess—5J 1
Elmcroft Clo. Felt—5D 84
Elmcroft Cres. NW11—5J 41
Elmcroft Cres. Harr—1L 37
Elmcroft Dri. Chess—5J 119
Elmcroft Gdns. NW9—3L 39
Elmcroft Rd. Orp—2E 128
Elmcroft St. E5—9G 45
Elmdale Rd. N13—5K 27
Elmdene. Surb—3A 120
Elmdene Av. Horn—3K 51
Elmdene Clo. Beck—1K 125
Elmdene Rd. SE18—6M 79
Elmdon Rd. Houn—1J 85
Elmdon Rd. Houn—2D 84
(Hatton)
Elm Dri. Harr—4M 37
Elm Dri. Sun—6G 101
Elm Dri. Swan—6B 114
Elm Dri. Wal X—1E 6
Elmer Av. Hav, Romf—3C 34
Elmer Clo. Enf—5K 15
Elmer Clo. Rain—3E 66
Elmer Gdns. Edgw—7M 23
Elmer Gdns. Iswth—2B 86
Elmer Gdns. Rain—3E 66
Elmer Rd. SE6—6A 94
Elmers Dri. Tedd—3F 102
Elmers End Rd. SE20 1-81 & 2-82
Beck remainder
—6G 109
Elmerside Rd. Beck—8J 109
Elmers Rd. SE25—2E 124
Elmfield Av. N8—3J 43
Elmfield Av. Mitc—5E 106
Elmfield Av. Tedd—2D 102
Elmfield Pk. Brom—7E 110
Elmfield Rd. E4—2A 30
Elmfield Rd. E17—4H 45
Elmfield Rd. N2—1B 42
Elmfield Rd. SW17—8E 90
Elmfield Rd. Brom—7E 110
Elmfield Rd. S'hall—4J 69
Elmfield Way. S Croy—1D 138
Elm Friars Wlk. NW1—3H 59
Elm Gdns. N2—1A 42
Elm Gdns. Enf—2B 16
Elm Gdns. Esh—8D 118
Elm Gdns. Mitc—8H 107
Elmgate Av. Felt—9G 85
Elmgate Gdns. Edgw—5A 24
Elm Grn. W3—9C 56
Elm Gro. N8—4J 43
Elm Gro. NW2—9M 41
Elm Gro. SE15—1D 92
Elm Gro. SW19—4J 105
Elm Gro. Eps—6A 134

Elm Gro. Eri—8B 82
Elm Gro. Harr—5L 37
Elm Gro. Horn—4J 51
Elm Gro. King—5J 103
Elm Gro. Orp—3D 128
Elm Gro. Sutt—6M 121
Elm Gro. Wat—1E 8
Elm Gro. W Dray—1K 143
Elm Gro. Wfd G—5D 30
Elmgrove Cres. Harr—3E 38
Elmgrove Gdns. Harr—3E 38
Elm Gro. Pde. Wall—5E 122
Elm Gro. Rd. SW13—1E 88
Elm Gro. Rd. W5—3J 71
Elmgrove Rd. Croy—2F 124
Elmgrove Rd. Harr—3D 38
Elmhall Gdns. E11—4F 46
Elmhurst. Belv—7J 81
Elmhurst Av. N2—1B 42
Elmhurst Av. Mitc—4F 106
Elmhurst Dri. E18—9E 30
Elmhurst Dri. Horn—6G 51
Elmhurst Rd. E7—3F 62
Elmhurst Rd. N17—9D 28
Elmhurst Rd. SE9—8J 95
Elmhurst Rd. Enf—1G 17
Elmhurst Rd. SW4—2H 91
Elmhurst Way. Lou—9K 19
Elmington Clo. Bex—5M 97
Elmington Rd. SE5—8B 76
Elmira St. SE13—2M 93
Elm La. SE6—8K 93
Elm Lawn Clo. Uxb—3C 142
Elmlea Dri. Hay—8C 52
Elmlee Clo. Chst—3K 111
Elmley Clo. E6—8J 63
Elmley St. SE18—5B 80
Elm M. Rich—5K 87
Elmore Rd. E11—8A 46
Elmore Rd. Enf—2H 17
Elmores. Lou—5L 19
Elmore St. N1—3B 60
Elm Pk. SW2—5K 91
Elm Pk. Stan—5F 22
Elm Pk. Av. N15—3D 44
Elm Pk. Av. Horn—9E 50
Elm Pk. Gdns. NW4—3H 41
Elm Pk. Gdns. SW10—6B 74
Elm Pk. Gdns. S Croy—2G 139
Elm Pk. La. SW3—6B 74
Elm Pk. Rd. E10—6J 45
Elm Pk. Rd. N3—7K 25
Elm Pk. Rd. N21—9A 16
Elm Pk. Rd. SE25—7D 108
Elm Pk. Rd. SW3—7B 74
Elm Pk. Rd. Pinn—9G 21
Elm Pas. Barn—6K 13
Elm Pl. SW7—6B 74
Elm Rd. E7—2D 62
Elm Rd. E11—7B 46
Elm Rd. E17—3A 46
Elm Rd. SW14—2A 88
Elm Rd. Barn—6K 13
Elm Rd. Beck—6K 109
Elm Rd. Chess—6J 119
Elm Rd. Dart—7H 99
Elm Rd. Eps—8D 120
Elm Rd. Eri—9E 82
Elm Rd. Esh—8D 118
Elm Rd. Felt—7B 84
Elm Rd. Houn—1J 85
Elm Rd. King—5K 103
Elm Rd. N Mald—7B 104
Elm Rd. Orp—9E 128
Elm Rd. Purl—5M 137
Elm Rd. Romf—9M 33
Elm Rd. Sidc—1E 112
Elm Rd. T Hth—8B 108
Elm Rd. Wall—3E 122
Elm Rd. Warl—9H 139
Elm Rd. Wemb—1J 55
Elm Rd. W. Sutt—2K 121
Elm Row. NW3—8A 42
Elms Av. N10—1F 42
Elms Av. NW4—3H 41
Elmscott Gdns. N21—8A 16
Elmscott Rd. Brom—2D 110
Elms Ct. Wemb—9E 38
Elms Cres. SW4—5G 91
Elmsdale Rd. E17—2K 45
Elms Farm Rd. Horn—1G 67
Elms Gdns. Dag—9K 49
Elms Gdns. Wemb—9E 38
Elmshaw Rd. SW15—4E 88
Elmshorn. Eps—8G 135
Elmshurst Cres. N2—2B 42
Elmside. Croy—8M 125
Elmside Rd. Wemb—8L 39
Elms La. Wemb—8E 38
Elmsleigh Av. Harr—2F 38
Elmsleigh Rd. Twic—8B 86
Elmslie Clo. Eps—6B 134
Elmslie Clo. Wfd G—6K 31

Elms M. W2—1B 74
Elms Pk. Av. Wemb—9E 38
Elms Rd. SW4—4G 91
Elms Rd. Harr—7C 22
Elmstead Av. Chst—2K 111
Elmstead Av. Wemb—6J 39
Elmstead Clo. N20—2L 25
Elmstead Clo. Eps—7C 120
Elmstead Gdns. Wor Pk
—5E 120
Elmstead Glade. Chst—3K 111
Elmstead La. Chst—4J 111
Elmstead Rd. Eri—9C 82
Elmstead Rd. Ilf—7C 48
Elmsted Cres. Well—7G 81
Elms, The. SW13—2D 88
Elmstone Rd. SW6—9L 73
Elm St. WC1—7K 59
Elmsworth Av. Houn—1M 85
Elm Ter. NW2—8L 41
Elm Ter. NW3—9C 42
Elm Ter. SE9—5L 95
Elm Ter. Harr—8B 22
Elm Ter. Stan—5G 23
Elmton Way. E5—8E 44
Elm Tree Av. Esh—2B 118
Elm Tree Clo. NW8—6B 58
Elm Tree Clo. N'holt—5K 53
Elmtree Rd. Tedd—1C 102
Elm Wlk. NW3—7L 41
Elm Wlk. SW20—8G 105
Elm Wlk. Orp—5K 127
Elm Wlk. Rad—1D 10
Elm Wlk. Romf—1E 50
Elm Way. N11—6E 26
Elm Way. NW10—9C 40
Elm Way. Eps—7B 120
Elm Way. Wor Pk—5G 121
Elmwood Av. N13—5J 27
Elmwood Av. Borwd—6M 11
Elmwood Av. Felt—8E 84
Elmwood Av. Harr—3E 38
Elmwood Clo. Asht—9H 133
Elmwood Clo. Wall—4F 122
Elmwood Ct. Wemb—8E 38
Elmwood Cres. NW9—2A 40
Elmwood Dri. Bex—6J 97
Elmwood Dri. Eps—8E 120
Elmwood Gdns. W7—9C 54
Elmwood Rd. SE24—4B 92
Elmwood Rd. W4—7A 72
Elmwood Rd. Croy—2M 123
Elmwood Rd. Mitc—7D 106
Elmworth Gro. SE21—8B 92
Elnathan M. W9—7M 57
Elphinstone Rd. E17—9K 29
Elphinstone St. N5—9M 43
Elrick Clo. Eri—7C 82
Elrington Rd. E8—2E 60
Elruge Clo. W Dray—4H 143
Elsa Rd. Well—1F 96
Elsa St. E1—8J 61
Elsdale St. E9—2G 61
Elsden M. E2—5G 61
Elsden Rd. N17—8D 28
Elsenham Rd. E12—1L 63
Elsenham St. SW18—7K 89
Elsham Rd. E11—9C 46
Elsham Rd. W14—3J 73
Elsiedene Rd. N21—9A 16
Elsiemaud Rd. SE4—4K 93
Elsie Rd. SE22—3D 92
Elsinge Rd. Enf—9B 6
Elsinore Av. Stai—6C 144
Elsinore Gdns. NW2—8H 41
Elsinore Rd. SE23—7J 93
Elsley Rd. SW11—2D 90
Elspeth Rd. SW11—3D 90
Elspeth Rd. Wemb—1J 55
Elsrick Av. Mord—9L 105
Elstan Way. Croy—2J 125
Elsted St. SE17—5B 76
Elstow Clo. SE9—4L 95
(in two parts)
Elstow Clo. Ruis—5H 37
Elstow Gdns. Dag—4J 65
Elstow Rd. Dag—4J 65
Elstree Gdns. N9—1F 28
Elstree Gdns. Belv—5J 81
Elstree Gdns. Ilf—1A 64
Elstree Hill. Brom—4C 110
Elstree Hill N. Borwd—7H 11
Elstree Hill S. Borwd—9H 11
Elstree Rd. Bush, Wat & Borwd
—9B 10
Elstree Way. Borwd—4M 11
Elswick Rd. SE13—1M 93
Elswick St. SW6—1A 90
Elsworthy. Th Dit—1C 118
Elsworthy Rise. NW3—3C 58
Elsworthy Rd. NW3—4C 58
Elsworthy Ter. NW3—3C 58
Elsynge Rd. SW18—4B 90

Eltham Grn. SE9—4H 95
Eltham Grn. Rd. SE9—3G 95
Eltham High St. SE9—5K 95
Eltham Hill. SE9—4H 95
Eltham Pal. Rd. SE9—5G 95
Eltham Pk. Gdns. SE9—3L 95
Eltham Rd.—4E 94
SE12 1-101 & 2-120
SE9 remainder
Elthiron Rd. SW6—9L 73
Elthorne Av. W7—3D 70
Elthorne Ct. Felt—7G 85
Elthorne Pk. Rd. W7—3E 70
Elthorne Rd. N19—7H 43
Elthorne Rd. NW9—5B 40
Elthorne Rd. Uxb—5B 142
Elthorne Way. NW9—4B 40
Elthruda Rd. SE13—5B 94
Eltisley Rd. Ilf—9M 47
Elton Av. Barn—7K 13
Elton Av. Gnfd—2D 54
Elton Av. Wemb—1F 54
Elton Clo. Tedd—4G 103
Elton Pl. N16—1C 60
Elton Rd. King—5K 103
Elton Rd. Purl—4G 137
Elton Way. Wat—4M 9
Eltringham St. SW18—3A 90
Elvaston M. SW7—4A 74
Elvaston Pl. SW7—4A 74
Elveden Pl. NW10—5L 55
Elveden Rd. NW10—5L 55
Elvendon Rd. N13—6J 27
Elver Gdns. E2—6E 60
Elverson Rd. SE8—1M 93
Elverton St. SW1—5H 75
Elvet Av. Romf—2G 51
Elvington Grn. Brom—9D 110
Elvington La. NW9—8C 24
Elvino Rd. SE26—2J 109
Elvis Rd. NW2—2G 57
Elwill Way. Beck—8A 110
Elwin St. E2—6E 60
Elwood St. N5—8M 43
Elwyn Gdns. SE12—6E 94
Ely Clo. Eri—1D 98
Ely Clo. N Mald—6D 104
Ely Gdns. Borwd—7B 12
Ely Gdns. Dag—8A 50
Ely Gdns. Ilf—5J 47
Elyne Rd. N4—4L 43
Ely Pl. EC1—8L 59
Ely Pl. Wfd G—6L 31
Ely Rd. E10—5A 46
Ely Rd. Croy—9B 108
Ely Rd. Houn—2G 85
Ely Rd. Houn—1D 84
(Hatton)
Elysian Rd. Orp—1D 128
Elysium Pl. SW6—1K 89
Elystan Clo. Wall—1G 137
Elystan Pl. SW3—6D 74
Elystan St. SW3—5C 74
Elystan Wlk. N1—4L 59
Emanuel Av. W3—9A 56
Embankment. SW15—1H 89
Embankment Gdns. SW3
—7D 74
Embankment Pl. WC2—2J 75
Embankment, The. Twic—7E 86
Embassy Ct. Sidc—9F 96
Embassy Ct. Well—2F 96
Emba St. SE16—3E 76
Ember Clo. Orp—2A 128
Embercourt Rd. Th Dit—1C 118
Ember Farm Av. E Mol—1B 118
Ember Farm Way. E Mol
—1B 118
Ember Gdns. Th Dit—2C 118
Ember La. Esh & E Mol—2B 118
Embleton Rd. SE13—3M 93
Embleton Rd. Wat—3E 20
Embleton Wlk. Hmptn—2K 101
Embry Clo. Stan—4E 22
Embry Dri. Stan—5E 22
Embry Way. Stan—4E 22
Emden St. SW6—9M 73
Emerald Gdns. Dag—6L 49
Emerald St. WC1—8K 59
Emerson Dri. Horn—5H 51
Emerson Gdns. Harr—4K 39
Emerson Rd. Ilf—5L 47
Emerson St. SE1—2A 76
Emery Hill St. SW1—4G 75
Emery St. SE1—4L 75
Emes Rd. Eri—8A 82
Emily Pl. N7—9J 43
Emlyn Gdns. W12—3C 72
Emlyn Rd. W12—3C 72
Emmanuel Rd. SW12—7G 91
Emmanuel Rd. N'wd—7D 20
Emma Rd. E13—5D 62

Emma St. E2—5F 60
Emmaus Way. Chig—5L 31
Emmett St. E14—1K 77
Emmott Av. Ilf—3A 48
Emmott Clo. E1—7J 61
Emmott Clo. NW11—4A 42
Emms Pas. King—6H 103
Emperor's Ga. SW7—4A 74
Empire Av. N18—5A 28
Empire Pde. N18—6B 28
Empire Rd. Gnfd—4F 54
Empire Way. Wemb—9K 39
Empire Wharf Rd. E14—5B 78
Empire Yd. N7—8J 43
Empress Av. E4—7M 29
Empress Av. E12—7G 47
Empress Av. Ilf—7K 47
Empress Av. Wfd G—7D 30
Empress Dri. Chst—3M 111
Empress Pl. SW6—6L 73
Empress St. SE17—7A 76
Empson St. E3—7M 61
Emsworth Clo. N9—1G 29
Emsworth Rd. Ilf—9M 31
Emsworth St. SW2—8K 91
Emu Rd. SW8—1F 90
Ena Rd. SW16—7J 107
Enbrook St. W10—6J 57
Endale Clo. Cars—4D 122
Endeavour Rd. Wal X—1E 6
Endeavour Way. SW19—1M 105
Endeavour Way. Bark—5E 64
Endeavour Way. Croy—2J 123
Endell St. WC2—9J 59
Enderby St. SE10—6C 78
Enderley Clo. Harr—9C 22
Enderley Rd. Harr—8C 22
Endersby Rd. Barn—7G 13
Endersleigh Gdns. NW4—2E 40
Endlebury Rd. E4—2A 30
Endlesham Rd. SW12—6E 90
Endsleigh Clo. S Croy—2G 139
Endsleigh Gdns. WC1—7H 59
Endsleigh Gdns. Ilf—7K 47
Endsleigh Gdns. Surb—1G 119
Endsleigh Gdns. W on T
—7G 117
Endsleigh Pl. WC1—7H 59
Endsleigh Rd. W13—1E 70
Endsleigh Rd. S'hall—5J 69
Endsleigh St. WC1—7H 59
End Way. Surb—2L 119
Endwell Rd. SE4—1J 93
Endymion Rd. N4—5L 43
Endymion Rd. SW2—5K 91
Enfield Clo. Uxb—5B 142
Enfield Rd. N1—3C 60
Enfield Rd. W3—3M 71
Enfield Rd. Bren—6H 71
Enfield Rd. Enf—6H 15
Enfield Rd. Houn—1C 84
Enfield Rd. E. Bren—6H 71
Enford St. W1—8D 58
Engadine Clo. Croy—5D 124
Engadine St. SW18—7L 89
Engate St. SE13—3A 94
Engayne Gdns. Upm—6M 51
Engel Pk. NW7—6G 25
Engineer Clo. SE18—7L 79
Engineers Dri. Bush, Wat—6L 9
Engineers Way. Wemb—9L 39
England's La. NW3—2D 58
Englands La. Lou—4L 19
Englefield Clo. Croy—1A 124
Englefield Clo. Enf—4L 15
Englefield Clo. Orp—8D 112
Englefield Cres. Orp—8D 112
Englefield Path. Orp—8E 112
Englefield Rd. N1—3B 60
Englehart Dri. Felt—5D 84
Engleheart Rd. SE6—6M 93
Englewood Rd. SW12—5F 90
English Grounds. SE1—2C 76
English St. E3—7K 61
Enid St. SE16—4D 76
Enkel St. N7—8K 43
Enmore Av. SE25—9E 108
Enmore Gdns. SW14—4B 88
Enmore Rd. SE25—9E 108
Enmore Rd. SW15—3G 89
Enmore Rd. S'hall—7L 53
Ennerdale Av. Horn—1E 66
Ennerdale Av. Stan—1G 39
Ennerdale Dri. NW9—3C 40
Ennerdale Gdns. Wemb—6G 39
Ennerdale Rd. Bexh—9L 81
Ennerdale Rd. Rich—1K 87
Ennersdale Rd. SE13—4B 94
Ennismore Av. W4—5D 72
Ennismore Av. Gnfd—2C 54
Ennismore Gdns. SW7—3C 74
Ennismore Gdns. Th Dit
—1C 118

Ennismore Gdns. M. SW7
—4C 74
Ennismore M. SW7—4C 74
Ennismore St. SW7—4C 74
Ennis Rd. N4—6L 43
Ennis Rd. SE18—7A 80
Ensign Clo. Stai—7B 144
Ensign Dri. N13—3A 28
Ensign St. E1—1E 76
Ensign Way. Stai—7B 144
Enslin Rd. SE9—6L 95
Ensor M. SW7—6B 74
Enstone Rd. Enf—5J 17
Enterprise Business Pk. E14
—3M 77
Enterprise Way. SW18—3L 89
Enterprise Way. Tedd—3D 102
Epirus M. SW6—8L 73
Epirus Rd. SW6—8K 73
Epping Clo. Romf—1M 49
Epping Glade. E4—8A 18
Epping New Rd. Buck H & Lou
—2F 30
Epping Pl. N1—2L 59
Epping Way. E4—8M 17
Epple Rd. SW6—9K 73
Epsom Clo. Bexh—2M 97
Epsom Clo. N'holt—1K 53
Epsom Gap. Lea—7F 132
Epsom Rd. E10—4A 46
Epsom Rd. Asht—9K 133
Epsom Rd. Croy—6J 123
Epsom Rd. Eps—3D 134
Epsom Rd. Ilf—4D 48
Epsom Rd. Sutt & Mord
—2K 121
Epsom Sq. Houn—1D 84
Epsom Way. Horn—9K 51
Epstein Rd. SE28—2E 80
Epworth Rd. Iswth—8F 70
Epworth St. EC2—7B 60
Erasmus St. SW1—5H 75
Erconwald St. W12—9D 56
Eresby Dri. Beck—3L 125
Eresby Pl. NW6—3L 57
Erica Ct. Swan—8C 114
Erica Gdns. Croy—5M 125
Erica St. W12—1E 72
Ericcson Clo. SW18—4L 89
Eric Rd. E7—9E 46
Eric Rd. NW10—2D 56
Eric Rd. Romf—5H 49
Eric St. E3—7K 61
Eridge Rd. W4—4B 72
Erin Clo. Brom—4C 110
Erindale. SE18—7B 80
Erindale Ter. SE18—7B 80
Eriswell Cres. W on T—5C 116
Eriswell Rd. W on T—7D 116
Erith Cres. Romf—8A 34
Erith High St. Eri—6C 82
Erith Rd. Belv & Eri—6M 81
Erith Rd. Bexh & Eri—8A 97
Erlanger Rd. SE14—9H 77
Erlesmere Gdns. W13—4E 70
Ermine Clo. Houn—1G 85
Ermine Clo. Wal X—4B 6
Ermine Rd. N15—4D 44
Ermine Rd. SE13—3M 93
Ermine Side. Enf—7E 16
Ermington Rd. SE9—8A 96
Ernald Av. E6—5J 63
Erncroft Way. Twic—5D 86
Ernest St. SE1—2M 107
Ernest Clo. Beck—9L 109
Ernest Gdns. W4—7M 71
Ernest Gro. Beck—9K 109
Ernest Rd. Horn—4J 51
Ernest Rd. King—6M 103
Ernest Sq. King—6M 103
Ernest St. E1—7H 61
Ernle Rd. SW20—4F 104
Ernshaw Pl. SW15—4J 89
Erpingham Rd. SW15—2G 89
Erridge Rd. SW19—6L 105
Errington Rd. W9—7K 57
Errol Gdns. Hay—7F 52
Errol Gdns. N Mald—8F 104
Erroll Rd. Romf—2D 50
Errol St. EC1—7A 60
Erskine Clo. Sutt—5C 122
Erskine Cres. N17—2F 44
Erskine Hill. NW11—2L 41
Erskine Rd. E17—2K 45
Erskine Rd. NW3—3D 58
Erskine Rd. Sutt—6B 122
Erwood Rd. SE7—6J 79
Esam Way. SW16—2L 107
Escott Gdns. SE9—1J 111
Escot Way. Barn—7G 13
Escreet Gro. SE18—5L 79
Esher Av. Romf—4A 50

Esher Av. Sutt—5H 121
Esher Av. W on T—2E 116
Esher By-Pass. Cob, Esh, Lea, & Chess—1A 132 to 5G 119
Esher Clo. Bex—7J 97
Esher Clo. Esh—7M 117
Esher Cres. Houn—1D 84
Esher Gdns. SW19—8H 89
Esher Grn. Esh—6M 117
Esher M. Mitc—7E 106
Esher Pk. Av. Esh—6A 118
Esher Pl. Av. Esh—6M 117
Esher Rd. E Mol—1B 118
Esher Rd. Ilf—8C 48
Esher Rd. W on T & Esh—7H 117
Eskdale Av. N'holt—4K 53
Eskdale Clo. Wemb—7H 39
Eskdale Gdns. Purl—6B 138
Eskdale Rd. Bexh—1L 97
Eskmont Ridge. SE19—4C 108
Esk Rd. E13—7F 62
Esk Way. Romf—7C 34
Esmar Cres. NW9—5E 40
Esmeralda Rd. SE1—5E 76
Esmond Clo. Rain—3F 66
Esmond Rd. NW6—4K 57
Esmond Rd. W4—5B 72
Esmond St. SW15—3J 89
Esparto St. SW18—6M 89
Essenden Rd. Belv—6L 81
Essenden Rd. S Croy—9C 124
Essendine Rd. W9—6L 57
Essex Av. Iswth—2C 86
Essex Clo. E17—2J 45
Essex Clo. Mord—2H 121
Essex Clo. Romf—2M 49
Essex Clo. Ruis—6H 37
Essex Ct. SW13—1D 88
Essex Gdns. N4—4M 43
Essex Gdns. Horn—3L 51
Essex Gro. SE19—3B 108
Essex La. K Lan & Abb L, Wat—6B 4
Essex Pk. N3—6M 25
Essex Pk. M. W3—2C 72
Essex Pl. W4—5A 72
Essex Pl. Sq. W4—5B 72
Essex Rd. E4—1C 30
Essex Rd. E10—4A 46
Essex Rd. E12—1J 63
Essex Rd. E17—4J 45
Essex Rd. E18—9F 30
Essex Rd. N1—4M 59
Essex Rd. NW10—3C 56
Essex Rd. W3—1A 72
Essex Rd. W4—5B 72
Essex Rd. Bark—3B 64
Essex Rd. Borwd—5L 11
Essex Rd. Dag—1A 66
Essex Rd. Dart—5H 99
Essex Rd. Enf—6B 16
Essex Rd. Romf—2M 49
Essex Rd. Romf—5G 49 (Chadwell Heath)
Essex Rd. Wat—4F 8
Essex Rd. S. E11—5B 46
Essex St. E7—1E 62
Essex St. WC2—1L 75
Essex Vs. W8—3L 73
Essex Wharf. E5—7H 45
Essian St. E1—8J 61
Essoldo Way. Edgw—1K 39
Estate Way. E10—6L 45
Estcourt Rd. SE25—1F 124
Estcourt Rd. SW6—8K 73
Estcourt Rd. Wat—5G 9
Estella Av. N Mald—8F 104
Estelle Rd. NW3—9D 42
Esterbrooke St. SW1—5H 75
Este Rd. SW11—2C 90
Esther Clo. N21—9L 15
Esther Rd. E11—5C 46
Estreham Rd. SW16—3H 107
Estridge Clo. Houn—3L 85
Eswyn Rd. SW17—1D 106
Etchingham Pk. Rd. N3—7M 25
Etchingham Rd. E15—9A 46
Eternit Wlk. SW6—9H 73
Etfield Gro. Sidc—2F 112
Ethelbert Clo. Brom—7E 110
Ethelbert Gdns. Ilf—3K 47
Ethelbert Rd. SW20—5H 105
Ethelbert Rd. Brom—7E 110
Ethelbert Rd. Dart—1J 115
Ethelbert Rd. Eri—8A 82
Ethelbert Rd. Orp—7H 113
Ethelbert St. SW12—7F 90
Ethelburga Rd. Romf—8K 35
Ethelburga St. SW11—9C 74
Etheldene Av. N10—2G 43
Etheldene Rd. W12—2F 72
Ethel Rd. E16—9F 62
Ethel St. SE17—5A 76

Etheridge Rd. NW4—5G 41
Etheridge Rd. Lou—4M 19
Etherley Rd. N15—3A 44
Etherow St. SE22—6E 92
Etherstone Grn. SW16—1L 107
Etherstone Rd. SW16—1L 107
Ethnard Rd. SE15—7F 76
Ethronvi Rd. Bexh—2J 97
Etloe Rd. E10—7L 45
Eton Av. N12—7A 26
Eton Av. NW3—3B 58
Eton Av. Barn—8C 14
Eton Av. Houn—7K 69
Eton Av. N Mald—9B 104
Eton Av. Wemb—9F 38
Eton Clo. SW18—9M 89
Eton College Rd. NW3—2D 58
Eton Garages. NW3—2C 58
Eton Gro. NW9—1L 39
Eton Gro. SE13—2C 94
Eton Pl. NW3—3E 58
Eton Rd. NW3—3D 58
Eton Rd. Hay—8D 68
Eton Rd. Ilf—9A 48
Eton Rd. Orp—6F 128
Eton St. Rich—4J 87
Eton Vs. NW3—2D 58
Etta St. SE8—7J 77
Etton Clo. Horn—7J 43
Ettrick St. E14—9A 62 (in two parts)
Etwell Pl. Surb—1K 119
Eugene Clo. Romf—2G 51
Eugenia Rd. SE16—5G 77
Eureka Rd. King—6L 103
Europa Pl. EC1—6A 60
Europa Trading Est. Eri—6B 82
Europe Rd. SE18—4K 79
Eustace Rd. E6—6J 63
Eustace Rd. SW6—8L 73
Eustace Rd. Romf—5H 49
Euston Av. Wat—7D 8
Euston Rd. NW1—6H 59
Euston Rd. Croy—3L 123
Euston Sq. NW1—6H 59
Euston Sta. Colonnade. NW1—6H 59
Euston St. NW1—6G 59
Evandale Rd. SW9—1L 91
Evangelist Rd. NW5—9F 42
Evans Av. Wat—8D 4
Evans Clo. E8—2D 60
Evansdale. Rain—6D 66
Evans Gro. Felt—8L 85
Evans Rd. SE6—8C 94
Evanston Av. E4—7A 30
Evanston Gdns. Ilf—4J 47
Eva Rd. Romf—5G 49
Evelina Rd. SE15—2G 93
Evelina Rd. SE20—4G 109
Eveline Rd. Mitc—5D 106
Evelyn Av. NW9—2B 40
Evelyn Av. Ruis—5C 36
Evelyn Clo. Twic—6M 85
Evelyn Ct. E8—9E 44
Evelyn Cres. Sun—5D 100
Evelyn Dri. Pinn—7H 21
Evelyn Gdns. SW7—6B 74
Evelyn Gdns. Rich—3J 87
Evelyn Gro. W5—2K 71
Evelyn Gro. S'hall—9K 53
Evelyn Rd. E16—2F 78
Evelyn Rd. E17—2A 46
Evelyn Rd. SW19—3M 105
Evelyn Rd. W4—4B 72
Evelyn Rd. Barn—6D 14
Evelyn Rd. Rich—2J 87
Evelyn Rd. Rich—9G 87 (Ham)
Evelyns Clo. Uxb—9E 142
Evelyn Sharp Clo. Romf—1H 51
Evelyn St. SE8—6J 77
Evelyn Ter. Rich—2J 87
Evelyn Wlk. N1—5B 60
Evelyn Way. Sun—5D 100
Evelyn Way. Wall—6H 123
Evelyn Yd. W1—9H 59
Evening Hill. Beck—4A 110
Evenwood Clo. SW15—4J 89
Everard Av. Brom—3E 126
Everard Way. Wemb—8J 39
Everdon Rd. SW13—7E 72
Everest Pl. E14—8A 62
Everest Pl. Swan—8B 114
Everest Rd. SE9—4K 95
Everest Rd. Stai—6B 144
Everett Clo. Pinn—1D 36
Everett Wlk. Belv—6K 81
Everglade. West—9H 141
Everglade Strand. NW9—8D 24
Evergreen Way. Hay—1D 68

Evering Rd.—8D 44
N16 1-183 & 2-158
E5 remainder
Everington St. N10—9D 26
Everington St. W6—7H 73
Everitt Rd. NW10—6B 56
Everleigh St. N4—6K 43
Eve Rd. E11—9C 46
Eve Rd. E15—5C 62
Eve Rd. N17—1C 44
Eve Rd. Iswth—3E 86
Eversfield Gdns. NW7—6C 24
Eversfield Rd. Rich—1K 87
Eversholt St. NW1—5G 59
Evershot Rd. N4—6K 43
Eversleigh Rd. E6—4H 63
Eversleigh Rd. N3—7K 25
Eversleigh Rd. SW11—2D 90
Eversleigh Rd. Barn—7A 14
Eversley Av. Bexh—1B 98
Eversley Av. Wemb—7L 39
Eversley Clo. N21—8K 15
Eversley Cres. N21—8L 15
Eversley Cres. Iswth—9B 70
Eversley Cres. Ruis—7C 36
Eversley Cross. Bexh—1C 98
Eversley Mt. N21—8K 15
Eversley Pk. SW19—2F 104
Eversley Pk. Rd. N21—8K 15
Eversley Rd. SE7—7F 78
Eversley Rd. SE19—4B 108
Eversley Rd. Surb—8K 103
Eversley Way. Croy—5L 125
Everthorpe Rd. SE15—2D 92
Everton Dri. Stan—1J 39
Everton Rd. Croy—3E 124
Evesham Av. E17—9L 29
Evesham Clo. Gnfd—5M 53
Evesham Clo. Sutt—9L 121
Evesham Grn. Mord—1M 121
Evesham Rd. E15—3D 62
Evesham Rd. N11—5G 27
Evesham Rd. W11—1H 73
Evesham Rd. Mord—1M 121
Evesham Wlk. SE5—1B 92
Evesham Wlk. SW9—1L 91
Evesham Way. SW11—2E 90
Evesham Way. Ilf—1L 47
Evry Rd. Sidc—3G 113
Ewald Rd. SW6—1K 89
Ewanrigg Ter. Wfd G—5G 31
Ewart Gro. N22—8L 27
Ewart Rd. SE23—6H 93
Ewe Clo. N7—2J 59
Ewell By-Pass. Eps—2E 134
Ewell Ct. Av. Eps—7C 120
Ewell Downs Rd. Eps—3E 134
Ewell Ho. Gro. Eps—2D 134
Ewellhurst Rd. Ilf—9J 31
Ewell Pk. Way. Eps—8E 120
Ewell Rd. Surb—2F 118
Ewell Rd. Surb—1J 119 (Long Ditton)
Ewell Rd. Sutt—9H 121
Ewelme Rd. SE23—7G 93
Ewen Cres. SW2—7L 91
Ewer St. SE1—2A 76
Ewhurst Av. S Croy—1D 138
Ewhurst Clo. Sutt—1G 135
Ewhurst Rd. SE4—5K 93
Exbury Rd. SE6—8L 93
Excelsior Clo. King—6L 103
Excelsior Gdns. SE13—1A 94
Exchange Bldgs. E1—9C 60
Exchange Ct. WC2—1J 75
Exchange Rd. Wat—6F 8
Exchange St. Romf—3C 50
Exeter Clo. E6—9K 63
Exeter Gdns. Ilf—6J 47
Exeter Rd. E16—8E 62
Exeter Rd. E17—3L 45
Exeter Rd. N9—2G 29
Exeter Rd. N14—1F 26
Exeter Rd. NW2—1J 57
Exeter Rd. SE15—9D 76
Exeter Rd. Croy—2C 124
Exeter Rd. Dag—2M 65
Exeter Rd. Enf—5H 17
Exeter Rd. Felt—9K 85
Exeter Rd. Harr—7J 37
Exeter Rd. Well—1D 96
Exeter St. WC2—1J 75
Exeter Way. SE14—8K 77
Exford Gdns. SE12—7F 94
Exford Rd. SE12—8F 94
Exhibition Clo. W12—1G 73
Exhibition Rd. SW7—3B 74
Exmoor St. W10—8H 57
Exmouth Mkt. EC1—7L 59
Exmouth Pl. E8—3F 60
Exmouth Rd. E17—3K 45
Exmouth Rd. Brom—7F 110

Exmouth Rd. Hay—6C 52
Exmouth Rd. Ruis—8G 37
Exmouth Rd. Well—9G 81
Exmouth St. E1—9G 61
Exning Rd. E16—7D 62
Exon St. SE17—6C 76
Explorer Av. Stai—7C 144
Exton Cres. NW10—3A 56
Exton Gdns. Dag—1G 65
Exton St. SE1—2L 75
Eyebright Clo. Croy—3H 125
Eyhurst Av. Horn—8E 50
Eyhurst Clo. NW2—7F 40
Eylewood Rd. SE27—2A 108
Eynella Rd. SE22—6D 92
Eynham Rd. W12—9G 57
Eynsford Clo. Orp—2A 128
Eynsford Cres. Sidc—7G 97
Eynsford Rise. Eyns, Dart—6D 131
Eynsford Rd. F'ham, Dart—3K 131
Eynsford Rd. Ilf—7C 48
Eynsford Rd. Sev & Eyns, Dart—9F 130
Eynsford Rd. Swan—1B 130
Eynsham Dri. SE2—5E 80
Eynswood Dri. Sidc—2F 112
Eyot Gdns. W6—6D 72
Eyot Grn. W4—6D 72
Eyre Clo. Romf—2G 51
Eyre Ct. NW8—5B 58
Eyre St. Hill. EC1—7L 59
Eythorne Rd. SW9—9L 75
Ezra St. SE5—9B 76
Ezra St. E2—6D 60

Faber Gdns. NW4—3E 40
Fabian Rd. SW6—8K 73
Fabian St. E6—7K 63
Factory La. N17—9D 28
Factory La. Croy—3L 123
Factory Pl. E14—6M 77
Factory Rd. E16—2J 79
Factory Sq. SW16—3J 107
Factory Yd. W7—2C 70
Faesten Way. Dart—9C 98
Fagg's Rd. Felt—3D 84
Fagus Av. Rain—6H 67
Faircacre. N Mald—7C 104
Fairacres. SW15—3E 88
Fairacres. Croy—1K 139
Fairacres. Ruis—5D 36
Fairbairn Grn. SW9—9M 75
Fairbank Av. Orp—4M 127
Fairbank Est. N1—5B 60
Fairbanks Rd. N17—1E 44
Fairbourne Rd. N17—1C 44
Fairbridge Rd. N19—7H 43
Fairbrook Clo. N13—5L 27
Fairbrook Rd. N13—6L 27
Fairburn Clo. Borwd—3L 11
Fairby Rd. SE12—4F 94
Fairchildes Av. Croy—4B 140
Fairchildes Rd. Warl—6B 140
Fairchild St. EC2—7C 60
Fair Clo. Bush, Wat—9M 9
Fairclough St. E1—9E 60
Faircross Av. Bark—2A 64
Faircross Av. Romf—7B 34
Fairdale Gdns. SW15—3F 88
Fairdale Gdns. Hay—3E 68
Fairdene Rd. Coul—9H 137
Fairey Av. Eps—1F 134
Fairfax Av. Eps—1F 134
Fairfax Clo. W on T—3F 116
Fairfax Gdns. SE3—9G 79
Fairfax Pl. NW6—3A 58
Fairfax Rd. N8—2L 43
Fairfax Rd. NW6—3A 58
Fairfax Rd. W4—4C 72
Fairfax Rd. Tedd—3E 102
Fairfield Av. NW4—4F 40
Fairfield Av. Edgw—6M 23
Fairfield Av. Ruis—5A 36
Fairfield Av. Twic—7M 85
Fairfield Av. Upm—8M 51
Fairfield Av. Wat—3G 21
Fairfield Clo. N12—4A 26
Fairfield Clo. Enf—6J 17
Fairfield Clo. Horn—7E 56
Fairfield Clo. N'wd—6A 20
Fairfield Clo. Rad—1C 10
Fairfield Clo. Sidc—5D 96
Fairfield Ct. NW10—4E 56
Fairfield Cres. Edgw—6M 23
Fairfield Dri. SW18—4M 89
Fairfield Dri. Gnfd—4G 55
Fairfield Dri. Harr—1A 38
Fairfield E. King—6J 103
Fairfield Gdns. N8—3J 43

Fairfield Gro. SE7—7H 79
Fairfield N. King—6J 103
Fairfield Path. Croy—5C 124
Fairfield Pl. King—7J 103
Fairfield Rd. E3—5L 61
Fairfield Rd. E17—9J 29
Fairfield Rd. N8—3J 43
Fairfield Rd. N18—4E 28
Fairfield Rd. W7—4E 70
Fairfield Rd. Beck—6L 109
Fairfield Rd. Bexh—1K 97
Fairfield Rd. Brom—4E 110
Fairfield Rd. Croy—5B 124
Fairfield Rd. Ilf—2M 63
Fairfield Rd. King—6J 103
Fairfield Rd. Orp—1B 128
Fairfield Rd. S'hall—9K 53
Fairfield Rd. Uxb—2B 142
Fairfield Rd. W Dray—1J 143
Fairfield Rd. Wfd G—6E 30
Fairfields Clo. NW9—3A 40
Fairfields Cres. NW9—3A 40
Fairfields S. King—6J 103
Fairfields Rd. Houn—2A 86
Fairfield St. SW18—4M 89
Fairfield Wlk. Wal X—1E 6
Fairfield Way. Barn—7L 13
Fairfield Way. Coul—6H 137
Fairfield Way. Eps—7C 120
Fairfield W. King—6J 103
Fairfolds. Wat—8J 5
Fairfoot Rd. E3—7L 61
Fairford Av. Bexh—9B 82
Fairford Av. Croy—9H 109
Fairford Clo. Croy—9J 109
Fairford Clo. Romf—6M 35
Fairford Gdns. Wor Pk—5D 120
Fairford Way. Romf—6M 35
Fairgreen. Barn—5D 14
Fairgreen E. Barn—5D 14
Fairgreen Rd. T Hth—9M 107
Fairhaven Av. Croy—1H 125
Fairhaven Cres. Wat—3E 20
Fairhazel Gdns. NW6—2M 57
Fairholme Av. Romf—3E 50
Fairholme. N3—2J 41
Fairholme Cres. Asht—9G 133
Fairholme Cres. Hay—7D 52
Fairholme Est. Felt—6B 84
Fairholme Gdns. N3—1J 41
Fairholme Rd. W14—6J 73
Fairholme Rd. Croy—2L 123
Fairholme Rd. Harr—3D 38
Fairholme Rd. Ilf—4L 47
Fairholme Rd. Sutt—8K 121
Fairholt Rd. N16—6B 44
Fairkytes Av. Horn—6H 51
Fairland Rd. E15—3D 62
Fairlands Av. Buck H—2E 30
Fairlands Av. Sutt—4L 121
Fairlands Av. T Hth—8K 107
Fairlands Ct. SE9—5L 95
Fairlawn. SE7—7G 79
Fairlawn Av. N2—2C 42
Fairlawn Av. W4—5A 72
Fairlawn Av. Bexh—1H 97
Fair Lawn Clo. Esh—8D 118
Fairlawn Clo. Felt—1K 101
Fairlawn Clo. King—3A 104
Fairlawn Dri. Wfd G—7E 30
Fairlawn Gdns. S'hall—1K 69
Fairlawn Gro. W4—5A 72
Fairlawn Gro. Bans—5B 136
Fairlawn Pk. SE26—2J 109
Fairlawn Rd. SW19—4K 105
Fairlawn Rd. Sutt—3A 136
Fairlawns. Pinn—9H 21
Fairlawns. Sun—7D 100
Fairlawns. Twic—5G 87
Fairlawns Clo. Horn—5K 51
Fairlea Pl. W5—7G 55
Fairley Way. Wal X—1B 6
Fairlie Gdns. SE23—6G 93
Fairlight Av. E4—2B 30
Fairlight Av. NW10—5C 56
Fairlight Av. Wfd G—6E 30
Fairlight Clo. E4—2B 30
Fairlight Clo. Wor Pk—6G 121
Fairlight Clo. SW17—1B 106
Fairline Ct. Beck—6A 110
Fairlop Clo. Horn—2F 66
Fairlop Gdns. Ilf—7A 32
Fairlop Rd. E11—5B 46
Fairlop Rd. Ilf—9A 32
Fairmark Dri. Uxb—2E 142
Fairmead. Brom—8B 111
Fairmead. Surb—3M 119
Fairmead Clo. Brom—8B 111
Fairmead Clo. Houn—8H 69
Fairmead Clo. N Mald—7B 104
Fairmead Cres. Edgw—3A 24

Fairmead Gdns. Ilf—3J 47
Fairmead Rd. N19—8J 43
Fairmead Rd. Croy—2K 123
Fairmead Rd. Lou—6F 18
Fairmeadside. Lou—7G 19
Fairmile Av. SW16—2H 107
Fairmount Rd. SW2—5K 91
Fairoak Clo. Kenl—7M 137
Fairoak Clo. Lea—4B 132
Fairoak Clo. Orp—2M 127
Fairoak Dri. SE9—4B 96
Fairoak Gdns. Romf—9C 34
Fairoak La. Lea & Chess
—4A 132
Fairseat Clo. Bush, Wat—2C 22
Fair St. SE1—3C 76
Fair St. Houn—2A 86
Fairthorn Rd. SE7—6E 78
Fairview. Eps—3G 135
Fairview. Eri—8D 82
Fairview Av. Rain—5H 67
Fairview Av. Wemb—2H 55
Fairview Clo. E17—8J 29
Fairview Clo. Chig—4C 32
Fairview Cres. Harr—6L 37
Fairview Dri. Chig—4C 32
Fairview Dri. Orp—6B 128
Fairview Dri. Wat—9C 4
Fairview Gdns. Wfd G—8F 30
Fairview Pl. SW2—6K 91
Fairview Rd. N15—4D 44
Fairview Rd. SW16—5K 107
Fairview Rd. Chig—4C 32
Fairview Rd. Enf—3L 15
Fairview Rd. Eps—3D 134
Fairview Rd. Sutt—7C 122
Fairview Way. Edgw—4L 23
Fairwater Av. Well—3E 96
Fairway. SW20—7G 105
Fairway. Bexh—4J 97
Fairway. Cars—3A 136
Fairway. Orp—9B 112
Fair Way. Wfd G—5G 31
Fairway Av. NW9—1M 39
Fairway Av. Borwd—4M 11
Fairway Av. W Dray—2G 143
Fairway Clo. NW11—5A 42
Fairway Clo. Croy—9J 109
Fairway Clo. Eps—6A 120
Fairway Clo. Houn—4G 85
Fairway Clo. St Alb—1M 5
Fairway Clo. W Dray—2H 143
Fairway Dri. Dart—6M 99
Fairway Dri. Gnfd—3A 54
Fairway Gdns. Ilf—1A 64
Fairways. Kenl—9A 138
Fairways. Stan—3J 23
Fairways. Tedd—4H 103
Fairways. Wal A—7L 7
Fairway, The. N13—3B 28
Fairway, The. N14—8G 15
Fairway, The. NW7—3B 24
Fairway, The. W3—9C 56
Fairway, The. Abb L, Wat—5B 4
Fairway, The. Barn—8M 13
Fairway, The. Brom—9K 111
Fairway, The. E Mol—7M 101
Fairway, The. N Mald—5B 104
Fairway, The. N'holt—2A 54
Fairway, The. N'wd—4C 20
Fairway, The. Ruis—9G 37
Fairway, The. Uxb—5D 142
Fairway, The. Wemb—7F 38
Fairweather Clo. N15—2C 44
Fairweather Rd. N16—4E 44
Fairwyn Rd. SE26—1J 109
Falcon Av. Brom—8J 111
Falcon Clo. SE1—2M 75
Falcon Clo. N'wd—7C 20
Falcon Ct. EC4—9L 59
Falcon Cres. Enf—8H 17
Falcon Dri. Stai—5B 144
Falconer Rd. Bush, Wat—8K 9
Falconer Rd. Ilf—5F 32
Falconer Wlk. N7—7K 43
Falcon Gro. SW11—2C 90
Falcon La. SW11—2D 90
Falcon Rd. SW11—1C 90
Falcon Rd. Enf—7H 17
Falcon Rd. Hmptn—4K 101
Falcon St. E13—7E 62
Falcon Ter. SW11—2C 90
Falcon Way. Felt—4F 84
Falcon Way. Harr—3G 39
Falcon Way. Rain—3E 66
Falcon Way. Shep—6C 100
Falcon Way. Wat—7J 5
Falconwood Av. Well—1B 96
Falconwood Pde. Well—3D 96
Falconwood Rd. Croy—1K 139
Falcourt Clo. Sutt—7M 121
Falkirk Clo. Horn—6L 51
Falkirk Gdns. Wat—5H 21

Falkirk St. N1—5C 60
Falkland Av. N3—7L 25
Falkland Av. N11—4F 26
Falkland Pk. Av. SE25—6C 108
Falkland Rd. N8—2L 43
Falkland Rd. NW5—1G 59
Falkland Rd. Barn—4J 13
Falling La. W Dray—1J 143
Falloden Way. NW11—2L 41
Fallow Clo. Chig—5D 32
Fallow Ct. Av. N12—6A 26
Fallowfield. Stan—3E 22
Fallowfield Ct. Stan—3E 22
Fallsbrook Rd. SW16—4G 107
Falmer Rd. E17—1M 45
Falmer Rd. N15—3B 44
Falmer Rd. Enf—6C 16
Falmouth Av. E4—5B 30
Falmouth Clo. N22—7K 27
Falmouth Clo. SE12—4D 94
Falmouth Gdns. Ilf—2H 47
Falmouth Rd. SE1—4A 76
Falmouth Rd. W on T—6G 117
Falmouth St. E15—1B 62
Fambridge Rd. SE26—1K 109
Fambridge Rd. Dag—6L 49
Famet Av. Purl—5A 138
Famet Clo. Purl—5A 138
Famet Gdns. Kenl—5A 138
Famet Wlk. Purl—5A 138
Fann St. EC1—7A 60
Fanshawe Av. Bark—2A 64
Fanshawe Cres. Dag—1K 65
Fanshawe Cres. Horn—4H 51
Fanshawe Rd. Rich—1G 103
Fanshaw St. N1—6C 60
Fanthorpe St. SW15—2G 89
Faraday Av. Sidc—8E 96
Faraday Clo. N7—2K 59
Faraday Clo. Wat—8B 8
Faraday Rd. E15—2D 62
Faraday Rd. SW19—3M 105
Faraday Rd. W3—1A 72
Faraday Rd. W10—8J 57
Faraday Rd. E Mol—8L 101
Faraday Rd. S'hall—1M 69
Faraday Rd. Well—2E 96
Faraday Way. SE18—4H 79
Faraday Way. Orp—8F 112
Fareham Rd. Felt—6G 85
Fareham St. W1—9H 59
Farewell Pl. Mitc—5C 106
Faringdon Av. Brom—2L 127
Faringdon Av. Romf—7H 35
Faringford Rd. E15—3C 62
Farington Acres. Wey—5B 116
Farjeon Rd. SE3—9H 79
Farleigh Av. Brom—2D 126
Farleigh Ct. Rd. Warl—6K 139
Farleigh Dean Cres. Croy
—3M 139
Farleigh Pl. N16—9D 44
Farleigh Rd. N16—9D 44
Farleigh Rd. Warl—9J 139
Farleton Clo. Wey—8B 116
Farley Dri. Ilf—6C 48
Farley Ho. SE26—9F 92
Farley Pl. SE25—8E 108
Farley Rd. S Croy—9F 124
Farlington Pl. SW15—6F 88
Farlow Rd. SW15—2H 89
Farlton Rd. SW18—7M 89
Farman Way. Wall—9H 123
Farmborough Clo. Harr—8C 38
Farm Av. NW2—8J 41
Farm Av. SW16—1J 107
Farm Av. Harr—4L 37
Farm Av. Swan—7A 114
Farm Av. Wemb—2G 55
Farm Clo. Barn—7G 13
Farm Clo. Buck H—3G 31
Farm Clo. Dag—3A 66
Farm Clo. S'hall—1M 69
Farm Clo. Sutt—9B 122
Farm Clo. Wall—2G 137
Farm Clo. Wal X—3C 6
Farm Clo. W Wick—5D 126
Farmcote Rd. SE12—7E 94
Farmdale Rd. SE10—6E 78
Farmdale Rd. Cars—9C 122
Farm Dri. Croy—4K 125
Farm Dri. Purl—3H 137
Farm End. E4—7C 18
Farmer Rd. E10—6M 45
Farmers Clo. Wat—6F 4
Farmers Ct. Wal A—6M 7
Farmer's Rd. SE5—8M 75
Farmer St. W8—2L 73
Farm Field. Wat—2C 8
Farmfield Rd. Brom—2C 110
Farm Fields. S Croy—3C 138
Farm Hill Rd. Wal A—6K 7

Farmhouse Rd. SW16—4G 107
Farmilo Rd. E17—5K 45
Farmington Av. Sutt—5B 122
Farmlands. Enf—3L 15
Farmlands. Pinn—2E 36
Farmlands, The. N'holt—2L 53
Farmland Wlk. Chst—2M 111
Farmleigh. N14—8E 14
Farmleigh Gro. W on T—7D 116
Farmleigh Rd. N14—9G 15
Farm Pl. W8—2L 73
Farm Pl. Dart—3E 98
Farm Rd. N21—1A 28
Farm Rd. Edgw—6M 23
Farm Rd. Esh—3M 117
Farm Rd. Houn—7J 85
Farm Rd. Mord—9M 105
Farm Rd. N'wd—5A 20
Farm Rd. Rain—6G 67
Farm Rd. Sutt—9B 122
Farmstead Rd. SE6—1M 109
Farmstead Rd. Harr—8B 22
Farm St. W1—1F 74
Farm Vale. Bex—5M 97
Farm Wlk. NW11—3K 41
Farm Way. Buck H—4G 31
Farm Way. Bush, Wat—6M 9
Farmway. Dag—8G 49
Farm Way. Horn—9G 51
Farm Way. N'wd—4C 20
Farm Way. Wor Pk—5G 121
Farnaby Rd. SE9—3G 95
Farnaby Rd. Brom—4B 110
Farnan Av. E17—9L 29
Farnan Rd. SW16—2J 107
Farnborough Av. E17—1J 45
Farnborough Av. S Croy
—9H 125
Farnborough Clo. Wemb
—8M 39
Farnborough Comn. Orp
—5K 127
Farnborough Cres. S Croy
—1J 139
Farnborough Hill. Orp—7B 128
(in two parts)
Farnborough Way. SE15
—8D 76
Farnborough Way. Orp
—6A 128
Farncombe St. SE16—3E 76
Farndale Av. N13—3M 27
Farndale Cres. Gnfd—6A 54
Farnell M. SW5—6M 73
Farnell Rd. Iswth—2B 86
Farnes Dri. Romf—9G 35
Farnham Clo. N20—9A 14
Farnham Gdns. SW20—6F 104
Farnham Pl. SE1—2M 75
Farnham Rd. Ilf—5D 48
Farnham Rd. Romf—5H 35
Farnham Rd. Well—1G 97
Farnham Royal. SE11—6K 75
Farningham Hill Rd. F'ham,
Dart—9G 115
Farningham Rd. N17—7E 28
Farnley Rd. E4—9C 18
Farnley Rd. SE25—8B 108
Farnol Rd. Dart—4L 99
Faro Clo. Brom—6L 111
Faroe Rd. W14—4H 73
Farorna Wlk. Enf—3L 15
Farquhar Rd. SE19—2D 108
Farquhar Rd. SW19—9L 89
Farquharson Rd. Croy—3A 124
Farraline Rd. Wat—6F 8
Farrance Rd. Romf—5J 49
Farrance St. E14—9L 61
Farrant Av. N22—9L 27
Farrant Clo. Orp—9E 128
Farrant Way. Borwd—3J 11
Farr Av. Bark—5E 64
Farren Rd. SE23—8J 93
Farrer M. N8—2G 43
Farrer Rd. N8—2G 43
Farrer Rd. Harr—3J 39
Farrier Clo. Sun—7E 100
Farrier Rd. N'holt—5L 53
Farrier St. NW1—3F 58
Farriers Way. Borwd—7B 12
Farringdon La. EC1—7L 59
Farringdon Rd. EC1—7L 59
Farringdon St. EC4—8M 59
Farrington Av. Orp—7F 112
Farrins Rents. SE16—2J 77
Farrow Pl. SE16—4J 77
Farr Rd. Enf—3B 16
Farthing All. SE1—3E 76
Farthing Barn La. Orp—1L 141

Farthing Clo. Dart—3K 99
Farthing Clo. Pinn—4F 36
Farthing Fields. E1—2F 76
Farthings Clo. E4—3C 30
Farthings Clo. Pinn—2E 36
Farthings, The. King—5L 103
Farthing St. Orp—9K 127
Farwell Rd. Sidc—1F 112
Farwig La. Brom—5D 110
Fashion St. E1—8D 60
Fashoda Rd. Brom—8H 111
Fassett Rd. E8—2E 60
Fassett Rd. King—8J 103
Fassett Sq. E8—2E 60
Fassnidge View. Uxb—3A 142
Fauconberg Rd. W4—7A 72
Faulkner's All. EC1—8M 59
Faulkners Rd. W on T—7G 117
Faulkner St. SE14—9G 77
Fauna Clo. Romf—4G 49
Faunce St. SE17—6M 75
Favart Rd. SW6—9L 73
Faversham Av. E4—1C 30
Faversham Av. Enf—8B 16
Faversham Clo. Chig—2F 32
Faversham Rd. SE6—7K 93
Faversham Rd. Beck—6K 109
Faversham Rd. Mord—1M 121
Fawcett Clo. SW11—1B 90
Fawcett Est. E5—6E 44
Fawcett Rd. NW10—3B 56
Fawcett Rd. Croy—5A 124
Fawcett St. SW10—7A 74
Fawcus Clo. Esh—8C 118
Fawe Pk. Rd. SW15—3K 89
Fawe St. E14—8M 61
Fawley Rd. N17—2E 44
Fawley Rd. NW6—1M 57
Fawnbrake Av. SE24—4A 92
Fawn Rd. E13—5G 63
Fawn Rd. Chig—5D 32
Fawns Mnr. Rd. Felt—7B 84
Fawood Av. NW10—3B 56
Faygate Cres. Bexh—4L 97
Faygate Rd. SW2—8K 91
Fay Grn. Abb L, Wat—6B 4
Fayland Av. SW16—2G 107
Fearnley Cres. Hmptn—3K 101
Fearnley St. Wat—6F 8
Fearon St. SE10—6E 78
Featherbed La. Croy & Warl
—1K 139
Featherbed La. Romf—1J 33
Feathers Pl. SE10—7B 78
Featherstone Av. SE23—8F 92
Featherstone Gdns. Borwd
—6A 12
Featherstone Industrial Est.
S'hall—4J 69
Featherstone Rd. NW7—6F 24
Featherstone Rd. S'hall—4J 69
Featherstone St. EC1—7B 60
Featherstone Ter. S'hall—4J 69
Featley Rd. SW9—2M 91
Federal Rd. Gnfd—4G 55
Federal Way. Wat—3G 9
Federation Rd. SE2—5F 80
Fee Farm Rd. Esh—9D 118
Felbridge Av. Stan—8E 22
Felbridge Clo. SW16—1L 107
Felbridge Clo. Sutt—1M 135
Felbrigge Rd. Ilf—7D 48
Felday Rd. SE13—5M 93
Felden Clo. Wat—7J 5
Felden St. SW6—9K 73
Feldman Clo. N16—6E 44
Feldon Clo. Pinn—7J 21
Felgate M. W6—5F 72
Felhampton Rd. SE9—9M 95
Felhurst Cres. Dag—9M 49
Felix Av. N8—4J 43
Felix La. Shep—1C 116
Felix Rd. W13—1E 70
Felix Rd. W on T—1E 116
Felixstowe Rd. N9—4E 28
Felixstowe Rd. N17—1D 44
Felixstowe Rd. NW10—6F 56
Felixstowe Rd. SE2—4F 80
Felix St. E2—5F 60
Fellbrigg Rd. SE22—4D 92
Fellbrigg St. E1—7F 60
Fellbrook. Rich—9F 86
Fellcott Clo. W on T—5G 117
Fellcott Rd. W on T—5G 117
Fellowes Clo. Hay—7H 53
Fellowes Rd. Cars—5C 122
Fellows Rd. NW3—3B 58
Fell Rd. Croy—5A 124
Felltram Way. SE7—6E 78
Fell Wlk. Edgw—8A 24

Felsberg Rd. SW2—6J 91
Fels Clo. Dag—8M 49
Fels Farm Av. Dag—8A 50
Felsham Rd. SW15—2G 89
Felspar Clo. SE18—6D 80
Felstead Av. Ilf—8L 31
Felstead Gdns. E14—6A 78
Felstead Rd. E11—5E 46
Felstead Rd. Eps—3B 134
Felstead Rd. Lou—9J 19
Felstead Rd. Orp—4E 128
Felstead Rd. Romf—7A 34
Felstead Rd. Wal X—5E 6
Felstead St. E9—2K 61
Felsted Rd. E16—9H 63
Feltham Av. E Mol—8C 102
Felthambrook Way. Felt
—9F 84
Felthamhill Rd. Ashf—2A 100
Felthamhill Rd. Felt—1E 100
Feltham Rd. Ashf—1A 100
Feltham Rd. Mitc—6E 106
Felton Clo. Borwd—2J 11
Felton Clo. Orp—1M 127
Felton Gdns. Bark—4C 64
Felton Lea. Sidc—2D 112
Felton Rd. W13—3G 71
Felton Rd. Bark—5C 64
Felton St. N1—4B 60
Fencepiece Rd. Chig & Ilf
—5A 32
Fenchurch Av. EC3—9C 60
Fenchurch Bldgs. EC3—9C 60
Fenchurch St. EC3—1C 76
Fen Ct. EC3—9C 60
Fendall Rd. Eps—7A 120
Fendall St. SE1—4C 76
Fendt Clo. E16—9D 62
Fendyke Rd. Belv—5H 81
Fenelon Pl. W14—5K 73
Fen Gro. Sidc—4D 96
Fenham Rd. SE15—8E 76
Fenman Ct. N17—8F 28
Fenn Clo. Brom—3E 110
Fennel Clo. Croy—3H 125
Fennells Mead. Eps—1D 134
Fennell St. SE18—7L 79
Fenner Clo. SE16—5F 76
Fenner Sq. SW11—2B 90
Fenning St. SE1—3C 76
Fenn St. E9—1G 61
Fenstanton Av. N12—6B 26
Fen St. E16—1D 78
Fens Way. Swan—3E 114
Fentiman Rd. SW8—7J 75
Fentiman Way. Horn—6J 51
Fenton Clo. E8—2D 60
Fenton Clo. SW9—1K 91
Fenton Clo. Chst—6K 111
Fenton Rd. N17—7A 28
Fentons Av. E13—6F 62
Fenton St. E1—9F 60
Fenton St. SE10—6C 78
Fenwick Clo. SE18—7L 79
Fenwick Gro. SE15—2E 92
Fenwick Path. Borwd—2K 11
Fenwick Pl. SW9—2J 91
Fenwick Rd. SE15—2E 92
Ferdinand Pl. NW1—3E 58
Ferdinand St. NW1—3E 58
Ferguson Av. Romf—9G 35
Ferguson Av. Surb—9K 103
Ferguson Ct. Romf—9H 35
Fergus Rd. N5—1M 59
Ferme Pk. Rd.—3J 43
N4 1-53 & 2-66a
N8 remainder
Fermor Rd. SE23—7J 93
Fermoy Rd. W9—7K 57
Fermoy Rd. Gnfd—7M 53
Fern Av. Mitc—8H 107
Fern Bank. Fyns, Dart—4K 131
Fernbank Av. Horn—9G 51
Fernbank Av. W on T—2J 117
Fernbank Av. Wemb—9D 38
Fernbrook Av. Sidc—4C 96
Fernbrook Dri. Harr—5M 37
Fernbrook Rd. SE13—5C 94
Ferncliff Rd. E8—1E 60
Fern Clo. Warl—9J 139
Ferncroft Av. N12—6D 26
Ferncroft Av. NW3—8L 41
Ferncroft Av. Ruis—7G 37
Ferndale. Brom—6G 111
Ferndale Av. E17—3B 46
Ferndale Av. Houn—2J 85
Ferndale Cres. Uxb—6A 142
Ferndale Rd. E7—3F 62
Ferndale Rd. E11—7C 46
Ferndale Rd. N15—4D 44
Ferndale Rd. SE25—9F 108
Ferndale Rd.—3J 91
SW4 1-169 & 2-172
SW9 remainder

Ferndale Rd. Bans—8K 135
Ferndale Rd. Enf—1J 17
Ferndale Rd. Romf—9A 34
Ferndale Ter. Harr—2D 38
Ferndale Way. Orp—7B 128
Ferndell Av. Bex—9B 98
Fern Dene. W13—8F 54
Ferndene Rd. SE24—3A 92
Fernden Way. Romf—4M 49
Ferndown. Horn—4K 51
Ferndown. N'wd—9E 20
Ferndown Av. Orp—3B 128
Ferndown Clo. Pinn—7J 21
Ferndown Clo. Sutt—8B 122
Ferndown Rd. SE9—6H 95
Ferndown Rd. Wat—4G 21
Fernes Clo. Uxb—9A 142
Ferney Rd. Barn—9E 14
Fern Gro. Felt—6F 84
Fernhall Dri. Ilf—3H 47
Fernham Rd. T Hth—7A 108
Fernhead Rd. W9—6K 57
Fernheath Way. Dart—2B 114
Fern Hill. Lea—6B 132
Fernhill Ct. E17—9B 30
Fernhill Gdns. King—2H 103
Fernhills. Abb L, Wat—6B 4
Fernhill St. E16—2K 79
Fernholme Rd. SE15—4H 93
Fernhurst Gdns. Edgw—6L 23
Fernhurst Rd. SW6—9J 73
Fernhurst Rd. Ashf—1A 100
Fernhurst Rd. Croy—3F 124
Fernie Clo. Chig—5E 32
Fernie Way. Chig—5E 32
Fern La. Houn—6K 69
Fernlea Rd. SW12—7F 90
Fernlea Rd. Mitc—6E 106
Fernleigh Clo. Croy—6L 123
Fernleigh Ct. Harr—9M 21
Fernleigh Ct. Wemb—7J 39
Fernleigh Rd. N21—2L 27
Fernsbury St. WC1—6L 59
Ferns Clo. Enf—9E 6
Ferns Clo. S Croy—2F 138
Fernshaw Rd. SW10—7A 74
Fernside. NW11—7L 41
Fern Side. Buck H—1F 30
Fernside Av. NW7—3B 24
Fernside Av. Felt—1F 100
Fernside Rd. SW12—7D 90
Ferns Rd. E15—2D 62
Fern St. E3—7L 61
Fernthorpe Rd. SW16—3G 107
Ferntower Rd. N5—1B 60
Fern Way. Wat—8F 4
Fernways. Ilf—9M 47
Fernwood. Croy—1J 139
Fernwood Av. SW16—1H 107
Fernwood Av. Wemb—2G 55
Fernwood Clo. Brom—6G 111
Fernwood Cres. N20—3D 26
Ferny Hill. Barn—2E 14
Ferranti Clo. SE18—5H 79
Ferraro Clo. Houn—7L 69
Ferrers Av. Wall—6H 123
Ferrers Av. W Dray—3H 143
Ferrers Rd. SW16—2H 107
Ferrestone Rd. N8—2K 43
Ferriby Clo. N1—3L 59
Ferrier St. SW18—3M 89
Ferrings. SE21—9C 92
Ferris Av. Croy—5K 125
Ferris Rd. SE22—3E 92
Ferron Rd. E5—8F 44
Ferro Rd. Rain—7E 66
Ferry App. SE18—4L 79
Ferryhills Clo. Wat—3H 21
Ferry La. N17—2E 44
Ferry La. SW13—7D 72
Ferry La. Bren—7J 71
Ferry La. Rain—9C 66
Ferry La. Rich—7K 71
Ferrymead Av. Gnfd—6L 53
Ferrymead Dri. Gnfd—5L 53
Ferrymead Gdns. Gnfd—5M 53
Ferrymoor. Rich—9F 86
Ferry Rd. SW13—8E 72
Ferry Rd. E Mol—7L 101
Ferry Rd. Tedd—2F 102
Ferry Rd. Th Dit—1F 118
Ferry Rd. Twic—7F 86
Ferry Sq. Bren—8J 71
Ferry Sq. Shep—2A 116
Ferry St. E14—6A 78
Festing Rd. SW15—2H 89
Festival Clo. Bex—7H 97
Festival Clo. Eri—8D 82
Festival Clo. Uxb—4F 142
Festival Wlk. Cars—7D 122
Fetter La. EC4—9L 59
Ffinch St. SE8—8L 77

Fiddicroft Av. Bans—6M 135
Fidler Pl. Bush, Wat—8M 9
Field Clo. E4—6M 29
Field Clo. Brom—6G 111
Field Clo. Buck H—3G 31
Field Clo. Chess—7G 119
Field Clo. Hay—4A 68
Field Clo. Houn—9F 68
Field Clo. Ruis—6A 36
Field Clo. S Croy—6F 138
Fieldcommon La. W on T
—3J 117
Field Ct. WC1—8K 59
Field End. Barn—6F 12
Field End. Coul—6H 137
Field End. N'holt—2J 53
Field End. Ruis—2G 53
Field End. Twic—1D 102
Field End Clo. Wat—9J 9
Fieldend Rd. SW16—5G 107
Field End Rd. Pinn & Ruis
—3F 36
Fieldfare Rd. SE28—1G 81
Fieldgate La. Mitc—6C 106
Fieldgate St. E1—8E 60
Fieldhouse Rd. SW12—7G 91
Fielding Av. Twic—9A 86
Fielding Rd. W4—4B 72
Fielding Rd. W14—4H 73
Fielding St. SE17—7A 76
Fieldings, The. SE23—7G 93
Field La. Bren—8G 71
Field La. Tedd—2E 102
Field Mead. NW9 & NW7—7C 24
Field Pl. N Mald—1D 120
Field Rd. E7—9E 46
Field Rd. N17—1B 44
Field Rd. SE28—1G 81
Field Rd. W6—6J 73
Field Rd. Felt—5F 84
Field Rd. Wat—8J 9
Fieldsend Rd. Sutt—7J 121
Fieldside Rd. Brom—2B 110
Fields Pk. Cres. Romf—3H 49
Field St. WC1—6K 59
Fieldview. SW18—7B 90
Field View. Felt—1B 100
Field View Rise. St Alb—2J 5
Field Way. NW10—3A 56
Field Way. Croy—9M 125
Fieldway. Dag—9G 49
Field Way. Gnfd—4M 53
Field Way. Orp—1B 128
Field Way. Ruis—6A 36
Fieldway Cres. N5—1L 59
Fiennes Clo. Dag—6G 49
Fife Rd. E16—8E 62
Fife Rd. N22—7M 27
Fife Rd. SW14—4A 88
Fife Rd. King—6J 103
Fife Ter. N1—5K 59
Fifield Path. SE23—9H 93
Fifth Av. E12—9K 47
Fifth Av. W10—6J 57
Fifth Av. Hay—2D 68
Fifth Av. Wat—8H 5
Fifth Cross Rd. Twic—8B 86
Fifth Way. Wemb—9M 39
Figges Rd. Mitc—4E 106
Filby Rd. Chess—8K 119
Filey Av. N16—6E 44
Filey Clo. Sutt—9A 122
Filey Waye. Ruis—7E 36
Fillebrook Av. Enf—4C 16
Fillebrook Rd. E11—6C 46
Filmer Rd. SW6—9K 73
Filston Rd. Eri—6A 82
Finborough Rd. SW10—7M 73
Finborough Rd. SW17—3D 106
Finchale Rd. SE2—4E 80
Fincham Clo. Uxb—8A 36
Finch Av. SE27—1B 108
Finch Clo. NW10—2B 56
Finchdean Way. SE15—8C 76
Finch Dri. Felt—6H 85
Finchingfield Av. Wfd G—7G 31
Finch La. EC3—9B 60
Finch La. Bush, Wat—6L 9
Finchley Clo. Dart—5L 99
Finchley Ct. N3—6M 25
Finchley La. NW4—2G 41
Finchley Pk. N12—4A 26
Finchley Pl. NW8—5B 58
Finchley Rd.—2K 41 to 4B 58
  NW8 1-97 & 2-82
  NW3 99-617 & 84-378
  NW2 619-707 & 380-450
  NW11 remainder
Finchley Way. N3—7L 25
Finch's Ct. E14—1M 77

Finck St. SE1—3K 75
Finden Rd. E7—1G 63
Findhorn Av. Hay—8F 52
Findhorn St. E14—9A 62
Findon Clo. SW18—5L 89
Findon Clo. Harr—8M 37
Findon Gdns. Rain—8F 66
Findon Rd. N9—1F 28
Findon Rd. W12—3E 72
Fine Bush La. Ruis—4A 36
Fingal St. SE10—6D 78
Finland Rd. SE4—2J 93
Finlay St. SW6—9H 73
Finnart Clo. Wey—6A 116
Finnemore Rd. Ilf—6E 32
Finnis St. E2—7F 60
Finnymore Rd. Dag—3J 65
Finsbury Av. EC2—8B 60
Finsbury Cir. EC2—8B 60
Finsbury Pk. Av. N4—4M 43
Finsbury Pk. Rd. N4—7M 43
Finsbury Pavement. EC2
—8B 60
Finsbury Rd. N22—7K 27
Finsbury Sq. EC2—8B 60
Finsbury St. EC2—8B 60
Finsen Rd. SE5—2A 92
Finstock Rd. W10—9H 57
Finucane Dri. Orp—2G 129
Finucane Gdns. Rain—2E 66
Finucane Rise. Bush, Wat
—2A 22
Firbank Clo. E16—8H 63
Firbank Clo. Enf—6A 16
Firbank Dri. Wat—9J 9
Firbank Rd. SE15—1F 92
Firbank Rd. Romf—5M 33
Fir Clo. W on T—2E 116
Fircroft Gdns. Harr—8C 38
Fircroft Rd. SW17—8D 90
Fircroft Rd. Chess—6K 119
Fir Dene. Orp—5L 127
Firdene. Surb—3A 120
Fire Bell All. Surb—1J 119
Firecrest Dri. NW3—8M 41
Firefly Clo. Wall—9J 123
Fire Sta. All. Barn—4J 13
Firfields. Wey—8A 116
Fir Grange Av. Wey—7A 116
Fir Gro. N Mald—1D 120
Firham Pk. Av. Romf—7L 35
Firhill Rd. SE6—1L 109
Firlands. Wey—8C 116
Firmingers Rd. Orp—7M 129
Firmin Rd. Dart—4G 99
Fir Rd. Felt—2H 101
Fir Rd. Sutt—3K 121
Firs Av. N10—1E 42
Firs Av. N11—6E 26
Firs Av. SW14—3A 88
Firsby Av. Croy—3H 125
Firsby Rd. N16—6E 44
Firs Clo. N10—2E 42
Firs Clo. SE23—6J 93
Firs Clo. Esh—9C 118
Firs Clo. Mitc—5F 106
Firs Croft. N13—3A 28
Firs Dri. Houn—8F 68
Firs Dri. Lou—3L 19
Firs La.—3A 28
  N21 1-253 & 2-144
  N13 remainder
Firs Pk. Av. N21—1B 28
Firs Pk. Gdns. N21—1B 28
Firs Rd. Kenl—7M 137
First Av. E12—9J 47
First Av. E13—6E 62
First Av. E17—3L 45
First Av. N18—4G 29
First Av. NW4—2G 41
First Av. SW14—2C 88
First Av. W3—2D 72
First Av. W10—7K 57
First Av. Dag—5M 65
First Av. E Mol—8K 101
First Av. Enf—7D 16
First Av. Eps—1C 134
First Av. Hay—2D 68
First Av. Romf—3G 49
First Av. W on T—1F 116
First Av. Wat—8G 5
First Av. Well—8G 81
First Av. Wemb—7H 39
First Clo. E Mol—7A 102
First Cross Rd. Twic—8C 86
Firs, The. N20—1B 26
Firs, The. W5—8H 55
Firs, The. Bex—7B 98
First Slip. Lea—9E 132

First St. SW3—5C 74
Firstway. SW20—6G 105
First Way. Wemb—9M 39
Firs Wlk. N'wd—6B 20
Firs Wlk. Wfd G—5E 30
Firswood Av. Eps—7D 120
Firth Gdns. SW6—9J 73
Firtree Av. Mitc—6E 106
Fir Tree Clo. Eps—7G 135
  (Nork)
Firtree Clo. Eps—6D 120
  (Stoneleigh)
Fir Tree Clo. Esh—7A 118
Firtree Clo. Orp—7D 128
Fir Tree Clo. Romf—1B 50
Firtree Ct. Borwd—6K 11
Firtree Gdns. Croy—6L 125
Fir Tree Gro. Cars—9D 122
Fir Tree Rd. Eps & Bans
—8F 134
Fir Tree Rd. Houn—3J 85
Fir Trees Clo. SE16—2J 77
Fir Tree Wlk. Dag—8A 50
Fir Tree Wlk. Enf—5B 16
Fir Wlk. Sutt—8G 121
Fisher Clo. Croy—3D 124
Fisher Clo. Gnfd—6L 53
Fisher Clo. W on T—6F 116
Fisherman Clo. Rich—1G 103
Fisherman's Pl. W4—7D 72
Fisher Rd. Harr—9D 22
Fishers Clo. Wal X—7G 7
Fishers Ct. SE14—9H 77
Fishers Dene. Esh—9E 118
Fishers La. W4—5B 72
Fisher St. E16—8E 62
Fisher St. WC1—8K 59
Fishers Way. Belv—2A 82
Fisherton St. NW8—7B 58
Fishponds Rd. SW17—1C 106
Fishponds Rd. Kes—7H 127
Fish St. Hill. EC3—1B 76
Fitzalan Rd. N3—1J 41
Fitzalan Rd. Esh—9C 118
Fitzalan St. SE11—5L 75
Fitzgeorge Av. W14—5J 73
Fitzgeorge Av. N Mald—5B 104
Fitzgerald·Av. SW14—2C 88
Fitzgerald Rd. E11—3E 46
Fitzgerald Rd. SW14—2B 88
Fitzgerald Rd. Th Dit—1E 118
Fitzhardinge St. W1—9E 58
Fitzherbert Ho. Rich—5K 87
Fitzhugh Gro. SW18—5B 90
Fitzilian Av. Romf—8K 35
Fitzjames Av. W14—5J 73
Fitzjames Av. Croy—4E 124
Fitzjohn Av. Barn—7J 13
Fitzjohn's Av. NW3—9A 42
Fitzmaurice Pl. W1—2F 74
Fitzneal St. W12—9D 56
Fitzroy Clo. N6—6D 42
Fitzroy Gdns. SE19—4C 108
Fitzroy Pk. N6—6D 42
Fitzroy Rd. NW1—4E 58
Fitzroy Sq. W1—7G 59
Fitzroy St. W1—7G 59
  (in two parts)
Fitzstephen Rd. Dag—1F 64
Fitzwarren Gdns. N19—6G 43
Fitzwilliam Av. Rich—1K 87
Fitzwilliam Ho. Rich—3H 87
Fitzwilliam Rd. SW4—2G 91
Fitz Wygram Clo. Hmptn
—2A 102
Five Acre. NW9—9D 24
Five Acres Av. St Alb—2K 5
Five Elms Rd. Brom—5G 127
Five Elms Rd. Dag—8K 49
Five Oaks La. Chig—6J 33
Fiveways Rd. SW9—1L 91
Five Wents. Swan—6E 114
Fladbury Rd. N15—4B 44
Fladgate Rd. E11—4C 46
Flag Clo. Croy—3H 125
Flagstaff Rd. Wal A—6H 7
Flambard Rd. Harr—4E 38
Flamborough Rd. Ruis—8E 36
Flamborough St. E14—9J 61
Flamingo Wlk. Rain—3E 66
Flamstead End Relief Rd. Wal X
—5A 6
Flamstead End Relief Rd. Wal X
Flamstead End Rd. Wal X—1B 6
Flamstead Gdns. Dag—3G 65
Flamstead Rd. Dag—3G 65
Flamsted Av. Wemb—2L 55
Flamsted Rd. SE7—6J 79
Flanchford Rd. W12—4D 72
Flanders Cres. SW17—4D 106
Flanders Rd. E6—5K 63

Flanders Rd. W4—5C 72
Flanders Way. E9—2H 61
Flank St. E1—1E 76
Flash La. Enf—1M 15
Flask Wlk. NW3—9A 42
Flaxey Rd. Mord—2M 121
Flaxman Rd. SE5—1M 91
Flaxman Ter. WC1—6H 59
Flaxton Rd. SE18—8C 80
Flecker Clo. Stan—5D 22
Fleece Rd. Surb—3G 119
Fleece Wlk. N7—2J 59
Fleetdale Pde. Dart—7M 99
Fleet La. EC4—9M 59
Floct La. E Mol—1K 117
Fleet Rd. NW3—1C 58
Fleet Rd. Dart—7M 99
Fleetside. E Mol—9K 101
Fleet Sq. WC1—6K 59
Fleet St. EC4—9L 59
Fleet St. Hill. E1—7E 60
Fleetwood Clo. E16—8H 63
Fleetwood Clo. Chess—9H 119
Fleetwood Rd. NW10—1E 56
Fleetwood Rd. King—7M 103
Fleetwood Sq. King—7M 103
Fleetwood St. N16—7C 44
Fleetwood Way. Wat—4G 21
Fleming Ct. Croy—7L 123
Fleming Mead. Mitc—4D 106
Fleming Rd. SE17—7M 75
Fleming Rd. S'hall—M1 53
Fleming Way. SE28—1H 81
Fleming Way. Iswth—2D 86
Flempton Rd. E10—6J 45
Fletcher La. E10—5A 46
Fletcher Path. SE8—8L 77
Fletcher Rd. W4—4A 72
Fletcher Rd. Chig—5D 32
Fletchers Clo. Brom—8F 110
Fletcher St. E1—1E 76
Fletching Rd. E5—8G 45
Fletching Rd. SE7—7H 79
Fletton Rd. N11—7J 27
Fleur de Lis St. E1—7D 60
Fleur Gates. SW19—6H 89
Flexmere Gdns. N17—8C 28
Flexmere Rd. N17—8B 28
Flight App. NW9—9D 24
Flimwell Clo. Brom—2C 110
Flintmill Cres. SE3—1J 95
Flinton St. SE17—6C 76
Flint St. SE17—5B·76
Flitcroft St. WC2—9H 59
Flockton St. SE16—3E·76
Flodden Rd. SE5—9A 76
Flood St. SW3—6C 74
Flood Wlk. SW3—7C 74
Flora Clo. E14—9M 61
Flora Gdns. W6—5F 72
Flora Gdns. Romf—4G 49
Floral Ct. Asht—9G 133
Floral St. WC2—1J 75
Flora St. Belv—6K 81
Florence Av. Enf—5A 16
Florence Av. Mord—9A 106
Florence Clo. Horn—7J 51
Florence Clo. W on T—2F 116
Florence Clo. Wat—8E 4
Florence Cotts. SE14—9K 77
Florence Dri. Enf—5A 16
Florence Gdns. W4—7A 72
Florence Rd. E6—4G 63
Florence Rd. E13—5E 62
Florence Rd. N4—5K 43
Florence Rd. SE2—5G 81
Florence Rd. SE14—9K 77
Florence Rd. SW19—3M 105
Florence Rd. W4—4B 72
Florence Rd. W5—1J 71
Florence Rd. Beck—6J 109
Florence Rd. Brom—5E 110·
Florence Rd. Felt—7F 84
Florence Rd. King—4K 103
Florence Rd. S Croy—1B 138
Florence Rd. W on T—2F 116
Florence St. E16—7D 62
Florence St. N1—3M 59
Florence Ter. SE14—9K 77
Florence Ter. SW15—9C 88
Florfield Rd. E8—2F 60
Florian Av. Sutt—6B 122
Florian Rd. SW15—3J 89
Florida Clo. Bush, Wat—2B 22
Florida Rd. T Hth—5M 107
Florida St. E2—6E 60
Floriston Av. Uxb—3A 52

Floriston Clo. Stan—8F 22
Floriston Gdns. Stan—8F 22
Floss St. SW15—1G 89
Flower & Dean Wlk. E1—8D 60
Flower Ho. Clo. SE6—2A 110
Flower Ho. Est. SE6—1A 110
Flower La. SW17—5D 24
Flowersmead. SW17—8E 90
Flower Wlk., The. SW7—3A 74
Floyd Rd. SE7—6G 79
Fludyer St. SE13—3C 94
Folair Way. SE16—6F 76
Foley Rd. Esh—9C 118
Foley Rd. West—9H 141
Foley St. W1—8G 59
Folgate St. E1—8C 60
Foliot St. W12—9D 56
Folkestone Rd. E6—5L 63
Folkestone Rd. E17—2M 45
Folkestone Rd. N18—4E 28
Folkingham La. NW9—8B 24
Folkington Corner. N12—5K 25
Follet Dri. Abb L, Wat—4D 4
Follett St. E14—9A 62
Follyfield Rd. Bans—6L 135
Folly La. E17—7K 29
Folly M. W11—9K 57
Folly Wall. E14—3A 78
Fontaine Rd. SW16—4K 107
Fontarabia Rd. SW11
—3E 90
Fontayne Av. Chig—4A 32
Fontayne Av. Rain—3C 66
Fontayne Av. Romf—9C 34
Fontenoy Rd. SW12—8F 90
Fonteyne Gdns. Wfd G—9H 31
Fonthill Clo. SE20—6E 108
Fonthill M. N4—7L 43
Fonthill Rd. N4—6K 43
Font Hills. N2—9A 26
Fontley Way. SW15—6E 88
Fontwell Clo. Harr—7C 22
Fontwell Clo. N'holt—2L 53
Fontwell Dri. Brom—9L 111
Football La. Harr—6D 38
Footbury Hill Rd. Orp—2E 128
Footpath, The. SW15—4E 88
Foots Cray High St. Sidc
—3G 113
Foots Cray La. Sidc—7G 97
Footscray Rd. SE9—5L 95
Forbes St. E1—9E 60
Forburg Rd. N16—6E 44
Fordbridge Rd. Shep & Sun
—1C 116
Ford Clo. Bush, Wat—6A 10
Ford Clo. Harr—5B 38
Ford Clo. Rain—3D 66
Ford Clo. T Hth—9M 107
Fordcroft Rd. Orp—9F 112
Forde Av. Brom—7G 111
Fordel Rd. SE6—7B 94
Ford End. Wfd G—6F 30
Fordham Clo. Barn—5C 14
Fordham Clo. W Dray—9D 142
Fordham Rd. Barn—5B 14
Fordham St. E1—9E 60
Fordhook Av. W5—1K 71
Fordingley Rd. W9—6K 57
Fordington Ho. SE26—9F 92
Fordington Rd. N6—3D 42
Ford La. Rain—3D 66
Fordmill Rd. SE6—8L 93
Ford Rd. E3 5K 61
Ford Rd. Dag—3K 65
Fords Gro. N21—1A 28
Fords Pk. Rd. E16—9E 62
Ford Sq. E1—8F 60
Ford St. E3—4J 61
(in two parts)
Ford St. E16—9D 62
Fordwich Clo. Orp—2D 128
Fordwych Rd. NW2—1J 57
Fordyce Rd. SE13—5A 94
Fordyke Rd. Dag—7K 49
Foreign St. SE5—1M 91
Foreland Ct. NW4—8H 25
Foreland St. SE18—5B 80
Foreman Ct. W6—5G 73
Foremark Clo. Ilf—5D 32
Foreshore. SE8—5K 77
Forest App. E4—9C 18
Forest App. Wfd G—7E 30
Forest Av. E4—9C 18
Forest Av. Chig—5L 31
Forest Clo. E11—3E 46
Forest Clo. Chst—5L 111
Forest Clo. Wal A—1F 18
Forest Clo. Wfd G—3F 30
Forest Ct. E4—1D 30
Forest Ct. E11—2C 46
Forest Cres. Asht—8L 133
Forestdale. N14—4H 27

Forestdale Centre, The. Croy
—9K 125
Forterie Gdns. Ilf—9E 48
Fortescue Av. E8—3F 60
Fortescue Av. Twic—9A 86
Fortescue Rd. SW19—4B 106
Fortescue Rd. Edgw—8B 24
Fortess Gro. NW5—1G 59
Fortess Rd. NW5—1F 58
Fortfield Rd. SW11—3E 90
Fortis Clo. E16—9G 63
Fortis Grn. N2 & N10—2C 42
Fortis Grn. Av. N2—1D 42
Fortis Grn. Rd. N10—1E 42
Fortismere Av. N10—1E 42
Fortnam Rd. N19—7H 43
Fortnums Acre. Stan—6D 22
Fort Rd. SE1—5D 76
Fort Rd. N'holt—3L 53
Fortrose Gdns. SW2—7J 91
Fort St. E1—8C 60
Fort St. E16—2F 78
Fortuna Clo. N7—2K 59
Fortune Ga. Rd. NW10—4C 56
Fortune Grn. Rd. NW6—9L 41
Fortune La. Borwd—8H 11
Fortunes Mead. N'holt—2J 53
Fortune St. EC1—7A 60
Forty Acre La. E16—8E 62
Forty Av. Wemb—8K 39
Forty Clo. Wemb—8K 39
Forty Footpath. SW14—2A 88
Forty Hill. Enf—2D 16
Forty La. Wemb—7M 39
Forumside. Edgw—6L 23
Forum, The. E Mol—8M 101
Forum Way. Edgw—6L 23
Forval Clo. Mitc—9D 106
Forward Dri. Harr—2D 38
Fosbury M. W2—1M 73
Foscote Rd. NW4—4F 40
Foscote Rd. NW4—4F 40
Foskett Rd. SW6—1K 89
Foss Av. Croy—7L 123
Fossdene Rd. SE7—6F 78
Fosse Way. W13—8E 54
Fossil Rd. SE13—2J 93
Fossington Rd. Belv—5H 81
Foss Rd. SW17—1B 106
Fossway. Dag—7G 49
Foster La. EC2—9A 60
Foster Pl. NW4—2G 41
Foster Rd. E13—7E 62
Foster Rd. W3—1C 72
Foster Rd. W4—6B 72
Fosters Clo. E18—8F 30
Fosters Clo. Chst—2K 111
Foster St. NW4—2G 41
Fothergill Clo. E13—5E 62
Fotheringham Rd. Romf—6D 16
Foubert's Pl. W1—9G 59
Foulden Rd. N16—9D 44
Foulis Ter. SW7—6B 74
Foulser Rd. SW17—9D 90
Foulsham Rd. T Hth—7B 108
Founders Gdns. SE19—4A 108
Foundry Clo. SE16—2J 77
Fountain Clo. Uxb—8A 52
Fountain Ct. EC4—1L 75
Fountain Dri. SE19—1D 108
Fountain Pl. SW9—9L 75
Fountain Pl. Wal A—7J 7
Fountain Rd. SW17—2B 106
Fountain Rd. T Hth—6A 108
Fountains Av. Felt—9K 85
Fountains Clo. Felt—8K 85
Fountains Cres. N14—9J 15
Fountayne Rd. N15—2E 44
Fountayne Rd. N16—7E 44
Fount St. SW8—8H 75
Fouracres. Enf—3J 17
Fourland Wlk. Edgw—6A 24
Fournier St. E1—8D 60
Four Seasons Cres. Sutt
—4K 121
Fourth Av. E12—9K 47
Fourth Av. W10—7J 57
Fourth Av. Hay—2D 68
Fourth Av. Romf—6B 50
Fourth Av. Wat—8H 5
Fourth Cross Rd. Twic—8B 86
Fourth Dri. Coul—8H 137
Fourth Way. Wemb—9A 40
Four Tubs, The. Bush, Wat
—9B 10
Four Wents. E4—2B 30
Fowey Av. Ilf—3H 47
Fowler Clo. SW11—2B 90
Fowler Rd. E7—9E 46
Fowler Rd. N1—4M 59
Fowler Rd. Ilf—6F 32
Fowler Rd. Mitc—6E 106
Fowler Rd. Sidc—2J 113

Fowler's Wlk. W5—7H 55
Fowley Clo. Wal X—7F 6
Fownes St. SW11—2C 90
Foxberry Rd. SE4—2J 93
Foxborough Gdns. SE4—4L 93
Foxbourne Rd. SW17—8E 90
Fox Burrow Rd. Chig—4H 33
Foxbury Av. Chst—3B 112
Foxbury Clo. Brom—3F 110
Foxbury Clo. Orp—7E 128
Foxbury Dri. Orp—8E 128
Foxbury Rd. Brom—3E 110
Fox Clo. E1—7G 61
Fox Clo. E16—8E 62
Fox Clo. Borwd—8H 11
Fox Clo. Orp—7E 128
Fox Clo. Romf—5M 33
Fox Clo. Wey—7B 116
Foxcombe. Croy—8M 125
(in two parts)
Foxcombe Clo. E6—5H 63
Foxcombe Rd. SW15—7E 88
Foxcroft Rd. SE18—9M 79
Foxdell. N'wd—6B 20
Foxearth Rd. S Croy—2G 139
Foxearth Spur. S Croy—1G 139
Foxes Dale. SE3—2E 94
Foxes Dale. Brom—7B 110
Foxfield Clo. N'wd—6D 20
Foxfield Rd. Orp—4B 128
Foxglove La. Chess—6L 119
Foxglove St. W12—1D 72
Foxgrove. N14—3J 27
Foxgrove Av. Beck—4M 109
Foxgrove Path. Wat—5H 21
Foxgrove Rd. Beck—4M 109
Foxhall Rd. Upm—1M 67
Foxham Rd. N19—8H 43
Fox Hill. SE19—4D 108
Fox Hill. Kes—7G 127
Foxhill. Wat—9E 4
Fox Hill Gdns. SE19—4D 108
Foxhole Rd. SE9—4J 95
Foxholes. Wey—7B 116
Foxholme Clo. Chst—3L 111
Foxholt Gdns. NW10—3A 56
Fox Ho. Rd. Belv—5M 81
Foxlands Cres. Dag—1A 66
Foxlands La. Dag—1B 66
Foxlands Rd. Dag—1A 66
Fox La. N13—2K 27
Fox La. W5—7J 55
Fox La. Kes—7F 126
Foxleas Ct. Brom—4D 110
Foxley Clo. E8—1E 60
Foxley Clo. Lou—4M 19
Foxley Gdns. Purl—5M 137
Foxley Hall. Purl—5L 137
Foxley Hill Rd. Purl—4L 137
Foxley La. Purl—3H 137
Foxley Rd. SW9—8L 75
Foxley Rd. Kenl—6M 137
Foxley Rd. T Hth—8M 107
Foxleys. Wat—3J 21
Foxley Sq. SW9—9M 75
Foxmore St. SW11—9D 74
Fox Rd. E16—8D 62
Fox's Path. Mitc—6C 106
Foxwarren. Esh—1D 132
Foxwell St. SE4—2J 93
Foxwood Clo. Felt—9F 84
Foxwood Rd. SE3—3D 94
Foyle Rd. N17—8E 28
Foyle Rd. SE3—7D 78
Framfield Clo. N12—3L 25
Framfield Rd. N5—1M 59
Framfield Rd. W7—9D 54
Framfield Rd. Mitc—4E 106
Framlingham Clo. E5—7G 45
Framlingham Cres. SE9
—1J 111
Frampton Clo. Sutt—9L 121
Frampton Pk. Est. E9—3G 61
Frampton Pk. Rd. E9—2G 61
Frampton Rd. Houn—4J 85
Frampton St. NW8—7B 58
Francemary Rd. SE4—4L 93
Frances Rd. E4—6L 29
Frances St. SE18—5K 79
Franche Ct. Rd. SW17—9A 90
Francis Av. Bexh—1L 97
Francis Av. Felt—9E 84
Francis Av. Ilf—7B 48
Franciscan Rd. SW17—2D 106
Francis Chichester Way. SW11
—9E 74
Francis Clo. Eps—6B 120
Francis Gro. SW19—3K 105
Francis Rd. E10—6A 46
Francis Rd. N2—2D 42
Francis Rd. Croy—2M 123
Francis Rd. Dart—4H 99
Francis Rd. Gnfd—4G 55

Francis Rd. Harr—3E 38
Francis Rd. Houn—1H 85
Francis Rd. Ilf—7B 48
Francis Rd. Orp—7H 113
Francis Rd. Pinn—3G 37
Francis Rd. Wall—8G 123
Francis Rd. Wat—6F 8
Francis St. E15—1C 62
Francis St. SW1—5G 75
Francis St. Ilf—7B 48
Francis Ter. N19—8G 43
Francklyn Gdns. Edgw—3L 23
Francombe Gdns. Romf—3E 50
Franconia Rd. SW4—4H 91
Frank Dixon Clo. SE21—7C 92
Frank Dixon Way. SE21—7C 92
Frankfurt Rd. SE24—4A 92
Frankham St. SE8—8L 77
Frankland Clo. Wfd G—5G 31
Frankland Rd. E4—5L 29
Frankland Rd. Rick—8A 8
Franklin Av. Wal X—3B 6
Franklin Clo. N20—9A 14
Franklin Clo. SE27—9M 91
Franklin Clo. King—7L 103
Franklin Cres. Mitc—8G 107
Franklin Pas. SE9—2J 95
Franklin Rd. SE20—4G 109
Franklin Rd. Bexh—9J 81
Franklin Rd. Horn—2G 67
Franklin Rd. Wat—4F 8
Franklin Sq. W14—6K 73
Franklin's Row. SW3—6D 74
Franklin St. E3—6M 61
Franklin St. N15—6A 44
Franklyn Gdns. Ilf—6B 32
Franklyn Rd. NW10—2D 56
Franklyn Rd. W on T—1F 116
Frank Martin Ct. Wal X—3B 6
Franks Av. N Mald—8A 104
Franks La. S Dar, Dart—9M 115
Frank St. E13—7E 62
Franks Wood Av. Orp—9A 112
Frank Towell Ct. Felt—6E 84
Franlaw Cres. N13—4A 28
Franmil Rd. Horn—6E 50
Fransfield Gro. SE26—9F 92
Frant Clo. SE20—4G 109
Franthorne Way. SE6—9M 93
Frant Rd. T Hth—9M 107
Fraser Clo. E6—9J 63
Fraser Clo. Bex—7A 98
Fraser Rd. E17—3M 45
Fraser Rd. N9—3F 28
Fraser Rd. Eri—6B 82
Fraser Rd. Gnfd—4G 55
Fraser Rd. Wal X—1E 6
Fraser St. W4—6C 72
Frating Cres. Wfd G—6F 30
Frays Av. W Dray—3H 143
Frays Clo. W Dray—4H 143
Frayslea. Uxb—5A 142
Frays Waye. Uxb—4A 142
Frazer Av. Ruis—1G 53
Frazier St. SE1—3L 75
Frean St. SE16—4E 76
Freda Corbett Clo. SE15—8E 76
Frederica Rd. E4—9B 18
Frederica St. N7—3K 59
Frederick Clo. W2—1C 74
Frederick Clo. Sutt—6K 121
Frederick Cres. SW9—8M 75
Frederick Cres. Enf—4G 17
Frederick Gdns. Sutt—7K 121
Frederick Pl. SE18—6M 79
Frederick Rd. Rain—5B 66
Frederick Rd. Sutt—7K 121
Frederick's Pl. EC2—9B 60
Fredericks Pl. N12—4A 26
Frederick's Row. EC1—6M 59
Frederick St. WC1—6K 59
Frederick Ter. E8—3D 60
Frederic St. E17—3J 45
Fredora Av. Hay—7D 52
Freeborne Gdns. Rain—2E 66
Freedom St. SW11—1D 90
Freedown La. Sutt—5M 135
Freegrove Rd. N7—1J 59
Freeland Ct. Sidc—9E 96
Freeland Pk. NW4—9J 25
Freeland Rd. W5—1K 71
Freelands Av. S Croy—1H 139
Freelands Gro. Brom—5F 110
Freelands Rd. Brom—5F 110
Freeling St. N1—3J 59
(in two parts)
Freeman Clo. N'holt—3J 53
Freeman Rd. Mord—9B 106
Freemans La. Hay—1C 68
Freemantle Av. Enf—7H 17
Freeman Way. Horn—4K 51
Freemasons Rd. E16—8F 62
Freemasons Rd. Croy—3C 124

Freesia Clo. Orp—7D 128
Freethorpe Clo. SE19—5C 108
Freke Rd. SW11—2E 90
Fremantle Rd. Belve—5L 81
Fremantle Rd. Ilf—9M 31
Fremantle St. SE17—6C 76
Fremont St. E9—4G 61
French Pl. E1—6C 60
French St. Sun—6G 101
Frendsbury Rd. SE4—3J 93
Frensham. Wal X—1A 6
Frensham Dri. SW15—9D 88
Frensham Dri. Croy—9A 126
Frensham Rd. SE9—8B 96
Frensham Rd. Kenl—6M 137
Frensham St. SE15—7E 76
Frensham Way. Eps—8G 135
Frere St. SW11—1C 90
Freshfield Av. Upm—1M 67
Freshfield Clo. SE13—2B 94
Freshfield Clo. SE13
Freshfield Dri. N14—9F 14
Freshfields. Croy—3K 125
Freshford St. SW18—9A 90
Fresh Mt. Gdns. Eps—3M 133
Freshwater Clo. SW17—3E 106
Freshwater Rd. SW17—3E 106
Freshwater Rd. Dag—6H 49
Freshwell Av. Romf—2G 49
Fresh Wharf Rd. Bark—4M 63
Freshwood Clo. Beck—5M 109
Freshwood Way. Wall—1F 136
Freston Gdns. Barn—7E 14
Freston Pk. N3—9K 25
Freston Rd. W10 & W11—1H 73
Freta Rd. Bexh—4K 97
Frewin Rd. SW18—7B 90
Friar M. SE27—9M 91
Friar Rd. Hay—7H 53
Friar Rd. Orp—9E 112
Friars Av. N20—3C 26
Friars Av. SW15—9D 88
Friars Clo. N'holt—6H 53
Friars Gdns. W3—9B 56
Friars La. Rich—4H 87
Friars Mead. E14—4A 78
Friars Pl. La. W3—1B 72
Friars Rd. E6—4H 63
Friars Stile Pl. Rich—5J 87
Friars Stile Rd. Rich—5J 87
Friars, The. Chig—4C 32
Friars Wlk. N14—9F 14
Friars Wlk. SE2—6H 81
Friars Way. W3—9B 56
Friars Way. Bush, Wat—3K 9
Friarswood. Croy—1J 139
Friary Clo. N12—5C 26
Friary La. Wfd G—4E 30
Friary Rd. N12—4B 26
Friary Rd. SE15—8E 76
Friary Rd. W3—9A 56
Friary Way. N12—4C 26
Friday Hill. E4—2C 30
Friday Hill E. E4—3C 30
Friday Hill W. E4—2C 30
Friday Rd. Eri—6B 82
Friday Rd. Mitc—4D 106
Friday St. EC4—1A 76
Frideswide Pl. NW5—1G 59
Friendly St. SE8—1L 93
Friendly St. M. SE8—1L 93
Friendship Wlk. N'holt—6H 53
Friendship Way. SW18—3M 89
Friends Rd. Croy—5B 124
Friends Rd. Purl—4M 137
Friend St. EC1—6M 59
Friends' Wlk. Uxb—3B 142
Friern Barnet La.—3B 26
  N11 1-71 & 2-80
  N20 remainder
Friern Barnet Rd. N11—5D 26
Friern Ct. N20—3B 26
Friern Mt. Dri. N20—9A 14
Friern Pk. N12—5A 26
Friern Rd. SE22—6E 92
Friern Watch Av. N12—4A 26
Frigate M. SE8—7L 77
Frimley Av. Horn—6L 51
Frimley Av. Wall—7K 123
Frimley Clo. SW19—8J 89
Frimley Clo. Croy—9A 126
Frimley Ct. Sidc—2G 113
Frimley Cres. Croy—9A 126
Frimley Gdns. Mitc—7C 106
Frimley Rd. Chess—7J 119
Frimley Rd. Ilf—8C 48
Frimley Way. E1—7H 61
Fringewood Clo. N'holt—8A 20
Frinsted Clo. Orp—8H 113
Frinsted Rd. Eri—6B 82
Frinton Clo. Wat—2F 20
Frinton Dri. Wfd G—7B 30
Frinton M. Ilf—4L 47

Frinton Rd. E6—6H 63
Frinton Rd. N15—4C 44
Frinton Rd. SW17—3E 106
Frinton Rd. Romf—7L 33
Frinton Rd. Sidc—8J 97
Friston Path. Chig—5C 32
Friston St. SW6—1M 89
Fritham Clo. N Mald—1C 120
Frith Ct. NW7—7J 25
Frith Knowle. W on T—8F 116
Frith La. NW7—7J 25
Frith Rd. E11—9A 46
Frith Rd. Croy—4A 124
Frith St. W1—9H 59
Frithville Gdns. W12—2G 73
Frithwood Av. N'wd—6C 20
Frizlands La. Dag—7M 49
Frobisher Clo. Kenl—9A 138
Frobisher Clo. Pinn—5H 37
Frobisher Cres. Stai—6C 144
Frobisher Gdns. Stai—6C 144
Frobisher Rd. N8—2L 43
Frobisher St. SE10—7C 78
Froghall La. Chig—4B 32
Frogley Rd. SE22—3D 92
Frogmore. SW18—4L 89
Frogmore Av. Hay—7C 52
Frogmore Clo. Sutt—5J 121
Frogmore Ct. S'hall—5K 69
Frogmore Gdns. Hay—7C 52
Frogmore Gdns. Sutt—6J 121
Frognal. NW3—1A 58
Frognal Av. Harr—2D 38
Frognal Av. Sidc—3E 112
Frognal Clo. NW3—1A 58
Frognal Ct. NW3—2A 58
Frognal Gdns. NW3—9A 42
Frognal La. NW3—1M 57
Frognal Pde. NW3—2A 58
Frognal Pl. Sidc—3E 112
Frognal Rise. NW3—9A 42
Frognal Way. NW3—9A 42
Froissart Rd. SE9—4H 95
Frome Rd. N15—1M 43
Frome St. N1—5A 60
Fromondes Rd. Sutt—7J 121
Frostic Wlk. E1—8E 60
Froude St. SW8—1F 90
Fruen Rd. Felt—6D 84
Fryatt Rd. N17—7B 28
  (in two parts)
Fryatt St. E14—9C 62
Fry Clo. Romf—5L 33
Fryent Clo. NW9—4L 39
Fryent Cres. NW9—4C 40
Fryent Fields. NW9—4C 40
Fryent Gro. NW9—4C 40
Fryent Way. NW9—3L 39
Frye's Bldgs. N1—5L 59
Fry Rd. E6—3H 63
Fry Rd. NW10—4D 56
Fryston Av. Coul—6F 136
Fryston Av. Croy—4E 124
Fuchsia St. SE2—6F 80
Fulbeck Dri. NW9—8C 24
Fulbeck Way. Harr—9A 22
Fulbourne Rd. E17—8A 30
Fulbourne St. E1—8F 60
Fulbrook M. N19—9G 43
Fulbrook Rd. N19—9G 43
Fulford Gro. Wat—2F 20
Fulford Rd. Eps—9B 120
Fulford St. SE16—3F 76
Fulham B'way. SW6—8L 73
Fulham Clo. Uxb—7A 52
Fulham High St. SW6—1J 89
Fulham Pal. Rd.—6G 73
  W6 55-211 & 2-284
  SW6 remainder
Fulham Pk. Gdns. SW6—1K 89
Fulham Pk. Rd. SW6—1K 89
Fulham Rd.—1J 89
  SW3 77-267 & 6-132
  SW10 273-459 & 134-366
  SW6 remainder
Fullbrooks Av. Wor Pk—3D 120
Fuller Clo. Orp—7D 128
Fuller Gdns. Wat—1F 8
Fuller Rd. Dag—8F 48
Fuller Rd. Wat—1F 8
Fullers Av. Surb—4K 119
Fullers Av. Wfd G—7D 30
Fullers Clo. Romf—7A 34
Fullers Clo. Wal A—6M 7
Fullers La. Romf—7A 34
Fullers Rd. E18—8D 30
Fuller St. E2—7E 60
Fuller St. NW4—2G 41
Fullers Way N. Surb—5K 119
Fullers Way S. Chess—6J 119
Fuller's Wood. Croy—7L 125
Fullerton Rd. Cars—1C 136

Fullerton Rd. Croy—2D 124
Fuller Way. Hay—6D 68
Fullwell Av. Ilf—8K 31
Fullwell Cross. Ilf—9B 32
Fullwood's M. N1—6B 60
Fulmar Rd. Rain—3E 66
Fulmead St. SW6—9M 73
Fulmer Clo. Hmptn—2J 101
Fulmer Rd. E16—8H 63
Fulmer Way. W13—4F 70
Fulready Rd. E10—3B 46
Fulstone Clo. Houn—3K 85
Fulthorp Rd. SE3—1E 94
Fulton Rd. Wemb—8L 39
Fulwell Pk. Av. Twic—8A 86
Fulwell Rd. Tedd—1B 102
Fulwich Rd. Dart—5K 99
Fulwood Av. Wemb—5K 55
Fulwood Clo. Hay—9D 52
Fulwood Gdns. Twic—5D 86
Fulwood Pl. WC1—8K 59
Fulwood Wlk. SW19—7J 89
Furber St. W6—4F 72
Furham Field. Pinn—7L 21
Furley Rd. SE15—8E 76
Furlong Clo. Wall—3F 122
Furlong Rd. N7—2L 59
Furmage St. SW18—6M 89
Furneaux Av. SE27—2M 107
Furner Clo. Dart—2D 98
Furness Rd. NW10—5E 56
Furness Rd. SW6—1M 89
Furness Rd. Harr—6M 37
Furness Rd. Mord—1M 121
Furness Way. Horn—1E 66
Furnival St. EC4—9L 59
Furrow La. E9—1G 61
Furrows, The. W on T—4G 117
Fursby Av. N3—6L 25
Further Acre. NW9—9D 24
Furtherfield. Abb L, Wat—5C 4
Further Grn. Rd. SE6—6C 94
Furzedown Dri. SW17—2F 106
Furzedown Rd. SW17—2F 106
Furzedown Rd. Sutt—3A 136
Furze Farm Clo. Romf—9J 33
Furze Field. Lea—5B 132
Furzefield. Wal X—1B 6
Furzefield Clo. Chst—3M 111
Furzefield Rd. SE3—8F 78
Furzeham Rd. W Dray—3J 143
Furze Hill. Purl—3J 137
Furze Hill. Purl—3J 137
Furzen Clo. Wat—5G 5
Furze Rd. T Hth—7A 108
Furze St. E3—8L 61
Furzewood. Sun—5E 100
Fyfe Way. Brom—6E 110
Fyfield Rd. E17—1B 46
Fyfield Rd. SW9—2L 91
Fyfield Rd. Enf—5C 16
Fyfield Rd. Rain—4D 66
Fyfield Rd. Wfd G—7G 31
Fynes St. SW1—5H 75

Gable Clo. Abb L, Wat—5C 4
Gable Clo. Dart—4E 98
Gable Clo. Pinn—7L 21
Gable Ct. SE26—1F 108
Gables Av. Borwd—5K 11
Gables, The. Bans—9K 135
Gabriel Clo. Felt—1J 101
Gabriel Clo. Romf—7A 34
Gabrielle Clo. Wemb—8K 39
Gabrielle Ct. NW3—2B 58
Gabriel St. SE23—6H 93
Gaddesden Av. Wemb—2K 55
Gaddesden Cres. Wat—7H 5
Gade Av. Wat—6C 8
Gadesden Rd. Eps—8A 120
Gade Side. Wat—8C 4
Gade View Gdns. K Lan—5A 4
Gadswell Clo. Wat—9J 5
Gadwall Way. SE28—3B 80
Gage Rd. E16—8C 62
Gage St. WC1—8J 59
Gainford St. N1—4L 59
Gainsborough Av. E12—1L 63
Gainsborough Av. Dart—4G 99
Gainsborough Clo. Beck
  —4L 109
Gainsborough Clo. Esh—3C 118
Gainsborough Ct. W on T
  —6E 116
Gainsborough Dri. S Croy
  —5E 138
Gainsborough Gdns. NW3
  —8B 42
Gainsborough Gdns. NW11
  —5K 41

Gainsborough Gdns. Edgw
  —9K 23
Gainsborough Gdns. Gnfd
  —1C 54
Gainsborough Gdns. Iswth
  —4B 86
Gainsborough M. SE26—9F 92
Gainsborough Rd. E11—5C 46
Gainsborough Rd. E15—6C 62
Gainsborough Rd. N12—5M 25
Gainsborough Rd. W4—5D 72
Gainsborough Rd. Dag—9F 48
Gainsborough Rd. Eps—2A 134
Gainsborough Rd. Hay—5A 52
Gainsborough Rd. N Mald
  —2B 120
Gainsborough Rd. Rain—4E 66
Gainsborough Rd. Rich—1K 87
Gainsborough Rd. Wfd G
  —6J 31
Gainsborough Sq. Bexh—2H 97
Gainsford Rd. E17—2K 45
Gainsford St. SE1—3D 76
Gairloch Rd. SE5—1C 92
Gaisford St. NW5—2G 59
Gaitskell Rd. SE9—7A 96
Galahad Rd. Brom—1E 110
Galata Rd. SW13—8E 72
Galatea Sq. SE15—2F 92
Galbraith St. E14—4A 78
Galdana Av. Barn—5A 14
Galeborough Av. Wfd G—7B 30
Gale Clo. Hmptn—3J 101
Gale Clo. Mitc—7B 106
Gale Cres. Bans—9L 135
Gale St. E3—8L 61
Gale St. Dag—1G 65
Gales Gdns. E2—6F 60
Gales Way. Wfd G—7J 31
Galgate Clo. SW19—7J 89
Gallants Farm Rd. Barn—9C 14
Gallery Gdns. N'holt—5H 53
Gallery Rd. SE21—7B 92
Galleyhill Rd. Wal A—5L 7
Galley La. Barn—2E 12
Galleywall Rd. SE16—5F 76
Galleywood Cres. Romf—6B 34
Galliard Clo. N9—8G 17
Galliard Ct. N9—8E 16
Galliard Rd. N9—9E 16
Gallia Rd. N5—1M 59
Gallions Clo. Bark—6E 64
Gallions Rd. E16—1M 79
Gallions Rd. SE7—5F 78
Gallon Clo. SE7—5G 79
Gallop, The. S Croy—9G 125
Gallop, The. Sutt—1B 136
Gallosson Rd. SE18—5C 80
Galloway Rd. W12—2E 72
Gallows Hill. K Lan—5A 4
Gallows Hill La. Abb L, Wat
  —5A 4
Gallus Clo. N21—8K 15
Gallus Sq. SE3—2F 94
Galpins Rd. T Hth—9J 107
Galsworthy Av. Romf—4F 48
Galsworthy Clo. SE28—2F 80
Galsworthy Cres. SE3—9G 79
Galsworthy Rd. NW2—9J 41
Galsworthy Rd. King—5M 103
Galsworthy Ter. N16—8C 44
Galton St. W10—6J 57
Galva Clo. Barn—6E 14
Galveston Rd. SW15—4K 89
Galway St. EC1—6A 60
Gambetta St. SW8—1F 90
Gambia St. SE1—2M 75
Gambole Rd. SW17—1C 106
Games Rd. Barn—5D 14
Gamlen Rd. SW15—3H 89
Gammons Farm Clo. Wat—9D 4
Gammons La. Wat—9D 4
Gander Grn. La. Sutt—4J 121
Ganders Ash. Wat—6E 4
Gant Ct. Wal A—7M 7
Ganton St. W1—1G 75
Ganton Wlk. Wat—4H 21
Gantshill Cres. Ilf—3L 47
Gants Hill Cross. Ilf—4L 47
Gap Rd. SW19—2L 105
Garage Rd. W3—9L 55
Garbrand Wlk. Eps—1D 134
Garbutt Pl. W1—8E 58
Garden Av. Bexh—4F 97
Garden Av. Mitc—4F 106
Garden City. Edgw—6L 23
Garden Clo. E4—5L 29
Garden Clo. SE12—9F 94
Garden Clo. SW9—2K 91
Garden Clo. SW15—6F 88
Garden Clo. Ashf—3A 100

Garden Clo. Bans—7L 135
Garden Clo. Hmptn—2K 101
Garden Clo. N'holt—4J 53
Garden Clo. Ruis—7C 36
Garden Clo. Wall—7J 123
Garden Clo. Wat—4D 8
Garden Ct. Rich—9K 71
Gardener's Rd. E3—5H 61
Gardeners Rd. Croy—3M 123
Gardenia Rd. Enf—8C 16
Garden La. SW2—7K 91
Garden La. Brom—3F 110
Garden M. W2—1L 73
Garden Pl. Dart—9H 99
Garden Rd. NW8—6A 58
Garden Rd. SE20—5G 109
Garden Rd. Abb L, Wat—4C 4
Garden Rd. Brom—4F 110
Garden Rd. Rich—2L 87
Garden Rd. W on T—1F 116
Gardens, The. SE22—3E 92
Gardens, The. Beck—6B 110
Gardens, The. Felt—5B 84
Gardens, The. Harr—4A 38
Gardens, The. Pinn—4K 37
Gardens, The. Wat—4D 8
Garden Row. SE1—4M 75
Garden Ter. SW1—6H 75
Garden Wlk. EC2—6C 60
Garden Wlk. Beck—5K 109
Gardenway. NW10—2A 56
Garden Way. Lou—2L 19
Gardiner Av. NW10—1G 57
Gardiner Clo. Orp—6G 113
Gardiner Ct. S Croy—8A 124
Gardner Clo. E11—4F 46
Gardner Gro. Felt—8K 85
Gardner Rd. E13—7F 62
Gardners La. EC4—1A 76
Gardnor Rd. NW3—9B 42
Gard St. EC1—6M 59
Garendon Gdns. Mord—2M 121
Garendon Rd. Mord—2M 121
Garenne Ct. Wal A—5L 7
Gareth Clo. Wor Pk—4H 121
Gareth Gro. Brom—1E 110
Garfield Rd. E4—1B 30
Garfield Rd. E13—7D 62
Garfield Rd. SW11—2E 90
Garfield Rd. SW19—2A 106
Garfield Rd. Enf—6G 17
Garfield Rd. Twic—7E 86
Garfield St. Wat—2F 8
Garford St. E14—1L 77
Garibaldi St. SE18—5C 80
Garland Rd. SE18—8B 80
Garland Rd. Stan—8J 23
Garland Way. Horn—2J 51
Garlichill Rd. Eps—9F 134
Garlick Hill. EC4—1A 76
Garlies Rd. SE23—9J 93
Garlinge Rd. NW2—2K 57
Garman Rd. N17—7G 29
Garnault Pl. EC1—6L 59
Garnault Rd. Enf—2D 16
Garner Rd. E17—8A 30
Garner St. E2—5E 60
Garnet Clo. St Alb—2K 5
Garnet Rd. NW10—2C 56
Garnet Rd. T Hth—8A 108
Garnet St. E1—1G 77
Garnett Clo. SE9—2K 95
Garnett Rd. NW3—1D 58
Garnet Way. E17—8J 29
Garnham Clo. N16—7D 44
Garnham St. N16—7D 44
Garnies Clo. SE15—8D 76
Garrad's Rd. SW16—9H 91
Garrard Clo. Bexh—2J 97
Garrard Clo. Chst—1M 111
Garrard Rd. Bans—8L 135
Garrard Wlk. NW10—2C 56
Garratt Clo. Croy—6J 123
Garratt La.—5M 89
  SW18 1-643 & 2-480
  SW17 remainder
Garratts La. Bans—8K 135
Garratts Rd. Bush, Wat—9A 10
Garratt Ter. SW17—1C 106
Garrett Rd. Edgw—7L 23
Garrett St. EC1—7A 60
Garrick Av. NW11—4J 41
Garrick Clo. SW18—3A 90
Garrick Clo. W5—7J 55
Garrick Clo. Iswth—2E 86
Garrick Clo. Rich—4H 87
Garrick Clo. W on T—6F 116
Garrick Cres. Croy—4C 124
Garrick Dri. NW4—9G 25
Garrick Gdns. E Mol—7L 101
Garrick Pk. NW4—9H 25
Garrick Rd. NW9—4D 40

Garrick Rd. Gnfd—7M 53
Garrick Rd. Rich—1L 87
Garrick St. WC2—1J 75
Garrick Way. NW4—2H 41
Garrison La. Chess—9H 119
Garrison Pde. Purf—5L 83
Garrows Field. Barn—7K 13
Garry Clo. Romf—7C 34
Garry Way. Romf—7C 34
Garside Clo. Hmptn—3M 101
Garsmouth Way. Wat—9H 5
Garson Rd. Esh—8K 117
Garston Cres. Wat—7G 5
Garston Dri. Wat—7G 5
Garston La. Kenl—6B 138
Garston La. Wat—7H 5
Garston Pk. Pde. Wat—7H 5
Garth Clo. W4—6B 72
Garth Clo. King—2K 103
Garth Clo. Mord—2H 121
Garth Clo. Ruis—6H 37
Garth Ct. W4—6B 72
Garthland Dri. Barn—7F 12
Garthorne Rd. SE23—6H 93
Garth Rd. NW2—7K 41
Garth Rd. W4—6B 72
Garth Rd. King—2K 103
Garth Rd. Mord—2H 121
Garthside—2J 103
Garth, The. Abb L. Wat—6B 4
Garth, The. Hmptn—3M 101
Garth, The. Harr—4K 39
Garthway. N12—6C 26
Gartlet Rd. Wat—5G 9
Gartmoor Gdns. SW19—7K 89
Gartmore Rd. Ilf—7D 48
Garton Pl. SW18—5A 90
Garvary Rd. E16—9F 62
Garway Rd. W2—9M 57
Gascoigne Gdns. Wfd G—7C 30
Gascoigne Pl. E2—6D 60
Gascoigne Rd. Bark—4A 64
Gascoigne Rd. Croy—2A 140
Gascony Av. NW6—3L 57
Gascoyne Dri. Dart—2D 98
Gascoyne Rd. E9—3H 61
Gaselee St. E14—1A 78
Gasholder Pl. SE11—6K 75
Gaskarth Rd. SW12—5F 90
Gaskarth Rd. Edgw—8A 24
Gaskell Rd. N6—4D 42
Gaskell St. SW4—1J 91
Gaskin St. N1—4M 59
Gaspar M. SW5—5M 73
Gassiot Rd. SW17—1D 106
Gassiot Way. Sutt—5B 122
Gastein Rd. W6—7H 73
Gaston Bell Clo. Rich—2K 87
Gaston Bri. Rd. Shep—1B 116
Gaston Rd. Mitc—7E 106
Gaston Way. Shep—9B 100
Gatcombe Ct. Beck—4L 109
Gatcombe Rd. N19—8H 43
Gate Centre, The. Bren—8E 70
Gate End. N'wd—7E 20
Gateforth St. NW8—7C 58
Gatehill Rd. N'wd—7D 20
Gatehouse Clo. King—4A 104
Gateley Rd. SW9—2K 91
Gatesborough St. EC2—7C 60
Gates Grn. Rd. W Wick & Kes
—5D 126
Gateshead Rd. Borwd—3K 11
Gateside Rd. SW17 9D 90
Gatestone Rd. SE19—3C 108
Gate St. WC2—9K 59
Gateway. NW10—6D 56
Gateway. SE17—7A 76
Gateway Clo. N'wd—6A 20
Gatfield Gro. Felt—8L 85
Gathorne Rd. N22—8L 27
Gathorne St. E2—5H 61
Gatley Av. Eps—7M 119
Gatliff Rd. SW1—6F 74
Gatling Rd. SE2—6E 80
Gatting Way. Uxb—2C 142
Gatton Clo. Sutt—1M 135
Gatton Rd. SW17—1C 106
Gattons Way. Sidc—1K 113
Gatward Clo. N21—8M 15
Gatward Grn. N9—2D 28
Gatwick Rd. SW18—6K 89
Gatwick Way. Horn—9K 51
Gauden Clo. SW4—2H 91
Gauden Rd. SW4—1H 91
Gauntlett Clo. N'holt—3J 53
Gauntlett Ct. Wemb—1F 54
Gauntlett Rd. Sutt—7B 122
Gaunt St. SE1—4A 76
Gautrey Rd. SE15—1G 93
Gautrey Sq. E6—9K 63
Gavel St. SE17—5B 76
Gaverick St. E14—5L 77

Gavestone Cres. SE12—6F 94
Gavestone Rd. SE12—6F 94
Gavina Clo. Mord—9C 106
Gawber St. E2—6G 61
Gawsworth Clo. E15—1D 62
Gawthorne Av. NW7—5J 25
Gay Clo. NW2—1F 56
Gaydon La. NW9—8C 24
Gayfere Rd. Eps—7E 120
Gayfere Rd. Ilf—1K 47
Gayfere St. SW1—4J 75
Gayford Rd. W12—3D 72
Gayhurst Rd. E8—3E 60
Gaylor Rd. N'holt—1K 53
Gaynes Ct. Upm—9M 51
Gaynesford Rd. SE23—8H 93
Gaynesford Rd. Cars—9D 122
Gaynes Hill Rd. Wfd G—6J 31
Gaynes Pk. Rd. Upm—9L 51
Gaynes Rd. Upm—7M 51
Gay Rd. E15—5B 62
Gaysham Av. Ilf—3L 47
Gaysham Hall. Ilf—1M 47
Gay St. SW15—2H 89
Gayton Cres. NW3—9B 42
Gayton Rd. NW3—9B 42
Gayton Rd. SE2—4G 81
Gayton Rd. Harr—4D 38
Gayville Rd. SW11—5D 90
Gaywood Av. Wal X—3D 6
Gaywood Clo. SW2—7K 91
Gaywood Rd. E17—1L 45
Gaywood St. SE1—4M 75
Gaza St. SE17—6M 75
Geariesville Gdns. Ilf—2M 47
Geary Rd. NW10—1E 56
Geary St. N7—1K 59
Geddes Rd. Bush, Wat
—6A 10
Gedeney Rd. N17—8A 28
Gedling Pl. SE1—4D 76
Geere Rd. E15—4D 62
Gees Ct. W1—9E 58
Geffrye Ct. N1—5C 60
Geffrye St. E2—5D 60
Geldart Rd. SE15—8F 76
Geldeston Rd. E5—7E 44
Gellatly Rd. SE14—1G 93
Gelsthorpe Rd. Romf—7M 33
General Gordon Pl. SE18
—5M 79
General's Wlk., The. Enf—1J 17
General Wolfe Rd. SE10—9B 78
Genesta Rd. SE18—7M 79
Geneva Clo. Shep—6C 100
Geneva Dri. SW9—3L 91
Geneva Rd. King—8J 103
Geneva Rd. T Hth—9A 108
Genever Clo. E4—5L 29
Genista Rd. N18—5F 28
Genoa Av. SW15—4G 89
Genoa Rd. SE20—5G 109
Genotin Rd. Enf—6B 16
Genotin Ter. Enf—6B 16
Gentian Row. SE13—9A 78
Gentlemans Row. Enf—5A 16
Gentry Gdns. E13—7E 62
Geoffrey Av. Romf—6L 35
Geoffrey Gdns. E6—5J 63
Geoffrey Rd. SE4—2K 93
George & Catherine Wheel All.
EC2—8C 60
George Cres. N10—7E 26
George V Av. Pinn—9K 21
George V Clo. Pinn—1L 37
George V Way. Gnfd—4F 54
George Inn Yd. SE1—2B 76
George La. E18—9E 30 & 1F 46
George La. SE13—5A 94
George La. Brom—3F 126
George Rd. E4—6L 29
George Rd. King—4M 103
George Rd. N Mald—8D 104
George Row. SE16—3E 76
Georges Clo. Orp—7G 113
George Sq. SW19—7L 105
George's Rd. N7—1K 59
George St. E16—9D 62
George St. W1—9D 58
George St. W7—2C 70
George St. Bark—3A 64
George St. Croy—4B 124
George St. Houn—1K 85
George St. Rich—4H 87
George St. Romf—4D 50
George St. S'hall—5J 69
George St. Sutt—7M 121
George St. Uxb—3B 142
George St. Wat—6G 9

Georgetown Clo. SE19—2C 108
Georgette Pl. SE10—8A 78
Georgeville Gdns. Ilf—2M 47
George Wyver Clo. SW19
—6J 89
George Yd. EC3—9B 60
George Yd. W1—1E 74
Georgiana St. NW1—4G 59
Georgian Clo. Brom—3F 126
Georgian Clo. N'wd—4C 20
Georgian Clo. Stan—7E 22
Georgian Ct. Barn—6A 14
Georgian Ct. Wemb—2M 55
Georgian Way. Harr—7B 38
Georgia Rd. T Hth—5M 107
Georgina Gdns. E2—6D 60
Geraint Rd. Brom—1E 110
Geraldine Rd. SW18—4A 90
Geraldine Rd. W4—7L 71
Geraldine St. SE11—4M 75
Gerald Rd. E16—7D 62
Gerald Rd. SW1—5E 74
Gerald Rd. Dag—6K 49
Geralds Gro. Bans—6H 135
Gerard Av. Houn—6L 85
Gerard Gdns. Rain—5C 66
Gerard Rd. SW13—9D 72
Gerard Rd. Harr—4E 38
Gerda Rd. SE9—8A 96
Gerdview Dri. Dart—1G 115
Germander Way. E15—6C 62
Gernon Clo. Rain—5H 67
Gernon Rd. E3—5J 61
Geron Way. NW2—7F 40
Gerpins La. Upm—5K 67
Gerrard Gdns. Pinn—3E 36
Gerrard Pl. W1—1H 75
Gerrard Rd. N1—5M 59
Gerrard St. W1—1H 75
Gerrards Clo. N14—7G 15
Gerridge St. SE1—4L 75
Gerry Raffles Sq. E15—3B 62
Gertrude Rd. Belv—5L 81
Gertrude St. SW10—7A 74
Gervase Clo. Wemb—8A 40
Gervase Rd. Edgw—8A 24
Gervase St. SE15—8F 76
Gew's Corner. Wal X—2D 6
Ghent St. SE6—8L 93
Giant Tree Hill. Bush, Wat
—1B 22
Gibbards Rd. Ilf—8M 47
Gibbins Rd. E15—3A 62
Gibbon Rd. SE15—1G 93
Gibbon Rd. W3—1C 72
Gibbon Rd. King—5J 103
Gibbons Clo. Borwd—3J 11
Gibbons Rd. NW10—2C 56
Gibbon Wlk. SW15—3E 88
Gibbs Av. SE19—2B 108
Gibbs Clo. SE19—2B 108
Gibbs Clo. Wal X—2D 6
Gibbs Couch. Wat—3H 21
Gibbs Grn. W14—6K 73
Gibbs Grn. Edgw—5A 24
Gibb's Rd. N18—4G 29
Gibbs Sq. SE19—2B 108
Gibraltar Cres. Eps—2C 134
Gibraltar Wlk. E2—6D 60
Gibson Clo. E1—7G 61
Gibson Clo. Chess—7G 119
Gibson Clo. Iswth—2C 86
Gibson Gdns. N16—7D 44
Gibson Rd. SE11—5K 75
Gibson Rd. Sutt—7M 121
Gibsons Hill. SW16—4L 107
Gibson Sq. N1—4L 59
Gibson St. SE10—6C 78
Gidd Hill. Coul—8E 136
Gidea Av. Romf—1E 50
Gidea Clo. Romf—1E 50
Gideon Clo. Belv—5M 81
Gideon Rd. SW11—2E 90
Giesbach Rd. N19—7H 43
Giffard Rd. N18—6C 28
Giffin St. SE8—8L 77
Gifford Gdns. W7—8B 54
Gifford St. N1—3J 59
Gift La. E15—4D 62
Giggs Hill. Orp—6E 112
Giggshill Gdns. Th Dit—3E 118
Giggshill Rd. Th Dit—2E 118
Gilbert Gro. Edgw—8B 24
Gilbert Pl. WC1—8J 59
Gilbert Rd. SE11—5L 75
Gilbert Rd. SW19—4A 106
Gilbert Rd. Belv—4L 81
Gilbert Rd. Brom—4E 110
Gilbert Rd. Pinn—2H 37
Gilbert Rd. Romf—2D 50
Gilbert St. E15—9C 46
Gilbert St. W1—9E 58

Gilbert St. Enf—1G 17
Gilbert St. Houn—2A 86
Gilbey Clo. Uxb—1F 142
Gilbey Rd. SW17—1C 106
Gilbourne Rd. SE18—7D 80
Gilda Av. Enf—7J 17
Gilda Cres. N16—6E 44
Gildea St. W1—8F 58
Gilden Cres. NW5—1E 58
Gildenhill Rd. Swan—4G 115
Gildersome St. SE18—7L 79
Gilders Rd. Chess—9K 119
Giles Clo. Rain—5H 67
Giles Coppice. SE19—1D 108
Gilfrid Clo. Uxb—9F 142
Gilhams Av. Bans—4H 135
Gilkes Cres. SE21—5C 92
Gilkes Pl. SE21—5C 92
Gillam Way. Rain—2E 66
Gill Av. E16—9E 62
Gillender St. E3—7A 62
E14 43-50
E3 remainder
Gillespie Rd. N5—8L 43
Gillett Av. E6—5J 63
Gillett Rd. T Hth—8B 108
Gillett St. N16—1C 60
Gilliam Gro. Purl—2L 137
Gillian Cres. Romf—9G 35
Gillian Grn. Bush, Wat—2A 22
Gillian Pk. Rd. Sutt—3K 121
Gillian St. SE13—4M 93
Gillies St. NW5—2E 58
Gilling Ct. NW3—2C 58
Gillingham M. SW1—5G 75
Gillingham Rd. NW2—8J 41
Gillingham Row. SW1—5G 75
Gillingham St. SW1—5G 75
Gillison Wlk. SE16—4F 76
Gillman Dri. E15—4D 62
Gillmans Rd. Orp—3F 128
Gills Hill La. Rad—1D 10
Gill St. E14—9K 61
Gillum Clo. Barn—1D 26
Gilmore Rd. SE13—3B 94
Gilmour Clo. Enf—8A 6
Gilpin Av. SW14—3B 88
Gilpin Cres. N18—5D 28
Gilpin Cres. Twic—6M 85
Gilpin Rd. E5—9J 45
Gilpin Way. Hay—8B 68
Gilroy Clo. Rain—2D 66
Gilroy Way. Orp—2F 128
Gilsland. Wal A—8L 7
Gilsland Rd. T Hth—8B 108
Gilstead Rd. SW6—1M 89
Gilston Rd. SW10—6A 74
Gilton Rd. SE6—9C 94
Giltspur St. EC1—9M 59
Gilwell Clo. E4—6M 17
Gilwell La. E4—6M 17
Gippeswyck Clo. Pinn—8H 21
Gipsy Corner. W3—8B 56
Gipsy Hill. SE19—2C 108
Gipsy La. SW15—2F 88
Gipsy La. Wey—4A 116
Gipsy Rd. SE27—1A 108
Gipsy Rd. Well—1H 97
Gipsy Rd. Gdns. SE27—1A 108
Giralda Clo. E16—8H 63
Giraud St. E14—9M 61
Girdler's Rd. W14—5H 73
Girdlestone Wlk. N19—7G 43
Girdwood Rd. SW18—6J 89
Girling Way. Felt—2E 84
Gironde Rd. SW6—8K 73
Girtin Rd. Bush, Wat—7M 9
Girton Av. NW9—1L 39
Girton Clo. N'holt—2A 54
Girton Gdns. Croy—5L 125
Girton Rd. SE26—2H 109
Girton Rd. N'holt—2A 54
Girton Vs. W10—9H 57
Girton Way. Rick—7A 8
Gisborne Gdns. Rain—6D 66
Gisburn Rd. N8—2K 43
Given Wilson Wlk. E13—5D 62
Gladbeck Way. Enf—6M 15
Gladding Rd. E12—9H 47
Glade Clo. Surb—4H 119
Glade Gdns. Croy—2J 125
Glade La. S'hall—3M 69
Gladeside. N21—8K 15
Gladeside. Croy—1H 125
Gladeside Clo. Chess—9H 119
Gladesmore Rd. N15—4D 44
Gladeswood Rd. Belv—5M 81
Glade, The. N21—9K 15
Glade, The. SE7—8G 79
Glade, The. Brom—6H 111
Glade, The. Croy—2J 125
Glade, The. Enf—4L 15
Glade, The. Eps—8E 121

Glade, The. Ilf—8K 31
Glade, The. Sutt—1J 135
Glade, The. W Wick—5M 125
Glade, The. Wfd G—3F 30
Gladeway, The. Wal A—6K 7
Gladiator St. SE23—6J 93
Glading Ter. N16—8D 44
Gladioli Clo. Hmptn—3L 101
Gladsdale Dri. Pinn—2F 36
Gladsmuir Clo. W on T—4G 117
Gladsmuir Rd. N19—6G 43
Gladsmuir Rd. Barn—4J 13
Gladstone Av. E12—3J 63
Gladstone Av. N22—9L 27
Gladstone Av. Felt—5E 84
Gladstone Av. Twic—8B 86
Gladstone M. SE20—4G 109
Gladstone Pk. Gdns. NW2
—8F 40
Gladstone Pl. Barn—6H 13
Gladstone Rd. SW19—4L 105
Gladstone Rd. W4—4B 72
Gladstone Rd. Buck H—1G 31
Gladstone Rd. Croy—2B 124
Gladstone Rd. Dart—5K 99
Gladstone Rd. King—7L 103
Gladstone Rd. Orp—7A 128
Gladstone Rd. S'hall—4J 69
Gladstone Rd. Surb—4J 119
Gladstone Rd. Wat—5G 9
Gladstone St. SE1—4M 75
Gladstone Ter. SW8—9F 74
Gladstone Way. Harr—1C 38
Gladwell Rd. N8—4K 43
Gladwell Rd. Brom—3E 110
Gladwyn Rd. SW15—2H 89
Gladys Rd. NW6—3L 57
Glamis Clo. Wal X—2A 6
Glamis Cres. Hay—4A 68
Glamis Dri. Horn—6J 51
Glamis Pl. E1—1G 77
Glamis Rd. E1—1G 77
Glamis Way. N'holt—2A 54
Glamorgan Clo. Mitc—7J 107
Glamorgan Rd. King—6G 103
Glanfield Rd. Beck—8K 109
Glanleam Rd. Stan—4H 23
Glanville Dri. Horn—6K 51
Glanville Rd. SW2—4J 91
Glanville Rd. Brom—7F 110
Glasbrook Av. Twic—7K 85
Glasbrook Rd. SE9—6H 95
Glaserton Rd. N16—5C 44
Glasford St. SW17—3D 106
Glasgow Rd. E13—5F 62
Glasgow Rd. N18—5F 28
Glasgow Ter. SW1—6G 75
Glasshill St. SE1—3M 75
Glasshouse Fields. E1—1H 77
Glasshouse St. W1—1G 75
Glasshouse Wlk. SE11—6K 75
Glasshouse Yd. EC1—7A 60
Glasslyn Rd. N8—3H 43
Glassmill La. Brom—6D 110
Glasson Clo. W Dray—3J 143
Glass St. E2—7F 60
Glastonbury Av. Wfd G—7H 31
Glastonbury Rd. N9—1E 28
Glastonbury Rd. Mord—2L 121
Glastonbury St. NW6—1K 57
Glaucus St. E3—8M 61
Glazbury Rd. W14—5J 73
Glazebrook Clo. SE21—8B 92
Glazebrook Rd. Tedd—4D 102
Glebe Av. Enf—5M 15
Glebe Av. Harr—2J 39
Glebe Av. Mitc—6C 106
Glebe Av. Ruis—2F 52
Glebe Av. Uxb—8A 36
Glebe Av. Wfd G—6E 30
Glebe Clo. S Croy—3D 138
Glebe Clo. Uxb—9A 36
Glebe Cotts. Felt—9L 85
Glebe Ct. Mitc—7D 106
Glebe Ct. Stan—5G 23
Glebe Cres. NW4—2G 41
Glebe Cres. Harr—1J 39
Glebe Gdns. N Mald—2C 120
Glebe Ho. Dri. Brom—3F 126
Glebe Hyrst. SE19—1C 108
Glebe Hyrst. S Croy—4D 138
Glebelands. Chig—3F 32
Glebelands. Dart—3D 98
Glebelands. E Mol—8M 101
Glebelands. Esh—1D 132
Glebelands Av. E18—9E 30
Glebelands Av. Ilf—5B 48
Glebelands Clo. SE5—2C 92
Glebelands Rd. Felt—7E 84
Glebe La. Barn—7E 12
Glebe La. Harr—2J 39

Glebe Path—Gordon Pl.

Glebe Path. Mitc—7D 106
Glebe Pl. SW3—7C 74
Glebe Rd. E8—3D 60
Glebe Rd. N3—8A 26
Glebe Rd. N8—2K 43
Glebe Rd. NW10—2D 56
Glebe Rd. SW13—1E 88
Glebe Rd. Asht—9H 133
Glebe Rd. Brom—5E 110
Glebe Rd. Cars—8D 122
Glebe Rd. Dag—2M 65
Glebe Rd. Hay—2D 68
Glebe Rd. Rain—6G 67
Glebe Rd. Stan—5G 23
Glebe Rd. Sutt—1J 135
Glebe Rd. Uxb—5A 142
Glebe Rd. Warl—9H 139
Glebe Side. Twic—5D 86
Glebe Sq. Mitc—7D 106
Glebe St. W4—6C 72
Glebe, The. SE3—2C 94
Glebe, The. SW16—1J 107
Glebe, The. Chst—5A 112
Glebe, The. Wat—6H 5
Glebe, The. W Dray—5K 143
Glebe, The. Wor Pk—3D 120
Glebe Way. Eri—7C 82
Glebe Way. Felt—9L 85
Glebe Way. Horn—5J 51
Glebe Way. S Croy—3D 138
Glebe Way. W Wick—4A 126
Glebe Way. Wfd G—5G 31
Gledhow Gdns. SW5—5A 74
Gledstanes Rd. W14—6J 73
Gledwood Av. Hay—8D 52
Gledwood Cres. Hay—8D 52
Gledwood Dri. Hay—8D 52
Gledwood Gdns. Hay—8D 52
Gleed Av. Bush, Wat—2B 22
Gleeson Dri. Orp—7D 128
Glegg Pl. SW15—3H 89
Glenaffric Av. E14—5B 78
Glen Albyn Rd. SW19—8H 89
Glenalla Rd. Ruis—5D 36
Glenalmond Rd. Harr—2J 39
Glenalvon Way. SE18—5J 79
Glena Mt. Sutt—6A 122
Glenarm Rd. E5—9G 45
Glen Av. Ashf—9E 144
Glenavon Clo. Esh—8E 118
Glenavon Lodge. Beck—4L 109
Glenavon Rd. E15—3C 62
Glenbarr Clo. SE9—2M 95
Glenbow Rd. Brom—3C 110
Glenbrook N. Enf—6K 15
Glenbrook Rd. NW6—1L 57
Glenbrook S. Enf—6K 15
Glenbuck Rd. Surb—1H 119
Glenburnie Rd. SW17—9D 90
Glencairn Dri. W5—7G 55
Glencairne Clo. E16—8H 63
Glencairn Rd. SW16—4J 107
Glencoe Av. Ilf—5C 48
Glencoe Dri. Dag—9L 49
Glencoe Rd. Bush, Wat—8L 9
Glencoe Rd. Hay—7H 53
Glencourse Grn. Wat—4H 21
Glen Cres. Wfd G—6F 30
Glendale. Swan—9D 114
Glendale Av. N22—7L 27
Glendale Av. Edgw—4K 23
Glendale Av. Romf—5G 49
Glendale Clo. SE9—2L 95
Glendale Dri. SW19—2K 105
Glendale Gdns. Wemb—6H 39
Glendale M. Beck—5M 109
Glendale Rise. Kenl—7M 137
Glendale Rd. Eri—5A 82
Glendale Wlk. Wal X—3E 6
Glendale Way. SE28—1G 81
Glendall St. SW9—3K 91
Glendarvon St. SW15—2H 89
Glendish Rd. N17—8F 28
Glendor Gdns. NW7—4B 24
Glendower Cres. Orp—1E 128
Glendower Gdns. SW14—2B 88
Glendower Pl. SW7—5B 74
Glendower Rd. E4—1B 30
Glendower Rd. SW14—2B 88
Glendown Rd. SE2—6E 80
Glendun Rd. W3—1C 72
Gleneagle M. SW16—2H 107
Gleneagle Rd. SW16—2H 107
Gleneagles. Stan—7F 22
Gleneagles Clo. Orp—3B 128
Gleneagles Clo. Romf—7K 35
Gleneagles Clo. Stai—5B 144
Gleneagles Clo. Wat—5H 21
Gleneagles Grn. Orp—3B 128
Gleneldon M. SW16—1J 107
Gleneldon Rd. SW16—1J 107
Glenelg Rd. SW2—4J 91
Glenesk Rd. SE9—2L 95
Glenfarg Rd. SE6—7A 94
Glenfield Cres. Ruis—5B 36
Glenfield Rd. SW12—7G 91
Glenfield Rd. W13—3F 70
Glenfield Rd. Ashf—3A 100
Glenfield Rd. Bans—7M 135
Glenfield Ter. W13—2F 70
Glenfinlas Way. SE5—8M 75
Glenforth St. SE10—6D 78
Glengall Causeway. E14—4L 77
Glengall Gro. E14—4A 78
Glengall Rd. NW6—4K 57
Glengall Rd. SE15—7D 76
Glengall Rd. Bexh—2J 97
Glengall Rd. Edgw—3M 23
Glengall Rd. Wfd G—6E 30
Glengall Ter. SE15—7D 76
Glen Gdns. Croy—6L 123
Glengarnock Av. E14—5B 78
Glengarry Rd. SE22—4C 92
Glenham Dri. Ilf—3M 47
Glenhaven Av. Borwd—5L 11
Glenhead Clo. SE9—2M 95
Glenhill Clo. N3—9L 25
Glenhouse Rd. SE9—4L 95
Glenhurst. Beck—5A 110
Glenhurst Av. NW5—9E 42
Glenhurst Av. Bex—7K 97
Glenhurst Av. Ruis—5A 36
Glenhurst Rise. SE19—4A 108
Glenhurst Rd. N12—5B 26
Glenhurst Rd. Bren—7G 71
Glenilla Rd. NW3—2C 58
Glenister Pk. Rd. SW16—4H 107
Glenister Rd. SE10—6D 78
Glenister St. E16—2L 79
Glenlea Rd. SE9—4K 95
Glenloch Rd. NW3—2C 58
Glenloch Rd. Enf—4G 17
Glenluce Rd. SE3—7E 78
Glenlyon Rd. SE9—4L 95
Glenmere Av. NW7—6E 24
Glenmore Lodge. Beck —5M 109
Glenmore Rd. NW3—2C 58
Glenmore Rd. Well—9D 80
Glenmore Way. Bark—5E 64
Glenmount Path. SE18—6A 80
Glenn Av. Purl—3M 137
Glennie Rd. SE27—9L 91
Glenny Rd. Bark—2A 64
Glenparke Rd. E7—2F 62
Glen Rise. Wfd G—6F 30
Glen Rd. E13—7G 63
Glen Rd. E17—3K 45
Glen Rd. End. Wall—1F 136
Glenrosa St. SW6—1A 90
Glenroy St. W12—9G 57
Glensdale Rd. SE4—2K 93
Glenshiel Rd. SE9—4L 95
Glenside. Chig—6M 31
Glentanner Way. SW17—9B 90
Glentham Gdns. SW13—7F 72
Glentham Rd. SW13—7F 72
Glen, The. Brom—6C 110
Glen, The. Croy—5H 125
Glen, The. Enf—6M 15
Glen, The. N'wd—7B 20
Glen, The. Orp—5L 127
Glen, The. Pinn—5J 37
Glen, The. Pinn—3F 36
(Eastcote Village)
Glen, The. Rain—7G 67
Glen, The. S'hall—6K 69
Glen, The. Wemb—9H 39
Glenthorne Av. Croy—3G 125
Glenthorne Clo. Sutt—3L 121
Glenthorne Clo. Uxb—6E 142
Glenthorne Gdns. Ilf—1M 47
Glenthorne Gdns. Sutt—3L 121
Glenthorne Rd. E17—3J 45
Glenthorne Rd. N11—5E 26
Glenthorne Rd. W6—5F 72
Glenthorne Rd. King—8K 103
Glenthorpe Rd. Mord—9H 105
Glenton Clo. Romf—7C 34
Glenton Rd. SE13—3C 94
Glenton Way. Romf—7C 34
Glentrammon Av. Orp—8D 128
Glentrammon Clo. Orp—7D 128
Glentrammon Gdns. Orp —8D 128
Glentrammon Rd. Orp—8D 128
Glentworth St. NW1—7D 58
Glenure Rd. SE9—4L 95
Glenview. SE2—7H 81
Glenview Rd. Brom—6H 111
Glenville Av. Enf—2A 16
Glenville Gro. SE8—8K 77
Glenville M. SW18—6M 89
Glenville Rd. King—5L 103
Glen Wlk. Iswth—4B 86
Glen Way. Wat—2C 8
Glenwood Av. NW9—6C 40
Glenwood Av. Rain—7E 66
Glenwood Clo. Harr—3D 38
Glenwood Dri. Romf—2E 50
Glenwood Gdns. Ilf—3L 47
Glenwood Gro. NW9—6A 40
Glenwood Rd. N15—3M 43
Glenwood Rd. NW7—3C 24
Glenwood Rd. SE6—7K 93
Glenwood Rd. Eps—8E 120
Glenwood Rd. Houn—2B 86
Glenwood Way. Croy—1H 125
Glenworth Av. E14—5B 78
Gliddon Rd. W14—5J 73
Glimpsing Grn. Eri—4J 81
Glisson Rd. Uxb—5E 142
Gload Cres. Orp—4H 129
Globe Pond Rd. SE16—2J 77
Globe Rd.—6G 61
E1 1-123 & 2-154a
E2 remainder
Globe Rd. E15—1D 62
Globe Rd. Horn—4E 50
Globe Rd. Wfd G—6G 31
Globe St. SE1—4B 76
Glossop Rd. S Croy—1B 138
Gloster Rd. N Mald—8C 104
Gloucester Av. NW1—3E 58
Gloucester Av. Horn—2L 51
Gloucester Av. Sidc—8C 96
Gloucester Av. Wal X—6E 6
Gloucester Av. Well—3D 96
Gloucester Cir. SE10—8A 78
Gloucester Clo. NW10—3B 56
Gloucester Clo. Th Dit—3E 118
Gloucester Ct. EC3—1C 76
Gloucester Ct. Rich—8L 71
Gloucester Cres. NW1—4F 58
Gloucester Dri. N4—7M 43
Gloucester Dri. NW11—2L 41
Gloucester Gdns. NW11—5K 41
Gloucester Gdns. W2—9A 58
Gloucester Gdns. Barn—6E 14
Gloucester Gdns. Ilf—5J 47
Gloucester Gdns. Sutt—4M 121
Gloucester Ga. NW1—5F 58
(in two parts)
Gloucester Ga. M. NW1—5F 58
Gloucester Gro. Edgw—8B 24
Gloucester M. W2—9A 58
Gloucester M. W. W2—9A 58
Gloucester Pde. Sidc—4E 96
Gloucester Pl.—7D 58
W1 1-127 & 10-118
NW1 remainder
Gloucester Pl. M. W1—8D 58
Gloucester Rd. E10—5L 45
Gloucester Rd. E11—3G 47
Gloucester Rd. E12—8K 47
Gloucester Rd. E17—9H 29
Gloucester Rd. N17—1B 44
Gloucester Rd. N18—5D 28
Gloucester Rd. SW7—4A 74
Gloucester Rd. W3—3A 72
Gloucester Rd. W13—3G 71
Gloucester Rd. Barn—7M 13
Gloucester Rd. Belv—6K 81
Gloucester Rd. Croy—2B 124
Gloucester Rd. Dart—6F 98
Gloucester Rd. Enf—2A 16
Gloucester Rd. Felt—7G 85
Gloucester Rd. Hmptn—4M 101
Gloucester Rd. Harr—3M 37
Gloucester Rd. Houn—3J 85
Gloucester Rd. King—6L 103
Gloucester Rd. Rich—8L 71
Gloucester Rd. Romf—4C 50
Gloucester Rd. Tedd—2C 102
Gloucester Rd. Twic—7A 86
Gloucester Sq. W2—9B 58
Gloucester St. SW1—6G 75
Gloucester Ter. W2—9M 57
Gloucester Wlk. W8—3L 73
Gloucester Way. EC1—6L 59
Glover Rd. Pinn—4H 37
Glovers Gro. Ruis—5A 36
Gloxinia Wlk. Hmptn—3L 101
Glycena Rd. SW11—2D 90
Glyn Av. Barn—6B 14
Glyn Clo. SE25—6C 108
Glyn Clo. Eps—1E 134
Glyndebourne Pk. Orp—4M 127
Glynde Rd. Bexh—2H 97
Glynde St. SE4—5K 93
Glyndon Rd. SE18—5A 80
Glyn Dri. Sidc—1F 112
Glynfield Rd. NW10—3C 56
Glynne Rd. N22—9L 27
Glyn Rd. E5—8H 45
Glyn Rd. Enf—6G 17
Glyn Rd. Wor Pk—4H 121
Glyn St. SE11—6K 75
Glynwood Dri. SE23—8G 93
Goat La. Enf—2D 16
Goat Rd. Mitc—2E 122
Goat Wharf. Bren—7J 71
Gobions Av. Romf—7B 34
Godalming Av. Wall—7J 123
Godalming Rd. E14—8M 61
Godbold Rd. E15—6C 62
Goddard Rd. Beck—8H 109
Goddington Chase. Orp —6F 128
Goddington La. Orp—5E 128
Godfrey Av. N'holt—4J 53
Godfrey Av. Twic—6B 86
Godfrey Hill. SE18—5J 79
Godfrey Rd. SE18—5K 79
Godfrey St. E15—5A 62
Godfrey St. SW3—6C 74
Godfrey Way. Houn—6K 85
Goding St. SE11—6K 75
Godley Rd. SW18—7B 90
Godliman St. EC4—9A 60
Godman Rd. SE15—1F 92
Godolphin Clo. Sutt—3K 135
Godolphin Rd. W12—3F 72
Godolphin Rd. Wey—8B 116
Godric Cres. Croy—2B 140
Godson Rd. Croy—5L 123
Godson St. N1—5L 59
Godstone Rd. Purl, Kenl & Whyt —4M 137
Godstone Rd. Sutt—6A 122
Godstone Rd. Twic—5F 86
Godstow Rd. SE2—3G 81
Godwin Rd. E7—9F 46
Godwin Rd. Brom—7G 111
Goffers Rd. SE3—9C 78
Goff's La. Wal X—2A 6
Goffs Rd. Ashf—3B 100
Goidel Clo. Wall—6H 123
Golborne Gdns. W10—7J 57
Golborne M. W10—8J 57
Golborne Rd. W10—8J 57
Golda Clo. Barn—8H 13
Goldbeaters Gro. Edgw—6C 24
Goldcliffe Clo. Mord—2L 121
Goldcrest Clo. E16—8H 63
Goldcrest Clo. SE28—1G 81
Goldcrest Way. Bush, Wat —1A 22
Goldcrest Way. Croy—1B 140
Goldcrest Way. Purl—2H 137
Golden Ct. Rich—4H 87
Golden Cres. Hay—2D 68
Golden Fleece Ct. EC3—9D 60
Golden La. EC1 & EC2—7A 60
Golden La. Est. EC1—7A 60
Golden Mnr. W7—1C 70
Golden Sq. W1—1G 75
Golders Clo. Edgw—5M 23
Golders Gdns. NW11—5J 41
Golders Grn. Cres. NW11 —5K 41
Golders Grn. Rd. NW11—4J 41
Golders Mnr. Dri. NW11—4H 41
Golders Pk. Clo. NW11—6L 41
Golders Rise. NW4—3H 41
Golders Way. NW11—5K 41
Goldfinch Clo. Orp—7E 128
Goldfinch Rd. SE28—4B 80
Goldfinch Rd. S Croy—2J 139
Goldhawk M. W12—3F 72
Goldhawk Rd.—5D 72
W12 1-309 & 2-310
W6 remainder
Gold Hill. Edgw—6B 24
Goldhurst Ter. NW6—3M 57
Goldingham Av. Lou—4M 19
Goldings Hill. Lou—1K 19
Goldings Rise. Lou—3L 19
Goldings Rd. Lou—3L 19
Golding St. E1—9E 60
Goldington Cres. NW1—5H 59
Goldington St. NW1—5H 59
Gold La. Edgw—6B 24
Goldman Clo. E2—7E 60
Goldney Rd. W9—7L 57
Goldrings Rd. Lea—5A 132
Goldsborough Cres. E4—2M 29
Goldsborough Rd. SW8—8H 75
Goldsdown Clo. Enf—4J 17
Goldsdown Rd. Enf—4H 17
Goldsel Rd. Swan—9B 114
Goldsmid St. SE18—6C 80
Goldsmith Av. E12—2J 63
Goldsmith Av. NW9—3C 40
Goldsmith Av. W3—1B 72
Goldsmith Av. Romf—5L 49
Goldsmith Clo. W3—2B 72
Goldsmith Clo. Harr—6M 37
Goldsmith La. NW9—2M 39
Goldsmith Rd. E10—6M 45
Goldsmith Rd. E17—9H 29
Goldsmith Rd. N11—5D 26
Goldsmith Rd. SE15—9E 76
Goldsmith Rd. W3—2B 72
Goldsmith's Row. E2—5E 60
Goldsmith's Sq. E2—5E 60
Goldsmith St. EC2—9A 60
Goldsworthy Gdns. SE16 —6G 77
Goldwell Rd. T Hth—8K 107
Goldwin Clo. SE14—9G 77
Golf Clo. Bush, Wat—5H 9
Golf Clo. Stan—7G 23
Golf Club Dri. King—4B 104
Golfe Rd. Ilf—8B 48
Golf Rd. W5—9K 55
Golf Rd. Brom—7L 111
Golf Rd. Kenl—9B 138
Golf Side. Sutt—3J 135
Golf Side. Twic—9B 86
Golfside Clo. N Mald—6C 104
Goliath Clo. Wall—9J 123
Gollogly Ter. SE7—7G 79
Gomer Gdns. Tedd—3E 102
Gomer Pl. Tedd—3E 102
Gomm Rd. SE16—4G 77
Gomshall Av. Wall—7J 123
Gomshall Gdns. Kenl—7C 138
Gomshall Rd. Sutt—2G 135
Gondar Gdns. NW6—1K 57
Gonson St. SE8—7M 77
Gonston Clo. SW19—8J 89
Gonville Cres. N'holt—2M 53
Gonville Rd. T Hth—9K 107
Gonville St. SW6—2J 89
Goodall Rd. E11—8A 46
Gooden Ct. Harr—8C 38
Goodenough Rd. SW19—4K 105
Goodge Pl. W1—8G 59
Goodge St. W1—8G 59
Goodhall St. NW10—6D 56
Goodhart Way. W Wick —2C 126
Goodinge Clo. N7—2J 59
Goodman Cres. SW2—8H 91
Goodman Rd. E10—5A 46
Goodman's Ct. E1—1D 76
Goodman's Stile. E1—9E 60
Goodman's Yd. E1—1D 76
Goodmayes Av. Ilf—6E 48
Goodmayes La. Ilf—8E 48
Goodmayes Rd. Ilf—6E 48
Goodmead Rd. Orp—2E 128
Goodrich Clo. Wat—8E 4
Goodrich Rd. SE22—5D 92
Goodson Rd. NW10—3C 56
Goods Way. NW1—4H 59
Goodway Gdns. E14—9B 62
Goodwin Ct. SW19—4C 106
Goodwin Dri. Sidc—9H 97
Goodwin Gdns. Croy—8M 123
Goodwin Rd. N9—1H 29
Goodwin Rd. W12—3E 72
Goodwin Rd. Croy—7M 123
Goodwin St. N4—7L 43
Goodwood Av. Enf—1G 17
Goodwood Av. Horn—9J 51
Goodwood Av. Wat—8C 4
Goodwood Clo. Mord—8L 105
Goodwood Dri. N'holt—2L 53
Goodwood Pde. Beck—8J 109
Goodwood Path. Borwd—4L 11
Goodwood Rd. SE14—8J 77
Goodwyn Av. NW7—5C 24
Goodwyns Vale. N10—8F 26
Goodyear Pl. SE5—7A 76
Goodyers Gdns. NW4—3H 41
Goosander Way. SE28—4B 80
Gooseacre La. Harr—3H 39
Goose Grn. Clo. Orp—6E 112
Gooseley La. E6—6L 63
(in two parts)
Goose Sq. E6—9K 63
Gooshays Dri. Romf—5J 35
Gooshays Gdns. Romf—6J 35
Gophir La. EC4—1B 76
Gopsall St. N1—4B 60
Gordon Av. E4—6C 30
Gordon Av. SW14—3C 88
Gordon Av. Horn—7D 50
Gordon Av. S Croy—2A 138
Gordon Av. Stan—7D 22
Gordon Av. Twic—4E 86
Gordonbrock Rd. SE4—4L 93
Gordon Clo. E17—4L 45
Gordon Clo. N19—7G 43
Gordon Ct. W12—9G 57
Gordon Cres. Croy—3D 124
Gordon Cres. Hay—5E 68
Gordondale Rd. SW19—8L 89
Gordon Gdns. Edgw—9M 23
Gordon Gro. SE5—1M 91
Gordon Hill. Enf—3A 16
Gordon Ho. Rd. NW5—9E 42
Gordon Pl. W8—3L 73

Gordon Rd. E4—9C 18
Gordon Rd. E11—4E 46
Gordon Rd. E15—9A 46
Gordon Rd. E18—8F 30
Gordon Rd. N3—7K 25
Gordon Rd. N9—2F 28
Gordon Rd. N11—7H 27
Gordon Rd. SE15—1F 92
Gordon Rd. W4—7M 71
Gordon Rd.—1F 70
  W5 1-95 & 2-84
  W13 remainder
Gordon Rd. Ashf—9C 144
Gordon Rd. Bark—4C 64
Gordon Rd. Beck—7K 109
Gordon Rd. Belv—5A 82
Gordon Rd. Cars—8D 122
Gordon Rd. Dart—6H 99
Gordon Rd. Enf—3A 16
Gordon Rd. Esh—9C 118
Gordon Rd. Harr—1C 38
Gordon Rd. Houn—3A 86
Gordon Rd. Ilf—8B 48
Gordon Rd. King—5K 103
Gordon Rd. Rich—1K 87
Gordon Rd. Romf—4K 49
Gordon Rd. Shep—1B 116
Gordon Rd. Sidc—4C 96
Gordon Rd. S'hall—5J 69
Gordon Rd. Surb—2K 119
Gordon Rd. Wal A—7G 7
Gordon Rd. W Dray—1J 143
Gordon Sq. WC1—7H 59
Gordon St. E13—6E 62
Gordon St. WC1—7H 59
Gordon Way. Barn—6K 13
Gore Ct. NW9—3L 39
Gorefield Pl. NW6—5L 57
Gore Rd. E9—4G 61
Gore Rd. SW20—6G 105
Goresbrook Rd. Dag—4F 64
Gore St. SW7—4A 74
Gorham Pl. W11—1J 73
Goring Clo. Romf—8A 34
Goring Gdns. Dag—9G 49
Goring Rd. N11—6J 27
Goring Rd. Dag—2B 66
Goring Way. Gnfd—5A 54
Gorle Clo. Wat—8E 4
Gorleston Rd. N15—3B 44
Gorleston St. W14—5J 73
Gorman Rd. SE18—5K 79
Gorringe Pk. Av. Mitc—4E 106
Gorse Hill. F'ham, Dart—1K 131
Gorse Rise. SW17—2E 106
Gorse Rd. Croy—6L 125
Gorse Rd. Orp—4L 129
Gorse Wlk. W Dray—9C 142
Gorseway. Romf—6C 50
Gorst Rd. NW10—7A 56
Gorst Rd. SW11—5D 90
Gorsuch Pl. E2—6D 60
Gorsuch St. E2—6D 60
Gosberton Rd. SW12—7E 90
Gosbury Hill. Chess—6J 119
Gosfield Rd. Dag—7L 49
Gosfield Rd. Eps—4B 134
Gosfield St. W1—8G 59
Gosford Gdns. Ilf—3K 47
Gosforth La. Wat—3E 20
Gosforth Path. Wat—3E 20
Goshawk Gdns. Hay—6C 52
Goslett Yd. WC2—9H 59
Gosling Grn. Gnfd—6L 53
Gosling Way. SW9—9L 75
Gospatrick Rd. N17—7A 28
Gospel Oak Est. NW5—1D 58
Gosport Dri. Horn—2G 67
Gosport Rd. E17—3K 45
Gosport Wlk. N17—2F 44
Gosport Way. SE15—8D 76
Gossage Rd. SE18—6B 80
Gossage Rd. Uxb—3D 142
Gossamers, The. Wat—8J 5
Gosset St. E2—6D 60
Goss Hill. Swan—3G 115
Gosshill Rd. Chst—6L 111
Gosterwood St. SE8—7J 77
Gostling Rd. Twic—7L 85
Goston Gdns. T Hth—7L 107
Goswell Rd. EC1—6M 59
Gothic Clo. Dart—9H 99
Gothic Ct. Hay—7B 68
Gothic Rd. Twic—8B 86
Goudhurst Rd. Brom—2C 110
Gough Rd. E15—9D 46
Gough Rd. Enf—4F 16
Gough Sq. EC4—9L 59
Gough St. WC1—7K 59
Gough Wlk. E14—9L 61
Gould Rd. Felt—6C 84
Gould Rd. Twic—7C 86
Gould's Grn. Uxb—1M 143

Gould Ter. E8—1F 60
Goulston St. E1—9D 60
Goulton Rd. E5—9F 44
Gourley Pl. N15—3C 44
Gourley St. N15—3C 44
Gourock Rd. SE9—4L 95
Govan St. E2—4E 60
Government Row. Enf—2L 17
Govett Av. Shep—9A 100
Govier Clo. E15—3C 62
Gowan Av. SW6—9J 73
Gowan Rd. NW10—2F 56
Gower Ct. WC1—7H 59
Gower M. WC1—8H 59
Gower Pl. WC1—7H 59
Gower Rd. E7—2E 62
Gower Rd. Iswth—7D 70
Gower Rd. Wey—8B 116
Gower St. WC1—7G 59
Gowers Wlk. E1—9E 60
Gowland Pl. Beck—6K 109
Gowlett Rd. SE15—2E 92
Gowrie Rd. SW11—2E 90
Graburn Way. E Mol—7B 102
Grace Av. Bexh—1K 97
Gracechurch St. EC3—1B 76
Gracedale Rd. SW16—2F 106
Gracefield Gdns. SW16—9J 91
Grace Path. SE26—1G 109
Grace Rd. Croy—1A 124
Grace's All. E1—1E 76
Grace's M. SE5—1C 92
Grace's Rd. SE5—1C 92
Grace St. E3—6M 61
Gradient, The. SE26—1E 108
Graeme Rd. Enf—4B 16
Graemesdyke Av. SW14
  —3M 87
Grafton Clo. W13—9E 54
Grafton Clo. Houn—7J 85
Grafton Clo. Wor Pk—5C 120
Grafton Cres. NW1—2F 58
Grafton Gdns. N4—4A 44
Grafton Gdns. Dag—7J 49
Grafton M. W1—7G 59
Grafton Pk. Rd. Wor Pk—5C 120
Grafton Pl. NW1—6H 59
Grafton Rd. NW5—1E 58
Grafton Rd. W3—1A 72
Grafton Rd. Croy—3L 123
Grafton Rd. Dag—7J 49
Grafton Rd. Enf—5K 15
Grafton Rd. Harr—3A 38
Grafton Rd. N Mald—7C 104
Grafton Rd. Wor Pk—5B 120
Grafton Sq. SW4—2G 91
Graftons, The. NW2—8L 41
Grafton St. W1—1F 74
Grafton Ter. NW5—1D 58
Grafton Way. W1—7G 59
Grafton Yd. NW5—2F 58
Graham Av. W13—3F 70
Graham Av. Mitc—5E 106
Graham Clo. Croy—4L 125
Grahame Pk. Way. NW9 & NW7
  —9D 24
Graham Gdns. Surb—3J 119
Graham Rd. E8—2E 60
Graham Rd. E13—7E 62
Graham Rd. N15—1M 43
Graham Rd. NW4—4F 40
Graham Rd. SW19—4K 105
Graham Rd. W4—4B 72
Graham Rd. Bexh—3K 97
Graham Rd. Hmptn—1L 101
Graham Rd. Harr—1C 38
Graham Rd. Mitc—5E 106
Graham Rd. Purl—5L 137
Graham St. N1—5M 59
Graham Ter. SW1—5E 74
Grainger Clo. N'holt—2A 54
Grainger Rd. N22—8A 28
Grainger Rd. Iswth—1D 86
Grainges Yd. Uxb—3A 142
Gramer Clo. E11—7B 46
Grampian Clo. Hay—8B 68
Grampian Clo. Orp—1D 128
Grampian Gdns. NW2—6J 41
Granada St. SW17—2D 106
Granard Av. SW15—4F 88
Granard Rd. SW12—6D 90
Granary St. NW1—4H 59
Granby Pk. Rd. Wal X—1A 6
Granby Rd. SE9—1K 95
Granby St. E2—7D 60
Granby Ter. NW1—5G 59
Grand Av. EC1—8M 59
Grand Av. N10—2E 42
Grand Av. Surb—9M 103
Grand Av. Wemb—1L 55
Grand Av. E. Wemb—1M 55
Grand Depot Rd. SE18—6L 79

Grand Dri. SW20—6G 105
Granden Rd. SW16—6J 107
Grandfield Av. Wat—3E 8
  (in two parts)
Grandison Rd. SW11—4D 90
Grandison Rd. Wor Pk—4G 121
Grand Pde. N4—3M 43
Grand Pde. M. SW15—4J 89
Grand Stand Rd. Eps—9D 134
Grand Union Industrial Est.
  NW10—5M 55
Grand View Av. West—8G 141
Grand Wlk. E1—7J 61
Granfield St. SW11—9B 74
Grange Av. N12—5A 26
Grange Av. N20—9J 13
Grange Av. SE25—6C 108
Grange Av. Barn—1C 26
Grange Av. Stan—9F 22
Grange Av. Twic—8C 86
Grange Av. Wfd G—7E 30
Grangecliffe Gdns. SE25
  —6C 108
Grange Clo. E Mol—8M 101
Grange Clo. Edgw—5A 24
Grange Clo. Hay—8C 52
Grange Clo. Houn—7K 69
Grange Clo. Sidc—9E 96
Grange Clo. Wfd G—7E 30
Grange Ct. WC2—9K 59
Grange Ct. Lou—7H 19
Grange Ct. N'holt—5G 53
Grange Ct. Wal A—7J 7
Grange Ct. W on t—4E 116
Grangecourt Rd. N16—6C 44
Grange Cres. SE28—9G 65
Grange Cres. Chig—5B 32
Grangedale Clo. N'wd—7C 20
Grange Dri. Chst—3J 111
Grange Farm Clo. Harr—7A 38
Grange Gdns. N14—1H 27
Grange Gdns. NW3—8M 41
Grange Gdns. SE25—6C 108
Grange Gdns. Bans—5M 135
Grange Gdns. Pinn—1J 37
Grange Gro. N1—2A 60
Grange Hill. SE25—6C 108
Grange Hill. Edgw—5A 24
Grangehill Rd. SE9—3K 95
Grange La. SE21—8D 92
Grange Mans. Eps—9D 120
Grange Meadow. Bans
  —5M 135
Grangemill Rd. SE6—9L 93
Grangemill Way. SE6—8L 93
Grange Pde. Hay—8C 52
Grange Pk. W5—2J 71
Grange Pk. Av. N21—8A 16
Grange Pk. Pl. SW20—5F 105
Grange Pk. Rd. E10—6M 45
Grange Pk. Rd. T Hth—8B 108
Grange Pl. NW6—3L 57
Grange Rd. E10—6L 45
Grange Rd. E13—6D 62
Grange Rd. E17—3J 45
Grange Rd. N6—4E 42
Grange Rd.—6E 28
  N17 1-51 & 2-10a
  N18 remainder
Grange Rd. NW10—2F 56
Grange Rd. SE1—4C 76
Grange Rd.—7B 108
  SE25 31-313 & 216-248
  SE19 315-361 & 250-352
  T Hth remainder
Grange Rd. SW13—9E 72
Grange Rd. W4—6M 71
Grange Rd. W5—2H 71
Grange Rd. Borwd—7K 11
Grange Rd. Chess—6J 119
Grange Rd. E Mol—8M 101
Grange Rd. Edgw—6B 24
Grange Rd. Harr—3E 38
Grange Rd. Harr—7B 38
  (Roxeth)
Grange Rd. Hay—9C 52
Grange Rd. Ilf—9M 47
Grange Rd. King—7J 103
Grange Rd. Orp—5A 128
Grange Rd. Romf—6F 34
Grange Rd. S'hall—3J 69
Grange Rd. S Croy—2A 138
Grange Rd. S Ock—2M 83
Grange Rd. Sutt—9L 121
Grange Rd. W on t—6J 117
Grange Rd. Wat—3B 10
Granger Way. Romf—4E 50
Grange St. N1—4B 60
Grange, The. SE1—4D 76
Grange, The. SW19—3H 105
Grange, The. Croy—4K 125
Grange, The. Wemb—5L 55
Grange, The. Wor Pk—6B 120
Grange Vale. Sutt—9M 121

Grangeview Rd. N20—1A 26
Grange Way. SE1—4C 76
Grange Way. N12—4M 25
Grange Way. NW6—3L 57
Grange Way. Eri—8F 82
Grange Way. Wfd G—4G 31
Grangeway, The. N21—8M 15
Grangewood. Bex—7K 97
Grangewood Av. Rain—7G 67
Grange Wood Clo. Pinn—3E 36
Grange Wood Dri. Sun—4D 100
Grange Wood La. Beck—3K 109
Grangewood St. E6—4H 63
Grange Yd. SE1—4D 76
Granham Gdns. N9—2D 28
Granite St. SE18—6D 80
Granleigh Rd. E11—7C 46
Gransden Av. E8—3F 60
Gransden Rd. W12—3D 72
Grantbridge St. N1—5M 59
Grant Clo. N14—9G 15
Grantham Clo. Edgw—3J 23
Grantham Gdns. Romf—5K 49
Grantham Grn. Borwd—7A 12
Grantham Pl. W1—2F 74
Grantham Rd. E12—9L 47
Grantham Rd. SW9—1J 91
Grantham Rd. W4—8C 72
Grantley Rd. Houn—1G 85
Grantley St. E1—6H 61
Grantock Rd. E17—8B 30
Granton Av. Upm—7K 51
Granton Rd. N16—5G 107
Granton Rd. Ilf—6E 48
Granton Rd. Sidc—3G 113
Grant Pl. Croy—3D 124
Grant Rd. SW11—3B 90
Grant Rd. Croy—3D 124
Grant Rd. Harr—1C 38
Grants Clo. NW7—7G 25
Grant St. E13—6E 62
Grant St. N1—5L 59
Grantully Rd. W9—6M 57
Granville Av. N9—3G 29
Granville Av. Felt—8E 84
Granville Av. Houn—4L 85
Granville Clo. Croy—4C 124
Granville Gdns. SW16—4K 107
Granville Gdns. W5—2K 71
Granville Gro. SE13—2A 94
Granville M. Sidc—1E 112
Granville Pk. SE13—2A 94
Granville Pl. N12—7A 26
Granville Pl. W1—9E 58
Granville Rd. E17—4M 45
Granville Rd. E18—9F 30
Granville Rd. N4—4K 43
Granville Rd. N12—7A 26
Granville Rd. N13—6K 27
Granville Rd. N22—8M 27
Granville Rd. NW2—7K 41
Granville Rd. NW6—5L 57
  (in two parts)
Granville Rd. SW18—6K 89
Granville Rd. SW19—4L 105
Granville Rd. Barn—5H 13
Granville Rd. Hay—5E 68
Granville Rd. Ilf—6M 47
Granville Rd. Sidc—1E 112
Granville Rd. Uxb—2F 142
Granville Rd. Wat—6G 9
Granville Rd. Well—2G 97
Granville Rd. Wey—9A 116
Granville Sq. WC1—6K 59
Granville St. WC1—6K 59
Grape St. WC2—9J 59
Grasdene Rd. SE18—8E 80
Grasmere Av. SW15—1B 104
Grasmere Av. SW19—7L 105
Grasmere Av. W3—1B 72
Grasmere Av. Houn—5M 85
Grasmere Av. Orp—5M 127
Grasmere Av. Ruis—5A 36
Grasmere Av. Wemb—5G 39
Grasmere Clo. Lou—4K 19
Grasmere Gdns. Harr—9E 22
Grasmere Gdns. Ilf—3K 47
Grasmere Gdns. Orp—5M 127
Grasmere Rd. E13—5E 62
Grasmere Rd. N10—8F 26
Grasmere Rd. N17—6E 28
Grasmere Rd. SE25—9F 108
Grasmere Rd. SW16—2K 107
Grasmere Rd. Bexh—1A 98
Grasmere Rd. Brom—5D 110
Grasmere Rd. Horn—2K 51
Grasmere Rd. Orp—5M 127
Grasmere Rd. Purl—3M 137
Grassington Clo. St Alb—3L 5
Grassington Rd. Sidc—1E 112
Grassmount. SE23—8F 92

Grassmount. Purl—2G 137
Grass Pk. N3—8K 25
Grass Way. Wall—6G 123
Grasvenor Av. Barn—7L 13
Grateley Way. SE15—8D 76
Gratton Rd. W14—4J 73
Gratton Ter. NW2—8H 41
Gravel Clo. Chig—2E 32
Graveley Av. Borwd—7A 12
Gravel Hill. N3—9K 25
Gravel Hill. Bexh—4M 97
Gravel Hill. Croy—8H 125
Gravel Hill. Lou—2E 18
Gravel Hill. Uxb—1B 142
Gravel Hill Clo. Bexh—4M 97
Gravel La. E1—9D 60
Gravel La. Chig—2E 32
Gravel Pit La. SE9—4M 95
Gravel Pits. Brom—7E 110
Gravel Rd. Brom—4J 127
Gravel Rd. Twic—7C 86
Gravelwood Clo. Chst—9A 96
Graveney Gro. SE20—4G 109
Graveney Rd. SW17—1C 106
Gravesend Rd. W12—1E 72
Gray Av. Dag—6K 49
Grayford Clo. E6—8H 63
Gray Gdns. Rain—2E 66
Grayham Cres. N Mald—8B 104
Grayham Rd. N Mald—8B 104
Grayland Clo. Brom—5H 111
Grayling Rd. N16—7B 44
Grayling Sq. E2—6E 60
Graylings, The. Abb L, Wat
  —6B 4
Grayscroft Rd. SW16—4H 107
Grays Farm Rd. Orp—5F 112
Grayshott Rd. SW11—2E 90
Gray's Inn Ct. WC1—8K 59
Gray's Inn Rd. WC1—6K 59
Gray's Inn Sq. WC1—8K 59
Grays La. Ashf—9F 144
Gray's Rd. Uxb—4C 142
Gray St. SE1—3M 75
Grayswood Gdns. SW20
  —6F 104
Graywood Ct. N12—7A 26
Grazebrook Rd. N16—7B 44
Grazeley Clo. Bexh—4M 97
Grazeley Ct. SE19—2C 108
Gt. Bell All. EC2—9B 60
Gt. Benty. W Dray—5J 143
Gt. Brownings. SE21—1D 108
Gt. Bushey Dri. N20—1M 25
Gt. Cambridge Rd.—7B 28 to
  1D 6
  N17—7B 28
  N18—6B 28
  N9—3B 28
  Enf—9D 16
  Wal X—5B 6
Gt. Castle St. W1—9G 59
Gt. Central Av. Ruis—1G 53
Gt. Central St. NW1—8D 58
Gt. Central Way. NW10—9A 40
Gt. Chapel St. W1—9H 59
Gt. Chertsey Rd. W4—9B &
  7D 72
Gt. Chertsey Rd. Felt & Twic
  —9K 85
Gt. Church La. W6—5H 73
Gt. College St. SW1—4J 75
Gt. Cross Av. SE10—8C 78
Gt. Cullings. Romf—7C 50
Gt. Cumberland M. W1—9D 58
Gt. Cumberland Pl. W1—9D 58
Gt. Dover St. SE1—4B 76
Greatdown Rd. W13—8D 54
Gt. Eastern Rd. E15—3B 62
Gt. Eastern St. EC2—7C 60
Gt. Ellshams. Bans—8L 135
Gt. Elms Rd. Brom—8G 111
Great Field. NW9—8C 24
Greatfield Av. E6—7K 63
Greatfield Clo. N19—9G 43
Gt. Field Clo. SE4—3L 93
Greatfields Dri. Uxb—8E 142
Greatfields Rd. Bark—4B 64
Great Gdns. Rd. Horn—4F 50
Gt. George St. SW1—3H 75
Great Gro. Bush, Wat—6M 9
Gt. Guildford St. SE1—2A 76
Greatham Rd. Bush, Wat
  —5H 9
Greatham Wlk. SW15—7E 88
Gt. Harry Dri. SE9—9L 95
Gt. James St. WC1—8K 59
Gt. Marlborough St. W1—9G 59
Gt. Maze Pond. SE1—3B 76
  (in two parts)
Gt. Nelmes Chase. Horn—3K 51
Gt. Newport St. WC2—1J 75
Gt. New St. EC4—9L 59

Gt. North Rd.—3C 42
  N6 2-66
  N2 remainder
Gt. North Rd. Barn—7L 13
  (High Barnet)
Gt. North Rd. Barn—4K 13
  (New Barnet)
Gt. North Way. NW4—9F 24
Gt. Oaks. Chig—4A 32
Greatorex St. E1—8E 60
Gt. Ormond St. WC1—8J 59
Gt. Owl Rd. Chig—3L 31
Gt. Percy St. WC1—6K 59
Gt. Peter St. SW1—4H 75
Gt. Portland St. W1—7F 58
Gt. Pulteney St. W1—1G 75
Gt. Queen St. WC2—3J 59
Gt. Queen St. Dart—5K 99
Gt. Russell St. WC1—9H 59
Gt. Saint Helen's. EC3—9C 60
Gt. Saint Thomas Apostle. EC4
—1A 76
Gt. Scotland Yd. SW1—2J 75
Gt. Smith St. SW1—4H 75
Gt. South West Rd. Felt & Houn
—6A 84
Gt. Spilmans. SE22—4C 92
Gt. Strand. NW9—8D 24
Gt. Suffolk St. SE1—2M 75
Gt. Sutton St. EC1—7M 59
Gt. Swan All. EC2—9B 60
Gt. Tattenhams. Eps—9H 135
Gt. Thrift. Orp—8A 112
Gt. Titchfield St. W1—8G 59
Gt. Tower St. EC3—1C 76
Gt. Trinity La. EC4—1A 76
Gt. Turnstile. WC1—8K 59
Gt. Western Industrial Pk.
  S'hall—3M 69
Gt. Western Rd.—8K 57
  W9 1-59 & 2-56
  W11 remainder
Gt. West Rd. W4 & W6—6D 72
Gt. West Rd. Houn, Iswth &
  Bren—1H 85
Gt. West Rd. Trading Est. Bren
—8F 70
Gt. Winchester St. EC2—9B 60
Gt. Windmill St. W1—1H 75
Greatwood. Chst—4L 111
Gt. Woodcote Dri. Purl—2H 137
Gt. Woodcote Pk. Purl—2H 137
Greaves Pl. SW17—1C 106
Grecian Cres. SE19—3M 107
Greek Ct. W1—9H 59
Greek St. W1—9H 59
Greenacre Clo. Barn—2K 13
Greenacre Clo. Swan—8C 114
Greenacres. SE9—5L 95
Greenacres. Bush, Wat—2B 22
Green Acres. Croy—5D 124
Greenacres Clo. Rain—6J 67
Greenacres Dri. Stan—7F 22
Greenacre Wlk. N14—3H 27
Greenall Clo. Wal X—3E 6
Green Av. NW7—4B 24
Green Av. W13—4F 70
Greenaway Gdns. NW3—9M 41
Green Bank. N12—4M 25
Greenbank. Wal X—1B 6
Greenbank Av. Wemb—1E 54
Greenbank Clo. E4—2A 30
Greenbank Clo. Romf—3H 35
Greenbank Cres. NW4—2J 41
Greenbank Rd. Wat—9B 4
Greenbanks. Dart—8J 99
Greenbay Rd. SE7—8H 79
Greenberry St. NW8—5C 58
Greenbrook Av. Barn—3A 14
Green Clo. NW9—4A 40
Green Clo. NW11—5A 42
Green Clo. Brom—7C 110
Green Clo. Cars—4D 122
Green Clo. Felt—2J 101
Green Clo. Wal X—4E 6
Greencoat Pl. SW1—5G 75
Greencoat Row. SW1—4G 75
Greencourt Av. Croy—4F 124
Greencourt Av. Edgw—8M 23
Greencourt Gdns. Croy—4F 124
Greencourt Rd. Orp—9C 112
Green Ct. Rd. Swan—9B 114
Greencrofts. Edgw—5A 24
Greencroft Av. Ruis—7G 37
Greencroft Clo. E6—8H 63
Greencroft Gdns. NW6—3M 57
Greencroft Gdns. Enf—5C 16
Greencroft Rd. Houn—9K 69
Green Curve. Bans—6K 135
Green Dale. SE22 & SE5—4C 92
Green Dale Clo. SE22—4C 92
Green Dragon La. N21—8L 15
Green Dragon La. Bren—6J 71

Green Dragon Yd. E1—8E 60
Green Dri. S'hall—2L 69
Green End. N21—2M 27
Green End. Chess—6J 119
Greenend Rd. W4—3C 72
Green Farm Clo. Orp—7D 128
Greenfell St. SE10—4C 78
Greenfield Av. Surb—2M 119
Greenfield Av. Wat—2H 21
Greenfield Gdns. NW2—7J 41
Greenfield Gdns. Dag—4H 65
Greenfield Gdns. Orp—2B 128
Greenfield Link. Coul—7J 137
Greenfield Pas. Barn—5J 13
Greenfield Rd. E1—9E 60
Greenfield Rd. N15—3C 44
Greenfield Rd. Dag—4G 65
Greenfield Rd. Dart—2B 114
Greenfields. Lou—6L 19
Greenfields. S'hall—9L 53
Greenfield St. Wal A—7J 7
Greenfield Way. Harr—1M 37
Greenford Av. W7—7C 54
Greenford Av. S'hall—1K 69
Greenford Gdns. Gnfd—6M 53
Greenford Grn. Gnfd—2C 54
Greenford Industrial Est.
  N'holt—3M 53
Greenford Rd. S'hall, Gnfd &
  Harr—1A 70
Greenford Rd. Sutt—6M 121
Green Gdns. Orp—7A 128
Greengate. Gnfd—2F 54
Greengate St. E13—5F 62
Green Glades. Horn—4L 51
Greenhalgh Wlk. N2—2A 42
Greenham Rd. N10—9E 26
Greenhayes Av. Bans—6L 135
Greenhayes Gdns. Bans
—7L 135
Greenheys Clo. N'wd—8C 20
Greenheys Dri. E18—1D 46
Green Hill. NW3—9B 42
Green Hill. SE18—6K 79
Greenhill. Buck H—1G 31
Green Hill. Orp—4K 141
Greenhill. Sutt—4A 122
Greenhill. Wemb—7M 39
Greenhill Cres. Wat—8C 8
Greenhill Gdns. N'holt—5K 53
Greenhill Gro. E12—9J 47
Green Hill La. Warl—9J 139
Greenhill Pk. NW10—4C 56
Greenhill Pk. Barn—7M 13
Greenhill Rd. NW10—4C 56
Greenhill Rd. Harr—4C 38
Greenhill's Rents. EC1—8M 59
Greenhills Ter. N1—2B 60
Greenhill Ter. N'holt—5K 53
Greenhill Way. Harr—4C 38
Greenhill Way. Wemb—7M 39
Greenhithe Clo. Sidc—6C 96
Greenholm Rd. SE9—4M 95
Green Hundred Rd. SE15—7E 76
Greenhurst Rd. SE27—2L 107
Greening St. SE2—5G 81
Greenland Cres. S'hall—4G 69
Greenland Pl. NW1—4F 58
Greenland Rd. NW1—4F 58
Greenland Rd. Barn—8G 13
Greenlands Rd. Wey—5A 116
Greenland St. NW1—4F 58
Green La. E4—3C 18
Green La. NW4—2H 41
Green La. SE9 & Chst—7M 95
Green La. SE20—4H 109
Green La. SW16 & T Hth
—4K 107
Green La. W7—3C 70
Green La. Asht—9G 133
Green La. Chess—1J 133
Green La. Chig—1A 32
Green La. E Mol—9M 101
Green La. Edgw—4K 23
Green La. Felt—2J 101
Green La. Harr—8C 38
Green La. Houn—2F 84
Green La. Ilf & Dag—7B 48
Green La. Mord—1L 121
Green La. N Mald—9A 104
Green La. N'wd—6B 20
Green La. Purl—3G 137
Green La. Shep—1A 116
Green La. Stan—4F 22
Green La. Sun—4D 100
Green La. Uxb—8A 52
Green La. W on T—8F 116
Green La. Warl—8J 139
Green La. Wat—9G 9
Green La. Wor Pk & Mord
—3E 120
Green La. Av. W on T—7G 117

Green La. Gdns. T Hth—6A 108
Green Lanes—6K 27
  N13 1-615 & 2-604
  N21 remainder
Green Lanes—2M 43
  N16 1-203 & 2-162
  N4 205-531 & 182-430
  N8 remainder
Green Lanes. Eps—1C 134
Greenlaw Gdns. N Mald
—2D 120
Green Lawns. Ruis—6G 37
Greenlaw St. SE18—4L 79
Greenleafe Dri. Ilf—1M 47
Greenleaf Rd. E6—4G 63
Greenleaf Rd. E17—1K 45
Greenlea Park Industrial Est.
  SW19—5B 106
Green Leas. Sun—4D 100
Greenleas. Wal A—7L 7
Greenleaves Ct. Ashf—3A 100
Green Man Gdns. W13—1E 70
Green Man La. W13—2E 70
Green Man La. Felt—3E 84
Green Man Pas. W13—2F 70
Greenman St. N1—4A 60
Green Moor Link. N21—9M 15
Greenmoor Rd. Enf—4G 17
Greenoak Way. SW19—1H 105
Greenock Rd. SW16—5H 107
Greenock Rd. W3—4M 71
Greenock Way. Romf—7C 34
Greenpark Ct. Gnfd—3G 55
Green Pl. Dart—4C 98
Green Pond Rd. E17—1J 45
Green Ride. Lou—6G 19
Green Rd. N14—8F 14
Green Rd. N20—3A 26
Greens Clo., The. Lou—4L 19
Green's End. SE18—5M 79
Greenshield Industrial Est.
  E16—3F 78
Greenside. Bex—7J 97
Greenside. Borwd—2L 11
Greenside. Dag—6G 49
Greenside. Swan—6B 114
Greenside Rd. W12—4E 72
Greenside Rd. Croy—2L 123
Greenstead Av. Wfd G—6G 31
Greenstead Clo. Wfd G—6G 31
Greenstead Gdns. SW15—4F 88
Greenstead Gdns. Wfd G
—6G 31
Greensted Rd. Lou—9J 19
Greenstone M. E11—4E 46
Green St.—2F 62
  E7 1-283 & 2-304
  E13 remainder
Green St. W1—1E 74
Green St. Enf—4G 17
Green St. Shen, Rad—1L 11
Green St. Sun—5E 100
Green Street Grn. Rd. Dart &
  Long, Dart—7M 99
Greensward. Bush, Wat—8M 9
Green, The. E4—1B 30
Green, The. E11—4F 46
Green, The. E15—2D 62
Green, The. N9—2E 28
Green, The. N14—3H 27
Green, The. N21—1L 27
Green, The. W3—9C 56
Green, The. W5—1H 71
Green, The. Bexh—9L 81
Green, The. Brom—9E 94
  (Grove Park)
Green, The. Brom—2E 126
  (Hayes)
Green, The. Cars—6E 122
Green, The. Croy—1K 139
Green, The. Eps—1E 134
Green, The. Esh—8D 118
Green, The. Felt—8F 84
Green, The. Houn—7L 69
Green, The. Mord—8J 105
Green, The. N Mald—7A 104
Green, The. Orp—7M 127
  (Farnborough)
Green, The. Orp—4F 112
  (St Paul's Cray)
Green, The. Rain—1J 83
Green, The. Rich—4H 87
Green, The. Shep—8C 100
Green, The. Sidc—1E 112
Green, The. S'hall—3K 69
Green, The. Sutt—5M 121
Green, The. Twic—8C 86
Green, The. Wal A—7J 7
Green, The. Wal X—1C 6
Green, The. Warl—9H 139
Green, The. Well—3C 96
Green, The. Wemb—7E 38
Green, The. W Dray—4H 143

Green, The. Wfd G—5E 30
Green Vale. W5—9K 55
Green Vale. Bexh—4H 97
Greenvale Rd. SE9—3K 95
Green Verges. Stan—7H 23
Green View. Chess—9K 119
Greenview Av. Beck—1J 125
Greenview Av. Croy—1J 125
Greenview Ct. Ashf—9D 144
Green Wlk. NW4—3H 41
Green Wlk. SE1—4C 76
Green Wlk. Dart—4D 98
Green Wlk. Hmptn—3K 101
Green Wlk. Lou—9J 19
Green Wlk. Ruis—6D 36
Green Wlk. S'hall—6L 69
Green Wlk. Wfd G—6J 31
Green Wlk., The. E4—1B 30
Greenway. N14—2J 27
Greenway. N20—2L 25
Greenway. SE9—4H 95
Greenway. SW20—8G 105
Green.Way. Brom—1J 127
Greenway. Chst—2L 111
Greenway. Dag—6G 49
Greenway. Harr—3J 39
Greenway. Hay—7F 52
Greenway. Pinn—9F 20
Greenway. Romf—6M 35
Green Way. Sun—8E 100
Greenway. Wall—6G 123
Green Way. Wfd G—5G 31
Greenway Av. E17—2B 46
Greenway Clo. N4—7A 44
Greenway Clo. N11—2E 26
Greenway Clo. N20—2L 25
Greenway Clo. NW9—9B 24
Greenway Gdns. NW9—9B 24
Greenway Gdns. Croy—5K 125
Greenway Gdns. Gnfd—6L 53
Green Way Gdns. Harr—9C 22
Greenways. Abb L, Wat—5C 4
Greenways. Beck—6L 109
Greenways. Esh—6C 118
Greenway, The. NW9—9B 24
Greenway, The. Enf—8D 6
Greenway, The. Eps—7L 133
Greenway, The. Houn—3K 85
Green Way, The. Harr—8C 22
Greenway, The. Orp—1F 128
Greenway, The. Pinn—4K 37
Greenway, The. Uxb—5B 142
Greenway, The. Uxb—7A 36
  (West Ruislip)
Greenwell St. W1—7F 58
Greenwich Chu. St. SE10
—7A 78
Greenwich High Rd. SE10
—8M 77
Greenwich Pk. St. SE10—7B 78
Greenwich S. St. SE10—9M 77
Greenwood Av. Dag—9M 49
Greenwood Av. Enf—3J 17
Greenwood Av. Wal X—4B 6
Greenwood Clo. Bush, Wat
—9C 10
Greenwood Clo. Mord—8J 105
Greenwood Clo. Orp—1C 128
Greenwood Clo. Sidc—8E 96
Greenwood Clo. Th Dit—3E 118
Greenwood Clo. Wal X—4B 6
Greenwood Dri. E4—5B 30
Greenwood Dri. Wat—7F 4
Greenwood Gdns. N13—3M 27
Greenwood Gdns. Ilf—7A 32
Greenwood Ho. N22—8L 27
Greenwood La. Hmptn
—2M 101
Greenwood Pk. King—4C 104
Greenwood Path. E13—5E 62
Greenwood Pl. NW5—1F 58
Greenwood Rd. E8—2E 60
Greenwood Rd. E13—5D 62
Greenwood Rd. Bex—1B 114
Greenwood Rd. Chig—4F 32
Greenwood Rd. Croy—2M 123
Greenwood Rd. Iswth—2D 86
Greenwood Rd. Mitc—7H 107
Greenwood Rd. Th Dit—4E 118
Greenwood Ter. NW10—5B 56
Green Wrythe Cres. Cars
—3C 122
Green Wrythe La. Cars—1B 122
Greenyard. Wal A—6J 7
Greer Rd. Harr—8A 22
Greet St. SE1—2L 75
Gregory Cres. SE9—6H 95
Gregory M. SE3—8F 78
Gregory Pl. W8—3M 73
Gregory Rd. Romf—2H 49
Gregory Rd. S'hall—4L 69
Gregson's Ride. Lou—2L 19
Greig Clo. N8—3J 43

Greig Ter. SE17—7M 75
Grenaby Av. Croy—2B 124
Grenaby Rd. Croy—2B 124
Grenada Rd. SE7—8G 79
Grenade St. E14—1K 77
Grenadier St. E16—2L 79
Grena Gdns. Rich—3K 87
Grena Rd. Rich—3K 87
Grendon Gdns. Wemb—7L 39
Grendon St. NW8—7C 58
Grenfell Av. Horn—6D 50
Grenfell Gdns. Harr—5J 39
Grenfell Gdns. Ilf—3D 48
Grenfell Rd. W11—1H 73
Grenfell Rd. Mitc—3D 106
Grenfell Tower. W11—1H 73
Grenfell Wlk. W11—1H 73
Grennell Clo. Sutt—4B 122
Grennell Rd. Sutt—4A 122
Grenoble Gdns. N13—6L 27
Grenside Rd. Wey—5A 116
Grenville Clo. Surb—3A 120
Grenville Clo. Wal X—5D 6
Grenville Gdns. Wfd G—7G 31
Grenville M. Hmptn—2M 101
Grenville Pl. NW7—5B 24
Grenville Pl. SW7—4A 74
Grenville Rd. N19—6J 43
Grenville Rd. Croy—1A 140
Grenville St. WC1—7J 59
Gresham Av. N20—4D 26
Gresham Clo. Bex—5K 97
Gresham Clo. Enf—5A 16
Gresham Dri. Romf—3F 48
Gresham Gdns. NW11—6J 41
Gresham Rd. E6—5K 63
Gresham Rd. E16—9F 62
Gresham Rd. NW10—1B 56
Gresham Rd. SE25—8E 108
Gresham Rd. SW9—2L 91
Gresham Rd. Beck—6J 109
Gresham Rd. Edgw—6K 23
Gresham Rd. Hmptn—3L 101
Gresham Rd. Houn—9A 70
Gresham Rd. Uxb—5E 142
Gresham St. EC2—9A 60
Gresham Way. SW19—9M 89
Gresley Clo. N15—2B 44
Gresley Ct. Enf—8C 6
Gresley Rd. N19—6G 43
Gressenhall Rd. SW18—5K 89
Gresse St. W1—9H 59
Greswell St. SW6—9H 73
Gretton Rd. N17—7D 28
Greville Av. S Croy—2H 139
Greville Pk. Av. Asht—9J 133
Greville Pk. Rd. Asht—9J 133
Greville Pk. Twic—6F 86
Greville Pl. NW6—5M 57
Greville Rd. E17—2A 46
Greville Rd. NW6—4M 57
Greville Rd. Rich—5K 87
Greville St. EC1—8L 59
Greycaine Rd. Wat—1H 9
Greycaine Trading Est. Wat
—1H 9
Grey Clo. NW11—4A 42
Greycoat Pl. SW1—4H 75
Greycoat St. SW1—4H 75
Greycot Rd. Beck—2L 109
Grey Eagle St. E1—7D 60
Greyfell Clo. Stan—5G 23
Greyfields Clo. Purl—5M 137
Greyfriars Pas. EC1—9M 59
Greyhound Ct. WC2—1K 75
Greyhound Hill. NW4—1F 40
Greyhound La. SW16—3H 107
Greyhound Rd. N17—1C 44
Greyhound Rd. NW10—6F 56
Greyhound Rd.—7H 73
  W6 1-183 & 2-136
  W14 remainder
Greyhound Rd. Sutt—7A 122
Greyhound Ter. SW16—5G 107
Greys Pk. Clo. Kes—7H 127
Greystead Rd. SE23—6G 93
Greystoke Av. Pinn—1L 37
Greystoke Gdns. W5—7J 55
Greystoke Gdns. Enf—6H 15
Greystoke Pk. Ter. W5—6H 55
Greystoke Pl. EC4—9L 59
Greystone Clo. S Croy—3G 139
Greystone Gdns. Harr—4G 39
Greystone Gdns. Ilf—9A 32
Greyswood St. SW16—3H 106
Grey Towers Av. Horn—6H 51
Grey Towers Gdns. Horn
—5G 51
Grice Av. West—5F 140
Gridiron Pl. Upm—7M 51
Grierson Rd. SE23—5H 93
Griffin Clo. NW10—1F 56

Griffin Mnr. Way. SE28—5B 80
Griffin Rd. N17—9C 28
Griffin Rd. SE18—6B 80
Griffin Way. Sun—6E 100
Griffiths Clo. Wor Pk—4F 120
Griffiths Rd. SW19—4L 105
Griggs App. Rd. Ilf—7A 48
Griggs Rd. E10—4A 46
Grimsby St. E2—7D 60
Grimsdyke Cres. Barn—5G 13
Grimsdyke Rd. Pinn—7J 21
Grimsell Path. SE5—8M 75
Grimstone Clo. Romf—6M 33
Grimston Rd. SW6—1K 89
Grimwade Av. Croy—5E 124
Grimwade Cres. SE15—2G 93
Grimwood Rd. Twic—6D 86
Grindal St. SE1—3L 75
Grinling Pl. SE8—7L 77
Grinstead Rd. SE8—6J 77
Grisedale Clo. Purl—6C 138
Grisedale Gdns. Purl—6C 138
Grittleton Av. Wemb—2M 55
Grittleton Rd. W9—7L 57
Grizedale Ter. SE23—8F 92
Grocer's Hall Ct. EC2—9B 60
Grogan Clo. Hmptn—3K 101
Groombridge Clo. W on T
—7F 116
Groombridge Clo. Well—4E 96
Groombridge Rd. E9—3H 61
Groom Cres. SW18—6B 90
Groomfield Clo. SW17—1E 106
Groom Pl. SW1—4E 74
Grosmont Rd. SE18—7D 80
Grosse Way. SW15—5F 88
Grosvenor Av. N5—1A 60
Grosvenor Av. SW14—2C 88
Grosvenor Av. Cars—8E 122
Grosvenor Av. Harr—4M 37
Grosvenor Av. Hay—5D 52
Grosvenor Av. K Lan—1A 4
Grosvenor Av. Rich—4J 87
Grosvenor Clo. Lou—3M 19
Grosvenor Cotts. SW1—5E 74
Grosvenor Ct. N14—9G 15
Grosvenor Cres. N14—7H 15
Grosvenor Cres. NW9—2L 39
Grosvenor Cres. SW1—3E 74
Grosvenor Cres. Dart—4H 99
Grosvenor Cres. Uxb—3F 142
Grosvenor Cres. M. SW1
—3E 74
Grosvenor Dri. Horn—6G 51
Grosvenor Dri. Lou—4M 19
Grosvenor Est. SW1—5H 75
Grosvenor Gdns. E6—6H 63
Grosvenor Gdns. N10—1G 43
Grosvenor Gdns. NW2—2G 57
Grosvenor Gdns. NW11—4K 41
Grosvenor Gdns. SW1—4F 74
Grosvenor Gdns. SW14—2C 88
Grosvenor Gdns. King—3H 103
Grosvenor Gdns. Wall—9G 123
Grosvenor Gdns. Wfd G—6E 30
Grosvenor Ga. W1—1E 74
Grosvenor Hill. SW19—3J 105
Grosvenor Hill. W1—1F 74
Grosvenor Pk. SE5—8A 76
Grosvenor Pk. Rd. E17—3M 45
Grosvenor Path. Lou—3M 19
Grosvenor Pl. SW1—3F 74
Grosvenor Pl. Houn—2A 86
Grosvenor Rise. E. E17—3M 45
Grosvenor Rd. E6—4H 63
Grosvenor Rd. E7—2F 62
Grosvenor Rd. E10—6A 46
Grosvenor Rd. E11—3F 46
Grosvenor Rd. N3—7K 25
Grosvenor Rd. N9—1F 28
Grosvenor Rd. N10—8F 26
Grosvenor Rd. SE25—8E 108
Grosvenor Rd. SW1—7F 74
Grosvenor Rd. W4—6M 71
Grosvenor Rd. W7—2E 70
Grosvenor Rd. Belv—7L 81
Grosvenor Rd. Bexh—4H 97
Grosvenor Rd. Borwd—5L 11
Grosvenor Rd. Bren—7H 71
Grosvenor Rd. Dag—6K 49
Grosvenor Rd. Houn—2K 85
Grosvenor Rd. Ilf—8A 48
Grosvenor Rd. N'wd—5D 20
Grosvenor Rd. Orp—1C 128
Grosvenor Rd. Rich—4J 87
Grosvenor Rd. Romf—5B 50
Grosvenor Rd. S'hall—4K 69
Grosvenor Rd. Twic—7E 86
Grosvenor Rd. Wall—8F 122
Grosvenor Rd. Wat—5G 9
Grosvenor Rd. W Wick
—4M 125
Grosvenor Sq. W1—1E 74

Grosvenor St. W1—1F 74
Grosvenor Ter. SE5—7A 76
Grosvenor Vale. Ruis—7D 36
Grosvenor Wharf Rd. E14
—5B 78
Grote's Bldgs. SE3—1C 94
Grote's Pl. SE3—1C 94
Groton Rd. SW18—8M 89
Grotto Ct. SE1—3A 76
Grotto Pas. W1—8E 58
Grotto Rd. Twic—8D 86
Grotto Rd. Wey—5A 116
Grove Av. N3—7L 25
Grove Av. N10—9G 27
Grove Av. W7—9C 54
Grove Av. Eps—5C 134
Grove Av. Pinn—2J 37
Grove Av. Sutt—8L 121
Grove Av. Twic—7D 86
Grovebury Clo. Eri—7B 82
Grovebury Ct. Bexh—4M 97
Grovebury Rd. SE2—3F 80
Grove Clo. SE23—7J 93
Grove Clo. Brom—4E 126
Grove Clo. Felt—1J 101
Grove Clo. King—8K 103
Grove Clo. Uxb—1E 142
Grove Ct. E Mol—9B 102
Grove Ct. Wal A—7H 7
Grove Cres. E18—9D 30
Grove Cres. NW9—2A 40
Grove Cres. SE5—1C 92
Grove Cres. Felt—1J 101
Grove Cres. King—7J 103
Grove Cres. W on T—2F 116
Grove Cres. Rd. E15—2B 62
Grovedale Clo. Wal X—3A 6
Grovedale Rd. N19—7H 43
Grove End. E18—9D 30
Grove End La. Esh—3B 118
Grove End Rd. NW8—6B 58
Grove Farm Industrial Est.
Mitc—9D 106
Grove Farm Pk. N'wd—5B 20
Grove Footpath. Surb—3J 103
Grove Gdns. E15—2C 62
Grove Gdns. NW4—3E 40
Grove Gdns. NW8—6C 58
Grove Gdns. Dag—8A 50
Grove Gdns. Enf—3H 17
Grove Gdns. Tedd—1E 102
Grove Grn. N'wd—5B 20
Grove Grn. Rd. E11—8A 46
Grove Hall Ct. NW8—6A 58
Grove Hall Rd. Bush, Wat—6J 9
Grove Hill. E18—9D 30
Grove Hill. Harr—5C 38
Grove Hill Rd. SE5—2C 92
Grove Hill Rd. Harr—5D 38
Grove Ho. Rd. N8—2J 43
Grove Ho. Rd. Bush, Wat—8K 9
Groveland Av. SW16—4K 107
Groveland Rd. Beck—7K 109
Grovelands. E Mol—8L 101
Grovelands Clo. SE5—1C 92
Grovelands Rd. N13—4K 27
Grovelands Rd. N15—4E 44
Grovelands Rd. Orp—4E 112
Grovelands Rd. Purl—4K 137
Groveland Way. N Mald
—9A 104
Grove La. SE5—9B 76
Grove La. Chig—3D 32
Grove La. Coul—6H 136
Grove La. King—8J 103
Grove La. Uxb—7D 142
Grove La. M. SE5—1C 92
Groveley Rd. Sun & Felt
—2D 100
Grove Mkt. Pl. SE9—5K 95
Grove M. W6—4G 73
Grove Mill La. Rick & Wat
—2A 8
Grove Pk. E11—3F 46
Grove Pk. NW9—2A 40
Grove Pk. SE5—1C 92
Grove Pk. Av. E4—7M 29
Grove Pk. Bri. W4—8A 72
Grove Pk. Gdns. W4—8A 72
Grove Pk. M. W4—8A 72
Grove Pk. Rd. N15—2C 44
Grove Pk. Rd. SE9—9G 95
Grove Pk. Rd. W4—8M 71
Grove Pk. Rd. Rain—4E 66
Grove Pk. Ter. W4—8M 71
Grove Pas. E2—5F 60
Grove Path. Wal X—4A 6
Grove Pl. NW3—8B 42
Grove Pl. W3—2A 72
Grove Pl. Bark—4A 64
Grove Pl. Wey—7A 116
Grove Rd. E3—4H 61
Grove Rd. E4—4A 30

Grove Rd. E11—5D 46
Grove Rd. E17—4M 45
Grove Rd. E18—9D 30
Grove Rd. N11—5F 26
Grove Rd. N12—5B 26
Grove Rd. N15—3C 44
Grove Rd. NW2—6C 57
Grove Rd. SW13—1D 88
Grove Rd. SW19—4A 106
Grove Rd. W3—2A 72
Grove Rd. W5—1H 71
Grove Rd. Barn—5C 14
Grove Rd. Belv—7K 81
Grove Rd. Bexh—3A 98
Grove Rd. Borwd—3L 11
Grove Rd. Bren—6G 71
Grove Rd. E Mol—8B 102
Grove Rd. Edgw—6L 23
Grove Rd. Eps—5C 134
Grove Rd. Houn—3L 85
Grove Rd. Iswth—9C 70
Grove Rd. Mitc—7E 106
Grove Rd. N'wd—5B 20
Grove Rd. Pinn—3K 37
Grove Rd. Rich—5K 87
Grove Rd. Romf—5F 48
Grove Rd. Shep—1A 116
Grove Rd. Surb—9H 103
Grove Rd. Sutt—8L 121
Grove Rd. T Hth—8L 107
Grove Rd. Twic—9B 86
Grove Rd. Uxb—3B 142
Grove Rd. W. Enf—1G 17
Grover Rd. Wat—9H 9
Groveside Rd. E4—2C 30
Grovestile Waye. Felt—6B 84
Grove St. N18—6D 28
Grove St. SE8—5K 77
Grove Ter. NW5—8F 42
Grove Ter. Tedd—1E 102
Grove, The. E15—2C 62
Grove, The. N3—8L 25
Grove, The. N4—5K 43
Grove, The. N6—6E 42
Grove, The. N8—3H 43
Grove, The. N13—4L 27
Grove, The. NW9—3B 40
Grove, The. NW11—5J 41
Grove, The. W5—1J 71
Grove, The. Bexh—3H 97
Grove, The. Coul—6H 137
Grove, The. Edgw—4M 23
Grove, The. Enf—4L 15
Grove, The. Eps—5C 134
Grove, The. Eps—2D 134
(Ewell)
Grove, The. Gnfd—9A 54
Grove, The. Iswth—9C 70
Grove, The. Sidc—1J 113
Grove, The. Swan—7D 114
Grove, The. Tedd—1E 102
Grove, The. Twic—5G 87
Grove, The. Upm—1M 67
Grove, The. Uxb—1E 142
Grove, The. W on T—2F 116
Grove, The. West—9J 141
Grove, The. W Wick—4A 126
Grove Vale. SE22—3D 92
Grove Vale. Chst—3L 111
Grove Vs. E14—1M 77
Groveway. SW9—9K 75
Groveway. Dag—9H 49
Grove Way. Esh—3A 118
Groveway. Wemb—1A 56
Grove Waye. Uxb—3B 142
Grovewood. Rich—9L 71
Grove Wood Hill. Coul—6G 137
Grummant Rd. SE15—9D 76
Grundy St. E14—9M 61
Gruneisen Rd. N3—7M 25
Gubbins La. Romf—7K 35
Gubyon Av. SE24—4M 91
Guerin Sq. E3—6K 61
Guernsey Clo. Houn—8L 69
Guernsey Gro. SE21—6A 92
Guernsey Ho. N1—2A 60
Guernsey Rd. E11—6B 46
Guibal Rd. SE12—6F 94
Guildersfield Rd. SW16—4J 107
Guildford Av. Felt—8D 84
Guildford Gdns. Romf—6J 35
Guildford Gro. SE10—9M 77
Guildford Rd. E6—9K 63
Guildford Rd. E17—8A 30
Guildford Rd. SW8—9J 75
Guildford Rd. Croy—1B 124
Guildford Rd. Ilf—7C 48
Guildford Rd. Romf—6J 35
Guildford Way. Wall—7J 123
Guildhall Yd. EC2—9A 60
Guildhouse St. SW1—5G 75
Guildown Av. N12—4M 25
Guild Rd. SE7—6H 79

Guild Rd. Eri—8D 82
Guildsway. E17—8K 29
Guilford Av. Surb—9K 103
Guilford Pl. WC1—7K 59
Guilford St. WC1—7J 59
Guillemot Pl. N22—9K 27
Guilsborough Clo. NW10
—3C 56
Guiness Trust Est. N16—6C 44
Guinness Clo. E9—3J 61
Guinness Clo. Hay—4B 68
Guinness Ct. NW8—4C 58
Guinness Sq. SE1—5C 76
Guion Rd. SW6—1K 89
Gulland Clo. Bush, Wat—7A 10
Gull Clo. Wall—9J 123
Gullet Wood Rd. Wat—8E 4
Gulliver Clo. N'holt—4K 53
Gulliver Rd. Sidc—8B 96
Gulliver St. SE16—4K 77
Gull Wlk. Rain—3F 66
Gumleigh Rd. W5—5G 71
Gumley Gdns. Iswth—2E 86
Gumping Rd. Orp—4A 128
Gundulph Rd. Brom—7G 111
Gunmaker's La. E3—4J 61
Gunner La. SE18—6L 79
Gunnersbury Av.—2K 71
  W5 1-119 & 2-114
  W3 127-143 & 144-248
  W4 remainder
Gunnersbury Clo. W4—6M 71
Gunnersbury Cres. W3—3L 71
Gunnersbury Dri. W5—3K 71
Gunnersbury Gdns. W3—3L 71
Gunnersbury La. W3—3L 71
Gunnersbury M. W4—6M 71
Gunners Gro. E4—3A 30
Gunners Rd. SW18—8B 90
Gunning St. SE18—5C 80
Gunstor Rd. N16—9C 44
Gun St. E1—8D 60
Gunter Gro. SW10—7A 74
Gunter Gro. Edgw—8B 24
Gunterstone Rd. W14—5J 73
Gunthorpe St. E1—8D 60
Gunton Rd. E5—7F 44
Gunton Rd. SW17—3E 106
Gurdon Rd. SE7—6E 78
Gurnard Clo. W Dray—1H 143
Gurnell Gro. W13—7D 54
Gurney Clo. E15—1C 62
Gurney Clo. Bark—2M 63
Gurney Cres. Croy—3K 123
Gurney Dri. N2—2A 42
Gurney Rd. E15—1C 62
Gurney Rd. Cars—6E 122
Gurney Rd. N'holt—6F 52
Guthrie St. SW3—6B 74
Gutter La. EC2—9A 60
Guyatt Gdns. Mitc—6E 106
Guy Rd. Wall—5H 123
Guyscliff Rd. SE13—4A 94
Guysfield Clo. Rain—4E 66
Guysfield Dri. Rain—4E 66
Guys Retreat. Buck H—9G 19
Guy St. SE1—3B 76
Gwalior Rd. SW15—3H 89
Gwendolen Av. SW15—3H 89
Gwendolen Clo. SW15—4H 89
Gwendoline Av. E13—4F 62
Gwendwr Rd. W14—6J 73
Gwent Clo. Wat—7H 5
Gwillim Clo. Sidc—4E 96
Gwydor Rd. Beck—7H 109
Gwydyr Rd. Brom—7D 110
Gwyn Clo. SW6—8A 74
Gwynne Av. Croy—2H 125
Gwynne Pk. Av. Wfd G—6K 31
Gwynne Pl. WC1—6K 59
Gwynne Rd. SW11—1B 90
Gyfford Wlk. Wal X—4B 6
Gylcote Clo. SE5—3B 92
Gyles Pk. Stan—8G 23
Gyllyngdune Gdns. Ilf—8D 48
Gypsy La. K Lan—8B 4

Hackney Rd. E2—6D 60
Hacton Dri. Horn—9H 51
Hacton La. Horn & Upm—7K 51
Hadden Rd. SE28—4C 80
Hadden Way. Gnfd—2B 54
Haddington Rd. Brom—9B 94
Haddon Clo. Borwd—5L 11
Haddon Clo. Enf—8E 16
Haddon Clo. N Mald—9D 104
Haddon Clo. Wey—5C 116
Haddon Gro. Sidc—6E 96
Haddon Rd. Orp—9G 113
Haddon Rd. Sutt—6M 121
Haddo St. SE10—7A 78
Hadfield Rd. Stai—5B 144
Hadleigh Clo. E1—7G 61
Hadleigh Rd. N9—9F 16
Hadleigh St. E2—6G 61
Hadleigh Wlk. E6—9J 63
Hadley Clo. N21—8L 15
Hadley Clo. Borwd—7K 11
Hadley Comn. Barn—4L 13
Hadley Ct. N16—6E 44
Hadley Gdns. W4—6B 72
Hadley Gdns. S'hall—6K 69
Hadley Grn. Rd. Barn—4K 13
Hadley Grn. W. Barn—4K 13
Hadley Gro. Barn—4J 13
Hadley Highstone. Barn—3K 13
Hadley Ridge. Barn—5K 13
Hadley Rd. Barn—5M 13
Hadley Rd. Barn & Enf—2D 14
Hadley Rd. Belv—5K 81
Hadley Rd. Mitc—8H 107
Hadley St. NW1—2F 58
Hadley Way. N21—8L 15
Hadley Wood Rise. Kenl
—7M 137
Hadlow Pl. SE19—4E 108
Hadlow Rd. Sidc—1E 112
Hadlow Rd. Well—8G 81
Hadrian Clo. Stai—6C 144
Hadrian Clo. Wall—9J 123
Hadrians Ride. Enf—7D 16
Hadrian St. SE10—6C 78
Hadrian Way. Stai—6B 144
(in two parts)
Hadyn Pk. Rd. W12—3E 72
Hafer Rd. SW11—3D 90
Hafton Rd. SE6—7C 94
Hagden La. Wat—7D 8
Haggard Rd. Twic—6F 86
Haggerston Rd. E8—3D 60
Haggerston Rd. Borwd—2J 11
Hague St. E2—6E 60
Ha Ha Rd. SE18—7K 79
Haig Rd. Stan—5G 23
Haig Rd. Uxb—8F 142
Haig Rd. West—9J 141
Haig Rd. E. E13—6G 63
Haig Rd. W. E13—6G 63
Haigville Gdns. Ilf—2M 47
Hailes Clo. SW19—3A 106
Haileybury Av. Enf—8D 16
Haileybury Rd. Orp—6E 128
Hailey Rd. Eri—3L 81
Hailsham Av. SW2—8K 91
Hailsham Clo. Romf—5G 35
Hailsham Clo. Surb—2H 119
Hailsham Gdns. Romf—5G 35
Hailsham Rd. SW17—3E 106
Hailsham Rd. Romf—5G 35
Hailsham Ter. N18—4B 28
Haimo Rd. SE9—4H 95
Hainault Gore. Romf—3J 49
Hainault Gro. Chig—4A 32
Hainault Rd. E11—6A 46
Hainault Rd. Chig—3M 31
Hainault Rd. Romf—9A 34
Hainault Rd. Romf—4K 49
(Chadwell Heath)
Hainault Rd. Romf—7F 32
(Little Heath)
Hainault St. SE9—7M 95
Hainault St. Ilf—7A 48
Haines Ct. Wey—7B 116
Haines St. SW8—8G 75
Haines Wlk. Mord—2M 121
Haines Way. Wat—7E 4
Hainthorpe Rd. SE27—9M 91
Hainton Clo. E1—9F 60
Halberd M. E5—7F 44
Halbutt Gdns. Dag—8K 49
Halbutt St. Dag—9K 49
Halcomb St. N1—4C 60
Halcot Av. Bexh—4M 97
Halcrow St. E1—8F 60
Halcyon Way. Horn—6K 51
Haldane Clo. N10—7F 26
Haldane Pl. SW18—7M 89
Haldane Rd. E6—6B 63
Haldane Rd. SE28—1H 81
Haldane Rd. SW6—8K 73

Havelock Rd. N17—9E 28
Havelock Rd. SW19—2A 106
Havelock Rd. Belv—5K 81
Havelock Rd. Brom—8G 111
Havelock Rd. Croy—4D 124
Havelock Rd. Dart—6F 98
Havelock Rd. Harr—1C 38
Havelock Rd. S'hall—4J 69
Havelock St. N1—4J 59
Havelock St. Ilf—7M 47
Havelock Ter. SW8—9F 74
Havelock Wlk. SE23—7G 93
Haven Clo. SW19—9H 89
Haven Clo. Hay—7C 52
Haven Clo. Swan—6D 114
Haven Grn. W5—9H 55
Havenhurst Rise. Enf—4L 15
Haven La. W5—9J 55
Haven Pl. W5—1H 71
Haven Rd. Ashf—9F 144
Haven St. NW1—3F 58
Haven Ter. W5—1H 71
Haven, The. Rich—2L 87
Havenwood. Wemb—8M 39
Haverfield Gdns. Rich—8L 71
Haverfield Rd. E3—6J 61
Haverford Way. Edgw—8K 23
Haverhill Rd. E4—1A 30
Haverhill Rd. SW12—7G 91
Havering Dri. Romf—2C 50
Havering Gdns. Romf—3H 49
Havering Rd. Romf—9B 34
Havering St. E1—9H 61
Havering Way. Bark—6F 64
Havers Av. W on T—7H 117
Haversham Clo. Twic—5H 87
Haverstock Ct. Orp—6E 112
Haverstock Hill. NW3—1C 58
Haverstock Rd. NW5—1E 58
Haverstock St. N1—5M 59
Haverthwaite Rd. Orp—5B 128
Havil St. SE5—8C 76
Hawarden Gro. SE21—6A 92
Hawarden Hill. NW2—8E 40
Hawarden Rd. E17—2H 45
Hawbridge Rd. E11—6B 46
Hawes Clo. N'wd—7D 20
Hawes La. E4—2A 18
Hawes La. W Wick—3A 126
Hawes Rd. N18—6F 28
Hawes Rd. Brom—5F 110
Hawes St. N1—3M 59
Hawfield Bank. Orp—5H 129
Hawgood St. E3—8L 61
Hawkdene. E4—8A 18
Hawke Pk. Rd. N22—1M 43
Hawke Rd. SE19—3C 108
Hawkesbury Rd. SW15—4F 88
Hawkesfield Rd. SE23—8J 93
Hawkesley Clo. Twic—1E 102
Hawkesmead Rd. Enf—9D 6
Hawkes Rd. Mitc—5D 106
Hawkesworth Clo. N'wd
—7C 20
Hawkewood Rd. Sun—7E 100
Hawkhirst Rd. Kenl—7B 138
Hawkhurst Gdns. Chess
—6J 119
Hawkhurst Gdns. Romf—5B 34
Hawkhurst Rd. SW16—5H 107
Hawkhurst Rd. Whyt—9C 138
Hawkhurst Way. N Mald
—9B 104
Hawkhurst Way. W Wick
—4M 125
Hawkinge Wlk. Orp—7F 112
Hawkinge Way. Horn—2G 67
Hawkins Clo. Harr—5B 38
Hawkins Rd. Tedd—3F 102
Hawkley Gdns. SE27—8M 91
Hawkridge Clo. Romf—4G 49
Hawksbrook La. Beck—1M 125
Hawkshaw Clo. SW2—7J 91
Hawkshead Clo. Brom—4C 110
Hawkshead Rd. NW10—3D 56
Hawkshead Rd. W4—3C 72
Hawkshill Clo. Esh—8L 117
Hawkshill Way. Esh—8K 117
Hawkslade Rd. SE15—4H 93
Hawksley Rd. N16—8C 44
Hawks M. SE10—8A 78
Hawksmoor Clo. E6—9J 63
Hawksmoor St. W6—7H 73
Hawksmouth. E4—9A 18
Hawks Rd. King—6K 103
Hawkstone Rd. SE16—5G 77
Hawkwood Cres. E4—8M 17
Hawkwood La. Chst—5A 112
Hawkwood Mt. E5—6F 44
Hawlands Dri. Pinn—5J 37
Hawley Clo. Hmptn—3K 101

Hawley Cres. NW1—3F 58
Hawley M. NW1—3F 58
Hawley Rd. NW1—3F 58
Hawley Rd. Dart—8J 99
Hawley St. NW1—3F 58
Hawstead La. Orp—7K 129
Hawstead Rd. SE6—5M 93
Hawsted. Buck H—9F 18
Hawsworth Clo. E13—5D 62
Hawthorn Av. N13—5J 27
Hawthorn Av. Cars—9E 122
Hawthorn Av. Rain—7F 66
Hawthorn Av. Rich—1J 87
Hawthorn Av. West—7H 141
Hawthorn Clo. N1—2C 60
Hawthorn Clo. Hmptn—2L 101
Hawthorn Clo. Orp—1B 128
Hawthorn Clo. Wat—2D 8
Hawthorndene Clo. Brom
—4D 126
Hawthorndene Rd. Brom
—4D 126
Hawthorn Dri. Harr—4L 37
Hawthorn Dri. Uxb—2A 142
Hawthorn Dri. W Wick—6C 126
Hawthorne Av. Harr—4E 38
Hawthorne Av. Mitc—6B 106
Hawthorne Av. Ruis—4F 36
Hawthorne Av. T Hth—5M 107
Hawthorne Av. Wal X—4B 6
Hawthorne Clo. SE15—1G 93
Hawthorne Clo. Brom—7K 111
Hawthorne Clo. S Croy—3G 139
Hawthorne Clo. Sutt—4A 122
Hawthorne Clo. Wal X—4B 6
Hawthorne Farm Av. N'holt
—4J 53
Hawthorne Gro. NW9—5A 40
Hawthorne Pl. Eps—4C 134
Hawthorne Rd. E17—1L 45
Hawthorne Rd. NW10—3E 56
Hawthorne Rd. Brom—7K 111
Hawthorn Gdns. W5—4H 71
Hawthorn Gro. SE20—5F 108
Hawthorn Gro. Enf—2B 16
Hawthorn Hatch. Bren—8F 70
Hawthorn M. NW7—8J 25
Hawthorn Pl. Hay—1D 68
Hawthorn Rd. N8—1H 43
Hawthorn Rd. N18—5D 28
Hawthorn Rd. Bexh—3K 97
Hawthorn Rd. Bren—8F 70
Hawthorn Rd. Buck H—4H 31
Hawthorn Rd. Dart—8H 99
Hawthorn Rd. Sutt—8C 122
Hawthorn Rd. Wall—9F 122
Hawthorns. Wfd G—3E 30
Hawthorns, The. Lou—6L 19
Hawthorn Wlk. W10—7J 57
Hawthorn Way. N9—2D 28
Hawthorn Way. Shep—8B 100
Hawtrey Av. N'holt—5H 53
Hawtrey Dri. Ruis—5E 36
Hawtrey Rd. NW3—5C 58
Haxted Rd. Brom—5F 110
Hayburn Way. Horn—6D 50
Hay Clo. E15—3C 62
Haycroft Gdns. NW10—4E 56
Haycroft Rd. SW2—4J 91
Haycroft Rd. Surb—4J 119
Hay Currie St. E14—9M 61
Hayday Rd. E16—8E 62
Haydens Clo. Orp—1E 128
Hayden's Pl. W11—9K 57
Hayden Way. Romf—9A 34
Haydn Av. Purl—6L 137
Haydn's M. W3—9A 54
Haydock Av. N'holt—2L 53
Haydock Clo. Horn—9K 51
Haydock Grn. N'holt—2L 53
Haydon Clo. NW9—2A 40
Haydon Dri. Pinn—2E 36
Haydon Pk. Rd. SW19—2L 105
Haydon Rd. Dag—7G 49
Haydon Rd. Wat—8J 9
Haydons Rd. SW19—2M 105
Haydon St. EC3—1D 76
Haydon Wlk. E1—9D 60
Hayes Chase. W Wick—1B 126
Hayes Clo. Brom—4E 126
Hayes Cres. NW11—3K 41
Hayes Cres. Sutt—6H 121
Hayes Dri. Rain—3F 66
Hayes End Clo. Hay—8B 52
Hayes End Dri. Hay—7B 52
Hayes End Rd. Hay—7B 52
Hayesford Pk. Dri. Brom
—9D 110
Hayes Garden. Brom—3E 126
Hayes Hill. Brom—3C 126
Hayes Hill Rd. Brom—3D 126
Hayes La. Beck—7A 110
Hayes La. Brom—9E 110

Hayes La. Kenl & Cat—8M 137
Hayes Mead. Brom—3C 126
Hayes Pl. NW1—7C 58
Hayes Rd. Brom—8E 110
Hayes Rd. S'hall—5F 68
Hayes St. Brom—3F 126
Hayes Way. Beck—8A 110
Hayes Wood Av. Brom—3F 126
Hayfield Clo. Bush, Wat—6M 9
Hayfield Pas. E1—7G 61
Hayfield Rd. Orp—9E 112
Haygarth Pl. SW19—2H 105
Haygreen Clo. King—3M 103
Hay Hill. W1—1F 74
Hayland Clo. NW9—2B 40
Hayles St. SE11—5M 75
Haylett Gdns. King—8H 103
Hayling Av. Felt—9E 84
Hayling Clo. N16—1C 60
Hayling Rd. Wat—3E 20
Hayman Cres. Hay—5B 52
Hayman St. N1—3M 59
Haymarket. SW1—1H 75
Haymeads Dri. Esh—8A 118
Haymer Gdns. Wor Pk—5E 120
Haymerle Rd. SE15—7E 76
Hayne Rd. Beck—6K 109
Haynes Clo. N17—7F 28
Haynes Clo. SE3—2C 94
Haynes La. SE19—3C 108
Haynes Rd. Horn—2H 51
Haynes Rd. Wemb—3J 55
Hayne St. EC1—8M 59
Haynt Wlk. SW20—7J 105
Hay's La. SE1—2C 76
Haysleigh Gdns. SE20—6E 108
Hay's M. W1—2F 74
Haysoms Clo. Romf—2C 50
Haystall Clo. Hay—5C 52
Hay St. E2—4E 60
Hays Wlk. Sutt—2H 135
Hayter Rd. SW2—4J 91
Hayton Clo. E8—2D 60
Hayward Clo. SW19—5M 105
Hayward Clo. Bex—4B 98
Hayward Gdns. SW15—5G 89
Hayward Rd. N20—2A 26
Hayward's Pl. EC1—7M 59
Haywood Clo. Pinn—9H 21
Haywood Ct. Wal A—7M 7
Haywood Rise. Orp—7C 128
Haywood Rd. Brom—8H 111
Hazel Av. W Dray—4L 143
Hazel Bank. Surb—3A 120
Hazelbank Rd. SE6—8B 94
Hazelbourne Rd. SW12—5F 90
Hazelbrouck Gdns. Ilf—7B 32
Hazelbury Av. Abb L, Wat
—5A 4
Hazelbury Grn. N9—3C 28
Hazelbury La. N9—3C 28
Hazel Clo. N13—3B 28
Hazel Clo. N19—7G 43
Hazel Clo. SE15—1E 92
Hazel Clo. Bren—8F 70
Hazel Clo. Horn—8F 50
Hazel Clo. Mitc—8H 107
Hazel Clo. Twic—6A 86
Hazel Croft. Pinn—6M 21
Hazeldean Ct. Kenl—7B 138
Hazeldene Dri. Pinn—1G 37
Hazeldene Gdns. Uxb—4A 52
Hazeldene Rd. NW10—3E 56
Hazeldene Rd. Ilf—7F 48
Hazeldene Rd. Well—1G 97
Hazeldon Rd. SE4—4J 93
Hazel Dri. Eri—9F 82
Hazeleigh Gdns. Wfd G—5J 31
Hazel End. Swan—9C 114
Hazel Gdns. Edgw—4M 23
Hazelgreen Clo. N21—1M 27
Hazel Gro. SE26—1H 109
Hazel Gro. Enf—8E 16
Hazel Gro. Orp—4M 127
Hazel Gro. Romf—1J 49
Hazel Gro. Wemb—4J 55
Hazelhurst. Beck—5B 110
Hazelhurst Rd. SW17—1B 106
Hazel La. Rich—8J 87
Hazell Cres. Romf—8M 33
Hazel Mead. Barn—7F 12
Hazel Mead. Eps—2E 134
Hazelmere Clo. Felt—5C 84
Hazelmere Clo. N'holt—5K 53
Hazelmere Dri. N'holt—5K 53
Hazelmere Gdns. Horn—3G 51
Hazelmere Rd. NW6—4L 57
Hazelmere Rd. SE5—9M 75
Hazelmere Rd. N'holt—5K 53
Hazelmere Rd. Orp—8A 112
Hazelmere Wlk. N'holt—5K 53
Hazelmere Way. Brom—1E 126

Hazel Rise. Horn—4G 51
Hazel Rd. NW10—6G 57
Hazel Rd. Dart—8H 99
Hazel Rd. Eri—9E 82
Hazel Rd. St Alb—1M 5
Hazeltree La. N'holt—6J 53
Hazel Tree Rd. Wat—9F 4
Hazelville Rd. N19—5H 43
Hazel Way. E4—6K 29
Hazel Way. SE1—5D 76
Hazelwood Av. Mord—8M 105
Hazelwood Clo. W5—3J 71
Hazel Wood Ct. NW10—8C 40
Hazelwood Ct. Surb—1J 119
Hazelwood Cres. N13—4L 27
Hazelwood Dri. Pinn—9F 20
Hazelwood Gro. S Croy
—5F 138
Hazelwood La. N13—4L 27
Hazelwood La. K Lan & Abb L,
Wat—5K 4
Hazelwood Rd. E17—3J 45
Hazelwood Rd. Enf—8D 16
Hazelwood Rd. Rick—8A 8
Hazlebury Rd. SW6—1M 89
Hazledean Rd. Croy—4B 124
Hazledene. Wal X—5E 6
Hazledene Rd. W4—7A 72
Hazlemere Gdns. Wor Pk
—3E 120
Hazlewell Rd. SW15—4G 89
Hazlewood. Lou—7H 19
Hazlewood Cres. W10—7J 57
Hazlitt Rd. W14—4J 73
Heacham Av. Uxb—7A 36
Headcorn Rd. N17—7D 28
Headcorn Rd. Brom—2D 110
Headcorn Rd. T Hth—8K 107
Headfort Pl. SW1—3E 74
Headington Rd. SW18—8A 90
Headlam Rd. SW4—6H 91
Headlam St. E1—7F 60
Headley App. Ilf—3M 47
Headley Av. Wall—7K 123
Headley Clo. Eps—8L 119
Headley Dri. Croy—9M 125
Headley Dri. Ilf—4M 47
Headley Rd. Eps—9M 133
Headley St. SE15—1F 92
Head's M. W11—9L 57
Headstone Dri. Harr—1B 38
Headstone Gdns. Harr—2A 38
Headstone La. Harr—2M 37
Headstone Rd. Harr—4C 38
Head St. E1—9H 61
(in two parts)
Headway Clo. Rich—1G 103
Headway, The. Eps—1D 134
Heald St. SE14—9J 77
Healey Rd. Wat—8D 8
Healey St. NW1—2F 58
Healy Dri. Orp—6D 128
Hearne Rd. W4—7L 71
Hearn Rise. N'holt—4H 53
Hearn Rd. Romf—4D 50
Hearn's Clo. Orp—8G 113
Hearn's Rise. Orp—8H 113
Hearn's Rd. Orp—8G 113
Hearnville Rd. SW12—7E 90
Heatham Pk. Twic—6D 86
Heath Av. Bexh—7H 81
Heathbourne Rd. Bush, Wat &
Stan—1C 22
Heath Brow. NW3—8A 42
Heath Clo. NW11—5M 41
Heath Clo. W5—7K 55
Heath Clo. Bans—6M 135
Heath Clo. Hay—8B 68
Heath Clo. Orp—2G 129
Heath Clo. Romf—1E 50
Heath Clo. Stai—5A 144
Heathclose Av. Dart—6F 98
Heathclose Rd. Dart—7E 98
Heathcote Av. Ilf—9K 31
Heathcote Gro. E4—3A 30
Heathcote Rd. Eps—6B 134
Heathcote Rd. Twic—5F 86
Heathcote St. WC1—7K 59
Heathcote Way. W Dray
—2H 143
Heathcroft. NW11—6M 41
Heathcroft. W5—7K 55
Heathcroft Av. Sun—4D 100
Heathdale Av. Houn—2J 85
Heathdene Dri. Belv—5M 81
Heathdene Rd. SW16—4K 107
Heathdene Rd. Wall—9F 122
Heath Dri. NW3—9M 41
Heath Dri. SW20—8G 105
Heath Dri. Romf—8E 34

Heath Dri. Sutt—1A 136
Heathedge. SE26—8F 92
Heathend Rd. Bex—7C 98
Heather Av. Romf—9B 34
Heatherbank. SE9—1K 95
Heatherbank. Chst—6L 111
Heather Clo. SW8—2F 90
Heather Clo. Hmptn—5K 101
Heather Clo. Iswth—4B 86
Heather Clo. Romf—8B 34
Heather Clo. Uxb—8D 142
Heatherdale Clo. King—3L 103
Heatherdene Clo. Mitc—8C 106
Heather Dri. Dart—6E 98
Heather Dri. Romf—9C 34
Heather End. Swan—8B 114
Heather Gdns. NW11—4J 41
Heather Gdns. Romf—9B 34
Heather Gdns. Sutt—8L 121
Heather Glen. Romf—9B 34
Heatherlands. Sun—3E 100
Heatherley Dri. Ilf—1J 47
Heather La. W Dray—9C 142
Heather Pk. Dri. Wemb—3L 55
Heather Pl. Esh—6M 117
Heather Rise. Bush, Wat—4K 9
Heather Rd. NW2—7D 40
Heather Rd. SE12—7E 94
Heatherset Gdns. SW16
—4K 107
Heatherside Rd. Eps—9B 120
Heatherside Rd. Sidc—9G 97
Heatherton Ter. N3—9M 25
Heather Wlk. W10—7J 57
Heather Wlk. Edgw—5M 23
Heather Way. Romf—8B 34
Heather Way. S Croy—1H 139
Heather Way. Stan—5D 22
Heatherwood Clo. E12—7G 47
Heath Farm Ct. Wat—1B 8
Heathfield. E4—3A 30
Heathfield. Chst—3A 112
Heathfield Av. SW18—6B 90
Heathfield Clo. E16—8H 63
Heathfield Clo. Kes—7G 127
Heathfield Ct. SE20—4G 109
Heathfield Ct. W4—6B 72
Heathfield Gdns. NW11—4H 41
Heathfield Gdns. SW18—5B 90
Heathfield Gdns. W4—6A 72
Heathfield La. Chst—3A 112
Heathfield N. Twic—6D 86
Heathfield Pk. NW2—2G 57
Heathfield Rise. Ruis—5A 36
Heathfield Rd. SW18—5B 90
Heathfield Rd. W3—3M 71
Heathfield Rd. Bexh—3K 97
Heathfield Rd. Brom—4D 110
Heathfield Rd. Bush, Wat—6J 9
Heathfield Rd. Croy—6B 124
Heathfield Rd. Kes—7G 127
Heathfield Rd. W on T—6J 117
Heathfield S. Twic—6D 86
Heathfield Sq. SW18—6B 90
Heathfield Ter. SE18—7C 80
Heathfield Ter. W4—6A 72
Heathfield Vale. S Croy
—1H 139
Heath Gdns. Twic—7D 86
Heathgate. NW11—4M 41
Heath Gro. SE20—4G 109
Heath Gro. Sun—4D 100
Heath Hurst Rd. NW3—9C 42
Heathland Rd. N16—6C 44
Heathlands Clo. Sun—6E 100
Heathlands Clo. Twic—7D 86
Heathlands Rise. Dart—5F 98
Heath La. SE3—1B 94
Heath La. (Lower). Dart—7G 99
Heath La. (Upper). Dart—8E 98
Heathlee Rd. SE3—3D 94
Heathley End. Chst—3A 112
Heathmans Rd. SW6—9K 73
Heath Mead. SW19—8H 89
Heath Pk. Ct. Romf—3E 50
Heath Pk. Rd. Romf—3E 50
Heath Rise. SW15—5H 89
Heath Rise. Brom—1D 126
Heath Rd. SW8—1F 90
Heath Rd. Bex—4A 98
Heath Rd. Dart—5D 98
Heath Rd. Harr—5A 38
Heath Rd. Houn—3M 85
Heath Rd. Lea—4A 132
Heath Rd. Romf—5H 49
Heath Rd. T Hth—7A 108
Heath Rd. Twic—7D 86
Heath Rd. Uxb—7A 52
Heath Rd. Wat—9H 9
Heath Side. NW3—9B 42
Heathside. Esh—5C 118
Heathside. Houn—6K 85
Heathside. Orp—2A 128

Higham Hill Rd. E17—8J 29
Higham Path. E17—1J 45
Higham Pl. E17—1J 45
Higham Rd. N17—1B 44
Higham Rd. Wfd G—6E 30
Highams Hill. Warl—4E 140
Higham Sta. Av. E4—6M 29
Higham St. E17—1J 45
Highbanks Clo. Well—8F 80
Highbanks Rd. Pinn—6M 21
Highbarrow Rd. Croy—3E 124
High Beech. S Croy—9C 124
High Beeches. Bans—6H 135
High Beeches. Orp—8E 128
High Beeches. Sidc—2J 113
High Beech Rd. Lou—6J 19
High Bri. SE10—6B 78
Highbridge Rd. Bark—4M 63
Highbridge St. Wal A—6H 7
(in two parts)
Highbrook Rd. SE3—2H 95
High Broom Cres. W Wick
—2M 125
Highbury Av. T Hth—6L 107
Highbury Clo. N Mald—8A 104
Highbury Clo. W Wick—4M 125
Highbury Cres. N5—1M 59
Highbury Gdns. Ilf—7C 48
Highbury Grange. N5—9A 44
Highbury Gro. N5—1M 59
Highbury Hill. N5—9M 43
Highbury M. N7—2L 59
Highbury New Pk. N5—1A 60
Highbury Pk. N5—9M 43
Highbury Pk. M. N5—9A 44
Highbury Pl. N5—2M 59
Highbury Quadrant. N5—8A 44
Highbury Rd. SW19—2J 105
Highbury Sta. Rd. N1—2L 59
Highbury Ter. N5—1M 59
Highbury Ter. M. N5—1M 59
High Canons. Borwd—1A 12
Highclere Clo. Kenl—7A 138
Highclere Rd. N Mald—7B 104
Highclere St. SE26—1J 109
Highcliffe Dri. SW15—5D 88
Highcliffe Gdns. Ilf—3J 47
Highcombe. SE7—7F 78
Highcombe Clo. SE9—7J 95
Highcroft. NW9—3C 40
Highcroft Av. Wemb—4L 55
Highcroft Gdns. NW11—4K 41
Highcroft Rd. N19—5J 43
High Cross Rd. N17—1E 44
Highcross Way. SW15—7E 88
Highdaun Dri. SW16—8K 107
Highdown. Wor Pk—4D 120
Highdown Rd. SW15—5F 88
High Dri. Lea—6B 132
High Dri. N Mald—5A 104
High Elms. Chig—4C 32
High Elms. Wfd G—5E 30
High Elms Clo. N'wd—6B 20
High Elms La. Wat—5H 5
High Elms La. Wat—4F 4
High Elms Rd. Orp—3L 141
Higher Dri. Bans—4H 135
Higher Dri. Purl—6L 137
Higher Grn. Eps—5E 134
Highfield. Bans—9C 136
Highfield. Felt—7E 84
Highfield Av. NW9—3A 40
Highfield Av. NW11—5H 41
Highfield Av. Eri—7M 81
Highfield Av. Gnfd—1C 54
Highfield Av. Orp—7D 128
Highfield Av. Pinn—3K 37
Highfield Av. Wemb—8K 39
Highfield Clo. NW9—3A 40
Highfield Clo. N'wd—8C 20
Highfield Clo. Romf—6A 34
Highfield Clo. Surb—9G 119
Highfield Ct. N14—8G 15
Highfield Cres. Horn—7K 51
Highfield Cres. N'wd—8C 20
Highfield Dri. Brom—8C 110
Highfield Dri. Eps—8D 120
Highfield Dri. W Wick—4M 125
Highfield Gdns. NW11—4J 41
Highfield Hill. SE19—4B 108
Highfield Link. Romf—6A 34
Highfield Rd. N21—2M 27
Highfield Rd. NW11—4J 41
Highfield Rd. W3—8M 55
Highfield Rd. Bexh—4K 97
Highfield Rd. Brom—8K 111
Highfield Rd. Chst—7D 112
Highfield Rd. Dart—6H 99
Highfield Rd. Felt—8E 84
Highfield Rd. Horn—7K 51
Highfield Rd. Iswth—9D 70
Highfield Rd. N'wd—8C 20

Highfield Rd. Purl—2K 137
Highfield Rd. Romf—7A 34
Highfield Rd. Sun—9D 100
Highfield Rd. Surb—2A 120
Highfield Rd. Sutt—7C 122
Highfield Rd. W on T—3E 116
Highfield Rd. West—9G 141
Highfield Rd. Wfd G—7J 31
Highfield Rd. N. Dart—5H 99
Highfield Way. Horn—7K 51
High Firs. Swan—8C 114
High Foleys. Esh—9F 118
High Gables. Lou—7H 19
High Garth. Esh—8A 118
Highgate Av. N6—5F 42
Highgate Clo. N6—5E 42
Highgate High St. N6—6E 42
Highgate Hill. N19—6F 42
Highgate Ho. SE26—9E 92
Highgate Rd. NW5—8E 42
Highgate W. Hill. N6—7E 42
High Gro. SE18—8B 80
Highgrove Clo. Chst—5J 111
Highgrove Ct. Beck—4L 109
Highgrove Rd. Dag—1G 65
Highgrove Way. Ruis—5E 36
High Hill Est. E5—6F 44
High Hill Ferry. E5—6F 44
High Hill Rd. Warl—7A 140
High Holborn. WC1—9J 59
Highland Av. W7—9C 54
Highland Av. Dag—8A 50
Highland Av. Lou—8J 19
Highland Cotts. Wall—6F 122
Highland Ct. E18—8F 30
Highland Croft. Beck—3M 109
Highland Dri. Bush, Wat—9A 10
Highland Pk. Felt—1D 100
Highland Rd. SE19—3C 108
Highland Rd. Bexh—4L 97
Highland Rd. Brom—5D 110
Highland Rd. N'wd—9D 20
Highland Rd. Purl—6L 137
Highlands. Wat—1G 21
Highlands Av. W3—1A 72
Highlands Clo. Houn—9M 69
Highlands Gdns. Ilf—6K 47
Highlands Heath. SW15—6G 89
Highlands Hill. Swan—5E 114
Highlands Rd. Barn—7L 13
Highlands Rd. Orp—2F 128
Highlands, The. Edgw—9M 23
High La. W7—1A 54
Highlea Clo. NW9—7C 24
High Level Dri. SE26—1E 108
Highlever Rd. W10—8G 57
Highmead. SE18—8D 80
High Mead. Chig—2A 32
High Mead. Harr—3C 38
High Mead. W Wick—4B 126
Highmead Cres. Wemb—3K 55
High Meadow Clo. Pinn—2G 37
High Meadow Cres. NW9
—3B 40
High Meadows. Chig—5B 32
Highmore Rd. SE3—8C 78
High Mt. NW4—4E 40
High Oaks. Enf—2K 15
High Pk. Av. Rich—9L 71
High Pk. Rd. Rich—9L 71
High Path. SW19—5M 105
High Pine Clo. Wey—7A 116
High Point. SE9—9M 95
Highridge Clo. Eps—6C 134
High Rd. Buck H & Lou
—2F 30
High Rd. Bushey Heath, Bush,
Wat—1B 22
High Rd. Chig—5L 31
High Rd. Cowley, Uxb—8A 142
High Rd. Dart—9G 99
High Rd. E. Finchley, N2—8B 26
High Rd. Harr—7C 22
High Rd. Ilf & Romf—7A 48
High Rd. Leavesden Green, Wat
—8D 4
High Rd. Leyton—4M 45
E15 1-185 & 2-164
E10 remainder
High Rd. Leytonstone, E11
—9C 46
High Rd. New Southgate, N11
—5F 26
High Rd. N. Finchley, N12
—4A 26
High Rd. South Woodford, E18
—8E 30
High Rd. Tottenham—2D 44
N15 1-363 & 2-344
N17 remainder
High Rd. Uxb—8A 36
High Rd. Wemb—1H 55

High Rd. Whetstone, N20
—9A 14
High Rd. Willesden, NW10
—2D 56
High Rd. Wood End Green, Hay
—8C 52
High Rd. Wfd G—6D 30
High Rd. Wood Green, N22
—8K 27
Highshore Rd. SE15—1D 92
High Silver. Lou—6H 19
Highstead Cres. Eri—9C 82
Highstone Av. E11—4E 46
High St. Abb L, Wat—4C 4
High St. Acton, W3—2M 71
High St. Bans—7L 135
High St. Barkingside, Ilf—1A 48
High St. Barn—5J 13
High St. Beck—6L 109
High St. Bedmond, Abb L,
Wat—1D 4
High St. Bren—8G 71
High St. Brom—6E 110
High St. Bush, Wat—8L 9
High St. Cars—6E 122
High St. Cheam, Sutt—8J 121
High St. Cheshunt, Wal X—1D 6
High St. Chst—3M 111
High St. Claygate, Esh—8D 118
High St. Colliers Wood. SW19
—4B 106
High St. Cowley, Uxb—7A 142
High St. Cranford, Houn—9E 68
High St. Croy—5A 124
High St. Dart—5J 99
High St. Downe, Orp—3L 141
High St. Ealing, W5—1H 71
High St. East Ham, E6—5K 63
High St. E Mol—8L 101
High St. Edgw—6L 23
High St. Elstree, Borwd—8H 11
High St. Eps—5B 134
High St. Esh—6M 117
High St. Ewell, Eps—1D 134
High St. Eyns, Dart—4J 131
High St. Farnborough, Orp
—7M 127
High St. F'ham, Dart—1K 131
High St. Felt—9D 84
High St. Green Street Green,
Orp—9D 128
High St. Hmptn—5A 102
High St. Hampton Hill, Hmptn
—3A 102
High St. Hampton Wick, King
—5G 103
High St. Harlesden, NW10
—5D 56
High St. Harrow on the Hill,
Harr—6C 38
High St. Hay—7B 68
High St. Horn—6H 51
High St. Hornsey, N8—2J 43
High St. Houn—2M 85
High St. King—7H 103
High St. Mill Hill, NW7—5F 24
High St. N Mald—8C 104
High St. N'wd—8D 20
High St. Orp—1G 129
High St. Oxshott, Lea—5B 132
High St. Penge, SE20—3G 109
High St. Pinn—1J 37
High St. Plaistow, E13—5E 62
High St. Ponders End, Enf
—7G 17
High St. Purf—6L 83
High St. Purl—3L 137
High St. Romf—3C 50
High St. Ruis—5C 36
High St. Saint Mary Cray, Orp
—1G 129
High St. Shep—1A 116
High St. S'hall—2K 69
High St. Southgate, N14—1H 27
High St. South Norwood, SE25
—8D 108
High St. Stanwell, Stai—5B 144
High St. Stratford, E15—5A 62
High St. Sutt—6M 121
(in four parts)
High St. Swan—8D 114
High St. Tedd—2D 102
High St. Th Dit—1E 118
High St. T Hth—8A 108
High St. Uxb—3A 142
(in three parts)
High St. Wal X—6E 6
(in two parts)
High St. Walthamstow, E17
—3J 45
High St. W on T—3E 116
High St. Wanstead, E11—3E 46
High St. Wat—6F 8

High St. Wealdstone, Harr
—9C 22
High St. Wembley Park, Wemb
—9K 39
High St. W Dray—7H 143
High St. W Wick—3M 125
High St. Whitton, Twic—6A 86
High St. Wimbledon. SW19
—2H 105
High St. Woolwich, SE18—4L 79
High St. Yiewsley, W Dray
—1H 143
High St. M. SW19—2J 105
High St. N.—1J 63
E6 1-239 & 2-226
E12 remainder
High St. S. E6—5K 63
High Timber St. EC4—1A 76
High Tor Clo. Brom—4F 110
High Trees. SW2—7L 91
High Trees. Barn—7C 14
High Trees. Croy—3J 125
Highview. NW7—3B 24
Highview. Pinn—1G 37
High View. Sutt—3K 135
High View. Wat—8D 8
Highview Av. Edgw—4A 24
Highview Av. Wall—7K 123
High View Clo. SE19—6D 108
High View Clo. Lou—7G 19
Highview Gdns. N3—1J 41
Highview Gdns. N11—5G 27
Highview Gdns. Edgw—4A 24
Highview Gdns. Upm—7M 51
High View Rd. E18—9D 30
Highview Rd. SE19—3B 108
Highview Rd. W13—9E 54
High View Rd. Orp—2L 141
High View Rd. Sidc—1F 112
Highway, The—1H 77
E1 1-485 & 2-388
E14 remainder
Highway, The. Orp—6G 129
Highway, The. Stan—7E 22
Highway, The. Sutt—1A 136
Highwold. Coul—9E 136
Highwood. Brom—7B 110
Highwood Av. N12—4A 26
Highwood Av. Bush, Wat—3K 9
Highwood Clo. Kenl—9A 138
Highwood Clo. Orp—4A 128
Highwood Dri. Orp—4A 128
Highwood Gdns. Ilf—3K 47
Highwood Gro. NW7—5B 24
Highwood Hill. NW7—2D 24
Highwood La. Lou—7L 19
Highwood Rd. N19—8J 43
High Worple. Harr—5J 37
Highworth Rd. N11—6H 27
Hilary Av. Mitc—7E 106
Hilary Clo. E11—3E 46
Hilary Clo. SW6—8M 73
Hilary Clo. Bexh—9A 82
Hilary Clo. Horn—1H 67
Hilary Rd. W12—1D 72
Hilbert Rd. Sutt—5H 121
Hilborough Clo. SW19—4A 106
Hilborough Way. Orp—7B 128
Hilda Ct. Surb—2H 119
Hilda May Av. Swan—6C 114
Hilda Rd. E6—3H 63
Hilda Rd. E16—7C 62
(in two parts)
Hilda Ter. SW9—1L 91
Hilda Vale Clo. Orp—6M 127
Hilda Vale Rd. Orp—6M 127
Hildenborough Gdns. Brom
—3C 110
Hilden Dri. Eri—8F 82
Hildenlea Pl. Brom—6C 110
Hilders, The. Asht—9M 133
Hilditch Ho. Rich—5K 87
Hildreth St. SW12—7F 90
Hildyard Rd. SW6—7L 73
Hiley Rd. NW10—6G 57
Hilfield La. Wat—3M 9
Hilfield La. S. Bush, Wat—8D 10
Hilgrove Rd. NW6—3A 58
Hiliary Gdns. Stan—9G 23
Hillars Heath Rd. Coul—7J 137
Hillary Cres. W on T—3G 117
Hillary Rise. Barn—6L 13
Hillary Rd. S'hall—4L 69
Hill Barn. S Croy—3C 138
Hillbeck Clo. SE15—8G 77
Hillbeck Way. Gnfd—4B 54
Hillborne Clo. Hay—6E 68
Hillbrook Rd. SW17—9D 90
Hill Brow. Brom—5H 111
Hill Brow. Dart—5D 98
Hillbrow. N Mald—7D 104
Hill Brow Clo. Bex—1B 114
Hillbrow Rd. Brom—3C 110

Hillbrow Rd. Esh—6A 118
Hillbury Av. Harr—3F 38
Hillbury Clo. Warl—9G 139
Hillbury Rd. SW17—9F 90
Hillbury Rd. Warl—9E 138
Hill Clo. NW2—8F 40
Hill Clo. NW11—4L 41
Hill Clo. Barn—7G 13
Hill Clo. Chst—2M 111
Hill Clo. Harr—8C 38
Hill Clo. Purl—5A 138
Hill Clo. Stan—4F 22
Hillcote Av. SW16—4L 107
Hill Ct. Romf—2D 50
Hillcourt Av. N12—6M 25
Hillcourt Est. N16—6B 44
Hillcourt Rd. SE22—5F 92
Hill Cres. N20—2M 25
Hill Cres. Bex—7A 98
Hill Cres. Harr—3E 38
Hill Cres. Horn—4G 51
Hill Cres. Surb—9K 103
Hill Cres. Wor Pk—4G 121
Hillcrest. N6—5E 42
Hillcrest. N21—9L 15
Hillcrest. Sidc—6E 96
Hillcrest. Wey—6A 116
Hillcrest Av. NW11—3K 41
Hillcrest Av. Edgw—4M 23
Hillcrest Av. Pinn—2H 37
Hillcrest Clo. SE26—1E 108
Hillcrest Clo. Beck—1K 125
Hillcrest Clo. Eps—7D 134
Hillcrest Gdns. N3—2J 41
Hill Crest Gdns. NW2—8E 40
Hillcrest Gdns. Esh—5D 118
Hillcrest Pde. Coul—6F 136
Hillcrest Rd. E17—9B 30
Hillcrest Rd. E18—9E 30
Hillcrest Rd. W3—2M 71
Hillcrest Rd. W5—8J 55
Hillcrest Rd. Brom—2E 110
Hillcrest Rd. Dart—6D 98
Hillcrest Rd. Horn—5E 50
Hillcrest Rd. Lou—8H 19
Hillcrest Rd. Orp—4E 128
Hillcrest Rd. Purl—2K 137
Hill Crest Rd. West—8H 141
Hillcrest Rd. Whyt—9D 138
Hillcrest Way. Beck—1K 125
Hillcroft. Lou—4L 19
Hillcroft Av. Pinn—4K 37
Hillcroft Av. Purl—5G 137
Hillcroft Cres. W5—9J 55
Hillcroft Cres. Ruis—8H 37
Hillcroft Cres. Wat—1F 20
Hillcroft Cres. Wemb—9K 39
Hillcroft Rd. E6—8M 63
Hillcroome Rd. Sutt—8B 122
Hillcross Av. Mord—1H 121
Hilldale Rd. Sutt—6K 121
Hilldene Av. Romf—6G 35
Hilldene Clo. Romf—5H 35
Hilldown Rd. SW16—4J 107
Hilldown Rd. Brom—3D 126
Hilldrop Cres. N7—1H 59
Hilldrop La. N7—1H 59
Hilldrop Rd. N7—1H 59
Hilldrop Rd. Brom—3E 110
Hillend. SE18—9L 79
Hill End. Orp—4D 128
Hillersdon Av. SW13—1E 88
Hillersdon Av. Edgw—5K 23
Hillery Clo. SE17—5B 76
Hill Farm Av. Wat—6E 4
Hill Farm Clo. Wat—6E 4
Hill Farm Rd. W10—8G 57
Hill Farm Rd. Uxb—9B 36
Hillfield Av. N8—3J 43
Hillfield Av. NW9—3C 40
Hillfield Av. Mord—1C 122
Hillfield Av. Wemb—3J 55
Hillfield Clo. Harr—2A 38
Hillfield Ct. NW3—1C 58
Hillfield Ct. Esh—7M 117
Hillfield Pk. N10—2F 42
Hillfield Pk. N21—2L 27
Hillfield Pk. M. N10—2F 42
Hillfield Rd. NW6—1K 57
Hillfield Rd. Hmptn—4K 101
Hillfoot Av. Romf—8A 34
Hillfoot Rd. Romf—8A 34
Hillgate Pl. W8—2L 73
Hillgate St. W8—2L 73
Hill Gro. Romf—1C 50
Hillhouse. Wal A—6M 7
Hill Ho. Av. Stan—7D 22
Hill Ho. Clo. N21—9L 15
Hill Ho. Rd. SW16—2K 107
Hilliard Rd. N'wd—8D 20
Hilliards Ct. E1—2G 77
Hilliards Rd. Uxb—9B 142

Hillier Clo. Barn—8M 13
Hillier Gdns. Croy—7L 123
Hillier Rd. SW11—5D 90
Hilliers Av. Uxb—6E 142
Hilliers La. Croy—5J 123
Hillingdale. West—9F 140
Hillingdon Av. Stai—7C 144
Hillingdon Hill. Uxb—6C 142
Hillingdon Rd. Bexh—2A 98
Hillingdon Rd. Uxb—4B 142
Hillingdon Rd. Wat—7E 4
Hillingdon St.—7M 75
  SE17 1-237 & 2-244
  SE5 remainder
Hillington Gdns. Wfd G—9H 31
Hill La. Ruis—6A 36
Hillman Clo. Horn—1H 51
Hillman Clo. Uxb—1C 142
Hillman St. E8—2F 60
Hillmarton Rd. N7—1J 59
Hillmead Dri. SW9—3M 91
Hillmont Rd. Esh—5C 118
Hillmore Gro. SE26—2J 109
Hill Oak Wlk. NW6—2K 57
Hillreach. SE18—6K 79
Hill Rise. N9—8F 16
Hill Rise. NW11—2M 41
Hill Rise. SE23—7F 92
Hill Rise. Esh—4F 118
Hill Rise. Gnfd—4A 54
Hill Rise. Rich—4H 87
Hill Rise. Ruis—6A 36
Hill Rise. Upm—7L 51
Hill Rise. W on T—2D 116
Hillrise Av. Wat—2H 9
Hillrise Rd. N19—5J 43
Hillrise Rd. Romf—6A 34
Hill Rd. N10—8D 26
Hill Rd. NW8—5A 58
Hill Rd. Cars—8C 122
Hill Rd. Dart—8J 99
Hill Rd. Harr—3E 38
Hill Rd. Mitc—5F 106
Hill Rd. N'wd—6B 20
Hill Rd. Pinn—3J 37
Hill Rd. Purl—4K 137
Hill Rd. Sutt—7M 121
Hill Rd. Wemb—8F 38
Hillsborough Grn. Wat—3E 20
Hillsborough Rd. SE22—4C 92
Hillside. NW9—2B 40
Hillside. NW10—3A 56
Hillside. SW19—3H 105
Hillside. Bans—7J 135
Hillside. Barn—7A 14
Hillside. F'ham, Dart—2K 131
Hillside. Romf—4H 35
Hillside Av. N11—6D 26
Hillside Av. Borwd—6M 11
Hillside Av. Purl—5M 137
Hillside Av. Wal X—4D 6
Hillside Av. Wemb—9K 39
Hillside Av. Wfd G—6G 31
Hillside Clo. NW8—5M 57
Hillside Clo. Abb L, Wat—5C 4
Hillside Clo. Bans—8J 135
Hillside Clo. Mord—8J 105
Hillside Clo. Wfd G—5G 31
Hillside Cres. Enf—2B 16
Hillside Cres. Harr—6A 38
Hillside Cres. N'wd—8E 20
Hillside Cres. Wal X—4D 6
Hillside Cres. Wat—8J 9
Hillside Dri. Edgw—6L 23
Hillside Est. N15—4D 44
Hillside Gdns. E17—1B 46
Hillside Gdns. N6—4F 42
Hillside Gdns. N11—6G 27
Hillside Gdns. Barn—6J 13
Hillside Gdns. Edgw—4K 23
Hillside Gdns. Harr—5J 39
Hillside Gdns. N'wd—7E 20
Hillside Gdns. Wall—9G 123
Hillside Gro. N14—9H 15
Hillside Gro. NW7—7E 24
Hillside La. Brom—4D 126
Hillside Pas. SW2—8K 91
Hillside Rise. N'wd—7E 20
Hillside Rd. N15—5C 44
Hillside Rd. SW2—8L 91
Hillside Rd. W5—8J 55
Hillside Rd. Asht—9K 133
Hillside Rd. Brom—7D 110
Hillside Rd. Bush, Wat—7J 9
Hillside Rd. Coul—9K 137
Hillside Rd. Croy—7M 123
Hillside Rd. Dart—5E 98
Hillside Rd. Eps—2G 135
Hillside Rd. N'wd & Pinn—7E 20
Hillside Rd. S'hall—7L 53
Hillside Rd. Surb—8L 103
Hillside Rd. Sutt—9K 121

Hillside, The. Orp—9F 128
Hills La. N'wd—8C 20
Hillsleigh Rd. W8—2K 73
Hillsmead Way. S Croy
  —5F 138
Hills Pl. W1—9G 59
Hills Rd. Buck H—1F 30
Hillstowe St. E5—8G 45
Hill St. W1—2E 74
Hill St. Rich—4H 87
Hill Top. NW11—2M 41
Hill Top. Lou—4L 19
Hill Top. Mord—1L 121
Hill Top. Sutt—2K 121
Hill Top. Wfd G—6K 31
Hill Top Clo. Lou—5L 19
Hilltop Gdns. NW4—9F 24
Hilltop Gdns. Dart—4K 99
Hilltop Gdns. Orp—4C 128
Hilltop Rd. NW6—3L 57
Hilltop Rd. K Lan—1B 4
Hilltop Rd. Whyt—9C 138
Hilltop Way. Stan—3E 22
Hillview. SW20—4F 104
Hillview Av. Harr—3J 39
Hillview Av. Horn—4G 51
Hillview Clo. Pinn—6K 21
Hillview Clo. Purl—3M 137
Hill View Cres. Ilf—4K 47
Hill View Cres. Orp—3D 128
Hill View Dri. Well—1C 96
Hillview Gdns. NW4—2H 41
Hillview Gdns. NW9—3B 40
Hillview Gdns. Harr—1L 37
Hill View Rd. NW7—4H 25
Hillview Rd. Chst—2L 111
Hill View Rd. Esh—9E 118
Hill View Rd. Orp—4D 128
Hillview Rd. Pinn—7K 21
Hill View Rd. Sutt—5A 122
Hill View Rd. Twic—5E 86
Hillway. N6—7E 42
Hillway. NW9—6C 40
Hillworth Rd. SW2—6L 91
Hillyard Rd. W7—8C 54
Hillyard St. SW9—9L 75
Hillyfield. E17—9J 29
Hillyfields. Lou—4L 19
Hilly Fields Cres. SE4—2L 93
Hilsea St. E5—9G 45
Hilton Av. N12—5B 26
Hilton Clo. Uxb—5A 142
Hilton Way. S Croy—7F 138
Hilversum Cres. SE22—4E 92
Himley Rd. SW17—2C 106
Hinchcliffe Clo. Wall—9K 123
Hinchley Clo. Esh—6D 118
Hinchley Dri. Esh—5D 118
Hinchley Way. Esh—5E 118
Hinckley Rd. SE15—3E 92
Hind Clo. Chig—5D 32
Hind Ct. EC4—9L 59
Hind Cres. Eri—7B 82
Hindes Rd. Harr—3B 38
Hinde St. W1—9E 58
Hind Gro. E14—9L 61
Hindhead Clo. N16—6C 44
Hindhead Clo. Uxb—8F 142
Hindhead Gdns. N'holt—4J 53
Hindhead Grn. Wat—5G 21
Hindhead Way. Wall—7J 123
Hindmans Rd. SE22—4E 92
Hindmans Way. Dag—7K 65
Hindmarsh Clo. E1—1E 76
Hindrey Rd. E5—1H 61
Hindsley's Pl. SE23—8H 93
Hinkler Clo. Wall—9J 123
Hinkler Rd. Harr—1H 39
Hinksey Path. SE2—3H 81
Hinstock Rd. SE18—8A 80
Hinton Av. Houn—3H 85
Hinton Clo. SE9—7J 95
Hinton Rd. N18—4C 28
Hinton Rd. SE24—2M 91
Hinton Rd. Uxb—4A 142
Hinton Rd. Wall—8G 123
Hippodrome Pl. W11—1J 73
Hitcham Rd. E17—5K 45
Hitchin Clo. Romf—4G 35
Hitchin Sq. E3—5J 61
Hitherbroom Rd. Hay—2E 68
Hitherfield Rd. SW16—9L 91
Hitherfield Rd. Dag—7J 49
Hither Grn. La. SE13—4A 94
Hitherwell Dri. Harr—8B 22
Hitherwood Clo. Horn—9H 51
Hitherwood Dri. SE19—1D 108
Hive Clo. Bush, Wat—2B 22
Hive Rd. Bush, Wat—2B 22
Hoadly Rd. SW16—9H 91
Hobart Clo. N20—2C 26
Hobart Gdns. T Hth—7B 108
Hobart Pl. SW1—4F 74

Hobart Pl. Rich—6K 87
Hobart Rd. Dag—9H 49
Hobart Rd. Hay—7H 53
Hobart Rd. Ilf—9A 32
Hobart Rd. Wor Pk—5F 120
Hobbayne Rd. W7—9B 54
Hobbes Wlk. SW15—4F 88
Hobbs Clo. Wal X—2D 6
Hobbs Grn. N2—1A 42
Hobbs Pl. N1—5C 60
Hobbs Rd. SE27—1A 108
Hobday St. E14—9M 61
Hobill Wlk. Surb—1K 119
Hoblands End. Chst—3C 112
Hobury St. SW10—7B 74
Hocker St. E2—6D 60
Hockett Clo. SE8—5J 77
Hockley Av. E6—5J 63
Hockley Dri. Romf—9G 35
Hocroft Av. NW2—8K 41
Hocroft Rd. NW2—8K 41
Hocroft Wlk. NW2—9J 41
Hodder Dri. Gnfd—5D 54
Hoddesdon Rd. Belv—6L 81
Hodford Rd. NW11—6K 41
Hodgkin Clo. SE28—1H 81
Hodister Clo. SE5—8A 76
Hodnet Gro. SE16—5H 77
Hodsoll Ct. Orp—9H 113
Hodson Clo. Harr—8K 37
Hodson Cres. Orp—9H 113
Hoe La. Enf—2E 16
Hoe La. Romf—1H 33
Hoe St. E17—2L 45
Hoe, The. Wat—2H 21
Hofland Rd. W14—4J 73
Hogan M. W2—8E 58
Hogan Way. E5—7E 44
Hogarth Av. Ashf—3A 100
Hogarth Clo. E16—8H 63
Hogarth Clo. W5—8J 55
Hogarth Ct. EC3—9C 60
Hogarth Ct. SE19—1D 108
Hogarth Ct. Bush, Wat—9M 9
Hogarth Cres. SW19—5B 106
Hogarth Cres. Croy—2A 124
Hogarth Gdns. Houn—8L 69
Hogarth Hill. NW11—2K 41
Hogarth La. W4—7C 72
Hogarth Rd. SW5—5M 73
Hogarth Rd. Edgw—9L 23
Hogarth Way. Hmptn—5A 102
Hoggin Rd. N9—2C 28
Hog Hill Rd. Romf—7K 33
Hog La. Borwd—6E 10
Hogsden Clo. N1—5A 60
Hogsmill Way. Eps—6A 120
Holbeach Gdns. Sidc—5D 96
Holbeach Rd. SE6—6L 93
Holbeck Row. SE15—8E 76
Holbein M. SW1—6E 74
Holbein Pl. SW1—5E 74
Holberton Gdns. NW10—6F 56
Holborn. EC1—8L 59
Holborn Cir. EC1—8L 59
Holborn Rd. E13—8F 62
Holborn Viaduct. EC1—8M 59
Holbrook Clo. N19—6F 43
Holbrook Clo. Enf—2E 16
Holbrooke Ct. N7—8J 43
Holbrooke Pl. Rich—4H 87
Holbrook La. Chst—4B 112
Holbrook Rd. E15—5D 62
Holbrook Way. Brom—1K 127
Holburne Clo. SE3—9G 79
Holburne Gdns. SE3—9H 79
Holburne Rd. SE3—9G 79
Holcombe Hill. NW7—3E 24
Holcombe Rd. N17—1E 44
Holcombe Rd. Ilf—5L 47
Holcombe St. W6—5F 72
Holcroft Rd. E9—3G 61
Holdbrook N. Wal X—7F 6
Holdbrook S. Wal X—7F 6
Holdbrook Way. Romf—9K 35
Holden Av. N12—5M 25
Holden Av. NW9—6A 40
Holdenby Rd. SE4—4J 93
Holden La. NW12—5M 25
Holden St. SW11—1E 90
Holdernesse Rd. SW17—8E 90
Holderness Way. SE27
  —2M 107
Holder's Hill Av. NW4—9H 25
Holder's Hill Cir. NW7—7J 25
Holder's Hill Cres. NW4—9H 25
Holder's Hill Dri. NW4—1H 41
Holders Hill Gdns. NW4—8J 25
Holders Hill Rd. NW4 & NW7
  —9H 25
Holdgate St. SE7—4H 79

Holecroft. Wal A—7L 7
Holford Pl. WC1—6K 59
Holford Rd. NW3—8A 42
Holford St. WC1—6L 59
Holgate Av. SW11—2B 90
Holgate Gdns. Dag—2L 65
Holgate Rd. Dag—1L 65
Holland Av. SW20—5D 104
Holland Av. Sutt—1L 135
Holland Clo. N20—9B 14
Holland Clo. Brom—4D 126
Holland Clo. Stan—5F 22
Holland Ct. NW7—6E 24
Holland Ct. Surb—2H 119
Holland Gdns. W14—4J 73
Holland Gdns. Wat—8G 5
Holland Gro. SW9—8L 75
Holland Pk. W11—2J 73
Holland Pk. Av. W11—2J 73
Holland Pk. Av. Ilf—4C 48
Holland Pk. Gdns. W14—3J 73
Holland Pk. M. W11—2K 73
Holland Pk. Rd. W14—4K 73
Holland Rd. E6—4K 63
Holland Rd. E15—6C 62
Holland Rd. NW10—4E 56
Holland Rd. SE25—9E 108
Holland Rd. W14—3J 73
Holland Rd. Wemb—2H 55
Hollands, The. Felt—1H 101
Hollands, The. Wor Pk—3D 120
Holland St. SE1—2M 75
Holland St. W8—3L 73
Holland Vs. Rd. W14—3J 73
Holland Wlk. N19—6H 43
Holland Wlk. W8—2K 73
Holland Wlk. Stan—5E 22
Holland Way. Brom—4D 126
Hollar Rd. N16—8D 44
Hollen St. W1—9H 59
Holles Clo. Hmptn—3L 101
Holles St. W1—9F 58
Holley Rd. W3—3C 72
Hollick Wood Av. N12—6D 26
Hollidge Way. Dag—3M 65
Hollies Av. Sidc—8D 96
Hollies Clo. Twic—8D 86
Hollies End. NW7—5F 24
Hollies Rd. W5—5G 71
Hollies, The. N20—1B 26
Hollies Way. SW12—6E 90
Holligrave Rd. Brom—5E 110
Hollingbourne Av. Bexh—9K 81
Hollingbourne Gdns. W13
  —8F 54
Hollingbourne Rd. SE24—4A 92
Hollingsworth Ct. Surb
  —2H 119
Hollingsworth Rd. Croy
  —8F 124
Hollington Cres. N Mald
  —1D 120
Hollington Rd. E6—6K 63
Hollington Rd. N17—9E 28
Hollingworth Rd. Orp—2M 127
Hollman Gdns. SW16—3M 107
Holloway La. W Dray—7J 143
Holloway Rd. E6—6K 63
Holloway Rd. E11—8C 46
Holloway Rd. N7—7H 43
  N7 31-479 & 2-596
  N19 remainder
Holloway St. Houn—2M 85
Hollowfield Wlk. N'holt—3J 53
Hollows, The. Bren—7K 71
Hollow, The. Wfd G—4D 30
Holly Av. Stan—9J 23
Holly Av. W on T—3H 117
Hollybank Clo. Hmptn—2L 101
Hollybrake Clo. Chst—4B 112
Hollybush Clo. E11—3E 46
Hollybush Clo. Harr—8C 22
Hollybush Gdns. E2—6F 60
Hollybush Hill. E11—4D 46
Holly Bush Hill. NW3—9A 42
Holly Bush La. Hmptn—4K 101
Holly Bush La. Orp—8L 129
Hollybush Pl. E2—6F 60
Hollybush Rd. King—2J 103
Hollybush St. E13—6F 62
Holly Bush Vale. NW3—9A 42
Holly Clo. NW10—3C 56
Holly Clo. Buck H—3H 31
Holly Clo. Felt—2J 101
Holly Cres. Beck—9K 109
Holly Cres. Wfd G—7B 30
Hollycroft Av. NW3—8L 41
Hollycroft Av. Wemb—8K 39
Hollycroft Clo. W Dray—7L 143
Hollycroft Gdns. W Dray
  —7L 143

Hollydale Dri. Brom—5K 127
Hollydale Rd. SE15—1G 93
Holly Dene. SE15—9F 76
Hollydown Way. E11—8B 46
Holly Dri. E4—9M 17
Hollyfarm Rd. S'hall—6J 69
Hollyfield Av. N11—5D 26
Hollyfield Rd. Surb—2K 119
Holly Gro. NW9—5A 40
Holly Gro. SE15—1D 92
Hollygrove. Bush, Wat—9B 10
Holly Hedge Ter. SE13—4B 94
Holly Hill. N21—8K 15
Holly Hill. NW3—9A 42
Holly Hill Dri. Bans—9L 135
Holly Hill Rd. Belv & Eri—6M 81
Holly La. Bans—8L 135
Holly La. E. Bans—8M 135
Holly La. W. Bans—9M 135
Holly Lodge Gdns. N6—7E 42
Hollymead. Cars—5D 122
Hollymoor La. Eps—2B 134
Holly Mt. NW3—9A 42
Hollymount Clo. SE10—9A 78
Holly Pk. N3—1K 41
Holly Pk. N4—5K 43
  (in two parts)
Holly Pk. Est. N4—5K 43
Holly Pk. Gdns. N3—1L 41
Holly Pk. Rd. N11—5E 26
Holly Pk. Rd. W7—2D 70
Holly Rd. E11—5D 46
Holly Rd. W4—5B 72
Holly Rd. Dart—7H 99
Holly Rd. Enf—9D 6
Holly Rd. Hmptn—3A 102
Holly Rd. Houn—3M 85
Holly Rd. Orp—9E 128
Holly Rd. Twic—7D 86
Holly St. E8—3D 60
Holly St. Est. E8—3D 60
Holly Ter. N6—6E 42
Holly Ter. N20—2A 26
Holly Tree Av. Swan—6C 114
Holly Tree Clo. SW19—7H 89
Holly Village. N6—7E 42
Holly Wlk. NW3—9A 42
Holly Wlk. Enf—5B 16
Holly Way. Mitc—8H 107
Hollywood Ct. Borwd—6L 11
Hollywood Gdns. Hay—9F 52
Hollywood M. SW10—7A 74
Hollywood Rd. E4—5J 29
Hollywood Rd. SW10—7A 74
Hollywoods. Croy—1K 139
Hollywood Way. Wfd G—7B 30
Holman Rd. SW11—1B 90
Holman Rd. Eps—7A 120
Holmbank Dri. Shep—8C 100
Holmbridge Gdns. Enf—6H 17
Holmbrook Dri. NW4—3H 41
Holmbury Clo. Bush, Wat
  —2C 22
Holmbury Ct. SW17—9D 90
Holmbury Ct. S Croy—7C 124
Holmbury Gdns. Hay—2D 68
Holmbury Gro. Croy—9K 125
Holmbury Pk. Brom—4J 111
Holmbury View. E5—6F 44
Holmbush Rd. SW15—5J 89
Holmcote Gdns. N5—1A 60
Holmcroft Way. Brom—9K 111
Holmdale Clo. Borwd—4K 11
Holmdale Gdns. NW4—3H 41
Holmdale Rd. NW6—1L 57
Holmdale Rd. Chst—2A 112
Holmdale Ter. N15—4C 44
Holmdene Av. NW7—6E 24
Holmdene Av. SE24—4A 92
Holmdene Av. Harr—1M 37
Holmdene Clo. Beck—6A 110
Holmead Rd. SW6—8M 73
Holme Chase. Wey—8A 116
Holme Clo. Wal X—4E 6
Holme Lacey Rd. SE12—5D 94
Holme Lea. Wat—7G 5
Holme Pk. Borwd—4K 11
Holme Rd. E6—4J 63
Holme Rd. Horn—6L 51
Holmes Av. E17—1K 45
Holmes Av. NW7—5J 25
Holmesdale. Wal X—8D 6
Holmesdale Av. SW14—3M 87
Holmesdale Clo. SE25—7D 108
Holmesdale Rd. N6—5F 42
Holmesdale Rd. SE25—9B 108
  SE25 45-387 & 62-326
  Croy remainder
Holmesdale Rd. Bexh—1H 97
Holmesdale Rd. Rich—9K 71
Holmesdale Rd. Tedd—4G 103
Holmesley Rd. SE23—5J 93
Holmes Pl. SW10—7A 74

Holmes Rd. NW5—1F 58
Holmes Rd. SW19—4A 106
Holmes Rd. Twic—8D 86
Holmeswood Ct. N22—9L 27
Holme Way. Stan—6D 22
Holmewood Gdns. SW2—6K 91
Holmewood Rd. SE25—7C 108
Holmewood Rd. SW2—6K 91
Holmfield. NW11—2L 41
Holmfield Av. NW4—3H 41
Holmfield Ct. NW3—2C 58
Holm Gro. Uxb—3E 142
Holmhurst Rd. Belv—6M 81
Holmleigh Av. Dart—4G 99
Holmleigh Rd. N16—6C 44
Holmoak Clo. SW15—5K 89
Holmoaks Ho. Beck—6A 110
Holmsdale Gro. Bexh—2C 98
Holmshaw Clo. SE26—1J 109
Holmshill La. Borwd—1C 12
Holmside Rise. Wat—3F 20
Holmside Rd. SW12—5E 90
Holmsley Clo. N Mald—2D 120
Holmstall Av. Edgw—1A 40
Holm Wlk. SE3—1E 94
Holmwood Av. S Croy—5D 138
Holmwood Clo. Harr—1A 38
Holmwood Clo. N'holt—2B 54
Holmwood Clo. Sutt—1H 135
Holmwood Gdns. N3—9L 25
Holmwood Gdns. Wall—8F 122
Holmwood Gro. NW7—5B 24
Holmwood Rd. Chess—7J 119
Holmwood Rd. Enf—9D 6
Holmwood Rd. Ilf—7C 48
Holmwood Rd. Sutt—1G 135
Holne Chase. N2—4A 42
Holne Chase. Mord—1K 121
Holness Rd. E15—2D 62
Holroyd Clo. Esh—1D 132
Holroyd Rd. SW15—3G 89
Holroyd Rd. Esh—1D 132
Holstein Way. Eri—4H 81
Holstock Rd. Ilf—7A 48
Holsworth Clo. Harr—3A 38
Holsworthy Ho. Romf—8H 35
Holsworthy Way. Chess
 —7G 119
Holt Clo. N10—2E 42
Holt Clo. SE28—1G 81
Holt Clo. Borwd—6K 11
Holton St. E1—7H 61
Holt Rd. E16—2J 79
Holt Rd. Wemb—8F 38
Holtsmere Clo. Wat—8G 5
Holt, The. Ilf—6A 32
Holt, The. Wall—6G 123
Holt Way. Chig—5D 32
Holtwhite's Av. Enf—4A 16
Holtwhite's Hill. Enf—3M 15
Holtwood Rd. Lea—5A 132
Holwell Pl. Pinn—2J 37
Holwood Clo. W on T—4G 117
Holwood Pk. Av. Orp—6K 127
Holwood Pl. SW4—3H 91
Holwood Rd. Brom—6E 110
Holybourne Av. SW15—6E 88
Holybush Wlk. SW9—3M 91
Holyfield Rd. Wal A—2J 7
Holyhead Clo. E3—6L 61
Holyoake Wlk. N2—1A 42
Holyoake Wlk. W5—7G 55
Holyoak Rd. SE11—5M 75
Holyport Rd. SW6—8H 73
Holyrood Av. Harr—9J 37
Holyrood Gdns. Edgw—1M 39
Holyrood Rd. Barn—8A 14
Holyrood St. SE1—2C 76
Holywell Clo. SE3—7E 78
Holywell Clo. Stai—7C 144
Holywell La. EC2—7C 60
Holywell Rd. Wat—7E 8
Holywell Row. EC2—7C 60
Holywell Way. Stai—7C 144
Home Clo. Cars—4D 122
Home Clo. N'holt—6K 53
Home Ct. Felt—7E 84
Homecroft Gdns. Lou—6M 19
Homecroft Rd. N22—8A 28
Homecroft Rd. SE26—2G 109
Home Farm Clo. Esh—9H 135
Home Farm Clo. Esh—8M 117
Home Farm Clo. Shep—8C 100
Homefarm Clo. Th Dit—2D 118
Home Farm Gdns. W on T
 —4G 117
Homefarm Rd. W7—9D 54
Home Field. Barn—7K 13
Homefield. Wal A—5M 7
Homefield. W on T—6H 117
Homefield Av. Ilf—3C 48
Homefield Clo. NW10—3A 56
Homefield Clo. Swan—7D 114

Homefield Gdns. N2—1B 42
Homefield Gdns. Mitc—6A 106
Homefield Pk. Sutt—8M 121
Homefield Rise. Orp—3E 128
Homefield Rd. SW19—3J 105
Homefield Rd. W4—6D 72
Homefield Rd. Brom—5G 111
Homefield Rd. Bush, Wat—7L 9
Homefield Rd. Edgw—6B 24
Homefield Rd. Rad—1D 10
Homefield Rd. W on T—2J 117
Homefield Rd. Wemb—9F 38
Homefield St. N1—5C 60
Home Gdns. Dag—8A 50
Home Gdns. Dart—5J 99
Home Hill. Swan—4D 114
Homeland Dri. Sutt—1M 135
Homelands Dri. SE19—4C 108
Home Lea. Orp—7D 128
Homeleigh Rd. SE15—4H 93
Home Mead. Stan—8G 23
Homemead Rd. Brom—9K 111
Homemead Rd. Croy—1G 123
Home Orchard. Dart—5J 99
Home Pk. Industrial Est. K Lan
 —4A 4
Home Pk. Rd. SW19—1K 105
Home Pk. Wlk. King—8H 103
Homer Ct. Bexh—9A 82
Homer Rd. SW11—1C 90
Homer Rd. E9—2J 61
Homer Rd. Croy—1H 125
Homer Row. W1—8C 58
Homersham Rd. King—6L 103
Homer St. W1—8C 58
Homerton Gro. E9—1H 61
Homerton High St. E9—1H 61
Homerton Rd. E9—1K 61
Homerton Row. E9—1K 61
Homerton Ter. E9—2G 61
Homesdale Clo. E11—3E 46
Homesdale Rd. Brom—8G 111
Homesdale Rd. Orp—2C 128
Homestall Rd. SE22—4G 93
Homestead Gdns. Esh—7C 118
Homestead Paddock. N14
 —7F 14
Homestead Pk. NW2—8D 40
Homestead Rd. SW6—8K 73
Homestead Rd. Dag—7K 49
Homestead Rd. Orp—9F 128
Homestead, The. Dart—5G 99
Homestead Way. Croy—3A 140
Homewaters Av. Sun—5D 100
Homeway. Romf—6M 35
Homewood Clo. Hmptn
 —3K 101
Homewood Cres. Chst—3C 112
Homildon Ho. SE26—9E 92
Honduras St. EC1—7A 60
Honeybourne Rd. NW6—1M 57
Honeybourne Way. Orp
 —3B 128
Honeybrook. Wal A—6L 7
Honeybrook Rd. SW12—6G 91
Honeycroft. Lou—6M 19
Honeycroft Hill. Uxb—3C 142
Honeyden Rd. Sidc—3J 113
Honey Hill. Uxb—3D 142
Honey La. Wal A—6L 7
Honeypot Clo. NW9—2K 39
Honeypot La. Stan & NW9
 —7H 23
Honeysett Rd. N17—9D 28
Honeysuckle Clo. Romf—6H 35
Honeysuckle Gdns. Croy
 —3H 125
Honeysuckle La. N22—9A 28
Honeywell Rd. SW11—5D 90
Honeywood Rd. NW10—5D 56
Honeywood Rd. Iswth—3E 86
Honeywood Wlk. Cars—6D 122
Honister Clo. Stan—8F 22
Honister Gdns. Stan—7F 22
Honister Heights. Purl—6B 138
Honister Pl. Stan—8F 22
Honiton Rd. NW6—5K 57
Honiton Rd. Romf—4B 50
Honiton Rd. Well—1D 96
Honley Rd. SE6—6M 93
Honor Oak Pk. SE23—5G 93
Honor Oak Rise. SE23—5G 93
Honor Oak Rd. SE23—7G 93
Hood Av. N14—8F 14
Hood Av. SW14—4A 88
Hood Av. Orp—9F 112
Hood Clo. Croy—3M 123
Hoodcote Gdns. N21—9M 15
Hood Rd. SW20—4D 104
Hood Rd. Rain—5D 66
Hood Wlk. Romf—8M 33
Hookers Rd. E17—1H 45

Hook Farm Rd. Brom—9H 111
Hookfield. Eps—5A 134
Hook Gate. Enf—1F 16
Hook Grn. La. Dart—9D 98
Hook Hill. S Croy—2C 138
Hooking Grn. Harr—3M 37
Hook La. Well—3D 96
Hook Rise N. Surb—5L 119
Hook Rise S. Surb—5L 119
Hook Rd. Chess—7H 119
Hook Rd. Eps—9A 120
Hook Rd. Surb—4J 119
Hooks Clo. SE15—9F 76
Hooks Hall Dri. Dag—8A 50
Hook, The. Barn—8B 14
Hook Wlk. Edgw—7A 24
Hooper Rd. E16—9E 62
Hooper's Ct. SW3—3D 74
Hooper St. E1—9F 60
Hoop La. NW11—5K 41
Hope Clo. SE12—9F 94
Hope Clo. Wfd G—6G 31
Hopedale Rd. SE7—7F 78
Hopefield Av. NW6—5J 57
Hope Grn. Wat—6E 4
Hope Pk. Brom—4D 110
Hope St. SW11—2B 90
Hopewell St. SE5—8B 76
Hop Gdns. WC2—1J 75
Hopgood St. W12—2G 73
Hopkinsons Pl. NW1—4E 58
Hopkins St. W1—9G 59
Hoppers Rd. N21—2L 27
Hoppett Rd. E4—2C 30
Hopping La. N1—2M 59
Hoppingwood Av. N Mald
 —7C 104
Hoppit Rd. Wal A—6H 7
Hoppner Rd. Hay—5B 52
Hopton Gdns. N Mald—1E 120
Hopton Rd. SW16—2J 107
Hopton St. SE1—2M 75
Hopwood Rd. SE17—7B 76
Hopwood Wlk. E8—3E 60
Horace Av. Romf—6A 50
Horace Rd. E7—9F 46
Horace Rd. Ilf—1A 48
Horace Rd. King—7K 103
Horatio St. E2—5E 60
Horatius Way. Croy—8K 123
Horbury Cres. W11—1L 73
Horbury M. W11—1K 73
Horder Rd. SW6—9J 73
Hordle Promenade E. SE15
 —8D 76
Hordle Promenade N. SE15
 —8D 76
Hordle Promenade S. SE15
 —8D 76
Hordle Promenade W. SE15
 —8C 76
Horizon Way. SE7—5F 78
Horley Clo. Bexh—4L 97
Horley Rd. SE9—1J 111
Hormead Rd. W9—7K 57
Hornbeam Av. Upm—9L 51
Hornbeam Clo. Borwd—3L 11
Hornbeam Cres. Bren—8F 70
Hornbeam Gro. E4—3C 30
Hornbeam La. E4—7C 18
Hornbeam La. Bexh—1A 98
Hornbeam Rd. Buck H—3H 31
Hornbeam Rd. Hay—8G 53
Hornbeams. St Alb—3K 5
Hornbeams Av. Enf—8C 6
Hornbeam Wlk. Rich—9K 87
Hornbeam Way. Brom—1L 127
Hornbill Clo. Uxb—9B 142
Hornbuckle Clo. Harr—7B 38
Hornby Clo. NW3—3C 58
Horncastle Clo. SE12—6E 94
Horncastle Rd. SE12—6E 94
Hornchurch Hill. Whyt—9D 138
Hornchurch Rd. Horn—6E 50
Horndean Clo. SW15—7E 88
Horndon Clo. Romf—8A 34
Horndon Grn. Romf—8A 34
Horndon Rd. Romf—8A 34
Hornets, The. Wat—6F 8
Horne Way. SW15—1G 89
Hornfair Rd. SE7—7H 79
Hornford Way. Romf—5C 50
Horniman Dri. SE23—7F 92
Horning Clo. SE9—1J 111
Horn La. SE10—5E 78
Horn La. W3—1A 72
Horn La. Wfd G—6E 30
Hornminster Glen. Horn—7L 51
Hornpark La. SE12—4F 94
Horns End Pl. Pinn—2G 37
Hornsey La. N6—6G 43
Hornsey La. Gdns. N6—5G 43
Hornsey Pk. Rd. N8—1K 43

Hornsey Rise. N19—5H 43
Hornsey Rise Gdns. N19—5H 43
Hornsey Rd.—7J 43
 N7 1-281 & 2-352
 N19 remainder
Hornsey St. N7—1K 59
Hornshay St. SE15—7G 77
Horns Rd. Ilf—3A 48
Hornton Pl. W8—3M 73
Hornton St. W8—3L 73
Horsa Clo. Wall—9J 123
Horsa Rd. SE12—6G 95
Horsa Rd. Eri—8A 82
Horsecroft. Bans—9K 135
Horsecroft Clo. Orp—3F 128
Horsecroft Rd. Edgw—7B 24
Horse Fair. King—6H 103
Horseferry Pl. SE10—7A 78
Horseferry Rd. SW1—5H 75
Horseguards Av. SW1—2J 75
Horse Guards Rd. SW1—2H 75
Horsell Rd. N5—1L 59
Horsell Rd. Orp—5F 112
Horselydown La. SE1—2D 76
Horsenden Av. Gnfd—1D 54
Horsenden Cres. Gnfd—1D 54
Horsenden La. N. Gnfd—2C 54
Horsenden La. S. Gnfd—4E 54
Horse Ride. Cars—3D 136
Horse Shoe Clo. NW2—7F 40
Horse Shoe Cres. N'holt—5L 53
Horse Shoe Grn. Sutt—4M 121
Horseshoe La. N20—1H 25
Horse Shoe La. Enf—5A 16
Horseshoe La. Wat—5F 4
Horseshoe, The. Bans—7L 135
Horseshoe, The. Coul—5H 137
Horsfeld Gdns. SE9—4J 95
Horsfeld Rd. SE9—4H 95
Horsford Rd. SW2—4K 91
Horsham Av. N12—5C 26
Horsham Clo. Orp—2D 128
Horsham Rd. Bexh—4L 97
Horsham Rd. Felt—5A 84
Horsley Clo. Eps—5B 134
Horsley Dri. Croy—9A 126
Horsley Rd. E4—2A 30
Horsley Rd. Brom—5F 110
Horsley St. SE17—7B 76
Horsman St. SE5—7A 76
Horsmonden Rd. SE4—5K 93
Hortensia Rd. SW10—8A 74
Horticultural Pl. W4—6B 72
Horton Av. NW2—9J 41
Horton Bri. Rd. W Dray—4H 143
Horton Clo. W Dray—2L 143
Horton Footpath. Eps—3A 134
Horton Gdns. Eps—3A 134
Horton Hill. Eps—3A 134
Horton La. Eps—3L 133
Horton Rd. E8—2F 60
Horton Rd. S Dar, Dart—8M 115
Horton Rd. W Dray—2J 143
Horton St. SE13—2M 93
Horton Way. F'ham, Dart
 —2K 131
Hortus Rd. E4—2A 30
Hortus Rd. S'hall—3K 69
Hosack Rd. SW17—8E 90
Hoser Av. SE12—8E 94
Hosier La. EC1—8M 59
Hoskins Clo. E16—9G 63
Hoskins Clo. Hay—6D 68
Hoskins St. SE10—6B 78
Hospital Bri. Rd. Twic—6M 85
Hospital La. Iswth—4D 86
Hospital Rd. Houn—2L 85
Hospital Rd. Sutt—3M 135
Hotham Clo. E Mol—7L 101
Hotham Rd. SW15—2G 89
Hotham Rd. SW19—4A 106
Hothfield Pl. SE16—4G 77
Hotspur Rd. N'holt—5L 53
Hotspur St. SE11—6L 75
Houblon Rd. Rich—4J 87
Houghton Clo. E8—2D 60
Houghton Clo. Hmptn—3J 101
Houghton Rd. N15—2D 44
Houghton St. WC2—9K 59
Houlder Cres. Croy—8M 123
Houndsden Rd. N21—8K 15
Houndsditch. EC3—9C 60
Houndsfield Rd. N9—9F 16
Hounslow Av. Houn—4M 85
Hounslow Gdns. Houn—4M 85
Hounslow Rd. Felt—7F 84
Hounslow Rd. Felt—1H 101
 (Hanworth)
Hounslow Rd. Twic—5M 85
Houseman Way. SE5—8B 76
Houston Rd. SE23—8J 93
Hove Av. E17—3K 45

Hoveden Rd. NW2—1J 57
Hove Gdns. Sutt—3M 121
Hoveton Rd. SE28—9G 65
Howard Av. Bex—7G 97
Howard Av. Eps—2E 134
Howard Clo. N11—2E 26
Howard Clo. NW2—9J 41
Howard Clo. W3—9M 55
Howard Clo. Bush, Wat—9C 10
Howard Clo. Hmptn—4A 102
Howard Clo. Sun—3D 100
Howard Clo. Wat—1E 8
Howard Dri. Borwd—6B 12
Howard Pl. SW1—4G 75
Howard Rd. E6—5K 63
Howard Rd. E11—8C 46
Howard Rd. E17—1M 45
Howard Rd. N15—4C 44
Howard Rd. N16—9B 44
Howard Rd. NW2—9H 41
Howard Rd. SE20—5G 109
Howard Rd. SE25—9E 108
Howard Rd. Bark—4B 64
Howard Rd. Brom—4E 110
Howard Rd. Coul—7G 137
Howard Rd. Dart—5L 99
Howard Rd. Ilf—9M 47
Howard Rd. Iswth—2D 86
Howard Rd. N Mald—7C 104
Howard Rd. S'hall—9M 53
Howard Rd. Surb—1K 119
Howard Rd. Upm—7M 51
Howards Clo. Pinn—9F 20
Howard's La. SW15—3F 88
Howards Rd. E13—6E 62
Howard St. Th Dit—2F 118
Howard Wlk. N2—2A 42
Howarth Rd. SE2—6E 80
Howberry Clo. Edgw—6H 23
Howberry Rd. Stan & Edgw
 —6H 23
Howberry Rd. T Hth—5B 108
Howbury La. Eri—1E 98
Howbury Rd. SE15—2G 93
Howcroft Cres. N3—7L 25
Howcroft La. Gnfd—6B 54
Howden Clo. SE28—1H 81
Howden Ho. Houn—6J 85
Howden Rd. SE25—6D 108
Howden St. SE15—2E 92
Howe Clo. Romf—8L 33
Howell Clo. Romf—3H 49
Howell Hill Clo. Eps—3G 135
Howell Hill Gro. Eps—2G 135
Howell Wlk. SE17—5M 75
Howfield Pl. N17—1D 44
Howgate Rd. SW14—2B 88
Howick Pl. SW1—4G 75
Howie St. SW11—8C 74
Howitt Rd. NW3—2C 58
Howland M. E. W1—8G 59
Howland St. W1—8G 59
How La. Coul—9E 136
Howletts La. Ruis—3A 36
Howlett's Rd. SE24—5A 92
Howley Pl. W2—8A 58
Howley Rd. Croy—5M 123
Hows Clo. Uxb—4A 142
Howsman Rd. SW13—7E 72
Howson Rd. SE4—3J 93
Howson Ter. Rich—5J 87
Hows Rd. Uxb—4A 142
How's St. E2—5D 60
Howton Pl. Bush, Wat—1B 22
How Wood. St Alb—1M 5
Hoxton Sq. N1—6C 60
Hoxton St. N1—4C 60
Hoylake Gdns. Mitc—7G 107
Hoylake Gdns. Romf—7L 35
Hoylake Gdns. Ruis—6F 36
Hoylake Gdns. Wat—4H 21
Hoylake Rd. W3—9C 56
Hoyland Clo. SE15—8F 76
Hoyle Rd. SW17—2C 106
Hoy St. E16—9D 62
Hubbard Rd. SE27—1A 108
Hubbards Chase. Horn—3L 51
Hubbards Clo. Horn—3L 51
Hubbard St. E15—4C 62
Hubert Gro. SW9—2J 91
Hubert Rd. E6—6H 63
Hubert Rd. Rain—6D 66
Hucknall Clo. Romf—6K 35
Huddart St. E3—8K 61
 (in two parts)
Huddlestone Rd. E7—9D 46
Huddlestone Rd. N7—8G 43
Huddlestone Rd. NW2—2F 56
Hudson Clo. Wat—9D 4
Hudson Pl. SE18—6A 80
Hudson Rd. Bexh—1K 97
Hudson Rd. Hay—7B 68
Hudson Rd. King—5J 103

Isleworth Promenade. Twic
—3F 86
Islington Grn. N1—4M 59
Islington High St. N1—5L 59
Islington Pk. St. N1—3L 59
Islip Gdns. Edgw—7B 24
Islip Gdns. N'holt—3J 53
Islip Mnr. Rd. N'holt—3J 53
Islip St. NW5—1G 59
Ismalia Rd. E7—3F 62
Isom Clo. E13—6F 62
Ivanhoe Clo. Uxb—8B 142
Ivanhoe Dri. Harr—1E 38
Ivanhoe Rd. SE5—2D 92
Ivanhoe Rd. Houn—2H 85
Ivatt Pl. W14—6K 73
Ivatt Way. N17—1M 43
Iveagh Av. NW10—5L 55
Iveagh Clo. E9 4H 61
Iveagh Clo. NW10—5L 55
Iveagh Ct. Beck—7A 110
Ivedon Rd. Well—1G 97
Ive Farm Clo. E10—7L 45
Ive Farm La. E10—7L 45
Iveley Rd. SW4—1G 91
Ivere Dri. Barn—8M 13
Iverhurst Clo. Bexh—4H 97
Iver La. Iver & Uxb—7A 142
Iverna Ct. W8—4L 73
Iverna Gdns. W8—4L 73
Iverna Gdns. Felt—4B 84
Iverson Rd. NW6—2K 57
Ivers Way. Croy—9M 125
Ives Gdns. Romf—2D 50
Ives Rd. E16—8C 62
Ives St. SW3—5C 74
Ivestor Ter. SE23—6G 93
Ivimey St. E2—6E 60
Ivinghoe Clo. Enf—3C 16
Ivinghoe Clo. Wat—8H 5
Ivinghoe Rd. Bush, Wat—9B 10
Ivinghoe Rd. Dag—1F 64
Ivor Gro. SE9—7M 95
Ivor Pl. NW1—7D 58
Ivor St. NW1—3G 59
Ivorydown. Brom—1E 110
Ivybridge La. WC2—1J 75
Ivychurch Clo. SE20—4G 109
Ivychurch La. SE17—6D 76
Ivy Clo. Dart—5L 99
Ivy Clo. Harr—9K 37
Ivy Clo. Pinn—5G 37
Ivy Clo. Sun—6G 101
Ivy Cres. W4—5A 72
Ivydale Rd. SE15—2H 93
Ivydale Rd. Cars—4D 122
Ivyday Gro. SW16—9K 91
Ivydene. E Mol—9K 101
Ivydene Clo. Sutt—6A 122
Ivydene Rd. E8—3E 60
Ivy Gdns. N8—4J 43
Ivy Gdns. Mitc—7H 107
Ivyhouse Rd. Dag—2H 65
Ivyhouse Rd. Uxb—8A 36
Ivy La. Houn—3K 85
Ivy Lodge La. Romf—8M 35
Ivymount Rd. SE27—9L 91
Ivy Rd. E16—9E 62
Ivy Rd. E17—4L 45
Ivy Rd. N14—9G 15
Ivy Rd. NW2—9G 41
Ivy Rd. SE4—3K 93
Ivy Rd. Houn—3M 85
Ivy Rd. Surb—3L 119
Ivy St. N1—5C 60
Ivy Wlk. Dag—2J 65
Ixworth Pl. SW3—6C 74
Izane Rd. Bexh—3K 97

Jackass La. Kes—7F 126
Jack Barnett Way. N22—9K 27
Jack Cornwell St. E12—9L 47
Jackets La. Uxb & N'wd—8A 20
Jacketts Field. Abb L, Wat
—4D 4
Jacklin Grn. Wfd G—4E 30
Jackman M. NW10—8C 40
Jackman St. E8—4F 60
Jackson Clo. Eps—6B 134
Jackson Clo. Uxb—3C 142
Jackson Rd. N7—9K 43
Jackson Rd. Bark—4B 64
Jackson Rd. Barn—8C 14
Jackson Rd. Brom—4K 127
Jackson Rd. Gnfd—4E 54
Jackson Rd. Uxb—3C 142
Jacksons Dri. Wal X—1A 6
Jacksons La. N6—5F 42
Jackson's Pl. Croy—3C 124
Jackson St. SE18—7L 79
Jackson Way. S'hall—3M 69
Jack Walker Ct. N5—9M 43

Jacob St. SE1—3E 76
Jacob's Well M. W1—9E 58
Jacqueline Clo. N'holt—4J 53
Jaffray Rd. Brom—8H 111
Jaggard Way. SW12—6D 90
Jago Clo. SE18—7A 80
Jago Wlk. SE5—8B 76
Jail La. West—7H 141
Jamacia Rd. T Hth—1M 123
Jamaica Rd. SE1 & SE16
—3D 76
Jamaica St. E1—8G 61
James Av. NW2—1G 57
James Av. Dag—6K 49
James Bedford Clo. Pinn
—9G 21
James Boswell Clo. SW16
—1L 10
James Clo. E13—5E 62
James Clo. NW11—4J 41
James Clo. Bush, Wat—7J 9
James Clo. Romf—3E 50
James Gdns. N22—7M 27
James La.—5A 46
E11 27-55
E10 remainder
Jameson St. W8—2L 73
James Pl. N17—8D 28
James Rd. Dart—6E 98
James's Cotts. Rich—8L 71
James St. W1—9E 58
James St. WC2—1J 75
James St. Bark—3A 64
James St. Enf—7D 16
James St. Houn—2B 86
Jamestown Rd. NW1—4F 58
Jane St. E1—9F 60
Janet St. E14—4L 77
Janeway Pl. SE16—3F 76
Janeway St. SE16—3E 76
Jansen Wlk. SW11—2B 90
Janson Clo. E15—1C 62
Janson Rd. E15—1C 62
Jansons Rd. N15—1C 44
Japan Cres. N4—5K 43
Japan Rd. Romf—4H 49
Jarrett Clo. SW2—7M 91
Jarrow Clo. Mord—9M 105
Jarrow Rd. N17—2F 44
Jarrow Rd. SE16—5G 77
Jarrow Rd. Romf—4G 49
Jarrow Way. E9—9K 45
Jarvis Clo. Barn—7H 13
Jarvis Rd. SE22—3C 92
Jarvis Rd. S Croy—8B 124
Jasmine Clo. Orp—4M 127
Jasmine Gdns. Croy—5M 125
Jasmine Gdns. Harr—7L 37
Jasmine Gro. SE20—5F 108
Jasmine Ter. W Dray—3L 143
Jasmine Way. E Mol—8C 102
Jasmin Rd. Eps—7M 119
Jason Clo. Wey—7A 116
Jason Wlk. SE9—1L 111
Jasper Clo. Enf—2G 17
Jasper Pas. SE19—3D 108
Jasper Rd. E16—6H 63
Jasper Rd. SE19—3D 108
Javelin Way. N'holt—6H 53
Jaycroft. Enf—3L 15
Jay M. SW7—3A 74
Jebb Av. SW2—5J 91
Jebb St. E3—5L 61
Jedburgh Rd. E13—6G 63
Jedburgh St. SW11—3E 90
Jeddo Rd. W12—3D 72
Jefferson Clo. W13—4F 70
Jefferson Clo. Ilf—3M 47
Jeffreys Rd. SW4—1J 91
Jeffreys Rd. Enf—6J 17
Jeffrey's St. NW1—3G 59
Jeffreys Wlk. SW4—1J 91
Jeffs Rd. Sutt—6K 121
Jeken Rd. SE9—3G 95
Jelf Rd. SW2—4L 91
Jellicoe Gdns. Stan—6E 22
(in two parts)
Jellicoe Rd. E13—7E 62
Jellicoe Rd. N17—7B 28
Jengar Clo. Sutt—6M 121
Jenkins Av. St Alb—3J 5
Jenkins La. Bark—5A 64
Jenkins Rd. E13—7E 62
Jenner Pl. SW13—7F 72
Jenner Rd. N16—8D 44
Jennett Rd. Croy—5L 123
Jennifer Rd. Brom—9D 94
Jennings Rd. SE22—5D 92
Jennings Way. Barn—5G 13
Jenningtree Rd. Eri—8F 82
Jenningtree Way. Belv—3A 82
Jenny Path. Romf—7H 35
Jenson Way. SE19—4D 108
Jenton Av. Bexh—1J 97

Jephson Rd. E7—3G 63
Jephson Rd. SE5—9B 76
Jephtha Rd. SW18—5L 89
Jeppos La. Mitc—8D 106
Jerdan Pl. SW6—8L 73
Jeremiah St. E14—9M 61
Jeremy's Grn. N18—4F 28
Jermyn St. SW1—2G 75
Jerningham Av. Ilf—9M 31
Jerningham Rd. SE14—1J 93
Jerome Cres. NW8—7C 58
Jerome St. E1—7D 60
Jerrard St. SE13—2M 93
Jerrold St. N1—5C 60
Jersey Av. Stan—9G 23
Jersey Dri. Orp—1B 128
Jersey Ho. N1—2A 60
Jersey Rd. E11—6B 46
Jersey Rd. E16—9F 62
Jersey Rd. SW17—3F 106
Jersey Rd. W7—3E 70
Jersey Rd. Houn & Iswth
—9M 69
Jersey Rd. Ilf—9M 47
Jersey Rd. Rain—3E 66
Jersey St. E2—6F 60
Jerusalem Pas. EC1—7M 59
Jervis Av. Enf—8E 6
Jerviston Gdns. SW16—3L 107
Jesmond Av. Wemb—2K 55
Jesmond Rd. Croy—2D 124
Jesmond Way. Stan—5J 23
Jessam Av. E5—6F 44
Jessamine Rd. W7—2D 70
Jessel Dri. Lou—3M 19
Jesse Rd. E10—6A 46
Jessica Rd. SW18—5A 90
Jessop Rd. SE24—3A 92
Jessops Way. Croy—1G 123
Jessup Clo. SE18—5A 80
Jetstar Way. N'holt—6J 53
Jevington Way. SE12—7F 94
Jewel Rd. E17—1L 45
Jewels Hill. Warl—4E 140
Jewry St. EC3—9D 60
Jew's Row. SW18—3A 90
Jews Wlk. SE26—1F 108
Jeymer Av. NW2—1F 56
Jeymer Dri. Gnfd—4A 54
(in two parts)
Jeypore Pas. SW18—5A 90
Jeypore Rd. SW18—5A 90
Jillian Clo. Hmptn—4L 101
Joan Cres. SE9—6H 95
Joan Gdns. Dag—7J 49
Joan Rd. Dag—7J 49
Joan St. SE1—2M 75
Jocelyn Rd. Rich—2J 87
Jockey's Fields. WC1—8K 59
Jodrell Rd. E3—4K 61
Joel St. N'wd & Pinn—1E 36
Johanna St. SE1—3L 75
John Adam St. WC2—1J 75
John Barnes Wlk. E15—2D 62
John Bradshaw Rd. N14—1H 27
John Burns Dri. Bark—3C 64
Johnby Clo. Enf—1J 17
John Campbell Rd. N16—1C 60
John Carpenter St. EC4—1M 75
John Felton Rd. SE16—3E 76
John Fisher St. E1—1E 76
John Islip St. SW1—5H 75
John McKenna Wlk. SE16
—4E 76
John Newton Ct. Well—2F 96
John Parker Clo. Dag—3M 65
John Parker Sq. SW11—2B 90
John Penn St. SE13—9M 77
John Perrin Pl. Harr—5J 39
John Prince's St. W1—9F 58
John Rennie Wlk. E1—2F 76
John Roll Way. SE16—4E 76
John Ruskin St. SE5—8M 75
John's Av. NW4—2G 41
John's Clo. Ashf—1A 100
Johns La. Mord—9A 106
John's M. WC1—7K 59
Johnson Clo. E8—4E 60
Johnson Rd. Brom—9H 111
Johnson Rd. Croy—2B 124
Johnson Rd. Houn—8G 69
Johnsons Clo. Cars—4D 122
Johnson's Ct. EC4—9L 59
Johnsons Dri. Hmptn—5A 102
Johnson's Pl. SW1—6G 75
Johnson St. E1—1G 77
Johnson St. S'hall—4G 69
Johnsons Way. NW10—7M 55
Johnson's Yd. Uxb—3A 142
John Spencer Sq. N1—2M 59
John's Pl. E1—9F 60
John's Ter. Croy—3C 124
John's Ter. Romf—6M 35

Johnstone Rd. E6—6K 63
Johnston Rd. Wfd G—6E 30
Johnston Ter. NW2—8H 41
John St. E15—4D 62
John St. SE25—8E 108
John St. WC1—7K 59
John St. Enf—7D 16
John St. Houn—1J 85
John Wilson St. SE18—4L 79
John Woolley Clo. SE13—3B 94
Joiner St. SE1—2B 76
Jollys La. Harr—6B 38
Jolly's La. Hay—8H 53
Jonathan St. SE11—6K 75
Jones Rd. E13—7F 62
Jones St. W1—1F 74
Jones Wlk. Rich—5K 87
Jonquil Gdns. Hmptn—3L 101
Jonson Clo. Hay—8E 52
Jonson Rd. Mitc—8F 106
Joram Way. SE16—6F 76
Jordan Clo. Dag—9M 49
Jordan Clo. Harr—8K 37
Jordan Clo. Iswth—9C 70
Jordan Clo. S Croy—3D 138
Jordan Clo. Wat—8D 4
Jordan Rd. Gnfd—4F 54
Jordans Clo. Stai—6A 144
Jordans Way. Rain—5H 67
Jordan's Way. St Alb—3K 5
Josephine Av. SW2—4K 91
Joseph Powell Clo. SW12
—5F 90
Joseph St. E3—7K 61
Joshua St. E14—9A 62
Joubert St. SW11—1D 90
Jowett St. SE15—8D 76
Joyce Av. N18—5D 28
Joyce Ct. Wal A—7K 7
Joyce Grn. La. Dart—9J 83
Joyce Grn. Wlk. Dart—3K 99
Joydens Wood Rd. Bex & Dart
—1B 114
Joydon Dri. Romf—4F 48
Jubb Powell Ho. N15—4C 44
Jubilee Av. E4—6A 30
Jubilee Av. Romf—3M 49
Jubilee Av. Twic—7A 86
Jubilee Clo. NW9—4B 40
Jubilee Clo. Pinn—9G 21
Jubilee Clo. Romf—3M 49
Jubilee Clo. Stai—6A 144
Jubilee Cres. E14—4A 78
Jubilee Cres. N9—1E 28
Jubilee Dri. Ruis—9H 37
Jubilee Gdns. Barn—6H 13
Jubilee Gdns. S'hall—8L 53
Jubilee Pl. SW3—6C 74
Jubilee Rd. Gnfd—4F 54
Jubilee Rd. Orp—8L 129
Jubilee Rd. Sutt—9H 121
Jubilee Rd. Wat—2E 8
Jubilee St. E1—9G 61
Jubilee Ter. N1—5B 60
Jubilee Way. SW19—5M 105
Jubilee Way. Chess—6L 119
Jubilee Way. Sidc—8E 96
Judd St. WC1—6J 59
Jude St. E16—9D 62
Judge Heath La. Hay—9A 52
Judge St. Wat—2F 8
Judges Wlk. NW3—8A 42
Judith Av. Romf—6M 33
Juer St. SW11—8C 74
Jug Hill. West—8H 141
Juglans Rd. Orp—3E 128
Julia Gdns. Bark—5H 65
Julian Av. W3—1M 71
Julian Clo. Barn—5M 13
Julian Hill. Harr—7C 38
Julian Pl. E14—6M 77
Julian Rd. Orp—8E 128
Julia St. NW5—9E 42
Julien Rd. W5—4G 71
Julien Rd. Coul—7H 137
Junction App. SE13—2A 94
Junction M. W2—9C 58
Junction Rd. E13—6F 62
Junction Rd. N9—1E 28
Junction Rd. N17—1E 44
Junction Rd. N19—8G 43
Junction Rd. W5—5G 71
Junction Rd. Ashf—2A 100
Junction Rd. Dart—5H 99
Junction Rd. Harr—4C 38
Junction Rd. Romf—2D 50
Junction Rd. S Croy—7B 124
Junction Rd. E. Romf—5J 49
Junction Rd. W. Romf—5J 49
June Clo. Coul—6F 136
Juniper Av. St Alb—4L 5
Juniper Clo. West—9J 141
Juniper Ct. Harr—8D 22

Juniper Gdns. SW16—5G 107
Juniper Gro. Wat—2E 8
Juniper Rd. Ilf—8L 47
Juniper St. E1—1G 77
Juniper Wlk. Swan—6B 114
Juniper Way. Hay—1B 68
Juniper Way. Romf—8J 35
Juno Way. SE14—7H 77
Jupiter Way. N7—2K 59
Jupp Rd. E15—3B 62
Jupp Rd. W. E15—4B 62
Justin Clo. Bren—8H 71
Justin Rd. E4—7L 29
Jute La. Enf—5J 17
Jutland Rd. E13—7E 62
Jutland Rd. SE6—6A 94
Jutsums Av. Romf—4M 49
Jutsums La. Romf—4M 49
Juxon Clo. Harr—8M 21
Juxon St. SE11—5K 75

Kaduna Clo. Pinn—3E 36
Kale Rd. Eri—4J 81
Kambala Rd. SW11—2B 90
Kangley Bri. Rd. SE26—2K 109
Karen Clo. Rain—5C 66
Kashgar Rd. SE18—5D 80
Kashmir Rd. SE7—8H 79
Kassala Rd. SW11—9D 74
Katherine Gdns. SE9—3H 95
Katherine Gdns. Ilf—7A 32
Katherine Rd. E6—2G 63
E6 1-239 & 2-224
E7 remainder
Katherine Rd. Twic—7E 86
Katherine St. Croy—5A 124
Kathleen Av. W3—8A 56
Kathleen Av. Wemb—3J 55
Kathleen Rd. SW11—2D 90
Kayemoor Rd. Sutt—8B 122
Kay Rd. SW9—1J 91
Kay St. E2—5E 60
Kay St. E15—3B 62
Kay St. Well—9F 80
Kean St. WC2—9K 59
Kearsley M. SW11—9D 74
Kearton Clo. Kenl—9A 138
Keats Av. Romf—7F 34
Keats Clo. Chig—6A 32
Keats Clo. Hay—8E 52
Keat's Gro. NW3—9C 42
Keats Rd. Belv—4A 82
Keats Rd. Well—9C 80
Keats Way. Croy—1G 125
Keats Way. Gnfd—8M 53
Keats Way. W Dray—5K 143
Keble Clo. N'holt—2A 54
Keble Clo. Wor Pk—3D 120
Keble St. SW17—1A 106
Keble Ter. Abb L, Wat—5D 4
Kechill Gdns. Brom—2E 126
Kedleston Dri. Orp—9D 112
Kedleston Wlk. E2—6F 60
Keedonwood Rd. Brom
—2C 110
Keeley Rd. Croy—4A 124
Keeley St. WC2—9K 59
Keeling Rd. SE9—4H 95
Keemor Clo. SE18—8L 79
Keens Rd. Croy—6A 124
Keen's Yd. N1—2M 59
Keep, The. SE3—1E 94
Keep, The. King—4K 103
Keeton's Rd. SE16—4F 76
Keevil Dri. SW19—6H 89
Keighley Clo. N7—9J 43
Keighley Rd. Romf—7J 35
Keightley Dri. SE9—7K 96
Keilder Clo. Uxb—5E 142
Keildon Rd. SW11—3D 90
Keir Hardie Way. Bark—3E 64
Keir Hardie Way. Hay—6E 52
Keith Av. S at H, Dart—3M 115
Keith Gro. W12—3E 72
Keith Pk. Cres. West—4F 140
Keith Pk. Rd. Uxb—3D 142
Keith Rd. E17—8K 29
Keith Rd. Bark—5B 64
Keith Rd. Hay—4C 68
Keith Way. Horn—5J 51
Kelbrook Rd. SE3—1J 95
Kelburn Way. Rain—6E 66
Kelceda Clo. NW2—7E 40
Kelday Rd. E9—3L 61
Kelf Gro. Hay—9D 52
Kelfield Gdns. W10—9G 57
Kelland Rd. E13—7E 62
Kellaway Rd. SE3—1H 95
Kellerton Rd. SE13—4C 94
Kellett Rd. SW2—3L 91
Kelling Gdns. Croy—2M 123

Kirby Clo. Lou—9J 19
Kirby Clo. N'wd—6D 20
Kirby Gro. SE1—3C 76
Kirby St. EC1—8L 59
Kirby Way. W on T—1G 117
Kirchen Rd. W13—1F 70
Kirkcaldy Grn. Wat—3G 21
Kirkdale. SE26—8F 92
Kirkdale Rd. E11—6C 46
Kirkham Rd. E6—9J 63
Kirkham St. SE18—7C 80
Kirkland Av. Ilf—9L 31
Kirkland Clo. Sidc—5C 96
Kirkland Wlk. E8—2D 60
kirkland Way. Orp—7H 113
Kirk La. SE18—7A 80
Kirklees Rd. Dag—1G 65
Kirklees Rd. Surb—3J 119
Kirklees Rd. T Hth—9L 107
Kirkley Rd. SW19—5L 105
Kirkly Clo. S Croy—1C 138
Kirkmichael Rd. E14—9A 62
Kirk Rd. E17—4K 45
Kirkside Rd. SE3—7E 78
Kirkstall Av. N17—2B 44
Kirkstall Gdns. SW2—7J 91
Kirkstall Rd. SW2—7H 91
Kirkstead Rd. Mord—3M 121
Kirkstone Way. Brom—4C 110
Kirkton Rd. N15—2C 44
Kirkwall Pl. E2—6G 61
Kirkwood Pl. NW1—3E 58
Kirkwood Rd. SE15—1F 92
Kirn Rd. W13—1F 70
Kirtley Rd. SE26—1J 109
Kirtling St. SW8—8G 75
Kirton Clo. W4—5B 72
Kirton Clo. Horn—2G 67
Kirton Gdns. E2—6D 00
Kirton Rd. E13—5G 63
Kirton Wlk. Edgw—7A 24
Kirwyn Way. SE5—8A 76
Kitcat Ter. E3—6L 61
Kitchener Rd. E7—2F 62
Kitchener Rd. E17—8M 29
Kitchener Rd. N2—1C 62
Kitchener Rd. N17—1C 44
Kitchener Rd. Dag—2A 66
Kitchener Rd. T Hth—7B 108
Kitley Gdns. SE19—1C 108
Kitson Rd. SE5—8B 76
Kitson Rd. SW13—9E 72
Kittiwake Clo. S Croy—2J 139
Kittiwake Rd. N'holt—6H 53
Kitto Rd. SE14—1H 93
Kitts End Rd. Barn—1J 13
Kiver Rd. N19—7H 43
Klea Av. SW4—5G 91
Knapdale Clo. SE23—8F 92
Knapmill Rd. SE6—8L 93
Knapmill Way. SE6—8M 93
Knapp Clo. NW10—2C 56
Knapp Rd. E3—7L 61
Knapp Rd. Ashf—9D 144
Knapton M. SW17—3E 106
Knaresborough Pl. SW5
—5M 73
Knatchbull Rd. NW10—4B 56
Knatchbull Rd. SE5—1M 91
Knebworth Av. E17—8L 29
Knebworth Path. Borwd—6B 12
Knebworth Rd. N16—9C 44
Knee Hill. SE2—5G 81
Knee Hill Cres. SE2—5G 81
Kneller Rd. SE4—3J 93
Kneller Rd. N Mald—2C 120
Kneller Rd. Twic—5A 86
Knightland Rd. E5—7F 44
Knighton Clo. Romf—4B 50
Knighton Clo. S Croy—1M 137
Knighton Dri. Wfd G—4F 30
Knighton Grn. Wfd G—4F 30
Knighton La. Buck H—2F 30
Knighton Pk. Rd. SE26—2H 109
Knighton Rd. E7—8E 46
Knighton Rd. Romf—4A 50
Knightrider St. EC4—9M 59
Knights Av. W5—3J 71
Knightsbridge. SW7—3D 74
SW1 1-161 & 2-124
SW7 remainder
Knightsbridge Gdns. Romf
—3B 50
Knightsbridge Grn. SW1
—3D 74
Knight's Clo. E9—1G 61
Knights Hill. SE27—2M 107
Knights Hill Sq. SE27—1M 107
Knights La. N9—3E 28
Knights Pk. King—7J 103
Knights Ridge. Orp—7F 128

Knight's Rd. E16—3E 78
Knights Rd. Stan—4G 23
Knight's Wlk. SE11—5M 75
Knightswood Clo. Edgw
—2A 24
Knightswood Ct. N6—5H 43
Knightswood Ho. N12—6A 26
Knightwood Cres. N Mald
—1C 120
Knivet Rd. SW6—7L 73
Knobs Hill Rd. E15—4M 61
Knockholt Rd. SE9—4H 95
Knole Clo. Croy—1G 125
Knole Rd. Dart—6E 98
Knole, The. SE9—1L 111
Knoll Cres. N'wd—8C 20
Knoll Dri. N14—9E 14
Knollmead. Surb—3A 120
Knoll Rise. Orp—3D 128
Knoll Rd. SW18—4A 90
Knoll Rd. Bex—6L 97
Knoll Rd. Sidc—2F 112
Knolls Clo. Wor Pk—5F 120
Knolls, The. Eps—8G 135
Knoll, The. W5—8G 55
Knoll, The. Beck—5M 109
Knoll, The. Brom—3E 126
Knollys Clo. SW16—9L 91
Knollys Rd. SW16—9L 91
Knottisford St. E2—6G 61
Knotts Grn. Rd. E10—4M 45
Knowle Av. Bexh—8J 81
Knowle Clo. SW9—2L 91
Knowle Rd. Brom—4K 127
Knowle Rd. Twic—7C 86
Knowles Hill Cres. SE13—4B 94
Knowles Wlk. SW4—2G 91
Knowl Pk. Borwd—7J 11
Knowlton Grn. Brom—9D 110
Knowl Way. Borwd—7K 11
Knowsley Av. S'hall—2M 69
Knowsley Rd. SW11—1D 90
Knox Rd. E7—2D 62
Knox St. W1—8D 58
Knoyle St. SE14—7J 77
Knutsford Av. Wat—2H 9
Kohat Rd. SW19—2M 105
Koh-i-noor Av. Bush, Wat—8L 9
Koonowla Clo. West—7H 141
Korda Clo. Shep—7D 144
Kossuth St. SE10—6C 78
Kotree Way. SE1—5E 76
Kramer M. SW5—6L 73
Kreisel Wlk. Rich—7K 71
Kuala Gdns. SW16—5K 107
Kuhn Way. E7—1E 62
Kydbrook Clo. Orp—2E 128
Kylemore Clo. E6—5H 63
Kylemore Rd. NW6—3L 57
Kymberley Rd. Harr—4C 38
Kyme Rd. Horn—4D 50
Kynance Clo. Romf—4G 35
Kynance Gdns. Stan—8G 23
Kynance M. SW7—4A 74
Kynance Pl. SW7—4A 74
Kynaston Av. N16—8D 44
Kynaston Av. T Hth—9A 108
Kynaston Clo. Harr—7B 22
Kynaston Cres. T Hth—9A 108
Kynaston Rd. N16—8C 44
Kynaston Rd. Brom—2E 110
Kynaston Rd. Enf—3B 16
Kynaston Rd. Orp—2F 128
Kynaston Rd. T Hth—9A 108
Kynaston Wood. Harr—7B 22
Kynnersley Clo. Cars—5D 122
Kynoch Rd. N18—4G 29
Kyrle Rd. SW11—5E 90
Kytes Dri. Wat—6H 5
Kytes Est. Wat—6H 5
Kyverdale Rd. N16—6D 44

Laburnam Clo. N11—6E 26
Laburnum Av. N9—2D 28
Laburnum Av. N17—7B 28
Laburnum Av. Dart—7G 99
Laburnum Av. Horn—7E 50
Laburnum Av. Sutt—5C 122
Laburnum Av. Swan—7B 114
Laburnum Av. W Dray—1K 143
Laburnum Clo. E4—6K 29
Laburnum Clo. SE15—8G 77
Laburnum Clo. Wal X—4D 6
Laburnum Ct. Stan—4G 23
Laburnum Cres. Sun—5F 100
Laburnum Gdns. N21—2A 28
Laburnum Gdns. Croy—3H 125
Laburnum Gro. N21—2A 28
Laburnum Gro. NW9—5A 40
Laburnum Gro. Houn—3K 85
Laburnum Gro. N Mald—6B 104

Laburnum Gro. Ruis—4B 36
Laburnum Gro. S'hall—7K 53
Laburnum Rd. SW19—4A 106
Laburnum Rd. Eps—5C 134
Laburnum Rd. Hay—5D 68
Laburnum Rd. Mitc—6E 106
Laburnum Wlk. Horn—1G 67
Laburnum Way. Brom—2C 127
Laburnum Way. Stai—7D 144
Lacey Dri. Edgw—4K 23
Lacey Dri. Hmptn—5K 101
Lacey Wlk. E3—5L 61
Lackford Rd. Coul—9D 136
Lackington St. EC2—8B 60
Lackmore Rd. Enf—8C 6
Lacock Clo. SW19—3A 106
Lacon Rd. SE22—3E 92
Lacy Rd. SW15—3H 89
Ladas Rd. SE27—1A 108
Ladbroke Cres. W11—9J 57
Ladbroke Gdns. W11—1K 73
Ladbroke Gro.—7H 57
W11 1-137 & 2-108
W10 remainder
Ladbroke M. W11—2J 73
Ladbroke Rd. W11—2K 73
Ladbroke Rd. Enf—8D 16
Ladbroke Rd. Eps—6B 134
Ladbroke Sq. W11—1K 73
Ladbroke Ter. W11—1K 73
Ladbroke Wlk. W11—2K 73
Ladbrook Clo. Pinn—3K 37
Ladbrooke Cres. Sidc—9H 97
Ladbrook Rd. SE25—8B 108
Ladderstile Ride. King—2M 103
Ladderswood Way. N11—5G 27
Ladds Way. Swan—8B 114
Ladycroft Gdns. Orp—7A 128
Ladycroft Rd. SE13—2M 93
Ladycroft Wlk. Stan—8H 23
Ladycroft Way. Orp—7A 128
Lady Dock Wlk. SE16—3J 77
Ladyfields. Lou—6M 19
Ladyfields Clo. Lou—6M 19
Ladygate La. Ruis—4A 36
Ladygrove. Croy—1J 139
Lady Hay. Wor Pk—4D 120
Lady Margaret Rd.—1G 59
NW5 1-83 & 2-70
N19 remainder
Lady Margaret Rd. S'hall
—1K 69
Lady's Clo. Wat—6G 9
Lady Shaw Ct. N13—2K 27
Ladyship Ter. SE22—6E 92
Ladysmith Av. E6—5J 63
Ladysmith Av. Ilf—5C 48
Ladysmith Rd. E16—6D 62
Ladysmith Rd. N17—9E 28
Ladysmith Rd. N18—5F 28
Ladysmith Rd. SE9—5L 95
Ladysmith Rd. Enf—5C 16
Ladysmith Rd. Harr—9C 22
Lady Somerset Rd. NW5
—9F 42
Ladywell Rd. SE13—4L 93
Ladywell St. E15—4D 62
Ladywood Av. Orp—9C 112
Ladywood Rd. Surb—4L 119
Lafone Av. Felt—8G 85
Lafone St. SE1—3D 76
Lagonda Av. Ilf—6D 32
Lagoon Rd. Orp—9G 113
Laing Clo. Ilf—6D 32
Laing Dean. N'holt—4G 53
Laings Av. Mitc—6D 106
Lainlock Pl. Houn—9M 69
Lainson St. SW18—6L 89
Lairdale Clo. SE21—7A 92
Lairs Clo. N7—1J 59
Laitwood Rd. SW12—7F 90
Lake Av. Brom—3E 110
Lake Av. Rain—5H 67
Lakedale Rd. SE18—7C 80
Lakefield Rd. N22—9M 27
Lakefields Clo. Rain—5H 67
Lake Footpath. SE2—3H 81
Lake Gdns. Dag—1L 65
Lake Gdns. Rich—8F 86
Lake Gdns. Wall—5F 122
Lakehall Gdns. T Hth—9M 107
Lakehall Rd. T Hth—9M 107
Lake Ho. Rd. E11—8E 46
Lakehurst Rd. Eps—7C 120
Lakeland Clo. Chig—4F 32
Lakeland Clo. Harr—6B 22
Lakenheath. N14—7H 15
Lake Rise. Romf—1D 50
Lake Rd. SW19—2K 105
Lake Rd. Croy—4K 125
Lake Rd. Romf—2H 49
Laker Pl. SW15—5J 89

Lakers Rise. Bans—8C 136
Lakeside. W13—9G 55
Lakeside. Beck—7M 109
Lakeside. Enf—6H 15
Lakeside. Rain—5J 67
Lakeside. Wall—6F 122
Lakeside. Wey—4C 116
Lakeside Av. Ilf—2H 47
Lakeside Clo. SE25—6E 108
Lakeside Clo. Ruis—2B 36
Lakeside Clo. Sidc—4G 97
Lakeside Ct. N4—7A 44
Lakeside Ct. Borwd—7L 11
Lakeside Cres. Barn—7D 14
Lakeside Dri. Brom—3J 127
Lakeside Dri. Esh—8A 118
Lakeside Rd. N13—4K 27
Lakeside Rd. W14—4H 73
Lakeside Rd. Wal X—1C 6
Lakeside Way. Wemb—9L 39
Lakes Rd. Kes—7G 127
Lake View. Edgw—5K 23
Lakeview Rd. SE27—2L 107
Lake View Rd. Well—3F 96
Lakewood Rd. Orp—1M 127
Lakis Clo. NW3—9A 42
Laleham Av. NW7—3B 24
Laleham Rd. SE6—6A 94
Lalor St. SW6—1J 89
Lambarde Av. SE9—1L 111
Lamberhurst Clo. Orp—3H 129
Lamberhurst Rd. SE27—1L 107
Lamberhurst Rd. Dag—6K 49
Lambert Av. Rich—2L 87
Lambert Clo. West—8H 141
Lambert Ct. Bush, Wat—6L 9
Lamberton Ct. Borwd—3L 11
Lambert Rd. E16—9F 62
Lambert Rd. N12—5A 26
Lambert Rd. SW2—4J 91
Lambert Rd. Bans—6L 135
Lamberts Pl. Croy—3B 124
Lamberts Rd. Surb—9K 103
Lambert St. N1—3L 59
Lambert Wlk. Wemb—8H 39
Lambert Way. N12—5A 26
Lambeth Bri. SW1 & SE1—5J 75
Lambeth High St. SE1—5K 75
Lambeth Hill. EC4—1A 76
Lambeth Pal. Rd. SE1—4K 75
Lambeth Rd. SE1—4K 75
Lambeth Rd. Croy—3L 123
Lambeth Wlk. SE1—5K 75
(in two parts)
Lamb La. E8—3F 60
Lamble St. NW5—1E 58
Lambley Rd. Dag—2F 64
Lambolle Pl. NW3—2C 58
Lambolle Rd. NW3—2C 58
Lambourn Clo. W7—3D 70
Lambourne Av. SW19—1K 105
Lambourne Cres. Chig—2F 32
Lambourne Gdns. E4—2L 29
Lambourne Gdns. Bark—3D 64
Lambourne Gdns. Enf—4D 16
Lambourne Gdns. Horn—7H 51
Lambourne Pl. SE3—9F 78
Lambourne Rd. E11—5A 46
Lambourne Rd. Bark—3C 64
Lambourne Rd. Chig—3D 32
Lambourne Rd. Ilf—7C 48
Lambourn Gro. King—6M 103
Lambourn Rd. SW4—2F 90
Lambrook Ter. SW6—9J 73
Lambs Clo. N9—2E 28
Lamb's Bldgs. EC1—7B 60
Lamb's Conduit Pas. WC1
—8K 59
Lamb's Conduit St. WC1
—7K 59
Lambscroft Av. SE9—9G 95
Lamb's La. Rain—8F 66
Lambs Meadow. Wfd G—9H 31
Lamb's M. N1—4M 59
Lamb's Pas. EC1—7B 60
Lamb's Pas. Bren—7K 71
Lambs Ter. N9—2B 28
Lamb St. E1—8D 60
Lamb's Wlk. Enf—4A 16
Lambton Av. Wal X—6D 6
Lambton Pl. W11—1K 73
Lambton Rd. N19—6J 43
Lambton Rd. SW20—5G 105
Lamb Wlk. SE1—3C 76
Lamerock Rd. Brom—1D 110
Lamerton Rd. Ilf—9M 31
Lamerton St. SE8—7L 77
Lamford Clo. N17—7B 28
Lamington St. W6—5F 72
Lamlash St. SE11—5M 75
Lammas Av. Mitc—6E 106
Lammas Grn. SE26—9F 92

Lammas La. Esh—7L 117
Lammas Pk. Gdns. W5—2G 71
Lammas Pk. Rd. W5—3H 71
Lammas Rd. E9—3H 61
Lammas Rd. E10—7J 45
Lammas Rd. Rich—1G 103
Lammas Rd. Wat—7G 9
Lammermoor Rd. SW12—6F 90
Lamont Rd. SW10—7A 74
Lamorbey Clo. Sidc—8D 96
Lamorna Clo. Orp—2E 128
Lamorna Gro. Stan—8H 23
Lampard Rd. N16—6D 44
Lampern Sq. E2—6E 60
Lampeter Sq. W6—7J 73
Lampmead Rd. SE12—4D 94
Lamport Clo. SE18—5K 79
Lampton Av. Houn—9M 69
Lampton Ho. Clo. SW19
—1H 105
Lampton Pk. Rd. Houn—1M 85
Lampton Rd. Houn—1M 85
Lamson Rd. Rain—8D 66
Lanacre Av. NW9—8C 24
Lanark Clo. W5—8G 55
Lanark Pl. W9—7A 58
Lanark Rd. W9—5M 57
Lanbury Rd. SE15—3H 93
Lancaster Av. E18—2F 46
Lancaster Av. SE27—8M 91
Lancaster Av. SW19—2H 105
Lancaster Av. Bark—3C 64
Lancaster Av. Barn—2B 14
Lancaster Av. Mitc—9J 107
Lancaster Clo. N17—7E 28
Lancaster Clo. SE27—8M 91
Lancaster Clo. Brom—8D 110
Lancaster Clo. Croy—4J 123
Lancaster Clo. King—2H 103
Lancaster Cotts. Rich—5J 87
Lancaster Ct. SW6—8K 73
Lancaster Ct. Bans—6K 135
Lancaster Ct. W on T—2E 116
Lancaster Dri. NW3—2C 58
Lancaster Dri. Horn—1F 66
Lancaster Garages. NW3
—2C 58
Lancaster Gdns. SW19—2J 105
Lancaster Gdns. W13—3F 70
Lancaster Gdns. King—2H 103
Lancaster Ga. W2—1A 74
Lancaster Gro. NW3—2B 58
Lancaster M. W2—1A 74
Lancaster M. Rich—5J 87
Lancaster Pk. Rich—4J 87
Lancaster Pl. SW19—2H 105
Lancaster Pl. WC2—1K 75
Lancaster Pl. Houn—1H 85
Lancaster Pl. Twic—5E 86
Lancaster Rd. E7—3E 62
Lancaster Rd. E11—7C 46
Lancaster Rd. E17—9H 29
Lancaster Rd. N4—5L 43
Lancaster Rd. N11—6H 27
Lancaster Rd. N18—5D 28
Lancaster Rd. NW10—1E 56
Lancaster Rd. SE25—6D 108
Lancaster Rd. SW19—2H 105
Lancaster Rd. W11—9J 57
Lancaster Rd. Barn—7B 14
Lancaster Rd. Enf—3B 16
Lancaster Rd. Harr—3L 37
Lancaster Rd. N'holt—2A 54
Lancaster Rd. S'hall—1J 69
Lancaster Rd. Uxb—2B 142
Lancaster St. SE1—3M 75
Lancaster Ter. W2—1B 74
Lancaster Wlk. W2 & SW7
—2A 74
Lancaster Wlk. Hay—9A 52
Lancefield St. W10—6K 57
(in two parts)
Lancell St. N16—7C 44
Lancelot Av. Wemb—9H 39
Lancelot Cres. Wemb—9H 39
Lancelot Gdns. Barn—9F 14
Lancelot Pl. SW7—3D 74
Lancelot Rd. Ilf—7C 32
Lancelot Rd. Well—3E 96
Lancelot Rd. Wemb—1H 55
Lance Rd. Harr—5A 38
Lancey Clo. SE7—5J 79
Lanchester Rd. N6—3D 42
Lancing Gdns. N9—1D 28
Lancing Rd. W13—1F 70
Lancing Rd. Croy—2K 123
Lancing Rd. Felt—8D 84
Lancing Rd. Ilf—4B 48
Lancing Rd. Orp—4E 128
Lancing Rd. Romf—7J 35
Lancing St. NW1—6H 59
Lancing Way. Rick—7A 8
Lancresse Clo. Uxb—2B 142

Landau Way—Lawrence Gdns.

Landau Way. Eri—6H 83
Landcroft Rd. SE22—4D 92
Landells Rd. SE22—5D 92
Landford Rd. SW15—2G 89
Landgrove Rd. SW19—2L 105
Landmann Way. SE14—6H 77
Landmead Rd. Wal X—2E 6
Landon Pl. SW1—4D 74
Landon Wlk. E14—1M 77
Landon Way. Ashf—3A 100
Landor Rd. SW9—2J 91
Landor Wlk. W12—3E 72
Landport Way. SE15—8D 76
Landra Gdns. N21—8M 15
Landridge Rd. SW6—1K 89
Landrock Rd. N8—4K 43
Landscape Rd. Wfd G—7F 30
Landseer Av. E12—1L 63
Landseer Clo. SW19—5A 106
Landseer Clo. Edgw—9L 23
Landseer Rd. N19—8J 43
Landseer Rd. Enf—7E 16
Landseer Rd. N Mald—2B 120
Landseer Rd. Sutt—8L 121
Landstead Rd. SE18—8B 80
Landway, The. Orp—7G 113
Lane App. NW7—5J 25
Lane Clo. NW2—8F 40
Lane End. Bexh—2M 97
Lane End. Eps—6M 133
Lane Gdns. Bush, Wat—9C 10
Lanercost Clo. SW2—8L 91
Lanercost Gdns. N14—9J 15
Lanercost Rd. SW2—8L 91
Laneside. Chst—2A 112
Laneside. Edgw—5A 24
Laneside Av. Dag—5K 49
Lane, The. NW8—5A 58
Lane, The. SE3—2E 94
Laneway. SW15—4F 88
Lanfranc Rd. E3—5J 61
Lanfrey Pl. W14—6K 73
Langbourne Av. N6—7E 42
Langbourne Way. Esh—8E 118
Langbrook Rd. SE3—2H 95
Langcroft Clo. Cars—5D 122
Langdale Av. Mitc—7D 106
Langdale Clo. SE17—7A 76
Langdale Clo. Orp—5M 127
Langdale Cres. Bexh—8L 81
Langdale Dri. Hay—5C 52
Langdale Gdns. Gnfd—6F 54
Langdale Gdns. Horn—1E 66
Langdale Gdns. Wal X—8D 6
Langdale Rd. SE10—8A 78
Langdale Rd. T Hth—8L 107
Langdale St. E1—9F 60
Langdon Ct. NW10—4C 56
Langdon Cres. E6—5L 63
Langdon Dri. NW9—6A 40
Langdon Pk. Rd. N6—5G 43
Langdon Pl. SW14—2A 88
Langdon Rd. E6—4L 63
Langdon Rd. Brom—7F 110
Langdon Rd. Mord—9A 106
Langdons Ct. S'hall—4L 69
Langdon Shaw. Sidc—2D 112
Langdon Wlk. Mord—9A 106
Langdon Way. SE1—5E 76
Langford Clo. E8—1E 60
Langford Clo. N15—4C 44
Langford Clo. NW8—5A 58
Langford Cres. Barn—6D 14
Langford Grn. SE5—2C 92
Langford Pl. NW8—5A 58
Langford Pl. Sidc—9E 96
Langford Rd. SW6—1M 89
Langford Rd. Barn—6D 14
Langford Rd. Wfd G—6G 31
Langfords. Buck H—2H 31
Langham Ct. Horn—5H 51
Langham Dene. Kenl—7M 137
Langham Dri. Romf—4F 48
Langham Gdns. N21—7L 15
Langham Gdns. W13—1F 70
Langham Gdns. Edgw—7A 24
Langham Gdns. Rich—1G 103
Langham Gdns. Wemb—7G 39
Langham Ho. Clo. Rich —1H 103
Langham Pl. N15—1M 43
Langham Pl. W1—8F 58
Langham Rd. N15—1M 43
Langham Rd. SW20—5G 105
Langham Rd. Edgw—6A 24
Langham Rd. Tedd—2F 102
Langham St. W1—8F 58
Langhedge Clo. N18—6D 28
Langhedge La. N18—6D 28
Langholm Clo. SW12—6H 91
Langholme. Bush, Wat—1A 22
Langhorne Rd. Dag—3L 65
Langland Ct. N'wd—7A 20
Langland Cres. E. Stan—9H 23
Langland Cres. W. Stan—9H 23
Langland Dri. Pinn—7J 21
Langland Gdns. NW3—1M 57
Langland Gdns. Croy—4K 125
Langlands Rise. Eps—5A 134
Langler Rd. NW10—5G 57
Langley Av. Ruis—7F 36
Langley Av. Surb—3H 119
Langley Av. Wor Pk—4H 121
Langleybury La. Wat & K Lan —9A & 7A 4
Langley Clo. Romf—7H 35
Langley Cres. E11—5G 47
Langley Cres. Dag—3G 65
Langley Cres. Edgw—3A 24
Langley Cres. Hay—8D 68
Langley Dri. E11—5F 46
Langley Dri. W3—3M 71
Langley Gdns. Brom—8G 111
Langley Gdns. Dag—3H 65
Langley Gdns. Orp—1M 127
Langley Gro. N Mald—6C 104
Langley La. SW8—7K 75
Langley La. Abb L, Wat—5D 4
Langley Oaks Av. S Croy —2E 138
Langley Pk. NW7—6C 24
Langley Pk. Rd. Sutt—8A 122
Langley Rd. SW19—5K 105
Langley Rd. Abb L, Wat—4C 4
Langley Rd. Beck—8J 109
Langley Rd. Iswth—1D 86
Langley Rd. S Croy—1H 139
Langley Rd. Surb—2J 119
Langley Rd. Wat—3E 8
Langley Rd. Well—7G 81
Langley St. WC2—9J 59
Langley Vale Rd. Eps—9C 134
Langley Way. Wat—4C 8
Langley Way. W Wick—3B 126
Langmead Dri. Bush, Wat —1C 22
Langmead St. SE27—1A 108
Langmore Ct. Bexh—2H 97
Langport Ct. W on T—3G 117
Langroyd Rd. SW17—8D 90
Langside Av. SW15—3E 88
Langside Cres. N14—3H 27
Lang St. E1—7G 61
Langthorne Rd. E11—8A 46
Langthorne St. SW6—8H 73
Langton Av. E6—6L 63
Langton Av. N20—9A 14
Langton Av. Eps—3D 134
Langton Clo. WC1—7K 59
Langton Gro. N'wd—5A 20
Langton Rise. SE23—6F 92
Langton Rd. NW2—8G 41
Langton Rd. SW9—8M 75
Langton Rd. E Mol—8A 102
Langton Rd. Harr—7A 22
Langton St. SW10—7A 74
Langton Way. SE3—9E 78
Langton Way. Croy—6C 124
Langtry Rd. NW8—4M 57
Langtry Rd. N'holt—5H 53
Langtry Wlk. NW8—4A 58
Langwood Chase. Tedd —3G 103
Langwood Gdns. Wat—3E 8
Langworth Clo. Dart—9H 99
Langworth Dri. Hay—9F 52
Langworthy. Pinn—6L 21
Lanhill Rd. W9—7L 57
Lanier Rd. SE13—5B 94
Lankaster Gdns. N2—8B 26
Lankers Dri. Harr—4K 37
Lankton Clo. Beck—5A 110
Lannock Rd. Hay—2D 68
Lannoy Rd. SE9—7A 96
Lanrick Rd. E14—9B 62
Lanridge Rd. SE2—4H 81
Lansbury Av. N18—5B 28
Lansbury Av. Bark—3E 64
Lansbury Av. Felt—5F 84
Lansbury Av. Romf—3J 49
Lansbury Clo. NW10—1A 56
Lansbury Cres. Dart—4L 99
Lansbury Dri. Hay—8D 52
Lansbury Est. E14—9M 61
Lansbury Gdns. E14—9B 62
Lansbury Rd. Enf—3H 17
Lansbury Way. N18—5C 28
Lanscombe Wlk. SW8—9J 75
Lansdell Rd. Mitc—6E 106
Lansdown Clo. W on T—3G 117
Lansdowne Av. Orp—3M 127
Lansdowne Av. Well—8H 81
Lansdowne Clo. SW20—4H 105
Lansdowne Clo. Twic—7D 86
Lansdowne Clo. Wat—8H 5
Lansdowne Ct. Purl—2M 137
Lansdowne Ct. Wor Pk—4E 120
Lansdowne Cres. W11—1J 73
Lansdowne Dri. E8—3E 60
Lansdowne Gdns. SW8—9J 75
Lansdowne Gro. NW10—9C 40
Lansdowne Hill. SE27—9M 91
Lansdowne La. SE7—6H 79
Lansdowne M. SE7—6H 79
Lansdowne M. W11—2K 73
Lansdowne Pl. SE1—4B 76
Lansdowne Pl. SE19—4D 108
Lansdowne Rise. W11—1J 73
Lansdowne Rd. E4—2L 29
Lansdowne Rd. E11—7D 46
Lansdowne Rd. E17—4L 45
Lansdowne Rd. E18—1E 46
Lansdowne Rd. N3—7L 25
Lansdowne Rd. N10—9G 27
Lansdowne Rd. N17—8E 28
Lansdowne Rd. SW20—4G 105
Lansdowne Rd. W11—1J 73
Lansdowne Rd. Brom—4E 110
Lansdowne Rd. Croy—4B 124
Lansdowne Rd. Eps—9B 120
Lansdowne Rd. Harr—5C 38
Lansdowne Rd. Houn—2M 85
Lansdowne Rd. Ilf—6D 48
Lansdowne Rd. Purl—4L 137
Lansdowne Rd. Stan—6G 23
Lansdowne Rd. Uxb—9A 52
Lansdowne Row. W1—2F 74
Lansdowne Ter. WC1—7J 59
Lansdowne Wlk. W11—2K 73
Lansdowne Way. SW8—9H 75
Lansdown Rd. E7—3G 63
Lansdown Rd. Sidc—9F 96
Lansfield Av. N18—4E 28
Lantern Clo. SW15—3E 88
Lantern Clo. Wemb—1H 55
Lant St. SE1—3A 76
Lanvanor Rd. SE15—1G 93
Lapford Clo. W9—7K 57
Lapponum Wlk. Hay—7H 53
Lapse Wood Wlk. SE23—8F 92
Lapstone Gdns. Harr—4G 39
Lapwing Clo. S Croy—2J 139
Lapworth Clo. Orp—4G 129
Lara Clo. Chess—9J 119
Larbert Rd. SW16—4G 107
Larby Pl. Eps—2C 134
Larch Av. W3—2C 72
Larch Av. St Alb—3J 5
Larch Clo. N11—7E 26
Larch Clo. SW12—8F 90
Larch Cres. Eps—8M 119
Larch Cres. Hay—8G 53
Larch Dene. Orp—4L 127
Larches Av. SW14—3B 88
Larches Av. Enf—8C 6
Larches, The. N13—3A 28
Larches, The. Uxb—5F 142
Larches, The. Wat—7H 9
Larch Grn. NW9—8C 24
Larch M. N19—7G 43
Larch Rd. NW2—9G 41
Larch Rd. Dart—6H 99
Larch Tree Way. Croy—5L 125
Larch Way. Brom—2L 127
Larch Way. Swan—6B 114
Larchwood Av. Romf—6M 33
Larchwood Clo. Bans—7J 135
Larchwood Clo. Romf—6A 34
Larchwood Rd. SE9—8M 95
Larcom St. SE17—5A 76
Larden Rd. W3—3C 72
Largewood Av. Surb—4L 119
Larkbere Rd. SE26—1J 109
Larken Dri. Bush, Wat—1A 22
Larkfield Av. Harr—1F 38
Larkfield Clo. Brom—4D 126
Larkfield Rd. Rich—3J 87
Larkfield Rd. Sidc—9D 96
Larkhall Clo. W on T—8G 117
Larkhall La. SW4—1H 91
Larkhall Rise. SW4—2G 91
Lark Row. E2—4G 61
Larksfield Gro. Enf—3F 16
Larkshall Ct. Romf—9A 34
Larkshall Cres. E4—4A 30
Larkshall Rd. E4—5A 30
Larkspur Clo. N17—7B 28
Larkspur Clo. Orp—4G 129
Larkspur Way. Eps—7A 120
Larkswood Ct. E4—5B 30
Larkswood Rise. Pinn—2G 37
Larkswood Rd. E4—4L 29
Larkway Clo. NW9—2B 40
Larmans Rd. Enf—9D 6
Larnach Rd. W6—7H 73
Larne Rd. Ruis—5D 36
Larner Rd. Eri—8C 82
Larpent Av. SW15—4G 89
Larsen Dri. Wal A—7K 7
Larwood Clo. Gnfd—1B 54
Lascelles Av. Harr—5B 38
Lascelles Clo. E11—7B 46
Lascotts Rd. N22—6K 27
Lassa Rd. SE9—4J 95
Lassell St. SE10—6B 78
Latchett Rd. E18—8F 30
Latchford Pl. Chig—4F 32
Latchingdon Gdns. Wfd G —6J 31
Latchmere Clo. Rich—2J 103
Latchmere La. King & Rich —3K 103
Latchmere Pas. SW11—1D 90
Latchmere Rd. SW11—1D 90
Latchmere Rd. King—4J 103
Latchmere St. SW11—1D 90
Lateward Rd. Bren—7H 71
Latham Clo. E6—8J 63
Latham Clo. Twic—6E 86
Latham Clo. West—8G 141
Latham Rd. Bexh—4L 97
Latham Rd. Twic—6D 86
Latham's Way. Croy—3J 123
Lathkill Clo. Enf—9E 16
Lathom Rd. E6—3J 63
Latimer Av. E6—4K 63
Latimer Clo. Pinn—8G 21
Latimer Clo. Wor Pk—6F 120
Latimer Gdns. Pinn—8G 21
Latimer Pl. W10—9G 57
Latimer Rd. E7—9F 46
Latimer Rd. N15—4C 44
Latimer Rd. SW19—3M 105
Latimer Rd. W10—8G 57
Latimer Rd. Barn—5M 13
Latimer Rd. Croy—5M 123
Latimer Rd. Tedd—2D 102
Latona Rd. SE15—7E 76
La Tourne Gdns. Orp—5A 128
Latton Clo. Esh—6M 117
Latton Clo. W on T—2J 117
Latymer Clo. Wey—6A 116
Latymer Ct. W6—5H 73
Latymer Gdns. N3—9J 25
Latymer Rd. N9—1D 28
Latymer Way. N9—2C 28
Lauder Clo. N'holt—5H 53
Lauder Ct. N14—9J 15
Lauderdale Dri. Rich—9H 87
Lauderdale Rd. W9—6M 57
Lauderdale Rd. K Lan—6A 4
Laud St. SE11—6K 75
Laud St. Croy—5A 124
Laughton Rd. N'holt—4H 53
Launcelot Rd. Brom—1E 110
Launcelot St. SE1—3L 75
Launceston Clo. Romf—8G 35
Launceston Gdns. Gnfd—3G 55
Launceston Pl. W8—4A 74
Launceston Rd. Gnfd—4G 55
Launch St. E14—4A 78
Launder's La. Rain—8J 67
Laundry Rd. E4—1B 30
Laundry Rd. W6—7J 73
Laura Clo. E11—3G 47
Laura Clo. Enf—7C 16
Lauradale Rd. N2—2D 42
Laura Dri. Swan—4E 114
Laura Pl. E5—9G 45
Laurel Av. Twic—7D 86
Laurel Bank Gdns. SW6—1K 89
Laurel Bank Rd. Enf—3B 16
Laurel Clo. N19—7G 43
Laurel Clo. Dart—7G 99
Laurel Clo. Ilf—6B 32
Laurel Clo. Sidc—9E 96
Laurel Cres. Croy—5L 125
Laurel Cres. Romf—6C 50
Laurel Dri. N21—9L 15
Laurel Gdns. E4—9M 17
Laurel Gdns. NW7—3B 24
Laurel Gdns. W7—2C 70
Laurel Gdns. Houn—3J 85
Laurel Gro. SE20—4G 109
Laurel Gro. SE26—1H 109
Laurel La. W Dray—5J 143
Laurel Lodge La. Barn—1G 13
Laurel Pk. Harr—7D 22
Laurel Rd. SW13—1E 88
Laurel Rd. SW20—5F 104
Laurel Rd. Tedd—2B 102
Laurels, The. Dart—9G 99
Laurels, The. Wey—5B 116
Laurel St. E8—2D 60
Laurel View. N12—3M 25
Laurel Way. E18—2D 46
Laurel Way. N20—3L 25
Laurence M. W12—3E 72
Laurence Pountney Hill. EC4 —1B 76
Laurence Pountney La. EC4 —1B 76
Laurie Gro. SE14—9J 77
Laurie Rd. W7—8C 54
Laurier Rd. NW5—8F 42
Laurier Rd. Croy—2D 124
Laurie Wlk. Romf—3C 50
Laurimel Clo. Stan—6F 22
Lauriston Rd. E9—3G 61
Lauriston Rd. SW19—3H 105
Lausanne Rd. N8—2L 43
Lausanne Rd. SE15—9G 77
Lauser Rd. Stai—6A 144
Lavell St. N16—9B 44
Lavender Av. NW9—6A 40
Lavender Av. Mitc—5C 106
Lavender Av. Wor Pk—5G 121
Lavender Clo. SW3—7B 74
Lavender Clo. Cars—6F 122
Lavender Clo. Romf—7H 35
Lavender Clo. Wal X—1A 6
Lavender Gdns. SW11—3D 90
Lavender Gdns. Enf—3M 15
Lavender Gro. E8—3E 60
Lavender Gro. Mitc—5C 106
Lavender Hill. SW11—2D 90
Lavender Hill. Enf—3L 15
Lavender Hill. Swan—7B 114
Lavender Rise. W Dray—3L 143
Lavender Rd. SE16—2J 77
Lavender Rd. SW11—2B 90
Lavender Rd. Cars—6E 122
Lavender Rd. Croy—1K 123
Lavender Rd. Enf—3B 16
Lavender Rd. Eps—7M 119
Lavender Rd. Sutt—6B 122
Lavender Rd. Uxb—8D 142
Lavender St. E15—2C 62
Lavender Sweep. SW11—3D 90
Lavender Ter. SW11—2C 90
Lavender Vale. Wall—8H 123
Lavender Wlk. SW11—3D 90
Lavender Wlk. Mitc—7E 106
Lavender Way. Croy—1H 125
Lavengro Rd. SE27—8A 92
Lavenham Rd. SW18—8K 89
Lavernock Rd. Bexh—1L 97
Lavers Rd. N16—8C 44
Laverstoke Gdns. SW15—6D 88
Laverton Pl. SW5—5M 73
Lavidge Rd. SE9—8J 95
Lavina Gro. N1—5K 59
Lavington Rd. W13—2F 70
Lavington Rd. Croy—5K 123
Lavington St. SE1—2M 75
Lavinia Av. Wat—7H 5
Lavinia Rd. Dart—5K 99
Lawdons Gdns. Croy—6M 123
Lawford Clo. Horn—9G 51
Lawford Clo. Wall—1J 137
Lawford Gdns. Dart—4G 99
Lawford Rd. NW5—2G 59
Lawford Rd. W4—8A 72
Lawless St. E14—1M 77
Lawley Rd. N14—9F 14
Lawley St. E5—9G 45
Lawn Av. W Dray—3G 143
Lawn Clo. N9—9D 16
Lawn Clo. Brom—4F 110
Lawn Clo. N Mald—6C 104
Lawn Clo. Ruis—8D 36
Lawn Clo. Swan—6A 114
Lawn Cres. Rich—1L 87
Lawn Farm Gro. Romf—2J 49
Lawn Gdns. W7—2C 70
Lawn La. SW8—7K 75
Lawn Rd. NW3—1D 58
Lawn Rd. Beck—4K 109
Lawn Rd. Uxb—3A 142
Lawnside. SE3—3D 94
Lawns, The. E4—5L 29
Lawns, The. SE3—2D 94
Lawns, The. SE19—5B 108
Lawns, The. Pinn—7M 21
Lawns, The. Sidc—1G 113
Lawns, The. Sutt—9J 121
Lawnsway. Romf—7A 34
Lawn Ter. SE3—2C 94
Lawn, The. S'hall—6L 69
Lawn Vale. Pinn—9J 21
Lawrence Av. E12—9L 47
Lawrence Av. E17—8M 29
Lawrence Av. N13—4M 27
Lawrence Av. NW7—4C 24
Lawrence Av. N Mald—1B 120
Lawrence Bldgs. N16—8D 44
Lawrence Campe Clo. N20 —3B 26
Lawrence Clo. E3—6L 61
Lawrence Clo. N15—1C 44
Lawrence Ct. NW7—5C 24
Lawrence Cres. Dag—8M 49
Lawrence Cres. Edgw—9L 23
Lawrence Dri. Uxb—9A 36
Lawrence Gdns. NW7—3D 24

Leyborne Av. W13—3F 70
Leyborne Pk. Rich—9L 71
Leybourne Clo. Brom—1E 126
Leybourne Rd. E11—6D 46
Leybourne Rd. NW1—3F 58
 (in two parts)
Leybourne Rd. NW9—3L 39
Leybourne Rd. Uxb—4A 52
Leybourne St. NW1—3F 58
Leybridge Ct. SE12—4E 94
Leyburn Clo. E17—2M 45
Leyburn Cres. Romf—7J 35
Leyburn Gdns. Croy—4C 124
Leyburn Gro. N18—6E 28
Leyburn Rd. N18—6E 28
Leyburn Rd. Romf—7J 35
Leycroft Clo. Lou—7L 19
Leycroft Gdns. Eri—9F 82
Leydenhatch La. Swan
 —5A 114
Leyden St. E1—8D 60
Leyes Rd. E16—9G 63
Leyfield. Wor Pk—3C 120
Leyhill Clo. Swan—8C 114
Leyland Av. Enf—4J 17
Leyland Clo. Wal X—2C 6
Leyland Gdns. Wfd G—5G 31
Leyland Rd. SE12—4E 94
Leylang Rd. SE14—8H 77
Ley Rd. Warl—9E 138
Leys Av. Dag—4A 66
Leys Clo. Dag—3A 66
Leys Clo. Harr—3B 38
Leysdown Av. Bexh—3A 98
Leysdown Rd. SE9—8J 95
Leysfield Rd. W12—4E 72
Leys Gdns. Barn—7E 14
Leyspring Rd. E11—6D 46
Leys Rd. Lea—4B 132
Leys Rd. E. Enf—3J 17
Leys Rd. W. Enf—3J 17
Leys Sq. N3—8M 25
Leys, The. N2—2A 42
Leys, The. Harr—4K 39
Ley St. Ilf—7M 47
Leyswood Dri. Ilf—3C 48
Leythe Rd. W3—3A 72
Leyton Ct. SE23—7G 93
Leyton Cross Rd. Dart—9D 98
Leyton Grange Est. E10—6M 45
Leyton Grn. Rd. E10—4A 46
Leyton Pk. Rd. E10—8A 46
Leyton Rd. E15—1A 62
Leyton Rd. SW19—4A 106
Leytonstone Rd. E15—1C 62
Leyton Way. E11—5C 46
Leywick St. E15—5C 62
Lezayre Rd. Orp—8D 128
Liardet St. SE14—7J 77
Liberia Rd. N5—2M 59
Liberty Av. SW19—5B 106
Liberty St. SW9—9K 75
Liberty, The. Romf—3C 50
Libra Rd. E3—5K 61
Libra Rd. E13—5E 62
Library Pl. E1—1F 76
Library St. SE1—3M 75
Lichfield Gdns. Rich—3J 87
Lichfield Gro. N3—8L 25
Lichfield Rd. E3—6J 61
Lichfield Rd. E6—6H 63
Lichfield Rd. N9—2E 28
Lichfield Rd. NW2—9J 41
Lichfield Rd. Dag—9F 48
Lichfield Rd. Houn—2G 85
Lichfield Rd. N'wd—1E 36
Lichfield Rd. Rich—9H 71
Lichfield Rd. Wfd G—4C 30
Lichfield Way. S Croy—2H 139
Lichlade Clo. Orp—6D 128
Lidbury Rd. NW7—6J 25
Lidcote Gdns. SW9—1L 91
Liddall Way. W Dray—2K 143
Liddell Gdns. NW10—5G 57
Liddell Rd. NW6—2L 57
Lidding Rd. Harr—3H 39
Liddington Rd. E15—4D 62
Liddon Rd. E13—6F 62
Liddon Rd. Brom—7G 111
Lidell Clo. Harr—1H 39
Lidfield Rd. N16—9B 44
Lidiard Rd. SW18—8A 90
Lidlington Pl. NW1—5G 59
Lidyard Rd. N19—6G 43
Liffler Rd. SE18—6C 80
Liffords Pl. SW13—1D 88
Lifford St. SW15—3H 89
Lightcliffe Rd. N13—4L 27
Lighterman's Rd. E14—3L 77
Lightfoot Rd. N8—3J 43
Lightley Clo. Wemb—4J 55
Ligonier St. E2—7D 60
Lilac Clo. E4—6K 29

Lilac Clo. Wal X—4B 6
Lilac Gdns. W5—4H 71
Lilac Gdns. Croy—5L 125
Lilac Gdns. Hay—9C 52
Lilac Gdns. Romf—6C 50
Lilac Gdns. Swan—7B 114
Lilac Pl. SE11—5K 75
Lilac Pl. W Dray—1K 143
Lilacs Av. Enf—9C 6
Lilac St. W12—1E 72
Lila Pl. Swan—8C 114
Lilburne Gdns. SE9—4J 95
Lilburne Rd. SE9—4J 95
Lilburne Wlk. NW10—2A 56
Lile Cres. W7—8C 54
Lilestone St. NW8—7C 58
Lilford Rd. SE5—1M 91
Lilian Board Way. Gnfd—1B 54
Lilian Clo. N16—8C 44
Lilian Gdns. Wfd G—8F 30
Lilian Rd. SW16—5G 107
Lillechurch Rd. Dag—2F 64
Lilley La. NW7—5B 24
Lillian Av. W3—3L 71
Lillian Rd. SW13—7F 72
Lillie Rd. SW6—7J 73
Lillie Rd. West—9H 141
Lillieshall Rd. SW4—2F 90
Lillieshall Rd. Mord—1B 122
Lillie Yd. SW6—7L 73
Lillington Gdns. Est. SW1
 —5G 75
Lilliput Av. N'holt—4J 53
Lilliput Ct. SE12—4F 94
Lilliput Rd. Romf—5B 50
Lillyville Rd. SW6—9K 73
Lily Clo. W14—5H 73
Lily Gdns. Wemb—5G 55
Lily Pl. EC1—8L 59
Lily Rd. E17—4L 45
Limbourne Av. Dag—5K 49
Limburg Rd. SW11—3C 90
Lime Av. Upm—9L 51
Lime Av. W Dray—1K 143
Lime Clo. Buck H—2H 31
Lime Clo. Cars—4D 122
Lime Clo. Romf—2A 50
Lime Clo. Wat—9H 9
Lime Cres. Sun—6G 101
Limecroft Clo. Eps—9B 120
Limedene Clo. Pinn—8H 21
Lime Gro. N20—1K 25
Lime Gro. W12—3G 73
Lime Gro. Hay—1B 68
Lime Gro. Ilf—6D 32
Lime Gro. N Mald—7B 104
Lime Gro. Orp—4M 127
Lime Gro. Ruis—4F 36
Lime Gro. Sidc—5D 96
Lime Gro. Twic—5D 86
Limeharbour. E14—4M 77
Limehouse Causeway. E14
 —1K 77
Limehouse Fields Est. E14
 —8J 61
Lime Meadow Av. S Croy
 —5E 138
Limerick Clo. SW12—6G 91
Lime Rd. Rich—3K 87
Lime Rd. Swan—7B 114
Lime Row. Eri—4K 81
Limerston St. SW10—7A 74
Limes Av. E11—2F 46
Limes Av. N12—4A 26
Limes Av. NW7—6C 24
Limes Av. NW11—5J 41
Limes Av. SE20—4F 108
Limes Av. SW13—1D 88
Limes Av. Cars—3D 122
Limes Av. Chig—5A 32
Limes Av. Croy—5L 123
Limes Av., The. N11—5G 27
Limesdale Gdns. Edgw—9A 24
Limes Field Rd. SW14—2C 88
Limesford Rd. SE15—3H 93
Limes Gdns. SW18—5L 89
Limes Gro. SE13—3A 94
Limes Pl. Croy—2B 124
Limes Rd. Beck—6M 109
Limes Rd. Croy—2B 124
Limes Rd. Wal X—5E 6
Limes, The. Brom—4J 127
Limestone Wlk. Eri—3H 81
Lime St. E17—2J 45
Lime St. EC3—1C 76
Lime St. Pas. EC3—9C 60
Limes Wlk. SE15—3G 93
Limes Wlk. W5—3H 71
Lime Ter. W7—1C 70
Lime Tree Av. SE20—5F 108
Lime Tree Av. Esh & Th Dit
 —3C 118
Limetree Clo. SW2—7K 91

Lime Tree Ct. Pinn—7L 21
Lime Tree Gro. Croy—5K 125
Lime Tree Pl. Mitc—5F 106
Lime Tree Rd. Houn—9M 69
Lime Tree Wlk. Bush, Wat
 —2C 22
Lime Tree Wlk. Enf—2A 16
Lime Tree Wlk. W Wick
 —6D 126
Lime Wlk. Uxb—1A 142
Limewood Clo. W13—9F 54
Limewood Rd. Eri—8A 82
Limpsfield Av. SW19—8H 89
Limpsfield Av. T Hth—5F 106
Limpsfield Av. S Croy & Warl
 —4E 138
Linacre Rd. NW2—2F 56
Linberry Wlk. SE8—5K 77
Linchmere Rd. SE12—6D 94
Lincoln Av. N14—3G 27
Lincoln Av. SW19—9H 89
Lincoln Av. Romf—6C 50
Lincoln Av. Twic—8A 86
Lincoln Clo. Eri—1D 98
Lincoln Clo. Gnfd—4A 54
Lincoln Clo. Harr—3K 37
Lincoln Clo. Horn—3L 51
Lincoln Ct. Borwd—7B 12
Lincoln Cres. Enf—7C 16
Lincoln Dri. Wat—3G 21
Lincoln Gdns. Ilf—5J 47
Lincoln Grn. Rd. Orp—9D 112
Lincoln M. NW6—4K 57
Lincoln Rd. E7—2H 63
Lincoln Rd. E13—7F 62
Lincoln Rd. E18—8E 30
Lincoln Rd. N2—1C 42
Lincoln Rd. SE25—7F 108
Lincoln Rd. Enf—6C 16
Lincoln Rd. Eri—1D 98
Lincoln Rd. Felt—9K 85
Lincoln Rd. Harr—3K 37
Lincoln Rd. Mitc—9J 107
Lincoln Rd. N Mald—7A 104
Lincoln Rd. N'wd—1D 36
Lincoln Rd. Sidc—2F 112
Lincoln Rd. Wemb—2H 55
Lincoln Rd. Wor Pk—3F 120
Lincoln's Inn Fields. WC2
 —9K 59
Lincolns, The. NW7—3D 24
Lincoln St. E11—7C 46
Lincoln St. SW3—5D 74
Lincoln Wlk. Eps—2B 134
 (in two parts)
Lincoln Way. Enf—7F 16
Lincoln Way. Sun—5C 100
Lincombe Rd. Brom—9D 94
Lindal Cres. Enf—6J 15
Lindal Rd. SE4—4K 93
Lindbergh Rd. Wall—9J 123
Linden Av. NW10—5H 57
Linden Av. Coul—8F 136
Linden Av. Dart—7G 99
Linden Av. Enf—3E 16
Linden Av. Houn—4M 85
Linden Av. Ruis—6E 36
Linden Av. T Hth—8M 107
Linden Av. Wemb—1K 55
Linden Clo. N14—8G 15
Linden Clo. Orp—7E 128
Linden Clo. Ruis—6E 36
Linden Clo. Stan—5F 22
Linden Clo. Th Dit—2D 118
Linden Ct. W12—2G 73
Linden Ct. Sidc—1C 112
Linden Cres. Gnfd—2D 54
Linden Cres. King—6K 103
Linden Cres. Wfd G—6F 30
Lindenfield. Chst—6M 111
Linden Gdns. W2—1L 73
Linden Gdns. W4—6C 72
Linden Gdns. Enf—3E 16
Linden Gro. SE15—2F 92
Linden Gro. SE26—3G 109
Linden Gro. N Mald—7C 104
Linden Gro. Tedd—2D 102
Linden Gro. W on T—4D 116
Linden Gro. Warl—9J 139
Linden Lea. N2—3A 42
Linden Lea. Wat—6E 8
Linden Leas. W Wick—4B 126
Linden M. W2—1L 73
Linden Pl. Eps—4C 134
Linden Rd. E17—3K 45
Linden Rd. N10—2F 42
Linden Rd. N11—2D 26
Linden Rd. N15—2A 44
Linden Rd. Hmptn—5L 101
Lindens Lawns. Wemb—9K 39
Lindens, The. W4—9A 72
Lindens, The. Croy—8A 126
Lindens The. Lou—7L 19

Linden St. Romf—2B 50
Linden Way. N14—8G 15
Linden Way. Purl—2G 137
Linden Way. Shep—9A 100
Lindfield Gdns. NW3—1A 58
Lindfield Rd. W5—7G 55
Lindfield Rd. Croy—1D 124
Lindfield Rd. Romf—5J 35
Lindfield St. E14—9L 61
Lindisfarne Rd. SW20—4E 104
Lindisfarne Rd. Dag—8G 49
Lindisfarne Way. E9—9J 45
Lindley Rd. E10—7A 46
Lindley Rd. W on T—4H 117
Lindley St. E1—8G 61
Lindore Rd. SW11—3D 90
Lindores Rd. Cars—3A 122
Lind Rd. Sutt—7A 122
Lindrop St. SW6—1A 90
Lindsay Clo. Chess—9J 119
Lindsay Clo. Eps—5A 134
Lindsay Clo. Stai—4B 144
Lindsay Dri. Harr—4J 39
Lindsay Dri. Shep—1B 116
Lindsay Rd. Hmptn—1M 101
Lindsay Rd. Wor Pk—4F 120
Lindsell St. SE10—9A 78
Lindsey Clo. Brom—7J 111
Lindsey Clo. Mitc—8J 107
Lindsey Gdns. Felt—6B 84
Lindsey M. N1—3A 60
Lindsey Rd. Dag—9G 49
Lindsey St. EC1—8M 59
Lindsey Way. Horn—3G 51
Lind St. SE8—1L 93
Lindum Rd. Tedd—4G 103
Lindway. SE27—2M 107
Linfield Clo. W on T—7F 116
Linford Rd. E17—1A 46
Linford St. SW8—9G 75
Lingards Rd. SE13—3A 94
Lingey Clo. Sidc—8D 96
Lingfield Av. Dart—6M 99
Lingfield Av. King—8J 103
Lingfield Av. Upm—8K 51
Lingfield Clo. Enf—8C 16
Lingfield Clo. N'wd—7C 20
Lingfield Cres. SE9—3B 96
Lingfield Gdns. N9—9F 16
Lingfield Rd. SW19—2H 105
Lingfield Rd. Wor Pk—5G 121
Lingham St. SW9—1J 91
Lingholm Way. Barn—7H 13
Lingmere Clo. Chig—2A 32
Ling Rd. E16—8E 62
Ling Rd. Eri—7A 82
Lingrove Gdns. Buck H—2F 30
Lings Coppice. SE21—8B 92
Lingwell Rd. SW17—9C 90
Lingwood. Bexh—1M 97
Lingwood Gdns. Iswth—8C 70
Lingwood Rd. E5—5E 44
Linhope St. NW1—7D 58
Linkfield. Brom—1E 126
Linkfield. E Mol—7M 101
Linkfield Rd. Iswth—1D 86
Link La. Wall—8H 123
Linklea Clo. NW9—7C 24
Link Rd. N8—1L 43
Link Rd. N11—4E 26
Link Rd. Dag—5M 65
Link Rd. Felt—6D 84
Link Rd. Wall—3E 122
Link Rd. Wat & Bush, Wat—4H 9
Links Av. Mord—8L 105
Links Av. Romf—9F 34
Links Clo. Asht—9G 133
Links Dri. N20—1L 25
Links Dri. Borwd—5K 11
Links Gdns. SW16—4L 107
Links Pl. Asht—9H 133
Links Rd. NW2—7D 40
Links Rd. SW17—3E 106
Links Rd. W3—9L 55
Links Rd. Asht—9G 133
Links Rd. Eps—5E 134
Links Rd. W Wick—3A 126
Links Rd. Wfd G—5E 30
Links Side. Enf—5L 15
Links, The. E17—2J 45
Links, The. W on T—4E 116
Link St. E9—2G 61
Links View. N3—7K 25
Links View. Dart—7G 99
Links View Clo. Stan—6E 22
Links View Rd. Croy—5L 125
Links View Rd. Hmptn—2A 102
Linksway. NW4—9H 25

Links Way. Beck—1L 125
Links Way. N'wd—7A 20
Links Way. Rick—5A 8
Link, The. W3—9M 55
Link, The. Enf—3J 17
Link, The. N'holt—1K 53
Link, The. Pinn—5G 37
Link, The. Wemb—6G 39
Linkway. N4—5A 44
Linkway. SW20—7F 104
Link Way. Brom—2J 127
Linkway. Dag—9G 49
Link Way. Horn—6J 51
Link Way. Pinn—8H 21
Linkway. Rich—8F 86
Linkway, The. Barn—8M 13
Linkway, The. Sutt—1A 136
Linley Cres. Romf—1M 49
Linley Rd. N17—9C 28
Linnell Clo. NW11—4M 41
Linnell Dri. NW11—4M 41
Linnell Rd. N18—5E 28
Linnell Rd. SE5—1C 92
Linnet Clo. SE28—1G 81
Linnet Clo. Bush, Wat—9A 10
Linnet Clo. S Croy—2H 139
Linnet M. SW12—6E 90
Linnett Clo. E4—4A 30
Linom Rd. SW4—3J 91
Linscott Rd. E5—9G 45
Linsdell Rd. Bark—4A 64
Linsey St. SE16—5E 76
 (in two parts)
Linslade Rd. Orp—8E 128
Linstead St. NW6—3L 57
Linstead Way. SW18—6J 89
Linster Gro. Borwd—7A 12
Lintaine Clo. W6—7J 73
Linthorpe Av. Wemb—2G 55
Linthorpe Rd. N16—5C 44
Linthorpe Rd. Barn—5C 14
Linton Av. Borwd—4K 11
Linton Clo. Well—9F 80
Linton Ct. Romf—9C 34
Linton Gdns. E6—8J 63
Linton Glade. Croy—1J 139
 (in two parts)
Linton Gro. SE27—2A 108
Linton Rd. Bark—3A 64
Lintons La. Eps—4C 134
Linton St. N1—4A 60
Lintott Ct. Stai—5B 144
Linver Rd. SW6—1L 89
Linwood Clo. E6—8K 63
Linzee Rd. N8—2J 43
Lion Av. Twic—7D 86
Lionel Gdns. SE9—4H 95
Lionel M. W10—8J 57
Lionel Rd. SE9—4H 95
Lionel Rd. Bren—4J 71
 (in two parts)
Lion Ga. Gdns. Rich—2K 87
Lion Grn. Rd. Coul—8H 137
Lion Pk. Av. Chess—6L 119
Lion Rd. N9—2E 28
Lion Rd. Bexh—3J 97
Lion Rd. Croy—9A 108
Lion Rd. Twic—7D 86
Lions Clo. SE9—9H 95
Lion Way. Bren—8H 71
Lion Wharf. Iswth—2F 86
Liphook Clo. Horn—9D 50
Liphook Cres. SE23—6G 93
Liphook Rd. Wat—4H 21
Lippitts Hill. Lou—3C 18
Lipsham Clo. Bans—5B 136
Lipton Clo. SE28—1G 81
Lipton Rd. E1—9H 61
Lisbon Av. Twic—8A 86
Lisburne Rd. NW3—9D 42
Lisford St. SE15—9D 76
Lisgar Ter. W14—5K 73
Liskeard Clo. Chst—3A 112
Liskeard Gdns. SE3—9E 78
Lisle St. WC2—1H 75
Lismore Clo. Iswth—1E 86
Lismore Rd. N17—1B 44
Lismore Rd. S Croy—8C 124
Lissenden Gdns. NW5—9E 42
Lisson Gro.—7B 58
 NW1 1-135 & 2-116
 NW8 remainder
Lisson St. NW1—8C 58
Liss Way. SE15—8D 76
Lister Gdns. N18—5A 28
Lister M. N7—9K 43
Lister Rd. E11—6C 46
Lister St. E13—6E 62
Lister Wlk. SE28—1H 81
Liston Rd. N17—8E 28
Liston Rd. SW4—2G 91
Liston Way. Wfd G—7G 31
Listowel Clo. SW9—8M 75

Listowel Rd. Dag—8L 49
Listria Pk. N16—7C 44
Litchfield Av. E15—2C 62
Litchfield Av. Mord—2K 121
Litchfield Gdns. NW10—2E 56
Litchfield Rd. Sutt—6A 122
Litchfield St. WC2—1H 75
Litchfield Way. NW11—3M 41
Lithgow's Rd. Houn—3C 84
Lithos Rd. NW3—2M 57
Lit. Acre. Beck—7L 109
Lit. Argyll St. W1—9G 59
Lit. Aston Rd. Romf—7K 35
Lit. Benty. W Dray—6H 143
Lit. Birches. Sidc—8C 96
Lit. Boltons, The. SW10—6M 73
Lit. Bornes. SE21—1C 108
Lit. Britain. EC1—8M 59
Littlebrook Gdns. Wal X—3D 6
—4L 99
Lit. Brownings. SE23—8F 92
Littlebury Rd. SW4—2H 91
Lit. Bury St. N9—9C 16
Lit. Bushey La. Bush, Wat—5L 9
Lit. Cedars. N12—4A 26
Lit. Chester St. SW1—4F 74
Lit. College St. SW1—4J 75
Littlecombe. SE7—7F 78
Littlecombe Clo. SW15—5H 89
Littlecote Clo. SW19—6J 89
Littlecote Pl. Pinn—8J 21
Little Ct. W Wick—4C 126
Littledale. SE7—2L 95
Lit. Dimocks. SW12—8F 90
Lit. Dorrit Ct. SE1—3A 76
Lit. Dragons. Lou—6H 19
Lit. Ealing La. W5—5G 71
Lit. Edward St. NW1—6F 58
Lit. Elms. Hay—8B 68
Lit. Ferry Rd. Twic—7F 86
Littlefield Clo. N19—9G 43
Littlefield Rd. Edgw—7A 24
Lit. Friday Hill. E4—2C 30
Lit. Gaynes Gdns. Upm—9M 51
Lit. Gaynes La. Upm—9L 51
Lit. Gearies. Ilf—2M 47
Lit. George St. SW1—3J 75
Lit. Gerpins La. Upm—4K 67
Lit. Graylings. Abb L, Wat—6C 4
Lit. Green. Rich—3H 87
Lit. Green La. Rick—5A 8
Lit. Green St. NW5—9F 42
Littlegrove. Barn—8E 14
Lit. Grove. Bush, Wat—6M 9
Lit. Heath. SE7—7J 79
Lit. Heath. Romf—2F 48
Lit. Heath Rd. Bexh—9K 81
Littleheath Rd. S Croy—9F 124
Lit. Holt. E11—3E 46
Lit. How Croft. Abb L, Wat
—4A 4
Lit. Ilford La. E12—9K 47
Lit. John Rd. W7—9D 54
Littlejohn Rd. Orp—1E 128
Lit. Martins. Bush, Wat—7M 9
Littlemead. Esh—6B 118
Littlemede. SE9—9K 95
Littlemoor Rd. Ilf—8B 48
Littlemore Rd. SE2—3E 80
Lit. Moss La. Pinn—9J 21
Lit. Newport St. WC2—1H 75
Lit. New St. EC4—9L 59
Lit. Orchard Clo. Pinn—9J 21
Lit. Oxhey La. Wat—5H 21
Lit. Park Dri. Felt—8J 85
Lit. Park Gdns. Enf—5B 16
Lit. Pluckett's Way. Buck H
—1H 31
Lit. Portland St. W1—9G 59
Lit. Potters. Bush, Wat—8F 10
Lit. Queen's Rd. Tedd—3D 102
Lit. Queen St. Dart—6K 99
Lit. Redlands. Brom—6J 111
Little Rd. Hay—3D 68
Lit. Roke Av. Kenl—6M 137
Lit. Roke Rd. Kenl—6A 138
Littlers Clo. SW19—5B 106
Lit. Russell St. WC1—8J 59
Lit. Saint James's St. SW1
—2G 75
Lit. Saint Leonard's. SW14
—2A 88
Lit. Sanctuary. SW1—3H 75
Lit. Smith St. SW1—4H 75
Lit. Somerset St. E1—9D 60
Littlestone Clo. Beck—3L 109
Lit. Strand. NW9—9D 24
Lit. Stream Clo. N'wd—5C 20
Lit. Thrift. Orp—8A 112
Lit. Titchfield St. W1—8G 59
Littleton Av. E4—1D 30

Littleton Cres. Harr—7D 38
Littleton Rd. Ashf—4A 100
Littleton Rd. Harr—7D 38
Littleton St. SW18—8A 90
Lit. Trinity La. EC4—1A 76
Lit. Venice. W2—8A 58
Littlewood. SE13—5A 94
Littlewood Clo. W13—4F 70
Lit. Woodcote La. Cars & Purl
—4F 136
Littleworth Av. Esh—7B 118
Littleworth Comn. Rd. Esh
—5B 118
Littleworth La. Esh—6B 118
Littleworth Rd. Esh—7B 118
Livermere Rd. E8—4D 60
Liverpool Gro. SE17—6B 76
Liverpool Rd. E10—4A 46
Liverpool Rd. E16—8C 62
Liverpool Rd.—2L 59
N1 1-393 & 2-296
N7 remainder
Liverpool Rd. W5—3H 71
Liverpool Rd. King—4L 103
Liverpool Rd. T Hth—7A 108
Liverpool Rd. Wat—7F 8
Liverpool St. EC2—8C 60
Livesey Pl. SE15—7E 76
Livingstone Pl. E14—6A 78
Livingstone Rd. E15—4A 62
Livingstone Rd. E17—4M 45
Livingstone Rd. N13—6J 27
Livingstone Rd. SW11—2B 90
Livingstone Rd. Houn—3A 86
Livingstone Rd. S'hall—1H 69
Livingstone Rd. T Hth—6B 108
Livingstone Ter. Rain—4C 66
Livonia St. W1—9G 59
Lizard St. EC1—6A 60
Lizban St. SE3—8F 78
Llanelly Rd. NW2—7K 41
Llanover Rd. SE18—7L 79
Llanover Rd. Wemb—8H 39
Llanthony Rd. Mord—9B 106
Llanvanor Rd. NW2—7K 41
Llewellyn St. SE16—3E 76
Lloyd Av. SW16—5J 107
Lloyd Av. Coul—6E 136
Lloyd Baker St. WC1—6L 59
Lloyd Ct. Pinn—3H 37
Lloyd Pk. Av. Croy—6D 124
Lloyd Rd. E6—4K 63
Lloyd Rd. E17—2H 45
Lloyd Rd. Dag—3K 65
Lloyd Rd. Wor Pk—5G 121
Lloyd's Av. EC3—9C 60
Lloyd's Pl. SE3—1C 94
Lloyd Sq. WC1—6L 59
Lloyd's Row. EC1—6L 59
Lloyd St. WC1—6L 59
Lloyds Way. Beck—9J 109
Loampit Hill. SE13—1L 93
Loampit Vale. SE13—2M 93
Loates La. Wat—5G 9
Loats Rd. SW2—5J 91
Local Board Rd. Wat—7G 9
Locarno Rd. W3—2A 72
Locarno Rd. Gnfd—7B 54
Lochaber Rd. SE13—3C 94
Lochaline St. W6—7G 73
Lochan Clo. Hay—7J 53
Lochinvar St. SW12—6F 90
Lochmere Clo. Eri—7M 81
Lochnagar St. E14—8A 62
Lock Chase. SE3—2C 94
Locke Clo. Rain—2D 66
Locker Wlk. Wemb—8H 39
Lockesley Dri. Orp—1D 128
Lockesley Sq. Surb—1H 119
Locket Rd. Harr—1C 38
Lockfield Av. Enf—4J 17
Lockhart Clo. N7—2K 59
Lockhart St. E3—7K 61
Lockhurst St. E5—9H 45
Lockington Rd. SW8—9F 74
Lockmead Rd. N15—4E 44
Lockmead Rd. SE13—2A 94
Lock Rd. Rich—1G 103
Locks La. Mitc—5E 106
Locksley Est. E14—9K 61
Locksley St. E14—8K 61
Locksmeade Rd. Rich—1G 103
Lockwood Clo. SE26—1H 109
Lockwood Sq. SE16—4F 76
Lockwood Wlk. Romf—3C 50
Lockwood Way. E17—9H 29
Lockwood Way. Chess—7L 119
Lockyer St. SE1—3B 76
Loddiges Rd. E9—3G 61
Loder St. SE15—8G 77
Lodge Av. SW14—2C 88
Lodge Av. Borwd—7K 11

Lodge Av. Croy—5L 123
Lodge Av. Dag—4E 64
Lodge Av. Dart—5G 99
Lodge Av. Harr—2J 39
Lodge Av. Romf—2E 50
Lodge Clo. N18—5A 28
Lodge Clo. Chig—3E 32
Lodge Clo. Edgw—6K 23
Lodge Clo. Iswth—9F 70
Lodge Clo. Orp—3F 128
Lodge Clo. Uxb—7A 142
Lodge Clo. Wall—3E 122
Lodge Ct. Horn—7J 51
Lodge Cres. Orp—3F 128
Lodge Cres. Wal X—7D 6
Lodge Dri. N13—4L 27
Lodge End. Rick—6B 8
Lodge Gdns. Beck—9K 109
Lodge Hill. Ilf—2J 47
Lodge Hill. Purl—7L 137
Lodge Hill. Well—8F 80
Lodge La. N12—5A 26
Lodge La. Bex—5H 97
Lodge La. Croy—8L 125
Lodge La. Romf—7L 33
Lodge La. Wal X—8K 7
Lodge Pl. Sutt—7M 121
Lodge Rd. NW4—2G 41
Lodge Rd. NW8—6B 58
Lodge Rd. Brom—4G 111
Lodge Rd. Croy—1M 123
Lodge Rd. Wall—7F 122
Lodge Vs. Wfd G—7D 30
Lodge Way. Ashf—8C 144
Lodge Way. Shep—6A 100
Lodore Gdns. NW9—3C 40
Lodore St. E14—9A 62
Loftie St. SE16—3F 76
Lofting Rd. N1—3L 59
Loftus Rd. W12—2F 72
Logan Clo. Enf—3H 17
Logan Clo. Houn—2K 85
Logan M. W8—5L 73
Logan Pl. W8—5L 73
Logan Rd. N9—2F 28
Logan Rd. Wemb—7H 39
Logs Hill. Chst—4J 111
Logs Hill Clo. Chst—5J 111
Lois Dri. Shep—9A 100
Lolesworth Clo. E1—8D 60
Lollard St. SE11—5K 75
Loman St. SE1—3M 75
Lomas Clo. Croy—9A 126
Lomas St. E1—8E 60
Lombard Av. Enf—3G 17
Lombard Av. Ilf—6C 48
Lombard Ct. EC3—1B 76
Lombard La. EC4—9L 59
Lombard Rd. N11—5F 26
Lombard Rd. SW11—1B 90
Lombard Rd. SW19—6M 105
Lombard St. EC3—9B 60
Lombard St. S Dar, Dart
—9M 115
Lombard Wall. SE7—4F 78
(in two parts)
Lombardy Pl. W2—1M 73
Lombardy Way. Borwd—3J 11
Lomond Clo. N15—3C 44
Lomond Clo. Wemb—3K 55
Lomond Gro. SE5—8B 76
Lomond Ho. SE15—8D 76
Loncroft Rd. SE5—7C 76
Londesborough Rd. N16
—9C 44
Londondale Clo. SE0 0H 06
London Bri. SE1 & EC4—2B 76
London Bri. St. SE1—2B 76
London Fields E. Side. E8
—3F 60
London Fields W. Side. E8
—3E 60
London Industrial Pk. E6
—8L 63
London La. E8—3F 60
London La. Brom—4D 110
London M. W2—9B 58
London Rd. E13—5E 62
London Rd. SE1—4M 75
London Rd. SE23—7F 92
London Rd.—5K 107
SW16 1102-1544 & 1109-1599
T Hth & Croy remainder
London Rd.—8C 106
SW17 1-59 & 2-66
Mitc remainder
London Rd. Ashf & Felt
—9A 144
London Rd. Bark—3M 63
London Rd. Brom—4D 110
London Rd. Bush, Wat—8J 9
London Rd. Dart—4B 98
London Rd. Dart, Grnh & Swans
—6M 99

London Rd. Enf—7B 16
London Rd. Eps & Wor Pk
—9E 120
London Rd. Harr—7C 38
London Rd. Houn, Iswth & Bren
—2A 86
London Rd. King—6K 103
London Rd. Mitc & Wall
—2E 122
London Rd. Mord—9L 105
London Rd. Purf & Grays
—6L 83
London Rd. Rain & Purf
—2K 83
London Rd. Romf—4L 49
London Rd. Sev—9J 129
London Rd. Shen, Rad & Borwd
—1A 12
London Rd. Stan—5G 23
London Rd. Swan—6B 114
London Rd. Swan & F'ham, Dart
—8D 114
London Rd. Twic—6E 86
Londons Clo. Upm—1M 67
London Stile. W4—6L 71
London St. EC3—1C 76
London St. W2—9B 58
London Wall. EC2—8A 60
Long Acre. WC2—1J 75
Long Acre. Orp—4H 129
Longacre Pl. Cars—8E 122
Longacre Rd. E17—8B 30
Long Barn Clo. Wat—5E 4
Longbeach Rd. SW11—2D 90
Longberrys. NW2—8K 41
Longbridge Rd. Bark & Dag
—2B 64
Longbridge Way. SE13—4A 94
Longbury Clo. Orp—7F 112
Longcliffe Path. Wat—3E 20
Longcroft. SE9—9K 95
Longcroft. Wat—9F 8
Longcroft Av. Bans—6A 136
Longcroft Dri. Wal X—7F 6
Longcrofte Rd. Edgw—7H 23
Longcroft Rise. Lou—7L 19
Longcrofts. Wal A—7L 7
Long Deacon Rd. E4—1C 30
Longdon Wood Av. Kes
—6J 127
Long Dri. W3—9C 56
Long Dri. Gnfd—4M 53
Long Dri. Ruis—9G 37
Long Elmes. Harr—8M 21
Long Elms. Abb L, Wat—6B 4
Long Elms Clo. Abb L, Wat
—6B 4
Longfellow Rd. E3—6J 61
Longfellow Rd. E17—4K 45
Longfellow Rd. Wor Pk—3E 120
Long Field. NW9—7C 24
Longfield. Brom—5D 110
Longfield. Lou—7H 19
Longfield Av. E17—2J 45
Longfield Av. NW7—7E 24
Longfield Av. W5—1G 71
Longfield Av. Enf—1G 17
Longfield Av. Horn—5D 50
Longfield Av. Wall—3E 122
Longfield Av. Wemb—6J 39
Longfield Cres. SE26—9G 93
Longdown La. N. Eps—6E 134
Longdown La. S. Eps—7E 134
Longdown Rd. SE6—1L 109
Longdown Rd. Eps—6E 134
Longfield Dri. SW14—4M 87
Longfield La. Wal X—1A 6
Longfield Rd. W5—9G 55
Longfield St. SW18—6L 89
Longfield Wlk. W5—9G 55
Longford Av. Felt—5C 84
Longford Av. S'hall—1M 69
Longford Av. Stai—7C 144
Longford Clo. Hmptn—1L 101
Longford Clo. Hay—1H 69
Longford Ct. Eps—6A 120
Longford Gdns. Hay—1H 69
Longford Gdns. Sutt—4A 122
Longford Rd. Twic—7M 85
Longford St. NW1—7F 58
Longford Wlk. SW2—6L 91
Longford Way. Stai—7C 144
Long Grn. Chig—4C 32
Long Grove Rd. Eps—2M 133
Longhayes Av. Romf—2H 49
Longheath Gdns. Croy—9G 109
Long Hedges. Houn—9L 69
Longhedge St. SW11—1E 90
Longhill Rd. SE6—8B 94
Longhook Gdns. N'holt—6F 52
Longhurst Rd. SE13—4B 94
Longhurst Rd. Croy—1F 124
Longland Ct. SE1—6E 76

Longland Dri. N20—3M 25
Longlands Av. Coul—6E 136
Longlands Clo. Wal X—5D 6
Longlands Pk. Cres. Sidc
—9C 96
Longlands Rd. Sidc—9C 96
Long La. EC1—8M 59
Long La.—8M 25
N3 1-223 & 2-280
N2 remainder
Long La. SE1—3B 76
Long La. Bexh—8H 81
Long La. Croy—1G 125
Long La. Stai—8D 144
Long La. Uxb—6E 142
Longleat Rd. Enf—7C 16
Longleat Way. Felt—6B 84
Longleigh La. SE2 & Bex H
—7G 81
Longley Av. Wemb—4K 55
Longley Rd. SW17—3C 106
Longley Rd. Croy—2M 123
Longley Rd. Harr—3A 38
Long Leys. E4—6A 30
Longley St. SE1—5E 76
Long Lodge Dri. W on T
—5G 117
Longmarsh View. S at H, Dart
—5M 115
Long Mead. NW9—8D 24
Longmead. Chst—6L 111
Longmead Dri. Sidc—8H 97
Longmead Ho. SE27—2A 108
Long Meadow. NW5—1H 59
Longmeadow Rd. Sidc—7C 96
Longmead Rd. SW17—2D 106
Longmead Rd. Eps—3B 134
Longmead Rd. Hay—1D 68
Longmead Rd. Th Dit—2C 118
Long Moor. Wal X—2E 6
Longmoore St. SW1—5G 75
Longmore Av. Barn—8A 14
Longmore Rd. W on T—6J 117
Longnor Est. E1—6H 61
Longnor Rd. E1—6H 61
Long Pond Rd. SE3—9C 78
Longport Clo. Ilf—6E 32
Long Reach Rd. Bark—7D 64
Longreach Rd. Eri—8F 82
Longridge La. S'hall—9M 53
Longridge Rd. SW5—5L 73
Long Rd. SW4—3G 91
Longshaw Rd. E4—3B 30
Longshore. SE8—5K 77
Longspring. Wat—1F 8
Longstaff Cres. SW18—6L 89
Longstaff Rd. SW18—5L 89
Longstone Av. NW10—3D 56
Longstone Rd. SW17—2F 106
Long St. E2—6D 60
(in two parts)
Longthornton Rd. SW16
—6G 107
Longton Av. SE26—1E 108
Longton Gro. SE26—1F 108
Longtown Clo. Romf—5G 35
Longtown Rd. Romf—5G 35
Longview Way. Romf—8B 34
Longville Rd. SE11—5M 75
Long Wlk. SE1—4C 76
Long Wlk. SE18—7M 79
Long Wlk. SW13—1D 88
Long Wlk. N Mald—7A 104
Long Wlk. Wal A—3G 7
Long Wall. E15—0D 62
Long Wlk. Wal A—3G 7
Longwood Clo. Upm—1M 67
Longwood Dri. SW15—5E 88
Longwood Gdns. Ilf—2K 47
Longwood Rd. Kenl—8B 138
Long Yd. WC1—7K 59
Loning, The. NW9—2D 40
Loning, The. Enf—2G 17
Lonsdale Av. E6—7H 63
Lonsdale Av. Romf—4A 50
Lonsdale Av. Wemb—1J 55
Lonsdale Clo. E6—7J 63
Lonsdale Clo. Pinn—7J 21
Lonsdale Clo. Uxb—8A 52
Lonsdale Ct. Surb—2H 119
Lonsdale Cres. Ilf—4M 47
Lonsdale Dri. Enf—6E 15
Lonsdale Gdns. T Hth—8K 107
Lonsdale M. Rich—9L 71
Lonsdale Pl. N1—3L 59
Lonsdale Rd. E11—5D 46
Lonsdale Rd. NW6—4K 57
Lonsdale Rd. SE25—8F 108
Lonsdale Rd. SW13—9D 72
Lonsdale Rd. W4—5D 72
Lonsdale Rd. W11—9K 57
Lonsdale Rd. Bexh—1K 97
Lonsdale Rd. S'hall—4H 69
Lonsdale Sq. N1—3L 59

Loobert Rd. N15—1C 44
Looe Gdns. Ilf—1M 47
Loom La. Rad—1D 10
Loom Pl. Rad—1E 10
Loop Rd. Chst—3A 112
Loop Rd. Eps—8A 134
Loop Rd. Wal A—5H 7
Lopen Rd. N18—4C 28
Loraine Clo. Enf—7G 17
Loraine Gdns. Asht—9J 133
Loraine Rd. N7—9K 43
Loraine Rd. W4—7M 71
Lord Av. Ilf—2K 47
Lord Chancellor Wlk. King
—5A 104
Lorden Wlk. E2—6E 60
Lord Gdns. Ilf—2J 47
Lord Hills Bri. W2—8M 57
Lord Hill's Rd. W2—8M 57
Lord Holland La. SW9—1L 91
Lord Knyvett Clo. Stai—5B 144
Lord Napier Pl. W6—6E 72
Lord North St. SW1—4J 75
Lord Roberts M. SW6—8M 73
Lord Robert's Ter. SE18—6L 79
Lordsbury Field. Wall—2G 137
Lord's Clo. SE21—8A 92
Lords Clo. Felt—8J 85
Lordship Gro. N16—7B 44
Lordship La.—9L 27
N17 1-421 & 2-470
N22 remainder
Lordship La. SE22—4D 92
Lordship Pk. N16—7A 44
Lordship Pk. M. N16—7A 44
Lordship Pl. SW3—7C 74
Lordship Rd. N16—6B 44
Lordship Rd. N'holt—3J 53
Lordship Rd. Wal X—3B 6
Lordship Ter. N16—7B 44
Lordsmead Rd. N17—9C 28
Lord St. E16—2J 79
Lord St. Wat—5G 9
Lord Warwick St. SE18—4K 79
Lorenzo St. WC1—6K 59
Loretto Gdns. Harr—2J 39
Lorian Clo. N12—4M 25
Loring Rd. N20—2C 26
Loring Rd. Iswth—1D 86
Loris Rd. W6—4G 73
Lorn Ct. SW9—9L 75
Lorne Av. Croy—2H 125
Lorne Clo. NW8—6C 58
Lorne Gdns. E11—2G 47
Lorne Gdns. W11—3J 73
Lorne Gdns. Croy—2H 125
Lorne Rd. E7—9F 46
Lorne Rd. E17—3L 45
Lorne Rd. N4—6K 43
Lorne Rd. Harr—9D 22
Lorne Rd. Rich—4K 87
Lorne Ter. N3—9K 25
Lorn Rd. SW9—1K 91
Lorraine Pk. Harr—7C 22
Lorrimore Rd. SE17—7M 75
Lorrimore Sq. SE17—7M 75
Losberne Way. SE16—6E 76
Loseberry Rd. Esh—7B 118
Lothair Rd. N4—5M 43
Lothair Rd. W5—3H 71
Lothair Rd. N. N4—4M 43
Lothbury. EC2—9B 60
Lothian Av. Hay—8F 52
Lothian Rd. SW9—9M 75
Lothrop St. W10—6J 57
Lots Rd. SW10—8A 74
Lotus Rd. West—9K 141
Loubet St. SW17—3D 106
Loudoun Av. Ilf—3M 47
Loudoun Rd. NW8—4A 58
Loudwater Clo. Sun—8E 100
Loudwater Rd. Sun—8E 100
Loughborough Pk. SW9
—3M 91
Loughborough Rd. SW9—1L 91
Loughborough St. SE11—6K 75
Lough Rd. N7—1K 59
Loughton Way. Buck H & Lou
—1H 31
Louisa St. E1—7H 61
Louise Ct. N22—8L 27
Louise Gdns. Rain—6C 66
Louise Rd. E15—2C 62
Louisville Rd. SW17—9E 90
Louvaine Rd. SW11—3B 90
Louvain Way. Wat—5F 4
Lovat Clo. NW2—8D 40
Lovat Clo. Edgw—6M 23
Lovat Dri. Ruis—3E 36
Lovat La. EC3—1C 76
Loveday Rd. W13—3F 70
Lovegrove St. SE1—6E 76

Lovekyn Clo. King—6J 103
Lovelace Av. Brom—1L 127
Lovelace Gdns. Bark—9E 48
Lovelace Gdns. Surb—2H 119
Lovelace Gdns. W on T—7G 117
Lovelace Grn. SE9—2K 95
Lovelace Rd. SE21—8A 92
Lovelace Rd. Barn—9C 14
Lovelace Rd. Surb—2G 119
Love La. EC2—9A 60
Love La. N17—7D 28
Love La. SE18—5L 79
Love La. SE25—7F 108
Love La. Abb L, Wat—3D 4
Love La. Bex—5K 97
Love La. Brom—6F 110
Love La. Mitc—7C 106
Love La. Mord—2L 121
Love La. Pinn—1J 37
Love La. S Ock—3M 83
Love La. Surb—4G 119
Love La. Sutt—8J 121
(in two parts)
Love La. Wfd G—6K 31
Lovel Av. Well—1E 96
Lovelinch Clo. SE15—7G 77
Lovell Pl. SE16—4J 77
Lovell Rd. Enf—8B 6
Lovell Rd. Rich—9G 87
Lovell Rd. S'hall—9M 53
Lovell Wlk. Rain—2E 66
Loveridge Rd. NW6—2K 57
Lovers Wlk. NW7—6K 25
Lovers Wlk. SE10—7B 78
Lovers Wlk. Romf—5B 34
Lovett Dri. Cars—2A 122
Lovett Way. NW10—1A 56
Love Wlk. SE5—1B 92
Lovibonds Av. Orp—5M 127
Lowbrook Rd. Ilf—9M 47
Low Cross Wood La. SE21
—9D 92
Lowdell Clo. W Dray—9C 142
Lowden Rd. N9—1F 28
Lowden Rd. SE24—3M 91
Lowden Rd. S'hall—1J 69
Lowe Av. E16—8E 62
Lowe Clo. Chig—5E 32
Lowell St. E14—9J 61
Lowen Rd. Rain—5B 66
Lwr. Addiscombe Rd. Croy
—3C 124
Lwr. Addison Gdns. W14
—3J 73
Lwr. Barn Rd. Purl—4A 138
Lwr. Bedfords Rd. Romf—6C 34
Lwr. Belgrave St. SW1—4F 74
Lwr. Boston Rd. W7—2C 70
Lwr. Broad St. Dag—4L 65
Lwr. Camden. Chst—4K 111
Lwr. Church St. Croy—4M 123
Lwr. Clapton Rd. E5—8F 44
Lwr. Common S. SW15—2F 88
Lwr. Coombe St. Croy—6A 124
Lwr. Court Rd. Eps—3A 134
Lwr. Croft. Swan—8D 114
Lwr. Downs Rd. SW20—5H 105
Lwr. Drayton Pl. Croy—4M 123
Lwr. Fore St. N9—4E 28
Lwr. George St. Rich—4H 87
Lwr. Gravel Rd. Brom—3J 127
Lwr. Green Rd. Esh—4M 117
Lwr. Green W. Mitc—7C 106
Lwr. Grosvenor Pl. SW1—4F 74
Lwr. Grove Rd. Rich—5K 87
Lwr. Hall La. E4—5J 29
Lwr. Hampton Rd. Sun—7G 101
Lwr. Ham Rd. King—3H 103
Lwr. High St. Wat—7H 9
Lwr. Hill Rd. Eps—4M 133
Lwr. Hythe St. Dart—4J 99
Lwr. Island Way. Wal A—8H 7
Lwr. James St. W1—1G 75
Lwr. John St. W1—1G 75
Lwr. Kenwood Av. Enf—7J 15
Lwr. Maidstone Rd. N11—6G 27
Lwr. Mall. W6—6F 72
Lwr. Mardyke Av. Rain—5A 66
Lwr. Marsh. SE1—3L 75
Lwr. Marsh La. King—8K 103
Lwr. Merton Rise. NW3—3C 58
Lwr. Morden La. Mord—1H 121
Lwr. Mortlake Rd. Rich—3J 87
Lwr. Noke Clo. Romf—2J 35
Lwr. Paddock Rd. Wat—8J 9
Lwr. Park Rd. N11—5F 26
Lwr. Park Rd. Bans—9C 136
Lwr. Park Rd. Belv—5B 81
Lwr. Park Rd. Lou—7J 19
Lwr. Pillory Downs. Coul &
Cars—5F 136
Lwr. Queen's Rd. Buck H
—2H 31

Lwr. Richmond Rd. SW15
—2F 88
Lwr. Richmond Rd. Rich & SW14
—2L 87
Lower Rd.—4G 77
SE16 1-245 & 2-196
SE8 remainder
Lower Rd. Belv & Eri—4M 81
Lower Rd. Harr—6B 38
Lower Rd. Kenl—5M 137
Lower Rd. Lou—3L 19
Lower Rd. Orp—1F 128
Lower Rd. Sutt—6A 122
Lower Rd. Swan—4E 114
Lwr. Sloane St. SW1—5E 74
Lower Sq. Iswth—2F 86
Lower Sq., The. Sutt—7M 121
Lwr. Station Rd. Dart—5C 98
Lwr. Strand. NW9—9D 24
Lwr. Sunbury Rd. Hmptn
—6K 101
Lwr. Tail. Wat—3J 21
Lwr. Teddington Rd. King
—5H 103
Lower Ter. NW3—8A 42
Lwr. Thames St. EC3—1C 76
Lower Tub. Bush, Wat—9B 10
Lwr. Wood Rd. Esh—8F 118
Lowestoft Rd. Wat—3F 8
Loweswater Clo. Wemb—7H 39
Lowe, The. Chig—5E 32
Lowfield Rd. NW6—3L 57
Lowfield Rd. W3—9A 56
Lowfield St. Dart—6J 99
Low Hall Clo. E4—9M 17
Lowhall La. E17—4J 45
Lowick Rd. Harr—2C 38
Lowlands Gdns. Romf—4M 49
Lowlands Rd. Harr—5C 38
Lowlands Rd. Pinn—4G 37
Lowlands Rd. S Ock—2M 83
Lowman Rd. N7—9K 43
Lowndes Clo. SW1—4E 74
Lowndes Pl. SW1—4E 74
Lowndes Sq. SW1—3D 74
Lowndes St. SW1—4E 74
Lownds Av. Brom—6E 110
Lowood St. E1—1F 76
Lowshoe La. Romf—4M 33
Lowson Gro. Wat—9J 9
Lowswood Clo. N'wd—8A 20
Lowther Clo. Borwd—7K 11
Lowther Dri. Enf—6J 15
Lowther Hill. SE23—6J 93
Lowther Rd. E17—9J 29
Lowther Rd. N7—1L 59
Lowther Rd. SW13—9D 72
Lowther Rd. King—5K 103
Lowther Rd. Stan—1K 39
Lowth Rd. SE5—1A 92
Loxford Av. E6—5H 63
Loxford La. Ilf—1A 64
Loxford Rd. Bark—2M 63
Loxham Rd. E4—7M 29
Loxham St. WC1—6J 59
Loxley Clo. SE9—2H 109
Loxley Rd. SW18—7B 90
Loxley Rd. Hmptn—1K 101
Loxton St. SE23—7H 93
Loxwood Clo. Orp—4H 129
Loxwood Rd. N17—1C 44
Lubbock Rd. Chst—4K 111
Lubbock St. SE14—8G 77
Lucan Pl. SW3—5C 74
Lucan Rd. Barn—5J 13
Lucas Av. E13—4F 62
Lucas Av. Harr—7L 37
Lucas Ct. Wal A—6M 7
Lucas Rd. SE20—3G 109
Lucas St. SE8—9L 77
Lucerne Clo. N13—3J 27
Lucerne Ct. Eri—4J 81
Lucerne Gro. E17—2B 46
Lucerne M. W8—2L 73
Lucerne Rd. N5—9M 43
Lucerne Rd. Orp—3D 128
Lucerne Rd. T Hth—8A 108
Lucerne Way. Romf—6H 35
Lucey Rd. SE16—4E 76
Lucey Way. SE16—4E 76
Lucien Rd. SW17—1E 106
Lucien Rd. SW19—8M 89
Lucknow St. SE18—8C 80
Lucorn Clo. SE12—5D 94
Luctons Av. Buck H—1G 31
Lucy Cres. W3—8A 56
Lucy Gdns. Dag—8K 49
Luddesdon Rd. Eri—8L 81
Ludford Clo. NW9—9C 24
Ludgate B'way. EC4—9M 59
Ludgate Cir. EC4—9M 59
Ludgate Hill. EC4—9M 59
Ludham Clo. SE28—9G 65

Ludlow Clo. Harr—9K 37
Ludlow Mead. Wat—3F 20
Ludlow Rd. W5—7G 55
Ludlow Rd. Felt—1E 100
Ludlow St. EC1—7A 60
Ludlow Way. N2—2A 42
Ludlow Way. Rick—6A 8
Ludovick Wlk. SW15—3C 88
Ludwick M. SE14—8J 77
Luffield Rd. SE2—4F 80
Luffman Rd. SE12—9F 94
Lugard Rd. SE15—1F 92
Luke St. EC2—7C 60
Lukin Cres. E4—3B 30
Lukin St. E1—9G 61
Lullarook Clo. West—8G 141
Lullingstone Av. Swan—7D 114
Lullingstone Clo. Orp—4F 112
Lullingstone Cres. Orp—4E 112
Lullingstone La. Eyns, Dart
—5G 131
Lullingstone Rd. Belv—7K 81
Lullington Garth. N12—5K 25
Lullington Garth. Borwd
—7M 11
Lullington Garth. Brom
—4C 110
Lullington Rd. SE20—4E 108
Lullington Rd. Dag—3J 65
Lulot Gdns. N19—7F 42
Lulworth Av. Houn—8A 70
Lulworth Av. Wemb—5G 39
Lulworth Clo. Harr—8K 37
Lulworth Dri. Pinn—5H 37
Lulworth Dri. Romf—5M 33
Lulworth Gdns. Harr—7J 37
Lulworth Rd. SE9—8J 95
Lulworth Rd. SE15—1F 92
Lulworth Rd. Well—1D 96
Lulworth Waye. Hay—6G 53
Lumley Clo. Belv—6L 81
Lumley Ct. WC2—1J 75
Lumley Gdns. Sutt—7J 121
Lumley Rd. Sutt—7J 121
Lumley St. W1—9E 58
Lunar Clo. West—8H 141
Luna Rd. T Hth—7A 108
Lundin Wlk. Wat—4H 21
Lundy Dri. Hay—5C 68
Lundy Wlk. N1—2A 60
Lunedale Rd. Dart—7M 99
Lunham Rd. SE19—3C 108
Lupin Clo. SW2—8M 91
Lupin Clo. Croy—3H 125
Lupin Clo. W Dray—6H 143
Lupton Clo. SE12—9F 94
Lupton St. NW5—9G 43
Lupus St. SW1—6F 74
Luralda Gdns. E14—6B 78
Lurgan Av. W6—7H 73
Lurgan St. W6—6H 73
Lurline Gdns. SW11—9E 74
Luscombe Ct. Brom—6G 110
Luscombe Way. SW8—8J 75
Lushes Rd. Lou—7M 19
Lushington Rd. NW10—5F 56
Lushington Rd. SE6—2M 109
Lushington Ter. E8—1E 60
Lusted Hall La. West—9H 141
Luther Clo. Edgw—2A 24
Luther Rd. Tedd—2D 102
Luton Pl. SE10—8A 78
Luton Rd. E17—1K 45
Luton Rd. Sidc—9G 97
Luton St. NW8—7B 58
Luttrell Av. SW15—4F 88
Lutwyche Rd. SE6—8K 93
Luxborough La. Chig—3J 31
Luxborough St. W1—8E 58
Luxemburg Gdns. W6—5H 73
Luxfield Rd. SE9—7J 95
Luxford St. SE16—5H 77
Luxmore Gdns. SE4—1K 93
Luxmore St. SE4—9K 77
Luxor St. SE5—2A 92
Luxted Rd. Orp—4L 141
Lyall Av. SE21—1C 108
Lyall M. SW1—4E 74
Lyall M. W. SW1—4E 74
Lyall St. SW1—4E 74
Lyal Rd. E3—5J 61
Lycett Pl. W12—3E 72
Lych Ga. Orp—3E 128
Lych Ga. Wat—6H 5
Lych Ga. Wlk. Hay—1D 68
(in two parts)
Lyconby Gdns. Croy—2J 125
Lydd Clo. Sidc—9C 96
Lydden Gro. SW18—6M 89
Lydden Rd. SW18—6M 89
Lydd Rd. Bexh—8K 81
Lydeard Rd. E6—3K 63
Lydford Rd. N15—3B 44

Lydford Rd. NW2—2H 57
Lydford Rd. W9—7K 57
Lydhurst Av. SW2—8K 91
Lydia Rd. Eri—7D 82
Lydney Clo. SE15—8C 76
Lydney Clo. SW19—8J 89
Lydon Rd. SW4—2G 91
Lydstep Rd. Chst—1L 111
Lye La. St Alb—3L 5
Lyfield. Lea—6A 132
Lyford Rd. SW18—6B 90
(in two parts)
Lygon Pl. SW1—4F 74
Lyham Clo. SW2—5J 91
Lyham Rd. SW2—4J 91
Lymbourne Clo. Sutt—2L 135
Lyme Farm Rd. SE12—3E 94
Lyme Gro. E9—3G 61
Lymer Av. SE19—2D 108
Lyme Regis Rd. Bans—9K 135
Lyme Rd. Well—9F 80
Lymescote Gdns. Sutt—4L 121
Lyme St. NW1—3G 59
Lyme Ter. NW1—3G 59
Lyminge Clo. Sidc—1D 112
Lyminge Gdns. SW18—7C 90
Lymington Av. N22—9L 27
Lymington Clo. SW16—6H 107
Lymington Dri. Ruis—7B 36
Lymington Gdns. Eps—7D 120
Lymington Rd. NW6—2M 57
Lymington Rd. Dag—6H 49
Lympstone Gdns. SE15—8E 76
Lynbridge Gdns. N13—4M 27
Lynbrook Clo. SE15—8C 76
Lynbrook Clo. Rain—5B 66
Lynch Clo. Uxb—3A 142
Lynchen Clo. Houn—9F 68
Lynch, The. Uxb—3A 142
Lynch Wlk. SE8—7K 77
Lyncott Cres. SW4—3F 90
Lyncroft Av. Pinn—3J 37
Lyncroft Gdns. NW6—1L 57
Lyncroft Gdns. W13—3G 71
Lyncroft Gdns. Eps—1D 134
Lyncroft Gdns. Houn—4A 86
Lyndale. NW2—9K 41
Lyndale Av. NW2—8K 41
Lyndale Clo. SE3—7D 78
Lynden Way. Swan—7A 114
Lyndhurst Av. N12—6D 26
Lyndhurst Av. NW7—6C 24
Lyndhurst Av. SW16—6H 107
Lyndhurst Av. Pinn—8F 20
Lyndhurst Av. S'hall—2M 69
Lyndhurst Av. Sun—7E 100
Lyndhurst Av. Surb—3M 119
Lyndhurst Av. Twic—7K 85
Lyndhurst Clo. NW10—8B 40
Lyndhurst Clo. Bexh—2M 97
Lyndhurst Clo. Croy—5D 124
Lyndhurst Ct. E18—8E 30
Lyndhurst Dri. E10—5A 46
Lyndhurst Dri. Horn—6G 51
Lyndhurst Dri. N Mald—2C 120
Lyndhurst Gdns. N3—8J 25
Lyndhurst Gdns. NW3—1B 58
Lyndhurst Gdns. Bark—2C 64
Lyndhurst Gdns. Enf—6C 16
Lyndhurst Gdns. Ilf—4B 48
Lyndhurst Gdns. Pinn—8F 20
Lyndhurst Gro. SE15—1C 92
Lyndhurst Rise. Chig—4L 31
Lyndhurst Rd. E4—7A 30
Lyndhurst Rd. N18—4E 28
Lyndhurst Rd. N22—6L 27
Lyndhurst Rd. NW3—1B 58
Lyndhurst Rd. Bexh—2M 97
Lyndhurst Rd. Coul—8E 136
Lyndhurst Rd. Gnfd—7M 53
Lyndhurst Rd. T Hth—8L 107
Lyndhurst Sq. SE15—9D 76
Lyndhurst Ter. NW3—1B 58
Lyndhurst Way. SE15—9D 76
Lyndhurst Way. Sutt—1L 135
Lyndon Av. Pinn—6J 21
Lyndon Av. Sidc—4D 96
Lyndon Av. Wall—5E 122
Lyndon Rd. Belv—5L 81
Lyne Cres. E17—8K 29
Lynegrove Av. Ashf—2A 100
Lyneham Wlk. E5—1J 61
Lynette Av. SW4—5G 91
Lynett Rd. Dag—7H 49
Lynford Clo. Edgw—7A 24
Lynford Gdns. Edgw—3M 23
Lynford Gdns. Ilf—7D 48
Lynford Ter. N9—9D 16
Lynhurst Cres. Uxb—3A 52
Lynhurst Rd. Uxb—3A 52
Lynmere Rd. Well—1F 96
Lynmouth Av. Enf—8D 16
Lynmouth Av. Mord—2H 121

Lynmouth Dri. Ruis—7F 36
Lynmouth Gdns. Gnfd—4F 54
Lynmouth Gdns. Houn—8H 69
Lynmouth Rise. Orp—8F 112
Lynmouth Rd. E17—4J 45
Lynmouth Rd. N2—2D 42
Lynmouth Rd. N16—6D 44
Lynmouth Rd. Gnfd—4F 54
Lynn Clo. Ashf—2B 100
Lynn Clo. Harr—9B 22
Lynne Clo. Orp—8D 128
Lynne Clo. S Croy—3G 139
Lynne Wlk. Esh—7A 118
Lynne Way. NW10—2C 56
Lynne Way. N'holt—5H 53
Lynn Rd. E11—7C 46
Lynn Rd. SW12—6F 90
Lynn Rd. Ilf—5B 48
Lynn St. Enf—3B 16
Lynross Clo. Romf—9K 35
Lynsted Clo. Bexh—4M 97
Lynsted Clo. Brom—6G 111
Lynsted Ct. Beck—6J 109
Lynsted Gdns. SE9—3H 95
Lynton Av. N12—4B 26
Lynton Av. NW9—2D 40
Lynton Av. W13—9E 54
Lynton Av. Orp—8F 112
Lynton Av. Romf—8M 33
Lynton Clo. Chess—6J 119
Lynton Clo. Iswth—3D 86
Lynton Cres. Ilf—4M 47
Lynton Gdns. Enf—9C 16
Lynton Mead. N20—3L 25
Lynton Rd. E4—5M 29
Lynton Rd. E11—9B 46
Lynton Rd. N8—3H 43
Lynton Rd. N11—6H 27
Lynton Rd. NW6—5K 57
Lynton Rd. SE1—5D 76
Lynton Rd. W3—1L 71
Lynton Rd. Croy—1L 123
Lynton Rd. Harr—7J 37
Lynton Rd. N Mald—9B 104
Lynton Wlk. Hay—6C 52
Lynwood Av. Coul—7F 136
Lynwood Av. Eps—6D 134
Lynwood Clo. E18—8G 31
Lynwood Clo. Romf—6M 33
Lynwood Clo. Ruis—8J 37
Lynwood Ct. King—6M 103
Lynwood Dri. N'wd—8D 20
Lynwood Dri. Romf—6M 33
Lynwood Dri. Wor Pk—4E 120
Lynwood Gdns. Croy—6K 123
Lynwood Gdns. S'hall—9G 53
Lynwood Gro. N21—1L 27
Lynwood Gro. Orp—2C 128
Lynwood Rd. SW17—1D 106
Lynwood Rd. W5—6J 55
Lynwood Rd. Eps—6D 134
Lynwood Rd. Th Dit—4D 118
Lyon Industrial Est. NW2
—7F 40
Lyon Meade. Stan—8G 23
Lyon Pk. Av. Wemb—2J 55
(in two parts)
Lyon Rd. SW19—5A 106
Lyon Rd. Harr—4D 38
Lyon Rd. Romf—5D 50
Lyon Rd. W on T—4J 117
Lyonsdown Av. Barn—8A 14
Lyonsdown Rd. Barn—8A 14
Lyons Pl. NW8—7B 58
Lyon St. N1—3K 59
Lyon Way. Gnfd—4C 54
Lyoth Rd. Orp—4A 128
Lyric Rd. SW13—9D 72
Lysander Gro. N19—6H 43
Lysander Rd. Croy—8K 123
Lysander Rd. Ruis—7B 36
Lysander Way. Orp—5A 128
Lysias Rd. SW12—5F 90
Lysia St. SW6—8H 73
Lysons Wlk. SW15—3E 88
Lytchet Rd. Brom—4F 110
Lytchet Way. Enf—3G 17
Lytchgate Clo. S Croy—9C 124
Lytcott Gro. SE22—6D 92
Lytham Av. Wat—5H 21
Lytham Gro. W5—6K 55
Lytham St. SE17—6B 76
Lyttelton Clo. NW3—3C 58
Lyttelton Rd. E10—8M 45
Lyttelton Rd. N2—3A 42
Lyttleton Rd. N8—1L 43
Lytton Av. N13—2L 27
Lytton Av. Enf—2J 17
Lytton Clo. N2—3B 42
Lytton Clo. N'holt—3K 53
Lytton Gdns. Wall—6H 123
Lytton Gro. SW15—4H 89
Lytton Rd. E11—5C 46

Lytton Rd. Barn—6A 14
Lytton Rd. Pinn—7J 21
Lytton Rd. Romf—3F 50
Lytton Strachey Path. SE28
—1F 80
Lyveden Rd. SE3—8F 78
Lyveden Rd. SW17—3D 106

Mabbutt Clo. St Alb—3J 5
Mabel Rd. Swan—3E 114
Maberley Cres. SE19—4E 108
Maberley Rd. SE19—5D 108
Maberley Rd. Beck—7H 109
Mabledon Pl. WC1—6H 59
Mablethorpe Rd. SW6—8J 73
Mabley St. E9—1J 61
McAdam Dri. Enf—4M 15
Macaret Way. N20—9A 14
Macarthur Ter. SE7—7H 79
Macaulay Rd. E6—5H 63
Macaulay Rd. SW4—2F 90
Macaulay Sq. SW4—3F 90
Macaulay Way. SE28—2F 80
Macaulay Av. Esh—4D 118
McAuley Clo. SE1—4L 75
McAuley M. SE13—1A 94
Macbean St. SE18—4M 79
Macbeth St. W6—6F 72
McCall Clo. SW4—1J 91
McCall Cres. SE7—6J 79
McCarthy Rd. Felt—2H 101
Macclesfield Rd. EC1—6A 60
Macclesfield Rd. SE25—9G 109
Macclesfield St. W1—1H 75
McClouds M. SW7—5M 73
MacCoid Way. SE1—3A 76
McCrone M. NW3—2B 58
McCullum Rd. E3—5K 61
McDermott Clo. SW11—2C 90
McDermott Rd. SE15—2E 92
Macdonald Av. Dag—8M 49
Macdonald Av. Horn—2J 51
Macdonald Rd. E7—9E 46
Macdonald Rd. E17—9A 30
Macdonald Rd. N11—5D 26
Macdonald Rd. N19—7G 43
Macdonald Way. Horn—2J 51
Macdonnell Gdns. Wat—8D 4
McDonough Clo. Chess
—6J 119
McDowall Rd. SE5—9A 76
McDowell Clo. E16—8D 62
Macduff Rd. SW11—9E 74
McEntee Av. E17—8J 29
Mace St. E2—5H 61
McEwan Way. E15—4B 62
Macfarlane Pl. W12—2G 73
Macfarlane Rd. W12—2G 73
Macfarren Pl. NW1—7E 58
McGrath Rd. E15—2D 62
McGredy. Wal X—2B 6
Macgregor Rd. E16—8G 63
McGregor Rd. W11—8K 57
Machell Rd. SE15—2G 93
McIntosh Clo. Romf—1C 50
McIntosh Clo. Wall—9J 123
McIntosh Rd. Romf—1C 50
Mackay Rd. SW4—2F 90
McKay Rd. SW20—4F 104
McKellar Clo. Bush, Wat—2A 22
Mackennal St. NW8—5C 58
Mackenzie Rd. N7—2K 59
Mackenzie Rd. Beck—6G 109
McKerrell Rd. SE15—9E 76
Mackeson Rd. NW3—9D 42
Mackie Rd. SW2—6L 91
Mackintosh La. E9—1H 61
Macklin St. WC2—9J 59
Mackrow Wlk. E14—1A 78
Mack's Rd. SE16—5E 76
Mackworth St. NW1—6G 59
Maclean Rd. SE23—5J 93
Maclennan Av. Rain—6H 67
McLeod Rd. SE2—5F 80
McLeod St. SE17—6A 76
Maclise Rd. W14—4J 73
Macmillan Gdns. Dart—3L 99
McMillan St. SE8—7L 77
McNeil Rd. SE5—1C 92
Macoma Rd. SE18—7B 80
Macoma Ter. SE18—7B 80
Macquarie Way. E14—5M 77
Macready Pl. N7—9J 43
Macroom Rd. W9—6K 57
Madans Wlk. Eps—6B 134
Mada Rd. Orp—5M 127
Maddams St. E3—7M 61
Maddison Clo. Tedd—3D 102
Maddocks Clo. Sidc—2J 113
Maddock Way. SE17—7M 75
Maddox St. W1—1F 74
Madeira Av. Brom—4C 110

Madeira Gro. Wfd G—6G 31
Madeira Rd. E11—6B 46
Madeira Rd. N13—3M 27
Madeira Rd. SW16—2J 107
Madeira Rd. Mitc—8D 106
Madeley Rd. W5—9J 55
Madeline Rd. SE20—4E 108
Madison Cres. Well—8G 81
Madison Gdns. Brom—7D 110
Madison Gdns. Well—8G 81
Madras Pl. N7—2L 59
Madras Rd. Ilf—9M 47
Madrid Rd. SW13—9E 72
Madron St. SE17—6C 76
Mafeking Av. E6—5J 63
Mafeking Av. Ilf—5B 48
Mafeking Rd. E16—7D 62
Mafeking Rd. N17—9E 28
Mafeking Rd. Bren—7J 71
Mafeking Rd. Enf—5D 16
Magdala Av. N19—7G 43
Magdala Rd. Iswth—2E 86
Magdala Rd. S Croy—9B 124
Magdalene Clo. SE15—1F 92
Magdalene Gdns. E6—7L 63
Magdalen Pas. E1—1D 76
Magdalen Rd. SW18—7A 90
Magdalen St. SE1—2C 76
Magee St. SE11—7L 75
Magnaville Rd. Bush, Wat
—9C 10
Magnin Clo. E8—4E 60
Magnolia Clo. King—3M 103
Magnolia Ct. SW4—4J 91
Magnolia Ct. Harr—5K 39
Magnolia Dri. West—8H 141
Magnolia Rd. W4—7M 71
Magnolia St. W Dray—5H 143
Magnolia Way. Eps—7A 120
Magnum Clo. Rain—7G 67
Magpie All. EC4—9L 59
Magpie Hall Clo. Brom—1J 127
Magpie Hall La. Brom—2J 127
Magpie Hall Rd. Bush, Wat
—2C 22
Maguire Dri. Rich—1G 103
Maguire St. SE1—3D 76
Mahlon Av. Ruis—1F 52
Mahogany Clo. SE16—2J 77
Maida Av. W2—8A 58
Maida Rd. Belv—4L 81
Maida Vale. W9—5M 57
Maida Vale Rd. Dart—4E 98
Maida Way. E4—9M 17
Maiden Erlegh Av. Bex—7J 97
Maiden La. NW1—3H 59
Maiden La. WC2—1J 75
Maiden La. Dart—2E 98
Maiden Rd. E15—3C 62
Maidenshaw Rd. Eps—4B 134
Maidenstone Hill. SE10—9A 78
Maids of Honour Row. Rich
—4H 87
Maidstone Av. Romf—9A 34
Maidstone Bldgs. SE1—2A 76
Maidstone Rd. N11—6H 27
Maidstone Rd. Sidc—3H 113
Mail Coach Yd. N1—6C 60
Main Av. Enf—7D 16
Main Av. N'wd—3A 20
Mainridge Rd. Chst—1L 111
Main Rd. F'ham, Dart—2L 131
Main Rd. Kes & West—5G 141
Main Rd. Orp—7G 113
Main Rd. Romf—2D 50
Main Rd. Sidc—9B 96
Main Rd. S at H, Dart—3M 115
Main Rd. Swan—1B 130
(Crockenhill)
Main Rd. Swan—4D 114
(Hextable)
Main St. Felt—2H 101
Maisie Webster Clo. Stai
—6A 144
Maismore St. SE15—8E 76
Maitland Clo. Houn—2K 85
Maitland Pk. Est. NW3—2D 58
Maitland Pk. Rd. NW3—2D 58
Maitland Pk. Vs. NW3—2D 58
Maitland Rd. E15—2D 62
Maitland Rd. SE26—3H 109
Maize Row. E14—1K 77
Majendie Rd. SE18—6B 80
Major Rd. E15—1B 62
Major Rd. SE16—4E 76
Makepeace Av. N6—7E 42
Makepeace Rd. N'holt—5J 53
Makins St. SW3—5C 74
Malabar St. E14—3L 77
Malam Gdns. E14—1M 77
Malan Clo. West—9J 141
Malan Sq. Rain—2F 66

Malbrook Rd. SW15—3F 88
Malcolm Ct. Stan—5G 23
Malcolm Cres. NW4—4E 40
Malcolm Dri. Surb—3H 119
Malcolm Pl. E2—7G 61
Malcolm Rd. E1—7G 61
Malcolm Rd. SE20—4G 109
Malcolm Rd. SE25—1E 124
Malcolm Rd. SW19—3J 105
Malcolm Rd. Coul—7H 137
Malcolm Way. E11—2E 46
Malden Av. SE25—7F 108
Malden Av. Gnfd—1C 54
Malden Ct. N Mald—7F 104
Malden Cres. NW1—2E 58
Malden Grn. Av. Wor Pk
—3D 120
Malden Hill. N Mald—7D 104
Malden Hill Gdns. N Mald
—7D 104
Malden Pk. N Mald—1D 120
Malden Rd. NW5—1E 58
Malden Rd. NW5—1E 58
Malden Rd. Borwd—5L 11
Malden Rd. N Mald & Wor Pk
—9C 104
Malden Rd. Sutt—6H 121
Malden Rd. Wat—2F 8
Malden Way N. Surb & N Mald
—2A 120
Malden Way S. Surb & Mald
—2A 120
Maldon Clo. N1—4A 60
Maldon Clo. SE5—2C 92
Maldon Rd. N9—3D 28
Maldon Rd. W3—1A 72
Maldon Rd. Romf—5A 50
Maldon Rd. Wall—7F 122
Maldon Wlk. Wfd G—6G 31
Malet Pl. WC1—7H 59
Malet St. WC1—7H 59
Maley Av. SE27—8M 91
Malford Ct. E18—9E 30
Malford Gro. E18—2D 46
Malfort Rd. SE5—2C 92
Malham Rd. SE23—7H 93
Malins Clo. Barn—7F 12
Mallams M. SW9—2M 91
Mallard Clo. Barn—8B 14
Mallard Clo. Twic—6L 85
Mallard Pl. N22—9K 27
Mallard Pl. Twic—9E 86
Mallard Rd. S Croy—2H 139
Mallard Wlk. Sidc—3G 113
Mallard Way. NW9—5A 40
Mallard Way. N'wd—7A 20
Mallard Way. Wat—1J 9
Mallet Dri. N'holt—1K 53
Mallet Rd. SE13—5B 94
Malling Clo. Croy—1G 125
Malling Gdns. Mord—1A 122
Malling Way. Brom—2D 126
Mallinson Rd. SW11—4C 90
Mallinson Rd. Croy—5H 123
Mallion Ct. Wal A—6H 7
Mallord St. SW3—7B 74
Mallory Clo. SE4—3J 93
Mallory Gdns. Barn—9E 14
Mallory St. NW8—7C 58
Mallow Clo. Croy—3H 125
Mallow Mead. NW7—7J 25
Mallows, The. Uxb—4A 36
Mallow St. EC1—7B 60
Mall Rd. W6—6F 72
Mall, The. E15—3B 62
Mall, The. N14—2J 27
Mall, The. SW1—2H 75
Mall, The. SW14—4A 88
Mall, The. W5—1J 71
Mall, The. Bexh—3L 97
Mall, The. Brom—7E 110
Mall, The. Croy—4A 124
Mall, The. Dag—2L 65
Mall, The. Harr—4K 39
Mall, The. St Alb—1M 5
Mall, The. Surb—1H 119
Malmains Clo. Beck—8B 110
Malmains Way. Beck—8A 110
Malmesbury Clo. Pinn—2E 36
Malmesbury Rd. E3—5K 61
Malmesbury Rd. E16—8C 62
Malmesbury Rd. E18—8D 30
Malmesbury Rd. Mord—2A 122
Malmesbury Ter. E16—8D 62
Malpas Dri. Pinn—3H 37
Malpas Rd. E8—1F 60
Malpas Rd. SE4—1K 93
Malpas Rd. Dag—2H 65
Malta Rd. E10—5L 45
Malta St. EC1—7M 59

Maltby Clo. Orp—3E 128
Maltby Rd. Chess—8L 119
Maltby St. SE1—3D 76
Malthouse Dri. Felt—2H 101
Malthus Path. SE28—2G 81
Maltings Clo. SW13—1D 88
Maltings Pl. SW6—9M 73
Maltings, The. K Lan—7A 4
Maltings, The. Orp—3D 128
Malton M. W10—9J 57
Malton Rd. W10—9J 57
Malton St. SE18—7C 80
Maltravers St. WC2—1K 75
Malt St. SE1—7E 76
Malva Clo. SW18—4M 89
Malvern Av. E4—7B 30
Malvern Av. Bexh—8J 81
Malvern Av. Ruis—8J 37
Malvern Clo. SE20—6E 108
Malvern Clo. W10—8K 57
Malvern Clo. Mitc—7G 107
Malvern Clo. Surb—3J 119
Malvern Dri. Felt—2H 101
Malvern Dri. Ilf—9D 48
Malvern Dri. Wfd G—5G 31
Malvern Gdns. NW2—7J 41
Malvern Gdns. NW6—5K 57
Malvern Gdns. Harr—2J 39
Malvern Gdns. Lou—8K 19
Malvern Ho. N16—6D 44
Malvern M. NW6—6L 57
Malvern Pl. NW6—6K 57
Malvern Rd. E6—4J 63
Malvern Rd. E8—3E 60
Malvern Rd. E11—7C 46
Malvern Rd. N8—1L 43
Malvern Rd. N17—1E 44
Malvern Rd. NW6—6L 57
Malvern Rd. Enf—9F 6
Malvern Rd. Hmptn—4L 101
Malvern Rd. Hay—8C 68
Malvern Rd. Horn—4E 50
Malvern Rd. Orp—6F 128
Malvern Rd. Surb—4J 119
Malvern Rd. T Hth—8L 107
Malvern Ter. N1—4L 59
Malvern Ter. N9—1D 28
Malvern Way. W13—8F 54
Malvern Way. Rick—7A 8
Malwood Rd. SW12—5F 90
Malyons Rd. SE13—4M 93
Malyons Rd. Swan—4D 114
Malyons Ter. SE13—4M 93
Managers St. E14—2A 78
Manaton Clo. SE15—2F 92
Manaton Cres. S'hall—9L 53
Manbey Gro. E15—2C 62
Manbey Pk. Rd. E15—2C 62
Manbey Rd. E15—2C 62
Manbey St. E15—2C 62
Manbrough Av. E6—6L 63
Manchester Dri. W10—7J 57
Manchester Gro. E14—6A 78
Manchester Rd. E14—6A 78
Manchester Rd. N15—4B 44
Manchester Rd. T Hth—7A 108
Manchester Sq. W1—9E 58
Manchester St. W1—8E 58
Manchester Way. Dag—9M 49
Manchuria Rd. SW11—5E 90
Manciple St. SE1—3B 76
Mandalay Rd. SW4—4G 91
Mandarin St. E14—1L 77
Mandela Clo. NW10—3A 56
Mandela St. NW1—4G 59
Mandeville Clo. SE3—8E 78
Mandeville Clo. Wat—2D 8
Mandeville Dri. Surb—3H 119
Mandeville Pl. W1—9E 58
Mandeville Rd. N14—2F 26
Mandeville Rd. Enf—9E 6
Mandeville Rd. Iswth—1E 86
Mandeville Rd. N'holt—3L 53
Mandeville St. E5—8J 45
Mandrake Rd. SW17—9D 90
Mandrell Rd. SW2—4J 91
Manette St. W1—9H 59
Manford Clo. Chig—4E 32
Manford Cross. Chig—5E 32
Manford Way. Chig—5C 32
Manfred Rd. SW15—4K 89
Manger Rd. N7—2J 59
Mangold Way. Eri—4H 81
Manilla St. E14—3L 77
Manister Rd. SE2—4E 80
Manley Ct. N16—8D 44
Manley St. NW1—4E 58
Manly Dixon Dri. Enf—1J 17
Manningford Clo. EC1—6M 59
Manning Gdns. Harr—5K 39
Manning Rd. E17—3J 45
Manning Rd. Dag—2L 65
Manning Rd. Orp—9H 113

Manning St. S Ock—2M 83
Manningtree Clo. SW19—7J 89
Manningtree Rd. Ruis—9F 36
Manningtree St. E1—9E 60
Mannin Rd. Romf—5F 48
Mannley's Yd. SW11—2E 90
Mannock Dri. Lou—4M 19
Mannock Rd. N22—1M 43
Mann's Clo. Iswth—4D 86
Manns Rd. Edgw—6L 23
Manoel Rd. Twic—8A 86
Manor Av. SE4—1K 93
Manor Av. Horn—3G 51
Manor Av. Houn—2H 85
Manor Av. N'holt—3K 53
Manor Brook. SE3—3E 94
Manor Chase. Wey—7A 116
Manor Clo. NW7—5B 24
Manor Clo. NW9—3M 39
Manor Clo. SE28—9G 65
Manor Clo. Barn—6J 13
Manor Clo. Dag—2B 66
Manor Clo. Dart—3B 98
(Crayford)
Manor Clo. Dart—9E 98
(Wilmington)
Manor Clo. Romf—3E 50
Manor Clo. Ruis—6D 36
Manor Clo. S Ock—2M 83
Manor Clo. Warl—9J 139
Manor Clo. Wor Pk—3C 120
Manor Cotts. N'wd—8D 20
Manor Cotts. App. N2—9A 26
Manor Ct. Enf—9B 6
Manor Ct. Twic—8A 86
Manor Ct. Wey—6A 116
Manor Ct. Wat. W7—1C 70
Manor Cres. Horn—3G 51
Manor Cres. Surb—1L 119
Manor Dene. SE28—9G 65
Manordeane Clo. Th Dit—3E 118
Manordene Rd. SE28—9H 65
Manor Dri. N14—1F 26
Manor Dri. N20—4C 26
Manor Dri. NW7—5B 24
Manor Dri. Eps—8C 120
Manor Dri. Esh—5D 118
Manor Dri. Felt—2H 101
Manor Dri. Sun—6E 100
Manor Dri. Surb—1K 119
Manor Dri. Wemb—9K 39
Manor Dri. N. N Mald & Wor Pk
—2B 120
Manor Dri., The. Wor Pk
—3D 120
Manor Farm Av. Shep—1A 116
Manor Farm Dri. E4—3C 30
Manor Farm Rd. SW16—6L 107
Manor Farm Rd. Enf—8B 6
Manor Farm Rd. Wemb—5H 55
Manor Fields. SW15—5H 89
Manor Gdns. N7—8J 43
Manor Gdns. SW20—6K 105
Manor Gdns. W3—5L 71
Manor Gdns. Hmptn—4M 101
Manor Gdns. Rich—8K 87
Manor Gdns. Ruis—1G 53
Manor Gdns. S Croy—8D 124
Manor Gdns. Sun—6E 100
Manor Ga. N'holt—3J 53
Manorgate Rd. King—5L 103
Manor Grn. Rd. Eps—5M 133
Manor Gro. SE15—7G 77
Manor Gro. Beck—6M 109
Manor Gro. Rich—3L 87
Manor Hall Av. NW4—9H 25
Manor Hall Dri. NW4—9H 25
Manorhall Gdns. E10—6L 45
Manor Hill. Bans—7D 136
Manor Ho. Ct. Eps—5A 134
Manor Ho. Ct. Shep—2A 116
Manor Ho. Dri. NW6—3H 57
Manor Ho. Gdns. Abb L, Wat
—4B 4
Manor La.—4C 94
SE13 1-59 & 2-86
SE12 remainder
Manor La. Felt—8E 84
Manor La. Hay—7B 68
Manor La. Sun—6E 100
Manor La. Sutt—7A 122
Manor La. Ter. SE13—4C 94
Manor M. SE4—1K 93
Manor Mt. SE23—7G 93
Manor Pk. SE13—3B 94
Manor Pk. Chst—6B 112
Manor Pk. Rich—3K 87
Manor Pk. Clo. W Wick—3M 125
Manor Pk. Cres. Edgw—6L 23
Manor Pk. Dri. Harr—1M 37
Manor Pk. Gdns. Edgw—5L 23
Manor Pk. Rd. E12—9H 47
Manor Pk. Rd. N2—1A 42

Manor Pk. Rd. NW10—4D 56
Manor Pk. Rd. Chst—5A 112
Manor Pk. Rd. Sutt—7A 122
Manor Pk. Rd. W Wick—3M 125
Manor Pl. SE17—6H 75
Manor Pl. Chst—6B 112
Manor Pl. Dart—7J 99
Manor Pl. Felt—7E 84
Manor Pl. Mitc—7G 107
Manor Pl. Sutt—6M 121
Manor Pl. W on T—2D 116
Manor Rd. E10—5L 45
Manor Rd.—7C 62
E15 1-347 & 2-118
E16 remainder
Manor Rd. E17—9J 29
Manor Rd. N16—6C 44
Manor Rd. N17—8E 28
Manor Rd. N22—6J 27
Manor Rd. SE25—8E 108
Manor Rd. SW20—6K 105
Manor Rd. W13—1E 70
Manor Rd. Bark—2D 64
Manor Rd. Barn—6J 13
Manor Rd. Beck—6M 109
Manor Rd. Bex—7M 97
Manor Rd. Dag—2A 66
Manor Rd. Dart—3C 98
Manor Rd. E Mol—8B 102
Manor Rd. Enf—4A 16
Manor Rd. Eri—7D 82
Manor Rd. Harr—4E 38
Manor Rd. Hay—9E 52
Manor Rd. Lou—8F 18
Manor Rd. Lou—3F 18
(High Beach)
Manor Rd. Mitc—8G 107
Manor Rd. Rich—3L 87
Manor Rd. Romf—3E 50
Manor Rd. Romf—4H 49
(Chadwell Heath)
Manor Rd. Romf—2G 33
(Lambourne End)
Manor Rd. Ruis—6B 36
Manor Rd. Sidc—9E 96
Manor Rd. Sutt—9K 121
Manor Rd. Tedd—2E 102
(in two parts)
Manor Rd. Twic—8A 86
Manor Rd. Wall—6F 122
Manor Rd. Wal A—6K 7
Manor Rd. W on T—2D 116
Manor Rd. Wat—3F 8
Manor Rd. W Wick—4M 125
Manor Rd. Wfd G & Chig—6K 31
Manor Rd. N. Esh & Th Dit
—5D 118
Manor Rd. N. Wall—6F 122
Manor Rd. S. Esh—6C 118
Manorside. Barn—6J 13
Manorside Clo. SE2—5G 81
Manor Sq. Dag—7H 49
Manor Vale. Bren—6G 71
Manor View. N3—9M 25
Manor Way. E4—4B 30
Manor Way. NW9—2C 40
Manor Way. SE3—3D 94
Manor Way. Bans—8D 136
Manor Way. Beck—6L 109
Manor Way. Bex—7L 97
Manor Way. Bexh—2B 98
Manor Way. Borwd—5A 12
Manor Way. Brom—1J 127
Manorway. Enf—9C 16
Manor Way. Harr—2M 37
Manor Way. Lea—8A 132
Manor Way. Mitc—7G 107
Manor Way. Orp—4A 112
Manor Way. Purl—4J 137
Manor Way. Rain—9C 66
Manor Way. Ruis—5C 36
Manor Way. S'hall—5H 69
Manor Way. S Croy—8C 124
Manor Way. Wal X—4E 6
Manor Way. Wfd G—5G 31
Manor Way. Wor Pk—3C 120
Manor Waye. Uxb—4B 142
Manorway Gdns. SE28—1G 81
Manor Way, The. Wall—6F 122
Manor Wood Rd. Purl—5J 137
Manresa Rd. SW3—6C 74
Mansard Beeches. SW17
—2E 106
Mansard Clo. Pinn—1H 37
Manse Clo. Hay—7B 68
Mansel Gro. E17—8L 29
Mansell Rd. W3—3B 72
Mansell Rd. Grnfd—8M 53
Mansell St. E1—9D 60
Mansel Rd. SW19—3J 105
Mansergh Clo. SE18—8J 79
Manse Rd. N16—8D 44
Manser Rd. Rain—6C 66

Manse Way. Swan—8E 114
Mansfield Av. N15—2B 44
Mansfield Av. Barn—8D 14
Mansfield Clo. N9—8E 16
Mansfield Clo. Orp—2H 129
Mansfield Dri. Hay—7C 52
Mansfield Gdns. Horn—7H 51
Mansfield Hill. E4—1M 29
Mansfield M. W1—8F 58
Mansfield Pl. NW3—9A 42
Mansfield Rd. E11—4F 46
Mansfield Rd. E17—2K 45
Mansfield Rd. NW3—1D 58
Mansfield Rd. W3—7M 55
Mansfield Rd. Chess—7G 119
Mansfield Rd. Ilf—7L 47
Mansfield Rd. S Croy—8B 124
Mansfield Rd. Swan—3C 114
Mansfield St. W1—8F 58
Mansford St. E2—5E 60
Manship Rd. Mitc—4E 106
Mansion Gdns. NW3—8M 41
Mansion Ho. Pl. EC4—9B 60
Manson M. SW7—5A 74
Manson Pl. SW7—5B 74
Manstead Gdns. Rain—9F 66
Mansted Gdns. Romf—5G 49
Manston Av. S'hall—5L 69
Manston Clo. SE20—5G 109
Manston Clo. Wal X—3C 6
Manstone Rd. NW2—1J 57
Manston Way. Horn—2F 66
Manthorp Rd. SE18—6A 80
Mantilla Rd. SW17—1E 106
Mantle Rd. SE4—2J 93
Manton Av. W7—3D 70
Manton Clo. Hay—1C 68
Manton Rd. SE2—5E 80
Mantua St. SW11—2B 90
Mantus Clo. E1—7G 61
Mantus Rd. E1—7G 61
Manus Way. N20—2A 26
Manville Gdns. SW17—9F 90
Manville Rd. SW17—8E 90
Manwood Rd. SE4—4K 93
Manwood St. E16—2K 79
Manygate La. Shep—2A 116
Manygates. SW12—8F 90
Mapesbury Rd. NW2—3J 57
Mape St. E2—7F 60
Maple Av. E4—5K 29
Maple Av. W3—2C 72
Maple Av. Harr—7M 37
Maple Av. Upm—8M 51
Maple Av. W Dray—1J 143
Maple Clo. N16—4E 44
Maple Clo. SW4—5H 91
Maple Clo. Buck H—3H 31
Maple Clo. Bush, Wat—4J 9
Maple Clo. Horn—8F 50
Maple Clo. Mitc—5F 106
Maple Clo. Orp—9B 112
Maple Clo. Ruis—4F 36
Maple Clo. Whyt—9D 138
Maple Ct. N Mald—7B 104
Maple Cres. Sidc—5E 96
Maplecroft Clo. E6—9H 63
Mapledale Av. Croy—4E 124
Mapledene. Chst—2A 112
Mapledene Rd. E8—3E 60
Maplefield. St Alb—2M 5
Maple Gdns. Edgw—7C 24
Maple Gro. NW9—5A 40
Maple Gro. W5—4H 71
Maple Gro. Bren—8F 70
Maple Gro. S'hall—8K 53
Maple Gro. Wat—3E 8
Maplehurst Clo. King—8J 103
Mapleleafe Gdns. Ilf—1M 47
Maple Pl. W1—8G 59
Maple Pl. Bans—6H 135
Maple Pl. W Dray—2J 143
Maple Rd. E11—4C 46
Maple Rd. SE20—5F 108
Maple Rd. Dart—7G 99
Maple Rd. Hay—6G 53
Maple Rd. Surb—1H 119
Maple Rd. Whyt—9D 138
Maplescombe La. Farn, Dart &
Sev—6M 131
Maples Pl. E1—8F 60
Maplestead Rd. SW2—6K 91
Maplestead Rd. Dag—4F 64
Maples, The. Bans—6M 135
Maple St. W1—8G 59
Maple St. Romf—2A 50
Maplethorpe Rd. T Hth
—8M 107
Mapleton Clo. Brom—1E 126
Mapleton Cres. SW18—5M 89
Mapleton Cres. Enf—2G 17
Mapleton Rd. E4—3A 30

Mapleton Rd. SW18—5M 89
Mapleton Rd. Enf—4F 16
Maple Wlk. W10—6H 57
Maple Wlk. Sutt—2M 135
Maple Way. Felt—9E 84
Maplin Clo. N21—8K 15
Maplin Rd. E16—9E 62
Maplin St. E3—7K 61
Mapperley Dri. Wfd G—7C 30
Maran Way. Eri—4H 81
Marban Rd. W9—6K 57
Marble Arch. W2—1D 74
Marble Clo. W3—2M 71
Marble Hill Clo. Twic—6F 86
Marble Hill Gdns. Twic—6F 86
Marbrook Ct. SE12—9G 95
Marcellina Way. Orp—5D 128
Marcet Rd. Dart—4G 99
Marchant Rd. E11—7B 46
Marchbank Rd. W14—7K 73
Marchmont Rd. Rich—4K 87
Marchmont Rd. Wall—9G 123
Marchmont St. WC1—7J 59
March Rd. Twic—6E 86
Marchwood Clo. SE5—8C 76
Marchwood Cres. W5—9H 55
Marcia Rd. SE1—5C 76
Marcilly Rd. SW18—4B 90
Marconi Way. S'hall—9M 53
Marcon Pl. E8—1F 60
Marco Rd. W6—4G 73
Marcus Ct. E15—4C 62
Marcus Garvey Way. SW9
—3L 91
Marcus Rd. Dart—6E 98
Marcus St. E15—4C 62
Marcus St. SW18—5M 89
Mardale Dri. NW9—3B 40
Mardell Rd. Croy—9H 109
Marden Av. Brom—1E 126
Marden Cres. Croy—1K 123
Marden Rd. N17—9C 28
Marden Rd. Croy—1K 123
Marden Rd. Romf—4C 50
Marden Sq. SE16—4F 76
Marder Rd. W13—3E 70
Marechal Niel Av. Sidc—9B 96
Mares Field. Croy—5C 124
Maresfield Gdns. NW3—1A 58
Mare St. E8—4F 60
Margaret Av. E4—8M 17
Margaret Bondfield Av. Bark
—3E 64
Margaret Bldgs. N16—6D 44
Margaret Clo. Romf—3F 50
Margaret Clo. Wal A—6K 7
Margaret Dri. Horn—6K 51
Margaret Rd. N16—6D 44
Margaret Rd. Barn—6B 14
Margaret Rd. Bex—5H 97
Margaret Rd. Romf—3F 50
Margaret Sq. Uxb—4A 142
Margaret St. W1—9G 59
Margaretta Ter. SW3—7C 74
Margaretting Rd. E12—6G 47
Margaret Way. Ilf—4J 47
Margate Rd. SW2—4J 91
Margeholes. Wat—2J 21
Margery Pk. Rd. E7—2E 62
Margery Rd. Dag—8H 49
Margery St. WC1—6L 59
Margin Dri. SW19—2H 105
Margravine Rd. W6—6H 73
Margravine Rd. W6—6H 73
Marham Gdns. SW18—7C 90
Marham Gdns. Mord—1A 122
Maria Clo. SE1—5E 76
Mariam Gdns. Horn—7K 51
Marian Clo. Hay—7H 53
Marian Ct. Sutt—7M 121
Marian Pl. E2—5F 60
Marian Way. SW16—5G 107
Marian St. E2—5F 60
Maria Ter. E1—8H 61
Maria Theresa Clo. N Mald
—9B 104
Maricas Av. Harr—8B 22
Marigold St. SE16—3F 76
Marigold Way. E4—6K 29
Marigold Way. Croy—3H 125
Marina Av. N Mald—9F 104
Marina Clo. Brom—7E 110
Marina Dri. Dart—7L 99
Marina Dri. Well—1C 96
Marina Gdns. Wal X—3C 6
Marina Way. Tedd—4H 103
Marine Dri. SE18—5K 79
Marinefield Rd. SW6—1M 89
Mariner Gdns. Rich—9G 87

Mariner Rd. E12—9L 47
Marine St. SE16—4E 76
Marion Av. Shep—9A 100
Marion Clo. Bush, Wat—3K 9
Marion Clo. Ilf—7B 32
Marion Cres. Orp—9E 112
Marion Gro. Wfd G—4C 30
Marion Rd. NW7—5E 24
Marion Rd. T Hth—9A 108
Marion Sq. E2—5F 60
Marischal Rd. SE13—2B 94
Maritime St. E3—7K 61
Marius Pas. SW17—8E 90
Marius Rd. SW17—8E 90
Marjorams Av. Lou—4L 19
Marjorie Gro. SW11—3D 90
Markab Rd. N'wd—5D 20
Mark Av. E4—8M 17
Mark Clo. Bexh—9J 81
Mark Clo. S'hall—1M 69
Marke Clo. Kes—6J 127
Markeston Grn. Wat—4H 21
Market Centre, The. S'hall
—5F 68
Market Entrance. SW8—8G 75
Market Hill. SE18—4L 79
Market La. Edgw—8A 24
Market Link. Romf—2C 50
Market Meadow. Orp—8G 113
Market M. W1—2F 74
Market Pl. N2—1C 42
Market Pl. NW11—2M 41
Market Pl. SE16—5E 76
Market Pl. W1—9G 59
Market Pl. W3—2A 72
Market Pl. Bexh—3L 97
Market Pl. Bren—8G 71
Market Pl. Dart—6J 99
Market Pl. Enf—5B 16
Market Pl. King—6H 103
Market Pl. Romf—3C 50
Market Rd. E14—1L 77
Market Rd. N7—2J 59
Market Rd. Rich—2L 87
Market Sq. E14—9M 61
Market Sq. N9—3E 28
Market Sq. Brom—6E 110
Market Sq. Uxb—3A 142
Market St. E6—5K 63
Market St. SE18—5L 79
Market St. Dart—6J 99
Market St. Wat—6F 8
Market Way. E14—9M 61
Markfield. Croy—2K 139
(in two parts)
Markfield Gdns. E4—9M 17
Markfield Rd. N15—2E 44
Markham Sq. SW3—6D 74
Markham St. SW3—6C 74
Markhole Clo. Hmptn—4K 101
Markhouse Av. E17—4J 45
Markhouse Rd. E17—4K 45
Mark La. EC3—1C 76
Markmanor Av. E17—5J 45
Mark Rd. N22—9M 27
Marksbury Av. Rich—2L 87
Marks Rd. Romf—3A 50
Marks Rd. Warl—9J 139
Mark St. E15—3C 62
Mark St. EC2—7G 60
Markway. Sun—6G 101
Mark Way. Swan—9E 114
Markwell Clo. SE26—1F 108
Markyate Rd. Dag—1F 64
Marlands Rd. Ilf—1J 47
Marlborough Av. E8—4E 60
(in three parts)
Marlborough Av. N14—3G 27
Marlborough Av. Edgw—3M 23
Marlborough Av. Ruis—4A 36
Marlborough Clo. N20—3D 26
Marlborough Clo. SE17—5A 76
Marlborough Clo. SW19
—3C 106
Marlborough Clo. Orp—2D 128
Marlborough Clo. W on T
—5H 117
Marlborough Cres. W4—4C 72
Marlborough Dri. Ilf—1J 47
Marlborough Dri. Wey—5A 116
Marlborough Gdns. N20—3D 26
Marlborough Gdns. Surb
—2H 119
Marlborough Gro. SE1—6E 76
Marlborough Hill. NW8—4A 58
Marlborough Hill. Harr—2C 38
Marlborough La. SE7—8G 79
Marlborough Pk. Av. Sidc
—6E 96
Marlborough Pl. NW8—5A 58
Marlborough Rd. E4—6M 29
Marlborough Rd. E7—3G 63
Marlborough Rd. E15—9C 46

Marlborough Rd. E18—9E 30
Marlborough Rd. N9—1D 28
Marlborough Rd. N19—7H 43
Marlborough Rd. N22—7K 27
Marlborough Rd. SW1—2G 75
Marlborough Rd. SW19
—3C 106
Marlborough Rd. W4—6A 72
Marlborough Rd. W5—3H 71
Marlborough Rd. Bexh—2H 97
Marlborough Rd. Brom
—8G 111
Marlborough Rd. Dag—9F 48
Marlborough Rd. Dart—5G 99
Marlborough Rd. Felt—8H 85
Marlborough Rd. Hmptn
—3L 101
Marlborough Rd. Iswth—9F 70
Marlborough Rd. Rich—5K 87
Marlborough Rd. Romf—2L 49
Marlborough Rd. S'hall—4G 69
Marlborough Rd. S Croy
—9A 124
Marlborough Rd. Sutt—4L 121
Marlborough Rd. Uxb—7F 142
Marlborough Rd. Wat—6F 8
Marlborough St. SW3—5C 74
Marlborough Yd. N19—7H 43
Marld, The. Asht—9K 133
Marle Gdns. Wal A—5J 7
Marler Rd. SE23—7J 93
Marlescroft Way. Lou—7M 19
Marley Av. Bexh—7H 81
Marley Clo. Gnfd—6L 53
Marlingdene Clo. Hmptn
—3L 101
Marlings Clo. Chst—8C 112
Marlings Clo. Whyt—9C 138
Marlings Pk Av Chst—8C 112
Marlin Sq. Abb L, Wat—4D 4
Marloes Clo. Wemb—9H 39
Marloes Rd. W8—4M 73
Marlow Clo. SE20—7F 108
Marlow Ct. NW9—1D 40
Marlow Cres. Twic—5D 86
Marlow Dri. Sutt—4H 121
Marlowe Clo. Chst—3B 112
Marlowe Clo. Ilf—8A 32
Marlowe Gdns. SE9—5L 95
Marlowe Gdns. Romf—6B 35
Marlowe Rd. E17—2A 46
Marlowe Sq. Mitc—8G 107
Marlowes, The. NW8—4B 58
Marlowes, The. Dart—3B 99
Marlow Gdns. Hay—4B 68
Marlow Rd. E6—6K 63
Marlow Rd. SE20—7F 108
Marlow Rd. S'hall—4K 69
Marlpit Av. Coul—9J 137
Marlpit La. Coul—8H 137
Marl Rd. SW18—3M 89
Marlton St. SE10—6D 78
Marlyon Rd. Ilf—5F 32
Marmadon Rd. SE18—5D 80
Marmion App. E4—4L 29
Marmion Av. E4—4K 29
Marmion Clo. E4—4K 29
Marmion M. SW11—2E 90
Marmion Rd. SW11—3E 90
Marmont Rd. SE15—9E 76
Marmora Rd. SE22—5G 93
Marmott Rd. Houn—2H 85
Marne Av. N11—4F 26
Marne Av. Well—2E 96
Marnell Way. Houn—2H 85
Marne St. W10—6J 57
Marney Rd. SW11—3E 90
Marneys Clo. Eps—7L 133
Marnham Av. NW2—9J 41
Marnham Cres. Gnfd—6M 53
Marnock Rd. SE4—4K 93
Maroon St. E14—8J 61
Maroons Way. SE6—2L 109
Marquess Rd. N1—2B 60
Marquis Clo. Wemb—3K 55
Marquis Rd. N4—6K 43
Marquis Rd. N22—6K 27
Marquis Rd. NW1—2H 59
Marrick Clo. SW15—3E 88
Marrilyne Av. Enf—2K 17
Marriots Clo. NW9—4D 40
Marriott Clo. Felt—5B 84
Marriott Rd. E15—4C 62
Marriott Rd. N4—6K 43
Marriott Rd. N10—8D 26
Marriott Rd. Barn—5H 13
Marriott Rd. Dart—6L 99
Marrowells. Wey—5D 16
Marryat Pl. SW19—1J 105
Marryat Rd. SW19—2H 105
Marryat Rd. Enf—8B 6
Marsala Rd. SE13—3M 93
Marsden Rd. N9—2F 28

Marsden St. NW5—2E 58
Marsden St. SE15—2D 92
Marsden Way. Orp—5D 128
Marshall Clo. SW18—5A 90
Marshall Clo. Harr—5B 38
Marshall Clo. Houn—4K 85
Marshall Dri. Hay—8D 52
Marshall Path. SE28—1F 80
Marshall Rd. N17—8B 28
Marshalls Clo. N11—4F 26
Marshalls Clo. Eps—5A 134
Marshalls Dri. Romf—1C 50
Marshall's Gro. SE18—5J 79
Marshalls Rd. Romf—2B 50
Marshall's Rd. Sutt—6M 121
Marshall St. W1—9G 59
Marshalsea Rd. SE1—3A 76
Marsham Clo. Chst—2M 111
Marsham St. SW1—4H 75
Marsh Av. Eps—2C 134
Marsh Av. Mitc—6D 106
Marsh Clo. NW7—3D 24
Marsh Clo. Wal X—6E 6
Marsh Ct. E8—3E 60
Marshcroft Dri. Wal X—3E 6
Marsh Dri. NW9—4D 40
Marsh Farm Rd. Twic—7D 86
Marshfield St. E14—4M 61
Marshgate La. E15—4M 61
Marshgate Path. SE28—4A 80
Marsh Grn. Rd. Dag—4L 65
Marsh Hill. E9—1J 61
Marsh Hill. Wal A—1L 7
Marsh La. E10—7K 45
Marsh La. N17—8F 28
Marsh La. NW7—3C 24
Marsh La. Stan—5G 23
Marsh Rd. Pinn—2J 37
Marsh Rd. Wemb—6H 55
Marsh St. E14—5M 77
(in two parts)
Marsh Wall. E14—2L 77
Marsland Clo. SE17—6M 75
Marston. Eps—3A 134
Marston Av. Chess—8J 119
Marston Av. Dag—7L 49
Marston Clo. NW6—3A 58
Marston Clo. Dag—8L 49
Marston Dri. Warl—9J 139
Marston Ho. SW9—1L 91
Marston Rd. Ilf—8J 31
Marston Rd. Tedd—2F 102
Marston Way. SE19—4A 108
Marsworth Av. Pinn—8H 21
Martaban Rd. N16—7D 44
Martello St. E8—3F 60
Martello Ter. E8—3F 60
Martell Rd. SE21—9B 92
Martel Pl. E8—2D 60
Marten Rd. E17—9L 29
Martens Av. Bexh—3M 97
Martens Clo. Bexh—3A 98
Martha Ct. E2—5F 60
Martha Rd. E15—2C 62
Martha St. E1—9G 61
Marthorne Cres. Harr—9B 22
Martinau Est. E1—9G 61
Martin Bowes Rd. SE9—2K 95
Martinbridge Trading Est. Enf
—7E 16
Martin Clo. S Crov—3H 139
Martin Clo. Warl—8F 138
Martin Cres. Croy—3L 123
Martindale. SW14—4A 88
Martindale Av. Orp—7E 128
Martindale Rd. SW12—6F 90
Martindale Rd. Houn—2J 85
Martin Dene. Bexh—4K 97
Martin Dri. N'holt—1K 53
Martin Dri. Rain—7F 66
Martineau Clo. Esh—6B 118
Martineau Rd. N5—9M 43
Martingale Clo. Sun—8E 100
Martingales Clo. Rich—9H 87
Martin Gdns. Dag—9H 49
Martin Gro. Mord—7L 105
Martin La. EC4—1B 76
Martin Rise. Bexh—4K 97
Martin Rd. Dag—9G 49
Martin Rd. Dart—9G 99
Martins Clo. Orp—7H 113
Martins Dri. Wal X—1E 6
Martins Mt. Barn—6L 13
Martins Rd. Brom—6D 110
Martins Wlk. N10—8E 26
Martin Way—7J 105
SW20 267-347 & 274-358
Mord remainder
Martlesham Clo. Horn—1G 67
Martlett Ct. WC2—9J 59
Martley Dri. Ilf—3M 47

Martock Clo. Harr—2E 38
Marton Clo. SE6—9L 93
Marton Rd. N16—8C 44
Mart St. WC2—1J 75
Marvell Av. Hay—8E 52
Marvels Clo. SE12—8F 94
Marvels La. SE12—8F 94
Marville Rd. SW6—8K 73
Marvin St. E8—2F 60
Marwood Clo. Well—2F 96
Marwood Way. SE16—6F 76
Mary Adelaide Clo. SW15
—1C 104
Mary Ann Gdns. SE8—7L 77
Maryatt Av. Harr—7M 37
Mary Bank. SE18—5K 79
Mary Clo. Stan—2K 39
Mary Datchelor Clo. SE5
—9B 76
Maryfield Clo. Bex—9C 98
Maryhill Clo. Kenl—9A 138
Maryland Pk. E15—1C 62
Maryland Rd. E15—1B 62
Maryland Rd. N22—6L 27
Maryland Rd. T Hth—5M 107
Maryland Sq. E15—1C 62
Marylands Rd. W9—7L 57
Maryland St. E15—1B 62
Maryland Way. Sun—6E 100
Marylebone Fly-over. W2 & NW1
—8C 58
Marylebone High St. W1
—8E 58
Marylebone La. W1—9E 58
Marylebone M. W1—8F 58
Marylebone Pas. W1—9G 59
Marylebone St. W1—8F 58
Marylce Way. SE11—5K 75
Maryon Gro. SE7—5J 79
Maryon M. NW3—9C 42
Maryon Rd. SE7 & SE18—5J 79
Mary Peters Dri. Gnfd—1B 54
Mary Pl. W11—1J 73
Mary Rose Clo. Hmptn—5L 101
Mary's Ter. Twic—6E 86
Mary St. E16—8D 62
Mary St. N1—4A 60
Mary Ter. NW1—4G 59
Maryville. Well—1D 96
Masbro' Rd. W14—4H 73
Mascalls Rd. SE7—7G 79
Mascotte Rd. SW15—3H 89
Mascotts Clo. NW2—8F 40
Masefield Av. Borwd—7M 11
Masefield Av. S'hall—1L 69
Masefield Av. Stan—5D 22
Masefield Clo. Eri—9D 82
Masefield Clo. Romf—8G 35
Masefield Ct. Surb—1H 119
Masefield Cres. N14—7G 15
Masefield Cres. Romf—8G 35
Masefield Gdns. E6—7L 63
Masefield La. Hay—7F 52
Masefield Rd. Dart—4M 99
Masefield Rd. Hmptn—1K 101
Masefield View. Orp—5A 128
Mashie Rd. W3—9C 56
Mashiters Hill. Romf—8B 34
Mashiters Wlk. Romf—1C 50
Maskell Clo. SW2—7L 91
Maskell Rd. SW17—9A 90
Maskelyne Clo. SW11—9C 74
Mason Clo. E16—1E 78
Mason Clo. Bexh—2M 97
Mason Clo. Hmptn—5K 101
Mason's Arms M. W1—9F 58
Masons Av. EC2—9B 60
Masons Av. Croy—5A 124
Masons Av. Harr—2D 38
Masons Grn. La. W5 & W3
—7L 55
Masons Hill. SE18—5M 79
Masons Hill. Brom—7F 110
Mason's Pl. EC1—6A 60
Masons Pl. Mitc—5D 106
Masons Rd. Enf—9B 6
Mason St. SE17—5R 76
Mason's Yd. SW1—2G 75
Mason's Yd. SW19—2H 105
Mason Way. Wal A—6L 7
Massey Clo. N11—5F 26
Massie Rd. E8—2E 60
Massinger St. SE17—5C 76
Massingham St. E1—7H 61
Masson Av. Ruis—2G 53
Master Gunners Pl. SE18
—8J 79
Masterman Rd. E6—6J 63
Master's St. E1—8H 61
Mast Ho. Ter. E14—5L 77
Mastmaker Rd. E14—3L 77

Maswell Pk. Cres. Houn—4A 86
Maswell Pk. Rd. Houn—4M 85
Matcham Rd. E11—8C 46
Matfield Clo. Brom—9E 110
Matfield Rd. Belv—7L 81
Matham Gro. SE22—3D 92
Matham Rd. E Mol—9B 102
Matheson Rd. W14—5K 73
Mathew Ct. E17—1A 46
Mathews Av. E6—5L 63
Mathews Pk. Av. E15—2D 62
Mathews Yd. WC2—9J 59
Mathias Clo. Eps—5A 134
Matlock Clo. SE24—3A 92
Matlock Cres. Sutt—6J 121
Matlock Cres. Wat—3G 21
Matlock Gdns. Horn—8J 51
Matlock Gdns. Sutt—6J 121
Matlock Pl. Sutt—6J 121
Matlock Rd. E10—4A 46
Matlock St. E14—9J 61
Matlock Way. N Mald—5B 104
Matrimony Pl. SW4—1G 91
Matthew Clo. W10—7H 57
Matthew Parker St. SW1
—3H 75
Matthews Clo. Romf—9K 35
Matthews Gdns. Croy—3B 140
Matthews Rd. Gnfd—1B 54
Matthews St. SW11—1D 90
Matthias Rd. N16—1C 60
Mattison Rd. N4—4L 43
Mattock La.—2F 70
W13 37-81
W5 remainder
Maude Cres. Wat—2F 8
Maude Rd. E17—3J 45
Maude Rd. SE5—9C 76
Maude Rd. Swan—3E 114
Maude Ter. E17—3J 45
Maud Gdns. E13—5D 62
Maud Gdns. Bark—5D 64
Maud Rd. E10—8A 46
Maud Rd. E13—5D 62
Maudslay Rd. SE9—2K 95
Maud St. E16—8D 62
Maudsville Cotts. W7—2C 70
Mauleverer Rd. SW2—4J 91
Maundeby Wlk. NW10—2C 56
Maunder Rd. W7—2D 70
Maunsel St. SW1—5H 75
Maureen Ct. Beck—6H 109
Maurice Av. N22—9M 27
Maurice Brown Clo. NW7
—5H 25
Maurice St. W12—9F 56
Maurice Wlk. NW11—2A 42
Maurier Clo. N'holt—4G 53
Mauritius Rd. SE10—5C 78
Maury Rd. N16—8E 44
Mavelstone Clo. Brom—5J 111
Mavelstone Rd. Brom—5J 111
Maverton Rd. E3—4L 61
Mavis Av. Eps—7C 120
Mavis Clo. Eps—7C 120
Mavis Gro. Horn—7J 51
Mawbey Pl. SE1—6D 76
Mawbey Pl. SW8—8J 75
Mawbey Rd. SE1—6D 76
Mawney Clo. Romf—9M 33
Mawney Rd. Romf—9M 33
Mawson Clo. SW20—6J 105
Mawson La. W4—7D 72
Maxey Gdns. Dag—9J 49
Maxey Rd. SE18—5A 80
Maxey Rd. Dag—9J 49
Maxilla Wlk. W11—9H 57
Maximfeldt Rd. Eri—6C 82
Maxim Rd. N21—8L 15
Maxim Rd. Dart—4C 98
Maxim Rd. Eri—5B 82
Maxted Pk. Harr—5C 38
Maxted Rd. SE15—2D 92
Maxwell Gdns. Orp—5D 128
Maxwell Rise. Wat—9J 9
Maxwell Rd. SW6—8M 73
Maxwell Rd. Ashf—3A 100
Maxwell Rd. Borwd—5M 11
Maxwell Rd. N'wd—7B 20
Maxwell Rd. Well—2D 96
Maxwell Rd. W Dray—5K 143
Maxwelton Av. NW7—5B 24
Maxwelton Clo. NW7—5B 24
Mayall Rd. SE24—4M 91
Maya Rd. N2—2A 42
May Av. Orp—9F 112
Maybank Av. E18—9F 30
Maybank Av. Horn—1F 66
Maybank Av. Wemb—1E 54
Maybank Gdns. Pinn—3E 36
Maybank Lodge. Horn—1G 67

Maybank Rd. E18—8F 30
Mayberry Pl. Surb—2K 119
Maybourne Clo. SE26—3F 108
Maybrick Rd. Horn—4G 51
Maybury Av. Dart—7M 99
Maybury Av. Wal X—1B 6
Maybury Clo. Orp—9M 111
Maybury Gdns. NW10—2F 56
Maybury Rd. E13—7G 63
Maybury Rd. Bark—5D 64
Maybury St. SW17—2C 106
Maychurch Clo. Stan—7H 23
May Clo. Chess—8K 119
Maycock Gro. N'wd—6D 20
Maycroft. Pinn—9F 20
Maycross Av. Mord—7K 105
Mayday Gdns. SE3—1J 95
Mayday Rd. T Hth—1M 123
Maydwell Lodge. Borwd
—4K 11
Mayerne Rd. SE9—4H 95
Mayesbrook Rd. Bark—4D 64
Mayesbrook Rd. Ilf & Dag
—8E 48
Mayes Clo. Swan—8E 114
Mayes Clo. Warl—9H 139
Mayesford Rd. Romf—5G 49
Mayes Rd. N22—9K 27
Mayeswood Rd. SE12—1G 111
Mayfair. Rick—7B 8
Mayfair Av. Bexh—9H 81
Mayfair Av. Ilf—7K 47
Mayfair Av. Romf—4H 49
Mayfair Av. Twic—6A 86
Mayfair Av. Wor Pk—3E 120
Mayfair Clo. Beck—5M 109
Mayfair Clo. Surb—3J 119
Mayfair Gdns. N17—6B 28
Mayfair Gdns. Wfd G—7E 30
Mayfair Pl. W1—2F 74
Mayfair Rd. Dart—4H 99
Mayfair Ter. N14—9H 15
Mayfield. Bexh—2K 97
Mayfield. Wal A—7K 7
Mayfield Av. N12—4A 26
Mayfield Av. N14—2H 27
Mayfield Av. W4—5C 72
Mayfield Av. W13—3F 70
Mayfield Av. Harr—3F 38
Mayfield Av. Orp—3D 128
Mayfield Av. Wfd G—6E 30
Mayfield Clo. E8—3D 60
Mayfield Clo. SE20—5F 108
Mayfield Clo. Th Dit—3F 118
Mayfield Clo. Uxb—6F 142
Mayfield Clo. W on T—6E 116
Mayfield Cres. N9—8F 16
Mayfield Cres. T Hth—8K 107
Mayfield Dri. Pinn—2K 37
Mayfield Gdns. NW4—4H 41
Mayfield Gdns. W7—9B 54
Mayfield Gdns. W on T—6E 116
Mayfield Rd. E4—2A 30
Mayfield Rd. E8—3D 60
Mayfield Rd. E13—7D 62
Mayfield Rd. E17—9J 29
Mayfield Rd. N8—3K 43
Mayfield Rd. SW19—5K 105
Mayfield Rd. W3—1M 71
Mayfield Rd. W12—3C 72
Mayfield Rd. Belv—5A 82
Mayfield Rd. Brom—9J 111
Mayfield Rd. Dag—6G 49
Mayfield Rd. Enf—4H 17
Mayfield Rd. S Croy—1B 138
Mayfield Rd. Sutt—8B 122
Mayfield Rd. T Hth—8K 107
Mayfield Rd. W on T—6E 116
Mayfields. Wemb—7L 39
Mayfields Clo. Wemb—7L 39
Mayflower Clo. Ruis—4A 36
Mayflower Rd. SW9—2J 91
Mayflower St. SE16—3G 77
Mayford Clo. SW12—6D 90
Mayford Clo. Beck—7H 109
Mayford Rd. SW12—6D 90
May Gdns. Wemb—6G 55
Maygoods Clo. Uxb—8B 142
Maygoods Grn. Uxb—8B 142
Maygoods La. Uxb—8B 142
Maygood St. N1—5L 59
Maygoods View. Uxb—8A 142
Maygreen Cres. Horn—5E 50
Maygrove Rd. NW6—2K 57
Mayhew Clo. E4—3M 29
Mayhill Rd. SE7—7F 78
Mayhill Rd. Barn—8J 13
Maylands Av. Horn—9F 50
Maylands Dri. Sidc—9H 97
Maylands Dri. Uxb—2D 142
Maylands Way. Wat—4G 21
Maylands Way. Romf—6M 35

Maynard Clo.—Merrilands Rd.

Maynard Clo. SW6—8M 73
Maynard Clo. Eri—8D 82
Maynard Ct. Wal A—7M 7
Maynard Rd. E17—3A 46
Maynards. Horn—5J 51
Mayo Clo. Wal X—1C 6
Mayo Ct. W13—4F 70
Mayola Rd. E5—9G 45
Mayo Rd. NW10—2C 56
Mayo Rd. Croy—9B 108
Mayo Rd. W on T—2D 116
Mayow Rd.—1H 109
 SE23 1-69 & 2-24
 SE26 remainder
Mayplace Av. Dart—3E 98
Mayplace Clo. Bexh—2M 97
Mayplace La. SE18—8M 79
Mayplace Rd. E. Bexh—2M 97
Mayplace Rd. W. Bexh—3L 97
Maypole Cres. Eri—7H 83
Maypole. Ilf—7B 32
Maypole Dri. Chig—3E 32
Maypole Rd. Orp—7K 129
May Rd. E4—6L 29
May Rd. E13—5E 62
May Rd. Dart—1K 115
May Rd. Twic—7C 86
Mayroyd Av. Surb—4L 119
Mays Ct. WC2—1J 75
Mays Hill Rd. Brom—6C 110
Mays La. Barn—9F 12
Maysoule Rd. SW11—3B 90
Mays Rd. Tedd—2B 102
May St. W14—6K 73
Mayswood Gdns. Dag—2A 66
Maythorne Clo. Wat—6C 8
Mayton St. N7—8K 43
Maytree Clo. Edgw—3A 24
Maytree Clo. Rain—5C 66
Maytree Ct. N'holt—6J 53
Maytree Cres. Wat—9D 4
May Tree La. Stan—7E 22
May Tree Wlk. SW2—8L 91
Mayville Rd. E11—7C 46
Mayville Rd. Ilf—1M 63
May Wlk. E13—5F 62
Maywater Clo. S Croy—3C 138
Maywin Dri. Horn—6K 51
Maywood Clo. Beck—4M 109
Maze Hill—7C 78
 SE10 1-119 & 2-40
 SE3 remainder
Mazenod Av. NW6—3L 57
Maze Rd. Rich—8L 71
Mead Clo. Harr—8B 22
Mead Clo. Romf—9E 34
Mead Clo. Swan—9E 114
Mead Ct. NW9—3B 40
Mead Ct. Wal A—7H 7
Mead Cres. E4—4A 30
Mead Cres. Dart—7H 99
Mead Cres. Sutt—5C 122
Meadcroft Rd. SE11—7M 75
Meade Clo. W4—7L 71
Mead End. Asht—9K 133
Meader Ct. SE14—8H 77
Meadfield. Edgw—2M 23
Meadfoot Rd. SW16—4H 107
Meadgate Av. Wfd G—5J 31
Mead Ho. Rd. Hay—7B 52
Meadlands Dri. Rich—8H 87
Meadow Av. Croy—1H 125
Meadoway. N14—2J 27
Meadow Bank. N21—8K 15
Meadowbank. NW3—3D 58
Meadow Bank. SE3—2D 94
Meadowbank. Surb—1K 119
Meadowbank. Wat—9G 9
Meadowbank Clo. SW6—8G 73
Meadowbank Gdns. Houn
—9F 68
Meadowbank Rd. NW9—5B 40
Meadow Clo. E4—1M 29
Meadow Clo. SE6—2L 109
Meadow Clo. SW20—8G 105
Meadow Clo. Barn—8K 13
Meadow Clo. Chst—2M 111
Meadow Clo. Enf—2J 17
Meadow Clo. Esh—5D 118
Meadow Clo. Houn—5L 85
Meadow Clo. N'holt—5L 53
Meadow Clo. Purl—5H 137
Meadow Clo. Rich—7J 87
Meadow Clo. Ruis—4D 36
Meadow Clo. Sutt—4A 122
Meadow Clo. W on T—6K 117
Meadow Ct. Eps—5B 134
Meadowcourt Rd. SE3—3D 94
Meadowcroft. Brom—7K 111
Meadowcroft Clo. N13—2M 27
Meadowcroft Rd. N13—2L 27
Meadowcross. Wal A—7L 7

Meadow Dri. N10—9F 26
Meadow Dri. NW4—9G 25
Meadow Gdns. Edgw—6M 23
Meadow Garth. NW10—2A 56
Meadow Hill. Coul & Purl
—6G 137
Meadow Hill. N Mald—1C 120
Meadowlands. Horn—5J 51
Meadow Leigh Clo. Wey
—5A 116
Meadow M. SW8—7K 75
Meadow Pl. SW8—8J 75
Meadow Rise. Coul—5H 137
Meadow Rd. SW8—8K 75
Meadow Rd. SW19—4A 106
Meadow Rd. Ashf—2B 100
Meadow Rd. Asht—9J 133
Meadow Rd. Bark—3D 64
Meadow Rd. Borwd—4M 11
Meadow Rd. Brom—6C 110
Meadow Rd. Bush, Wat—7M 9
Meadow Rd. Dag—2K 65
Meadow Rd. Esh—8C 118
Meadow Rd. Felt—8J 85
Meadow Rd. Lou—7J 19
Meadow Rd. Pinn—2H 37
Meadow Rd. Romf—6A 50
Meadow Rd. S'hall—1K 69
Meadow Rd. Sutt—6C 122
Meadow Rd. Wat—7E 4
Meadow Row. SE1—4A 76
Meadows Clo. E10—7L 45
Meadows End. Sun—5E 100
Meadowside. SE9—3G 95
Meadowside. Dart—7H 99
Meadowside. W on T—4G 117
Meadowside Rd. Sutt—1J 135
Meadowside Rd. Upm—1M 67
Meadows, The. Orp—8G 129
Meadow Stile. Croy—5A 124
Meadow, The. Chst—3A 112
Meadow View. Orp—7G 113
Meadow View. Sidc—6F 96
Meadowview Rd. SE6—2L 109
Meadowview Rd. Bex—5J 97
Meadowview Rd. Eps—1C 134
Meadow View Rd. Hay—7B 52
Meadow View Rd. T Hth
—9M 107
Meadow Wlk. E18—2E 46
Meadow Wlk. Dag—2K 65
Meadow Wlk. Dart—1G 115
Meadow Wlk. Eps—8C 120
Meadow Wlk. Wall—5F 122
Meadow Way. NW9—3B 40
Meadow Way. Abb L, Wat
—1D 4
Meadow Way. Chess—7J 119
Meadow Way. Chig—3A 32
Meadow Way. Dart—6M 99
Meadow Way. Orp—5L 127
Meadow Way. Ruis—4F 36
Meadow Way. Tad—9J 135
Meadow Way. Upm—8M 51
Meadow Way. Wemb—9H 39
Meadow Waye. Houn—7J 69
Meadow Way, The. Harr—8C 22
Mead Path. SW17 & SW19
—1A 106
Mead Pl. E9—2G 61
Mead Pl. Croy—3A 124
Mead Plat. NW10—2A 56
Mead Rd. Chst—3A 112
Mead Rd. Dart—7H 99
Mead Rd. Edgw—6L 23
Mead Rd. Rich—9G 87
Mead Rd. Uxb—3B 142
Mead Rd. W on T—6J 117
Mead Row. SE1—4L 75
Meads La. Ilf—5C 48
Meads Rd. N22—9M 27
Meads Rd. Enf—3J 17
Meads, The. Edgw—6B 24
Meads, The. St Alb—3L 5
Meads, The. Sutt—5J 121
Meads, The. Uxb—7C 142
Mead, The. N2—9A 26
Mead, The. W13—8F 54
Mead, The. Beck—5A 110
Mead, The. Wall—8H 123
Mead, The. Wal X—2C 6
Mead, The. Wat—3J 21
Mead, The. W Wick—3B 126
Meadvale Rd. W5—7F 54
Meadvale Rd. Croy—2D 124
Meadway. NW11—4M 41
Meadway. SW20—8G 105
Meadway. Ashf—9E 144
Meadway. Barn—6L 13
Meadway. Beck—5A 110
Mead Way. Brom—1D 126
Mead Way. Bush, Wat—4J 9
Mead Way. Coul—9J 137

Mead Way. Croy—4J 125
Meadway. Enf—9C 6
Meadway. Eps—4A 134
Meadway. Esh—9M 117
Meadway. Ilf—9C 48
Meadway. Lea—6C 132
 (Oxshott)
Meadway. Orp—8F 128
Meadway. Romf—9E 34
Mead Way. Ruis—4B 36
Meadway. Surb—3A 120
Meadway. Twic—7B 86
Meadway. Warl—8G 139
Mead Way. Wfd G—5G 31
Meadway Clo. NW11—4M 41
Meadway Clo. Barn—6L 13
Meadway Clo. Pinn—6M 21
Meadway Ct. Dag—7K 49
Meadway Gdns. Ruis—4B 36
Meadway Ga. NW11—4L 41
Meadway, The. SE3—1B 94
Meadway, The. Buck H—1H 3
Meadway, The. Lou—8K 19
Meaford Way. SE20—4F 108
Meakin Est. SE1—4C 76
Meanley Rd. E12—9J 47
Meard St. W1—9H 59
Meath Clo. Orp—9F 112
Meath Rd. E15—5D 62
Meath Rd. Ilf—8A 48
Meath St. SW11—9F 74
Mechanic's Path. SE18—8L 77
Mecklenburgh Pl. WC1—7K 59
Mecklenburgh Sq. WC1—7K 59
Mecklenburgh St. WC1—7K 59
Medburn St. NW1—5H 59
Medcalfe Pl. N1—5L 59
Medcalf Rd. Enf—1K 17
Medcroft Gdns. SW14—3A 88
Medebourne Clo. SE3—2E 94
Medesenge Way. N13—6M 27
Medfield St. SW15—6F 88
Medhurst Rd. E3—5J 61
Median Rd. E5—1G 61
Medina Av. Esh—5C 118
Medina Gro. N7—8L 43
Medina Rd. N7—8L 43
Medland Clo. Wall—3E 122
Medlar Clo. N'holt—5H 53
Medlar St. SE5—9A 76
Medley Rd. NW6—2L 57
Medman Clo. Uxb—5A 142
Medora Rd. SW2—6K 91
Medora Rd. Romf—2B 50
Medusa Rd. SE6—5M 93
Medway Clo. Croy—1G 125
Medway Clo. Ilf—1A 64
Medway Clo. Wat—7G 5
Medway Dri. Gnfd—5D 54
Medway Gdns. Wemb—9E 38
Medway M. E3—5J 61
Medway Pde. Gnfd—5D 54
Medway Rd. E3—5J 61
Medway Rd. Dart—2E 98
Medway St. SW1—4H 75
Meerbrook Rd. SE3—2G 95
Meeson Rd. E15—3D 62
Meeson St. E5—9J 45
Meeting Field Path.E9—2G 61
Meetinghouse All. E1—2F 76
Meeting Ho. La. SE15—9F 76
Mehetabel Rd. E9—1G 61
Melancholy Wlk. Rich—8G 87
Melanda Clo. Chst—2K 111
Melanie Clo. Bexh—9J 81
Melba Way. SE13—9M 77
Melbourne Av. N13—6K 27
Melbourne Av. W13—2E 70
Melbourne Av. Pinn—1M 37
Melbourne Clo. SE20—4E 108
Melbourne Clo. Orp—2C 128
Melbourne Clo. Wall—7G 123
Melbourne Gdns. Romf—3J 49
Melbourne Gro. SE22—3C 92
Melbourne M. SW9—9L 75
Melbourne Pl. WC2—9K 59
Melbourne Rd. E6—5K 63
Melbourne Rd. E10—5M 45
Melbourne Rd. E17—2J 45
Melbourne Rd. SW19—5L 105
Melbourne Rd. Bush, Wat
—8M 9
Melbourne Rd. Ilf—6M 47
Melbourne Rd. Tedd—3G 103
Melbourne Rd. Wall—7F 122
Melbourne Sq. SW9—9L 75
Melbourne Way. Enf—8D 16
Melbury Av. S'hall—4M 69
Melbury Clo. Chst—3K 111
Melbury Clo. Esh—8F 118
Melbury Ct. W8—4L 73
Melbury Dri. SE5—8C 76

Melbury Gdns. SW20—5F 104
Melbury Rd. W14—4K 73
Melbury Rd. Harr—3K 39
Melbury Ter. NW1—7C 58
Melcombe Gdns. Harr—4K 39
Melcombe Pl. NW1—8D 58
Melcombe St. NW1—7D 58
Meldon Clo. SW6—9M 73
Meldrum Clo. Orp—1G 129
Meldrum Rd. Ilf—7E 48
Melfield Gdns. SE6—2A 110
Melford Av. Bark—2C 64
Melford Rd. E6—6K 63
Melford Rd. E11—7C 46
Melford Rd. E17—2K 45
Melford Rd. SE22—6E 92
Melford Rd. Ilf—7B 48
Melfort Av. T Hth—7M 107
Melfort Rd. T Hth—7M 107
Melgund Rd. N5—1L 59
Melina Clo. Hay—8B 52
Melina Pl. NW8—6B 58
Melina Rd. W12—3F 72
Melior Pl. SE1—3C 76
Melior St. SE1—3C 76
Meliot Rd. SE6—8B 94
Melksham Clo. Romf—7K 35
Melksham Dri. Romf—7K 35
Melksham Gdns. Romf—7J 35
Melksham Grn. Romf—7K 35
Meller Clo. Croy—5J 123
Melling St. SE18—7C 80
Mellish Clo. Bark—4D 64
Mellish St. E14—4L 77
Mellison Rd. SW17—2C 106
Mellitus St. W12—9D 56
Mellor Clo. W on T—2K 117
Mellow Clo. Bans—6M 135
Mellow La. E. Hay—7A 52
Mellow La. W. Uxb—6A 52
Mellows Rd. Ilf—1K 47
Mellows Rd. Wall—7H 123
Mells Cres. SE9—1K 111
Mell St. SE10—6C 78
Melody Rd. SW18—4A 90
Melody Rd. W4—6M 71
Melody Rd. West—9G 141
Melon Pl. W8—3L 73
Melon Rd. SE15—9E 76
Melrose Av. N22—8M 27
Melrose Av. NW2—1F 56
Melrose Av. SW16—7L 107
Melrose Av. SW19—8K 89
Melrose Av. Borwd—7M 11
Melrose Av. Gnfd—5M 53
Melrose Av. Mitc—4F 106
Melrose Av. Twic—6M 85
Melrose Clo. SE12—7E 94
Melrose Clo. Gnfd—5M 53
Melrose Clo. Hay—8E 52
Melrose Cres. Orp—6B 128
Melrose Dri. S'hall—2L 69
Melrose Gdns. W6—4G 73
Melrose Gdns. Edgw—9M 23
Melrose Gdns. N Mald—7B 104
Melrose Gdns. W on T—7G 117
Melrose Pl. Wat—2D 8
Melrose Rd. SW13—1D 88
Melrose Rd. SW18—5K 89
Melrose Rd. SW19—6L 105
Melrose Rd. W3—4A 72
Melrose Rd. Coul—7F 136
Melrose Rd. Pinn—2K 37
Melrose Rd. West—8G 141
Melrose Ter. W6—4G 73
Melsa Rd. Mord—1A 122
Melstock Av. Upm—9M 51
Meltham Way. SE16—6F 76
Melthorne Dri. Ruis—8G 37
Melthorpe Gdns. SE3—9J 79
Melton Clo. Ruis—6G 37
Melton Ct. SW7—5B 74
Melton Gdns. Romf—5D 50
Melton Pl. Eps—1B 134
Melton St. NW1—6H 59
Melville Av. SW20—4E 104
Melville Av. Gnfd—1D 54
Melville Av. S Croy—7D 124
Melville Clo. Uxb—7B 36
Melville Gdns. N13—5M 27
Melville Rd. E17—1K 45
Melville Rd. NW10—3B 56
Melville Rd. SW13—9E 72
Melville Rd. Rain—7E 66
Melville Rd. Romf—8M 33
Melville Rd. Sidc—8G 97
Melville St. N1—3A 60
Melville Vs. Rd. W3—2B 72
Melvin Rd. SE20—5G 109
Melyn Clo. N7—9G 43
Memel St. EC1—7A 60
Memess Path. SE18—7L 79
Memorial Av. E15—6C 62

Memorial Clo. Houn—7K 69
Mendip Clo. SE26—1G 109
Mendip Clo. SW19—8J 89
Mendip Clo. Hay—8B 68
Mendip Dri. NW2—7J 41
Mendip Rd. SW11—2A 90
Mendip Rd. Bexh—9C 82
Mendip Rd. Bush, Wat—8A 10
Mendip Rd. Horn—5E 50
Mendip Rd. Ilf—3C 48
Mendora Rd. SW6—8J 73
Mendoza Clo. Horn—3J 51
Menelik Rd. NW2—9J 41
Menlo Gdns. SE19—4B 108
Menotti St. E2—7E 60
Menthone Pl. Horn—5H 51
Mentmore Clo. Harr—4G 39
Mentmore Ter. E8—3F 60
Meon Ct. Iswth—1C 86
Meon Rd. W3—3A 72
Meopham Rd. Mitc—5G 107
Mepham Cres. Harr—7A 22
Mepham Gdns. Harr—7A 22
Mepham St. SE1—2L 75
Mera Dri. Bexh—3L 97
Mercator Rd. SE13—3B 94
Mercer Av. WC2—9J 59
Mercer Clo. Th Dit—2D 118
Merceron St. E1—7F 60
Mercer Pl. Pinn—9G 21
Mercers Clo. SE10—5D 78
Mercers Pl. W6—5G 73
Mercers Rd. N19—8H 43
Mercer St. WC2—9J 59
Mercer Wlk. Uxb—3A 142
Merchant Industrial Ter. NW10
—7A 56
Merchant St. E3—6K 61
Merchiston Rd. SE6—8B 94
Merchland Rd. SE9—7A 96
Mercia Gro. SE13—3A 94
Mercier Rd. SW15—4J 89
Mercury Gdns. Romf—3C 50
Mercury Rd. Bren—6G 71
Mercury Way. SE14—7H 77
Mercy Ter. SE13—4M 93
Merebank La. Croy—7K 123
Mere Clo. SW15—6H 89
Mere Clo. Orp—4L 127
Meredith Av. NW2—1G 57
Meredith Clo. Pinn—7H 21
Meredith St. E13—6E 62
Meredith St. EC1—6M 59
Meredyth Rd. SW13—1E 88
Mere End. Croy—2H 125
Mere Rd. Shep—1A 116
Mere Rd. Wey—5B 116
Mere Side. Orp—4L 127
Meretone Clo. SE4—3J 93
Merevale Cres. Mord—1A 122
Mereway Rd. Twic—7B 86
Merewood Clo. Brom—6L 111
Merewood Rd. Bexh—1A 98
Mereworth Clo. Brom—9D 110
Mereworth Dri. SE18—8M 79
Merganser Gdns. SE28—8B 80
Meriden Clo. Brom—4H 111
Meriden Clo. Ilf—8A 32
Meriden Way. Wat—9J 5
Meridian Rd. SE7—8H 79
Meridian View. E14—2A 78
Meridian Wlk. N17—6C 28
Merifield Rd. SE9—3G 95
Merino Pl. Sidc—5C 96
Merivale Rd. SW15—3J 89
Merivale Rd. Harr—5A 38
Merlewood Dri. Chst—5K 111
Merlewood Pl. SE9—5K 95
Merley Ct. NW9—6A 40
Merlin Clo. Croy—6C 124
Merlin Clo. Ilf—5G 33
Merlin Clo. N'holt—6G 53
Merlin Clo. Romf—6B 34
Merlin Ct. Brom—8D 110
Merlin Cres. Edgw—8K 23
Merlin Gdns. Brom—9E 94
Merlin Gdns. Romf—6B 34
Merlin Gro. Beck—8K 109
Merlin Gro. Ilf—7M 31
Merlin Rd. E12—7H 47
Merlin Rd. Romf—6B 34
Merlin Rd. Well—3E 96
Merlin Rd. N. Well—3E 96
Merlins Av. Harr—8K 37
Merlin St. WC1—6L 59
Mermagen Dri. Rain—3F 66
Mermaid Ct. SE1—3B 76
Merredene St. SW2—5K 91
Merrick Rd. S'hall—4K 69
Merrick Sq. SE1—4B 76
Merridene. N21—8M 15
Merrielands Cres. Dag—5K 65
Merrilands Rd. Wor Pk—3G 121

Merrilees Rd. Sidc—6C 96
Merrilyn Clo. Esh—8E 118
Merriman Rd. SE3—9G 79
Merrington Rd. SW6—7L 73
Merrion Av. Stan—5H 23
Merritt Rd. SE4—4K 93
Merrivale. N14—8H 15
Merrivale Av. Ilf—2H 47
Merrow Rd. Sutt—1H 135
Merrows Clo. N'wd—6A 20
Merrow St. SE17—6B 76
Merrow Wlk. SE17—6B 76
Merrow Way. Croy—8A 126
Merrydown Way. Chst—5J 111
Merryfield. SE3—1D 94
Merryfield Gdns. Stan—5G 23
Merryfields. Uxb—5B 142
(in two parts)
Merryhill Clo. E4—9M 17
Merry Hill Mt. Bush, Wat
—1M 21
Merry Hill Rd. Bush, Wat—8K 9
Merryhills Clo. West—8H 141
Merryhills Ct. N14—7G 15
Merryhills Dri. Enf—6H 15
Merry Meet. Bans—6D 136
Mersey Rd. E17—1K 45
Mersham Dri. NW9—3L 39
Mersham Rd. T Hth—6B 108
Merten Ter. SW13—7F 72
Merthyr Ter. SW13—7F 72
Merton Av. W4—5D 72
Merton Av. N'holt—1A 54
Merton Av. Uxb—3F 142
Merton Gdns. Orp—9M 111
Merton Hall Gdns. SW20
—5J 105
Merton Hall Rd. SW19—5J 105
Merton High St. SW19—4M 105
Merton La. N6—7D 42
Merton Mans. SW20—6H 105
Merton Rise. NW3—3C 58
Merton Rd. E17—3A 46
Merton Rd. SE25—9E 108
Merton Rd. SW18—5L 89
Merton Rd. SW19—4M 105
Merton Rd. Bark—3D 64
Merton Rd. Enf—2B 16
Merton Rd. Harr—6A 38
Merton Rd. Ilf—5D 48
Merton Rd. Wat—6F 8
Merton Way. E Mol—8M 101
Merton Way. Uxb—3F 142
Merttins Rd. SE15—4H 93
Mervan Rd. SW2—3L 91
Mervyn Av. SE9—9A 96
Mervyn Rd. W13—4E 70
Meryfield Rd. Borwd—4K 11
Messaline Av. W3—9A 56
Messent Rd. SE9—4G 95
Messeter Pl. SE9—5L 95
Messina Av. NW6—3L 57
Metcalfe Wlk. Felt—1J 101
Metcalf Rd. Ashf—2A 100
Meteor St. SW11—3E 90
Meteor Way. Wall—9J 123
Metheringham Way. NW9
—8C 24
Methley St. SE11—6L 75
Methuen Clo. Edgw—7L 23
Methuen Pk. N10—1F 42
Methuen Rd. Belv—5M 81
Methuen Rd. Bexh—3K 97
Methuen Rd. Edgw—7L 23
Methwold Rd. W10—8H 57
Meux Clo. Wal X—4A 6
Mews End. West—9H 141
Mews St. E1—2E 76
Mews, The. N1—4A 60
Mews, The. Ilf—3H 47
Mews, The. Romf—2C 50
Mews, The. Twic—5F 86
Mexfield Rd. SW15—4K 89
Meyer Gro. Enf—2E 16
Meyer Rd. Eri—7B 82
Meymott St. SE1—2M 75
Meynell Cres. E9—3H 61
Meynell Gdns. E9—3H 61
Meynell Rd. E9—3H 61
Meynell Rd. Romf—7F 34
Meyrick Rd. NW10—2E 56
Meyrick Rd. SW11—2B 90
Mezen Clo. N'wd—5B 20
Miall Wlk. SE26—1J 109
Micawber Av. Uxb—7E 142
Micawber St. N1—6A 60
Michael Gdns. Horn—2H 51
Michael Gaynor Dri. W7—2D 70
Michael Rd. E11—6D 46
Michael Rd. SE25—7C 108
Michael Rd. SW6—9M 73
Michael's Clo. SE13—3C 94

Michdever Rd. SE12—5D 94
Michelham Gdns. Twic—9D 86
Michel's Row. Rich—3J 87
Michigan Av. E12—9J 47
Mickleham Clo. Orp—6D 112
Mickleham Gdns. Sutt—8J 121
Mickleham Rd. Orp—5D 112
Mickleham Way. Croy—9B 126
Micklethwaite Rd. SW6—7L 73
Midcroft. Ruis—6C 36
Middle Clo. Eps—4C 134
Middle Dene. NW7—3B 24
Middle Field. NW8—4B 58
Middlefielde. W13—8F 54
Middlefields. Croy—1J 139
Middle Furlong. Bush, Wat
—6M 9
Middle Grn. Clo. Surb—1K 119
Middleham Gdns. N18—6E 28
Middleham Rd. N18—6E 28
Middle La. N8—3J 43
Middle La. Eps—4C 134
Middle La. Tedd—3D 102
Middle Ope. Wat—1F 8
Middle Pk. Av. SE9—5H 95
Middle Path. Harr—6B 38
Middle Rd. E13—5E 62
Middle Rd. SW16—6H 107
Middle Rd. Barn—8C 14
Middle Rd. Harr—7B 38
Middle Rd. Wal A—5H 7
Middle Row. W10—7J 57
Middlesborough Rd. N18
—6E 28
Middlesex Ct. W4—6D 72
Middlesex Rd. Mitc—9J 107
Middlesex St. E1—8C 60
Middlesex Wharf. E5—7G 45
Middle St. EC1—8A 60
Middle St. Croy—4A 124
Middle Temple La. EC4—9L 59
Middleton Av. E4—4K 29
Middleton Av. Gnfd—5B 54
Middleton Av. Sidc—3G 113
Middleton Clo. E4—3K 29
Middleton Dri. Pinn—1E 36
Middleton Gdns. Ilf—4M 47
Middleton Gro. N7—1J 59
Middleton M. N7—1J 59
Middleton Rd. E8—3D 60
Middleton Rd. NW11—5L 41
Middleton Rd. Eps—2B 134
Middleton Rd. Hay—8B 52
Middleton Rd. Mord & Cars
—1M 121
Middleton Rd. N Mald—6A 104
Middleton St. E2—6F 60
Middleway. SE13—3B 94
Middleway. NW11—3M 41
Middle Way. SW16—6H 107
Middle Way. Hay—7G 53
Middle Way, The. Harr—9D 22
Middle Yd. SE1—2C 76
Midfield Av. Bexh—2A 98
Midfield Av. Swan—3E 114
Midfield Pde. Bexh—2A 98
Midfield Way. Orp—5F 112
Midford Pl. W1—7G 59
Midholm. NW11—2M 41
Midholm. Wemb—6L 39
Midholm Clo. NW11—2M 41
Midhope St. WC1—6J 59
Midhurst Av. N10—1E 42
Midhurst Av. Croy—2L 123
Midhurst Clo. Horn—9E 50
Midhurst Gdns. Uxb—4A 52
Midhurst Hill. Bexh—5L 97
Midhurst Rd. W13—3E 70
Midland Pl. E14—6A 78
Midland Rd. E10—5A 46
Midland Rd. NW1—5H 59
Midland Ter. NW2—8H 41
Midland Ter. NW10—7C 56
Midmoor Rd. SW12—7G 91
Midmoor Rd. SW19—5J 105
Midstrath Rd. NW10—9C 40
Midsummer Av. Houn—3K 85
Midway. Sutt—2K 121
Midway. W on T—4F 116
Midwood Clo. NW2—8F 40
Miena Way. Asht—9H 133
Miers Clo. E6—4L 63
Mighell Av. Ilf—3H 47
Milborne Gro. SW10—6A 74
Milborne St. E9—2G 61
Milborough Cres. SE12—5C 94
Milbourne La. Esh—8A 118
Milbrook. Esh—8A 118
Milburn Wlk. Eps—7C 134

Milby Ct. Borwd—3K 11
Milcote St. SE1—3M 75
Mildenhall Rd. E5—9G 45
Mildmay Av. N1—2B 60
Mildmay Gro. N1—1B 60
(in two parts)
Mildmay Pk. N1—1B 60
Mildmay Rd. N1—1B 60
Mildmay Rd. Ilf—8M 47
Mildmay Rd. Romf—3A 50
Mildmay St. N1—1B 60
Mildred Av. Borwd—6L 11
Mildred Av. Hay—5B 68
Mildred Av. N'holt—1M 53
Mildred Av. Wat—6D 8
Mildred Clo. Dart—5L 99
Mildred Rd. Eri—6D 82
Mile Clo. Wal A—6J 7
Mile End Pl. E1—7H 61
Mile End Rd. E1 & E3—8G 61
E1 1-357 & 2-510
E3 remainder
Mile End, The. E17—8H 29
Mile Rd. Wall—3F 122
Milespit Hill. NW7—5F 24
Miles Pl. Surb—8K 103
Miles Rd. N8—1J 43
Miles Rd. Eps—4B 134
Miles Rd. Mitc—7C 106
Miles St. SW8—7J 75
(in two parts)
Milestone Clo. Sutt—9B 122
Milestone Rd. SE19—3D 108
Milestone Rd. Dart—5M 99
Miles Way. N20—2C 26
Milfoil St. W12—1E 72
Milford Clo. SE2—7J 81
Milford Gdns. Edgw—7L 23
Milford Gdns. Wemb—1H 55
Milford Gro. Sutt—6A 122
Milford La. WC2—1L 75
Milford M. SW16—9K 91
Milford Rd. W13—2F 70
Milford Rd. S'hall—1L 69
Milford Towers. SE6—6M 93
Milford Way. SE15—9D 76
Milking La. Kes—3H 141
Milking La. Orp—4J 141
Milk St. E16—2M 79
Milk St. EC2—9A 60
Milk St. Brom—3F 110
Milkwell Gdns. Wfd G—7F 30
Milkwood Rd. SE24—4M 91
Milk Yd. E1—1G 77
Millais Av. E12—1L 63
Millais Gdns. Edgw—9L 23
Millais Rd. E11—9A 46
Millais Rd. Enf—7D 16
Millais Rd. N Mald—2C 120
Millais Way. Eps—6A 120
Millard Clo. N16—1C 60
Millard Ter. Dag—2L 65
Mill Av. Uxb—5A 142
Millbank. SW1—5J 75
Millbank Way. SE12—4E 94
Millbourne Rd. Felt—1J 101
Mill Bridge. Barn—8K 13
Millbro. Swan—5E 114
Millbrook. Wey—6C 116
Millbrook Av. Well—3B 96
Millbrook Gdns. Romf—7L 23
Millbrook Gdns. Romf—4K 49
(Chadwell Heath)
Millbrook Rd. N9—1F 28
Millbrook Rd. SW9—2M 91
Millbrook Rd. Bush, Wat—3K 9
Mill Brook Rd. Orp—8G 113
Mill Clo. Cars—4E 122
Mill Clo. W Dray—4H 143
Mill Corner. Barn—3K 13
Mill Ct. E10—8A 46
Mill Dri. SW16—7K 107
Millender Wlk. SE16—5G 77
Miller Clo. Pinn—9G 21
Miller Rd. SW19—3B 106
Miller Rd. Croy—3K 123
Millers Av. E8—1D 60
Miller's Clo. Chig—2F 32
Miller's Ct. W6—6D 72
Millers Grn. Enf—5M 15
Miller's La. Chig—1F 32
Millers Ter. E8—1D 60
Miller St. NW1—5G 59
Millet Rd. Gnfd—6M 53
Mill Farm Av. Sun—4C 100
Mill Farm Clo. Pinn—9G 21
Mill Farm Cres. Houn—7J 85
Millfield. Sun—5B 100
Millfield Av. E17—8J 29
Millfield La. N6—7D 42
Millfield Pl. N6—7E 42
Millfield Rd. Edgw—9A 24
Millfield Rd. Houn—7J 85

Millfields Clo. Orp—8F 112
Millfields Rd. E5—9G 45
Mill Gdns. SE26—9F 92
Mill Grn. Rd. Mitc—2E 122
Millgrove St. SW11—1E 90
Millharbour. E14—4L 77
Mill Hill Cir. NW7—5D 24
Mill Hill Gro. W3—2M 71
Mill Hill Rd. SW13—1E 88
Mill Hill Rd. W3—3M 71
Mill Hill Ter. W3—2M 71
Millhoo Ct. Wal A—7M 7
Millhouse La. Abb L, Wat
—1E 4
Millhouse Pl. SE27—1M 107
Millicent Rd. E10—6K 45
Milligan St. E14—1L 77
Milling Rd. Edgw—7B 24
Millington Rd. Hay—4C 68
Mill La. E4—5M 17
Mill La. NW6—1K 57
Mill La. SE18—6L 79
Mill La. Cars—6D 122
Mill La. Croy—5K 123
Mill La. Eps—1D 134
Mill La. Eyns, Dart—3J 131
Mill La. Orp—2L 141
Mill La. Romf—4J 49
(Chadwell Heath)
Mill La. Wal X—1E 6
Mill La. Wfd G—5D 30
Millman M. WC1—7K 59
Millman St. WC1—7K 59
Millmark Gro. SE14—1J 93
Millmarsh La. Enf—4K 17
Millmead Industrial Centre.
N17—1F 44
Mill Mead Rd. N17—1F 44
Mill Pk. Av. Horn—7J 51
Mill Pl. E14—9J 61
Mill Pl. Chst—5M 111
Mill Pl. Dart—3E 98
Mill Pl. King—7K 103
Mill Plat. Iswth—1E 86
Mill Plat Av. Iswth—1E 86
Mill Pond Rd. Dart—5J 99
Mill Ridge. Edgw—5K 23
Mill Rd. E16—2F 78
Mill Rd. SE13—2A 94
Mill Rd. SW19—4A 106
Mill Rd. Dart—1K 115
Mill Rd. Eps—4D 134
Mill Rd. Eri—8A 82
Mill Rd. Esh—4L 117
Mill Rd. Ilf—8L 47
Mill Rd. Purf—7M 83
Mill Rd. S Ock—1M 83
Mill Rd. Twic—3A 86
Mill Rd. W Dray—4G 143
Mill Row. N1—4C 60
Mills Clo. Uxb—5E 142
Mills Gro. E14—9A 62
Mills Gro. NW4—1H 41
Mill Shot Clo. SW6—9G 73
Millside. Cars—4D 122
Millsmead Way. Lou—4K 19
Millson Clo. N20—2B 26
Mills Rd. W on T—5B 72
Mills Rd. W on T—7G 117
Mills Row. W4—5B 72
Millstream Rd. SE1—3D 76
Mill St. SE1—3D 76
Mill St. W1—1G 75
Mill St. King—7J 103
Mill Vale. Brom—6D 110
Mill View Gdns. Croy—5H 125
Mill Way. NW7—4C 24
Mill Way. Bush, Wat—4J 9
Mill Way. Felt—4F 84
Millway Gdns. N'holt—2K 53
Millwell Cres. Chig—5B 32
Millwood Rd. Hqun—4A 86
Millwood Rd. Orp—7G 113
Millwood St. W10—8J 57
Milman Clo. Pinn—1H 37
Milman Rd. NW6—5J 57
Milman's St. SW10—7B 74
Milne Fst SE18—5K 79
Milne Feild. Pinn—7L 21
Milne Gdns. SE9—4J 95
Milne Pk. E. Croy—3B 140
Milne Pk. W. Croy—3B 140
Milner Clo. Wat—7F 4
Milner Ct. Bush, Wat—8M 9
Milner Dri. Twic—5B 86
Milner Pl. N1—4M 59
Milner Pl. Cars—6E 122
Milner Rd. E15—6C 62
Milner Rd. SW19—5M 105
Milner Rd. Dag—7G 49
Milner Rd. King—7H 103
Milner Rd. Mord—9B 106

Milner Rd. T Hth—7B 108
Milner Sq. N1—3M 59
Milner St. SW3—5D 74
Milnthorpe Rd. W4—7B 72
Milo Rd. SE22—5D 92
Milroy Wlk. SE1—2M 75
Milson Rd. W14—4H 73
Milton Av. E6—3H 63
Milton Av. N6—5G 43
Milton Av. NW9—1A 40
Milton Av. NW10—4A 56
Milton Av. Barn—7K 13
Milton Av. Croy—2B 124
Milton Av. Horn—7D 50
Milton Av. Sutt—5B 122
Milton Clo. N2—3A 42
Milton Clo. Hay—9E 52
Milton Clo. Pinn—7J 21
Milton Clo. Sutt—5B 122
Milton Ct. EC2—8B 60
Milton Ct. Uxb—8A 36
Milton Ct. Wal A—7J 7
Milton Ct. Rd. SE14—7J 77
Milton Cres. Ilf—5A 48
Milton Dri. Borwd—7M 11
Milton Gdns. Eps—6C 134
Milton Gro. N11—5G 27
Milton Gro. N16—9C 44
Milton Pk. N6—5G 43
Milton Pl. N7—1L 59
Milton Rd. E17—2L 45
Milton Rd. N6—5G 43
Milton Rd. N15—2M 43
Milton Rd. NW7—5E 24
Milton Rd. NW9—5E 40
Milton Rd. SE24—4M 91
Milton Rd. SW14—2B 88
Milton Rd. SW19—3A 106
Milton Rd. W3—2B 72
Milton Rd. W7—1D 70
Milton Rd. Belv—5L 81
Milton Rd. Croy—2B 124
Milton Rd. Hmptn—4L 101
Milton Rd. Harr—2C 38
Milton Rd. Mitc—4E 106
Milton Rd. Romf—4E 50
Milton Rd. Sutt—5L 121
Milton Rd. Uxb—9A 36
Milton Rd. Wall—8G 123
Milton Rd. W on T—5H 117
Milton Rd. Well—9D 80
Milton St. EC2—8B 60
Milton St. Wal A—7J 7
Milton St. Wat—3F 8
Milton Way. W Dray—5K 143
Milverton Dri. Uxb—9A 36
Milverton Gdns. Ilf—7D 48
Milverton Rd. NW6—3G 57
Milverton St. SE11—6L 75
Milverton Way. SE9—1L 111
Milward St. E1—8F 60
Milward Wlk. SE18—7L 79
Mimosa Clo. Orp—4G 129
Mimosa Clo. Romf—7G 35
Mimosa Rd. Hay—8G 53
Mimosa St. SW6—9K 73
Minard Rd. SE6—6C 94
Mina Rd. SE17—6C 76
Mina Rd. SW19—5L 105
Minchenden Cres. N14—3H 27
Mincing La. EC3—1C 76
Minden Rd. SE20—5F 108
Minehead Rd. SW16—2K 107
Minehead Rd. Harr—8L 37
Mineral St. SE18—5C 80
Minera M. SW1—5E 74
Minerva Clo. SW9—1L 91
Minerva Dri. Wat—9C 4
Minerva Rd. E4—7M 29
Minerva Rd. NW10—7A 56
Minerva Rd. King—6K 103
Minerva Rd. Sidc—1C 112
Minerva St. E2—5F 60
Minet Av. NW10—5C 56
Minet Dri. Hay—2E 68
Minet Gdns. NW10—5C 56
Minet Gdns. Hay—2F 68
Minet Rd. SW9—1M 91
Minford Gdns. W14—3H 73
Mingard Wlk. N7—7K 43
Ming St. E14—1L 77
Mink Ct. Houn—1G 85
Minniedale. Surb—9K 103
Minnow Wlk. SE17—5C 76
Minories. EC3—9D 60
Minshull St. SW8—9H 75
Minson Rd. E9—4H 61
Minstead Gdns. SW15—6D 88
Minstead Way. N Mald—1C 120
Minster Av. Sutt—4L 121
Minster Dri. Croy—6C 124
Minster Gdns. E Mol—8K 101
Minsterley Av. Shep—8C 100
Minster Rd. NW2—1J 57

Minster Rd. Brom—4F 110
Minster Wlk. N8—2J 43
Minster Way. Horn—6K 51
Minstrel Gdns. Surb—8K 103
Mintern Clo. N13—3M 27
Minterne Av. S'hall—5L 69
Minterne Rd. Harr—3K 39
Minterne Waye. Hay—9G 53
Mintern St. N1—5B 60
Minton M. NW6—2M 57
Mint Rd. Bans—8A 136
Mint Rd. Wall—6F 122
Mint St. SE1—3A 76
Mint Wlk. Croy—5A 124
Mint Wlk. Warl—9H 139
Mirabel Rd. SW6—8K 73
Miramar Way. Horn—1H 67
Miranda Rd. N19—6G 43
Mirfield St. SE7—5H 79
Miriam Rd. SE18—6C 80
Mirror Path. SE9—9G 95
Misbourne Rd. Uxb—5E 142
Miskin Rd. Dart—6G 99
Missenden Gdns. Mord
—1A 122
Mission Gro. E17—3J 45
Mission Pl. SE15—9E 76
Mission Sq. Bren—7J 71
Mistletoe Clo. Croy—3H 125
Mitcham Garden Village. Mitc
—9E 106
Mitcham La. SW16—3F 106
Mitcham Pk. Mitc—8C 106
Mitcham Rd. E6—6J 63
Mitcham Rd. SW17—2D 106
Mitcham Rd. Croy—1J 123
Mitcham Rd. Ilf—5D 48
Mitchell Clo. SE2—5G 81
Mitchell Clo. Dart—8J 99
Mitchell Rd. N13—5A 28
Mitchell Rd. Orp—6D 128
Mitchell St. EC1—7A 60
Mitchell Wlk. E6—8H 63
Mitchell Way. NW10—2A 56
Mitchell Way. Brom—5E 110
Mitchison Rd. N1—2B 60
Mitchley Av. Purl & S Croy
—5B 138
Mitchley Gro. S Croy—5E 138
Mitchley Hill. S Croy—5D 138
Mitchley Rd. N17—1E 44
Mitchley View. S Croy—5E 138
Mitford Rd. N19—7J 43
Mitre Clo. Sutt—9A 122
Mitre Rd. E15—5C 62
Mitre Rd. SE1—3L 75
Mitre Sq. EC3—9C 60
Mitre St. EC3—9C 60
Mitre, The. E14—1K 77
Mixbury Gro. Wey—8B 116
Moat Clo. Bush, Wat—7M 9
Moat Ct. Asht—9J 133
Moat Cres. N3—1M 41
Moat Dri. E13—5G 63
Moat Dri. Harr—2A 38
Moat Dri. Ruis—5C 36
Moat Farm Rd. N'holt—2K 53
Moatfield Rd. Bush, Wat—7M 9
Moat La. Eri—9E 82
Moat Pl. SW9—2K 91
Moat Pl. W3—9M 55
Moatside. Enf—6H 17
Moatside. Felt—1G 101
Moat, The. N Mald—5C 104
Moberley Rd. SW4—6H 91
Modbury Gdns. NW5—2E 58
Modder Pl. SW15—3H 89
Model Cotts. SW14—3A 88
Model Cotts. W13—3F 70
Model Farm Clo. SE9—9J 95
Moelwyn Hughes Ct. N7—1H 59
Moelyn M. Harr—3E 38
Moffat Gdns. Mitc—7C 106
Moffat Rd. N13—6J 27
Moffat Rd. SW17—1D 106
Moffat Rd. T Hth—6A 108
Mogden La. Iswth—4D 86
Moiety Rd. E14—3L 77
Moira Clo. N17—9C 28
Moira Rd. SE9—3K 95
Moir Clo. S Croy—1E 138
Molash Rd. Orp—8H 113
Mole Abbey Gdns. E Mol
—7M 101
Mole Ct. Eps—6A 120
Molember Rd. E Mol—9C 102
Mole Rd. W on T—7H 117
Molescroft. SE9—9A 96
Molesey Av. E Mol—9C 102
Molesey Clo. W on T—6J 117
Molesey Dri. Sutt—4J 121
Molesey Pk. Av. E Mol—9M 101

Molesey Pk. Clo. E Mol—9A 102
Molesey Pk. Rd. E Mol—9M 101
Molesey Rd. W on T & E Mol
—7H 117
Molesford Rd. SW6—9L 73
Molesham Clo. E Mol—7M 101
Molesham Way. E Mol—7M 101
Moles Hill. Lea—3B 132
Molesworth St. SE13—2A 94
Moliner Ct. Beck—4L 109
Mollison Av. Enf—6J 17
Mollison Dri. Wall—9H 123
Mollison Way. Edgw—9K 23
Molteno Rd. Wat—3E 8
Molyneux St. W1—8C 58
Monahan Av. Purl—4K 137
Monarch Clo. Felt—6C 84
Monarch Clo. W Wick—6D 126
Monarch Rd. Belv—4L 81
Monarchs Way. Ruis—6C 36
Monarchs Way. Wal X—6E 6
Mona Rd. SE15—1G 93
Monastery Gdns. Enf—4B 16
Mona St. E16—8D 62
Monaveen Gdns. E Mol
—7M 101
Monck St. SW1—4H 75
Monclar Rd. SE5—3B 92
Moncorvo Clo. SW7—3C 74
Moncrieff Clo. E6—9J 63
Moncrieff St. SE15—1E 92
Monega Rd.—2G 63
E7 1-203 & 2-204
E12 remainder
Money La. W Dray—4H 143
Mongers La. Eps—2D 134
Monica James Ho. Sidc—9E 96
Monical Clo. Wat—4G 9
Monier Rd. E3—3L 61
Monivea Rd. Beck—4K 109
Monkchester Clo. Lou—3K 19
Monk Dri. E16—1E 78
Monkfrith Av. N14—8F 14
Monkfrith Clo. N14—9F 14
Monkfrith Way. N14—9E 14
Monkham's Av. Wfd G—5F 30
Monkham's Dri. Wfd G—5F 30
Monkham's La. Buck H—3F 30
Monkham's La. Wfd G—4F 30
Monkleigh Rd. Mord—7J 105
Monks Av. Barn—8A 14
Monks Av. E Mol—9K 101
Monks Clo. SE2—5H 81
Monks Clo. Enf—4A 16
Monks Clo. Ruis—9H 37
Monks Cres. W on T—3F 116
Monksdene Gdns. Sutt
—5M 121
Monks Dri. W3—8L 55
Monksgrove. Lou—7L 19
Monksmead. Borwd—6A 12
Monks Orchard. Dart—8H 99
Monks Orchard Rd. Beck
—3L 125
Monks Pk. Wemb—2M 55
Monks Pk. Gdns. Wemb
—3M 55
Monks Rd. Bans—M 135
Monks Rd. Enf—4A 16
Monk St. SE18—5L 79
Monks Way. Beck—1L 125
Monks Way. Orp—3A 128
Monks Way. W Dray—7J 143
Monkswood Av. Wal A—6K 7
Monkswood Gdns. Borwd
—7B 12
Monkswood Gdns. Ilf—1L 47
Monkton Rd. Well—1D 96
Monkton St. SE11—5L 75
Monkville Av. NW11—2K 41
Monkwell Sq. EC2—8A 60
Monmouth Av. E18—1F 46
Monmouth Av. King—4G 103
Monmouth Clo. Mitc—8J 107
Monmouth Clo. Well—3E 96
Monmouth Rd. E6—6K 63
Monmouth Rd. N9—2F 28
Monmouth Rd. W2—9L 57
Monmouth Rd. Dag—1K 65
Monmouth Rd. Hay—5G 68
Monmouth Rd. Wat—5F 8
Monmouth St. WC2—9J 59
Monnery Rd. N19—8G 43
Monnow Rd. SE1—5E 76
Mono La. Felt—8F 84
Monoux Gro. E17—8L 29
Monpelier Rd. Purl—2M 137
Monroe Cres. Enf—3F 16
Monroe Dri. SW14—4M 87
Monro Gdns. Harr—7C 22
Monsell Rd. N4—8M 43
Monson Rd. NW10—5E 56
Monson Rd. SE14—8H 77

Mons Way. Brom—1J 127
Montacute Rd. SE6—6K 93
Montacute Rd. Bush, Wat
—9C 10
Montacute Rd. Croy—1A 140
Montacute Rd. Mord—1B 122
Montagu Cres. N18—4F 28
Montague Av. SE4—3K 93
Montague Av. W7—2D 70
Montague Av. S Croy—4C 138
Montague Clo. SE1—2B 76
Montague Clo. W on T—2E 116
Montague Gdns. W3—1L 71
Montague Pl. WC1—8H 59
Montague Rd. E8—1E 60
Montague Rd. E11—7D 46
Montague Rd. N8—3K 43
Montague Rd. N15—2E 44
Montague Rd. SW19—4M 105
Montague Rd. W7—3D 70
Montague Rd. W13—9F 54
Montague Rd. Croy—3M 123
Montague Rd. Houn—2M 85
Montague Rd. Rich—5J 87
Montague Rd. S'hall—5J 69
Montague Rd. Swan—8D 114
Montague Rd. Uxb—3B 142
Montague Sq. SE15—8G 77
Montague St. WC1—8J 59
Montague Waye. S'hall—4J 69
Montagu Gdns. N18—4F 28
Montagu Gdns. Wall—6G 123
Montagu Mans. W1—8D 58
Montagu M. N. W1—8D 58
Montagu M. S. W1—9D 58
Montagu M. W. W1—9D 58
Montagu Pl. W1—8D 58
Montagu Rd.—5F 28
N18 1-219 & 2-228
N9 remainder
Montagu Rd. NW4—4E 40
Montagu Row. W1—8D 58
Montagu Sq. W1—8D 58
Montagu St. W1—9D 58
Montalt Rd. Wfd G—5D 30
Montana Clo. S Croy—2B 138
Montana Rd. SW17—9E 90
Montana Rd. SW20—5G 105
Montayne Rd. Wal X—5D 6
Montbelle Rd. SE9—9M 95
Montcalm Clo. Brom—1E 126
Montcalm Clo. Hay—6F 52
Montcalm Rd. SE7—8H 79
Montclare St. E2—7D 60
Monteagle Av. Bark—2A 64
Monteagle Ct. N1—5C 60
Monteagle Way. E5—8E 44
Monteagle Way. SE15—2F 92
Montefiore St. SW8—1F 90
Monteith Rd. E3—4K 61
Montem Rd. SE23—6K 93
Montem Rd. N Mald—8C 104
Montem St. N4—6K 43
Montenotte Rd. N8—3G 43
Monterey Clo. Bex—8A 98
Montesole Ct. Pinn—9G 21
Montford Pl. SE11—6L 75
Montford Rd. Sun—8E 100
Montfort Gdns. Ilf—6A 32
Montfort Pl. SW19—7H 89
Montgolfier Wlk. N'holt—6J 53
Montgomery Av. Esh—4C 118
Montgomery Clo. Mitc—8J 107
Montgomery Clo. Sidc—5D 96
Montgomery Cres. Romf
—5G 35
Montgomery Dri. Wal X—1E 6
Montgomery Rd. W4—5A 72
Montgomery Rd. Edgw—6K 23
Montholme Rd. SW11—5D 90
Monthope Rd. E1—8E 60
Montolieu Gdns. SW15—4F 88
Montpelier Av. W5—8G 55
Montpelier Av. Bex—6H 97
Montpelier Clo. Uxb—4E 142
Montpelier Gdns. E6—6H 63
Montpelier Gdns. Romf—5G 49
Montpelier Gro. NW5—1G 59
Montpelier M. SW7—4C 74
Montpelier Pl. SW7—4C 74
Montpelier Rise. NW11—5J 41
Montpelier Rise. Wemb—6H 39
Montpelier Rd. N3—8A 26
Montpelier Rd. SE15—9F 76
Montpelier Rd. W5—8H 55
Montpelier Rd. Sutt—6A 122
Montpelier Row. SE3—1D 94
Montpelier Row. Twic—6D 86
Montpelier Sq. SW7—3C 74
Montpelier St. SW7—4C 74
Montpelier Ter. SW7—3C 74
Montpelier Vale. SE3—1D 94
Montpelier Wlk. SW7—4C 74

Montpelier Way. NW11—5J 41
Montrave Rd. SE20—3G 109
Montreal Pl. WC2—1K 75
Montreal Rd. Ilf—5A 48
Montrell Rd. SW2—7J 91
Montrose Av. NW6—5J 57
Montrose Av. Edgw—9A 24
Montrose Av. Romf—9G 35
Montrose Av. Sidc—6E 96
Montrose Av. Twic—6M 85
Montrose Av. Well—2B 96
Montrose Clo. Ashf—3A 100
Montrose Clo. Well—2D 96
Montrose Clo. Wfd G—4E 30
Montrose Ct. SW7—3B 74
Montrose Cres. N12—6A 26
Montrose Cres. Wemb—2J 55
Montrose Gdns. Lea—4B 132
Montrose Gdns. Mitc—6D 106
Montrose Gdns. Sutt—4M 121
Montrose Pl. SW1—3E 74
Montrose Rd. Felt—5B 84
Montrose Rd. Harr—9C 22
Montrose Way. SE23—7H 93
Montrouge Cres. Eps—8G 135
Montserrat Av. Wfd G—7B 30
Montserrat Clo. SE19—2B 108
Montserrat Rd. SW15—3J 89
Monument Hill. Wey—6A 116
Monument Rd. Wey—6A 116
Monument St. EC3—1B 76
Monument Way. N17—1D 44
Monza St. E1—1G 77
Moodkee St. SE16—4G 77
Moody St. E1—6H 61
Moon La. Barn—5K 13
Moon St. N1—4M 59
Moorcroft La. Uxb—8E 142
Moorcroft Rd. SW16—9J 91
Moorcroft Way. Pinn—3J 37
Moordown. SE18—9M 79
Moore Clo. SW14—2A 88
Moore Clo. Mitc—6F 106
Moore Clo. Wall—9J 123
Moore Cres. Dag—4F 64
Moorehead Way. SE3—2F 94
Mooreland Rd. Brom—4D 110
Moor End Rd. Twic—5E 86
Moore Pk. Rd. SW6—8M 73
Moore Rd. SE19—3A 108
Moore St. SW3—5D 74
Moore Wlk. E7—9E 46
Moorey Clo. E15—4D 62
Moorfield Av. W5—7H 55
Moorfield Rd. N17—9D 28
Moorfield Rd. Chess—7J 119
Moorfield Rd. Enf—3G 17
Moorfield Rd. Orp—2E 128
Moorfield Rd. Uxb—9B 142
Moorfields. EC2—8B 60
Moorgate. EC2—9B 60
Moorhouse Rd. W2—9L 57
Moorhouse Rd. Harr—1H 39
Moorland Clo. Romf—7M 33
Moorland Clo. Twic—6L 85
Moorland Rd. SW9—3M 91
Moorland Rd. W Dray—7G 143
Moorlands Av. NW7—6F 24
Moorland Rd. SW9—3M 91
Moor La. EC2—8B 60
Moor La. Chess—6J 119
Moor La. Rick—1A 20
Moor La. W Dray—7G 143
Moor La. Crossing. Wat—9A 8
Moormead Dri. Eps—7C 120
Moor Pk. Rd. N'wd—6B 20
Moor Pl. EC2—8B 60
Moorside Rd. Brom—9C 94
Moorview Way. Coul—9H 137
Moor St. W1—9H 59
Moortown Rd. Wat—4G 21
Moor View. Wat—8E 8
Moot Ct. NW9—3L 39
Morant Gdns. Romf—5M 33
Morant Pl. N22—8K 27
Morant St. E14—1L 77
Mora Rd. NW2—9G 41
Mora St. EC1—6A 60
Morat St. SW9—9K 75
Moravian Pl. SW10—7B 74
Moravian St. E2—6G 61
Moray Av. Hay—2D 68
Moray Clo. Romf—7C 34
Moray M. N7—7K 43
Moray Rd. N4—7K 43
Moray Way. Romf—7B 34
Mordaunt Gdns. Dag—3J 65
Mordaunt Rd. NW10—4B 56
Mordaunt St. SW9—2K 91
Morden Ct. Mord—8M 105
Morden Gdns. Gnfd—1D 54
Morden Gdns. Mitc—8B 106
Morden Hall Rd. Mord—7M 105
Morden Hill. SE13—1A 94

Morden La. SE13—9A 78
Morden Rd. SE3—1E 94
Morden Rd. SW19—5M 105
Morden Rd. Mord & Mitc
—8A 106
Morden Rd. Romf—5J 49
Morden Rd. M. SE3—1E 94
Morden St. SE13—9M 77
Morden Way. Sutt—2L 121
Morden Wharf Rd. SE10—4C 78
Mordon Rd. Ilf—5D 48
Mordred Rd. SE6—8C 94
Morecambe Clo. E1—8H 61
Morecambe Clo. Horn—1F 66
Morecambe Gdns. Stan—4H 23
Morecambe St. SE17—6A 76
Morecambe Ter. N18—4B 28
More Clo. E16—9D 62
More Clo. W14—5H 73
More Clo. Purl—3L 137
Morecoombe Clo. King
—4M 103
Moree Way. N18—4E 28
Moreland Clo. NW11—6M 41
Moreland St. EC1—6M 59
Moreland Way. E4—3A 30
More La. Esh—5M 117
Morella Rd. SW12—6D 90
Morello Av. Uxb—8F 142
Moremead Rd. SE6—1K 109
Morena St. SE6—6M 93
Moresby Av. Surb—2M 119
Moresby Rd. E5—5F 44
Moresby Wlk. SW8—1G 91
Moretaine Rd. Ashf—9B 144
Moreton Av. Iswth—9C 70
Moreton Clo. E5—7F 44
Moreton Clo. N15—4B 44
Moreton Clo. Swan—6C 114
Moreton Clo. Wal X—1B 6
Moreton Gdns. Wfd G—5J 31
Moreton Pl. SW1—6G 75
Moreton Rd. N15—4B 44
Moreton Rd. S Croy—7B 124
Moreton Rd. Wor Pk—4E 120
Moreton St. SW1—6G 75
Moreton Ter. SW1—6G 75
Moreton Ter. M. N. SW1—6G 75
Moreton Ter. M. S. SW1—6G 75
Morford Clo. Ruis—5F 36
Morford Way. Ruis—5F 36
Morgan Av. E17—2B 46
Morgan Clo. Dag—3L 65
Morgan Clo. N'wd—6D 20
Morgan Rd. N7—1L 59
Morgan Rd. W10—8K 57
Morgan Rd. Brom—4E 110
Morgan's La. SE1—2C 76
Morgan's La. Hay—8B 52
Morgan St. E3—6J 61
Morgan St. E16—8D 62
Morgan Way. Rain—6G 67
Morgan Way. Wfd G—6J 31
Morie St. SW18—4M 89
Morieux Rd. E10—6K 45
Moring Rd. SW17—1E 106
Morkyns Wlk. SE21—9C 92
Morland Av. Croy—3C 124
Morland Clo. Hmptn—2K 101
Morland Gdns. NW10—3B 56
Morland Gdns. S'hall—2M 69
Morland M. N1—3L 59
Morland Rd. E17—3H 45
Morland Rd. SE20—3H 109
Morland Rd. Croy—3C 124
Morland Rd. Dag—3L 65
Morland Rd. Dart—4F 98
Morland Rd. Harr—3J 39
Morland Rd. Ilf—7M 47
Morland Rd. Sutt—7A 122
Morland Way. Wal X—1E 6
Morley Av. E4—7B 30
Morley Av. N18—4E 28
Morley Av. N22—9L 27
Morley Clo. Orp—4M 127
Morley Clo. Ruis—7G 37
Morley Ct. Brom—8D 110
Morley Cres. Edgw—2A 24
Morley Cres. E. Stan—9G 23
Morley Cres. W. Stan—1G 39
Morley Hill. Enf—2B 16
Morley Rd. E10—6A 46
Morley Rd. E15—5D 62
Morley Rd. SE13—3A 94
Morley Rd. Bark—4B 64
Morley Rd. Chst—5A 112
Morley Rd. Romf—3J 49
Morley Rd. S Croy—2D 138
Morley Rd. Sutt—3K 121
Morley Rd. Twic—5H 87
Morley St. SE1—4L 75
Mormead. Wal A—6K 7

Morna Rd. SE5—1A 92
Morning La. E9—2G 61
Morningside Rd. Wor Pk
—4G 121
Mornington Av. W14—5N 73
Mornington Av. Brom—7G 111
Mornington Av. Ilf—5L 47
Mornington Clo. Wfd G—4E 30
Mornington Ct. Bex—7B 98
Mornington Cres. NW1—5G 59
Mornington Cres. Houn—9F 68
Mornington Gro. E3—6L 61
Mornington M. SE5—9A 76
Mornington Pl. NW1—5G 59
Mornington Rd. E4—9B 18
Mornington Rd. E11—5D 46
Mornington Rd. SE8—8K 77
Mornington Rd. Ashf—2A 100
Mornington Rd. Gnfd—8M 53
Mornington Rd. Lou—5M 19
Mornington Rd. Wfd G—4D 30
Mornington St. NW1—5F 58
Mornington Ter. NW1—5F 58
Mornington Wlk. Rich—1G 103
Morocco St. SE1—3C 76
Morpeth Av. Borwd—2K 11
Morpeth Gro. E9—4H 61
Morpeth Rd. E9—4H 61
Morpeth St. E2—6H 61
Morpeth Ter. SW1—4G 75
Morpeth Wlk. N17—7F 28
Morrab Gdns. Ilf—8D 48
Morrell Clo. Barn—5A 14
Morris Av. E12—1K 63
Morris Clo. Orp—5C 128
Morris Ct. Wal A—7M 7
Morris Gdns. SW18—6L 89
Morris Gdns. Dart—4L 99
Morrish Rd. SW2—6J 91
Morrison Av. N17—1C 44
Morrison Rd. Bark—5J 65
Morrison Rd. Hay—6F 52
Morrison St. SW11—2E 90
Morris Pl. N4—7L 43
Morris Rd. E14—8M 61
Morris Rd. E15—9C 46
Morris Rd. Dag—7K 49
Morris Rd. Iswth—2D 86
Morris Rd. Romf—7F 34
Morris St. E1—9F 60
Morriston Clo. Wat—5G 21
Morse Clo. E13—6E 62
Morshead Rd. W9—6L 57
Morston Gdns. SE9—1K 111
Morten Clo. SW4—5H 91
Morteyne Rd. N17—8B 28
Mortham St. E15—4C 62
Mortimer Clo. NW2—7K 41
Mortimer Clo. SW16—8H 91
Mortimer Clo. Bush, Wat—8M 9
Mortimer Cres. NW6—4M 57
Mortimer Cres. Wor Pk—5B 120
Mortimer Mkt. WC1—7G 59
Mortimer Pl. NW6—4M 57
Mortimer Rd. E6—6K 63
Mortimer Rd. N1—3C 60
Mortimer Rd. NW10—6G 57
Mortimer Rd. W13—9G 55
Mortimer Rd. Eri—7B 82
Mortimer Rd. Mitc—5D 106
Mortimer Rd. Orp—3E 128
Mortimer Rd. West—4G 141
Mortimer Sq. W11—1H 73
Mortimer St. W1—8G 59
Mortimer Ter. NW5—9F 42
Mortlake Clo. Croy—5J 123
Mortlake High St. SW14—2B 88
Mortlake Rd. E16—9F 62
Mortlake Rd. Ilf—9A 48
Mortlake Rd. Rich—8L 71
Mortlock Clo. SE15—9F 76
Mortlock Ct. E12—9H 47
Morton Cres. N14—4H 27
Morton Gdns. Wall—7G 123
Morton Pl. SE1—4L 75
Morton Rd. E15—3D 62
Morton Rd. N1—3A 60
Morton Rd. Mord—9B 106
Morton Way. N14—3G 27
Morvale Clo. Belv—5K 81
Morval Rd. SW2—4L 91
Morven Rd. SW17—9D 90
Morvi!le St. E3—5L 61
Morwell St. WC1—8H 59
Moscow Pl. W2—1M 73
Moscow Rd. W2—1L 73
Moselle Av. N22—9L 27
Moselle Clo. N8—1K 43
Moselle Rd. West—9J 141
Moselle St. N17—7D 28
Mospey Cres. Eps—7D 134
Mossborough Clo. N12—6M 25
Mossbury Rd. SW11—2C 90

Moss Clo. E1—8E 60
Moss Clo. Pinn—9K 21
Mossdown Clo. Belv—5L 81
Mossford Ct. Ilf—1M 47
Mossford Grn. Ilf—1M 47
Mossford La. Ilf—9M 31
Mossford St. E3—7K 61
Moss Gdns. S Croy—9H 125
Moss Hall Cres. N12—6M 25
Moss Hall Gro. N12—6M 25
Mossington Gdns. SE16—5G 77
Moss La. Pinn—8J 21
Moss La. Romf—4D 50
Mosslea Rd. SE20—3G 109
Mosslea Rd. Brom—9H 111
Mosslea Rd. Orp—5A 128
Mosslea Rd. Whyt—8D 138
Mossop St. SW3—5C 74
Moss Rd. Dag—3L 65
Moss Rd. Wat—7F 4
Moss Side. St Alb—3K 5
Mossville Gdns. Mord—7K 105
Moston Clo. Hay—6D 68
Mostyn Av. Wemb—1K 55
Mostyn Gdns. NW10—6H 57
Mostyn Gro. E3—5L 61
Mostyn Rd. SW9—9L 75
Mostyn Rd. SW19—5K 105
Mostyn Rd. Bush, Wat—7A 10
Mostyn Rd. Edgw—7C 24
Mosul Way. Brom—1J 127
Mosyer Dri. Orp—4H 129
Motcomb St. SW1—4E 74
Motspur Pk. N Mald—1D 120
Mottingham Rd. N9—8H 17
Mottingham Rd. SE9—0J 95
Mottisfont Rd. SE2—4E 80
Mott St. E4 & Lou—2B 18
Mouchotte Clo. West—4F 140
Moulins Rd. E9—3H 61
Moultain Hill. Swan—8E 114
Moulton Av. Houn—1J 85
Moundfield Rd. N16—4E 44
Mound, The. SE9—9L 95
Mountacre Clo. SE26—1E 108
Mountague Pl. E14—1A 78
Mt. Adon Pk. SE22—6E 92
Mt. Angelus Rd. SW15—6D 88
Mt. Ararat Rd. Rich—3J 87
Mt. Ash Rd. SE26—9F 92
Mount Av. E4—3L 29
Mount Av. W5—8G 55
Mount Av. Romf—6M 35
Mount Av. S'hall—9L 53
Mountbatten Clo. SE18—7C 80
Mountbatten Clo. SE19
—2C 108
Mountbatten M. SW18—6A 90
Mountbel Rd. Stan—9E 22
Mount Clo. Barn—6E 14
Mount Clo. Brom—5J 111
Mount Clo. Cars—1E 136
Mount Clo. Kenl—8B 138
Mount Ct. W Wick—4C 126
Mt. Culver Av. Sidc—3H 113
Mount Dri. Bexh—4J 97
Mount Dri. Harr—3K 37
Mount Dri. Wemb—7A 40
Mountearl Gdns. SW16—9K 91
Mt. Echo Av. E4—1M 29
Mt. Echo Dri. E4—1M 29
Mt. Ephraim La. SW16—9H 91
Mt. Ephraim Rd. SW16—9H 91
Mt. Felix. W on T—2D 116
Mountfield Rd. E6—5L 63
Mountfield Rd. N3—1K 41
(in two parts)
Mountfield Rd. W5—9H 55
Mountfield Way. Orp—8G 113
Mountfort Cres. N1—3L 59
Mountfort Ter. N1—3L 59
Mount Gdns. SE26—9F 92
Mount Gro. Edgw—3A 24
Mountgrove Rd. N5—8A 44
Mounthurst Rd. Brom—2D 126
Mountjoy Clo. SE2—3F 80
Mt. Mills. EC1—6M 59
Mt. Nod Rd. SW16—9K 91
Mt. Olive Ct. W7—3C 70
Mount Pk. Cars—1E 136
Mount Pk. Av. Harr—7B 38
Mount Pk. Av. S Croy—1M 137
Mount Pk. Cres. W5—9H 55
Mount Pk. Rd. W5—8H 55
Mount Pk. Rd. Harr—8B 38
Mount Pk. Rd. Pinn—3E 36
Mt. Pleasant. SE27—1A 108

Mt. Pleasant. WC1—7L 59
Mt. Pleasant. Barn—6D 14
Mt. Pleasant. Eps—2D 134
Mt. Pleasant. Ruis—7G 37
Mt. Pleasant. Wemb—4J 55
Mt. Pleasant. West—9H 141
Mt. Pleasant Cres. N4—5K 43
Mt. Pleasant Hill. E5—7G 45
Mt. Pleasant La. E5—7F 45
Mt. Pleasant La. St Alb—3J 5
Mt. Pleasant Rd. E17—9J 29
Mt. Pleasant Rd. N17—9C 28
Mt. Pleasant Rd. NW10—3G 57
Mt. Pleasant Rd. SE13—5M 93
Mt. Pleasant Rd. W5—7G 55
Mt. Pleasant Rd. Chig—4B 32
Mt. Pleasant Rd. Dart—5K 99
Mt. Pleasant Rd. N Mald
—7A 104
Mt. Pleasant Rd. Romf—6B 34
Mt. Pleasant Vs. N4—5K 43
Mt. Pleasant Wlk. Bex—4A 98
Mount Rd. NW2—8G 41
Mount Rd. NW4—4E 40
Mount Rd. SW19—8L 89
Mount Rd. Barn—7C 14
Mount Rd. Bexh—4H 97
Mount Rd. Chess—7K 119
Mount Rd. Dag—6K 49
Mount Rd. Dart—5D 98
Mount Rd. Felt—9J 85
Mount Rd. Hay—3E 68
Mount Rd. Ilf—1M 63
Mount Rd. Mitc—6B 106
Mount Rd. N Mald—7B 104
Mount Row. W1—1F 74
Mountsfield Ct. SE13—5B 94
Mountside. Stan—8E 22
Mounts Pond Rd. SE3—1B 94
Mount Sq., The. NW3—8A 42
Mt. Stewart Av. Harr—5H 39
Mount St. W1—1E 74
Mount, The. N20—2A 26
Mount, The. NW3—9A 42
Mount, The. Coul—6F 136
Mount, The. Eps—2D 134
Mount, The. Esh—8L 117
Mount, The. N Mald—7D 104
Mount, The. Romf—3G 35
Mount, The. Wemb—7A 40
Mount, The. Wey—4C 116
Mount, The. Wor Pk—6F 120
Mt. Vernon. NW3—9A 42
Mount View. NW7—3B 24
Mount View. Enf—2K 15
Mount View. N'wd—6D 20
Mountview Ct. N15—2M 43
Mt. View·Rd. E4—9B 18
Mt. View Rd. N4—5J 43
Mt. View Rd. NW9—3B 40
Mt. View Rd. Esh—9F 118
Mountview Rd. Orp—2E 128
Mount Vs. SE27—9M 91
Mount Way. Cars—1E 136
Mount Wood. E Mol—7M 101
Mountwood Clo. S Croy
—2F 138
Movers La. Bark—4B 64
Mowatt Clo. N19—7H 43
Mowbray Pde. Edgw—4L 23
Mowbray Rd. NW6—3J 57
Mowbray Rd. SE19—5D 108
Mowbray Rd. Barn—2A 14
Mowbray Rd. Edgw 4L 23
Mowbray Rd. Rich—9G 87
Mowbrays Clo. Romf—8A 34
Mowbrays Rd. Romf—9A 34
Mowlem St. E2—5F 60
Mowlem Trading Est. N17
—7G 29
Mowll St. SW9—8L 75
Moxon Clo. E13 5D 62
Moxon St. W1—8E 58
Moxon St. Barn—5K 13
Moye Clo. E2—5E 60
Moyers Rd. E10—5A 46
Moylan Rd. W6—7J 73
Moyne Pl. NW10—5L 55
Moyser Rd. SW16—2F 106
Mozart St. W10—6K 57
Muchelney Rd. Mord—1A 122
Muddy La. Dart—6M 99
Muggeridge Rd. Dag—9M 49
Muirdown Av. SW14—3B 88
Muirfield. W3—9C 56
Muirfield Clo. Wat—5G 21
Muirfield Grn. Wat—4F 20
Muirfield Rd. Wat—4F 20
Muirkirk Rd. SE6—7A 94
Muir Rd. E5—9E 44
Muir St. E16—2K 79
Mulberry Av. Stai—7C 144
Mulberry Clo. E4—2L 29

Mulberry Clo. NW3—9B 42
Mulberry Clo. NW4—1G 41
Mulberry Clo. SW16—1G 107
Mulberry Clo. N'holt—5J 53
Mulberry Clo. Romf—2G 51
Mulberry Clo. St Alb—1M 5
Mulberry Clo. Wey—5A 116
Mulberry Ct. Bark—3D 64
Mulberry Ct. Surb—2H 119
Mulberry Cres. Bren—8G 71
Mulberry Cres. W Dray—3L 143
Mulberry Dri. Purf—5K 83
Mulberry La. Croy—3D 124
Mulberry M. Wall—4G 123
Mulberry Pl. W6—6E 72
Mulberry St. E1—9E 60
Mulberry Trees. Shep—2B 116
Mulberry Wlk. SW3—7B 74
Mulberry Way. E18—9F 30
Mulberry Way. Belv—3A 82
Mulberry Way. Ilf—2A 48
Mulgrave Rd. NW10—9D 40
Mulgrave Rd. SW6—7K 73
Mulgrave Rd. W5—7H 55
Mulgrave Rd. Croy—5B 124
Mulgrave Rd. Harr—7E 38
Mulgrave Rd. Sutt—9K 121
Mulholland Clo. Mitc—6E 106
Mulkern Rd. N19—6H 43
Muller Rd. SW4—5H 91
Mullins Path. SW14—2B 88
Mullion Clo. Harr—8M 21
Mullion Wlk. Wat—4H 21
Mulready St. NW8—7C 58
Multi Way. W3—3C 72
Multon Rd. SW18—6B 90
Mulvaney Way. SE1—3B 76
Mumford Ct. EC2—9A 60
Mumford Rd. SE24—4M 91
Muncaster Rd. SW11—4D 90
Munday Rd. E16—1E 78
Munden Dri. Wat—1J 9
Munden Gro. Wat—2G 9
Munden St. W14—5J 73
Mundesly Clo. Wat—4G 21
Mundford Rd. E5—7G 45
Mundon Gdns. Ilf—6B 48
Mund St. W14—6K 73
Mundy St. N1—6C 60
Mungo Pk. Clo. Bush, Wat
—2A 22
Mungo Pk. Rd. Rain—2E 66
Mungo Pk. Way. Orp—2G 129
Munnings Gdns. Iswth—4B 86
Munro Dri. N11—6G 27
Munro M. W10—8J 57
Munro Rd. Bush, Wat—7M 9
Munro Ter. SW10—7B 74
Munster Av. Houn—4J 85
Munster Gdns. N13—4M 27
Munster Rd. SW6—8J 73
Munster Rd. Tedd—3G 103
Munster Sq. NW1—7F 58
Munton Rd. SE17—5A 76
Murchison Av. Bex—7H 97
Murchison Rd. E10—7A 46
Murdock Clo. E16—9E 62
Murdock Cotts. E3—6J 61
Murdock St. SE15—7F 76
Murfett Clo. SW19—8J 89
Murfitt Way. Upm—9L 51
Muriel Av. Wat—7M 9
Muriel St. N1—5K 59
(in two parts)
Murillo Rd. SE13—3B 94
Murphy St. SE1—3L 75
Murray Av. Brom—7F 110
Murray Av. Houn—4M 85
Murray Ct. Twic—8B 86
Murray Cres. Pinn—8H 21
Murray Gro. N1—5A 60
Murray M. NW1—3H 59
Murray Rd. SW19—3H 105
Murray Rd. W5—5G 71
Murray Rd. N'wd—7C 20
Murray Rd. Orp—7F 112
Murray Rd. Rich—8G 87
Murray Sq. E16—9E 62
Murray St. NW1—3H 59
Murray Ter. NW3—9D 42
Murtwell Dri. Chig—6A 33
Musard Rd. W6—7J 73
Musbury St. E1—9G 61
Muschamp Rd. SE15—2D 92
Muschamp Rd. Cars—4C 122
Muscovy St. EC3—1C 76
Museum Pas. E2—6G 61
Museum St. WC1—8J 59
Musgrave Clo. Barn—3A 14
Musgrave Cres. SW6—9L 73
Musgrave Rd. Iswth—9D 70
Musgrove Rd. SE14—9H 77
Musjid Rd. SW11—1B 90

Musquash Way. Houn—1G 85
Muston Rd. E5—7F 44
Muswell Av. N10—8F 26
Muswell Hill. N10—1F 42
Muswell Hill B'way. N10—1F 42
Muswell Hill Pl. N10—2F 42
Muswell Hill Rd.—4E 42
N6 1 & 2-40
N10 remainder
Muswell M. N10—1F 42
Muswell Rd. N10—1F 42
Mutchetts Clo. Wat—6J 5
Mutrix Rd. NW6—4L 57
Mutton Pl. NW1—2E 58
Muybridge Rd. N Mald—6A 104
Myatt Rd. SW9—9M 75
Mycenae Rd. SE3—8E 78
Myddelton Av. Enf—2C 16
Myddelton Clo. Enf—3D 16
Myddelton Gdns. N21—9A 16
Myddelton Pk. N20—3B 26
Myddelton Pas. EC1—6L 59
Myddelton Rd. N8—2J 43
Myddelton Sq. EC1—6L 59
Myddelton St. EC1—6L 59
Myddleton Path. Wal X—4B 6
Myddleton Rd. N22—7J 27
Myddleton Rd. Uxb—4A 142
Mygrove Clo. Rain—5H 67
Mygrove Gdns. Rain—5H 67
Mygrove Rd. Rain—5H 67
Mylis Clo. SE26—1F 108
Mylne St. EC1—6L 59
Mynn's Clo. Eps—6M 133
Myra St. SE2—5E 80
Myrdle St. E1—8E 60
Myrna Clo. Mitc—4C 106
Myron Pl. SE13—2A 94
Myrtle Av. Felt—4C 84
Myrtle Av. Ruis—5E 36
Myrtle Clo. Barn—1D 26
Myrtle Clo. Eri—8C 82
Myrtle Clo. Uxb—8D 142
Myrtle Clo. W Dray—4K 143
Myrtledene Rd. SE2—6E 80
Myrtle Gdns. W7—2C 70
Myrtle Gro. Enf—2B 16
Myrtle Gro. N Mald—6A 104
Myrtle Gro. S Ock—3M 83
Myrtle Rd. E6—4J 63
Myrtle Rd. E17—4J 45
Myrtle Rd. N13—3A 28
Myrtle Rd. W3—2A 72
Myrtle Rd. Croy—5L 125
Myrtle Rd. Dart—7H 99
Myrtle Rd. Hmptn—3A 102
Myrtle Rd. Houn—1A 86
Myrtle Rd. Ilf—7M 47
Myrtle Rd. Romf—6G 35
Myrtle Rd. Sutt—7A 122
Myrtleside Clo. N'wd—7B 20
Myrtle Wlk. N1—5C 60
Mysore Rd. SW11—3D 90
Myton Rd. SE21—9B 92

Nadine St. SE7—6G 79
Nagle Clo. E17—9B 30
Nags Head La. Upm & Brtwd
—8M 35
Nags Head La. Well—2F 96
Nags Head Rd. Enf—6G 17
Nairne Gro. SE24—4B 92
Nairn Grn. Wat—3E 20
Nairn Rd. Ruis—2G 53
Nairn St. E14—8A 62
Naish Ct. N1—4J 59
Nallhead Rd. Felt—2G 101
Namton Dri. T Hth—8K 107
Nan Clark's La. NW7—2D 24
Nancy Downs. Wat—9G 9
Nankin St. E14—9L 61
Nansen Rd. SW11—2E 90
Nansen Village. N12—4M 25
Nantes Clo. SW18—3A 90
Nantes Pas. E1—8D 60
Nant Rd. NW2—7K 41
Nant St. E2—6F 60
Napier Av. SW6—2K 89
Napier Clo. SE8—8K 77
Napier Clo. W14—4K 73
Napier Dri. Bush, Wat—6J 9
Napier Gro. N1—5A 60
Napier Pl. W14—4K 73
Napier Rd. E6—4L 63
Napier Rd. E11—9C 46
Napier Rd. E15—5C 62
Napier Rd. N17—1C 44
Napier Rd. NW10—6F 56
Napier Rd. SE25—8F 108
Napier Rd. W14—4K 73
Napier Rd. Ashf—4B 100
Napier Rd. Belv—5K 81

Napier Rd. Brom—8F 110
Napier Rd. Enf—7H 17
Napier Rd. Houn—9H 143
Napier Rd. Iswth—3E 86
Napier Rd. S Croy—9B 124
Napier Rd. Wemb—2H 55
Napier Rd. W Dray—4K 143
Napier Ter. N1—3M 59
Napoleon Rd. E5—8F 44
Napoleon Rd. Twic—6F 86
Napton Clo. Hay—7J 53
Narbonne Av. SW4—4G 91
Narboro Ct. Romf—4E 50
Narborough Clo. Uxb—7A 36
Narborough St. SW6—1M 89
Narcissus Rd. NW6—1L 57
Nare Rd. S Ock—1M 83
Naresby Fold. Stan—6G 23
Narford Rd E5—8F 44
Narrow St. E14—1J 77
Narrow St. W3—2M 71
Narrow Way. Brom—1J 127
Nascot Pl. Wat—4F 8
Nascot Rd. Wat—4F 8
Nascot St. W12—9G 57
Nascot St. Wat—4F 8
Nascot Wood Rd. Wat—1D 8
Naseby Clo. NW6—3A 58
Naseby Clo. Iswth—9C 70
Naseby Ct. W on T—4G 117
Naseby Rd. SE19—3B 108
Naseby Rd. Dag—8L 49
Naseby Rd. Ilf—8K 31
Nash Clo. Borwd—6K 11
Nash Grn. Brom—3E 110
Nash La. Kes—9E 126
Nash Rd. N9—2G 29
Nash Rd. SE4—4J 93
Nash Rd. Romf—2H 49
Nash St. NW1—6F 58
Nash's Yd. Uxb—3B 142
Nasmyth St. W6—4F 72
Nassau Path. SE28—2G 81
Nassau Rd. SW13—9D 72
Nassau St. W1—8G 59
Nassington Rd. NW3—9D 42
Natalie Clo. Felt—6B 84
Natal Rd. N11—6J 27
Natal Rd. SW16—3H 107
Natal Rd. Ilf—9M 47
Natal Rd. T Hth—7B 108
Nathaniel Clo. E1—8D 60
Nathans Rd. Wemb—6G 39
Nathan Way. SE28, Eri & Belv
—5C 80
Nation Way. E4—1A 30
Naval Row. E14—1A 78
Navarino Gro. E8—2E 60
Navarino Rd. E8—2E 60
Navarre Gdns. Romf—5M 33
Navarre Rd. E6—5J 63
Navarre St. E2—7D 60
Navenby Wlk. E3—7L 61
Navestock Clo. E4—3A 30
Navestock Cres. Wfd G—7G 31
Navy St. SW4—2H 91
Naylor Gro. Enf—7H 17
Naylor Rd. N20—2A 26
Naylor Rd. SE15—8F 76
Nazeing Wlk. Rain—3D 66
Neagle Clo. Borwd—3A 12
Neal Av. S'hall—7K 53
Neal Clo. N'wd—8E 20
Neal Ct. Wal A—6M 7
Nealden St. SW9—2K 91
Neale Clo. N2—1A 42
Neal St. WC2—9J 59
Neal St. Wat—7G 9
Neal's Yd. WC2—9J 59
Near Acre. NW9—8D 24
Neasden Clo. NW10—1C 56
Neasden La. NW10—9C 40
(in two parts)
Neasden La. N. NW10—8B 40
Neasham Rd. Dag—1F 64
Neate St. SE5—7C 76
Neath Gdns. Mord—1A 122
Neathouse Pl. SW1—5G 75
Neats Acre. Ruis—5B 36
Neatscourt Clo. E6—8H 63
Neave Cres. Romf—6K 35
Nebraska St. SE1—3B 76
Neckinger. SE1—4D 76
Neckinger St. SE1—3D 76
Nectarine Way. SE13—1M 93
Needham Rd. W11—9L 57
Needham Ter. NW2—8H 41
Neela Clo. Uxb—9A 36
Neeld Cres. NW4—3F 40
Neeld Cres. Wemb—1L 55
Neil Clo. Ashf—2A 100
Nelgarde Rd. SE6—6L 93
Nella Rd. W6—7H 73

Nelldale Rd. SE16—5G 77
Nellgrove Rd. Uxb—7A 52
Nell Gwynne Av. Shep—1B 116
Nelmes Clo. Horn—3K 51
Nelmes Cres. Horn—3K 51
Nelmes Rd. Horn—5J 51
Nelmes Way. Horn—2J 51
Nelson Clo. Croy—3M 123
Nelson Clo. Romf—8M 33
Nelson Clo. Uxb—6F 142
Nelson Clo. W on T—3F 116
Nelson Clo. West—9J 141
Nelson Gdns. E2—6E 60
Nelson Gdns. Houn—5L 85
Nelson Gro. Rd. SW19—5A 106
Nelson Industrial Est. SW19
—5M 105
Nelson La. Uxb—6F 142
Nelson Pas. EC1—6A 60
Nelson Pl. N1—5M 59
Nelson Pl. W3—2M 71
Nelson Pl. Sidc—1E 112
Nelson Rd. E4—6M 29
Nelson Rd. E11—2E 46
Nelson Rd. N8—3K 43
Nelson Rd. N9—2F 28
Nelson Rd. N15—2C 44
Nelson Rd. SE10—7A 78
Nelson Rd. SW19—4A 106
Nelson Rd. Belv—6K 81
Nelson Rd. Brom—8G 111
Nelson Rd. Dart—5G 99
Nelson Rd. Enf—8H 17
Nelson Rd. Harr—6C 38
Nelson Rd. Houn—9K 143
Nelson Rd. Houn & Twic—5L 85
Nelson Rd. N Mald—9B 104
Nelson Rd. Rain—5D 66
Nelson Rd. Sidc—1E 112
Nelson Rd. Stan—6G 23
Nelson Rd. Uxb—6F 142
Nelson Sq. SE1—3M 75
Nelson's Row. SW4—3H 91
Nelson St. E1—9F 60
Nelson St. E6—5K 63
(in two parts)
Nelson St. E16—1D 78
(in two parts)
Nelson Ter. N1—5M 59
Nelson Wlk. SE16—2J 77
Nelwyn Av. Horn—3K 51
Nemoure Rd. W3—1A 72
Nene Gdns. Felt—8K 85
Nene Rd. Houn—9M 143
Nepaul Rd. SW11—2C 90
Nepean St. SW15—5E 88
Neptune Rd. Harr—4B 38
Neptune Rd. Houn—9A 68
Neptune St. SE16—4G 77
Nesbit Clo. SE3—2C 94
Nesbit Rd. SE9—3H 95
Nesbitts All. Barn—5K 13
Ness Rd. Eri—7H 83
Ness St. SE16—4E 76
Nesta Rd. Wfd G—6C 30
Nestles Av. Hay—4D 68
Neston Rd. Wat—1G 9
Neston St. SE16—3G 77
Nestor Av. N21—8M 15
Nethan Dri. S Ock—1M 83
Netheravon Rd. W7—2D 70
Netheravon Rd. N. W4—5D 72
Netheravon Rd. S. W4—6D 72
Netherbury Rd. W5—4H 71
Netherby Gdns. Enf—6J 15
Netherby Pk. Wey—7C 116
Netherby Rd. SE23—6G 93
Nether Clo. N3—7L 25
Nethercourt Av. N3—6L 25
Netherfield Gdns. Bark—3B 64
Netherfield Rd. N12—5M 25
Netherfield Rd. SW17—9E 90
Netherford Rd. SW4—1G 91
Netherhall Gdns. NW3—2A 58
Netherhall Way. NW3—1A 58
Netherlands Rd. Barn & Ald
—8B 14
Netherleigh Clo. N6—6G 43
Netherpark Dri. Romf—9D 34
Nether St.—8L 25
N12 1-175 & 2-124
N3 remainder
Netherton Gro. SW10—7A 74
Netherton Rd. N15—4B 44
Netherton Rd. Twic—4E 86
Netherwood Rd. W14—4H 73
Netherwood St. NW6—3K 57
Netley Clo. Croy—9A 126
Netley Clo. Sutt—7H 121
Netley Dri. W on T—2H 117
Netley Gdns. Mord—2A 122
Netley Rd. E17—3K 45
Netley Rd. Bren—7J 71

Netley Rd. Houn—9B 68
Netley Rd. Ilf—3B 48
Netley Rd. Mord—2A 122
Netley St. NW1—6G 59
Nettlecombe Clo. Sutt—1M 135
Nettleden Av. Wemb—2L 55
Nettlefold Pl. SE27—9M 91
Nettlestead Clo. Beck—4K 109
Nettleton Rd. SE14—9H 77
Nettleton Rd. Houn—9M 143
Nettlewood Rd. SW16—4H 107
Neuchatel Rd. SE6—8K 93
Nevada St. SE10—7A 78
Nevern Pl. SW5—5L 73
Nevern Rd. SW5—5L 73
Nevern Sq. SW5—5L 73
Neville Av. N Mald—5B 104
Neville Clo. E11—8D 46
Neville Clo. NW1—5H 59
Neville Clo. NW6—5K 57
Neville Clo. SE15—9E 76
Neville Clo. W3—3A 72
Neville Clo. Esh—8K 117
Neville Clo. Houn—1M 85
Neville Clo. Sidc—1D 112
Neville Dri. N2—4A 42
Neville Gdns. Dag—8H 49
Neville Gill Clo. SW18—5L 89
Neville Pl. N22—8K 27
Neville Rd. E7—3E 62
Neville Rd. NW6—5K 57
Neville Rd. W5—7H 55
Neville Rd. Croy—2B 124
Neville Rd. Dag—8H 49
Neville Rd. Ilf—8A 32
Neville Rd. King—6L 103
Neville Rd. Rich—9G 87
Nevilles Ct. NW2—8E 40
Neville St. SW7—6B 74
Neville Ter. SW7—6B 74
Neville Wlk. Cars—2C 122
Nevill Gro. Wat—3F 8
Nevill Rd. N16—9C 44
Nevill Way. Lou—4J 19
Nevin Dri. E4—1M 29
Nevis Clo. Romf—6C 34
Nevis Rd. SW17—8E 90
Newall Rd. Houn—9A 68
Newark Ct. W on T—3G 117
Newark Cres. NW10—6B 56
Newark Grn. Borwd—5L 12
Newark Rd. S Croy—8B 124
Newark St. E1—8F 60
(in two parts)
Newark Way. NW4—2E 40
New Ash Clo. N2—1B 42
New Barn La. West & Sev
—9M 141
New Barn La. Whyt—8C 138
New Barn Rd. Swan—5C 114
New Barns Av. Mitc—4H 107
New Barn St. E13—7E 62
New Barns Way. Chig—3M 31
New Berry La. W on T—7H 117
Newbery Rd. Eri—9D 82
Newbiggin Path. Wat—4G 21
Newbolt Av. Sutt—7G 121
Newbolt Rd. Stan—5D 22
New Bond St. W1—9F 58
Newborough Grn. N Mald
—8B 104
New Brent St. NW4—3G 41
New Bri. St. EC4—9M 59
New Broad St. EC2—8C 60
New B'way. W5—1H 71
Newburgh Rd. W3—2A 72
Newburgh St. W1—9G 59
New Burlington M. W1—1G 75
New Burlington Pl. W1—1G 75
New Burlington St. W1—1G 75
Newburn St. SE11—6K 75
Newbury Av. Enf—2F 17
Newbury Clo. N'holt—2K 53
Newbury Clo. Romf—6H 35
Newbury Gdns. Eps—6D 120
Newbury Gdns. Romf—6H 35
Newbury Gdns. Upm—4K 51
Newbury M. NW5—2E 58
Newbury Rd. E4—6A 30
Newbury Rd. Brom—7E 110
Newbury Rd. Houn—9K 143
Newbury Rd. Ilf—4C 48
Newbury Rd. Romf—6H 35
Newbury St. EC1—8A 60
Newbury Wlk. Romf—5H 35
Newbury Way. N'holt—2J 53
New Butt La. SE8—8L 77
Newby Clo. Enf—4C 16
Newby St. E14—1A 78
Newby St. SW8—2F 91
Newcastle Av. Ilf—6E 32
Newcastle Clo. EC4—9M 59
Newcastle Pl. W2—8B 58

Newcastle Row. EC1—7L 59
New Cavendish St. W1—8E 58
New Change. EC4—9A 60
New Chapel Sq. Felt—7F 84
New Chu. Rd. SE5—8B 76
New City Rd. E13—6G 63
New Clo. SW19—7A 106
New Clo. Felt—2J 101
New College M. N1—3L 59
Newcombe Gdns. SW16
—1J 107
Newcombe Pk. NW7—5C 24
Newcombe Pk. Wemb—4K 55
Newcombe St. W8—2L 73
Newcomen Rd. E11—8D 46
Newcomen Rd. SW11—2B 90
Newcomen St. SE1—3B 76
New Compton St. WC2—9H 59
New Ct. Dart—5J 99
Newcourt. Uxb—8A 142
Newcourt St. NW8—5C 58
New Coventry St. W1—1H 75
Newcroft Clo. Uxb—8D 142
New Cross Rd. SE14—8H 77
Newdales Clo. N9—2E 28
Newdene Av. N'holt—5H 53
Newell St. E14—9K 61
New End. NW3—8A 42
New End Sq. NW3—9B 42
Newent Clo. SE15—8C 76
Newent Clo. Cars—3D 122
New Farm Av. Brom—8E 110
New Farm La. N'wd—6C 20
New Fetter La. EC4—9L 59
Newfield Clo. Hmptn—5L 101
Newfield Rise. NW2—8F 40
New Ford Rd. Wal X—7F 6
New Forest La. Chig—6L 31
Newgale Gdns. Edgw—8K 23
New Garden Dri. W Dray
—3J 14
Newgate. Croy—3A 124
Newgate Clo. Felt—9J 85
Newgate St. E4—3C 30
Newgate St. EC1—9M 59
New Goulston St. E1—9D 60
New Hall Ct. Wal A—6M 7
New Hall Dri. Romf—8J 35
Newham's Row. SE1—3C 76
Newham Way—8D 62
E16 55-413
E6 remainder
Newhaven Clo. Hay—5D 68
Newhaven Cres. Ashf—2B 100
Newhaven Gdns. SE9—3H 95
Newhaven Rd. SE25—9B 108
New Heston Rd. Houn—8K 69
Newhouse Av. Romf—1H 49
Newhouse Clo. N Mald—2C 120
Newhouse Cres. Wat—5F 4
Newhouse Wlk. Mord—2A 122
Newick Clo. Bex—5M 97
Newick Rd. E5—9F 44
Newing Grn. Brom—4H 111
Newington Barrow Way. N7
—8K 43
Newington Butts—5M 75
SE1 2-22
SE11 remainder
Newington Causeway. SE1
—4A 76
Newington Grn. N1 & N16
—1B 60
Newington Grn. Rd. N1—1B 60
New Inn B'way. EC2—7C 60
New Inn Pas. EC2—7C 60
New Inn St. EC2—7C 60
New Inn Yd. EC2—7C 60
New Kent Rd. SE1—5A 76
New Kings Rd. SW6—1K 89
New King St. SE8—7L 77
Newland Clo. Pinn—6J 21
Newland Dri. Enf—3F 16
Newland Gdns. W13—3E 70
Newland Rd. N8—1J 43
Newlands Av. Th Dit—3C 118
Newlands Clo. Edgw—3J 23
Newlands Clo. S'hall—6J 69
Newlands Clo. W on T—6J 117
Newlands Clo. Wemb—2G 55
Newlands Ct. SE9—5L 95
Newlands Pk. SE26—3G 109
Newlands Pl. Barn—7H 13
Newlands Rd. SW16—6J 107
Newlands Rd. Wfd G—2D 30
Newlands, The. Wall—9H 123
Newland St. E16—2J 79
Newlands Wlk. Wat—6H 5
Newlands Way. Chess—7G 119
Newlands Wood. Croy—1K 139
Newling Clo. E6—9K 63
New Lydenburgh St. SE7
—4G 79
Newlyn Clo. St Alb—3J 5

Newlyn Clo. Uxb—8E 142
Newlyn Gdns. Harr—5K 37
Newlyn Rd. N17—8D 28
Newlyn Rd. Barn—6K 13
Newlyn Rd. Well—1D 96
Newman Clo. Horn—3J 51
New Mnr. Rd. E15—5C 62
Newman Pas. W1—8G 59
Newman Rd. E13—6F 62
Newman Rd. E17—3H 45
Newman Rd. Brom—5E 110
Newman Rd. Croy—3K 123
Newman Rd. Hay—1F 68
Newmans Clo. Lou—5L 19
Newmans Row. WC2—8K 59
Newman's Way. Barn—3A 14
Newman Yd. W1—9H 59
Newmarket Av. N'holt—1L 53
Newmarket Grn. SE9—6H 95
Newmarket Way. Horn—9J 51
Newminster Rd. Mord—1A 122
New Mount St. E15—3B 62
Newnes Path. SW15—3F 88
Newnham Av. Ruis—6G 37
Newnham Clo. Lou—8H 19
Newnham Clo. N'holt—2A 54
Newnham Clo. T Hth—6A 108
Newnham Gdns. N'holt—2A 54
Newnham Ho. Lou—8H 19
Newnham Pde. Wal X—3D 6
Newnham Rd. N22—8K 27
Newnhams Clo. Brom—7K 111
Newnham Ter. SE1—4L 75
Newnham Way. Harr—3J 39
New North Pl. EC2—7C 60
New North Rd. N1—3A 60
New North Rd. Ilf—7B 32
New North St. WC1—8K 59
Newton Clo. N4—5B 44
New Oak Rd. N2—9B 26
New Orleans Wlk. N19—5H 43
New Oxford St. WC1—9H 59
New Pk. Av. N13—3A 28
New Pk. Clo. N'holt—2J 53
New Pk. Rd. SW2—7H 91
New Pk. Rd. Ashf—2A 100
New Peachey La. Uxb—9B 142
Newpiece. Lou—5M 19
New Pl. Croy—8L 125
New Pl. Sq. SE16—4F 76
New Plaistow Rd. E15—4C 62
Newport Av. E13—7F 62
Newport Ct. WC2—1H 75
Newport Mead. Wat—4H 21
Newport Pl. W1—1H 75
Newport Rd. E10—7A 46
Newport Rd. E17—2J 45
Newport Rd. SW13—9E 72
Newport Rd. Hay—8B 52
Newport Rd. Houn—9L 143
Newports. Swan—2B 130
Newport St. SE11—5K 75
Newquay Cres. Harr—7J 37
Newquay Gdns. Wat—2F 20
Newquay Rd. SE6—8M 93
New Quebec St. W1—9D 58
New River Ct. Wal X—4B 6
New River Cres. N13—4M 27
New River Wlk. N1—2A 60
New Rd. E1—8F 60
New Rd. E4—4M 29
New Rd. N8—3J 43
New Rd. N9—3E 28
New Rd. N17—8D 28
New Rd. N22—8A 28
New Rd. NW7—7J 25
(Bittacy Hill)
New Rd. NW7—9D 12
(Hendon Wood La.)
New Rd. SE2—5H 81
New Rd. Borwd—8H 11
New Rd. Bren—7H 71
New Rd. Dag & Rain—5L 65
New Rd. E Mol—8L 101
New Rd. Esh—5A 118
New Rd. Felt—7F 84
New Rd. Felt—5B 84
(Bedfont)
New Rd. Felt—2J 101
(Hanworth)
New Rd. Harr—9D 38
New Rd. Hay—8A 68
New Rd. Houn—3M 85
New Rd. Ilf—7C 48
New Rd. King—4L 103
New Rd. Lea—3D 132
New Rd. Mitc—3E 122
New Rd. Orp—2E 128
New Rd. Rad—1C 10
New Rd. Rich—1G 103
New Rd. Rick—8A 8

New Rd. Shep—7A 100
New Rd. Swan—7D 114
New Rd. Swan—4D 114
 (Hextable)
New Rd. Uxb—7A 52
New Rd. Wat—6G 9
New Rd. Wat—3C 10
 (Letchmore Heath)
New Rd. Well—1F 96
New Rochford St. NW5—1D 58
New Row. WC2—1J 75
Newry Rd. Twic—4E 86
Newsam Av. N15—3B 44
New Spring Gdns. Wlk. SE11
—6J 75
Newstead Av. Orp—5B 128
Newstead Rd. SE12—6D 94
Newstead Way. SW19—1J 105
New Sq. WC2—9L 59
New St. EC2—8C 60
New St. Wat—6G 9
New St. Hill. Brom—2F 110
New St. Sq. EC4—9L 59
Newteswell Dri. Wal A—5K 7
Newton Av. N10—8E 26
Newton Av. W3—3A 72
Newton Gro. W4—5C 72
Newton Rd. E15—1B 62
Newton Rd. N15—3E 44
Newton Rd. NW2—9G 41
Newton Rd. SW19—4J 105
Newton Rd. W2—9M 57
Newton Rd. Chig—5F 32
Newton Rd. Harr—9C 22
Newton Rd. Iswth—1D 86
Newton Rd. Purl—4G 137
Newton Rd. Well—2E 96
Newton Rd. Womb 3K 55
Newtons Clo. Rain—3D 66
Newton St. WC2—9J 59
Newton's Yd. SW18—4L 89
Newton Wlk. Edgw—8M 23
Newton Way. N18—5A 28
Newton Wood Rd. Asht
—8K 133
Newtown Rd. Uxb—2A 142
Newtown St. SW11—9F 74
New Union Clo. E14—4A 78
New Union St. EC2—8B 60
New Wanstead. E11—4D 46
New Way Rd. NW9—2C 40
New Wharf Rd. N1—5J 59
New Windsor St. Uxb—4A 142
New Zealand Av. W on T
—3D 116
New Zealand Way. W12—1F 72
New Zealand Way. Rain—6D 66
Niagara Av. W5—5G 71
Niagara Clo. Wal X—2D 6
Nibthwaite Rd. Harr—4C 38
Nicholas Clo. Gnfd—5M 53
Nicholas Clo. Wat—1F 8
Nicholas Gdns. W5—3H 71
Nicholas La. EC4—1B 76
Nicholas Rd. E1—7G 61
Nicholas Rd. Borwd—7K 11
Nicholas Rd. Croy—6J 123
Nicholas Rd. Dag—7K 49
Nicholas Way. N'wd—4B 20
Nicholay Rd. N19—6H 43
Nichol Clo. N14—1H 27
Nicholes Rd. Houn—3L 85
Nichol La. Brom—4E 110
Nicholls Av. Uxb—7E 142
Nicholls St. E2—4E 60
Nicholson Rd. Croy—3D 124
Nicholson St. SE1—2M 75
Nichol's Sq. E2—5D 60
Nickleby Clo. Uxb—9F 142
Nicola Clo. Harr—9B 22
Nicola Clo. S Croy—8A 124
Nicol Clo. Twic—5F 86
Nicoll Pl. NW4—4F 40
Nicoll Rd. NW10—4C 56
Nicoll Way. Borwd—7B 12
Nicolson Dri. Bush, Wat—2A 22
Nicolson Rd. Orp—2H 129
Nicosia Rd. SW18—6C 90
Niederwald Rd. SE26—1J 109
Nield Rd. Hay—3D 68
Nigel Clo. N'holt—4J 53
Nigel M. Ilf—9M 47
Nigel Playfair Av. W6—6F 72
Nigel Rd. E7—1G 63
Nigel Rd. SE15—2E 92
Nigeria Rd. SE7—8H 79
Nightingale Av. E4—5C 30
Nightingale Clo. E4—4C 30

Nightingale Clo. W4—7A 72
Nightingale Clo. Cars—4E 122
Nightingale Dri. Eps—8M 119
Nightingale Gro. SE13—4B 94
Nightingale Gro. Dart—3L 99
Nightingale La. E11—3F 46
Nightingale La. N8—2J 43
Nightingale La.--6D 90
 SW4 1-25
 SW12 remainder
Nightingale La. Brom—6G 111
Nightingale La. Rich—6J 87
Nightingale Pl. SE18—7L 79
Nightingale Rd. E5—8F 44
Nightingale Rd. N9—8G 17
Nightingale Rd. N22—7J 27
Nightingale Rd. NW10—5D 56
Nightingale Rd. W7—2D 70
Nightingale Rd. Bush, Wat
—7L 9
Nightingale Rd. Cars—5D 122
Nightingale Rd. E Mol—9M 101
Nightingale Rd. Esh—8K 117
Nightingale Rd. Hmptn—2L 101
Nightingale Rd. Orp—1A 128
Nightingale Rd. S Croy—3H 139
Nightingales. Wal A—7L 7
Nightingale Sq. SW12—6E 90
Nightingale Vale. SE18—7L 79
Nightingale Wlk. SW4—5F 90
Nightingale Way. Swan
—7C 114
Nile Path. SE18—7L 79
Nile Rd. E13—5G 63
Nile St. N1—6B 60
Nile Ter. SE15—6D 76
Nimbus Rd. Eps—2B 134
Nimegan Way. SE22—4C 92
Nimmo Dri. Bush, Wat—9B 10
Nimrod Clo. N'holt—GII 53
Nimrod Rd. SW16—3F 106
Nine Acres Clo. E12—1J 63
Nine Elms Av. Uxb—8B 142
Nine Elms Clo. Uxb—8B 142
Nine Elms La. SW8—8G 75
Ninefields. Wal A—6M 7
Nineteenth Rd. Mitc—8J 107
Ninhams Wood. Orp—6L 127
Ninth Av. Hay—1E 68
Nithdale Rd. SE18—8M 79
Nithsdale Gro. Uxb—8A 36
Niton Clo. Barn—8H 13
Niton Rd. Rich. C 87
Niton St. SW6—8H 73
Noak Hill Rd. Romf—4G 35
Nobel Rd. N18—5G 29
Noble St. EC2—9A 60
Noel Pk. Rd. N22—9J 27
Noel Rd. E6—7J 63
Noel Rd. N1—5M 59
Noel Rd. W3—1L 71
Noel Sq. Dag—9G 49
Noel St. W1—9G 59
Noke La. St Alb—1K 5
Nolan Way. E5—9E 44
Nolton Pl. Edgw—8K 23
Nonsuch Clo. Ilf—6M 31
Nonsuch Ct. Av. Eps—2F 134
Nonsuch Industrial Est. Eps
—3C 134
Nonsuch Wlk. Sutt—2H 135
 (in two parts)
Nora Gdns. NW4—2H 41
Nora Ter. Harr—6C 38
Norbiton Av. King—6L 103
Norbiton Comn. Rd. King
—7M 103
Norbiton Rd. E14—9K 61
Norbreck Gdns. NW6—5K 55
Norbreck Pde. W5—6J 55
Norbroke St. W12—1D 72
Norburn St. W10—8J 57
Norbury Av.—5K 107
 SW16 245-319 & 236-328
 T Hth remainder
Norbury Av. Houn—3B 86
Norbury Clo. SW16—5L 107
Norbury Ct. Rd. SW16—6J 107
Norbury Cres. SW16—5K 107
Norbury Cross. SW16—7J 107
Norbury Gdns. Romf—3H 49
Norbury Gro. NW7—3C 24
Norbury Hill. SW16—3L 107
Norbury Rise. SW16—7J 107
Norbury Rd. E4—5L 29
Norbury Rd. T Hth—6A 108
Norbury Trading Est. SW16
—6K 107
Norcombe Gdns. Harr—4G 39
Norcott Clo. Hay—7G 53
Norcott Rd. N16—7E 44
Norcroft Gdns. SE22—6E 92
Norcutt Rd. Twic—7C 86

Nordenfeldt Rd. Eri—6B 82
Norfield Rd. Dart—1A 114
Norfolk Av. N13—6M 27
Norfolk Av. N15—4D 44
Norfolk Av. S Croy—2E 138
Norfolk Av. Wat—2G 9
Norfolk Clo. N2—1C 42
Norfolk Clo. N13—6M 27
Norfolk Clo. Barn—6E 14
Norfolk Cres. W2—9C 58
Norfolk Cres. Sidc—6C 96
Norfolk Gdns. Bexh—9K 81
Norfolk Gdns. Borwd—6B 12
Norfolk Gdns. Houn—4K 85
Norfolk Ho. Rd. SW16—9H 91
Norfolk Pl. W2—9B 58
Norfolk Pl. Well—1E 96
Norfolk Rd. E6—4K 63
Norfolk Rd. E17—9H 29
Norfolk Rd. NW8—4B 58
Norfolk Rd. NW10—3C 56
Norfolk Rd. SW19—4C 106
Norfolk Rd. Bark—3C 64
Norfolk Rd. Barn—5L 13
Norfolk Rd. Dag—1M 65
Norfolk Rd. Enf—7F 16
Norfolk Rd. Esh—7C 118
Norfolk Rd. Felt—7G 85
Norfolk Rd. Harr—3M 37
Norfolk Rd. Ilf—6C 48
Norfolk Rd. Romf—4A 50
Norfolk Rd. T Hth—7A 108
Norfolk Rd. Upm—8L 51
Norfolk Rd. Uxb—2B 142
Norfolk Row. SE11—5K 75
Norfolk Sq. W2—9B 58
Norfolk St. E7—1E 62
Norfolk Ter. W6—6J 73
Norgrove St. SW12—6E 90
Norheads La. Warl & West
—9F 140
Norhyrst Av. SE25—7D 108
Nork Gdns. Bans—6J 135
Nork Rise. Bans—8H 135
Nork Way. Bans—8G 135
Norland Pl. W11—2J 73
Norland Rd. W11—2H 73
Norlands Cres. Chst—5M 111
Norland Sq. W11—2J 73
Norley Vale. SW15—7E 88
Norlington Rd.—6A 46
 E11 1-55 & 2-28
 E10 remainder
Norman Av. N22—8A 28
Norman Av. Eps—4D 134
Norman Av. Felt—8J 85
Norman Av. S'hall—1A 69
Norman Av. Twic—6G 87
Normanby Clo. SW15—4K 89
Normanby Rd. NW10—9D 40
Norman Clo. N22—8A 28
Norman Clo. Orp—5A 128
Norman Clo. Romf—8M 33
Norman Clo. Wal A—6K 7
Norman Ct. N4—5L 43
Norman Ct. Ilf—5B 48
Norman Cres. Houn—8H 69
Norman Cres. Pinn—8G 21
Normand M. W14—7J 73
Normand Rd. W14—7K 73
Normandy Av. Barn—7K 13
Normandy Dri. Hay—9A 52
Normandy Rd. SW9—9L 75
Normandy Ter. E16—9F 62
Normandy Way. Eri—9C 82
Norman Gro. E3—5J 61
Normanhurst Av. Well & Bex H
—9H 81
Normanhurst Dri. Twic—4F 86
Normanhurst Rd. SW2—8K 91
Normanhurst Rd. Orp—6F 112
Normanhurst Rd. W on T
—4H 117
Norman Rd. E6—7K 63
Norman Rd. E11—7B 46
Norman Rd. N15—3D 44
Norman Rd. SE10—8M 77
Norman Rd. SW19—4A 106
Norman Rd. Ashf—3B 100
Norman Rd. Belv—4M 81
Norman Rd. Dart—7J 99
Norman Rd. Horn—6E 50
Norman Rd. Ilf—1M 63
Norman Rd. Sutt—7L 121
Norman Rd. T Hth—9M 107
Norman's Bldgs. EC1—6A 60
Normans Clo. NW10—2B 56
Norman's Clo. Uxb—7D 142
Normansfield Av. Tedd—4G 103
Normansfield Clo. Bush, Wat
—9M 9

Normanshire Av. E4—4A 30
Normanshire Dri. E4—4L 29
Normans Mead. NW10—2B 56
Norman St. EC1—6A 60
Norman Ter. NW6—1K 57
Normanton Av. SW19—8L 89
Normanton Pk. E4—2C 30
Normanton Rd. S Croy—8C 124
Normanton St. SE23—8H 93
Norman Way. N14—2J 27
Norman Way. W3—8M 55
Normington Clo. SW16—2L 107
Norrice Lea. N2—3B 42
Norris St. SW1—1H 75
Norris Way. Dart—2D 98
Norroy Rd. SW15—3H 89
Norry's Clo. Barn—6D 14
Norry's Rd. Barn—6D 14
Norseman Way. Gnfd—4M 53
Norstead Pl. SW15—8E 88
N. Access Rd. E17—4H 45
North Acre. NW9—8C 24
North Acre. Bans—8K 135
N. Acton Rd. NW10—5B 56
Northallerton Way. Romf
—5H 35
Northall Rd. Bexh—1A 98
Northampton Gro. N1—1B 60
Northampton Pk. N1—2A 60
Northampton Rd. EC1—7L 59
Northampton Rd. Croy—4E 124
Northampton Rd. Enf—6J 17
Northampton Sq. EC1—6M 59
Northampton St. N1—3A 60
Northanger Rd. SW16—3J 107
North App. N'wd—2A 20
North App. Wat—7E 4
N. Audley St. W1—1E 74
North Av. N18—4E 28
North Av. W13—8F 54
North Av. Cars—9E 122
North Av. Harr—4M 37
North Av. Hay—1E 68
North Av. Rich—9L 71
North Av. S'hall—1K 69
North Av. W on T—9C 116
North Bank. NW8—6C 58
Northbank Rd. E17—9A 30
N. Birkbeck Rd. E11—8B 46
Northborough Rd. SW16
—7H 107
Northbourne. Brom—2E 126
Northbourne Rd. SW4—4H 91
Northbrook Dri. N'wd—8C 20
Northbrook Rd. N22—7J 27
Northbrook Rd. SE13—4C 94
Northbrook Rd. Barn—8J 13
Northbrook Rd. Croy—9B 108
Northbrook Rd. Ilf—7L 47
Northburgh St. EC1—7M 59
Northchurch. SE17—6B 76
Northchurch Rd. N1—3B 60
 (in two parts)
N. Church Rd. Wemb—2L 55
Northchurch Ter. N1—3C 60
N. Circular Rd. E4—7K 29
N. Circular Rd. E6—3J 63
N. Circular Rd. E18—9D 30
N. Circular Rd. N13—5L 27
N. Circular Rd. 6K 55 to
7E 26
 NW10—6K 55
 NW2—8C 40
 NW4—6F 40
 NW11—4H 41
 N3—2K 41
 N12—8B 26
Northcliffe Clo. Wor Pk
—5C 120
Northcliffe Dri. N20—1K 25
North Clo. Barn—7G 13
North Clo. Bexh—3H 97
North Clo. Chig—5E 32
North Clo. Dag—4L 65
North Clo. Felt—5B 84
North Clo. Mord—8J 105
North Comn. Wey—6A 116
N. Common Rd. W5—1J 71
N. Common Rd. Uxb—1B 142
Northcote. Lea—7A 132
Northcote Av. W5—1J 71
Northcote Av. Iswth—4E 86
Northcote Av. S'hall—1J 69
Northcote Av. Surb—2M 119
Northcote Rd. E17—2J 45
Northcote Rd. NW10—3C 56
Northcote Rd. SW11—4C 90
Northcote Rd. Croy—1B 124
Northcote Rd. N Mald—7C 104
Northcote Rd. Sidc—1C 112
Northcote Rd. Twic 4E 86
Northcott Av. N22—8J 27

N. Countess Rd. E17—8K 29
North Ct. W1—8G 59
N. Cray Rd. Sidc & Bex—3J 113
North Cres. N3—9K 25
North Cres. WC1—8H 59
Northcroft Rd. W13—3F 70
Northcroft Rd. Eps—9C 120
North Crofts. SE23—7F 92
N. Cross Rd. SE22—4D 92
N. Cross Rd. Ilf—2A 48
North Dene. NW7—3B 24
Northdene. Chig—5B 32
North Dene. Houn—9M 69
Northdene Gdns. N15—4D 44
North Down. S Croy—3C 138
Northdown Clo. Ruis—8D 36
Northdown Gdns. Ilf—3C 48
Northdown Rd. Horn—5F 50
Northdown Rd. Sutt—2L 135
Northdown Rd. Well—1F 96
N. Downs Cres. Croy—2M 139
 (in two parts)
N. Downs Rd. Croy—2M 139
Northdown St. N1—5K 59
North Dri. SW16—1G 107
North Dri. Houn—1A 86
North Dri. Orp—6C 128
North Dri. Romf—1G 51
North End. NW3—7A 42
North End. Croy—4A 124
North End. Buck H—9G 19
North End. Croy—4A 124
N. End Av. NW3—7A 42
N. End Cres. W14—5K 73
N. End La. Orp—3L 141
N. End Rd. NW11—6L 41
N. End Rd.—5J 73
 W14 1-311 & 2-234
 SW6 remainder
Northend Rd. Eri—9D 82
N. End Rd. Wemb—8L 39
N. End Way. NW3—7A 42
Northern Av. N9—2D 28
Northernhay Wlk. Mord
—8J 105
Northern Perimeter Rd. Houn
—9M 143
Northern Perimeter Rd. W. Houn
—9J 143
Northern Rd. E13—5F 62
Northey Av. Sutt—2H 135
N. Eyot Gdns. W6—6D 72
Northey St. E14—1J 77
N. Feltham Trading Est. Felt
—4F 84
Northfield Av.—2F 70
 W13 1-249 & 2-242
 W5 remainder
Northfield Av. Orp—1G 129
Northfield Av. Pinn—2H 37
Northfield Clo. Hay—4D 68
Northfield Cres. Sutt—6J 121
Northfield Gdns. Dag—9K 49
Northfield Gdns. Wat—1G 9
Northfield Industrial Est.
 NW10—6L 55
Northfield Industrial Est.
 Wemb—4L 55
Northfield Pde. Hay—4C 68
Northfield Pk. Hay—4D 68
Northfield Path. Dag—9K 49
Northfield Pl. Wey—9A 116
Northfield Rd. E6—3K 63
Northfield Rd. N16—5C 44
Northfield Rd. W13—3F 70
Northfield Rd. Barn—5C 14
Northfield Rd. Borwd—3M 11
Northfield Rd. Dag—9K 49
Northfield Rd. Enf—7F 16
Northfield Rd. Houn—7H 69
Northfield Rd. Wal X—5E 6
Northfields. SW18—3L 89
Northfields Rd. W3—8M 55
N. Flock St. SE16—3E 76
North Gdns. SW19—4B 106
Northgate. N'wd—2A 20
Northgate Path. Borwd—2K 11
North Glade, The. Bex—7K 97
N. Gower St. NW1—6G 59
North Grn. NW9—7C 24
North Gro. N6—5E 42
North Gro. N15—3B 44
N. Hatton Rd. Houn—9B 68
North Hill. N6—4D 42
N. Hill Av. N6—4E 42
N. Hill Dri. Romf—4H 35
N. Hill Grn. Romf—4H 35
N. Hyde Gdns. Hay—5E 68
N. Hyde La. S'hall & Houn
—6J 69
N. Hyde Rd. Hay—4C 68
 (in two parts)
Northiam. N12—4L 25
Northiam St. E8—4F 60

Northington St. WC1—7K 59
N. Kent Gro. SE18—5K 79
Northlands Av. Orp—6C 128
Northlands St. SE5—1A 92
North La. Tedd—3D 102
N. Lodge Clo. SW15—4H 89
North Mall. N9—2F 28
North M. WC1—7K 59
Northolm. Edgw—4B 24
Northolme Gdns. Edgw—8L 23
Northolme Rise. Orp—4C 128
Northolme Rd. N5—9A 44
Northolt Av. Ruis—1F 52
Northolt Gdns. Gnfd—1D 54
Northolt Rd. Harr—9M 37
Northolt Rd. Houn—9H 143
Northolt Way. Horn—2G 67
N. Orbital Rd. Wat—6H 5
N. Orbital Rd. Wat & St Alb
—4H 5
Northover. Brom—9D 94
North Pde. Chess—7K 119
North Pk. SE9—5K 95
N. Park Av. NW10 & NW2
—1F 56
North Pas. SW18—3L 89
North Pl. Mitc—4D 106
North Pl. Tedd—3D 102
North Pl. Wal A—6H 7
N. Pole La. Kes—8D 126
N. Pole Rd. W10—8G 57
Northport St. N1—4B 60
N. Riding. St Alb—3L 5
North Rd. N6—5E 42
North Rd. N7—2J 59
North Rd. N9—1F 28
North Rd. SE18—5C 80
North Rd. SW19—3A 106
North Rd. W5—4H 71
North Rd. Belv—4M 81
North Rd. Bren—7J 71
North Rd. Brom—5F 110
North Rd. Dart—5D 98
North Rd. Edgw—8M 23
North Rd. Felt—5B 84
North Rd. Hav, Romf—3C 34
North Rd. Hay—8B 52
North Rd. Ilf—7C 48
North Rd. Purf—5M 83
North Rd. Rich—2L 87
North Rd. Romf—3J 49
North Rd. Ruis—5C 36
North Rd. S'hall—1L 69
North Rd. Surb—1H 119
North Rd. Wal X—6E 6
North Rd. W on T—7G 117
North Rd. W Dray—4K 143
North Rd. W Wick—3M 125
North Row. W1—1D 74
North Several. SE3—1B 94
Northside Rd. Brom—5E 110
Northspur Rd. Sutt—5L 121
North Sq. N9—2F 28
North Sq. NW11—3L 41
Northstead Rd. SW2—8L 91
North St. E13—5F 62
North St. NW4—3G 41
North St. SW4—2G 91
North St. Bark—3M 63
North St. Bexh—3L 97
North St. Brom—5E 110
North St. Cars—5D 122
North St. Dart—6H 99
North St. Horn—6H 51
North St. Iswth—2E 86
North St. Romf—1B 50
North St. Pas. E13—5F 62
N. Tenter St. E1—9D 60
North Ter. SW3—4C 74
Northumberland All. EC3
—9C 60
Northumberland Av. E12
—6G 47
Northumberland Av. WC2
—2J 75
Northumberland Av. Enf
—3F 16
Northumberland Av. Horn
—3G 51
Northumberland Av. Iswth
—9D 70
Northumberland Av. Well
—2C 96
Northumberland Clo. Eri
—8A 82
Northumberland Clo. Stai
—5C 144
Northumberland Cres. Felt
—5C 84
Northumberland Gdns. N9
—3D 28
Northumberland Gdns. Iswth
—8E 70

Northumberland Gdns. Mitc
Northumberland Gro. N17
—7F 28
Northumberland Pk. N17
—7E 28
Northumberland Pk. Eri—8A 82
Northumberland Pl. W2—9L 57
Northumberland Pl. Rich
—4H 87
Northumberland Rd. E6—9K 63
Northumberland Rd. E17
—5L 45
Northumberland Rd. Barn
—8A 14
Northumberland Rd. Harr
—3K 37
Northumberland Row. Twic
—7C 86
Northumberland St. WC2
—2J 75
Northumberland Way. Eri
—9A 82
Northumbria St. E14—9L 61
N. Verbena Gdns. W6—6E 72
North View. SW19—2G 105
North View. W5—7G 55
North View. Ilf—7E 32
North View. Pinn—5G 37
Northview. Swan—6C 114
N. View Cres. NW10—9D 40
N. View Cres. Eps—9G 135
N. View Dri. Wfd G—9H 31
N. View Rd. N8—1H 43
North Vs. NW1—2H 59
North Wlk. Croy—8M 125
(in two parts)
North Wlk. Sutt—3H 135
(in two parts)
North Way. N9—2H 29
North Way. N11—6G 27
North Way. NW9—1M 39
Northway. NW11—3M 41
Northway. Mord—8J 105
North Way. Pinn—2H 37
North Way. Uxb—3C 142
Northway. Wall—6G 123
Northway Cir. NW7—4B 24
Northway Cres. NW7—4B 24
Northway Gdns. NW11—3M 41
Northway Rd. SE5—2A 92
Northway Rd. Croy—1D 124
N. Western Av. Wat—8C 4
Northwest Pl. N1—5L 59
N. Wharf Rd. W2—8B 58
Northwick Av. Harr—4E 38
Northwick Circ. Harr—4G 39
Northwick Clo. NW8—7B 58
Northwick Pk. Rd. Harr—4D 38
Northwick Rd. Wat—4G 21
Northwick Rd. Wemb—4H 55
Northwick Sq. Houn—9A 68
Northwick Ter. NW8—7B 58
Northwick Wlk. Harr—5D 38
Northwold Dri. Pinn—9G 21
Northwold Est. E5—7K 44
Northwold Rd.—7D 44
N16 1-67 & 2-34
E5 remainder
Northwood Av. Horn—9E 50
Northwood Av. Purl & Kenl
—5L 137
N. Wood Ct. SE25—7E 108
Northwood Gdns. N12—5B 26
Northwood Gdns. Gnfd—1D 54
Northwood Gdns. Ilf—2L 47
Northwood Pl. Eri—4K 81
Northwood Rd. N6—5F 42
Northwood Rd. SE23—7K 93
Northwood Rd. Cars—8E 122
Northwood Rd. Houn—9H 143
Northwood Rd. T Hth—6A 108
Northwood Way. SE19—3B 108
Northwood Way. N'wd—7E 20
N. Woolwich Rd. E16—2F 78
(in two parts)
N. Worple Way. SW14—2B 88
Norton Av. Surb—2M 119
Norton Clo. E4—5L 29
Norton Clo. Enf—4F 16
Norton Folgate. E1—8C 60
Norton Gdns. SW16—6J 107
Norton Rd. E10—6K 45
Norton Rd. Dag—2B 66
Norton Rd. Uxb—6B 142
Norton Rd. Wemb—2H 55
Norval Rd. Wemb—7F 38
Norway Pl. E14—9K 61
Norway St. SE10—7M 77
Norway Wlk. Rain—7G 67
Norwich Av. Ilf—6E 48
Norwich Pl. Bexh—3L 97
Norwich Rd. E7—1E 62
Norwich Rd. Dag—5L 65

Norwich Rd. Gnfd—4M 53
Norwich Rd. N'wd—1D 36
Norwich Rd. T Hth—7A 108
Norwich St. EC4—9L 59
Norwich Wlk. Edgw—7A 24
Norwich Way. Rick—5A 8
Norwood Av. Romf—5C 50
Norwood Av. Wemb—4K 55
Norwood Clo. S'hall—5L 69
Norwood Cres. Houn—9A 68
Norwood Dri. Harr—4L 37
Norwood Gdns. Hay—7G 53
Norwood Gdns. S'hall—5K 69
Norwood Grn. Rd. S'hall—5L 69
Norwood High St. SE27—9M 91
Norwood Pk. Rd. SE27—2A 108
Norwood Rd.—7M 91
SE24 1-339 & 2-150
SE27 remainder
Norwood Rd. S'hall—4J 69
Noss Clo. Sutt—7C 122
Notley St. SE5—8B 76
Notson Rd. SE25—8F 108
Notting Barn Rd. W10—7H 57
Nottingham Av. E16—8G 63
Nottingham Clo. Wat—6E 4
Nottingham Ct. WC2—9J 59
Nottingham Pl. W1—8E 58
Nottingham Rd. E10—4A 46
Nottingham Rd. SW17—7D 90
Nottingham Rd. Iswth—1D 86
Nottingham Rd. S Croy
—7A 124
Nottingham St. W1—8E 58
Notting Hill Ga. W11—2L 73
Nova M. Sutt—3J 121
Novar Clo. Orp—2D 128
Nova Rd. Croy—2M 123
Novar Rd. SE9—7A 96
Novello St. SW6—9L 73
Nowell Rd. SW13—7E 72
Nower Hill. Pinn—2K 37
Noyna Rd. SW17—9D 90
Nuding Clo. SE13—2L 93
Nuffield Lodge. N6—4F 42
Nuffield Rd. Swan—3E 114
Nugent Industrial Pk. Orp
—8G 113
Nugent Rd. N19—6J 43
Nugent Rd. SE25—7D 108
Nugents Pk. Pinn—8J 21
Nugent Ter. NW8—5A 58
Nuneaton Rd. Dag—3J 65
Nunhead Cres. SE15—2F 92
Nunhead Grn. SE15—2F 92
Nunhead Gro. SE15—2G 93
Nunhead La. SE15—2F 92
Nunnington Clo. SE9—9J 95
Nunns Rd. Enf—4A 16
Nupton Dri. Barn—8G 13
Nursery App. N12—6C 26
Nursery Av. N3—9A 26
Nursery Av. Bexh—2K 97
Nursery Av. Croy—4H 125
Nursery Clo. SW15—3H 89
Nursery Clo. Croy—4H 125
Nursery Clo. Enf—3H 17
Nursery Clo. Eps—2C 134
Nursery Clo. Felt—6F 84
Nursery Clo. Orp—2E 128
Nursery Clo. Romf—4H 49
Nursery Clo. Swan—6A 114
Nursery Clo. Wfd G—5F 30
Nursery Ct. N17—7D 28
Nursery Gdns. Enf—3H 17
Nursery Gdns. Sun—6D 100
Nursery La. E7—2E 62
Nursery La. W10—8G 57
Nursery La. Uxb—7B 142
Nursery Rd. E9—2G 61
Nursery Rd. N2—8B 26
Nursery Rd. N14—9G 15
Nursery Rd. SW9—3K 91
Nursery Rd. SW19—6M 105
(Merton)
Nursery Rd. SW19—4J 105
(Wimbledon)
Nursery Rd. Lou—7G 19
Nursery Rd. Lou—3G 19
(High Beach)
Nursery Rd. Pinn—1G 37
Nursery Rd. Sun—6C 100
Nursery Rd. Sutt—6A 122
Nursery Rd. T Hth—8B 108
Nursery Row. Barn—5J 13
Nursery St. N17—7D 28
Nursery, The. Eri—8D 82
Nursery Wlk. NW4—1G 41
Nursery Wlk. Romf—5B 50
Nursery Waye. Uxb—4B 142
Nurstead Rd. Eri—8L 81
Nutbourne St. W10—6J 57
Nutbrook St. SE15—2E 92

Nutbrowne Rd. Dag—4K 65
Nutcroft Rd. SE15—8F 76
Nutfield Clo. N17—6E 28
Nutfield Gdns. Ilf—7E 48
Nutfield Gdns. N'holt—5G 53
Nutfield Rd. E15—9A 46
Nutfield Rd. NW2—8E 40
Nutfield Rd. SE22—3D 92
Nutfield Rd. Coul—8E 136
Nutfield Rd. T Hth—8M 107
Nutfield Way. Orp—4M 127
Nutford Pl. W1—9D 58
Nuthatch Gdns. SE28—3B 80
Nuthatch M. SE28—3B 80
Nuthurst Av. SW2—8K 91
Nutley Clo. Swan—5D 114
Nutley Ter. NW3—2A 58
Nutmead Clo. Bex—7A 98
Nuttall St. N1—5C 60
Nutter La. E11—4G 47
Nuttfield Clo. Rick—8A 8
Nutt Gro. Edgw—2H 23
Nut Tree Clo. Orp—5H 129
Nutt St. SE15—8D 76
Nutty La. Shep—7A 100
Nutwell St. SW17—2C 106
Nuxley Rd. Belv—7K 81
Nyanza St. SE18—7B 80
Nylands Av. Rich—1L 87
Nymans Gdns. SW20—7F 104
Nynehead St. SE14—8J 77
Nyon Gro. SE6—8K 93
Nyssia Clo. Wfd G—6K 31
Nyton Clo. N19—6J 43

Oakapple Clo. S Croy—6F 138
Oak Av. N8—2J 43
Oak Av. N10—7F 26
Oak Av. N17—7B 28
Oak Av. Croy—4L 125
Oak Av. Enf—2K 15
Oak Av. Hmptn—2J 101
Oak Av. Houn—8H 69
Oak Av. St Alb—3L 5
Oak Av. Upm—8M 51
Oak Av. Uxb—7A 36
Oak Av. W Dray—4L 143
Oak Bank. Croy—8A 126
Oakbank Av. W on T—2K 117
Oakbank Gro. SE24—3A 92
Oakbrook Clo. Brom—1F 110
Oakbury Rd. SW6—1M 89
Oak Clo. N14—9F 14
Oak Clo. Sutt—4A 122
Oak Clo. Wal A—7K 7
Oakcombe Clo. N Mald—5C 104
Oak Cottage Clo. SE6—7D 94
Oak Cotts. W7—3C 70
Oak Cres. E16—8C 62
Oakcroft Clo. Pinn—9F 20
Oakcroft Rd. SE13—1B 94
Oakcroft Rd. Chess—6K 119
Oakcroft Vs. Chess—6K 119
Oakdale. N14—1F 26
Oakdale Av. Harr—3J 39
Oakdale Av. N'wd—9E 20
Oakdale Clo. Wat—4G 21
Oakdale Rd. E7—3F 62
Oakdale Rd. E11—7B 46
Oakdale Rd. E18—9F 30
Oakdale Rd. N4—4A 44
Oakdale Rd. SE4—2G 93
Oakdale Rd. SW16—2J 107
Oakdale Rd. Eps—1B 134
Oakdale Rd. Wat—4G 21
Oak Dene. SE15—9F 76
Oakdene. W13—8F 54
Oakdene. Wal X—3E 6
Oakdene Av. Chst—2L 111
Oakdene Av. Eri—7A 82
Oakdene Av. Th Dit—3E 118
Oakdene Clo. Horn—4F 50
Oakdene Clo. Pinn—7K 21
Oakdene Dri. Surb—2A 120
Oakdene Pk. N3—7K 25
Oakdene Rd. Orp—9D 112
Oakdene Rd. Uxb—5F 142
Oakdene Rd. Wat—9F 4
Oakden St. SE11—5L 75
Oaken Dri. Esh—8D 118
Oaken La. Esh—6C 118
Oakenshaw Clo. Surb—2J 119
Oakes Clo. E6—9K 63
Oakeshott Av. N6—7E 42
Oakey La. SE1—4L 75
Oak Farm. Borwd—7A 12
Oakfield. E4—5M 29
Oakfield Av. Harr—1F 38
Oakfield Clo. N Mald—9D 104
Oakfield Clo. Wey—6A 116
Oakfield Ct. N8—5J 43
Oakfield Gdns. N18—4C 28

Oakfield Gdns. SE19—2D 108
(in two parts)
Oakfield Gdns. Beck—9M 109
Oakfield Gdns. Cars—3C 122
Oakfield Gdns. Gnfd—7B 54
Oakfield Glade. Wey—6A 116
Oakfield La. Dart—8D 98
Oakfield La. Kes—6G 127
Oakfield Pk. Rd. Dart—8H 99
Oakfield Pl. Dart—8H 99
Oakfield Rd. E6—4J 63
Oakfield Rd. E17—9J 29
Oakfield Rd. N3—8M 25
Oakfield Rd. N4—4L 43
Oakfield Rd. N14—2J 27
Oakfield Rd. SE20—4F 108
Oakfield Rd. SW19—9H 89
Oakfield Rd. Asht—9J 133
Oakfield Rd. Croy—3A 124
Oakfield Rd. Ilf—8M 47
Oakfield Rd. Orp—2E 128
Oakfield Rd. Th Dit—9D 102
Oakfields. W on T—3E 116
Oakfields Rd. NW11—4J 41
Oakfield St. SW10—7A 74
Oakford Rd. NW5—9G 43
Oak Gdns. Croy—4L 125
Oak Gdns. Edgw—9M 23
Oak Glade. N'wd—8A 20
Oak Glen. Horn—1J 51
Oak Grn. Abb L, Wat—5C 4
Oak Grn. Way. Abb L, Wat—5C 4
Oak Gro. NW2—9J 41
Oak Gro. Ruis—5F 36
Oak Gro. Sun—4F 100
Oak Gro. W Wick—3A 126
Oak Gro. SE20—5G 109
Oakhall Dri. Sun—2D 100
Oak Hall Rd. E11—4F 46
Oakham Clo. SE6—8K 93
Oakham Dri. Brom—8D 110
Oakhampton Rd. NW7—7H 25
Oak Hill. Eps—8B 134
Oakhill. Esh—8E 118
Oak Hill. Surb—2J 119
Oak Hill. Wfd G—7B 30
Oakhill Av. NW3—9M 41
Oakhill Av. Pinn—9J 21
Oak Hill Clo. Wfd G—7B 30
Oakhill Ct. E11—4F 46
Oak Hill Cres. Surb—2J 119
Oak Hill Cres. Wfd G—7B 30
Oakhill Dri. Surb—2J 119
Oakhill Gdns. Wey—4C 116
Oak Hill Gdns. Wfd G—8C 30
Oakhill Gro. Surb—1J 119
Oak Hill Pk. NW3—9M 41
Oak Hill Pk. M. NW3—9A 42
Oakhill Path. Surb—1J 119
Oakhill Pl. SW15—4L 89
Oakhill Rd. SW15—4K 89
Oakhill Rd. SW16—5K 107
Oakhill Rd. Asht—9G 133
Oakhill Rd. Beck—6A 110
Oakhill Rd. Orp—3D 128
Oakhill Rd. Romf—1B 34
Oakhill Rd. Surb—1J 119
Oakhill Rd. Sutt—5M 121
Oak Hill Way. NW3—9M 41
Oakhouse Rd. Bexh—4L 97
Oakhurst Av. Barn—9C 14
Oakhurst Av. Bexh—8J 81
Oakhurst Clo. E17—2C 46
Oakhurst Clo. Tedd—2C 102
Oakhurst Gdns. E4—1D 30
Oakhurst Gdns. E17—2C 46
Oakhurst Gdns. Bexh—8J 81
Oakhurst Gro. SE22—3E 92
Oakhurst Rise. Cars—2C 136
Oakhurst Rd. Enf—9D 6
Oakhurst Rd. Eps—8B 120
Oakington Av. Harr—5L 37
Oakington Av. Hay—5B 68
Oakington Av. Wemb—8K 39
Oakington Dri. Sun—6G 101
Oakington Mnr. Dri. Wemb
—1L 55
Oakington Rd. W9—7L 57
Oakington Way. N8—5J 43
Oaklands. N21—2K 27
Oaklands. Beck—5M 109
Oaklands. Kenl—6A 138
Oaklands Av. N9—8F 16
Oaklands Av. Esh—3B 118
Oaklands Av. Iswth—7D 70
Oaklands Av. Romf—1C 50
Oaklands Av. Sidc—6D 96
Oaklands Av. T Hth—8L 107
Oaklands Av. Wat—1F 20
Oaklands Av. W Wick—5M 125
Oaklands Clo. Bexh—4K 97
Oaklands Clo. Orp—1C 128

Oaklands Clo. Wemb—1H 55
Oaklands Ct. Wat—3E 8
Oaklands Ct. Wemb—1H 55
Oaklands Dri. Twic—6A 86
Oaklands Gdns. Kenl—6A 138
Oaklands Ga. N'wd—6C 20
Oaklands Gro. W12—2E 72
Oaklands La. Barn—6F 12
Oaklands La. West—5F 140
Oaklands Pk. Av. Ilf—7A 48
Oaklands Pl. SW4—3G 91
Oaklands Rd. N20—9K 13
Oaklands Rd. NW2—9H 41
Oaklands Rd. SW14—2B 88
Oaklands Rd. W7—3D 70
Oaklands Rd. Bexh—3K 97
Oaklands Rd. Brom—4C 110
Oaklands Rd. Dart—7M 99
Oakland Way. Eps—8C 120
Oak La. E14—1K 77
Oak La. N2—9B 26
Oak La. N11—6H 27
Oak La. Iswth—3C 86
Oak La. Twic—6E 86
Oak La. Wfd G—4D 30
Oaklawn Rd. Lea—9C 132
Oakleafe Gdns. Ilf—1M 47
Oaklea Pas. King—7H 103
Oakleigh Av. N20—2B 26
Oakleigh Av. Edgw—9M 23
Oakleigh Av. Surb—3L 119
Oakleigh Clo. N20—3D 26
Oakleigh Ct. Edgw—9A 24
Oakleigh Cres. N20—3C 26
Oakleigh Dri. Rick—8A 8
Oakleigh Gdns. N20—1A 26
Oakleigh Gdns. Edgw—5K 23
Oakleigh Gdns. Orp—6C 128
Oakleigh M. N20—1A 26
Oakleigh Pk. Av. Chst—5L 111
Oakleigh Pk. N. N20—1B 26
Oakleigh Pk. S. N20—1C 26
Oakleigh Rd. Pinn—6K 21
Oakleigh Rd. Uxb—3A 52
Oakleigh Rd. N. N20—2B 26
Oakleigh Rd. S. N11—3E 26
Oakleigh Way. Mitc—5F 106
Oakleigh Way. Surb—3L 119
Oakley Av. W5—1L 71
Oakley Av. Bark—3D 64
Oakley Av. Croy—6K 123
Oakley Clo. E4—3A 30
Oakley Clo. E6—9J 63
Oakley Clo. W7—1C 70
Oakley Clo. Iswth—9B 70
Oakley Cres. EC1—5M 59
Oakley Dri. SE9—7B 96
Oakley Dri. Brom—5J 127
Oakley Dri. Romf—5L 35
Oakley Gdns. N8—3K 43
Oakley Gdns. SW3—7C 74
Oakley Gdns. Bans—7M 135
Oakley Pk. Sidc—6G 97
Oakley Pl. SE1—6D 76
Oakley Rd. N1—3B 60
Oakley Rd. SE25—9F 108
Oakley Rd. Brom—5J 127
Oakley Rd. Harr—4C 38
Oakley Rd. Warl—9E 138
Oakley Sq. NW1—5G 59
Oakley St. SW3—7C 74
Oakley Wlk. W6—7H 73
Oak Lodge. E11—4E 46
Oak Lodge Av. Chig—5D 32
Oak Lodge Clo. Stan—5G 23
Oak Lodge Clo. W on T—7G 117
Oak Lodge Dri. W Wick
—2M 125
Oakmead Av. Brom—1E 126
Oak Meade. Pinn—6L 21
Oakmead Gdns. Edgw—4B 24
Oakmead Rd. SW12—7F 90
Oakmead Rd. Croy—1H 123
Oakmere Rd. SE2—7E 80
Oakmont Pl. Orp—3B 128
Oakmoor Way. Chig—5C 32
Oakridge Dri. N2—1B 42
Oakridge La. Wat & St Alb
—1B 10
Oakridge Rd. Brom—1C 110
Oak Rise. Buck H—3H 31
Oak Rd. W5—1H 71
Oak Rd. Eri—8A 82
(Northumberland Heath)
Oak Rd. Eri—1E 98
(Slade Green)
Oak Rd. N Mald—6B 104
Oak Rd. Orp—9E 128
Oak Rd. Romf—8K 35
Oak Row. SW16—6G 107
Oaks Av. SE19—2C 108
Oaks Av. Felt—8J 85
Oaks Av. Romf—9A 34

Oaks Av. Wor Pk—5F 120
Oaksford Av. SE26—9F 92
Oaks Gro. E4—2C 30
Oakshade Rd. Brom—1B 110
Oakshade Rd. Lea—6A 132
Oakshaw Rd. SW18—6M 89
Oakside. Uxb—2A 142
Oaks La. Croy—5G 125
Oaks La. Ilf—3C 48
Oaks Rd. Croy—7F 124
Oaks Rd. Kenl—6M 137
Oaks Rd. Stai—5B 144
Oaks, The. N12—4M 25
Oaks, The. SE18—6A 80
Oaks, The. Eps—6C 134
Oaks, The. Hay—5A 52
Oaks, The. Ruis—5C 36
Oaks, The. Wfd G—7C 30
Oaks Track. Cars & Wall
—3D 136
Oaks Way. Cars—9D 122
Oaks Way. Kenl—6A 138
Oaksway. Surb—3H 119
Oakthorpe Pk. Est. N13—5A 28
Oakthorpe Rd. N13—5L 27
Oak Tree Clo. W5—9G 55
Oak Tree Clo. Stan—7G 23
Oak Tree Ct. N'holt—5H 53
Oak Tree Dell. NW9—3B 40
Oak Tree Dri. N20—1M 25
Oak Tree Gdns. Brom—2F 110
Oak Tree Rd. NW8—6C 58
Oakview Gdns. N2—2B 42
Oakview Gro. Croy—3J 125
Oakview Rd. SE6—2M 109
Oak Village. NW5—9E 42
Oak Way. N14—9F 14
Oakway. SW20—8G 105
Oak Way. W3—2C 72
Oak Way. Asht—8L 133
Oakway. Brom—6B 110
Oak Way. Croy—1H 125
Oakway. Felt—7C 84
Oakway Clo. Bex—5J 97
Oakways. SE9—5M 95
Oakwood. Wall—1F 136
Oakwood. Wal A—7L 7
Oakwood Av. N14—9H 15
Oakwood Av. Beck—6A 110
Oakwood Av. Borwd—6M 11
Oakwood Av. Brom—7F 110
Oakwood Av. Mitc—6B 106
Oakwood Av. Purl—4M 137
Oakwood Av. S'hall—1L 69
Oakwood Chase. Horn—5K 51
Oakwood Clo. N14—8G 15
Oakwood Clo. Chst—3K 111
Oakwood Clo. Dart—7M 99
Oakwood Clo. Wfd G—6J 31
Oakwood Ct. W14—4K 73
Oakwood Cres. N21—8J 15
Oakwood Cres. Gnfd—2E 54
Oakwood Dri. SE19—3B 108
Oakwood Dri. Bexh—3A 98
Oakwood Dri. Edgw—6A 24
Oakwood Gdns. Ilf—7D 48
Oakwood Gdns. Orp—4A 128
Oakwood Gdns. Sutt—4L 121
Oakwood Hill. Lou—8K 19
Oakwood Hill Industrial Est.
Lou—7M 19
Oakwood La. W14—4K 73
Oakwood Pde. Enf—7D 16
Oakwood Pk. Rd. N14—8J 15
Oakwood Pl. Croy—1L 123
Oakwood Rd. NW11—3L 41
Oakwood Rd. SW20—5E 104
Oakwood Rd. Croy—1L 123
Oakwood Rd. Orp—4A 128
Oakwood Rd. Pinn—9F 20
Oakwood Rd. St Alb—2K 5
Oakwood View. N14—8H 15
Oakworth Rd. W10—8H 57
Oasthouse Way. Orp—8F 112
Oates Rd. Romf—5M 33
Oatfield Rd. Orp—3D 128
Oatland Rise. E17—9J 29
Oatlands Av. Wey—7B 116
Oatlands Chase. W on T
—5C 116
Oatlands Dri. Wey—6A 116
Oatlands Grn. Wey—6A 116
Oatlands Mere. Wey—5B 116
Oatlands Rd. Enf—3G 17
Oat La. EC2—9A 60
Oban Rd. E13—6G 63
Oban Rd. SE25—8B 108
Oban St. E14—9B 62
Oberstein Rd. SW11—3B 90
Oborne Clo. SE24—4M 91

Observatory Gdns. W8—3L 73
Observatory Rd. SW14—3A 88
Occupation La. SE18—9M 79
Occupation La. W5—5H 71
Occupation Rd. SE17—6A 76
Occupation Rd. W7—5E 70
Occupation Rd. W13—3F 70
Occupation Rd. Wat—7F 8
Ocean Est. E1—8J 61
(in two parts)
Ocean St. E1—8H 61
Ockendon Rd. N1—2B 60
Ockham Dri. Orp—4E 112
Ockley Rd. SW16—1J 107
Ockley Rd. Croy—2K 123
Octavia Clo. Mitc—9C 106
Octavia Rd. Iswth—2C 86
Octavia St. SW11—9C 74
Octavia Way. SE28—1F 80
Octavius St. SE8—8L 77
Odard Rd. E Mol—8L 101
Oddesey Rd. Borwd—3M 11
Odessa Rd. E7—9D 46
Odessa Rd. NW10—5E 56
Odessa St. SE16—3K 77
Odger St. SW11—1D 90
Offa's Mead. E9—9K 45
Offenham Rd. SE9—1K 111
Offerton Rd. SW4—2G 91
Offham Slope. N12—5K 25
Offley Rd. SW9—8L 75
Offord Clo. N17—6E 28
Offord Rd. N1—3K 59
Offord St. N1—3K 59
Ogilby St. SE18—5K 79
Oglander Rd. SE15—2D 92
Ogle St. W1—8G 59
Oglethorpe Rd. Dag—8L 49
Ohio Rd. E13—7D 62
Oil Mill La. W6—6E 72
£2 1-211 & 2-232
E3 remainder
Okeburn Rd. SW17—2E 106
Okehampton Clo. N12—5B 26
Okehampton Cres. Well—9F 80
Okehampton Rd. NW10—4G 57
Okehampton Rd. Romf—6G 35
Okehampton Sq. Romf—6G 35
Okemore Gdns. Orp—8G 113
Olaf St. W11—1H 73
Old Av. Wey—9A 116
Old Bailey. EC4—9M 59
Old Barn Clo. Sutt—9J 121
Old Barn La. Whyt—8D 138
Old Barn Rd. Eps—9A 134
Old Barn Way. Bexh—3B 98
Old Barrack Yd. SW1—3E 74
Old Barrowfield. E15—4C 62
Oldberry Rd. Edgw—6B 24
Old Bethnal Grn. Rd. E2—6E 60
Old Bexley La. Bex & Dart
—8B 98
Old Bond St. W1—1G 75
Oldborough Rd. Wemb—8G 39
Old Brewer's Yd. WC2—9J 59
Old Brewery M. NW3—9B 42
Old Bri. Clo. N'holt—5L 53
Old Bri. St. King—6H 103
(in two parts)
Old Broad St. EC2—9B 60
Old Bromley Rd. Brom—2B 110
Old Brompton Rd.—6M 73
SW7 1-125 & 2-146
SW5 remainder
Old Burlington St. W1—1G 75
Oldbury Clo. Orp—8G 113
Oldbury Pl. W1—8F 58
Oldbury Rd. Enf—4E 16
Old Castle St. E1—9D 60
Old Cavendish St. W1—9F 58
Old Chapel Rd. Swan—2A 130
Old Charlton Rd. Shep—9A 100
Old Chestnut Av. Esh—8L 117
Oldchurch Gdns. Romf—5B 50
Old Chu. La. NW9—7B 40
Old Chu. La. Gnfd—6E 54
Old Chu. La. Stan—5F 22
Old Chu. Path. Esh—6A 118
Oldchurch Rise. Romf—5C 50
Old Chu. Rd. E1—9H 61
Old Chu. Rd. E4—4L 29
Oldchurch Rd. Romf—5B 50
Old Chu. St. SW3—6B 74
Old Claygate La. Esh—8E 118
Old Compton St. W1—1H 75
Old Cote Dri. Houn—7L 69
Old Ct. Pl. W8—3M 73
Old Deer Pk. Gdns. Rich—2J 87
Old Devonshire Rd. SW12
—6F 90
Old Dock Clo. Rich—7L 71
Old Dover Rd. SE3—8E 78
Oldenburgh Av. N12—7A 26
Olden La. Purl—4L 137
Old Esher Clo. W on T—7H 117
Old Esher Rd. W on T—7H 117

Old Esher Rd. W on T—7H 117
Old Farleigh Rd. S Croy & Warl
—2G 139
Old Farm Av. N14—9G 15
Old Farm Av. Sidc—7B 96
Old Farm Clo. Houn—3K 85
Old Farm Gdns. Swan—7D 114
Old Farm Ho. Dri. Lea—7B 132
Old Farm Pas. Hmptn—5A 102
Old Farm Rd. N2—8B 26
Old Farm Rd. Hmptn—3K 101
Old Farm Rd. W Dray—3H 143
Old Farm Rd. E. Sidc—8E 96
Old Farm Rd. W. Sidc—8D 96
Oldfield Clo. Brom—8K 111
Oldfield Clo. Gnfd—1C 54
Oldfield Clo. Stan—5E 22
Oldfield Clo. Wal X—1E 6
Oldfield Dri. Wal X—1E 6
Oldfield Farm Gdns. Gnfd
—4B 54
Oldfield Gro. SE16—5H 77
Oldfield La. N. Gnfd—4B 54
Oldfield La. S. Gnfd—6A 54
Oldfield M. N6—5G 43
Oldfield Rd. N16—8C 44
Oldfield Rd. NW10—3D 56
Oldfield Rd. SW18—3M 89
Oldfield Rd. SW19—3J 105
Oldfield Rd. W3—3D 72
Oldfield Rd. Bexh—1J 97
Oldfield Rd. Brom—8K 111
Oldfield Rd. Hmptn—5K 101
Oldfields Cir. N'holt—2A 54
Oldfields Rd. Sutt—5K 121
Old Fold Clo. Barn—3K 13
Old Fold La. Barn—3K 13
Old Fold View. Barn—5G 13
Old Ford Rd.—5G 61
E2 1-211 & 2-232
E3 remainder
Old Forge Clo. Stan—4E 22
Old Forge Clo. Wat—6E 4
Old Forge Cres. Shep—1A 116
Old Forge Rd. Enf—2D 16
Old Forge Way. Sidc—1F 112
Old Gannon Clo. N'wd—4A 20
Old Gloucester St. WC1—8J 59
Old Hall Clo. Pinn—8J 21
Old Hall Dri. Pinn—8J 21
Oldhams Ter. W3—3A 72
Old Hatch Mnr. Ruis—5E 36
Old Hill. Chst—5L 111
Old Hill. Orp—8B 128
Oldhill St. N16—6E 44
Old Homesdale Rd. Brom
—8G 111
Old Ho. Clo. SW19—2J 105
Old Ho. Clo. Eps—2D 134
Old Jamaica Rd. SE16—4E 76
Old James St. SE15—2F 92
Old Jewry. EC2—9B 60
Old Kenton La. NW9—3M 39
Old Kent Rd. SE1—5C 76
Old Kingston Rd. Wor Pk
—5A 120
Old Lodge La. Purl & Kenl
—5K 137
Old Lodge Way. Stan—5E 22
Old London Rd. Eps—9E 134
Old Maidstone Rd. Sidc
—4K 113
Old Malden La. Wor Pk—4B 120
Old Mnr. Rd. Iswth—5A 86
Old Mnr. Way. Bexh—1B 98
Old Mnr. Yd. SW5—5M 73
Old Marylebone Rd. NW1
—8C 58
Old Mill Clo. E18—1G 47
Old Mill La. Uxb—9A 142
Old Mill Rd. SE18—7B 80
Old Mill Rd. K Lan—7A 4
Old Mitre Ct. EC4—9L 59
Old Montague St. E1—8E 60
Old Nichol St. E2—7D 60
Old Oak Common La.—8C 56
W3 51-189 & 82-240
NW10 remainder
Old Oak La. NW10—6C 56
Old Oak Rd. W3—1D 72
Old Orchard. Sun—6G 101
Old Orchard, The. NW3—9D 42
Old Pal. Gdns. Wey—5H 116
Old Pal. La. Rich—4G 87
Old Pal. Rd. Croy—5A 124
Old Pal. Ter. Rich—4H 87
Old Pal. Yd. SW1—4J 75
Old Pal. Yd. Rich—4H 87
Old Paradise St. SE11—5K 75
Old Pk. Av. SW12—5E 90
Old Pk. Av. Enf—6A 16
Old Pk. Gro. Enf—6A 16
Old Pk. La. W1—2F 74

Old Pk. M. Houn—8K 69
Oldpark Ride. Wal X—6A 6
Old Pk. Ridings. N21—8M 15
Old Pk. Rd. N13—4K 27
Old Pk. Rd. SE2—6E 80
Old Pk. Rd. Enf—5M 15
Old Pk. Rd. S. Enf—6M 15
Old Pk. View. Enf—5L 15
Old Perry St. Chst—3C 112
Old Pye St. SW1—4H 75
Old Quebec St. W1—9D 58
Old Queen St. SW1—3H 75
Old Rectory Gdns. Edgw—6L 23
Old Redding. Harr—5M 21
Oldridge Rd. SW12—6E 90
Old Rd. SE13—3C 94
Old Rd. Dart—4B 98
Old Rd. Enf—3G 17
Old Ruislip Rd. N'holt—5G 53
Olds App. Wat—1A 20
Old Schools La. Eps—1D 134
Old Seacoal La. EC4—9M 59
Old S. Lambeth Rd. SW8—8J 75
Old Sq. WC2—9L 59
Old Sta. Rd. Hay—4D 68
Old Sta. Rd. Lou—7J 19
Oldstead Rd. Brom—1B 110
Old Stockley Rd. W Dray
—3M 143
Old St. E13—5G 63
Old St. EC1—7A 60
Old Swan Yd. Cars—6D 122
Old Town. SW4—2G 91
Old Town. Croy—5M 123
Old Tye Av. West—8J 141
Old Watford Rd. St Alb—3J 5
Old Woolwich Rd. SE10—7B 78
Oleander Clo. Orp—7B 128
O'Leary Sq. E1—8G 61
Olga St. E3—5J 61
Olinda Rd. N16—4D 44
Oliphant St. W10—6H 57
Oliver Av. SE25—7D 108
Oliver Clo. E10—7M 45
Oliver Clo. W4—7M 71
Oliver Ct. SE18—5A 80
Oliver Cres. F'ham, Dart
—2K 131
Oliver Gdns. E6—8J 63
Oliver Gro. SE25—8D 108
Olive Rd. E13—6G 63
Olive Rd. NW2—9G 41
Olive Rd. SW19—4A 106
Olive Rd. W5—4H 71
Olive Rd. Dart—7H 99
Oliver Rd. E10—7M 45
Oliver Rd. E17—3A 46
Oliver Rd. N Mald—6A 104
Oliver Rd. Rain—4D 66
Oliver Rd. Sutt—6B 122
Oliver Rd. Swan—7B 114
Olivers Yd. EC1—7B 60
Olivette St. SW15—3H 89
Ollard's Gro. Lou—6H 19
Ollerton Grn. E3—4K 61
Ollerton Rd. N11—5H 27
Olley Clo. Wall—9J 123
Ollgar Clo. W12—2D 72
Olliffe St. E14—4A 78
Olmar St. SE1—7E 76
Olney Rd. SE17—7M 75
Olron Cres. Bexh—4H 97
Olven Rd. SE18—7A 80
Olveston Wlk. Cars—1B 122
Olyffe Av. Well—1E 96
Olyffe Dri. Beck—5A 110
Olympia Way. W14—4J 73
Olympia Yd. W2—1M 73
Olympic Industrial Est. Wemb
—9M 39
Olympic Way. Gnfd—4A 54
Olympic Way. Wemb—8L 39
Olympus Sq. E5—8E 44
Oman Av. NW2—9F 40
O'Meara St. SE1—2A 76
Omega St. SE14—9J 77
Ommaney Rd. SE14—9H 77
Ondine Rd. SE15—3D 92
O'Neill Path. SE18—7L 79
One Tree Clo. SE23—5G 93
Ongar Clo. Romf—3G 49
Ongar Rd. SW6—7L 73
Ongar Way. Rain—4C 66
Onra Rd. E17—5L 45
Onslow Av. Rich—4J 87
Onslow Av. Sutt—2K 135
Onslow Clo. E4—2A 30
Onslow Clo. Th Dit—3C 118
Onslow Cres. Chst—5M 111
Onslow Dri. Sidc—8H 97
Onslow Gdns. E18—1F 46
Onslow Gdns. N10—3F 42

Oxleys Rd. NW2—8F 40
Oxlip Clo. Croy—3H 125
Oxlow La. Dag—9K 49
Oxonian St. SE22—3D 92
Oxshott Rd. Lea—8D 132
Oxted Clo. Mitc—7B 106
Oxtoby Way. SW16—5H 107
Ozolins Way. E16—9E 62

Pachesham Dri. Lea—8D 132
Pachesham Pk. Lea—8E 132
Pacific Rd. E16—9E 62
Packet Boat La. Uxb—9A 140
Packhorse La. Borwd—1C 12
Packington Rd. W3—4A 72
Packington Sq. N1—4A 60
Packington St. N1—4M 59
Packmores Rd. SE9—4B 96
Padbury Ct. E2—6D 60
Padcroft Rd. W Dray—2H 143
Paddenswick Rd. W6—4E 72
Paddington Clo. Hay—7H 53
Paddington Grn. W2—8B 58
Paddington St. W1—8E 58
Paddock Clo. SE3—2E 94
Paddock Clo. SE26—1H 109
Paddock Clo. Harr—9M 37
Paddock Clo. N'holt—5L 53
Paddock Clo. Orp—6M 127
Paddock Clo. Wor Pk—3C 120
Paddock Gdns. SE19—3C 108
Paddock Rd. NW2—8E 40
Paddock Rd. Bexh—3J 97
Paddock Rd. Ruis—8H 37
Paddocks Clo. Orp—4H 129
Paddocks, The. Barn—5D 14
Paddocks, The. Croy—8L 125
Paddocks, The. Wemb—7M 39
Paddocks, The. Wey—5C 116
Paddock, The. Uxb—9A 36
Paddock Way. Chst—4B 112
Padfield Rd. SE5—2A 92
Padnall Rd. Romf—1H 49
Padstow Rd. Enf—4M 15
Padua Rd. SE20—5G 109
Pagden St. SW8—9F 74
Pageant Wlk. Croy—5C 124
Page Clo. Hmptn—3J 101
Page Clo. Harr—4K 39
Page Cres. Croy—7M 123
Page Cres. Eri—8D 82
Page Grn. N15—3D 44
Page Grn. Rd. N15—3E 44
Page Heath La. Brom—7H 111
Page Heath Vs. Brom—7H 111
Pagehurst Rd. Croy—2F 124
Page Meadow. NW7—7E 24
Page Pl. E1—9F 60
Page Rd. Felt—5B 84
Pages Hill. N10—9E 26
Pages La. N10—9E 26
Page St. NW7—8E 24
Page St. SW1—5H 75
Page's Wlk. SE1—5C 76
Pages Yd. W4—7C 72
Paget Av. Sutt—5B 122
Paget Clo. Hmptn—1B 102
Paget Gdns. Chst—5M 111
Paget Rise. SE18—7L 79
Paget Rd. N16—6B 44
Paget Rd. Ilf—9M 47
Paget Rd. Uxb—7A 52
Paget St. EC1—6M 59
Paget Ter. SE18 7M 79
Pagnell St. SE14—8K 77
Pagoda Av. Rich—2K 87
Pagoda Gdns. SE3—1B 94
Pagoda Vista. Rich—9K 71
Paignton Rd. N15—4C 44
Paignton Rd. Ruis—8E 36
Paines Brook Rd. Romf—6K 35
Paines Brook Way. Romf
—6K 35
Paines Clo. Pinn—1J 37
Paines La. Pinn—8J 21
Pain's Clo. Mitc—6F 106
Painsthorpe Rd. N16—8C 44
Painters La. Enf—8E 6
Painters Rd. Ilf—1D 48
Paisley Rd. N22—8M 27
Paisley Rd. Cars—3B 122
Pakeman St. N7—8K 43
Pakenham Clo. SW12—7E 90
Pakenham St. WC1—7K 59
Palace Av. W8—3M 73
Palace Ct. NW3—1M 57
Palace Ct. W2—1M 73
Palace Ct. Harr—4J 39
Palace Ct. Gdns. N10—2G 43
Palace Gdns. Buck H—1H 31
Palace Gdns. Enf—6B 16
Palace Gdns. M. W8—2M 73

Palace Gdns. Ter. W8—2L 73
Palace Ga. W8—3A 74
Palace Gates Rd. N22—8H 27
Palace Grn. W8—2M 73
Palace Grn. Croy—9K 125
Palace Gro. SE19—4D 108
Palace Gro. Brom—5F 110
Palace M. Enf—5B 16
Palace Rd. N8—3H 43
(in two parts)
Palace Rd. N11—7J 27
Palace Rd. SE19—4D 108
Palace Rd. SW2—7K 91
Palace Rd. Brom—5F 110
Palace Rd. E Mol—7B 102
Palace Rd. King—8H 103
Palace Rd. Ruis—9J 37
Palace Sq. SE19—4D 108
Palace St. SW1—4G 75
Palace View. SE12—8E 94
Palace View. Brom—7F 110
Palace View. Croy—6K 125
Palace View Rd. E4—5M 29
Palamos Rd. E10—6L 45
Palatine Av. N16—9C 44
Palatine Rd. N16—9C 44
Palermo Rd. NW10—5E 56
Palestine Gro. SW19—5B 106
Palewell Clo. Orp—6F 112
Palewell Comn. Dri. SW14
—4B 88
Palewell Pk. SW14—4B 88
Paley Gdns. Lou—5M 19
Palfrey Pl. SW8—8K 75
Palgrave Av. S'hall—1L 69
Palgrave Rd. W12—4D 72
Palissy St. E2—6D 60
Pallant Way. Orp—5L 127
Pallet Way. SE18—9J 79
Palliser Rd. W14—6J 73
Pall Mall. SW1—2G 75
Pall Mall E. SW1—2H 75
Palmar Cres. Bexh—2L 97
Palmar Rd. Bexh—1L 97
Palmarsh Clo. Orp—8H 113
Palm Av. Sidc—3H 113
Palmeira Rd. Bexh—2H 97
Palmer Av. Bush, Wat—7M 9
Palmer Av. Sutt—6G 121
Palmer Clo. Houn—9L 69
Palmer Cres. King—7J 103
Palmer Pl. N7—1L 59
Palmer Rd. E13—7F 62
Palmer Rd. Borwd—3M 11
Palmersfield Rd. Bans—6L 135
Palmers Gdns. Barn—7H 13
Palmers Gro. E Mol—8L 101
Palmers La. Enf—3F 16
Palmers Pas. SW14—2A 88
Palmer's Rd. E2—5H 61
Palmer's Rd. N11—5G 27
Palmers Rd. SW14—2A 88
Palmers Rd. SW16—6K 107
Palmerston Ct. Surb—2H 119
Palmerston Cres. N13—5K 27
Palmerston Cres. SE18—7A 80
Palmerston Gro. SW19—4L 105
Palmerston Rd. E7—2F 62
Palmerston Rd. E17—2K 45
Palmerston Rd. N22—7K 27
Palmerston Rd. NW6—3K 57
(in two parts)
Palmerston Rd. SW14—3A 88
Palmerston Rd. SW19—4L 105
Palmerston Rd. W3—4A 72
Palmerston Rd. Buck H—2F 30
Palmerston Rd. Cars—6D 122
Palmerston Rd. Harr—1D 38
Palmerston Rd. Orp—7A 128
Palmerston Rd. Rain—5G 67
Palmerston Rd. Sutt—7A 122
Palmerston Rd. T Hth—9B 108
Palmerston Rd. Twic—5D 86
Palmerston Way. SW8—8G 75
Palmer St. SW1—4H 75
Palmers Way. Wal X—2E 6
Palm Gro. W5—4J 71
Palm Rd. Romf—3A 50
Pamber St. W10—9H 57
Pamela Gdns. Pinn—3F 36
Pamela Wlk. E8—4E 60
Pampisford Rd. Purl & S Croy
—3L 137
Pam's Way. Eps—7B 120
Pancras La. EC4—9A 60
Pancras Rd. NW1—5H 59
Pandora Rd. NW6—2L 57
Panfield M. Ilf—4L 47
Panfield Rd. SE2—4E 80
Pangbourne Av. W10—8G 57
Pangbourne Dri. Stan—5H 23
Panhard Pl. S'hall—1M 69

Pank Av. Barn—7A 14
Panmuir Rd. SW20—5F 104
Panmure Clo. N5—9M 43
Panmure Rd. SE26—9F 92
Pansy Gdns. W12—1E 72
Panter's. Swan—4D 114
Pantile Rd. Wey—6B 116
Pantiles, The. Bexh—8K 81
Pantiles, The. Brom—7J 111
Pantiles, The. Bush, Wat—1B 22
Pantiles Wlk. Uxb—3A 142
Panton St. SW1—1H 75
Papillons Wlk. SE3—2E 94
Papworth Gdns. N7—1K 59
Papworth Way. SW2—6L 91
Parade M. SE27—8M 91
Parade, The. N4—6L 43
Parade, The. SW11—8D 74
Parade, The. Dart—4D 98
Parade, The. Eps—5C 134
Parade, The. Esh—8C 118
Parade, The. Romf—6M 35
Parade, The. Sun—4D 100
Parade, The. Wat—5F 8
Parade, The. Wat—3J 21
(Carpenders Park)
Parade, The. Wat—3H 21
(South Oxhey)
Paradise Clo. Wal X—1B 6
Paradise Pas. N7—1L 59
Paradise Pl. SE18—5J 79
Paradise Rd. SW4—1J 91
Paradise Rd. Rich—4J 87
Paradise Rd. Wal A—7J 7
Paradise Wlk. SE16—3F 76
Paradise Wlk. SW3—7D 74
Paragon All. SE1—4C 76
Paragon Gro. Surb—1K 119
Paragon M. SE1—5R 76
Paragon Pl. SE3—1D 94
Paragon Pl. Surb—1K 119
Paragon Rd. E9—2G 61
Paragon Row. SE17—5B 76
Paragon, The. SE3—1E 94
Parbury Rise. Chess—8J 119
Parbury Rd. SE23—5J 93
Parchmore Rd. T Hth—6M 107
Parchmore Way. T Hth
—6M 107
Pardoner St. SE1—4B 76
Pardon St. EC1—7M 59
Parfett St. E1—8E 60
Par Four Dri. Kenl—8A 138
Parfrey St. W6—7G 73
Parham Dri. Ilf—4M 47
Parham Way. N10—9G 27
Parisfal Rd. NW6—1L 57
Paris Garden. SE1—2M 75
Parish Ga. Dri. Sidc—5C 96
Parish La. SE20—3H 109
Park App. SE16—4F 76
Park App. Well—3F 96
Park Av. E6—4L 63
Park Av. E15—2C 62
Park Av. N3—8M 25
Park Av. N13—3L 27
Park Av. N18—4E 28
Park Av. N22—9J 27
Park Av. NW10—1F 56
(Dudden Hill)
Park Av. NW10—5K 55
(Park Royal)
Park Av. NW11—6M 41
Park Av. SW14—3A 88
Park Av. SW14—3B 88
Park Av. Bark—2A 64
Park Av. Brom—3D 110
Park Av. Bush, Wat—4J 9
Park Av. Cars—8E 122
Park Av. Enf—7B 16
Park Av. Houn—5M 85
Park Av. Ilf—6L 47
Park Av. Mitc—4F 106
Park Av. Orp—4E 128
Park Av. Orp—5C 127
(Locksbottom)
Park Av. Ruis—4B 36
Park Av. S'hall—3K 69
Park Av. Wat—6E 8
Park Av. W Wick—4A 126
Park Av. E. Eps—8E 120
Park Av. M. Mitc—4F 106
Park Av. N. N8—2H 43
Park Av. N. NW10—7F 28
Park Av. S. N8—2H 43
Park Av. W. Eps—8E 120
Park Boulevd. Romf—8D 34
Park Chase. Wemb—9K 39
Park Clo. E9—4G 61
Park Clo. NW2—8F 40
Park Clo. NW10—6K 55
Park Clo. SE7—6J 79
Park Clo. SW1—3D 74

Park Clo. W4—6B 72
Park Clo. W14—4K 73
Park Clo. Bush, Wat—5H 9
Park Clo. Cars—8D 122
Park Clo. Esh—8L 117
Park Clo. Hmptn—5A 102
Park Clo. Harr—8C 22
Park Clo. Houn—4A 86
Park Clo. Rick—4A 20
Park Clo. W on T—4D 116
Park Ct. N17—7E 28
Park Ct. Harr—5J 39
Park Ct. King—5G 103
Park Ct. N Mald—8B 104
Park Ct. Wemb—1J 55
Park Cres. N3—7A 26
Park Cres. W1—7F 58
Park Cres. Borwd—5K 11
Park Cres. Enf—6B 16
Park Cres. Eri—7A 82
Park Cres. Harr—8C 22
Park Cres. Horn—5E 50
Park Cres. Twic—7B 86
Park Cres. M. E. W1—7F 58
Park Cres. M. W. W1—7F 58
Parkcroft. Edgw—8A 24
Parkcroft Rd. SE12—6D 94
Parkdale Cres. Wor Pk—5B 120
Parkdale Rd. SE18—6C 80
Park Dri. N21—8A 16
Park Dri. NW11—6M 41
Park Dri. SE7—7J 79
Park Dri. SW14—4B 88
Park Dri. W3—4L 71
Park Dri. Asht—9L 133
Park Dri. Dag—8A 50
Park Dri. Harr—6B 22
(Harrow Weald)
Park Dri. Harr—5L 37
(Rayners Lane)
Park Dri. Romf—2B 50
Park Dri. Upm—9M 51
Park End. NW3—9C 42
Park End. Brom—5D 110
Park End Rd. Romf—2C 50
Parker Clo. E16—2J 79
Parke Rd. SW13—9E 72
Parke Rd. Sun—8E 100
Parker Rd. Croy—6A 124
Parkers Row. SE1—3D 76
Parker St. E16—2J 79
Parker St. WC2—9J 59
Parker St. Wat—3F 8
Parkes Rd. Chig—5C 32
Park Farm Clo. N2—1A 42
Park Farm Clo. Pinn—3F 36
Park Farm Rd. Brom—5H 111
Park Farm Rd. King—4J 103
Park Farm Rd. Upm—1K 67
Parkfield Av. SW14—3C 88
Parkfield Av. Felt—9E 84
Parkfield Av. Harr—9A 22
Parkfield Av. N'holt—5H 53
Parkfield Av. Uxb—6F 142
Parkfield Clo. Edgw—6M 23
Parkfield Clo. N'holt—5J 53
Parkfield Cres. Felt—9E 84
Parkfield Cres. Harr—9A 22
Parkfield Cres. Ruis—7J 37
Parkfield Dri. N'holt—5H 53
Parkfield Gdns. Harr—1M 37
Parkfield Rd. NW10—3F 56
Parkfield Rd. SE14—9K 77
Parkfield Rd. Felt—9E 84
Parkfield Rd. Harr—8A 38
Parkfield Rd. N'holt—5J 53
Parkfield Rd. Ruis—7A 36
Parkfields. SW15—3G 89
Parkfields. Croy—3K 125
Parkfields. Lea—3B 132
Park Fields Rd. King—2K 103
Parkfield St. N1—5L 59
Parkfield Way. Brom—1K 127
Park Gdns. NW9—1M 39
Park Gdns. Eri—5B 82
Park Gdns. King—2K 103
Park Ga. N2—1B 42
Park Ga. N21—9K 15
Park Ga. SE3—2D 94
Park Ga. W5—8H 55
Parkgate Av. Barn—3A 14
Park Ga. Clo. King—3M 103
Parkgate Cres. Barn—3A 14
Parkgate Gdns. SW14—4B 88
Parkgate Rd. SW11—8C 74
Parkgate Rd. Orp—6M 129
Parkgate Rd. Wall—7F 122
Parkgate Rd. Wat—1G 9
Park Gro. E15—4E 62
Park Gro. N11—7H 27
Park Gro. Bexh—3A 98

Park Gro. Brom—5F 110
Park Gro. Edgw—5K 23
Park Gro. Rd. E11—7C 46
Park Hall Rd. N2—2C 42
Park Hall Rd. SE21—9B 92
Park Hall Rd. SW11—9C 74
Park Hill. SE23—7F 92
Park Hill. SW4—4H 91
Park Hill. W5—8H 55
Park Hill. Brom—8J 111
Park Hill. Cars—8C 122
Park Hill. Lou—7H 19
Park Hill. Rich—5K 87
Park Hill Clo. Cars—7C 122
Parkhill Clo. Horn—7G 51
Park Hill Ct. SW17—9D 90
Park Hill Rise. Croy—4C 124
Parkhill Rd. E4—9A 18
Parkhill Rd. NW3—1D 58
Parkhill Rd. Bex—6K 97
Park Hill Rd. Brom—6C 110
Park Hill Rd. Croy—6C 124
Parkhill Rd. Eps—3D 134
Park Hill Rd. Sidc—9C 96
Park Hill Rd. Wall—9F 122
Parkhill Wlk. NW3—1D 58
Parkholme Rd. E8—2E 60
Park Ho. N21—9K 15
Park Ho. Gdns. Twic—4G 87
Parkhouse St. SE5—8B 76
Parkhurst. Eps—2A 134
Parkhurst Gdns. Bex—6L 97
Parkhurst Rd. E12—9L 47
Parkhurst Rd. E17—2J 45
Parkhurst Rd. N7—9J 43
Parkhurst Rd. N11—5E 26
Parkhurst Rd. N17—9E 28
Parkhurst Rd. N22—6K 27
Parkhurst Rd. Bex—6L 97
Parkhurst Rd. Sutt—6B 122
Parking Ct. E6—9J 63
Parkland Av. Romf—9D 34
Parkland Av. Upm—1M 67
Parkland Gro. Ashf—9E 144
Parkland Rd. N22—9K 27
Parkland Rd. Ashf—9E 144
Parkland Rd. Wfd G—7F 30
Parklands. Chig—3A 32
Parklands. Surb—9K 103
Parklands. Wal A—5K 7
Parklands Clo. Chig—3A 32
Parklands Ct. Houn—1H 85
Parklands Dri. N3—1J 41
Parklands Pde. Houn—1H 85
Parklands Rd. SW16—2F 106
Parklands Way. Wor Pk
—4C 120
Park La. E15—4B 62
Park La. N9—3D 28
Park La. N17—7E 28
Park La. W1—1D 74
Park La. Cars & Wall—7E 122
Park La. Croy—5B 124
Park La. Harr—8M 37
Park La. Hay—8C 52
Park La. Horn—4D 50
Park La. Horn—2F 66
(Elm Park)
Park La. Houn—8E 68
Park La. Rich—3H 87
Park La. Romf—4H 49
Park La. Sutt—8J 121
Park La. Swan—6G 115
Park La. Tedd—3D 102
Park La. Wal X—6C 6
Park La. Wal X—1B 6
(Flamstead End)
Park La. Wemb—1J 55
Park La. Clo. N17—7E 28
Parklawn Av. Eps—5M 133
Park Lawn Rd. Wey—6A 116
Park Lawns. Wemb—9K 39
Parklea Clo. NW9—8C 24
Parkleigh Rd. SW19—6M 105
Parkleys. Rich—1H 103
Parkmead. SW15—5F 88
Park Mead. Harr—8M 37
Parkmead. Lou—7L 19
Park Mead. Sidc—4F 96
Parkmead Gdns. NW7—6D 24
Parkmore Clo. Wfd G—4E 30
Park Nook Gdns. Enf—1B 16
Park Pde. NW10—5D 56
Park Pde. W5—4L 71
Park Pl. SW1—2G 75
Park Pl. W3—5L 71
Park Pl. W5—2H 71
Park Pl. Hmptn—3A 102
Park Pl. Wemb—9K 39
Park Pl. Gdns. W2—8A 58
Park Pl. Vs. W2—8A 58
Park Ridings. N8—1L 43

Pelton Av. Sutt—2M 135
Pelton Rd. SE10—6C 78
Pembar Av. E17—1J 45
Pember Rd. NW10—6H 57
Pemberton Av. Romf—1F 50
Pemberton Gdns. N19—8G 43
Pemberton Gdns. Romf—3J 49
Pemberton Gdns. Swan
—7C 114
Pemberton Pl. E9—3G 61
Pemberton Rd. N4—3L 43
Pemberton Rd. E Mol—8A 102
Pemberton Ter. N19—8G 43
Pemberton Row. EC4—9L 59
Pembrey Way. Horn—2G 67
Pembridge Av. Twic—7K 85
Pembridge Cres. W11—1L 73
Pembridge Gdns. W2—1L 73
Pembridge M. W11—1L 73
Pembridge Pl. W2—1L 73
Pembridge Rd. W11—1L 73
Pembridge Sq. W2—1L 73
Pembridge Vs. W11—1L 73
Pembroke Av. Enf—3F 16
Pembroke Av. Harr—1E 38
Pembroke Av. Surb—9M 103
Pembroke Av. W on T—6H 117
Pembroke Clo. SW1—3E 74
Pembroke Clo. Bans—9M 135
Pembroke Clo. Horn—2K 51
Pembroke Gdns. W8—5K 73
Pembroke Gdns. Dag—8M 49
Pembroke Gdns. Clo. W8
—4L 73
Pembroke M. W8—4L 73
Pembroke Pl. W8—4L 73
Pembroke Pl. Edgw—7L 23
Pembroke Pl. Iswth—1C 86
Pembroke Pl. S at H, Dart
—5M 115
Pembroke Rd. E17—3M 45
Pembroke Rd. N8—2J 43
Pembroke Rd. N10—8E 26
Pembroke Rd. N13—3A 28
Pembroke Rd. N15—3D 44
Pembroke Rd. SE25—8C 108
Pembroke Rd. W8—5L 73
Pembroke Rd. Brom—6G 111
Pembroke Rd. Eri—6A 82
Pembroke Rd. Gnfd—7M 53
Pembroke Rd. Ilf—6D 48
Pembroke Rd. Mitc—6E 106
Pembroke Rd. N'wd—3A 20
Pembroke Rd. Ruis—6D 36
Pembroke Rd. Wemb—8H 39
Pembroke Sq. W8—4L 73
Pembroke St. N1—3J 59
Pembroke Vs. W8—5L 73
Pembroke Vs. Rich—3H 87
Pembroke Wlk. W8—5L 73
Pembury Av. Wor Pk—2E 120
Pembury Clo. Brom—2D 126
Pembury Clo. Coul—6E 136
Pembury Ct. Hay—7B 68
Pembury Cres. Sidc—8J 97
Pembury Pl. E5—1F 60
Pembury Rd. E5—1F 60
Pembury Rd. N17—8G 28
Pembury Rd. SE25—8E 108
Pembury Rd. Bexh—8J 81
Pemdevon Rd. Croy—2L 123
Pemell Clo. E1—7G 61
Pemerich Clo. Hay—6D 68
Penally Pl. N1—4B 60
Penang St. E1—2F 76
Penarth St. SE15—7G 77
Penberth Rd. SE6—8A 94
Penbury Rd. S'hall—6K 69
Pencombe M. W11—1K 73
Pencraig Way. SE15—7F 76
Penda Rd. Eri—8M 81
Pendarves Rd. SW20
—5G 105
Penda's Mead. E9—9J 45
Pendell Av. Hay—8D 68
Pendennis Rd. N17—1B 44
Pendennis Rd. SW16—1J 107
Pendennis Rd. Orp—4G 129
Penderel Rd. Houn—4L 85
Penderry Rise. SE6—8B 94
Penderyn Way. N7—9H 43
Pendle Ho. SE26—9E 92
Pendle Rd. SW16—3F 106
Pendlestone Rd. E17—3M 45
Pendragon Rd. Brom—9D 94
Pendrell Rd. SE4—1J 93
Pendrell St. SE18—7B 80
Pendula Dri. Hay—7H 53
Penerley Rd. SE6—7M 93
Penerley Rd. Rain—8F 66
Penfold La. Bex—8H 97
Penfold Pl. NW1—8C 58
Penfold Rd. N9—1H 29

Penfold St.—7B 58
NW1 1-11 & 2-28
NW8 remainder
Penford Gdns. SE9—2H 95
Penford St. SE5—1M 91
Pengarth Rd. Bex—5H 97
Penge La. SE20—4G 109
Pengelly Clo. Wal X—3B 6
Penge Rd. E13—4G 63
Penge Rd.—7E 108
SE25 1-81 & 2-70
SE20 remainder
Penhall Rd. SE7—5H 79
Penhill Rd. Bex—5G 97
Penhurst Rd. Ilf—7M 31
Penifather La. Gnfd—6B 54
Peninsular Clo. Felt—5B 84
Penistone Rd. SW16—4J 107
Penistone Wlk. Romf—6G 35
Penketh Dri. Harr—8B 38
Penmon Rd. SE2—4E 80
Pennack Rd. SE15—7D 76
Pennant M. W8—5M 73
Pennant Ter. E17—9K 29
Pennard Rd. W12—3G 73
Pennards, The. Sun—7G 101
Penn Clo. Gnfd—5M 53
Penn Clo. Harr—2G 39
Penn Clo. Uxb—7B 142
Penner Clo. SW19—8J 89
Pennethorne Clo. E9—4G 61
Pennethorne Rd. SE15—8F 76
Penney Clo. Dart—6H 99
Penn Gdns. Chst—6M 111
Penn Gdns. Romf—7L 33
Pennine Dri. NW2—7H 41
Pennine La. NW2—7J 41
Pennine Way. Bexh—9C 82
Pennine Way. Hay—8B 68
Pennington Clo. SE27—1B 108
Pennington Dri. Wey—5C 116
Pennington St. E1—1F 76
Penn La. Bex—5H 97
Penn Rd. N7—1J 59
Penn Rd. St Alb—1M 5
Penn Rd. Wat—3F 8
Penn St. N1—4B 60
Pennycroft. Croy—1J 139
Pennyfields. E14—1L 77
Penny La. Shep—2C 116
Pennymoor Wlk. W9—6K 57
Penny Rd. NW10—6M 55
Penpoll La. Well—2F 96
Penrhyn Av. E17—8L 29
Penrhyn Cres. E17—8L 29
Penrhyn Cres. SW14—3A 88
Penrhyn Gro. E17—8L 29
Penrhyn Rd. King—8J 103
Penrith Clo. SW15—4J 89
Penrith Clo. Beck—5M 109
Penrith Clo. Uxb—3B 142
Penrith Cres. Horn—1E 66
Penrith Pl. SE27—8M 91
Penrith Rd. N15—3B 44
Penrith Rd. N Mald—8B 104
Penrith Rd. Romf—6L 35
Penrith Rd. T Hth—6A 108
Penrith St. SW16—3G 107
Penrose Av. Wat—2J 21
Penrose Gro. SE17—6A 76
Penrose St. SE17—6A 76
Penryn St. NW1—5H 59
Penry St. SE1—5C 76
Pensbury Pl. SW8—1G 91
Pensbury St. SW8—1G 91
Penscroft Gdns. Borwd—6B 12
Pensford Av. Rich—1L 87
Penshurst Gdns. Edgw—5M 23
Penshurst Grn. Brom—9D 110
Penshurst Rd. E9—3H 61
Penshurst Rd. N17—7D 28
Penshurst Rd. Bexh—9K 81
Penshurst Rd. T Hth—9M 107
Penshurst Wlk. Brom—9D 110
Penshurst Way. Sutt—1L 135
Pentelow Gdns. Felt—5E 84
Pentire Rd. E17—8B 30
Pentland Clo. NW11—7J 41
Pentland Gdns. SW18—5A 90
Pentland Rd. Bush, Wat—8A 10
Pentlands Clo. Mitc—7F 106
Pentland St. SW18—5A 90
Pentland Way. Uxb—8A 36
Pentlow St. SW15—2G 89
Pentlow Way. Buck H—9J 19
Pentney Rd. E4—1B 30
Pentney Rd. SW12—7G 91
Pentney Rd. SW19—5J 105
Penton Dri. Wal X—2D 6

Penton Gro. N1—5L 59
Penton Pl. SE17—6M 75
Penton Rise. WC1—6K 59
Penton St. N1—5L 59
Pentonville Rd. N1—5K 59
Pentrich Av. Enf—2E 16
Pentridge St. SE15—8D 76
Pentyre Av. N18—5B 28
Penwerris Av. Iswth—8A 70
Penwith Rd. SW18—8M 89
Penwortham Ct. N22—9K 27
Penwortham Rd. SW16
—3G 107
Penwortham Rd. S Croy
—2B 138
Penylan Pl. Edgw—7L 23
Penywern Rd. SW5—6L 73
Penzance Gdns. Romf—6L 35
Penzance Pl. W11—2J 73
Penzance Rd. Romf—6L 35
Penzance St. W11—2J 73
Peony Ct. Wfd G—7C 30
Peony Gdns. W12—1E 72
Peploe Rd. NW6—5H 57
Pepper All. Lou—4D 18
Pepper St. SE1—3A 76
Pepys Clo. Asht—9L 133
Pepys Clo. Dart—3L 99
Pepys Cres. Barn—7G 13
Pepys Rise. Orp—3D 128
Pepys Rd. SE14—9H 77
Pepys Rd. SW20—5G 105
Pepys St. EC3—1C 76
Perceval Av. NW3—1C 58
Percheron Rd. Borwd—8B 12
Perch St. E8—9D 44
Percival Ct. N17—7D 28
Percival Gdns. Romf—4H 49
Percival Rd. SW14—3A 88
Percival Rd. Enf—6D 16
Percival Rd. Felt—8D 84
Percival Rd. Horn—4G 51
Percival Rd. Orp—4M 127
Percival St. EC1—7M 59
Percival Way. Eps—6B 120
Percy Bryant Rd. Sun—4C 100
Percy Cir. WC1—6K 59
Percy Gdns. Enf—7H 17
Percy Gdns. Hay—6C 52
Percy Gdns. Iswth—2E 86
Percy Gdns. Wor Pk—3C 120
Percy Rd. E11—5C 46
Percy Rd. E16—8C 62
Percy Rd. N12—5A 26
Percy Rd. N21—9A 16
Percy Rd. NW6—6L 57
Percy Rd. SE20—5H 109
Percy Rd. SE25—9E 108
Percy Rd. W12—3E 72
Percy Rd. Bexh—1J 97
Percy Rd. Dag—7L 65
Percy Rd. Hmptn—4L 101
Percy Rd. Ilf—5E 48
Percy Rd. Iswth—3E 86
Percy Rd. Mitc—2E 122
Percy Rd. Romf—1M 49
Percy Rd. Twic—7M 85
Percy Rd. Wat—6F 8
Percy Way. Twic—7A 86
Percy St. W1—8H 59
Percy Yd. WC1—6K 59
Peregrine Clo. Wat—7J 5
Peregrine Rd. Ilf—5F 32
Peregrine Rd. Sun—6D 100
Peregrine Way. SW19—4G 105
Perham Rd. W14—6J 73
Perifield. SE21—7A 92
Perimeade Rd. Gnfd—5G 55
Periton Rd. SE9—3H 95
Perivale Gdns. W13—7F 54
Perivale Gdns. Wat—7F 4
Perivale Industrial Pk. Gnfd
—4F 54
Perivale La. Gnfd—6E 54
Perkin Clo. Wemb—1F 54
Perkin's Rents. SW1—4H 75
Perkins Rd. Ilf—3B 48
Perks Clo. SE3—2C 94
Perpins Rd. SE9—5C 96
Perran Rd. SW2—7M 91
Perran Wlk. Bren—6J 71
Perren St. NW5—2F 58
Perrers Rd. W6—5F 72
Perrin Rd. Wemb—9F 38
Perrin's La. NW3—9A 42
Perrin's Wlk. NW3—9A 42
Perrott St. SE18—5A 80
Perry Av. W3—9B 56
Perry Clo. Rain—8B 66
Perry Clo. Uxb—9F 142
Perry Ct. N15—4C 44
Perryfield Way. NW9—4D 40
Perryfield Way. Rich—9F 86

Perry Gdns. N9—3B 28
Perry Garth. N'holt—4G 53
Perry Gro. Dart—3L 99
Perry Hall Rd. Orp—1D 128
Perry Hill. SE6—9K 93
Perry How. Wor Pk—3D 120
Perrymans Farm Rd. Ilf—4B 48
Perry Mead. Bush, Wat—8A 10
Perry Mead. Enf—4M 15
Perrymead St. SW6—9M 73
Perryn Rd. W3—2B 72
Perry Oaks Dri. W Dray & Houn
—1A 144
Perry Rise. SE23—9J 93
Perry Rd. S Ock—1M 83
Perry's Pl. W1—9H 59
Perry St. Chst—3B 112
Perry St. Dart—3C 98
Perry St. Gdns. Chst—3C 112
Perry St. Shaw. Chst—4C 112
Perry Vale. SE23—8G 93
Persant Rd. SE6—8C 94
Perseverance Pl. Rich—3J 87
Persfield Clo. Eps—2E 134
Pershore Clo. Ilf—3M 47
Pershore Gro. Cars—1B 122
Pert Clo. N10—6F 26
Perth Av. NW9—5B 40
Perth Av. Hay—7G 53
Perth Clo. SW20—6E 104
Perth Rd. E10—6J 45
Perth Rd. E13—5F 62
Perth Rd. N4—6L 43
Perth Rd. N22—8M 27
Perth Rd. Bark—4B 64
Perth Rd. Beck—6A 110
Perth Rd. Ilf—4F 47
Perth Ter. Ilf—5A 48
Perwell Av. Harr—6K 37
Peter Av. NW10—3F 56
Peterborough Ct. EC4—9L 59
Peterborough Gdns. Ilf—5J 47
Peterborough M. SW6—1L 89
Peterborough Rd. E10—3A 46
Peterborough Rd. SW6—1L 89
Peterborough Rd. Cars—1C 122
Peterborough Rd. Harr—6C 38
Peterborough Vs. SW6—9M 73
Petergate. SW11—3A 90
Peters Clo. Stan—6H 23
Petersfield Av. Romf—6J 35
Petersfield Clo. N18—5A 28
Petersfield Clo. Romf—6L 35
Petersfield Cres. Coul—7J 137
Petersfield Rise. SW15—7F 88
Petersfield Rd. W3—3A 72
Petersham Clo. Rich—8H 87
Petersham Clo. Sutt—7L 121
Petersham Dri. Orp—6D 112
Petersham Gdns. Orp—6D 112
Petersham La. SW7—4A 74
Petersham M. SW7—4A 74
Petersham Pl. SW7—4A 74
Petersham Rd. Rich—5H 87
Peters Hill. EC4—1A 76
Peter's La. EC1—8M 59
Peter's Path. SE26—1F 108
Peterstone Rd. SE2—3F 80
Peterstow Clo. SW19—8J 89
Peter St. W1—1H 75
Petherton Rd. N5—1A 60
Petley Rd. W6—7H 73
Peto Pl. NW1—7F 58
Peto St. N. E16—9D 62
Peto St. S. E16—1D 78
Petrie Clo. NW2—2J 57
Petten Clo. Orp—3H 129
Petten Gro. Orp—3G 129
Petters Rd. Asht—8K 133
Petticoat La. E1—8C 60
Petticoat Sq. E1—9D 60
Pettits Boulevd. Romf—8C 34
Pettits Clo. Romf—9C 34
Pettits La. Romf—9C 34
Pettits La. N. Romf—8B 34
Pettits Pl. Dag—1L 65
Pettits Rd. Dag—1L 65
Pettiward Clo. SW15—3G 89
Pettley Gdns. Romf—3B 50
Pettman Cres. SE28—4B 80
Pettsgrove Av. Wemb—1G 55
Pett's Hill. N'holt—1M 53
Pett St. SE18—5J 79
Petts Wood Rd. Orp—9B 112
Petty France. SW1—4G 75
Petworth Clo. N'holt—3K 53
Petworth Clo. Coul—1G 151
Petworth Gdns. SW20—7F 104
Petworth Gdns. Uxb—4A 52
Petworth Rd. N12—5C 26
Petworth Rd. Bexh—4L 97
Petworth St. SW11—9C 74

Petworth Way. Horn—9D 50
Petyt Pl. SW3—7C 74
Petyward. SW3—5C 74
Pevensey Av. N11—5H 27
Pevensey Av. Enf—4C 16
Pevensey Clo. Iswth—8A 70
Pevensey Rd. E7—9D 46
Pevensey Rd. SW17—1B 106
Pevensey Rd. Felt—7J 85
Peverett Clo. N11—5F 26
Peveril Dri. Tedd—2B 102
Pewsey Clo. E4—5L 29
Peyton Pl. SE10—8A 78
Pheasant Clo. Purl—5M 137
Phelp St. SE17—7B 76
Phelps Way. Hay—5D 68
Phene St. SW3—7C 74
Philan Way. Romf—6B 34
Philbeach Gdns. SW5—6L 73
Philchurch Pl. E1—9E 60
Philip Av. Romf—6B 50
Philip Av. Swan—8B 114
Philip Clo. Romf—6B 50
Philip Gdns. Croy—4K 125
Philip La. N15—2B 44
Philpot Path. SE9—5K 95
Philippa Gdns. SE9—4H 95
Philip Rd. SE15—2E 92
Philip Rd. Rain—6C 66
Philip St. E13—7E 62
Philip Wlk. SE15—2F 92
Phillida Rd. Romf—9L 35
Phillimore Gdns. NW10—4G 57
Phillimore Gdns. W8—3L 73
Phillimore Gdns. Clo. W8
—4L 73
Phillimore Pl. W8—3L 73
Phillimore Pl. Rad—1C 10
Phillimore Wlk. W8—4L 73
Phillippers. Wat—8J 5
Phillip St. N1—4C 60
Phillips Clo. Dart—5F 98
Philpot La. EC3—1C 76
Philpot Path. Ilf—8A 48
Philpots Clo. W Dray—1H 143
Philpot Sq. SW6—2M 89
Philpot St. E1—9F 60
(in two parts)
Phineas Pett Rd. SE9—2J 95
Phipps Bri. Rd.—6A 106
SW19 97-273 & 84-176
Mitc remainder
Phipps Hatch La. Enf—2A 16
Phipp's M. SW1—5F 74
Phipp St. EC2—7C 60
Phoebeth Rd. SE4—4L 93
Phoenix Dri. Kes—6H 127
Phoenix Pl. Dart—6H 99
Phoenix Rd. NW1—6H 59
Phoenix Rd. SE20—3G 109
Phoenix St. WC2—9H 59
Phoenix Trading Pk. Bren
—6H 71
Phoenix Way. Houn—7H 69
Phoenix Way. N'wd—4D 20
Phyllis Av. N Mald—9F 104
Picardy Manorway. Belv
—4M 81
Picardy Rd. Belv—6L 81
Picardy St. Belv—4L 81
Piccadilly. W1—2F 74
Piccadilly Cir. W1—1H 75
Pickard St. EC1—6M 59
Pickering Av. E6—5L 63
Pickering M. W2—9M 57
Pickering St. N1—4M 59
Pickets Clo. Bush, Wat—1B 22
Pickets St. SW12—6F 90
Pickett Croft. Stan—8H 23
Picketts Lock La. N9—2H 29
Pickford Clo. Bexh—1J 97
Pickford La. Bexh—1J 97
Pickford Rd. Bexh—2J 97
Pickfords Yd. N17—6D 28
Pick Hill. Wal A—5M 7
Pickhurst Grn. Brom—2D 126
Pickhurst La. W Wick & Brom
—9C 110
Pickhurst Mead. Brom—2D 126
Pickhurst Pk. Brom—9C 110
Pickhurst Rise. W Wick
—3B 126
Pickle Herring St. SE1—2C 76
Pickwick M. N18—5C 28
Pickwick Pl. Harr—5C 38
Pickwick Rd. SE21—6B 92
Pickwick St. SE1—3A 76
Pickwick Way. Chst—3A 112
Pickworth Clo. SW8—8J 75
Picquets Way. Bans—9K 135
Picton Pl. W1—9E 58
Picton St. SE5—8B 76
Piedmont Rd. SE18—6B 80

Pield Heath Av. Uxb—7E 142
Pield Heath Rd. Uxb—7C 142
Piermont Rd. SE22—4F 92
Pierrepoint Rd. W3—1M 71
Pier Rd. E16—3L 79
Pier Rd. Eri—7C 82
(in two parts)
Pier Rd. Felt—4F 84
Pier St. E14—5A 78
Pier Ter. SW18—3M 89
Pigeon La. Hmptn—1L 101
Pigott St. E14—9L 61
Pike Clo. Brom—2F 110
Pike Rd. NW7—4B 24
Pike's End. Pinn—2F 36
Pikes Hill. Eps—5C 134
Pikestone Clo. Hay—7J 53
Pilgrimage St. SE1—3B 76
Pilgrim Hill. SE27—1A 108
Pilgrims Clo. Wat—6H 5
Pilgrim's La. NW3—9B 42
Pilgrim's Pl. NW3—9B 42
Pilgrims Rise. Barn—7C 14
Pilgrim St. EC4—9M 59
Pilgrims Way. N19—6H 43
Pilgrims Way. Dart—7L 99
Pilgrims Way. S Croy—7D 124
Pilgrim's Way. Wemb—6M 39
Pilkington Rd. SE15—1F 92
Pilkington Rd. Orp—4A 128
Pillions, The. Hay—7B 52
Pillmans Clo. Sidc—3G 113
Pilot Industrial Centre. NW10
—7B 56
Pilsden Clo. SW19—7H 89
Piltdown Rd. Wat—4H 21
Pimlico Rd. SW1—6E 74
Pimlico Wlk. N1—6C 60
Pimpernel Way. Romf—6H 35
Pinchbeck Rd. Orp—8D 128
Pinchin St. E1—1E 76
Pincott Rd. SW19—4A 106
Pincott Rd. Bexh—4L 97
Pindar St. EC2—8C 60
Pindock M. W9—7M 57
Pine Av. W Wick—3M 125
Pine Clo. N14—9G 15
Pine Clo. N19—7G 43
Pine Clo. Kenl—9B 138
Pine Clo. Stan—4F 22
Pine Clo. Swan—8D 114
Pine Clo. Wal X—1D 6
Pine Coombe. Croy—6H 125
Pine Ct. N'holt—7J 53
Pine Ct. Upm—9M 51
Pine Cres. Cars—3B 136
Pine Dene. SE15—9F 76
Pinefield Clo. E14—1L 77
Pine Gdns. Ruis—6F 36
Pine Gdns. Surb—1L 119
Pine Glade. Orp—6K 127
Pine Gro. N4—7J 43
Pine Gro. N20—1K 25
Pine Gro. SW19—2K 105
Pine Gro. Bush, Wat—4K 9
Pine Gro. St Alb—3K 5
Pine Gro. M. Wey—7A 116
Pine Gro. M. Wey—7A 116
Pine Hill. Eps—7B 134
Pinehurst Wlk. Orp—3C 128
Pine Pl. Bans—6H 135
Pine Pl. Hay—7D 52
Pine Ridge. Cars—1E 136
Pine Rd. N11—2E 26
Pine Rd. NW2—9G 41
Pines Av. Enf—9C 6
Pines Clo. N'wd—6C 20
Pines Rd. Brom—6J 111
Pines, The. Coul—9F 136
Pines, The. Purl—5A 138
Pines, The. Sun—7E 100
Pines, The. Wfd G—3E 30
Pine St. EC1—7L 59
Pine Tree Clo. Houn—9F 68
Pine Wlk. Bans—9D 136
Pine Wlk. Cars—2B 136
Pine Wlk. Surb—1L 119
Pine Wlk. E. Cars—3B 136
Pine Wlk. W. Cars—2B 136
Pine Wood. Sun—5E 100
Pinewood Av. Pinn—6M 21
Pinewood Av. Rain—7F 66
Pinewood Av. Sidc—7C 96
Pinewood Av. Uxb—9D 142
Pinewood Clo. Borwd—3B 12
Pinewood Clo. Croy—5J 125
Pinewood Clo. Orp—3B 128
Pinewood Clo. Pinn—6M 21
Pinewood Dri. Orp—7C 128
Pinewood Gro. W5—9G 55
Pinewood Rd. SE2—7H 81
Pinewood Rd. Brom—8E 110
Pinewood Rd. Felt—9F 84

Pinewood Rd. Hav, Romf
—4A 34
Pinfold Rd. SW16—1J 107
Pinfold Rd. Bush, Wat—4K 9
Pinglestone Clo. W Dray
—8J 143
Pinkcoat Clo. Felt—9F 84
Pinkerton Pl. SW16—1H 107
Pinkham Way. N11—7E 26
Pinks Hill. Swan—9C 114
Pinkwell Av. Hay—5B 68
Pinkwell La. Hay—5A 68
Pinley Gdns. Dag—4F 64
Pinnacle Hill. Bexh—3M 97
Pinnacle Hill N. Bexh—3M 97
Pinnacles. Wal A—7L 7
Pinn Clo. Uxb—9B 142
Pinnell Rd. SE9—3H 95
Pinner Grn. Pinn—9G 21
Pinner Gro. Pinn—2J 37
Pinner Hill. Pinn—7F 20
Pinner Hill Rd. Pinn—7F 20
Pinner Pk. Av. Harr—1M 37
Pinner Pk. Gdns. Harr—9A 22
Pinner Rd. N'wd & Pinn—8D 20
Pinner Rd. Pinn & Harr—2K 37
Pinner Rd. Wat—8H 9
Pinner View. Harr—2A 38
Pinn Way. Ruis—5B 36
Pintail Rd. Wfd G—7F 30
Pinto Clo. Borwd—8B 12
Pinto Way. SE3—3F 94
Piper Clo. N7—1K 59
Piper Rd. King—7L 103
Pipers Grn. NW9—3A 40
Pipers Grn. La. Edgw—3J 23
Pipewell Rd. Cars—1C 122
Pippin Clo. Croy—3K 125
Pippins Clo. W Dray—4H 143
Piquet Rd. SE20—6G 109
Pirbright Cres. Croy—8A 126
Pirbright Rd. SW18—7K 89
Pirie St. E16—2F 78
Pitcairn Clo. Romf—2L 49
Pitcairn Rd. Mitc—4D 106
Pitchford St. E15—3B 62
Pitfield St. N1—6C 60
Pitfield Way. NW10—2A 56
Pitfield Way. Enf—3G 17
Pitfold Clo. SE12—5F 94
Pitfold Rd. SE12—5E 94
Pitlake. Croy—4M 123
Pitman St. SE5—8A 76
Pitsea Pl. E1—9H 61
Pitsea St. E1—9H 61
Pitshanger La. W5—7F 54
Pitt Cres. SW19—1M 105
Pitt Pl. Eps—6C 134
Pitt Rd. Eps—6C 134
Pitt Rd. Orp—6A 128
Pitt Rd. T Hth—9A 108
Pitt's Head M. W1—2E 74
Pittsmead Av. Brom—2E 126
Pitt St. SE15—9D 76
Pitt St. W8—3L 73
Pittville Gdns. SE25—7E 108
Pixley St. E14—9K 61
Pixton Way. Croy—1J 139
Place Farm Av. Orp—3B 128
Plaistow Gro. E15—4D 62
Plaistow Gro. Brom—4F 110
Plaistow La. Brom—4F 110
Plaistow Pk. Rd. E13—5F 62
Plaistow Rd. E15—4D 62
Plane St. SE26—9F 92
Plane Tree Cres. Felt—9F 84
Plane Tree Wlk. SE19—3C 108
Plantagenet Clo. Wor Pk
—6B 120
Plantagenet Gdns. Romf
—5H 49
Plantagenet Pl. Romf—5H 49
Plantagenet Rd. Barn—6A 14
Plantain Pl. SE1—3B 76
Plantation Dri. Orp—3H 129
Plantation Rd. Eri—9E 82
Plantation Rd. Swan—4E 114
Plantation, The. SE3—1E 94
Plashet Gro. E6—4G 63
Plashet Rd. E13—4E 62
Plassy Rd. SE6—6M 93
Platford Grn. Horn—2J 51
Plato Rd. SW2—3J 91
Platts Av. Wat—5F 8
Platt's La. NW3—8L 41
Platts Rd. Enf—3G 17
Platt St. NW1—5H 59
Platt, The. SW15—2H 89
(in two parts)
Plawsfield Rd. Beck—5H 109
Plaxtol Clo. Brom—5G 111
Plaxtol Rd. Eri—8L 81
Playfield Av. Romf—8A 34

Playfield Cres. SE22—4D 92
Playfield Rd. Edgw—9A 24
Playford Rd. N4—7K 43
(in two parts)
Playgreen Way. SE6—9L 93
Playground Clo. Beck—6H 109
Playhouse Yd. EC4—9M 59
Pleasance Rd. SW15—4F 88
Pleasance Rd. Orp—6F 112
Pleasance, The. SW15—3F 88
Pleasant Gro. Croy—5K 125
Pleasant Pl. N1—3M 59
Pleasant Pl. Harr—7B 38
Pleasant Pl. W on T—8G 117
Pleasant Row. NW1—4F 58
Pleasant View. Eri—6C 82
Pleasant View Pl. Orp—7M 127
Pleasant Way. Wemb—5G 55
Pleasure Pit Rd. Asht—9M 133
Plender St. NW1—4G 59
Pleshey Rd. N7—9H 43
Plesman Way. Wall—1J 137
Plevna Cres. N15—4C 44
Plevna Rd. N9—3E 28
Plevna Rd. Hmptn—5M 101
Plevna St. E14—4A 78
Pleydell Av. SE19—4D 108
Pleydell Av. W6—5D 72
Plimsoll Clo. E14—9M 61
Plimsoll Rd. N4—8M 43
Plough Ct. EC3—1B 76
Plough Farm Clo. Ruis—4B 36
Plough La. SE22—5D 92
Plough La.—2M 105
SW19 2-56
SW17 remainder
Plough La. Purl—1K 137
Plough La. Wall—6J 123
Plough La. Clo. Wall—7J 123
Ploughmans Clo. NW1—4H 59
Ploughmans End. Iswth—4B 86
Plough Pl. EC4—9L 59
Plough Rd. SW11—2B 90
Plough Rd. Eps—1B 134
Plough Ter. SW11—3B 90
Plough Way. SE16—5H 77
Plough Yd. EC2—7C 60
Plumber's Row. E1—9E 60
Plumbridge St. SE10—9A 78
Plum Garth. Bren—5H 71
Plum La. SE18—8M 79
Plummer La. Mitc—6D 106
Plummer Rd. SW4—6H 91
Plumpton Av. Horn—9J 51
Plumpton Clo. N'holt—2L 53
Plumpton Way. Cars—5C 122
Plumstead Comn. Rd. SE18
—7M 79
Plumstead High St. SE18
—5B 80
Plumstead Rd. SE18—5M 79
Plumtree Clo. Wall—9H 123
Plumtree Clo. Dag—9M 65
Plumtree Mead. Lou—5L 19
Plybrook Rd. Sutt—5L 121
Plymouth Rd. E16—8E 62
Plymouth Rd. Brom—5F 110
Plympton Av. NW6—3K 57
Plympton Pl. NW8—7C 58
Plympton Rd. NW6—3K 57
Plympton St. NW8—7C 58
Plymstock Rd. Well—8G 81
Pocklington Clo. NW9—9C 24
Pocock St. SE1—3M 75
Podmore Rd. SW18—3A 90
Poets' Corner. SW1—4J 75
Poet's Rd. N5—1B 60
Pointalls Clo. N3—9A 26
Point Clo. SE10—9A 78
Pointers Cotts. Rich—8G 87
Point Hill. SE10—9A 78
Point Pleasant. SW18—3L 89
Point, The. Ruis—9E 36
Poland St. W1—9G 59
Polebrook Rd. SE3—2G 95
Pole Cat All. Brom—4D 126
Polecroft La. SE6—8K 93
Pole Hill Rd. E4—9A 18
Pole Hill Rd. Uxb—7F 142
Polesden Gdns. SW20—6F 104
Polesteeple Hill. West—9H 141
Polesworth Rd. Dag—3H 65
Police Sta. La. Bush, Wat—9M 9
Police Sta. Rd. W on T—8G 117
Pollard Clo. E16—1E 78
Pollard Clo. N7—9K 43
Pollard Clo. Chig—5E 32
Pollard Rd. N20—2C 26
Pollard Rd. Mord—9B 106
Pollard Row. E2—6E 60
Pollards Clo. Lou—7G 19
Pollards Cres. SW16—7J 107
Pollards Hill E. SW16—7K 107

Pollards Hill N. SW16—7J 107
Pollards Hill S. SW16—7J 107
Pollards Hill W. SW16—7K 107
Pollard St. E2—6E 60
Pollards Wood Rd. SW16
—7J 107
Pollard Wlk. Sidc—3G 113
Pollen St. W1—9G 59
Pollitt Dri. NW8—7B 58
Pollyhaugh. Eyns, Dart—5J 131
Polperro Clo. Orp—1D 128
Polsted Rd. SE6—6K 93
Polthorne Gro. SE18—5B 80
Polworth Rd. SW16—2J 107
Polygon Rd. NW1—5H 59
Polygon, The. SW4—3G 91
Polytechnic St. SE18—5L 79
Pomell Way. E1—9D 60
Pomeroy Cres. Wat—9F 4
Pomeroy St. SE14—8G 77
Pomfret Rd. SE5—2A 92
Pond Clo. SE3—1D 94
Pond Clo. W on T—8E 116
Pond Cotts. SE21—7C 92
Pond Grn. Ruis—7C 36
Pondhead La. W on T—9D 116
Pond Hill Gdns. Sutt—8J 121
Ponder St. N7—3K 59
Pondfield Ho. SE27—2A 108
Pondfield Rd. Brom—3C 126
Pondfield Rd. Dag—1M 65
Pondfield Rd. Kenl—8M 137
Pondfield Rd. Orp—5M 127
Pondhead La. W on T—9D 116
Pond Piece. Lea—5A 132
Pond Pl. SW3—5C 74
Pond Pl. Asht—9J 133
Pond Rd. E15—5C 62
Pond Rd. SE3—1D 94
Pondside Clo. Hay—7B 68
Pond Sq. N6—6E 42
Pond St. NW3—1C 58
Pond Way. Chst—3M 111
Pond Way. Tedd—3G 103
Pondwood Rise. Orp—2C 128
Ponler St. E1—9F 60
Ponsard Rd. NW10—6F 56
Ponsford St. E9—2G 61
Ponsonby Pl. SW1—6H 75
Ponsonby Rd. SW15—6F 88
Ponsonby Ter. SW1—6H 75
Pontefract Rd. Brom—2D 110
Ponton Rd. SW8—8H 75
Pont St. SW1—4D 74
Pont St. M. SW1—4D 74
Pontypool Wlk. Romf—6G 35
Pool Clo. Beck—2L 109
Pool Clo. E Mol—9K 101
Poole Clo. Ruis—7C 36
Poole Ct. Rd. Houn—1J 85
Poole Rd. E9—2H 61
Poole Rd. Eps—8B 120
Poole Rd. Horn—5K 51
Pooles Cotts. Rich—8H 87
Pooles La. SW10—8A 74
Pooles La. Dag—5J 65
Pooles Pk. N4—7L 43
Poole St. N1—4B 60
Poole Way. Hay—6C 52
Pool Rd. E Mol—9K 101
Poolsford Rd. NW9—2C 40
Poonah St. E1—9G 61
Pope Rd. Brom—9H 111
Popes Av. Twic—8C 86
Pope's Dri. N3—8L 25
Popes Gro. Croy—5K 125
Popes Gro. Twic—8D 86
Pope's Head All. EC3—9B 60
Popes La. W5—4H 71
Popes La. Wat—2F 8
Pope's Rd. SW9—2L 91
Pope's Rd. Abb L, Wat—4C 4
Pope St. SE1—3C 76
Popham Clo. Felt—9K 85
Popham Gdns. Rich—2L 87
Popham Rd. N1—4A 60
(in two parts)
Popham St. N1—4A 60
Poplar Av. Mitc—5D 106
Poplar Av. Orp—4M 127
Poplar Av. S'hall—4M 69
Poplar Av. W Dray—1K 143
Poplar Bath St. E14—1M 77
Poplar Clo. Pinn—8H 21
Poplar Ct. SW19—2L 105
Poplar Cres. Eps—8A 120
Poplar Dri. Bans—6J 135
Poplar Farm Clo. Eps—8A 120
Poplar Gdns. SE28—9G 65
Poplar Gdns. N Mald—6B 104
Poplar Gro. N11—6E 26

Poplar Gro. W6—3G 73
Poplar Gro. N Mald—6B 104
Poplar Gro. Wemb—8A 40
Poplar High St. E14—1M 77
Poplar Mt. Belv—5A 82
Poplar Pl. SE28—2G 81
Poplar Pl. W2—1M 73
Poplar Pl. Hay—1E 68
Poplar Rd. SE24—3A 92
Poplar Rd. SW19—6L 105
Poplar Rd. Ashf—2A 100
Poplar Rd. Sutt—3K 121
Poplar Rd. Uxb—2A 142
Poplar Rd. S. SW19—7L 105
Poplars Av. NW2—2G 57
Poplars Clo. Ruis—6C 36
Poplars Clo. Wat—5F 4
Poplar Shaw. Wal A—6M 7
Poplars Rd. E17—4M 45
Poplars, The. N14—7F 14
Poplar St. Romf—2A 50
Poplar Wlk. SE24—3A 92
Poplar Wlk. Croy—3A 124
Poplar Way. Felt—9F 84
Poplar Way. Ilf—2A 48
Poppins Ct. EC4—9M 59
Poppleton Rd. E11—4C 46
Poppy La. Croy—3G 125
Porchester Clo. SE5—3B 92
Porchester Clo. Horn—4J 51
Porchester Gdns. W2—1M 73
Porchester Gdns. M. W2
—9M 57
Porchester Mead. Beck
—3L 109
Porchester M. W2—9M 57
Porchester Pl. W2—9C 58
Porchester Rd. W2—9M 57
Porchester Rd. King—6M 103
Porchester Sq. W2—9M 57
Porchester Ter. W2—1A 74
Porchester Ter. N. W2—9M 57
Porchfield Clo. Sutt—2M 135
Porch Way. N20—3D 26
Porcupine Clo. SE9—8J 95
Porden Rd. SW2—3K 91
Porlock Av. Harr—6A 38
Porlock Ho. SE26—9E 92
Porlock Rd. Enf—9D 16
Porlock St. SE1—3B 76
Porrington Clo. Chst—5L 111
Portal Clo. SE27—9L 91
Portal Clo. Ruis—9E 36
Portal Clo. Uxb—3C 142
Portbury Clo. SE15—9E 76
Port Cres. E13—7F 62
Portcullis Lodge Rd. Enf—5B 16
Portelet Rd. E1—6H 61
Porten Rd. W14—4J 73
Porter Rd. E6—9K 63
Porters Av. Dag—2F 64
Porter St. W1—8D 58
Porters Way. W Dray—4K 143
Porteus Rd. W2—8A 58
Portgate Clo. W9—7K 57
Porthcawe Rd. SE26—1J 109
Porthkerry Av. Well—3E 96
Portia Way. E3—7K 61
Portinscale Rd. SW15—4J 89
Portland Av. N16—5D 44
Portland Av. N Mald—2D 120
Portland Av. Sidc—5C 96
Portland Cres. SE9—8J 95
Portland Cres. Felt—1B 100
Portland Cres. Gnfd—8M 53
Portland Cres. Stan—9H 23
Portland Dri. Wal X—4A 6
Portland Gdns. N4—4M 43
Portland Gdns. Romf—3H 49
Portland Gro. SW8—9K 75
Portland Pl. W1—8F 58
Portland Pl. Eps—6C 134
Portland Rise. N4—6M 43
Portland Rise. Est. N4—6A 44
Portland Rd. N15—2D 44
Portland Rd. SE9—8J 95
Portland Rd. SE25—8E 108
Portland Rd. W11—1J 73
Portland Rd. Ashf—9C 144
Portland Rd. Brom—1G 111
Portland Rd. Hay—6C 52
Portland Rd. King—7J 103
Portland Rd. Mitc—6C 106
Portland Rd. S'hall—4K 69
Portland St. SE17—6B 76
Portland Ter. Rich—3H 87
Portman Av. SW14—2B 88
Portman Clo. W1—9E 58
Portman Clo. Bex—7C 98
Portman Clo. Bexh—2J 97
Portman Dri. Wfd G—9H 31
Portman Gdns. NW9—9B 24
Portman M. S. W1—9E 58

Portman Pl. E2—6G 61
Portman Rd. King—6K 103
Portman Sq. W1—9E 58
Portman St. W1—9E 58
Portmeadow Wlk. SE2—3H 81
Portmeers Clo. E17—4K 45
Portmore Gdns. Romf—5L 33
Portnall Rd. W9—6K 57
Portnalls Clo. Coul—8F 136
Portnalls Rise. Coul—8G 137
Portnalls Rd. Coul—9F 136
Portnoi Clo. Romf—9B 34
Portobello M. W11—1L 73
Portobello Rd.—8J 57
  W11 1-275 & 2-262
  W10 remainder
Portpool La. EC1—8L 59
Portree Clo. N22—7K 27
Portree St. E14—9B 62
Portsdown. Edgw—5L 23
Portsdown Av. NW11—4K 41
Portsea Pl. W2—9C 58
Portslade Rd. SW8—1G 91
Portsmouth Av. Th Dit—2E 118
Portsmouth Rd. SW15—6F 88
Portsmouth Rd. Cob & Esh
  —9K 117
Portsmouth Rd. Esh, Th Dit,
  Surb & King—8L 117
Portsmouth St. WC2—9K 59
Portsoken St. E1—1D 76
Portswood Pl. SW15—6D 88
Portugal Gdns. Twic—8A 86
Portugal St. WC2—9K 59
Portway. E15—4D 62
Portway. Eps—1E 134
Portway Cres. Eps—1E 134
Portway Gdns. SE18—8H 79
Postern Grn. Enf—5L 15
Post La. Twic—7B 86
Post Office All. Hmptn—6M 101
Post Office App. E7—1F 62
Post Office Way. SW8—7H 75
Postway M. Ilf—8M 47
  (in two parts)
Potier St. SE1—4B 76
Potter Clo. Mitc—6F 106
Potterne Clo. SW19—6H 89
Potters Clo. Lou—4J 19
Potters' Fields. SE1—2C 76
Potters Gro. N Mald—8A 104
Potters Heights Clo. Pinn
  —7F 20
Potter's La. SW16—3H 107
Potters La. Barn—6L 13
Potters La. Borwd—3A 12
Potters Rd. Barn—6M 13
Potter St. N'wd & Pinn—8E 20
Potter St. Hill. Pinn—6F 20
Pottery La. W11—2J 73
Pottery Rd. Bex—8A 98
Pottery Rd. Bren—7J 71
Pottery St. SE16—3F 76
Pott St. E2—6F 60
Poulett Gdns. Twic—7E 86
Poulett Rd. E6—5K 63
Poulner Way. SE15—8D 76
Poulters Wood. Kes—7H 127
Poulton Av. Sutt—5B 122
Poulton Clo. E8—2F 60
Poultry. EC2—9B 60
Pound Clo. Orp—4B 128
Pound Clo. Surb—3G 119
Pound Ct. Dri. Orp—4B 128
Poundfield. Wat—8D 4
Poundfield Rd. Lou—7L 19
Pound La. NW10—2E 56
Pound La. Eps—3B 134
  (in two parts)
Pound Pk. Rd. SE7—5H 79
Pound Pl. SE9—5L 95
Pound Rd. Bans—9K 135
Pound St. Cars—7D 122
Pountney Rd. SW11—2E 90
Poverest Rd. Orp—9D 112
Powder Mill La. Dart—8J 99
Powder Mill La. Twic—6K 85
Powdermill La. Wal A—6H 7
Powdermill Way. Wal A—6H 7
Powell Clo. Edgw—6K 23
Powell Clo. Wall—9J 123
Powell Gdns. Dag—9L 49
Powell Rd. E5—8F 44
Powell Rd. Buck H—9G 19
Powell's Wlk. W4—7C 72
Power Industrial Est. Eri
  —9E 8
Power Rd. W4—5L 71
Powers Ct. Twic—6H 87
Powerscroft Rd. E5—9G 45
Powerscroft Rd. Sidc—3G 113
Powis Gdns. NW11—5K 41
Powis Gdns. W11—9K 57

Powis M. W11—9K 57
Powis Pl. WC1—7J 59
Powis Rd. E3—6M 61
Powis Sq. W11—9K 57
Powis St. SE18—4L 79
Powis Ter. W11—9K 57
Powlett Pl. NW1—3F 58
Pownall Gdns. Houn—3M 85
Pownall Rd. E8—4E 60
Pownall Rd. Houn—3M 85
Powster Rd. Brom—2E 110
Powys Clo. Bexh—7H 81
Powys Ct. N13—5J 27
Powys La.—4J 27
  N14 2-46
  N13 remainder
Poynders Gdns. SW4—6G 91
Poynders Rd. SW4—5G 91
Poynings Clo. Orp—4G 129
Poynings Rd. N19—8G 43
Poynings Way. N12—5L 25
Poynings Way. Romf—8J 35
Poyntell Cres. Chst—5B 112
Poynter Rd. Enf—7E 16
Poynton Rd. N17—9E 28
Poyntz Rd. SW11—1D 90
Poyser St. E2—5F 60
Praed M. W2—9B 58
Praed St. W2—9B 58
Pragel St. E13—5G 63
Pragnell Rd. SE12—8F 94
Prague Pl. SW2—4J 91
Prah Rd. N4—7L 43
Prairie St. SW8—1F 90
Pratt M. NW1—4G 59
Pratts La. W on T—6H 117
Pratt St. NW1—4G 59
Pratt Wlk. SE11—5K 75
Prayle Gro. NW2—6H 41
Prebend Gdns.—5D 72
  W4 1-37 & 2-40
  W6 remainder
Prebend St. N1—4A 60
Precinct Rd. Hay—1E 68
Premier Lodge. N3—8L 25
Prendergast Rd. SE3—2C 94
Prentis Rd. SW16—1H 107
Prentiss Ct. SE7—5H 79
Presburg Rd. N Mald—9C 104
Prescelly Pl. Edgw—8K 23
Prescot St. E1—1D 76
Prescott Clo. SW16—4J 107
Prescott Grn. Lou—5M 19
Prescott Pl. SW4—3H 91
Prescott Rd. Wal X—1E 6
Press Rd. NW10—8B 40
Press Rd. Uxb—2B 142
Prestage St. E14—1B 78
Prestbury Cres. Bans—8D 136
Prestbury Rd. E7—3G 63
Prestbury Sq. SE9—1K 111
Prested Rd. SW11—3C 90
Preston Av. E4—6B 30
Preston Clo. SE1—5C 76
Preston Clo. Twic—9C 86
Preston Ct. W on T—3G 117
Preston Dri. E11—3G 47
Preston Dri. Bexh—9H 81
Preston Dri. Eps—8C 120
Preston Gdns. NW10—2C 56
Preston Gdns. Enf—1J 17
Preston Gdns. Ilf—4J 47
Preston Gro. Asht—9G 133
Preston Hill. Harr—5J 39
Preston Pl. NW2—2E 56
Preston Pl. Rich—4J 87
Preston Rd. E11—4C 46
Preston Rd. SE19—3M 107
Preston Rd. SW20—4D 104
Preston Rd. Romf—4H 35
Preston Rd. Wemb & Harr
  —7J 39
Preston's Rd. E14—1A 78
Prestons Rd. Brom—5E 126
Preston Waye. Harr—6J 39
Prestwick Rd. Wat—5F 20
Prestwood Av. Harr—2F 38
Prestwood Clo. Harr—2F 38
Prestwood Dri. Romf—5A 34
Prestwood Gdns. Croy—2A 124
Prestwood St. N1—5A 60
Pretoria Av. E17—2J 45
Pretoria Clo. N17—7D 28
Pretoria Cres. E4—1A 30
Pretoria Rd. E4—1A 30
Pretoria Rd. E11—6B 46
Pretoria Rd. E16—7D 62
Pretoria Rd. N17—7D 28
Pretoria Rd. SW16—3F 106
Pretoria Rd. Ilf—1M 63
Pretoria Rd. Romf—2A 50
Pretoria Rd. Wat—6E 8

Pretoria Rd. N. N18—6D 28
Prevost Rd. N11—2E 26
Price Clo. NW7—6J 25
Price Clo. SW17—9D 90
Price Rd. Croy—7M 123
Price's St. SE1—2M 75
Price's Yd. N1—4K 59
Price Way. Hmptn—3J 101
Pricklers Hill. Barn—8M 13
Prickley Wood. Brom—3D 126
Priddy's Yd. Croy—4A 124
Prideaux Pl. WC1—6K 59
Prideaux Rd. SW9—2J 91
Pridham Rd. E . T Hth—8B 108
Priestfield Rd. SE23—9J 93
Priestlands Pk. Rd. Sidc—9D 96
Priestley Clo. N16—5D 44
Priestley Gdns. Romf—4F 48
Priestley Rd. Mitc—6E 106
Priestley St. E9—1H 61
Priestley Way. E17—1H 45
Priestley Way. NW2—6E 40
Priests Av. Romf—9B 34
Priests Bri.—2C 88
  SW15 2-20
  SW14 remainder
Prima Rd. SW9—8L 75
Primrose Av. Enf—3C 16
Primrose Av. Romf—5F 48
Primrose Clo. Harr—8K 37
Primrose Gdns. NW3—2C 58
Primrose Gdns. Bush, Wat
  —9M 9
Primrose Gdns. Ruis—1G 53
Primrose Glen. Horn—2J 51
Primrose Hill. EC4—9L 59
Primrose Hill. K Lan—2A 4
Primrose Hill Rd. NW3—3D 58
Primrose La. Croy—3H 125
Primrose Path. Wal X—4A 6
Primrose Rd. E10—6M 45
Primrose Rd. E18—9F 30
Primrose W. on T—7G 117
Primrose St. EC2—8C 60
Primrose Way. Wemb—5H 55
Primula St. W12—9E 56
Prince Albert Rd.—5C 58
  NW1 1-23
  NW8 remainder
Prince Arthur M. NW3—9A 42
Prince Arthur Rd. NW3—1A 58
Prince Charles Dri. NW4—5G 41
Prince Charles Rd. SE3—1D 94
Prince Charles Way. Wall
  —5F 122
Prince Consort Dri. Chst
  —5B 112
Prince Consort Rd. SW7—4B 74
Princedale Rd. W11—2J 73
Prince Edward Rd. E9—2K 61
Prince George Av. N14—7H 15
Prince George Rd. N16—9C 44
Prince George's Av. SW20
  —6G 105
Prince George's Rd. SW19
  —5B 106
Prince Henry Rd. SE7—8H 79
Prince Imperial Rd. SE18
  —9K 79
Prince Imperial Rd. Chst
  —4M 111
Prince John Rd. SE9—4J 95
Princelet St. E1—8D 60
Prince of Orange La. SE10
  —8A 78
Prince of Wales Clo. NW4
  —2F 40
Prince of Wales Dri. SW11 &
  SW8—9D 74
Prince of Wales Footpath. Enf
  —2J 17
Prince of Wales Rd. E16—9G 63
Prince of Wales Rd. NW5
  —2E 58
Prince of Wales Rd. SE3—9D 78
Prince of Wales Rd. Sutt
  —4B 122
Prince of Wales Ter. W4—6C 72
Prince of Wales Ter. W8
  —3M 73
Prince Regent La.—6F 62
  E13 1-279 & 2-250
  E16 remainder
Prince Regent Rd. Houn—2A 86
Prince Rd. SE25—9C 108
Prince Rupert Rd. SE9—3K 95
Princes Av. N3—8L 25
Princes Av. N10—1F 42
Princes Av. N13—5L 27
Princes Av. N22—8H 27
Princes Av. NW9—2L 39
Princes Av. W3—4L 71
Princes Av. Cars—9D 122

Princes Av. Dart—7M 99
Princes Av. Enf—9E 6
Prince's Av. Gnfd—9M 53
Princes Av. Orp—9C 112
Prince's Av. S Croy—7F 138
Prince's Av. Surb—3L 119
Prince's Av. Wat—7D 8
Prince's Av. Wfd G—4F 30
Princes Clo. NW9—2L 39
Princes Clo. Edgw—5L 23
Princes Clo. Sidc—9H 97
Princes Clo. S Croy—7F 138
Prince's Clo. Tedd—1B 102
Princes Ct. Wemb—1J 55
Princes Dri. Harr—1C 38
Prince's Dri. Lea—4C 132
Princes Gdns. SW7—4B 74
Prince's Gdns. W3—8L 55
Princes Gdns. W5—7G 55
Prince's Ga. SW7—3B 74
  (in three parts)
Prince's Ga. Ct. SW7—3B 74
Prince's Ga. M. SW7—4B 74
Princes La. N10—1F 42
Prince's M. W2—1M 73
Princes Pk. Rain—3E 66
Princes Pk. Av. NW11—4J 41
Princes Pk. Av. Hay—1B 68
Princes Pk. Circ. Hay—1B 68
Princes Pk. Clo. Hay—1B 68
Princes Pk. La. Hay—1B 68
Princes Pk. Pde. Hay—1B 68
Prince's Pl. W11—2J 73
Prince's Plain. Brom—2J 127
Prince's Rise. SE13—1A 94
Princes Rd. N18—4G 29
Princes Rd. SE20—3H 109
Princes Rd. SW14—2B 88
Prince's Rd. SW19—3L 105
Princes Rd. W13—2F 70
Princes Rd. Buck H—2G 31
Princes Rd. Dart—5E 98
Princes Rd. Felt—9D 84
Princes Rd. Ilf—2B 48
Princes Rd. King—4L 103
Princes Rd. Rich—4K 87
Princes Rd. Rich—9K 71
  (Kew)
Prince's Rd. Romf—3E 50
Princes Rd. Tedd—1B 102
Princes Rd. Wey—7A 116
Princess Av. Wemb—7J 39
Princess Ct. N6—5G 43
Princess Cres. N4—7M 43
Princess May Rd. N16—9C 44
Princess M. NW3—1B 58
Princess Pde. Orp—5L 127
Prince's Sq. W2—1M 73
Princess Rd. NW1—4E 58
Princess Rd. NW6—5L 57
Princess Rd. Croy—1A 124
Princess Rd. Swan—3E 114
Princess St. SE1—4M 75
Prince's St. EC2—9B 60
Princes St. N17—6C 28
Princes St. W1—9F 58
Princes St. Bexh—3K 97
Princes St. Rich—3J 87
Princes St. Sutt—6B 122
Princes Ter. E13—4F 62
Prince St. SE8—7K 77
Prince St. Wat—5G 9
Princes View. Dart—7L 99
Princes Way. SW19—6H 89
Princes Way. Buck H—2G 31
Princes Way. Croy—7K 123
Princes Way. Ruis—9J 37
Princes Way. W Wick—6D 126
Princethorpe Rd. SE26—1H 109
Princeton St. WC1—8K 59
Pringle Gdns. SW16—1G 107
  (in two parts)
Printer St. EC4—9L 59
Printinghouse La. Hay—3C 68
Printing Ho. Yd. E2—6C 60
Priolo Rd. SE7—6G 79
Prior Av. Sutt—9C 122
Prior Bolton St. N1—2M 59
Prioress Rd. SE27—9M 91
Prioress St. SE1—4C 76
Priors Croft. E17—9J 29
Priorsford Av. Orp—8E 112
Priors Field. N'holt—2J 53
Priors Gdns. Ruis—1G 53
Priors Mead. Enf—3C 16
Priors Pk. Horn—8G 51
Prior St. SE10—8A 78
Priory Av. E4—3K 29
Priory Av. E17—3L 45
Priory Av. N8—2H 43
Priory Av. W4—5C 72
Priory Av. Orp—1B 128
Priory Av. Sutt—6H 121

Priory Av. Wemb—9D 38
Priory Clo. E4—3K 29
Priory Clo. E18—8E 30
Priory Clo. N3—8K 25
Priory Clo. N14—7F 14
Priory Clo. N20—1K 25
Priory Clo. SW19—5M 105
Priory Clo. Beck—7J 109
Priory Clo. Chst—5K 111
Priory Clo. Dart—4H 99
Priory Clo. Hmptn—5K 101
Priory Clo. Ruis—6D 36
Priory Clo. Stan—3D 22
Priory Clo. Sun—4E 100
Priory Clo. W on T—5E 116
Priory Clo. Wemb—9D 38
Priory Ct. E17—9E 29
Priory Ct. SW8—9H 75
Priory Ct. Est. E17—9H 29
Priory Cres. SE19—4A 108
Priory Cres. Sutt—6H 121
Priory Cres. Wemb—8E 38
Priory Dri. SE2—6H 81
Priory Dri. Stan—3D 22
Priory Gdns. N6—4F 42
Priory Gdns. SW13—2D 88
Priory Gdns. W4—5C 72
Priory Gdns. W5—6J 55
Priory Gdns. Dart—4H 99
Priory Gdns. Hmptn—4K 101
Priory Gdns. Wemb—9E 38
Priory Gro. SW8—9J 75
Priory Hill. Dart—5H 99
Priory Hill. Wemb—9E 38
Priory La. SW15—5C 88
Priory La. E Mol—8M 101
Priory La. F'ham, Dart—3K 131
Priory La. Rich—8L 71
Priory M. SW8—9H 75
Priory Pk. SE3—2D 94
Priory Pk. Rd. NW6—4K 57
Priory Pk. Rd. Wemb—9E 38
Priory Path. Romf—3J 35
Priory Pl. Dart—5H 99
Priory Rd. E6—4H 63
Priory Rd. N8—2H 43
Priory Rd. NW6—4M 57
Priory Rd. SW19—4B 106
Priory Rd. W4—4B 72
Priory Rd. Bark—3B 64
Priory Rd. Chess—5J 119
Priory Rd. Croy—2L 123
Priory Rd. Dart—4H 99
  (in two parts)
Priory Rd. Hmptn—5K 101
Priory Rd. Houn—4A 86
Priory Rd. Lou—6J 19
Priory Rd. Rich—7L 71
Priory Rd. Romf—3J 35
Priory Rd. Sutt—6H 121
Priory St. E3—6M 61
Priory Ter. NW6—4M 57
Priory Ter. Sun—4E 100
Priory, The. SE3—3D 94
Priory View. Bush, Wat—9C 10
Priory Wlk. SW10—6A 74
Priory Way. Harr—2M 37
Priory Way. S'hall—4H 69
Priory Way. W Dray—7J 143
Pritchard's Rd. E2—5E 60
Priter Rd. SE16—4E 76
Priter Way. SE16—4E 76
Private Rd. Enf—7B 16
Probert Rd. SW2—4L 91
Probyn Rd. SW2—8M 91
Proctor Clo. SE16—4E 76
Proctors Clo. Felt—7E 84
Proctors Rd. SE16—4E 76
Profumo Rd. W on T—7H 117
Progress Way. N22—8L 27
Progress Way. Croy—4K 123
Progress Way. Enf—7E 16
Promenade App. Rd. W4
  —8C 72
Promenade de Verdun. Purl
  —3H 137
Promenade, The. W4—9C 72
Prospect Clo. SE26—1F 108
Prospect Clo. Belv—5L 81
Prospect Clo. Houn—9K 69
Prospect Clo. Ruis—5H 37
Prospect Cotts. SW18—3L 89
Prospect Cres. Twic—5A 86
Prospect Hill. E17—2M 45
Prospect Pl. N2—2B 42
Prospect Pl. N7—7C 28
Prospect Pl. NW2—8K 41
Prospect Pl. W4—6B 72
Prospect Pl. Brom—7F 110
Prospect Pl. Eps—4C 134
Prospect Pl. Romf—9A 34
Prospect Ring. N2—1B 42
Prospect Rd. NW2—8K 41

223

Prospect Rd. Barn—6L 13
Prospect Rd. Horn—1K 51
Prospect Rd. Surb—1G 119
Prospect Rd. Wal X—2C 6
Prospect Rd. Wfd G—6G 31
Prospect St. SE16—4F 76
Prospect Vale. SE18—5J 79
Prospero Rd. N19—6H 43
Protheroe Rd. SW6—8K 73
Prothero Gdns. NW4—3F 40
Prout Gro. NW10—9C 40
Prout Rd. E5—8F 44
Provence St. N1—5A 60
Providence Ct. W1—1E 74
Providence La. Hay—8B 68
Providence Pl. N1—4M 59
Providence Pl. Eps—4C 134
Providence Pl. Romf—9K 33
Providence Rd. W Dray—2J 143
Provident Industrial Est. Hay
—3E 68
Provost Rd. NW3—3D 58
Provost St. N1—6B 60
Prowse Av. Bush, Wat—1A 22
Prowse Pl. NW1—3G 59
Pruden Clo. N14—2G 27
Prusom St. E1—2F 76
Pryor Clo. Abb L, Wat—5D 4
Pryors, The. NW3—8B 42
Puck La. Wal A—2L 7
Pudding La. EC3—1B 76
Pudding La. Chig—1D 32
Pudding Mill La. E15—4M 61
Puddle Dock. EC4—1M 75
Puddledock La. Dart & Swan
—2C 114
Pulborough Rd. SW18—6K 89
Pulborough Way. Houn—3G 85
Pulford Rd. N15—4B 44
Pulham Av. N2—2A 42
Puller Rd. Barn—4J 13
Pulleyns Av. E6—6J 63
Pullman Gdns. SW15—5G 89
Pulross Rd. SW9—2K 91
Pulteney Clo. E3—4K 61
Pulteney Rd. E18—1F 46
Pulteney Ter. N1—4K 59
Pulton Pl. SW6—8L 73
Puma Ct. E1—8D 60
Pump All. Bren—8H 71
Pump Clo. N'holt—5I. 53
Pump Ct. EC4—9L 59
Pump Hill. Lou—4K 19
Pumping Sta. Rd. W4—8C 72
Pump La. Hay—3D 68
Pump La. Orp—7M 129
Pump Pail N. Croy—5A 124
Pump Pail S. Croy—5A 124
Punderson's Gdns. E2—6F 60
Purbeck Av. N Mald—1D 120
Purbeck Dri. NW2—7H 41
Purbeck Rd. Horn—5E 50
Purberry Gro. Eps—2D 134
Purbrock Av. Wat—9G 5
Purbrook St. SE1—4C 76
Purcell Clo. Borwd—3H 11
Purcell Cres. SW6—8J 73
Purcell Rd. Gnfd—8M 53
Purcells Av. Edgw—5L 23
Purcell St. N1—5C 60
Purchese St. NW1—5H 59
Purdy St. E3—7M 61
Purfleet By-Pass. Purf—5M 83
Purfleet Rd. S Ock—3L 83
Purland Clo. Dag—6K 49
Purland Way. SE28—3D 80
Purleigh Av. Wfd G—6J 31
Purley Av. NW2—7J 41
Purley Bury Av. Purl—3A 138
Purley Bury Clo. Purl—3A 138
Purley Clo. Ilf—9L 31
Purley Downs Rd. Purl & S Croy
—2A 138
Purley Hill Rd. Purl—4M 137
Purley Knoll. Purl—3K 137
Purley Oaks Rd. S Croy
—1B 138
Purley Pk. Rd. Purl—2M 137
Purley Pl. N1—3M 59
Purley Rise. Purl—4K 137
Purley Rd. N9—3C 28
Purley Rd. Purl—3L 137
Purley Rd. S Croy—9B 124
Purley Vale. Purl—5M 137
Purley Way. Croy & Purl
—2K 123
Purlings Rd. Bush, Wat—7M 9
Purneys Rd. SE9—3H 95
Purrett Rd. SE18—6D 80
Purser's Cross Rd. SW6—9K 73
Pursewardens Clo. W13—2G 71
Pursley Gdns. Borwd—2L 11
Pursley Rd. NW7—7F 24

Purves Rd. NW10—5F 56
Putney Bri. SW15 & SW6—2J 89
Putney Bri. App. SW6—2J 89
Putney Bri. Rd.—3J 89
  SW18 1-73 & 2-114
  SW15 remainder
Putney Comn. SW15—2G 89
Putney Heath. SW15—5F 88
Putney Heath La. SW15—5H 89
Putney High St. SW15—3J 89
Putney Hill. SW15—5H 89
Putney Pk. Av. SW15—3E 88
Putney Pk. La. SW15—3F 88
Putney Rd. Enf—9D 6
Puttenham Clo. Wat—3G 21
Pyecombe Corner. N12—4K 25
Pylbrook Rd. Sutt—5L 121
Pymers Mead. SE21—7A 92
Pym Clo. Barn—7B 14
Pym Ho. SW9—1L 91
Pymmes Clo. N13—5K 27
Pymmes Gdns. N. N9—3D 28
Pymmes Gdns. S. N9—3D 28
Pymmes Grn. Rd. N11—4F 26
Pymmes Rd. N13—6J 27
Pymms Brook Dri. Barn—6C 14
Pyne Rd. Surb—3L 119
Pynest Grn. La. Wal A—2E 18
Pynham Clo. SE2—4F 80
Pynnacles Clo. Stan—5F 22
Pyrcroft La. Wey—7A 116
Pyrland Rd. N5—1B 60
Pyrland Rd. Rich—5K 87
Pyrles Grn. Lou—3M 19
Pyrles La. Lou—4M 19
Pyrmont Gro. SE27—9M 91
Pyrmont Rd. W4—7L 71
Pytchley Cres. SE19—3A 108
Pytchley Rd. SE5—2C 92

Quadrant Arc. Romf—3C 50
Quadrant Gro. NW5—1D 58
Quadrant Rd. Rich—3H 87
Quadrant Rd. T Hth—8M 107
Quadrant, The. NW4—2G 41
Quadrant, The. SW20—5J 105
Quadrant, The. Bexh—8H 81
Quadrant, The. Purf—5M 83
Quadrant, The. Rich—3J 87
Quadrant, The. Sutt—8A 122
Quaggy Wlk. SE3—3E 94
Quail Gdns. S Croy—2J 139
Quainton St. NW10—8B 40
Quaker La. Iswth—8E 70
  (in two parts)
Quaker La. S'hall—4L 69
Quaker La. Wal A—7J 7
Quakers Course. NW9—8D 24
Quaker St. E1—7D 60
Quakers Wlk. N21—8B 16
Quantock Clo. Hay—8B 68
Quantock Gdns. NW2—7H 41
Quantock Rd. Bexh—1C 98
Quarles Clo. Romf—7L 33
Quarley Way. SE15—8D 76
Quarrendon St. SW6—1L 89
Quarr Rd. Cars—1C 122
Quarry Pk. Rd. Sutt—8K 121
Quarry Rise. Sutt—8K 121
Quarry Rd. SW18—5A 90
Quarter Mile La. E10 & E15
—9M 45
Quebec M. W1—9D 58
Quebec Rd. Hay—1G 69
Quebec Rd. Ilf—5M.47
Quebec Way. SE16—3J 77
Queen Adelaide Ct. SE20
—3G 109
Queen Adelaide Rd. SE20
—4G 109
Queen Anne Av. N15—3D 44
Queen Anne Av. Brom—7D 110
Queen Anne Dri. Esh—9C 118
Queen Anne M. W1—8F 58
Queen Anne Rd. E9—2H 61
Queen Anne's Clo. Twic—9B 86
Queen Anne's Gdns. W4—4C 72
Queen Anne's Gdns. W5—3J 71
Queen Anne's Gdns. Enf—8C 16
Queen Anne's Gdns. Mitc
—7D 106
Queen Anne's Ga. SW1—3H 75
Queen Anne's Ga. Bexh—2H 97
Queen Anne's Gro. W4—4C 72
Queen Anne's Gro. W5—3J 71
Queen Anne's Gro. Enf—9B 16
Queen Anne's Pl. Enf—8D 16
Queen Anne St. W1—8F 58
Queenborough Gdns. Ilf—2L 47
Queen Caroline St. W6—6G 73
Queen Elizabeth Gdns. Mord
—8L 105

Queen Elizabeth Ho. SW12
—6E 90
Queen Elizabeth Rd. E17—1J 45
Queen Elizabeth Rd. King
—6K 103
Queen Elizabeth's Clo. N16
—7B 44
Queen Elizabeth's Dri. N14
—1J 27
Queen Elizabeth's Dri. Croy
—1B 140
Queen Elizabeth's Gdns. Croy
—2B 140
Queen Elizabeth St. SE1—3D 76
Queen Elizabeth's Wlk. N16
—7B 44
Queen Elizabeth Wlk. SW13
—9F 72
Queen Elizabeth Wlk. Wall
—6H 123
Queenhill Rd. S Croy—2F 138
Queenhithe. EC4—1A 76
Queen Margaret's Gro. N1
—1C 60
Queen Mary Av. Mord—9H 105
Queen Mary Rd. SE19—3M 107
Queen Mary Rd. Shep—6A 100
Queen Mary's Av. Cars—9D 122
Queen Mary's Av. Wat—6C 8
Queens Acre. Sutt—9J 121
Queens Av. N3—7A 26
Queens Av. N10—1E 42
Queens Av. N20—2B 26
Queens Av. N21—1M 27
Queens Av. Felt—1G 101
Queen's Av. Gnfd—9M 53
Queen's Av. Stan—1G 39
Queen's Av. Wat—6D 8
Queen's Av. Wfd G—5F 30
Queensberry M. W. SW7
—5B 74
Queensberry Pl. SW7—5B 74
Queensberry Way. SW7—5B 74
Queensborough M. W2—1A 74
Queensborough Ter. W2
—1M 73
Queensbridge Pk. Iswth—5C 86
Queensbridge Rd.—2D 60
  E2 1-173 & 2-120
  E8 remainder
Queensbury Ho. Rich—4H 87
Queensbury Rd. NW9—5B 40
Queensbury Rd. Wemb—5K 55
Queensbury Sta. Pde. Edgw
—1K 39
Queensbury St. N1—3A 60
Queen's Cir. SW8—8F 74
Queens Clo. Edgw—5L 23
Queens Clo. Esh—6M 117
Queen's Clo. Wall—7F 122
Queen's Club Gdns. W14—7J 73
Queens Ct. SE23—8G 93
Queens Ct. Harr—9G 23
Queens Ct. Rich—5K 87
Queenscourt. Wemb—9J 37
Queens Ct. Wey—8C 116
Queen's Cres. NW5—2E 58
Queen's Cres. Rich—4K 87
Queenscroft Rd. SE9—5H 95
Queensdale Cres. W11—2H 73
Queensdale Pl. W11—2J 73
Queensdale Rd. W11—2J 73
Queensdale Wlk. W11—2J 73
Queensdown Rd. E5—9F 44
Queens Dri. E10—5L 45
Queens Dri. N4—7M 43
Queens Dri. W3—9K 55
Queens Dri. Abb L, Wat—5D 4
Queen's Dri. Lea—3A 132
Queen's Dri. Surb—2L 119
Queen's Dri. Th Dit—1E 118
Queen's Dri. Wal X—6F 7
Queen's Elm Sq. SW3—6B 74
Queensferry Wlk. N17—2F 44
Queen's Gdns. NW4—3G 41
Queen's Gdns. SW1—3G 75
Queen's Gdns. W2—1A 74
Queen's Gdns. W5—7G 55
Queens Gdns. Dart—7M 99
Queen's Gdns. Houn—9J 69
Queen's Gdns. Rain—5B 66
Queen's Ga. SW7—4A 74
Queen's Ga. Gdns. SW7—4A 74
Queens Ga. Gdns. SW15—3F 88
Queensgate Gdns. Chst
—5B 112
Queen's Ga. M. SW7—4A 74
Queensgate Pl. NW6—3L 57
Queen's Ga. Pl. SW7—4A 74
Queen's Ga. Pl. M. SW7—4A 74
Queen's Ga. Ter. SW7—4A 74
Queen's Gro. NW8—4B 58
Queens Gro. Rd. E4—1B 30

Queen's Head St. N1—4M 59
Queen's Ho. Tedd—3D 102
Queensland Av. N18—6A 28
Queensland Av. SW19—5M 105
Queensland Pl. N7—9L 43
Queensland Rd. N7—9L 43
Queens La. N10—1F 42
Queens La. Ashf—9D 144
Queensmead. NW8—4B 58
Queens Mead Rd. Brom
—6D 110
Queensmere Clo. SW19—8H 89
Queensmere Rd. SW19—8H 89
Queensmill Rd. SW6—8H 73
Queens Pde. N8—2M 43
Queen's Pde. N11—5D 26
Queens Pde. W5—9K 55
Queen's Pk. Gdns. Felt—9D 84
Queen's Pk. Rd. Romf—8L 35
Queen's Pl. Mord—8L 105
Queen's Pl. Wat—5G 9
Queen's Promenade. King
—8H 103
Queen Sq. WC1—7J 59
Queens Ride. SW13 & SW15
—2E 88
Queens Rise. Rich—5K 87
Queens Rd. E11—5C 46
Queen's Rd. E13—4F 62
Queen's Rd. E17—4K 45
Queen's Rd. N3—8A 26
Queen's Rd. N9—2F 28
Queen's Rd. N11—7J 27
Queen's Rd. NW4—3G 41
Queen's Rd.—9F 76
  SE15 1-289 & 2-222
  SE14 remainder
Queen's Rd. SW14—2B 88
Queen's Rd. SW19—3L 105
Queen's Rd. W5—9J 55
Queens Rd. Bark—3A 64
Queens Rd. Barn—5H 13
Queens Rd. Beck—6J 109
Queen's Rd. Brom—6E 110
Queen's Rd. Buck H—2F 30
Queen's Rd. Chst—3M 111
Queen's Rd. Croy—1M 123
Queen's Rd. Enf—6C 16
Queen's Rd. Eri—7C 82
Queen's Rd. Felt—7F 84
Queen's Rd. Hmptn—1M 101
Queen's Rd. Hay—9C 52
Queen's Rd. Houn—2M 85
Queen's Rd. King—4L 103
Queen's Rd. Lou—5J 19
Queen's Rd. Mitc—7B 106
Queen's Rd. Mord—8L 105
Queen's Rd. N Mald—8D 104
Queen's Rd. Rich—6K 87
Queen's Rd. Sutt—3L 135
Queen's Rd. Tedd—3D 102
Queen's Rd. Th Dit—9D 102
Queen's Rd. Twic—7E 86
Queen's Rd. Uxb—6A 142
Queen's Rd. Wall—7F 122
Queen's Rd. Wal X—6E 6
Queen's Rd. W on T—7F 116
Queen's Rd. Wat—5G 9
  (in two parts)
Queen's Rd. Well—1F 96
Queen's Rd. W Dray—3K 143
Queens Rd. Wey & W on T
—7A 116
Queens Rd. W. E13—5E 62
Queen's Row. SE17—7B 76
Queen's St. Eri—7C 82
Queen's Ter. E13—4F 62
Queen's Ter. NW8—5B 58
Queens Ter. Iswth—3E 86
Queen's Ter. Cotts. W7—3C 70
Queensthorpe Rd. SE26
—1H 109
Queenstown Gdns. Rain—6D 66
Queenstown Rd. SW8—2F 90
Queen St. EC4—1A 76
Queen St. N17—6C 28
Queen St. Bexh—2K 97
Queen St. Croy—6A 124
Queen St. Romf—4B 50
Queen St. Mayfair. W1—2F 74
Queen St. Pl. EC4—1A 76
Queensville Rd. SW12—6H 91
Queens Wlk. E4—1B 30
Queens Wlk. NW9—7A 40
Queen's Wlk. SW1—2G 75
Queen's Wlk. W5—7G 55
Queen's Wlk. Ashf—9H 144
Queens Wlk. Harr—2C 38
Queens Wlk. Ruis—7G 37
Queen's Way. NW4—3G 41

Queensway. W2—9M 57
Queensway. Croy—7K 123
Queensway. Enf—6F 16
Queens Way. Felt—1G 101
Queensway. Orp—9A 112
Queensway. Sun—6E 100
Queensway. Wal X—7F 6
Queensway. W Wick—6D 126
Queensway. N W on T—6G 117
Queensway. S W on T—7G 117
  (in two parts)
Queenswell Av. N20—4C 26
Queenswood Av. E17—8A 30
Queenswood Av. Hmptn
—3M 101
Queenswood Av. Houn—1K 85
Queenswood Av. T Hth—9L 107
Queenswood Av. Wall—6H 123
Queenswood Ct. SE27—1B 108
Queenswood Cres. Wat—6E 4
Queenswood Gdns. E11—6F 46
Queenswood Pk. N3—9J 25
Queens Wood Rd. N10—4F 42
Queenswood Rd. SE23—9H 93
Queenswood Rd. Sidc—5D 96
Queen Victoria Av. Wemb
—3H 55
Queen Victoria St. EC4—1M 75
Quemerford Rd. N7—1K 59
Quendon Dri. Wal A—6K 7
Quentin Pl. SE13—2C 94
Quentin Rd. SE13—2C 94
Quernmore Clo. Brom—3E 110
Quernmore Rd. N4—4L 43
Quernmore Rd. Brom—3E 110
Querrin St. SW6—1A 90
Quex M. NW6—4L 57
Quex Rd. NW6—4L 57
Quick Pl. N1—4M 59
Quick Rd. W4—6C 72
Quicksilver Pl. N22—9K 27
Quicks Rd. SW19—4M 105
Quick St. N1—5M 59
Quickswood. NW3—3C 58
Quiet Nook. Kes—5H 127
Quill La. SW15—3H 89
Quillot, The. W on T—7D 116
Quilp St. SE1—3A 76
Quilter Gdns. Orp—3G 129
Quilter Rd. Orp—3G 129
Quilter St. E2—6E 60
Quinta Dri. Barn—7F 12
Quintin Av. SW20—5K 105
Quinton Clo. Beck—7A 110
Quinton Clo. Wall—6F 122
Quinton Rd. Th Dit—3E 118
Quinton St. SW18—8A 90
Quinton Way. Wal A—8J 7
Quixley St. E14—9J 61
Quorn Rd. SE22—3C 92

Rabbit La. W on T—9E 116
Rabbit Row. W8—2L 73
Rabbits Rd. E12—9J 47
Rabbs Mill Ho. Uxb—5A 142
Raby Rd. N Mald—8B 104
Raby St. E14—9J 61
Raccoon Way. Houn—1G 85
Racton Rd. SW6—7L 73
Radbourne Av. W5—5G 71
Radbourne Clo. E5—9H 45
Radbourne Cres. E17—1B 46
Radbourne Rd. SW12—6G 91
Radcliffe Av. NW10—5E 56
Radcliffe Av. Enf—3A 16
Radcliffe Gdns. Cars—9C 122
Radcliffe Rd. N21—1M 27
Radcliffe Rd. Croy—4D 124
Radcliffe Rd. Stan—9E 22
Radcliffe Sq. SW15—5H 89
Radcliffe Way. N'holt—6H 53
Radcot St. SE11—6L 75
Raddington Rd. W10—8J 57
Radfield Way. Sidc—6B 96
Radford Rd. SE13—5A 94
Radford Way. Bark—6D 64
Radipole Rd. SW6—9K 73
Radland Rd. E16—9D 62
Radlett Av. SE26—8F 92
Radlett Clo. E7—2D 62
Radlett Pl. NW8—4C 58
Radlett Rd. Wat—5G 9
Radlett Rd. Wat—2M 9
  (Aldenham)
Radley Av. Ilf—9E 48
Radley Gdns. Harr—2J 39
Radley M. W8—4M 73
Radley Rd. N17—9C 28
Radley's La. E18—9E 30
Radleys Mead. Dag—2M 65
Radley Sq. E5—7G 45
Radlix Rd. E10—6L 45

Redbury Clo. Rain—7G 67
Redcar Clo. N'holt—1M 53
Redcar Rd. Romf—5K 35
Redcar St. SE5—8A 76
Redcastle Clo. E1—1G 77
Red Cedars Rd. Orp—2C 128
Redchurch St. E2—7D 60
Redcliffe Gdns. SW10—6M 73
Redcliffe Gdns. Ilf—6L 47
Redcliffe M. SW10—6M 73
Redcliffe Pl. SW10—7A 74
Redcliffe Rd. SW10—7A 74
Redcliffe Sq. SW10—6M 73
Redcliffe St. SW10—7M 73
Redclose Av. Mord—9L 105
Redclyffe Rd. E6—4G 63
Redcroft Rd. S'hall—1A 70
Redden Ct. Rd. Romf—1J 51
Reddings Av. Bush, Wat—7M 9
Reddings Clo. NW7—4D 24
Reddings, The. NW7—3D 24
Reddings, The. Borwd—5K 11
Reddington Clo. S Croy
—1B 138
Reddins Rd. SE15—8E 76
Reddons Rd. Beck—4J 109
Reddown Rd. Coul—9H 137
Reddy Rd. Eri—7D 82
Rede Pl. W2—9L 57
Redesdale Gdns. Iswth—8E 70
Redesdale St. SW3—7D 74
Redfern Av. Houn—6L 85
Redfern Clo. Uxb—4A 142
Redfern Gdns. Romf—9H 35
Redfern Rd. NW10—3C 56
Redfern Rd. SE6—6A 94
Redfield La. SW5—5L 73
Redford Av. Coul—7F 136
Redford Av. T Hth—8K 107
Redford Av. Wall—8J 123
Redford Way. Uxb—3B 142
Redgate Dri. Brom—4F 126
Redgate Ter. SW15—5H 89
Redgrave Rd. SW15—2H 89
Redheath Clo. Wat—8D 4
Red Hill. Chst—2M 111
Redhill Ct. SW2—8L 91
Redhill Dri. Edgw—9A 24
Redhill St. NW1—5F 58
Red Ho. La. Bexh—3J 97
Red Ho. La. W on T—4E 116
Redhouse Rd. Croy—1H 123
Redington Gdns. NW3—9M 41
Redington Rd. NW3—8M 41
Redlands. Coul—8J 137
Redlands Ct. Brom—4D 110
Redlands Gdns. E Mol—8K 101
Redlands Rd. Enf—3J 17
Redlands Way. SW2—6K 91
Red La. Esh—8E 118
Redlaw Way. SE16—6E 76
Redleaf Clo. Belv—7L 81
Redleaves Av. Ashf—3A 100
Redlees Clo. Iswth—3E 86
Red Lion Clo. Orp—1G 129
Red Lion Ct. EC4—9L 59
Red Lion Hill. N2—9B 26
Red Lion La. SE18—9L 79
Red Lion Pl. SE18—9L 79
Red Lion Rd. Surb—4K 119
Red Lion Sq. WC1—8K 59
Red Lion St. WC1—8K 59
Red Lion St. Rich—4H 87
Red Lion Way. SE17—7A 76
Red Lion Yd. Wat—6G 9
Red Lodge Cres. Bex—9C 98
Red Lodge Rd. Bex—9B 98
Red Lodge Rd. W Wick—2A 126
Redmans La. Sev—8A 130
Redman's Rd. E1—8G 61
Redmead La. E1—2E 76
Redmead Rd. Hay—5C 68
Redmore Rd. W6—5F 72
Red Oak Clo. Orp—4M 127
Red Pl. W1—1E 74
Redpoll Way. Eri—4H 81
Red Post Hill—3B 92
  SE21 1-9 & 2-12
  SE24 remainder
Redriffe Rd. E13—4D 62
Redriff Rd. SE16—4H 77
Redriff Rd. Romf—9M 33
Red Rd. Borwd—5K 11
Redruth Clo. N22—7K 27
Redruth Gdns. Romf—5K 35
Redruth Rd. E9—4G 61
Redruth Rd. Romf—5K 35
Redruth Wlk. Romf—5K 35
Redstart Clo. Croy—2B 140
Redston Rd. N8—2H 43
Redvers Rd. N22—9L 27
Redvers St. N1—6C 60

Redwald Rd. E5—9H 45
Redway Dri. Twic—6A 86
Redwing Clo. S Croy—3H 139
Redwing Path. SE28—4B 80
Redwood Clo. N14—9H 15
Redwood Clo. SE16—2J 77
Redwood Clo. Kenl—6A 138
Redwood Clo. Uxb—5F 142
Redwood Clo. Wat—4H 21
Redwood Ct. N'holt—6J 53
Redwood Ct. Surb—2H 119
Redwood Est. Houn—7F 68
Redwood Gdns. Chig—5E 32
Redwood Rise. Borwd—1L 11
Redwoods. SW15—7E 88
Reece M. SW7—5B 74
Reed Av. Orp—5C 128
Reed Clo. E16—8E 62
Reed Clo. SE12—4E 94
Reede Gdns. Dag—1M 65
Reede Rd. Dag—2L 65
Reede Way. Dag—2M 65
Reedham Clo. N17—2F 44
Reedham Clo. St Alb—2L 5
Reedham Dri. Purl—5K 137
Reedham Pk. Av. Purl—8L 137
Reedham Rd. SE15—2E 92
Reedholm Vs. N16—9B 44
Reed Pond Wlk. Romf—9D 34
Reed Rd. N17—9D 28
Reedsfield Rd. Ashf—9F 144
Reed's Pl. NW1—3G 59
Reedworth St. SE11—5L 75
Reenglass Rd. Stan—4H 23
Rees Gdns. Croy—1D 124
Reesland Clo. E12—2L 63
Rees St. N1—4A 60
Reets Farm Clo. NW9—4C 40
Reeves Av. NW9—5B 40
Reeves Corner. Croy—4M 123
Reeves Cres. Swan—7B 114
Reeves M. W1—1E 74
Reeves Path. Hay—6D 68
Reeves Rd. E3—7M 61
Reeves Rd. SE18—7M 79
Reform Row. N17—9D 28
Reform St. SW11—1D 90
Regal Clo. E1—8E 60
Regal Clo. W5—8H 55
Regal Ct. N18—5D 28
Regal Cres. Wall—5F 122
Regal La. NW1—4E 58
Regal Way. Harr—4J 39
Regan Way. N1—5C 60
Regarder Rd. Chig—5F 32
Regarth Av. Romf—4C 50
Regency Clo. W5—9J 55
Regency Clo. Chig—5A 32
Regency Clo. Hmptn—2K 101
Regency Dri. Ruis—6C 36
Regency M. Iswth—4C 86
Regency Pl. SW1—5H 75
Regency St. SW1—5H 75
Regency Wlk. Croy—1K 125
Regency Way. Bexh—2H 97
Regent Av. Uxb—3F 142
Regent Clo. N12—5A 26
Regent Clo. Harr—4J 39
Regent Clo. Houn—9F 68
Regent Ct. N20—2A 26
Regent Pl. W1—1G 75
Regent Pl. Croy—3D 124
Regent Rd. SE24—4M 91
Regent Rd. Surb—9K 103
Regents Av. N13—5L 27
Regents Clo. S Croy—8C 124
Regents Clo. Whyt—9D 138
Regents Ct. Edgw—4J 23
Regents Dri. Kes—7H 127
Regents M. NW8—5A 58
Regent's Pk. Gdns. M. NW1
—4E 58
Regents Pk. Rd. N3—1K 41
Regent's Pk. Rd. NW1—4D 58
Regent's Pk. Rd. NW1—4F 58
Regent's Pl. SE3—1E 94
Regent Sq. E3—6M 61
Regent Sq. WC1—6J 59
Regent Sq. Belv—5M 81
Regent's Row. E8—4E 60
Regent St. NW10—6H 57
Regent St.—9F 58
  SW1 1-37 & 2-36
  W1 remainder
Regent St. W4—6L 71
Regent St. Wat—2F 8
Regina Clo. Barn—5H 13
Reginald Rd. E7—2E 62
Reginald Rd. SE8—8L 77
Reginald Rd. N'wd—8D 20
Reginald Rd. Romf—8L 35
Reginald Sq. SE8—8L 77

Regina Rd. N4—6K 43
Regina Rd. SE25—7E 108
Regina Rd. W13—2E 70
Regina Rd. S'hall—5J 69
Regina Ter. W13—2F 70
Regis Rd. NW5—1F 58
Reid Clo. Pinn—2E 36
Reidhaven Rd. SE18—5C 80
Reigate Av. Sutt—3L 121
Reigate Av. Brom—9D 94
Reigate Rd. Eps & Tad—2E 134
Reigate Rd. Ilf—7D 48
Reigate Way. Wall—7J 123
Reighton Rd. E5—8E 44
Relay Rd. W12—2G 73
Relf Rd. SE15—2E 92
Relko Ct. Eps—3B 134
Relko Gdns. Sutt—7B 122
Relton M. SW7—4C 74
Rembrandt Rd. SE13—3C 94
Rembrandt Rd. Edgw—9L 23
Rembrandt Way. W on T
—4F 116
Remington Rd. E6—9J 63
Remington Rd. N15—4B 44
Remington St. N1—5M 59
Rempstone M. N1—5B 60
Remus Rd. E3—3L 61
Rendlesham Av. Rad—1D 10
Rendlesham Rd. E5—9E 44
Rendlesham Rd. Enf—3M 15
Renforth St. SE16—3G 77
Renfrew Clo. E6—1L 79
Renfrew Ct. Houn—1J 85
Renfrew Rd. SE11—5M 75
Renfrew Rd. Houn—1J 85
Renfrew Rd. King—4M 103
Renmans, The. Asht—8K 133
Renmuir St. SW17—3D 106
Rennell St. SE13—2A 94
Renness Rd. E17—1J 45
Rennets Clo. SE9—4C 96
Rennets Wood Rd. SE9—4B 96
Rennie Clo. Ashf—9B 144
Rennies Est. SE16—5F 76
Rennie St. SE1—2M 75
Renown Clo. Croy—3M 123
Renown Clo. Romf—8L 33
Rensburg Rd. E17—4H 45
Renshaw Clo. Belv—7K 81
Renters Av. NW4—4G 41
Renton Dri. Orp—2H 129
Renwick Clo. Orp—8H 113
Renwick Rd. Bark—7F 64
Repens Way. Hay—7H 53
Rephidim St. SE1—4C 76
Replingham Rd. SW18—7K 89
Reporton Rd. SW6—8J 73
Repository Rd. SE18—7K 79
Repton Av. Hay—5B 68
Repton Av. Wemb—9G 39
Repton Clo. Cars—7C 122
Repton Ct. Beck—5M 109
Repton Ct. Ilf—8K 31
Repton Dri. Romf—2E 50
Repton Gdns. Romf—1E 50
Repton Gro. Ilf—8K 31
Repton Rd. Harr—2K 39
Repton Rd. Orp—5E 128
Repton St. E14—9J 61
Repulse Clo. Romf—8L 33
Reservoir Rd. N14—7G 15
Reservoir Rd. SE4—1J 93
Reservoir Rd. Lou—3F 18
Reservoir Rd. Ruis—2B 36
Resolution Wlk. SE18—4K 79
Restell Clo. SE3—7C 78
Reston Clo. Borwd—2L 11
Reston Path. Borwd—2L 11
Reston Pl. SW7—3A 74
Restons Cres. SE9—5B 96
Restormel Clo. Houn—4L 85
Retcar Clo. N19—7F 42
Retford Clo. Romf—6L 35
Retford Path. Romf—6L 35
Retford Rd. Romf—6K 35
Retford St. N1—5C 60
Retingham Way. E4—2M 29
Retreat Clo. Harr—3G 39
Retreat Pl. E9—2G 61
Retreat Rd. Rich—4H 87
Retreat, The. NW9—3B 40
Retreat, The. SW14—2C 88
Retreat, The. Abb L, Wat—4A 4
Retreat, The. Harr—5L 37
Retreat, The. Orp—8F 128
Retreat, The. Surb—1K 119
Retreat, The. T Hth—8B 108
Retreat, The. Wor Pk—5F 120
Retreat Way. Chig—3F 32
Revell Rise. SE18—7D 80

Revell Rd. King—6M 103
Revell Rd. Sutt—8K 121
Revelon Rd. SE4—2J 93
Revelstoke Rd. SW18—8K 89
Reventlow Rd. SE9—7A 96
Reverdy Rd. SE1—5E 76
Revesby Rd. Cars—1C 122
Review Rd. NW2—7D 40
Review Rd. Dag—5M 65
Rewell St. SW6—8A 74
Rewley Rd. Cars—1B 122
Rex Clo. Romf—7M 33
Rex Pl. W1—1E 74
Reydon Av. E11—4G 47
Reynard Clo. Brom—7K 111
Reynard Dri. SE19—4D 108
Reynardson Rd. N17—7A 28
Reynards Way. St Alb—2K 5
Reynolds Av. E12—1L 63
Reynolds Av. Chess—9J 119
Reynolds Av. Romf—5G 49
Reynolds Clo. NW11—5M 41
Reynolds Clo. Cars—3D 122
Reynolds Dri. Edgw—1K 39
Reynold's Pl. SE3—8F 78
Reynolds Pl. Rich—5K 87
Reynolds Rd. SE15—3G 93
Reynolds Rd. W4—4A 72
Reynolds Rd. Hay—7G 53
Reynolds Rd. N Mald—2B 120
Reynolds Way. Croy—6C 124
Rheidol M. N1—5A 60
Rheidol Ter. N1—4A 60
Rheingold Way. Wall—1J 137
Rheola Clo. N17—8D 28
Rhoda St. E2—7D 60
Rhodes Av. N22—8G 27
Rhodesia Rd. E11—7B 46
Rhodesia Rd. SW9—1J 91
Rhodesmoor Ho. Ct. Mord
—1L 121
Rhodes St. N7—1K 59
Rhodes Way. Wat—4H 9
Rhodeswell Rd. E14—9K 61
Rhodrons Av. Chess—7J 119
Rhondda Gro. E3—6J 61
Rhyl Rd. Gnfd—5D 54
Rhyl St. NW5—2E 58
Rhys Av. N11—7H 27
Rialto Rd. Mitc—6E 106
Ribble Clo. Wfd G—6G 31
Ribblesdale Av. N'holt—2M 53
Ribblesdale Rd. N8—2K 43
Ribblesdale Rd. SW16—3F 106
Ribblesdale Rd. Dart—7M 99
Ribchester Av. Gnfd—6D 54
Ribston Clo. Brom—3K 125
Ricardo Path. SE28—2G 81
Ricardo St. E14—9M 61
Ricards Rd. SW19—2C 105
Richard Clo. SE18—5J 79
Richards Av. Romf—4A 50
Richards Clo. Harr—3E 38
Richards Clo. Hay—7B 68
Richards Clo. Uxb—4E 142
Richardson Rd. E15—5C 62
Richards Pl. E17—1L 45
Richard's Pl. SW3—5C 74
Richard St. E1—9F 60
(in two parts)
Richbell Clo. Asht—9H 133
Richbell Pl. WC1—8K 59
Richborne Ter. SW8—8K 75
Richborough Clo. Orp—8H 113
Richborough Rd. NW2—9J 41
Riches Rd. Ilf—7A 48
Richfield Rd. Bush, Wat—9A 10
Richford Rd. E15—4D 62
Richford St. W6—3G 73
Richland Av. Coul—6E 136
Richlands Av. Eps—6E 120
Rich La. SW5—6M 73
Richmer Rd. Eri—8E 82
Richmond Av. E4—5B 30
Richmond Av. N1—4K 59
Richmond Av. NW10—2G 57
Richmond Av. SW20—5J 105
Richmond Av. Uxb—2F 142
Richmond Br. Twic & Rich
—5H 87
Richmond Bldgs. W1—9H 59
Richmond Clo. E17—4K 45
Richmond Clo. Eps—6C 134
Richmond Clo. Wal X—2C 6
Richmond Cres. E4—5B 30
Richmond Cres. N1—4L 59
Richmond Cres. N9—1E 28
Richmond Dri. Shep—1B 116
Richmond Dri. Wat—4C 8
Richmond Gdns. NW4—3E 40
Richmond Gdns. Harr—7D 22
Richmond Grn. Croy—5J 123
Richmond Gro. N1—3M 59

Richmond Gro. Surb—1K 119
Richmond Hill. Rich—5J 87
Richmond Hill Ct. Rich—5J 87
Richmond M. W1—9H 59
Richmond M. Tedd—2D 102
Richmond Pk. Rd. SW14—4A 88
Richmond Pk. Rd. King—4J 103
Richmond Pl. SE18—5A 80
Richmond Rd. E4—1B 30
Richmond Rd. E7—1F 62
Richmond Rd. E8—3D 60
Richmond Rd. E11—7B 46
Richmond Rd. N2—9A 26
Richmond Rd. N11—6J 27
Richmond Rd. N15—4C 44
Richmond Rd. SW20—5F 104
Richmond Rd. W5—3J 71
Richmond Rd. Barn—7M 13
Richmond Rd. Coul—7F 136
Richmond Rd. Croy—5J 123
Richmond Rd. Ilf—8A 48
Richmond Rd. Iswth—2E 86
Richmond Rd. King—2H 103
Richmond Rd. Romf—4D 50
Richmond Rd. T Hth—7M 107
Richmond Rd. Twic—6F 86
Richmond St. E13—5E 62
Richmond Ter. SW1—3J 75
Richmond Ter. M. SW1—3J 75
Richmond Way. E11—7E 46
Richmond Way—3H 73
  W12 1-15 & 2-52
  W14 remainder
Richmount Gdns. SE3—2E 94
Rich St. E14—1K 77
Rickard Clo. SW2—7L 91
Rickard Clo. W Dray—4H 143
Rickards Clo. Surb—3J 119
Ricketts Hill Rd. West—9H 141
Rickett St. SW6—7L 73
Rickfields. Harr—7B 38
Rickman Hill. Coul—9F 136
Rickman Hill Rd. Coul—9F 136
Rickman St. E1—7G 61
Rickmansworth Rd. N'wd
—5A 20
Rickmansworth Rd. Pinn
—9F 20
Rickmansworth Rd. Wat—6C 8
Rickthorne Rd. N19—7J 43
Rickyard Path. SE9—3J 95
Riddlesdown Av. Purl—4A 138
Riddlesdown Rd. Purl & Kenl
—3A 138
Riddons Rd. SE12—9G 95
Rideout St. SE18—5K 79
Rider Clo. Sidc—5C 96
Ride, The. Bren—6F 70
Ride, The. Enf—6H 17
Ridge Av. N21—9A 16
Ridge Av. Dart—5D 98
Ridgebrook Rd. SE3—2H 95
Ridge Clo. NW4—9H 25
Ridge Clo. NW9—2B 40
Ridge Crest. Enf—3K 15
Ridgecroft Clo. Bex—7A 98
Ridgedale St. E3—5M 61
Ridge Hill. NW11—6J 41
Ridgehurst Av. Wat—7D 4
Ridge La. Wat—1D 8
Ridge Langley. S Croy—2E 138
Ridgemont Gdns. Edgw—4A 24
Ridgemount. Wey—4C 116
Ridgemount Av. Coul—9F 136
Ridgemount Av. Croy—3H 125
Ridgemount Clo. SE20—4F 108
Ridgemount Gdns. Enf—4M 15
Ridge Pk. Purl—2H 137
Ridge Rd. N8—4K 43
Ridge Rd. N21—1A 28
Ridge Rd. NW2—8K 41
Ridge Rd. Mitc—4F 106
Ridge Rd. Sutt—3J 121
Ridge St. Wat—2F 8
Ridge, The. Barn—7K 13
Ridge, The. Bex—6K 97
Ridge, The. Coul—6J 137
Ridge, The. Eps—9A 134
Ridge, The. Orp—4B 128
Ridge, The. Purl—2H 137
Ridge, The. Surb—9L 103
Ridge, The. Twic—6B 86
Ridgeview Clo. Barn—8H 13
Ridgeview Rd. N20—3M 25
Ridge Way. SE19—3C 108
Ridgeway. Brom—4E 126
Ridge Way. Dart—5D 98
  (Crayford)
Ridgeway. Eps—4A 134
Ridge Way. Felt—9J 85
Ridge Way. Wfd G—4G 31

Ridgeway Av. Barn—8D 14
Ridgeway Clo. Lea—6A 132
Ridgeway Cres. Orp—5C 128
Ridgeway Cres. Gdns. Orp
—5C 128
Ridgeway Dri. Brom—2F 110
Ridgeway E. Sidc—4D 96
Ridgeway Gdns. Ilf—3J 47
Ridgeway Rd. Iswth—8C 70
Ridgeway Rd. N. Iswth—8C 70
Ridgeway, The. E4—1A 30
Ridgeway, The. N3—7M 25
Ridgeway, The. N11—4D 26
Ridgeway, The. N14—2J 27
Ridgeway, The. NW7—4F 24
Ridgeway, The. NW9—2B 40
Ridgeway, The. NW11—6K 41
Ridgeway, The. W3—4L 71
Ridgeway, The. Croy—5K 123
Ridgeway, The. Enf & Pot B
—4M 15
Ridgeway, The. Harr—4G 39
(Kenton)
Ridgeway, The. Harr—3K &
5M 37
(North Harrow)
Ridgeway, The. Lea—6A 132
(Oxshott)
Ridgeway, The. Rad—1E 10
Ridgeway, The. Romf—2E 50
Ridgeway, The. Romf—8K 35
(Harold Wood)
Ridgeway, The. Ruis—5E 36
Ridge Way, The. S Croy—2C 138
Ridgeway, The. Stan—6G 23
Ridgeway, The. Sutt—8B 122
Ridgeway, The. W on T—3D 116
Ridgeway W. Sidc—4C 96
Ridgewell Clo. N1—1A 60
Ridgewell Clo. Dag—4M 65
Ridgmount Gdns. WC1—8H 59
Ridgmount Pl. WC1—8H 59
Ridgmount Rd. SW18—4M 89
Ridgmount St. WC1—8H 59
Ridgway. SW19—4G 105
Ridgway Gdns. SW19—4H 105
Ridgway Pl. SW19—3J 105
Ridgway Rd. SW9—2M 91
Ridgwell Rd. E16—8G 63
Riding Hill. S Croy—5E 138
Riding Ho. St. W1—8G 59
Ridings Av. N21—7A 16
Ridings Clo. N6—5G 43
Ridings, The. W5—7K 55
Ridings, The. Asht—9H 133
Ridings, The. Barn—9B 14
Ridings, The. Eps—7C 134
Ridings, The. Sun—5E 100
Ridings, The. Surb—9L 103
Ridings, The. West—9J 141
Riding, The. NW11—5K 41
Ridler Rd. Enf—2C 16
Ridley Av. W13—4F 70
Ridley Clo. Romf—8F 34
Ridley Rd. E7—9G 47
Ridley Rd. E8—1D 60
Ridley Rd. NW10—5E 56
Ridley Rd. SW19—4M 105
Ridley Rd. Brom—7D 110
Ridley Rd. Well—9F 80
Ridley Several. SE1—5A 44
Ridsdale Rd. SE20—5F 108
Riefield Rd. SF9—3A 96
Riesco Dri. Croy—8G 125
Riffel Rd. NW2—1G 57
Rifle Butts All. Eps—7D 134
Rifle Ct. SE11—7L 75
Rifle Pl. W11—2H 73
Rifle St. E14—8M 61
Rigault Rd. SW6—1J 89
Rigby Clo. Croy—5L 123
Rigby La. Hay—3A 68
Rigby M. Ilf—7L 47
Rigden St. E14—9M 61
Rigeley Rd. NW10—6E 56
Rigg App. E10—6H 45
Rigge Pl. SW4—3H 91
Riggindale Rd. SW16—2H 107
Riley Rd. SE1—4D 76
Riley Rd. Enf—2G 17
Riley St. Sw10—8B 74
Ring Clo. Brom—4F 110
Ringcroft St. N7—1L 59
Ringers Rd. Brom—7E 110
Ringford Rd. SW18—4K 89
Ringlewell Clo. Enf—4F 16
Ringmer Av. SW6—9J 73
Ringmer Gdns. N19—7J 43
Ringmer Pl. N21—7B 16
Ringmer Way. Brom—9K 111
Ringmore Rise. SF23—6F 92
Ringmore Rd. W on T—5G 117

Ringshall Rd. Orp—7E 112
Ringslade Rd. N22—9K 27
Ringstead Rd. SE6—6M 93
Ringstead Rd. Sutt—6B 122
Ring, The. W2—2C 74
Ring Way. N11—6G 27
Ringway. S'hall—6J 69
Ringway Rd. St Alb—1M 5
Ringwold Clo. Beck—4J 109
Ringwood Av. N2—9D 26
Ringwood Av. Croy—2J 123
Ringwood Av. Horn—7H 51
Ringwood Clo. Pinn—1G 37
Ringwood Gdns. SW15—7E 88
Ringwood Rd. E17—4K 45
Ringwood Way. N21—9M 15
Ringwood Way. Hmptn
—1L 101
Ripley Clo. Brom—9K 111
Ripley Clo. Croy—8A 126
Ripley Gdns. SW14—2B 88
Ripley Gdns. Sutt—6A 122
Ripley Rd. E16—9G 63
Ripley Rd. Belv—5L 81
Ripley Rd. Enf—3A 16
Ripley Rd. Hmptn—4L 101
Ripley Rd. Ilf—7D 48
Ripley View. Lou—2M 19
Ripley Way. Wal X—3B 6
Ripon Clo. N'holt—2L 53
Ripon Gdns. Chess—7H 119
Ripon Rd. N9—9F 16
Ripon Rd. N17—1B 44
Ripon Rd. SE18—7M 79
Ripon Way. Borwd—7B 12
Rippersley Rd. Well—9E 80
Ripple Rd. Bark & Dag—4B 64
Ripplevale Gro. N1—3K 59
Rippolson Rd. SE18—6D 80
Rippon Cdns. Ilf—5J 47
Ripston Rd. Ashf—2B 100
Risborough Dri. N Mald
—2E 120
Risborough St. SE1—3M 75
Risdon St. SE16—3G 77
Risebridge Chase. Romf
—7D 34
Risebridge Rd. Romf—9D 34
Risedale Rd. Bexh—2A 98
Riseholme St. E9—2K 61
Riseldine Rd. SE23—5J 93
Rise Pk. Boulevd. Romf—8D 34
Rise Pk. Pde. Romf—9C 34
Rise, The. E11—3E 46
Rise, The. N13—4L 27
Rise, The. NW7—6D 24
Rise, The. NW10—9B 40
Rise, The. Bex—6G 97
Rise, The. Borwd—7K 11
Rise, The. Buck H—9H 19
Rise, The. Dart—3D 98
Rise, The. Edgw—5M 23
Rise, The. Eps—2D 134
Rise, The. Gnfd—1E 54
Rise, The. S Croy—1G 139
Rise, The. Uxb—5D 142
Rising Hill Clo. N'wd—4A 20
Risinghill St. N1—5L 59
Rising Holme Clo. Bush, Wat
—9M 9
Risingholme Clo. Harr—8C 22
Risingholme Rd. Harr—9C 22
Risings, The. E17—2B 46
(in two parts)
Risley Av. N17—8A 28
Rita Rd. SW8—7J 75
Ritches Rd. N15—3A 44
Ritchie Rd. Croy—1F 124
Ritchie St. N1—5L 59
Ritchings Av. E17—2J 45
Ritherdon Rd. SW17—8E 90
Ritson Rd. E8—2F 60
Ritter St. SE18—7L 79
Rivaz Pl. E9—2G 61
Rivenhall Gdns. E18—2D 46
River Av. N13—2M 27
River Av. Th Dit—2E 118
River Bank. N21—9A 16
River Bank. E Mol—7C 102
River Bank. E Mol—7L 101
(West Molesey)
River Bank. Th Dit—9D 102
River Barge Clo. E14—3A 78
River Clo. E11—4G 47
River Clo. Rain—4D 36
River Clo. Ruis—4D 36
River Clo. Wal X—7G 7
Rivercourt Rd. W6—5F 72
Riverdale. SE13—2A 94
Riverdale Gdns. Twic—4G 87
Riverdale Rd. SE18—6D 80
Riverdale Rd. Bex—6K 97
Riverdale Rd. Eri—6M 81

Riverdale Rd. Felt—1K 101
Riverdale Rd. Twic—5G 87
Riverdene. Edgw—3A 24
Riverdene Industrial Est.
W on T—7H 117
Riverdene Rd. Ilf—8L 47
River Front. Enf—5C 16
River Gdns. Cars—4E 122
River Gdns. Felt—4F 84
River Gro. Pk. Beck—5K 109
Riverhead Clo. E17—9H 29
Riverholme Dri. Eps—1C 134
River Ho. SE26—9F 92
River Meads Av. Twic—9M 85
River Mt. W on T—2D 116
Rivernook Clo. W on T—9G 101
River Pk. Gdns. Brom—4B 110
River Pk. Rd. N22—9K 27
River Pl. N1—3A 60
River Reach. Tedd—2G 103
River Rd. Bark—5C 64
River Rd. Buck H—1J 31
Riversdale Rd. N5—8M 43
Riversdale Rd. Romf—7M 33
Riversdale Rd. Th Dit—1E 118
Riversfield Rd. Enf—5C 16
Riverside. NW4—5F 40
Riverside. SE7—4G 79
Riverside. Eyns, Dart—4H 131
Riverside. Rich—4H 87
Riverside. Shep—2C 116
Riverside. Twic—7F 86
Riverside Av. E Mol—9B 102
River Side Av. Rich—8J 71
Riverside Clo. W7—7C 54
Riverside Clo. King—8H 103
Riverside Clo. Wall—5F 122
Riverside Ct. SW8—7H 75
Riverside Dri. NW11—4J 41
Riverside Dri. W4—8B 72
Riverside Dri. Esh—6L 117
Riverside Dri. Mitc—9C 106
Riverside Dri. Rich—9F 86
Riverside Gdns. W6—6F 72
Riverside Gdns. Enf—4B 16
Riverside Gdns. Wemb—5J 55
Riverside Industrial Est. Enf
—8J 17
Riverside Industrial Est. Dart
—5D 86
Riverside Path. Wal X—2C 6
Riverside Pl. Stai—5B 144
Riverside Rd. E15—5A 62
Riverside Rd. N15—4E 44
Riverside Rd. Stan—1M 105
Riverside Rd. Sidc—9J 97
Riverside Rd. Stai—4B 144
(Stanwell)
Riverside Rd. W on T—6J 117
Riverside Rd. Wat—8F 8
Riverside Wlk. N12 & N20
—3M 25
Riverside Wlk. SE1—2K 75
Riverside Wlk. Barn—8H 13
Riverside Wlk. Iswth—2C 86
Riverside Way. Dart—4J 99
Riverside Way. Uxb—4A 142
River St. EC1—6L 59
River Ter. W6—6G 73
Riverton Clo. W9—6K 57
River View. Enf—5A 16
Riverview Gdns. SW13—7F 72
River View Gdns. Twic—8D 86
Riverview Gro. W4—7M 71
Riverview Rd. W4—8M 71
Riverview Rd. Eps—6A 120
River Wlk. Uxb—1A 142
River Wlk. W on T—1E 116
Riverway. N13—4L 27
River Way. SE10—4D 78
River Way. Eps—7B 120
River Way. Lou—8K 19
River Way. Twic—8M 85
Riverwood La. Chst—6B 112
Rivington Av. Wfd G—9H 31
Rivington Bldgs. EC2—6C 60
Rivington Ct. NW10—4E 56
Rivington Cres. NW7—7D 24
Rivington Pl. EC2—6C 60
Rivington St. EC2—6C 60
Rivington Wlk. E8—4E 60
Rivulet Rd. N17—7A 28
Rixsen Rd. E12—1J 63
Roach Rd. E3—3L 61
Roads Pl. N19—7J 43
Roan St. SE10—8M 77
Robbins Ct. Beck—6B 110
Robb Rd. Stan—6F 22
Robert Adam St. W1—9E 58
Roberta St. E2—6E 60
Robert Clo. W9—7A 58

Robert Clo. Chig—5D 32
Robert Clo. W on T—7F 116
Robert Dashwood Way. SE17
—5A 76
Robert Keen Clo. SE15—9E 76
Robert Lowe Clo. SE14—8H 77
Roberton Dri. Brom—5G 111
Roberts All. W5—3H 71
Robertsbridge Rd. Cars
—2A 122
Roberts Clo. Romf—8F 34
Roberts Clo. Stai—5A 144
Roberts Clo. Sutt—9H 121
Roberts Clo. W Dray—2J 143
Roberts M. SW1—4E 74
Robertson St. SW8—2F 90
Roberts Pl. EC1—7L 59
Roberts Rd. E17—8M 29
Roberts Rd. NW7—6J 25
Roberts Rd. Belv—6L 81
Roberts Rd. Wat—7G 9
Robert St. E16—2M 79
Robert St. NW1—6F 58
Robert St. SE18—6B 80
Robert St. WC2—1J 75
Robert St. Croy—5A 124
Robeson St. E3—8K 61
Robina Clo. Bexh—3H 97
Robina Clo. Ilf—6C 32
Robin Clo. Romf—7B 34
Robin Gro. N6—7E 42
Robin Gro. Bren—7G 71
Robin Gro. Harr—4K 39
Robin Hill Dri. Chst—3J 111
Robinhood Clo. Mitc—7G 107
Robin Hood Dri. Bush, Wat
—3K 9
Robin Hood Dri. Harr—7D 22
Robin Hood Grn. Orp—9E 112
Robin Hood La. E14—1A 78
Robin Hood La. SW15—1C 104
Robin Hood La. Bexh—4J 97
Robin Hood Rd. SW19—2E 104
Robinhood La. Mitc—7G 107
Robin Hood La. Sutt—7L 121
Robin Hood Rd. SW19—2E 104
Robin Hood Way. SW15 & SW20
—2C 104
Robin Hood Way. Gnfd—2D 54
Robins Clo. Uxb—8A 142
Robins Ct. SE12—9G 95
Robins Gro. W Wick—5E 126
Robinson Cres. Bush, Wat
—1A 22
Robinson Rd. E2—5G 61
Robinson Rd. SW17—3C 106
Robinson Rd. Dag—9L 49
Robinson's Clo. W13—8E 54
Robinson St. SW3—7D 74
Robins Way. Wal A—7L 7
Robinsway. W on T—6G 117
Robin Way. Orp—7F 112
Robinwood Pl. SW15—1B 104
Roborough Wlk. Horn—2G 67
Robsart St. SW9—1L 91
Robson Av. NW10—4E 56
Robson Clo. Enf—4M 15
Robson Clo. E6—9J 63
Robson Rd. SE27—9A 92
Robsons Clo. Wal X—2C 6
Roch Av. Edgw—9K 23
Rochdale Rd. E17—5L 45
Rochdale Rd. SE2—6F 80
Rochdale Way. SE8—8L 77
Rochello Clo. SW11—3D 90
Rochelle St. E2—6D 60
Roche Rd. SW16—5K 107
Rochester Av. E13—4G 63
Rochester Av. Brom—6F 110
Rochester Av. Felt—8D 84
Rochester Clo. SE3—2G 95
Rochester Clo. SW16—4J 107
Rochester Clo. Enf—3C 16
Rochester Clo. Sidc—5F 96
Rochester Dri. Bex—5L 97
Rochester Dri. Pinn—3H 37
Rochester Gdns. Croy—5C 124
Rochester Gdns. Ilf—5K 47
Rochester M. NW1—3G 59
Rochester Pl. NW1—2G 59
(in two parts)
Rochester Rd. NW1—2G 59
Rochester Rd. Cars—6D 122
Rochester Rd. Dart—6L 99
Rochester Row. SW1—5G 75
Rochester Sq. NW1—3G 59
Rochester St. SW1—5H 75
Rochester Ter. NW1—2G 59
Rochester Way.—9F 78
SE3 1-325 & 2-364
SE9 remainder
Rochester Way. Bex & Dart
—6C 98

Roche Wlk. Cars—1B 122
Rochford Av. Lou—5M 19
Rochford Av. Romf—3G 49
Rochford Av. Wal A—7K 7
Rochford Clo. E6—5H 63
Rochford Clo. Horn—2F 66
Rochford Grn. Lou—5M 19
Rochford Wlk. E8—3E 60
Rochford Way. Croy—1J 123
Rock Av. SW14—2B 88
Rockbourne Rd. SE23—7H 93
Rockchase Gdns. Horn—4J 51
Rockell's Pl. SE22—5F 92
Rockford Av. Gnfd—5F 54
Rock Gdns. Dag—1M 65
Rockhall Rd. NW2—9H 41
Rockhampton Clo. SE27
—1L 107
Rockhampton Rd. SE27
—1L 107
Rockhampton Rd. S Croy
—8C 124
Rock Hill. SE26—1D 108
Rock Hill. Orp—8M 129
Rockingham Av. Horn—4F 50
Rockingham Clo. SW15—3D 88
Rockingham Clo. Uxb—4A 142
Rockingham Pde. Uxb—3A 142
Rockingham Rd. Uxb—4A 142
Rockingham St. SE1—4A 76
Rockland Rd. SW15—3J 89
Rocklands Dri. Stan—9F 22
Rockley Rd. W14—3H 73
Rockmount Rd. SE18—6D 80
Rockmount Rd. SE19—3B 108
Rocks La. SW13—2E 88
Rock St. N4—7L 43
Rockware Av. Gnfd—4B 54
Rockways. Barn—8D 12
Rockwell Rd. Dag—1M 65
Rockwood Pl. W12—3G 73
Rocliffe St. N1—5M 59
Rocombe Cres. SE23—6G 93
Rocque La. SE3—2D 94
Rodborough Rd. NW11—6L 41
Roden Gdns. Croy—1C 124
Rodenhurst Rd. SW4—5G 91
Roden St. N7—8K 43
Roden St. Ilf—8L 47
Roderick Rd. NW3—9D 42
Rodgers Ct. Swan—8E 114
Roding Av. Wfd G—6J 31
Roding La. Buck H & Chig
—1J to 2M 31
Roding La. N. Wfd G—9H 31
Roding La. S. Ilf & Wfd G
—2H 47
Roding Rd. E5—9H 45
Roding Rd. E6—8M 63
Roding Rd. Lou—7J 19
Rodings, The. Wfd G—6G 31
Roding Trading Est. Bark
—3M 63
Roding View. Buck H—1H 31
Roding Way. Rain—5H 67
Rodmarton St. W1—8D 58
Rodmell Slope. N12—5K 25
Rodmere St. SE10—6C 78
Rodmill La. SW2—6J 91
Rodney Clo. Croy—3M 123
Rodney Clo. N Mald—9C 104
Rodney Clo. Pinn—5J 37
Rodney Clo. W on T—3G 117
Rodney Ct. Barn—5K 13
Rodney Gdns. Pinn—3F 36
Rodney Gdns. W Wick—6E 126
(in two parts)
Rodney Grn. W on T—4G 117
Rodney Pl. E17—9J 29
Rodney Pl. SE17—5A 76
Rodney Pl. SW19—5A 106
Rodney Rd. E11—2F 46
Rodney Rd. SE17—5B 76
Rodney Rd. Mitc—7C 106
Rodney Rd. N Mald—9C 104
Rodney Rd. Twic—5L 85
Rodney Rd. W on T—4G 117
Rodney St. N1—5K 59
Rodney Way. Romf—8M 33
Rodsley St. SE1—7E 76
Rodway Rd. SW15—6E 88
Rodway Rd. Brom—5F 110
Rodwell Clo. Ruis—6G 37
Rodwell Rd. SE22—5D 92
Roebourne Way. E16—2L 79
Roebuck Clo. Felt—1F 100
Roebuck La. N17—6D 28
Roebuck La. Buck H—9G 19
Roebuck Rd. Chess—7L 119
Roebuck Rd. Ilf—6F 32
Roedean Av. Enf—3G 17
Roedean Clo. Enf—3G 17
Roedean Cres. SW15—5C 88

Routledge Clo. N19—6H 43
Rover Av. Ilf—6D 32
Rowallan Rd. SW6—8J 73
Rowan Av. E4—6K 29
Rowan Clo. SW16—5G 107
Rowan Clo. W5—3J 71
Rowan Clo. N Mald—6C 104
Rowan Clo. St Alb—4L 5
Rowan Clo. Wemb—8E 38
Rowan Cres. SW16—5G 107
Rowan Cres. Dart—7G 99
Rowan Dri. NW9—1E 40
Rowan Gdns. Croy—5D 124
Rowan Grn. Wey—6B 116
Rowan Pl. Hay—1D 68
Rowan Rd. SW16—6G 107
Rowan Rd. W6—5H 73
Rowan Rd. Bexh—2J 97
Rowan Rd. Bren—8F 70
Rowan Rd. Swan—7B 114
Rowan Rd. W Dray—5H 143
Rowans, The. N13—3A 28
Rowans, The. Sun—2D 100
Rowantree Clo. N21—1B 28
Rowantree Rd. N21—1B 28
Rowantree Rd. Enf—4M 15
Rowan Wlk. N2—3A 42
Rowan Wlk. N19—7G 43
Rowan Wlk. W10—7J 57
Rowan Wlk. Brom—5K 127
Rowan Wlk. Horn—2H 51
Rowanway. Lou—6K 19
Rowan Way. Romf—1E 49
Rowben Clo. N20—1M 25
Rowberry Clo. SW6—8G 73
Rowcross St. SE1—6D 76
Rowdell Rd. N'holt—4L 53
Rowden Rd. E4—6M 29
Rowden Rd. Beck—5J 109
Rowden Rd. Eps—6M 119
Rowditch La. SW11—1E 90
Rowdon Av. NW10—3F 56
Rowdown Cres. Croy—1B 140
Rowdowns Rd. Dag—4K 65
Rowe Gdns. Bark—5D 64
Rowe La. E9—1G 61
Rowena Cres. SW11—1C 90
Rowe Wlk. Harr—8L 37
Rowfant Rd. SW17—7E 90
Rowhill Rd. E5—9F 44
Rowhill Rd. Dart & Swan
—3D 114
Rowhurst Av. Lea—9D 132
Rowington Clo. W2—8M 57
Rowland Av. Harr—1G 39
Rowland Ct. E16—7D 62
Rowland Cres. Chig—4C 32
Rowland Gro. SE26—9F 92
Rowland Hill Av. N17—7A 28
Rowland Hill St. NW3—1C 58
Rowlands Av. Pinn—6L 21
Rowlands Clo. NW7—7E 24
Rowlands Clo. Wal X—3D 6
Rowlands Fields. Wal X—3D 6
Rowlands Rd. Dag—7K 49
Rowland Wlk. Hav, Romf
—3C 34
Rowland Way. SW19—5M 105
Rowland Way. Ashf—4A 100
Rowlatt Clo. Dart—5C 115
Rowlatt Rd. Dart—1G 115
Rowley Av. Sidc—6F 96
Rowley Clo. Wat—8J 9
Rowley Clo. Wemb—3K 55
Rowley Gdns. N4—5A 44
Rowley Gdns. Wal X—1D 6
Rowley Grn. Rd. Barn—7E 12
Rowley Industrial Pk. W3
—4M 71
Rowley La. Barn—6C 12
Rowley La. Borwd—3B 12
Rowley Rd. N15—3A 44
Rowley Way. NW8—4M 57
Rowlheys Pl. W Dray—4J 143
Rowlls Rd. King—7K 103
Rowney Gdns. Dag—2G 65
Rowney Rd. Dag—2F 64
Rowntree Path. SE28—2F 80
Rowntree Rd. Twic—7C 84
Rowse Clo. E15—4A 62
Rowsley Av. NW4—1G 41
Rowstock Gdns. N7—1H 59
Rowton Rd. SE18—8A 80
Rowzill Rd. Swan—3D 114
Roxborough Av. Harr—5C 38
Roxborough Av. Iswth—8D 70
Roxborough Pk. Harr—5C 38
Roxborough Rd. Harr—4B 38
Roxbourne Clo. N'holt—2J 53
Roxburgh Rd. SE27—2M 107
Roxburn Way. Ruis—8D 36
Roxby Pl. SW6—7L 73
Roxeth Grn. Av. Harr—8M 37

Roxeth Gro. Harr—9M 37
Roxeth Hill. Harr—7B 38
Roxford Clo. Shep—9C 100
Roxley Rd. SE13—5M 93
Roxton Gdns. Croy—7L 125
Roxwell Rd. W12—3E 72
Roxwell Rd. Bark—5E 64
Roxwell Trading Pk. E10—5J 45
Roxwell Way. Wfd G—7G 31
Roxy Av. Romf—5G 49
Royal Av. SW3—6D 74
Royal Av. Wal X—6E 6
Royal Av. Wor Pk—4C 120
Royal Cir. SE27—9L 91
Royal Clo. Uxb—9D 142
Royal Clo. Wor Pk—4C 120
Royal College St. NW1—3G 59
Royal Cres. W11—2H 73
Royal Cres. Ruis—9J 37
Royal Gdns. W7—4E 70
Royal Hill. SE10—8A 78
Royal Hospital Rd. SW3—7D 74
Royal La. Uxb & W Dray
—8D 142
Royal London Est. N17—6F 28
Royal London Industrial Est.
NW10—5B 56
Royal Mint St. E1—1D 76
Royal Oak Rd. E8—2F 60
Royal Oak Rd. Bexh—3K 97
Royal Opera Arc. SW1—2H 75
Royal Pde. SE3—1D 94
Royal Pde. W5—6J 55
Royal Pde. Chst—4A 112
Royal Pl. SE10—8A 78
Royal Rd. E16—9H 63
Royal Rd. SE17—7M 75
Royal Rd. Dart—2L 115
Royal Rd. Sidc—9H 97
Royal Rd. Tedd—2B 102
Royal Route. Wemb—9L 39
Royal St. SE1—4K 75
Royal Victoria Patriotic
Building. SW18—5B 90
Royal Victor Pl. E3—5H 61
Royal Wlk. Wall—4F 122
Roycraft Av. Bark—5D 64
Roycroft Clo. E18—8F 30
Roycroft Clo. SW2—7L 91
Roydene Rd. SE18—7C 80
Roydon Clo. Lou—9J 19
Roy Gdns. Ilf—2C 48
Roy Gro. Hmptn—3M 101
Royle Clo. Romf—3F 50
Royle Cres. W13—7E 54
Roy Rd. N'wd—7D 20
Royston Av. E4—5L 29
Royston Av. Sutt—5B 122
Royston Av. Wall—6H 123
Royston Clo. Houn—9F 68
Royston Clo. W on T—3E 116
Royston Ct. SE24—5A 92
Royston Ct. Rich—9K 71
Royston Gdns. Ilf—4H 47
Royston Gdns. Pinn—6L 21
Royston Pk. Rd. Pinn—6K 21
Royston Rd. SE20—5H 109
Royston Rd. Dart—5D 98
Royston Rd. Rich—4J 87
Royston Rd. Romf—7L 35
Roystons, The. Surb—9M 103
Royston St. E2—5G 61
Rozel Rd. SW4—2G 91
(in two parts)
Rubastic Rd. S'hall—4G 69
Rubens Rd. N'holt—5G 53
Rubens St. SE6—8K 93
Ruberoid Rd. Enf—5K 17
Ruby Rd. E17—1L 45
Ruby St. SE15—7F 76
Ruby Triangle. SE15—7F 76
Ruckholt Clo. E10—8M 45
Ruckholt Rd. E10—9M 45
Rucklidge Av. NW10—5D 56
Rudall Cres. NW3—9B 42
Ruddy Way. NW7—6D 24
Ruden Way. Eps—8F 134
Rudland Rd. Bexh—2M 97
Rudloe Rd. SW12—6G 91
Rudolph Rd. E13—5D 62
Rudolph Rd. NW6—5L 57
Rudolph Rd. Bush, Wat—8L 9
Rudost Pl. SE18—5M 79
Rudyard Gro. NW7—6A 24
Rue de St Lawrence. Wal A
—7J 7
Ruffetts Clo. S Croy—9F 124
Ruffetts, The. S Croy—9F 124
Rufford Clo. Harr—4E 38
Rufford St. N1—4J 59
Rufus Clo. Ruis—8J 37
Rufus St. N1—6C 60
Rugby Av. N9—1D 28

Rugby Av. Gnfd—2B 54
Rugby Av. Wemb—1F 54
Rugby Clo. Harr—2C 38
Rugby Gdns. Dag—2G 65
Rugby La. Sutt—1H 135
Rugby Rd. NW9—2M 39
Rugby Rd. W4—3C 72
Rugby Rd. Dag—3F 64
Rugby Rd. Twic & Iswth—5C 86
Rugby St. WC1—7K 59
Rugg St. E14—1L 77
Ruislip Clo. Gnfd—7M 53
Ruislip Rd. N'holt & Gnfd
—4G 53
Ruislip St. SW17—1D 106
Rumbold Rd. SW6—8M 73
Rum Clo. E1—1G 77
Rumsey Clo. Hmptn—3K 101
Rumsey Rd. SW9—2K 91
Runbury Circ. NW9—7B 40
Runcorn Clo. N17—2F 44
Runcorn Pl. W11—1J 73
Rundell Cres. NW4—3F 40
Runnel Field. Harr—8C 38
Running Horse Yd. Bren—7J 71
Runnymede. SW19—5B 106
Runnymede Clo. Twic—5M 85
Runnymede Cres. SW16
—5H 107
Runnymede Gdns. Gnfd—5C 54
Runnymede Gdns. Twic
—5M 85
Runnymede Rd. Twic—5M 85
Runway, The. Ruis—1F 52
Rupack St. SE16—3G 77
Rupert Av. Wemb—1J 55
Rupert Ct. W1—1H 75
Rupert Gdns. SW9—1M 91
Rupert Rd. N19—8H 43
(in two parts)
Rupert Rd. NW6—5K 57
Rupert Rd. W4—4C 72
Rupert St. W1—1H 75
Rural Way. SW16—4F 106
Ruscoe Rd. E16—9D 62
Ruscombe Way. Felt—6D 84
Rusham Rd. SW12—5D 90
Rushbrook Cres. E17—8A 30
Rushbrook Rd. SE9—8A 96
Rushcroft Rd. E4—7M 29
Rushcroft Rd. SW2—3L 91
Rushdene. SE2—4H 81
Rushdene Av. Barn—9C 14
Rushdene Clo. N'holt—5G 53
Rushdene Cres. N'holt—5F 52
Rushdene Rd. Pinn—4H 37
Rushdene Wlk. West—9H 141
Rushden Gdns. NW7—6G 25
Rushden Gdns. Ilf—1L 47
Rushen Wlk. Cars—3B 122
Rushes Mead. Uxb—4A 142
Rushet Rd. Orp—6E 112
Rushett Clo. Th Dit—3F 118
Rushett La. Chess—3G 133
Rushett Rd. Th Dit—2F 118
Rushey Clo. N Mald—8B 104
Rushey Grn. SE6—6M 93
Rushey Hill. Enf—6K 15
Rushey Mead. SE4—4L 93
Rushford Rd. SE4—5K 93
Rush Grn. Gdns. Romf—6A 50
Rush Grn. Rd. Romf—6A 50
Rushgrove Av. NW9—3C 40
Rushgrove Pde. NW9—3C 40
Rushgrove St. SE18—5K 79
Rush Hill Rd. SW11—2E 90
Rushleigh Av. Wal X—4D 6
Rushley Clo. Kes—6H 127
Rushmead. E2—6F 60
Rushmead. Rich—9F 86
Rushmead Clo. Croy—6D 124
Rushmead Clo. Edgw—2M 23
Rushmoor Clo. Pinn—2F 36
Rushmore Clo. Brom—7J 111
Rushmore Ct. Wor Pk—4E 120
Rushmore Cres. E5—9H 45
Rushmore Rd. E5—9G 45
Rusholme Av. Dag—8L 49
Rusholme Gro. SE19—2C 108
Rusholme Rd. SW15—5H 89
Rushout Av. Harr—4F 38
Rushton Av. Wat—8E 4
Rushton St. N1—5B 60
Rushworth Av. NW4—1E 40
Rushworth Gdns. NW4—2E 40
Rushworth St. SE1—3M 75
Ruskin Av. E12—2J 63
Ruskin Av. Felt—5D 84

Ruskin Av. Rich—8L 71
Ruskin Av. Wal A—7L 7
Ruskin Av. Well—1E 96
Ruskin Clo. NW11—4M 41
Ruskin Dri. Orp—5C 128
Ruskin Dri. Well—2E 96
Ruskin Dri. Wor Pk—4F 120
Ruskin Gdns. W5—7H 55
Ruskin Gdns. Harr—3K 39
Ruskin Gdns. Romf—7F 34
Ruskin Gro. Dart—4L 99
Ruskin Gro. Well—1E 96
Ruskin Pk. Ho. SE5—2B 92
Ruskin Rd. N17—8D 28
Ruskin Rd. Belv—5L 81
Ruskin Rd. Cars—7E 122
Ruskin Rd. Croy—4M 123
Ruskin Rd. Iswth—2D 86
Ruskin Rd. S'hall—1J 69
Ruskin Wlk. N9—2E 28
Ruskin Wlk. SE24—4A 92
Ruskin Wlk. Brom—1K 127
Ruskin Way. SW19—5B 106
Rusland Av. Orp—5B 128
Rusland Pk. Rd. Harr—2C 38
Rusper Clo. Stan—4G 23
Rusper Rd. N22—1A 44
Rusper Rd. Dag—2G 65
Russell Av. N22—9M 27
Russell Clo. NW10—3A 56
Russell Clo. SE7—8G 79
Russell Clo. Beck—7A 110
Russell Clo. Bexh—3L 97
Russell Clo. Dart—3E 98
Russell Clo. Ruis—7G 37
Russell Ct. N14—8H 15
Russell Ct. St Alb—3L 5
Russell Ct. Wat—8D 4
Russell Dri. Stai—5B 144
Russell Gdns. N20—2C 26
Russell Gdns. NW11—4J 41
Russell Gdns. W14—4J 73
Russell Gdns. Rich—8G 87
Russell Gdns. W Dray—6L 143
Russell Gdns. M. W14—4J 73
Russell Grn. Clo. Purl—2L 137
Russell Gro. NW7—4C 24
Russell Gro. SW9—8L 75
Russell Hill. Purl—2K 137
Russell Hill Pl. Purl—3L 137
Russell Hill Rd. Purl—3L 137
Russell La. N20—2C 26
Russell La. Wat—9B 4
Russell Pl. S at H, Dart—5L 115
Russell Rd. E4—4K 29
Russell Rd. E10—4M 45
Russell Rd. E16—9E 62
Russell Rd. E17—1K 45
Russell Rd. N8—4H 43
Russell Rd. N13—6K 27
Russell Rd. N15—3C 44
Russell Rd. N20—2C 26
Russell Rd. NW9—4D 40
Russell Rd. SW19—4L 105
Russell Rd. W14—4J 73
Russell Rd. Buck H—1G 31
Russell Rd. Enf—2D 16
Russell Rd. Mitc—7C 106
Russell Rd. N'holt—1A 54
Russell Rd. N'wd—4A 20
Russell Rd. Shep—2A 116
Russell Rd. Twic—5D 86
Russell Rd. W on T—1E 116
Russell's Footpath. SW16
—2J 107
Russell Sq. WC1—8J 59
Russell's Ride. Wal X—4E 6
Russell St. WC2—1J 75
Russell Wlk. Rich—5K 87
Russet Clo. Uxb—7A 52
Russet Cres. N7—1K 59
Russets Clo. E4—4B 30
Russett Clo. Orp—7F 128
Russett Way. SE13—1M 93
Russett Way. Swan—5B 114
Russia Dock Rd. SE16—2J 77
Russia La. E2—5G 61
Russia Row. EC2—9A 60
Russington Rd. Shep—1B 116
Rusthall Av. W4—5B 72
Rusthall Clo. Croy—1G 125
Rustic Av. SW16—4F 106
Rustic Pl. Wemb—9H 39
Rustington Wlk. Mord—2K 121
Ruston Av. Surb—2M 119
Ruston M. W11—9J 57
Ruston St. E3—4K 61
Rust Sq. SE5—8B 76
Rutford Rd. SW16—2J 107
Ruth Clo. Stan—2K 39
Ruthen Clo. Eps—6M 133
Rutherford Clo. Sutt—8B 122
Rutherford St. SW1—5H 75

Rutherford Way. Bush, Wat
—1B 22
Rutherford Way. Wemb—9L 39
Rutherglen Rd. SE2—7E 80
Rutherwick Rise. Coul—9J 137
Rutherwyke Clo. Eps—8E 120
Ruthin Rd. SE3—7E 78
Ruthven Av. Wal X—6D 6
Ruthven St. E9—4H 61
Rutland App. Horn—3L 51
Rutland Av. Sidc—6E 96
Rutland Clo. SW14—2A 88
Rutland Clo. SW19—4C 106
Rutland Clo. Bex—7H 97
Rutland Clo. Chess—8K 119
Rutland Clo. Dart—6H 99
Rutland Clo. Eps—2B 134
Rutland Dri. Horn—3L 51
Rutland Dri. Mord—1K 121
Rutland Dri. Rich—7J 87
Rutland Gdns. N4—4M 43
Rutland Gdns. SW7—3C 74
Rutland Gdns. W13—8E 54
Rutland Gdns. Croy—6C 124
Rutland Gdns. Dag—1G 65
Rutland Gdns. M. SW7—3C 74
Rutland Ga. SW7—3C 74
Rutland Ga. Belv—6M 81
Rutland Ga. Brom—8D 110
Rutland Gro. W6—6F 72
Rutland M. NW8—4M 57
Rutland Pk. NW2—2G 57
Rutland Pk. SE6—8K 93
Rutland Pl. EC1—8M 59
Rutland Pl. Bush, Wat—1B 22
Rutland Rd. E7—3H 63
Rutland Rd. E9—4H 61
Rutland Rd. E11—3F 46
Rutland Rd. E17—4L 45
Rutland Rd. SW19—4C 106
Rutland Rd. Harr—4A 38
Rutland Rd. Hay—5B 68
Rutland Rd. Ilf—8M 47
Rutland Rd. S'hall—8L 53
Rutland Rd. Twic—8B 86
Rutland St. SW7—4C 74
Rutland Wlk. SE6—8K 93
Rutland Way. Orp—1G 129
Rutley Clo. SE17—7M 75
Rutlish Rd. SW19—5L 105
Rutter Gdns. Mitc—8A 106
Rutters Clo. W Dray—3L 143
Rutts, The. Bush, Wat—1B 22
Ruvigny Gdns. SW15—2H 89
Ruxley Clo. Eps—7M 119
Ruxley Clo. Sidc—3J 113
Ruxley Corner Industrial Est.
Sidc—3H 113
Ruxley Cres. Esh—9F 118
Ruxley La. Eps—8M 119
Ruxley Ridge. Esh—9E 118
Ruxton Clo. Swan—7C 114
Ryan Clo. SE3—3G 95
Ryarsh Cres. Orp—6C 128
Rycott Path. SE22—6E 92
Rycroft Way. N17—1D 44
Ryculf Sq. SE3—1D 94
Rydal Clo. NW4—9H 25
Rydal Clo. Purl—5B 138
Rydal Cres. Gnfd—6F 54
Rydal Dri. Bexh—9L 81
Rydal Gdns. NW9—3C 40
Rydal Gdns. SW15—2C 104
Rydal Gdns. Houn—5M 85
Rydal Gdns. Wemb—6G 39
Rydal Rd. SW16—1H 107
Rydal Way. Enf—8G 17
Rydal Way. Ruis—9G 37
Rydens Av. W on T—4G 117
Rydens Clo. W on T—4G 117
Rydens Gro. W on T—6H 117
Rydens Pk. W on T—4H 117
Rydens Rd. W on T—5F 116
Ryder Clo. Brom—2F 110
Ryder Clo. Bush, Wat—8M 9
Ryder Gdns. Rain—2D 66
Ryders Ter. NW8—5A 58
Ryder St. SW1 2G 75
Ryder Yd. SW1—2G 75
Ryde Vale Rd. SW12—8G 91
Rydons Clo. SE9—2J 95
Rydon St. N1—4A 60
Rydston Clo. N7—3J 59
Ryebridge Clo. Lea—9E 132
Ryebrook Rd. Lea—9E 132
Rye Clo. Bex—5M 97
Rye Clo. Horn—1G 67
Ryecotes Mead. SE21—7C 92
Rye Cres. Orp—3G 129
Rycroft Av. Ilf—9M 31
Ryecroft Av. Twic—7M 85
Ryecroft Cres. Barn—7F 12

Ryecroft Rd.—St John's Rd.

Ryecroft Rd. SE13—4A 94
Ryecroft Rd. SW16—3L 107
Ryecroft Rd. Orp—1B 128
Ryecroft St. SW6—9M 73
Ryedale. SE22—5F 92
Rye Field. Orp—3H 129
Ryefield Av. Uxb—3F 142
Ryefield Cres. N'wd—9E 20
Ryefield Path. SW15—7E 88
Ryefield Rd. SE19—3A 108
Rye Hill Pk. SE15—3G 93
Ryeland Clo. W Dray—9C 142
Ryelands Cres. SE12—5G 95
Rye La. SE15—1E 92
Rye Rd. SE15—3H 93
Rye, The. N14—9G 15
Rye Wlk. SW15—4H 89
Rye Way. Edgw—6K 23
Ryfold Rd. SW19—9L 89
Ryhope Rd. N11—4F 26
Ryland Clo. Felt—1D 100
Rylandes Rd. NW2—8E 40
Rylandes Rd. S Croy—2F 138
Ryland Rd. NW5—2F 58
Rylett Cres. W12—4D 72
Rylett Rd. W12—3D 72
Rylston Rd. N13—3B 28
Rylston Rd. SW6—7K 73
Rymer Rd. SW18—4A 90
Rymer Rd. Croy—2C 124
Rymer St. SE24—5M 91
Rymill St. E16—2L 79
Rysbrack St. SW3—4D 74
Rythe Ct. Th Dit—2E 118
Rythe Rd. Esh—7B 118

Sabbarton St. E16—9D 62
Sabella Ct. E3—5K 61
Sabine Rd. SW11—2D 90
Sable Clo. Houn—2G 85
Sable St. N1—3M 59
Sach Rd. E5—7F 44
Sackville Av. Brom—3E 126
Sackville Clo. Harr—8B 38
Sackville Cres. Romf—8J 35
Sackville Gdns. Ilf—6K 47
Sackville Rd. Dart—8J 99
Sackville Rd. Sutt—9L 121
Sackville St. W1—1G 75
Saddlers Clo. Borwd—7B 12
Saddlers Clo. Pinn—6L 21
Saddlers M. Wemb—9D 38
Saddler's Pk. Eyns, Dart —5H 131
Saddlers Ride E Mol—7M 101
Saddlescombe Way. N12 —5L 25
Saddleworth Rd. Romf—6G 35
Saddleworth Sq. Romf—6G 35
Sadler Clo. Mitc—6D 106
Saffron Clo. NW11—3K 41
Saffron Hill. EC1—8L 59
Saffron Rd. Romf—9B 34
Saffron St. EC1—8L 59
Saffron Way. Surb—3H 119
Sage St. E1—1G 77
Saigasso Clo. E16—9H 63
Sail St. SE11—5K 75
Sainfoin Rd. SW17—8E 90
Sainsbury Rd. SE19—2C 108
St Agatha's Dri. King—3K 103
St Agatha's Gro. Cars—3D 122
St Agnes Clo. E9—4G 61
St Agnes Pl. SE11—7M 75
St Aidan's Rd. SE22—5F 92
St Aidan's Rd. W13—3F 70
St Alban's Av. E6—6L 63
St Alban's Av. W4—4B 72
St Albans Av. Felt—2H 101
St Albans Clo. NW11—6L 41
St Alban's Cres. N22—8L 27
St Alban's Cres. Wfd G—7E 30
St Alban's Gdns. Tedd—2E 102
St Alban's Gro. W8—4M 73
St Alban's Gro. Cars—2C 122
St Albans La. NW11—6L 41
St Alban's M. W2—8B 58
St Alban's Pl. N1—4M 59
St Alban's Rd. NW5—8E 42
St Albans Rd. NW10—4C 56
St Albans Rd. Barn—1G 13
St Alban's Rd. Dart—5K 99
St Albans Rd. Ilf—6D 48
St Alban's Rd. King—3J 103
St Alban's Rd. Sutt—6K 121
St Albans Rd. Wat—4F 8
St Alban's Rd. Wfd G—7E 30
St Alban's St. SW1—1H 75
St Alban's Ter. W6—7J 73
St Alfege Pas. SE10—7A 78
St Alfege Rd. SE7—7H 79
St Alphage Garden. EC2—8A 60
St Alphage Wlk. Edgw—9A 24
St Alphege Rd. N9—9G 17
St Alphonsus Rd. SW4—3G 91
St Amunds Clo. SE6—1L 109
St Andrew's Av. Horn—1D 66
St Andrew's Av. Wemb—9E 38
St Andrew's Clo. N12—4A 26
St Andrew's Clo. NW2—8F 40
St Andrew's Clo. Iswth—9C 70
St Andrew's Clo. Ruis—7H 37
St Andrew's Clo. Shep—8B 100
St Andrew's Clo. Stan—9G 23
St Andrew's Ct. SW18—8A 90
St Andrew's Dri. Orp—2F 128
St Andrew's Dri. Stan—8G 23
St Andrew's Gro. N16—6B 44
St Andrew's Hill. EC4—9M 59
St Andrew's M. N16—6C 44
St Andrew's M. SE3—8E 78
St Andrew's Pl. NW1—7F 58
St Andrew's Rd. E11—4C 46
St Andrew's Rd. E13—6F 62
St Andrew's Rd. E17—9H 29
St Andrew's Rd. N9—9G 17
St Andrew's Rd. NW9—6B 40
St Andrew's Rd. NW10—2F 56
St Andrew's Rd. NW11—4K 41
St Andrew's Rd. W3—1C 72
St Andrew's Rd. W7—3C 70
St Andrew's Rd. W14—7J 73
St Andrew's Rd. Cars—5C 122
St Andrew's Rd. Coul—8E 136
St Andrew's Rd. Croy—6A 124
St Andrew's Rd. Enf—5B 16
St Andrew's Rd. Ilf—5K 47
St Andrew's Rd. Romf—4B 50
St Andrew's Rd. Sidc—9H 97
St Andrew's Rd. Surb—1H 119
St Andrew's Rd. Uxb—4C 142
St Andrew's Rd. Wat—3H 21
St Andrew's Sq. Surb—1H 119
St Andrew St. EC4—8L 59
St Anne's Av. Stai—6B 144
St Anne's Clo. N6—8E 42
St Anne's Clo. Wal X—1A 6
St Anne's Ct. W1—9H 59
St Anne's Ct. W Wick—6C 126
St Anne's Pas. E14—9K 61
St Anne's Rd. E11—7B 46
St Anne's Rd. Wemb—1H 55
St Anne's Row. E14—9K 61
St Anne St. E14—9K 61
St Ann's. Bark—4A 64
St Ann's Cres. SW18—5A 90
St Ann's Gdns. NW5—2E 58
St Ann's Gdns. NW10—6K 55
St Ann's Hill. SW18—5M 89
St Ann's La. SW1—4H 75
St Ann's Pk. Rd. SW18—5A 90
St Ann's Pas. SW13—2C 88
St Ann's Rd. N9—1D 28
St Ann's Rd. N15—3A 44
St Ann's Rd. SW13—1D 88
St Ann's Rd. W11—1H 73
St Ann's Rd. Bark—4A 64
St Ann's Rd. Harr—4C 38
St Ann's St. SW1—4H 75
St Ann's Ter. NW8—5B 58
St Ann's Vs. W11—2H 73
St Ann's Way. S Croy—8M 123
St Anselm's Pl. W1—1F 74
St Anselm's Rd. Hay—3D 68
St Anthony's Av. Wfd G—6G 31
St Anthony's Clo. E1—2E 76
St Anthony's Clo. SW17—8C 90
St Anthony's Way. Felt—3D 84
St Antony's Rd. E7—3F 62
St Arvan's Clo. Croy—5C 124
St Asaph Rd. SE4—2H 93
St Aubyn's Av. SW19—2K 105
St Aubyn's Av. Houn—4L 85
St Aubyn's Clo. Orp—5D 128
St Aubyn's Gdns. Orp—5D 128
St Aubyn's Rd. SE19—3D 108
St Audrey Av. Bexh—1L 97
St Augustine's Av. W5—5J 55
St Augustine's Av. Brom —9J 111
St Augustine's Av. S Croy
St Augustine's Av. Wemb
St Augustine's Rd. NW1—3H 59
St Augustine's Rd. Belv—5K 81
St Austell Clo. Edgw—9K 23
St Austell Rd. SE13—1A 94
St Awdry's Rd. Bark—3B 64
St Awdry's Wlk. Bark—3A 64
St Barnabas Clo. Beck—6A 110
St Barnabas Rd. E17—4L 45
St Barnabas Rd. Mitc—4E 106
St Barnabas Rd. Sutt—7B 122
St Barnabas Rd. Wfd G—8F 30
St Barnabas St. SW1—6E 74
St Barnabas Ter. E9—1H 61
St Barnabas Vs. SW8—9J 75
St Bartholomew's Clo. SE26 —1G 109
St Bartholomew's Rd. E6 —5K 63
St Benedict's Clo. SW17 —2E 106
St Benet's Clo. SW17—8C 90
St Benet's Gro. Cars—2A 122
St Benet's Pl. EC3—1C 76
St Bernards. Croy—5C 124
St Bernard's Clo. SE27—1B 108
St Bernard's Rd. E6—4H 63
St Blaise Av. Brom—6F 110
St Botolph Row. EC3—9D 60
St Botolph St. EC3—9D 60
St Bride's Av. Edgw—8K 23
St Bride's Clo. Eri—3H 81
St Bride St. EC4—9M 59
St Catherine's Clo. SW17 —8C 90
St Catherine's Dri. SE14—1H 93
St Catherine's Farm Ct. Ruis —4A 36
St Catherine's Rd. E4—2L 29
St Catherine's Rd. Ruis—4B 36
St Chad's Gdns. Romf—5J 49
St Chad's Pl. WC1—6K 59
St Chad's Rd. Romf—5J 49
St Chad's St. WC1—6J 59
St Charles Pl. W10—8J 57
St Charles Sq. W10—8J 57
St Christopher Rd. Uxb —9B 142
St Christopher's Clo. Iswth —9C 70
St Christopher's Pl. W1—9E 58
St Clair Dri. Wor Pk—5F 120
St Claire Clo. Ilf—9K 31
St Clair Rd. E13—5F 62
St Clair's Rd. Croy—4C 124
St Clare St. EC3—9D 60
St Clement Clo. Uxb—9B 142
St Clement's Heights. SE26 —9E 92
St Clement's La. WC2—9K 59
St Clement St. N7—3L 59
St Cloud Rd. SE27—1A 108
St Crispin's Clo. NW3—9C 42
St Crispin's Clo. S'hall—9K 53
St Cross St. EC1—8L 59
St Cuthbert's Gdns. Pinn —7K 21
St Cuthbert's Rd. NW2—2K 57
St Cuthbert's Wlk. NW6—2K 57
St Cyprian's St. SW17—1D 106
St David Clo. Uxb—8B 142
St David's. Coul—9K 137
St David's Clo. Wemb—8A 40
St David's Clo. W Wick —2M 125
St David's Dri. Edgw—8K 23
St David's Pl. NW4—5F 40
St David's Rd. Swan—3D 114
St Denis Rd. SE27—1B 108
St Dionis Rd. SW6—1K 89
St Donatt's Rd. SE14—9K 77
St Dunstan's Av. W3—1B 72
St Dunstan's Clo. Hay—6D 68
St Dunstan's Ct. EC4—9L 59
St Dunstan's Gdns. W3—1B 72
St Dunstan's Hill. EC3—1C 76
St Dunstan's Hill. Sutt—8J 121
St Dunstan's La. EC3—1C 76
St Dunstan's La. Beck—1A 126
St Dunstan's Rd. E7—2G 63
St Dunstan's Rd. SE25—8D 108
St Dunstan's Rd. W6—6H 73
St Dunstan's Rd. W7—3C 70
St Dunstan's Rd. Felt—9D 84
St Dunstan's Rd. Houn—1G 85
St Edmund's Av. Ruis—4B 36
St Edmund's Clo. NW8—4D 58
St Edmund's Clo. SW17—8C 90
St Edmund's Clo. Eri—3H 81
St Edmund's Dri. Stan—8E 22
St Edmund's La. Twic—6M 85
St Edmund's Rd. N9—9E 16
St Edmund's Rd. Dart—3L 99
St Edmund's Rd. Ilf—4K 47
St Edmund's Ter. NW8—4C 58
St Edward's Clo. NW11—4L 41
St Edward's Clo. Croy—3B 140
St Edward's Way. Romf—3B 50
St Egbert's Way. E4—1A 30
St Elmo Rd. W12—3D 72
St Erkenwald Rd. Bark—4B 64
St Ervan's Rd. W10—8K 57
St Faith's Clo. Enf—3A 16
St Faith's Rd. SE21—7M 91
St Fidelis Rd. Eri—5B 82
St Fillans Rd. SE6—7A 94
St Francis Clo. Orp—1C 128
St Francis Clo. Wat—1F 20
St Francis Rd. SE22—3C 92
St Francis Rd. Eri—5B 82
St Gabriel's Rd. NW2—1H 57
St George's Av. E7—3F 62
St George's Av. N7—9H 43
St George's Av. NW9—2B 40
St George's Av. W5—3H 71
St George's Av. Horn—5K 51
St George's Av. S'hall—1K 69
St George's Av. Wey—8A 116
St George's Bldgs. SE1—3A 76
St George's Cir. SE1—4M 75
St George's Clo. NW11—4K 41
St George's Clo. Wemb—8E 38
St George's Clo. Wey—7A 116
St George's Ct. E6—7K 63
St George's Dri. SW1—5F 74
St George's Dri. Wat—3J 21
St George's Fields. W2—9C 58
St George's Gdns. Eps—6D 134
St George's Gdns. Surb —4M 119
St George's Gro. SW17—9B 90
St George's Lodge. Wey —7B 116
St George's M. NW1—3D 58
St George's Rd. E7—3F 62
St George's Rd. E10—8A 46
St George's Rd. N9—3E 28
St George's Rd. N13—2K 27
St George's Rd. NW11—4K 41
St George's Rd. SE1—4M 75
St George's Rd. SW19—3K 105
St George's Rd. W4—3B 72
St George's Rd. W7—2D 70
St George's Rd. Beck—5M 109
St George's Rd. Brom—6K 111
St George's Rd. Dag—1J 65
St George's Rd. Enf—2D 16
St George's Rd. Felt—1H 101
St George's Rd. Ilf—5K 47
St George's Rd. King—4L 103
St George's Rd. Mitc—7F 106
St George's Rd. Orp—1B 128
St George's Rd. Rich—2K 87
St George's Rd. Sidc—3H 113
St George's Rd. Swan—8D 114
St George's Rd. Twic—4F 86
St George's Rd. Wall—7F 122
St George's Rd. Wat—2F 8
St George's Rd. Wey—8B 116
St George's Rd. W. Brom —6J 111
St George's Sq. E7—3F 62
St George's Sq. SW1—6H 75
St George's Sq. N Mald—7C 104
St George's Sq. M. SW1—6H 75
St George's Stairs. SE16 —5K 77
St George's Ter. NW1—3D 58
St George St. W1—1F 74
St George's Wlk. Croy—5A 124
St George's Way. SE15—7C 76
St Gerard's Clo. SW4—4G 91
St German's Pl. SE3—9E 78
St German's Rd. SE23—7J 93
St Giles Av. Dag—3M 65
St Giles Av. Uxb—9A 36
St Giles Cir. W1, WC1 & WC2 —9H 59
St Giles Clo. Dag—3M 65
St Giles Clo. Orp—7B 128
St Giles Ct. Enf—8C 6
St Giles High St. WC2—9H 59
St Giles Ho. Barn—6A 14
St Giles Rd. SE5—8C 76
St Gothard Rd. SE27—1B 108
St Helena Rd. SE16—5H 77
St Helena St. WC1—6L 59
St Helen Clo. Uxb—8B 142
St Helen's Ct. Rain—7E 66
St Helen's Cres. SW16—5K 107
St Helen's Gdns. W10—9H 57
St Helen's Pl. EC3—9C 60
St Helen's Rd. SW16—5K 107
St Helen's Rd. W13—2G 71
St Helen's Rd. Eri—3H 81
St Helen's Rd. Ilf—4K 47
St Helier Av. Mord—2A 122
St Helier's Av. Houn—4L 85
St Helier's Rd. E10—4A 46
St Hilda's Clo. NW6—4H 57
St Hilda's Clo. SW17—8C 90
St Hilda's Rd. SW13—7F 72
St Hughe's Clo. SW17—8C 90
St Hughes Rd. SE20—5F 108
St Ivian's Dri. Romf—1E 50
St James Av. N20—3C 26
St James Av. W13—2E 70
St James Av. Eps—3D 134
St James Av. Sutt—7L 121
St James Clo. N20—3C 26
St James Clo. SE18—6A 80
St James Clo. Eps—6C 134
St James Clo. N Mald—9D 104
St James Clo. Ruis—7G 37
St James' Ct. SW1—4G 75
St James' Gdns. Wemb—3J 55
St James Ga. NW1—3H 59
St James Gro. SW11—1D 90
St James Pl. Dart—5H 99
St James' Rd. E15—1D 62
St James' Rd. N9—2F 28
St James Rd. Cars—5C 122
St James Rd. King—6H 103
St James Rd. Mitc—4E 106
St James Rd. Purl—5A 138
St James Rd. Sutt—7L 121
St James Rd. Wat—7F 8
St James's. SE14—9J 77
St James's Av. E2—5G 61
St James's Av. Beck—7J 109
St James's Av. Hmptn—2A 102
St James's Clo. SW17—8D 90
St James's Cotts. Rich—4H 87
St James's Cres. SW9—2L 91
St James's Dri. SW17—7D 90
St James's Gdns. W11—2J 73
St James's La. N10—2F 42
St James's Mkt. SW1—1H 75
St James's Pk. Croy—2A 124
St James's Pl. SW1—2G 75
St James's Rd.—4E 76
SE16 1-167 & 2-144
SE1 remainder
St James's Rd. Croy—2A 124
St James's Rd. Hmptn—2M 101
St James's Rd. Surb—1H 119
St James's Row. EC1—7M 59
St James's Sq. SW1—2G 75
St James's St. SW1—2G 75
St James's Ter. M. NW8—4D 58
St James St. E17—3J 45
St James St. W6—6G 73
St James's Wlk. EC1—7M 59
St James Way. Sidc—2J 113
St Jerome's Gro. Hay—9A 52
St Joan's Rd. N9—2D 28
St John's Av. N11—5D 26
St John's Av. NW10—4D 56
St John's Av. SW15—4H 89
St John's Av. Eps—4E 134
St John's Chu. Rd. E9—1G 61
St John's Clo. Rain—3E 66
St John's Clo. Uxb—4A 142
St John's Clo. Wemb—1J 55
St John's Cotts. SE20—4G 109
St John's Ct. Buck H—1F 30
St John's Ct. Iswth—1D 86
St John's Ct. N'wd—8C 20
St John's Cres. SW9—2L 91
St John's Dri. SW18—7M 89
St John's Dri. W on T—3G 117
St John's Est. N1—5B 60
St John's Gdns. W11—1K 73
St John's Gro. N19—7G 43
St John's Gro. Rich—3J 87
St John's Hill. SW11—3B 90
St John's Hill. Coul—9L 137
St John's Hill. Purl—8L 137
St John's Hill Gro. SW11—3B 90
St John's La. EC1—7M 59
St John's Pk. SE3—8D 78
St John's Pas. SW19—3J 105
St John's Pl. EC1—7M 59
St John's Rd. E4—4M 29
St John's Rd. E6—4J 63
St John's Rd. E16—9E 62
St John's Rd. E17—9M 29
St John's Rd. N15—4C 44
St John's Rd. NW11—4K 41
St John's Rd. SE20—3G 109
St John's Rd. SW11—3C 90
St John's Rd. SW19—4J 105
St John's Rd. Bark—4C 64
St John's Rd. Cars—5C 122
St John's Rd. Croy—5M 123
St John's Rd. Dart—6M 99
St John's Rd. E Mol—8B 102
St John's Rd. Eri—6B 82
St John's Rd. Felt—1J 101
St John's Rd. Harr—4D 38
St John's Rd. Ilf—5C 48
St John's Rd. Iswth—1D 86
St John's Rd. King—6G 103
St John's Rd. Lou—4K 19
St John's Rd. N Mald—7A 104
St John's Rd. Orp—1B 128
St John's Rd. Rich—3J 87
St John's Rd. Romf—5A 34
St John's Rd. Sidc—1F 112
St John's Rd. S'hall—4J 69
St John's Rd. Sutt—4M 121
St John's Rd. Uxb—4A 142
St John's Rd. Wat—4F 8

St John's Rd.—Salisbury Rd.

St John's Rd. Well—2F 96
St John's Rd. Wemb—9H 39
St John's Sq. EC1—7M 59
St John's Ter. E7—2F 62
St John's Ter. SE18—7A 80
St John's Ter. W10—7H 57
St John's Ter. Enf—1B 16
St John St. EC1—6M 59
St John's Vale. SE8—1L 93
St John's Vs. N19—7H 43
St John's Way. N19—7G 43
St John's Wood High St. NW8 —5C 58
St John's Wood Pk. NW8 —4B 58
St John's Wood Rd. NW8 —7B 58
St John's Wood Ter. NW8 —5C 58
St John's Yd. N17—7D 28
St Joseph's Clo. Orp—5D 128
St Joseph's Dri. S'hall—2J 69
St Joseph's Rd. N9—9F 16
St Joseph's Rd. Wal X—6E 6
St Joseph's St. SW8—9F 74
St Jude's Rd. E2—5F 60
St Jude St. N16—1C 60
St Julian's Clo. SW16—1L 107
St Julian's Farm Rd. SE27 —1L 107
St Julian's Rd. NW6—4L 57
St Justin Clo. Orp—7H 113
St Katharine's Precinct. NW1 —5F 58
St Katharine's Way. E1—2D 76
St Katherine's Rd. Eri—3H 81
St Keverne Rd. SE9—1J 111
St Kilda Rd. W13—3E 70
St Kilda Rd. Orp—3D 128
St Kilda's Rd. N16—6B 44
St Kilda's Rd. Harr—4C 38
St Kitts Ter. SE19—2C 108
St Laurence Clo. Orp—7H 113
St Laurence's Clo. NW6—4H 57
St Lawrence Clo. Abb L, Wat —3C 4
St Lawrence Clo. Edgw—7K 23
St Lawrence Clo. Uxb—8A 142
St Lawrence Dri. Pinn—3F 36
St Lawrence Rd. Upm—7M 51
St Lawrence St. E14—2A 78
St Lawrence Ter. W10—8J 57
St Lawrence Way. SW9—1L 91
St Lawrence Way. St Alb—3K 5
St Leonard's Av. E4—6B 30
St Leonard's Av. Harr—3G 39
St Leonard's Clo. Bush, Wat —6J 9
St Leonard's Clo. Well—2E 96
St Leonard's Gdns. Houn —9J 69
St Leonard's Gdns. Ilf—1A 64
St Leonard's Rise. Orp—6C 128
St Leonard's Rd. E14—8M 61
(in two parts)
St Leonard's Rd. NW10—7B 56
St Leonard's Rd. SW14—2A 88
St Leonard's Rd. W13—1G 71
St Leonard's Rd. Croy—5M 123
St Leonard's Rd. Esh—8D 118
St Leonard's Rd. Surb—9H 103
St Leonard's Rd. Th Dit—2E 118
St Leonard's Sq. Surb—9H 103
St Leonard's St. E3—6M 61
St Leonard's Ter. SW3—6D 74
St Leonard St. NW5—2E 58
St Leonard's Wlk. SW16 —4K 107
St Loo Av. SW3—7C 74
St Louis Rd. SE27—1B 108
St Loy's Rd. N17—9C 28
St Luke Clo. Uxb—9B 142
St Luke's Av. SW4—3H 91
St Luke's Av. Enf—2B 16
St Luke's Av. Ilf—1M 63
St Luke's Clo. EC1—7A 60
St Luke's Clo. SE25—1F 124
St Luke's M. W11—9K 57
St Luke's Pas. King—5K 103
St Luke's Path. Ilf—1M 63
St Luke's Rd. W11—8K 57
St Luke's Rd. Uxb—3C 142
St Luke's Rd. Whyt—9D 138
St Luke's Sq. E16—9D 62
St Luke's St. SW3—6C 74
St Luke's Yd. W9—5K 57
St Malo Av. N9—3G 29
St Margaret's. Bark—4B 64
St Margaret's Av. N15—2M 43
St Margaret's Av. N20—1A 26
St Margaret's Av. Ashf —2A 100
St Margaret's Av. Harr—8A 38
St Margaret's Av. Sidc—9B 96
St Margaret's Av. Sutt
St Margaret's Av. Uxb—7E 142
St Margaret's Clo. Orp—6F 128
St Margaret's Ct. N11—4E 26
St Margaret's Ct. SE1—2B 76
St Margaret's Cres. SW15 —4F 88
St Margaret's Dri. Iswth—4F 86
St Margaret's Gro. SE18—7A 80
St Margaret's Gro. Twic—5E 86
St Margaret's Pas. SE13—2C 94
St Margaret's Rd. E12—7G 47
St Margaret's Rd. N17—1C 44
St Margaret's Rd. NW10—6G 57
St Margaret's Rd. SE4—3K 93
St Margaret's Rd. W7—3C 70
St Margaret's Rd. Beck —8H 109
St Margaret's Rd. Edgw —5M 23
St Margaret's Rd. Ruis—4B 36
St Margaret's Rd. Twic—3F 86
St Margaret's Sq. SE4—3K 93
St Margaret's Ter. SE18—6A 80
St Margaret St. SW1—3J 75
St Mark's Clo. SE10—8A 78
St Mark's Clo. W11—9J 57
St Mark's Clo. Barn—5M 13
St Mark's Cres. NW1—4E 58
St Mark's Ga. E9—3K 61
St Mark's Gro. SW10—7M 73
St Mark's Hill. Surb—1J 119
St Mark's Pl. SW19—3K 105
St Mark's Pl. W11—9J 57
St Mark's Rise. E8—1D 60
St Mark's Rd. SE25—8E 108
St Mark's Rd. W5—2J 71
St Mark's Rd. W7—3C 70
St Mark's Rd.—8H 57
W11 1-53a & 2-22
W10 remainder
St Mark's Rd. Brom—7F 110
St Mark's Rd. Enf—8D 16
St Mark's Rd. Mitc—6D 106
St Mark's Rd. Tedd—4F 102
St Mark's Sq. NW1—4E 58
St Mark St. E1—9D 60
St Martin Clo. Uxb—9B 142
St Martin's App. Ruis—5C 36
St Martin's Av. E6—5H 63
St Martin's Av. Eps—6C 134
St Martin's Clo. NW1—4G 59
St Martin's Clo. Enf—3F 16
St Martin's Clo. Eps—5D 134
St Martin's Clo. Eri—3H 81
St Martin's Clo. W Dray —4G 143
St Martin's Ct. WC2—1J 75
St Martin's Dri. Eyns, Dart —5H 131
St Martin's Dri. W on T—5G 117
St Martin's La. WC2—1J 75
St Martin's le Grand. EC1 —9A 60
St Martin's Pl. WC2—1J 75
St Martin's Rd. N9—2F 28
St Martin's Rd. SW9—1K 91
St Martin's Rd. Dart—5K 99
St Martin's Rd. W Dray—4H 143
St Martin's St. WC2—1H 75
St Martin's Way. SW17—9A 90
St Mary Abbot's Pl. W8—4K 73
St Mary Abbot's Ter. W14 —4K 73
St Mary at Hill. EC3—1C 76
St Mary Av. Wall—5F 122
St Mary Axe. EC3—9C 60
St Marychurch St. SE16—3G 77
St Mary Rd. E17—2L 45
St Mary's. Bark—4B 64
St Mary's App. E12—1K 63
St Mary's Av. E11—5F 46
St Mary's Av. N3—9J 25
St Mary's Av. Brom—7C 110
St Mary's Av. N'wd—5C 20
St Mary's Av. S'hall—5M 69
(in two parts)
St Mary's Av. Stai—6B 144
St Mary's Av. Tedd—3D 102
St Mary's Clo. N17—8E 28
St Mary's Clo. Chess—9K 119
St Mary's Clo. Eps—9D 120
St Mary's Clo. Orp—6G 113
St Mary's Clo. Stai—6B 144
St Mary's Clo. Sun—8E 100
St Mary's Clo. Wat—6G 9
St Mary's Ct. E6—7K 63
St Mary's Ct. SE7—8H 79
St Mary's Ct. W5—3H 71
St Mary's Cres. NW4—1F 40
St Mary's Cres. Hay—1D 68
St Mary's Cres. Iswth—8B 70
St Mary's Cres. Stai—6B 144
St Mary's Dri. Felt—6A 84
St Mary's Gdns. SE11—5L 75
St Mary's Grn. N2—9A 26
St Mary's Grn. West—9G 141
St Mary's Gro. N1—2M 59
St Mary's Gro. SW13—2F 88
St Mary's Gro. W4—7M 71
St Mary's Gro. Rich—3K 87
St Mary's Gro. West—9G 141
St Mary's La. Upm & Brtwd —7M 51
St Mary's Mans. W2—8B 58
St Mary's M. NW6—3M 57
St Mary's Path. N1—4M 59
St Mary's Rd. E10—8A 46
St Mary's Rd. E13—5F 62
St Mary's Rd. N8—2J 43
St Mary's Rd. N9—1F 28
St Mary's Rd. NW10—4C 56
St Mary's Rd. NW11—5J 41
St Mary's Rd. SE15—9G 77
St Mary's Rd. SE25—7C 108
St Mary's Rd. SW19—2J 105
St Mary's Rd. W5—3H 71
St Mary's Rd. Barn—9D 14
St Mary's Rd. Bex—7A 98
St Mary's Rd. E Mol—9B 102
St Mary's Rd. Hay—1D 68
St Mary's Rd. Ilf—7B 48
St Mary's Rd. S Croy—1B 138
St Mary's Rd. Surb—1H 119
St Mary's Rd. Surb—2G 119
(Long Ditton)
St Mary's Rd. Swan—8B 114
St Mary's Rd. Wal X—2C 6
St Mary's Rd. Wat—6F 8
St Mary's Rd. Wey—6B 116
St Mary's Rd. Wor Pk—4C 120
St Mary's Sq. W2—8B 58
St Mary's Ter. W2—8B 58
St Mary St. SE18—5K 79
St Mary's Wlk. SE11—5L 75
St Mary's Wlk. Hay—1D 68
St Mary's Way. Chig—5L 31
St Matthew Clo. Uxb—9B 142
St Matthew's Av. Surb—3J 119
St Matthew's Clo. Rain—3E 66
St Matthew's Clo. Wat—8H 9
St Matthew's Dri. Brom —7K 111
St Matthew's Rd. SW2—4K 91
St Matthew's Rd. W5—2J 71
St Matthew's Row. E2—7E 60
St Matthew St. SW1—4H 75
St Matthias Clo. NW9—3D 40
St Maur Rd. SW6—9K 73
St Merryn Clo. SE18—8B 80
St Merryn Ct. Beck—4L 109
St Michael's All. EC3—9B 60
St Michael's Av. N9—9G 17
St Michael's Av. Wemb—2L 55
St Michael's Clo. N3—9K 25
St Michael's Clo. N12—5C 26
St Michael's Clo. Brom—7J 111
St Michael's Clo. Eri—3H 81
St Michael's Clo. W on T —4G 117
St Michael's Cres. Pinn—4J 37
St Michael's Gdns. W10—8J 57
St Michael's Rise. Well—9F 80
St Michael's Rd. NW2—9G 41
St Michael's Rd. SW9—1K 91
St Michael's Rd. Croy—3A 124
St Michael's Rd. Wall—8G 123
St Michael's Rd. Well—2F 96
St Michael's St. W2—9B 58
St Michael's Ter. N22—8J 27
St Mildred's Ct. EC2—9B 60
St Mildred's Rd. SE12—6D 94
St Neot's Rd. Romf—7K 35
St Nicholas Av. Horn—8E 50
St Nicholas Clo. Borwd—8H 11
St Nicholas Clo. Uxb—9B 142
St Nicholas Glebe. SW17 —2E 106
St Nicholas Rd. SE18—6D 80
St Nicholas Rd. Sutt—7M 121
St Nicholas Rd. Th Dit—1D 118
St Nicholas St. SE8—9K 77
St Nicholas Way. Sutt—6M 121
St Nicolas La. Chst—5J 111
St Norbert Grn. SE4—3J 93
St Norbert Rd. SE4—4H 93
St Norman's Way. Eps—2E 134
St Olaf's Rd. SW6—8J 73
St Olave's Ct. EC2—9B 60
St Olave's Gdns. SE11—5L 75
St Olave's Rd. E6—4L 63
St Olave's Wlk. SW16—6G 107
St Oswald's Pl. SE11—6K 75
St Oswald's Rd. SW16—5M 107
St Pancras Ct. N2—9B 26
St Pancras Way. NW1—3G 59
St Patrick's Ct. Wfd G—7C 30
St Paul Clo. Uxb—8B 142
St Paul's Av. NW2—2G 57
St Paul's Av. SE16—2H 77
St Paul's Av. Harr—2K 39
St Paul's Chyd. EC4—9M 59
St Paul's Clo. W5—3K 71
St Paul's Clo. Ashf—2A 100
St Paul's Clo. Cars—3C 122
St Paul's Clo. Chess—6H 119
St Paul's Clo. Hay—6B 68
St Paul's Clo. Houn—1J 85
St Paul's Clo. S Ock—1M 83
St Paul's Cray Rd. Chst—5B 112
St Paul's Cres. NW1—3H 59
St Paul's Dri. E15—1B 62
St Paul's Pl. N1—2B 60
St Paul's Rd. N1—2M 59
St Paul's Rd. N11—5F 26
St Paul's Rd. N17—8E 28
St Paul's Rd. Bark—4A 64
St Paul's Rd. Bren—7H 71
St Paul's Rd. Eri—8A 82
St Paul's Rd. Rich—2K 87
St Paul's Rd. T Hth—7A 108
St Paul's Sq. Brom—6D 110
St Paul St. N1—4A 60
(in two parts)
St Paul's Wlk. King—4L 103
St Paul's Way. E3—8K 61
St Paul's Way. N3—7M 25
St Paul's Way. Wat—4G 9
St Paul's Wood Hill. Orp —6C 112
St Peter's Av. E2—5E 60
St Peter's Av. E17—2C 46
St Peter's Av. N18—4E 28
St Petersburgh M. W2—1M 73
St Petersburgh Pl. W2—1M 73
St Peter's Clo. E2—5E 60
St Peter's Clo. SW17—8C 90
St Peter's Clo. Barn—7F 12
St Peter's Clo. Bush, Wat —1B 22
St Peter's Clo. Chst—4B 112
St Peter's Clo. Ilf—2D 48
St Peter's Clo. Ruis—7H 37
St Peter's Ct. NW4—3G 41
St Peter's Gdns. SE27—9L 91
St Peter's Gro. W6—5E 72
St Peter's Rd. N9—1F 28
St Peter's Rd. W6—6E 72
St Peter's Rd. Croy—6B 124
St Peter's Rd. E Mol—8L 101
St Peter's Rd. Iswth—4F 86
St Peter's Rd. King—6L 103
St Peter's Rd. S'hall—8L 53
St Peter's Rd. Uxb—8B 142
St Peter's Sq. E2—5E 60
St Peter's Sq. W6—6E 72
St Peter's St. N1—4M 59
St Peter's St. S Croy—7B 124
St Peter's Ter. SW6—8K 73
St Peter's Vs. W6—5E 72
St Peter's Way. N1—3C 60
St Peter's Way. W5—8H 55
St Peter's Way. Hay—6B 68
St Philip's Av. Wor Pk—4F 120
St Philip's Pl. W2—8B 58
St Philip Sq. SW8—1F 90
St Philip's Rd. E8—2E 60
St Philip's Rd. Surb—1H 119
St Philip St. SW8—1F 90
St Philip's Way. N1—4A 60
St Quentin Rd. Well—2D 96
St Quintin Av. W10—8G 57
St Quintin Gdns. W10—8G 57
St Quintin Rd. E13—6F 62
St Raphael's Way. NW10 —1A 56
St Regis Clo. N10—9F 26
St Regis Heights. NW3—8M 41
St Ronan's Clo. Barn—2B 14
St Ronan's Cres. Wfd G—7E 30
St Rule St. SW8—1G 91
St Saviour's Rd. SW2—4K 91
St Saviour's Rd. Croy—1A 124
Saints Dri. E7—1H 63
St Silas Pl. NW5—2E 58
St Simon's Av. SW15—4G 89
St Stephen's Av. E17—3A 46
St Stephen's Av. W12—3F 72
St Stephen's Av. W13—9F 54
St Stephen's Av. Asht—8J 133
St Stephen's Clo. E17—3M 45
St Stephen's Clo. NW8—4C 58
St Stephen's Clo. S'hall—8L 53
St Stephen's Cres. W2—9L 57
St Stephen's Cres. T Hth —7L 107
St Stephen's Gdns. SW15 —4K 89
St Stephen's Gdns. W2—9L 57
(in two parts)
St Stephen's Gdns. Twic —5G 87
St Stephen's Gro. SE13—2A 94
St Stephen's M. W2—8L 57
St Stephen's Pas. Twic—5G 87
St Stephen's Rd. E3—4J 61
St Stephen's Rd. E6—3G 63
St Stephen's Rd. E17—3M 45
St Stephen's Rd. W13—9F 54
St Stephen's Rd. Barn—7H 13
St Stephen's Rd. Enf—1H 17
St Stephen's Rd. Houn—5L 85
St Stephen's Rd. W Dray —2H 143
St Stephen's Ter. SW8—8K 75
St Stephen's Wlk. SW7—5A 74
St Swithin's La. EC4—1B 76
St Swithun's Rd. SE13—5B 94
St Theresa's Rd. Felt—3D 84
St Thomas Ct. Bex—6L 97
St Thomas Dri. Orp—3A 128
St Thomas' Dri. Pinn—8J 21
St Thomas Gdns. Bark—2A 64
St Thomas Rd. E16—9E 62
St Thomas Rd. N14—9H 15
St Thomas Rd. W4—7A 72
St Thomas Rd. Belv—3A 82
St Thomas's Gdns. NW5—2E 58
St Thomas's Pl. E9—3G 61
St Thomas's Rd. N4—7L 43
St Thomas's Rd. NW10—4C 56
St Thomas's Sq. E9—3G 61
St Thomas St. SE1—2B 76
St Thomas's Way. SW6—8K 73
St Ursula Gro. Pinn—3H 37
St Ursula Rd. S'hall—9L 53
St Vincent Rd. Twic—5A 86
St Vincent Rd. W on T—5F 116
St Vincent's Av. Dart—4L 99
St Vincent's Rd. Dart—5L 99
St Vincent St. W1—8E 58
St Wilfrid's Clo. Barn—7C 14
St Wilfrid's Rd. Barn—7C 14
St Winefride's Av. E12—1K 63
St Winifred's Clo. Chig—5A 32
St Winifred's Rd. Tedd—3F 102
St Winifred's Rd. West—9K 141
Saladin Dri. Purf—5L 83
Salamanca Pl. SE1—5K 75
Salamanca St. SE1 & SE11 —5K 75
Salamons Way. Rain—9C 66
Salcombe Dri. Mord—3H 121
Salcombe Dri. Romf—4K 49
Salcombe Gdns. NW7—6G 25
Salcombe Rd. E17—5K 45
Salcombe Rd. N16—1C 60
Salcombe Rd. Ashf—9C 144
Salcombe Way. Hay—6C 52
Salcombe Way. Ruis—7E 36
Salcot Cres. Croy—2A 140
Salcott Rd. SW11—4C 90
Salcott Rd. Croy—5J 123
Salehurst Clo. Harr—3J 39
Salehurst Rd. SE4—5K 93
Salem Pl. Croy—5A 124
Salem Rd. W2—1M 73
Sale Pl. W2—9C 58
Sale St. E2—7E 60
Salford Rd. SW2—7H 91
Salhouse Clo. SE28—9G 65
Salisbury Av. N3—1K 41
Salisbury Av. Bark—3B 64
Salisbury Av. Sutt—8K 121
Salisbury Av. Swan—8E 114
Salisbury Clo. SE17—5B 76
Salisbury Clo. Wor Pk—5D 120
Salisbury Ct. EC4—9M 59
Salisbury Cres. Wal X—5D 6
Salisbury Gdns. SW19—4J 105
Salisbury Gdns. Buck H—2H 31
Salisbury Hall Gdns. E4—7L 29
Salisbury M. SW6—8K 73
Salisbury Pl. W1—8D 58
Salisbury Rd. E4—3L 29
Salisbury Rd. E7—2E 62
Salisbury Rd. E10—7A 46
Salisbury Rd. E12—1H 63
Salisbury Rd. E17—3A 46
Salisbury Rd. N4—3M 43
Salisbury Rd. N9—3E 28
Salisbury Rd. N22—9M 27
Salisbury Rd. SE25—1E 124
Salisbury Rd. SW19—4J 105
Salisbury Rd. W13—3F 70
Salisbury Rd. Bans—6M 135
Salisbury Rd. Barn—5J 13
Salisbury Rd. Bex—7L 97
Salisbury Rd. Brom—9J 111
Salisbury Rd. Cars—8D 122
Salisbury Rd. Dag—2M 65

Salisbury Rd. Enf—1K 17
Salisbury Rd. Felt—7G 85
Salisbury Rd. Harr—3B 38
Salisbury Rd. Houn—2G 85
Salisbury Rd. Ilf—7C 48
Salisbury Rd. N Mald—7B 104
Salisbury Rd. Pinn—2E 36
Salisbury Rd. Rich—3J 87
Salisbury Rd. Romf—3F 50
Salisbury Rd. S'hall—5J 69
Salisbury Rd. Uxb—5A 142
Salisbury Rd. Wat—2F 8
Salisbury Rd. Wor Pk—6B 120
Salisbury Sq. EC4—9L 59
Salisbury St. NW8—7C 58
Salisbury Ter. SE15—2G 93
Salisbury St. W3—3A 72
Salisbury Wlk. N19—7G 43
Salix Clo. Sun—4F 100
Salliesfield. Twic—5B 86
Salmen Rd. E13—5D 62
Salmond Clo. Stan—6E 22
Salmon La. E14—9J 61
Salmon Rd. Belv—6G 81
Salmons Rd. N9—1E 28
Salmons Rd. Chess—8J 119
Salmon St. NW9—6M 39
Salomons Rd. E13—8G 63
Salop Rd. E17—4H 45
Saltash Clo. Sutt—6K 121
Saltash Rd. Ilf—7B 32
Saltash Rd. Well—9G 81
Saltbox Hill. West—5F 140
Saltcoats Rd. W4—3C 72
Saltcroft Clo. Wemb—6M 39
Salterford Rd. SW17—3E 106
Salter Rd. SE16—2H 77
Salters Hill. SE19—2B 108
Salters Rd. E17—2B 46
Salters Rd. W10—7H 57
Salter St. E14—1L 77
Salter St. NW10—6E 56
Salterton Rd. N7—8K 43
Saltford Clo. Eri—6C 82
Salt Hill Clo. Uxb—1C 142
Saltoun Rd. SW2—3L 91
Saltram Clo. N15—2D 44
Saltram Cres. W9—6K 57
Saltwell St. E14—1L 77
Saltwood Clo. Orp—6G 129
Saltwood Gro. SE17—6B 76
Salusbury Rd. NW6—4J 57
Salvador. SW17—2C 106
Salva Gdns. Gnfd—5E 54
Salvin Rd. SW15—2H 89
Salway Clo. Wfd G—7E 30
Salway Pl. E15—2B 62
Salway Rd. E15—2B 62
Samantha Clo. E17—5K 45
Samantha M. Hav. Romf—3C 34
Sam Bartram Clo. SE7—6G 79
Samels Ct. W6—6E 72
Samford St. NW8—7C 58
Samos Rd. SE20—6F 108
Sampson Av. Barn—7H 13
Sampson St. E1—2E 76
Samson St. E13—5G 63
Samuda Est. E14—4A 78
Samuel Clo. E8—4D 60
Samuel Johnson Clo. SW16
—1K 107
Samuel St. SE18—5K 79
Sancroft Clo. NW2—8F 40
Sancroft Rd. Harr—9D 22
Sancroft St. SE11—6K 75
Sanctuary Clo. Dart—5G 99
Sanctuary St. SE1—3A 76
Sanctuary. The. Bex—5H 97
Sanctuary. The. Mord—1L 121
Sandale Clo. N16—8B 44
Sandall Clo. W5—7J 55
Sandall Rd. NW5—2G 59
Sandall Rd. W5—7J 55
Sandal Rd. N18—5E 28
Sandal Rd. N Mald—8C 104
Sandal St. E15—4C 62
Sandalwood Clo. E1—7J 61
Sandalwood Rd. Felt—9F 84
Sandbach Pl. SE18—6A 80
Sandbourne Av. SW19
—6M 105
Sandbourne Rd. SE4—1J 93
Sandbrook Clo. Edgw—6B 24
Sandbrook Rd. N16—8C 44
Sandby Grn. SE9—2J 95
Sandcliff Rd. Eri—5B 82
Sandell's Av. Ashf—1A 100
Sandell St. SE1—3L 75
Sanderling Ct. SE28—1G 81
Sanders Clo. Hmptn—2A 102
Sandersfield Gdns. Bans
—7L 135
Sandersfield Rd. Bans—6M 135

Sanders La. NW7—7J 25
Sanderson Clo. NW5—9F 42
Sanderson Cres. Gnfd—5E 54
Sanderstead Av. NW2—7J 41
Sanderstead Clo. SW12—6G 91
Sanderstead Ct. Av. S Croy
—5E 138
Sanderstead Hill. S Croy
—3C 138
Sanderstead Rd. E10—6J 45
Sanderstead Rd. Orp—1F 128
Sanderstead Rd. S Croy
—9B 124
Sanders Way. N19—6H 43
Sandfield Gdns. T Hth—7M 107
Sandfield Rd. T Hth—7M 107
Sandford Av. N22—8A 28
Sandford Av. Lou—5M 19
Sandford Clo. E6—7K 63
Sandford Rd. E6—6J 63
Sandford Rd. Bexh—3J 97
Sandford Rd. Brom—8E 110
Sandford St. SW6—8M 73
Sandgate Rd. Well—8G 81
Sandgate St. SE15—7F 76
Sandhills. Wall—6H 123
Sandhills Rd. SW6—9M 73
Sandhurst Av. Harr—4M 37
Sandhurst Av. Surb—2M 119
Sandhurst Clo. NW9—1L 39
Sandhurst Clo. S Croy—1C 138
Sandhurst Dri. Ilf—9D 48
Sandhurst Rd. N9—8G 17
Sandhurst Rd. NW9—1L 39
Sandhurst Rd. SE6—7B 94
Sandhurst Rd. Bex—4H 97
Sandhurst Rd. Orp—5E 128
Sandhurst Rd. Sidc—9E 96
Sandhurst Way. S Croy
—9C 124
Sandiford Rd. Sutt—4K 121
Sandiland Cres. Brom—4D 126
Sandilands. Croy—4E 124
Sandilands Rd. SW6—9M 73
Sandison St. SE15—2E 92
Sandland St. WC1—8K 59
Sandling Rise. SE9—9L 95
Sandlings, The. N22—1M 43
Sandmere Rd. SW4—3J 91
Sandon Clo. Esh—2B 118
Sandon Rd. Wal X—3C 6
Sandow Cres. Hay—4D 68
Sandown Av. Dag—2A 66
Sandown Av. Esh—7A 118
Sandown Av. Horn—7H 51
Sandown Clo. Houn—9E 68
Sandown Dri. Cars—1E 136
Sandown Industrial Pk. Esh
—4L 117
Sandown Rd. SE25—9F 108
Sandown Rd. Coul—8E 136
Sandown Rd. Esh—6A 118
Sandown Rd. Wat—2G 9
Sandown Way. N'holt—2J 53
Sandpiper Rd. S Croy—3H 139
Sandpit Rd. SE7—6J 79
Sandpit Rd. Brom—2C 110
Sandpit Rd. Dart—3G 99
Sandpits Rd. Croy—4E 124
Sandpits Rd. Rich—8H 87
Sandra Clo. N22—8A 28
Sandra Clo. Houn—4M 85
Sandridge Clo. Harr—2C 38
Sandringham Av. SW20
—6J 105
Sandringham Clo. Enf—4C 16
Sandringham Clo. Ilf—1A 48
Sandringham Ct. Sutt—1L 135
Sandringham Ct. Uxb—7A 52
Sandringham Cres. Harr
—7L 37
Sandringham Dri. Well—1C 96
Sandringham Gdns. N8—4J 43
Sandringham Gdns. N12
—6B 26
Sandringham Gdns. Houn
—9E 68
Sandringham Gdns. Ilf—1A 48
Sandringham M. W5—1H 71
Sandringham Rd. E7—1G 63
Sandringham Rd. E8—1D 60
Sandringham Rd. E10—4B 46
Sandringham Rd. N22—9A 28
Sandringham Rd. NW2—2F 56
Sandringham Rd. NW11—5J 41
Sandringham Rd. Bark—2D 64
Sandringham Rd. Brom
—2E 110
Sandringham Rd. Houn
—4C 144
Sandringham Rd. N'holt—3L 53
Sandringham Rd. T Hth
—9A 108
Sandringham Rd. Wat—1G 9

Sandringham Rd. Wor Pk
—5E 120
Sandringham Way. Wal X
—7D 6
Sandrock Pl. Croy—6H 125
Sandrock Rd. SE13—2L 93
Sand's End La. SW6—9M 73
Sandstone Pl. N19—7F 42
Sandstone Rd. SE12—8F 94
Sands Way. Wfd G—6K 31
Sandtoft Rd. SE7—7F 78
Sandway Rd. Orp—8G 113
Sandwell Cres. NW6—2L 57
Sandwich St. WC1—6J 59
Sandy Bury. Orp—5B 128
Sandycombe Rd. Felt—7E 84
Sandycombe Rd. Rich—2L 87
Sandycombe Rd. Twic—5G 87
Sandycroft. SE2—7E 80
Sandy Dri. Felt—7C 84
Sandy Hill Av. SE18—6M 79
Sandy Hill Rd. SE18—6M 79
Sandyhill Rd. Ilf—9M 47
Sandy Hill Rd. Wall—1G 137
Sandy La. Bush, Wat & Wat
—5A 10
Sandy La. Harr—4K 39
Sandy La. Mitc—5E 106
Sandy La. N'wd—2D 20
Sandy La. Orp—2E 128
Sandy La. Orp & Sidc—6H 113
Sandy La. Rain & S Ock—1K 83
Sandy La. Rich—8G 87
Sandy La. Sutt—1J 135
Sandy La. Tedd & King—4E 102
Sandy La. W on T—1F 116
Sandy La. N. Wall—7H 123
Sandy La. S. Wall—1G 137
Sandy Lodge La. N'wd—2B 20
Sandy Lodge Rd. Rick—2A 20
Sandy Lodge Way. N'wd
—5C 20
Sandymount Av. Stan—5G 23
Sandy Ridge. Chst—3L 111
Sandy Rd. NW3—7M 41
Sandys Row. E1—8C 60
Sandy Way. Croy—5K 125
Sandy Way. W on T—3D 116
Sanford Clo. Ruis—4A 36
Sanford La. N16—7D 44
Sanford St. SE14—7J 77
Sanford Ter. N16—8D 44
Sanford Wlk. N16—7D 44
Sanford Wlk. SE14—7J 77
Sanger Av. Chess—7J 119
Sangley Rd. SE6—6M 93
Sangley Rd. SE25—8C 108
Sangora Rd. SW11—3B 90
Sansom Rd. E11—7D 46
Sansom St. SE5—9B 76
Sans Wlk. EC1—7L 59
Santley St. SW4—3K 91
Santos Rd. SW18—4L 89
Santway, The. Stan—5C 22
Sapcote Trading Est. NW10
—2D 56
Saphora Clo. Orp—7B 128
Sapphire Rd. SE8—5J 77
Saracen Clo. Croy—1B 124
Saracen St. E14—9J 61
Sarah St. N1—6C 60
Saratoga Rd. E5—9G 45
Sargeant Clo. Uxb—6B 142
Sarita Clo. Harr—9B 22
Sarjant Path. SW19—8H 89
Sark Clo. Houn—8L 69
Sark Wlk. E16—9F 62
Sarnesfield Rd. Enf—6B 16
Sarre Av. Horn—2G 67
Sarre Rd. NW2—1K 57
Sarre Rd. Orp—9G 113
Sarsen Av. Houn—1L 85
Sarsfeld Rd. SW12—7D 90
Sarsfield Rd. Gnfd—5F 54
Sartor Rd. SE15—3H 93
Sarum Grn. Wey—5C 116
Satchell Mead. NW9—8D 24
Satchwell Rd. E2—6E 60
Sauls Grn. E11—8C 46
Saunders Ness Rd. E14—6A 78
Saunders Rd. SE18—6D 80
Saunders Rd. Uxb—3D 142
Saunders Way. SE28—1F 80
Saunderton Rd. Wemb—1F 54
Saunton Av. Hay—8D 68
Saunton Rd. Horn—7E 50
Savage Gdns. E6—9K 63
Savage Gdns. EC3—1C 76
Savernake Rd. N9—8E 16
Savernake Rd. NW3—9D 42
Savile Clo. N Mald—9C 104
Savile Gdns. Croy—4D 124

Savile Row. W1—1G 75
Saville Cres. Ashf—3B 100
Saville Rd. E16—2J 79
Saville Rd. W4—4B 72
Saville Rd. Romf—4H 49
Saville Rd. Twic—7D 86
Saville Row. Enf—4H 17
Savill Gdns. SW20—7E 104
Savill Row. Wfd G—6D 30
Savona Clo. SW19—4H 105
Savona St. SW8—8G 75
Savoy Av. Hay—6C 68
Savoy Clo. E15—4C 62
Savoy Clo. Edgw—5L 23
Savoy Ct. NW3—8M 41
Savoy Ct. WC2—1K 75
Savoy Hill. WC2—1K 75
Savoy Pde. Enf—5C 16
Savoy Pl. WC2—1J 75
Savoy Rd. Dart—4H 99
Savoy St. WC2—1K 75
Sawkins Clo. SW19—8J 89
Sawley Rd. W12—2E 72
Sawtry Clo. Cars—2C 122
Sawyers Hill. Rich—6K 87
Sawyers La. Borwd—3F 10
Sawyers Lawn. W13—9E 54
Sawyer St. SE1—3A 76
Saxby Rd. SW2—6J 91
Saxham Rd. Bark—4C 64
Saxlingham Rd. E4—3B 30
Saxon Av. Felt—8J 85
Saxonbury Av. Sun—7F 100
Saxonbury Clo. Mitc—7B 106
Saxonbury Gdns. Surb—3G 119
Saxon Clo. Uxb—8D 142
Saxon Clo. Romf—9K 35
Saxon Ct. Borwd—3J 11
Saxon Dri. W3—9L 55
Saxon Gdns. S'hall—1J 69
Saxon Pl. S Dar, Dart—9M 115
Saxon Rd. E3—5K 61
Saxon Rd. E6—7K 63
Saxon Rd. N22—8M 27
Saxon Rd. SE25—9B 108
Saxon Rd. Ashf—3B 100
Saxon Rd. Brom—4D 110
Saxon Rd. Dart—1J 115
Saxon Rd. Ilf—2M 63
Saxon Rd. S'hall—1J 69
Saxon Rd. W on T—4H 117
Saxon Rd. Wemb—8A 40
Saxon Wlk. Sidc—3G 113
Saxon Way. N14—8H 15
Saxon Way. Wal A—6J 7
Saxon Way. W Dray—7G 143
Saxony Pde. Hay—8A 52
Saxton Clo. SE13—2B 94
Saxville Rd. Orp—7F 112
Sayer's Wlk. Rich—6K 87
Sayes Ct. SE8—6K 77
Sayes Ct. Rd. Orp—8E 112
Sayes Ct. St. SE8—7K 77
Scads Hill Clo. Orp—1D 128
Scala St. W1—8G 59
Scales Rd. N17—1E 44
Scampston M. W10—9H 57
Scampton Rd. Houn—5D 144
Scandrett St. E1—2F 76
Scarborough Clo. Sutt—3K 135
Scarborough Rd. E11—6B 46
Scarborough Rd. N4—6L 43
Scarborough Rd. N9—9G 17
Scarborough St. E1—9D 60
Scarbrook Rd. Croy—5A 124
Scarle Rd. Wemb—2H 55
Scarlet Rd. SE6—9C 94
Scarlette Mnr. Way. SW2
—6L 91
Scarsbrook Rd. SE3—2H 95
Scarsdale Pl. W8—4M 73
Scarsdale Rd. Harr—8A 38
Scarsdale Vs. W8—4L 73
Scarth Rd. SW13—2D 88
Scawen Rd. SE8—6J 77
Scawfell St. E2—5D 60
Sceptre Rd. E2—6G 61
Sceynes Link. N12—4L 25
Schofield Wlk. SE3—8F 78
Scholars Rd. E4—1B 30
Scholars Rd. SW12—7G 91
Scholefield Rd. N19—7H 43
School All. Twic—7E 86
School App. E2—6C 60
School Ho. La. E1—1H 77
School Ho. La. Tedd—4F 102
School La. SE23—8F 92
School La. Bush, Wat—9M 9
School La. Dag—8G 49
School La. King—5G 103
School La. Pinn—2J 37

School La. Shep—1A 116
School La. Surb—3L 119
School La. Swan—5F 114
School La. Wat & St Alb—7K 5
School La. Well—2F 96
School Mead. Abb L, Wat—5C 4
School Pas. S'hall—1K 69
School Rd. E12—9K 47
School Rd. NW10—7B 56
School Rd. Ashf—3A 100
School Rd. Chst—5A 112
School Rd. Dag—4L 65
School Rd. E Mol—8B 102
School Rd. Hmptn—3A 102
School Rd. Houn—2A 86
School Rd. King—5G 103
School Rd. W on T—7D 116
School Rd. W Dray—7H 143
School Rd. Av. Hmptn—3A 102
School Wlk. Sun—8D 100
School Way. N12—6B 26
Schubert Rd. SW15—4K 89
Schubert Rd. Borwd—8H 11
Sclater St. E1—7D 60
Scoble Pl. N16—9D 44
Scoles Cres. SW2—7L 91
Scoresby St. SE1—2M 75
Scorton Av. Gnfd—5E 54
Scotch Comn. W13—8E 54
Scoter Clo. Wfd G—7F 30
Scotland Grn. N17—9E 28
Scotland Grn. Rd. Enf—7H 17
Scotland Grn. Rd. N. Enf—6J 17
Scotland Pl. SW1—2J 75
Scotland Rd. Buck H—1G 31
Scotney Wlk. Horn—1G 67
Scots Clo. Stai—7B 144
Scotsdale Clo. Orp—8C 112
Scotsdale Clo. Sutt—9J 121
Scotsdale Rd. SE12—4F 94
Scotshall La. Warl—7A 140
Scotswood St. EC1—7L 59
Scotswood Wlk. N17—7E 28
Scott Clo. SW16—5K 107
Scott Clo. Eps—7A 120
Scott Clo. W Dray—5K 143
Scott Cres. Eri—9D 82
Scott Cres. Harr—6M 37
Scott Ellis Gdns. NW8—6B 58
Scottes La. Dag—6H 49
Scott Gdns. Houn—8H 69
Scott Gro. Pinn—7H 21
Scott Lidgett Cres. SE16—3E 76
Scotts Av. Brom—6B 110
Scotts Av. Sun—4C 100
Scotts Clo. Horn—1G 67
Scotts Dri. Hmptn—4M 101
Scotts Farm Dri. Eps—8A 120
Scotts La. Brom—7B 110
Scotts La. W on T—6H 117
Scott's Rd. E10—6A 46
Scotts Rd. W12—3F 72
Scotts Rd. Brom—4E 110
Scott's Rd. S'hall—4G 69
Scott St. E1—7F 60
Scotts Way. Sun—4C 100
Scottswood Clo. Bush, Wat
—4J 9
Scottswood Rd. Bush, Wat
—4J 9
Scoulding Rd. E16—9E 62
Scouler St. E14—1B 78
Scout App. NW10—9C 40
Scout La. SW4—2G 91
Scout Way. NW7—4B 24
Scovell Rd. SE1—3A 76
Scrattons Ter. Bark—4H 65
Scriven St. E8—4D 60
Scrooby St. SE6—5M 93
Scrubs La. NW10—6E 56
Scrutton Clo. SW12—6H 91
Scrutton St. EC2—7C 60
Scudamore La. NW9—2A 40
Scutari Rd. SE22—4G 93
Scylla St. SE15—2F 92
(in two parts)
Scylla Rd. Houn—5F 144
Seabright St. E2—6F 60
Seabrook Dri. W Wick—4C 126
Seabrook Gdns. Romf—5L 49
Seabrook Rd. Dag—8H 49
Seaburn Clo. Rain—6C 66
Seacoal La. EC4—9M 59
Seacourt Rd. SE2—3H 81
Seacroft Gdns. Wat—3H 21
Seafield Rd. N11—4H 27
Seaford Clo. Ruis—7B 36
Seaford Rd. E17—1M 45
Seaford Rd. N15—3B 44
Seaford Rd. W13—2F 70
Seaford Rd. Enf—6C 16
Seaford St. WC1—6J 59

Seaforth Av. N Mald—9F 104
Seaforth Clo. Romf—7C 34
Seaforth Cres. N5—1A 60
Seaforth Dri. Wal X—7D 6
Seaforth Gdns. N21—9K 15
Seaforth Gdns. Eps—6D 120
Seaforth Gdns. Wfd G—5G 31
Seager Pl. E3—8K 61
Seagrave Rd. SW6—7L 73
Seagry Rd. E11—4E 46
Sealand Rd. Houn—5E 144
Sealand Wlk. N'holt—6H 53
Seal St. E8—9D 44
Searches La. Abb L, Wat
—1F 4
Searchwood Rd. Warl—9F 138
Searle Pl. N4—6K 43
Searles Clo. SW11—8C 74
Searles Rd. SE1—5B 76
Sears St. SE5—8B 76
Seasprite Clo. N'holt—6H 53
Seaton Av. Ilf—1D 64
Seaton Clo. E13—7E 62
Seaton Clo. SE11—6L 75
Seaton Clo. SW15—7F 88
Seaton Clo. Twic 5B 86
Seaton Dri. Ashf—8C 144
Seaton Gdns. Ruis—8E 36
Seaton Rd. Dart—6E 98
Seaton Rd. Hay—5B 68
Seaton Rd. Mitc—6C 106
Seaton Rd. Twic—5A 86
Seaton Rd. Well—8G 81
Seaton Rd. Wemb—5J 55
Seaton St. N18—5E 28
Sebastian St. EC1—6M 59
Sebastopol Rd. N9—4E 28
Sebbon St. N1—3M 59
Sebert Rd. E7—1F 62
Sebright Pas. E2—5E 60
Sebright Rd. Barn—4H 13
Secker Cres. Harr—8A 22
Secker St. SE1—2L 75
Second Av. E12—9J 47
Second Av. E13—6E 62
Second Av. E17—3L 45
Second Av. N18—4G 29
Second Av. NW4—2H 41
Second Av. SW14—2C 88
Second Av. W3—2D 72
Second Av. W10—7J 57
Second Av. Dag—5M 65
Second Av. Enf—7D 16
Second Av. Hay—2D 68
Second Av. Romf—3G 49
Second Av. W on T—1F 116
Second Av. Wat—8H 5
Second Av. Wemb—7H 39
Second Clo. E Mol—8A 102
Second Cross Rd. Twic—8C 86
Second Way. Wemb—9M 39
Sedan Way. SE17—6C 76
Sedcombe Clo. Sidc—1G 113
Sedcote Rd. Enf—7H 17
Sedding St. SW1—5E 74
Seddon Rd. Mord—9B 106
Seddon St. WC1—6K 59
Sedgebrook Rd. SE3—2H 95
Sedgecombe Av. Harr—3G 39
Sedgefield Clo. Romf—4K 35
Sedgefield Cres. Romf—4K 35
Sedgeford Rd. W12—2D 72
Sedgehill Rd. SE6—1L 109
Sedgemere Av. N2—1A 42
Sedgemere Rd. SE2—4G 81
Sedgemoor Dri. Dag—9L 49
Sedgeway. SE6—7D 94
Sedgewick Av. Uxb—3F 142
Sedgewood Clo. Brom—2D 126
Sedgmoor Pl. SE5—8C 76
Sedgwick Rd. E10—7A 46
Sedgwick St. E9—1H 61
Sedleigh Rd. SW18—5K 89
Sedlescombe Rd. SW6—7L 73
Sedley Pl. W1—9F 58
Sedley Rise. Lou—4K 19
Seeley St. SE21—1C 108
Seelig Av. NW9—5E 40
Seely Rd. SW17—3E 106
Seething La. EC3—1C 76
Seething Wells La. Surb
—1G 119
Sefton Av. NW7—5B 24
Sefton Av. Harr—8B 22
Sefton Clo. Orp—8D 112
Sefton Rd. Croy—3E 124
Sefton Rd. Eps—2B 134
Sefton Rd. Orp—8D 112
Sefton St. SW15—2G 89
Sefton Way. Uxb—9A 142
Segal Clo. SE23—6J 93
Sekforde St. EC1—7M 59
Selan Gdns. Hay—8F 52

Selbie Av. NW10—1D 56
Selborne Av. E12—9L 47
Selborne Av. Bex—7J 97
Selborne Gdns. NW4—2E 40
Selborne Gdns. Gnfd—5E 54
Selborne Rd. E17—3K 45
Selborne Rd. N14—3J 27
Selborne Rd. N22—8K 27
Selborne Rd. Croy—5C 124
Selborne Rd. Ilf—7L 47
Selborne Rd. N Mald—6C 104
Selborne Rd. Sidc—1F 112
Selbourne Av. Surb—4K 119
Selby Chase. Ruis—7F 36
Selby Clo. E6—8J 63
Selby Clo. Chess—9J 119
Selby Clo. Chst—3L 111
Selby Gdns. S'hall—7L 53
Selby Grn. Cars—2C 122
Selby Rd. E11—8C 46
Selby Rd. E13—8F 62
Selby Rd. N17—7C 28
Selby Rd. SE20—6E 108
Selby Rd. W5—7F 54
Selby Rd. Ashf—3A 100
Selby Rd. Cars—2C 122
Selby St. E1—7E 60
Selcroft Rd. Purl—4M 137
Selden Rd. SE15—1G 93
Selincourt Rd. SW17—2C 106
Sellindge Clo. Beck—4K 109
Sellon M. SE11—5K 75
Sellons Av. NW10—4D 56
Sellwood Dri. Barn—7H 13
Selsdon Av. S Croy—8B 124
Selsdon Clo. Romf—8A 34
Selsdon Clo. Surb—9J 103
Selsdon Cres. S Croy—1G 139
Selsdon Pk. Rd. S Croy & Croy
—1H 139
Selsdon Rd. E11—5E 46
Selsdon Rd. E13—4G 63
Selsdon Rd. NW2—7D 40
Selsdon Rd. SE27—9L 91
Selsdon Rd. S Croy—7B 124
Selsea Pl. N16—1C 60
Selsey Cres. Well—9H 81
Selsey St. E14—8L 61
Selvage La. NW7—5B 24
Selway Clo. Pinn—1F 36
Selwin Clo. Houn—3J 85
Selwood Clo. Stai—5A 144
Selwood Gdns. Stai—5A 144
Selwood Pl. SW7—6B 74
Selwood Rd. Chess—6H 119
Selwood Rd. Croy—4F 124
Selwood Rd. Sutt—3K 121
Selwood Ter. SW7—6B 74
Selworthy Clo. E11 -3E 46
Selworthy Rd. SE6—9K 93
Selwyn Av. E4—6A 30
Selwyn Av. Ilf—4D 48
Selwyn Av. Rich—2J 87
Selwyn Ct. Edgw—7M 23
Selwyn Cres. Well—2F 96
Selwyn Pl. Orp—7F 112
Selwyn Rd. E3—5K 61
Selwyn Rd. E13—4F 62
Selwyn Rd. NW10—3C 56
Selwyn Rd. N Mald—9B 104
Semley Ga. E9—2K 61
Semley Pl. SW1—5E 74
Semley Rd. SW16—6J 107
Senate St. SE15—1G 93
Seneca Rd. SW4—3J 91
Seneca Rd. T Hth—8A 108
Senga Rd. Wall—3E 122
Senhouse Rd. Sutt—5H 121
Senior St. W2—8M 57
Senlac Rd. SE12—7F 94
Sennen Rd. Enf—9D 16
Senrab St. E1—9H 61
Sentinel Sq. NW4—2G 41
September Way. Stan—6F 22
Septimus Pl. Enf—7E 16
Sequoia Clo. Bush, Wat—1B 22
Sequoia Gdns. Orp—2D 128
Sequoia Pk. Pinn—6M 21
Serbin Clo. E10—5A 46
Serjeant's Inn. EC4—9L 59
Serle St. WC2—9K 59
Sermon Dri. Swan—7A 114
Serpentine Rd. W2—2C 74
Serviden Dri. Brom—5H 111

Setchell Rd. SE1—5D 76
Setchell Way. SE1—5D 76
Seth St. SE16—3G 77
Seton Gdns. Dag—3G 65
Settle Rd. E13—5E 62
Settle Rd. Romf—4L 35
Settles St. E1—8E 60
Settrington Rd. SW6—1M 89
Seven Dials. WC2—9J 59
Seven Hills Clo. W on T—9C 116
Seven Hills Rd. W on T & Cob
—9C 116
Seven Kings Rd. Ilf—7D 48
Sevenoaks Clo. Bexh—3M 97
Sevenoaks Clo. Romf—4G 35
Sevenoaks Ct. N'wd—7A 20
Sevenoaks Rd. SE4—5J 93
Sevenoaks Rd. Orp & Sev
—6D 128
Sevenoaks Way. Orp & Sidc
—4G 113
Sevenoaks Way Industrial Est.
Orp—7G 113
Seven Sisters Rd.—8K 43
N7 1a-163 & 2-188a
N4 105-437 & 190-486
N15 remainder
Seventh Av. E12—9K 47
Seventh Av. Hay—2E 68
Severn Av. Romf—1F 50
Severn Dri. Enf—2E 16
Severn Dri. Esh—4E 118
Severn Dri. W on T—4H 117
Severn Way. NW10—1D 56
Severn Way. Wat—7G 5
Severus Rd. SW11—3C 90
Seville St. SW1—3D 74
Sevington Rd. NW4—4F 40
Sevington St. W9—7M 57
Seward Rd. W7—3E 70
Seward Rd. Beck—6H 109
Sewardstone Gdns. E4—7M 17
Sewardstone Rd. E2—5G 61
Sewardstone Rd. E4 & Wal A
—9M 17
Sewardstone St. Wal A—6J 7
Seward St. EC1—6A 60
Sewdley St. E5—9H 45
Sewell Rd. SE2—4E 80
Sewell St. E13—6E 62
Sexton Clo. Rain—4D 66
Seymer Rd. Romf—1B 50
Seymour Av. N17—9E 28
Seymour Av. Eps—1F 134
Seymour Av. Mord—2H 121
Seymour Clo. EC1—7M 59
Seymour Clo. E Mol—9A 102
Seymour Clo. Pinn—8K 21
Seymour Ct. E4—2D 30
Seymour Ct. NW2—7F 40
Seymour Gdns. Felt—1G 101
Seymour Gdns. Ilf—6K 47
Seymour Gdns. Ruis—6H 37
Seymour Gdns. Surb—9K 103
Seymour Gdns. Twic—6F 86
Seymour M. W1—9E 58
Seymour Pl. SE25—8F 108
Seymour Pl. W1—8D 58
Seymour Rd. E4—1M 29
Seymour Rd. E6—5H 63
Seymour Rd. E10—6K 45
Seymour Rd. N3—7M 25
Seymour Rd. N8—3L 43
Seymour Rd. N9—2F 28
Seymour Rd. SW18—5K 89
Seymour Rd. SW19—9H 89
Seymour Rd. W4—5A 72
Seymour Rd. Cars—7E 122
Seymour Rd. E Mol—9A 102
Seymour Rd. Hmptn—2A 102
Seymour Rd. King—5H 103
Seymour Rd. Mitc—2E 122
Seymours, The. Lou—3L 19
Seymour St.—9D 58
W1 1-61 & 2-68
W2 remainder
Seymour Ter. SE20—5F 108
Seymour Vs. SE20—5F 108
Seymour Wlk. SW10—7A 74
Seymour Way. Sun—4C 100
Seysell St. E14—5A 78
Shaa Rd. W3—1B 72
Shacklegate La. Tedd—1C 102
Shackleton Clo. SE23—8F 92
Shackleton Rd. S'hall—1K 69
Shacklewell Grn. E8—9D 44
Shacklewell La. E8—1D 60
Shacklewell Rd. N16—9D 44
Shacklewell Row. E8—9D 44
Shacklewell St. E2—6D 60
Shadbolt Clo. Wor Pk—4D 120
Shad Thames. SE1—3D 76
Shadwell Dri. N'holt—6K 53

Shadwell Pierhead. E1—1G 77
Shadwell Pl. E1—1G 77
Shadybush Clo. Bush, Wat
—9A 10
Shady La. Wat—4F 8
Shaef Way. Tedd—4E 102
Shafter Rd. Dag—2A 66
Shaftesbury. Lou—5H 19
Shaftesbury Av.—1H 75
W1 1-111 & 2-136
WC2 remainder
Shaftesbury Av. Barn—6A 14
Shaftesbury Av. Enf -4H 17
Shaftesbury Av. Felt—5E 84
Shaftesbury Av. Harr—6M 37
Shaftesbury Av. Harr—3H 39
(Kenton)
Shaftesbury Av. S'hall—4L 69
Shaftesbury La. Dart—3M 99
Shaftesbury Rd. E4—1B 30
Shaftesbury Rd. E7—3G 63
Shaftesbury Rd. E10—6L 45
Shaftesbury Rd. E17—4M 45
Shaftesbury Rd. N18—6C 28
Shaftesbury Rd. N19—6J 43
Shaftesbury Rd. Beck—6K 109
Shaftesbury Rd. Cars—2B 122
Shaftesbury Rd. Rich—2J 87
Shaftesbury Rd. Romf—4D 50
Shaftesbury Rd. Wat—5G 9
Shaftesburys, The. Bark—5A 64
Shaftesbury St. N1—5A 60
Shaftesbury Way. K Lan—1A 4
Shaftesbury Way. Twic—9B 86
Shaftesbury Waye. Hay—9G 53
Shafto M. SW1—4D 74
Shafton Rd. E9—4H 61
Shafts Ct. EC3—9C 60
Shakespeare Av N11—5G 27
Shakespeare Av. NW10—4B 56
Shakespeare Av. Felt—5E 84
Shakespeare Av. Hay—9E 52
(in two parts)
Shakespeare Ct. Barn—5M 13
Shakespeare Cres. E12—2K 63
Shakespeare Cres. NW10
—4B 56
Shakespeare Dri. Harr—4K 39
Shakespeare Gdns. N2—2D 42
Shakespeare Rd. E17—9H 29
Shakespeare Rd. N3—8L 25
Shakespeare Rd. NW7—4E 24
Shakespeare Rd. SE24—4M 91
Shakespeare Rd. W3—2A 72
Shakespeare Rd. W7—1D 70
Shakespeare Rd. Bexh—9J 81
Shakespeare Rd. Dart—3L 99
Shakespeare Rd. Romf—4D 50
Shakespeare Sq. Ilf—6A 32
Shakespeare St. Wat—2F 8
Shakespeare Way. Felt
—1G 101
Shakspeare Wlk. N16—9C 44
Shalcomb St. SW10—7A 74
Shalcross Dri. Wal X—3F 6
Shaldon Dri. Mord—9J 105
Shaldon Dri. Ruis—8G 37
Shaldon Rd. Edgw—9K 23
Shaldon Way. W on T—5G 117
Shalfleet Dri. W10—1H 73
Shalford Clo. Orp—6A 128
Shalimar Gdns. W3—1A 72
Shalimar Rd. W3—1A 72
Shallons Rd. SE9—1M 111
Shalstone Rd. SW14—2M 87
Shalston Vs. Surb—1K 119
Shamrock Rd. Croy—1K 123
Shamrock St. SW4—2H 91
Shamrock Way. N14—1F 26
Shandon Rd. SW4—5G 91
Shand St. SE1—3C 76
Shandy St. E1—8H 61
Shanklin Gdns. Wat—4G 21
Shanklin Rd. N8—3H 43
Shanklin Rd. N15—2E 44
Shanklin Way. SE15—8D 76
Shannon Clo. S'hall—6H 69
Shannon Gro. SW9—3K 91
Shannon Pl. NW8—5C 58
Shannon Way. S Ock—1M 83
Shannon Way. Beck—3M 109
Shap Cres. Cars—3D 122
Shap St. E2—5D 60
(in two parts)
Shardcroft Av. SE24—4M 91
Shardeloes Rd. SE14—1K 93
Shard's Sq. SE15—7E 76
Sharman Ct. Sidc—1E 112
Sharnbrooke Clo. Well—2G 97
Sharon Clo. Eps—5A 134
Sharon Clo. Surb—3H 119
Sharon Gdns. E9—4G 61
Sharon Rd. W4—6B 72

Sharon Rd. Enf—4J 17
Sharpleshall St. NW1—3D 58
Sharp's La. Ruis—5B 36
Sharp Way. Dart—2K 99
Sharratt St. SE15—7G 77
Sharsted St. SE17—6M 75
Sharvel La. N'holt—4F 52
Shaw Av. Bark—5J 65
Shawbrooke Rd. SE9—4H 95
Shawbury Rd. SE22—4D 92
Shaw Clo. SE28—2F 80
Shaw Clo. Bush, Wat—2B 22
Shaw Clo. Eps—3D 134
Shaw Clo. S Croy—4D 138
Shaw Clo. Wal X—1C 6
Shaw Cres. S Croy—4D 138
Shawfield Pk. Brom—6H 111
Shawfield St. SW3—6C 74
Shawford Ct. SW15—6E 88
Shawford Rd. Eps—8B 120
Shaw Gdns. Bark—5J 65
Shawley Cres. Eps—9G 135
Shawley Way. Eps—9F 134
Shaw Rd. Brom—9D 94
Shaw Rd. Enf—3H 17
Shaw Sq. E17—8J 29
Shaw Way. Wall—9J 123
Shaxton Cres. Croy—1A 140
Shearing Dri. Cars—2A 122
Shearling Way. N7—2J 59
Shearman Rd. SE3—3D 94
Shearwood Cres. Dart—2E 98
Sheath's La. Lea—5A 132
Sheaveshill Av. NW9—2C 40
Sheba St. E1—7D 60
Sheen Comn. Dri. Rich—3L 87
Sheen Ct. Rd. Rich—3L 87
Sheendale Rd. Rich—3K 87
Sheenewood. SE26—1F 108
Sheen Ga. Gdns. SW14—3A 88
Sheen Gro. N1—4L 59
Sheen La. SW14—4A 88
Sheen Pk. Rich—3K 87
Sheen Rd. Orp—8D 112
Sheen Rd. Rich—4J 87
Sheen Way. Wall—7K 123
Sheen Wood. SW14—4A 88
Sheepbarn La. Warl—4D 140
Sheepcot Dri. Wat—7G 5
Sheepcote Clo. Houn—8E 68
Sheepcote La. SW11—1D 90
Sheepcote Rd. Harr—4D 38
Sheepcotes Rd. Romf—2J 49
Sheepcot La. Wat—6E 4
(in two parts)
Sheephouse Way. N Mald
—2C 120
Sheep La. E8—4F 60
Sheep Wlk. M. SW19—3J 105
Sheerwater Rd. E16—8H 63
Sheffield Dri. Romf—5L 35
Sheffield Gdns. Romf—5L 35
Sheffield Sq. E3—6K 61
Sheffield St. WC2—9K 59
Sheffield Ter. W8—2L 73
Shefton Rise. N'wd—7E 20
Sheila Clo. Romf—7M 33
Sheila Rd. Romf—7M 33
Sheilings, The. Horn—3K 51
Shelbourne Clo. Pinn—1K 37
Shelbourne Rd. N17—8F 28
Shelburne Rd. N7—9K 43
Shelbury Clo. Sidc—9E 96
Shelbury Rd. SE22—4F 92
Sheldon Av. N6—5C 42
Sheldon Av. Ilf—9M 31
Sheldon Clo. SE20—5F 108
Sheldon Rd. N18—4C 28
Sheldon Rd. NW2—9H 41
Sheldon Rd. Bexh—9K 81
Sheldon Rd. Dag—3J 65
Sheldon St. Croy—5A 124
Sheldrake Pl. W8—3L 73
Sheldrick Clo. Mitc—6B 106
Shelford Pl. N16—8B 44
Shelford Rise. SE19—4D 108
Shelford Rd. Barn—8G 13
Shelgate Rd. SW11—4C 90
Shell Clo. Brom—1J 127
Shelley Av. E12—2J 63
Shelley Av. Gnfd—6B 54
Shelley Av. Horn—7D 50
Shelley Clo. Bans—7J 135
Shelley Clo. Edgw—4L 23
Shelley Clo. Gnfd—6B 54
Shelley Clo. Hay—8E 52
Shelley Clo. N'wd—5D 20
Shelley Clo. Orp—5C 128
Shelley Clo. Houn—9H 69
Shelley Cres. S'hall—9K 53
Shelley Dri. Well—9C 80

Shelley Gdns. Wemb—7G 39
Shelley Gro. Lou—6K 19
Shellness Rd. E5—1F 60
Shell Rd. SE13—2M 93
Shellwood Rd. SW11—1D 90
Shelmerdine Clo. E3—8L 61
Shelson Av. Felt—9D 84
Shelton Av. Warl—9G 139
Shelton Av. Warl—9H 19
Shelton Clo. Warl—9G 139
Shelton Rd. SW19—5L 105
Shelton St. WC2—9J 59
  (in two parts)
Shenfield Rd. Wfd G—7F 30
Shenfield St. N1—5C 60
Shenley Av. Ruis—7D 36
Shenley Rd. SE5—9C 76
Shenley Rd. Borwd—6L 11
Shenley Rd. Dart—5L 99
Shenley Rd. Houn—9J 69
Shenstone Clo. Dart—3B 98
Shenstone Gdns. Romf—8G 35
Shepherdess Pl. N1—6B 60
Shepherdess Wlk. N1—5A 60
Shepherd Mkt. W1—2F 74
Shepherd's Bush Centre. W12
  —3H 73
Shepherd's Bush Grn. W12
  —3G 73
Shepherd's Bush Mkt. W12
  —3G 73
Shepherd's Bush Pl. W12
  —3H 73
Shepherd's Bush Rd. W6
  —5G 73
Shepherd's Clo. N6—4F 42
Shepherd's Clo. Orp—5D 128
Shepherds Clo. Romf—3H 49
Shepherds Clo. Uxb—7A 142
Shepherds Grn. Chst—4B 112
Shepherd's Hill. N6—4F 42
Shepherds Hill. Romf—9L 35
Shepherd's La. E9—2H 61
Shepherd's La. Dart—7E 98
Shepherds Pl. W1—1E 74
Shepherd's Rd. Wat—6D 8
Shepherd St. W1—2F 74
Shepherd's Wlk. NW3—1B 58
Shepherds Way. S Croy
  —9H 125
Shepiston La. W Dray & Hay
  —5M 143
Shepley Clo. Cars—5E 122
Shepley Clo. Horn—1H 67
Sheppard Clo. Enf—3F 16
Sheppard Clo. King—8J 103
Sheppard St. E16—7D 62
Shepperton Clo. Borwd—3B 12
Shepperton Rd. N1—4B 60
Shepperton Rd. Orp—1A 128
Sheppey Clo. Eri—8F 82
Sheppey Gdns. Dag—3G 65
Sheppey Rd. Dag—3F 64
Sheppey's La. K Lan & Abb L,
  Wat—2A 4
Sheppey Wlk. N1—2A 60
Sherard Rd. SE9—4J 95
Sheraton Clo. Borwd—7K 11
Sheraton Dri. Eps—5A 134
Sheraton St. W1—9H 59
Sherborne Av. Enf—4G 17
Sherborne Av. S'hall—5L 69
Sherborne Cres. Cars—2C 122
Sherborne Gdns. NW9—1L 39
Sherborne Gdns. W13—8F 54
Sherborne Gdns. Romf—5L 33
Sherborne La. EC4—1B 76
Sherborne Rd. Chess—7J 119
Sherborne Rd. Felt—7B 84
Sherborne Rd. Orp—9D 112
Sherborne Rd. Sutt—4L 121
Sherborne St. N1—4B 60
Sherborne Way. Rick—7A 8
Sherbourne Clo. Eps—9G 135
Sherbrooke Clo. Bexh—3L 97
Sherbrooke Rd. SW6—8J 73
Sherbrook Gdns. N21—9M 15
Shere Av. Sutt—2G 135
Shereboro Rd. N15—4D 44
Shere Clo. Chess—7H 119
Sheredan Rd. E4—5C 30
Shere Rd. Ilf—3L 47
Sherfield Gdns. SW15—5D 88
Sheridan Clo. Romf—7G 35
Sheridan Clo. Swan—8D 114
Sheridan Clo. Uxb—7A 52
Sheridan Ct. Dart—3L 99
Sheridan Cres. Chst—6M 111
Sheridan Gdns. Harr—4H 39
Sheridan Pl. Hmptn—5M 101
Sheridan Rd. E7—8D 46
Sheridan Rd. E12—1J 63
Sheridan Rd. SW19—5K 105
Sheridan Rd. Belv—5L 81

Sheridan Rd. Bexh—2J 97
Sheridan Rd. Rich—9G 87
Sheridan Rd. Wat—9H 9
Sheridan St. E1—9F 60
Sheridan Ter. N'holt—1M 53
Sheridan Wlk. NW11—4L 41
Sheridan Wlk. Cars—7D 122
Sheriff Way. Wat—6E 4
Sheringham Av. E12—9K 47
Sheringham Av. N14—7H 15
Sheringham Av. Felt—9E 84
Sheringham Av. Romf—4A 50
Sheringham Av. Twic—7L 85
Sheringham Dri. Bark—1D 64
Sheringham Rd. N7—2L 59
Sheringham Rd. SE20—7G 109
Sherington Av. Pinn—7L 21
Sherington Rd. SE7—7F 78
Sherland Rd. Twic—7D 86
Sherlies Av. Orp—4C 128
Sherlock M. W1—8E 58
Shermanbury Pl. Eri—8D 82
Sherman Rd. Brom—5E 110
Shernbroke Rd. Wal A—7M 7
Shernhall St. E17—1A 46
Sherrard Rd.—2G 63
  E7 1-195 & 2-210
  E12 remainder
Sherrards Way. Barn—7L 13
Sherrick Grn. Rd. NW10—1F 56
Sherriff Rd. NW6—2L 57
Sherringham Av. N17—9E 28
Sherrock Gdns. NW4—2E 40
Sherwin Rd. SE14—9H 77
Sherwood Av. E18—1F 46
Sherwood Av. SW16—4H 107
Sherwood Av. Gnfd—2C 54
Sherwood Av. Hay—7F 52
Sherwood Av. Ruis—4C 36
Sherwood Clo. SW15—2F 88
Sherwood Clo. W13—2F 70
Sherwood Clo. Bex—5G 97
Sherwood Gdns. Bark—3B 64
Sherwood Pk. Av. Sidc—6E 96
Sherwood Pk. Rd. Mitc—8G 107
Sherwood Pk. Rd. Sutt—7L 121
Sherwood Rd. NW4—1G 41
Sherwood Rd. SW19—4K 105
Sherwood Rd. Coul—8G 137
Sherwood Rd. Croy—2F 124
Sherwood Rd. Hmptn—2A 102
Sherwood Rd. Harr—7A 38
Sherwood Rd. Ilf—2B 48
Sherwood Rd. Well—1C 96
Sherwoods Rd. Wat—9J 9
Sherwood St. N20—3B 26
Sherwood St. W1—1G 75
Sherwood Ter. N20—3B 26
Sherwood Way. W Wick
  —4A 126
Shetland Clo. Borwd—8B 12
Shetland Rd. E3—5K 61
Shield Dri. Bren—7E 70
Shieldhall St. SE2—5G 81
Shield Rd. Ashf—1A 100
Shilliber Wlk. Chig—3D 32
Shillingford St. N1—3M 59
Shillitoe Rd. N13—5A 28
Shinfield St. W12—9G 57
Shinford Path. SE23—9H 93
Shingle Ct. Wal A—6M 7
Shingle End. Bren—8G 71
Shinglewell Rd. Eri—8L 81
Ship & Half Moon Pas. SE18
  —4M 79
Ship & Mermaid Row. SE1
  —3B 76
Shipka Rd. SW12—7F 90
Ship La. SW14—1A 88
Ship La. S at H, Dart—5H 115
Shipman Rd. E16—9F 62
Shipman Rd. SE23—8H 93
Ship St. SE8—9L 77
Ship Tavern Pas. EC3—1C 76
Shipton Clo. Dag—8H 49
Shipton Pl. NW5—2E 58
Shipton St. E2—6D 60
Shipway Ter. N16—8D 44
Shipwright Rd. SE16—3J 77
Shirbutt St. E14—1M 77
Shirebrook Rd. SE3—2H 95
Shirehall Clo. NW4—4H 41
Shirehall Gdns. NW4—4H 41
Shirehall La. NW4—4H 41
Shirehall Pk. NW4—4H 41
Shirehall Rd. Dart—2G 115
Shire La. Kes & Orp—9K 127
Shire La. Orp—7C 128
Shiremeade. Borwd—7K 11
Shires, The. Rich—1J 103
Shirland M. W9—6K 57
Shirland Rd. W9—6K 57
Shirley Av. Bex—6H 97

Shirley Av. Croy—3G 125
Shirley Av. Sutt—6B 122
Shirley Av. Sutt—1K 135
  (Belmont)
Shirley Chu. Rd. Croy—5H 125
Shirley Clo. E17—3M 45
Shirley Clo. Dart—3G 99
Shirley Clo. Houn—4A 86
Shirley Clo. Wal X—2C 6
Shirley Ct. Lou—4K 19
Shirley Cres. Beck—8J 109
Shirley Dri. Houn—4A 86
Shirley Gdns. W7—2D 70
Shirley Gdns. Bark—2C 64
Shirley Gdns. Horn—7G 51
Shirley Gro. N9—9H 17
Shirley Gro. SW11—2E 90
Shirley Heights. Wall—1G 137
Shirley Hills Rd. Croy—7G 125
Shirley Ho. Dri. SE7—8G 79
Shirley Oaks Rd. Croy—3H 125
Shirley Pk. Rd. Croy—3F 124
Shirley Rd. E15—3C 62
Shirley Rd. W4—3B 72
Shirley Rd. Abb L, Wat—5D 4
Shirley Rd. Croy—2F 124
Shirley Rd. Enf—5A 16
Shirley Rd. Sidc—9C 96
Shirley Rd. Wall—1G 137
Shirley St. E16—9D 62
Shirley Way. Croy—5J 125
Shirlock Rd. NW3—9D 42
Shobden Rd. N17—8B 28
Shoebury Rd. E6—3K 63
Shoe La. EC4—9L 59
Sholden Gdns. Orp—9G 113
Shooters Av. Harr—2G 39
Shooters Hill. SE18 & Well
  —9L 79
Shooters Hill Rd.—9B 78
  SE3 1-311 & 2-238
  SE18 remainder
Shooters Rd. Enf—3M 15
Shoot up Hill. NW2—1J 57
Shord Hill. Kenl—8B 138
Shore Clo. Felt—6E 84
Shore Clo. Hmptn—3J 101
Shoreditch High St. E1—7C 60
Shore Gro. Felt—8L 85
Shoreham Clo. SW18—4M 89
Shoreham Clo. Bex—7H 97
Shoreham Clo. Croy—9G 109
Shoreham La. Orp—8L 129
Shoreham Rd. Orp—6F 112
Shoreham Rd. E. Houn—4C 144
Shoreham Rd. W. Houn—4C 144
Shoreham Way. Brom—1E 126
Shore Pl. E9—3G 61
Shore Rd. E9—3G 61
Shorncliffe Rd. SE1—6D 76
Shorndean St. SE6—7A 94
Shorne Clo. Orp—8H 113
Shorne Clo. Sidc—5F 96
Shornefield Clo. Brom—7L 111
Shornells Way. SE2—6G 81
Shorrold's Rd. SW6—8K 73
Shortcroft Rd. Eps—9D 120
Shortcrofts Rd. Dag—2K 65
Shorter St. E1—1D 76
Short Rd. E11—7C 46
Short Rd. E15—4B 62
Short Rd. W4—7C 72
Short Rd. Houn—5C 144
Shorts Croft. NW9—2M 39
Shorts Gdns. WC2—9J 59
Shorts Rd. Cars—6C 122
Short St. NW4—2G 41
Short St. SE1—3L 75
Short Wall. E15—6A 62
Short Way. N12—6C 26
Short Way. SE9—2J 95
Short Way. Twic—6A 86
Shortwood Av. Ashf—9A 144
Shotfield. Wall—8F 122
Shotfield Av. SW14—3C 88
Shottendane Rd. SW6—9L 73
Shottery Clo. SE9—9J 95
Shoulder of Mutton All. E14
  —1J 77
Silbury Ho. SE26—9E 92

Shouldham St. W1—8C 58
Showers Way. Hay—2E 68
Shrapnel Clo. SE18—8J 79
Shrapnel Rd. SE9—2K 95
Shrewsbury Av. SW14—3B 88
Shrewsbury Av. Harr—2J 39
Shrewsbury Clo. Surb—4J 119
Shrewsbury Cres. NW10
  —4B 56
Shrewsbury La. SE18—9M 79
Shrewsbury Rd. E7—1H 63
Shrewsbury Rd. N11—6H 27
Shrewsbury Rd. W2—9L 57
Shrewsbury Rd. Beck—7J 109
Shrewsbury Rd. Cars—2C 122
Shrewsbury Wlk. Iswth—2E 86
Shrewton Rd. SW17—4D 106
Shroffold Rd. Brom—1C 110
Shropshire Clo. Mitc—8J 107
Shropshire Pl. WC1—7G 59
Shropshire Rd. N22—7K 27
Shroton St. NW1—8C 58
Shrubberies, The. E18—9E 30
Shrubberies, The. Chig—5A 32
Shrubbery Gdns. N21—9M 15
Shrubbery Rd. N9—2E 28
Shrubbery Rd. SW16—1J 107
Shrubbery Rd. S'hall—2L 69
Shrubbery, The. Upm—8M 51
Shrubland Gro. Wor Pk
  —5G 121
Shrubland Rd. E8—4E 60
Shrubland Rd. E10—5L 45
Shrubland Rd. E17—3L 45
Shrubland Rd. Bans—8K 135
Shrublands Av. Croy—5L 125
Shrublands Clo. N20—1B 26
Shrublands Clo. Chig—6A 32
Shuna Wlk. N1—2B 60
Shurland Av. Barn—8B 14
Shurland Gdns. SE15—8D 76
Shurlock Av. Swan—6B 114
Shurlock Dri. Orp—6A 128
Shuttle Clo. Sidc—6D 96
Shuttlemead. Bex—6K 97
Shuttle Rd. Dart—2E 98
Shuttle St. E1—7E 60
Shuttleworth Rd. SW11—1C 90
Sibella Rd. SW4—1H 91
Sibley Clo. Bexh—4J 97
Sibley Gro. E12—3J 63
Sibthorpe Rd. SE12—6F 94
Sibthorp Rd. Mitc—6D 106
Sibton Rd. Cars—2C 122
Sickert Ct. N1—3A 60
Sickle Corner. Dag—7M 65
Sidbury St. SW6—9J 73
Sidcup By-Pass. Sidc—9B 96
Sidcup High St. Sidc—1E 112
Sidcup Hill. Sidc—1F 112
Sidcup Hill Gdns. Sidc—2G 113
Sidcup Rd.—5G 95
  SE12 1-59 & 2-188
  SE9 remainder
Siddons La. NW1—7D 58
Siddons Rd. N17—8E 28
Siddons Rd. SE23—8J 93
Siddons Rd. Croy—5L 123
Side Rd. E17—3K 45
Sidewood Rd. SE9—7B 96
Sidford Pl. SE1—4L 75
Sidings, The. E11—6B 46
Sidmouth Av. Iswth—1C 86
Sidmouth Clo. Wat—2F 20
Sidmouth Dri. Ruis—8E 36
Sidmouth Rd. E10—8A 46
Sidmouth Rd. NW2—3G 57
Sidmouth Rd. SE15—9D 76
Sidmouth Rd. Orp—9F 112
Sidmouth Rd. Well—8G 81
Sidmouth St. WC1—6K 59
Sidney Av. N13—5K 27
Sidney Elson Way. E6—5L 63
Sidney Gdns. Bren—7H 71
Sidney Gro. EC1—5N 59
Sidney Rd. E7—8E 46
Sidney Rd. N22—7K 27
Sidney Rd. SE25—9E 108
Sidney Rd. SW9—1K 91
Sidney Rd. Beck—6J 109
Sidney Rd. Harr—1A 38
Sidney Rd. Twic—5E 86
Sidney Rd. W on T—2E 116
Sidney Sq. E1—8G 61
Sidney St. E1—8G 61
Sidney St. Est. E1—8G 61
  (in two parts)
Sidworth St. E8—3F 60
Siebert Rd. SE3—7E 78
Siemens Rd. SE18—4H 79
Sigdon Rd. E8—1E 60
Sigers, The. Pinn—4F 36

Silbury St. N1—6B 60
Silchester Rd. W10 & W11
  —9H 57
Silecroft Rd. Bexh—9L 81
Silesia Bldgs. E8—3F 60
Silex St. SE1—3M 75
Silkin Clo. SE12—4E 94
Silkin Clo. SE12—4E 94
Silk Mill Ct. Wat—9F 8
Silk Mill Rd. Wat—9F 8
Silk Mills Path. SE13—1A 94
Silkmill Way. Wat—9F 8
Silkstream Rd. Edgw—8A 24
Silk St. EC2—8A 60
Silsoe Rd. N22—9K 27
Silver Birch Av. E4—6K 29
Silverbirch Clo. N11—6E 26
Silver Birch Clo. Dart—1C 114
Silverbirch Clo. Uxb—1C 142
Silvercliffe Gdns. Barn—6C 14
Silver Clo. Harr—7B 22
Silver Cres. W4—5M 71
Silverdale. SE26—1G 109
Silverdale. Enf—6J 15
Silverdale Av. Ilf—3C 48
Silverdale Av. Lea—6A 132
Silverdale Av. W on T—4D 116
Silverdale Clo. W7—2D 70
Silverdale Clo. N'holt—1K 53
Silverdale Clo. Sutt—6K 121
Silverdale Dri. Horn—1F 66
Silverdale Dri. Sun—6E 100
Silverdale Gdns. Hay—3E 68
Silverdale Rd. E4—6B 30
Silverdale Rd. Bexh—1M 97
Silverdale Rd. Bush, Wat—7J 9
Silverdale Rd. Croy—5M 123
Silverdale Rd. Hay—3D 68
Silverdale Rd. Orp—8A 112
  (Petts Wood)
Silverdale Rd. Orp—7E 112
  (St Mary Cray)
Silver Dell. Wat—9D 4
Silverhall St. Iswth—2E 86
Silver Hill. Borwd—1A 12
Silverholme. Harr—5J 39
Silver Jubilee Way. Houn
  —1F 84
Silverland St. E16—2K 79
Silver La. Purl—4H 137
Silver La. W Wick—4B 126
Silverleigh Rd. T Hth—8K 107
Silvermere Av. Romf—6M 33
Silvermere Rd. SE6—6M 93
Silver Rd. W12—1H 73
Silver Spring Clo. Eri—7M 81
Silverston Way. Stan—6G 23
Silver St. N18—4B 28
Silver St. Enf—5B 16
Silver St. Wal A—7J 7
Silverthorne Gdns. E4—2L 29
Silverthorne Rd. SW8—1F 90
Silverton Rd. W6—7H 73
Silvertown By-Pass. E16—2H 79
Silvertown Way. E16—9D 62
Silver Tree Clo. W on T—5E 116
Silvertree La. Gnfd—6B 54
Silver Wlk. SE16—2K 77
Silver Way. Romf—1M 49
Silverwood Clo. Beck—4L 109
Silverwood Clo. N'wd—8A 20
Silvester Rd. SE22—4D 92
Silvester St. SE1—3B 76
Silwood St. SE16—5G 77
Simla Clo. SE14—7J 77
Simmil Rd. Esh—7C 118
Simmonds Clo. N20—2C 26
Simmons La. E4—2B 30
Simmons Rd. SE18—6M 79
Simmons Way. N20—2C 26
Simms Clo. Cars—4C 122
Simms Rd. SE1—5E 76
Simnel Rd. SE12—6F 94
Simon Clo. W11—1K 73
Simon Ct. Bush, Wat—8L 9
Simonds Rd. E10—7L 45
Simone Clo. Brom—5J 111
Simone Dri. Kenl—8A 138
Simon Peter Ct. Enf—4M 15
Simons Wlk. E15—1B 62
Simpson Rd. Houn—5K 85
Simpson Rd. Rain—2D 66
Simpson Rd. Rich—1G 103
Simpson's Rd. E14—1M 77
Simpsons Rd. Brom—7E 110
Simpson St. SW11—1C 90
Simrose Ct. SW18—4L 89
Sims Clo. Romf—2D 50
Sims Wlk. SE3—3D 94
Sinclair Ct. Croy—4D 124
Sinclair Gdns. W14—3H 73
Sinclair Rd. W11—4H 41
Sinclair Rd. E4—5K 29

Sinclair Rd. W14—3H 73
Sinclare Clo. Enf—3D 16
Sindall Rd. Gnfd—5F 54
Sinderby Clo. Borwd—3K 11
Singapore Rd. W13—2E 70
Singer St. EC2—6B 60
Single St. West—7M 141
Singleton Clo. SW17—4D 106
Singleton Clo. Croy—2A 124
Singleton Clo. Horn—9D 50
Singleton Rd. Dag—1K 65
Singleton Scarp. N12—5L 25
Singret Pl. Uxb—7A 142
Sinnott Rd. E17—8H 29
Sion Rd. Twic—7F 86
Sipson Clo. W Dray—7L 143
Sipson La. W Dray—8L 143
Sipson La. W Dray & Hay
—7L 143
Sipson Rd. W Dray—4K to
8M 143
Sir Alexander Clo. W3—2D 72
Sir Alexander Rd. W3—2D 72
Sirdar Rd. N22—1M 43
Sirdar Rd. W11—1H 73
Sirdar Rd. Mitc—3E 106
Sirus Rd. N'wd—5E 20
Sisley Rd. Bark—4C 64
Sispara Gdns. SW18—5K 89
Sissinghurst Rd. Croy—2E 124
Sister Mabel's Way. SE15
—8E 76
Sisters Av. SW11—2D 90
Sistova Rd. SW12—7F 90
Sittingbourne Av. Enf—8B 16
Sitwell Gro. Stan—5D 22
Siverst Clo. N'holt—2M 53
Siviter Way. Dag—3M 65
Siward Rd. N17—8B 28
Siward Rd. SW17—9A 90
Siward Rd. Brom—7F 110
Sixth Av. E12—9K 47
Sixth Av. W10—6J 57
Sixth Av. Hay—2D 68
Sixth Av. Wat—8H 5
Sixth Cross Rd. Twic—9A 86
Skardu Rd. NW2—1J 57
Skarning Ct. Wal A—6M 7
Skeena Hill. SW18—6J 89
Skeet Hill La. Orp—4J 129
Skeffington Rd. E6—4K 63
Skelbrook St. SW18—8A 90
Skelgill Rd. SW15—3K 89
Skelley Rd. E15—3D 62
Skelton Clo. E8—2D 60
Skelton Rd. E7—2E 62
Skelton's La. E10—5M 45
Skelwith Rd. W6—7G 73
Sketchley Gdns. SE16—6H 77
Sketty Rd. Enf—5D 16
Skibbs La. Orp—7J 129
Skid Hill La. Warl—5D 140
Skiers St. E15—4C 62
Skiffington Clo. SW2—7L 91
Skinner St. E2—5F 60
Skinners Clo. SE25—9E 108
Skinners La. EC4—1A 76
Skinners La. Asht—9H 133
Skinner's Row. SW19—9M 77
Skinner St. EC1—7L 59
Skipsey Av. E6—6K 63
Skipton Dri. Hay—4A 68
Skipton St. SE1—4M 75
Skipworth Rd. E9—4G 61
Skomer Wlk. N1—2A 60
Sky Peals Rd. Wfd G—7B 30
Skyport Dri. W Dray—8H 143
Sladebrook Rd. SE3—2H 95
Sladedale Rd. SE18—6C 80
Slade Gdns. Eri—9D 82
Slade Grn. Rd. Eri 8E 82
Slade Grn. Rd. Eri
Sladen Pl. E5—9F 44
Slades Clo. Enf—5L 15
Slades Dri. Chst—1A 112
Slades Gdns. Enf—5L 15
Slades Hill. Enf—5L 15
Slades Rise. Enf—5L 15
Slade, The. SE18 7C 80
Slade Wlk. SE17—7A 76
Slagrove Pl. SE4 & SE13—4L 93
Slaidburn St. SW10—7A 74
Slaithwaite Rd. SE13—3A 94
Slaney Rd. N7—1L 59
Sleaford Grn. Wat—3H 21
Sleaford St. SW8—8G 75
Slewins Clo. Horn—3G 51
Slewins La. Horn—3G 51
Slindon Ct. N16—8D 44
Slingsby Pl. WC2—1J 75
Slippers Pl. SE16—4F 76
Sloane Av. SW3—5C 74
Sloane Ct. E. SW3—6E 74

Sloane Ct. W. SW3—6E 74
Sloane Gdns. SW1—5E 74
Sloane Gdns. Orp—5A 128
Sloane Sq. SW1—5D 74
Sloane St. SW1—4D 74
Sloane Ter. SW1—5E 74
Sloane Wlk. Croy—1K 125
Slocum Clo. SE28—1G 81
Slough La. NW9—3A 40
Sly St. E1—9F 60
Smallberry Av. Iswth—1D 86
Smallbrook M. W2—9B 58
Smalley Clo. N16—8D 44
Smallholdings Rd. Eps—6G 135
(in two parts)
Smallwood Rd. SW17—1B 106
Smardale Rd. SW18—4A 90
Smarden Clo. Belv—6L 81
Smarden Gro. SE9—1K 111
Smart Clo. Romf—8F 34
Smart's La. Lou—6H 19
Smarts Pl. N18—5E 28
Smart's Pl. WC2—9J 59
Smart St. E2—6H 61
Smeaton Rd. SW18—6L 89
Smeaton Rd. Wfd G—5K 31
Smedley St.—1H 91
SW8 1-3
SW4 remainder
Smeed Rd. E3—3L 61
Smitham Bottom La. Purl
—3G 137
Smitham Downs Rd. Purl
—5H 137
Smithfield St. EC1—8M 59
Smithies Rd. SE2—5F 80
Smithson Rd. N17—8B 28
Smith Sq. SW1—4J 75
Smith St. SW3—6D 74
Smith St. Surb—1K 119
Smith St. Wat—6G 9
Smith Ter. SW3—6D 74
Smithwood Clo. SW19—7J 89
Smithy St. E1—8G 61
Smock Wlk. Croy—1A 124
Smug Oak La. St Alb—3M 5
Smyrk's Rd. SE17—6C 76
Smyrna Rd. NW6—3L 57
Smythe Rd. S at H, Dart—5L 115
Smythe St. E14—1M 77
Snakes La. Barn—5F 14
Snakes La. E. Wfd G—6G 31
Snakes La. W. Wfd G 6E 30
Snaresbrook Dri. Stan—4H 23
Snaresbrook Rd. E11—2C 46
Snarsgate St. W10—8G 57
Sneath Av. NW11—5K 41
Snellings Rd. W on T—7G 117
Snells Pk. N18—6D 28
Sneyd Rd. NW2—1G 57
Snodland Clo. Orp—2L 141
Snowbury Rd. SW6—1M 89
Snowden Av. Uxb—5F 142
Snowden Cres. Hay—4A 68
Snowden St. EC2—7C 60
Snowdrop Clo. Hmptn—3L 101
Snowdrop Path. Romf—7H 35
Snow Hill. EC1—8M 59
Snow Hill Ct. EC1—9M 59
Snowsfields. SE1—3B 76
Snowshill Rd. E12—1J 63
Soames St. SE15—2D 92
Soames Wlk. N Mald 5C 104
Socket La. Brom—1F 126
Soham Rd. Enf—1K 17
Soho Sq. W1—9H 59
Soho St. W1—9H 59
Solebay St. E1—7J 61
Solent Rd. NW6—1L 57
Solent Rd. Houn—5D 144
Soley M. WC1—6L 59
Solna Av. SW15—4G 89
Solna Rd. N21—1B 28
Solomon's Pas. SE15—3F 92
Solomons Ter. N20—2A 26
Soloms Ct. Rd. Bans—9B 136
Solon New Rd. SW4—3J 91
Solon Rd. SW2—3J 91
Solway Clo. Houn—2J 85
Solway Rd. N22—8M 27
Solway Rd. SE22—3E 92
Somaford Gro. Barn—8B 14
Somali Rd. NW2—1K 57
Somerby Rd. Bark—3B 64
Somercoates Clo. Barn—5C 14
Somerden Rd. Orp—2H 129
Somerfield Rd. N4—7M 43
Somerford Clo. Pinn—2E 36
Somerford Est. N16—9D 44
Somerford Gro. N16—9D 44
Somerford Gro. N17—7E 28
Somerford St. E1—7F 60
Somerford Way. SE16—3J 77

Somerhill Av. Sidc—6F 96
Somerhill Rd. Well—1F 96
Somerleyton Rd. SW9—3L 91
Somersby Gdns. Ilf—3K 47
Somers Clo. NW1—5H 59
Somers Cres. W2—9C 58
Somerset Av. SW20—6F 104
Somerset Av. Chess—6H 119
Somerset Av. Well—3D 96
Somerset Clo. Eps—1B 134
Somerset Clo. N Mald—1C 120
Somerset Clo. W on T—7F 116
Somerset Clo. Wfd G—8E 30
Somerset Gdns. N6—5E 42
Somerset Gdns. SE13—1M 93
Somerset Gdns. SW16—7K 107
Somerset Gdns. Horn—6L 51
Somerset Gdns. Tedd—2C 102
Somerset Rd. E17—4L 45
Somerset Rd. N17—1D 44
Somerset Rd. N18—5D 28
Somerset Rd. NW4—2G 41
Somerset Rd. SW19—9H 89
Somerset Rd. W4—4B 72
Somerset Rd. W13—2G 71
Somerset Rd. Barn—7M 13
Somerset Rd. Bren—7G 71
Somerset Rd. Dart—5F 98
Somerset Rd. Enf—2K 17
Somerset Rd. Harr—3A 38
Somerset Rd. King—6K 103
Somerset Rd. Orp—2E 128
Somerset Rd. S'hall—8L 53
Somerset Rd. Tedd—2C 102
Somerset Sq. W14—3J 73
Somerset Way. Houn—7J 69
Somersham Rd. Bexh—1J 97
Somers M. W2—9C 58
Somers Pl. SW2—6K 91
Somers Rd. E17—2K 45
Somers Rd. SW2—5K 91
Somers Way. Bush Wat—9A 10
Somerton Av. Rich—2M 87
Somerton Clo. Purl—8L 137
Somerton Rd. NW2—8J 41
Somerton Rd. SE15—3F 92
Somertrees Av. SE12—8F 94
Somervell Rd. Harr—1K 53
Somerville Rd. SE20—4H 109
Somerville Rd. Dart—5K 99
Somerville Rd. Romf—4G 49
Sonderburg Rd. N7—7K 43
Sondes St. SE17—7B 76
Sonia Ct. Harr—4D 38
Sonia Gdns. N12—4A 26
Sonia Gdns. NW10—9D 40
Sonia Gdns. Houn—8L 69
Sonning Rd. SE25—1E 124
Sophia Clo. N7—2K 59
Sophia Rd. E10—6M 45
Sophia Rd. E16—9F 62
Sopwith Av. Chess—7J 119
Sopwith Rd. Houn—8G 69
Sopwith Way. Wall—9H 123
Sorrel Bank. Croy—1J 139
Sorrel Clo. SE28—2E 80
Sorrell Clo. SW9—1L 91
Sorrel Wlk. Romf—1D 50
Sorrento Rd. Sutt—5M 121
Sotheran Rd. SW6—8M 73
Sotheron Rd. Wat—5G 9
Soudan Rd. SW11—9D 74
Souldern Rd. W14—4H 73
Souldern St. Wat—7F 8
Sounds Lodge. Swan—1A 130
S. Access Rd. E17—5J 45
South Acre. NW9—9D 24
Southacre Way. Pinn—8G 21
S. Africa Rd. W12—2F 72
Southall La. Houn & S'hall
7F 68
Southall Pl. SE1—3B 76
Southampton Bldgs. WC2
—8L 59
Southampton Gdns. Mitc
—9J 107
Southampton Pl. WC1—8J 59
Southampton Rd. NW5—1D 58
Southampton Rd. Houn
—5C 144
Southampton Row. WC1
—8J 59
Southampton St. WC2—1J 75
Southampton Way. SE5—8B 76
Southam St. W10—7J 57
S. Approach. N'wd—3B 20
S. Audley St. W1—1E 74
South Av. E4—9M 17
South Av. Cars—9E 122
South Av. Rich—1L 87
South Av. S'hall—1K 69
South Av. Gdns. S'hall—1K 69
South Bank. Chst—1A 112

South Bank. Surb—1J 119
Southbank. Th Dit—2F 116
S. Bank Ter. Surb—1J 119
S. Birkbeck Rd. E11—8B 46
S. Black Lion La. W6—6E 72
S. Bolton Gdns. SW5—6A 74
S. Border, The. Purl—3J 137
Southborough Clo. Surb
—3H 119
Southborough La. Brom
—9J 111
Southborough Rd. E9—4H 61
Southborough Rd. Brom
—7J 111
Southborough Rd. Surb
—3J 119
Southbourne. Brom—2E 126
Southbourne Av. NW9—9A 24
Southbourne Clo. Pinn—5J 37
Southbourne Cres. NW4—2J 41
Southbourne Gdns. SE12
—4F 94
Southbourne Gdns. Ilf—1A 64
Southbourne Gdns. Ruis
—6F 36
Southbridge Pl. Croy—6A 124
Southbridge Rd. Croy—6A 124
Southbridge Way. S'hall
—3J 69
Southbrook Dri. Wal X—1D 6
Southbrook M. SE12—5D 94
Southbrook Rd. SE12—5D 94
Southbrook Rd. SW16—5J 107
Southbury Av. Enf—6E 16
Southbury Clo. Horn—1H 67
Southbury Rd. Enf—5C 16
S. Carriage Dri. SW7 & SW1
—3B 74
Southchurch Rd. E6—5K 63
South Clo. N6—4F 42
South Clo. Barn—5K 13
South Clo. Bexh—3H 97
South Clo. Dag—4L 65
South Clo. Mord—1L 121
South Clo. Pinn—8H 21
(Pinner Green)
South Clo. Pinn—5K 37
(Rayners Lane)
South Clo. Twic—9L 85
South Clo. W Dray—4K 143
Southcombe St. W14—5J 73
S. Common Rd. Uxb—2C 142
Southcote Av. Felt—8E 84
Southcote Av. Surb—2M 119
Southcote Rise. Ruis—5B 36
Southcote Rd. E17—3H 45
Southcote Rd. N19—9G 43
Southcote Rd. SE25—1F 124
Southcote Rd. S Croy—2C 138
S. Countess Rd. E17—1K 45
Southcroft Av. Well—2C 96
Southcroft Av. W Wick
—4A 126
Southcroft Rd.—3E 106
SW17 1-161 & 2-248
SW16 remainder
Southcroft Rd. Orp—5C 128
S. Cross Rd. Ilf—3A 48
S. Croxted Rd. SE21—9D 92
Southdale. Chig—6B 32
Southdean Gdns. SW19—8K 89
South Dene. NW7—3B 24
Southdown Av. W7 4E 70
Southdown Cres. Harr—6A 38
Southdown Cres. Ilf—3C 48
Southdown Dri. SW20—4H 105
Southdown Rd. SW20—4H 105
Southdown Rd. Cars—1E 136
Southdown Rd. Horn—5F 50
Southdown Rd. W on T—6J 117
South Dri. Bans—5C 136
South Dri. Coul—7H 137
South Dri. Orp—7C 128
South Dri. Romf—1G 51
South Dri. Ruis—6C 36
South Dri. Sutt—2J 135
S. Ealing Rd. W5 & Bren—3H 71
S. Eastern Av. N9—3D 28
S. Eaton Pl. SW1—5E 74
S. Eden Pk. Rd. Beck—1M 125
S. Edwardes Sq. W8—4L 73
South End. W8—4M 73
South End. Croy—6A 124
Southend Arterial Rd. Romf,
Horn & Upm—9H 35
S. End Clo. NW3—9C 42
Southend Clo. SE9—5M 95
S. End Grn. NW3—9C 42
Southend La.—1K 109
SE6 1-299 & 2-298
SE26 remainder
Southend Rd. E6—3K 63

Southend Rd. E17—8B 30
Southend Rd. E18—8E 30
S. End Rd. NW3—9C 42
Southend Rd. Beck—5L 109
S. End Rd. Rain & Horn—4E 66
Southend Rd. Wfd G—9H 31
S. End Row. W8—4M 73
Southerland Clo. Wey—6A 116
Southern Av. SE25—7D 108
Southern Av. Felt—7E 84
Southern Clo. E8—4E 60
Southern Dri. Lou—8K 19
Southern Gro. E3—6K 61
Southernhay. Lou—7H 19
Southern Perimeter Rd. Houn &
Stai—4C 144
Southern Pl. Swan—8B 114
Southern Rd. E13—5F 62
Southern Rd. N2—2D 42
Southern Row. W10—7J 57
Southern St. N1—5K 59
Southern Way. Romf—4L 49
Southerton Rd. W6—5G 73
S. Esk Rd. E7—2G 63
Southey Rd. N15—3C 44
Southey Rd. SE20—4H 109
Southey Rd. SW9—9L 75
Southey Rd. SW19—4L 105
Southfield. Barn—8H 13
Southfield Av. Wat—2G 9
Southfield Clo. Uxb—7E 142
Southfield Cotts. W7—3D 70
Southfield Ct. E11—8B 46
Southfield Gdns. Twic—1D 102
Southfield Pk. Harr—2M 37
Southfield Pl. Wey—9A 116
Southfield Rd. N17—9C 28
Southfield Rd. W4—3B 72
Southfield Rd. Chst—7E 112
Southfield Rd. Enf—8F 16
Southfield Rd. Wal X—5E 6
Southfields. NW4—1F 40
Southfields. E Mol—1C 118
Southfields Av. Ashf—3A 100
Southfields Pas. SW18—5L 89
Southfields Rd. SW18—5L 89
Southfleet Rd. Orp—5C 128
South Gdns. SW19—4B 106
Southgate Av. Felt—1B 100
Southgate Cir. N14—1H 27
Southgate Gro. N1—3B 60
Southgate Rd. N1—4B 60
S. Gipsy Rd. Well—2H 97
South Glade, The. Bex—7K 97
South Grn. NW9—8C 24
South Gro. E17—3K 45
South Gro. N6—6E 42
South Gro. N15—3B 44
S. Hall Clo. F'ham, Dart—2K 131
S. Hall Dri. Rain—8F 66
South Hill. Chst—3K 111
S. Hill Av. Harr—8A 38
S. Hill Gro. Harr—9C 38
S. Hill Pk. NW3—9C 42
S. Hill Pk. Gdns. NW3—9C 42
S. Hill Rd. Brom—7C 110
Southill La. Pinn—2F 36
Southill Rd. Chst—4J 111
S. Island Pl. SW9—9L 75
S. Lambeth Pl. SW8—7J 75
S. Lambeth Rd. SW8—7J 75
Southland Rd. SE18—8D 80
Southlands Av. Orp—6C 128
Southlands Clo. Coul—9K 137
Southlands Gro. Brom—7J 111
Southlands Rd. Brom—8H 111
Southland Way. Houn—4B 86
South La. King—7H 103
South La. N Mald—8B 104
South La. W. N Mald—8B 104
S. Lodge Av. Mitc—8J 107
S. Lodge Cres. Enf—6H 15
(in two parts)
S. Lodge Dri. N14—6H 15
S. Lodge Rd. W on T—9E 116
Southly Clo. Sutt—5L 121
South Mall, The. N9—3E 28
South Mead. NW9—8D 24
S. Mead. Eps—9D 120
Southmead Cres. Wal X—3E 6
S. Meadows. Wemb—1K 55
Southmead Rd. SW19—7J 89
S. Molton La. W1—1F 74
S. Molton Rd. E16—9E 62
S. Molton St. W1—9F 58
Southmont Rd. Esh—4C 118
Southmoor Way. E9—2K 61
S. Norwood Hill. SE25—5C 108
S. Oak Rd. SW16—1K 107
Southold Rise. SE9—9K 95
Southolm St. SW11—9F 74
Southover. N12—3L 25
Southover. Brom—2E 110

South Pde. SW3—6B 74
South Pde. W4—5B 72
South Pde. Wal A—6J 7
S. Park Cres. SE6—7D 94
S. Park Cres. Ilf—8B 48
S. Park Dri. Bark & Ilf—1C 64
S. Park Gro. N Mald—8A 104
S. Park Hill Rd. S Croy—7B 124
S. Park Rd. SW19—3L 105
S. Park Rd. Ilf—8B 48
S. Park Ter. Ilf—8C 48
S. Park Way. Ruis—2G 53
South Pl. EC2—8B 60
South Pl. Enf—7G 17
South Pl. Surb—2K 119
South Pl. M. EC2—8B 60
Southport Rd. SE18—5B 80
S. Riding. St Alb—3L 5
South Rise. Cars—1C 136
South Rd. N9—1E 28
South Rd. SE23—8H 93
South Rd. SW19—3A 106
South Rd. W5—5H 71
South Rd. Edgw—8M 23
South Rd. Eri—8D 82
South Rd. Felt—2H 101
South Rd. Hmptn—3J 101
South Rd. Romf—4J 49
(Chadwell Heath)
South Rd. Romf—3G 49
(Little Heath)
South Rd. S'hall—3K 69
South Rd. Twic—9B 86
South Rd. W Dray—4L 143
South Rd. Wey—7A 116
South Row. SE1—1D 94
Southsea Av. Wat—6E 8
Southsea Rd. King—8J 103
South Side. W6—4D 72
Southside Comn. SW19
—3G 105
Southspring. Sidc—6B 96
South Sq. NW11—4M 41
South Sq. WC1—8L 59
South St. W1—2E 74
South St. Brom—6E 110
South St. Enf—7G 17
South St. Eps—5B 134
South St. Iswth—2E 86
South St. Rain—5A 66
South St. Romf—3C 50
S. Tenter St. E1—1D 76
South Ter. SW7—5C 74
South Ter. Surb—1J 119
South Vale. SE19—3C 108
South Vale. Harr—9C 38
Southvale Rd. SE3—1C 94
Southview. Brom—6G 111
Southview Av. NW10—1D 56
Southview Clo. Bex—5K 97
Southview Clo. Swan—8E 114
Southview Cotts. Mitc—6D 106
Southview Cres. Ilf—4M 47
S. View Dri. E18—1F 46
S. View Dri. Upm—8L 51
Southview Gdns. Wall—9G 123
S. View Rd. N8—1H 43
Southview Rd. Brom—1B 110
S. View Rd. Dart—9H 99
S. View Rd. Lou—8K 19
S. View Rd. Pinn—6F 20
Southviews. S Croy—1H 139
South Vs. NW1—2H 59
Southville. Eps—1B 134
Southville Clo. Felt—7C 84
Southville Cres. Felt—7C 84
Southville Rd. Felt—7C 84
Southville Rd. Th Dit—2F 118
South Wlk. Hay—8B 52
South Wlk. W Wick—5C 126
Southwark Bri. SE1 & EC4
—1A 76
Southwark Bri. Rd. SE1—3A 76
Southwark Gro. SE1—2A 76
Southwark Pk. Rd. SE16
—5D to 4F 76
Southwark Pl. Brom—7K 111
Southwark St. SE1—2M 75
Southwater Clo. E14—9K 61
South Way. N9—2G 29
South Way. N11—6G 27
Southway. NW11—4M 41
Southway. SW20—8G 105
South Way. Brom—2E 126
South Way. Croy—5J 125
South Way. Harr—2L 37
South Way. K Lan & Abb L, Wat
—6B 4
South Way. Sutt—2B 136
Southway. Wall—6G 123
South Way. Wal A—1M 17

South Way. Wemb—1L 55
Southweald Dri. Wal A—6K 7
Southwell Av. N'holt—2M 53
Southwell Gdns. SW7—4A 74
Southwell Gro. Rd. E11—7C 46
Southwell Rd. SE5—2A 92
Southwell Rd. Croy—1L 123
Southwell Rd. Harr—4H 39
S. Western Rd. Twic—5E 86
Southwest Rd. E11—6B 46
S. Wharf Rd. W2—9B 58
Southwick M. W2—9B 58
Southwick Pl. W2—9C 58
Southwick St. W2—9C 58
Southwold Dri. Bark—1E 64
Southwold Rd. E5—7F 44
Southwold Rd. Bex—5M 97
Southwold Rd. Wat—1G 9
Southwood Av. N6—5F 42
Southwood Av. Coul—9G 137
Southwood Av. King—5A 104
Southwood Clo. Brom—8K 111
Southwood Clo. Wor Pk
—3H 121
Southwood Dri. Surb—2A 120
Southwood Gdns. Esh—5E 118
Southwood Gdns. Ilf—2M 47
Southwood Hall. N6—4F 42
Southwood La. N6—5E 42
Southwood Lawn Rd. N6
—5F 42
Southwood Pk. N6—5E 42
Southwood Rd. SE9—8M 95
Southwood Rd. SE28—2F 80
S. Worple Av. SW14—2C 88
S. Worple Way. SW14—2B 88
Sovereign Clo. W5—8G 55
Sovereign Clo. Ruis—6C 36
Sowerby Clo. SE9—4K 95
Sowrey Av. Rain—2D 66
Space Way. Felt—4F 84
Spa Clo. SE25—5C 108
Spa Dri. Eps—6L 133
Spa Hill. SE19—5B 108
Spalding Rd. NW4—5G 41
Spalding Rd. SW17—2F 106
Spanby Rd. E3—7L 61
Spaniards Clo. NW11—6B 42
Spaniards End. NW3—6A 42
Spaniards Rd. NW3—7A 42
Spanish Pl. W1—9E 58
Spanish Rd. SW18—4A 90
Spanswick Lodge. N15—2M 43
Spareleaze Hill. Lou—6K 19
Sparepenny La. Eyns & F'ham
Dart—4H 131
Sparkbridge Rd. Harr—2C 38
Sparks Clo. Hmptn—3J 101
Spa Rd. SE16—4D 76
Sparrick's Row. SE1—3B 76
Sparrow Dri. Orp—3B 128
Sparrow Farm Dri. Felt—6G 85
Sparrow Farm Rd. Eps—6E 120
Sparrow Grn. Dag—8M 49
Sparrows Herne. Bush, Wat
—9M 9
Sparrows La. SE9—7A 96
Sparrows Way. Bush, Wat
—9A 10
Sparsholt Rd. N19—6K 43
Sparsholt Rd. Bark—4C 64
Sparta St. SE10—9A 78
Spearman St. SE18—7L 79
Spear M. SW5—5L 73
Spearpoint Gdns. Ilf—3D 48
Spears Rd. N19—6J 43
Speart La. Houn—8J 69
Spedan Clo. NW3—8A 42
Speedwell Pl. SE8—8L 77
Speer Rd. Th Dit—1D 118
Speirs Clo. N Mald—1D 120
Speke Hill. SE9—9K 95
Speke Rd. T Hth—6B 108
Speldhurst Clo. Brom—9D 110
Speldhurst Rd. E9—3H 61
Speldhurst Rd. W4—4B 72
Spellbrook Wlk. N1—4A 60
Spelman St. E1—8E 60
Spelthorne Gro. Sun—4D 100
Spelthorne La. Ashf—5A 100
Spencer Av. N13—6K 27
Spencer Av. Hay—8E 52
Spencer Clo. N3—9L 25
Spencer Clo. NW10—6K 55
Spencer Clo. Croy—2B 124
Spencer Clo. Orp—4C 128
Spencer Clo. Uxb—6A 142
Spencer Clo. Wfd G—5G 31
Spencer Dri. N2—4A 42
Spencer Gdns. SE9—4K 95
Spencer Gdns. SW14—4A 88
Spencer Hill. SW19—3J 105
Spencer M. W6—7J 73

Spencer Pk. SW18—4B 90
Spencer Rise. NW5—8F 42
Spencer Rd. E6—4H 63
Spencer Rd. E17—9A 30
Spencer Rd. N8—3K 43
(in two parts)
Spencer Rd. N11—4F 26
Spencer Rd. N17—8E 28
Spencer Rd. SW18—4B 90
Spencer Rd. SW20—5F 104
Spencer Rd. W3—2A 72
Spencer Rd. W4—8A 72
Spencer Rd. Brom—4D 110
Spencer Rd. E Mol—8A 102
Spencer Rd. Harr—9C 22
Spencer Rd. Ilf—6D 48
Spencer Rd. Iswth—9A 70
Spencer Rd. Mitc—7E 106
Spencer Rd. Mitc—2E 122
(Beddington Corner)
Spencer Rd. Rain—6B 66
Spencer Rd. S Croy—7C 124
Spencer Rd. Twic—9C 86
Spencer Rd. Wemb—7G 39
Spencer St. EC1—6M 59
Spencer St. S'hall—3H 69
Spencer Wlk. SW15—3H 89
Spenser Cres. Upm—5M 51
Spenser Gro. N16—9C 44
Spenser Rd. SE24—4M 91
Spenser St. SW1—4G 75
Spensley Wlk. N16—8B 44
Speranza St. SE18—6D 80
Sperling Rd. N17—9C 28
Spert St. E14—1J 77
Spey Side. N14—8G 15
Spey St. E14—8A 62
Spey Way. Romf—7C 34
Spezia Rd. NW10—5E 56
Spicer Clo. SW9—1M 91
Spicers Field. Lea—5B 132
Spice's Yd. Croy—6A 124
Spielman Rd. Dart—3K 99
Spigurnell Rd. N17—8B 28
Spikes Bri. Rd. S'hall—1J 69
Spilsby Clo. NW9—8C 24
Spilsby Rd. Romf—7H 35
Spindlewood Gdns. Croy
—6C 124
Spinel Clo. SE18—6D 80
Spingate Clo. Horn—1G 67
Spinnells Rd. Harr—6K 37
Spinney Clo. N Mald—9C 104
Spinney Clo. W Dray—1J 143
Spinney Dri. Felt—6A 84
Spinney Gdns. SE19—2D 108
Spinney Gdns. Dag—1J 65
Spinney Oak. Brom—6J 111
Spinneys, The. Brom—6K 111
Spinney, The. N21—9L 15
Spinney, The. SW16—9G 91
Spinney, The. Barn—4M 13
Spinney, The. Brtwd—8A 10
Spinney, The. Purl—3M 137
Spinney, The. Sidc—2J 113
Spinney, The. Stan—4J 23
Spinney, The. Sun—5E 100
Spinney, The. Sutt—6G 121
Spinney, The. Wat—3E 8
Spinney, The. Wemb—8E 38
Spires, The. Dart—8H 99
Spital Sq. E1—8C 60
Spital St. E1—8E 60
Spital St. Dart—5H 99
Spital Yd. E1—8C 60
Spitfire Rd. Houn—5A 84
Spitfire Way. Houn—6G 69
Spode Wlk. NW6—1M 57
Spondon Rd. N15—2E 44
Spooners Dri. St Alb—1M 5
Spooner Wlk. Wall—7J 123
Sportsbank St. SE6—6A 94
Spottons Grn. N17—8A 28
Spout Hill. Croy—7L 125
Spout La. N. Stai—3A 144
Spratt Hall Rd. E11—4E 46
Spray La. Twic—5C 86
Spray St. SE18—5M 79
Spreighton Rd. E Mol—8M 101
Sprimont Pl. SW3—5D 74
Springall St. SE15—8F 76
Spring Bank. N21—8K 15
Springbank Av. Horn—1G 67
Springbank Rd. SE13—5B 94
Springbank Wlk. NW1—3H 59
Springbourne Ct. Beck—5A 110
Spring Bri. M. W5—1H 71
Springbridge Rd. W5—1H 71
Spring Clo. Borwd—3L 11
Spring Clo. La. Sutt—8J 121
Spring Corner. Felt—9E 84
Spring Cotts. Surb—9H 103
Spring Ct. Eps—1D 134

Spring Ct. Rd. Enf—2L 15
Springcroft Av. N2—2D 42
Spring Crofts. Bush, Wat—7L 9
Springdale Rd. N16—9B 44
Spring Dri. Pinn—4E 36
Springfield. E5—6F 44
Springfield. Bush, Wat—1B 22
Springfield Av. N10—1G 43
Springfield Av. SW20—7K 105
Springfield Av. Hmptn
—3M 101
Springfield Av. Swan—8D 114
Springfield Clo. Rick—7A 8
Springfield Clo. Stan—3E 22
Springfield Dri. Ilf—3A 48
Springfield Gdns. E5—6F 44
Springfield Gdns. NW9—3B 40
Springfield Gdns. Brom
—8K 111
Springfield Gdns. Ruis—6F 36
Springfield Gdns. Upm—8M 51
Springfield Gdns. W Wick
—4M 125
Springfield Gdns. Wfd G—7G 31
Springfield Gro. SE7—7G 79
Springfield Gro. Sun—5E 100
Springfield La. NW6—4M 57
Springfield Mt. NW9—3C 40
Springfield Rise. SE26—9F 92
Springfield Rd. E4—1C 30
Springfield Rd. E6—3K 63
Springfield Rd. E15—6C 62
Springfield Rd. E17—4K 45
Springfield Rd. N11—2E 26
Springfield Rd. N15—2E 44
Springfield Rd. NW8—4A 58
Springfield Rd. SE26—2F 108
Springfield Rd. SW19—2K 105
Springfield Rd. W7—2C 70
Springfield Rd. Bexh—3M 97
Springfield Rd. Brom—8K 111
Springfield Rd. Eps—2G 135
Springfield Rd. Harr—4C 38
Springfield Rd. Hay—2G 69
Springfield Rd. King—7J 103
Springfield Rd. Tedd—2E 102
Springfield Rd. T Hth—5A 108
Springfield Rd. Twic—7L 85
Springfield Rd. Wall X—5E 6
Springfield Rd. Wat—7F 4
Springfield Rd. Wfd G—7G 31
Springfields. Wal A—7L 7
Spring Gdns. N5—1A 60
Spring Gdns. SW1—2H 75
Spring Gdns. E Mol—9M 101
Spring Gdns. Horn—8F 128
Spring Gdns. Romf—3A 50
Spring Gdns. Wall—7G 123
Spring Gdns. Wat—8G 5
Spring Gdns. West—9G 141
Spring Gdns. Wfd G—7G 31
Spring Gro. SE19—4D 108
Spring Gro. W4—6L 71
Spring Gro. Hmptn—5M 101
Spring Gro. Lou—8H 19
Spring Gro. Cres. Houn—9A 70
Spring Gro. Rd. Houn & Iswth
Spring Gro. Rd. Rich—4K 87
Springhead Rd. Eri—7D 82
Spring Hill. E5—5E 44
Spring Hill. SE26—1G 109
Springhill Clo. SE5—2B 92
Springholm Clo. West—9G 141
Spring Lake. Stan—4F 22
Spring La. E5—5F 44
Spring La. SE25—1F 124
Spring M. W1—8D 58
Spring Pk. Av. Croy—4H 125
Spring Pk. Dri. N4—6A 44
Spring Pk. Rd. Croy—4H 125
Spring Pl. NW5—1F 58
Springpond Rd. Dag—1J 65
Springrice Rd. SE13—5B 94
Spring Rd. Felt—9D 84
Spring St. W2—9B 58
Spring St. Eps—1D 134
Spring Ter. Rich—4J 87
Spring Vale. Bexh—3M 97
Spring Vale Av. Bren—6J 71
Spring Vale N. Dart—6H 99
Spring Vale S. Dart—6H 99
Spring Vale Ter. W14—4H 73
Springvale Way. Orp—7G 113
Springvilla Rd. Edgw—7L 23
Springwater Clo. SE18—9L 79
Springwell Av. NW10—4D 56
Springwell Clo. SW16—1K 107

Springwell Ct. Houn—1H 85
Springwell Rd. SW16—1L 107
Springwell Rd. Houn—9H 69
Springwood Ct. S Croy—6C 124
Springwood Cres. Edgw
—2M 23
Springwood Way. Romf—3E 50
Sprowston M. E7—2E 62
Sprowston Rd. E7—1E 62
Sprucedale Gdns. Croy
—6H 125
Sprucedale Gdns. Wall—1J 137
Spruce Hills Rd. E17—9A 30
Spruce Rd. West—8H 141
Sprules Rd. SE4—1J 93
Spur Clo. Abb L, Wat—6B 4
Spurfield. E Mol—7M 101
Spurgeon Av. SE19—5B 108
Spurgeon Rd. SE19—5B 108
Spurgeon St. SE1—4B 76
Spurling Rd. SE22—3D 92
Spurling Rd. Dag—2K 65
Spurrell Av. Bex—1B 114
Spur Rd. N15—2B 44
Spur Rd. SW1—3G 75
Spur Rd. Edgw—4J 23
Spur Rd. Felt—3F 84
Spur Rd. Iswth—8F 70
Spur Rd. Orp—4E 128
Spurstowe Rd. E8—1F 60
Spurstowe Ter. E8—2F 60
Squadrons App. Horn—2G 67
Square, The. Cars—7E 122
Square, The. Ilf—5L 47
Square, The. Rich—4H 87
Square, The. Wat—1F 8
Square, The. Wey—7A 116
Square, The. Wfd G—5E 30
Squarey St. SW17—9A 90
Squires La. N3—9M 25
Squires M. NW3—8B 42
Squires Way. Bex—1B 114
Squires Wood Dri. Chst
—4J 111
Squirrel Clo. Houn—2G 85
Squirrels Clo. N12—4A 26
Squirrels Clo. Uxb—3E 142
Squirrels Grn. Wor Pk—4D 120
Squirrels Heath Av. Romf
—1F 50
Squirrels Heath La. Romf &
Horn—2G 51
Squirrels Heath Rd. Romf
—1J 51
Squirrels, The. Bush, Wat
—8B 10
Squirrels, The. Pinn—1K 37
Squirrels Way. Eps—7B 134
Squirries St. E2—6E 60
Stable Clo. N'holt—5L 53
Stable M. SE27—2A 108
Stables End. Orp—5A 128
Stables, The. Buck H—9G 19
Stables Way. SE11—6L 75
Stable, Wlk. N2—8B 26
Stable Way. W10—9G 57
Stable Yd. Rd. SW1—3G 75
Stacey Av. N18—4G 29
Stacey Clo. E10—3B 46
Stacey St. WC2—9H 59
Stacy Path. SE5—8C 76
Stadium Rd. NW4—5E 40
Stadium Rd. SE18—8K 79
Stadium Rd. Dart—4C 98
Stadium St. SW10—8A 74
Stadium Way. Wemb—9L 39
Staffa Rd. E10—6J 45
Stafford Av. Horn—1H 51
Stafford Av. Ilf—9L 31
Stafford Clo. N14—7G 15
Stafford Clo. NW6—6L 57
Stafford Clo. Sutt—8J 121
Stafford Clo. Wal X—2B 6
Stafford Gdns. Croy—7K 123
Stafford M. Rich—6K 87
Stafford Pl. SW1—4G 75
Stafford Rd. E3—5K 61
Stafford Rd. E7—2H 63
Stafford Rd. NW6—6L 57
Stafford Rd. Harr—7A 22
Stafford Rd. N Mald—7A 104
Stafford Rd. Ruis—9D 36
Stafford Rd. Sidc—1C 112
Stafford Rd. Wall & Croy
—8G 123
Staffordshire St. SE15—9E 76
Stafford Sq. Wey—6B 116
Stafford St. W1—2G 75
Stafford Ter. W8—3L 73
Staff St. EC1—6B 60
Stag Clo. Edgw—9M 23
Stag Ct. Eps—3D 134

Staggart Grn. Chig—6D 32
Stagg Hill. Barn—1C 14
Stag La. SW15—9D 88
Stag La. Edgw—9M 23
Stag Pl. SW1—4G 75
Stags Way. Iswth—7D 70
Stainbank Rd. Mitc—7F 106
Stainby Clo. W Dray—4J 143
Stainby Rd. N15—2D 44
Stainer Rd. Borwd—3H 11
Stainer St. SE1—2B 76
Staines Av. Sutt—4H 121
Staines Rd. Felt & Houn
—7F 144
Staines Rd. Ilf—1A 64
Staines Rd. Twic—9M 85
Staines Rd. E. Sun—4E 100
Staines Rd. W. Ashf & Sun
—4A 100
Staines Wlk. Sidc—3G 113
Stainforth Clo. Ashf—2B 100
Stainforth Rd. E17—2L 45
Stainforth Rd. Ilf—5B 48
Staining La. EC2—9A 60
Stainmore Clo. Chst—5B 112
Stainsbury St. E2—5G 61
Stainsby Pl. E14—9L 61
Stainsby Rd. E14—9L 61
Stains Clo. Wal X—1E 6
Stainton Rd. SE6—5B 94
Stainton Rd. Enf—3G 17
Stalbridge St. NW1—8C 58
Stalham St. SE16—4F 76
Stalisfield Pl. Orp—2L 141
Stambourne Way. SE19
—4C 108
Stambourne Way. W Wick
—4A 126
Stamford Brook Av. W6—4D 72
Stamford Brook Rd. W6—4D 72
Stamford Clo. N15—3E 44
Stamford Clo. Harr—7C 22
Stamford Clo. S'hall—1L 69
Stamford Dri. Brom—8D 110
Stamford Gdns. Dag—3G 65
Stamford Grn. Rd. Eps—5M 133
Stamford Gro. E. N16—6E 44
Stamford Gro. W. N16—6E 44
Stamford Hill. N16—7D 44
Stamford Hill Est. N16—6D 44
Stamford Rd. E6—4J 63
Stamford Rd. N1—3C 60
Stamford Rd. N15—3E 44
Stamford Rd. Dag—4F 64
Stamford Rd. W on T—5H 117
Stamford St. SE1—2L 75
Stamp Pl. E2—5D 60
Stanborough Av. Borwd
—1L 11
Stanborough Clo. Borwd
—2L 11
Stanborough Clo. Hmptn
—3K 101
Stanborough Rd. Houn—2B 86
Stanbridge Rd. SW15—2G 89
Stanbrook Rd. SE2—3F 80
Stanbury Av. Wat—1C 8
Stanbury Rd. SE15—1F 92
Stancroft. NW9—3C 40
Standale Gro. Ruis—3A 36
Standard Clo. N16—5C 44
Standard Industrial Est. E16
—3K 79
Standard Rd. NW10—7A 56
Standard Rd. Belv—6L 81
Standard Rd. Bexh—3J 97
Standard Rd. Enf—1J 17
Standard Rd. Houn—2J 85
Standard Rd. Orp—2L 141
Standen Av. Horn—8J 51
Standen Rd. SW18—6K 89
Standfield. Abb L, Wat—4C 4
Standfield Gdns. Dag—2L 65
Standfield Rd. Dag—1L 65
Standish Rd. W6—5E 72
Stane Clo. SW19—4M 105
Stane Pas. SW16—2J 107
Stane Way. SE18—8H 79
Stane Way. Eps—2E 134
Stanfield Rd. E3—5J 61
Stanford Clo. Hmptn—3K 101
Stanford Clo. Romf—4M 49
Stanford Clo. Wfd G—5J 31
Stanford Ct. SW6—9M 73
Stanford Ct. Wal A—6M 7
Stanford Pl. SE17—5C 76
Stanford Rd. N11—5D 26
Stanford Rd. SW16—6H 107
Stanford Rd. W8—4M 73
Stanford St. SW1—5H 75
Stanford Way. SW16—6H 107

Stangate Cres. Borwd—7B 12
Stangate Gdns. Stan—4F 22
Stanger Rd. SE25—8E 108
Stanham Pl. Dart—3E 98
Stanham Rd. Dart—4G 99
Stanhope Av. N3—1K 41
Stanhope Av. Brom—3E 126
Stanhope Av. Harr—8B 22
Stanhope Gdns. N4—4M 43
Stanhope Gdns. N6—4G 43
Stanhope Gdns. NW7—5D 24
Stanhope Gdns. SW7—5A 74
Stanhope Gdns. Dag—8K 49
Stanhope Gdns. Ilf—6K 47
Stanhope Ga. W1—2E 74
Stanhope Gro. Beck—9K 109
Stanhope Heath. Stai—5A 144
Stanhope M. E. SW7—5A 74
Stanhope M. S. SW7—5A 74
Stanhope M. W. SW7—5A 74
Stanhope Pk. Rd. Gnfd—7A 54
Stanhope Pl. W2—1D 74
Stanhope Rd. E17—3M 45
Stanhope Rd. N6—4G 43
Stanhope Rd. N12—5A 26
Stanhope Rd. Barn—8H 13
Stanhope Rd. Bexh—-1J 97
Stanhope Rd. Cars—9E 122
Stanhope Rd. Croy—5C 124
Stanhope Rd. Dag—7K 49
Stanhope Rd. Gnfd—8A 54
Stanhope Rd. Rain—5E 66
Stanhope Rd. Sidc—1E 112
Stanhope Row. W1—2F 74
Stanhope St. NW1—6G 59
(in two parts)
Stanhope Ter. W2—1B 74
Stanhope Way. Stai—5A 144
Stanier Clo. W14—6K 73
Stanlake M. W12—2G 73
Stanlake Rd. W12—2G 73
Stanlake Vs. W12—2G 73
Stanley Av. Bark—5D 64
Stanley Av. Beck—7A 110
Stanley Av. Dag—6K 49
Stanley Av. Gnfd—4A 54
Stanley Av. N Mald—9E 104
Stanley Av. Romf—2E 50
Stanley Av. Wemb—3J 55
Stanley Clo. SW8—7K 75
Stanley Clo. Coul—9K 137
Stanley Clo. Horn—7G 51
Stanley Clo. Romf—2E 50
Stanley Clo. Uxb—4B 142
Stanley Clo. Wemb—3J 55
Stanley Cres. W11—1K 73
Stanleycroft Clo. Iswth—9C 70
Stanley Gdns. NW2—1G 57
Stanley Gdns. W3—3C 72
Stanley Gdns. W11—1K 73
Stanley Gdns. Borwd—3J 11
Stanley Gdns. Mitc—3E 106
Stanley Gdns. S Croy—4E 138
Stanley Gdns. Wall—8G 123
Stanley Gdns. Rd. Tedd—2C 102
Stanley Gro. N17—7D 28
Stanley Gro. SW8—1E 90
Stanley Gro. Croy—1L 123
Stanley Pk. Dri. Wemb—4K 55
Stanley Pk. Rd. Cars—9D 122
Stanley Pk. Rd. Wall—8F 122
Stanley Pas. NW1—5J 59
Stanley Rd. E4—1B 30
Stanley Rd. E10—4M 45
Stanley Rd. E12—1J 63
Stanley Rd. E15—4B 62
Stanley Rd. E18—8D 30
Stanley Rd. N2—1B 42
Stanley Rd. N9—2D 28
Stanley Rd. N10—7F 26
Stanley Rd. N11—6H 27
Stanley Rd. N15—2M 43
Stanley Rd. NW9—5E 40
Stanley Rd. SW14—3M 87
Stanley Rd. SW19—3L 105
Stanley Rd. W3—4A 72
Stanley Rd. Brom—8G 111
Stanley Rd. Cars—9E 122
Stanley Rd. Croy—2L 123
Stanley Rd. Enf—5C 16
Stanley Rd. Harr—7A 38
Stanley Rd. Horn—7G 51
Stanley Rd. Houn—3A 86
Stanley Rd. Ilf—7B 48
Stanley Rd. Mitc—4E 106
Stanley Rd. Mord—8L 105
Stanley Rd. N'wd—8E 20
Stanley Rd. Orp—3E 128
Stanley Rd. Sidc—9E 96
Stanley Rd. S'hall—1F 69
Stanley Rd. Sutt—8M 121
Stanley Rd. Twic & Tedd
—9B 86

Stanley Rd. Wat—6G 9
Stanley Rd. Wemb—2K 55
Stanley Rd. N. Rain—4C 66
Stanley Rd. S. Rain—5D 66
Stanley Sq. Cars—1D 136
Stanley St. SE8—8K 77
Stanley Ter. N19—7J 43
Stanley Way. Orp—9F 112
Stanmer St. SW11—1C 90
Stanmore Gdns. Rich—2K 87
Stanmore Gdns. Sutt—5A 122
Stanmore Hill. Stan—3E 22
Stanmore Pl. NW1—4F 58
Stanmore Rd. E11—6D 46
Stanmore Rd. N15—2M 43
Stanmore Rd. Belv—5A 82
Stanmore Rd. Rich—2K 87
Stanmore Rd. Wat—3F 8
Stanmore St. N1—4K 59
Stanmore Ter. Beck—6L 109
Stanmore Way. Lou—3L 19
Stannard Cres. E6—9L 63
Stannard Rd. E8—2E 60
Stannary St. SE11—7L 75
Stannington Path. Borwd
—3L 11
Stansfeld Rd. E16 & E6—8H 63
Stansfield Rd. SW9—2K 91
Stansfield Rd. Houn—1F 84
Stansgate Rd. Dag—8L 49
Stanstead Clo. Brom—1D 126
Stanstead Cres. Bex—7H 97
Stanstead Gro. SE6—7K 93
Stanstead Mnr. Sutt—8L 121
Stanstead Rd. E11—3F 46
Stanstead Rd.—7H 93
 SE23 1-319 & 2-302
 SE6 remainder
Stansted Clo. Horn—2F 66
Stanswood Gdns. SE5—8C 76
Stanthorpe Clo. SW16—2J 107
Stanthorpe Rd. SW16—2J 107
Stanton Av. Tedd—3C 102
Stanton Clo. Eps—7M 119
Stanton Clo. Wor Pk—3H 121
Stanton Rd. SE26—1K 109
Stanton Rd. SW13—1D 88
Stanton Rd. SW20—5H 105
Stanton Rd. Croy—2A 124
Stanton St. SE15—9E 76
Stanton Way. SE26—1K 109
Stanway Clo. Chig—5C 32
Stanway Ct. N1—5C 60
Stanway Gdns. W3—2L 71
Stanway Gdns. Edgw—5A 24
Stanway St. N1—5C 60
Stanwell Clo. Stai—5B 144
Stanwell Gdns. Stai—5B 144
Stanwell Moor Rd. Stai &
 W Dray—5A 144
Stanwell Rd. Ashf—9C 144
Stanwell Rd. Felt—6F 144
Stanwick Rd. W14—5K 73
Stanworth St. SE1—4D 76
Stanwyck Dri. Chig—5A 32
Stanwyck Gdns. Romf—5F 34
Stapenhill Rd. Wemb—8F 38
Staple Clo. Bex—9B 98
Staplefield Clo. SW2—7J 91
Staplefield Clo. Pinn—7J 21
Stapleford Av. Ilf—3C 48
Stapleford Clo. E4—3A 30
Stapleford Clo. SW19—6J 89
Stapleford Clo. King—6L 103
Stapleford Gdns. Romf—6L 33
Stapleford Rd. Wemb—3H 55
Stapleford Way. Bark—6F 64
Staplehurst Rd. SE13—4C 94
Staplehurst Rd. Cars—9C 122
Staple Inn Bldgs. WC1—8L 59
Staples Clo. SE16—2J 77
Staples Corner. NW2—6F 40
Staples Rd. Lou—5H 19
Stapleton Cres. Rain—2E 66
Stapleton Gdns. Croy—7L 123
Stapleton Hall Rd. N4—5K 43
Stapleton Rd. SW17—9E 90
Stapleton Rd. Bexh—8K 81
Stapleton Rd. Borwd—2L 11
Stapleton Rd. Orp—5D 128
Stapley Rd. Belv—6L 81
Stapylton Rd. Barn—5J 13
Star & Garter Hill. Rich—7J 87
Starboard Way. E14—4L 77
Starch Ho. La. Ilf—9B 32
Starcross St. NW1—6G 59
Starfield Rd. W12—3E 72
Star Hill. Dart—4C 98
Starkleigh Way. SE16—6F 76
Star La. E16—7C 62
Star La. Orp—8G 113

Starling Clo. Buck H—1E 30
Starling Clo. Pinn—1G 37
Starling' M. SE28—3B 80
Star Rd. W14—7K 73
Star Rd. Iswth—1B 86
Star Rd. Uxb—7A 52
Star St. E16—8D 62
Star St. W2—9C 58
Starts Clo. Orp—5L 127
Starts Hill Av. Orp—6M 127
Starts Hill Rd. Orp—5L 127
Star Yd. WC2—9L 59
State Farm Av. Orp—6M 127
Staten Gdns. Twic—7D 86
Statham Gro. N16—9B 44
Statham Gro. N18—5C 28
Station App. E7—9F 46
Station App. E11—3E 46
Station App. N11—5F 26
Station App. NW10—6D 56
Station App. SE26—1G 109
Station App. SW6—2J 89
Station App. SW16—2H 107
Station App. W7—2C 70
Station App. Ashf—9D 144
Station App. Bex—7L 97
Station App. Bexh—1A 98
 (Barnehurst)
Station App. Bexh—1J 97
 (Bexleyheath)
Station App. Brom—3E 126
Station App. Buck H—4H 31
Station App. Chst—5L 111
Station App. Chst—3J 111
 (Elmstead Woods)
Station App. Coul—8H 137
Station App. Coul—9D 136
 (Chipstead)
Station App. Dart—5J 99
Station App. Dart—5D 98
 (Crayford)
Station App. Eps—5B 134
Station App. Eps—2F 134
 (Ewell East)
Station App. Eps—1D 134
 (Ewell West)
Station App. Eps—7E 120
 (Stoneleigh)
Station App. Esh—5D 118
Station App. Harr—5C 38
Station App. Hay—4D 68
Station App. King—6L 103
Station App. Lou—7J 19
Station App. Lou—6M 19
 (Debden)
Station App. N'wd—7C 20
Station App. Orp—4D 128
Station App. Orp—7F 128
 (Chelsfield)
Station App. Orp—8F 112
 (St Mary Cray)
Station App. Pinn—1J 37
Station App. Rich—9L 71
Station App. Ruis—6C 36
Station App. Ruis—1F 52
 (South Ruislip)
Station App. Shep—9A 100
Station App. S Croy—1B 138
Station App. Sun—5E 100
Station App. Sutt—9J 121
Station App. Swan—8C 114
Station App. Wal X—7E 6
Station App. Wat—6D 8
Station App. Wat—3H 21
 (Carpenders Park)
Station App. Well—1E 96
Station App. Wemb—2F 54
Station App. Whyt—9E 138
Station App. N. Sidc—8E 96
Station App. Rd. W4—8A 72
Station App. N. Sidc—8E 96
Station Av. SW9 2M 91
Station Av. Eps—1C 134
Station Av. N Mald—7C 104
Station Av. Rich—9L 71
Station Av. W on T—6E 116
Station Clo. N3—8L 25
Station Clo. Hmptn—5M 101
Station Cres. N15—3B 44
Station Crcs. SE3—6E 78
Station Cres. Ashf—9B 144
Station Cres. Wemb—2F 54
Stationer's Hall Ct. EC4—9M 59
Station Est. Beck—8H 109
Station Est. Rd. Felt—7F 84
Station Garage M. SW16
—3H 107
Station Gdns. W4—8A 72
Station Gro. Wemb—2J 55
Station Hill. Brom—4E 126
Station La. Horn—8H 51
Station Pdc. E11—3E 46
Station Pde. NW2—2G 57

Station Pde. Bark—3A 64
Station Pde. Felt—7F 84
Station Pde. Horn—9F 50
Station Pde. Rich—9L 71
Station Pl. N4—1B 30
Station Rise. SE27—8M 91
Station Rd. E4—1B 30
Station Rd. E7—9E 46
Station Rd. E10—8A 46
Station Rd. E12—9J 47
Station Rd. E17—4J 45
Station Rd. N3—8L 25
Station Rd. N11—5F 26
Station Rd. N17—1E 44
Station Rd. N18—5D 28
Station Rd. N19—8G 43
Station Rd. N21—1M 27
Station Rd. N22—7J 27
 (Bowes Park)
Station Rd. N22—9K 27
 (Wood Green)
Station Rd. NW4—4E 40
Station Rd. NW7—6C 24
Station Rd. NW10—5D 56
Station Rd. SE20—3G 109
Station Rd. SE25—8D 108
Station Rd. SW13—1D 88
Station Rd. SW19—5A 106
Station Rd. W5—9K 55
Station Rd. W7—2C 70
Station Rd. Ashf—9D 144
Station Rd. Barn—7M 13
Station Rd. Belv—4L 81
Station Rd. Bexh—2J 97
Station Rd. Borwd—6L 11
Station Rd. Brom—5E 110
Station Rd. Brom—6C 110
 (Shortlands)
Station Rd. Cars—6D 122
Station Rd. Chess—7J 119
Station Rd. Chig—3M 31
Station Rd. Croy—4B 124
 (East Croydon)
Station Rd. Croy—3A 124
 (West Croydon)
Station Rd. Dart—6D 98
Station Rd. Edgw—6L 23
Station Rd. Eri—6C 82
Station Rd. Esh—7C 118
 (Claygate)
Station Rd. Esh—4B 118
 (Esher)
Station Rd. Esh—2D 118
 (Thames Ditton)
Station Rd. Eyns, Dart—5H 131
Station Rd. Hmptn—5L 101
Station Rd. Harr—2D 38
Station Rd. Harr—3M 37
 (North Harrow)
Station Rd. Hay—5C 68
Station Rd. Houn—3M 85
Station Rd. Ilf—8M 47
Station Rd. Ilf—1B 48
 (Barkingside)
Station Rd. Kenl—6A 138
Station Rd. K Lan—2A 4
Station Rd. King—5H 103
 (Hampton Wick)
Station Rd. King—5L 103
 (Norbiton)
Station Rd. Lou—7J 19
Station Rd. N Mald—9F 104
Station Rd. Orp—4D 128
Station Rd. Orp—8G 113
 (St Mary Cray)
Station Rd. Romf—5H 49
 (Chadwell Heath)
Station Rd. Romf—2F 50
 (Gidea Park)
Station Rd. Romf—8K 35
 (Harold Wood)
Station Rd. St Alb—4L 5
Station Rd. Shep—9A 100
Station Rd. Sidc—8E 96
Station Rd. Sun—4E 100
Station Rd. Sutt—2L 135
Station Rd. S at H & S Dar,
 Dart—6M 115
Station Rd. Swan—8C 114
Station Rd. Tedd—2D 102
Station Rd. Th Dit—2D 118
Station Rd. Twic—7D 86
Station Rd. Upm—7M 51
Station Rd. Uxb—7B 142
Station Rd. Wal A—7G 7
Station Rd. Wat—4F 8
Station Rd. W Dray—3J 143
Station Rd. W Wick—3A 126
Station Rd. Whyt—9D 138
Station Rd. N. Belv—4M 81
Station Sq. SE26—1K 109
Station Sq. Orp—9A 112
 (Petts Wood)

Station Sq.—Stroud Grn. Gdns.

Station Sq. Orp—8F 112
(St Mary Cray)
Station St. E15—3B 62
Station St. E16—2M 79
Station Ter. NW10—5H 57
Station Ter. SE5—9A 76
Station View. Gnfd—4B 54
Station Way. Buck H—4G 31
Station Way. Eps—5B 134
Station Way. Esh—8C 118
Station Way. Sutt—9J 121
Station Yd. Twic—6E 86
Staunton Rd. King—3J 103
Staunton St. SE8—7K 77
Staveley Clo. E9—1G 61
Staveley Clo. N7—9J 43
Staveley Clo. SE15—9G 77
Staveley Gdns. W4—9B 72
Staveley Rd. W4—7A 72
Staveley Rd. Ashf—3B 100
Staverton Rd. NW2—3G 57
Staverton Rd. Horn—4H 51
Stave Yd. Rd. SE16—2J 77
Stavordale Rd. N5—9M 43
Stavordale Rd. Cars—2A 122
Stayners Rd. E1—7H 61
Stayton Rd. Sutt—5L 121
Stead St. SE17—5B 76
Steam Farm La. Felt—3D 84
Stean St. E8—4D 60
Stebbing Way. Bark—5E 64
Stebondale St. E14—5A 78
Stedman Clo. Bex—9C 98
Steedman St. SE17—5A 76
Steeds Rd. N10—8D 26
Steeds Way. Lou—5J 19
Steele Rd. E11—9C 46
Steele Rd. N17—1C 44
Steele Rd. NW10—5A 56
Steele Rd. W4—4A 72
Steele Rd. Iswth—3E 86
Steele's M. NW3—2D 58
Steele's Rd. NW3—2D 58
Steel's La. E1—9G 61
Steel's La. Lea—6A 132
Steen Way. SE22—4C 92
Steep Clo. Orp—8D 128
Steep Hill. SW16—9H 91
Steep Hill. Croy—6C 124
Steeplands. Bush, Wat—9M 9
Steeple Clo. SW6—1J 89
Steeple Clo. SW19—2J 105
Steeplestone Clo. N18—5A 28
Steerforth St. SW18—8A 90
Steers Mead. Mitc—5D 106
Stella Rd. SW17—3D 106
Stelling Rd. Eri—8B 82
Stellman Clo. E5—8E 44
Stembridge Rd. SE20—6F 108
Stephan Clo. E8—4E 60
Stephen Av. Rain—2E 66
Stephen Clo. Orp—5D 128
Stephendale Rd. SW6—1M 89
Stephen M. W1—8H 59
Stephen Rd. Bexh—2A 98
Stephens Clo. Romf—5G 35
Stephenson Rd. W7—9D 54
Stephenson Rd. Twic—6L 85
Stephenson St. E16—7C 62
Stephenson St. NW10—6C 56
Stephenson Way. NW1—7G 59
Stephen's Rd. E15—4C 62
Stephen St. W1—8H 59
Stepney Causeway. E1—9H 61
Stepney Grn. E1—8H 61
Stepney High St. E1—8H 61
Stepney Way. E1—8F 60
Sterling Av. Edgw—4K 23
Sterling Av. Wal X—7D 6
Sterling Rd. Enf—3B 16
Sterling St. SW7—4C 74
Sterling Way. N18—5B 28
Sterndale Rd. W14—4H 73
Sterndale Rd. Dart—6K 99
Sterne St. W12—3H 73
Sternhall La. SE15—2E 92
Sternhold Av. SW2—8H 91
Sterry Cres. Dag—1L 65
Sterry Dri. Eps—6C 120
Sterry Dri. Th Dit—1C 118
Sterry Gdns. Dag—2L 65
Sterry Rd. Bark—4D 64
Sterry Rd. Dag—9L 49
Sterry St. SE1—3B 76
Steugers La. SE23—7J 93
Steve Biko La. SE6—1L 109
Stevedale Rd. Well—1G 97
Stevenage Cres. Borwd—3J 11
Stevenage Rd. E6—2L 63
Stevenage Rd. SW6—9H 73
Stevens Av. E9—2G 61
Stevens Clo. Beck—3L 109
Stevens Clo. Bex—1B 114
Stevens Clo. Eps—5C 134
Stevens Clo. Hmptn—2J 101
Stevens Clo. Pinn—3G 37
Stevens Grn. Bush, Wat—1A 22
Stevens La. Esh—9E 118
Stevenson Clo. Eri—8F 82
Stevens Rd. Dag—8F 48
Stevens St. SE1—4C 76
Stevens Way. Chig—4C 32
Steventon Rd. W12—1D 72
Steward Clo. Wal X—3E 6
Stewards Holte Wlk. N11 —4F 26
Steward St. E1—8C 60
Stewards Wlk. Romf—3C 50
Stewart Av. Upm—8M 51
Stewart Clo. NW9—4A 40
Stewart Clo. Hmptn—3J 101
Stewart Rd. E15—9B 46
Stewartsby Clo. N18—5A 28
Stewart's Gro. SW3—6B 74
Stewart's Rd. SW8—8G 75
Stewart St. E14—3A 78
Steyne Rd. W3—2M 71
Steyning Clo. Kenl—8M 137
Steyning Gro. SE9—1K 111
Steynings Way. N12—5L 25
Steyning Way. Houn—3G 85
Steynton Av. Bex—8H 97
Stickland Rd. Belv—5L 81
Stickleton Clo. Gnfd—6M 53
Stilecroft Gdns. Wemb—8F 38
Stile Hall Gdns. W4—6L 71
Stile Path. Sun—8E 100
Stiles Clo. Brom—1K 127
Stillingfleet Rd. SW13—7E 72
Stillington St. SW1—5G 75
Stillness Rd. SE23—5J 93
Stilton Cres. NW10—3B 56
Stilton Path. Borwd—2L 11
Stipularis Dri. Hay—7H 53
Stirling Clo. Bans—9K 135
Stirling Clo. Rain—6F 66
Stirling Clo. Uxb—6A 142
Stirling Corner. Borwd & Barn —8B 12
Stirling Dri. Orp—7F 128
Stirling Rd. E13—5F 62
Stirling Rd. E17—1J 45
Stirling Rd. N17—8E 28
Stirling Rd. N22—8M 27
Stirling Rd. SW9—1J 91
Stirling Rd. W3—4M 71
Stirling Rd. Harr—1D 38
Stirling Rd. Hay—1F 68
Stirling Rd. Houn—5D 144
Stirling Rd. Twic—6L 85
Stirling Rd. Path. E17—1J 45
Stirling Wlk. Surb—1M 119
Stirling Way. Borwd—8B 12
Stirling Way. Croy—2J 123
Stiven Cres. Harr—8K 37
Stoats Nest Rd. Coul—6J 137
Stoats Nest Village. Coul —7J 137
Stockbury Rd. Croy—1G 125
Stockdale Rd. Dag—7K 49
Stockdove Way. Gnfd—6D 54
Stockfield Rd. SW16—9K 91
Stockfield Rd. Esh—7C 118
Stock Hill. West—8H 141
Stockholm Rd. SE16—6G 77
Stockhurst Clo. SW15—1H 89
Stockingswater La. Enf—5K 17
Stockland Rd. Romf—4B 50
Stock La. Dart—9G 99
Stockley Clo. W Dray—3M 143
Stockley Farm Rd. W Dray —4M 143
Stockley Rd. Uxb & W Dray —9E 142
Stock Orchard Cres. N7—1K 59
Stock Orchard St. N7—1K 59
Stockport Rd. SW16—5H 107
Stocksfield Rd. E17—1A 46
Stocks Pl. E14—1K 77
Stock St. E13—5E 62
Stockton Gdns. N17—7A 28
Stockton Gdns. NW7—3C 24
Stockton Rd. N17—7A 28
Stockton Rd. N18—6E 28
Stockwell Av. SW9—2K 91
Stockwell Clo. Wal X—1A 6
Stockwell Gdns. SW9—9K 75
Stockwell Grn. SW9—1K 91
Stockwell La. SW9—1K 91
Stockwell La. Wal X—1A 6
Stockwell Pk. Cres. SW9 —1K 91
Stockwell Pk. Rd. SW9—9K 75
Stockwell Pk. Wlk. SW9—2L 91
Stockwell Rd. SW9—1K 91
Stockwell St. SE10—7A 78
Stockwell Ter. SW9—9K 75
Stodart Rd. SE20—5G 109
Stofield Gdns. SE9—9H 95
Stoford Clo. SW19—7J 89
Stoke Av. Ilf—6E 32
Stokenchurch St. SW6—9M 73
Stoke Newington Chu. St. N16 —8B 44
Stoke Newington Comn. N16 —7D 44
Stoke Newington High St. N16 —8D 44
Stoke Newington Rd. N16 —1D 60
Stoke Pl. NW10—6D 56
Stoke Rd. King—4A 104
Stoke Rd. Rain—5H 67
Stoke Rd. W on T—5G 117
Stokesby Rd. Chess—6M 119
Stokes Cotts. Ilf—8A 32
Stokesheath Rd. Lea—3A 132
Stokesley St. W12—9D 56
Stokes Rd. E6—7J 63
Stokes Rd. Croy—1H 125
Stompond La. W on T—4E 116
Stoms Path. SE6—2L 109
Stonard Rd. N13—3L 27
Stonard Rd. Dag—9F 48
Stonards Hill. Lou—8K 19
Stondon Pk. SE23—5J 93
Stondon Wlk. E6—5H 63
Stonebridge Pk. NW10—3B 56
Stonebridge Rd. N15—3D 44
Stonebridge Way. Wemb —2M 55
Stone Clo. Dag—7K 49
Stone Clo. W Dray—2K 143
Stonecot Clo. Sutt—3J 121
Stonecot Hill. Sutt—3J 121
Stonecroft Rd. Eri—8A 82
Stonecroft Way. Croy—2J 123
Stonecutter St. EC4—9M 59
Stonefield Clo. Bexh—2L 97
Stonefield Clo. Ruis—1J 53
Stonefield St. N1—4L 59
Stonefield Way. SE7—8H 79
Stonefield Way. Ruis—9J 37
Stonegate Clo. Orp—7G 113
Stonegrove. Edgw—4J 23
Stonegrove Gdns. Edgw —5K 23
Stonehall Av. Ilf—4J 47
Stone Hall Rd. N21—9K 15
Stoneham Rd. N11—5G 27
Stonehill Clo. SW14—4B 88
Stonehill Rd. SW14—4B 88
Stonehill Rd. W4—6L 71
Stonehills Ct. SE21—9C 92
Stonehorse Rd. Enf—7G 17
Stoneleigh Av. Enf—3F 16
Stoneleigh Av. Wor Pk—6E 120
Stoneleigh Clo. Wal X—6D 6
Stoneleigh Cres. Eps—7D 120
Stoneleigh Pk. Wey—8A 116
Stoneleigh Pk. Av. Croy —1H 125
Stoneleigh Pk. Rd. Eps—8D 120
Stoneleigh Pl. W11—1H 73
Stoneleigh Rd. N17—1D 44
Stoneleigh Rd. Cars—2C 122
Stoneleigh Rd. Ilf—1J 47
Stoneleigh St. W11—1H 73
Stoneleigh Ter. N19—7F 42
Stonell's Rd. SW11—5D 90
Stonenest St. N4—6K 43
Stone Pk. Av. Beck—8L 109
Stone Pl. Wor Pk—4E 120
Stone Rd. Brom—9D 110
Stones All. Wat—6F 8
Stones Cross Rd. Swan —9A 114
Stones End St. SE1—3A 76
Stones Rd. Eps—4C 134
Stone St. Croy—7L 123
Stonewold Ct. W5—9H 55
Stonewood Rd. Eri—6C 82
Stoney All. SE18—1L 95
Stoneyard La. E14—1M 77
Stoneycroft Clo. SE12—6D 94
Stoneycroft Rd. Wfd G—6J 31
Stoneydeep. Tedd—1E 102
Stoneydown. E17—2J 45
Stoneydown Av. E17—2J 45
Stoneyfield Rd. Coul—9K 137
Stoneyfields Gdns. Edgw —4A 24
Stoneyfields La. Edgw—4A 24
Stoney La. E1—9C 60
Stoney La. SE19—3D 108
Stoney St. SE1—2B 76
Stonhouse St. SW4—3H 91
Stonny Croft. Asht—9K 133
Stonor Rd. W14—5K 73
Stony Hill. Esh—9K 117
Stony Path. Lou—3K 19
Stonyshotts. Wal A—7L 7
Stopford Rd. E13—4E 62
Stopford Rd. SE17—6M 75
Store Rd. E16—3L 79
Store St. E15—1B 62
Store St. WC1—8H 59
Storey Rd. E17—2K 45
Storey Rd. N6—4D 42
Storey's Ga. SW1—3H 75
Storey St. E16—2L 79
Stories Rd. SE5—2C 92
Stork Rd. E7—2E 62
Storksmead Rd. Edgw—7C 24
Stork's Rd. SE16—4E 76
Stormont Rd. N6—5D 42
Stormont Rd. SW11—2E 90
Stormont Way. Chess—7G 119
Stormount Dri. Hay—3A 68
Storrington Rd. Croy—3D 124
Story St. N1—3K 59
Stothard Pl. EC2—8C 60
Stothard St. E1—7G 61
Stoughton Av. Sutt—7H 121
Stoughton Clo. SE11—5K 75
Stoughton Clo. SW15—7E 88
Stour Av. S'hall—4L 69
Stourcliffe St. W1—9D 58
Stour Clo. Kes—6G 127
Stourhead Clo. SW19—6H 89
Stourhead Gdns. SW20 —7E 104
Stour Rd. E3—3L 61
Stour Rd. Dag—7L 49
Stour Rd. Dart—2E 98
Stourton Av. Felt—1K 101
Stowage. SE8—7M 77
Stow Cres. E17—7J 29
Stowe Cres. Ruis—4A 36
Stowe Gdns. N9—1D 28
Stowell Av. Croy—2B 140
Stowe Pl. N15—1C 44
Stowe Rd. W12—3F 72
Stowe Rd. Orp—6F 128
Stowting Rd. Orp—6C 128
Stoxmead. Harr—8B 22
Stracey Rd. E7—9E 46
Stracey Rd. NW10—4B 56
Strachan Pl. SW19—3G 105
Stradbroke Dri. Chig—6M 31
Stradbroke Gro. Buck H—1H 31
Stradbroke Gro. Ilf—1J 47
Stradbroke Rd. N5—9A 44
Stradella Rd. SE24—5A 92
Strafford Rd. W3—3A 72
Strafford Rd. Barn—5J 13
Strafford Rd. Houn—2K 85
Strafford Rd. Twic—6E 86
Strafford St. E14—3L 77
Strahan Rd. E3—6J 61
Straight Rd. Romf—5F 34
Straightsmouth. SE10—8A 78
Straight, The. S'hall—3J 69
Strait Rd. E6—1J 79
Straits, The. Wal A—5H 7
Straker's Rd. SE15—3F 92
Strand. WC2—1J 75
Strand Ct. SE18—6C 80
Strandfield Clo. SE18—6C 80
Strand La. WC2—1K 75
Strand on the Grn. W4—7L 71
Strand Pl. N18—4C 28
Strand School App. W4—7L 71
Strangeways. Wat—9C 4
Strangways Ter. W14—4K 73
Stranraer Rd. Houn—5C 144
Stranraer Way. N1—3K 59
Stratfield Rd. Borwd—5L 11
Stratford Av. W8—4L 73
Stratford Av. Uxb—5D 142
Stratford Clo. Bark—3E 64
Stratford Clo. Dag—3A 66
Stratford Ct. N Mald—8B 104
Stratford Gro. SW15—3H 89
Stratford Pl. W1—9F 58
Stratford Rd. E13—4D 62
Stratford Rd. W8—4L 73
Stratford Rd. Hay—7F 52
Stratford Rd. S'hall—5J 69
Stratford Rd. T Hth—8L 107
Stratford Rd. Wat—4E 8
Stratford Shopping Centre. E15 —3B 62
Stratford Vs. NW1—3H 59
Stratford Way. Wat—4D 8
Strathan Clo. SW18—5K 89
Strathaven Rd. SE12—5F 94
Strathblaine Rd. SW11—3B 90
Strathbrook Rd. SW16—4K 107
Strathcona Rd. Wemb—7H 39
Strathdale. SW16—2K 107
Strathdon Dri. SW17—9B 90
Strathearn Av. Hay—8D 68
Strathearn Av. Twic—7M 85
Strathearn Pl. W2—9C 58
Strathearn Rd. SW19—2L 105
Strathearn Rd. Sutt—7L 121
Stratheden Rd. SE3—8E 78
Strathfield Gdns. Bark—2B 64
Strathleven Rd. SW2—4J 91
Strathmore Gdns. N3—8M 25
Strathmore Gdns. W8—2L 73
Strathmore Gdns. Edgw —9M 23
Strathmore Gdns. Horn—6D 50
Strathmore Rd. SW19—9L 89
Strathmore Rd. Croy—2B 124
Strathmore Rd. Tedd—1C 102
Strathnairn St. SE1—5E 76
Strathray Gdns. NW3—2C 58
Strath Ter. SW11—3C 90
Strathville Rd. SW18—8L 89
Strathyre Av. SW16—7L 107
Stratton Av. Enf—1B 16
Stratton Av. Wall—1H 137
Stratton Clo. SW19—6L 105
Stratton Clo. Bexh—2J 97
Stratton Clo. Edgw—6K 23
Stratton Clo. Houn—9L 69
Stratton Clo. W on T—3G 117
Strattondale St. E14—4A 78
Stratton Dri. Bark—1D 64
Stratton Gdns. S'hall—9K 53
Stratton Rd. SW19—6L 105
Stratton Rd. Bexh—2J 97
Stratton Rd. Romf—5L 35
Stratton Rd. Sun—6D 100
Stratton St. W1—2F 74
Stratton Wlk. Romf—5L 35
Strauss Rd. W4—3B 72
Strawberry Hill. Twic—9D 86
Strawberry Hill Clo. Twic —9D 86
Strawberry Hill Rd. Twic —9D 86
Strawberry La. Cars—5E 122
Strawberry Vale. N2—8B 26
Strawberry Vale. Twic—9E 86
(in two parts)
Strayfield Rd. Enf—1L 15
Streamdale. SE2—7F 80
Stream La. Edgw—5M 23
Streamside Clo. Brom—8E 110
Stream Way. Belv—7L 81
Streatfeild Av. E6—4K 63
Streatfield Rd. Harr—1G 39
Streatham Clo. SW16—8J 91
Streatham Comn. N. SW16 —2J 107
Streatham Comn. S. SW16 —3J 107
Streatham High Rd. SW16 —1J 107
Streatham Hill. SW2—8J 91
Streatham Pl. SW2—6J 91
Streatham Rd.—5E 106
SW16 225-263 & 228-260
Mitc remainder
Streatham St. WC1—9J 59
Streatham Vale. SW16—5G 107
Streathbourne Rd. SW17—9E 90
Streatley Pl. NW3—9A 42
Streatley Rd. NW6—3K 57
Streetfield M. SE3—2E 94
Street, The. S Dar, Dart—8M 115
Streimer Rd. E15—5A 62
Strelley Way. W3—1C 72
Stretton Rd. Croy—2C 124
Stretton Rd. Rich—8G 87
Stretton Way. Borwd—2J 11
Strickland Av. Dart—2K 99
(in two parts)
Strickland Row. SW18—6B 90
Strickland St. SE8—9L 77
Strickland Way. Orp—6D 128
Stride Rd. E13—5D 62
Strode Clo. N10—7E 26
Strode Rd. E7—9E 46
Strode Rd. N17—9C 28
Strode Rd. NW10—2E 56
Strode Rd. SW6—8J 73
Strone Rd.—2G 63
E7 1-209 & 2-216
E12 remainder
Strongbow Cres. SE9—4K 95
Strongbow Rd. SE9—4K 95
Strongbridge Clo. Harr—6L 37
Stronsa Rd. W12—3D 72
Strood Av. Romf—6B 50
Stroud Cres. SW15—9E 88
Stroudes Clo. Wor Pk—2D 120
Stroud Field. N'holt—2J 53
Stroud Ga. Harr—9M 37
Stroud Grn. Gdns. Croy —2G 125

Stroud Grn. Rd. N4—6K 43
Stroud Grn. Way. Croy—2F 124
Stroudley Wlk. E3—6M 61
Stroud Rd. SE25—1E 124
Stroud Rd. SW19—9L 89
Stroudwater Pk. Wey—8A 116
Stroud Way. Ashf—3A 100
Strouts Pl. E2—6D 60
Strutton Ground. SW1—4H 75
Strype St. E1—8D 60
Stuart Av. NW9—5E 40
Stuart Av. W5—2K 71
Stuart Av. Brom—3E 126
Stuart Av. Harr—8K 37
Stuart Av. W on T—3F 116
Stuart Clo. Swan—4D 114
Stuart Clo. Uxb—2E 142
Stuart Ct. Borwd—8H 11
Stuart Cres. N22—8K 27
Stuart Cres. Croy—5K 125
Stuart Cres. Hay—9A 52
Stuart Evans Clo. Well—2G 97
Stuart Gro. Tedd—2C 102
Stuart Mantle Way. Eri—8C 82
Stuart Pl. Mitc—5D 106
Stuart Rd. NW6—6L 57
Stuart Rd. SE15—3G 93
Stuart Rd. SW19—9L 89
Stuart Rd. W3—2A 72
Stuart Rd. Bark—3D 64
Stuart Rd. Barn—9C 14
Stuart Rd. Harr—1D 38
Stuart Rd. Rich—8F 86
Stuart Rd. T Hth—8A 108
Stuart Rd. Well—9F 80
Stuart Way. Wal X—4B 6
Stubbs Way. SW19—5B 106
Stucley Pl. NW1—3F 58
Stucley Rd. Houn—8A 70
Studdridge St. SW6—1L 89
Studd St. N1—4M 59
Stud Grn. Wat—5E 4
Studholme Ct. NW3—9L 41
Studholme St. SE15—8F 76
Studios, The. Bush, Wat—8L 9
Studio Way. Borwd—4A 12
Studland Clo. Sidc—9D 96
Studland Rd. SE26—2H 109
Studland Rd. W7—9B 54
Studland Rd. King—3J 103
Studland St. W6—5F 72
Studley Av. E4—7B 30
Studley Clo. E5—1J 61
Studley Ct. Sidc—2F 112
Studley Dri. Ilf—4H 47
Studley Grange Rd. W7—3C 70
Studley Rd. E7—2F 62
Studley Rd. SW4—9J 75
Studley Rd. Dag—3H 65
Stukeley Rd. E7—3F 62
Stukeley St. WC2—9J 59
Stumps Hill La. Beck—3L 109
Stumps La. Whyt—9C 138
Sturdy Rd. SE15—1F 92
Sturge Av. E17—9M 29
Sturgeon Rd. SE17—6A 76
Sturges Field. Chst—3B 112
Sturgess Av. NW4—5F 40
Sturge St. SE1—3A 76
Sturlas Way. Wal X—6D 6
Sturmer Way. N7—1K 59
Sturrock Clo. N15—2B 44
Sturry St. E14—9M 61
Sturt St. N1—5A 60
Stutfield St. E1—9E 60
Styles Gdns. SW9—2M 91
Styles Way. Beck—8A 110
Sudbourne Rd. SW2—4J 91
Sudbrooke Rd. SW12—5D 90
Sudbrook Gdns. Rich—9H 87
Sudbrook La. Rich—8J 87
Sudbury Av. Wemb—8G 39
Sudbury Ct. Dri. Harr—8D 38
Sudbury Ct. Rd. Harr—8E 38
Sudbury Cres. Brom—3E 110
Sudbury Cres. Wemb—1F 54
Sudbury Gdns. Croy—6C 124
Sudbury Gro. Wemb—9D 38
Sudbury Heights Av. Gnfd
—1D 54
Sudbury Hill. Harr—8C 38
Sudbury Hill Clo. Wemb—8D 38
Sudbury Rd. Bark—1D 64
Sudeley St. N1—5M 59
Sudicamps Ct. Wal A—6M 7
Sudlow Rd. SW18—4L 89
Sudrey St. SE1—3A 76
Suez Av. Gnfd—5D 54
Suez Rd. Enf—6J 17
Suffield Clo. S Croy—4H 139
Suffield Rd. E4—4M 29
Suffield Rd. N15—3D 44
Suffield Rd. SE20—6G 109

Suffolk Clo. Borwd—7B 12
Suffolk Ct. E10—5L 45
Suffolk La. EC4—1B 76
Suffolk Pk. Rd. E17—2J 45
Suffolk Pl. SW1—2H 75
Suffolk Rd. E13—6E 62
Suffolk Rd. N15—3B 44
Suffolk Rd. NW10—3C 56
Suffolk Rd. SE25—8D 108
Suffolk Rd. SW13—8D 72
Suffolk Rd. Bark—3B 64
Suffolk Rd. Dag—1A 66
Suffolk Rd. Dart—5J 99
Suffolk Rd. Enf—7F 16
Suffolk Rd. Harr—4K 37
Suffolk Rd. Ilf—4C 48
Suffolk Rd. Sidc—3G 113
Suffolk Rd. Wor Pk—4D 120
Suffolk St. E7—9E 46
Suffolk St. SW1—1H 75
Sugar Ho. La. E15—5A 62
Sugar Loaf Wlk. E2—6G 61
Sugden Rd. SW11—2E 90
Sugden Rd. Th Dit—3F 118
Sugden Rd. SE5—7B 76
Sugden Way. Bark—5D 64
Sulgrave Rd. W6—4G 73
Sulina Rd. SW2—6J 91
Sulivan Ct. SW6—1L 89
Sulivan Rd. SW6—2L 89
Sullivan Av. E16—8H 63
Sullivan Clo. SW11—2C 90
Sullivan Clo. E Mol—7M 101
Sullivan Rd. SE11—5M 75
Sullivan Way. Borwd—8G 11
Sultan Rd. E11—2F 46
Sultan St. SE5—8A 76
Sultan St. Beck—6H 109
Sumatra Rd. NW6—1L 57
Sumburgh Rd. SW12—5E 90
Summer Av. E Mol—9C 102
Summercourt Rd. E1—9G 61
Summerfield Av. NW6—5J 57
Summerfield La. Surb—4H 119
Summerfield Rd. W5—7F 54
Summerfield Rd. Lou—8H 19
Summerfield Rd. Wat—8E 4
Summerfield St. SE12—6D 94
Summer Gdns. E Mol—9C 102
Summer Gro. Borwd—8H 11
Summer Hill. Borwd—7L 11
Summer Hill. Chst—6L 111
Summerhill Clo. Orp—5C 128
Summerhill Gro. Enf—8C 16
Summerhill Rd. N15—2B 44
Summerhill Rd. Dart—6H 99
Summerhill Vs. Chst—5L 111
Summerhouse Av. Houn
—9J 69
Summerhouse Dri. Bex & Swan
—1B 114
Summerhouse La. Wat—3A 10
Summerhouse La. W Dray
—7H 143
Summerhouse Rd. N16—7C 44
Summerhouse Way. Abb L, Wat
—3D 4
Summerland Gdns. N10—1F 42
Summerlands Av. W3—1A 72
Summerlee Av. N2—2D 42
Summerlee Gdns. N2—2D 42
Summerley St. SW18—8M 89
Summer Rd. E Mol & Th Dit
—9C 102
Summersby Rd. N6—4F 42
Summers Clo. Wemb—6M 39
Summers Ct. Sutt—9L 121
Summers La. N12—7B 26
Summers Row. N12—6C 26
Summers St. EC1—7L 59
Summerstown. SW17—1A 106
Summer Trees. Sun—5F 100
Summerville Gdns. Sutt
—8K 121
Summerwood Rd. Iswth
—4D 86
Summit Av. NW9—3B 40
Summit Clo. N14—2G 27
Summit Clo. NW2—1J 57
Summit Clo. NW9—3B 40
Summit Clo. Edgw—7L 23
Summit Dri. Wfd G—9H 31
Summit Rd. E17—2M 45
Summit Rd. N'holt—3L 53
Summit, The. Lou—3K 19
Summit Way. N14—2F 26
Summit Way. SE19—4C 108
Sumner Av. SE15—9D 76
Sumner Clo. Orp—6A 128
Sumner Gdns. Croy—3M 123
Sumner Pl. SW7—5B 74
Sumner Pl. M. SW7—5B 74

Sumner Rd. SE15—8D 76
Sumner Rd. Croy—3M 123
Sumner Rd. Harr—5A 38
Sumner Rd. S. Croy—3L 123
Sumner St. SE1—2M 75
Sumpter Clo. NW3—2A 58
Sun All. Rich—3J 87
Sunbeam Rd. NW10—7A 56
Sunbury Av. NW7—5B 24
Sunbury Av. SW14—3B 88
Sunbury Ct. Rd. Sun—6G 101
Sunbury Cres. Felt—1D 100
Sunbury Cross Shopping
Centre. Sun—4D 100
Sunbury Gdns. NW7—5B 24
Sunbury La. SW11—9B 74
Sunbury La. W on T—1E 116
Sunbury Rd. Felt—9D 84
Sunbury Rd. Sutt—5J 121
Sunbury St. SE18—4K 79
Sunbury Way. Felt—2G 101
Suncourt. Eri—1D 98
Suncroft Pl. SE26—9G 93
Sundale Av. S Croy—2G 139
Sunderland SE23—7H 93
Sunderland Rd. W5—4H 71
Sunderland Rd. Houn—5C 144
Sunderland Ter. W2—9M 57
Sunderland Way. E12—7H 47
Sundew Av. W12—1E 72
Sundial Av. SE25—7D 108
Sundown Av. S Croy—3D 138
Sundown Rd. Ashf—2A 100
Sundra Wlk. E1—7H 61
Sundridge Av. Brom & Chst
—5H 111
Sundridge Av. Well—1B 96
Sundridge Clo. Dart—5L 99
Sundridge Pl. Croy—3E 124
Sundridge Rd. Croy—3D 124
Sunfields Pl. SE3—8F 78
Sunflower Way. Romf—8H 35
Sunkist Way. Wall—1J 137
Sunland Av. Bexh—3J 97
Sunleigh Rd. Wemb—4J 55
Sunley Gdns. Gnfd—4E 54
Sunmead Rd. Sun—7E 100
Sunna Gdns. Sun—6F 100
Sunningdale. N14—5H 27
Sunningdale Av. W3—1C 72
Sunningdale Av. Bark—3B 64
Sunningdale Av. Felt—8J 85
Sunningdale Av. Rain—7F 66
Sunningdale Av. Ruis—6G 37
Sunningdale Clo. Stan—7E 22
Sunningdale Gdns. NW9
—3A 40
Sunningdale Rd. Brom—8J 111
Sunningdale Rd. Rain—3E 66
Sunningdale Rd. Sutt—6K 121
Sunningfields Cres. NW4
—9F 24
Sunningfields Rd. NW4—1F 40
Sunninghill Rd. SE13—1M 93
Sunningvale Av. West—7G 141
Sunningvale Clo. West—7H 141
Sunny Bank. SE25—7E 108
Sunnybank. Eps—8A 134
Sunnybank. Warl—9J 139
Sunny Cres. NW10—3A 56
Sunnycroft Rd. SE25—8E 108
Sunnycroft Rd. Houn—1M 85
Sunnycroft Rd. S'hall—8L 53
Sunnydale. Orp—4L 127
Sunnydale Gdns. NW7—6B 24
Sunnydale Rd. SE12—4F 94
Sunnydene Av. E4—5B 30
Sunnydene Av. Ruis—6E 36
Sunnydene Clo. Romf—7K 35
Sunnydene Gdns. Wemb
—2G 55
Sunnydene Rd. Purl—5M 137
Sunnydene St. SE26—1J 109
Sunnyfield. NW7—4D 24
Sunnyfield Rd. Chst—7E 112
Sunny Gdns. Rd. NW4—9F 24
Sunny Hill. NW4—1F 40
Sunnyhill Rd. SW16—1J 107
Sunnyhurst Clo. Sutt—5L 121
Sunnymead Av. Mitc—7H 107
Sunnymead Rd. NW9—5B 40
Sunnymead Rd. SW15—4F 88
Sunnymede. Chig—3F 32
Sunnymede Av. Cars—3B 136
Sunnymede Av. Eps—1C 134
Sunnymede Dri. Ilf—2M 47
Sunny Nook Gdns. S Croy
—8B 124
Sunny Rd., The. Enf—3H 17
Sunnyside. NW2—8K 41
Sunnyside. SW19—3J 105

Sunny Side. W on T—9G 101
Sunnyside Dri. E4—9A 18
Sunnyside Gdns. Upm—8M 51
Sunnyside Pas. SW19—3J 105
Sunnyside Rd. E10—6L 45
Sunnyside Rd. N19—5H 43
Sunnyside Rd. W5—2H 71
Sunnyside Rd. Ilf—8A 48
Sunnyside Rd. Tedd—1B 102
Sunnyside Rd. E. N9—3E 28
Sunnyside Rd. N. N9—3E 28
Sunnyside Rd. S. N9—3D 28
Sunny View. NW9—3B 40
Sunny Way. N12—7C 26
Sunray Av. SE24—3B 92
Sunray Av. Brom—1J 127
Sunray Av. Surb—4M 119
Sunray Av. W Dray—3H 143
Sunrise Av. Horn—8G 51
Sunrise Clo. Felt—9K 85
Sun Rd. W14—6K 73
Sunset Av. E4—1M 29
Sunset Av. Wfd G—4D 30
Sunset Dri. Hav, Romf—5F 34
Sunset Gdns. SE25—6D 108
Sunset Rd. SE5—3A 92
Sunset View. Barn—4J 13
Sunshine Way. Mitc—6D 106
Sun St. EC2—8B 60
Sun St. Wal A—6J 7
Sunwell Clo. SE15—9F 76
Surbiton Ct. Surb—1H 119
Surbiton Cres. King—8J 103
Surbiton Hall Clo. King—8J 103
Surbiton Hill Pk. Surb—9K 103
Surbiton Hill Rd. Surb—9J 103
Surbiton Rd. King—8J 103
Surlingham Clo. SE28—1H 81
Surrendale Pl. W9—7L 57
Surrey Canal Rd. SE15 & SE14
—7G 77
Surrey Cres. W4—6L 71
Surrey Dri. Horn—2L 51
Surrey Gro. SE17—6C 76
Surrey La. SW11—9C 74
Surrey M. SE27—1C 108
Surrey Mt. SE23—7F 92
Surrey Rd. SE15—4H 93
Surrey Rd. Bark—3C 64
Surrey Rd. Dag—1M 65
Surrey Rd. Harr—3A 38
Surrey Rd. W Wick—3M 125
Surrey Row. SE1—3M 75
Surrey Sq. SE17—6C 76
Surrey St. E13—6F 62
Surrey St. WC2—1K 75
Surrey St. Croy—5A 124
Surrey Ter. SE17—6C 76
Surridge Clo. Rain—6G 67
Surridge Gdns. SE19—3B 108
Surr St. N7—1J 59
Susan Clo. Romf—1A 50
Susannah St. E14—9M 61
Susan Rd. SE3—1F 94
Susan Wood. Chst—5L 111
Sussex Av. Iswth—2C 86
Sussex Av. Romf—7K 35
Sussex Clo. N19—7J 43
Sussex Clo. Ilf—3K 47
Sussex Clo. N Mald—8C 104
Sussex Clo. Twic—5H 87
Sussex Cres. N'holt—2L 53
Sussex Gdns. N4—3A 44
Sussex Gdns. N6—3D 42
Sussex Gdns. W2—9B 58
Sussex Gdns. Chess—8H 119
Sussex Pl. NW1—7D 58
(in two parts)
Sussex Pl. W2—9B 58
Sussex Pl. W6—6G 73
Sussex Pl. Eri—8M 81
Sussex Pl. N Mald—8C 104
Sussex Ring. N12—5L 25
Sussex Rd. E6—4L 63
Sussex Rd. Cars—8D 122
Sussex Rd. Dart—6L 99
Sussex Rd. Eri—8M 81
Sussex Rd. Harr—3A 38
Sussex Rd. Mitc—9J 107
Sussex Rd. N Mald—8C 104
Sussex Rd. Orp—1G 129
Sussex Rd. Sidc—2F 112
Sussex Rd. S'hall—4H 69
Sussex Rd. S Croy—8B 124
Sussex Rd. Uxb—9A 36
Sussex Rd. Wat—2E 8
Sussex Rd. W Wick
—3M 125
Sussex Sq. W2—1B 74
Sussex St. E13—6F 62
Sussex St. SW1—6F 74
Sussex Wlk. SW9—3M 91

Sussex Way—6J 43
N7 1-131 & 2-130
N19 remainder
Sussex Way. Barn—7F 14
Sutcliffe Clo. NW11—3M 41
Sutcliffe Clo. Bush, Wat—6A 10
Sutcliffe Rd. SE18—7C 80
Sutcliffe Rd. Well—1G 97
Sutherland Av. W9—7L 57
Sutherland Av. W13—9F 54
Sutherland Av. Hay—5E 68
Sutherland Av. Orp—1D 128
Sutherland Av. Sun—6D 100
Sutherland Av. Well—3C 96
Sutherland Av. West—9H 141
Sutherland Clo. Barn—6J 13
Sutherland Ct. NW9—3M 39
Sutherland Dri. SW19—5B 106
Sutherland Gdns. SW14—2C 88
Sutherland Gdns. Sun—6D 100
Sutherland Gdns. Wor Pk
—3F 120
Sutherland Gro. SW18—5J 89
Sutherland Gro. Tedd—2C 102
Sutherland Pl. W2—9L 57
Sutherland Rd. E3—5K 61
Sutherland Rd. E17—1H 45
Sutherland Rd. N9—1F 28
Sutherland Rd. N17—8E 28
Sutherland Rd. W4—7C 72
Sutherland Rd. W13—9E 54
Sutherland Rd. Belv—4L 81
Sutherland Rd. Croy—2G 123
Sutherland Rd. Enf—8H 17
Sutherland Rd. Path. E17
—1H 45
Sutherland Row. SW1—6F 74
Sutherland Sq. SE17—6A 76
Sutherland St. SW1—6F 74
Sutherland Wlk. SE17—6A 76
Sutlej Rd. SE7—8G 79
Sutterton St. N7—2K 59
Sutton Arc. Sutt—7M 121
Sutton Clo. Beck—5M 109
Sutton Clo. Lou—9J 19
Sutton Clo. Pinn—3E 36
Sutton Comn. Rd. Sutt—2K 121
Sutton Ct. W4—7A 72
Sutton Ct. Rd. E13—6G 63
Sutton Ct. Rd. W4—8A 72
Sutton Ct. Rd. Sutt—8A 122
Sutton Ct. Rd. Uxb—4F 142
Sutton Cres. Barn—7H 13
Sutton Dene. Houn—9M 69
Sutton Est. W10—8G 57
Sutton Gdns. Bark—4C 64
Sutton Gdns. Croy—9D 108
Sutton Gro. Sutt—7B 122
Sutton Hall Rd. Houn—8L 69
Sutton La. Houn—1K 85
Sutton La. Sutt & Bans
—3M 135
Sutton La. N. W4—6A 72
Sutton La. S. W4—7A 72
Sutton Pk. Rd. Sutt—8M 121
Sutton Path. Borwd—5L 11
Sutton Pl. E9—1G 61
Sutton Rd. E13—7D 62
Sutton Rd. E17—8H 29
Sutton Rd. N10—8E 26
Sutton Rd. Bark—4C 64
Sutton Rd. Houn—9L 69
Sutton Rd. Wat—5G 9
(in two parts)
Sutton Row. W1—9H 59
Suttons Av. Horn—8G 51
Suttons Gdns. Horn—8H 51
Suttons La. Horn—1H 67
Sutton Sq. Houn—9K 69
Sutton St. E1—1G 77
Sutton Way. W10—7G 57
Sutton Way. Houn—9K 69
Swaby Rd. SW18—7A 90
Swaffham Way. N22—7M 27
Swaffield Rd. SW18—6M 89
Swain Clo. W Dray—3J 143
Swain Rd. T Hth—9A 108
Swains La. N6—8E 42
Swainson Rd. W3—3D 72
Swains Rd. SW17—4D 106
Swaisland Dri. Dart—4D 98
Swaisland Rd. Dart—5F 98
Swakeleys Dri. Uxb—1E 142
Swakeleys Rd. Uxb—8A 36 &
1C 142
Swalecliffe Rd. Belv—6M 81
Swale Rd. S Ock—9M 67
Swaledale Rd. Dart—7M 99
Swale Rd. Dart—3E 98
Swallands Rd. SE6—1M 109
(in two parts)
Swallow Clo. SE14—9H 77

Swallow Clo. Bush, Wat—1M 21
Swallow Ct. Ilf—3M 47
Swallowdale. S Croy—1H 139
Swallow Dri. N'holt—5L 53
Swallowfield Rd. SE7—6F 78
Swallowfield Way. Hay—3B 68
Swallow Pl. W1—9F 58
Swallow St. W1—1G 75
Swallow Wlk. Rain—2F 66
Swanage Rd. E4—7A 30
Swanage Rd. SW18—5A 90
Swanage Waye. Hay—9G 53
Swan & Pike Rd. Enf—2L 17
Swanbourne Dri. Horn—1H 67
Swanbridge Rd. Bexh—9L 81
Swan Clo. Felt—1J 101
Swan Clo. Orp—7E 112
Swanfield Rd. Wal X—6E 6
Swanfield St. E2—6D 60
Swan La. EC4—1B 76
Swan La. N20—3A 26
Swan La. Dart—6D 98
Swanley By-Pass. Swan
—6A 114
Swanley Centre. Swan—7C 114
Swanley La. Swan—7D 114
Swanley Rd. Well—9G 81
Swanley Village Rd. Swan
—5F 114
Swan Mead. SE1—4C 76
Swan SW9—9K 75
Swan Pl. SW13—1D 88
Swan Rd. SE16—3G 77
Swan Rd. SE18—4H 79
Swan Rd. Felt—2J 101
Swan Rd. S'hall—9M 53
Swan Rd. W Dray—3H 143
Swanscombe Rd. W4—6C 72
Swanscombe Rd. W11—2H 73
Swansea Rd. Enf—6G 17
Swanshope. Lou—4M 19
Swansland Gdns. E17—8J 29
Swanston Path. Wat—3G 21
Swan St. SE1—4A 76
Swan St. Iswth—2F 86
Swanton Gdns. SW19—7H 89
Swanton Rd. Eri—8L 81
Swan Wlk. SW3—7D 74
Swan Wlk. Romf—3C 50
Swan Way. Enf—4H 17
Swanwick Clo. SW15—6D 88
Swan Yd. N1—2M 59
Sward Rd. Orp—1E 128
Swaton Rd. E3—7L 61
Swaylands Rd. Belv—7L 81
Swedenborg Gdns. E1—1F 76
Sweeney Cres. SE1—3D 76
Sweeps La. Orp—9H 113
Sweet Briar Grn. N9—3D 28
Sweet Briar Gro. N9—3D 28
Sweet Briar La. Eps—6B 134
Sweet Briar Wlk. N18—4D 28
Sweetcroft La. Uxb—3E 142
Sweetland Ct. Dag—2F 64
Sweetmans Av. Pinn—1H 37
Sweets Way. N20—2B 26
Swetenham Wlk. SE18—6A 80
Swete St. E13—5E 62
Sweyn Pl. SE3—1E 94
Swievelands Rd. West—9G 141
Swift Clo. Harr—7M 37
Swift Clo. Hay—9D 52
Swift Ct. Sutt—9M 121
Swift Rd. Felt—1H 101
Swift Rd. S'hall—4L 69
Swiftsden Way. Brom—3C 110
Swift St. SW6—9K 73
Swift Way. Wall—1H 137
Swinbrook Rd. W10—8J 57
Swinburne Cres. Croy—1G 125
Swinburne Rd. SW15—3E 88
Swinderby Rd. Wemb—2J 55
Swindon Clo. Ilf—7C 48
Swindon Clo. Romf—5K 35
Swindon Gdns. Romf—5K 35
Swindon La. Romf—5K 35
Swindon St. W12—2G 73
Swinfield Clo. Felt—9J 85
Swinford Gdns. SW9—2M 91
Swingate La. SE18—7C 80
Swinnerton St. E9—1J 61
Swinton Clo. Wemb—6M 39
Swinton Pl. WC1—6K 59
Swinton St. WC1—6K 59
Swires Shaw. Kes—7H 127
Swiss Av. Wat—5C 8
Swiss Clo. Wat—5C 8
Swiss Ter. NW6—3B 58
Swithland Gdns. SE9—1L 111
Swyncombe Av. W5—5F 70
Sybourn St. E17—5K 45
Sycamore App. Rick—7A 8
Sycamore Av. W5—4H 71

Sycamore Av. Hay—1C 68
Sycamore Av. Sidc—5D 96
Sycamore Av. Upm—8L 51
Sycamore Clo. E16—8C 62
Sycamore Clo. Barn—8B 14
Sycamore Clo. Bush, Wat—4J 9
Sycamore Clo. Cars—6D 122
Sycamore Clo. Felt—9E 84
Sycamore Clo. N'holt—4J 53
Sycamore Clo. Wat—8F 4
Sycamore Clo. W Dray—1K 143
Sycamore Dri. Swan—7C 114
Sycamore Gdns. W6—4F 72
Sycamore Gdns. Mitc—6B 106
Sycamore Gro. NW9—5A 40
Sycamore Gro. SE20—5E 108
Sycamore Gro. N Mald—7B 104
Sycamore Rise. Bans—6H 135
Sycamore Rd. SW19—3G 105
Sycamore St. EC1—7A 60
Sycamore Wlk. W10—7J 57
Sycamore Wlk. Ilf—2A 48
Sycamore Way. T Hth—9L 107
Sydcote. SE21—7A 92
Sydenham Av. SE26—2F 108
Sydenham Hill—1D 108
SE26 1-135 & 2-48
SE23 remainder
Sydenham Pk. SE26—9G 93
Sydenham Pk. Rd. SE26—9G 93
Sydenham Pl. SE27—9M 91
Sydenham Rise. SE23—8F 92
Sydenham Rd. SE26—1G 109
Sydenham Rd. Croy—3B 124
Sydner M. N16—9D 44
Sydner Rd. N16—9D 44
Sydney Av. Purl—4K 137
Sydney Clo. SW3—5B 74
Sydney Gro. NW4—3G 41
Sydney M. SW3—5B 74
Sydney Pl. SW7—5B 74
Sydney Rd. E11—4F 46
Sydney Rd. N8—2L 43
Sydney Rd. N10—8F 26
Sydney Rd. SE2—4H 81
Sydney Rd. SW20—6H 105
Sydney Rd. W13—2E 70
Sydney Rd. Bexh—3H 97
Sydney Rd. Enf—6B 16
Sydney Rd. Felt—7E 84
Sydney Rd. Ilf—9A 32
Sydney Rd. Rich—3J 87
Sydney Rd. Sidc—1C 112
Sydney Rd. Sutt—6L 121
Sydney Rd. Tedd—2D 102
Sydney Rd. Wat—7C 8
Sydney Rd. Wfd G—4E 30
Sydney St. SW3—6C 74
Sylvana Clo. Uxb—4D 142
Sylvan Av. N3—9L 25
Sylvan Av. N22—7K 27
Sylvan Av. NW7—6D 24
Sylvan Av. Horn—4J 51
Sylvan Av. Romf—4K 49
Sylvan Clo. S Croy—2F 138
Sylvan Ct. N12—3M 25
Sylvan Gdns. Surb—2H 119
Sylvan Gro. SE15—7F 76
Sylvan Hill. SE19—5C 108
Sylvan Rd. E7—2E 62
Sylvan Rd. E11—3E 46
Sylvan Rd. E17—3L 45
Sylvan Rd. SE19—5D 108
Sylvan Way. Chig—3F 32
Sylvan Way. Dag—9F 48
Sylvan Way. W Wick—6C 126
Sylverdale Rd. Purl—5M 137
Sylvester Gdns. Ilf—5F 32
Sylvester Path. E8—2F 60
Sylvester Rd. E8—2F 60
Sylvester Rd. E17—5K 45
Sylvester Rd. N2—9B 26
Sylvester Rd. Wemb—1G 55
Sylvestrus Clo. King—5L 103
Sylvia Av. Pinn—6J 21
Sylvia Gdns. Wemb—3M 55
Symons St. SW3—5D 74
Syon Ga. Way. Bren—8E 70
Syon La. Iswth—7D 70
Syon Pk. Gdns. Iswth—8D 70
Syon Vista. Rich—9J 71
Syracuse Av. Rain—6J 67

Tabard St. SE1—3B 76
Tabarn Way. Eps—8G 135
Tabernacle Av. E13—7E 62
Tabernacle St. EC2—7B 60
Tableer Av. SW4—4H 91
Tabley Rd. N7—9J 43

Tabor Gdns. Sutt—8K 121
Tabor Gro. SW19—4K 105
Tabor Rd. W6—4F 72
Tachbrook Est. SW1—6H 75
Tachbrook M. SW1—5G 75
Tachbrook Rd. Felt—6D 84
Tachbrook Rd. S'hall—5H 69
Tachbrook Rd. Uxb—5A 142
Tachbrook Rd. W Dray—2J 143
Tachbrook St. SW1—5G 75
Tack M. SE4—2L 93
Tadema Rd. SW10—8A 74
Tadlows Clo. Upm—1M 67
Tadmor Clo. Sun—8D 100
Tadmor St. W12—2H 73
Tadworth Av. N Mald—9D 104
Tadworth Pde. Horn—9F 50
Tadworth Rd. NW2—7E 40
Taffy's How. Mitc—7C 106
Taft Way. E3—6M 61
Tait Rd. Croy—2C 124
Takeley Clo. Romf—9B 34
Takeley Clo. Wal A—6K 7
Talacre Rd. NW5—2E 58
Talbot Av. N2—1B 42
Talbot Av. Wat—9J 9
Talbot Clo. N15—2D 44
Talbot Cres. NW4—3E 40
Talbot Gdns. Ilf—7E 48
Talbot Pl. SE3—1C 94
Talbot Rd. E6—5L 63
Talbot Rd. E7—9E 46
Talbot Rd. N6—4E 42
Talbot Rd. N15—2D 44
Talbot Rd. N22—9G 27
Talbot Rd.—9K 57
W2 1-97 & 2-102
W11 remainder
(in two parts)
Talbot Rd. W13—2E 70
Talbot Rd. Brom—7F 110
Talbot Rd. Cars—7E 122
Talbot Rd. Dag—2K 65
Talbot Rd. Harr—9D 22
Talbot Rd. Iswth—3E 86
Talbot Rd. S'hall—5J 69
Talbot Rd. T Hth—8B 108
Talbot Rd. Twic—7C 86
Talbot Rd. Wemb—2H 55
Talbot Wlk. NW10—2C 56
Talbot Yd. SE1—2B 76
Talcott Path. SW2—7L 91
Talfourd Pl. SE15—9D 76
Talfourd Rd. SE15—9D 76
Talgarth Rd.—6H 73
W14 1-155
W6 remainder
Talisman Sq. SE26—1E 108
Talisman Way. Eps—8G 135
Talisman Way. Wemb—8K 39
Tallack Clo. Harr—7C 22
Tallack Rd. E10—6K 45
Tall Elms Clo. Brom—9D 110
Tallis Gro. SE7—7F 78
Tallis St. EC4—1L 75
Tallis Way. Borwd—3H 11
Talma Gdns. Twic—5C 86
Talman Gro. Stan—6H 23
Talma Rd. SW2—3L 91
Talwin St. E3—6M 61
Tamar Dri. S Ock—9M 67
Tamarisk Sq. W12—1D 72
Tamar Sq. Wfd G—6F 30
Tamar Way. N17—1E 44
Tamesis Gdns. Wor Pk—4C 120
Tamian Way. Houn—3G 85
Tamworth Av. E4—6C 30
Tamworth La. Mitc—6F 106
Tamworth Pk. Mitc—7F 106
Tamworth Pl. Croy—4A 124
Tamworth Rd. Croy—4M 123
Tamworth St. SW6—7L 73
Tamworth Vs. Mitc—8G 107
Tancred Rd. N4—4M 43
Tandridge Dri. Orp—3B 128
Tandridge Gdns. S Croy
—5E 138
Tandridge Pl. Orp—3B 128
Tanfield Av. NW2—9C 40
Tanfield Rd. Croy—6A 124
Tangent Rd. Romf—8H 35
Tangier Rd. Rich—3L 87
Tangier Way. Tad—9J 135
Tangier Wood. Tad—9J 135
Tanglewood Clo. Croy—5G 125
Tanglewood Clo. Felt—9F 84
Tanglewood Clo. Stan—2C 22
Tanglewood Clo. Uxb—6E 142
Tangley Gro. SW15—5D 88
Tangley Pk. Rd. Hmptn—2K 101
Tangmere Cres. Horn—2F 66

Tangmere Gdns. N'holt—5G 53
Tangmere Way. NW9—9C 24
Tanhurst Wlk. SE2- 4H 81
Tankerton Rd. Surb—4K 119
Tankerton St. WC1—6J 59
Tankerville Rd. SW16—4H 107
Tank Hill Rd. Purf—5L 83
Tank La. Purf—5L 83
Tankridge Rd. NW2—7F 40
Tanners End La. N18—5C 28
Tanner's Hill. SE8—9K 77
Tanners Hill. Abb L, Wat—4D 4
Tanners La. Ilf—1A 48
Tanner St. SE1—3C 76
Tanner St. Bark—2A 64
Tanners Wood. Abb L, Wat
—5C 4
Tannery Clo. Beck—9H 109
Tannery Clo. Dag—8M 49
Tannsfeld Rd. SE26—2H 109
Tansley Clo. N7—1H 59
Tansy Clo. Romf—6J 35
Tantallon Rd. SW12—7E 90
Tant Av. E16—9D 62
Tantony Gro. Romf—1H 49
Tanworth Clo. N'wd—6A 20
Tanworth Gdns. Pinn—9G 21
Tanza Rd. NW3—9D 42
Tapestry Clo. Sutt—9M 121
Taplow St. N1—5A 60
Tappesfield Rd. SE15—2G 93
Tapp St. E1—7F 60
Tapster St. Barn—6K 13
Tarbert Rd. SE22—4C 92
Tarbert Wlk. E1—1G 77
Target Clo. Felt—5C 84
Tariff La. N17—6E 28
Tariff Rd. N17—6E 28
Tarleton Ct. N22—9L 27
Tarleton Gdns. SE23—8F 92
Tarling Clo. Sidc—9F 96
Tarling Rd. E16—9D 62
Tarling Rd. N2—9A 26
Tarling St. E1—9G 61
Tarling St. Est. E1—9G 61
Tarn Bank. Enf—7J 15
Tarnwood Pk. SE9—7K 95
Tarporley Clo. SW16—9H 91
Tarragon Clo. SE14—9H 77
Tarry La. SE8—5J 77
Tarver Rd. SE17—6M 75
Tarves Way. SE10—8M 77
Tash Pl. N11—5F 26
Tasker Rd. NW3—1D 58
Tasman Ct. Ashf—4C 100
Tasmania Ter. N18—6A 28
Tasman Rd. SW9—2J 91
Tasman Wlk. E16—9H 63
Tasso Rd. W6—7J 73
Tatam Rd. NW10—3B 56
Tate Rd. E16—2K 79
Tate Rd. Sutt—7L 121
Tatnell Rd. SE23—5J 93
Tattenham Corner Rd. Eps
—9D 134
Tattenham Cres. Eps—9F 134
Tattenham Way. Tad—9J 135
Tattersall Clo. SE9—4J 95
Tatton Cres. N16—5D 44
Tatum St. SE17—5B 76
Taunton Av. SW20—6F 104
Taunton Av. Houn—1A 86
Taunton Clo. Bexh—1B 98
Taunton Clo. Sutt—3L 121
Taunton Dri. Enf—5L 15
Taunton M. NW1—7D 58
Taunton Pl. NW1—7D 58
Taunton Rd. SE12—4C 94
Taunton Rd. Gnfd—4M 53
Taunton Rd. Romf—4G 35
Taunton Way. Stan—9J 23
Taverners Clo. W11—2J 73
Taverner Sq. N5—9A 44
Taverners Way. E4—1C 30
Tavern La. SW9—1L 91
Tavistock Av. E17—1H 45
Tavistock Av. Gnfd—5E 54
Tavistock Clo. N16—1C 60
Tavistock Clo. Romf—8H 35
Tavistock Cres. W11—8K 57
Tavistock Cres. Mitc—8J 107
Tavistock Gdns. Ilf—9C 48
Tavistock Gro. Croy—2B 124
Tavistock M. E18—1E 46
Tavistock Pl. E18—1E 46
Tavistock Pl. N14—9F 14
Tavistock Pl. WC1—7J 59
Tavistock Rd. E7—9D 46
Tavistock Rd. E15—2D 62
Tavistock Rd. E18—1E 46
Tavistock Rd. N4—4B 44
Tavistock Rd. NW10—5D 56
Tavistock Rd. W11—9K 57

Tavistock Rd. Brom—8D 110
Tavistock Rd. Cars—3B 122
Tavistock Rd. Croy—3B 124
Tavistock Rd. Edgw—8L 23
Tavistock Rd. Uxb—1B 52
Tavistock Rd. Wat—3H 9
Tavistock Rd. Well—9G 81
Tavistock Rd. W Dray—2H 143
Tavistock Sq. WC1—7H 59
Tavistock St. WC2—1J 75
Tavistock Ter. N19—8H 43
Tavistock Wlk. Cars—3B 122
Taviton St. WC1—7H 59
Tavy Bri. SE2—3G 81
Tavy Bri. Centre. SE2—3G 81
Tawney Rd. SE28—1F 80
Tawny Av. Upm—1M 67
Tawny Way. SE16—5H 77
Tayben Av. Twic—5C 86
Taybridge Rd. SW11—2E 90
Tayburn Clo. E14—9A 62
Tayles Hill. Eps—2D 134
Taylor Av. Rich—1M 87
Taylor Clo. N17—7E 28
Taylor Clo. Hmptn—2A 102
Taylor Clo. Orp—6D 128
Taylor Clo. Romf—7L 33
Taylor Rd. Asht—9H 133
Taylor Rd. Mitc—4C 106
Taylor Rd. Wall—7F 122
Taylors Bldgs. SE18—5M 79
Taylors Clo. Sidc—1D 112
Taylors Grn. W3—9C 56
Taylors La. NW10—3C 56
Taylor's La. Barn—3K 13
Taylor's La. SE26—1F 108
Taylor St. SE18—5M 79
Taymount Rise. SE23—8G 93
Tayport Clo. N1—3K 59
Tay Way. Romf—8D 34
Taywood Rd. N'holt—6K 53
Teak Clo. SE16—2J 77
Teal Clo. E16—9J 63
Teal Clo. S Croy—3H 139
Teale St. E2—5E 60
Tealing Dri. Eps—6B 120
Teasel Clo. Croy—3H 125
Teasel Way. E15—6C 62
Tebworth Rd. N17—7D 28
Tedder Clo. Chess—7G 119
Tedder Clo. Ruis—1E 52
Tedder Clo. Uxb—3D 142
Tedder Rd. S Croy—9H 125
Teddington Clo. Eps—2B 134
Teddington Pk. Tedd—2D 102
Teddington Pk. Rd. Tedd
—1D 102
Tedworth Sq. SW3—6D 74
Tees Av. Gnfd—5D 54
Teesdale Av. Iswth—9E 70
Teesdale Clo. E2—5F 60
Teesdale Gdns. SE25—6C 108
Teesdale Gdns. Iswth—9E 70
Teesdale Rd. E11—5D 46
Teesdale Rd. Dart—7M 99
Teesdale St. E2—5F 60
Tees Dri. Romf—3H 35
Tee, The. W3—9C 56
Teevan Clo. Croy—2E 124
Teevan Rd. Croy—2E 124
Teignmouth Clo. SW4—3H 91
Teignmouth Clo. Edgw—9K 23
Teignmouth Gdns. Gnfd—5E 54
Teignmouth Rd. NW2—1H 57
Teignmouth Rd. Well—1G 97
Telcote Way. Ruis—5G 37
Telegraph Hill. NW3—8M 41
Telegraph La. Esh—7D 118
Telegraph M. Ilf—6E 48
Telegraph Pl. E14—5M 77
Telegraph Rd. SW15—6F 88
Telegraph St. EC2—9B 60
Telegraph Track. Cars & Wall
—3E 136
Teleman Sq. SE3—3F 94
Telephone Pl. SW6—7K 73
Telferscot Rd. SW12—7H 91
Telford Av. SW2—7H 91
Telford Clo. SE19—3D 108
Telford Clo. Wat—8H 5
Telford Rd. N11—5G 27
Telford Rd. SE9—8B 96
Telford Rd. W10—8J 57
Telford Rd. S'hall—1M 69
Telford Rd. Twic—6L 85
Telford Rd. W3—8C 56
Telham Rd. E6—5L 63
Tell Gro. SE22—3D 92
Tellisford. Esh—6M 117
Tellson Av. SE18—9H 79
Telscombe Clo. Orp—4C 128
Temeraire St. SE16—3G 77
Temperley Rd. SW12—6E 90
Tempest Way. Rain—2E 66
Templar Ho. NW2—2K 57

Templar Pl.—Thurlby Rd.

Templar Pl. Hmptn—4L 101
Templars Av. NW11—4K 41
Templars Cres. N3—9L 25
Templars Dri. Harr—6B 22
Templars Ho. E15—1M 61
Templar St. SE5—1M 91
Temple Av. EC4—1L 75
Temple Av. N20—9B 14
Temple Av. Croy—4K 125
Temple Av. Dag—6L 49
Temple Clo. N3—9K 25
Temple Clo. Wal X—4A 6
Temple Clo. Wat—4D 8
Templecombe Rd. E9—4G 61
Templecombe Way. Mord —9J 105
Templecroft. Ashf—3B 100
Temple Fortune Hill. NW11 —3L 41
Temple Fortune La. NW11 —4L 41
Temple Fortune Pde. NW11 —3K 41
Temple Gdns. N21—2M 27
Temple Gdns. NW11—4K 41
Temple Gdns. Dag—8H 49
Temple Gdns. Rick—4A 20
Temple Gro. NW11—4L 41
Temple Gro. Enf—5M 15
Temple Hall Ct. E4—2B 30
Temple Hill. Dart—5K 99
Temple Hill Sq. Dart—4K 99
Templehof Av. NW4—5G 41
Temple La. EC4—9L 59
Templeman Clo. Purl—8M 137
Templeman Rd. W7—8D 54
Templemead Clo. W3—9C 56
Temple Mead Clo. Stan—6F 22
Templemere. Wey—5K 116
Temple Mills La. E15—9M 45
Temple Mills Rd. E15—9L 45
Temple Pk. Uxb—6E 142
Temple Pl. WC2—1K 75
Temple Rd. E6—4J 63
Temple Rd. N8—2K 43
Temple Rd. NW2—9G 41
Temple Rd. W4—4A 72
Temple Rd. W5—4H 71
Temple Rd. Croy—6B 124
Temple Rd. Eps—4B 134
Temple Rd. Houn—3M 85
Temple Rd. Rich—1K 87
Temple Rd. West—9H 141
Temple Sheen. SW14—4A 88
Temple Sheen Rd. SW14 —3M 87
Temple St. E2—5F 60
Templeton Av. E4—4L 29
Templeton Clo. N15—4B 44
Templeton Clo. N16—1C 60
Templeton Clo. SE19—5B 108
Templeton Pl. SW5—5L 73
Templeton Rd. N15—4B 44
Temple Way. Sutt—5B 122
Templewood. W13—8F 54
Templewood Av. NW3—8M 41
Templewood Gdns. NW3 —8M 41
Tempsford Av. Borwd—6B 12
Tempsford Clo. Enf—5A 16
Temsford Clo. Harr—9A 22
Tenbury Clo. E7—1H 63
Tenbury Ct. SW2—7H 91
Tenby Av. Harr—9F 22
Tenby Clo. N15—2D 44
Tenby Clo. Romf—4J 49
Tenby Gdns. N'holt—2L 53
Tenby Rd. E17—3J 45
Tenby Rd. Edgw—8K 23
Tenby Rd. Enf—6G 17
Tenby Rd. Romf—4J 49
Tenby Rd. Well—9H 81
Tench St. E1—2F 76
Tenda Rd. SE16—5F 76
Tendring Way. Romf—3G 49
Tenham Av. SW2—8H 91
Tenison Ct. W1—1G 75
Tenison Way. SE1—2L 75
Tenniel Clo. W2—1A 74
Tennis Ct. La. Th Dit—8D 102
Tennison Av. Borwd—7M 11
Tennison Rd. SE25—8D 108
Tennis St. SE1—3B 76
Tenniswood Rd. Enf—3C 16
Tennyson Av. E11—5E 46
Tennyson Av. E12—3J 63
Tennyson Av. NW9—1A 40
Tennyson Av. N Mald—9F 104
Tennyson Av. Twic—7D 86
Tennyson Av. Wal A—7L 7
Tennyson Clo. Felt—5D 84
Tennyson Clo. Well—9C 80
Tennyson Rd. E10—6M 45
Tennyson Rd. E15—3C 62
Tennyson Rd. E17—4K 45
Tennyson Rd. NW6—4K 57
Tennyson Rd. NW7—5E 24
Tennyson Rd. SE20—4H 109
Tennyson Rd. SW19—3A 106
Tennyson Rd. W7—1D 70
Tennyson Rd. Dart—4L 99
Tennyson Rd. Houn—1A 86
Tennyson Rd. Romf—7G 35
Tennyson St. SW8—1F 90
Tennyson Way. Horn—6D 50
Tensing Rd. S'hall—4L 69
Tentelow La. S'hall—6L 69
Tenterden Clo. NW4—1H 41
Tenterden Clo. SE9—1K 111
Tenterden Dri. NW4—1H 41
Tenterden Gdns. NW4—1H 41
Tenterden Gdns. Croy—2E 124
Tenterden Gro. NW4—1H 41
Tenterden Rd. N17—7D 28
Tenterden Rd. Croy—2E 124
Tenterden Rd. Dag—7K 49
Tenterden St. W1—9F 58
Tenter Ground. E1—8D 60
Tent St. E1—7F 60
Terborch Way. SE22—4C 92
Tercel Path. Chig—4F 32
Teresa Wlk. N10—3F 42
Terling Clo. E11—8D 46
Terling Rd. Dag—7L 49
Terminus Pl. SW1—4F 74
Terrace Gdns. SW13—1D 88
Terrace Gdns. Wat—4F 8
Terrace La. Rich—5J 87
Terrace Rd. E9—3H 61
Terrace Rd. E13—4E 62
Terrace Rd. W on T—2E 116
Terrace, The. N3—9K 25
Terrace, The. NW6—4L 57
Terrace, The. SE8—5K 77
Terrace, The. SW1—3J 75
Terrace, The. SW13—1C 88
Terrace, The. Wfd G—6E 30
Terrace Wlk. Dag—1J 65
Terrapin Rd. SW17—9F 90
Terretts Pl. N1—3M 59
Terrick Rd. N22—8J 27
Terrick St. W12—9F 56
Terrilands. Pinn—1K 37
Terront Rd. N15—2A 44
Testerton Wlk. W11—1H 73
Tetbury Pl. N1—4M 59
Tetcott Rd. SW10—8A 74
Tetherdown. N10—1E 42
Tetterby Way. SE16—6E 76
Tetty Way. Brom—6E 110
Teversham La. SW8—9J 75
Teviot Clo. Well—9F 80
Teviot St. E14—8A 62
Tewkesbury Av. SE23—6F 92
Tewkesbury Av. Pinn—3J 37
Tewkesbury Clo. N15—4B 44
Tewkesbury Gdns. NW9—1M 39
Tewkesbury Rd. N15—4B 44
Tewkesbury Rd. W13—2E 70
Tewkesbury Rd. Cars—3B 122
Tewkesbury Ter. N11—6G 27
Tewson Rd. SE18—6C 80
Teynham Av. Enf—8B 16
Teynham Grn. Brom—9E 110
Teynton Ter. N17—8A 28
Thackeray Av. N17—9E 28
Thackeray Clo. SW19—4H 105
Thackeray Clo. Harr—6L 37
Thackeray Clo. Uxb—9F 142
Thackeray Dri. Romf—5E 48
Thackeray Rd. E6—5H 63
Thackeray Rd. SW8—1F 90
Thackeray St. W8—4M 73
Thakeham Clo. SE26—2F 108
Thalia Clo. SE10—7B 78
Thames Av. Dag—7M 65
Thames Av. Gnfd—5G 55
Thames Bank. SW14—1A 88
Thames Clo. Hmptn—6M 101
Thames Clo. Rain—9F 66
Thames Dri. Ruis—4A 36
Thamesfield Ct. Shep—2A 116
Thamesfield M. Shep—2A 116
Thamesgate Clo. Rich—1F 102
Thameshill Av. Romf—9A 34
Thameside. Tedd—4H 103
Thameside Industrial Est. E16 —3H 79
Thamesmead. W on T—2E 116
Thames Meadow. E Mol —6L 101
Thames Pl. E14—1K 77
Thames Rd. E16—2H 79
Thames Rd. W4—7L 71
Thames Rd. Bark—6D 64
Thames Rd. Dart—1D 98
Thames Side. King—5H 103
Thames St. SE10—7M 77
Thames St. Hmptn—6M 101
Thames St. King—6H 103
Thames St. Shep—4A 116
Thames St. Sun—8F 100
Thames St. W on T—2D 116
Thamesvale Clo. Houn—1L 85
Thames Village. W4—9A 72
Thanescroft Gdns. Croy —5C 124
Thanet Dri. Kes—5H 127
Thanet Pl. Croy—6A 124
Thanet Rd. Bex—6L 97
Thanet Rd. Eri—8C 82
Thanet St. WC1—6J 59
Thane Vs. N7—8K 43
Tharp Rd. Wall—7H 123
Thatcham Gdns. N20—9A 14
Thatcher Clo. W Dray—3J 143
Thatcher Ct. Dart—6H 99
Thatchers Clo. Lou—4M 19
Thatchers Way. Iswth—4B 86
Thatches Gro. Romf—2J 49
Thavies Inn. EC1—9L 59
Thaxted Ho. Dag—3M 65
Thaxted Pl. SW20—4H 105
Thaxted Rd. SE9—8A 96
Thaxted Rd. Buck H—9J 19
Thaxted Wlk. Rain—3C 66
Thaxted Way. Wal A—6K 7
Thaxton Rd. W14—7K 73
Thayers Farm Rd. Beck —5J 109
Thayer St. W1—9E 58
Theatre St. SW11—2D 90
Theberton St. N1—4L 59
Theed St. SE1—2L 75
Thelma Gdns. SE3—9H 79
Thelma Gro. Tedd—3E 102
Theobald Cres. Harr—8A 22
Theobald Rd. E17—5L 45
Theobald Rd. Croy—4M 123
Theobalds Av. N12—4A 26
Theobalds La. Wal X—5B 6
Theobalds Pk. Rd. Enf—1M 15
Theobald's Rd. WC1—8K 59
Theobald St. Rad & Borwd —1G 11
Theodore Rd. SE13—5B 94
Therapia La. Croy—2H 123 (in two parts)
Therapia Rd. SE22—5G 93
Theresa Rd. W6—5E 72
Theresa's Wlk. S Croy—1B 138
Thermopylae Ga. E14—5M 77
Thesiger Rd. SE20—4H 109
Thessaly Rd. SW8—8G 75
Thetford Clo. N13—6M 27
Thetford Gdns. Dag—3J 65
Thetford Rd. Ashf—9C 144
Thetford Rd. Dag—3H 65
Thetford Rd. N Mald—1B 120
Thetis Ter. Rich—7L 71 (in two parts)
Theydon Gdns. Rain—3C 66
Theydon Gro. Wfd G—6G 31
Theydon Rd. E5—7G 45
Theydon St. E17—5K 45
Thicket Cres. Sutt—6A 122
Thicket Gro. Dag—2G 65
Thicket Rd. SE20—4E 108
Thicket Rd. Sutt—6A 122
Thicket, The. W Dray—9C 142
Third Av. E12—9J 47
Third Av. E13—6E 62
Third Av. E17—3L 45
Third Av. W3—2D 72
Third Av. W10—6J 57
Third Av. Dag—4M 65
Third Av. Enf—7D 16
Third Av. Hay—2D 68
Third Av. Romf—4G 49
Third Av. Wat—8H 5
Third Av. Wemb—7H 39
Third Clo. E Mol—8A 102
Third Cross Rd. Twic—8B 86
Third Way. Wemb—9M 39
Thirleby Rd. SW1—4G 75
Thirleby Rd. Edgw—8B 24
Thirlmere Av. Gnfd—6G 55
Thirlmere Gdns. N'wd—5A 20
Thirlmere Gdns. Wemb—6G 39
Thirlmere Rise. Brom—3D 110
Thirlmere Rd. N10—8F 26
Thirlmere Rd. SW16—1H 107
Thirlmere Rd. Bexh—9A 82
Thirsk Clo. N'holt—2L 53
Thirsk Rd. SE25—8B 108
Thirsk Rd. SW11—2E 90
Thirsk Rd. Borwd—1L 11
Thirsk Rd. Mitc—4E 106
Thirza Rd. Dart—5K 99
Thistlebrook. SE2—3G 81
Thistlecroft Gdns. Stan—9H 23
Thistlecroft Rd. W on T—6G 117
Thistledene. Th Dit—1C 118
Thistledene Av. Harr—8J 37
Thistledene Av. Romf—5M 33
Thistle Gro. SW10—6A 74
Thistlemead. Chst—6M 111
Thistle Mead. Lou—5L 19
Thistlewaite Rd. E5—8F 44
Thistlewood Clo. N7—7K 43
Thistlewood Cres. Croy —4B 140
Thistleworth Clo. Iswth—8B 70
Thomas a' Beckett Clo. Wemb —9D 38
Thomas Baines Rd. SW11 —2B 90
Thomas Doyle St. SE1—4M 75
Thomas La. SE6—6L 93
Thomas More St. E1—2E 76
Thomas More Way. N2—1A 42
Thomas Rd. E14—9K 61
Thomas Sims Ct. Horn—1F 66
Thomas St. SE18—5M 79
Thompson Av. Rich—2L 87
Thompson Rd. SE22—5D 92
Thompson Rd. Dag—8K 49
Thompson Rd. Uxb—3C 142
Thompson's Av. SE5—8A 76
Thompson's La. Lou—2E 18
Thompson Way. Ilf—7M 47
Thomson Cres. Croy—3L 123
Thomson Rd. Harr—1C 38
Thorburn Sq. SE1—5E 76
Thorburn Way. SW19—5B 106
Thoresby St. N1—6A 60
Thorkhill Gdns. Th Dit—3E 118
Thorkhill Rd. Th Dit—3F 118
Thornaby Gdns. N18—5E 28
Thorn Av. Bush, Wat—1A 22
Thornbury Av. Iswth—8B 70
Thornbury Gdns. Borwd —6A 12
Thornbury Rd. SW2—5J 91
Thornbury Rd. Iswth—8B 70
Thornby Rd. E5—8G 45
Thorncliffe Rd. SW2—5J 91
Thorncliffe Rd. S'hall—6K 69
Thorn Clo. Brom—1L 127
Thorn Clo. N'holt—6K 53
Thorncombe Rd. SE22—4C 92
Thorncroft. Horn—4F 50
Thorncroft Rd. Sutt—7M 121
Thorncroft St. SW8—8J 75
Thorndean St. SW18—8A 90
Thorndene. SE28—1G 81
Thorndene Av. N11—1E 26
Thorndike Av. N'holt—4H 53
Thorndike Clo. SW10—8A 74
Thorndon Clo. Orp—6D 112
Thorndon Gdns. Eps—7C 120
Thorndon Rd. Orp—6D 112
Thorndyke Ct. Pinn—7K 21
Thorne Clo. E11—9C 46
Thorne Clo. E16—9E 62
Thorne Clo. Ashf—4A 100
Thorne Clo. Eri—7M 81
Thorne Clo. N Mald—8A 104
Thorneloe Gdns. Croy—7L 123
Thorne Pas. SW13—1C 88
Thorne Rd. SW8—8J 75
Thorne Rd. N Mald—8A 104
Thornes Clo. Beck—7A 110
Thorne St. SW13—2C 88
Thornet Wood Rd. Brom —7L 111
Thorney Cres. SW11—8B 74
Thorney Hedge Rd. W4—5M 71
Thorney Mill Rd. Iver & W Dray —4G 143
Thorney St. SW1—5J 75
Thornfield Av. NW7—8J 25
Thornfield Rd. W12—3F 72
Thornfield Rd. Bans—9L 135
Thornford Rd. SE13—4A 94
Thorngate Rd. W9—7L 57
Thorngrove Rd. E13—4F 62
Thornham Gro. E15—1B 62
Thornham St. SE10—7M 77
Thornhaugh M. WC1—7H 59
Thornhaugh St. WC1—7H 59
Thornhill Av. SE18—8C 80
Thornhill Av. Surb—4J 119
Thornhill Cres. N1—3K 59
Thornhill Gdns. E10—7M 45
Thornhill Gdns. Bark—3C 64
Thornhill Gro. N1—3K 59
Thornhill Rd. E10—7M 45
Thornhill Rd. N1—3L 59
Thornhill Rd. Croy—2A 124
Thornhill Rd. N'wd—4A 20
Thornhill Rd. Surb—4J 119
Thornhill Sq. N1—3K 59
Thorn La. Rain—5H 67
Thornlaw Rd. SE27—1L 107
Thornley Clo. N17—7F 28
Thornley Dri. Harr—7M 37
Thornley Pl. SE10—6C 78
Thornsbeach Rd. SE6—7A 94
Thornsett Pl. SE20—6F 108
Thornsett Rd. SE20—6F 108
Thornsett Rd. SW18—7M 89
Thornton Av. SW2—7H 91
Thornton Av. W4—5C 72
Thornton Av. Croy—1K 123
Thornton Av. W Dray—4K 143
Thornton Clo. W Dray—4K 143
Thornton Dene. Beck—6L 109
Thornton Gdns. SW12—7H 91
Thornton Gro. Pinn—6L 21
Thornton Hill. SW19—4J 105
Thornton Pl. W1—8D 58
Thornton Rd. E11—7B 46
Thornton Rd. SW12—6H 91
Thornton Rd. SW14—3B 88
Thornton Rd. SW19—3H 105
Thornton Rd. Barn—5J 13
Thornton Rd. Belv—5M 81
Thornton Rd. Brom—2E 110
Thornton Rd. Cars—3B 122
Thornton Rd. Croy & T Hth —1K 123
Thornton Rd. Ilf—9M 47
Thornton Rd. E. SW19—3H 105
Thornton Row. T Hth—9L 107
Thornton's Farm Av. Romf —6B 50
Thornton St. SW9—1L 91
Thornton Way. NW11—3M 41
Thorntree Rd. SE7—6H 79
Thornville St. SE8—9L 77
Thornwood Clo. E18—9F 30
Thornwood Rd. SE13—4C 94
Thorogood Gdns. E15—1C 62
Thorogood Way. Rain—4C 66
Thorold Clo. S Croy—2H 139
Thorold Rd. N22—7J 27
Thorold Rd. Ilf—7M 47
Thorparch Rd. SW8—9H 75
Thorpebank Rd. W12—2E 72
Thorpe Clo. W10—9J 57
Thorpe Clo. Croy—3A 140
Thorpe Clo. Orp—4C 128
Thorpe Cres. E17—9K 29
Thorpe Cres. Wat—9G 9
Thorpedale Gdns. Ilf—2L 47
Thorpedale Rd. N4—6J 43
Thorpe Hall Rd. E17—8A 30
Thorpe Lodge. Horn—5H 51
Thorpe Rd. E6—4K 63
Thorpe Rd. E7—9D 46
Thorpe Rd. E17—9A 30
Thorpe Rd. N15—4C 44
Thorpe Rd. Bark—3B 64
Thorpe Rd. King—4J 103
Thorpewood Av. SE26—8F 92
Thorpland Av. Uxb—8A 36
Thorsden Way. SE19—2C 108
Thorverton Rd. NW2—8J 41
Thoydon Rd. E3—5J 61
Thrale Rd. SW16—2G 107
Thrale St. SE1—2A 76
Thrawl St. E1—8D 60
Threadneedle St. EC2—9B 60
Three Colts La. E2—7F 60
Three Colt St. E14—9K 61
Three Corners. Bexh—1M 97
Three Kings Rd. Mitc—7E 106
Three Kings Yd. W1—1F 74
Three Mill La. E3—6A 62
Three Oak La. SE1—3D 76
Threshers Pl. W11—1J 73
Thriffwood. SE23—9H 93
Thrift Farm La. Borwd—4A 12
Thrigby Rd. Chess—8K 119
Thrisk Rd. SW11—2E 90
Throckmorten Rd. E16—9F 62
Throgmorton Av. EC2—9B 60
Throgmorton St. EC2—9B 60
Throwley Clo. SE2—4G 81 (in two parts)
Throwley Rd. Sutt—7M 121
Throwley Way. Sutt—6M 121
Thrums, The. Wat—1F 8
Thrupp Clo. Mitc—6F 106
Thrupp's Av. W on T—7H 117
Thrupp's La. W on T—7H 117
Thrush St. SE17—6A 76
Thruxton Way. SE15—8D 76
Thurbarn Rd. SE6—2M 109
Thurland Rd. SE16—4E 76
Thurlby Clo. Harr—4E 38
Thurlby Clo. Wfd G—5K 31
Thurlby Rd. SE27—1L 107
Thurlby Rd. Wemb—2H 55

Thurleigh Av. SW12—5E 90
Thurleigh Rd. SW12—5D 90
Thurleston Av. Mord—9J 105
Thurlestone Av. N12—6D 26
Thurlestone Av. Ilf—9D 48
Thurlestone Rd. SE27—1L 107
Thurloe Clo. SW7—5C 74
Thurloe Gdns. Romf—4D 50
Thurloe Pl. SW7—5B 74
Thurloe Sq. SW7—5C 74
Thurloe St. SW7—5B 74
Thurlow Gdns. Ilf—6B 32
Thurlow Gdns. Wemb—1H 55
Thurlow Hill. SE21—7A 92
Thurlow Pk. Rd. SE21—8M 91
Thurlow Rd. NW3—1B 58
Thurlow Rd. W7—3E 70
Thurlow St. SE17—6B 76
Thurlow Ter. NW5—2D 58
Thurlow Wlk. SE17—6C 76
Thurlstone Clo. Shep—1A 116
Thurlston Rd. Ruis—8E 36
Thursland Rd. Sidc—2J 113
Thursley Cres. Croy—9B 126
Thursley Gdns. SW19—8H 89
Thursley Rd. SE9—9K 95
Thurso Clo. Romf—6M 35
Thurso St. SW11—1B 106
Thurstan Rd. SW20—4F 104
Thurston Path. Borwd—4L 11
Thurston Rd. SE13—1M 93
Thurston Rd. S'hall—9K 53
Thurtle Rd. E2—5D 60
Thwaite Clo. Eri—7A 82
Thyer Clo. Orp—6A 128
Thyra Gro. N12—6M 25
Tibbatts Rd. E3—7M 61
Tibbenham Wlk. E13—5D 62
Tibberton Sq. N1—3A 60
Tibbet's Clo. SW19—7H 89
Tibbet's Corner. SW19—7H 89
Tibbet's Ride. SW15—6H 89
Tibbles Clo. Wat—8J 5
Tibbs Hill Rd. Abb L, Wat—3D 4
Ticehurst Rd. SE23—8J 93
Tichmarsh. Eps—3A 134
Tickford Clo. SE2—3G 81
Tidal Basin Rd. E16—1D 78
Tidenham Gdns. Croy—5C 124
Tideswell Rd. SW15—3G 89
Tideswell Rd. Croy—5L 125
Tideway Clo. Rich—1F 102
Tideway Wlk. SW8—7G 75
Tidey St. E3—8L 61
Tidford Rd. Well—1D 96
Tidworth Rd. E3—7L 61
Tiepigs La. W Wick—4C 126
Tierney Ct. Croy—4D 124
Tierney Rd. SW2—7J 91
Tiger Bay. SE16—4H 77
Tiger La. Brom—8F 110
Tiger Way. E5—9F 44
Tilbrook Rd. SE3—2G 95
Tilbury Clo. SE15—8D 76
Tilbury Clo. Orp—6F 112
Tilbury Rd. E6—5K 63
Tilbury Rd. E10—5A 46
Tildesley Rd. SW15—5G 89
Tile Farm Rd. Orp—5B 128
Tilehurst Rd. SW18—7B 90
Tilehurst Rd. Sutt—7J 121
Tile Kiln La. N6—6G 43
Tile Kiln La. N13—5A 28
Tile Kiln La. Bex—8A 98
Tile Kiln La. Dart—9C 98
Tile Kiln La. Uxb—5A 36
Tile Kiln Studios. N6—6G 43
Tile Yd. E14—9K 61
Tileyard Rd. N7—3J 59
Tilford Av. Croy—1A 140
Tilford Gdns. SW19—7H 89
Tilia Rd. E5—9F 44
Till Av. F'ham, Dart—2K 131
Tiller Rd. E14—4L 77
Tillet Clo. NW10—2A 56
Tillet Way. E2—6E 60
Tillingbourne Gdns. N3—1K 41
Tillingbourne Grn. Orp—8E 112
Tillingbourne Way. N3—2K 41
Tillingham Ct. Wal A—6M 7
Tillingham Way. N12—4L 25
Tilling Rd. NW4—6G 41
Tillman St. E1—9F 60
Tilloch St. N1—3K 59
Tillotson Rd. N9—2D 28
Tillotson Rd. Harr—7M 21
Tillotson Rd. Ilf—5L 47
Tilmans Mead. F'ham, Dart
—2L 131
Tilney Ct. EC1—7A 60
Tilney Dri. Buck H—2E 30
Tilney Gdns. N1—2B 60
Tilney Rd. Dag—2K 65

Tilney Rd. S'hall—5G 69
Tilney St. W1—2E 74
Tilson Gdns. SW2—6J 91
Tilson Rd. N17—8E 28
Tilton St. SW6—7J 73
Tiltwood, The. W3—1A 72
Tilt Yd. App. SE9—5K 95
Timber Clo. Chst—6L 111
Timbercroft. Eps—6C 120
Timbercroft La. SE18—7C 80
Timberdene. NW4—9H 25
Timberland Rd. E1—9F 60
Timberling Gdns. S Croy
—2B 138
Timbermill Way. SW4—2H 91
Timberslip Dri. Wall—1H 137
Timber St. EC1—7A 60
Timbertop Rd. West—9G 141
Timberwharf Rd. N16—4E 44
Times Sq. Sutt—7M 121
Timsbury Wlk. SW15—7E 88
Tindale Clo. S Croy—3B 138
Tindall Clo. Romf—9K 35
Tindal St. SW9—9M 75
Tinderbox All. SW14—2B 88
Tine Rd. Chig—5C 32
Tinsley Rd. E1—8G 61
Tintagel Clo. Eps—6D 134
Tintagel Cres. SE22—3D 92
Tintagel Dri. Stan—4H 23
Tintagel Rd. Orp—4G 129
Tintern Av. NW9—1M 39
Tintern Clo. SW15—4J 89
Tintern Clo. SW19—3A 106
Tintern Gdns. N14—9J 15
Tintern Rd. N22—8A 28
Tintern Rd. Cars—3B 122
Tintern St. SW4—3J 91
Tintern Way. Harr—6M 37
Tinto Rd. E16—7E 62
Tinworth St. SE11—6J 75
Tippetts Clo. Enf—3A 16
Tipthorpe Rd. SW11—2E 90
Tipton Dri. Croy—6C 124
Tiptree Clo. E4—3A 30
Tiptree Clo. Horn—6L 51
Tiptree Cres. Ilf—1L 47
Tiptree Dri. Enf—6B 16
Tiptree Rd. Ruis—9F 36
Tirlemont Rd. S Croy—9A 124
Tirrell Rd. Croy—1A 124
Tisbury Rd. SW16—6J 107
Titchborne Row. W2—9C 58
Titchfield Rd. NW8—5D 58
Titchfield Rd. Cars—3B 122
Titchfield Rd. Enf—1J 17
Titchfield Wlk. Cars—2B 122
Titchwell Rd. SW18—7B 90
Tite St. SW3—7D 74
Tithe Barn Clo. King—5K 103
Tithe Barn Way. N'holt—5F 52
Tithe Clo. NW7—8E 24
Tithe Farm Av. Harr—8L 37
Tithe Farm Clo. Harr—8L 37
Tithepit Shaw La. Warl
—9F 138
Tithe Wlk. NW7—8E 24
Titian Av. Bush, Wat—9C 10
Titley Clo. E4—5L 29
Titmus Clo. Uxb—9A 52
Titmuss Av. SE28—1F 80
Titmuss St. W12—3F 72
Tiverton Av. Ilf—1L 47
Tiverton Dri. SE9—7A 96
Tiverton Gro. Romf—5L 35
Tiverton Rd. N15—4B 44
Tiverton Rd. N18—5C 28
Tiverton Rd. NW10—4H 57
Tiverton Rd. Edgw—9K 23
Tiverton Rd. Houn—1A 86
Tiverton Rd. Ruis—8E 36
Tiverton Rd. T Hth—9L 107
Tiverton Rd. Wemb—5J 55
Tiverton St. SE1—4A 76
Tiverton Way. Chess
—7H 119
Tivoli Gdns. SE18—5J 79
Tivoli Rd. N8—3H 43
Tivoli Rd. SE27—2A 108
Tivoli Rd. Houn—3J 85
Tobago St. E14—3L 77
Tobin Clo. NW3—3C 58
Toby La. E1—7J 61
Todds Wlk. N7—7K 43
Tokenhouse Yd. EC2—9B 60
Tokyngton Av. Wemb—2L 55
Toland Sq. SW15—4E 88
Tolcarne Dri. N'wd—9E 20
Toley Av. Wemb—5J 39
Tollesbury Gdns. Ilf—1B 48
Tollet St. E1—7H 61
Tollgate Dri. SE21—8C 92
Tollgate Gdns. NW6—5M 57

Tollgate Rd.—8G 63
 E16 1-153 & 2-130
 E6 remainder
Tollgate Rd. Wal X—8D 6
Tollhouse Way. N19—7G 43
Tollington Pk. N4—7K 43
Tollington Pl. N4—7K 43
Tollington Rd. N7—9K 43
Tollington Way. N7—8J 43
Tolmers Sq. NW1—7G 59
Tolpits Clo. Wat—7D 8
Tolpits La. Wat—1A 20
Tolsford Rd. E5—1F 60
Tolson Rd. Iswth—2E 86
Tolverne Rd. SW20—5G 105
Tolworth Clo. Surb—3M 119
Tolworth Gdns. Romf—3H 49
Tolworth Pk. Rd. Surb—4K 119
Tolworth Rise N. Surb
—3M 119
Tolworth Rise S. Surb
—3M 119
Tolworth Rd. Surb—4J 119
Tom Coombs Clo. SE9—3J 95
Tom Cribb Rd. SE28—4A 80
Tomkins Clo. Borwd—3J 11
Tomlins All. Twic—7E 94
Tomlin's Gro. E3—6L 61
Tomlinson Clo. E2—6D 60
Tomlinson Clo. W4—6M 71
Tomlins Orchard. Bark—4A 64
Tomlins Ter. E14—9J 61
Tomlins Wlk. N7—7K 43
Tom Mann Clo. Bark—4C 64
Tompion St. EC1—6M 59
Tom's La. K Lan & Abb L, Wat
—2A 4
Tom Smith Clo. SE10—7C 78
Tomswood Ct. Ilf—8A 32
Tomswood Hill. Ilf—7M 31
Tomswood Rd. Chig—6L 31
Tonbridge Clo. Bans—6D 58
Tonbridge Cres. Harr—2J 39
Tonbridge Rd. E Mol—8K 101
Tonbridge Rd. Romf—7H 35
Tonbridge St. WC1—6J 59
Tonfield Rd. Sutt—3K 121
Tonge Clo. Beck—9L 109
Tonsley Hill. SW18—4M 89
Tonsley Pl. SW18—4M 89
Tonsley Rd. SW18—4M 89
Tonsley St. SW18—4M 89
Tonstall Rd. Eps—2B 134
Tonstall Rd. Mitc—6E 106
Tony Law Ho. SE20—5F 108
Tooke Clo. Pinn—8J 21
Toorack Rd. Harr—9B 22
Tooley St. SE1—2C 76
Tooting Bec Gdns. SW16
 (in two parts)—1H 107
Tooting Bec Rd. SW17 & SW16
—9E 90
Tooting B'way. SW17—2D 106
Tooting Gro. SW17—2C 106
Tooting High St. SW17—2C 106
Tootswood Rd. Brom—9C 110
Topaz St. SE11—5K 75
Topcliffe Dri. Orp—6B 128
Top Dartford Rd. Swan
—4D 114
Topham Sq. N17—8A 28
Topham St. EC1—7L 59
Top Ho. Rise. E4—9A 18
Topiary Sq. Rich—2K 87
Toplands Rd. S Ock—2M 83
Topley St. SE9—3G 95
Top Pk. Beck—9C 110
Topp Wlk. NW2—7G 41
Topsfield Rd. N8—3J 43
Topsham Rd. SW17—9D 90
Torbay Rd. NW6—3K 57
Torbay Rd. Harr—7J 37
Torbay St. NW1—3F 58
Torbridge Clo. Edgw—7J 23
Torbrook Clo. Bex—5J 97
Torcross Dri. SE23—8G 93
Torcross Rd. Ruis—8F 36
Tor Gdns. W8—3L 73
Tor Ho. N6—4F 42
Torland Dri. Lea—5B 132
Tormead Clo. Sutt—8L 121
Tormount Rd. SE18—7C 80
Toronto Av. E12—9K 47
Toronto Rd. E11—9B 46
Toronto Rd. Ilf—6M 47
Torquay Gdns. Ilf—2H 47
Torquay St. W2—8M 57
Torrance Clo. Horn—6G 51
Torrens Rd. E15—2D 62
Torrens Rd. SW2—4K 91
Torrens Sq. E15—2D 62
Torrens St. EC1—5M 59

Torre Wlk. Cars—3C 122
Torriano Av. NW5—1H 59
Torriano Cotts. NW5—1G 59
Torridge Gdns. SE15—3G 93
Torridge Rd. T Hth—9M 107
Torridon Rd.—6B 94
 SE13 1 & 3
 SE6 remainder
Torrington Av. N12—5B 26
Torrington Clo. Esh—8C 118
Torrington Dri. Harr—8M 37
Torrington Dri. Lou—6M 19
Torrington Gdns. N11—6G 27
Torrington Gdns. Gnfd—3G 55
Torrington Gro. N12—5C 26
Torrington Pk. N12—5A 26
Torrington Pl. WC1—8H 59
Torrington Rd. E18—1E 46
Torrington Rd. Dag—6K 49
Torrington Rd. Esh—8C 118
Torrington Rd. Gnfd—4G 55
Torrington Rd. Ruis—8D 36
Torrington Sq. WC1—7H 59
Torrington Way. Mord—1L 121
Tor Rd. Well—9G 81
Torr Rd. SE20—4H 109
Torver Rd. Harr—2C 38
Torver Way. Orp—5B 128
Torwood Rd. SW15—4E 88
Torworth Rd. Borwd—3K 11
Tothill St. SW1—3H 75
Totnes Rd. Well—8F 80
Totnes Wlk. N2—2B 42
Tottenhall Rd. N13—6L 27
Tottenham Ct. Rd. W1—7G 59
Tottenham Grn. E. N15—2D 44
 (in two parts)
Tottenham Grn. E. S. Side. N15
—2D 44
Tottenham La. N8—3J 43
Tottenham M. W1—8G 59
Tottenham Rd. N1—2C 60
Tottenham St. W1—8G 59
Totterdown St. SW17—1D 106
Totteridge Comn. N20—2E 24
Totteridge Grn. N20—2L 25
Totteridge La. N20—2L 25
Totteridge Rd. Enf—1H 17
Totteridge Village. N20—1J 25
Totternhoe Clo. Harr—3G 39
Totton Rd. T Hth—7L 107
Totty St. E3—5J 61
Toulmin St. SE1—3A 76
Toulon St. SE5—8A 76
Tournay Rd. SW6—8K 73
Toussaint Wlk. SE16—4E 76
Tovil Clo. SE20—6F 108
Towcester Rd. E3—7A 62
Tower Bri. SE1 & E1—2D 76
Tower Bri. App. E1—1D 76
Tower Bri. Rd. SE1—4C 76
Tower Hill. EC3—1D 76
Tower M. E17—2L 45
Tower Rise. Rich—2J 87
Tower Rd. NW10—3E 56
Tower Rd. Belv—5A 82
Tower Rd. Bexh—3L 97
Tower Rd. Grnh—5G 99
Tower Rd. Orp—4D 128
Tower Rd. Twic—9D 86
Tower Royal. EC4—1B 76
Towers Av. Uxb—6A 52
Towers Pl. Rich—4J 87
Towers Rd. Pinn—8J 21
Towers Rd. S'hall—7L 53
Towers, The. Kenl—7A 138
Tower St. WC2—9J 59
Tower Wlk. Wey—8A 116
Tower Ter. N22—9K 27
Tower View. Croy—2J 125
Tower Yd. Rich—4K 87
Towfield Av. Felt—8K 85
Towgar St. N20—9A 14
Towncourt Cres. Orp—9A 112
Towncourt La. Orp—1B 128
Towncourt Path. N4—6A 44
Towney Mead. N'holt—5K 53
Townfield Rd. Hay—1D 68
Townfield Sq. Hay—1D 68
Town Hall App. Rd. N15—2D 44
Town Hall Rd. SW11—2D 90
Townholm Cres. W7—4D 70
Town La. Stai—5B 144
Townley Ct. E15—2D 62

Townley Rd. SE22—4C 92
Townley Rd. Bexh—4K 97
Townley St. SE17—6B 76
 (in two parts)
Town Mead. Bren—7H 71
Townmead Rd. SW6—2M 89
Townmead Rd. Rich—1M 87
Townmead Rd. Wal A—7J 7
Town Quay. Bark—4M 63
Town Rd. N9—2F 28
Townsend Av. N14—4H 27
Townsend Industrial Est. NW10
—5A 56
Townsend La. NW9—5B 40
Townsend Rd. N15—3D 44
Townsend Rd. S'hall—2J 69
Townsend St. SE17—5C 76
Townsend Way. N'wd—7D 20
Townsend Yd. N6—6F 42
Townshend Rd. NW8—4C 58
Townshend Rd. Chst—2M 111
Townshend Rd. Rich—3K 87
Townshend Ter. Rich—3K 87
Townson Av. N'holt—5E 52
Townson Way. N'holt—5E 52
Town Sq. Eri—7C 82
Town, The. Enf—5B 16
Town Wharf. Iswth—2F 86
Towton Rd. SE27—8A 92
Toynbee Rd. SW20—5J 105
Toynbee St. E1—8D 60
Toyne Way. N6—4D 42
Tracery, The. Bans—7M 135
Tracey Av. NW2—1G 57
Tracey St. SE11—5L 75
 (in two parts)
Tracy Ct. Stan—7G 23
Tradescant Rd. SW8—8J 75
Trading Est. Rd. NW10—7A 56
Trafalgar Av. N17—6C 28
Trafalgar Av. SE15—6D 76
Trafalgar Av. Wor Pk—3H 121
Trafalgar Dri. W on T—5F 116
Trafalgar Gdns. E1—8H 61
Trafalgar Gro. SE10—7B 78
Trafalgar Pl. N18—5E 28
Trafalgar Rd. SE10—7B 78
Trafalgar Rd. SW19—4A 106
Trafalgar Rd. Dart—4J 99
Trafalgar Rd. Rain—5D 66
Trafalgar Rd. Twic—8B 86
Trafalgar Sq. WC2 & SW1
—2H 75
Trafalgar St. SE17—6B 76
Trafalgar Ter. Harr—6C 38
Trafford Clo. E15—1M 61
Trafford Rd. T Hth—9K 107
Tramway Av. E15—3B 62
Tramway Av. N9—9G 17
Tramway Path. Mitc—8C 106
 (in two parts)
Tranby Pl. E9—1H 61
Tranley M. NW3—9C 42
Tranmere Rd. N9—9D 16
Tranmere Rd. SW18—8A 90
Tranmere Rd. Twic—6M 85
Tranquil Pas. SE3—1D 94
Tranquil Rise. Eri—6C 82
Tranquil Vale. SE3—1C 94
Transay Wlk. N1—2B 60
Transept St. NW1—8C 58
Transmere Clo. Orp—1A 128
Transmere Rd. Orp—1A 128
Transport Av. Bren—6F 70
Tranton Rd. SE16—4E 76
Trap's Hill. Lou—5K 19
Traps La. N Mald—5C 104
Travellers Way. Houn—1G 85
Travers Rd. N7—8L 43
Treacy Clo. Bush, Wat—2A 22
Treadgold St. W11—1H 73
Treadway St. E2—5F 60
Treadwell Rd. Eps—8C 134
Treaty Rd. Houn—2M 85
Treaty St. N1—4K 59
Trebeck St. W1—2F 74
Trebovir Rd. SW5—6L 73
Treby St. E3—7K 61
Trecastle Way. N7—9H 43
Tredegar Rd. E3—5K 61
Tredegar Rd. Dart—9E 98
Tredegar Sq. E3—6K 61
Tredegar Ter. E3—6K 61
Trede Rd. N11—7H 27
Trederwen Rd. E8—4E 60
Tredown Rd. SE26—2G 109
Tredwell Clo. Brom—8J 111
Tredwell Rd. SE27—1M 107
Treebourne Rd. West—9G 141
Tree Clo. Rich—7H 87
Treemount Ct. Eps—5C 134
Treen Av. SW13—2D 88
Tree Rd. E16—9G 63

Treeside Clo.—Tysoe St.

Treeside Clo. W Dray—5H 143
Treetops Clo. SE2—6J 81
Treetops Clo. N'wd—5B 20
Treewall Gdns. Brom—1F 110
Trefgarne Rd. Dag—7L 49
Trefil Wlk. N7—9J 43
Trefoil Rd. SW18—4A 90
Trefusis Wlk. Wat—3C 8
Tregaron Av. N8—4J 43
Tregaron Gdns. N Mald —8C 104
Tregarvon Rd. SW11—3E 90
Tregenna Av. Harr—9L 37
Tregenna Clo. N14—7G 15
Trego Rd. E9—3L 61
Tregothnan Rd. SW9—2J 91
Tregunter Rd. SW10—7A 74
Trehearn Rd. Ilf—7B 32
Treherne Ct. SW9—9M 75
Treherne Ct. SW17—1E 106
Trehern Rd. SW14—2B 88
Trehurst St. E5—1J 61
Trelawney Est. E9—2G 61
Trelawney Rd. Ilf—7B 32
Trelawn Rd. E10—8A 46
Trelawn Rd. SW2—4L 91
Trellis Sq. E3—6K 61
Treloar Gdns. SE19—3B 108
Tremadoc Rd. SW4—3H 91
Tremaine Clo. SE4—1L 93
Tremaine Rd. SE20—6F 108
Tremlett Gro. N19—8G 43
Tremlett M. N19—8G 43
Trenance Gdns. Ilf—8E 48
Trenchard Av. Ruis—9F 36
Trenchard Clo. Stan—6E 22
Trenchard Clo. W on T—7G 117
Trenchard Ct. NW4—3E 40
Trenchard Ct. Mord—1L 121
Trenchard St. SE10—6D 78
Trenchold St. SW8—7J 75
Trenham Dri. Warl—8G 139
Trenholme Clo. SE20—4F 108
Trenholme Rd. SE20—4F 108
Trenholme Ter. SE20—4F 108
Trenmar Gdns. NW10—6F 56
Trent Av. W5—4G 71
Trent Gdns. N14—8F 14
Trentham Dri. Orp—8E 112
Trentham St. SW18—7L 89
Trent Rd. SW2—4K 91
Trent Rd. Buck H—1F 30
Trent Way. Hay—5C 52
Trent Way. Wor Pk—5G 121
Trentwood Side. Enf—5K 15
Treport St. SW18—6M 89
Tresco Clo. Brom—3C 110
Trescoe Gdns. Harr—5J 37
Trescoe Gdns. Romf—5A 34
Tresco Gdns. Ilf—7E 48
Tresco Rd. SE15—3F 92
Tresham Cres. NW8—7C 58
Tresham Rd. Bark—3D 64
Tresham Wlk. E9—1G 61
Tressell Clo. N1—3M 59
Tressillian Cres. SE4—2L 93
Tressillian Rd. SE4—3K 93
Trestis Clo. Hay—7H 53
Treswell Rd. Dag—4J 65
Tretawn Gdns. NW7—4C 24
Tretawn Pk. NW7—4C 24
Trevanion Rd. W14—6J 73
Treve Av. Harr—5B 38
Trevellance Way. Wat—6H 5
Trevelyan Av. E12—9K 47
Trevelyan Clo. Dart—3K 99
Trevelyan Cres. Harr—5H 39
Trevelyan Gdns. NW10—4G 57
Trevelyan Rd. E15—9D 46
Trevelyan Rd. SW17—3C 106
Treveris St. SE1—2M 75
Treverton St. W10—7H 57
Treville St. SW15—6F 88
Treviso Rd. SE23—8H 93
Trevithick Dri. Dart—3K 99
Trevithick St. SE8—7L 77
Trevone Gdns. Pinn—4J 37
Trevor Clo. Barn—8B 14
Trevor Clo. Brom—2D 126
Trevor Clo. Harr—7D 22
Trevor Clo. Iswth—4D 86
Trevor Clo. N'holt—5G 53
Trevor Cres. Ruis—9D 36
Trevor Gdns. Edgw—8B 24
Trevor Gdns. N'holt—5G 53
Trevor Pl. SW7—3C 74
Trevor Rd. SW19—4J 105
Trevor Rd. Edgw—8B 24
Trevor Rd. Hay—3C 68
Trevor Rd. Wfd G—7E 30
Trevor Sq. SW7—3D 74
Trevor St. SW7—3C 74
Trevose Rd. E17—8B 30
Trevose Way. Wat—3G 21
Trewenna Dri. Chess—7H 119
Trewince Rd. SW20—5G 105
Trewint St. SW18—8A 90
Trewsbury Rd. SE26—2H 109
Triandra Way. Hay—8H 53
Triangle Ct. E16—8G 63
Triangle Pas. Barn—6A 14
Triangle Pl. SW4—3H 91
Triangle Rd. E8—4F 60
Triangle, The. E8—4F 60
Triangle, The. N13—4L 27
Triangle, The. Bark—2A 64
Triangle, The. King—6A 104
Trident Rd. Wat—7D 4
Trident St. SE16—5H 77
Trident Way. S'hall—4F 68
Trig La. EC4—1A 76
Trigo Ct. Eps—3B 134
Trigon Rd. SW8—8K 75
Trilby Rd. SE23—8H 93
Trimmer Wlk. Bren—7J 71
Trinder Gdns. N19—6J 43
Trinder Rd. N19—6J 43
Trinder Rd. Barn—7G 13
Tring Av. W5—2K 71
Tring Av. S'hall—9K 53
Tring Av. Wemb—2L 55
Tring Clo. Ilf—3B 48
Tring Clo. Romf—4K 35
Tring Gdns. Romf—4J 35
Tring Grn. Romf—4J 35
Tring Wlk. Romf—4J 35
Trinidad Gdns. Dag—3B 66
Trinidad St. E14—1K 77
Trinity Av. N2—1B 42
Trinity Av. Enf—8D 16
Trinity Chu. Rd. SW13—7F 72
Trinity Chu. Sq. SE1—4A 76
Trinity Clo. E11—7C 46
Trinity Clo. SE13—3B 94
Trinity Clo. Brom—3J 127
Trinity Clo. Houn—3J 85
Trinity Clo. N'wd—6C 20
Trinity Clo. S Croy—1C 138
Trinity Clo. Stai—5A 144
Trinity Cotts. Rich—2K 87
Trinity Ct. N1—4C 60
Trinity Ct. Croy—4A 124
Trinity Cres. SW17—8D 90
Trinity Gdns. E16—8D 62
Trinity Gdns. SW9—3K 91
Trinity Gro. SE10—9A 78
Trinity Hall Clo. Wat—5G 9
Trinity La. Wal X—5E 6
Trinity Pl. EC3—1D 76
Trinity Pl. Bexh—3K 97
Trinity Rise. SW2—7L 91
Trinity Rd. N2—1B 42
Trinity Rd. N22—7J 27
Trinity Rd.—3A 90
SW17 1-259 & 4-226
SW18 remainder
Trinity Rd. SW19—3L 105
Trinity Rd. Ilf—1A 48
Trinity Rd. Rich—2K 87
Trinity Rd. S'hall—2J 69
Trinity Sq. EC3—1D 76
Trinity St. E16—8D 62
Trinity St. SE1—3A 76
Trinity St. Enf—4A 16
Trinity Wlk. NW3—2A 58
Trinity Way. W3—1C 72
Trio Pl. SE1—3A 76
Tristan Sq. SE3—2C 94
Tristram Clo. E17—1B 46
Tristram Rd. Brom—1D 110
Triton Sq. NW1—7G 59
Tritton Av. Croy—6J 123
Tritton Rd. SE21—9B 92
Triumph Clo. Hay—9A 68
Trojan Way. Croy—5K 123
Troon St. E1—9J 61
Trosley Rd. Belv—7L 81
Trossachs Rd. SE22—4C 92
Trothy Rd. SE1—5E 76
Trotters Bottom. Borwd—1E 12
Trott Rd. N10—7D 26
Trott St. SW11—9C 74
Trotwood. Chig—6B 32
Troughton Rd. SE7—6F 78
Troutbeck Rd. SE14—9J 77
Trout La. W Dray—1G 143
Trout Rd. W Dray—2H 143
Trouville Rd. SW4—5G 91
Trowbridge Rd. E9—2K 61
Trowbridge Rd. Romf—6H 35
Trowley Rise. Abb L, Wat—4C 4
Trowlock Av. Tedd—3G 103
Trowlock Way. Tedd—3H 103
Troy Rd. SE19—3B 108
Troy Town. SE15—2E 92
Truesdale Rd. E6—9K 63
Trulock Rd. N17—7E 28
Truman's Rd. N16—1C 60
Trumble Gdns. T Hth—8M 107
Trumpers Way. W7—4C 70
Trumper Way. Uxb—4A 142
Trumpington Rd. E7—9D 46
Trump St. EC2—9A 60
Trundlers Way. Bush, Wat —1C 22
Trundley's Rd. SE8—6H 77
Trundley's Ter. SE8—5H 77
Trunks All. Swan—6M 113
Truro Gdns. Ilf—5J 47
Truro Rd. E17—2K 45
Truro Rd. N22—7J 27
Truro St. NW5—2E 58
Truro Wlk. Romf—6G 35
Truro Way. Hay—6C 52
Truslove Rd. SE27—2L 107
Trussley Rd. W6—4G 73
Truston's Gdns. Horn—5E 50
Trust Rd. Wal X—7E 6
Trust Wlk. SE21—7M 91
Tryfan Clo. Ilf—3H 47
Tryon St. SW3—6D 74
Trystings Clo. Esh—8E 118
Tuam Rd. SE18—7B 80
Tubbenden Clo. Orp—5C 128
Tubbenden Dri. Orp—6B 128
Tubbenden La. Orp—6B 128
Tubbenden La. S. Orp—7B 128
Tubbs Rd. NW10—5D 56
Tucker St. Wat—7G 9
Tuck Rd. Rain—2E 66
Tuckton Wlk. SW15—6D 88
Tudor Av. Hmptn—4L 101
Tudor Av. Romf—1E 50
Tudor Av. Wal X—4A 6
Tudor Av. Wat—2H 9
Tudor Av. Wor Pk—5F 120
Tudor Clo. N6—5G 43
Tudor Clo. NW3—1C 58
Tudor Clo. NW7—6E 24
Tudor Clo. NW9—7A 40
Tudor Clo. Ashf—9C 144
Tudor Clo. Bans—7J 135
Tudor Clo. Chess—7J 119
Tudor Clo. Chig—4L 31
Tudor Clo. Chst—5K 111
Tudor Clo. Dart—5F 98
Tudor Clo. Pinn—3E 36
Tudor Clo. S Croy—7F 138
Tudor Clo. Sutt—7H 121
Tudor Clo. Wall—9G 123
Tudor Clo. Wal X—4B 6
Tudor Clo. Wfd G—5F 30
Tudor Ct. E17—5K 45
Tudor Ct. Borwd—4J 11
Tudor Ct. Felt—1G 101
Tudor Ct. Romf—6M 35
Tudor Ct. N. Wemb—1L 55
Tudor Ct. S. Wemb—1L 55
Tudor Cres. Enf—3A 16
Tudor Cres. Ilf—6M 31
Tudor Dri. King—2H 103
Tudor Dri. Mord—1H 121
Tudor Dri. Romf—2E 50
Tudor Dri. W on T—3H 117
Tudor Dri. Wat—2H 9
Tudor Gdns. NW9—7A 40
Tudor Gdns. SW13—2C 88
Tudor Gdns. W3—8L 55
Tudor Gdns. Harr—9B 22
Tudor Gdns. Romf—2E 50
Tudor Gdns. Twic—7D 86
Tudor Gdns. Upm—7M 51
Tudor Gdns. W Wick—5A 126
Tudor Gro. E9—3G 61
Tudor Pl. Mitc—4C 106
Tudor Rd. E4—6M 29
Tudor Rd. E6—4G 63
Tudor Rd. E9—4F 60
Tudor Rd. N9—9F 16
Tudor Rd. SE19—4D 108
Tudor Rd. SE25—9F 108
Tudor Rd. Ashf—3B 100
Tudor Rd. Bark—4D 64
Tudor Rd. Barn—5L 13
Tudor Rd. Beck—7A 110
Tudor Rd. Hmptn—4L 101
Tudor Rd. Harr—9B 22
Tudor Rd. Hay—9B 52
Tudor Rd. Houn—3B 86
Tudor Rd. King—4L 103
Tudor Rd. Pinn—9G 21
Tudor Rd. S'hall—1J 69
Tudor Sq. Hay—8B 52
Tudor St. EC4—1L 75
Tudor Wlk. Bex—5J 97
Tudor Wlk. Wat—1H 9
Tudor Wlk. Wey—5A 116
Tudor Way. N14—1H 27
Tudor Way. W3—3L 71
Tudor Way. Orp—1B 128
Tudor Way. Uxb—2E 142
Tudor Way. Wal A—6K 7
Tudor Well Clo. Stan—5F 22
Tudway Rd. SE3—2F 94
Tufnail Rd. Dart—5K 99
Tufnell Pk. Rd.—9G 43
N7 1-217 & 2-210
N19 remainder
Tufter Rd. Chig—5D 32
Tufton Gdns. E Mol—6M 101
Tufton Rd. E4—4L 29
Tufton St. SW1—4J 75
Tugela Rd. Croy—1B 124
Tugela St. SE6—8K 93
Tulip Clo. Croy—3H 125
Tulip Clo. Hmptn—3K 101
Tulip Clo. Romf—6H 35
Tulip Ct. Pinn—1G 37
Tuliptree Av. Rich—9J 71
Tulse Clo. Beck—7A 110
Tulse Hill. SW2—5L 91
Tulsemere Rd. SE27—8A 92
Tumblewood Rd. Bans—8J 135
Tumbling Bay. W on T—1E 116
Tuncombe Rd. N18—4C 28
Tunis Rd. W12—2G 73
Tunley Grn. E14—8K 61
Tunley Rd. NW10—4C 56
Tunley Rd. SW17—8E 90
Tunmarsh La. E13—6G 63
Tunnel App. E14—1J 77
Tunnel App. SE10—3C 78
Tunnel Av. SE10—3B 78
(in two parts)
Tunnel Gdns. N11—7G 27
Tunnel Rd. SE16—3G 77
Tunnel Wood Clo. Wat—1D 8
Tunnel Wood Rd. Wat—1D 8
Tunstall Av. Ilf—6E 32
Tunstall Clo. Orp—6C 128
Tunstall Rd. SW9—3K 91
Tunstall Rd. Croy—3C 124
Tunstall Wlk. Bren—7J 71
Tunworth Clo. NW9—4A 40
Tunworth Cres. SW15—5D 88
Turenne Clo. SW18—3A 90
Turin Rd. N9—1G 29
Turin St. E2—6E 60
Turkey Oak Clo. SE19—5C 108
Turkey St. Enf—9A 6
Turks Clo. Uxb—6E 142
Turk's Head Yd. EC1—8M 59
Turks Row. SW3—6D 74
Turle Rd. N4—7K 43
Turle Rd. SW16—6J 107
Turley Clo. E15—4C 62
Turnage Rd. Dag—6J 49
Turnberry Way. Orp—3B 128
Turnchapel M. SW4—2F 90
Turner Av. N15—2C 44
Turner Av. Mitc—5D 106
Turner Av. Twic—9A 86
Turner Clo. NW11—4M 41
Turner Clo. Hay—5A 52
Turner Dri. NW11—4M 41
Turner Rd. E17—1A 46
Turner Rd. Bush, Wat—6A 10
Turner Rd. Edgw—4J 23
Turner Rd. N Mald—2B 120
Turner Rd. West—4G 141
Turner's All. EC3—1C 76
Turner's Hill. Wal X—2D 6
Turners La. W on T—8F 116
Turner's Rd. E3—8K 61
Turner St. E1—8F 60
Turner St. E16—9D 62
Turners Wood. NW11—5A 42
Turneville Rd. W14—7K 73
Turney Rd. SE21—6A 92
Turnham Grn. Ter. W4—5C 72
Turnham Grn. Ter. M. W4 —5C 72
Turnham Rd. SE4—4J 93
Turnmill St. EC1—8M 59
Turnpike Clo. SE8—8K 77
Turnpike La. N8—2K 43
Turnpike La. Uxb—5C 142
Turnpike Link. Croy—4C 124
Turnpin La. SE10—7A 78
Turnstone Clo. S Croy—2J 139
Turnstones, The. Wat—9J 5
Turpentine La. SW1—6F 74
Turpin Av. Romf—7L 33
Turpington Clo. Brom—2J 127
Turpington La. Brom—2J 127
Turpin Rd. Felt—5D 84
Turpin's La. Wfd G—5K 31
Turpin Way. N19—7H 43
Turpin Way. Wall—9F 122
Turquand St. SE17—5A 76
Turret Gro. SW4—2G 91
Turtleway Clo. N4—6K 43
Turton Rd. Wemb—1J 55
Turville St. E2—7D 60
Tuscan Rd. SE18—6B 80
Tuskar St. SE10—7C 78
Tustin Est. SE15—7G 77
Tuttlebee La. Buck H—2E 30
Tuxford Clo. Borwd—2J 11
Tweeddale Gro. Uxb—8A 36
Tweeddale Rd. Cars—3B 122
Tweed Glen. Romf—7B 34
Tweed Grn. Romf—7B 34
Tweedmouth Rd. E13—5F 62
Tweed Way. Romf—7B 34
Tweedy Rd. Brom—5E 110
Twelvetrees Cres. E3—7A 62
Twentyman Clo. Wfd G—5E 30
Twickenham Bri. Twic & Rich —4G 87
Twickenham Clo. Croy—5K 123
Twickenham Gdns. Gnfd —1E 54
Twickenham Gdns. Harr —7C 22
Twickenham Rd. E11—7B 46
Twickenham Rd. Felt—9K 85
Twickenham Rd. Iswth—4E 86
Twickenham Rd. Rich—3G 87
Twickenham Rd. Tedd—1E 102
(in two parts)
Twickenham Trading Est. Iswth —5D 86
Twigg Clo. Eri—8C 82
Twilley St. SW18—6M 89
Twineham Grn. N12—4L 25
Twining Av. Twic—9A 86
Twinn Rd. NW7—6J 25
Twisden Rd. NW5—9F 42
Twitton La. Sev—7B 140
Twybridge Way. NW10—3A 56
Twyford Abbey Rd. NW10 —6K 55
Twyford Av. N2—1D 42
Twyford Av. W3—1L 71
Twyford Cres. W3—2L 71
Twyford Pl. WC2—9K 59
Twyford Rd. Cars—3B 122
Twyford Rd. Harr—6M 37
Twyford Rd. Ilf—1A 64
Twyford St. N1—4K 59
Tyas Rd. E16—7D 62
Tybenham Rd. SW19—7L 105
Tyberry Rd. Enf—5G 17
Tyburn La. Harr—5D 38
Tyburn Way. W1—1D 74
Tycehurst Hill. Lou—6K 19
Tye La. Orp—7A 128
Tyers Ga. SE1—3C 76
Tyers St. SE11—6K 75
Tyers Ter. SE11—6K 75
Tyeshurst Clo. SE2—6J 81
Tyfield Clo. Wal X—3C 6
Tykeswater La. Borwd—4G 11
Tylecroft Rd. SW16—6J 107
Tyle Grn. Horn—2J 51
Tylehurst Gdns. Ilf—1A 64
Tyler Gro. Dart—3K 99
Tylers Clo. Lou—9J 19
Tylers Cres. Horn—1G 67
Tylers Ga. Harr—4J 39
Tylers Grn. Rd. Swan—2A 130
Tylers Path. Cars—6D 122
Tyler St. SE10—6C 78
Tylers Way. Wat—6B 10
Tylney Av. SE19—2D 108
Tylney Rd. E7—9G 47
Tylney Rd. Brom—6H 111
Tynan Clo. Felt—7E 84
Tyndale La. N1—3M 59
Tyndale Ter. N1—3M 59
Tyndall Rd. E10—7A 46
Tyndall Rd. Well—2D 96
Tyneham Rd. SW11—1E 90
(in two parts)
Tynemouth Dri. Enf—2E 16
Tynemouth Rd. N15—2D 44
Tynemouth Rd. Mitc—4E 106
Tynemouth St. SW6—1A 90
Tyne St. E1—9D 60
Tynwald Ho. SE26—9E 92
Type St. E2—5H 61
Tyrawley Rd. SW6—9M 73
Tyrell Clo. Harr—9C 38
Tyrell Ct. Cars—6D 122
Tyrells Clo. Upm—7M 51
Tyrone Rd. E6—5K 63
Tyron Way. Sidc—1C 112
Tyrrell Av. Well—4E 96
Tyrrell Rd. SE22—3E 92
Tyrrel Way. NW9—5D 40
Tyrwhitt Rd. SE4—2L 93
Tysea Hill. Romf—1D 34
Tysoe Av. Enf—9F 6
Tysoe St. EC1—6L 59

Tyson Rd. SE23—6G 93
Tyssen Pas. E8—2D 60
Tyssen Rd. N16—8D 44
Tyssen St. E8—2D 60
Tytherton Rd. N19—8H 43

Uamvar St. E14—8M 61
Uckfield Gro. Mitc—5E 106
Uckfield Rd. Enf—1H 17
Udall Gdns. Romf—6L 33
Udall St. SW1—5G 75
Udney Pk. Rd. Tedd—3E 102
Uffington Rd. NW10—4E 56
Uffington Rd. SE27—1L 107
Ufford Clo. Harr—7M 21
Ufford Rd. Harr—7M 21
Ufford St. SE1—3L 75
Ufton Gro. N1—3B 60
Ufton Rd. N1—3C 60
Ullathorne Rd. SW16—1G 107
Ulleswater Rd. N14—3J 27
Ullin St. E14—8A 62
Ullswater Clo. SW15—1B 104
Ullswater Clo. Brom—4C 110
Ullswater Clo. Hay—5C 52
Ullswater Cres. SW15—1B 104
Ullswater Cres. Coul—8J 137
Ullswater Rd. SE27—8M 91
Ullswater Rd. SW13—8E 72
Ullswater Way. Horn—1E 66
Ulster Gdns. N13—4A 28
Ulster Pl. NW1—7F 58
Ulundi Rd. SE3—7C 78
Ulva Rd. SW15—4H 89
Ulverscroft Rd. SE22—4E 92
Ulverstone Rd. SE27—8M 91
Ulverston Rd. E17—9B 30
Ulysses Rd. NW6—1K 57
Umberston St. E1—9E 60
Umbria St. SW15—5E 88
Umfreville Rd. N4—4M 43
Underbridge Way. Enf—5J 17
Undercliffe Rd. SE13—2L 93
Underhill. Barn—7L 13
Underhill Rd. SE22—4E 92
Underhill St. NW1—4F 58
Underne Av. N14—2F 26
Undershaft. EC3—9C 60
Undershaw Rd. Brom—9D 94
Underwood. Croy—7A 126
Underwood Rd. E1—7E 60
Underwood Rd. E4—5M 29
Underwood Row. N1—6A 60
Underwood St. N1—6A 60
Underwood, The. SE9—9K 95
Undine St. SW17—2D 106
Uneeda Dri. Gnfd—4B 54
Unicorn Pas. SE1—2C 76
Union Cotts. E15—3C 62
Union Ct. Rich—4J 87
Union Dri. E1—7J 61
Union Gro. SW8—1H 91
Union Rd. N11—6H 27
Union Rd.—1H 91
  SW4 1-93 & 2-102
  SW8 remainder
Union Rd. Brom—9H 111
Union Rd. Croy—2A 124
Union Rd. N'holt—5L 53
Union Rd. Wemb—2J 55
Union Sq. N1—4A 60
Union St. E15—4A 62
Union St. SE1—2M 75
Union St. Barn—5J 13
Union St. King—6H 103
Union Wlk. E2—6C 60
Union Yd. W1—9F 58
Unity Rd. Enf—1G 17
Unity Way. SE18—4H 79
University Clo. NW7—7D 24
University Pl. Eri—8A 82
University Rd. SW19—3B 106
University St. WC1—7G 59
Unwin Av. Felt—4B 84
Unwin Clo. SE15—7E 76
Unwin Rd. Iswth—2C 86
Upbrook M. W2—9A 58
Upcerne Rd. SW10—8A 74
Upchurch Clo. SE20—4F 108
Upcroft Av. Edgw—5A 24
Updale Rd. Sidc—1D 112
Upfield. Croy—5F 124
Upfield Rd. W13—8D 54
Upgrove Mnr. Way. SW2
  —6L 91
Uphall Rd. Ilf—1M 63
Upham Pk. Rd. W4—5C 72
Uphill Dri. NW7—5C 24
Uphill Dri. NW9—3A 40
Uphill Gro. NW7—4C 24
Uphill Rd. NW7—4C 24
Upland Ct. Romf—9K 35

Upland Rd. E13—7E 62
Upland Rd. SE22—6E 92
Upland Rd. Bexh—2K 97
Upland Rd. S Croy—7B 124
Upland Rd. Sutt—9B 122
Uplands. Beck—6L 109
Uplands Av. E17—9H 29
Uplands Clo. SW14—4M 87
Uplands End. Wfd G—7J 31
Uplands Pk. Rd. Enf—4L 15
Uplands Rd. N8—3K 43
Uplands Rd. Barn—1E 26
Uplands Rd. Kenl—8A 138
Uplands Rd. Orp—3F 128
Uplands Rd. Romf—1H 49
Uplands Rd. Wfd G—7J 31
Uplands, The. Lou—5K 19
Uplands, The. Ruis—5E 36
Uplands, The. St Alb—3J 5
Uplands Way. N21—7L 15
Upland Way. Eps—9G 135
Upminster. Horn & Upm
  —7K 51
Upminster Rd. N. Rain—6G 67
Upminster Rd. S. Rain—7E 66
Upney Clo. Horn—1G 67
Upney La. Bark—2C 64
Upnor Way. SE17—6C 76
Uppark Dri. Ilf—4A 48
Up. Abbey Rd. Belv—5K 81
Up. Addison Gdns. W14—3J 73
Up. Austin Lodge Rd. Eyns,
  Dart & Sev—6H 131
Up. Belgrave St. SW1—4E 74
Up. Berkeley St. W1—9D 58
Up. Beulah Hill. SE19—5C 108
Up. Brentwood Rd. Romf
  —2G 51
Up. Brighton Rd. Surb—1H 119
Up. Brockley Rd. SE4—1K 93
Up. Brook St. W1—1E 74
Up. Butts. Bren—7G 71
Up. Cavendish Av. N3—1L 41
Up. Cheyne Row. SW3—7C 74
Up. Clapton Rd. E5—7F 44
Up. Court Rd. Eps—3A 134
Upper Dri. West—9G 141
Up. Elmers End Rd. Beck
  —8J 109
Up. Farm Rd. E Mol—8K 101
Up. Fore St. N18—6D 28
Up. Green E. Mitc—7D 106
Up. Green W. Mitc—6D 106
Up. Grosvenor St. W1—1E 74
Up. Grotto Rd. Twic—8D 86
Up. Ground. SE1—2L 75
Up. Gulland Rd. SE25—8D 108
Up. Grove Rd. Belv—7K 81
Up. Halliford By-Pass. Shep
  —9C 100
Up. Halliford Grn. Shep
  —8C 100
Up. Halliford Rd. Shep—7C 100
Up. Ham Rd. Rich—1H 103
Up. Harley St. NW1—7E 58
Up. High St. Eps—5C 134
Up. Highway. K Lan & Abb L,
  Wat—6B 4
Up. Hitch. Wat—1J 21
Up. Holly Hill Rd. Belv—6M 81
Up. James St. W1—1G 75
Up. John St. W1—1G 75
Up. Mall. W6—6E 72
Up. Marsh. SE1—4K 75
Up. Montagu St. W1—8D 58
Up. Mulgrave Rd. Sutt—9J 121
Up. North St. E14—8L 61
Up. Paddock Rd. Wat—8J 9
Up. Palace Rd. E Mol—7B 102
Upper Pk. Lou—6H 19
Up. Park Rd. N11—5G 27
Up. Park Rd. NW3—1D 58
Up. Park Rd. Belv—5M 81
Up. Park Rd. Brom—5F 110
Up. Park Rd. King—3L 103
Up. Phillimore Gdns. W8—3L 73
Up. Pillory Downs. Cars
  —5E 136
Up. Pines. Bans—9D 136
Up. Rainham Rd. Horn—6D 50
Up. Richmond Rd. SW15
  —3D 88
Up. Richmond Rd. W. Rich &
  SW14—3L 87
Upper Rd. E13—6E 62
Upper Rd. Wall—7H 123
Up. Saint Martin's La. WC2
  —1J 75
Up. Selsdon Rd. S Croy
  —1D 138
Up. Sheridan Rd. Belv—5L 81
Up. Shirley Rd. Croy—4G 125
Upper Sq. Iswth—2E 86

Upper St. N1—5M 59
Up. Sunbury Rd. Hmptn
  —5J 101
Up. Sutton La. Houn—9L 69
Up. Tachbrook St. SW1—5G 75
Up. Tail. Wat—3J 21
Up. Teddington Rd. King
  —5G 103
Upper Ter. NW3—8A 42
Up. Thames St. EC4—1M 75
Up. Tollington Pk. N4—6L 43
  (in two parts)
Upperton Rd. Sidc—2D 112
Upperton Rd. E. E13—6G 63
Upperton Rd. W. E13—6G 63
Up. Tooting Pk. SW17—8D 90
Up. Tooting Rd. SW17—1D 106
Up. Town Rd. Gnfd—7M 53
Up. Tulse Hill. SW2—6K 91
Up. Vernon Rd. Sutt—7B 122
Upper Wlk., The. Sutt—7M 121
Up. Walthamstow Rd. E17
  —1B 46
Up. Wickham La. Well—1F 96
Up. Wimpole St. W1—8E 58
Up. Woburn Pl. WC1—6H 59
Up. Woodcote Village. Purl
  —4H 137
Uppingham Av. Stan—8F 22
Upsdell Av. N13—6L 27
Upshire Rd. Wal A—5M 7
Upstall St. SE5—9M 75
Upton Av. E7—3E 62
Upton Clo. Bex—5K 97
Upton Dene. Sutt—9M 121
Upton Gdns. Harr—3F 38
Upton La. E7—3E 62
Upton Lodge Clo. Bush, Wat
  —9A 10
Upton Pk. Rd. E7—3F 62
Upton Rd. N18—5F 28
Upton Rd. SE18—7A 80
Upton Rd. Bexh & Bex—3J 97
Upton Rd. Houn—2L 85
Upton Rd. T Hth—6B 108
Upton Rd. Wat—5F 8
Upton Rd. S. Bex—5K 97
Upway. N12—6C 26
Upwood Rd. SE12—5E 94
Upwood Rd. SW16—5J 107
Urban Av. Horn—8G 51
Urlwin St. SE5—7A 76
Urlwin Wlk. SW9—9L 75
Urmston Dri. SW19—7J 89
Ursula St. SW11—9C 74
Urswick Gdns. Dag—3J 65
Urswick Rd. E9—1G 61
Urswick Rd. Dag—3H 65
Usher Rd. E3—5K 61
  (in two parts)
Usk Rd. SW11—3A 90
Usk Rd. S Ock—9M 67
Usk St. E2—6H 61
Usk St. E16—1D 78
Uvedale Clo. Croy—3B 140
Uvedale Cres. Croy—3B 140
Uvedale Rd. Dag—8L 49
Uvedale Rd. Enf—7B 16
Uverdale Rd. SW10—8A 74
Uxbridge Rd. W5 & W3—1J 71
Uxbridge Rd. W12—2E 72
Uxbridge Rd. W13 & W5—2F 70
Uxbridge Rd. Felt—8G 85
Uxbridge Rd. Hmptn—1L 101
Uxbridge Rd. King—8H 103
Uxbridge Rd. Pinn, Harr & Stan
  —9H 21
Uxbridge Rd. S'hall—2L 69
Uxbridge Rd. Uxb & Hay
  —6E 142
Uxbridge St. W8—2L 73
Uxendon Cres. Wemb—6J 39
Uxendon Hill. Wemb—6K 39

Vaillant Rd. Wey—6A 116
Valance Av. E4—1C 30
Valan Leas. Brom—7C 110
Vale Av. Borwd—7M 11
Vale Border. Croy & S Croy
  —3H 139
Vale Clo. W9—6A 58
Vale Clo. Coul—6J 137
Vale Clo. Orp—6L 127
Vale Clo. Wey—5B 116
Vale Cotts. Brom—7E 110
Vale Ct. Wey—5B 116
Vale Cres. SW15—1C 104
Vale Croft. Pinn—3J 37
Vale Dri. Barn—6K 13
Vale End. SE22—3D 92
Vale Gro. N4—5A 44
Vale Gro. W3—3B 72

Vale Industrial Pk. Rick—9A 8
Vale La. W3—8L 55
Valence Av. Dag—6H 49
Valence Cir. Dag—8J 49
Valence Rd. Eri—8B 82
Valence Wood Rd. Dag—8H 49
Valencia Rd. Stan—4G 23
Valency Clo. N'wd—4D 20
Valentia Pl. SW9—3L 91
Valentine Av. Bex—7J 97
Valentine Pl. SE1—3M 75
Valentine Rd. E9—2H 61
Valentine Rd. Harr—8M 37
Valentine Row. SE1—3M 75
Valentines Rd. Ilf—6M 47
Valentine's Way. Romf—7C 50
Vale Pl. W14—4H 73
Valerian Way. E15—6C 62
Vale Rise. NW11—6K 41
Vale Rd. E7—2F 62
Vale Rd. N4—5A 44
Vale Rd. Brom—5L 111
Vale Rd. Bush, Wat—7J 9
Vale Rd. Dart—7F 98
Vale Rd. Esh—1C 132
Vale Rd. Mitc—8H 107
Vale Rd. Sutt—6M 121
Vale Rd. Wey—5B 116
Vale Rd. Wor Pk & Eps—5D 120
Vale Rd. N. Surb—4J 119
Vale Rd. S. Surb—4J 119
Vale Row. N5—8M 43
Vale Royal. N7—3J 59
Valeswood Rd. Brom—2D 110
Vale Ter. N4—4A 44
Vale, The. N10—8E 26
Vale, The. N14—8K 15
Vale, The. NW11—7J 41
Vale, The. SW3—7B 74
Vale, The. W3—2D 72
Vale, The. Coul—6J 137
Vale, The. Croy—4H 125
Vale, The. Felt—5F 84
Vale, The. Houn—7J 69
Vale, The. Ruis—9G 37
Vale, The. Sun—3E 100
Vale, The. Wfd G—7E 30
Valetta Gro. E13—5E 62
Valetta Rd. W3—3C 72
Valette St. E9—2G 61
Valiant Clo. N'holt—6H 53
Valiant Clo. Romf—9M 33
Vallance Rd.—7E 60
  E1 1-121 & 2-168
  E2 remainder
Vallance Rd. N22—9G 27
Vallentin Rd. E17—2A 46
Valley Av. N12—4B 26
Valley Clo. Dart—5D 98
Valley Clo. Lou—8K 19
Valley Clo. Pinn—9F 20
Valley Clo. Wal A—5J 7
Valley Dri. NW9—4L 39
Valleyfield Rd. SW16—2K 107
Valley Fields Cres. Enf—4L 15
Valley Gdns. SW19—4B 106
Valley Gdns. Wemb—3K 55
Valley Gro. SE7—6G 79
Valley Hill. Lou—8J 19
Valley M. Twic—8D 86
Valley Rise. Wat—6F 4
Valley Rd. SW16—2K 107
Valley Rd. Belv—5M 81
Valley Rd. Brom—6C 110
Valley Rd. Dart—5D 98
Valley Rd. Eri—5B 82
Valley Rd. Kenl—7B 138
Valley Rd. Orp—5F 112
Valley Rd. Uxb—5C 142
Valley Side. E4—2L 29
Valley View. Barn—8J 13
Valley View. West—9G 141
Valley View Gdns. Kenl
  —7C 138
Valley View Ter. F'ham, Dart
  —3K 131
Valley Wlk. Croy—4G 125
Valley Wlk. Rick—7A 8
Valliere Rd. NW10—6E 56
Valliers Wood Rd. Sidc
  —7C 96
vallis Way. W13—8E 54
Vallis Way. Chess—6H 119
Valmar Rd. SE5—9A 76
Valnay St. SW17—2D 106
Valognes Av. E17—8J 29
Valonia Gdns. SW18—5K 89
Vambery Rd. SE18—7A 80
Vanbrough Cres. N'holt—4G 53
Vanbrugh Clo. E16—8H 63
Vanbrugh Fields. SE3—8D 78

Vanbrugh Hill—6D 78
  SE3 1-31 & 2-44
  SE10 remainder
Vanbrugh Pk. SE3—8D 78
Vanbrugh Pk. Rd. SE3—8D 78
Vanbrugh Pk. Rd. W. SE3
  —8D 78
Vanbrugh Rd. W4—4B 72
Vanbrugh Ter. SE3—9D 78
Vanburgh Clo. Orp—3C 128
Vancouver Clo. Eps—3A 134
Vancouver Rd. SE23—8J 93
Vancouver Rd. Edgw—8M 23
Vancouver Rd. Hay—7F 52
Vancouver Rd. Rich—1G 103
Vanderbilt Rd. SW18—7A 90
Vandome Clo. E16—9F 62
Vandon Pas. SW1—4G 75
Vandon St. SW1—4G 75
Van Dyck Av. N Mald—2B 120
Vandyke Clo. SW15—5H 89
Vandyke Cross. SE9—4J 95
Vandy St. EC2—7C 60
Vane Clo. NW3—9B 42
Vane Clo. Harr—4K 39
Vanessa Clo. Belv—6L 81
Vanessa Way. Bex—9B 98
Vane St. SW1—5G 75
Vanguard Clo. Croy—3M 123
Vanguard Clo. Romf—9M 33
Vanguard St. SE8—9L 77
Vanguard Way. Wall—9J 123
Vanoc Gdns. Brom—1E 110
Vansittart Rd. E7—9D 46
Vansittart St. SE14—7J 77
Vanston Pl. SW6—8L 73
Vant Rd. SW17—2D 106
Varcoe Rd. SE16—6F 76
Vardens Rd. SW11—3B 90
Varden St. E1—9F 60
Varley Pde. NW9—2C 40
Varley Rd. E16—9F 62
Varna Rd. SW6—8J 73
Varna Rd. Hmptn—5M 101
Varndell St. NW1—6G 59
Varney Clo. Wal X—1A 6
Vartry Rd. N15—4B 44
Vassall Rd. SW9—8L 75
Vauban St. SE16—4D 76
Vaughan Av. NW4—3E 40
Vaughan Av. W6—5D 72
Vaughan Av. Horn—9H 51
Vaughan Clo. Hmptn—3J 101
Vaughan Gdns. Ilf—5K 47
Vaughan Rd. E15—2D 62
Vaughan Rd. SE5—1A 92
Vaughan Rd. Harr—5A 38
Vaughan Rd. Th Dit—2F 118
Vaughan Rd. Well—1D 96
Vaughan Williams Clo. SE8
  —8L 77
Vaux Cres. W on T—8F 116
Vauxhall Bri. SW1 & SE1
  —6J 75
Vauxhall Bri. Rd. SW1—5G 75
Vauxhall Gdns. S Croy—8A 124
Vauxhall Gro. SW8—7K 75
Vauxhall Pl. Dart—6J 99
Vauxhall St. SE11—6K 75
Vauxhall Wlk. SE11—6K 75
Vawdrey Clo. E1—7G 61
Vectis Gdns. SW17—3F 106
Vectis Rd. SW17—3F 106
Veda Rd. SE13—3L 93
Vega Cres. N'wd—5D 20
Vega Rd. Bush, Wat—9A 10
Velde Way. SE22—4C 92
Venables St. NW8—7B 58
Vencourt Pl. W6—5E 72
Venetian Rd. SE5—1A 92
Venetia Rd. N4—4M 43
Venetia Rd. W5—3H 71
Venette Clo. Rain—8F 66
Venner Rd. SE26—3G 109
Venners Clo. Bexh—1C 98
Venn St. SW4—3G 91
Ventnor Dri. N20—3M 25
Ventnor Gdns. Bark—2C 64
Ventnor Rd. SE14—8H 77
Ventnor Rd. Sutt—9M 121
Venture Clo. Bex—6J 97
Venue St. E14—8A 62
Venus Rd. SE18—4K 79
Veny Cres. Horn—1H 67
Vera Av. N21—7L 15
Vera Ct. Wat—9H 9
Vera Rd. SW6—9J 73
Verbena Clo. W Dray—6H 143
Verbena Gdns. W6—6E 72
Verdant La. SE6—6C 94
Verdayne Av. Croy—3H 125

Verdayne Gdns. Warl—8G 139
Verderers Rd. Chig—4E 32
Verdun Rd. SE18—7E 80
Verdun Rd. SW13—7E 72
Vereker Dri. Sun—7E 100
Vereker Rd. W14—6J 73
Vere Rd. Lou—6M 19
Vere St. W1—9F 58
Verity Clo. W11—1J 73
Vermont Rd. SE19—3C 108
Vermont Rd. SW18—5M 89
Vermont Rd. Sutt—5M 121
Verney Gdns. Dag—9J 49
Verney Pl. SE16—6F 76
Verney Rd. Dag—9J 49
 (in two parts)
Verney St. NW10—8B 40
Verney Way. SE16—6F 76
Vernham Rd. SE18—7A 80
Vernon Av. E12—9K 47
Vernon Av. SW20—6H 105
Vernon Av. Enf—9E 6
Vernon Av. Wfd G—7F 30
Vernon Clo. Eps—8A 120
Vernon Clo. Orp—7F 112
Vernon Ct. W5—1G 71
Vernon Ct. Stan—8F 22
Vernon Cres. Barn—8E 14
Vernon Dri. Stan—8E 22
Vernon Pl. WC1—8J 59
Vernon Rise. WC1—6K 59
Vernon Rise. Gnfd—1B 54
Vernon Rd. E3—5K 61
Vernon Rd. E11—7C 46
Vernon Rd. E15—3C 62
Vernon Rd. E17—3K 45
Vernon Rd. N8—1L 43
Vernon Rd. SW14—2B 88
Vernon Rd. Bush. Wat—7J 9
Vernon Rd. Felt—8D 84
Vernon Rd. Ilf—6D 48
Vernon Rd. Romf—5A 34
Vernon Rd. Sutt—7B 122
Vernon Sq. WC1—6K 59
Vernon St. W14—5J 73
Vernon Yd. W11—1K 73
Veroan Rd. Bexh—1J 97
Verona Clo. Uxb—8A 142
Verona Dri. Surb—4J 119
Verona Rd. E7—3E 62
Veronica Clo. Romf—7G 35
Veronica Rd. SW17—8F 90
Veronique Gdns. Ilf—3A 48
Verran Rd. SW12—6F 90
Versailles Rd. SE19—4E 108
Verulam Av. E17—5K 45
Verulam Av. Purl—4G 137
Verulam Pas. Wat—4F 8
Verulam Rd. Gnfd—7L 53
Verulam St. WC1—8L 59
Verwood Rd. Harr—9A 22
Vesey Path. E14—9M 61
Vespan Rd. W12—3E 72
Vesta Rd. SE4—1J 93
Vestris Rd. SE23—8H 93
Vestry M. SE5—9C 76
Vestry Rd. E17—2M 45
Vestry Rd. SE5—9C 76
Vestry St. N1—6B 60
Vevey St. SE6—8K 93
Veysey Gdns. Dag—8L 49
Viaduct Bldgs. EC1—8L 59
Viaduct Pl. E2—6F 60
Viaduct St. E2—6F 60
Viaduct, The. E18—9F 30
Vian Av. Enf—8E 6
Vian St. SE13—2M 93
Vibart Gdns. SW2—6K 91
Vicarage Av. SE3—8E 78
Vicarage Clo. Eri—7A 82
Vicarage Clo. N'holt—3K 53
Vicarage Clo. Ruis—5B 36
Vicarage Ct. W8—3M 73
Vicarage Ct. Felt—6A 84
Vicarage Ct. Ilf—1M 63
Vicarage Cres. SW11—9B 74
Vicarage Dri. SW14—4B 88
Vicarage Dri. Bark—3A 64
Vicarage Farm Rd. Houn
 —1J 85
Vicarage Fields. W on T
 —1G 117
Vicarage Gdns. W8—2L 73
Vicarage Gdns. Mitc—7C 106
Vicarage Ga. W8—2M 73
Vicarage Gro. SE5—9B 76
Vicarage La. E6—6K 63
Vicarage La. E15—3C 62
Vicarage La. Chig—2A 32
Vicarage La. Eps—1E 134
Vicarage La. Ilf—6B 48
Vicarage Pk. SE18—6A 80
Vicarage Path. N8—5H 43

Vicarage Rd. E10—5L 45
Vicarage Rd. E15—3D 62
Vicarage Rd. N17—8E 28
Vicarage Rd. NW4—4E 40
Vicarage Rd. SE18—6A 80
Vicarage Rd. SW14—4B 88
Vicarage Rd. Bex—7M 97
Vicarage Rd. Croy—5L 123
Vicarage Rd. Dag—3M 65
Vicarage Rd. Horn—6E 50
Vicarage Rd. King—6H 103
Vicarage Rd. King—5G 103
 (Hampton Wick)
Vicarage Rd. Sun—2D 100
Vicarage Rd. Sutt—5M 121
Vicarage Rd. Tedd—2E 102
Vicarage Rd. Twic—8C 86
Vicarage Rd. Twic—5A 86
 (Whitton)
Vicarage Rd. Wat—8E 8
Vicarage Rd. Wfd G—7J 31
Vicarage Wlk. SW11—9B 74
Vicarage Way. Harr—5L 37
Vicar's Clo. E9—4G 61
Vicars Clo. E15—4E 62
Vicars Clo. Enf—4C 16
Vicar's Hill. SE13—3M 93
Vicars Moor La. N21—9M 15
Vicars Oak Rd. SE19—3C 108
Vicar's Rd. NW5—1E 58
Vicars Wlk. Dag—8F 48
Viceroy Ct. Croy—3B 124
Viceroy Rd. SW8—9J 75
Vickers Rd. Eri—6B 82
Victor App. Horn—6H 51
Victor Clo. Horn—6H 51
Victor Gdns. Horn—6H 51
Victor Gro. Wemb—3J 55
Victoria Av. E6—4H 63
Victoria Av. EC2—8C 60
Victoria Av. N3—8K 25
Victoria Av. Barn—6B 14
Victoria Av. E Mol—7M 101
Victoria Av. Houn—4L 85
Victoria Av. Romf—6M 33
Victoria Av. S Croy—2A 138
Victoria Av. Surb—1H 119
Victoria Av. Uxb—2F 142
Victoria Av. Wall—5E 122
Victoria Av. Wemb—2M 55
Victoria Clo. Barn—6B 14
Victoria Clo. E Mol—7L 101
Victoria Clo. Hay—9B 52
Victoria Clo. Wey—5B 116
Victoria Cotts. Rich—9K 71
Victoria Ct. Wemb—2L 55
Victoria Cres. N15—3C 44
Victoria Cres. SE19—3C 108
Victoria Cres. SW19—4K 105
Victoria Dock Rd. E16—9C 62
Victoria Dri. SW19—6H 89
Victoria Embkmt. SW1, WC2 &
 EC4—3J 75
Victoria Gdns. W11—2L 73
Victoria Gdns. Houn—9J 69
Victoria Gdns. West—7G 141
Victoria Gro. N12—5B 26
Victoria Gro. W8—4A 74
Victoria Hill Rd. Swan—5E 114
Victoria La. Barn—6K 13
Victoria La. Hay—6A 68
Victoria M. NW6—4L 57
Victoria M. SW4—3F 90
Victorian Gro. N16—8C 44
Victorian Rd. N16—8D 44
Victoria Pk. Rd. E9—4G 61
Victoria Pk. Sq. E2—6G 61
Victoria Pas. Wat—6F 8
Victoria Pl. Eps—4C 134
Victoria Pl. Rich—4H 87
Victoria Rise. SW4—2F 90
Victoria Rd. E4—1C 30
Victoria Rd. E11—9C 46
Victoria Rd. E13—5E 62
Victoria Rd. E17—9A 30
Victoria Rd. E18—1F 46
Victoria Rd. N4—5K 43
Victoria Rd. N15—2E 44
Victoria Rd.—4D 28
 N18 1-55
 N9 remainder
Victoria Rd. N22—8G 27
Victoria Rd. NW4—2G 41
Victoria Rd. NW6—5K 57
Victoria Rd. NW7—5D 24
Victoria Rd. SW14—2B 88
Victoria Rd. W3—8B 56
Victoria Rd. W5—8F 54
Victoria Rd. W8—4A 74
Victoria Rd. Bark—2M 63
Victoria Rd. Barn—6B 14
Victoria Rd. Bexh—3L 97

Victoria Rd. Brom—9H 111
Victoria Rd. Buck H—2H 31
Victoria Rd. Bush, Wat—1M 21
Victoria Rd. Chst—2L 111
Victoria Rd. Coul—7H 137
Victoria Rd. Dag—1M 65
Victoria Rd. Dart—4H 99
Victoria Rd. Eri—7C 82
Victoria Rd. Felt—7F 84
Victoria Rd. King—6K 103
Victoria Rd. Mitc—4C 106
Victoria Rd. Romf—4D 50
Victoria Rd. Ruis—6E 36
Victoria Rd. Sidc—9D 96
Victoria Rd. S'hall—4K 69
Victoria Rd. Surb—1H 119
Victoria Rd. Sutt—7B 122
Victoria Rd. Tedd—3D 102
Victoria Rd. Twic—6F 86
Victoria Rd. Uxb—3A 142
Victoria Rd. Wal A—7J 7
Victoria Rd. Wat—2F 8
Victoria Rd. Wey—5B 116
Victoria Scott Ct. Dart—2D 98
Victoria Sq. SW1—4F 74
Victoria St. E15—3C 62
Victoria St. SW1—4G 75
Victoria St. Belv—6K 81
Victoria Ter. N4—6L 43
Victoria Ter. Harr—6C 38
Victoria Vs. Rich—3K 87
Victoria Way. SE7—6F 78
Victoria Way. Wey—5B 116
Victor Rd. NW10—6F 56
Victor Rd. SE20—4H 109
Victor Rd. Harr—1A 38
Victor Rd. Tedd—1C 102
Victors Dri. Hmptn—3J 101
Victor Wlk. Horn—6H 51
Victory Av. Mord—9A 106
Victory Pl. SE17—5B 76
Victory Pl. SE19—4C 108
Victory Rd. SW19—4A 106
Victory Rd. Rain—5E 66
Victory Sq. SE5—7B 76
Victory Wlk. SE8—9L 77
Victory Way. SE16—3J 77
Victory Way. Houn—6G 69
Victory Way. Romf—9M 33
View Clo. N6—5D 42
View Clo. Chig—5B 32
View Clo. Harr—2B 38
View Clo. West—8G 141
Viewfield Rd. SW18—5K 89
Viewfield Rd. Sidc—7G 97
Viewland Rd. SE18—6D 80
View Rd. N6—5D 42
View, The. SE2—6J 81
Viga Rd. N21—8L 15
Vigilant Clo. SE26—1E 108
Vignoles Rd. Romf—5L 49
Vigo St. W1—1G 75
Viking Rd. S'hall—1J 69
Villacourt Rd. SE18—8E 80
Village Clo. E4—5A 30
Village Grn. Av. West—9J 141
Village Grn. Rd. Dart—3E 98
Village Grn. Way. West—9J 141
Village Rd. N3—9J 25
Village Rd. Enf—9B 16
Village Row. Sutt—9L 121
Village, The. SE7—7H 79
Village Way. NW10—9B 40
Village Way. SE21—5B 92
Village Way. Ashf—9D 144
Village Way. Beck—6L 109
Village Way. Pinn—5J 37
Village Way. S Croy—5E 138
Village Way E. Harr—5L 37
Villa Rd. SW9—2L 91
Villas Rd. SE18—5A 80
 (in two parts)
Villa St. SE17—6B 76
Villa Wlk. SE17—6B 76
Villiers Av. Surb—9K 103
Villiers Av. Twic—7K 85
Villiers Clo. E10—7L 45
Villiers Clo. Surb—8K 103
Villiers Path. Surb—9J 103
Villiers Rd. NW2—2E 56
Villiers Rd. Beck—6H 109
Villiers Rd. Iswth—1C 86
Villiers Rd. King—8K 103
Villiers Rd. S'hall—2K 69
Villiers Rd. Wat—8J 9
Villiers St. WC2—2J 75
Villier St. Uxb—5B 142
Vincam Clo. Twic—6L 85
Vincent Av. Cars—3B 136
Vincent Av. Surb—4A 120
Vincent Clo. SE16—3J 77
Vincent Clo. Barn—5M 13

Vincent Clo. Brom—8F 110
Vincent Clo. Esh—5M 117
Vincent Clo. Ilf—6A 32
Vincent Clo. Sidc—7C 96
Vincent Clo. Wal X—1E 6
Vincent Clo. W Dray—7L 143
Vincent Dri. Shep—7C 100
Vincent Gdns. NW2—8D 40
Vincent Rd. E4—6B 30
Vincent Rd. N15—2A 44
Vincent Rd. N22—9L 27
Vincent Rd. SE18—5M 79
Vincent Rd. W3—4A 72
Vincent Rd. Coul—8G 137
Vincent Rd. Croy—2C 124
Vincent Rd. Dag—3J 65
Vincent Rd. Houn—2H 85
Vincent Rd. Iswth—9B 70
Vincent Rd. King—7L 103
Vincent Rd. Rain—7G 67
Vincent Rd. Wemb—3K 55
Vincent Row. Hmptn—3A 102
Vincent Sq. SW1—5H 75
Vincent Sq. West—5G 141
Vincent St. E16—8D 62
Vincent St. SW1—5H 75
Vincent Ter. N1—5M 59
Vince St. EC1—6B 60
Vine Clo. Surb—1K 119
Vine Clo. Sutt—5A 122
Vine Clo. W Dray—5L 143
Vine Ct. E1—8E 60
Vine Ct. Harr—4J 39
Vinegar All. E17—2M 45
Vine Gdns. Ilf—1A 64
Vine Gro. Uxb—3E 142
Vine Hill. EC1—7L 59
Vine La. SE1—2C 76
Vine La. Uxb—4D 142
Vine Pl. Houn—3M 85
Vineries Bank. NW7—5F 24
Vineries Clo. Dag—2K 65
Vineries Clo. W Dray—7L 143
Vineries, The. N14—8G 15
Vineries, The. SE6—7L 93
Vineries, The. Enf—5C 16
Vine Rd. E15—3D 62
Vine Rd. SW13—2D 88
Vine Rd. E Mol—8A 102
Vine Rd. Orp—8D 128
Vines Av. N3—8M 25
Vine St. E3—1D 76
 (in two parts)
Vine St. W1—1G 75
Vine St. Romf—2A 50
Vine St. Uxb—4B 142
Vine St. Bri. EC1—7L 59
Vineyard Av. NW7—7J 25
Vineyard Clo. SE6—7L 93
Vineyard Hill Rd. SW19
 —1L 105
Vineyard Pas. Rich—4J 87
Vineyard Path. SW14—2B 88
Vineyard Rd. Felt—9E 84
Vineyard Row. King—5G 103
Vineyard, The. Rich—4J 87
Vineyard Wlk. EC1—7L 59
Viney Bank. Croy—1K 139
Viney Rd. SE13—2M 93
Vining St. SW9—3L 91
Vinson Clo. Orp—3E 128
Vintners Pl. EC4—1A 76
Viola Av. SE2—5F 80
Viola Av. Felt—5G 85
Viola Av. Stai—7C 144
Viola Sq. W12—1D 72
Violet Av. Enf—2B 16
Violet Av. Uxb—8D 142
Violet Gdns. Croy—7M 123
Violet Hill. NW8—5A 58
Violet La. Croy—7M 123
Violet Rd. E3—7M 61
Violet Rd. E17—4L 45
Violet Rd. E18—9F 30
Violet St. E2—7F 60
Virgil Pl. W1—8D 58
Virgil St. SE1—4K 75
Virginia Gdns. Ilf—9B 32
Virginia Rd. E2—6D 60
Virginia Rd. T Hth—5M 107
Virginia St. E1—1E 76
Virginia Wlk. SW2—5K 91
Viscount Gro. N'holt—6H 53
Viscount Rd. Stai—7C 144
Viscount St. EC1—7A 60
Viscount Way. Houn—3C 84
Vista Av. Enf—4H 17
Vista Dri. Ilf—3H 47
Vista, The. SE9—5H 95
Vista, The. Sidc—2D 112
Vista Way. Harr—4J 39
Viveash Clo. Hay—4D 68
Vivian Av. NW4—3F 40

Vivian Av. Wemb—1L 55
Vivian Clo. Wat—1E 20
Vivian Gdns. Wat—1E 20
Vivian Gdns. Wemb—1L 55
Vivian Rd. E3—5J 61
Vivian Sq. SE15—2F 92
Vivian Way. N2—3B 42
Vivien Clo. Chess—9J 119
Vivienne Clo. Twic—5H 87
Voce Rd. SE18—8B 80
Voewood Clo. N Mald—1D 120
Voltaire Rd. SW4—2H 91
Voltaire Way. Hay—1C 68
Voluntary Pl. E11—4E 46
Vorley Rd. N19—7G 43
Voss Ct. SW16—3J 107
Voss St. E2—6E 60
Vulcan Clo. Wall—9K 123
Vulcan Ga. Enf—4L 15
Vulcan Rd. SE4—1K 93
Vulcan Ter. SE4—1K 93
Vulcan Way. N7—2K 59
Vulcan Way. Croy—2C 140
Vyner Rd. W3—1B 72
Vyner St. E2—4F 60
Vyner's Way. Uxb—1E 142
Vyne, The. Bexh—2M 97
Vyse Clo. Barn—6G 13

Wadding St. SE17—5B 76
Waddington Rd. E15—1B 62
Waddington St. E15—2B 62
Waddington Way. SE19
 —4A 108
Waddon Clo. Croy—5L 123
Waddon Ct. Rd. Croy—5L 123
Waddon Marsh Way. Croy
 —3K 123
Waddon New Rd. Croy
 —5M 123
Waddon Pk. Av. Croy—6L 123
Waddon Rd. Croy—5L 123
Waddon Way. Croy—8L 123
Wade Av. Orp—2H 129
Wade Rd. E16—9G 63
Wades Gro. N21—9L 15
Wades Hill. N21—8L 15
Wades La. Tedd—2E 102
Wadeson St. E2—5F 60
Wade's Pl. E14—1M 77
Wadeville Av. Romf—5K 49
Wadeville Clo. Belv—6L 81
Wadham Av. E17—7M 29
Wadham Clo. Shep—2A 116
Wadham Gdns. NW3—3C 58
Wadham Gdns. Gnfd—2B 54
Wadham Rd. E17—8M 29
Wadham Rd. SW15—9J 75
Wadham Rd. Abb L, Wat—4D 4
Wadhurst Clo. SE20—6F 108
Wadhurst Rd. SW8—9G 75
Wadhurst Rd. W4—8A 72
Wadley Rd. E11—5C 46
Wadsworth Clo. Enf—7H 17
Wadsworth Clo. Gnfd—5G 55
Wadsworth Rd. Gnfd—5F 54
Wager St. E3—7K 61
Waggon La. N17—6E 28
Waggon Rd. Barn—1A 14
Waghorn Rd. E13—4G 63
Waghorn Rd. Harr—1H 39
Waghorn St. SE15—2F 92
Wagner St. SE15—8G 77
Wagon Rd. Barn—1M 13
Wagtail Gdns. S Croy—2J 139
Waid Clo. Dart—5K 99
Waights Ct. King—5J 103
Wainfleet Av. Romf—9A 34
Wainford Clo. SW19—7H 89
Wainwright Gro. Iswth—3B 86
Waite Davies Rd. SE12—6D 94
Waite St. SE15—7D 76
Wakefield Gdns. SE19—4C 108
Wakefield Gdns. Ilf—4J 47
Wakefield M. WC1—6J 59
Wakefield Rd. N11—5H 27
Wakefield Rd. N15—3D 44
Wakefield Rd. Rich—4H 87
Wakefield St. E6—4H 63
Wakefield St. N18—5E 28
Wakefield St. WC1—7J 59
Wakefields Wlk. Wal X—4E 6
Wakehams Hill. Pinn—1K 37
Wakeham St. N1—2B 60
Wakehurst Rd. SW11—4C 90
Wakeling Rd. W7—8D 54
Wakeling St. E14—9J 61
Wakelin Rd. E15—5C 62
Wakeman Rd. NW10—6G 57
Wakemans Hill Av. NW9
 —3B 40
Wakerfield Clo. Horn—3K 51

Wakering Rd. Bark—2A 64
Wakerley Clo. E6—9K 63
Wake Rd. Lou—2G 19
Wakley St. EC1—6M 59
Walberswick St. SW8—8J 75
Walbrook. EC4—1B 76
Walburgh St. E1—9F 60
Walburton Rd. Purl—5G 137
Walcorde Av. SE17—5A 76
Walcot Rd. Enf—4K 17
Walcot Sq. SE11—5L 75
Walcott St. SW1—5G 75
Waldeck Gro. SE27—9M 91
Waldeck Rd. N15—2M 43
Waldeck Rd. SW14—2A 88
Waldeck Rd. W4—7L 71
Waldeck Rd. W13—9F 54
Waldeck Rd. Dart—5L 99
Waldegrave Av. Tedd—2D 102
Waldegrave Gdns. Twic—9D 86
Waldegrave Gdns. Upm
—6M 51
Waldegrave Pk. Twic—1D 102
Waldegrave Rd. N8—1L 43
Waldegrave Rd. SE19—4D 108
Waldegrave Rd. W5—1K 71
Waldegrave Rd. Brom—8J 111
Waldegrave Rd. Dag—7G 49
Waldegrave Rd. Twic & Tedd
—1D 102
Waldegrove. Croy—6D 124
Waldemar Av. SW6—9J 73
Waldemar Av. W13—2G 71
Waldemar Rd. SW19—2L 105
Walden Av. N13—4A 28
Walden Av. Chst—1K 111
Walden Av. Rain—5B 66
Walden Clo. Belv—6K 81
Walden Gdns. T Hth—7K 107
Waldenhurst Rd. Orp—2H 129
Walden Rd. N17—8B 28
Walden Rd. Horn—4H 51
Waldens Clo. Orp—2H 129
Waldenshaw Rd. SE23—7G 93
Waldens Rd. Orp—2J 129
Walden St. E1—9F 60
Walden Way. NW7—6H 25
Walden Way. Horn—4H 51
Walden Way. Ilf—7C 32
Waldo Pl. Mitc—4C 106
Waldorf Clo. S Croy—1M 137
Waldo Rd. NW10—6E 56
Waldo Rd. Brom—7H 111
Waldram Cres. SE23—7G 93
Waldram Pk. Rd. SE23—7H 93
Waldram Pl. SE23—7G 93
Waldron Gdns. Brom—7B 110
Waldronhyrst. Croy—6M 123
Waldron M. SW3—7B 74
Waldron Rd. SW18—9A 90
Waldron Rd. Harr—6C 38
Waldron's Path. S Croy
—6A 124
Waldrons, The. Croy—6M 123
Waldrons Yd. Harr—7B 38
Waleran Clo. Stan—5D 22
Walerand Rd. SE13—1A 94
Wales Av. Cars—7C 122
Wales Farm Rd. W3—8B 56
Waley St. E1—8J 61
Walfield Av. N20—9M 13
Walford Rd. N16—9C 44
Walford Rd. Uxb—5A 142
Walfrey Gdns. Dag—3J 65
Walham Gro. SW6—8L 73
Walham Rise. SW19—3J 105
Walham Yd. SW6—8L 73
Walkden Rd. Chst—2L 111
Walker Clo. SE18—5A 80
Walker Clo. Dart—2D 98
Walker Clo. Hmptn—3K 101
Walkerscroft Mead. SE21
—7A 92
Walkers Pl. SW15—3J 89
Walkford Way. SE15—8D 76
Walkley Rd. Dart—4F 98
Walk, The. Horn—7K 51
Walk, The. Sun—4D 100
Wallace Clo. SE28—1H 81
Wallace Clo. Shep—8B 100
Wallace Cres. Cars—7D 122
Wallace Fields. Eps—5E 134
Wallace Rd. N1—2A 60
Wallbutton Rd. SE4—1J 93
Wall Clo. Uxb—5C 142
Wallcote Av. NW2—6H 41
Wall End Rd. E6—3L 63
Wallenger Av. Romf—1F 50
Waller Dri. N'wd—9E 20
Waller Rd. SE14—9H 77
Wallers Clo. Wfd G—6K 31

Waller's Hoppet. Lou—4K 19
Wallflower St. W12—1D 72
Wallgrave Rd. SW5—5M 73
Wallhouse Rd. Eri—8F 82
Wallingford Av. W10—9H 57
Wallingford Rd. Uxb—5A 142
Wallington Clo. Ruis—4A 36
Wallington Rd. Ilf—5D 48
Wallington Sq. Wall—8G 123
Wallis Clo. SW11—2B 90
Wallis Clo. Dart—9D 98
Wallis Rd. E9—2K 61
Wallis Rd. S'hall—9M 53
Wallorton Gdns. SW14—3B 88
Wall St. N1—2B 60
Wallwood Rd. E11—5B 46
Wallwood St. E14—8K 61
Walmar Clo. Barn—2C 14
Walmer Clo. Romf—9M 33
Walmer Gdns. W13—3E 70
Walmer Rd. W11—1J 73
Walmer St. W1—8D 58
Walmer Ter. SE18—5A 80
Walmgate Rd. Gnfd—4F 54
Walmington Fold. N12—6L 25
Walm La. NW2—2G 57
Walney Wlk. N1—2A 60
Walnut Av. W Dray—4L 143
Walnut Clo. Cars—7D 122
Walnut Clo. Eps—7D 134
Walnut Clo. Hay—1C 68
Walnut Clo. Ilf—2A 48
Walnut Ct. W5—3J 71
Walnut Grn. Bush, Wat—4K 9
Walnut Gro. Enf—7B 16
Walnut M. Sutt—9A 122
Walnuts Rd. Orp—3F 128
Walnuts, The. Orp—3E 128
Walnut Tree Av. Dart—8J 99
Walnut Tree Av. Mitc—7C 106
Walnut Tree Clo. SW13—9D 72
Walnut Tree Clo. Bans—4J 135
Walnut Tree Clo. Chst—5B 112
Walnut Tree Clo. Shep—7A 100
Walnut Tree Cotts. SW19
—2J 105
Walnut Tree Rd. SE10—6C 78
Walnut Tree Rd. Bren—7J 71
Walnut Tree Rd. Dag—7J 49
Walnut Tree Rd. Eri—6C 82
Walnut Tree Rd. Houn—7K 69
Walnut Tree Rd. Shep—6A 100
Walnut Tree Wlk. SE11—5L 75
Walnut Way. Buck H—3H 31
Walnut Way. Ruis—2G 53
Walnut Way. Swan—6B 114
Walpole Av. Rich—1K 87
Walpole Clo. W13—3G 71
Walpole Clo. Pinn—6L 21
Walpole Cres. Tedd—2D 102
Walpole Gdns. W4—6A 72
Walpole Gdns. Twic—8C 86
Walpole Pl. Tedd—2D 102
Walpole Rd. E6—3G 63
Walpole Rd. E17—2K 45
Walpole Rd. E18—8D 30
Walpole Rd. N17—1A 44
(in two parts)
Walpole Rd. SW19—3B 106
Walpole Rd. Brom—9H 111
Walpole Rd. Croy—4B 124
Walpole Rd. Surb—1J 119
Walpole Rd. Tedd—2D 102
Walpole Rd. Twic—8C 86
Walpole St. SW3—6D 74
Walpole Way. Barn—7G 13
Walrond Av. Wemb—1J 55
Walsham Clo. N16—6E 44
Walsham Clo. SE28—1H 81
Walsham Rd. SE14—1H 93
Walsham Rd. Felt—6F 84
Walsh Cres. Croy—4C 140
Walshford Way. Borwd—2L 11
Walsingham Gdns. Eps
—6C 120
Walsingham Pk. Chst—6B 112
Walsingham Rd. E5—8E 44
Walsingham Rd. W13—2E 70
Walsingham Rd. Croy—2A 140
Walsingham Rd. Enf—7B 16
Walsingham Rd. Mitc—9D 106
Walsingham Rd. Orp—5F 112
Walsingham Wlk. Belv—7L 81
Walters Mead. Asht—9J 133
Walters Rd. SE25—8C 108
Walters Rd. Enf—6G 17
Walter St. E2—6H 61
Walter St. King—5J 103
Walters Yd. Brom—6E 110
Walter Ter. E1—9H 61
Walterton Rd. W9—7K 57
Walter Wlk. Edgw—6A 24

Waltham Av. NW9—4L 39
Waltham Av. Hay—4A 68
Waltham Clo. Dart—5E 98
Waltham Clo. Orp—3H 129
Waltham Dri. Edgw—9L 23
Waltham Gdns. Enf—9C 6
Waltham Pk. Way. E17—8L 29
Waltham Rd. Cars—2B 122
Waltham Rd. S'hall—4J 69
Waltham Rd. Wfd G—6J 31
Walthamstow Av. E4—6J 29
Waltham Way. E4—3K 29
Waltheof Av. N17—8B 28
Waltheof Gdns. N17—8B 28
Walton Av. Harr—1K 53
Walton Av. N Mald—8D 104
Walton Av. Sutt—5K 121
Walton Bri. Shep & W on T
—2C 116
Walton Bri. Rd. Shep—2C 116
Walton Clo. E5—8H 45
Walton Clo. NW2—7F 40
Walton Clo. SW8—8J 75
Walton Clo. Harr—2B 38
Walton Dri. Harr—2B 38
Walton Gdns. W3—8M 55
Walton Gdns. Felt—1D 100
Walton Gdns. Wemb—7J 39
Walton Grn. Croy—9A 126
Walton La. Shep—2B 116
Walton La. Wey—4A 116
Walton Pk. W on T—4H 117
Walton Pk. La. W on T—4H 117
Walton Pl. SW3—4D 74
Walton Rd. E12—9L 47
(in two parts)
Walton Rd. E13—5G 63
Walton Rd. N15—2D 44
Walton Rd. Bush, Wat—6H 9
Walton Rd. Eps—9D 134
(Epsom Downs)
Walton Rd. Harr—2B 38
Walton Rd. Romf—8K 33
Walton Rd. Sidc—9F 96
Walton Rd. W on T & E Mol
—9G 101
Walton St. SW3—5C 74
Walton St. Enf—3B 16
Walton Way. W3—8M 55
Walton Way. Mitc—8G 107
Walverns Clo. Wat—8G 9
Walworth Pl. SE17—6A 76
Walworth Rd.—5A 76
SE1 2-96
SE17 remainder
Walwyn Av. Brom—7H 111
Wanborough Dri. SW15—7F 88
Wandle Bank. SW19—4B 106
Wandle Bank. Croy—5J 123
Wandle Ct. Eps—6A 120
Wandle Ct. Gdns. Croy—5J 123
Wandle Pk. Trading Est. Croy
—3L 123
Wandle Rd. SW17—8C 90
Wandle Rd. Croy—5A 124
Wandle Rd. Croy—5J 123
(Beddington)
Wandle Rd. Mord—8A 106
Wandle Rd. Wall—4F 122
Wandle Side. Croy—5K 123
Wandle Side. Wall—5F 122
Wandle Way. SW18—7M 89
Wandle Way. Mitc—9D 106
Wandon Rd. SW6—8M 73
Wandsworth Bri. SW6 & SW18
—2M 89
Wandsworth Bri. Rd. SW6
—9M 73
Wandsworth Comn. N. Side.
SW18—4B 90
Wandsworth Comn. W. Side.
SW18—4A 90
Wandsworth High St. SW18
—4L 89
Wandsworth Plain. SW18
—4M 89
Wandsworth Rd. SW8—2F 90
Wangey Rd. Romf—5H 49
Wanless Rd. SE24—2A 92
Wanley Rd. SE5—3B 92
Wanlip Rd. E13—7F 62
Wannock Gdns. Ilf—7M 31
Wansbeck Rd. E9—3K 61
Wansbury Way. Swan—9E 114
Wansdown Pl. SW6—8M 73
Wansey St. SE17—5A 76
Wansford Pk. Borwd—6J 12
Wansford Rd. Wfd G—8G 31
Wanstead Clo. Brom—6G 111
Wanstead Gdns. Ilf—4H 47
Wanstead La. Ilf—4J 47
Wanstead Pk. Av. E12—7H 47

Wanstead Pk. Rd. Ilf—5J 47
Wanstead Pl. E11—4E 46
Wanstead Rd. Brom—6G 111
Wansunt Rd. Bex—7A 98
Wantage Rd. SE12—4D 94
Wantz La. Rain—7F 66
Wantz Rd. Dag—9M 49
Wapping Dock St. E1—2F 76
Wapping High St. E1—2E 76
Wapping La. E1—1F 76
Wapping Pier Head. E1—2F 76
Wapping Wall. E1—2G 77
Warbank Clo. Croy—2C 140
Warbank Cres. Croy—2C 140
Warbank La. King—4D 104
Warbeck Rd. W12—3F 72
Warberry Rd. N22—8K 27
Warboys App. King—3M 103
Warboys Cres. E4—5A 30
Warboys Rd. King—3M 103
Warburton Clo. Harr—6B 22
Warburton Rd. E8—4F 60
Warburton Rd. Twic—7M 85
Warburton Ter. E17—9M 29
Wardale Clo. SE16—4F 76
Ward Clo. Eri—7B 82
Wardell Clo. NW7—7C 24
Wardell Field. NW9—8C 24
Warden Av. Harr—6K 37
Warden Av. Romf—5A 34
Warden Rd. NW5—2E 58
Wardens Gro. SE1—2A 76
Ward La. Warl—9H 139
Wardle St. E9—1H 61
Wardley St. SW18—6M 89
Wardo Av. SW6—9J 73
Wardour St. W1—9G 59
Ward Rd. E15—4B 62
Ward Rd. N19—8G 43
Ward Rd. SW19—5A 106
Wards La. Borwd—4D 10
Wards Rd. Ilf—5B 48
Ware Ct. Sutt—6K 121
Wareham Clo. Houn—3M 85
Waremead Rd. Ilf—3M 47
Warenford Way. Borwd—3L 11
Warfield Rd. NW10—6H 57
Warfield Rd. Felt—6C 84
Warfield Rd. Hmptn—5M 101
Wargrave Av. N15—4D 44
Wargrave Rd. Harr—8A 38
Warham Rd. N4—3L 43
Warham Rd. Harr—9D 22
Warham Rd. Croy & S Croy
—7M 123
Warham St. SE5—8M 75
(in two parts)
Waring Clo. Orp—8D 128
Waring Dri. Orp—8D 128
Waring Rd. Sidc—3G 113
Waring St. SE27—1A 108
Warkworth Gdns. Iswth—8E 70
Warkworth Rd. N17—7B 28
Warland Rd. SE18—8B 80
Warley Av. Dag—5K 49
Warley Av. Hay—9E 52
Warley Clo. E10—6K 45
Warley Rd. N9—2G 29
Warley Rd. Hay—9E 52
Warley Rd. Ilf—8L 31
Warley Rd. Wfd G—7F 30
Warley St. E2—6H 61
Warlingham Rd. T Hth—8M 107
Warlock Rd. W9—7K 57
Warlters Clo. N7—9J 43
Warlters Rd. N7—9J 43
Warltersville Rd. N19—5J 43
Warmington Rd. SE24—5A 92
Warminster Gdns. SE25
—6E 108
Warminster Rd. SE25—7E 108
Warminster Sq. SE25—6E 108
Warminster Way. Mitc—5F 106
Warndon St. SE16—5H 77
Warneford Pl. Wat—6J 9
Warneford Rd. Harr—1H 39
Warneford St. E9—4F 60
Warner Av. Sutt—4J 121
Warner Clo. E15—1C 62
Warner Clo. NW9—5D 40
Warner Clo. Hay—8B 68
Warner Clo. Wfd G—5E 30
Warner Pde. Hay—8B 68
Warner Pl. E2—5E 60
Warner Rd. E17—2J 45
Warner Rd. N8—2H 43
Warner Rd. SE5—9A 76
Warner Rd. Brom—4D 110
Warners La. Rich & King
—1H 103
Warners Path. Wfd G—5E 30
Warner St. EC1—7L 59
Warnford Rd. Orp—7D 128

Warnham Ct. Rd. Cars—9D 122
Warnham Rd. N12—5C 26
Warple Way. SW18—3M 89
Warple Way. W3—3C 72
Warren Av. E10—8A 46
Warren Av. Brom—4C 110
Warren Av. Orp—7D 128
Warren Av. Rich—3M 87
Warren Av. S Croy—9H 125
Warren Av. Sutt—2K 135
Warren Clo. N9—9H 17
Warren Clo. SE21—6A 92
Warren Clo. Bexh—4L 97
Warren Clo. Esh—6M 117
Warren Clo. Wemb—7H 39
Warren Ct. Beck—4L 109
Warren Ct. Chig—4B 32
Warren Cres. N9—9D 16
Warren Cutting. King—4B 104
Warrender Rd. N19—9G 43
Warrender Way. Ruis—5E 36
Warren Dri. Gnfd—7M 53
Warren Dri. Horn—9E 50
Warren Dri. Orp—7F 128
Warren Dri. Ruis—5H 37
Warren Dri. N. Surb—3M 119
Warren Dri. S. Surb—3A 120
Warren Dri., The. E11—5G 47
Warreners La. Wey—8A 116
Warrenfield Clo. Wal X—4A 6
Warren Footpath. Twic—7G 87
Warren Gdns. E15—1B 62
Warren Gdns. Orp—7E 128
Warren Gro. Borwd—6B 12
Warren Hill. Eps—8B 134
Warren Hill. Lou—7G 19
Warren La. SE18—4M 79
Warren La. Lea—3A 132
Warren La. Stan—2E 22
Warren Mead. Bans—7G 135
Warren M. W1—7G 59
Warren Pk. King—3A 104
Warren Pk. Warl—9H 139
Warren Pk. Rd. Sutt—8C 122
Warren Pond Rd. E4—1D 30
Warren Rise. N Mald—5B 104
Warren Rd. E4—2A 30
Warren Rd. E10—8A 46
Warren Rd. E11—4G 47
Warren Rd. NW2—7D 40
Warren Rd. SW19—3C 106
Warren Rd. Ashf—4C 100
Warren Rd. Bans—6G 135
Warren Rd. Bexh—4L 97
Warren Rd. Brom—4E 126
Warren Rd. Bush, Wat—1A 22
Warren Rd. Croy—3D 124
Warren Rd. Dart—9J 99
Warren Rd. Ilf—3B 48
Warren Rd. King—3A 104
Warren Rd. Orp—7D 128
Warren Rd. Purl—4M 137
Warren Rd. Sidc—9G 97
Warren Rd. Twic—5A 86
Warren Rd. Uxb—1C 142
Warrens Shawe La. Edgw
—2M 23
Warren St. W1—7G 59
Warren Ter. Romf—2H 49
Warren, The. E12—9J 47
Warren, The. Cars—2C 136
Warren, The. Hay—9E 52
Warren, The. Houn—8K 69
Warren, The. Wor Pk—5B 120
Warren Wlk. SE7—7G 79
Warren Way. NW7—6J 25
Warren Way. Wey—8A 116
Warren Wood Clo. Brom
—4D 126
Warriner Av. Horn—7H 51
Warriner Gdns. SW11—9D 74
Warrington Cres. W9—7A 58
Warrington Gdns. W9—7A 58
Warrington Gdns. Horn—4G 51
Warrington Pl. E14—2A 78
Warrington Rd. Croy—5M 123
Warrington Rd. Dag—7H 49
Warrington Rd. Harr—3C 38
Warrington Rd. Rich—4H 87
Warrington Sq. Dag—7H 49
Warrior Sq. E12—9L 47
Warsaw Clo. Ruis—2F 52
Warspite Rd. SE18—4J 79
Warton Rd. E15—3A 62
Warwick Av.—7M 57
W2 1-5a & 2-16
W9 remainder
Warwick Av. Edgw—3M 23
Warwick Av. Harr—9K 37
Warwick Clo. Barn—7B 14
Warwick Clo. Bush, Wat—9C 10
Warwick Clo. Hmptn—4A 102
Warwick Clo. Orp—-5E 128

Warwick Ct.—Wellington Way

Warwick Ct. WC1—8K 59
Warwick Cres. W2—8A 58
Warwick Cres. Hay—7D 52
Warwick Dene. W5—2J 71
Warwick Dri. SW15—2F 88
Warwick Dri. Wal X—1D 6
Warwick Est. W2—8M 57
Warwick Gdns. N4—3A 44
Warwick Gdns. W14—5K 73
Warwick Gdns. Asht—9G 133
Warwick Gdns. Ilf—6M 47
Warwick Gdns. Romf—1G 51
Warwick Gdns. Th Dit—9D 102
Warwick Gdns. T Hth—8L 107
Warwick Gro. E5—6F 44
Warwick Gro. Surb—2K 119
Warwick Ho. St. SW1—2H 75
Warwick La. EC4—9M 59
Warwick La. Rain & Upm —5K 67
Warwick Pl. W5—3H 71
Warwick Pl. W9—8A 58
Warwick Pl. Uxb—3A 142
Warwick Pl. N. SW1—5G 75
Warwick Rd. E4—5L 29
Warwick Rd. E11—3F 46
Warwick Rd. E12—1J 63
Warwick Rd. E15—2D 62
Warwick Rd. E17—8K 29
Warwick Rd. N11—6H 27
Warwick Rd. N18—4C 28
Warwick Rd. SE20—7F 108
Warwick Rd.—5K 73
SW5 1-133 & 2-76
W14 remainder
Warwick Rd. W5—3H 71
Warwick Rd. Barn—6M 13
Warwick Rd. Borwd—5B 12
Warwick Rd. Coul—6G 137
Warwick Rd. Enf—1K 17
Warwick Rd. Houn—2F 84
Warwick Rd. King—5G 103
Warwick Rd. N Mald—7A 104
Warwick Rd. Rain—7G 67
Warwick Rd. Sidc—2F 112
Warwick Rd. S'hall—4K 69
Warwick Rd. Sutt—6A 122
Warwick Rd. Th Dit—9D 102
Warwick Rd. T Hth—7L 107
Warwick Rd. Twic—7C 86
Warwick Rd. Well—2G 97
Warwick Rd. W Dray—2J 143
Warwick Row. SW1—4G 75
Warwickshire Path. SE8 —8K 77
Warwick Sq. EC4—9M 59
Warwick Sq. SW1—6G 75
Warwick Sq. M. SW1—5G 75
Warwick St. W1—1G 75
Warwick Ter. SE18—7B 80
Warwick Way. SW1—6F 74
Warwick Way. Rick—6A 8
Warwick Yd. EC1—7A 60
Washington Av. E12—9J 47
Washington Rd. E6—3G 63
Washington Rd. E18—9D 30
Washington Rd. SW13—8E 72
Washington Rd. King—6L 103
Washington Rd. Wor Pk —4F 120
Washpond La. Warl—9A 140
Wastdale Rd. SE23—7H 93
Watchfield Ct. W4—6A 72
Watcombe Cotts. Rich—7L 71
Watcombe Pl. Croy—8F 108
Watcombe Rd. SE25—9F 108
Waterbank Rd. SE6—1A 110
Waterbeach Dri. NW9—9C 24
Waterbeach Rd. Dag—2G 65
Water Brook La. NW4—3G 41
Waterdale Rd. SE2—7E 80
Waterden Rd. E15—1L 61
Waterer Gdns. Tad—9J 135
Waterer Rise. Wall—8H 123
Waterfall Clo. N14—3G 27
Waterfall Cotts. SW19—3B 106
Waterfall Rd.—4F 26
N11 1-27 & 2-46
N14 remainder
Waterfall Rd. SW19—3B 106
Waterfall Ter. SW17—3C 106
Waterfall Wlk. N14—1F 26
Waterfield Clo. SE28—2F 80
Waterfield Gdns. SE28—2F 80
Waterflow Rd. N19—6G 43
Waterford Rd. SW6—8M 73
Water Gdns. Stan—6F 22
Watergate. EC4—1M 75
Watergate St. SE8—7L 77
Watergate, The. Wat—2H 21
Watergate Wlk. WC2—2J 75
Waterhall Av. E4—4C 30
Waterhead Clo. Eri—8C 82
Waterhouse Clo. E16—8H 63
Waterhouse Clo. NW3—1B 58
Waterhouse Clo. W6—5H 73
Water La. E15—2C 62
Water La. Ilf—8D 48
Water La. K Lan—2A 4
Water La. King—5H 103
Water La. Rich—4H 87
Water La. Sidc—9K 97
Water La. Twic—7E 86
Water La. Wat—6G 9
Waterloo Bri. WC2 & SE1 —1K 75
Waterloo Gdns. E2—5G 61
Waterloo Gdns. Romf—4B 50
Waterloo Pas. NW6—3K 57
Waterloo Pl. SW1—2H 75
Waterloo Pl. Rich—3J 87
Waterloo Rd. E6—3G 63
Waterloo Rd. E7—1D 62
Waterloo Rd. E10—5L 45
Waterloo Rd. NW2—6E 40
Waterloo Rd. SE1—3L 75
Waterloo Rd. Eps—8B 134
Waterloo Rd. Ilf—9A 32
Waterloo Rd. Romf—4C 50
Waterloo Rd. Sutt—7B 122
Waterloo Rd. Uxb—4A 142
Waterloo Ter. N1—3M 59
Waterman Clo. Wat—8F 8
Watermans Clo. King—4J 103
Waterman's Sq. SE20—4G 109
Waterman St. SW15—2H 89
Watermans Wlk. SE16—4J 77
Waterman's Yd. Wat—6G 9
Watermead. Felt—7C 84
Watermead La. Cars—2D 122
Watermead Rd. SE6—1A 110
Watermill Clo. Rich—9G 87
Watermill La. N18—5C 28
Water Mill Way. Felt—8K 85
Water Mill Way. S Dar, Dart —6M 115
Water Rd. Wemb—4K 55
Watersedge. Eps—6A 120
Watersfield Way. Edgw—7H 23
Waters Gdns. Dag—1L 65
Waterside. Beck—5K 109
Waterside. Dart—4C 98
Waterside. Uxb—8A 142
Waterside Clo. SE16—3E 76
Waterside Pl. NW1—4E 58
Waterside Rd. S'hall—4L 69
Waterson St. E2—6D 60
Watersplash La. Hay & Houn —5E 68
(in two parts)
Waters Rd. SE6—9C 94
Waters Rd. King—6M 103
Waters Sq. King—7M 103
Water Tower Clo. Uxb—1C 142
Water Tower Hill. Croy—6B 124
Waterville Rd. N17—8A 28
Waterworks La. E5—7H 45
Waterworks Rd. SW2—5K 91
Waterworks Yd. Croy—5A 124
Watery La. SW20—6K 105
Watery La. Hay—6C 68
Watery La. N'holt—5G 53
Watery La. Sidc—3F 112
Wates Way. Mitc—1D 122
Watford By-Pass. Borwd—9F 10
Watford By-Pass. Edgw—2J 23
Watford Clo. SW11—9C 74
Watford Field Rd. Wat—7G 9
Watford Heath. Wat—9H 9
Watford Rd. E16—8E 62
Watford Rd. Borwd—8F 10
Watford Rd. Harr & Wemb —5E 38
Watford Rd. K Lan—5A 4
Watford Rd. N'wd—6D 20
Watford Rd. Rad—1C 10
Watford Rd. Rick—8A 8
Watford Way—4C 24
NW4 1-103, 171-487 &
2-46, 190-402
NW7 remainder
Watkin Rd. Wemb—8M 39
Watkinson Rd. N7—2K 59
Watling Av. Edgw—8A 24
Watling Farm Clo. Stan—1G 23
Watling St. EC4—9A 60
Watling St. Bexh—3M 97
Watling St. Dart & Grav—6M 99
Watling St. St Alb, Rad & Borwd—1F 10
Watlington Gro. SE26—2J 109
Watney Mkt. E1—9F 60
Watney Rd. SW14—2A 88
Watney's Rd. Mitc—9H 107
Watney St. E1—9F 60
Watson Av. E6—3L 63
Watson Av. Sutt—4J 121
Watson Clo. N16—1B 60
Watson Clo. SW19—3C 106
Watson Rd. Gnfd—5E 54
Watson's M. W1—8C 58
Watsons Rd. N22—8K 27
Watson's St. SE8—8L 77
Watson St. E13—5F 62
Watsons Yd. NW2—7E 40
Wattendon Rd. Kenl—8M 137
Wattisfield Rd. E5—8G 45
Watts Bri. Rd. Eri—7D 82
Watts Gro. E3—8M 61
Watts La. Chst—5M 111
Watts La. Tedd—2E 102
Watts Rd. Th Dit—2E 118
Watts St. E1—2F 76
Wat Tyler Rd. SE10—1A 94
Wauthier Clo. N13—5M 27
Wavell Clo. Wal X—1E 6
Wavell Dri. Sidc—5C 96
Wavel M. NW6—3M 57
Wavendon Av. W4—6B 72
Waveney Av. SE15—3F 92
Waverley Av. E4—4K 29
Waverley Av. E17—1B 46
Waverley Av. Kenl—8C 138
Waverley Av. Surb—1M 119
Waverley Av. Sutt—4M 121
Waverley Av. Twic—7K 85
Waverley Av. Wemb—1K 55
Waverley Clo. E18—8G 31
Waverley Clo. Brom—9H 111
Waverley Clo. Hay—5B 68
Waverley Ct. SE26—2G 109
Waverley Cres. SE18—6B 80
Waverley Cres. Romf—7G 35
Waverley Gdns. NW10—5K 55
Waverley Gdns. Bark—5C 64
Waverley Gdns. Ilf—9A 32
Waverley Gdns. N'wd—8E 20
Waverley Gro. N3—1H 41
Waverley Pl. N4—6M 43
Waverley Pl. NW8—5B 58
Waverley Rd. E17—1A 46
Waverley Rd. E18—8G 31
Waverley Rd. N8—4J 43
Waverley Rd. N17—7F 28
Waverley Rd. SE18—6B 80
Waverley Rd. SE25—8F 108
Waverley Rd. Cob & Lea —6A 132
Waverley Rd. Enf—5M 15
Waverley Rd. Eps—7F 120
Waverley Rd. Harr—6J 37
Waverley Rd. Rain—7F 66
Waverley Rd. S'hall—1L 69
Waverley Vs. N17—9D 28
Waverley Way. Cars—8C 122
Waverton Rd. SW18—6A 90
Waverton St. W1—2F 74
Wavertree Rd. E18—9E 30
Wavertree Rd. SW2—7K 91
Waxlow Cres. S'hall—9L 53
Waxlow Rd. NW10—5A 56
Waxwell Clo. Pinn—9H 21
Waxwell La. Pinn—9H 21
Waxwell Ter. SE1—3K 75
Waybourne Gro. Ruis—4A 36
Waye Av. Houn—9E 68
Wayfarer Rd. N'holt—7H 53
Wayfield Link. SE9—5B 96
Wayford St. SW11—1C 90
Wayland Av. E8—1E 60
Waylands. Swan—8D 114
Waylands Mead. Beck —5M 109
Waylett Pl. SE27—9M 91
Waylett Pl. Wemb—9H 39
Wayne Clo. Orp—5D 128
Wayneflete Av. Croy—5M 123
Wayneflete Tower Av. Esh —5L 117
Waynflete Sq. W10—1H 73
Waynflete St. SW18—8A 90
Wayside. NW11—6J 41
Wayside. SW14—4A 88
Wayside. Croy—8M 125
Wayside Av. Bush, Wat—8B 10
Wayside Av. Horn—7H 51
Wayside Clo. N14—8G 15
Wayside Clo. Romf—1D 50
Wayside Ct. Twic—5G 87
Wayside Ct. Wemb—8L 39
Wayside Gdns. SE9—1K 111
Wayside Gdns. Dag—1L 65
Wayside Gro. SE9—1K 111
Wayside M. Ilf—3L 47
Wayville Rd. Dart—6M 99
Weald Clo. Brom—4J 127
Weald La. Harr—9B 22
Weald Rise. Harr—7D 22
Weald Rd. Brtwd—1K 35
Weald Rd. Uxb—5E 142
Weald Sq. E5—7F 44
Wealdstone Rd. Sutt—4K 121
Weald, The. Chst—3K 111
Weald Way. Hay—6C 52
Weald Way. Romf—4M 49
Wealdwood Gdns. Pinn—6M 21
Weale Rd. E4—3B 30
Weall Grn. Wat—5F 4
Weardale Gdns. Enf—3B 16
Weardale Rd. SE13—3B 94
Wear Pl. E2—6F 60
Wearside Rd. SE13—3M 93
Weatherley Clo. E3—8K 61
Weavers Clo. Iswth—3C 86
Weaver's La. SE1—2C 76
Weaver St. E1—7E 60
Weavers Way. NW1—4H 59
Weaver Wlk. SE27—1A 108
Webber Clo. Borwd—8H 11
Webber Clo. Eri—8F 82
Webber Row. SE1—3M 75
Webber St. SE1—3L 75
Webb Est. E5—5E 44
Webb Gdns. E13—7E 62
Webb Rd. SE3—7D 78
Webb's Rd. SW11—4D 90
Webbs Rd. Hay—6F 52
Webb St. SE1—4C 76
Webster Clo. Lea—6A 132
Webster Clo. Wal A—6M 7
Webster Gdns. W5—2H 71
Webster Rd. E11—8A 46
Webster Rd. SE16—4E 76
Wedderburn Rd. NW3—1B 58
Wedderburn Rd. Bark—4C 64
Wedgewood Clo. N'wd—7A 20
Wedgewood Way. SE19 —4A 108
Wedgwood M. W1—9H 59
Wedgwood Wlk. NW6—1M 57
Wedlake Clo. Horn—6J 51
Wedlake St. W10—7J 57
Wedmore Av. Ilf—8L 31
Wedmore Gdns. N19—7H 43
Wedmore M. N19—8H 43
Wedmore Rd. Gnfd—6B 54
Wedmore St. N19—8H 43
Wednesbury Gdns. Romf —7K 35
Wednesbury Grn. Romf—7K 35
Wednesbury Rd. Romf—7K 35
Weech Rd. NW6—9L 41
Weedington Rd. NW5—1E 58
Weekley Sq. SW11—2B 90
Weigall Rd. SE12—4E 94
Weighhouse St. W1—9E 58
Weighton M. SE20—6F 108
Weighton Rd. SE20—6F 108
Weighton Rd. Harr—8B 22
Weihurst Gdns. Sutt—7B 122
Weimar St. SW15—2J 89
Weirdale Av. N20—2D 26
Weir Hall Av. N18—6B 28
Weir Hall Gdns. N18—5B 28
Weir Hall Rd.—5B 28
N17 1-35 & 2-34
N18 remainder
Weir Rd. SW12—6G 91
Weir Rd. SW19—9M 89
Weir Rd. Bex—6M 97
Weir Rd. W on T—1E 116
Weir's Pas. NW1—6H 59
Weiss Rd. SW15—2H 89
Welbeck Av. Brom—1E 110
Welbeck Av. Hay—7F 52
Welbeck Av. Sidc—7E 96
Welbeck Clo. N12—5B 26
Welbeck Clo. Borwd—5L 11
Welbeck Clo. Eps—9E 120
Welbeck Clo. N Mald—9D 104
Welbeck Rd. E6—6H 63
Welbeck Rd. Barn—8C 14
Welbeck Rd. Harr—6M 37
Welbeck Rd. Sutt & Cars —4B 122
Welbeck St. W1—8E 58
Welbeck Wlk. Cars—3B 122
Welbeck Way. W1—9F 58
Welby St. SE5—9M 75
Welch Pl. Pinn—8G 21
Welcomes Rd. Kenl—9B 138
Weldon Clo. Ruis—2F 52
Weld Pl. N11—5F 26
Welfare Rd. E15—3C 62
Welford Clo. E5—8H 45
Welford Pl. SW19—1J 105
Welham Rd.—2E 106
SW16 1-129 & 2-34
SW17 remainder
Welhouse Rd. Cars—3C 122
Wellacre Rd. Harr—4F 38
Wellan Clo. Well—4F 96
Welland Gdns. Gnfd—5D 54
Wellands Clo. Brom—6K 111
Welland St. SE10—7A 78
Well App. Barn—7G 13
Wellbrook Rd. Orp—6L 127
Well Clo. Ruis—8J 37
Wellclose Sq. E1—1E 76
Wellclose St. E1—1E 76
Wellcome Av. Dart—3J 99
Well Cottage Clo. E11—4G 47
Well Ct. EC4—9A 60
Welldon Cres. Harr—3C 38
Well End Rd. Borwd—1A 12
Wellers Ct. N1—5J 59
Wellers Gro. Wal X—1A 6
Weller St. SE1—3A 76
Wellesford Clo. Bans—9K 135
Wellesley Av. W6—4F 72
Wellesley Av. N'wd—5D 20
Wellesley Ct. Rd. Croy—4B 124
Wellesley Cres. Twic—8C 86
Wellesley Gro. Croy—4B 124
Wellesley Rd. E11—3E 46
Wellesley Rd. E17—4L 45
Wellesley Rd. N22—9L 27
Wellesley Rd. NW5—1E 58
Wellesley Rd. W4—6L 71
Wellesley Rd. Croy—3A 124
Wellesley Rd. Harr—3C 38
Wellesley Rd. Ilf—7M 47
Wellesley Rd. Sutt—8A 122
Wellesley Rd. Twic—9C 86
Wellesley St. E1—8H 61
Wellesley Ter. N1—6A 60
Wellfield Av. N10—1F 42
Wellfield Rd. SW16—1J 107
Wellfields Rd. Lou—5L 19
Wellfield Wlk. SW16 —1K 107
Wellfit St. SE24—2M 91
Wellgarth. Gnfd—2F 54
Wellgarth Rd. NW11—6M 41
Well Hall Rd. SE9—2J 95
Well Hill. Orp—8M 129
Well Hill La. Orp—8M 129
Wellhouse La. Barn—6G 13
Wellhouse Rd. Beck—8L 109
Welling High St. Well—2F 96
Wellington Av. E4—2L 29
Wellington Av. N9—2F 28
Wellington Av. N15—4D 44
Wellington Av. Houn—4L 85
Wellington Av. Pinn—8K 21
Wellington Av. Sidc—5E 96
Wellington Av. Wor Pk—5G 121
Wellington Bldgs. SW1—6E 74
Wellington Clo. SE14—9H 77
Wellington Clo. W11—9L 57
Wellington Clo. Dag—3A 66
Wellington Cres. N Mald —7A 104
Wellington Dri. Dag—3A 66
Wellington Est. E2—5G 61
Wellington Gdns. SE7—6G 79
Wellington Gdns. Twic—1B 102
Wellington Hill. Lou—1E 18
Wellingtonia Av. Hav, Romf —4A 34
Wellington Pk. Est. NW2—7E 40
Wellington Pl. E11—3E 46
Wellington Pl. NW8—6B 58
Wellington Rd. E6—4K 63
Wellington Rd. E7—9D 46
Wellington Rd. E10—6J 45
Wellington Rd. E11—3E 46
Wellington Rd. E17—2J 45
Wellington Rd. NW8—5B 58
Wellington Rd. NW10—6H 57
Wellington Rd. SW19—8L 89
Wellington Rd. W5—4G 71
Wellington Rd. Belv—6K 81
Wellington Rd. Bex—4H 97
Wellington Rd. Brom—8G 111
Wellington Rd. Croy—2M 123
Wellington Rd. Dart—5G 99
Wellington Rd. Enf—7C 16
Wellington Rd. Felt—4C 84
Wellington Rd. Hmptn & Twic —1B 102
Wellington Rd. Harr—1C 38
Wellington Rd. Orp—1F 128
Wellington Rd. Pinn—8K 21
Wellington Rd. Uxb—4A 142
Wellington Rd. Wat—4F 8
Wellington Rd. N. Houn—2K 85
Wellington Rd. S. Houn—3K 85
Wellington Row. E2—6D 60
Wellington Sq. SW3—6D 74
Wellington St. SE18—5L 79
Wellington St. WC2—1K 75
Wellington St. Bark—4A 64
Wellington Ter. Harr—6B 38
Wellington Way. E3—6L 61

Westminster Rd. N9—1F 28
Westminster Rd. W7—2C 70
Westminster Rd. Sutt—4B 122
W. Moat Clo. Beck—4A 110
Westmont Rd. Esh—4C 118
Westmoor Gdns. Enf—4H 17
Westmoor Rd. Enf—4H 17
Westmoor St. SE7—4H 79
Westmoreland Av. Horn
—3G 51
Westmoreland Av. Well—3C 96
Westmoreland Bldgs. EC1
—8A 60
Westmoreland Dri. Sutt
—9M 121
Westmoreland Pl. SW1—6F 74
Westmoreland Pl. W5—8H 55
Westmoreland Rd. NW9—1K 39
Westmoreland Rd. SE17
—7B 76
Westmoreland Rd. SW13
—9D 72
Westmoreland Rd. Brom
—9C 110
Westmoreland St. W1—8E 58
Westmoreland Ter. SW1
—6F 74
Westmorland Clo. E12—7H 47
Westmorland Clo. Eps—2C 134
Westmorland Clo. Twic—5F 86
Westmorland Ct. Surb—2H 119
Westmorland Rd. E17—4L 45
Westmorland Rd. Harr—3M 37
Westmorland Way. Mitc
—9J 107
Westmount Rd. SE9—1K 95
West Oak. Beck—5B 110
Westoe Rd. N9—2F 28
Weston Av. E Mol—8J 101
Weston Av. Th Dit—2C 118
Weston Dri. Stan—8F 22
Weston Gdns. Iswth—9C 70
Weston Grn. Dag—9K 49
Weston Grn. Th Dit—3C 118
(in two parts)
Weston Grn. Rd. Esh & Th Dit
—3B 118
Weston Gro. Brom—5D 110
Weston Pk. N8—4J 43
Weston Pk. King—6J 103
Weston Pk. Th Dit—3C 118
Weston Pk. Clo. Th Dit—3C 118
Weston Rise. WC1—6K 59
Weston Rd. W4—4A 72
Weston Rd. Brom—4D 110
Weston Rd. Dag—9J 49
Weston Rd. Enf—4B 16
Weston Rd. Th Dit—3C 118
Weston St. SE1—3C 76
Weston St. SE19—3C 108
Weston Wlk. E9—3F 60
Weston Yd. SE1—3B 76
Westover Clo. Sutt—1M 135
Westover Hill. NW3—7L 41
Westover Rd. SW18—6A 90
Westow Hill. SE19—3C 108
W. Palace Gdns. Wey—5A 116
West Pk. SE9—8J 95
W. Park Av. Rich—9M 71
W. Park Clo. Romf—3H 49
W. Park Rd. Eps—4K 133
W. Park Rd. Rich—9L 71
West Pier. E1—2E 76
West Pl. SW19—2G 105
Westpoint Trading Est. W3
—8L 55
Westpole Av. Barn—6E 14
Westport Rd. E13—7F 62
Westport St. E1—9H 61
W. Poultry Av. EC1—8M 59
W. Quarters. W12—9E 56
West Ramp. Houn—9L 143
W. Ridge Gdns. Gnfd—5A 54
W. Riding. St Alb—3K 5
West Rd. E15—4D 62
West Rd. N17—6F 28
West Rd. SW3—7D 74
West Rd. SW4—4H 91
West Rd. W5—8J 55
West Rd. Barn—1E 26
West Rd. Chess—6G 133
West Rd. Felt—5B 84
West Rd. King—5A 104
West Rd. Romf—4H 49
(Chadwell Heath)
West Rd. Romf—5B 50
(Rush Green)
West Rd. W Dray—4K 143
West Rd. Wey—9A 116
Westrow. SW15—5G 89
West Row. W10—7J 57
Westrow Dri. Bark—2D 64
Westrow Gdns. Ilf—7D 48

W. Sheen Vale. Rich—3K 87
West Side. NW4—9F 24
W. Side Comn. SW19—2G 105
W. Smithfield. EC1—8M 59
West Sq. SE11—4M 75
West St. E2—5F 60
West St. E11—8C 46
West St. E17—3M 45
West St. WC2—9H 59
West St. Bexh—2K 97
West St. Bren—7G 71
West St. Brom—5E 110
West St. Cars—5D 122
West St. Croy—6A 124
West St. Eps—5A 134
West St. Eps—2C 134
(Ewell)
West St. Eri—5B 82
West St. Harr—6B 38
West St. Sutt—7M 121
West St. Wat—4F 8
West St. La. Cars—6D 122
W. Temple Sheen. SW14
—4M 87
W. Tenter St. E1—1D 76
West Towers. Pinn—4H 37
West View. NW4—2G 41
West View. Felt—6A 84
West View. Lou—5K 19
W. View Clo. NW10—1D 56
W. View Ct. Borwd—8H 11
W. View Cres. N9—9C 16
Westview Dri. Wfd G—9H 31
W. View Gdns. Borwd—8H 11
W. View Rd. Dart—5K 99
W. View Rd. Swan—8E 114
W. View Rd. Swan—1B 130
(Crockenhill)
Westville Rd. W12—3E 72
Westville Rd. Th Dit—2E 118
West Wlk. W5—8J 55
West Wlk. Barn—9E 14
West Wlk. Hay—2E 68
W. Walkway, The. Sutt—7M 121
Westward Rd. E4—5K 29
Westward Way. Harr—4J 39
W. Warwick Pl. SW1—5G 75
Westway.—1D 72
Westway. N18—4B 28
West Way. NW10—8B 40
Westway. SW20—8F 104
West Way. Cars—2B 136
West Way. Croy—4J 125
West Way. Edgw—6M 23
West Way. Houn—9K 69
Westway. Orp—9B 112
West Way. Pinn—2H 37
West Way. Ruis—6D 36
West Way. Shep—1B 116
West Way. Wal A—9H 7
West Way. W Wick—1B 126
Westway Clo. SW20—7F 104
W. Way Gdns. Croy—4H 125
Westways. Eps—6D 120
Westwell Clo. Orp—3H 129
Westwell M. SW16—3J 107
Westwell Rd. SW16—3J 107
Westwell Rd. App. SW16
—3J 107
Westwick Gdns. W14—3H 73
Westwick Gdns. Houn—1F 84
Westwood Av. SE19—4B 108
Westwood Av. Harr—9M 37
Westwood Clo. Brom—7H 111
Westwood Clo. Esh—5B 118
Westwood Clo. Ruis—4B 36
Westwood Gdns. SW13—2D 88
Westwood Hill. SE26—2E 108
Westwood La. Well & Sidc
—2D 96
Westwood Pk. SE23—6F 92
Westwood Rd. E16—2F 78
Westwood Rd. SW13—2D 88
Westwood Rd. Coul—9H 137
Westwood Rd. Ilf—6D 48
W. Woodside. Bex—7J 97
Wetheral Dri. Stan—8F 22
Wetherby Clo. N'holt—2M 53
Wetherby Gdns. SW5—5A 74
Wetherby M. SW5—6M 73
Wetherby Pl. SW7—5A 74
Wetherby Rd. Borwd—3J 11
Wetherby Rd. Enf—3A 16
Wetherby Way. Chess—9J 119
Wetherden St. E17—5A 45
Wetherell Rd. E9—4H 61
Wetherill Rd. N10—8E 26
Wettern Clo. S Croy—2C 138
Wexford Rd. SW12—6D 90
Weybourne St. SW18—8A 90
Weybridge Rd. T Hth—8L 107
Wey Ct. Eps—6A 120

Weydown Clo. SW19—7J 89
Weyhill Rd. E1—9E 60
Weylond Rd. Dag—8K 49
Weyman Rd. SE3—9G 79
Weymouth Av. NW7—5C 24
Weymouth Av. W5—4G 71
Weymouth Ct. Sutt—9L 121
Weymouth M. W1—8F 58
Weymouth Rd. Hay—6C 52
Weymouth St. W1—8E 58
Weymouth Ter. E2—5D 60
(in two parts)
Weymouth Wlk. Stan—6E 22
Whadcoat St. N4—7L 43
Whalebone Av. Romf—4K 49
Whalebone Gro. Romf—4K 49
Whalebone La. E15—3C 62
Whalebone La. N. Romf—7J 33
Whalebone La. S. Romf & Dag
—5K 49
Wharfdale Rd. N1—5J 59
Wharfedale Gdns. T Hth
—8K 107
Wharfedale St. SW10—6M 73
Wharf La. Twic—7E 86
Wharf Pl. E2—4F 60
Wharf Rd. E15—4B 62
Wharf Rd. N1—5A 60
Wharf Rd. Enf—8J 17
Wharfside Rd. E16—9C 62
Wharf St. E16—8C 62
Wharncliffe Dri. S'hall—2B 70
Wharncliffe Gdns. SE25
—6C 108
Wharton Clo. NW10—2C 56
Wharton Rd. Brom—5F 110
Wharton St. WC1—6K 59
Whateley Rd. SE20—4H 109
Whateley Rd. SE22—4D 92
Whatley Av. SW20—7H 105
Whatman Rd. SE23—6H 93
Wheatcroft. Wal X—1B 6
Wheatfields. Enf—3J 17
Wheathill Rd. SE20—7F 108
Wheat Knoll. Kenl—8A 138
Wheatlands. Houn—7L 69
Wheatlands Rd. SW17—9E 90
Wheatley Clo. NW4—9E 24
Wheatley Cres. Hay—1E 68
Wheatley Gdns. N9—2C 28
Wheatley Rd. Iswth—2D 86
Wheatley St. W1—8E 58
Wheatley Ter. Rd. Eri—7D 82
Wheatsheaf La. SW6—8G 73
Wheatsheaf La. SW8—8J 75
Wheatsheaf Rd. Romf—4D 50
Wheatsheaf Ter. SW6—8K 73
Wheelers Cross. Bark—5B 64
Wheelers Dri. Ruis—4A 36
Wheelers La. Eps—6M 133
Wheel Farm Dri. Dag—8A 50
Wheel Wright Clo. Bush, Wat
—9M 9
Wheelwright St. N7—3K 59
Whelan Way. Wall—5H 123
Wheler St. E1—7D 60
Whellock Rd. W4—4C 72
Whenman Av. Bex—9A 98
Whernside Clo. SE28—1G 81
Whetstone Clo. N20—2B 26
Whetstone Pk. WC2—9K 59
Whetstone Rd. SE3—1G 95
Whewell Rd. N19—7J 43
Whidborne St. WC1—6J 59
Whimbrel Clo. SE28—1G 81
Whimbrel Clo. S Croy—3b 138
Whinfell Clo. SW16—2H 107
Whinyates Rd. SE9—2J 95
Whippendell Clo. Orp—5F 112
Whippendell Rd. Wat—7C 8
Whippendell Way. Orp—5F 112
Whipps Cross. E17—3B 46
Whipps Cross Rd. E17—3B 46
Whiskin St. EC1—6M 59
Whistler Gdns. Edgw—9K 23
Whistlers Av. SW11—8B 74
Whistler St. N5—1M 59
Whistler Wlk. SW10—8B 74
Whiston Rd. E2—4D 60
Whitakers Way. Lou—3K 19
Whitbread Clo. N17—8E 28
Whitbread Rd. SE4—3J 93
Whitburn Rd. SE13—3A 94
Whitby Av. NW10—6M 55
Whitby Ct. N7—9J 43
Whitby Gdns. NW9—1L 39
Whitby Gdns. Sutt—4B 122
Whitby Rd. SE18—5K 79
Whitby Rd. Harr—8A 38
Whitby Rd. Ruis—8F 36
Whitby Rd. Sutt—4B 122
Whitby St. E1—7D 60

Whitcher Clo. SE14—7J 77
Whitcher Pl. NW1—2G 59
Whitchurch Av. Edgw—7K 23
Whitchurch Gdns. Edgw
—6K 23
Whitchurch La. Edgw—7H 23
Whitchurch Rd. W11—1H 73
Whitchurch Rd. Romf—4H 35
Whitcomb St. WC2—1H 75
White Acre. NW9—9C 24
Whitear Wlk. E15—2B 62
Whitebarn La. Dag—4L 65
Whitebeam Av. Brom—2L 127
Whitebeam Clo. SW9—8K 75
Whitebridge Clo. Felt—5D 84
White Butts Rd. Ruis—8H 37
Whitechapel High St. E1—9D 60
Whitechapel Rd. E1—8E 60
White Chu. La. E1—9E 60
White City Clo. W12—1G 73
White City Rd. W12—1F 72
White Conduit St. N1—5L 59
Whitecote Rd. S'hall—9A 54
White Craig Clo. Pinn—5L 21
Whitecroft Clo. Beck—8B 110
Whitecroft Way. Beck—8A 110
Whitecross Pl. EC2—8B 60
Whitecross St. EC1 & EC2
—7A 60
Whitefield Av. NW2—6G 41
Whitefield Av. Purl—8L 137
Whitefield Clo. SW18—5J 89
Whitefield Clo. Orp—7G 113
Whitefields Rd. Wal X—1C 6
Whitefoot La. Brom—1A 110
Whitefoot Ter. Brom—9D 94
Whitefriars Av. Harr—9C 22
Whitefriars Dri. Harr—9C 22
Whitefriars St. EC4—9L 59
White Gdns. Dag—2L 65
Whitegate Gdns. Harr—7D 22
Whitehall. SW1—2J 75
Whitehall Clo. Chig—3E 32
Whitehall Clo. Uxb—4A 142
Whitehall Ct. SW1—2J 75
Whitehall Cres. Chess—7H 119
Whitehall Gdns. E4—1C 30
Whitehall Gdns. W3—2L 71
Whitehall Gdns. W4—7M 71
Whitehall La. Eri—1D 98
Whitehall Pk. N19—6G 43
Whitehall Pk. Rd. W4—7M 71
Whitehall Pl. E7—1E 62
Whitehall Pl. SW1—2J 75
Whitehall Pl. Wall—6F 122
Whitehall Rd. E4 & Wfd G
—2C 30
Whitehall Rd. Brom—9H 111
Whitehall Rd. Harr—5C 38
Whitehall Rd. T Hth—9L 107
Whitehall Rd. Uxb—4B 142
Whitehall St. N17—7D 28
White Hart Clo. Hay—7B 68
White Hart La. N17—7A 28
White Hart La. N22—8L 27
White Hart La. NW10—2D 56
White Hart La. SW13—2C 88
White Hart La. Romf—8L 33
White Hart Rd. SE18—5C 80
White Hart Rd. Orp—2E 128
White Hart Slip. Brom—6E 110
White Hart St. SE11—6L 75
White Hart Yd. SE1—2B 76
Whitehaven Clo. Brom—8E 110
Whitehaven St. NW8—7C 58
Whitehead Clo. SW18—6A 90
Whitehead Clo. Dart—9G 99
Whitehead's Gro. SW3—5C 74
White Heart Av. Uxb—8A 52
Whiteheath Av. Ruis—5A 36
White Hill. Rick—5A 20
White Hill. S Croy—2B 138
Whitehill Rd. Dart—4E 98
Whitehills Rd. Lou—5L 19
White Horse Dri. Eps—6A 134
White Horse Hill. Chst—1L 111
White Horse La. E1—8H 61
Whitehorse La. SE25—8B 108
White Horse Rd. E1—9J 61
(in two parts)
White Horse Rd. E6—6K 63
Whitehorse Rd. Croy & T Hth
—2A 124
White Horse St. W1—2F 74
White Horse Yd. EC2—9B 60
Whitehouse Av. Borwd—5M 11
White Ho. Dri. Stan—4G 23
Whitehouse La. Abb L, Wat
—1G 5

Whitehouse La. Enf—3A 16
Whitehouse Way. N14—2F 26
White Kennett St. E1—9D 60
White Knights La. Wey—9A 116
Whitelands Way. Romf—8H 35
Whiteledges. W13—9G 55
Whitelegg Rd. E13—5D 62
Whiteley Rd. SE19—2B 108
Whiteley Way. Felt—9L 85
White Lion Hill. EC4—1M 75
White Lion St. N1—5L 59
White Lodge. SE19—4M 107
White Lodge Clo. N2—4B 42
White Lodge Clo. Sutt—9A 122
White Oak Dri. Beck—6A 110
Whiteoaks La. Gnfd—6B 54
White Orchards. N20—9K 13
White Orchards. Stan—5E 22
White Post Hill. F'ham, Dart
—2L 131
White Post La. E9—2L 61
Whitepost La. SE13—2L 93
White Post St. SE15—8G 77
White Rd. E15—3C 62
Whites Av. Ilf—4C 48
White's Grounds. SE1—3C 76
White's Row. E1—8D 60
White's Sq. SW4—3H 91
Whitestile Rd. Bren—6G 71
Whitestone La. NW3—8A 42
White St. S'hall—1A 70
White Swan M. W4—7C 72
Whitethorn Av. Coul—7E 136
Whitethorn Av. W Dray—1J 143
Whitethorn Gdns. Croy—4F 124
Whitethorn Gdns. Enf—7B 16
Whitethorn Gdns. Horn—4G 51
Whitethorn Pl. W Dray—2K 143
Whitethorn St. E3—8L 61
Whitewebbs La. Enf—8A 6
Whitewebbs Way. Orp—5D 112
Whitfield Rd. E6—3G 63
Whitfield Rd. SE3—9B 78
Whitfield Rd. Bexh—8K 81
Whitfield St. W1—7G 59
Whitford Gdns. Mitc—7D 106
Whitgift Av. S Croy—7A 124
Whitgift Centre. Croy—4A 124
Whitgift Sq. Croy—4A 124
Whitgift St. SE11—5K 75
Whitgift St. Croy—5A 124
Whiting Av. Bark—3M 63
Whitings Rd. Barn—7G 13
Whitings Way. E6—8L 63
Whitland Rd. Cars—3B 122
Whitley Clo. Stai—5C 144
Whitley Rd. N17—9C 28
Whitlock Dri. SW19—6J 89
Whitman Rd. E3—7J 61
Whitmead Clo. S Croy—8C 124
Whitmore Clo. N11—5F 26
Whitmore Gdns. NW10—5G 57
Whitmore Rd. N1—4C 60
Whitmore Rd. Beck—7K 109
Whitmore Rd. Harr—5A 38
Whitmores Clo. Eps—7A 134
Whitnell Way. SW15—4G 89
Whitney Av. Ilf—2H 47
Whitney Rd. E10—5M 45
Whitney Wlk. Sidc—3J 113
Whitstable Clo. Beck—5K 109
Whitstable Clo. Ruis—7C 36
Whittaker Av. Rich—4H 87
Whittaker Rd. E6—3H 63
Whittaker Rd. Sutt—5K 121
Whittaker St. SW1—5E 74
Whittaker Way. SE1—5E 76
Whitta Rd. E12—9H 47
Whittell Gdns. SE26—9G 93
Whittingstall Rd. SW6—9K 73
Whittington Av. EC3—9C 60
Whittington Av. Hay—8D 52
Whittington Rd. N22—7J 27
Whittington Way. Pinn—3J 37
Whittlebury Clo. Cars—9D 122
Whittle Clo. S'hall—9M 53
Whittle Rd. Houn—8G 69
Whittlesea Clo. Harr—7A 22
Whittlesea Path. Harr—8A 22
Whittlesea Rd. Harr—8A 22
Whittlesey St. SE1—2L 75
Whitton Av. E. Gnfd—1D 54
Whitton Av. W. N'holt & Gnfd
—1M 53
Whitton Clo. Gnfd—2F 54
Whitton Dene. Houn & Iswth
—4A 86
Whitton Dene. Iswth—5B 86
Whitton Dri. Gnfd—2E 54
Whitton Mnr. Rd. Iswth—5A 86
Whitton Rd. Houn—3M 85
Whitton Rd. Twic—5C 86
Whitton Wlk. E3—6L 61

Whitton Waye. Houn—5L 85
Whitwell Rd. E13—6E 62
Whitwell Rd. Wat—8H 5
Whitworth Rd. SE18—8L 79
Whitworth Rd. SE25—7C 108
Whitworth St. SE10—6C 78
Whorlton Rd. SE15—2F 92
Whybridge Clo. Rain—4D 66
Whynark Av. N22—1M 43
Whytecliffe Rd. Purl—3L 137
Whytecroft. Houn—8H 69
Whyteleafe Hill. Whyt—9D 138
Whyteville Rd. E7—2F 62
Wichling Clo. Orp—3H 129
Wickersley Rd. SW11—1E 90
Wickers Oake. SE19—1D 108
Wicker St. E1—9F 60
Wicket, The. Croy—7L 125
Wickford Clo. Romf—5K 35
Wickford Dri. Romf—5K 35
Wickford St. E1—7G 61
Wickford Way. E17—2H 45
Wickham Av. Croy—4J 125
Wickham Av. Sutt—7C 120
Wickham Chase. W Wick
—3B 126
Wickham Clo. Enf—5G 17
Wickham Clo. N Mald—9D 104
Wickham Ct. Rd. W Wick
—4A 126
Wickham Cres. W Wick
—4A 126
Wickham Gdns. SE4—2K 93
Wickham La. SE2—6E 80
Wickham M. SE4—1K 93
Wickham Rd. E4—7A 30
Wickham Rd. SE4—2K 93
Wickham Rd. Beck—6M 109
Wickham Rd. Croy—4H 125
Wickham Rd. Harr—9B 22
Wickham Rd. SE11—6K 75
Wickham St. Well—1C 96
Wickham Way. Beck—8A 110
Wick La. E3—4L 61
(in two parts)
Wickliffe Av. N3—9J 25
Wickliffe Gdns. Wemb—7M 39
Wicklow St. WC1—6K 59
Wick Rd. E9—2H 61
Wick Rd. Tedd—4F 102
Wick Sq. E9—2K 61
Wicksteed Clo. Bex—9B 98
Wickwood St. SE5—1M 91
Widdecombe Av. Harr—7J 37
Widdenham Rd. N7—9K 43
Widdin St. E15—3C 62
Widecombe Clo. Romf—8H 35
Widecombe Gdns. Ilf—2J 47
Widecombe Rd. SE9—9J 95
Widecombe Way. N2—2B 42
Widegate St. E1—8C 60
Widenham Clo. Pinn—3G 37
Wide Way. Mitc—7H 107
Widgeon Way. Wat—1J 9
Widley Rd. W9—6L 57
Widmore Lodge Rd. Brom
—6H 111
Widmore Rd. Brom—6E 110
Widmore Rd. Uxb—7F 142
Wieland Rd. N'wd—7E 20
Wigan Ho. E5—6F 44
Wigeon Path. SE28—4B 80
Wiggenhall Rd. Wat—7F 8
Wiggington Av. Wemb—2M 55
Wiggins Mead. NW9—7D 24
Wightman Rd. N8—2L 43
Wigley Rd. Felt—8H 85
Wigmore Pl. W1—9F 58
Wigmore Rd. SE24—2A 92
Wigmore Rd. Cars—4B 122
Wigmore St. W1—9E 58
Wigmore Wlk. Cars—4B 122
Wigram Rd. E11—4G 47
Wigram Sq. E17—1A 46
Wigston Rd. E13—7F 62
Wigton Gdns. Stan—8J 23
Wigton Pl. SE11—6L 75
Wigton Rd. E17—8K 29
Wigton Rd. Romf—4J 35
Wigton Way. Romf—4J 35
Wilberforce Rd. N4—7M 43
Wilberforce Rd. NW9—4E 40
Wilberforce Way. SW19
—3H 105
Wilbraham Pl. SW1—5D 74
Wilbury Av. Sutt—2K 135
Wilbury Way. N18—5B 28
Wilby M. W11—2K 73
Wilcot Av. Wat—9J 9
Wilcox Clo. SW8—8J 75
Wilcox Clo. Borwd—3A 12
Wilcox Pl. SW1—4G 75

Wilcox Rd. SW8—8J 75
Wilcox Rd. Sutt—6M 121
Wilcox Rd. Tedd—1B 102
Wild Ct. WC2—9K 59
Wildcroft Gdns. Edgw—6H 23
Wildcroft Mnr. SW15—6G 89
Wildcroft Rd. SW15—6G 89
Wilde Clo. E8—4E 60
Wilde Pl. N13—6M 27
Wilderness Rd. Chst—4M 111
Wilderness, The. Hmptn
—1M 101
Wilderton Rd. N16—5C 44
Wildfell Rd. SE6—6M 93
Wild Goose Dri. SE14—9G 77
Wild Hatch. NW11—4L 41
Wild Oaks Clo. N'wd—6D 20
Wild's Rents. SE1—4C 76
Wild St. WC2—9J 59
Wildwood. N'wd—6B 20
Wildwood Av. St Alb—3K 5
Wildwood Clo. SE12—6D 94
Wildwood Ct. Kenl—7B 138
Wildwood Gro. NW3—6A 42
Wildwood Rise. NW11—6A 42
Wildwood Rd. NW11—4A 42
Wilford Clo. Enf—5B 16
Wilford Clo. N'wd—7B 20
Wilfred Av. Rain—8E 66
Wilfred St. SW1—4G 75
Wilfrid Gdns. W3—8A 56
Wilkes St. E1—8D 60
(in two parts)
Wilkins Clo. Hay—6D 68
Wilkinson Clo. Dart—3K 99
Wilkinson Rd. E16—9G 63
Wilkinson St. SW8—8K 75
Wilkinson Way. W4—3B 72
Wilkin St. NW5—2F 58
Wilkin St. M. NW5—2F 58
Wilks Pl. N1—5C 60
Willan Rd. N17—9C 28
Willan Wall. E16—1D 78
Willard St. SW8—2F 90
Willcocks Clo. Chess—5J 119
Willcott Rd. W3—2M 71
Willcrooks Gdns. SE9—3H 95
Willenhall Av. Barn—8A 14
Willenhall Rd. SE18—6M 79
Willersley Av. Orp—5B 128
Willersley Av. Sidc—7D 96
Willersley Clo. Sidc—7D 96
Willesden La.—2G 57
NW6 1-221 & 2-218
NW2 remainder
Willes Rd. NW5—2F 58
Willet Clo. N'holt—6G 53
Willett Clo. Orp—1C 128
Willett Pl. T Hth—9L 107
Willett Rd. T Hth—9L 107
Willett Way. Orp—9B 112
Willet Way. SE16—6F 76
William Barefoot Dri. SE9
—1L 111
William Booth Rd. SE20
—5E 108
William Clo. Romf—8B 34
William Cory Prom. Eri—6C 82
William Ct. W5—8G 55
William Covell Clo. Enf—2K 15
William Ellis Way. SE16—4E 76
William Gdns. SW15—4F 88
William Gunn Ho. NW3—1C 58
William Guy Gdns. E3—6M 61
William Margrie Clo. SE15
—1E 92
William M. SW1—3D 74
William Morley Clo. E6—4H 63
William Morris Clo. E17—1K 45
William Pl. Orp—8G 113
William Rd. NW1—6G 59
William Rd. SW19—4J 105
William Rd. Sutt—7A 122
Williams Av. E17—8K 29
William's Bldgs. E2—7G 61
Williams Gro. N22—8L 27
William's La. SW14—2A 88
Williams La. Mord—9A 106
Williamson Clo. SE10—6D 78
Williamson Rd. N4—4M 43
Williamson St. N7—9J 43
Williamson Way. NW7—6J 25
Williams Rd. W13—2E 70
Williams Rd. S'hall—5J 69
Williams Ter. Croy—8L 123
William St. E10—4M 45
William St. N17—7D 28
William St. SW1—3D 74
William St. Bark—3A 64
William St. Bush, Wat—5H 9
William St. Cars—5C 122
Willifield Way. NW11—2K 41

Willingale Clo. Wfd G—6G 31
Willingale Rd. Lou—3M &
5M 19
Willingdon Rd. N22—9M 27
Willinghall Clo. Wal A—5C 7
Willingham Clo. NW5—1G 59
Willingham Ter. NW5—1G 59
Willingham Way. King—7L 103
Willington Rd. SW9—2J 91
Willis Av. Sutt—8C 122
Willis Clo. Eps—6M 133
Willis Rd. Croy—2A 124
Willis Rd. Eri—5B 82
Willis St. E14—9M 61
Willmore End. SW19—5M 105
Willoughby Av. Croy—6K 123
Willoughby Gro. N17—7F 28
Willoughby La. N17—6F 28
Willoughby Pk. Rd. N17—7F 28
Willoughby Rd. N8—1L 43
Willoughby Rd. NW3—8B 42
Willoughby Rd. King—5K 103
Willoughby Rd. Rain—3C 66
Willoughby Rd. Twic—4G 87
Willow Av. SW13—1D 88
Willow Av. Sidc—5E 96
Willow Av. Swan—8D 114
Willow Av. Uxb—2A 142
Willow Av. W Dray—1K 143
Willow Bank. Rich—9F 86
Willow Bri. Rd. N1—2A 60
Willowbrook Rd. SE15—7D 76
Willowbrook Rd. S'hall—4L 69
Willowbrook Rd. Stai—8C 144
Willow Clo. Bex—5K 97
Willow Clo. Bren—7G 71
Willow Clo. Brom—9K 111
Willow Clo. Buck H—3H 31
Willow Clo. Horn—8F 50
Willow Clo. Orp—2F 128
Willow Cotts. N16—7D 44
Willow Cotts. Rich—7L 71
Willow Ct. Edgw—4J 23
Willowcourt Av. Harr—3F 38
Willow Cres. E. Uxb—1A 142
Willow Cres. W. Uxb—1A 142
Willowdene. N6—5D 42
Willow Dene. Bush, Wat—9C 10
Willow Dene. Pinn—9H 21
Willowdene Clo. Twic—6A 86
Willow Dri. Barn—6J 13
Willow End. N20—2L 25
Willow End. Surb—3J 119
Willow Gdns. Houn—9L 69
Willow Gdns. Ruis—7D 36
Willow Grange. Sidc—9F 96
Willow Grn. NW9—8C 24
Willow Grn. Borwd—7B 12
Willow Gro. Chst—3L 111
Willow Gro. Ruis—7D 36
Willow Hayne Rd. W on T
—2F 116
Willow Hayne Gdns. Wor Pk
—6G 121
Willowherb Wlk. Romf—7G 35
Willow La. Mitc—9D 106
Willow La. Wat—7E 8
Willow La. Industrial Est.
Mitc—1D 122
Willow Mead. Chig—3E 32
Willowmead Clo. W5—8H 55
Willow Mere. Esh—6A 118
Willow Mt. Croy—5C 124
Willow Path. Wal A—7L 7
Willow Pl. SW1—5G 75
Willow Rd. NW3—9B 42
Willow Rd. W5—3J 71
Willow Rd. Dart—7G 99
Willow Rd. Enf—5C 16
Willow Rd. Eri—9E 82
Willow Rd. N Mald—8A 104
Willow Rd. Romf—4J 49
Willow Rd. Wall—9F 122
Willows Av. Mord—9M 105
Willows Clo. Pinn—9G 21
Willows Path. Eps—6M 133
Willows, The. Wat—9F 8
Willow St. E4—1B 30
Willow St. EC2—7C 60
Willow St. Romf—2A 50
Willow Tree Clo. SW18—7M 89
Willowtree Clo. Hay—7G 53
Willowtree Clo. Uxb—8A 36
Willow Tree La. Hay—7G 53
Willow Vale. W12—2E 72
Willow Vale. Chst—3M 111
Willow View. SW19—5B 106
Willow Wlk. E17—3K 45
Willow Wlk. N2—9B 26
Willow Wlk. N15—2M 43
Willow Wlk. N21—8K 15
Willow Wlk. SE1—5C 76

Willow Wlk. Dart—3G 99
Willow Wlk. Orp—5M 127
Willow Wlk. Sutt—5K 121
Willow Way. N3—7M 25
Willow Way. SE26—9G 93
Willow Way. Eps—8B 120
Willow Way. Rad—1D 10
Willow Way. Romf—6M 35
Willow Way. Sun—8E 100
Willow Way. Twic—8M 85
Willow Way. Wemb—8E 38
Willow Wood Cres. SE25
—1C 124
Willrose Cres. SE2—6F 80
Wills Cres. Houn—5M 85
Wills Gro. NW7—5E 24
Wilman Gro. E8—3E 60
Wilmar Clo. Hay—7B 52
Wilmar Clo. Uxb—3B 142
Wilmar Gdns. W Wick—3M 125
Wilmer Clo. King—2K 103
Wilmer Cres. King—2K 103
Wilmer Gdns. N1—4C 60
(in two parts)
Wilmerhatch La. Eps—9M 133
Wilmer Lea Clo. E15—3B 62
Wilmer Way. N14—5H 27
Wilmington Av. W4—8B 72
Wilmington Av. Orp—4G 129
Wilmington Ct. Rd. Dart—9E 98
Wilmington Gdns. Bark—2B 64
Wilmington Sq. WC1—6L 59
Wilmington St. WC1—6L 59
Wilmot Clo. N2—9A 26
Wilmot Clo. SE15—8E 76
Wilmot Pl. NW1—3G 59
Wilmot Pl. W7—2C 70
Wilmot Rd. E10—7M 45
Wilmot Rd. N17—1B 44
Wilmot Rd. Cars—7D 122
Wilmot Rd. Dart—4F 98
Wilmot Rd. Purl—4L 137
Wilmot St. E2—7F 60
Wilmot Way. Bans—6L 135
Wilmount St. SE18—5M 79
Wilna Rd. SW18—6A 90
Wilsham St. W11—2J 73
Wilshaw St. SE14—9L 77
Wilsmere Dri. Harr—7C 22
Wilsmere Dri. Ruis—1J 53
Wilson Av. Mitc—5C 106
Wilson Gdns. Harr—5A 38
Wilson Gro. SE16—3F 76
Wilson Rd. E6—6H 63
Wilson Rd. SE5—9C 76
Wilson Rd. Chess—8K 119
Wilson Rd. Ilf—5K 47
Wilson's Pl. E14—9K 61
Wilson St. E17—3A 46
Wilson St. EC2—8B 60
Wilson St. N21—9L 15
Wilson Av. W4—6C 72
Wilton Cres. SW1—3E 74
Wilton Cres. SW19—5K 105
Wilton Dri. Romf—7A 34
Wilton Gdns. E Mol—7L 101
Wilton Gdns. W on T—3H 117
Wilton Gro. SW19—5K 105
Wilton Gro. N Mald—1D 120
Wilton M. SW1—4E 74
Wilton Pl. SW1—3E 74
Wilton Rd. N10—9E 26
Wilton Rd. SE2—5G 81
Wilton Rd. SW1—5G 75
Wilton Rd. SW19—4C 106
Wilton Rd. Barn—6D 14
Wilton Rd. Houn—2H 85
Wilton Row. SW1—3E 74
Wilton Sq. N1—4B 60
Wilton St. SW1—4F 74
Wilton Ter. SW1—4E 74
Wilton Way. E8—2E 60
Wiltshire Av. Horn—2K 51
Wiltshire Clo. SW3—5D 74
Wiltshire Gdns. Twic—7A 86
Wiltshire La. Pinn—1D 36
Wiltshire Rd. SW9—2L 91
Wiltshire Rd. Orp—2E 128
Wiltshire Rd. T Hth—7L 107
Wiltstone Clo. Hay—7J 53
Wilverley Cres. N Mald
—1C 120
Wimbart Rd. SW2—6K 91
Wimbledon Hill Rd. SW19
—3J 105
Wimbledon Pk. Rd.—8J 89
SW18 1-257 & 2-218
SW19 remainder
Wimbledon Pk. Side. SW19
—8H 89
Wimbledon Rd. SW17—1A 106

Wimbolt St. E2—6E 60
Wimborne Av. Hay—9F 52
Wimborne Av. Orp & Chst
—8D 112
Wimborne Av. S'hall—5L 69
Wimborne Clo. SE12—4D 94
Wimborne Clo. Buck H—2F 30
Wimborne Clo. Eps—5D 134
Wimborne Clo. Wor Pk—3G 121
Wimborne Dri. NW9—1L 39
Wimborne Dri. Pinn—5H 37
Wimborne Gdns. W13—8F 54
Wimborne Gro. Wat—1C 8
Wimborne Rd. N9—2E 28
Wimborne Rd. N17—9C 28
Wimborne Way. Beck—7H 109
Wimbourne St. N1—5B 60
Wimpole Clo. King—6K 103
Wimpole M. W1—8F 58
Wimpole Rd. W Dray—2H 143
Wimpole St. W1—8F 58
Winans Wlk. SW9—1L 91
Wincanton Cres. N'holt—1L 53
Wincanton Gdns. Ilf—9M 31
Wincanton Rd. SW18—6K 89
Wincanton Rd. Romf—3H 35
Winchat Rd. SE28—4B 80
Winchcombe Gdns. SE9—2H 95
Winchcombe Rd. Cars—2B 122
Winchelsea Av. Bexh—8K 81
Winchelsea Clo. SW15—4H 89
Winchelsea Rd. E7—9E 46
Winchelsea Rd. N17—1C 44
Winchelsea Rd. NW10—4B 56
Winchelsey Rise. S Croy
—8D 124
Winchendon Rd. SW6—9K 73
Winchendon Rd. Tedd—1B 102
Winchester Av. NW6—4J 57
Winchester Av. NW9—1L 39
Winchester Av. Houn—7K 69
Winchester Clo. E6—9K 63
Winchester Clo. SE17—5M 75
Winchester Clo. Brom—7D 110
Winchester Clo. Enf—8C 16
Winchester Clo. Esh—6L 117
Winchester Clo. King—4M 103
Winchester Dri. Pinn—3H 37
Winchester Pk. Brom—7D 110
Winchester Pl. E8—1D 60
Winchester Pl. N6—6F 42
Winchester Rd. E4—7A 30
Winchester Rd. N6—5F 42
Winchester Rd. N9—1D 28
Winchester Rd. NW3—3B 58
Winchester Rd. Bexh—1H 97
Winchester Rd. Brom—7D 110
Winchester Rd. Felt—9K 85
Winchester Rd. Harr—2J 39
Winchester Rd. Hay—8C 68
Winchester Rd. Ilf—8B 48
Winchester Rd. N'wd—1E 36
Winchester Rd. Orp—6G 129
Winchester Rd. Twic—5F 86
Winchester Rd. W on T—3E 116
Winchester St. SW1—6F 74
Winchester St. W3—3A 72
Winchester Wlk. SE1—2B 76
Winchester Way. Rick—7A 8
Winchet Wlk. Croy—1G 125
Winchfield Clo. Harr—4G 39
Winchfield Rd. SE26—2J 109
Winchilsea Cres. E Mol
—6A 102
Winchmore Hill Rd.—1H 27
N14 1-173 & 2-136
N21 remainder
Winckley Clo. Harr—3K 39
Wincott St. SE11—5L 75
Wincrofts Dri. SE9—3B 96
Windborough Rd. Cars—9E 122
Windermere Av. N3—1L 41
Windermere Av. NW6—4J 57
Windermere Av. SW19
—7M 105
Windermere Av. Horn—1E 66
Windermere Av. Ruis—5G 37
Windermere Av. Wemb—5G 39
Windermere Clo. Dart—7F 98
Windermere Clo. Orp—5M 127
Windermere Ct. Kenl—7M 137
Windermere Gdns. Ilf—3J 47
Windermere Gro. Wemb—6G 39
Windermere Ho. Barn—6M 13
Windermere Rd. N10—8F 26
Windermere Rd. N19—7G 43
Windermere Rd. SW15—1C 104
Windermere Rd. SW16—5G 107
Windermere Rd. W5—4G 71
Windermere Rd. Bexh—1A 98
Windermere Rd. Coul—7J 137
Windermere Rd. Croy—3D 124
Windermere Rd. S'hall—8K 53

Windermere Rd. W Wick
—4C 126
Winders Rd. SW11—1C 90
Windfield Clo. SE26—1H 109
Windham Av. Croy—2B 140
Windham Rd. Rich—2K 87
Windings, The. S Croy—3D 138
Winding Way. Dag—8G 49
Winding Way. Harr—9C 38
Windlass Pl. SE8—5J 77
Windlesham Gro. SW19—7H 89
Windley Clo. SE23—8G 93
Windmill Av. Eps—3D 134
Windmill Clo. SE1—5E 76
Windmill Clo. Eps—4D 134
Windmill Clo. Sun—4C 100
Windmill Clo. Surb—3G 119
Windmill Clo. Upm—7L 51
Windmill Clo. Wal A—7L 7
Windmill Ct. NW2—2J 57
Windmill Dri. SW4—4F 90
Windmill Dri. Kes—6G 127
Windmill End. Eps—4D 134
Windmill Gdns. Enf—5L 15
Windmill Gro. Croy—1A 124
Windmill Hill. NW3—8A 42
Windmill Hill. Enf—5M 15
Windmill Hill. Ruis—5D 36
Windmill La. E15—2B 62
Windmill La. Barn—8D 12
Windmill La. Bush—1C 22
Windmill La. Eps—4D 134
Windmill La. Gnfd—8A 54
Windmill La. S'hall & Iswth
—3A 70
Windmill La. Surb—2F 118
Windmill La. Wal X—3E 6
Windmill M. W4—5C 72
Windmill Pas. W4—5C 72
Windmill Rd. N18—4B 28
Windmill Rd. SW18—5B 90
Windmill Rd. SW19—8F 88
Windmill Rd. W4—5C 72
Windmill Rd.—5G 71
W5 143a-245 & 158-366
Bren remainder
Windmill Rd. Croy—2A 124
Windmill Rd. Hmptn—2M 101
Windmill Rd. Mitc—9G 107
Windmill Rd. Sun—5C 100
Windmill Rd. W. Sun—6C 100
Windmill Row. SE11—6L 75
Windmill St. W1—8H 59
(in two parts)
Windmill St. Bush. Wat—1C 22
Windmill Wlk. SE1—2L 75
Windmill Way. Ruis—6D 36
Windover Av. NW9—2B 40
Windrush. SE28—2F 80
Windrush Clo. SW11—3B 90
Windrush Clo. W4—9A 72
Windrush La. SE23—9H 93
Windsor Av. E17—9J 29
Windsor Av. SW19—5A 106
Windsor Av. E Mol—7L 101
Windsor Av. Edgw—4M 23
Windsor Av. N Mald—9A 104
Windsor Av. Sutt—5J 121
Windsor Av. Uxb—4F 142
Windsor Clo. N3—9J 25
Windsor Clo. Borwd—3L 11
Windsor Clo. Bren—7F 70
Windsor Clo. Harr—8L 37
Windsor Clo. N'wd—9E 20
Windsor Clo. Wal X—3A 6
Windsor Ct. N14—9G 15
Windsor Ct. Sun—4E 100
Windsor Cres. Harr—8L 37
Windsor Cres. Wemb—8M 39
Windsor Dri. Ashf—9B 144
Windsor Dri. Barn—8D 14
Windsor Dri. Dart—5E 98
Windsor Dri. Orp—8E 128
Windsor Gdns. W9—8L 57
Windsor Gdns. Hay—4B 68
Windsor Gro. SE27—1A 108
Windsor Pk. Rd. Hay—8D 68
Windsor Pl. SW1—5G 75
Windsor Rd. E4—4M 29
Windsor Rd. E7—1F 62
Windsor Rd. E10—7M 45
Windsor Rd. E11—7E 46
Windsor Rd. N7—8J 43
Windsor Rd. N13—3L 27
Windsor Rd. N17—9E 28
Windsor Rd. NW2—2F 56
Windsor Rd. W5—1J 71
Windsor Rd. Barn—8H 13
Windsor Rd. Bexh—3J 97
Windsor Rd. Dag—8J 49
Windsor Rd. Enf—9D 6
Windsor Rd. Harr—8B 22

Windsor Rd. Horn—5G 51
Windsor Rd. Houn—1G 85
Windsor Rd. IIf—9M 47
Windsor Rd. King—4J 103
Windsor Rd. Rich—1K 87
Windsor Rd. Sidc—3F 112
Windsor Rd. S'hall—4K 69
Windsor Rd. Sun—3E 100
Windsor Rd. Tedd—2B 102
Windsor Rd. T Hth—6M 107
Windsor Rd. Wat—2G 9
Windsor Rd. Wor Pk—4E 120
Windsor St. N1—4M 59
Windsor St. Uxb—3A 142
(in two parts)
Windsor Ter. N1—6A 60
Windsor Wlk. SE5—1B 92
Windsor Wlk. Wey—7A 116
Windspoint Dri. SE15—7F 76
Windus Rd. N16—6D 44
Windus Wlk. N16—6D 44
Windward Clo. Enf—8D 6
Windy Ridge. Brom—5J 111
Windy Ridge Clo. SW19
—2H 105
Wine Clo. E1—1G 77
Wine Office Ct. EC4—9L 59
Winforton St. SE10—9A 78
Winfred Gro. SW11—3D 90
Winfrith Rd. SW18—7A 90
Wingate Cres. Croy—1J 123
Wingate Rd. W6—4F 72
Wingate Rd. IIf—1M 63
Wingate Rd. Sidc—3G 113
Wingfield Rd. E15—1C 62
Wingfield Rd. E17—3M 45
Wingfield Rd. King—3L 103
Wingfield St. SE15—2E 92
Wingfield Way. Ruis—2F 52
Wingford Rd. SW2—5J 91
Wingletye La. Horn—2K 51
Wingrave Rd. W6—7G 73
Wingrove Rd. SE6—8C 94
Winifred Av. Horn—9H 51
Winifred Rd. SW19—5L 105
Winifred Rd. Coul—8E 136
Winifred Rd. Dag—7J 49
Winifred Rd. Dart—4F 98
Winifred Rd. Eri—6C 82
Winifred Rd. Hmptn—1L 101
Winifred St. E16—2K 79
Winifred Ter. Enf—9D 16
Winkfield Rd. E13—5F 62
Winkfield Rd. N22—8L 27
Winkley St. E2—5F 60
Winkworth Pl. Bans—6K 135
Winkworth Rd. Bans—6K 135
Winlaton Rd. Brom—1B 110
Winmill Rd. Dag—8K 49
Winnett St. W1—1H 75
Winnington Clo. N2—4B 42
Winnington Rd. N2—4B 42
Winnington Rd. Enf—2G 17
Winnock Rd. W Dray—2H 143
Winn Rd. SE12—7E 94
Winns Av. E17—1K 45
Winns Comn. Rd. SE18—7C 80
Winns M. N15—2C 44
Winns Ter. E17—1L 45
Winsbeach. E17—9B 30
Winscombe Cres. W5—7H 55
Winscombe St. N19—7F 42
Winscombe Way. Stan—5E 22
Winsford Rd. SE6—9K 93
Winsford Ter. N18—5D 28
Winsham Gro. SW11—4E 90
Winslade Rd. SW2—4J 91
Winslade Way. Se6—6M 93
Winsland M. W2—9B 58
Winsland St. W2—9B 58
Winsley St. W1—9G 59
Winslow Clo. NW10—8C 40
Winslow Gro. E4—2C 30
Winslow Rd. W6—7G 73
Winslow Way. Felt—9J 85
Winslow Way. W on T—5G 117
Winsor Ter. E6—8L 63
Winstanley Rd. SW11—2B 90
Winstead Gdns. Dag—1A 66
Winston Av. NW9—5C 40
Winston Clo. Harr—6D 22
Winston Clo. Romf—2M 49
Winston Ct. Harr—7M 21
Winston Rd. N16—9B 44
Winston Wlk. W4—5B 72
Winston Way. IIf—8M 47
Winstre Rd. Borwd—3L 11
Winter Av. E6—4J 63
Winterborne Av. Orp—5B 128
Winterbourne Gro. Wey
—8A 116
Winterbourne Rd. SE6—7K 93

Winterbourne Rd. Dag—7G 49
Winterbourne Rd. T Hth
—8L 107
Winter Box Wlk. Rich—4K 87
Winterbrook Rd. SE24—5A 92
Winterdown Gdns. Esh—8K 117
Winterdown Rd. Esh—8K 117
Winterfold Clo. SW19—8J 89
Winters Rd. Th Dit—2F 118
Winterstoke Gdns. NW7—5E 24
Winterstoke Rd. SE6—7K 93
Winters Way. Wal A—6M 7
Winterton Ct. SE20—6E 108
Winterton Pl. SW10—7A 74
Winterwell Rd. SW2—4J 91
Winthorpe Rd. SW15—3J 89
Winthrop St. E1—8F 60
Winthrop Wlk. Wemb—8J 39
Winton App. Rick—7A 8
Winton Av. N11—7G 27
Winton Clo. N9—9H 17
Winton Cres. Rick—7A 8
Winton Dri. Rick—7A 8
Winton Dri. Wal X—2E 6
Winton Gdns. Edgw—7K 23
Winton Rd. Orp—6M 127
Winton Way. SW16—2L 107
Wirrall Ho. SE26—9E 92
Wisbeach Rd. Croy—9B 108
Wisborough Rd. S Croy
—1D 138
Wisdons Clo. Dag—6M 49
Wise La. NW7—5E 24
Wise La. W Dray—4H 143
Wiseman Rd. E10—7L 45
Wise Rd. E15—4B 62
Wiseton Rd. SW17—7C 90
Wishart Rd. SE3—1H 95
Wishford Ct. Asht—9K 133
Wisley Rd. SW11—4E 90
Wisley Rd. Orp—4E 112
Wistaria Clo. Orp—4M 127
Wisteria Gdns. Swan—6B 114
Wisteria Rd. SE13—3B 94
Witan St. E2—6F 60
Witham Clo. Lou—8J 19
Witham Rd. SE20—7G 109
Witham Rd. W13—2E 70
Witham Rd. Dag—1L 65
Witham Rd. Iswth—9B 70
Witham Rd. Romf—3F 50
Withens Clo. Orp—8G 113
Witherby Clo. Croy—6C 124
Witherfield Way. SE16—6F 76
Witherings, The. Horn—3J 51
Witherington Rd. N5—1L 59
Withers Mead. NW9—8D 24
Withers Pl. EC1—7A 60
Witherston Way. SE9—8L 95
Withycombe Rd. SW19—6H 89
Withy La. Ruis—3A 36
Withy Mead. E4—3B 30
Witley Cres. Croy—8A 126
Witley Gdns. S'hall—5K 69
Witley Rd. N19—7G 43
Witney Clo. Pinn—6K 21
Witney Path. SE23—9H 93
Wittenham Way. E4—3B 30
Wittering Way. Horn—2G 67
Wittersham Rd. Brom—2D 110
Wivenhoe Clo. SE15—2F 92
Wivenhoe Ct. Houn—3K 85
Wivenhoe Rd. Bark—5E 64
Wiverton Rd. SE26—3G 109
Wix Rd. Dag—4H 65
Wix's La. SW4—2F 90
Woburn Av. Horn—9E 50
Woburn Av. Purl—3L 137
Woburn Clo. SW19—3A 106
Woburn Clo. Bush, Wat—8A 10
Woburn Pl. WC1—7J 59
Woburn Rd. Cars—3C 122
Woburn Rd. Croy—3A 124
Woburn Sq. WC1—7H 59
Woburn Wlk. WC1—6H 59
Woffington Clo. King—5G 103
Woking Clo. SW15—3D 88
Woldham Rd. Brom—8G 111
Wolds Dri. Orp—6L 127
Wolfe Clo. Brom—1E 126
Wolfe Clo. Hay—6F 52
Wolfe Cres. SE7—6H 79
Wolfe Gdns. E15—2D 62
Wolferton Rd. E12—9K 47
Wolfington Rd. SE27—1M 107
Wolfram Clo. SE13—4C 94
Wolftencroft Clo. SW11—2C 90
Wollaston Clo. SE1—5A 76
Wolmer Clo. Edgw—4L 23
Wolmer Gdns. Edgw—3L 23
Wolseley Av. SW19—8L 89
Wolseley Gdns. W4—7M 71
Wolseley Rd. E7—3F 62

Wolseley Rd. N8—4H 43
Wolseley Rd. N22—8K 27
Wolseley Rd. W4—5A 72
Wolseley Rd. Harr—1C 38
Wolseley Rd. Mitc—2E 122
Wolseley Rd. Romf—5B 50
Wolseley St. SE1—3E 76
Wolsey Av. E6—6L 63
Wolsey Av. E17—1K 45
Wolsey Av. Th Dit—9D 102
Wolsey Av. Wal X—2A 6
Wolsey Clo. SW20—4F 104
Wolsey Clo. Houn—3A 86
Wolsey Clo. King—5M 103
Wolsey Clo. S'hall—4A 70
Wolsey Clo. Wor Pk—6E 120
Wolsey Cres. Croy—1A 140
Wolsey Cres. Mord—2J 121
Wolsey Dri. King—2J 103
Wolsey Dri. W on T—3H 117
Wolsey Gdns. IIf—6M 31
Wolsey Gro. Edgw—7B 24
Wolsey Gro. Esh—6M 117
Wolsey M. NW5—2G 59
Wolsey Rd. N1—1B 60
Wolsey Rd. E Mol—8B 102
Wolsey Rd. Enf—4F 16
Wolsey Rd. Esh—6M 117
Wolsey Rd. Hmptn—3M 101
Wolsey Rd. N'wd—2A 20
Wolsey Rd. Sun—4D 100
Wolsey St. E1—8G 61
Wolsey Way. Chess—7L 119
Wolsley Clo. Dart—4C 98
Wolstonbury. N12—5L 25
Wolvercote Rd. SE2—3H 81
Wolverley St. E2—6F 60
Wolverton. SE17—6C 76
Wolverton Av. King—5L 103
Wolverton Gdns. W5—1K 71
Wolverton Gdns. W6—5H 73
Wolverton Rd. Stan—6F 22
Wolverton Way. N14—7G 15
Wolves La.—7L 27
N13 1-37 & 2-40
N22 remainder
Womersley Rd. N8—4K 43
Wonersh Way. Sutt—1H 135
Wonford Clo. King—5C 104
Wontford Rd. Purl—7M 137
Wontner Rd. SW17—8D 90
Wooburn Clo. Uxb—7F 142
Woodall Clo. E14—1M 77
Woodall Rd. Enf—8H 17
Wood Av. Purf—5M 83
Woodbank Rd. Brom—9D 94
Woodbastwick Rd. SE26
—2H 109
Woodberry Av. N21—2L 27
Woodberry Av. Harr—2A 38
Woodberry Clo. Sun—3E 100
Woodberry Cres. N10—1F 42
Woodberry Down. N4—5A 44
Woodberry Gdns. N12—6A 26
Woodberry Gro. N4—5A 44
Woodberry Gro. N12—6A 26
Woodberry Gro. Bex—9B 98
Woodberry Way. E4—9A 18
Woodberry Way. N12—6A 26
Woodbine Clo. Twic—8B 86
Woodbine Gro. SE20—4F 108
Woodbine Gro. Enf—2B 16
Woodbine La. Wor Pk—5G 121
Woodbine Pl. E11—4E 46
Woodbine Rd. Sidc—7C 96
Woodbines Av. King—7H 103
Woodbine Ter. E9—2G 61
Woodborough Rd. SW15
—3F 88
Woodbourne Av. SW16—9H 91
Woodbourne Dri. Esh—8D 118
Woodbourne Gdns. Wall
—9F 122
Woodbridge Av. Lea—9E 132
Woodbridge Clo. N7—7K 43
Woodbridge Clo. Romf—4H 35
Woodbridge Ct. Wfd G—7J 31
Woodbridge Gro. Lea—9E 132
Woodbridge La. Romf—3H 35
Woodbridge Rd. Bark—1D 64
Woodbridge St. EC1—7M 59
Woodbrook Gdns. Wal A—6L 7
Woodbrook Rd. SE2—7E 80
Woodburn Clo. NW4—3H 41
Woodbury Clo. E11—2F 46
Woodbury Clo. Croy—4D 124
Woodbury Dri. Sutt—2A 136
Woodbury Hill. Lou—5J 19
Woodbury Hollow. Lou—4J 19
Woodbury Rd. SE26—9E 92
Woodbury Pk. Rd. W13—7F 54
Woodbury Rd. E17—2M 45
Woodbury St. SW17—2C 106

Woodchester Sq. W2—8M 57
Woodchurch Clo. Sidc—9C 96
Woodchurch Dri. Brom—4H 111
Woodchurch Rd. NW6—3M 57
Wood Clo. E2—7E 60
Wood Clo. NW9—5B 40
Wood Clo. Bex—9C 98
Wood Clo. Harr—5B 38
Woodclyffe Dri. Chst—6L 111
Woodcock Dell Av. Harr
—5H 39
Woodcock Hill. Borwd—8K 11
Woodcock Hill. Harr—3G 39
Woodcombe Cres. SE23—7G 93
Woodcote Av. NW7—6G 25
Woodcote Av. Horn—9E 50
Woodcote Av. T Hth—8M 107
Woodcote Av. Wall—1F 136
Woodcote Clo. Enf—8G 17
Woodcote Clo. Eps—6B 134
Woodcote Clo. King—6J 103
Woodcote Clo. Wal X—3C 6
Woodcote Dri. Orp—2B 128
Woodcote Dri. Purl—2H 137
Woodcote End. Eps—7B 134
Woodcote Grn. Wall—1G 137
Woodcote Grn. Rd. Eps
—7A 134
Woodcote Gro. Cars—4F 136
Woodcote Gro. Rd. Coul
—7H 137
Woodcote Hurst. Eps—8A 134
Woodcote La. Purl—3H 137
Woodcote M. Wall—8F 122
Woodcote Pk. Av. Purl—4G 137
Woodcote Pk. Rd. Eps—7A 134
Woodcote Pl. SE27—2M 107
Woodcote Rd. E11—5E 46
Woodcote Rd. Eps—6B 134
Woodcote Rd. Wall & Purl
—8F 122
Woodcote Side. Eps—7M 133
Woodcote Valley Rd. Purl
—5H 137
Woodcrest Rd. Purl—5J 137
Woodcroft. N21—1L 27
Woodcroft. SE9—9K 95
Woodcroft. Gnfd—2E 54
Woodcroft Av. NW7—6C 24
Woodcroft Av. Stan—8E 22
Woodcroft Cres. Uxb—4F 142
Woodcroft Rd. T Hth—9M 107
Wood Dri. Chst—3J 111
Woodedge Clo. E4—1D 30
Woodend. SE19—3A 108
Woodend. Esh—4A 118
Wood End. St Alb—1M 5
Woodend. Sutt—4A 122
Wood End Av. Harr—9M 37
Wood End Clo. N'holt—1A 54
Woodend Gdns. Enf—6J 15
Wood End Gdns. N'holt—1A 54
Wood End Grn. Rd. Hay—8B 52
Wood End La. N'holt—1M 53
Woodend Rd. E17—9A 30
Wood End Rd. Harr—9B 38
Woodend, The. Wall—1F 136
Woodend Way. Mord—8K 105
Wood End Way. N'holt—1A 54
Wooder Gdns. E7—9E 46
Woodfall Av. Barn—7K 13
Woodfall Rd. N4—7L 43
Woodfall St. SW3—6D 74
Woodfarrs. SE5—3B 92
Woodfield. Asht—9H 133
Woodfield Av. NW9—2C 40
Woodfield Av. SW16—9H 91
Woodfield Av. W5—7G 55
Woodfield Av. Cars—8E 122
Woodfield Av. N'wd—4C 20
Woodfield Av. Wemb—8G 39
Woodfield Clo. SE19—4A 108
Woodfield Clo. Asht—9H 133
Woodfield Cres. W5—7H 55
Woodfield Dri. Barn—1E 26
Woodfield Dri. Romf—2E 50
Woodfield Gdns. W9—8L 57
Woodfield Gdns. N Mald
—9D 104
Woodfield Gro. SW16—9H 91
Woodfield La. SW16—9H 91
Woodfield La. Asht—9J 133
Woodfield Pl. W9—7K 57
Woodfield Rise. Bush, Wat
—9B 10
Woodfield Rd. W5—7G 55
Woodfield Rd. W9—8K 57
Woodfield Rd. Asht—9H 133
Woodfield Rd. Houn—1F 84
Woodfield Rd. Th Dit—4D 118
Woodfields, The. S Croy
—3D 138

Every possible care has been taken to ensure that the information given in this atlas is accurate and whilst the publishers would be grateful to learn of any errors, they regret they can accept no responsibility for any expense or loss thereby caused.

The representation on the maps of a road, track or footpath is no evidence of the existence of a right of way.

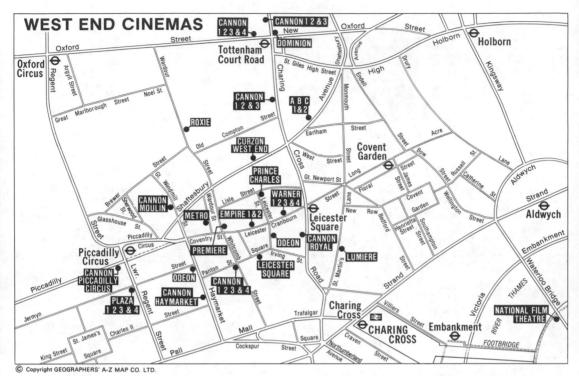

WEST END CINEMAS

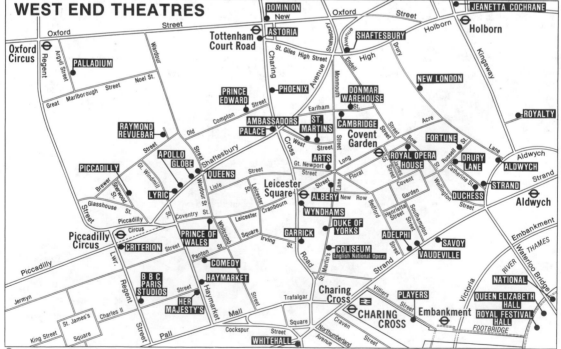

WEST END THEATRES

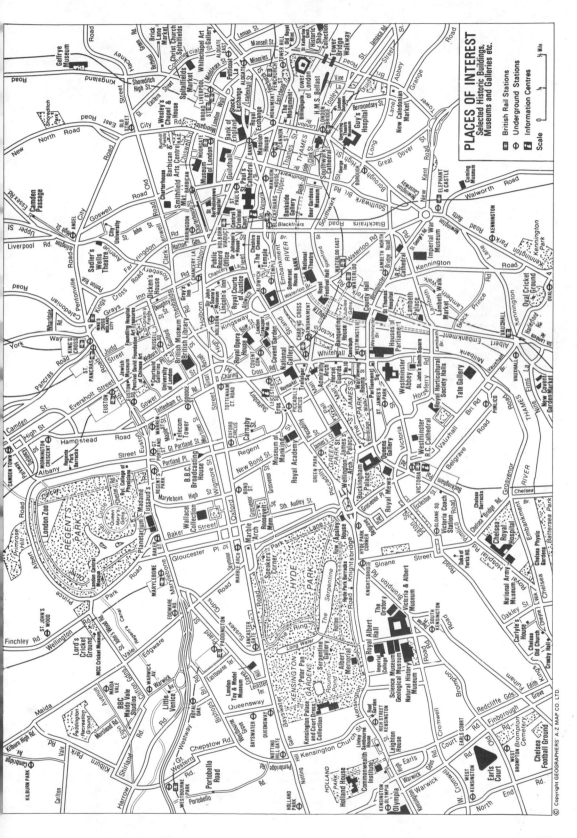

Maps printed in Great Britain by
Cripplegate Printing Co. Ltd., Fircroft Way, Edenbridge, Kent.

Index printed and atlas bound in Great Britain by
Mackays of Chatham Ltd., Lordswood, Chatham, Kent.